Buddhist Phenomenology

General Editors:

Charles S. Prebish and Damien Keown

The Curzon Critical Studies in Buddhism Series is a comprehensive study of the Buddhist tradition. The series explores this complex and extensive tradition from a variety of perspectives, using a range of different methodologies.

The Series is diverse in its focus, including historical studies, textual translations and commentaries, sociological investigations, bibliographic studies, and considerations of religious practice as an expression of Buddhism's integral religiosity. It also presents materials on modern intellectual historical studies, including the role of Buddhist thought and scholarship in a contemporary, critical context and in the light of current social issues. The series is expansive and imaginative in scope, spanning more than two and a half millennia of Buddhist history. It is receptive to all research works that inform and advance our knowledge and understanding of the Buddhist tradition.

THE REFLEXIVE NATURE OF AWARENESS
Paul Williams

BUDDHISM AND HUMAN RIGHTS
Edited by Damien Keown, Charles Prebish, Wayne Husted

ALTRUISM AND REALITY
Paul Williams

WOMEN IN THE FOOTSTEPS OF THE BUDDHA
Kathryn R. Blackstone

THE RESONANCE OF EMPTINESS
Gay Watson

IMAGING WISDOM
Jacob N. Kinnard

AMERICAN BUDDHISM
Edited by Duncan Ryuken Williams and Christopher Queen

PAIN AND ITS ENDING
Carol S. Anderson

THE SOUND OF LIBERATING TRUTH
Edited by Sallie B. King and Paul O. Ingram

BUDDHIST THEOLOGY
Edited by Roger R. Jackson and John J. Makransky

EMPTINESS APPRAISED
David F. Burton

THE GLORIOUS DEEDS OF PŪRṆA
Joel Tatelman

CONTEMPORARY BUDDHIST ETHICS
Edited by Damien Keown

INNOVATIVE BUDDHIST WOMEN
Edited by Karma Lekshe Tsomo

TEACHING BUDDHISM IN THE WEST
Edited by V.S. Hori, R.P. Hayes and J.M. Shields

EMPTY VISION
David L. McMahan

SELF, REALITY AND REASON IN TIBETAN PHILOSOPHY
Thupten Jinpa

BUDDHIST PHENOMENOLOGY
Dan Lusthaus

Buddhist Phenomenology

A Philosophical Investigation of Yogācāra Buddhism and the *Ch'eng Wei-shih lun*

Dan Lusthaus

RoutledgeCurzon
Taylor & Francis Group
LONDON AND NEW YORK

First published 2002
by RoutledgeCurzon
2 Park Square, Milton Park, Abingdon, Oxon OX14 4RN

Simultaneously published in the USA and Canada
by RoutledgeCurzon
270 Madison Ave, New York, NY 10016

Reprinted 2003

RoutledgeCurzon is an imprint of the Taylor & Francis Group

Transferred to Digital Printing 2006

British Library Cataloguing in Publication Data
A catalogue record of this book is available from the British Library

Library of Congress Cataloging in Publication Data
A catalog record for this book has been requested

ISBN10: 0–7007–1186–4 (hbk)
ISBN10: 0–415–40610–2 (pbk)

ISBN13: 978–0–7007–1186–4 (hbk)
ISBN13: 978–0–415–40610–9 (pbk)

Table of Contents

Preface

Yogācāra Buddhism as a distinct and important school first attracted the attention of Western scholars early in the Twentieth century. The enormity and complexity of Yogācāra has posed a daunting, but rewarding challenge to the Western scholars who have attempted to tackle it.

At the beginning of the Twentieth century many of the seminal Indian Yogācāra texts were no longer extant in their original Sanskrit but only in Chinese or Tibetan translations. With intrepid determination, already in the nineteenth century scholars such as Pelliot, Stein, and Lévy, scoured India and Central Asia searching for ancient, forgotten sites and texts, often successfully relying on the travelogue composed by Hsüan-tsang in the seventh century—the *Hsi yu chi* (Record of Western Lands)—to locate and identify such places. Propelled by the discovery of long lost Sanskrit manuscripts (e.g., Sylvain Lévy's discovery in Nepal and subsequent publishing of Asaṅga's *Mahāyānasūtralaṃkāra* and Sthiramati's commentary on Vasubandhu's *Triṃśikā*)[1] and the monumental translation efforts of Louis de la Vallée Poussin (especially the *Ch'eng wei-shih lun* and, from Hsüan-tsang's Chinese rendering, the related *Abhidharmakośa* of Vasubandhu, before the Sanskrit text was rediscovered),[2] and reaching a culmination in Étienne Lamotte's French translation of Asaṅga's *Mahāyānasaṃgraha* with the commentaries of Vasubandhu and *Asvabhāva using the Chinese and Tibetan versions (the Sanskrit is still lost),[3] scholars began making available, in Western language translations, extended examples of the Yogācāra system with all its categorial and terminological complexity. This phase of Western Yogācāra studies primarily employed philological and historical methodologies developed in European Nineteenth century biblical studies.

In the latter half of the Twentieth century, scholars became more modest in their efforts. Philological work continued (critical editions, concordances, etc.), but little appeared in English; certainly nothing to rival the early achievements of Vallée Poussin and Lamotte.[4] Attention focused more on the relatively short works of Vasubandhu, some of which have been translated several times (e.g., Anacker, Kochumuttom, Wood, etc.; see Bibliography).[5]

The Yogācāra school appeared relatively late in the development of Indian Buddhism (ca. fifth century), seeing itself as a continuation or fulfillment of all the earlier developments rather than as a radical departure. It incorporated virtually everything that previous Buddhist schools had developed, from intricate abhidharmic systems with elaborate technical vocabularies, to detailed expositions of all the theoretical and practical issues entailed in each of the many stages along the path to Awakening; from reevaluations of sundry major and minor doctrinal disputes in the light of reason and an expanding scriptural canon, to innovative models that recontextualized—while largely preserving and absorbing—the full gamut of Buddhist thought and practice that had preceded Yogācāra. The profound influence of Yogācāra on subsequent Buddhist developments in East Asia and Tibet still remains largely unacknowledged and unexplored by Western scholars. Yogācāra sits at the hub of Buddhism, absorbing most of what came before it, and influencing (directly and indirectly) much of what came after.

Some of the early scholars did concern themselves with the philosophical significance of the Yogācāra material, but with less impressive results than they demonstrated with their philological acumen. Stcherbatsky, for instance, recognized some affinities between Yogācāra (primarily in its later developments in Buddhist logic) and Kant's critical philosophy in that both paid enormous attention to the activities of cognitive construction through which the world appears to us as it does. But there were major differences between Yogācāra and Kant. Some examples: For Kant a thing in-itself is ultimately unknowable as it is in itself; i.e., it is noumenal. For Yogācāra the way things happen (*yathābhūtam*) is eminently knowable, and seeing things as they truly are is one of the goals of the system. For Kant, we subliminally intuit things in-themselves,[6] but never actually perceive anything beyond our own mental representations (*Vorstellungen*); for Yogācāra eliminating precisely this sort of narcissistic cognitive closure (*vijñapti-mātra*), so that one's cognitions (*jñāna*) are open to everything beyond ourselves, like a mirror (*ādarśa*), is the cognitive shift (*āśraya-parāvṛtti*) necessary to become Awakened (*bodhi*). That while Stcherbatsky was writing, contemporary developments in Western philosophy—particularly Husserl and the phenomenologists—were practicing a brand of philosophical investigation much closer to Yogācāra than was Kant, largely escaped his attention.

Vallée Poussin was enamored of Idealism, as were many of his contemporaries who harbored religious and spiritual interests. For him and many subsequent scholars, Yogācāra represented one of the great Indian Idealist systems. That interpretation will be challenged in the present work.

The Indian Yogācāra authors wrote in several genres, each genre presenting its own special type of difficulty for the modern interpreter. These ranged from concise, terse verse texts (*Triṃśikā, Trisvabhāvanirdeśa*, etc.) that sought to encapsulate complicated analyses and systematic refinements in a few words, to verse texts expanded by explanatory commentaries (*Viṃśatikā-vṛtti, Madhyānta-vibhāga-bhāṣya*, etc.), to extended essays on critical themes (*Karmasiddhi-prakaraṇa, Pañcaskandhaka prakaraṇa*, etc.), to massive compendiums that delved into the minutia of seemingly interminable models and specialized vocabulary (e.g., *Yogācārabhūmi, Mahāyānasaṃgraha, Abhidharmasamuccaya*, etc.).

The present study deals with texts of the first and last genres mentioned above. Vasubandhu's *Triṃśikā*, as its title states, consists of thirty verses. Despite its brevity it manages to engage a broad spectrum of issues, virtually all the core Yogācāra issues, in a sophisticated and detailed manner. Among the topics it discusses are the eight consciousnesses, *trisvabhāva* theory, the one hundred dharma system and its categories, *vijñapti-mātra*, and the stages of the Bodhisattva path. Part Four will present the Sanskrit text along with two Chinese translations, one by Paramārtha and the other by Hsüan-tsang. Each is accompanied by an English translation. A comparative analysis is also offered.

The *Triṃśikā* provided the skeletal core for Hsüan-tsang's *Ch'eng wei-shih lun* (Treatise Establishing Vijñapti-mātra), a ten fascicle work traditionally believed to be a collation and translation of ten separate Indian commentaries. Chapter Fifteen will cast some doubt on this traditional attribution. In any event, this text is unlike any other produced by Hsüan-tsang, since it was neither a strict translation of a single text, nor a totally original composition.[7]

Typically Western studies of Yogācāra employ one of the following approaches:

1) A diachronic study of a term or concept, tracing it from pre-Yogācāric roots through a series of Yogācāra texts, usually with the implication that the order in which the texts are discussed represents their historical sequence.
2) A translation and/or critical edition of a text or series of texts, often drawing on Sanskrit, Chinese and Tibetan versions when these are available.
3) Contextual studies, primarily dealing with schools and texts most proximate in time and conceptualization to Yogācāra, such as Sarvāstivādin Abhidharma.
4) Comparative philosophical analysis, comparing and contrasting Yogācāra or some aspects of Yogācāra with a Western school or thinker.

Since the present work does not follow one of these approaches, readers accustomed to more conventional Buddhological works may find this book unusual. Therefore it may be helpful to the reader if I explain what it is I have attempted to do here, and the reasons for it.

The conventional approaches lean heavily toward philology and history. While the present work does concern itself with philological and historical matters, these have remained largely in the background. Nor is this a work of comparative philosophy. I have not taken Husserl and phenomenology on one side, and compared point for point and issue for issue Yogācāra counterparts on the other side, the reason being that Husserlian phenomenology and Yogācāra are not isomorphic systems, nor should one expect them to be. When one compares two systems as distinct from each other in time, space, language, and history as are Yogācāra from phenomenology, it is as if one assumes that one can occupy a privileged third system, or an objective vantage point external to both of them.

Yet even when not wishing to go to such a place, one can find oneself there. Husserl, et al., do not provide us with an exact correlation to Yogācāra. For example, the husserlian terms *noesis* (the constructive knower) and *noema* (the 'known' object constructed by noesis) are useful for pointing out aspects of Yogācāra that also deal with how the noema—the meaningful cognitive object—is constructed by noesis (i.e., "noetically constituted"). But which

Yogācāra term best corresponds to noesis-noema? *Darśana* and *nimitta*? *Grāhaka* and *grāhya*? *Ālambaka* and *ālambana*? *Ātman* and *dharmas*? This list could easily expand to a dozen or more items. The Yogācāra vocabulary, in fact, is far richer and more intricate than the husserlian version, though the latter cannot be accused of lacking in carefully etched distinctions expressed in a rich vocabulary of its own. Simply put, Yogācāra makes numerous distinctions that Western phenomenologists ignore or have failed to adequately thematize (e.g., causal analysis, karmic analysis, clearly demarcated levels of noetic-noemic interaction, etc.).

If the match between Buddhism and Western phenomenology is not perfect, why did I choose it as the target idiom into which to "translate" Buddhism and Yogācāra? After all, few Buddhologists study Husserl, Sartre, Merleau-Ponty, Lacan, Lyotard, Derrida, et al., in detail. Wouldn't this be a sterile exercise, rendering the abstruse terminological details of one system—already difficult enough to comprehend in it own terms—into another system equally difficult? Given the prominence of Anglo-American philosophy in English-speaking academia today, and its virtual hostility to "continental" thought, wouldn't this be a futile exercise?

Granted Western phenomenology is not identical to Yogācāra, but its models and concerns provide the closest form of Western philosophy we currently have. When looking at something unfamiliar, one tends to notice those aspects reminiscent of things familiar while overlooking other aspects that one's prior experience (or lack of experience) has not prepared one to notice. Phenomenology affords us some sensitivities with which to notice aspects of Yogācāra that otherwise we might overlook. Perhaps, when Western philosophy progresses further, new approaches will emerge that will bring us even closer.

In fact, a sizable number of English-speaking philosophers, well-trained in phenomenology and other forms of "continental" thought, also maintains an interest in Buddhism. There are also many students who, while studying Buddhism, also find themselves stimulated by Western philosophy and are seeking ways to bridge the cultural gap, since they recognize that these two systems have great potential to become allies. This book is intended to help them forge these bridges It is also designed to help facilitate a conversation between Buddhologists and Western philosophers. We all have much to learn from each other. This is only a starting effort. Hopefully others will carry this type of project further, and explore the possibilities opened here in greater depth and detail.

Phenomenology and Buddhism both take the whys and hows of *human experience* as their starting and concluding points. Both focus on similar epistemological issues, such as perception, sensation, cognition, noetic construction, embodied conditioning, and the overcoming of embodied ways of seeing the world. Both propose, through methodic investigation of the way we cognize, to resolve the most fundamental human dilemmas and problems.

For Husserl, 'returning to the things themselves'—i.e., recovering the essences of things lost to Western metaphysics since Kant put noumenal reality out of the reach of phenomenal experience—could be accomplished through rigorous, methodic attention to phenomena, i.e., what appears in cognition; with the proper methods (bracketing, eidetic variation, phenomenological reduction, transcendental reduction, etc.) the essences—or invariant structures—of things would be disclosed. By revealing the apodictic truths made intersubjectively evident through the phenomenological method, Husserl offered not only self-understanding but an epistemological foundation for the European sciences (*Wissenschaften*) which, according to Husserl, were in crisis precisely because they lacked such grounding. Key to the phenomenological project is an understanding of how intentionality constitutes meaning (*Sinn*). Merleau-Ponty deepened Husserl's description with his own description of the 'intentional arc' in which the mutual intentionalities of lived-bodies and perceptual fields constitute meanings out of a region of ambiguity through which they interact and mutually influence each other. In short, through corrected cognition presuppositions, conditioned historical views, 'sediments,' and so on, are replaced by a life grounded in *Evidenz.*

For Buddhism, the root of all human problems lies in ignorance, i.e., the mis-cognition and misperception of 'things as they become' (*yathābhūtam*). Buddhist practice provides methodic and rigorous attention to the facts of experience. Cognitive acuity is sharpened through various means, from meditation and epistemological rigor, to affective and ethical betterment. Key to the Buddhist project is an understanding of how desire (intent) constitutes life-forms. In short, Buddhism aims at removing the deep-seated proclivities (*anuśaya*), views (*dṛṣṭi*), and mental disturbances (*kleśa*) that hinder correct cognition and produce binding karma; removing these obstructions is Awakening.

What I have set out to do here is express Buddhism phenomenologically, since, as this book argues and demonstrates, it is a type of phenomenology; Yogācāra even moreso. That claim will no longer sound odd or need defending if this book is successful.

I have attempted to offer a *philosophical translation* of Yogācāra into the idiom of phenomenology (and vice versa). By "translation" I don't mean strictly the rendering of an Asian text into a Western language, though my translations do utilize phenomenological terms. Instead, I have tried to translate Buddhism, and especially Yogācāra, into phenomenology. Many of the best known and oft-repeated Buddhist models and doctrines are phenomenological, i.e., concerned with noetic constitution, how we cognize, and the construction of *meaning.* This will be discussed and illustrated in Part Two.

The *Ch'eng wei-shih lun* is an encyclopedic text, covering not only the full spectrum of Yogācāric issues, but also expositions and critiques of other schools, Buddhist and non-Buddhist. Too many complex issues are dealt with in it for me to air them all in this book. Instead I have concentrated on those sections of the *Ch'eng wei-shih lun* most relevant to a philosophical understanding of Yogācāra. Many issues—such as the distinctive seed theory of the *Ch'eng wei-shih lun*, disputes in Abhidharmic classifications, the more elaborate treatments of types of causes, and so on—must await another occasion. Philosophical sections, such as the *Ch'eng wei-shih lun*'s treatment of language, vijñapti-mātra, the four causes, the criteria of reality, and the proper understanding of rūpa (sensorial materiality), are explored.

The move from philology to philosophy does not entail a rejection of philology. On the contrary, philology is one of the necessary foundations on which philosophical investigations into systems remote in time and language stand. Without carefully establishing realistic and judicious limits through meticulous philological and historical work on the range of hermeneutic possibilities offered by a bare text, philosophical speculation can easily lead itself astray. Nonetheless, it is also necessary to eventually go beyond merely doing philology, in order to explore what a text *means* rather than merely collating it with materials related to it, or assigning it an historical spot, or detailing its social significance and context.

Yogācāra is sometimes treated by Buddhologists as if it were a unique school, a notion that gets reinforced when scholars concentrate exclusively on the *novel* concepts associated with Yogācāra, such as the eight consciousnesses, the ālaya-vijñāna, trisvabhāva, and vijñapti-mātra. Yogācārin texts deal with many other topics as well, and when these are ignored, not only do the novel concepts risk being misunderstood by becoming decontextualized, but Yogācāra itself becomes more *novel*, more isolated from other forms of Buddhism. Even when Yogācāra materials are contextualized by those schools most proximate to it, such as Sarvāstivāda, it risks being understood under the same isolation, since, sadly, many Buddhologists are not as conversant with Sarvāstivāda and Abhidharma as perhaps they should be. In order to counter the propensity to treat Yogācāra as a school apart from other Buddhist schools, I have gone back to the early and medieval Pāli materials instead of restricting myself to texts like the *Abhidharmakośa* and *Mahāvibhāṣa*. Most of the questions and problems that Yogācāra wrestled with have their roots there. As Parts Two and Three show, Buddhism was phenomenological from the outset. It becomes easier to understand a text like the *Ch'eng wei-shih lun* when the pre-Yogācāric phenomenological basis on which it draws has already been spelled out. Since nowhere else has this been spelled out, I devote a major portion of this book to providing this necessary context. Most Buddhologists believe they know the models discussed in Part Two well, possibly even intimately. Perhaps they will find some food for thought there nonetheless.

In November of 1998, the first session of the AAR Yogācāra Seminar was held at the American Academy of Religion Annual Meeting. Papers by John Cha, Matthew Kapstein, Parimal Patil and Jeffrey Hopkins on Vasubandhu and Sthiramati, Vasubandhu's arguments against atomism, Ratnakīrti's epistemology, and Tsong-ka-pa's analysis of Asaṅga, respectively, had precirculated among the seminar members. John Dunne and I were the respondents.[8] Lively discussion of the papers at the meeting was followed up by an email discussion between the seminar members. I had noticed that even though the papers dealt with disparate figures from different times with ostensibly different agendas and approaches, the texts dealt with in all of the papers, even in the different manners that this distinct group of scholars interpreted and presented them, seemed to share a common core structure. I summarized that observation this way in the email discussion.[9]

> In my response I suggested that it may be time to replace the standard 'textbook' synopsis of Yogācāra—namely, an enumeration of 8 consciousnesses and 3 svabhāvas—and instead develop something that I argue is structurally at the core of each of the papers, to wit:
>
> Starting with the assumption that
>
> (1) some sort of untainted cognitive activity free from erroneous qualities is accessible to humans—the nature and characteristics of which may or may not differ across the papers
> (2) various sorts of discriminations and linguistic-conceptual additions are introduced that complicate cognitive activity, so much so that
> (3) the problems these complications produce must be overcome.
> (4) The method or recommendations for overcoming these problems, again, may or may not be the same for all the texts and thinkers presented or represented by these papers, but one problem that emerges with the discriminative, linguistic-conceptual problems is the notion—and even phenomenological experience—of externality.
>
> Is this a better structural introduction to Yogācāra than the eight consciousnesses and three svabhāvas? (i.e., does it explain why they develop those—and all the additional categories, from 100 dharmas abhidharma, to vijñapti-mātra, to rigorous epistemology and logic, etc.—in the first place?)

The reader may wish to keep these questions and points in mind while reading this book. Externality will be discussed in Chapter Nineteen.

There are many who as teachers, colleagues, friends, and students have contributed in countless ways to what appears in the following pages. Richard Robinson, my first academic teacher of Buddhism, provided such an inspiring model that decades later I find myself engaged in the same career. If in some small measure the present work can be seen as a corollary to his *Early Mādhyamika in India and China*, only this time with Yogācāra, then I will have repaid at least a small part of the debt I owe him. Antonio de Nicolas taught me to think, the centrality of epistemology, that philosophy is something philosophers *do* rather than think about, and that philosophy done well has no "East" or "West." Sung-bae Park introduced me to East Asian Buddhism and the Chinese language. Thomas Altizer challenged, encouraged, and befriended me; Robert Neville taught me the "process" of Wu style Taiji and the contours of Religious Thought. For training in phenomenology and poststructuralism I am indebted to Hugh Silverman, David Allison, and Ed Casey. Norbert Samuelson presided over a small group meeting weekly at his home that worked methodically through Spinoza's *Ethics* in Latin; after seven years we were almost to the end of bk. IV! Tom Dean embodied a Heideggerian mind more open and adventurous than Heidegger's. Bibhuti Yadav and Charles Wei-Hsun Fu, sadly no longer with us, were both master philosophers and teachers, equally adept in the languages and thought of Asia and the West. I first read the *Ch'eng wei-shih lun* in a graduate seminar devoted to it by Dr. Fu, and have been studying it ever since. Dr. Yadav was a living embodiment of Candrakīrti, as caring for students as he was sharp in argument. Philosophy gushed from his pores, rendering systems that others might consider remote and abstract palpably vital and pertinent, including Yogācāra. Jitendranath Mohanty dispelled the pervasive myth that Anglo-American philosophy and Continental Philosophy are incommensurate and even hostile to each other by becoming a noted authority on and in both, respected by both camps; as if that were not enough, he is also recognized as a leading authority on Indian Philosophy, specializing in Navya-nyāya no less! His clear yet gentle logical mind made his seminars on Husserl, Frege, Heidegger and Hegel lucid joys. Through his auspices several of us were fortunate to study Indian philosophy with Bimal K. Matilal shortly before Matilal succumbed to illness.

Robert Buswell afforded me the opportunity to spend a year as a visiting professor at UCLA, where I benefited greatly from the feedback I received on earlier drafts of Parts Two and Three from the graduate students in my two quarter seminar on Chinese Buddhism. I spent a year as visiting faculty at the University of Illinois, Champaign-Urbana, in part due to Peter Gregory, who also kindly provided critical comments on earlier drafts of some sections of this book, especially Chapter Fifteen. I am grateful for the continuous support and encouragement offered by John Strong, for whom I filled in at Bates College as a two-year visiting professor while he was on sabbatical; incidentally that was where I met my wife, Hiromi, who was filling in for John's wife, Sarah, at the same time. Hiromi helped with some of the typing of this book.

Others whom I would like to thank for directly or indirectly encouraging this project and my research over the years include Leslie Kawamura, Collett Cox, David Kolb, John Keenan, Steve Heine, Charles Muller, Kathleen Erndl, Chen-kuo Lin, Russell Kirkland, Joe Wilson, Jan Nattier, John McRae, Alan Sponberg, Richard Hayes, David Loy, and Bill Waldron. Whatever faults remain in this book are entirely my responsibility.

My dissertation, the distant ancestor of this book, was generously supported by a scholarship from the China Times Cultural Foundation, the first such scholarship awarded to a non-Chinese.

Finally I wish to thank my parents whose constant love and encouragement have sustained me during times of adversity.

I dedicate this work to Charles Fu and Bibhuti Yadav, without whom it would never have been written.

Notes

1 Lévy, Sylvain. *Matériaux pour l'étude du systeme Vijñaptimātra.* Paris: Bibliothèque de l'École des Hautes Études, 1925, and *Mahāyāna-Sūtrālaṃkāra, exposé de la doctrine du Grand Vehicule selon le système Yogācāra.* Ed. et tr. d'apres un manuscrit rapporte du Nepal, par Sylvain Lévi. Paris: H. Champion, Bibliothèque de l'École des Hautes Études, 1907-11, 2 vols

2 Louis de la Vallée Poussin. *Vijñaptimātratāsiddhi: La Siddhi de Hiuan-Tsang.* 2 vols., Paris, 1928, and *L'Abhidharmakośa de Vasubandhu,* traduit et annoté par Louis de la Vallée Poussin. Paris: Paul Greuthner, 1931, 7 vols

3 Étienne Lamotte, *La Somme du Grand Véhicule d'Asaṅga,* 2 vols., Louvaine: Institut Orientaliste, 1973 rpt of 1938 ed

4 The leading Western work on Yogācāra in the first half of the Twentieth century appeared in French; in the late Twentieth century it has been in German, especially the works of Lambert Schmithausen and Ernst Steinkellner. In the States, Alex Wayman and a few others published important articles on aspects of Yogācāra and its early figures.

5 For a more comprehensive overview of twentieth century Yogācāra studies in the West, see my "A Brief Retrospective of Western Yogācāra Scholarship of the 20th Century," on the Yogācāra Buddhism Research Association website: <http://www.uncwil.edu/p&r/yogacara/ISCP_99_Yogacara_retro2.html>.

6 This 'intuition' is mentioned briefly at the beginning of Kant's *Critique of Pure Reason* as a stimulus that provokes the cognitive overlay blocking direct access to the noumena, but he never develops or clarify the nature of this intuition, so that it remains, in his system, merely a vague and ambiguous notion, one which was nonetheless necessary for Kant to maintain a realist foundation.

7 For a complete annotated list of all of Hsüan-tsang's works, see Appendix Four. Aside from the *Ch'eng wei-shih lun,* all of these works are translations of single texts, plus two original compositions: the aforementioned *Hsi yu chi* (Record of Western Lands) and the *Pa-shih kuei-chu sung* (Verses on the Structure of the Eight Consciousnesses). In all, Hsüan-tsang produced seventy-seven works, including some of the largest texts in the Chinese Buddhist canon.

8 Dunne was unable to attend, so his response was read by Sara McClintock.

9 The full discussion can be found on the Studies in Yogācāra Buddhism website maintained for the Seminar by Joe Wilson: <http://www.uncwil.edu/p&r/yogacara/TSN/Spring99.html> All the papers mentioned, including one by me on the notion of 'externality' in Yogācāra can be accessed on the Seminar website at <http://www.uncwil.edu/p&r/yogacara/External_Objects/index.html>.

Part One

Buddhism and Phenomenology

Chapter One

Buddhism and Phenomenology

From its inception, Buddhism reminds us that we are sentient beings. 'Sentient' means to have senses, to feel, to perceive, to cognize. We are constituted by how we respond to and interpret our sensations. There is no thought, feeling, idea, memory, or knowledge of any kind that does not come to us through our senses. You are aware of nothing whatsoever apart from what you have discerned (*vijñapti*) through the sensorium, the domain of sensory experience. The mind, according to Buddhism, is simply another sense, one that cognizes its own specific sort of sense-objects, called dharmās (factors of experience, thoughts).

Buddhism contends that we habitually and incessantly misinterpret our experience, due to a lack of insight into the conditions of experience. Our misinterpretations are driven by our desires, fears and anxieties. According to Yogācāra our mental experience is changing, altering (*pariṇāma, pravṛtti*) every moment. In this fluctuating stream (*vijñāna-santāna*) we tend to posit two constants against which and through which we cognize and evaluate all that we experience. We interpret the varying alterations of our mental experience in terms of *ātman* (an independent, unchanging observer or witness) and *dharmas* (affective, thetic, and 'objective' circumstances). Forgetting that these posited constants are constructions fabricated (*parikalpita*) through our attempt to suppress the anxieties and fears which change, impermanence, uncertainty, instability, and death arouse in us, we invest our invented constants with ultimate sanctity and significance. Desire—which is always the expression of a thirst that what now is should become otherwise at some future point—formulates these constants to which it can anchor itself and measure its progress toward that 'otherwise.'

Our actions, emotions, concerns, and orientation are shaped by how we experience, how we cognize. Cognition, we mistakenly believe, consists in the observer 'grasping' (*grāhaka*) or appropriating (*upādāna*) his/her circumstances (*grāhya, viṣaya, gocara*). The problem is not primarily that we grasp physical objects, but rather that we grasp and cling to ideas, theories (*dṛṣṭi*); and those theories invisibly shape and orient the way we confront our experience. In fact, we grasp physical objects precisely because of the theories we have of them and ourselves; theories by which we give value and identity to ourselves through the values and identities we project on the objects. We define ourselves in terms of what we own, what is our own; by our property, just as a thing is defined in physics by its properties. We are our cars, our opinions and beliefs, our clothes, our nationality, our religion, our habits. We think what we possess (physical objects, but especially ideas) makes us what we are. Cognition is a kind of eating, a taking in and swallowing, or appropriation, of what we experience—and, as Fueuerbach wryly remarked, we are what we 'eat.'

Yogācāra does not talk about 'subject and object,' but about 'graspers and what is grasped' (*grāhaka-grāhya*). We project our theories onto our experience in the form of ātman and dharmas in order to maintain an appropriational circuit. We appropriate because we desire, and desire stems from a sense of lack: to desire one must sense that what is desired is presently lacking or not yet fully possessed. According to Buddhism what we fundamentally lack is a 'self,' and our frantic search and grasping for 'things' is at once a sign of our sense of this lack—a way of masking, suppressing or diverting the painful awareness of that lack—and a desperate attempt to fill the void with an acquirable 'identity,' a self which one owns—one's own self. Religions such as Hinduism may formalize and valorize this frantic pursuit, but the same dynamic also drives our most mundane, everyday pursuits, those things we do in order to have or be ourselves. The world that the unenlightened experience is the projection (*pratibimba*) of their own desires and anxieties (Pāli, *āsava*; Skt., *āśrava*). We forge our sense and meaning of the world in our own image and then devote our lives to pursuing and clinging to it. We create our-*selves* through our own projections, and are defined precisely by whatever it is that we are most attached to, such as religious and national allegiances. That is why the easiest way to intensely upset and anger someone is to challenge his/her most cherished beliefs; few subjects elicit as much rancor and passion as religion and politics. Challenging someone's views threatens their very identity, i.e., what it is that they identify themselves to be, what the world and their position within it is, such that it *makes sense* to them. One clings to those identities as an expression of a deep-seated desire for permanence, stability, as a shielding from death. These identities, which are ideas that each individual appropriates through his/her senses, through his/her cognitions, through his/her experience, are the theories each of us lives by, the grounding orientations through and by which we experience the world as we do. When one's ground—the precise ideological soil on which we stand and in which our living orientation to the world and ourselves is nourished and produced—becomes threatened, that disturbs the sense of order and meaning that one projects on the world, an order that one has grasped, apprehended, and now clings to. The more insecure one's hold on those theories, the more intolerant of opposing views one will be, and the more zealously one will advocate one's own view.

Buddhism notes that no matter how seamlessly we seem to project our desires and anxieties, eventually our experience itself challenges us. Everything is impermanent, and whatever is living must inevitably succumb to sickness, old age and/or death. We are driven to be other than we are (i.e., to "improve") and, simultaneously, to maintain ourselves permanently (i.e., to be an immortal soul). We are caught in the incoherence of these two mutually exclusive, opposing drives: We want to change, become otherwise, improve ourselves, and, on the other hand, we want to maintain our-selves as unalterable, immutable, immortal. We want *difference* and *identity* to coincide. Some religions attempt to ameliorate the tension between these two incommensurate impulses by yoking the former into the service of the latter. One strives to improve *in order to* achieve or acquire some desired immutable condition, to find one's way back to a Garden of Eden and recover the fruit of the Tree of (Eternal) Life. One strives to control *change* in order to reach a *changeless* state. In this way of thinking and acting, changelessness becomes the telos of change, thus relativizing and contextualizing all manner of change. The invariant becomes the context, origin, and telos of the variable. While, as we will see in later chapters, some forms of Buddhism also succumbed to this tempting solution, in its more radical and fundamental formulations, Buddhism consistently challenged and critiqued the motives and methods that religions and philosophies used to promote these illusory goals. Rather, one trains oneself to recognize and accept radical variability, especially in its implication that no permanent, immutable *self* has ever or will ever exist. That realization, when experienced at the root of all one's cognitive activities and abilities (*mūla-vijñāna*), is liberation; the after-effect of this realization is nirvāṇa, providing calm and unhindered modes of cognition while one is alive, and freedom from any return to enslaving habits or attachments, and thus freedom from all *saṃsāra*.

Psychologically, pursuit of the *same* involves habitual attachment to repetition and the familiar status quo, while pursuit of *difference* involves restlessness, a craving for new sensations, and novelty. Either extreme harbors dangers, and neither can be maintained indefinitely. Radical change disrupts what we are used to, while routine deadens our senses. We resist changes to the status quo because the illusion of its permanence gives us comfort, and we grow bored and depressed by routinized sameness because we thirst for the excitement and stimulation of novelty. According to Yogācāra, these extremes do not reflect objective circumstances, but rather reveal our interpretive enterprise: To fail to cognize changes with acceptance due to our expectations and frustrations on the one hand, and to fail to see the uniqueness of each and every moment on the other. Caught between these extremes of our own devising (*parikalpita*), we suppress our dissatisfactions, only to reproject them into one set of circumstances after another (*saṃsāra*). For Yogācāra, the appropriational circuit running between grasper and grasped signifies that we are locked inside the narcissism of our own habits (*karma*). Rather than seeing, hearing, smelling, tasting, touching, and thinking our relation to the world in the manner it becomes (*yathābhūtaṃ, tathatā*), we perpetually grasp at our own reflections, mistaking the images (*pratibimba*) in our self-constructed mirror for what is other than ourself. Ironically, in order that our projected images and ideas become graspable and appropriatable, we have to dispossess them, i.e., disown and disavow them as our own projections. If we recognized them as already ours, pursuing them further would be redundant. Only by pretending that they are not ours, can we appropriate them. We use all the means and strategies at our cognitive disposal—such as language, sensation, reason, belief, willful ignorance, hedonistic tone—to maintain this pretense.

To see clearly requires rectifying the way we experience, and to rectify the way we experience requires understanding the *causes and conditions* of experience. To see things as they are actually becoming (*yathābhūtaṃ*) is to be Enlightened or Awakened (*bodhi*). Buddha is the 'Enlightened One' or 'Awakened One,' a human sentient being who achieved the ability to see clearly, and thus he became an exemplar for other sentient beings to emulate. Through insight (*jñāna*), our deepest incessant misinterpretations (*prapañca*) are extinguished, put to rest (*prapañcopaśama*), and experience becomes peaceful. Buddhism is a method (*mārga*) for rectifying our cognitive activities.

To that end, Buddhism has focused on issues of cognition, psychology, epistemology, soterics and ethics. Dharmas are factors of experience, or the phenomena which constitute experience. Therefore the investigation of dharmas can be called 'Buddhist phenomenology.' As we shall see, the affinities between Buddhist phenomenologists and Western phenomenologists are at times striking.

Buddhist phenomenology reached its peak in the Yogācāra school. Yogācārins examined the structure and function of cognition from epistemological, logical, psychological, ethical, and soteric perspectives, and they saw that it was precisely in the realm of cognition that the key problematic diagnosed by Buddhist thought was situated. That problematic is the karmic economy driven by appropriational habits.

What is(n't) Yogācāra?

What is Yogācāra? It has generally been mislabeled as 'idealism.' Many scholars, including D.T. Suzuki, Edward Conze,[1] and others, have constructed elaborate interpretations of its supposed idealistic premises: One Mind creating and tending the whole world, the flat denial that anything whatsoever exists outside the mind, an *ālaya-vijñāna* (warehouse-consciousness) that functions like Jung's collective unconscious, etc.

Technically speaking, the label 'idealism' is too vague to be meaningful. In its broadest usage, the term 'idealism' includes *everything* other than or opposed to materialism, 'materialism' being the belief that matter is the most fundamental reality lying behind everything. Thus 'idealism' includes the full spectrum of philosophical and religious positions distinguishable from materialism, including virtually everything from Deism, Theism, Monotheism, Pantheism, etc., through Monism, Pluralism, Transcendental Idealism, Critical Realism, Rationalism, Vitalism, etc. For previous generations of scholars what was usually meant when Yogācāra was labeled idealism was that it paralleled the metaphysical idealism of the Bradleyan or Vedāntic kind. In the West, the label 'idealism' has been used commonly to highlight three positions or commitments:[2]

1) The mind or some supermental, non-material entity or force *creates* all that exists. This is *metaphysical idealism.*
2) The ultimate ground of all that is or can be conceived is the cognizing subject, such that the subjective self is the one epistemological non-reducible factor. This is a different form of metaphysical idealism, closer to *epistemological idealism.*
3) *Critical epistemological idealism*, as opposed to metaphysical idealism, need not insist on metaphysical or ontological implications, but merely claims that the cognizer shapes his/her experience to such an extent that s/he will never be able to extricate what s/he brings to an experience from what is other to the cognizer. Like can only know like, so what is truly other is essentially and decisively unknowable precisely because it is other, foreign, alien, inscrutable.

As the present work intends to argue, these idealistic positions are thoroughly inappropriate for Yogācāra. Rather than claiming that a cosmic mind creates the universe, they assert, on the contrary, that one only comes to see things as they actually become by 'abandoning' or destroying (*vyāvṛti*) the mind.[3] Rather than holding the self or subject as non-reducible, their project aims precisely at the deconstruction and overthrowing of the cognitive conditions that give rise to the delusion of self-hood. Rather than declare the Other essentially unknowable, Yogācāra invites us to erase the mirror that blocks our view, and thus see the Other completely and unobstructedly, which is to say, no longer as an Other at all.

However, the initial stages of their analysis follow a similar trajectory to that typically found in epistemological idealism. Like critical epistemological idealists, such as Kant, Husserl , and Merleau-Ponty, they insist that we not lose sight of the fact that everything we know, everything we consider or posit, everything we affirm and deny, occurs to us *in consciousness.* The status and value that we attribute to those things which appear in consciousness, therefore, depends on consciousness, so that even the notion that "things exist external to my consciousness" is a notion conceived, affirmed, or denied in consciousness.

This, however, does not lead Yogācāra to the conclusion that consciousness itself is *ultimately* real (*paramārtha-sat*), much less the *only* reality. On the contrary, it is precisely this closure or narcissistic self-referentiality of consciousness that they identify as our most fundamental problem, and the formidable system they have erected aims at the disruption and elimination of that closure. *For Yogācāra 'mind' is the problem, not the solution.* What is reduced in consciousness is not simply and purely consciousness itself, as the French phenomenologists Merleau-Ponty and Levinas repeatedly remind us. Thus the key Yogācāric phrase *vijñapti-mātra* does not mean (as is often touted in scholarly literature) that 'consciousness alone exists,' but rather that 'all our efforts to get beyond ourselves are nothing but projections of our consciousness.' Yogācārins treat the term *vijñapti-mātra* as an epistemic caution, not an ontological pronouncement. Having suspended the ontological query that leads either to idealism or materialism, they instead are interested in uncovering why we generate and attach to such positions in the first place. Insofar as either position might lead to attachment, Yogācāra clearly and forthrightly rejects both of them. Subsequent chapters will delve into this further.

While it is not uncommon for Western philosophical systems to begin with ontological commitments or assumptions (this is especially true in Theological philosophy, but generally true in other forms as well, including Analytic Philosophy which has bestowed a virtual ontological status on language and 'statements') and secondarily to generate epistemological criteria and methods whereby those commitments or assumptions can be verified, in India the situation is reversed. Indian philosophers, including the theologians, begin with epistemology (*pramāṇa*), and only once they have satisfactorily established the criteria for valid means of knowledge can they move on to making ontological, metaphysical or ethical claims. The various Indian schools and sects, Buddhist as well as non-Buddhist, spent at least as much time arguing over what constituted valid means of knowledge as they did arguing about other matters. Yogācāra's central concern with epistemological issues, then, should be seen in this light. All Indian schools accepted the proposition that if one relied on invalid *pramāṇa*, then whatever one proposed or accepted consequently would be invalid as well. Yogācāra argued that the errors made by its opponents were rooted in faulty epistemology, and therefore the Yogācārins concentrated their efforts there. More importantly, since the soteric efficacy of Buddhism itself rested on the question of correct cognition, there could be no more momentous endeavor than epistemology. Again, since all Indian thinkers agreed on the fundamental and primary role of epistemology, this alone does not distinguish Yogācāra from them, nor does it justify calling Yogācārins idealists. What does differentiate Yogācāra from the other Indian schools is its rigorous insistence that the very endeavor of epistemology is itself always an act of cognitive constitution, as are whatever ontological and ethical norms emerge as its consequence. We shall have occasion in later chapters to discuss Yogācāra epistemology more thoroughly.

If they are not idealists, what are they? What do they posit as real, if anything? Part Five will address these questions in depth.

Alterity

As to the 'identity' of Yogācāra, like the self and dharmas Yogācārins deconstruct, the Yogācāric identity displays an alterity (*anyathātvam*). No single monolithic doctrinal system can univocally answer, by itself, to the name Yogācāra. Many texts and doctrinal positions, disseminated throughout a number of cultures in a variety of languages, identified themselves or may be identified by us as Yogācāric or Yogācāra-influenced. The fictitious 'origins of Yogācāra' story relayed by tradition that traces its origins to two half-brothers, Asaṅga and Vasubandhu, and the former's 'teacher', Maitreya,[4] does not explain the existence of texts such as the *Saṅdhinirmocana Sūtra*, certain *Prajñā-pāramitā Sūtras*, etc., which were already circulating all the 'characteristic' Yogācāra doctrines a century or more before these two half-brothers lived. Moreover, to assume a conceptual identity between Asaṅga and Vasubandhu, much less between either or both of them and their later commentators and interpreters (Sthiramati, Dharmapāla, Hsüan-tsang, etc.) is to risk egregiously misunderstanding one or all of them.

After Vasubandhu Yogācāra developed in two distinct directions:

1) A logico-epistemic tradition, exemplified by such thinkers as Dignāga, Dharmakīrti, Śāntarakṣita, and Ratnakīrti;
2) An Abhidharmic psychology, exemplified by such thinkers as Sthiramati, Dharmapāla, Hsüan-tsang, and Vinītadeva.

Several Yogācāra notions were severely attacked by other Buddhists, especially the notion of *ālaya-vijñāna*, which was denounced as something akin to the Hindu notions of *ātman* (permanent, invariant self) and *prakṛti* (primordial substrative nature from which all mental, emotional and physical things evolve). Eventually the critiques became so entrenched that the Abhidharma direction atrophied, and by the eighth century had been eclipsed by (1) the logico-epistemic tradition (which had the good sense to use the term *citta-santāna*, "mind-stream," instead of *ālaya-vijñāna*, for what amounted to a streamlined version of the same idea) as well as (2) a hybrid school that combined basic Yogācāra doctrines with Tathāgatagarbha thought. Key works of the hybrid school include the *Laṅkāvatāra Sūtra*, *Ratnagotravibhāga* (*Uttaratantra*), and in China the *Awakening of Faith.*

In the sixth and seventh centuries Chinese Buddhism was dominated by several competing forms of Yogācāra. A major schism during those centuries between orthodox versions of Yogācāra and Tathāgatagarbha hybrid versions was finally settled in the eighth century, the century following Hsüan-tsang, in favor of a hybrid version that became doctrinally definitive for all subsequent forms of East Asian Buddhism. Yogācāra ideas were also studied and classified in Tibet. The Nyingma and Dzog Chen schools settled on a hybrid version similar to the Chinese Tathāgatagarbha hybrid; the Gelugpas subdivided Yogācāra into a number of different types and considered them preparatory teachings for studying Prāsaṅgika Madhyamaka, which Gelugpa's ranked as the highest Buddhist teaching. The Tibetans, however, tended to view the logico-epistemological tradition as distinct from Yogācāra proper.

The problem of trying to treat Yogācāra thought as univocal and homogenous is compounded by the lack of agreement between the Chinese and Tibetan traditions on whom to consider to be the authors of various seminal Yogācāra texts, especially in relation to the question of Maitreya. Some Chinese and Central Asian Buddhists,[5] it seems, were attracted to the notion of an ontological Buddha-nature which they associated with the *tathāgata-garbha* (potential for Buddhahood). Originally tathāgatagarbha seems to have signified the 'embryonic' potential for Buddhahood inherent in sentient beings; the term functioned as a guarantee that merely by being a sentient being one had the capacity to reach enlightenment and become a Buddha. This was because Buddhahood signified that one had reached a complete understanding of what it means to be a sentient being (and, arguably, that is all that Awakening means). Thus any sentient being capable of analyzing its own situation had the raw materials required to Awaken (*bodhi*). As Tathāgatagarbha thought developed it was transformed into a notion of the pristine original nature of Reality. Texts of this latter tradition, such as the *Ratnagotravibhāga*, were eventually ascribed by the Central Asians to Maitreya, thus combining and blending Tathāgatagarbha thought with the authors and thought of Yogācāra.[6] Authorship and author-ity are inseparable in religious traditions, hence the common practice of introducing pseudepigraphic or 'apocryphal' texts to lend authority and history to novel claims. The Chinese tradition follows an earlier Central Asian tradition, reported by Fa-tsang, ascribing the *Ratnagotra* to Sāramati,[7] not Maitreya. Yogācāra's self-alterity is marked by such conflicts of ascription and interpretation.

Philosophically speaking, the key insight that Yogācāra introduced to Indian Buddhism was the deconstruction of identity into alterity. In disputes between previous Buddhist schools, there emerged a seemingly perpetual vacillation between notions of immutable identities and continuities on the one hand, and radical difference and discontinuity on the other hand.[8] Buddhism thus presented Yogācāra with the dilemma of deciding whether to privilege identity or difference. Since Buddhism had always emphasized impermanence, the scales were slightly tipped in favor of differentialism. However, Buddhism also adhered to the principle of a Middle Way between extremes, and thus neither the continuous nor discontinuous could be given final imprimatur. Yogācāra resolved the problem by displacing identity with the notion of alterity. As we shall see later, what makes this move so intriguing to (post-)modern readers is not simply that Yogācāra anticipated the readings and critiques of Husserlian phenomenology proposed by Levinas, Derrida, et al., but that it conceived of alterity in *causal terms*. This is significant, since German and French phenomenology has by and large ignored or bracketed the question of causality altogether, perhaps to its own detriment.

When the *Ch'eng wei-shih lun* appeared in 659, a number of competing Yogācāric schools in China were battling out doctrines based on what Hsüan-tsang rightly considered deficient and misleading translations. For example, the types of Yogācāra that arose in the sixth century from the translations of Bodhiruci, Ratnamati, and Paramārtha, especially the influential works of the latter's school (such as the *Awakening of Faith*) were attempts at blending Yogācāric notions such as the *ālaya-vijñāna* (warehouse consciousness) with *tathāgata-garbha* thought. The *Ch'eng wei-shih lun* displaces Tathāgatagarbha ideology by deploying 'orthodox' Yogācāra categories to account for the sorts of issues that had come to be associated with Tathāgatagarbha.[9] In fact the term 'tathāgatagarbha' never occurs in the *Ch'eng wei-shih lun.*

The *Ch'eng wei-shih lun* is only one of seventy seven texts that Hsüan-tsang introduced to rectify Chinese deviance from "authentic" Buddhism. It forms part of a sizable collection of texts by Hsüan-tsang and, in a larger scope, part of a larger body of Yogācāric Chinese texts produced over a number of centuries by many translators, many of whom championed viewpoints at odds with each other. In an even larger scope, it is one text among an even larger number of texts in a variety of languages that appeared from the third or fourth century until today, all of which may be called Yogācāra. No single text would or should pretend to speak for all of them. Many directly confront and oppose the stated positions of other Yogācāra texts. One may even argue that the *Ch'eng wei-shih lun* is not definitive for Hsüan-tsang's own thought, that other texts, for instance the *Yogācārabhūmi* or *Prajñāpāramitā* texts such as the *Heart Sutra*, were much closer to his heart and his way of thinking.[10]

Despite this alterity and proliferation of Yogācāric 'identities,' Yogācāra does display a certain methodological consistency, and it is this methodology that I characterize as 'phenomenology.'

Notes

1 In fact, Conze's treatment of 'The Yogācārins' in his *Buddhist Thought In India*, chapter III.3, is mostly drawn from Suzuki. However even while Suzuki understands Yogācāra as a form of idealism, he sees it as inferior to Zen and the teachings of the *Laṅkāvatāra Sūtra* since it falls short of what he calls their "absolute idealism" (*Studies in the Laṅkāvatāra Sūtra*, Boulder: Prajñā Press, 1981 rpt. of the 1930 edition, pp. 102-3 and *passim*).

2 For a more detailed discussion of these points see my article on 'Yogācāra Buddhism' in the *Routledge Encyclopedia of Philosophy*, 1998.

3 Scholars have argued the meaning of *vyāvṛti* in *Triṃśikā* verse 5 (*Tasya vyāvṛtir-arhattve...*), and without entering the full spectrum of that debate, I cite some of the meanings offered in Monier-Williams' *Sanskrit-English Dictionary*, p. 1039:

> to become separated or singled out from... to be dispersed (as an army)... to turn away from, part from, get rid of... to diverge from... to turn around, revolve... to sink (as the sun)... to come to an end, cease, perish, disappear... to destroy or annul (an enemy or rule)... to wish or intend to liberate one's self from or get rid of...

None of these alternatives would allow one to construe the *vyāvṛti* of consciousness as either a valorization or reification of consciousness or mind.

4 Whether this Maitreya is a real person (= human), or a *nirmāṇa-kāya* manifestation that 'inspired' Asaṅga in some less than (or more than, depending on your perspective) in-the-flesh manner is still argued by scholars. No position on that will be taken here.

5 The role of Central Asian Buddhists in the development of Tathāgatagarbha thought is still unclear, as unfortunately is much of Central Asian Buddhism. It has been speculated that due to their location they could have been recipients and transmitters of Gnostic, Manichean and Nestorian ideas; and there are some significant similarities between Tathāgatagarbha thought and those systems. A predominant number of the important Buddhist missionaries and early Chinese Buddhist thinkers either came from Central Asia or were of Central Asian descent, among the best known being Kumārajīva, Ratnamati, Chi-tsang, Fa-tsang, etc.

6 On the *Ratnagotra*, cf. *Uttaratantra or Ratnagotravibhāga: The Sublime Science of the Great Vehicle to Salvation*, tr. from Tibetan by E. Obermiller (Talent, OR: Canon Publications, 1984), rpt. of *Acta Orientalia*, IX, 1931, which follows the Tibetan tradition; and TAKASAKI Jikido, *A Study on the Ratnagotravibhāga (Uttaratantra) Being a Treatise on the Tathāgatagarbha Theory of Mahāyāna Buddhism* (Rome: Instituto Italiano per Il Medio Ed Estremo Oriente, 1966), which focuses on the Chinese version. Incidentally, the *Ratnagotra* is the only major *Tathāgatagarbha* text (as opposed to hybrid Yogācāra-Tathāgatagarbha works such as the *Laṅkāvatāra Sūtra*) for which we have the original Sanskrit version. It was rediscovered in this century, and is available in a critical edition: *The Ratnagotravibhāga Mahāyānottaratantraśāstra*, ed. by E.H. Johnston (Patna: T. Chowdhury, 1950).

7 Takasaki, *op. cit.*, writes (p. 9):

> Fa-tsang... said... that... Sāramati,... wrote *the Ratnagotravibhāga...* . This report, heard by Fa-tsang from Devaprajña... a monk... from Khotan, is reliable to some extent.

Later, the Central Asians assigned authorship to Maitreya (see *ibid.*, p. 7).

8 Pudgalavādins had argued for some sort of stable personal identity; Sarvāstivādins argued that the essence or self-nature (*svabhāva, svarūpa*) of dharmas existed at all times, past, present and future; Sautrāntikas argued that each moment was radically discrete, and that the seeming continuity between one moment and the next was a fictitious mental interpolation; etc. We will discuss some of the early disputes on continuity and discontinuity preserved in the *Kathā vatthu* in a later chapter.

9 The mixing of the two streams already begins in such texts as the *Laṅkāvatāra sūtra*, but Paramārtha and the translators of his day introduced such a strong version of the blend, that it eventually became fundamental for East Asian Buddhism. Part of Fa-tsang's rejection of Hsüan-tsang, and thus the Hua-yen critique of so-called *fa-hsiang*, revolves around the absence of tathāgata-garbha in their system. The *Ch'eng wei-shih lun* uses the notion of seeds (*bījā*) to describe the sort of metapsychological dynamic that Chinese Buddhists associated with Tathāgatagarbha. The term *tathāgatagarbha* (*ju-lai-tsang* 如來藏) occurs only four times in Hsüan-tsang's translations—T.7.220.921b18;T.31.1597.344a5;T.31.1598.406b28; T.31.1598.416b15 —and not at all in the *Ch'eng wei-shih lun.*

10 We will argue in a later chapter that this text may have assumed its present importance *after* Hsüan-tsang's death and that it was Hsüan-tsang's successor, K'uei-chi, who gave the text its preeminent status.

Chapter Two

Husserl and Merleau-Ponty

Yogācāra is Buddhist phenomenology. The term 'phenomenology' already appeared in the works of Kant and Hegel, but it is the system developed by Edmund Husserl , along with elaborations by his German and French disciples, that generally receives the name Phenomenology in philosophic circles today. The Husserlian and post-husserlian sense of Phenomenology is what the present work follows.

Husserl defined his phenomenology as a Transcendental Idealism, a term Kant had applied to his own philosophy. It meant a critical concern with epistemological issues, a recognition that knowledge comes through cognition, but without implying any metaphysical statement about the nature of reality as dependent on or created by mind. This idealism was 'transcendental' in the sense that its objects of investigation were the transcendental conditions of experience—'transcendental' here meaning nothing more than *what constitutes experience without giving itself as an object in that experience.* For instance, the eye is transcendental to seeing, since though one sees through the eye, the eye does not see itself when looking at things. The eye constitutes vision, but does not show itself in the act of seeing. Even more transcendental to vision is the brain that processes excitations of the optic nerves and constructs the colors and shapes that present themselves to us as what we 'see.' There is nothing either mysterious or ineffable about these transcendentals; they are knowable, understandable, accessible, though we may have to study their structure and functions in detail before reaching adequate or full understanding of them. More importantly, while they are operating transcendentally they may go unnoticed, forgotten, lying in the background, shaping and constructing experiences in which they do not present themselves, like a presupposition. By 'idealism' Husserl meant the region of ideas, thoughts, feelings, etc., in other words, the total spectrum of conscious experience as it is constituted and present to us. 'Transcendental Idealism' thus signifies an investigation of those conditions through which we experience and think that are not readily apparent while we are experiencing and thinking. Husserl's philosophy, therefore, strove to be 'presuppositionless.' Yogācāra shares Husserl's concern with epistemic questions, namely the search for the cognitive roots of knowledge (and ignorance), as should any Buddhist.

Husserl labeled his philosophy 'Transcendental Idealism' based on ontological commitments not shared by Yogācāra. One cannot imagine, for instance, a Yogācārin taking 'zu Sachen selbst' (to the things themselves) as his rallying cry. Husserl was comfortable with the 'idealism' label, but Yogācāra, for reasons already stated, would not be. While insisting that all our knowledge and the very 'sense' we make of anything utterly depends on consciousness, Yogācāra, for instance, accepted and employed the category of *rūpa* (sensate material stuff), which, if they were the sort of thoroughgoing idealists they are usually imputed to be, they should reject. They do seek to remind us that all our theories and sensibilities *about* rūpa occur within consciousness. Since we only know rūpa through our theories of it, i.e., actual perception instantiates embodied conditioning, what we know *as* rūpa is largely our own projection. Since this issue is pivotal to our understanding of Yogācāra's actual intent, it requires careful investigation. We will pick up the Yogācārin discussion of this in a later chapter. We will set the stage for that by turning, in a moment, to the parallel issue as it appears in Husserl's work and the work of some subsequent phenomenologists.

The reader will discover phenomenological and deconstructive terminology liberally spread throughout this work. In fact, a number of key Yogācāra terms have been rendered into the vocabulary of Husserl , Merleau-Ponty, and Derrida. A few words of explanation and caution are thus necessary if the reader is to avoid misunderstanding the purpose of this terminological 'conversion.'

These 'translations' or 'substitutions' should not be taken as a claim that Yogācāra as such and Phenomenology (or Deconstruction, etc.) are interchangeable or neatly reducible to each other, such that one entire system, or even a constellation of concepts and terms from one system can be carried over into the other painlessly and without shedding a drop of doctrinal blood. Husserl is Husserl and Yogācāra is Yogācāra. But 'identity' does not operate that simply. "Husserl" (1859-1938) is a name, a heuristic concatenation, a *prajñapti*, for a stream of writings and formulations, the majority of which remain unpublished, that emerged as a distinct philosophical position (and subsequently a school) around the year 1900 with the publication of the *Logical Investigations*, and continues through his death and post-humous publications, from the extensive Husserlian archives at Louvain to the appropriations and disseminations of his thoughts and formulations by his 'successors,' from Heidegger, Fink, Sartre, and Merleau-Ponty, to the undergraduate reading "Husserl" for the first time. The specific ideas that he advanced altered as he reflected on them—and in Husserl's case in particular his virtual neurosis for rewriting and re-editing make it a marvel that he managed to publish at all; he would continue to revise even his published pieces, as extensive writing in the margins of his own works in his personal library indicate. Thus, despite a general continuity of concerns and a certain continuity of methodology, the term or name "Husserl" does not refer to a monolithic, stable set of propositions or positions, but rather denotes a trajectory within which certain 'characteristic' moves occur; and these characteristics may temporally and/or logically oppose each other. We 'know' Husserl precisely to the degree that we can recite these characteristics and their alterations.

Since Husserl is not even self-identical with himself, meaning that his thinking continued to change, how much less could Yogācāra be self-identical to Husserl? Nonetheless Yogācāra is a form of phenomenology, with affinities to Husserl, Merleau-Ponty, etc., if not identities. Similarities and differences will be pointed out in the text as occasion for explication arises. For now a few of the crucial terms from Husserl , et al., that will be used need to be explained, especially as to the sense(s) in which I use them.

The problem of what a consciousness knows that is not strictly of itself, or put another way, what appears in a specific consciousness that is not reducible to that consciousness itself, arises in Husserl's thought under the name of *hyle*, an ancient Greek term for 'matter' or 'primordial stuff.'

The *Hyle*

As Husserl says at the very beginning of *The Idea of Phenomenology*[1]

> *Natural thinking* in science and everyday life is untroubled by the difficulties concerning the possibility of cognition. *Philosophical thinking* is circumscribed by one's position toward the problems concerning the possibility of cognition.

Husserl immediately locates the philosophical enterprise squarely within the epistemic domain. All other philosophic concerns, such as ontology, metaphysics, ethics, aesthetics, etc., are derivative and will stand (or fall) on epistemic foundations. Specifically, what differentiates the philosophical attitude from the 'natural' or naive attitude is that philosophers *question* why and how cognition is possible, while the naive viewpoint leaves such things unquestioned.

To get to the essence of the 'real' (*reeller*) components of cognition, Husserl proposes a series of 'reductions,' whose nature and relationship will vary in subsequent reformulations through the next few decades; these changes thus constitute one of the variables in the durational alterations known by the name "Husserl." In *Ideas I*, revising his earlier formulations in the *Logical Investigations*, Husserl offers a number of cognitive elements in a less than crystal clear manner. Noesis becomes his term for the psyche, i.e., mentation whose essence is intentionality.[2] Intentionality means that consciousness is driven by an intent, a being-directed-towards, which Husserl describes with the well-known phrase "consciousness is always consciousness of." What this means is that consciousness is never blank or "pure," but always *of* something—a table, an image, a color, an idea. Intentionality also implies for Husserl that the intent of consciousness is the recovery or constitution of meaning (*Sinn*). The essence of a cognition, Husserl argues, is its meaning. But that meaning is noetically constituted, i.e., constituted by the activity of noesis. Noesis is a Greek term related to gnosis, 'knowledge.' For Husserl, noesis signifies an intent-toward-meaning, a movement from a transcendental subject towards an object of cognition.

In secs. 85, 86, 97 and 98 of *Ideas I*, he paints the following picture: Drawing upon the Aristotelean notion of Form and Matter, Husserl says that noesis gives ("animates," "bestows") meaning to raw sensate material (e.g., colors, texture, sounds, etc.), called hyle. The hyle, he says, is *not* intentional. Intentionality constitutes or appropriates what is non-intentional, and thereby imbues it with 'meaning' (*Sinn*). The noetic constitution or appropriation of 'hyletic data' is what produces the noema, or the object as it is cognized.

The notion of the hyle signifies what an individual consciousness encounters that cannot, in some important sense, be reduced to that consciousness, and yet which never appears anywhere else except in a consciousness. This notion, then, is the crux for determining the extent to which Husserlian Phenomenology is idealism. On the one hand Husserl seems to treat the hyle as something objective, something which in itself contributes its essence to an instance of cognition.[3] On the other hand, he declares it a part of the noetic side of cognition.

Husserl's discussion of the hyle has frustrated virtually every commentator, and many applaud his abandonment of the term in his later writings. Though the word 'hyle' disappears, the problematic remained in nearly the same language, indicating it expressed a problem that his phenomenology couldn't 'think' without.[4] For our purposes we will briefly examine its treatment in earlier works.

In the *Idea of Phenomenology*, a series of lectures he gave in 1907 which previewed some of what was to appear in 1913 in *Ideas I* as his revised phenomenology, he states succinctly the issue within which the problem of the hyle arises, in language similar to that which he will use in *Ideas I* when beginning his discussion of the hyle there:[5]

> ...the phenomena of sound perception, even as evident and reduced, demands within the immanent a distinction between *appearance* and *that which appears*. We thus have two absolute data, the givenness of the appearing and the givenness of the object; and the object within this immanence is not immanent in the sense of genuine immanence; it is not a concrete part (*Stück*) of the appearance, i.e., the past phases of the enduring sound are now still objective and yet they are not genuinely contained in the present moment of the appearance. Therefore, we also find in the case of the phenomenon of perception what we found in the case of consciousness of universals, namely, that it is a consciousness which constitutes something self-given which is not contained within what is occurring [in the world] and is not at all found as *cogitatio*.

Within the immanent (i.e., within an experienced, cognitive moment) there are two absolute data: What actually appears in/as cognition and the object imputed to lie behind it. The former is "concrete," while the later is a construction derived from the former. The appearance is always immediately present, here, now. The notion of an object extends through time, and in the example of sound, takes its significance from its temporal context. The *note* G will sound like a tonic if in the key of G or G minor. It will sound like a minor third if in the key E or E minor. It will sound like a fifth in the key of C, and so on. The 'meaning' of the note G, i.e., how it actually sounds and is perceived, is shaped by what has preceded and what will follow it. The note G is "that which appears," i.e., it is an 'object' that is temporally or contextually defined. However, the *tone* G, i.e., the raw sensate appearance that impinges on our awareness, is the hyle. It may be loud or soft, shrill or harmonic. As it impinges on us, we 'fill' it with meaning, which means we reduce it to an object situated in a meaningful context (a melody). 'Reduce' does not necessarily mean 'to lessen' in Husserl's vocabulary, but, reflecting his mathematical background, it denotes performing an operation on something that converts it into something simpler, more basic. The note is 'simpler' than the tone because it seems to carry a context, a ready-made ordering system that assigns it a precise meaning. A tone, because it lacks such a context, carries an air of ambiguity and mystery, a richness that is anything but simple. What is initially encountered in a *moment* of auditory cognition is a tone, but the tone is perceived *as* a note, as a part of a succession of other notes that temporally and logically precede and succeed it. Yet, in actuality, tones only 'appear' (or better put, tones only appear as notes), it is we who 'hear' them as notes. The "perceptual object" is the note, something meaningfully constructed or constituted by noesis. We, the listeners, constitute the context, just as we can scarcely avoid hearing a note occurring in musical passage as part of a melody. In fact, within experience *tones* per se are hard to hear. To hear them one must resist hearing them as a notes. Even playing them in isolation is only to insert them into another type of context, and thus still hearing them as notes.

To restate this for non-musicians, the hyle would be, for Husserl , only what is immediately present. And only what is immediately present is "genuine." The example Husserl offers of a non-genuine cognitive object, namely a 'past' object, is strikingly Yogācāric. Yogācāra also accepts only a present object as genuine, as real. Objects from the past and future are never immediately given, or even remotely given; they are, according to Yogācāra, cognitive constructions (*parikalpita*), which is to say, they are mental fictions.

In *Ideas I* the hyle is described as[6]

> unitary "*sensile*" experiences, "*sensory contents*" such as the data of color, touch, sound, and the like, which we shall no longer confuse with the appearing phases of things, their colour-quality, their roughness, and so forth...

Unlike "the appearing phases of things" (i.e., "that which appears") which are *interpreted* sensations, the hyle are raw, discrete, "unitary," sensate contents, the data that cognition interprets. In experience sounds, colors and so forth appear. We interpret them as signifying things, and then determine that such appearances are the variable 'masks' or 'signs' of a determinate object that lies behind them. That determination is a mental construction, or in Husserl's language, it is noetically constituted. The notion that there are self-identical objects that 'appear' through various phases while in-themselves remaining identical and the same, is not given immediately in experience. Only raw sensate variable data impinges on us, moment after moment. The idea of a self-same object is a 'meaning' that we project; we provide a sense of constancy that is never actually present in sensation. We 'fill' the hyle with our projections, and thereby perceive a meaningful object, i.e., a noema.

A few pages later Husserl offers the following paragraphs, the first of which is entirely in italics:[7]

> The stream of phenomenological being has a twofold bed: a material and a noetic.
>
> Phenomenological reflexions and analyses which specifically concern the material may be called hyletically phenomenological, as, on the other side, those that relate to noetic phases may be referred to as noetically phenomenological. The incomparably more important and fruitful analyses belong to the noetical side.

Yet, in a discussion of the noema, Robert Solomon observes (in parentheses):[8]

> (It is important to stress, even though it is not our topic, that the sensory matter or "hyletic data" of perception are not introduced on the noematic side of the act but rather in the noesis itself. The purpose of this move is precisely to avoid making the sensory into an object.)

Even though this seems to fly in the face of the passage just quoted from Husserl , a case can be made for it; though obviously an opposing case could be made as well.[9]

Noesis is consciousness intending toward its object/meaning. It reacts to and acts upon hyle, and constitutes the noema or noemata (meaningful objects) out of that encounter. The noema is noetically constituted. Husserl's initial phenomenological project was the description and analysis of this process of constitution, and he explored its nuances at great length. His famous *epoche* (bracketing whether the object under consideration exists or not) and the various reductions (eidetic, phenomenological, transcendental) were the methodological tools of that investigation. Put in plain language, Husserl examined how we come to know the world and ourselves in the ways that we do. As an epistemologist, he was also concerned with what are the correct ways to cognize, and how to avoid cognitive errors. His data were never exclusively propositions or mere verbal formulations; instead he repeatedly pushed philosophy to return to the raw sense of experiencing this or that, whether of tactile or imaginary objects (for Husserl unicorns are viable phenomenological objects, since, like everything else he subjected to reductions, whether they exist or not is bracketed). In his phrase, philosophy must return "to the things themselves" (*zum Sachen selbst*).

Returning to Solomon's observation, in part what Solomon contends could be true because, for Husserl , it would be impossible for the noema to ground the hyle, since the hyle and the noesis are 'real' (*reelles*), whereas the noema is the unreal byproduct of their interaction (*Ideas I*, sec. 97). Thus the opposition hyle/noesis is primary to the opposition noesis/noema. The hyle is that which participates with the noesis in the constitution of a noema by allowing itself to be appropriated and reduced by the noesis. But this would still be far less than saying that the hyle is *in* the noetic; it seems that for Husserl this would be too reductionistic.

We needn't wade any further into this hermeneutic morass, since our purpose is an exposition of Yogācāra and not to take sides in controversies over interpretations of Husserlian ideas. But this obvious conflict was introduced to highlight the problems of the hyle. When arriving at the notion of hyle, many commentators suddenly feel that this is their opportunity to decry whatever they see as fundamentally lacking or unsatisfactory in Husserl's thought in general. The hyle becomes their occasion to complain. For instance, while discussing Husserl's notions of 'filling,' self-evidence and time-consciousness, Izchak Miller complains:[10]

> The trouble is that Husserl himself does not pursue the notion of "filling" very far. He seems to be, simply, more comfortable discussing the difference between memory (retention), perception (primal-impression), and anticipation (protention) in terms of the difference in their strength of "self-evidence," or its absence altogether. This is a pity. The connection between Husserl's notion of "hyle" and sensory "filling," on the one hand, and the *experience of causation* (in the primitive, pre-theoretical sense of the latter), on the other, is strong. Pursuing that connection might have yielded a better explication of the notions "hyle" and "filling," notions which still remain for the most part obscure. Perhaps even more importantly, it might have yielded a *phenomenological* account of our experience of causation, an account which is sorely missing in Husserl's theory of our empirical experience.

Rather than perform his own phenomenological investigation of 'causality,' Miller bemoans its conspicuous absence in Husserlian thought because of the strong "connection between" the hyle and our basic sense of cause and effect. Husserl would probably argue that there is no such thing as a "primitive, pre-theoretical sense of" causation, and like Hume, he would see causality as an inferential imputation incommensurate with immediate experience. Causality, in anything other than the formal sense, implies a relationship between two entities across time. If only the present is real and genuinely present in a cognitive act, causality, since it requires the linking of a past object with a future object (one or the other might be present, but never both), can never be given evidentially in perception, but only cognitively constructed, inferred. However, we shall see later that Buddha (if not all Buddhists) *did* argue that efficient causal relationships are capable of being immediately cognized. The Theravādin interpretation of Buddha's enlightenment experience, viz. that he perceived the causes which produce and end 'suffering,' must insist that they are.

Miller associates 'impinging' with the noema, pointing out that at any moment a vast array of 'objects' may be impinging, although we don't perceive them all as objects; i.e., some are background while we gestalt others.[11] But elsewhere[12] Miller characterizes the hyle as "constraints," and again elsewhere[13] he characterizes it as an imposition that, e.g., limits my cognition by making a certain object feel smooth, even if I anticipated it would be rough, or vice versa. Thus the hyle, in principle, serves the function of empirically impelling one to revise one's beliefs and theories. Miller, too, registers his complaint against Husserl's hyle:[14]

> Reasonable as is its role, the notion of hyle is a component of Husserl's account of perception which is most difficult to accommodate within that theory...

We turn to Donn Welton for another example of such complaints:[15]

> As long as the coincidence between *Darstellungsinhalt* [presentational contents] and the given was adequate and as long as meaning, logically characterized, was considered symmetrical with the unmodalized [i.e., athetic, not thetic: thetic = species of cognition, e.g., perceiving, willing, believing, remembering, etc.] perceptual object fulfilling or ratifying it, Husserl had no reason to be concerned with the unique structure of the perceptual object. But once it is seen as inadequate, even for the immanent sphere, we are left with a nasty split between intentional and perceptual object, between "mental" object and concrete object. And second, rather than giving full range to the unique and different way in which a perceptual noema functions, the sense is still characterized as that which the act must animate and bestow [i.e., the noema acts as 'form' to the non-intentional 'matter;' it in-forms it].[16] And as a result we are left with the puzzling problem of how that which we do not directly intend is nevertheless seen and how it can itself initiate a perceptual act. [square brackets mine]

In other words, if Husserl is an ontological dualist, such that an irremediable rift separates the object as I experience it from the object as it is in-itself, then a number of familiar philosophical problems emerge, beginning with the Kantian in-itself that forever remains noumenous and hence finally unknowable. Knowledge, in some sense, becomes paradoxically grounded in the unknowable. Husserl's project of 'returning to the things themselves,' his promise of disclosing and recovering 'essences' would be completely thwarted.

Other incoherencies intrude into his formulations. If 'knowing' is grounded in a consciousness whose immediate experience is essentially intentional (i.e., "consciousness of"), how do non-intentional things announce themselves, and in what way are they given or give themselves to the intentional economy, and by what means might one clearly know what relation obtains between the non-intentional object as cognized (i.e., as appropriated by an intentionality) and the object in itself? That question lies at the crux of Ricouer's and Welton's comments. If meaning (*Sinn*) is 'given' to an object by the noesis, i.e., it is noetically constituted, in what sense (*Sinn*) can one say that the meaning is *of* the object? Do objects (*Stoffe*, 'material [fabric or matter], substance, subject-matter') announce their meanings (and to whom or what?) or are all meanings gifts from noesis? What do the sensory (*sensuelle*) and the sensible (*sinnliche*) finally mean? Does the form-matter model solve or perpetuate these difficulties? Further, if we perceive non-intentional objects as such, then consciousness is not essentially intentional, but only partially intentional,[17] a possibility that some readers of Husserl maintain he advocated.

The notion of the *ālaya-vijñāna* or 'warehouse consciousness' in Yogācāra thought posed some of the same problems. It was considered the fundamental consciousness that acted as a basis for the other seven consciousnesses in the Yogācāra system. The other seven were considered thoroughly intentional, driven by karmic intentionality, but the *ālaya-vijñāna* was considered non-intentional (*anivṛta, avyākta*) even though its major function was to appropriate the karmic consequences of the other seven consciousnesses. Thus the Yogācāra consciousness system (*citta-kalāpa*) consists of seven intentionalities grounded in non-intentionality. Though the non-intentional component here is neither an object as such nor a hyle, the problem of the relation between intentional and non-intentional components of cognition is similar. This problem in its Yogācāric context will be addressed in a later chapter.[18]

Returning to Husserl , as Welton points out, many other technical problems emerge as well. He continues:[19]

> These difficulties also have a disturbing effect on Husserl's discussion of sensation and sense-data. In *Ideas* the hyletic data are considered to be a formless, timeless, immanent, noetic content of consciousness which the act then animates with a representative function. They accounted for the fact that we see the same color, for example, with different intensities and textures—for what Husserl spoke of as adumbrations of profiles. What is amazing, however, is that Husserl considered them not something excluded by the transcendental reduction but rather a noetic "residue" to which we have immediate access from within the reduction. This creates not merely an insurmountable methodological problem, but it also seems to transpose—once the split between intentional object and real object is forced—all the problems of Hume's empiricism into a transcendental phenomenalism.

For Husserl , the 'adumbrations of profiles' are not excluded by bracketing precisely because they constitute experience concretely: We perceive various shades of red "as red," various sweet tastes "as sweet," etc. To dismiss that essential aspect of a perceptual act is to denude perception of something that is evidential within it. Until light is diminished to the point where an object appears grey, a red object will appear 'red' to a perceiver; in fact, that the shades of red differ is usually *not* apparent to a perceiver until some technique or experiment demonstrates the variance and the reliance of color perception on different types of lighting. Is the hyle the raw redness that occurs in a perception of any shade of red? Or is each shade, no matter how slight the chromatic shift, a different hyle? But Welton's criticism is not merely empirical, but systemic. The problem Welton discerns is that Husserl at various times treats hyle as that which initiates noetic activity (by being what the noetic act acts upon), and at other times he treats it as the "residue" within a noetic act. It is as if the hyle both preceded the noetic act and was also produced by or in conjunction with it. This means that the hyle "red" might be considered, in one context, to be the particular sensation of a given moment, and in another context, the 'redness' that subtends differing perceptions of a red object. Husserl , thus, seems to be employing a single term to denote intrinsically opposed notions. Sometimes hyle carries particularistic implications, at other times it functions as a type of universal. Sometimes it assumes a type of primacy, at other times it seems derivative.

A Buddhist might retort that what drives Husserl to insist that these "residues" be retained within the reduction is his presupposed commitment to the metaphysical integrity of the 'object' as such. In other words, Husserl is assuming that the *variations* produced by altering perspectives (or by applying the recommended reductions) are variations of an integral identity; these variations in perspective display modalities of an 'invariant essence' of which these variations are themselves aspects. Since Buddhists deny such essentialism, they would say that a red sun and a red apple are entirely discrete and distinct, not merely as nouns, but adjectivally as well. The red of the apple and the red of the sun are only metaphorically or tropologically identifiable and collapsible one into the other; in actuality, what we call 'red' in each case is different. Even the redness of an apple changes (as lighting conditions change, etc.), and each shade and type of 'red' is distinct. The same is true of a 'red' sun. Each perceptual variation signifies a unique, discrete particular situation. There is, then, no such inherent or universal property or class called 'redness' in which particular things participate; there are only momentary, discrete cognitions of red-things, blue-things, etc. Nor is the 'object,' or noun, detachable from its adjective. The red-apple is not a red-sun, just as it is not a green-apple. Without the apple, the red does not appear; without the red, the apple does not appear. The separation of 'red' from 'apple' is a deceptive trick of language, arising from our ability to separate the words 'red' and 'apple' from each other while overlooking that the term 'red apple' is really a tautology. The apparent separability of the two terms conceals an actual inseparability that may only be 'separated' in language.

Welton, however, suggests a different way of formulating the difficulty he has located in Husserl , and describes the "insurmountable methodological problem" in a note:[20]

> Asemissen has described this problem with clarity and force: "Without the corporeality of the body (*Leiblichkeit*) the sensations are absolutely nothing. The body (*Leib*) is the medium of their being. In that Husserl bracketed the body in the reduction in order to gain the pure ego and pure consciousness as the proper domain of phenomenology, he, at the same time, without knowing it, also bracketed the sensations.... Just as the pure ego does not have a body, so it also does not have and cannot have sensations. And just as the body is not an

immanent (*reel*) content of consciousness, so neither can the sensation be such. Husserl's talk of sensations after the bracketing of the body as content of pure consciousness is not a phenomenological discovery." Herman Asemissen, *Strukturanalytische Probleme der Wahrnehmung in der Phänomenologie Husserls*, Kantstudien Erg. H. (Cologne, 1957), 73:34.

In other words, deprived of a body, the transcendental ego also loses the sensorium, the stuff from which noesis constructs meaning. It would thereby be left to perceive nothing but empty, nonsensate formalities. One can, however, imagine Husserl replying that this criticism begs the question, and invites a chicken-and-egg dilemma. What, after all, guarantees the body as either the medium or necessary a priori condition of sensation? Through what is that known? The body's necessary role may be established a posteriori, but its givenness is only self-evident, if at all, after reflection. The evidence is not unquestionably self-evident, since most people seem completely unaware that *everything* they know, think, experience, etc. has come to them through/as the sensorium (especially if we grant with the Buddhists that the mind is only another sense, functioning in a similar manner to the other sense organs). The necessity of the body for experience was clearly not self-evident to Plato, nor to most Christian theologians. They argued that the cognition of ideas involved an entirely different order of experience than 'sensation' (which is restricted to the five senses), distinguishable mainly because ideas could be constant, eternally true, whereas sensations were always temporally subject to generation and decay. Actually the ideas *qua* cognition were conceded to arise and cease temporally, but the *essence* of the idea, that essence which the idea is about (e.g., a geometric theorem) was eternal, always already true whether or not cognized at such and such a time by anyone or not. While sensory objects are fleeting, ephemeral, ideational objects are eternal. Since these two types of objects are of such radically different orders, the faculty through which the ideational type of cognition occurs had to be radically different from the sensory cognizer, and thus divorceable from the body as such. Hence I can know true things without recourse to my body.

In opposition to this sort of idealistic epistemological claim, Husserl's phenomenology denies that knowledge can arise anywhere else than in experience.[21]

The determination that the body is always present during sensation is arrived at in reflection, by a reduction which exposes its ubiquity. To insist beforehand, as Asemissen is doing, that the body must remain non-bracketed, is to naively buy into a causal theory of sensation, or some such theoretical construction before it has been phenomenologically grounded. Simply put, to a large extent, the body remains transcendentally poised through much of the experience for which it is the ground. The reductions and bracketing are advocated by Husserl precisely to establish the body as a transcendental ground (transcendental = constituting experience, though not itself given in experience). Not only do we become oblivious to basic sensations (such as the pressure of your chair or seat against your backside as you have been reading this) which involves being unaware of the full role of the body in constituting the experience of reading, but we can sit, for instance, in a movie house, and not only lose track of our bodily sensations as such, but forget we are physically in a movie house, in such and such a seat, in such and such a city, etc. We may become so engrossed in the film, so deeply identified with one of the characters, that we literally forget we are anywhere other than a ghostly witness to the world of the movie. The body through which we are participating in the film has become entirely transcendental. Husserl's reduction aims at bringing us back to an awareness of body.

One may refocus Asemmisen's criticism, arguing that the problem is not directly the failure to recognize the importance of the body, but rather that in some of the later developments in Husserl's thinking, particularly in *Cartesian Meditations*, where he explicitly announces that the transcendentals he is seeking through his method are specifically the transcendental ego and the transcendental object, his agenda obscures rather discloses the importance of body. This criticism would have some legitimacy, but it would need to be balanced against such bodily-related issues in the later Husserl as the history of ideas becoming embodied conditioning, 'sediments.' Such reflections indicate that Husserl's notion of body was much more deeply contextual than the mere mechanical explanation for sensation. It is that which embodies what has preceded it, which is why we today 'perceive' the world in largely Cartesian terms, for instance, without always recognizing that as such.

A loss of the role of the body, it should be pointed out, never occurs in Buddhism. Even in its most idealistic strains, Buddhism remains committed to at least a Dharma-*kāya*, i.e., a dharma-*body* that interacts with the dharma-dhātu (the field of experience). Even texts are considered em-bodied (*nikāya*).

The force of Asemissen's argument lies in the epistemic chicken and egg. If consciousness requires the body in order to sense, then a pure consciousness or a pure ego would be unable to ground or recover the transcendental body, since the very sensations that the consciousness would have to reflect upon are always already bodily sensations that have not yet been bracketed, and that once bracketed can now be said to 'belong' to consciousness and not to the body per se. The body can only ground itself tautologically, in which case the role of consciousness as something other or at least distinguishable from body becomes problematic. And even if consciousness and body are equated in some sense, as Merleau-Ponty reads Husserl as doing, the problem of grounding remains, and another issue arises: Why then does consciousness know itself as other than body, and why can body be conceived as other than consciousness?

It is ironic that the attack against Husserl here focuses on the body, since ironically the body's importance was one of the revelations that Husserl gave us. Though the rediscovery of the body is often associated with Buytendjik or Husserl's leading French disciple, Merleau-Ponty, already in *Ideas II*, completed sometime before 1925,[22] Husserl delved deeply into the question of the body, though it is true that through it he tried to approach the pure-ego, pure consciousness, *Geist* and the transcendental self that is further quested after in the *Cartesian Meditations* (1928-31).

Levinas, who studied with both Husserl and Heidegger in Germany and introduced their thought to France, characterizes this aspect of Husserl's thought thus:[23]

> ...Concrete life is not the solipsist's life of a consciousness closed upon itself. Concrete being is not what exists for only one consciousness. In the very idea of concrete being is contained the idea of an intersubjective world. If we limit ourselves to describing the constitution of objects in an individual consciousness, in an *ego*, we will never reach objects as they are in concrete life but will reach only an abstraction. The reduction of an *ego*, the *egological reduction*, can only be a first step toward phenomenology. We must also discover "others" and the intersubjective world. A phenomenological intuition of the life of others, a reflection by *Einfühlung* [empathy, sympathetic understanding] opens the field of transcendental intersubjectivity and completes the work of the philosophical intuition of subjectivity. Here again, the problems of the constitution of the world will arise. [square brackets mine]

Interestingly, although what he says here is faithful to Husserl's texts, his predictions about the direction in which Phenomenology would have to go reveals more about where Levinas himself has gone—i.e., to an interpersonal ethic 'otherwise than being'—than Husserl , who doggedly pursued the transcendental ego in his *Cartesian Meditations* and sought to discover it still constituting the Lived-World (*Lebenswelt*) in *The Crisis of European Sciences.*[24]

Levinas continues:[25]

> The works of Husserl published so far make only very brief mentions of an intersubjective reduction.[26] We can do no more than repeat what Husserl has said. However, we believe that this intersubjective reduction and all the problems that arise from it have much preoccupied Husserl . He has studied the *Einfühlung*, the intuition through which intersubjectivity becomes accessible; he has described the role played in the *Einfühlung* by the perception of our body and its analogy with the body of others; he has analyzed the life which manifests in this other body a type of existence analogous to mine. Finally, he has examined the characteristic of the constitution proper to intersubjectivity, the conscious reality without which no existence at all would be possible. Although his unpublished works have been very influential, we are not authorized to use them prior to their publication[27]

Ricouer's essay summarizing *Ideas II* fleshes out some of the then 'unpublished' details.[28]

> As phenomenology reaches for its heights, the hyle is forgotten, buried beneath transcendental egos, intersubjective empathies, personal and cultural bodies, and a reflectivity so intent on catching itself in the act of intending that

it virtually overlooks that which it originally intended toward. Why then, should I want to pick up this obscure, difficult term "hyle" for a discussion of Yogācāra, which has more than enough of its own obscurities?

Ricouer notes that kinesthetic sensations, such as eye or hand movements, differ from "the sensations of color, roughness or warmth that immediately constitute the aspects of the thing itself." The "apprehensions" or intentive "meanings" which pass through these two types of sensation differ: The hyletic sensations, in some sense, are transitive, i.e., they go into the object itself, even if abstractly.[29]

> But on the other hand, kinesthetic sensations do not go beyond themselves into the thing itself but rather reveal my corporeal existence to me. And yet this revelation of the body still remains a function of the percept, no longer as hyle—as brute matter—it is true, but rather as "motivating" circumstance in the course of perception. The thing can appear to me in this way if I turn my head or my eyes, or if I extend my hand. Thus, the same course of perception refers in a polar manner back to a stream of kinesthetic subjective processes as a typical group of circumstances, for the relation of motivation, the lived-through reference to a motivated order of appearances, still plays a part in the apprehension of "things." And since it is possible for all other sensations to be "motivated" in a spontaneous motion of my body, the totality of sensoriality appears as a unique operation with a double pole. At one end, sensoriality goes beyond itself into the spatial [? *sic*] order of the things; at the other end, it is motivated in the free spontaneity of a course of conscious processes.

The dividing line, as Ricouer sketches it, runs between sensation in a sensory world, presumably 'constrained' and 'resistant' to being otherwise than it is, and a mental, noetic realm of 'free spontaneity.' Husserl's possible dualism has become here only bipolar, and that bipolarity is determined by the direction of intent in terms of the body: If it intends outward, externally, it is (merely) sensory; if it folds back into the body and the noetic processes which constitute it, then it is 'kinesthetic.'

Despite the neatness, this again smacks of platonism as it involves the separation of intellect from sensation, assigning each the same platonic hierarchical values, viz., sensation is mundane while *Geist cum Nous cum ésprit* is freedom, even though 'mind' is here at least nominally classified as 'sensation' as well. This, as was the case with Levinas, is more indicative of Ricouer's own characteristic issues than a totally fair depiction of Husserl , though, again, like Levinas, the basic details here *are accurate*.

In these texts by Levinas and Ricouer that are designed to serve as expository presentations of Husserl's thought rather than platforms for their own philosophizing, it is precisely at the point where the hyle or its substitute appears that those concerns most intimately connected with the philosophies that they subsequently developed emerge. In the place of the hyle, instead of becoming constrained by it, new philosophies emerge through its critique. Even

Miller envisions here an opening for a new philosophy, a phenomenology of causality, though, unlike Ricoeur of Levinas, he laments Husserl's failure to develop it rather than seizing that as an occasion to pursue it himself.

In Ricouer's case, a new manner of describing the possibilities of noetic constitution elevates its status. As will, as spontaneous, as capable of becoming free from hyletic restraints, the role of the noesis is displaced by the sensor, that which can determine how everything in its orbit is motivated. It spills over into the 'space' beyond it, imbuing meaning. The unintentional is now at most an invisible, unimportant blank screen to be filled with intentionality, with meaning, by an in-forming noesis. And, for Ricouer, this sensor will soon play background to the self's self-reflection. In Ricouer's hands, noesis becomes more and more autonomous, liberated from hyletic restraints. For Ricouer, freedom and narcissism seem to converge. That the self's freedom remains perpetually challenged by the 'unwilling,' the 'involuntary,' the 'unconscious'—in other words, one is always opposed and constrained by things one can never fully control by deliberate, conscious decisions—became the fundamental problematic that Ricouer wrestled with in many of his works.

If meaning is not simply an invention of noetic intentionality, what is its source? It should not be shocking then that in his latest writings Husserl turns to history, for, with the empty selfhood that he was etching through his narrowed search for a transcendental ego, where else could he go for constitutive meanings? The self's structures, its meanings, are, as Husserl points out in his later writings, sedimented meanings, embodied history. In later chapters we will see that these sedimentations are called *bījās* (seeds) and *vāsanā* (perfumings; habitual residue) by Yogācāra.

We note as a point of interest that for both Husserl and Yogācāra the present moment alone was real, and yet the present is never anything other than an embodied history. Phenomenology reached history through the moment by an innovative method of reflection on and description of that moment. Conversely, Yogācāra arose out of a history, namely, Buddhist tradition, that carried a karmic theory of historical embodiment (see Part Three). The primacy of the moment was bequeathed to them through that history; and they reinterpreted that history in the light of an epistemology that, like Husserl , scrutinizes the structure of a moment of cognition in order to recover its context and horizons.[30] For both Husserl and Yogācāra understanding involves a leap from the present as mere presence to embodied history, to the uncovering and reworking of habitual sedimentations—and in the case of Yogācāra, the ultimate elimination of habit (*karma*) altogether.

Even when Husserl's interpreters substitute another term for 'hyle,' its basic function seems to be retained. It is that *within* consciousness that remains irreducible (at least in its entirety) to consciousness itself. While it is *in* consciousness (i.e., cognized), it announces itself as an impingement, a constraint; it conveys a 'sense' of arriving from without. It is that which "demands within the immanent a distinction between *appearance* and *that which appears*." The relation between consciousness and the hyle is neither genitive nor ablative; whether it is locative, instrumental or dative is arguable and unclear; it is accusative.

Curiously, as we have seen, the notion of the hyle has become emblematic of an epistemological object that not only provokes the deepest concerns of different writers (e.g., Levinas and Ricouer), but that also seems to simultaneously conceal itself while revealing itself. Even as it poses itself as an object for interpretation, authors envelop it in their own projections, interpreting and contextualizing it according to their own presuppositions and agendas. While it presents itself as that in cognition which resists being reduced to a subjective whim, its epistemological ambiguity (is it noetic? noemic? something other? etc.) invites interpretive reductions. For Levinas it became emblematic of the Other; for Ricoueur it marked the unwilling that confronts the individual will; for Miller, it is symptomatic of a failure to grapple with realist and causal issues; etc. Each takes the hyletic object and reduces it to a noema, all the while claiming that it is the hyle, not the noema, that they are grappling with, or as Nietzsche might say, they have reduced so-called reality to their interpretations of reality and now mistake their interpretations for reality itself.

It is the effort to avoid that sort of cognitive reductionism, rather than ontological idealism, that lies behind the Yogācāra focus on cognitive closure (*vijñapti-mātra*). Yogācāra proposes a hermeneutics not just for reading or even perception, but for experience in general. Since the problem lies in the propensities and compulsions that impel us to attribute some status or another to the 'objects' we cognize and experience, Yogācāra suggests that it would be more useful and soterically pertinent to examine the causes which produce those impulses—with an aim towards erasing them—than to endlessly insist on the metaphysical validity of one theory after another. Their use of the term *vijñapti-mātra* is thus hermeneutical and soteric, since its aim is the rupture and definitive overcoming of cognitive closure, not its reification.

As propounded by Husserl, the hyle confounds any attempt to determine whether it is or is not idealistic. That it is appropriated by consciousness, though not created by consciousness, implies that it is not idealistic. That it functions in the noetic reductions, even if as a "residue," implies idealistic affinities. Some would try to sort this ambivalence out by claiming that Husserl's position is epistemic idealism, mixed with a metaphysical realism, a categorization to which Husserl would not be totally averse. But that does little to really resolve the ambivalence which intensifies when we note that the key term, 'constitution,' was also treated ambiguously by Husserl , indicating both (1) formulated by, and (2) appropriated by. Thus for something to be 'noetically constituted' could mean either to be constructed wholly or partly by the noetic act, or it could mean that noesis has taken something in to work it over and imbue it with 'meaning.'

Those who followed Husserl were glad to see him finally abandon the term. But the hyle is not so easily abandoned. It forms the limit case, that which makes the perception of a red shirt *as* red imperative.[31] It also implies something stubbornly irreducible to the capricious consciousness that would make it over entirely in its (i.e., the consciousness') own image. It is through the hyle, moreover, that the other, including the other mind, is known—whether by analogy or in some other fashion. The *Ch'eng wei-shih lun* will introduce the hyle at just such junctures. I will use it to translate the Chinese character *chih* 質, which means 'matter, substance.'

Before turning to Merleau-Ponty's reworking of the problem of the hyle, let me summarize what has been argued so far.

1) The hyle is for phenomenology a marginal concern that paradoxically stands at its heart. It is the ontological pivot of the phenomenological rallying cry "to the things themselves" (*zum Sachen selbst*), insofar as those things are conceived to be 'essences.' The ontological meaning (*Sinn*) of 'essence' epistemologically hinges on the status of the hyle. Hence, for instance, even the slight confusion as to whether the hyle is to be situated on the noetic side or the 'objective' side—compounded with the epistemic dependency of the noema on the noesis—puts Husserl's notion of a transcendental object into question. What in experience, aside from a hyle, would announce that something not given in experience is actually constituting it? The methodology with which Husserl attempts to recover the thing itself, namely transcendental objects, is finally and simply *imputational.* Through correlations by way of eidetic variations and the various reductions suggested by Husserl , his method promises in a quasi-mathematical manner that the route to the thing itself consists of reducing the range of cognitive possibilities to their *common denominator*, which is their "essence," and that this cognitively constructed and/or recovered "essence" is the *meaning* (*Sinn*) of the 'thing,' such that the thing itself qua referent of a cognitive act (*Bedeutung*) is nothing other than this *Sinn.* But what sort of thing has Husserl returned to? The answer to that lies in precisely how we choose to define the hyle! Its supposed non-intentional status, its objective resistance (i.e., it imposes some limits on the ability of a consciousness to manipulate or reconfigure it), and so on, sets, within Husserl's system, the limit of what can be called 'objective.'
2) The notion of the hyle arises, as the examples I've offered illustrate, at precisely the key moments in the reflections of Husserl's interpreters where their own most distinctive views emerge. Further, these moments, in their most profound sense, mark and define the exact points at which these interpretations begin to grow away from Husserl . Levinas' *autre/autrui* (other/Other), Ricouer's *involontaire* (unwilling), etc., are notions that sprout from reflections on Husserl's hyle, and thus put them at once in proximity to and at a distance from Husserl . This notion of distance became thematic for Levinas, whose work has influenced Derrida's ruminations on that very theme. The Freudian 'anxiety of influence' that Harold Bloom has applied to reading and thinking in general draws on a similar problematic.

As such, the hyle becomes not only a thematic for the notion of intersubjectivity in phenomenology, but a crucial instantiation of Husserlian intersubjectivity in relation to his interpreters. Vasubandhu's *Viṃśatikā* (Twenty Verses) repeatedly emphasizes in a variety of ways that karma is intersubjective and that the course of each and every stream of consciousness (*vijñāna-santāna*, i.e., the changing individual) is profoundly influenced by its relations with other consciousness streams. We will see in a later chapter how the *Ch'eng wei-shih lun* adopts some of Vasubandhu's arguments from the *Viṃśatikā* to develop this theme.

3) The hyle provides Husserl's transcendental idealism with something that allows it to claim that it is *more* than idealism. It provides a grain of 'realism.' It announces, in as muted a tone as can be mustered, that the other can never be truly and fully reduced to one's self, i.e., you are never simply and exclusively my idea of you (and vice versa). Thus Husserl's 'idealism' should be seen as an epistemological idealism that contextualizes itself by emphatically *denying* ontological or metaphysical idealism.

Given that all cognitive claims must survive or perish on the tenability of their epistemological foundations, any system seeking to give itself a stable foundation from which to make claims must begin by establishing criteria for valid cognitions. Since cognition, as both Husserl and Yogācāra argue, is constituted through *consciousness of* as its absolutely necessary condition (without a notion of consciousness, the notion of a cognitive claim becomes absurd), a cognitive foundation that remains faithful to this epistemological demand must, at least initially, begin as some sort of epistemological idealism. The history of philosophy, both East and West, seems to bear this out: Whether Descartes' grounding of certainty in thinking, Buddha's grounding of his claims in cognitive experience, or Mencius' grounding of the Confucian ethos in a theory of Mind Nature, etc. From there one may either 'leap' to a realism, as for instance Russell does when he concedes that solipsism is an air-tight argument to be rejected not because it is logically untenable, but because, in his view, more is to be gained by *assuming* that a real, non-mental world exists than by assuming its opposite. Or one may try to construct an epistemological bridge from cognitive idealism to some sort of realism (or a 'beyond idealism' or 'otherwise than idealism'), as Kant, Husserl, etc. attempted. One can seek to establish a method that goes from cognitive experience to apodictic truths to veridical truth: That is precisely what Husserl attempted with his notion of "Evidence."

Yogācāra, on the other hand, views such bridge-building as unnecessary and irrelevant, since what is required is an Awakening from the muddled-headed dream state within which such bridges are designed. Epistemological bridge-building within a dream does not awaken one from the dream. It merely provides the dream with a certain type of content. Yogācāra's focus remains the karmic problem, a problem they describe as cognitive closure (*saṃvṛti*). Awakened cognition requires more than a program that 'redefines' cognition; it follows from a radical turnaround of the way we cognize (*āśraya-paravṛtti*).

The Husserlian pursuit of 'Evidence' is one approach for correcting cognitive problems. Another possibility is the Yogācāra option, which is (1) to recognize and explore the issue of cognitive criteria along with their attendant problems, (2) to demonstrate the untenability of any cognitive closure that follows from accepting an ontological commitment, (3) to offer a methodology for the erasure of that closure, and yet (4) to resist either positing or committing to any ontological 'position' or 'definitive/definable' reality 'otherwise than' the cognitive dimension. They resist since to define or describe something requires immediately inducting that 'something' into a cognitive, linguistic sphere from which that definition or description, qua definition/description, can never escape. Like Mādhyamika and many important Twentieth Century Western thinkers, Yogācāra contends that language never directly refers to anything but itself.

By refusing to entertain "the split between intentional object and real object," the problems which Welton expressed as having "a disturbing effect" on Husserl's epistemology are avoided. Thus, Yogācārins distinguish eight modalities of consciousness, the first seven of which are intentional, while the eighth or root consciousness, the *ālaya-vijñāna*, is non-intentional, but appropriative of the other seven. For Yogācāra, appropriation (*upādāna*) is a more fundamental category than intentionality. It is precisely this appropriational aspect that needs to be neutralized, according to their view.

The Intentional Arc

As we have seen, for Husserl the interplay between *what is perceived* and *that which perceives*, along with the demand for a distinction between *an appearance* and *that which appears*, was situated in philosophically difficult waters. By emphasizing the noetic constitution of experience over the hyletic contribution, his transcendental idealism talked about materiality but never took matter seriously, either on a causal or ontological level. His attempts in his later writings to overcome the problems of this interplay by recourse to the notions of the sensorial body, intersubjectivity (cf. *Ideen II*), and intentionality as a process of historical sedimentations (cf. *The Crisis of European Sciences*), i.e., *historical intentionality*, proliferated a sophisticated grid of concepts and descriptive terms that brought a degree of clarity to the experiencer-experienced issues without solving them altogether. To the end he maintained the primacy of noesis in the constitution of experience, and even with his elaborations of the historical origins of attitudes and their intentionalities, he still treated the transcendental subject as the ultimate source of consciousness, and, thus, all experience.

With the transcendental ego as its source, intentionality reached out toward its intentional objects, reducing the 'hyletic data' to noemata, unified perceptual contents. Often Husserl seems to presuppose an analogy to a spotlight or beacon that shines on ("animates," "bestows") a certain hyletic field, and by illuminating it making it accessible to perceptual apprehension (*auffassung*).

Bouncing off a realm of transcendental objects, noesis constitutes a noema, a reductive, synthetic representation that cojoins the transcendental object with the transcendental subject at once *in* consciousness and *as* consciousness.

By criticizing the beacon model, which seemed to posit the source of the intentional act as originating each moment in the transcendental subject, Merleau-Ponty utilized other Husserlian elements to 'solve' some of the husserlian dilemmas by reconfiguring them through the notion of the 'intentional arc,' a term he borrowed from others. The term itself occurs only twice in *The Phenomenology of Perception*, both in the same paragraph. He writes:[32]

> Beneath intelligence as beneath perception, we discover a more fundamental function, 'a vector mobile in all directions like a searchlight, one through which we can direct ourselves toward anything, in or outside ourselves, and display a form of behavior in relation to that object'.[33] Yet the analogy of the searchlight is inadequate, since it presupposes given objects on to which the beam plays, whereas the nuclear function to which we refer, before bringing objects to our sight or knowledge, makes them exist in a more intimate sense, for us. Let us therefore say rather, borrowing a term from other works,[34] that the life of consciousness—cognitive life, the life of desire or perceptual life—is subtended by an 'intentional arc' which projects round about us our past, our future, our human setting, our physical, ideological and moral situation, or rather which results in our being situated in all these respects. It is this intentional arc which brings about the unity of the senses, of intelligence, of sensibility and motility. And it is this which 'goes limp' in illness.

Such a potent unitary force, in order to be understood more clearly, obviously requires some unpacking. To simplify to the extreme, according to Merleau-Ponty our body is a lived-body, meaning that it *is not* a material entity but a sensorially, cognitively charged intending movement (the cogito is not an "I think," *je pense*, but an "I can," *je peux*). The limits of the body are not epidermal, but cognitive. I live the feelings of my body, such that my body at this moment includes my inner feelings (memories, discomforts, kinesthetic perceptions, etc.) as well as the time and space in which I am located. My lived-body is as large as the room, or ideational space it occupies at any moment. The visualizing aspect of my body is not limited to the tissues and humours of my eyes, but includes my intent-to-see and extends through my current field of vision, and likewise for all my senses. What my body perceives is called by Merleau-Ponty the 'perceptual field.' The field is a complex network of embodied intentionalities, i.e., potential and actual meanings, primarily characterizable through the distinction between foreground or *Gestalt*, and background or *Ganzfeld.* My lived-body intends towards my perceptual field, shifting focus so that various gestalts arise from and return to their background. So far this accords fully with Husserl's analysis and seems to be another variation of the searchlight model. But Merleau-Ponty reminds us that the perceptual field also embodies intentionalities. Thus, it is not simply that we, as transcendental subjects, or even lived-bodies always initiate intentionality and hence acts of cognition. The perceptual field also intends toward us. As we reach towards it, it is also reaching toward us. I condition my world as it is conditioning me. Intentionality is, then, not a unilinear act projected outwards that bounces back and reflects itself into the form of a noema. Intentionality circulates in a circuit that flows from the world into me, from me into the world, and back again and again. My subjectivity is a cognitive location in an intentional circuit, its center to be sure, but not its only source.

Since my lived-body includes all that I perceive through my body at any moment, it coincides hyletically with the perceptual field, and yet *in perception* there clearly exists a palpable distinction between the lived-body and the perceptual field. This elusive but real margin—which always places itself between my lived-body and my perceptual field—is the region of ambiguity in which 'meanings' are forged. Meanings, for Merleau-Ponty, are our attempts to tame and curtail this foundational ambiguity.

Thus, Merleau-Ponty solves Husserl's hyletic problematic dialectically. This interaction between body, field and the intentional consciousness which arises through their 'contact' (*sparśa*) is also foundational for Buddhism. The *Ch'eng wei-shih lun* in fact sees the world as constituted precisely of this arc, as we will see in later chapters.

Once the region of consciousness becomes the critical region of inquiry—and any type of thought which attempts to ground itself in actual experience has no choice but to begin with such inquiries—certain consequences logically follow. Merleau-Ponty begins the third section of his *Phenomenology of Perception*, entitled "The Thing and the Natural World," with the following paragraph:[35]

> A THING has 'characteristics' or 'properties' which are stable, even if they do not entirely serve to define it, and we propose to approach the phenomenon of reality by studying perceptual constants. A thing has in the first place *its* size and *its* shape throughout variations of perspective which are merely apparent. We do not attribute these appearances to the object itself, but regard them as an accidental feature of our relations with it, and not as being of it. What do we mean by this, and on what basis do we judge that form or size are the form and size *of the object*?

Here is evident also a seeming reduction to the noetic side of experience. But something new has been emphasized. What is of import for our study is not how momentarily Merleau-Ponty will demonstrate that these and other seeming constants are not constant at all, but rather the necessary and radical move of bracketing the object as such from being a substance in which perceptible properties inhere (a point, I argued above, also made by Buddhism).

The move he makes—reemphasizing something already in Husserl but sometimes obscured or overlooked in Husserl's metalogical language—points to the fact that all experience is interpretation. To perceive, to cognize is to interpret. He challenges the naiveté with which we appropriate the world through experience. Thus, he proposes a *hermeneutics of cognition.* This, too, is the Yogācāra proposal.

A thing is a thing precisely insofar as it is a thing *for me*, or for a lived-body. Whatever does not enter the cognitive sphere(s) in one form or another simply does not exist; or better put, cognition is always potentially cognition of all that can be. The thing, thus, is always a correlate of my (or someone's) body.

Merleau-Ponty writes:[36]

> However, we have not exhausted the meaning of the 'thing' by defining it as the correlative of our body and our life. After all, we grasp the unity of our body only in that of the thing, and it is by taking things as our starting point that our hands, eyes and all our sense-organs appear to us as so many interchangeable instruments. The body by itself, the body at rest is merely an obscure mass, and we perceive it as a precise and identifiable being when it moves towards a thing, and in so far as it is intentionally projected outwards, and even then this perception is never more than incidental and marginal to consciousness, the centre of which is occupied with things and the world. One cannot, as we have said, conceive any perceived thing without someone to perceive it. But the fact remains that the thing presents itself to the person who perceives it as a thing in itself, and thus poses the problem of the genuine *in-itself-for-us...* The thing holds itself aloof from us and remains self-sufficient. This will become clear if we suspend our ordinary preoccupations and pay a metaphysical and disinterested attention to it. It is then hostile and alien, no longer an interlocuter, but a resolutely silent Other, a Self which evades us no less than does intimacy with an outside consciousness. The thing and the world... are offered to perceptual communication as is a familiar face with an expression which is immediately understood.[37] But then a face expresses something only through the arrangements of the colours and the lights which make it up, the meaning of the gaze being not behind the eyes, but in them, and a touch of colour more or less is all the painter needs in order to transform the facial expression of a portrait. In the work of his earlier years, Cézanne tried to paint the expression first and foremost, and that is why he never caught it. He gradually learned that expression is the language of the thing itself and springs from its configuration.

While the thing is always *of my experience*, it nonetheless has an integrity of its own. There is no 'red' per se, only specific things with specific textures, sensory configurations, etc. that are or aren't red, in such a way that the red itself is always a specific red, a 'woolen red' or 'sunset red,' etc. Most importantly, it always gives itself to me in some configurational combination. Not only is there no red per se, but there is no isolated object per se either. Each specific thing is embedded in a perceptual context. The depths of meaning are, like "the meaning of the gaze," not buried behind appearance, but expressed, disclosed in the appearance itself. This is why painting, drama, and other representational arts, when well crafted, can evoke the deepest resonances from an audience or viewer. A person's comportment, gestures, mannerisms, facial expressions, etc., reveal meanings that, because they are being revealed at the very moment they are occurring, are not hidden at all (except to those who fail to recognize and respond to them). To know the thing beyond a merely psychological sphere of fleeting subjective impressions means not to construct an ideological representation, but rather to take account of the full range of its possibilities, i.e., its configurational limits through an circuit of intentionalities flowing between a lived-body and a perceptual field.

This, for Merleau-Ponty, takes us beyond the usual attempts to 'define' a certain thing, to delimit it and reduce it to its definition; in a move prefiguring the poststructuralist thinkers to come twenty or more years later, Merleau-Ponty calls this quality of a thing its 'style'.[38]

> What needs to be elucidated, then, is this primary comprehension of the world. The natural world, we said, is the schema of intersensory relations.... The world has its unity, although the mind may not have succeeded in inter-relating its facets and in integrating them into the conception of a flat projection. This unity is comparable with that of an individual whom I recognize because he is recognizable in an unchallengeably self-evident way, before I ever succeed in stating the formula governing his character, because he retains the same style in everything he says and does, even though he may change his place or his opinions. A style is a certain manner of dealing with situation, which I identify or understand in an individual or in a writer, by taking over that manner myself in a sort of imitative way, even though I may be quite unable to define it; and in any case a definition, correct though it may be, never provides an exact equivalent, and is never of interest to any but those who have already had the actual experience. I experience the unity of the world as I recognize a style. Yet even so the style of a person, or a town, does not remain constant for me. After ten years of friendship, even independently of any changes brought about by age, I seem to be dealing with a different person, and after ten years of living in a district, it is as if I were in a different one.

The world seems to change, but what of the self that cognizes it? Neither, finally, can the world or myself be seen as ineluctably constant. For me to perceive the world or things within it as changing, I must fix myself as the constant against which their variations and alterations are measured. In order to see the variability of my inner world, the world (e.g., notions of role, gender, religious affiliation, age, profession, psychological values, etc.) must be fixed as constant. Both change, but their changes must be temporarily suspended in order that either be known. In order to see variables, constants must be fixed. This is an invariant epistemological axiom. Thus, knowledge at its roots is constituted by a kind of blindness, an imaginary pretending that fixes constants out of variables.

Later, again prefiguring the deconstructive poststructural notion of alterity (first brought to the forefront of French thinking by Levinas), particularly of the self and consciousness, Merleau-Ponty, striking a non-Wittgensteinian stance, writes:[39]

> To ask oneself whether the world is real is to fail to understand what one is asking, since the world is not a sum of things which might always be called into question, but the inexhaustible reservoir from which things are drawn.... There could not possibly be error where there is not yet truth, but reality, and not yet necessity, but facticity. Correspondingly, we must refuse to attribute to perceptual consciousness the full possession of itself, and that immanence which would rule out any possible illusion. If hallucinations are to be possible, it is necessary that consciousness should, at some moment, cease to know what it is doing, otherwise it would be conscious of constituting an illusion, and would not stand by it, so there would no longer be any illusion at all. And if, as we have said, the illusory thing and the true thing do not have the same structure, for the patient to assent to the illusion, he must forget or repress the true world, and cease to refer back to it, and retain at least the ability to revert to the primitive confusion of the true and the false.

Merleau-Ponty has here broached, in a style very like Yogācāra Buddhism, the problem of cognitive closure. We will look at how he treats closure momentarily, but first let us finish out this passage, to see what he says about alterity.

> Yet we do not cut consciousness off from itself, which would preclude all progress of knowledge beyond primary opinion, and especially the philosophic examination of primary opinion as the basis of knowledge. All that is required is that the coincidence of myself with myself, as it is achieved in the *cogito*, shall never be a real coincidence, but merely an intentional and presumptive one.[40] In fact, between myself who have just thought this, and myself who am thinking that I have thought it, there is interposed already a thickness of duration, so that I may always doubt whether that thought which has already passed was indeed such as I now see it to have been. Since, furthermore, I have no other evidence of my past than present testimony and yet do have the idea of a past, I have no reason to set the unreflective, as an unknowable, over against the reflection which I bring to bear on it. But my confidence in reflection amounts in the last resort to my accepting and acting on the fact of temporality, and the fact of the world as the invariable framework of all illusion and all disillusion: I know myself only in so far as I am inherent in time and in the world, that is, I know myself only in my ambiguity.

My self is my self-otherness, and between my lived-body and 'myself' as a perceptual field I always approach myself through the region of ambiguity.

But the 'confidence,' the self-evidential appearance that hinges on the blind spots in my consciousness, envelops me. In the following two passages, Merleau-Ponty suggests how cognitive closure functions. Curiously, in both passages which are separated by more than fifty pages in the English translation, he makes reference to Spinoza.

> My thought, my self-evident truth is not one fact among others, but a value-fact which envelops and conditions every other possible one. There is no other world

> possible in the sense in which mine is, not because mine is necessary as Spinoza thought, but because any 'other world' that I might try to conceive would set limits to this one, would be found on its boundaries, and would consequently merely fuse with it.[41]
>
> Between this experience of red which I have, and that about which other people speak to me, no direct comparison will ever be possible. I am here in my own point of view, and since all experience, in so far as it derives from impression, is in the same way strictly my own, it seems that a unique and unduplicated subject enfolds them all. Suppose I formulate a thought, the God of Spinoza, for example: this thought as it is in my living experience is a certain landscape to which no one will ever have access, even if, moreover, I manage to enter into a discussion with a friend on the subject of Spinoza's God.... [However,] my thought about the God of Spinoza is only apparently a strictly unique experience, for it is the concretion of a certain cultural world, the Spinozist philosophy, or of a certain philosophic style in which I immediately recognize a 'Spinozist' idea.[42]

Closure consists of a boundary to which, in the profoundest sense, there can never be an outside. What lies beyond the horizons of my experience is not simply unknown—since within the closure there is a category for 'unknowns' into which notions of the unknown can be classified and placed. The 'beyond' simply does not occur in any way whatsoever. Should something not already inside the boundaries of the closure make an appearance, it "would consequently merely fuse with it," i.e., take up some place within the closure, even if by doing so it reconfigures the closure and its borders.

While I have seemingly set out the phenomenological positions of two Western philosophers, the reader will discover in later chapters that we have in fact set the stage for a proper appreciation of Yogācāra. If there is one striking difference between Husserl and Merleau-Ponty on the one hand and Yogācāra Buddhism on the other, it would concern the function and type or 'reductions' employed by each.

Though one may find glimpses of Husserl's eidetic reduction, phenomenological reduction, transcendental reduction, etc., in Yogācāra, one will find a reduction in Yogācāra not readily evident as such in the Western phenomenologists. I shall call this the 'karmic reduction.'

Consequent on the preeminent function already assigned, at Buddhism's inception, to consciousness in the Buddhist analysis of karma, Yogācāra's emphasis on 'nothing but cognition' (*vijñapti-mātra*) serves to highlight a reductive description and analysis of the human condition to a moral sphere of advantageous (*kuśala*) and disadvantageous (*akuśala*) actions and attitudes (*kāya-vāc-manas karma*). Further, while causality is conspicuously absent from Husserl's reductions, it lies at the core of Yogācāra phenomenology. Yogācāra put forth the notion of psychosophic closure (*vijñapti-mātra*) as a way of making us aware that our karmic dilemma only occurs in that sphere; that positing a sense of externality to things is only the most basic of the self-blinding moves that keeps us enmeshed in the appropriational web we conceive of as a world. Their denial of externality does not entail the reification of that denial into an ontological position; it is rather an existential disruptive force. Yogācāra attempted something which has not yet been successfully accomplished in Western thought, which is *epistemo-ethics,* i.e., a liberational ethics fully derived from a coherent epistemology grounded in radical experience. They displace ontology and thus ground ethics in something other than metaphysics—in fact, they ground it in the very necessity of bracketing metaphysics. This will become clearer in later chapters.

We next turn to those basic Buddhist models which served as the soil from which the seed of Yogācāra grew.

Notes

1 *The Idea of Phenomenology*, tr. by William Alston and George Nakhnikian (Hague: Martinus Nijhoff, 1964), p. 1.

2 He says 'noesis' is preferable to 'psyche' because the latter may include or allude to aspects of consciousness which are non-intentional. *Ideas*, tr. by W.R. Boyce Gibson (NY: Collier Books, 1962), Sec. 85, p. 230.

3 This is a difficult characterization in part because Husserl claims that objectivity itself is noetically constituted.

4 Ricouer, for instance, discussing *Ideas II,* writes:

> At this point in our analysis, the question of the "reality" of the psyche is raised again. If the unformed hyle is the localizable face of consciousness, then is not the whole unity to be found on the side of the body-thing that, somehow, is the place of implantation for this strange reverse side of consciousness? We find once more that [we come to] the problem of the quasi-reality of the psychic... with the resources of a new analysis of the localized psyche.
>
> Husserl presents the problem in the following terms: "How is the content of sensation linked to the constituted thing, and how does the body, which is a material thing, have the contents of sensations in and of itself (*in und auf sich*)?" (II, p. 154). This way of putting the question is striking. The problem is to know what the attribution of psychic qualities to the body understood as a thing signifies. [This is] a question of taking up the physicalistic understanding of the body in order to attribute sensations to it. In what sense does the body have the property of sensing? In what sense does sensibility belong to the body? Thus, the possibility of psycho-physics and psycho-physiology is in question and not the situating of an irreducible existential experience.

In other words, one's own consciousness alone does not solipsistically construct the world. Hence the question arises as to how what is other than consciousness, e.g., the physical body, becomes involved in the conscious, sensorial world. Posed as such, the question is of course very Cartesian. Ricouer continues:

> ... Husserl... considers the psycho-physical problem of the concomitant variations of a series of mechanical stimuli and of a series of localized tactile sensations. The example presupposes that the thing perceived is grasped on the most objective level, since the "stimulus" in terms of physics is related to the body as a field of sensations. Under this condition a relation of dependence is instituted between "states" and "circumstances," which is, as we know, the essential thing for objective thought. And since the field of localized sensations is always occupied by sensations, the variations of the stimulus bring about variations of "states," a

permanent "property" of being-affected. Thus, "sensoriality (*Empfindsamkeit*) is constituted entirely as a 'conditioned' or psycho-physical property" (II, p. 155).

Thus, to perceive a body as a thing is also "to co-apprehend" (*Mit-auffassung*) its sensoriality, for certain sensorial fields belong to this body-thing. This belonging is not an existential phenomenon external to the series of appearances but rather is an application of the relation of dependence (*wenn-so*).... Hence, Husserl sees no opposition between the body as a thing and the body as lived through. To understand and animate body is to grasp a... concrete unity in respect to which the physical and the aesthetic are only abstractions.

Paul Ricouer, *Husserl: An Analysis of His Phenomenology*, tr. by Edward Ballard and Lester Embree (Evanston: Northwestern University Press, 1967), pp. 62-63. This leads to the problem of intersubjectivity, where the problem of the hyle is now displaced by the problem of knowing another person. Broached in *Ideas I*, expanded in *Ideas II*, deepened in the Fifth of the *Cartesian Meditations* and opened to all of history in *The Crisis of European Sciences*, 'intersubjectivity' becomes pivotal to phenomenological thinking.

5 *Op. cit.*, p. 9. He reiterates the same basic themes, in greater detail, in *Ideas I*. Cf. especially sec. 85.

6*Ideas*, p. 226.

7*Ibid.*, p. 230.

8 Robert C. Solomon, "Husserl's Concept of the Noema," in *Husserl: Expositions and Appraisals*, eds. Frederick Elliston and Peter McCormick (Notre Dame: University of Notre Dame Press, 1977), p. 170.

9 The references Solomon directs us to as support for his contention are secondary sources, not Husserl's own texts. His note reads:

> See Gurwitsch, "On the Intentionality of Consciousness," in *Studies* [*in Phenomenology and Psychology* (Evanston: Northwestern University Press, 1966]; A. Lingis, "Hyletic Data," in *Analecta Husserliana* (Dordrecht, Holland: D. Reidel, 1972), 2: 96-103...

and he concludes with a reference to Frege's "On Sense and Reference." *Ibid.*, p. 180 n. 23.

10Izchak Miller, *Husserl: Perception & Temporal Awareness* (Cambridge, MA: MIT Press, 1984), p. 135.

11*Ibid.*, p. 136.

12*Ibid.*, p. 129.

13*Ibid.*, pp. 52-53.

14 *Ibid.*, p. 53.

15 "Structure and Genesis in Husserl's Phenomenology," in *Husserl: Expositions and Appraisals*, p. 57.

16Cf. *Ideas I*, sec. 85; *Ibid.*, esp. pp. 226-227.

17 How that which we don't intend *intrudes* on us is discussed at great length by Paul Ricoeur in his *Freedom and Nature* (the French title literally means: The Voluntary and the Involuntary, or the Willing and the Unwilling).

18 See Part V, ch. 20.

19 "Structure and Genesis...," *op. cit.*

20*Ibid.*, p. 68 n. 13.

21 Already in his earliest work, *Philosophy of Arithmetic*, he rejected the Platonic interpretation of numbers and mathematical entities as existents or essences apart from experience; for Husserl, mathematical truths are *constructed*, not eternal verities. This is, however, another thorny area where Husserlian scholars lock horns. Husserl attempted to avoid both the extreme of platonism and its opposing extreme (at that time) of psychologism. Logicists and platonists accused him of psychologism, and psychologistics accused him of logicism and 'realistic platonism.' This is not the place to explore this problem. Cf. J.N. Mohanty's *Husserl & Frege* (Bloomington: University of Indiana Press, 1982), esp. ch 2; Also Emmanuel Levinas, *The Theory of Intuition in Husserl's Phenomenology*, tr. by André Orianne (Evanston: Northwestern University Press, 1973), esp. ch. 6.

22 Published posthumously as *Phänomenologische Untersuchungen zur Konstitution*, in *Husserliana IV*, ed. Walter Biemel (Hague, 1952), and later a revised version by Karl Schuhmann was released

(*HusserlianasIII,* 1 and 2, 1976). *Ideas II* has been translated into English by R. Rojcewicz and A. Schuwer, *Ideas Pertaining to a Pure Phenomenology and to a Phenomenological Philosophy: Second Book,* (Dordrecht: Kluwer Academic Publishers, 1989). Kluwer also offers F. Kersten's translation of *Ideas I,* which provides a useful counterpoint to Gibson's earlier version.

23 Levinas, *op. cit.*, p. 150f.

24 Levinas is undoubtedly the leading phenomenological ethicist. His works have only in recent years received serious attention in the States. His *Totality and Infinity: an Essay on Exteriority,* tr. by Alphonso Lingis (Pittsburgh: Duquesne University Press, 1969) "distinguish[es] between the idea of totality and the idea of infinity, and affirm[s] the philosophical primacy of the idea of infinity" (p. 26). Subjectivity is presented "as welcoming the Other, as hospitality" (p. 27). While Heidegger only initially saw things ready-at-hand, Levinas sees the self as originarily embedded in an alien world, a place of Others.

> But the world as I originally experience it is not a logical system [of objective impartial relations]... in which no term takes precedence over the rest. My primary experience is definitely biased and egocentric. I take precedence over the various objects I find around me, and in so far as my experience is normal, I learn to manipulate and control them to my advantage, either as a member of a group which I identify with myself or simply as myself alone. In general, these objects are at my disposal, and I am free to play with them, live on them, and to enjoy them at my pleasure.
>
> Levinas finds that this primordial experience of enjoyment (*jouissance*) has been neglected by Heidegger and other phenomenologists. (p. 12, from John Wild's introduction).

It could be the source of enjoyment of the other, but it is also the root of abuse, oppression, war and exploitation. Thus his book is about how to relate to the Other. The theme is continued and expanded in *Otherwise than Being or Beyond Essence,* tr. by A. Lingis (The Hague: Martinus Nijhoff, 1981), in which he makes it even clearer that ethics is primary to ontology.

In the last decade or so more of his works have been translated into English, and the effort continues: *Existence and Existents,* tr. A. Lingis (The Hague: Martinus Nijhoff, 1978); *Discovering Existence with Husserl,* tr. Richard Cohen (Bloomington: Indiana University Press, 1988); *Ethics and Infinity: Conversations with Philippe Nemo,* tr. Richard Cohen (Pittsburgh: Dusquesne University Press, 1985); *Time and the Other,* tr. Richard Cohen (Pittsburgh: Duquesne University Press, 1987); and *Nine Talmudic Readings,* tr. Annette Aronowicz (Bloomington: Indiana University Press, 1990); *Collected Philosophical Works,* tr. Alphonso Lingis (Dordrecht: Kluwer Academic Publishers, 1993; *Beyond the Verse: Talmudic Readings and Lectures,* tr. Gary D. Mole (Bloomington: Indiana University Press, 1994); *In the Time of the Nations,* tr. Michael B. Smith (Bloomington: Indiana University Press, 1994); *Difficult Freedom,* tr. Seán Hand (Baltimore: Johns Hopkins University Press, 1990); *Outside the Subject,* tr. Michael B. Smith (Stanford: Stanford University Press, 1993). For selections, cf. *The Levinas Reader,* ed. Sean Hand (Oxford and Cambridge: Blackwell, 1992) and *Basic Philosophical Writings,* ed. Adriaan T. Peperzak, Simon Churchill, Robert Bernasconi (Bloomington: Indiana University Press, 1996). A few insightful secondary works, primarily collections of essays, have also appeared: *The Provocation of Levinas - Rethinking the Other,* eds. Robert Bernasconi and David Wood (London & New York: Routledge, 1988) [includes recent bibliography of translations of Levinas' essays and secondary works]; *Face to Face with Levinas,* ed. Richard Cohen (Albany: SUNY Press, 1986); *Re-Reading Levinas,* ed. Robert Bernasconi and Simon Critchley (Bloomington: Indiana University Press, 1991).

25 *The Theory of Intuition...* , p. 151.

26 Levinas cites *Ideas I,* secs. 29, 45, 48, 49, 66; and "Philosophie als strenge Wissenschaft," in *Logos,* I (1910), p. 313, translated by Quentin Lauer, in *Edmund Husserl: Phenomenology and the Crisis of Philosophy* (NY: Harper & Row, 1965), p. 108.

27 In the light of this summary of Husserl's notion of intersubjectivity, Wild's remarks in his introduction to Levinas' Totality and Infinity are pertinent:

The other person as he comes before me in a face to face encounter is not an *alter ego*, another self with different properties and accidents but in all essential respects like me. This may be the expression of an optimistic hope from a self-centered point of view which is often verified. The other may, indeed, turn out to be, on the surface at least, merely an analogue of myself. But not necessarily! I may find him to be inhabiting a world that is basically other than mine and to be essentially different from me... .

... these traditional theories are one-sidedly egocentric and reductive. None of them does justice to the other as I meet him for the first time in his strangeness face to face. I see this countenance before me nude and bare. He is present in the flesh. But as Levinas points out in his revealing description, there is also a sense of distance and even absence in his questioning glance.... Of course, I may simply treat him as a different version of myself, or, if I have the power, place him under my categories and use him for my purposes. But this means reducing him to what he is not. How can I coexist with him and still leave his otherness intact? (p. 13)

28 Paul Ricouer, *Husserl: An Analysis of His Phenomenology, op. cit.*, Ch. 3.

29 *Ibid.*, p. 46f.

30 In Buddhist thought Vasubandhu's follower, Dignāga, honed this epistemology and its logic into a finely tuned instrument. In the West, Derrida challenged Husserl's moment of presence by deconstructing it into its différance, its alterity. As I will argue in a later chapter, Yogācāra also ultimately deconstructs the present into a flow of alterity.

31 Yogācāra and the Ch'eng wei-shih lun correctly argue that color is not a property inhering in a thing, but a contribution of the mind to perception. Locke argued similarly in his distinction of primary and secondary qualities. Modern empirical studies have shown that there is no one-to-one correspondence between light frequencies and the perception of specific colors, and that colors are codings of visual data which happen in the brain, not in the things. The first chapter of Merleau-Ponty's Phenomenology of Perception argues the case well, and physical studies done since only further confirm the empirical research he cites.

32 Phenomenology of Perception, tr. by Colin Smith (London: Routledge & Kegan Paul, 1978), p. 135f. In this chapter my discussion of Merleau-Ponty will be confined to statements found in that text. However, recognizing that this early text was not his final word, that many of the notions introduced there, such as the tacit cogito and the body image, were later radically reshaped or abandoned, and that later notions, such as the chiasm and 'wild ontology,' redefine the scope and application of earlier concepts, the use of Merleau-Ponty in the following chapters will treat his work from this 'revised' reading.

33 He cites Hochheimer, [Analyse eines Seeleblinden von der Sprache,] p. 69. No other publication data is given.

34 He gives this note: "Cf. Fischer, Raum-Zeitstruktur und Denkstörung in der Schizophrenie, p. 250." His bibliography offers the following data: "Ztschr, f. d. ges. Neurologie und Psychiatrie, 1930."

35 Op. cit., p. 299.

36 Ibid., p. 322.

37 It is noteworthy that the 'face' became important in the philosophy of Levinas due to the sort of primacy that Merleau-Ponty is recognizing in it here. For Levinas, the face carries not only ontological primacy, but more importantly ethical primacy—since I respond to the face as an Other who embodies and presents itself to me as a person to whom I have responsibilities. Levinas' reflections on the face serve as a foundational cornerstone in his arguments for the primacy of ethics over ontology.

38 Ibid., p. 327.

39 Ibid., pp. 344f.

40 He is alluding to the Hegelian notion of authentic self as coincidence of the self with the self, which Hegel deems possible, and yet defers to the end of history (implying it is not yet achievable).

41 Ibid., p. 398.

42 Ibid., p. 451.

Part Two

The Four Basic Buddhist Models in India

What is it that the common people take for knowledge? What do they want when they want "knowledge" ? Nothing more than this: Something strange is to be reduced to something *familiar*... the will to uncover under everything strange, unusual, and questionable something that no longer disturbs us. Is it not the *instinct of fear* that bids us to know? And is the jubilation of those who attain knowledge not the jubilation over the restoration of a sense of security?

... To become the founder of a religion one must be psychologically infallible in one's knowledge of a certain average type of souls who have not yet *recognized* that they belong together. It is he that brings them together. The founding of a religion therefore always becomes a long festival of recognition.

Nietzsche, *Joyous Wisdom* (#355 and #353)

Now I know well that when I approached various large assemblies, even before I had sat down there or had spoken or begun to talk to them, whatever might have been their sort I made myself of like sort, whatever their language so was my language. And I rejoiced them with talk on Dhamma, made it acceptable to them, set them on fire, gladdened them.

Dīgha-Nikāya II, 109

Indeed, the designation "name and clan" in this world, arisen here and there, was settled by convention.
The ignorant declare to us this groundless opinion, unknowingly, latent so long: "One is a Brahmin by birth".
One becomes neither a Brahmin nor non-Brahmin by birth, one becomes a Brahmin by *kamma* [i.e., by what one does]; one becomes a non-Brahmin by *kamma*...
Thus the wise truly see *kamma*. Seers of conditioned co-arising, those who know *kammic*-results (*kammavipāka*):
The world fares on by *kamma*. Mankind fares on by *kamma*, *kamma* [actions] binds beings, as a linchpin the quickly moving chariot.

Samyutta-Nikāya 648-650, 653-654

Introduction

Buddhism founded itself on the observation that something was wrong, something was unsatisfactory with the human condition—*as lived.* Further, it observed that we are all aware on some level of this unsatisfactoriness, and most acutely aware of it in moments of crisis. This sense of unsatisfactoriness, of dis-ease, Buddha called *duḥkha.* Through study, self-investigation, and resolute perseverance, Siddhārtha Gotama 'Awakened' (*Bodhi*) to the source of *duḥkha* and the means to its eradication. Through various methods, models and arguments Buddha (lit. 'The Awakened') endeavored to enable others to also 'Awaken.'[1] How his followers have appropriated and utilized these methods, models and arguments—augmenting, elaborating, and altering them—and the schisms that arose out of differing interpretations, constitutes the 'Buddhist Tradition.'

In order to examine how Yogācāra appropriated and presented Buddha's teaching, in this Part certain terms and concepts which became crucial for Yogācāra will be examined. In the next Part we will trace out how some of these issues developed into Yogācāra. Since our tracings will lead us from the early Pāli texts up to the writings of Vasubandhu,[2] what follows cannot be exhaustive, as any one of the terms to be considered could rightfully be made the subject of a number of separate works.[3]

It is possible to generate Buddhism, in all its complexity and variant developments, out of four basic and somewhat overlapping models. These four, well-known to all students of Buddhism, are: 1. the five *skandhas* ; 2. the twelve links of *pratītya-samutpāda*; 3. the *tri-dhātu* ; and 4. the trialectic praxis of *śīla, samādhi,* and *prajñā.* This does not mean that other models could not serve the same function. I have selected these four because (a) they are all basic Buddhist models, utilized by all Buddhist schools (though different schools may interpret or emphasize them differently), (b) these four models are distinctly Buddhist in that they are exclusively associated with Buddhism, whereas many other familiar Buddhist doctrines are shared by non-Buddhist schools (e.g., *duḥkha* and *kleśa* are also main features in Sāṃkhya thought, etc.), (c) these four not only overlap with each other, but overlap with virtually every other model common to all the schools, and hence, by extension, may be taken to connote the vast range of other Buddhist models, (d) these four, either explicitly or implicitly, underpin the Abhidharmic project upon which Yogācāra is built, and (e) taken together they can be made to generate the full range of Buddhist philosophical, psychological, existential, linguistic, cognitive, ethical, cosmological, and disciplinary-pedagogic (i.e., practice) observations or theories through which Buddhism has constructed itself.[4]

A brief account of each will be given in this Part. Instead of diachronically tracing the development of each model and term, a largely generic account will be offered, one that most, and sometimes all, Indian Buddhists would subscribe to. If a significant variation exists amongst Indian Buddhist schools on a certain term or model, the 'generic' version presented here will be one in accord at least with usage in Pāli texts and Yogācāra. One aim of this Part is to demonstrate the conceptual proximity of Yogācāra thought with early Buddhist thinking. Too often modern scholarship has contextualized Yogācāra with the materials and schools closest to it historically, such as the Sanskrit abhidharma schools, Madhyamaka, and so on. While such an approach is warranted and necessary, it tends to obscure how faithful Yogācāra thought is to early Buddhist thinking. Divorced from this context, it then becomes easy to paint Yogācāra as a school with doctrines vastly different from the doctrines of its Buddhist predecessors. That conclusion becomes intensified when what is presented to the modern reader in the name of Yogācāra is restricted to the few distinctively Yogācāric concepts—such as the eight consciousnesses, trisvabhāva, etc.—as if those ideas, and those ideas alone, were of interest to Yogācārins. At the very least, such impressions are highly misleading. Despite Yogācāra's detailed discussions of the terms and arguments developed by later schools, its orientation in most cases proves consistent in large part with the thinking of the Pāli Nikāyas.[5] Since Yogācāra frequently treats later developments in a way that realigns them with earlier versions of Buddhist doctrines, we may conclude that one of Yogācāra's agendas was to reorient the later refinements, in all their minute complexities, so that they accorded doctrinally with the earliest Buddhist doctrines.

The Part Three will examine aspects of the treatment of these models in the Pāli and Abhidharmic texts, particularly in relation to the problem of karma,[6] and the manner in which this problematic helped shape the Yogācāric system.

It will become evident that these models display a strong phenomenological orientation, i.e., a fundamental concern with the conditions of cognition, perception, thinking and the constitution of experience. Those familiar with the Buddhist literature being drawn on here will recognize that the proximity of this sort of Buddhist discourse to phenomenology is not derived through a reductionistic interpretation of Buddhism, but rather reflects quite accurately Buddhist discourse itself.

Notes

1 This is a recapitulation of what is traditionally called the Four Noble Truths, which constitute the cornerstone of Buddhism, viz.: 1. *duḥkha*, 2. its cause, 3. its extinction, and 4. the method. I have not included the Four Noble Truths in the list of four basic Buddhist models, because, in a most profound sense, it is the meta-model on which all the rest of Buddhism hangs. It is the Four Noble Truths that serve as a constant reminder that everything Buddhists do, everything they study, everything they analyze, everything they institutionalize, has the sole purpose of

disclosing and elimination duḥkha. In other words, Buddhists engage in all Buddhist practices, whether meditation, philosophical analysis, ethical behavior, etc., due to an underlying soteric purpose. Buddhism, therefore, in its most basic sense, is therapy.

2 The two-Vasubandhu theory is ludicrous, and arises from historical and chronological discrepancies between secondary sources (such as Paramārtha's biography of Vasubandhu) rather than from a serious reading of the primary texts themselves. Textually it seems clear to me that Vasubandhu undergoes precisely the type of evolution of thinking that one would expect from someone starting in Sarvāstivādin thought, moving through Sautrāntika and related critiques, and finally settling in Yogācāra. Two quick examples: (1) Vasubandhu's 'Mahāyānic' works are as concerned with Abhidharmic categories as is the *Abhidarmakośa*. His works exhibit a progressional unfolding. His *Pañcaskandha prakāraṇa* deals with a dharma list that is somewhere between the seventy-five list (the *kośa* list) and the hundred list (the doctrinal Yogācāric account)(see appendices); and the same could be said for the *Triṃśikā* (though the *Ch'eng Wei-shih lun* attempts to account for both lists). His *One-hundred Dharma Treatise* (T.31.1624) gives the mature account. (2) The *Triṃśikā* mentions *arhats* but not *bodhisattvas,* indicating, at the least, that Vasubandhu was still thinking in 'pre-Mahāyānic' categories while writing it. Though A. K. Warder, Amar Singh and their followers have remained steadfast in their insistence that we should sharply distinguish between two Vasubandhus, Frauwallner, the most important voice originally arguing for two Vasubandhus, has recanted and finally accepted that there was only one.

3 Two such works have appeared. One is James McDermott's *Developments in the Early Buddhist Concept of Kamma/Karma* (Princeton, 1970), though it only covers the development of 'karma' up to the *Abhidharmakośa*. The other is Paul Griffith's dissertation, reworked and published as *On Being Mindless: Buddhist Meditation and the Mind-body Problem* (La Salle, IL: Open Court, 1987), which addresses the issue of the absence and reemergence of *citta* in *nirodha-samāpatti* (the temporary 'attainment of cessation [of mental activity]'). The range of texts he examines together with his philosophical approach make this an important contribution, though some of his assertions and conclusions are less than satisfactory (e.g., equating *nirodha-samāpatti* with 'catalepsy,' or presuming and subsequently reading in a form of the mind-body problem that seems inappropriate for Buddhist thought). Griffith's book nonetheless moves the examination and discussion of these issues into a new and welcome arena.

4 This book will not attempt to demonstrate all these points exhaustively, since that would require reconstituting the whole of Buddhism, in all its detailed, historical embellishments. Rather I will be suggesting general aspects that bear directly on the development of a Yogācāric philosophical sensibility and orientation, since the aim of this work is finally to clarify that orientation.

5 One of the few to notice Yogācāra's faithfulness to the orientation of the Pāli Nikāyas was Walpola Rahula, who in "A Comparative Study of Dhyānas according to Theravāda, Sarvāstivāda and Mahāyāna" in *Zen and the Taming of the Bull* (London: Gordon Fraser, 1978), pp. 10-109, repeatedly points out how Asaṅga's *Abhidharmasamuccaya* is invariably closer to the Nikāyas than are the Theravādin Abhidhamma texts.

6 Since the Sanskrit terms are generally more familiar to English readers than their Pāli equivalents (e.g. *karma* instead of *kamma*, or *nirvāṇa* instead of *nibbāna*) general discussion will use the Sanskrit terms *except* (1) when citing or quoting a Pāli text, (2) when the context demands a distinction be drawn between Pāli and Sanskrit usage (e.g., when comparing or contrasting how different texts define terms), and (3) during the first major occurrence of a term in this text, if its Pāli form is pertinent that will be given in parenthesis, prefixed with 'P.'; ex: *kleśa* (P. *kilesa*). If the Pāli term occurs first, the Sanskrit will be given in parenthesis; ex.: *dhamma* (S. *dharma*). Also it should be pointed out that several Sanskrit and/or Pāli terms will be used throughout the text in anglicized adjectival forms, such as 'karmic,' 'svabhāvic,' etc.

Two more points about the use of Sanskrit and/or Pāli terms and concepts should be noted: (1) for clarity, some terms which grammatically should be compounded will sometimes be given in non-compounded form (i.e., ignoring saṅdhi rules) to enable the English reader to quickly identify the respective terms (e.g., *kleśa-āvaraṇa* instead of *kleśāvaraṇa*); (2) varying translations or equivalents will be used interchangeably to emphasize the semantic spread of some terms (e.g., see how *sparśa, saṃskāra* and *prajñapti* are treated in Part Two). Since Sanskrit notions and terms stubbornly resist being reduced to English equivalents this becomes necessary. Insistence on strict one-to-one correspondences is not only unfeasible, but when attempted often leads to erroneous and nonsensical English expositions, as for instance A. K. Warder's use of "principle" for *dharma* throughout his *Indian Buddhism.*

Chapter Three

Model One: The Five Skandhas

Denying the existence of any permanent, invariant, unchanging, substantial 'self' or 'I' (*anātman*, P. *anatta*), Buddha analyzed what we perceive to be a self as a collection or concatenation of five 'aggregates' (*skandha;* P. *khandha*). When these five aggregate, there is a person; when they are disbanded, there is no longer any person. These five are subdivided into two types, (1) *rūpa* (sensorial materiality) and (2) *nāma* (*nomi*-nal foci), which, as aggregated, are together called *nāma-rūpa.*

The five *skandhas* are:

1) *Rūpa*—though usually translated as "form" or "matter," in most Indian thought rūpa denotes a materiality *capable of being sensed.*[1] Matter was not considered as the antipode to consciousness, but rather as what offers 'resistance' (*pratigha*) to a sensorial body (*saviññāṇaka kāya*). Resistance means both (i) that which appears as a cognitive object because it resists a sensory probe (e.g., I see the wall because it 'blocks' my vision from seeing further; I feel the book because it resists letting my hand occupy its space, etc.), as well as (ii) the physical resistance between two objects such that they can not occupy the same space at the same time. Rūpa's secondary meaning is '[what is] visible,' 'color-datum,' etc., reinforcing its sensorial characteristic. In the earlier texts it is generally glossed as the four sensory qualities of hardness/softness, fluidity, temperature and movement; or their 'abstractions,' the four Great Elements (*mahābhūta*) of Earth, Water, Fire and Air. Note the sensorial qualities are not considered properties of material entities, but, quite to the contrary, *material entities are considered concretized instantiations of sensorial 'textures.'* We will have occasion to investigate *rūpa* more thoroughly later;

2) *Vedanā*—the three hedonic modalities through which we cognize anything, viz. as pleasurable (*sukha*), as painful (*dukkha*, S. *duḥkha*) or as neutral (*upekkhā*, S. *upekṣa*). As modern psychology reiterates, these modalities condition how we perceive and respond to all experience. There is no moment, Buddhism asserts, in which one is not engaged in at least one of those modalities. Moreover, through them we become conditioned in regard to future experiences.

On the simplest level, 'pleasurable' experiences condition us to desire their prolongment or reoccurrence, while 'unpleasurable' experiences generate the desire to terminate present 'pain' and avert future occurrences. Put another way, what is pleasurable we either want to hold on to and continue, or, should it stop, we desire its return. Painful experiences or sensations we wish to stop, and once they have ceased, we desire to avoid their reoccurrence. Hence, for instance, we repeatedly eat foods that taste 'good' (= pleasurable taste) to us, and try to avoid 'bad' (= painful) tasting food. This process, which produces and conditions our eating *habits* (= karma), although seemingly overt, is to some extent subliminal, particularly in the manner that it forms habits that may become intractable. That East Asians desire (some would say 'require') rice at every meal (or at least noodles), while most Westerners would consider that sort of diet too redundant, reflects differences in cultural conditioning, differences shaped by each's previous pleasurable or painful experiences. On a more complicated subliminal level *vedanā* determines, to greater and lesser extents, how we actually perceive experiences. When hearing a spokesman express an opinion that we also hold, we may feel and even 'judge' him to be 'right' and 'speaking honestly,' while when hearing someone express a position significantly opposed to our own, we may feel and judge that this person is not only 'wrong' but 'speaking deceitfully.' If listening to the latter is sufficiently 'painful' we may even *perceive* the perverse motives behind his declarations as he utters them, as if they were written on his face or inscribed in his voice, that is, as if they were really *in him* instead of arising as a projection of our own mind.

Inanimate objects can be infused with living meanings through associations we make with previous experiences. For instance, a certain object associated with a traumatic experience can, just by its mere presence, recreate some of the affective ambiance of the original experience, such that we perceive the object as possessing properties that empirically are not intrinsic to the object. Similarly a certain song or place or smell may regenerate old familiar feelings, our associations with previous experiences of that event producing affective corollaries such as moods, inner comfort or discomfort, and perhaps even details long forgotten. We call such feelings, whether pleasant or unpleasant, "familiar" precisely because they had been temporarily forgotten, absent from experience, and now those associative feelings have re-emerged. It is not uncommon to attribute the source of those feelings, thoughts, remembrances, etc. to the object, as if we perceive them directly *as* the object ("what a depressing song" or "that picture *carries memories* of my childhood," etc.). *Vedanā*, though, is simply the perceptual modalities of pleasure, pain, and neutral (sometimes rendered "indifference") apart from these associational embellishments.

3) *saṁjñā* (P. *saññā*)—involves subjecting pain-pleasure-neutral perceptions to further 'conceptualizations.' In part, *saṁjñā* signifies the webs of association and relation through which vedanic experience is strung together (*saṁ-* = to put together + *jñā* = knowing, hence 'knowledge which puts together' or 'associational knowledge'). The acquiring of a habit

requires repeated pleasurable and/or painful experiences that somehow become psychologically associated or mutually related. In a more general sense *saṁjñā* involves and includes most of what we would mean by 'thinking' or 'rational-izing.'

These cognitive associations occur in several ways. (1) A percept always arises in and from a background, a *Ganzfeld,* which means each distinct object arises in association with a perceptual background. While focusing on a specific object, such as a book, the background (the furniture, space, and things surrounding the book) might be ignored or overlooked, but the background helps constitute the perception of the book and actually is part of the perception, even when ignored. We visually see the surrounding space, furniture, etc., even while failing to pay attention to them. (2) Cognition, especially when it involves recognition, invariably requires a historical context, viz. previous experience. To perceive a book *as* a book requires that I have previously seen a book and that I associate my current percept (embedded in its background) with that previous cognition. I perceive *this* as a book because I have previously seen *other* books, and I associate this book with them. (3) All 'thinking' is comparative, i.e., thinking requires comparing and contrasting something with something else (or something with itself). An object under observation and scrutiny must be associated with other things in terms of its similarity and difference from them. The red pencil I now hold is 'perceived' as a "red pencil" because I 'know it by associating' (*saṁjñā*) it with other experiences I have had of red objects and of pencils. The recognition not only requires that the red pencil be associated with other experiences of color and pencil-like *objects,* but the *categories* 'red' and 'pencil' must also be associated or related to each other. In part I know this is a pencil because it is not (i.e., it is different from) a pen. Of course, all these associations would take place in such a way that the cognizer generally remains unaware of the web of associations or relations that cooperate and converge to co-produce (*samutpāda*) the perception. Similar webs are involved in more abstract cognitive activities as well. To think about concepts such as 'peace,' 'flexibility,' 'hypotenuse,' etc., requires associationally relating various other things or concepts, e.g., triangles with their qualities and theorems in the case of 'hypotenuse.'

Hence *saṁjñā* means perception (the relational matrix through which an object becomes identified as such), thinking or conceptualization. The notion of *saṁjñā* acts as a perpetual reminder that neither perception nor thinking may be divorced from the conditions of association which produce them.

4) *saṃskāra* (P. *saṅkhāra*)—'embodied conditioning.' These are the karmic latencies that predispose us to perceive or react in certain ways. They are karmic insofar as they are the product of previous vedanic experience, now latent, and insofar as they condition how we re-act or will re-act to present or future vedanic experience. If you meet someone for the first time, and have one of the most enjoyable, pleasing, stimulating conversations you have ever had, you will become happy the moment you spy that person

again; a smile will likely break out on your face, and your voice and manner will become cordial and friendly. Conversely, if your interaction with that person the first time you met had been painful—the most excruciating, uncomfortable, awkward conversation you have ever had—not only will you not look forward to seeing that person again, but should you notice that person on the street or elsewhere you may even take great lengths to try to avoid making eye contact or otherwise acknowledge that you notice that person. We, of course, think that it is we, as autonomous beings, who *decide* who and what we like, but, in reality, that decision is reached by the accumulation of painful and pleasurable experiences, i.e., conditioning. The reason we found that person's conversation either inspiring or insipid in the first place would be due to the fact that our preferences were already conditioned by previous experiences. If the person was, for instance, ranting in racist, misogynist tones, whether one would find such conversation pleasant or offensive would depend completely on one's prior conditioning concerning matters of race and gender. One usually does not think about the history of one's preferences while one is reacting; one rather experiences such things as if they were tastes, natural predilections, or, most fundamentally, as forms of pleasure and pain. We react similarly to similar things. We are all bundles of such habitual predilections; the patterns of those predilections together constitute our personalities, i.e., how and what we are. I have translated *saṃskāra* as *embodied conditioning* because such predilections are always already inscribed in our flesh, in our very way of being in the world, even while we ignore—or remain ignorant of—the causes and conditions that have given rise to them.

Later Buddhists both restricted and expanded the meaning of *saṃskāra*. The restriction, already evident in some Nikāyas and highlighted in the Pāli Abhidhamma, treated *saṃskāra* as virtually synonymous with 'intention' and 'volition' (*cetanā*). One's previous conditioning becomes active and takes effect the moment it arises as a volition to do or avoid something. While saṃskāras are generally latent and hence go unnoticed, during a moment of volition they *may* be noticed (if one is paying proper attention rather than merely acting on one's predilections, or deluding oneself into thinking that the volitional moment was generated more or less ex nihilo by oneself, the autonomous 'decider'). Volitions and intents are forms of desire. Observing them provides not only access to one's desires, but to one's subliminal, unconscious motivations as well, since it is during such moments that latent tendencies—each with a history of conditioning—reveal themselves. That moment of revelation can be used to disclose one's most basic conditioning. The implications of defining volitions or intentionality in terms of latent conditioning, particularly as that affects ethical considerations, will be discussed later.

The expansion, primarily evident in later Abhidharmic literature, opened *saṃskāra* into a broad category that contained many sub-categories (e.g., all the *viprayukta-saṃskāra-dharmas*). For Yogācāra *all* dharmas in their list of 100 dharmas (see appendix) were, in part, reducible to *citta* (mental operations), and at the same time a large portion of those one hundred dharmas were also classified as *saṃskāras*. Thus saṃskāra virtually rivals citta in importance. Why this is the case will be examined later.

5) *vijñāna* (P. *viññāṇa*)—'consciousness;' that which cognizes (*-jñāna*) through bifurcation (*vi-*). Consciousness takes the activities of each of the other skandhas for its objects. It can also cognize its own activities, though a major debate developed in the medieval period as to whether consciousness can be reflexive, that is, know itself (*svasamveda*), and if so, how.[2] The type of Yogācāra typified by Hsüan-tsang asserted that consciousness does know itself. For reasons which will become apparent as we progress, 'consciousness,' of all the skandhas, was selected for the most thorough and rigorous scrutiny and elaboration by all Buddhist schools.

The first skandha is rūpic, while numbers two through five are nominal (*nāma*). For now we may call this model a phenomenological description of the psycho-physical organism. When conditions are such that these aggregates arise together, there is an 'individual' (*bhāva, sattva,* etc.); with the absence of any of these conditions or at their dissolution, no individual exists. Also, as the contents of the aggregates change, so does the individual. Hence no enduring, unchanging 'self' exists.

This almost simplistic model carried such complex implications, that one might be tempted to claim that Buddhism is the systematic unpacking of this model's ramifications. This is undeniably the case with Abhidharma, Sarvāstivāda, and Yogācāra.[3] This will be demonstrated shortly.

The Pāli texts generally discuss the khandhas as *upādānakkhandhas*, 'appropriational aggregations.'[4] We will examine *upādāna* as it occurs in the next model, and return to implications of *appropriational aggregations* at the end of Part Two.

The *skandha* model in several ways overlaps the next model to be presented. Not only do they share some of the same key terms, though each model distributes these terms differently, but they may also be understood as addressing the same concern, the second model offering an expanded analysis or description of what the skandhic model has outlined.

Notes

1 For an informative discussion of *rūpa* in the Theravāda tradition, cf. Y. Karunadasa, *Buddhist Analysis of Matter* (Singapore: The Buddhist Research Society, 1989, 2nd ed.). While the

early Buddhist materials entertain rūpa theories quite different from atomism, the Indians, possibly as a result of their contacts with Hellenic culture, eventually developed several atomic theories of matter. The most prominent atomic theory belonged to the Hindu Vaiśeṣikas, but many Buddhist groups also adopted comparable theories, though, as Yogācāra texts such as *Viṃśatikā* demonstrate, Yogācārins rejected atomism as incoherent.

2 For an in-depth discussion of this debate in Tibet, see Paul Williams, *The Reflexive Nature of Awareness* (London: Curzon, 1998).

3 Part II aims at demonstrating the validity of this claim for this, as well as the other three models to be treated here. While the presentation just given of the skandhas emphasized the psychological aspects, the description of *pratītya-samutpāda* which follows will begin to open the discussion into a more philosophic discourse. This should not be understood as implying that one model is more philosophical or more psychological than the other. Either model could be presented in either a philosophic or psychological discourse exclusively (as well as within other discursive realms, e.g., devotional, cosmological, etc.). As a result of the Renaissance and reinforced by Nineteenth and Twentieth Century Liberalism, Western thought has advocated and insisted upon a sharp distinction between 'philosophy' *qua Wissenschaften* (the hard and soft sciences) and its supposed nemesis 'religion' ("that irrational bundle of superstitions").

Similarly a line has been drawn, particularly by the modern Analytic tradition following Frege's rejection of *psychologism*, between 'psychology' and what they would like to think of as 'philosophy proper.' Despite whatever political or ideological purposes such a distinction may serve today, blind adherence to it can distort our view of non-Western or pre-Renaissance thought, where no such demarcation between philosophy and psychology is countenanced. In modern philosophy this almost irrational fear of psychology has forced an otherwise usually clear-headed discipline into avoiding any radical encounters with the most fundamental epistemological issues, seemingly out of fear that such investigations may border on psychology. Even exemplary rationalist efforts, such as the later books of Spinoza's *Ethics*, are today typically viewed as "weak" because they indulge in psychological categories.

Whatever their current status, for Indian thought, particularly Buddhist thought, philosophy and psychology are deemed inseparable. To mark this inseparability, highlighting both the logical rigor needed to do proper psychology while maintaining awareness of the psychological aspects at play in philosophizing, I have coined the term *Psychosophy*. This word has the advantage of eliminating the *logos* from psycho-*logy* while sedating the rapturous hyperbole of the *philo-* in philo-sophy. The de-theologizing aspect (exclusion of *logos*) of this term is completely appropriate within the Buddhist context. While Yogācāra is perhaps the psychosophic system *sine qua non*, no doubt many other traditions, Western as well as Eastern, could be more adequately interpreted through this term.

4 For a good overview of the skandhas in the early Pāli texts, one that takes issue with labeling them "psycho-physical," see Rupert Gethin's "The Five Khandhas: Their Treatment in the Nikāyas and Early Abhidhamma," *Journal of Indian Philosophy*, 14 (1986) pp. 35-53, and the sources cited there. This article will be discussed near the end of Part II.

Chapter Four

Model Two: *Pratītya-samutpāda* (P. *paṭicca-samuppāda*)

Generally considered the most fundamental or central doctrine in Buddhism, 'conditioned co-arising' is often held to be the actual content of Buddha's Awakening in the third watch of the night under the Bodhi-tree.[1] As such, all schools of Buddhism have been compelled to develop their own interpretations of this doctrine in the light of their specific concerns and emphases. Here I shall offer a basic, generic description of conditioned co-arising in terms of the twelve links (*nidāna* or *aṅga*).[2] Aspects of this model which assumed prominence in Yogācāra, however, will be highlighted.

1. *avidyā* (P. *avijjā*)—A basic and ubiquitous 'nescience,' the fundamental 'non-knowing' due to which beings are bound in saṃsāra (the habitual repetition of 'experienc-ing'). Exact definitions of precisely what constitutes *avidyā* vary from text to text and school to school,[3] but everywhere it is taken to be indicative of the root problem of the human condition. In the early Pāli texts it is connected with the notions of *āsava* (root psychosophic problems)[4] and *anusaya* (latent tendencies). Both are fundamentally karmic.

Avidyā eventually comes to be glossed as the more radical of the two primary *āvaraṇas*,[5] namely the *jñeyāvaraṇa* (*jñeya* + *āvaraṇa*, obstruction by what is [mistakenly] known). The stage in the development of Buddhist thought where *jñeyāvaraṇa* is separated from *kleśāvaraṇa* (*kleśa* + *āvaraṇa*, obstruction by mental disturbances) marks a separation of emotional-cognitive problems (*kleśa*) from intellective-cognitive problems (*jñeya*, lit. 'what is known'; *jñāna*, cognition, etc.). Originally Buddhism made no such sharp separation, and *avidyā* was understood to involve both. This later privileging of the intellective, a key characteristic of Indian Mahāyāna, will be given fuller treatment in Part Three.

Jñeyāvaraṇa itself was often glossed as a synonym for *ātma-dṛṣṭi* (belief that a self exists) or *sat-kāya-dṛṣṭi* (belief in substantialistic selves and entities). However, originally *avidyā* carried additional connotations. Whether taken to be something specific—a particular nescience of some particular insight or principle, e.g., lack of insight into the Four Noble Truths, as Theravādins and Sarvāstivādins contend—or as a more general non-knowing, *avidyā* signifies the absence of precisely that knowledge which would prevent one from becoming conditioned (*saṃskṛta*). Inversely, in the absence of *avidyā* conditioning ceases (*asaṃskṛta*). However, because there is nescience, there arises

2. *saṃskāra* (P. *saṅkhāra*)—As in the skandhic model, it here stands for 'embodied conditioning.' Inclusive of all the psycho-physical conditioning that each sentient being carries from the past—whether what we today would call "evolutionary inheritances" (all humans embody conditioning that re-acts in certain conditioned ways, such as the 'flinching reflex,' or eyes that only react to certain wavelengths of the electromagnetic spectrum and not others, etc.), or predilections and predispositions, etc.

Saṃskāras are latent and usually subconscious. For this reason initially Yogācāra viewed *saṃskāra* as *citta-viprayukta*, i.e., not directly accessible to conscious mental processes. Rather than cognizable within immediate, direct perception, it is only known inferentially, insofar as it constitutes experience but does not give itself *as itself* in experience. The conditioning makes itself known *as* volitions, as specific desires to do certain things under certain circumstances. *Viprayukta* in this context is similar to Husserl's notion of 'transcendental.' For instance, 'aging' or 'numericality' are not immediately given in perception, but the manner in which they influence perception can be ascertained through reflection.

Saṃskāra covers a wide field inclusive of cognitive, dispositional and psychological tendencies, from 'presuppositions'—especially insofar as these are suppositions or assumptions which operate prior to our being conscious of them or outside the range in which we apply conscious scrutiny—to subconscious motivations. Thus the term carries cognitive as well as affective implications.

A major thrust of Pāli abhidhammic psychology hinges on the manner *saṅkhāras* and volitions (*cetanā*) are reducible to or distinguishable from each other. Kalupahana contends[6] that there is no notion of an 'unconscious' in Pāli Buddhism. I disagree, and find myself closer to de Silva who sees strong corollaries between Pāli Buddhist psychology and Freud.[7] The operations of an unconscious are clearly evident in discussions of *āsavas, anusayas, saṅkhāra,* etc. Structurally and functionally, these are motivational 'drives' that are basic to human cognition, attitudes, etc. Further, these drives are identified by Buddhist psychology as *the fundamental, root problems.* Moreover, the *āsavas,* etc., operate *outside* the purview of normal consciousness, and indeed, for early Buddhist psychology, the prime imperative is to bring these dangerous operations into the light of awareness so as to undo and eliminate them. They are, in other words, the most deep-seated and urgent of all psychological problems, and they operate outside the scope of normal awareness, while shaping and affecting that same normal consciousness. Along with categorizing the components of conscious and unconscious experience (*citta-cetasika*), Buddhist psychology focuses on the mechanics of how actual experiences become latent and influential; how later they burst into awareness as *cetanā* (volitions), flavored by prior *vedanā* (pain and pleasure sensations) while flavoring the *vedanā* of present and future experiences, and so on.; and, most importantly, the karmic dimensions of those mechanical operations. In a later chapter we will offer further evidence of the importance of *saṅkhāra* in Theravādin psychology.

Mahāyānic psychology emphasizes how the cognitive (presuppositions), affective (motivations) and even physical (*rūpa*) *saṃskāras* collapse into each other, being merely alternate modes of observing the same type of karmic operations.[8] Again, *saṃskāra* is entirely karmic, and could perhaps be translated as 'latent karma.'

A discussion of the centrality of saṃskāra for the Theravāda soteric system will be offered later. While, as mentioned above, saṃskāra initially signified a range of unconscious and inferential activities, the *Ch'eng wei-shih lun* will finally declare that all saṃskāras are linguistic fictions (*prajñapti*), and not real. Since for Theravāda the uncovering and elimination of saṃskāras constituted the theoretical and practical basis of the pursuit of Awakening, the *Ch'eng wei-shih lun*'s revaluation obviously marked a radically different approach to the problem of Awakening. Later chapters shall develop this issue further.

3. *vijñāna* (P. *viññāṇa*)—'Consciousness,' which becomes crucial to the Abhidhammic and Abhidharmic systems as well as Yogācāra, will be treated thoroughly later so that here we may merely note its position as mediating between *saṃskāra* and

4. *nāma-rūpa* (P. *nāma-rūpa*)—Literally 'name-and-form,' *nāma-rūpa* implies the five skandhas. Again, it may be understood as a 'psycho-physical' organism, or as a phenomenal 'body' (*kāya*) consisting of psycho-cognitive and physical components.[9] It denotes both sensorial capacity and the physico-cognitive structures necessary to interpret the sensorium. Significantly *nāma-rūpa* precedes both the actual differentiation of sense-organs (*nidāna* #5) as well as any actual sensorial 'contact' with the sensorium (*nidāna* #6), indicating that we are predisposed (*saṃskāra*) to interpret—and in fact are already interpreting—prior to (again *saṃskāra*) any particular sensation. Hence Buddhism, like Sāṃkhya, claims it is not because there are sounds that our ears hear, but rather that it is because we have ears (which are embodiments of an intentionality to hear) that there are sounds (and likewise for the other senses).[10]

Rūpa was never understood in the way 'matter' is sometimes currently conceived in the West. For instance, the 'ear' as a physical, sensory organ was not regarded as inert matter, but as an intentional, charged mechanism always already embodying the characteristics of hearing (elsewise it is considered defective). Thus the ear, or any sensory organ, is not reducible to the status of a mere physical object (size, shape, tactile structures, etc.). Rūpa senses, and is sensed. The sense organs are essentially *sensorial*. For this reason, even physically speaking, the ear is primarily understood to be an *auditory condition*.

Nāma denotes not only the four nāmic *skandhas*, but the entire psycho-linguistic sphere, and thus implies such terms as *prajñapti* (P. *paññati*, 'designation,' or more accurately language's nominalistic pretext towards referentiality,[11] accomplished by as-signing an identity to disparate conditions through the sheer power of uniting them under a single name) and *prapañca* (P. *papañca*, a multivalent term connoting something like the psycho-linguistic proliferation of cognitive-conative projections onto experience; or the linguistic "excess" responsible for and resulting from mistaking interpretation for 'reality'[12]).

5. *ṣaḍ-āyatana* (P. *saḷāyatana*)—The enumeration 'six sense-bases' is curious. This is generally understood to signify the six sense-organs, viz. eye, ear, nose, tongue, body, and mind—mind (*manas*) being considered the sixth sense, its 'sense-objects' being *dhammā* (S. *dharmā*), i.e., ideas, thoughts, experiential components, etc. However in Buddhist texts, usually the word *indriya*, not *āyatana*, is used to denote the six sense organs. The term *indriya* signifies that they are faculties, *capacities*, thus reinforcing that sensation is an active, constructive process and not a passive reception of such things as external 'sense-data.'

The term *āyatana* usually denotes the twelve sensory bases or domains, i.e., the six kinds of sensory organs along with their respective six kinds of sensory objects. The eye sees 'visibles' (*rūpa*), the ear hears 'audibles' (*śabda*), etc. The twelve *āyatana* are regarded as the twelve 'bases' upon which the six types of consciousness arise, viz. when the eye-organ and a 'visible' (*rūpa*) come into contact, visual consciousness arises, and when the ear-organ and a sound make contact, auditory consciousness arises, etc. Each of these six consciousnesses (five physical senses and a psycho-cognitive 'sense') is discrete and occurs separately from the others, though the sixth consciousness (*mano-vijñāna*) to some extent appropriates and interprets the other five.[13]

indriya (sense organ; faculty; capacity)	*viṣaya* (sensory object)	*vijñāna* (consciousness)
1. eye	7. visibles (*rūpa*)	13. visual consciousness
2. ear	8. audibles	14. auditory consciousness
3. nose	9. smells	15.olfactory consciousness
4. tongue	10. tastes	16.gustatory consciousness
5. body/skin	11. touchables (*sparśa*)	17. tactile consciousness
6. mind (*manas*)	12. *dharmas*	18. *mano-vijñāna*

|———*indriya*———|

|——————— *āyatana* ———————|

|———————————————*dhātu* ———————————————|

The twelve *āyatanas* are 1 through 12, grouped as 1 with 7, 2 with 8, 3 with 9, etc. The six sense-organs, with their six respective types of objects, along with the six types of consciousnesses they engender all together constitute the Eighteen *Dhātus.*

These eighteen *dhātus* constitute the sensorium, and according to Buddhism the sensorium is all-inclusive. Buddha forcefully makes that point in the *Sabba sutta* of the *Saṃyutta Nikāya* (4.15). When asked 'What is everything?' (*sabba*), i.e., describe what is the case exhaustively and inclusively, Buddha replied as follows:[14]

> At Sāvatthī... the Exalted One said:—
>
> 'Brethren, I will teach you 'the all' [*sabba*]. Do listen to it.
>
> And what, brethren, is the all? It is the eye and visibles, ear and sound, nose and scent, tongue and savor, body and tangible things, mind and mental-states. That, brethren, is called "the all."
>
> Whoso, brethren, should say: 'Rejecting this all, I will proclaim another all,—it would be mere talk [*vāca-vatthu*, lit. "a linguistic matter," i.e., having only words, not things as a referent] on his part, and when questioned he could not make good his boast, and further would come to an ill pass. Why so? Because, brethren, it would be beyond his scope to do so.'

Given the sort of theosophical metaphysics that extol what lies beyond the senses while denigrating the sensory realm, a metaphysic commonly propounded by spiritual systems (including some later advocates of Buddhism), this passage is striking. The 'all' is simply the sensorium: sensory organs and sensory objects. The twelve *āyatanas* (as enumerated in this passage) are synonymous with the eighteen *dhātus* because the six dhātus not mentioned (#13-#18) are the effects or products of the interaction of the first twelve. When the eye comes into contact with a visible object, visual consciousness arises. In the absence of those precipitating conditions (the sense organ, the sense object and their contact), no consciousness arises. It is as if Buddha intentionally omits the six consciousnesses precisely because consciousness is frequently associated by claimants to "another all" with that all beyond sensation. These fields, viz. the sensorium, are *everything* (*sabba*). The cognitive sensorium is all-inclusive. Nothing whatsoever exists outside the eighteen dhātus. This should be kept in mind by scholars who try to impose some 'ineffable' extra-sensory or non-sensory 'reality' into Buddhist thought.

Note also the consequences Buddha assigns to holding or promoting an erroneous view. (1) That view will be unsupportable, indefensible in the face of a critical challenge ("could not make good on his boast"). (2) It is "beyond his scope," i.e., not only does it entail holding to a position one is incapable of defending, but it would require making claims about what lies entirely outside one's experience and knowledge. (3) Most importantly, it leads to disadvantageous karmic consequences ("would come to an ill pass"). Holding false views, then, is not a neutral or harmless affair. Rather, such views harbor dire consequences. This *power* inherent in attaching to 'views' becomes a crucial focus for Mahāyānic soterics, but its *classicus locus* is already found in the first text of the Pāli *Dīgha Nikāya*, the *Brahmajāla sutta*, in which dozens of wrong views are laid out and critiqued.

Scholars frequently lose sight of the fact that even while Yogācāra presents the motto *vijñapti-mātra*, it neither rejects nor deviates from this causative model of consciousness (cf., e.g., *Madhyānta-vibhāga* v. 9, and Sthiramati's *-ṭīkā* to verses 6 and 7). Even for Yogācāra, *vijñāna* is *produced* by sensory activity. In order to explore those processes not immediately tied to the sensation of a present moment (such as memory, latent tendencies, etc.), they expand the sixth sphere (i.e., *dhātus* #6,#12 and #18; *manas, dharmas* and *mano-vijñāna*) to two new forms of consciousness—making *mano-vijñāna* the sense organ of the sixth consciousness (rather than its conscious byproduct), elevating *manas* to the cognitive organ of a seventh consciousness (whose cognitive object is either the eighth consciousness or the lower six, depending on which text one reads), and introducing an eighth consciousness, the *ālaya-vijñāna*, or 'warehouse consciousness,' which is a revaluated version of *saṃskāra* as a fundamental (*mūla*), fluctuating, momentary stream (*santāna*) of karmic accumulation (*cīyate, vipāka, sarva-bījā-vijñāna*, etc.) and karmic projection (cf. *Triṃśikā* vs. 3 and 4). This will be examined more fully in the Section on the *Triṃśikā.*

According to Buddhism, each sensory realm (vision, audition, etc.) constitutes a perceptual domain distinct and discrete from each of the other sensory domains. To say that we *see* a "tasty object" entails a category error, since we neither taste visibles nor see gustatory sensations. Only mentally do we construct a referent as the identical 'source' for both sensory realms. Although each sense constitutes an entirely separate domain and occurs independently of the other five senses, such that taste is taste and always radically different from and nonreducible to, for example, a sound, nonetheless mental-consciousness (*mano-vijñāna*) *interprets* these discrete sensations as if they were unified, thus mistakenly constructing a unified subject as well as a unified object. Hence the 'red' seen, the 'sweetness' tasted, the 'smooth solidity' felt, the 'tart aroma' smelled, the 'tearing noise' heard become properties of a single, unified apple that I, as agent and locale of these perceptions, am eating. Not only do simultaneous sensations get blurred together as referring to unified objects and subjects, but temporally discrete sensations also become 'unified.' For instance the belief arises that the apple I picked up and bit is the *same* apple I continue to eat, and finally the eaten apple was one integral object just as the eater was one integral subject.

These psycho-linguistic cognitive errors are errors precisely because they are inferences displacing actual perception, i.e., inferences masquerading as perceptions. The statement or belief, 'I ate an apple,' is an expression of a set of inferences based on discrete sensations in which, technically speaking, in the absence of those inferences, no "I" or "apple" occur. The error arises when the inference substitutes itself for the sensation in such a way as to mask the inferential origins. Inferential aggregations come to be experienced as perceived 'identities' (*ātmadharma-svabhāva*). Recognizing that "I" and "apple" in the statement "I ate an apple" are valid only heuristically or nominally (*prajñapti*), but not actually (*paramārtha*), is to see things as they actually become (*yathābhūtam*), error-free (*abhrānta*).

Buddhism further argues that these cognitive displacements are symptomatic of one's deep desire to be a (universalizable) self (*ātma-dṛṣṭi*), to be a permanent identity not subject to the limitations and vicissitudes of mortality or the loneliness of a finite spatio-temporal horizon. We are driven to expand our horizon, to universalize our 'self,' not only by attaching to theories that offer communal identities larger than any individual (e.g., a tradition, a religion, a family or clan, a political movement, a God, etc.); more radically the very structures through which those theories arise—such as language, perception, and action—carry the signs of this anxious displacement. Anxiety encodes itself within or as these human structures. Moreover *perception*, insofar as it is a constructive enterprise, is regarded as an *action*. This simultaneously implicates and is implicated by the presuppositional belief (*saṃskāra*) that language (*nāma*) always *refers* to non-linguistic objects (*āyatana*); that action (*karma*) is everywhere invisibly mediated by a language that 'refers' subjects to objects, and vice versa. From this it follows that action has a 'grammar,' a discernible structure through which it is 'articulated.' Since a self acting *towards an object* follows the same propositional structure as that of a signifier signifying towards a signified, language and action (*karma*) share the same grammar, the identical structure.[15] One step further and all nominalizations (*prajñapti*, i.e., psycho-linguistic approximations) that can be said to be empirically demonstrated (or otherwise 'validated') may come to be taken as substantives, since one may forget that the validated referent is a linguistic event, not a substantial entity. One may conceive of two types of referents: (1) *Referent qua object*, for which one assumes that the referent of a linguistic expression is an actual, non-linguistic object. (2) *Referent qua referent*, in which a referent is never considered to be anything other than a linguistic component of a linguistic expression. For Madhyamakans, Sautrāntikas, and Yogācārins, *a referent never occurs elsewhere than in an act of referring*. To claim the referent *refers* to some object outside the act of reference is to invite an infinite regress. Hence a substantialized nominalization, conjured in an act of reference, which presents itself as an *identity* (i.e., 'referent *qua* object') exceeds its determination as a constituent of an act of reference, though as 'referent *qua* referent' it can never be found elsewhere than *in* that act, rendering any notion of the referentiality of 'objects' questionable. The act of reference operates by foisting the illusion that what is being referred to 'exists' outside the realm of language. Similarly, Yogācāra will argue that a comparable illusion accompanies all acts of consciousness, i.e., consciousness cognizes 'objects' *as if* they existed outside consciousness, while, in actuality, those objects *as cognized* appear no where else than *within* consciousness.[16]

That, ironically, precisely in their capacity to seemingly *refer*, both language and action cannot escape their horizons, i.e., they cannot refer beyond themselves, I will here call *closure*. Language and action are both closed systems, self-referential, whose perpetuation constitutes and is constituted by repetition. In Buddhist terminology karmic closure is called *saṃsāra*, the reiterative repetition of birth and death[17] or 'arising and ceasing,' a repetition impelled by the desire to substantially embody as a permanent entity in spite of the variable, fluxational impermanence (*anitya*) that invariably characterizes all conditioned things (*saṃskṛta-lakṣaṇa*). Hence one prapañcically arrives at substantial selves and objects.

To quickly summarize what has been discussed up to this point: Embodied conditioning (*saṃskāra*) continues to en-act and unfurl due to the absence of some basic insight (*avidyā*). Hence cognizance (*vijñāna*) arises as a lived-body (*nāma-rūpa*) bursting with sensorial capacity (*āyatana*). At this stage, the circuits between organs and objects that result in the sensory consciousnesses constitute a kind of 'intentional arc.'[18] This sets the basis for the Buddhist version of *intentionality*. Because sensation, according to Buddhism, is always already intentional, at each and every moment it involves

6) *sparśa* (P. *phassa*)—Literally 'touch' or 'sensory contact.' This term accrued varied usages in later Indian thought, but here it simply means that the sense organs are 'in contact with' sensory objects. The circuit of intentionality, or to borrow Merleau-Ponty's term *intentional arc*, is operational. This term could be translated as 'sensation' as long as this is qualified as a constructional, active process[19] that is invariably contextualized within its psycho-cognitive dimensions. For Buddhists, sensation can be neither passive nor purely a physical or neurological matter. When the proper sensorial conditions aggregate, i.e., come into contact with each other, sensation occurs. These proper conditions include a properly functioning sense organ and a cognitive-sensory object, which already presuppose a linguistically-complex conscious body (*nāma-rūpa*).

Further, there is no moment when 'contact' does not occur. At least one of the six senses (and in this model the mind is treated as a sense), if not all of them, is in contact with its cognitive object at any given moment. Hence each moment constitutes and is constituted by intentionalities inhabiting one or several of the sensory domains.[20] Put another way, *experience is always in and of the sensorium*. This carries implications similar to those drawn by the existential-phenomenologists who claim man is never other than being-in-the-world. The psycho-cognitive dimensions of sensation are reinforced by the next *nidāna*.

7) *vedanā*—As in the *skandhic* model *vedanā* here means the three initial interpretive modes of any experience, viz. pleasure, pain, and neutral. Every instance of 'contact' is immediately perceived as either pleasure, pain or neutral. The person (*pudgala*, P. *puggala*)—insofar as 'person' is merely a designatory label (*prajñapti*) for the karmic stream (*santāna*) produced by and producing pain and pleasure—develops and is conditioned by the

repeated experiences of these positive and negative reinforcements, viz. enjoyment and hurt, reward and punishment, etc.

To some extent Buddhism and Behaviorism concur on the nature of the self. For both, the self is considered merely a nominal substitute for behavior (= karma), derived through pleasure/pain conditioning. They diverge on the importance of non-apparent 'behavior,' or the unconscious processes (*saṃskāra*) that underpin and actually operate the conditioning. Behaviorism is content to note that pleasurable stimulus X, when sufficiently reinforced or repeated produces behavioral action Y. Buddhism, on the other hand, holds that not only must 'unconscious motivations' be reducible to empirical conditioning, but that empirical conditioning is only efficacious because of latent, previously embodied conditioning, and that these latencies are therefore more radically significant, since they are temporally, logically and psychologically prior to any single empirically observable occurrence of that conditioned behavior.[21] Hence when a behaviorist claims that in order to modify behavior one must find an appropriate reinforcement (e.g., while a cookie might work for a young child, an adult might require a salary incentive), he will nonetheless regard the selection of an appropriate reinforcement as a purely random, pragmatic affair;[22] whatever works for a subject, works. For the Behaviorist the 'general' principle overrides in importance its application in particular circumstances. The Buddhist is more interested in concrete particularities. Each individual's conditioning is the primary issue; the *principle* of conditioning alone has no immediate soteric value (some Buddhist rhetoric to the contrary not withstanding). Rather Buddhism is nothing more than a method that facilitates the unraveling and overcoming, *by each individual*, of each's distinctive configuration of conditioning. The soteric dimension can only be effective to the extent that it addresses and alleviates the particular, distinct situations of individuals. *Upāya* (beneficent deception) means the ability to devise such individualized therapeutic aids for the benefit of specific individuals in specific situations. Sautrāntic Buddhism will go so far as to emphasize discrete, momentary particularity while utterly rejecting universality of any sort. By the same token, in the Pāli texts Buddha emphasized that teaching must be geared to the capacities of particular audiences. To know there is such a thing as conditioning may lead one to metaphysicalize; and what is worse, such 'knowledge' does not offer any leverage into resolving one's own embodied conditioning. Each person must uncover his own conditioning, and not be content with theoretical panaceas. Most significantly, while the Behaviorist is content to substitute one form of conditioning (behavior) for another, the Buddhist attempts to overcome the conditioning process itself. The Buddhist is more interested in (a) *why* someone responds as he/she does to certain things, and (b) why pain and pleasure are so ubiquitous and radically constitutive.

The issue of latency was crucial because it helped explain how discrete experiences of pleasure and pain, through reiteration, formed habits (some scholars have translated *saṃskāra* as 'habit-formations'). In other words, karma was understood as a designatory label for the process of pleasure/pain/neutral conditioning. That which gives me pleasure I wish to experience again (*rāga*), while that which causes pain I wish to continually avoid (*pratigha*). Hence my behavior (*karma*) arises from what I do positively or negatively to reiterate pain and pleasure. As this shapes my actions (*karma*), it is called

8) *tṛṣṇa* (P. *taṇhā*)—'Desire' or more literally 'thirst.' In a Buddhist context 'desire' connotes more than just lust, wanting, or craving. As previous vedānic experiences simmer and coalesce (*saṃskāra*), they come to actualize as specific intentions (*cetanā*). The movement by which tendencies and predispositions become teleologically focused—in other words, when intentions cathex on goals—is called 'desire.'

Desire is a fixation on an object or idea (*artha*), a fixation through which one orients oneself *towards* that object or idea. 'Thirst' means the fixation can become obsessional, laced with a sense of need or necessity, as when a thirsty person, stranded in a desert, can think of nothing more pressing or urgent than alleviating his/her thirst. All other possible 'enticements' lose their allure; one would forego money, pass over sexual opportunities, and sacrifice anything in order to procure some water. Thus, one orients one's values, one's priorities, according to the dictates of one's thirst.

Desire may be a positive desire *for* something, or a negative desire to *avoid* something. It is important to keep in mind that for Buddhism, the problem is *not* desire for material things; more fundamentally, desire is a thirst for ideas, theories (*dṛṣṭi*), since it is these that give us a sense of identity and define the values we impute to material things, such that we then find them desirable. We pursue certain fashions, certain automobiles, certain signs of sophistication or success, etc., *not* because of the materiality of such objects, but rather because of the ideas and values that we and others impute to them. Owning a Porsche instead of a Honda says something about one's *idea* about status rather than expressing anything about the material composition of either car, since either will convey one to one's destination. Those ideas, theories (*dṛṣṭi*) are part of the play of a linguistic-cognitive web of closure (*prapañca, āsava, anuśaya, saṃvṛti*, etc.).

Desire, then, is expressed in our basic intentions toward the world and ourselves. According to Merleau-Ponty, intentionality involves a *directed towardness* of a lived-body toward a perceptual field, and vice versa, or in Husserl's phrase "consciousness is always *consciousness of*." Particularly in Merleau-Ponty's reading, this indicated the simultaneity of consciousness being (i) of an object *and* (ii) of a subject, this simultaneity constituted by and constitutive of the mutual influences and appropriations of the lived-body and the perceptual field.

While the previous *nidānas* were more concerned with the engendering of *possibilities* (the nescience that underpins and makes possible the dynamics of being-in-the-world, the process of embodiment and the further possibilities and limitations which that entails), desire and the subsequent *nidānas* are more concerned with *actualizations*.

In the cardinal doctrine of Buddhism called the Four Noble Truths, 'desire' is often cited as the cause of *duḥkha* (this is the second of the Four truths). But since even the earliest texts claim that the overcoming of *duḥkha* involves knowledge or special modes of knowing (*jñāna* or *prajñā*, P. *aññā* or *paññā*), it quickly became standard practice to assert a kind of parity between *avidyā* (nescience) and *tṛṣṇa* (desire) as co-causes of *duḥkha*. Sometimes this was treated as a parity between cognitive and affective root problematics. However affective disorders (*kleśa*) were seen by Buddhists as derivative of cognitive disorders. With nescience considered more radical and fundamental than desire, the parity was disrupted. While feelings (*vedanā*) played a crucial role in the formation of karmic tendencies, it was nescience that allowed these feelings to engender habitual continuity, that allowed them, as it were, to take on a life of their own. One can only be conditioned by positive and negative reinforcement when, on some level, one is unaware of or overlooks the process of conditioning as it happens. Hence while affective correctives were beneficial, particularly in the moral and ethical spheres, the truly radical remedy to the duḥkhic dilemma was correct knowledge.

Initially correct knowledge was encapsulated as four items in the Noble Eightfold Path (which is itself a corollary to the fourth Noble Truth), viz. *sammā-diṭṭhi, sammā-saṃkappa, sammā-sati* and *sammā-samādhi* (S. *samyagdṛṣṭi, samyaksaṃkalpa, samyaksmṛti* and *samyaksamādhi*) meaning 'correct perspective, correct thought or consideration, correct mindfulness or recollection, and correct meditation,' respectively. The first two items involve theoretic orientation, while the second two items emphasize attitudinal focus and context.[23] As Buddhist theory grew more intricate and diverse, the scope of correct knowledge accordingly expanded, eventually encompassing the vast complex of Abhidharmic speculation and categorization. Mahāyāna, in one stroke, attempted to resimplify correct knowledge, asserting that it involved exposing (1) a false deep inner conviction that eternal essences exist, particularly as *as-signed* to selves (*ātman*) and events (*dharmas*) under the rubric of 'intrinsic natures' (*svabhāva*), (2) a false sense of the continuous in the discontinuous, and (3) the underlying dualistic extremism of all attempted theories (*dṛṣṭi*). By exposing these problems one is enabled to follow a middle way between extremes.[24]

The issues only broached here go to the heart of much of the development of Buddhist theory. The emphasis on 'knowledge-remedies' led Buddhism to become a major spearhead in the development of logic in India and to produce some of India's finest logicians. Dignāga goes so far as to declare in the dedicatory verse to his *Pramāṇasamuccaya* that Buddha is *pramāṇa*, i.e., Buddha and his Awakening are nothing but euphemisms for cognizing correctly. Buddha's axiom *"ehipassiko"* ('come and see')—meaning don't believe anything that your own experience doesn't confirm, no matter who says it—established a critical stance that fluctuated between empiricism[25] and onto-theological skepticism (e.g., Prāsaṅghika-Mādhyamika). This overemphasis on rationalism had its backlashes, and was often mediated by devotional movements, the East Asian Pure Land traditions being the best known.

The schematic complexities of Abhidharmic thought, while relished by such schools such as the Sarvāstivādins and Theravādins (the latter particularly as its doctrines came to be codified in the fifth century by Buddhaghosa), invited attack from other schools, notably Mādhyamika and Sautrāntika, who in their respective manners attempted to simplify if not entirely jettison it. Yogācāra forges a kind of curious middle way between these extremes. While Asaṅga endeavored to develop a distinctly Mahāyānic Abhidharma that grew increasingly more comprehensive and complex (e.g., his *Yogācārabhūmi śāstra*), Vasubandhu's works display a gradual but definite simplification of this enterprise. In the *Triṃśikā*, while he still enumerates the standard dharmic categories like a good Abhidharmist, after verse 17 he reduces them to linguistic euphemisms for the operations of *vijñapti* (Sthiramati's commentary is particularly emphatic about this point). If, as many scholars believe, the *Trisvabhāvanirdeśa* Treatise[26] was his last, most mature work, we can say that in the end he abandons Abhidharmic architectonics for the dialectical interpretation of *pratītya-samutpāda* introduced in the *Madhyānta-vibhāga*.[27]

After Vasubandhu, Yogācāra splinters into (1) a streamlined Abhidharmic school, exemplified by Sthiramati, Dharmapāla and Hsüan-tsang, and (2) a school of critical epistemo-logic, exemplified by Dignāga and Dharmakīrti, that concerned itself less with Abhidharmic categories and more with epistemological issues. To say that this latter school rejected the Abhidharmic form of Yogācāra is not to say that they are Sautrāntikas, as some scholars have held. At the core of both approaches lay a concern with cognition and conditions of knowing, aimed at correcting cognitive errors. The abhidharmic approach was more psychological, the epistemo-logical approach was more epistemological, but the goal was the same for both.

As for the issue of continuity and discontinuity, this debate raged on many fronts throughout Buddhist history. While on the one hand, rubrics were offered that warned against seeing something permanent in the impermanent (one of the four[28] *viparyāsas*), it became difficult to account for moral responsibility or karmic continuity if all conditioned things, including the self, are to be understood as momentary and radically discontinuous. If the act performed by P at $time_1$ does not consequentially inhere in that same P at $time_2$, then it becomes difficult either to hold P responsible for that act after he has committed it, or to assert that the consequences of acts done at $time_1$ come to fruition in or for P at $time_2$. Buddhist karmic theory requires holding both to be the case.[29] Also, causality, especially efficient causality—which is the only form that really interested the Indian Buddhists—also becomes problematic if one adheres to an ontology so radically discontinuous that time and temporality are rejected as misconstrued notions. On the other hand, continuity implies permanent or at least stable *identities*, since to say that X is continuous means that there is an X such that at $time_1$ and at $time_2$ X is the same, i.e., *identical*. But it is precisely this notion of identity that the Buddhist doctrines of *anātman* (no-self) and *anitya* (impermanence) wish to put into question. This controversy, especially as developed between the Sarvāstivādins (on the side of continuity) and the Sautrāntikas (on the side of discontinuity), served as a catalytic condition for Vasubandhu's eventual embracing of Yogācāra and its notion of the ālaya-vijñāna as a solution. 'What is a person if neither a continuous entity nor something discontinuous?' became a basic problematic for Buddhism since many of its doctrines, such as karma and rebirth, presuppose some form of temporally continuous identity. They risk becoming incoherent without it. The various attempts to answer this question contributed to many of the early schisms that resulted in a plethora of schools, such as the Puggalavādins, Paññattivādins, etc. We will return to these questions later while discussing the *Kathā-vatthu.*

Returning to the 'desire' *nidāna*, once again the term used, *tṛṣṇa* (lit. 'thirst'), evokes the sense of a man stranded in the desert, whose sole guiding passion and concern is the alleviation of his thirst. This thirst obstructs and trivializes any other competing concerns. Driven by desires, we formulate and project expectations and aspirations. The success or failure of our attempts to reach our 'objectives' (i.e., those desires which have projected and objectified themselves, transferring[30] their charge to the desired object so as to cathex or teleologize themselves) encourages or frustrates further efforts, hence this too is subject to *vedanic* cataloging and conditioning. The 'successful' precipitates the 'successive.' More importantly, the so-called 'objects' of our world of experience become a thick texture of teleologically cathexed desires, bristling with the same allure and exclusivistic attraction that a mirage holds for the desperate thirsty man lost in his desert. Even the 'objective scientist,' who supposedly observes objects and events dispassionately, has actually cathexed his desire for hypothetical verifications, principles, and understanding onto the events he observes and manipulates. Buddhism reasserts the parity between *avidyā* and *tṛṣṇa* by arguing, as did Kierkegaard,[31] that reason itself is a passion, an expression of desire.

It is the situation and consequence of this projective operation that Yogācāra wishes to highlight by the doctrine of *vijñapti-mātra*, as will be demonstrated later. According to Yogācāra the texture of these projections becomes so thick that nothing else is experienced; hence *vijñapti* (that which causes cathexic objects to be cognized) 'only' (*mātra*) is experienced. This is the 'closure' that psycho-sophically encloses (*saṃvṛti*) the human horizon.

While the dyad of *avidyā-tṛṣṇa* is much discussed, a lesser appreciated but equally important dyad remains virtually unnoticed in much of the secondary literature. The interaction of *saṃskāra* and *vedanā* mirrors to some extent the interaction of the *avidyā-tṛṣṇa* dyad. While the first term of each pair (*avidyā* and *saṃskāra*) primarily involves subliminal or unconscious conditions, the second terms (*vedanā* and *tṛṣṇa*) primarily concern the processes through which the latencies of the first terms become conscious. Also as *avidyā* is the condition upon which *saṃskāra* arises, so is *vedanā* the condition upon which *tṛṣṇa* arises. The Abhidhammic literature especially grounds its analyses on the interrelation of *vedanā* and *saṅkhāra.* Its kammic analysis is rooted in descriptions of how *vedanic* activities latently develop and ultimately reiterate themselves saṅkhārically as they come to fruition (*vipāka*).

As *avidyā* came to be glossed as the fundamental cognitive error under the term *jñeya-āvaraṇa*, *tṛṣṇa* was glossed as the fundamental affective error under the term *kleśa-āvaraṇa. Kleśa* (P. *kilesa*), often translated as 'defilements,' 'afflictions,' 'evil passions,' etc., means *mental disturbances*, i.e., those things which disturb a healthy mental condition.[32] Their specific enumeration varies from text to text and school to school.[33] Yogācāra was one of a number of schools that redefined *avidyā* and *tṛṣṇa* as the two root causes of duḥkha in terms of *jñeyāvaraṇa* and *kleśāvaraṇa* respectively.

9) *upādāna*—'Appropriation' arises with the movement of *saṃskāras* through sensorially operative lived-bodies, conditioned by pleasure/pain. What is pleasurable I desire to repeat; what is painful I desire to avoid. To repeatedly reach out and grasp for what has given me pleasure, or to negatively seize on ways to avoid what has given pain, is called *appropriation.* Its enactment presupposes the prior establishment of a teleological, referential relationship between X and Y such that X has desired Y, has in some manner made it his goal, and now has succeeded in attaining it.

Appropriation also involves a kind of accrual (*prāpti*) onto or into the self. Only that which in some sense is *external* to me can be appropriated. If it were already internal, intrinsic, I could not *take* it; it would already be mine. Even my innermost feelings and thoughts can only be appropriated when they are elsewhere or otherwise then how and where I presently find myself. That which is already mine, according to Buddhism, likewise should not be seen as *essentially* or *intrinsically* mine (*sva-bhāva*), but as products and fruits of prior appropriative acts. We appropriate in order to expand, strengthen and affirm our selves. Self-definition, self-identification arises through appropriation. What is *other* either becomes *mine*, or else it serves as the boundary marker that circumscribes my limits, and thus what I am. The 'more' I *possess*, the 'greater' I *am.*

Conversely the corollary, negative appropriation, defines me by what I reject.[34] Negative appropriation consists of attempting to eject out from myself that which I carry with me always, viz. the memories of previous pains.[35] However it shares the same objectives as positive appropriation, viz. to expand, strengthen and affirm the self, but in these instances, by the avoidance of that which opposes or hinders, i.e., hurts, the self's efforts at self-perpetuation.[36]

Appropriation thus sets and defines the limits of my 'self' while simultaneously striving to always alter it. As I accrue or divest, I expand or contract my self, my horizons. Appropriating ideas, things, people, relationships, personal biography, beliefs, the sensations and feelings which are *mine*, etc., I become the person who, after the fact, can be pointed to as who "I" am. And this "identification" is always retrospective and constructed.

Whereas desire (*tṛṣṇa*) affectively establishes goals and objectives, appropriation (*upādāna*) actively grasps and clings to them. Appropriation is the behavioral correlate to desire. They are two aspects of a conational drive, with desire primarily a mental aspect and appropriation primarily an enactment in action. Desire is an intent; appropriation is the effort to fulfill that intent. They overlap, since the conative is always constituted by affective as well as active aspects—or as Buddhists might put it, since karma is the 'activity of *body, mind, and speech,*' desire and appropriation, insofar as they are sensorial, cognitive and linguistic affects/actions, karmically share the same conative structure.

For the Yogācāra school the 'appropriation' *nidāna* is the most crucial. Vasubandhu's doctrine of *vijñapti-mātra* identified the root problematic as the objectification and subjectification of appropriation (*grāhya-grāhaka*). Unlike many Western commentators, Vasubandhu rarely talks about 'subject' and 'object' but rather describes *grāhaka* ('that which appropriates,' which will be translated subsequently as *noesis* in order to emphasize its intentional, appropriating structure) and *grāhya* ('that which is appropriated,' to be translated *noema*). The movement through which noemata are noetically constituted is appropriation. It is within the circuit of intentionality as it constitutes a world in which noetic subjectivities attempt to project and locate themselves within and toward noemata that Vasubandhu attempts to rupture karmic continuity.

As an instantiation of conditioned desires, appropriation infuses the subjects and objects of experience.[37] Eventually the *activity* of appropriating (the making of karma) supplants and represses the *conditions* for appropriating (the experiential enactment of *pratītya-samutpāda*), establishing a self-perpetuating appropriational dynamic. This dynamic, when self-perpetuating, is called

10) *bhāva* (P. *bhava*)—Here this term should be translated 'impetus' or 'impulse,' or perhaps 'motiv-ation.' *Bhāva*, which sometimes means 'an existent,' is usually translated in the *pratītya-samutpāda* model as 'becoming,' since it derives from the root √*bhū*, 'to become.'[38] Becoming, if taken as a bare concept stripped of its philosophical and metaphysical baggage, conveys the basic sense. Perhaps the best rendering would be "the Ongoing." *Bhāva* overlaps the notion of active inertia. It signifies the fact that there is always already something *going on*. We are impelled to always take a next breath; atoms are in constant motion; the heart keeps beating; even the corpse as a bundle of materiality is fully active and engaged in decompositional transformation; each thought and sensation gives way to a subsequent thought or sensation. Everything is driven, moved (motiv-ated) by an impetus into the next moment, constantly. This concrescence of the previous *nidānas* is never a terminus. It is ongoing, though durational (in Bergson's sense of the term). As the ongoing duration of types of activities, *bhāva* may be called 'behavior.' As that which can be said to always keep the world in motion, it may be called 'motive force.' However, as our description of the previous *nidānas* should indicate, this

'force' is understood in Buddhism as primarily psychological—the implementation of formalized tendencies—and not metaphysical.

For Theravāda, liberation from *saṃsāra* means the 'stopping' of *bhāva*, i.e., the cessation of the 'ongoing,' or bringing *bhāva* to rest. As *bhāvāsava*, the *āsava* of craving existence or lust for life, it is one of the subtle, basic underlying karmic problems that must be overcome in order to Awaken. One of the most common euphemisms for Awakening in the Pāli literature is 'overcoming the āsavas' (*āsavakkhaya*). The Buddha and Arhats are called *khāṇāsava*, 'one who has overcome or destroyed the āsavas.' Thus, *bhāva* cannot be a perpetual metaphysical condition, but rather something personal (or intrapersonal) that ceases to continue at the culmination of the *mārga* (method, path).

As the durational instantiation of appropriational modalities, it is always intentional and hence directional, that is, aimed toward something. This directionality signals *bhāva* as radically temporal, suggesting that time itself functions through motives, or that time is nothing other than a way of measuring the im-pulses.[39] These impulses coalesce as

11) *jāti*—birth (or arising due to conditions), and

12) *mārana* (P. *maraṇa*)—death. Sometimes this last *nidāna* is called 'sickness, old age and death,' evoking three of the four signs prince Gotama saw before leaving home to become the Buddha.[40]

Birth and death, in the Buddhist context, mean more than simply the birth and death of an individual. They signify the arising and ceasing of all conditioned things (*saṃskṛta*), each and every moment. 'Arising and ceasing' signifies the perpetuating, impermanent coursing of *saṃsāra* as well as the arising and ceasing of objects, thoughts, persons, moments, etc. within it. By designating this coursing as 'arising and ceasing' Buddhism seeks to emphasize that everything relies on conditions in order to come into or go out of existence, and further, that all conditioned things inevitably cease or die. Hence 'arising and ceasing' mark the inseparability of life and death as well as highlighting the simple but dialectical fact that the full power and vitality that each and every thing enjoys at the peak of its coming into existence always already marks the limits, boundaries, ends and death of that thing and its power. That is the doctrine of impermanence.

Though we have presented the twelve *nidānas* in the order most typically found in modern sources, traditionally other arrangements of the model were employed, and often considered *more* important. For instance, when *pratītya-samutpāda* is taken as a circle (known as the *bhavacakka*, S. *bhāvacakra*, 'impetus-wheel'), #12 (death) and #1 (nescience) become contiguous. As the first and last *nidānas* of the standard formulation, they occupy highly significant positions. In the circular version of the model death leads to ignorance (i.e., one forgets everything from previous experiences and lives, hence failing to recognize the causes of the same patterns as they appear in present situations).

The 'cause' of ignorance, then, is death, or more specifically forgetfulness, which is to say, lack of effective mindfulness.

In one frequently cited exposition of *pratītya-samutpāda*[41] Buddha is depicted as gaining Awakening, and discovering the process of *pratītya-samutpāda,* by asking himself "Why is there death?" The answer is 'birth.' Birth is the number-one cause of death. Death follows ineluctably from birth. Whatever is born, dies. He then asks, "Why is there birth?" Through a process of deduction, he reasons there is death because there is birth, and there is birth because there is *bhāva,* etc., until he uncovers all twelve *nidānas* culminating in nescience. The listing of the links in their order of 'discovery,' i.e., from #12 to #11, #11 to #10, all the way to #1, is called *pratiloma* (order of discovery) or *sammāpatipadā* (correct methodology). He then further reasons that if nescience is extinguished, *saṃskāras* likewise will be extinguished, and if *saṃskāras* are extinguished then consciousness will be eliminated, and so on, until death itself is extinguished. The standard order, starting with #1 and culminating in #12 is called *anuloma* (preparational or sequential order).

Another text, ascribed to Nāgārjuna, the *Pratītya-samutpāda hṛdaya kārikā,* offers "an exegetical attempt to reconcile the traditional *dvādaśāṅgaḥ pratītya-samutpāda* [i.e., as the twelve links] with the *śūnyatā*-doctrine."[42] A partial translation is given by L. Jamspal and Peter Della Santini.[43] The Jamspal-Della Santini text consists of seven kārikās which divide the twelve links into 3 parts, viz. the 1st, 8th, and 9th links = 'afflictions' (*kleśa* or *vikalpa*)[44]; the 2nd and 10th = deeds (*karma*); and the remaining seven = sufferings (*duḥkha* or *janman*). Though Lindtner argues that this should be accepted as an authentic Nāgārjunic text, its reliance on Abhidharmic theory and such Yogācāra texts as the *Daśabhūmi-sūtra* leaves this conclusion suspect. The *Ch'eng wei-shih lun* follows these same three divisions in its discussion of *pratītya-samutpāda.*[45]

Significantly Nāgārjuna in his *Mūlamadhyamaka kārikā,* in the chapter on *pratītya-samutpāda* (ch. 26), not only chose to repeat the standard twelve-link version of the formula verbatim, but more surprisingly, he utterly neglected to negate or even challenge this formula or the manner of its formulation—which is something that cannot be said for virtually every other Buddhist doctrine he treated, including nirvāṇa and Tathāgata.

We may point out here a feature of the *nidānas* in general. *Prajñapti* in part indicates the reduction of complex factors to a single word or phrase which can then become a kind of conventional shorthand or heuristic. The word "person" evokes an endless list of characteristics and qualities, and any particular person is an intersection of myriads of causal chains, from his/her ancestors, to the cultural notions and products that have nourished and sustained him/her, etc. The danger of *prajñapti* is that users of a prajñaptic term will think that it has an actual integral referent *apart from* those causal chains, and thus overlook the diverse conditions it has heuristically simplified and supplemented.[46]

In the same manner, each of the *nidānas* functions as a heuristic or conventional supplement for the interrelations between the others. This is most clearly seen when a *nidāna* is deconstructed into its contiguous *nidānas.* For example, there is actually no independent or self-functioning thing called 'desire' (#8). Desire is a verbal substitute for saying 'the interrelationship of *vedanā* (#7) and appropriation (#9).' Based on particular experiences of pleasure and pain, there will be a tendency to appropriate particular things. That 'tendency' is desire. Similarly, *nāma-rūpa* ('name and form,' lived-body, #4) is shorthand for *vijñāna* (consciousness, #3) and its relation to *āyatana* (sensorial capacity, #5), i.e., the relation (*nāma*) to *rūpa*. Or, consciousness (#3) is shorthand for the relation between *saṃskāras* (embodied conditioning, #2) and *nāma-rūpa* (#4), i.e., the cognizance suspended between embodied unconscious dispositions and psycho-physical structures. This exercise could be applied to any of the *nidānas*: they all reduce to their contiguous neighbors.[47]

Thus, "embodied conditioning" (#2) is shorthand for 'nescience' (#1) emerging into consciousness (#3); consciousness is 'embodied conditioning' instantiating as a sensorial body (#4); the sensorial body is consciousness channeled into the six sensorial realms (#5); the six sensorial realms are a way of speaking about a sensorial body experiencing sensory contact (#6); sensory contact consists of the six sense spheres engaged in pleasurable, painful, or neutral sensations (#7); *vedanā* is the precipitation of sensory contact *as* desires (#8); desire is a euphemism for how pleasurable and painful conditioning manifests as appropriational activities (#9); Appropriation describes how desire becomes on-going behavior (#10); the on-going coalesces, giving birth (#11) to consequences of appropriational trajectories; birth is the on-going leading to its inevitable conclusion, death (#12). Under careful scrutiny, each link disappears into its surrounding links. There is no such "thing" as "ignorance," "desire," etc.; each term is a prajñapti for certain aspects of the conditioning dynamics called *pratītya-samutpāda*. Throughout the Nikāyas, Buddha resorts to *pratītya-samutpāda* to explain and eliminate all sorts of misunderstandings, and he does not always offer the full list of twelve links. Sometimes other links (e.g., *āsavas*) are substituted for one or more of the standard twelve. This should remind us not to freeze our understanding of *pratītya-samutpāda* to these twelve "things," but rather to use them as an access route into the conditional dynamics these 'co-arising' links allude to.

Moreover, this mutual reductionism can be expanded, so that all the *nidānas* reduce to all the others. Hence Buddhists claim that they are always simultaneous, that each moment is constituted by the full twelve *nidānas*, and that this model is merely a heuristic, though an extremely efficacious one.

While the root *problematic* is nescience, the root *problem* is death. While the former is the (indirect) cause of the latter, the dilemma of the latter is what instigates the investigation that uncovers the former. When the former is eliminated, the latter also disappears.

Since knowledge of some sort (*jñāna*) is necessary to eliminate nescience, nothing is more vitally important, valuable or useful for overcoming life's problems. Thus Buddhist praxis inevitably centers on the clear, insightful seeing (*vipaśyanā*) of things in the way they become (*yathābhūtam*). The development of this insight (*jñāna*) is called *prajñā*. Moreover, as the problem of death is not merely an intellectual or abstract problem, but involves powerful and even terrifying existential and psychological dimensions, Buddhist 'reason' endeavors to existentialize and psychologize the intellectual, while simultaneously rigorously reasoning through the psychological and existential. This marks the psychosophic project of all schools of Buddhism, no matter which method or approach they take to this problem.

Before moving on to the next model, it should be noted that although throughout Buddhist history the *pratītya-samutpāda* model has been used and explicated in countless and diverse ways, primarily they boil down to six basic paradigmatic interpretations, several of which have been suggested during the course of this exposition.

(1) It is often treated as a *sequential series* of twelve links, link #1 leading to link #2, etc. This is usually stated through the conditional causal formula '[when] X exists, Y comes to exist' or 'dependent on X, there is Y.' Typically these formulae occur in the following forms: *avijjāpaccayā saṅkhāra*, '[given the] condition nescience, embodied-conditioning [arises]'; or the formula in *M* I.262-64:

> *Imasmiṃ sati idaṃ hoti, imassa upādā idaṃ uppajjati. Imasmiṃ asati idaṃ na hoti, imassa nirodhā idaṃ nirujjhati.*
>
> When that exists, this comes to be; on the arising of that, this arises. When that does not exist, this does not come to be; on the cessation of that, this ceases.'

This meant, given link #1, link #2 arose, and given link #2, link #3 arose, etc., all the way up to link #12. By extinguishing link #1, link #2 also ceases, and so on. *Pratītya-samutpāda* was also treated as bi-directional, i.e., as #1 up to #12 (called *anuloma*, 'conforming' or *micchāpatipadā*, 'erroneous methodology') as well as from #12 down to #1 (called *pratiloma* or *sammāpatipadā*). The *Saṃyutta Nikāya*, in the *sal-āyatana* section, claims that the *anuloma* version is 'incorrect' (*micchāpatipadā*, lit. 'erroneous method'), whereas its negative counterpart ('when nescience does not exist, embodied-conditioning ceases, etc.') is 'correct' (*sammāpatipadā*, lit. 'correct method'). Hence the positive enumeration is 'erroneous' while the negational enumeration is 'correct.'

Frequently modern writers fail to appreciate the cogency and coherency of *pratītya-samutpāda* simply because the ascending causal sequence puzzles them. They wonder, for instance, Why should birth (#11) come so late in the sequence? The order of discovery, i.e., the order in which Buddha supposedly discovered the twelve links, however, is not the ascending order (#1→#12), but rather the descending order (#12→#1). As stated above, he asked, 'Why is there Death?' (#12), and answered, 'Because there is Birth' (#11). 'Why is there Birth? Because there is Impetus/impetuousness (#10, *bhāva*),' and so on until he 'discovered' Nescience (#1). Viewed in this way with a little careful reflection, the twelve links become eminently reasonable.

(2) For several reasons, including the overlap of connotations between the various *nidānas*, the fact that each can be seen as a mere nominalization of the

dynamics of the others, that each *nidāna* functions as a cause for the others, and that they are thus mutually dependent, led to the conclusion that rather than being treated as a sequence, more properly they should be understood as *simultaneous.* Once the Mādhyamika doctrine of *śūnyatā* took hold—namely that all things lack a self-creating, self-defining, independent essence (*svabhāva*)—no single thing, much less a single *nidāna,* could be postulated as causally efficient in and of itself. Since the 'others' upon which anything depends are in turn also devoid of self-essence, things were all to be regarded as mutually dependent, i.e., mutually conditioned and conditioning. Since no thing and no moment could be given primacy, all were evened-out into a simultaneous synchronicity which itself had no self-essence. Since even the nomenclature 'simultaneous synchronicity' becomes meaningless without its diachronic counterpoint, *pratītya-samutpāda* came to be regarded, as Candrakīrti writes in the *Prasannapadā,* as *pratyayatā matreṇa* ('utter conditionality')[48].

(3) It came also to be treated as a sophisticated and intricate *causal nexus.* This genre of interpretation is best represented by Abhidharma literature and Buddhaghosa's *Visuddhimagga.*[49]

(4) When applied as a methodological tool for analyzing how, in terms of conditioning, no thing has a self or essence, *pratītya-samutpāda* enables the *dialectical and deconstructive de-nominalization* of all 'theories' (*dṛṣṭi*) of reality. This usage was most consistently carried out by the Mādhyamika school. It also shows up in other writings, particularly when the entire list of twelve links becomes subsumed under the dialectical tension of some particular pair. The most frequently encountered example of a dialectical dyad metonymically substituting itself for the full formula, is the birth-death pair, which as stated above came to stand for the entire realm of *saṃsāra,* as did *pratītya-samutpāda* itself. The pair *vijñāna* and *nāma-rūpa* also emerged sporadically in various manifestations of the mind-body problem. When Buddhism psychologized, usually the *vedanā-tṛṣṇa* pair took center stage; and when it moralized, the *tṛṣṇa-upādāna* dyad became prominent. Incidentally the highly moralistic content of much Yogācāra material derives from the preeminence this last dyad enjoys in their system, particularly the latter term.

(5) When applied to an individual, it could also give an account of his/her experience of the cycle of rebirth. Buddhaghosa's formulation of this is the best known. He claimed that #1, #2 and half of #3 signified one's past life; the other half of #3 through half of #10 signified one's present life; and the last half of #10 through #12 signified one's future life. Conze believed that the twelve links version developed as the *pratītya-samutpāda* doctrine came to be applied to the problem of rebirth.

(6) It can also be used to highlight what each school considered paradigmatic of Buddhism. Generally the claim is that though all twelve nidānas are simultaneous and all together condition each moment, in terms of how someone experiences the effects from moment to moment, usually one or the other nidāna predominates in a person's awareness. For instance, when I am desiring, I may 'forget' the other conditions, such as the sensations, previous

vedanic experiences and their saṃskāric consequences, etc., though these are all operative in that moment of desire. As pointed out, the desire itself could be reduced to the confluence of those other conditions. Similarly, in a moment of sensation (*sparśa*) I may forget or overlook the cognitive and affective components which go into making that sensory moment (the field of 'philosophy of perception' in the West sometimes myopically exemplifies this). Based on this, various schools have argued that certain nidānas are more efficacious for entry into, clarification, and resolution of the karmic dilemma, due to such factors as the ability of those nidānas to more efficiently evoke awareness of the others, the degree of each's cognitive ubiquity, their amenability to conscious alteration, their ability to positively influence the remaining nidānas, etc.

The predominance of one nidāna also shows itself in the central concerns of the various Buddhist schools. While some focus more on 'desire' as a root problematic, others focus more on 'nescience,' or the problems of cognitive dissonance due to improper or imperfect sensation (*sparśa*), etc. One may even systematically group or categorize the various schools and thinkers by determining which nidāna predominates or is central in their philosophy (though, of course, all the nidānas will be utilized in some form). As an example, I have compiled the following correlations, which are merely provisional illustrations, admittedly controversial and subject to revision or reevaluation. On the left are the names of the nidānas and on the right the school(s) or thinker(s) who most exemplifies a basic concern or central preoccupation with that nidāna (with their key doctrines in parentheses).

1. *avidyā*	Nāgārjuna (*śūnya-dṛṣṭi, prapañcopaśama*)
2. *saṃskāra*	Candrakīrti (*prapañca*)
3. *vijñāna*	*Sākāravāda-Vijñānavāda;* Paramārtha's *āmala-vijñāna*
4. *nāma-rūpa*	Tantra; Buddhaghosa
5. *āyatana*	Sautrāntika (*samyakpramāṇa*)
6. *sparśa*	Dignāga (*pratyakśa*)
7. *vedanā*	Buddhaghosa (*Visuddhimagga*)
8. *tṛṣṇa*	Theravāda
9. *upādāna*	Vasubandhu (*vijñapti-mātra*)
10. *bhāva*	Sarvāstivāda; Tathāgatagarba
11. *jāti*	Pure Land
12. *mārana*	Dōgen; Han-shan te-ching

In this list Buddhaghosa appears twice. He is associated with *vedanā* since the most often studied portion of his *Visuddhimagga* is the meditation section, which emphasizes a kind of alternating adhesion/aversion therapy. One practices and cultivates good virtues, while one overcomes, for instance, lust for women by visualizing them as putrefying corpses, etc. This is a kind of self-imposed operant conditioning designed to intercept and alter the manner in which one classifies various experiences vedānically. I have also included him under *nāma-rūpa* because the fundamental question underlying the *Visuddhimagga* is 'What is *nāma-rūpa,*' i.e., how does it become reborn, what are the kammic factors, etc.? Dōgen and Han-shan are grouped under *mārana* because (1) their underlying existential issues concern impermanence (e.g., Dōgen's revaluation of satori as *Uji*, 'Being-Time,' affectively cultivated through *Genjōkōan*, 'Real-izing the kōan,' etc.), and (2) both—as did many other Buddhists, particularly in the Zen tradition—were driven to seek answers from Buddhism due to the deaths of their parents (particularly mothers) when they were very young. Hsüan-tsang also exhibits some of this when he gets the Emperor to foot the bill for his mother's reburial after his triumphant return to China from India. The other correlations should be self-explanatory.

Though we have barely scratched the surface in our exploration of *pratītya-samutpāda* , it is now time to turn to the next model.

Notes

1 The most common traditional account of Buddha's Awakening claims that it occurred at night, and describes three sequential insights which respectively occupied the three 'watches' of the night (i.e., roughly three-hour periods, approximately corresponding to 9-12 p.m., 12-3 a.m., and 3-6 a.m.). In the first watch Buddha saw his own karmic continuity, i.e., all his previous lives, actions, thoughts, etc., the interaction of each action with those that preceded it and those which followed from it, and how all these had led him to this particular moment under the Bodhi tree. In the second watch his insight extended to the past and future actions and conditions of all sentient beings, how each and every situation arises due to previous actions and conditions and how this subsequently conditions the arising of further actions. In other words, he 'saw' the principle of karma, not as a universalistic 'principle,' but in or as its particular operations. In the third watch he observed *pratītya-samutpāda,* which held the key to unraveling karmic bondage (i.e., *duḥkha*). He achieved Awakening (*bodhi*) just as the dawn broke. According to the opening section of the *Mahāvagga* in the Pāli Vinaya, Buddha spent the seven days following his Awakening enjoying the bliss of liberation while contemplating again and again the details of *pratītya-samutpāda.*

That the elements of this story are so mythologically perfect has led some scholars to question its authenticity. These doubts are buttressed by the occurrence in the Pāli *suttas* of significantly different versions of Buddha's Awakening, which vary on such things as the relevance of its relation to conditioned co-arising, some concurring with the above version of the story and others contradicting it, though many of these accounts are supposed to represent Buddha's own words (there are also second-hand accounts by his contemporaries). See D. M. Williams, "The *Paṭiccasamuppāda* : A Developed Formula," *Religious Studies*, 14, March 1978, pp. 35-56, esp. pp. 38-40, for a discussion of some of these variants. Also see the excellent study by Étienne Lamotte, "Conditioned Co-production and Supreme Enlightenment," in *Buddhist Studies in Honor of Walpola Rahula* (London: Gordon Frazer) 1980, pp. 118-132. We need not here go further into the question of the authenticity of this story. For our purposes it should be sufficient to point out that the tripartite knowledge acquired during the three watches—knowing one's own karma, the karma of others, and reaching the insight that precipitates Awakening—is also found repeated in other contexts, and hence probably represents an early tradition of what, for Buddhists, was both fundamental and *unique* to Buddhism in their own eyes. For instance, the *Tevijja-vacchagotta sutta* in *Majjhima Nikāya* has Buddha deny the claim that he is omniscient, that rather he possesses three kinds of special knowledge (*tevijja*), viz. (1) When he wishes, he can look back into all his past lives and see who and what he was, the situations he had been in, etc., (2) when he wishes, he can see the past, present and future lives of all beings, their dispositions, if they are happy or sad, and the conditions which produce those dispositions, etc., and (3) he knows the means of cutting off the *āsavas* ('outflows,' 'cankers,' 'festering karmic predilections') and *āvaraṇas* (cognitive and conative obstructions), he has already done this, and 'knows how to enter therein' (i.e., into the condition devoid of *āsavas* and *āvaraṇas*). Cutting off the *āsavas* is synonymous in Pāli texts with achieving Awakening. Here cutting off the *āsavas*, etc., may also be taken as a synonym for understanding conditioned co-arising. However, see *Majjhima Nikāya* I.21-22 for perhaps a different implication.

2 The Pāli texts contain formulations that omit certain *nidānas*, and there are also instances in which terms not part of the standard list are included (e.g., *āsavas, papañca*, etc.) On this, see Conze, *Buddhist Thought in India*, pp. 156-158; D. M. Williams, "The *Paṭiccasamuppāda* : A Developed Formula," *op. cit.*, pp. 35-56; also see TAKEUCHI Yoshinori, *The Heart of Buddhism*, esp. pp. 63-126, for an attempt to philosophically investigate these discrepancies, utilizing not only a close reading of the texts but also ideas culled from Kant, Husserl, Heidegger and other European thinkers. It should also be noted that as schismatic disputes developed, almost any " typical" Buddhist position drew counterpositions, all of which had their adherents and schools. The *Kathā vatthu* and *Abhidharmakośa* with their commentaries are just two of the better known compendiums of these disputes. This plurality of positions should be kept in mind while reading the following exposition of *pratītya-samutpāda*. Many of the positions given here have their Buddhist opponents. I am interested in giving a sense of the issues with which Yogācāra was concerned, though the exposition is not confined to their position alone, nor does it present their position fully.

3 We will shortly offer a description that accords with the *Abhidharmakośa* and general Yogācāra theory.

4 The Pāli texts sometimes list three *āsavas* and sometimes four: 1. *kāmāsava* (karmic propensity for pleasure), 2. *bhavāsava* (karmic propensity for existence), 3. *ditthāsava* (karmic propensity for a viewpoint or perspective), 4. *avijjāsava* (karmic propensity for nescience). Sometimes the third (*ditthāsava*) is omitted, and sometimes another *āsava*, namely *abhavāsava* (karmic propensity for non-existence) is included. The "destruction of the *āsavas*" is a euphemism or synonym for complete Awakening. Scholars have debated how to translate *āsava* for over a century now (e.g., 'outflows, intoxicants, cankers,' etc.), but despite many poignant and creative efforts, none are fully satisfactory. The term was originally appropriated from the Jains, who used it in a more concrete sense (the flow of karmic particles attracted to a being performing an action), but Buddhists sharply rejected Jaina theories on karma. Some examples of the Buddhist-Jaina disputes on karma will be offered later.

5 For the other *āvaraṇa*, i.e., *kleśa-āvaraṇa*, see the description of the eighth *nidāna* below. The theory of two *āvaraṇas* is a later innovation, thoroughly entrenched by the time the Yogācāra school emerges. In the earlier texts, such as the Pāli *suttas* and *Abhidhamma*, more often a list of *five āvaraṇas*, or *nīvaraṇas* (*pañcanīvaraṇā*) is encountered, though, by most accounts, these are usually confronted and overcome early in one's practice, rather than signifying the culmination of practice (but cf. Nyanatiloka's *Buddhist Dictionary*, Kandy: Buddhist Publication Society, 1980, 4th revised ed., pp. 129f.). Gunaratana gives the following description of the *pañcanīvaraṇā*:

> The five hindrances (*pañcanīvaraṇā*) are sensual desire, ill will, sloth and torpor, restlessness and worry, and doubt... They receive the name "hindrances" because they hinder and *envelop* the mind... (*The Path of Serenity and Insight*, pp. 28f; emphasis added)

They 'enclose' or effect mental *closure*. Cf. the notion of *saṃvṛti* (enclosure) to be discussed in Chapter Four. This list of five later becomes part of the dispute between the 75 dharma scheme of the *Abhidharmakośa* and the 100 dharma scheme of Yogācāra, i.e., whether to classify them as *kleśa dharma, aniyata dharma*, etc. See appendices for those respective lists.

6 *The Principles of Buddhist Psychology* (Albany: SUNY Press, 1987).

7 Padmasiri de Silva, *Buddhist and Freudian Psychology* (NY: Barnes and Noble, 1979).

8 As we will see, in the Pāli Abhidhamma the term *cetanā* (volition or motivation) is frequently substituted for *saṃskāra*. In Mahāyāna, this collapsing of saṃskāric strata is perhaps most evident in the writings of Vasubandhu (who subsumes it under the rubric of 'appropriation,' *upādāna*) and Candrakīrti (who sees these strata as similar expressions of prapañcic anxieties, i.e., as psycho-linguistic projections attempting to mask duḥkhic dis-ease). For both Vasubandhu as a Yogācārin and Candrakīrti as a Madhyamakan, *saṃskāra* is merely a nominalistic method of describing the basic psycho-cognitive disorders that characterize human existence. Vasubandhu calls these basic disorders *vijñapti* while Candrakīrti calls them *prapañca*. Cf., e.g. Candrakīrti's *Prasannapadā* for kārikā 18.9 where he defines *prapañca* as *vāk* ('discourse') and *vikalpa* as *citta-pracāra* ('the play-ground of thought').

Probably precisely because *saṃskāra* is a nominalistic recounting of subconscious operations of consciousness, Vasubandhu in his *Triṃśikā*—the core text behind the *Ch'eng wei-shih lun*—chose to bypass listing or describing the *saṃskāras* usually included in the Yogācāric list of 100 dharmas. This list is given below in an appendix. After describing how consciousness operates (*vipāka, pariṇāma, pravṛtti*, etc.), a separate discussion of *saṃskāra* would have been redundant. Perhaps the text that most explicitly collapses these categories is the *Laṅkāvatāra Sūtra*; cf., e.g., *sagātakam* section, vs. 683 and 718.

9 *Kāya* (body) is, in Buddhism, a larger notion than *nāma-rūpa*, since there are bodies entirely independent of *rūpa*, such as the *mano-maya-kāya* (body produced by mind). Also see Rupert Gethin's "The Five Khandhas...," *op. cit.*

10 The notion of senses actively *intending* or constituting (or even 'constructing') objects became virtually axiomatic for many Indian schools, not only Sāṃkhya and Buddhism. It can even be found as late as Svapneśvara's commentary (18th century ?) to Śāṇḍilya's *Bhakti-sūtra*; see Cowell's translation, ch. 1, p. 4 and n. 3 (*Bibliotheca Indica*, v. 84, 1981, W. German rpt. of the 1878 Calcutta ed.)

11 Stated another way, many Buddhists contend that language does not refer to things, but only to other words, i.e., language is self-referential. The 'tree' indicated by that word is not any actual physical object, but rather a set of linguistic conceptions—for example, roots, organic, shade, wood, green, brown, branches, photosynthesis, elm, oak, willow, characteristics of chemistry, physics, literature, etc. One superimposes such concepts onto certain sensory precepts or imaginary constructions so seamlessly that whatever might lie outside language's closure becomes thoroughly obscured.

12 Prapañca is often used in both Pāli and Mādhyamika texts to signify the root problematic, the erasure of which eliminates duḥkhic ensnarement. Yogācāra also uses this term, though its use there is not as prominent as in these two other schools. See the excellent examination of prapañca by Bhikkhu Ñāṇananda, *Concept and Reality in Early Buddhist Thought: an Essay on 'Papañca' and 'Papañca-Saññā-Saṅkhā'*. On p. 130 Ñāṇananda correctly warns "to equate [*papañca*] to '*nāmarūpa*'... would be to obscure an important segment of the philosophy of early Buddhism." Though he says this in the context of extricating the distinctively Buddhistic use of the term from its later appropriation and redesignation by other systems, notably Vedānta, this may also caution us against treating these terms as synonyms.

They cannot be fully reduced to each other, though their semantic spread does overlap. The same caution applies to the other terms being listed here as implicated by *nāma-rūpa.*

Moreover the observation that prapañca implies that something extra is generated and remains—that even as these terms overlap, that overlap itself creates new resonances, connotations, evocations, a psycho-linguistic *excess* that helps to establish the conditions for the further generation of further terms, which require *more* clarification, etc. -- also applies to the overlapping of the four models being articulated here. For instance, some Buddhist schools might claim that only the first and fourth models are reducible to the second, i.e., *pratītya-samutpāda.* We will soon demonstrate that the third can also be reduced to the second -- in fact the Pāli texts have already substituted and interchanged them in the most critical and significant contexts. Nonetheless, by virtue of the excess alluded to here, these models can never be entirely reduced to each other. To a certain extent, this notion of 'excess' and the notion of *prapañca* also 'overlap' in this same manner. *Prapañca*, particularly in its aspect as 'proliferating,' tellingly intersects what we, following suggestions in the writings of Bataille, Derrida, et al., have described as excess.

13 The difficulty of accounting for this special function of *mano-vijñāna* both logically and epistemologically contributed to the Yogācāra attempt to supplement the six *vijñānas* with two additional *vijñānas*, making eight in all.

14 *The Book of Kindred Sayings*, tr. by F.L. Woodward, v.4, p. 8.

15 This line of reasoning, though already present in the earliest texts, became most clearly articulated in Dharmottara's -*ṭīkā* to Dharmakīrti's *Nyāyabīndu*. It is also echoed in the opening pages of Kamalaśīla's commentary to the *Tattvasaṃgraha*. The point in these texts, as in the early texts, is that this psycho-linguistic overlay (= imaginative conceptualization, *savikalpa-jñāna*) obstructs direct cognition of the non-conceptualized sensorium (*nirvikalpa-jñāna*—though Dharmottara's position is a bit more complex; for him a valid cognition must be distinct and 'reach' its object, hence it must be definite, *savikalpa*, and by definition cannot be indefinite or indistinct, *nirvikalpa*. In the text however this is not as clear as I am stating it here and it may be fair to say that he equivocates on this issue).

This debate grew out of Dharmakīti's revision of Dignāga's definition of 'valid perception.' While Dignāga defined valid perception as *kalpanāpoḍha* (i.e., 'devoid of conceptual construction' or *avikalpa* 'without constructive imagination') Dharmakīrti added that it must also be *abhrānta* 'free of error'. To be free of error, it was assumed and argued, implied being definite and non-ambiguous, and thus Dharmottara's position. For an insightful discussion of this issue, with special reference to the problem of cognitive errors (mirages, eye-sickness, etc.) see Eli Franco's "Once Again on Dharmakīrti's Deviation from Dignāga on *Pratyakṣābhāsa*," *Journal of Indian Philosophy*, 14 (1986) pp. 79-97. For a related discussion on the criteria of veridical perception, this time between Yogācāra and Sautrāntika, see Bimal Matilal's " Error and Truth - Classical Indian Theories," *Philosophy East and West*, 31, 2 (1981) pp. 215-224.

Though this fact sometimes is obscured or lost amidst the intricacies and complexities of philosophic debate, it cannot be overemphasized: the 'ineffability' of reality derives not from reality being somewhere other than experience, but simply from the fact that sensation, as sensation, is always verbally 'silent'. *Prapañca* is the discourse (*vāk*—see above) that *supplements* it; it is the linguistic web that accompanies sensation, infiltrating it, finally substituting *itself* for the actual sensations.

Literature is the attempt to fill the gap between sensation and discourse with *meaning*, an activity that is both a reduction of sensation to language and an evocation of sensation by language. It could be argued that beginning with the *Prajñāpāramitā* literature, the Buddhist theory of verbal and textual authority (*śruti*) hinges on the ability of fictitious literature (i.e., the *sūtras* of a Buddha who does not speak; cf. *Kathā vatthu* XVIII.2 and similar statements in the *Laṅkāvatāra sūtra, Lotus sūtra,* etc.) to evoke soterically expedient sensations.

16 The "illusion" of externality will be discussed more fully in chapter 19.

17 How this psycho-linguistic closure comes to reiterate itself will be outlined and examined in what is to follow. It is the formative question for Abhidharma Buddhism. In Chinese *saṃsāra* is translated 生滅 *sheng-mieh* which means 'birth and destruction,' 'arising and ceasing,' or 'life and death,' implying the repetitions of rebirth through multiple lives and deaths.

18 See Part I for a comparison between the three types of components in a *dhātu*—viz. organ, object and consciousness—and Merleau-Ponty's notion of the 'intentional arc.'

19 Merleau-Ponty also refutes the notion of sensation as a passive process, and even rejects the term 'sensation,' offering in its stead *le sentir. Sentir* is the infinitive meaning 'to sense' and *le* treats the verb as if it were a noun, hence this would be literally translated as 'the to-sense,' evoking the active, intentional character of sensing. On his refutation of the theories of passive perception, particularly as they presuppose the 'constancy hypothesis' (i.e., there is a one-to-one correspondence between actual objects and our perceptions of them) see ch. 1 of his *Phenomenology of Perception.* On *le sentir* see *ibid.* ch. 2.

20 Cf. Sthiramati's commentary to v.15 of the *Triṃśikā*; and ch. 1 of the *Abhidharmakośa.*

21 Thus, while on the one hand Abhidharma thought is concerned with the description and analysis of conscious experience (*citta* and *caitta*, i.e., apperception and its cognitive fields), this concern is always the context for, as well as contextualized by, the unconscious conditions (*saṃskāra; citta-viprayukta saṃskāra*, etc.). The desire to identify concrete latencies even went so far as the positing of rūpic intentional structures, such as *avijñapti-rūpa* and *vijñapti-rūpa* by the Sarvāstivādins. The notion of a latent conditioning that is 'deeper' or (logically) prior to empirical conditioning is discussed in Yogācāra as *bījās* (seeds), of which there are two types: (1) acquired seeds - corollaries to the 'empirical conditioning' discussed, and (2) 'beginningless' seeds - those seeds or conditioning factors and structures which have always already underpinned the process of conditioning.

'Beginningless' is a commonly misunderstood Buddhist term that simply means, much as the term "transcendental" meant for Husserl, that which *constitutes* experience *though not* itself *given* in the actual moment of experience. It was their admittedly sloppy way (since it confuses, among other things, logical and temporal priority) of circumventing the chicken-and-egg problem. If how I am conditioned now depends on my previous conditioning, what initially conditioned me to be susceptible to conditioning at all? Moreover, what originally differentiated my conditioning from someone else's, such that mine has been advantageous (*kuśala*) and hers disadvantageous (*akuśala*), or *vice versa*?

The notion of an unconscious assumes that certain forces must always already be in operation, whether libidinal forces, or "seeds." Hence the interpretation of Freud's notion of 'drives' (*trauben*) by the American Freudians as "instincts" derived naturally, if mistakenly, from the original concept of the unconscious as operations always already in play. The problem of the 'origins' of the karmic consciousness stream became a kind of Buddhist psycho-epistemological parallel to the Western theological problem of the first cause or prime mover. We will examine how Hsüan-tsang treated this controversy, which became quite heated in China, later when dealing with the *Ch'eng wei-shih lun* in Part Five.

22 This is to a large extent a consequence of Behaviorism's radical empiricism, i.e., its desire that everything it describes and asserts be 'objectively' observable. Since choosing what would give John pleasure or Mary pain involves to some extent John's and Mary's subjective dispositions, the Behaviorist strives to avoid basing his science on such 'non-publicly observables'. Hence he avoids difficult issues, such as the fact that the same object (e.g., a pornographic movie) might give John pleasure and at the same time give Mary pain (or *vice versa*). Thus pain and pleasure are not intrinsic properties of an object, but depend on the dispositions of the perceiver. For the Behaviorist, whether such a movie causes someone pain or pleasure should be ascertained by observing empirical behavior, not by an appeal to subjective states. For good introductions to Behaviorism, see e.g., John B. Watson's *Behaviorism* (NY: Norton Library) 1970 rpt. of 1924 ed.; or B. F. Skinner's *About*

Behaviorism (NY: Vintage) 1976. For a step-by-step manual of how operant conditioning is implemented, see Luke S. Watson, Jr.'s *Child Behavior Modification: A Manual for Teachers, Nurses, and Parents* (NY: Pergamon Press) 1973; For some of Skinner's responses to the critique I have suggested here, see his "Humanism and Behaviorism" in *Reflections*, VIII, no. 3, 1973, pp. 1-8. This attitude for avoiding 'subjectivistic' or 'psychologistic' explanations is also echoed in most twentieth century Analytic Philosophy, particularly in the area of what is perhaps currently mislabeled 'philosophy of mind'. Did the logical and evidential difficulties of 'psychologism,' the anxiety of ambiguity, prove too *painful*, leading to this 'aversion' (*pratigha*)?

In contemporary European philosophy one of the more interesting attempts to deal with this issue, particularly in light of the Buddhist notion of *saṃskāra* as latent and yet related to volition, is that of Paul Ricouer, especially the first volume of his 'philosophy of will' trilogy, *Le Volontaire et l'involontaire* (Paris: 1950), tr. into English by Erazim Kohak as *Freedom and Nature: The Voluntary and the Involuntary* (Evanston: Northwestern UP, 1966). However Buddhists would be extremely critical of several elements in Ricouer's attempt to reconcile the decisive, effort-making, consenting will with the 'involuntary' resistances of personal character, the unconscious and "the brute fact of organic life." First, Ricouer's wish to salvage and preserve the "I" (like many others, he takes Descartes' salvaging of the Cogito as a decisive and positive historical moment for philosophy), particularly the I as *appropriator* of life and world, simultaneously confounds freedom with bondage (we shall see later that the issue of appropriation is central to Yogācāra's analysis of *saṃsāra*) as well as confusing the notions of agent and action. 'Will,' for Buddhism, is a *prajñapti* for the coalescence of saṃskāric latencies; the activity of deciding is not the expression of a self (*ātman*) or will, but the expression of compulsive and impulsive forces -- at least in the case of we nonenlightened ones; but a fully awakened Buddha must be devoid of will, since will implies a *desire* that arises from a perceived lack, and the Buddha must be beyond this; which is why Mahāyāna Buddhism insists on limiting one's progress to the highest Bodhisattva realm such that one always intentionally falls short of becoming a full Buddha precisely so that one can 'will' to help other sentient beings -- hence the agent is (a euphemism for) latent tendencies, not a quasi-docetic 'incarnating Cogito'. This is not the place to develop a point by point Buddhist critique of Ricouer's project (which would include his notions of body, Transcendence, fault, consent, preformed emotions, etc.). His later revisions when confronting Freud already indicate that he himself saw a need to modify his position in the face of saṃskāric complexities. Here we need only reiterate that when he offers arguments like "the act of deciding is the central and constitutive act of my mode of being" (*Freedom and Nature*, p. xviii, translator's intro) because "a decision intends its object as something *to be done by me...* [and] *is within my power*" (*ibid.*), this indicates an attempt at self-affirmation, not because there is a self which is free in virtue of that affirmation, as Ricouer maintains, but because the sheer fact of this attempt signifies that the desire for self-affirmation already concedes the absence of any self, such that a self must be constructed in the place of this absence. Since this need, like all needs, "is not self-explanatory but is a lack and a desire which acquire[s] definitive direction only as appropriated by a will" (*ibid.*, p. xix), Ricouer's resolution of the tension between self and object, appropriator and appropriated, will and unwilling, becomes a mere nominalistic victory of the will over the unwilling which, in spite of its nominalistic supplementarity (see above) or perhaps even because of it, has already conceded itself to the saṃskāric forces it intends to subdue with its 'consent' treaty. This deserves further investigation, but that must await another occasion. All in all, Ricouer's work is one of the most sustained wrestlings with this problematic in the twentieth century.

23 The assigning of *samādhi* to the category of knowledge rather than maintaining it as a distinct category may be a bit controversial. On these categories, see the discussion below on the *śīla, samādhi, prajñā* model in chapter six.

24 In Yogācāra this is most clearly exemplified by the characterization of Awakening as an exchanging of *vi-jñāna* (bifurcating cognition) for *jñāna* (non-dual, immediate knowing).

25 On early Buddhism as a logical, empirical enterprise, see Jayatilleke's classic *Early Buddhist Theory of Knowledge.*

26 This text was never translated into Chinese. English translations from the Sanskrit and Tibetan are found in Kochumuttom and Anacker.

27 On both the implicit and explicit uses of *pratītya-samutpāda* in the *Madhyānta-vibhāga*, see Appendix 3 to my dissertation, *A Philosophic Investigation of the* Ch'eng wei-shih lun.

28 The four *viparyāsas* are: 1. seeing permanence in the impermanent, 2. seeing self in the selfless, 3. seeing purity in the impure, 4. seeing happiness (*sukha*) in *duḥkha.*

29 But cf. Nāgārjuna's MMK 17, the chapter on *karma-phala* (karmic consequences) in which Nāgārjuna negates these positions.

30 The idea here is very close to the Freudian notion of Transference.

31 Kierkegaard, *Philosophical Fragments,* ch. III. However, Buddhism would not agree that the appropriate response to this state of affairs is to reject reason for a 'leap of faith.' Rather the 'poison' of reason can be turned into 'medicine.'

32 Cf. Anacker's discussion in *Seven Works of Vasubandhu,* pp. 146f n. 43.

33 Two such lists are translated as appendices to the present work.

34 Spinoza, particularly in bk. IV of his *Ethics,* is very sensitive to this issue. The seeds of the dialectical method later developed by Hegel, who was profoundly influenced by Spinoza, are to be found in Spinoza's treatment of pleasure (*Lætitia*) and pain (*Tristitia*), which, like Buddhism, he also examines in relation to desire (*Cupiditas*). Spinoza claims that moral values have a utilitarian basis, i.e., what we call 'good' and 'bad' are actually what gives us pleasure or pain, which he defines as that which increases the self (pleasure) or decreases the self (pain) in its conative efforts to persevere and perfect itself. An equivocation in his treatment of the notions 'good' and 'bad' is dialectically suggestive. At first Spinoza claims that pain is bad and pleasure is good. IVp41: *Lætitia directe mala non est, sed bona; Tristitia autem contra directe est mala* ; "Pleasure is not in itself bad, but good. On the other hand, pain is in itself bad" (Shirley's translation). This receives an important qualification later. Though pain signals the bad, or what obstructs one's efforts at perfectability, it sometimes proves more ethically efficacious—and hence 'good'—because it can generate enough discomfort that one will make an effort to improve; whereas pleasure has a tendency to make one complacent and arrogant (cf. E-IVp58sch). Though this formulation is not yet quite fully dialectical, the shifting value of pain as bad and good (and likewise for pleasure), especially given the pivotal role this plays in the *Ethics* on the turn from bondage to freedom, invites a dialectical interpretation.

This rejection of pain for being intrinsically bad, though sometimes morally expedient, opens an interesting avenue for comparing Spinoza, Nietzsche and Buddhism on their shared condemnation of self-abasement and asceticism, a condemnation common to all three.

35 Along with similar notions in Western philosophy, such as Hegel's observation that I define myself through the other, or Whitehead's 'negative prehensions,' a most fruitful inquiry into the economy of 'negative appropriation' might begin with Freud's theory of defense mechanisms. Defense mechanisms are unconscious, reiterative operations which at once *repeat and distort* 'threatening' psychic episodes. In order to avoid certain unpleasant situations, these mechanisms psychologically displace the pain elsewhere only to reinvest a new center or locality with a distorted repetition of the situation from which they fled, so that they must attempt again to break away, and in so doing consistently (re-)define and (re-)determine the self and its actions as the locale of these 'neurotic' displacements. These 'defensive' maneuvers come very close to the Buddhist notion of the saṃskāric operations behind *upādāna* as well as offering an illustration of the tenacious reiterability of *saṃsāra.*

The work by deSilva and others to compare Freud and Buddhism has barely begun to reveal the deeply penetrating lights they can shine on each other.

36 Cf. the Freudian theory of projection, and Spinoza's discussion of pain alluded to above. Whitehead's notion of negative prehension also offers some interesting parallels.

37 Yogācāra will go one step further and insist that subjects and objects are themselves nothing but instantiated conditioned desires. That which is untainted (*anuśrava*) by appropriation is no longer available to description, since description itself, as a mode of psycho-linguistic appropriation, automatically 'taints' whatever it *takes* to be a referent. Discussing Freud's chagrin and resistance to the mounting evidence that the traumatic childhood experiences his patients reported were in fact fictions, not actual events, J. H. Van Den Berg writes:

> If every patient and every normal person relates events, and even serious, very serious, events from his past which actually never happened, then something is wrong with that past. The past has become talkative, but it is talking nonsense, it is playing the fool.

A comparison of this notion of "talkative" with the notion of *prapañca* may not be inappropriate. Van Den Berg continues:

> For each fact in the present, the past is giving history, but a history which never was, which evidently was made up quickly; the past is fabricating history, it is making up astounding events and indelible experiences. The past would not do this if it had not been forced to do it... Is the past not obliged to talk and talk and talk, if the idea that everything has a past is allowed no exception? Apparently there was every reason to make this rule absolute; nineteenth-century man was afraid, he found safety if the "meaning" of things was located in the past. But the past was not ready for this task, it was just being built; nonetheless it had to produce a "meaning" for everything. Is it surprising that at the end of the nineteenth century the past started to make up stories?
>
> ...In our day [the past] no longer produces hastily fabricated fantasies. The modern fantasies are much better constructed; so well constructed, in fact, that it is hardly possible to unmask them, if at all.

Of course, contemporary fantasies are always harder to identify, to become aware of, than those of the past. The conditioning most difficult to see is inevitably our own.

> ...Everything is "past"; nothing is "present". Since the present was made uninhabitable by the signs pointing to the past, the past had to take over the task which had been entrusted to the present for as long as man could remember. The past did take over the task; now we are living in the past.
>
> ...He who, on principle, resorts to the past is obliged to retreat ever deeper there. For the past has once been present, and for that reason was part of the dangers which exist in the present. Only when the past loses itself in primeval ages, in other words, only when the character of the present has been substantially erased from the past -- only when the past has been made entirely imaginary and so unreal -- only then is the regression halted. ("Neurosis or Sociosis", pp. 56-58, in Harold Bloom's [ed.] *Sigmund Freud: Modern Critical Views*)

If we carry this analysis a few steps further, and note that not only is the 'neurotic trauma' a fictionalized past constructed in the present, but the present also, insofar as it is influenced and shaped by this construction, is also fictitious -- which means that the oppositions of past/present and fiction/actuality are not as neat as Van Den Berg suggests -- and that this "talkative" propensity (*prapañca*) displaces both present and past with its interpretive jabber, a jabber that assumes a mythic, deep-seated, symbolic 'reality,' then we begin to approach the Yogācāra notion of *vijñapti.*

38 Alex Wayman, on the basis of some Tibetan texts, has suggested *bhāva* be translated as 'gestation' (see his "Dependent Origination - The Indo-Tibetan Tradition", rpt. in his *Buddhist*

Insight, pp. 163-192). Though perhaps adequate for when *pratītya-samutpāda* is strictly used to refer to the human condition or the organic conditions of sentient beings, 'gestation' is too limited. *Bhāva* here signifies something like a state of Nature. It is analogous to the notion of a 'Cosmic Verb,' though either of these suggestions should be taken merely as heuristics; *bhāva* should not be interpreted in such a metaphysical way.

39 In later Indian Philosophy, particularly Kashmir Śaivism, this notion of the cosmic pulse of the world, compounded with a rich philosophy of language, reached prominence as the *unmeśa* and *nimeśa* (uncovering and concealing) of spanda (the cosmic vibrating Pulse).

40 Raised in a very sheltered life, he had never been allowed to see any suffering. When nearly thirty he sneaked out of the palace with his charioteer and saw, much to his horror and shock, a grossly ill man, a withered decrepit old man, and a several day old corpse, each on successive nights. This so disturbed him that when on the following night he saw a wandering mendicant seeking Dharma, he vowed to also follow that path and overcome the outrage of *duḥkha*.

41 *S.* XII,7.65ff. See also the discussion of this formulation in R. Robinson's *The Buddhist Religion* (first ed.), pp. 21f and in Takeuchi, *op. cit.*, pp. 84ff.

42 Lindtner, *Nagarjuniana*, p. 171.

43 "The Heart of Interdependent Origination of Acarya Nāgārjuna with Commentary by the Author: Translated into English from the Tibetan", *Buddhist Studies,* (Delhi) March 1974, pp. 17-31 [includes introduction, English tr., an Eng/Tib/Skt glossary, and a reconstructed Sanskrit text in Devanāgri].

44 Cf. Lindtner, *ibid.*

45 But see Lindtner's arguments, *ibid.* Cf. Dragonetti's response to the claim of Nāgārjuna's authorship in his "Some Notes on the *Pratītyasamutpāda hṛdayakārikā* and the *Pratītyasamutpāda hṛdayakārikāvyākhyāna* Attributed to Nāgārjuna", *Buddhist Studies* (Delhi) no. 6, 1979, pp. 70-73. In this response to Jamspal and Della Santini, Dragonetti claims that Sanskrit citations exist for more of the text than they thought, and that the probable author was Suddhamati.

46 Cf. e.g., *Madhyamaka-kārikā* 22.10-11:

> 10. Thus, altogether empty are appropriation and the appropriator (*śūnyam upādānam upādātā*); How can an empty-Tathāgata [qua 'appropriated object'] be made known (*prajñapyate*) by an empty [appropriator] (*śūnyena*).
>
> 11. "Empty," "non-empty," "both," "neither" should not be asserted (*na vaktavyam*); these [terms] are expounded (*kathyate*) only to communicate (lit. "to heuristically designate a referent," *prajñaptyartham*).

47 This raises the possibility of an interesting interpretation of *avidyā*. Since *pratītya-samutpāda* is usually treated as a circle, the twelfth link and the first link are contiguous. Hence (#1) nescience 'reduces' to (#12) Death and (#2) embodied conditioning. What does that mean ? Conditioning only accrues and remains as a continuous underpinning if one *dies* after each moment or experience, i.e., in a profound and radical way one *forgets* the conditions constituting one's experiences so that when subsequent conditions make these latencies (= [temporarily] forgotten experiences) emerge into actuality, one acts 'impulsively' with no idea where the feeling or disposition originated. This is something like the guy who comes home from a miserable day at work and yells at his wife. He may even think and feel that she is the cause of his anger, when actually the real causes are his previous experiences. The *Abhidharmakośa* does in fact suggest that *avidyā* is a kind of breach or rupture in memory. If *avidyā* is this kind of radical discontinuity, one in which conditioning continues precisely because we don't see the conditioning connections between temporally discrete actions, then the cure for *avidyā* is memory, i.e., *smṛti* (lit. 'memory'), a steady and aware 'mindfulness'

(another translation of *smṛti*); a memory both in the here and now, such that I am fully aware of what I am doing (*karma*) and in what context (*dharma*), and one which recovers the seeds of my karmic conditioning. For most Buddhists this recovery would not involve a primordial *arché*, but rather the etiological roots of my particular situation, i.e., the unraveling of my conditioning. However, particularly in East Asian Buddhism, there are elements of arché-recovery, notably in the theories of Buddha-nature and Original Mind. In Yogācāra this controversy took the form of an argument about whether the seeds (*bījā*) in the *ālaya-vijñāna* are beginningless (i.e., have always been there) or whether they are all acquired through experience. According to the *Ch'eng wei-shih lun* different groups held different opinions, with one position (attributed by K'uei-chi to Dharmapāla) contending that the *ālaya-vijñāna* contains both types of seed.

If this theory of *avidyā* is examined closely however, a most striking paradox emerges. The *continuity* of karmic conditioning is grounded on the *discontinuity* of memory about the formative events that constitute that conditioning. Moreover, the solution to this misplaced sense of continuity consists precisely in rectifying the memory, such that it becomes continuous in order to reveal a discontinuous universe (the Sautrāntika doctrine of momentariness posits that reality is composed of absolutely discrete individual moments, *kṣanika,* which *are* efficient causes—*karaṇā*—but since that causal force does not extend past the moment in which it is being discharged, all moments are rendered radically discontinuous). From a continuous universe (or rather, plura-verse) and discontinuous mindfulness/memory to a discontinuous plura-verse and continuous mindfulness/memory -- this reversal of continuity/discontinuity nonetheless maintains an unquestioned dichotomy between an ontology and the way that that ontology is viewed. As stated earlier, Mahāyāna aimed at erasing bifurcational thinking, particularly dichotomies of such fundamental metaphysical gravitude, and therefore it is not surprising that this paradigm was rejected by them as "Hīnayānic." For our purposes, it is important to note that this paradigm's 'solution' suggested that the overcoming of *duḥkha* was primarily the rectification of a mental problem, and that this rectification results in a continuous, all-embracing memory/mindfulness. Certain Sautrāntika elements of the Yogācāra school retained this paradigm, though altering its terminology (e.g., they were called *sākāra-vijñānavādins*, 'the school [holding that enlightened] consciousness retains mental representations'). Further, this element also fueled the Buddhist controversy on the omniscience of the Buddha, supporting the doctrine that Buddha knows all things, i.e., has total mindfulness *and* total memory.

48 Sprung, p. 49.

49 An excellent exposition of *pratītya-samutpāda* from the perspective of Theravāda, and the *Visuddhimagga* in particular, is given in the *pratītya-samutpāda* essay in *Nava-Nalanda* I (Patna: n.d.) pp. 179-239.

Chapter Five

Model Three: Tridhātu

The model of the "three realms" or "three existential horizons" involves some of the most intricate and hair-splitting distinctions in Buddhist doctrine. It has been applied to cosmology, classifications of meditation levels, rebirth schema, and the hierarchical categorizing of psychological situations. As with the previous model, the description here will be far from exhaustive, but rather will aim at orienting the reader toward very basic but significant issues that will help prepare the way for understanding how this model came to be appropriated and utilized by Yogācāra.

The three realms are (1) the realm of desire (*kāma-dhātu*), (2) the formal or material realm (*rūpa-dhātu*), and (3) the formless or immaterial realm (*ārūpya-dhātu*).

As humans we "live" primarily in the desire realm. The word for desire here is *kāma*, not *taṇhā* or *tṛṣṇa* as in the *pratītya-samutpāda* model. Its closest equivalent term would be the Greek word *Eros*, meaning not just what we today would consider "erotic," but the entire domain of sensorial pleasure, particularly as that domain involves the pleasure principle as a motive for all action and interpretation. To say we primarily live in the desire realm means that to us life and its meanings generally derive from how, by way of pleasant and painful experiences, we *interpret* the world through our senses. Moreover the will-to-meaning and the will-to-life are derivative processes of a fundamental desire or urge that there be a world of objects so constituted that this desire can locate and attempt to satisfy itself within such a world, constructing and interpreting the world to 'be' what this desire desires. The pursuit of pleasure (*kāma*), worldly success (*artha*) and ethical betterment (*dharma*) all derive through this 'desire' and help establish its horizons. The horizons of our experience (*dhātu*) are constituted by the 'erotic sensorium' (*kāma*).

Rūpa-dhātu is hard to render accurately in English. *Rūpa,* though generally translated as 'form' or 'materiality,' in this model displays few of the characteristics usually associated with 'matter' in Buddhist thought. If anything, it denotes a realm whose properties are best understood as *formal thought.* The modern notion of Formal Logic as a logic radically separated from any empirical content would be located, by the Buddhist, in this *rūpa-dhātu.* Since the term *rūpa* functions in this model in a manner inconsistent with its more common usage as 'sensorial materiality,' it has engendered a great deal of hermeneutic difficulty for Buddhists in all subsequent interpretative traditions. The *rūpa* of the five skandhas (see above) has little in common with this *rūpa* either in terms of definition or function. The Abhidhammic attempts to conflate these two *rūpas* only generated further obfuscations, and in the end led Buddhaghosa, as the leading compiler and codifier of Theravāda doctrine, to severely violate and contradict the original Abhidhammic doctrines.[1]

The meaning of *rūpa* in this model may become more evident if we turn to the next realm, the formless *(arūpa)* realm. The *ārūpya-dhātu* is described as a series of ever expansive boundless realms, i.e., as one progresses through the formless realm, boundaries or restrictions are stripped away. As we shall see in a moment, successively vaster and more inclusive horizonal margins are uncovered and stripped away. One's awareness becomes coterminal with the full expanse of each realm as one sees how each underpins the preceding realm, and the defining margins of each level are erased in turn until one achieves direct experience of marginality itself.

The first *ārūpya* horizon is *ākāśa* or 'spatiality.' Thus the rūpa-dhātu may be seen as underpinned by or presupposing 'spatiality.' In this context, *rūpa*, as the contrary of *ārūpya*, would signify a (mentally) limited or restricted realm. This implies that early on Buddhists understood *rūpa* by the formal definition that became prominent later in the scholastic period, viz. "what offers resistance" or "what obstructs space," rather than simply as the material 'Great Elements' (*mahābhūta*). The *Potthapāda sutta* of the *Dīgha Nikāya* does in fact suggest such an understanding, when, while describing how a meditator advances from the rūpa-dhātu to the ārūpya-dhātu, it says:

> The Bhikkhu, by passing beyond the consciousness of rūpa, *by putting an end to the sense of resistance*, by paying no heed to the idea of distinction, thinking: 'The space is infinite,' reaches up to and remains in the mental state in which the mind is concerned only with the consciousness of the infinity of space." (T.W. Rhys David's tr., slightly modified, emphasis added)

Each of the three realms is subdivided into various levels, which vary slightly in different traditions. In cosmological versions of the tridhātu each level is treated as a separate 'rebirth' realm in which various kinds of beings are born and live and die. The desire realm includes the hells, animals, ghostly spirits, and humans, as well as some lower heavens. The formal realm contains various higher heavens, and the formless realm is abodeless (though some sources correlate the ārūpya levels with the abodes of rebirth for advanced practitioners).

I will not give a detailed description of this scheme since such descriptions are available elsewhere[2] and need not be repeated here. Rather a generic, skeletal description will be offered, along with an attempt to suggest some of the critical issues which came to bear on Yogācāra theory.

Kāma-dhātu

Kāma-dhātu is generally subdivided into five regions:

1. *Naraka* (P. *niraya*)—The hellish regions. Buddhist cosmology conceived of many types of hells: cold ones, hot ones, desolate ones, ones with multiple tortures, etc., which vary from text to text and tradition to tradition.[3] As Conze points out[4] "since life in hell comes to an end some day, they are more like the Purgatory of the Catholic Church, than like the Hell in orthodox Christianity." Vasubandhu seems to suggest in the *Viṃśatika* that the hells are not ontological regions awaiting denizens, but are produced, intersubjectively, by the collective karma of those whose actions project the requisite tendencies. Hell, in particular, is a paranoid projection in which the hell denizens unwittingly torture themselves by imagining all sorts of tormenting guards that are not really there. If the karmic habits which lead to hellish experiences would cease, so would the hells they inhabit. Hsüan-tsang rejects this idea, and argues in *Ch'eng wei-shih lun* that the various realms exist even when no one lives there.
2. *Tiryagyoni* (P. *tiracchānayoni*)—The animal world. Any one or anything can be born as anything else. The chain of saṃsāra involves all sentient beings. People may be reborn as animals, and *vice versa*. In fact, since there is no abiding self, it would be improper to say a 'person' was reborn as an animal (or *vice versa*) since the animal, despite his past karma, is now fully an animal, just as a person is now fully a person. There is no 'person-self' that takes on different forms, since there is no permanent self. Nonetheless in popular thinking, such intra-life 'relationships' are contemplated. Hence the Buddhist notion of *ahiṃsā*, the non-harming of any sentient being, extends to animals, since the cow or ox or cockroach you abuse may be a (former) member of your family. Buddhists have also produced a rich literature of legends and fables detailing what kind of personality traits lead to what kind of animal rebirth. Stubbornness may lead to being born as an ass, cleverness may lead to life as a fox, etc. These stories have always been popular, even in Zen.[5]
3. *Preta* (P. *petta* or *pettivisaya*, '*preta* sense-field')—The hungry ghosts. There are several versions of what exactly a preta is, and like most other features of Buddhist cosmology, they are not original to Buddhism. Originally pretas were the "fathers" (*pitṛ*, cognate to Latin *pater*), i.e., parents who had recently died and were believed to spend a year in limbo as ghosts awaiting arrival in some other destiny. Offerings were made to appease them, since, reflecting their unsure and unstable status, they could become dangerous. Failure to appease them could have dire consequences both for the ghost and the surviving family members. Since the *petas* are not mentioned in some of the early Pāli listings of *gatis* (rebirth locations[6]), it is likely that they were late additions to the early Buddhist cosmology. Eventually, they came to be described as ghostly figures with perpetually ravenous appetites

who are somehow constituted in a way that makes satisfying and gratifying those appetites impossible. One version asserts that they have large, insatiable stomachs, and mouths the size of pin-pricks, making the act of eating virtually impossible. Another asserts that their throats are too narrow to actually swallow anything. When food or drink comes within their grasp, it turns to pus or blood or other noxious and disgusting materials. A preta's immediately previous life was almost definitely human, and even more than with animals, they are commonly considered to be recently departed relatives. There is an annual festival in most Buddhist countries where food is put out for them by their living relatives, and on that day they can eat. Pretas are victims of frustrated desires which they could not overcome while human. Like the hells, and all the other *gatis* or rebirth realms, existence as a *preta* is not permanent, and eventually leads to rebirth elsewhere.

4. *Manuṣya* (P. *manussa-loka* , 'human world')—The human realm. As the middle way between those realms beneath it and those above it, Buddhism considers this the most auspicious realm in which to be born. It is neither too hellish or unpleasant to keep one constantly distracted or preoccupied with animal needs (as in the lower realms), nor is it so unimaginably pleasant that the thought of self-improvement or untangling the saṃsāric knot would never occur to one (as in the divine realms). Its auspiciousness is matched by the difficulty of being born in it. Rahula paraphrases the *Majjhima Nikāya* thus:[7]

> Suppose a yoke with a single hole is cast into the great ocean where it is tossed about by the winds that blow in all directions, and that in this same ocean lives a one-eyed turtle who comes up once in a hundred years to catch a glimpse of the heavens. Is it possible that this one-eyed turtle would ever chance to look at the sky through the hole in the yoke?... it is even more difficult... to be born a man.

Significantly, Buddhism generally holds that complete unexcelled Awakening (*anuttara samyak saṃbodhi*) is only attainable in the human realm. Gods can progress on the path of Dharma, but even they need to be reborn as humans in order to achieve Nirvāṇa. Later, some Mahāyāna speculation reversed this, claiming that one could be reborn in certain Buddha-Lands, such as Amitābha's Western Paradise, and achieve enlightenment there without returning to the human realm. Similar speculations appear in Buddhaghosa and the *Abhidharmakośa,* though without reference to Amitābha, of course. Buddhaghosa, for instance, says a Non-returner who fails to achieve Arhathood during their last human life will be born in a deva realm and from there go on to Nibbāna—non-returning to human existence.

5. *Kāmadeva* (P. *kāmavacara sugatibhūmi*)—The divine Kāma realm. In this realm the various traditions and texts begin to exhibit significant divergences. For instance, in the Pāli tradition, particularly following Buddhaghosa, the *kāmavacara sugatibhūmi* (lit. 'pleasant [reward] stage of

the eros field') includes the human realm as well as the divine kāma heavens. Among other things, this indicates that desire (*kāma*) per se is not taken to signify an a priori evil, since even within the realm of desire, certain desires may yield pleasant and beneficial fruits.

Texts also diverge as to how many levels to assign to the *kāma-dhātu*. Sometimes instead of dividing it into five parts, a sixth is posited, viz. the Āsuras who are comparable to the Greek titans, i.e., divine beings coarser than the higher divinities who jealously wrangle with their superiors. The Āsuras are sometimes placed below the human realm, and sometimes above it; sometimes they are included in the divine realms (though on the lowest rung), and sometimes they are completely ignored in the tabulations.

Even without the Āsuras, this fifth level is usually subdivided into six regions, which from lowest to highest are:

[a] the realm of the four great kings (*caturmahārājakāyika;* P. *cātummahārājikā devaloka*);[8]
[b] The realm of the thirty-three gods (*Trāyastriṃśa*, P. *tāvatiṃsa*);
[c] The Yama realm (in Hinduism, Yama is the god of death);
[d] The realm of delight, i.e., Tuṣita heaven. This 'heaven' becomes most important in Yogācāra thinking, since it is considered the abode of Maitreya, the future Buddha who, according to tradition, dictated the Yogācāra sūtras to Asaṅga, Vasubandhu's half-brother, while Asaṅga visited Tuṣita through meditation.[9]
[e] The realm of gods who rejoice in their own creations (*Nirmāṇarati,* P. *nimmāṇarati*);
[f] The realm of gods who lord over the creations of others (*Paranirmatavaśavatin,* P. *paranimmitavasavatti*).

As pointed out, these five 'worlds' (*loka*) are accessible through rebirth and meditation. Since 'desire' may lead to propitious or inauspicious situations, Buddhists distinguish between two types of desire: *kusala* (beneficial) and *akusala* (non-beneficial, harmful). Morally and ethically these terms may also be rendered 'good' and 'bad,' or 'wholesome' and 'unwholesome,' etc.

Akusala-karma—constituted by and constitutive of *akusala* desires—results (*vipāka*) in the first three worlds (hells, animals and pretas); and *kusala-karma* results in the upper two worlds (human and *kāmadeva*). Of course, in practice this is an oversimplification, since in any of these realms some traces of the inverse karma (*kusala* or *akusala*) are also found, though perhaps temporarily latent.

It is interesting to note that these kinds of heavenly rebirths, no matter how good (*kusala*) or noble the intent, are still considered to be within the desire-realm (*kāma-dhātu*), and hence relatively low-level accomplishments. Even the desire for Awakening or nirvāṇa may limit one to rebirth (i.e., the existential horizon toward which one's actions generate anticipations and expectations) in the desire-realm. Further, since all the realms into which one could be born are impermanent, as is one's duration within them, whichever rebirth status one attains can only be temporary. As in ordinary life, success and failure dialectically grow out of each other. The nicer one's current life, the more attached one will become to it. Hence leaving that life—which is necessary since all the realms are impermanent and therefore one will eventually die and leave it—will be painful, and the inevitable pains of the subsequent life will seem, by contrast, that much more outrageous and frustrating. Conversely, to be 'upwardly mobile' transmigrationally necessarily involves desiring, to some extent, the pleasures of betterment and comfort. Hence even seeking betterment leads to the karmic trap of attachment to pleasure through desire. None of these realms, moreover, can guarantee absolute security, since they are impermanent. Since the movement from life to life, according to most Buddhist thought, is merely an extension of the movement from moment to moment within a life, this rebirth schema should also (and some schools would argue primarily) be understood as a description of how the dynamics of one's current existential circumstance tends to predict and predispose one towards future existential circumstances, from moment to moment, hour to hour, day to day, year to year, and life to life, as well as a reminder that one has arrived at this moment through a history that the moment and oneself embodies.

As for the Maitreya heaven, the Tuṣita, one desired rebirth there in order to study Dharma directly with Maitreya and his retinue in order to advance toward the attainment of the complete Awakening which one could not reach in the present life, and thus to return to earth with Maitreya when he returns as the next Buddha, at which time Awakening will be achieved all sentient beings. For Mahāyāna Buddhists Maitreya functions very much like a Buddhist messianic figure. Maitreya cults reached their popular peak in the seventh century in China, only to be superseded by Amita cults in which one seeks rebirth in Amitābha's Western Pure Land. Vestiges of Maitreya worship can still be found in East Asia, especially in Korea.

Rūpa-dhātu

Rūpa-dhātu is subdivided into either four or five levels.[10] Buddhist discourses on this dhātu primarily concern meditation, though rebirth fields are also associated with each of the levels.[11]

As meditational strata, each of the levels is defined by the conditions and factors that cause it to arise. That is, when certain specific conditions coalesce, a meditative level defined as the concurrence of those conditions occurs. Since these are important practices, one might expect that the literature would offer precise definitions. Unfortunately the Pāli Abhidhamma texts, notably the *Dhammasaṅgaṇi* and *Vibhaṅga*, differentiate between two models, one ascribed to the *suttas* and the other to the *Abhidhamma* itself. These models differ on precisely the question of which factors constitute each level. Moreover, the conditions which the Abhidhamma texts cite as representing the sutta version do not coincide with what is actually found in the suttas. The origin of the Abhidhamma models and how they came to diverge from the original models of the suttas is unknown. Apparently by the time the Abhidhamma texts were codified, such supplementary models were common and accepted.[12]

Buddhaghosa, the great Theravādin codifier and commentator, who probably lived in the fourth or fifth century (ca. a century or more after Asaṅga and Vasubandhu, and ca. a century or two before Hsüan-tsang), opted for the abhidhammic version. Since his work, the *Visuddhimagga,* became the definitive Theravādin textbook for meditative practice, particularly as it applies to the *rūpa-dhātu,* to find a modern source that does not reiterate (sometimes blindly) Buddhaghosa's interpretations and conclusions is rare. Unfortunately this makes critical appraisals of this model, such as those by Rahula and Wayman[13], even rarer, since Buddhaghosa's late interpretations often impose an order and structure on the original texts not readily evident there.

Curiously, though the Sarvāstivāda and Yogācāra schools are usually described by scholars as abhidharmic in orientation, rather than sūtric, the rūpa-dhātu models found in both these schools are closer to the Pāli suttas than to the Abhidhamma.

What makes the abhidhammic version attractive is its neatness and symmetry. Each succeeding level consists in the dropping of conditions present in the immediately previous level. The sutta version is more ambiguous, and the Sarvāstivāda and Yogācāra texts which follow it closely are less symmetrical than Buddhaghosa's account.

Since an examination of the differences between these two models has already been commendably executed by others[14], we will only give a bare skeletal description here and refer the interested reader to those other works.

The Rūpa-dhātu, divided into four levels (i.e., the sutta version), called *jhānas* (S. *dhyāna*, 'meditative situational contexts'), is enumerated as follows, going from lowest to highest:

1. The first dhyāna involves the following four components:
   (a) *vitakka* (S. *vitarka*)—initial mental application, or initial intellectual investigative intent, i.e., the initial focusing of consciousness on a mental object.
   (b) *vicāra*—subsequent discursive reasoning and thought, i.e., investigating what has been focused on by *vitakka. Vitakka* may be compared to striking a bell, and *vicāra* to the subsequent resonance;
   (c) *pīti*—intense joy; and
   (d) *sukha*—intense pleasure and enjoyment.[15]
2. The second dhyāna involves the subsiding (*vūpasamā*) of *vitakka* and *vicāra* which leads to
   (a) *ajjhattaṃ sampasāda* (S. *adhyātmasamprasāda*) inner serenity,
   (b) *pīti,*
   (c) *sukha* and

(d) *cetaso ekodibhāvaṃ* or *cittassa ekaggatā* (S. *cittaikāgratā*) 'one-pointedness of mind' arising through samādhi (meditative concentration).[16]

3. The third dhyāna consists of detaching (*virāgā*) from *pīti* (intense joy), leading to

(a) *upekkhā* (S. *upekṣā*) 'equanimitous neutrality' implying neutrality between the pain and pleasure of vedanā previously discussed in the skandha and pratītya-samutpāda models,

(b) *sati* (S. *smṛti*) 'recollective mindfulness.'

(c) *sampajañña* (S. *samprajanya*) 'discerning awareness' which the *Vibhaṅga* says is synonymous with *paññā* (S. *prajñā*),

(d) *sukhañ ca kāyena paṭisaṃvedeti* (S. *kāya-sukha saṃveda*) 'enjoying bodily happiness and pleasure.' This is paraphrased as "dwelling in equanimity, mindfulness and happiness."[17]

4. The fourth dhyāna climaxes the process by

(a) abandoning (*pahānā*) both *sukha* and *dukkha*, i.e., overcoming pleasure and pain,

(b) and by eliminating (*atthaṅgamā*) delight and sadness (*somanassa domanassānaṃ*) one reaches

(c) purified [vedānically] neutralized recollective-mindfulness (*upekkhā sati pārisuddhi*, S. *upekṣā smṛti pāriśuddhi*).[18]

The neater, symmetrical fivefold scheme of the Abhidhamma organizes this as follows[19]:

1st Jhāna	*vitakka*	*vicāra*	*pīti*	*sukha*	*ekaggatā*
2nd Jhāna	———	*vicāra*	*pīti*	*sukha*	*ekaggatā*
3rd Jhāna	———	———	*pīti*	*sukha*	*ekaggatā*
4th Jhāna	———	———	———	*sukha*	*ekaggatā*
5th Jhāna	———	———	———	*upekkhā*	*ekaggatā*

Whether we follow the fourfold scheme or the fivefold scheme, certain aspects remain constant. The jhānas begin with an initial mental effort (*vitakka vicāra*) that is accompanied by pleasant feelings (*pīti sukha*). As the effort subsides, the intensity of the pleasurable feelings decreases until finally pleasure itself is sublimated into an equanimitous neutrality.

In a sense, the rūpa-dhātu is a formal abstraction from the kāma-dhātu. Whereas the kāma-dhātu operates as and through an appropriational desire predicated on and conditioned by vedanic experience (pleasure, pain, neutral), the rūpa-dhātu involves the neutralization of this conditioning. As the conative force becomes less emotive and affective, it becomes more intentional and formal. The charged appropriational milieu of kāma-dhātu gradually gives way to a clarified, purified (*suddha*) formal mental realm removed from hedonic bipolarities such as pain and pleasure or sadness and delight (*dukkha sukha*, *domanassa somanassa*). One reaches equanimity by divesting bipolarity. The formula in the suttas for this stage is: "by abandoning happiness and suffering (*sukha dukkha*), by the elimination of delight and sadness, [arises] the fourth jhāna, which is neither happiness nor suffering and which is clarified-purified equanimity and recollective-mindfulness." Mindfulness in this jhāna is an alert, relaxed awareness detached from positive and negative conditioning.[20]

We will return to this, but first we will outline the next realm.

Ārūpya-dhātu (P. arūpa-dhātu)

Ārūpya-dhātu—As stated previously, this realm involves the progressive erasure of formal boundaries. As with the rūpa-dhātu the most commonly encountered interpretation of this realm is that advanced by Buddhaghosa in his *Visuddhimagga.* In his account each of the four levels of the ārūpya-dhātu is reached by taking its immediately antecedent level—which up to this point appears to be an all-encompassing horizon—and first turning into a contemplative object, after which it dissolves or disappears to reveal a more rarefied level that becomes a new lived horizon. His interpretation can be read as treating this progression as a kind of crude Hegelian *aufhebung*, each level sequentially negating its immediate antecedent level while simultaneously retaining it as an objectified 'concept.'[21] Following his idea, I will offer a slightly different interpretation.

There is much ambivalence in Buddhist literature about the status of the ārūpya dhyānas. Without entering into the full web of these complexities, a few comments are in order. First, they are sometimes not treated as dhyānas of a distinct, arūpic realm, but as adjuncts or corollaries of the fourth (or fifth) dhyāna of the rūpa-dhātu. To be more precise, while the suttas enumerate them as ārūpya jhānas, the Pāli Abhidhamma considers them to be aspects of rūpa jhāna since the conditions which form them are identical to the (abhidhammic version of the) constitutive conditions of the fourth rūpa dhyāna (i.e., *upekkhā* and *ekagattā*).[22] For this reason, the meditative levels associated with ārūpya-dhātu are sometimes technically *not* called jhānas or dhyānas, so that the term jhāna becomes reserved exclusively for descriptions of meditation within the rūpa-dhātu. Nonetheless, I will apply the term jhāna/dhyāna to the ārūpya levels in the following discussion. Secondly, while the rūpic dhyānas are considered necessary prerequisites for the ārūpic dhyānas, these latter are sometimes considered to be unnecessary, digressional practices, useful perhaps for developing spiritual powers (especially the *iddhis*[23] and *abhiññā*[24]), but inconsequential in the pursuit of Awakening.

The four *ārūpya dhyānas* are:

1) *Ākāśānantya* (P. *ākāsānañca* or *ākāsanañcāyatana*)—Gunaratana translates this as 'boundless space,' while Guenther translates it 'infinite space.' Technically, *anta-* (related to the English "anti-") means 'other,' 'side,' or

'limiting border;' *ananta* means 'without sides,' 'without limits,' 'without being closed in,' 'without an end,' etc. Hence something *'ananta'* would seem to be devoid of a limiting margin or absolute circumference: Without bounds, without limits, infinitely expansive, a range non-obstructed on any side, with limitless scope. As we shall see shortly, this seeming boundlessness actually only marks a temporary inscription. Each of the boundless realms dissolves into another, more radical "seemingly" boundless realm. This shedding of horizonal margins finally leads to utter marginality, to an aporia or undecidability whose teetering locates itself in, or more accurately *as* a margin. This will be clearer presently.

Ākāśa does not really imply the common notion of 'space' that we usually oppose to 'time' (in Sanskrit, that 'space' would be *deśa*); it is closer to the alchemical notion of ether, an all-pervading space-ness or spatiality *in which* everything, including space, may be located. *Ākāśānanta* means that in which one is aware (*citta*) of *ākāśa* and nothing other than *ākāśa*. It is not a mere abstract formulation, but an experience seemingly unbound by any horizon. The *ā-rūpya-dhātu* or *non*-rūpic realm begins here since, whereas rūpa signified 'resistance' (*pratigha*) and sensorial obstruction—i.e., what obstructs space such that two rūpic things may not occupy the same space simultaneously—*ākāśānanta* unobstructedly opens out without circumference or center. The 'resistance' characteristic of the rūpic realm (*pratigha* means both 'resistance' in the sense of physics, as well as 'aversion or hatred' psychologically)—the limits which demarcate and isolate one object from another, one view from its contrary—dissolve away, and with the dissolving of the limits, the rūpic gives way to the ārūpic. Moreover, just as spatiality is seen to be the grounding condition for space and whatever might occupy it, ārūpya is the grounding cognitive condition for rūpa, since rūpa occupies (and displaces) space. *Ārūpya* is the background, or radical *Ganzfeld*, within which any formal, specific content may arise. It is the necessary condition for the arising of formal structures. In this sense Guenther is justified in translating *ārūpya* as 'non-Gestalt.'[25] It simultaneously erases the formal realm (*rūpa-dhātu*) while presenting itself as the ground, or field of possibilities through which that realm comes to be constituted. Stated more simply, the contents, images, sensations, and formal structures of the cathexic (*kāma-dhātu*) and the formal (*rūpa-dhātu*) realms dissolve into a non-conditioning neutrality and mental equanimity (*avyākta upekṣā*)[26] which itself engenders an awareness of the ethereal matrix through which those realms arise. The life-condition infused with manifold desires quiets into a formal equanimity, which allows an expanded equanimous awareness of possibilities unconstrained by demarcations.

Later Buddhist thought, especially in certain Mahāyānic strains, come to treat *ākāśa* as a synonym for *śūnyatā* (emptiness), i.e., a ubiquitous, pervasive ground synonymous with Original Awakening or Buddha-Nature. The Chinese translation of *ākāśa* as *k'ung-hsü* 空虛 lent some force to this conflation since *k'ung* also became the Chinese term for *śūnyatā*, implying a cognate terminological affinity that the terms lacked in Sanskrit.

2) *Vijñānānantya* (P. *viññāṇañca* or *viññāṇañcāyatana*)—Having become aware of *ākāśa* as the ubiquitous ground of the 'erotic' and formal sensorium, *ākāśa* itself is emptied, revealing the ground on which it arises, namely 'boundless (*ananta*) consciousness (*vijñāna*).'

In terms of Yogācāra, it should be noted that had Yogācāra indeed wished to present itself as a form of idealism, basing all 'reality' in the mind, it should have chosen to call its philosophy *vijñānānanta* and not *vijñapti-mātra.* While the former term carries a positive connotation *vis-à-vis* the presence of 'consciousness,' the latter is more negative and ironical, as we will argue later. Since the model of the ārūpya-dhātu clearly indicates that becoming aware of the ubiquity of consciousness is an important, but nonetheless *transitive* experience, Yogācāra would be in violation of basic Buddhist doctrine if it held to the position that 'consciousness alone' is real. One of the points I will strive to prove in the course of this work is that Yogācāra, at least in the forms advocated by Vasubandhu and Hsüan-tsang, in no way attempted to violate basic Buddhist doctrine nor did it contemplate any form of metaphysical idealism.

'Boundless consciousness' involves awareness of the fact that wherever awareness occurs, such that it may (dis-)locate itself anywhere, awareness is always within or of consciousness. While 'things' may be located in *ākāśa,* which stands for the raw possibilities of the arising of things,[27] being aware of boundless *ākāśa* is an act that takes place in consciousness, i.e., it is always *of* experience. Without consciousness there could be no such awareness, and hence consciousness is given primacy as a cognitive condition. In the awareness of boundless consciousness, *ākāśa* has become nothing more than one type of potential cognitive object. It is the ubiquity and limitless abilities of consciousness that one becomes aware of. These are, one must not forget, descriptive maps of meditative *experiences.* The Indians held that whatever is or is not the case can not to be determined abstractly or simply by abstract means and instruments. Rather what is or isn't the case must be known to be such because it is *cognized* 'as such' (*tathatā*). Hence the ubiquity of consciousness should be understood phenomenologically, not metaphysically.

3) *Akiṃcanya* (P. *ākiñcañña* or *akiñcaññāyatana*)—If *ākāśa* underpins the structures by which we perceive the world(s), and that in turn is underpinned by consciousness, what underpins consciousness? *Akiṃcanya* means 'nothing.' Notice the suffix *-ananta* ('unbounded') is absent from the title of this dhyāna, since this 'nothing' is not a "nothing-ness" or "void" for which spatial qualities—like being 'boundless' or expansive—can be predicated. Rather it entails an awareness that consciousness is always contingent. Whatever "is" might be otherwise, or might not be at all. Consciousness arises through the contact between sense organ and sense object. In any conscious moment, the functioning quality of the organ or the object might have been different. One aspect of the Ganzfeld might have emerged as a Gestalt rather than another. Whatever occurs in awareness does so arising within this sea of contingency.

This 'nothing' can be understood as implying death, i.e., the possibility of not-being. Consciousness, far from being ubiquitous and eternal, exists only within the parameters of its possibility for not existing. Each cognitive moment is in flux, which is to say, it occurs within a stream of 'becoming otherwise.' Cognitive objects are in flux, changing; and the cognitive subject, too, is perpetually undergoing alterations. The sensorial impact that produces a moment of presence instantaneously ceases, and turns to nothing. The sound of the word "now" ceases even as its meaning is comprehended; it slips away, as did the printed word scanned just a moment ago. To look at it again is not to see the same word, but to engage in a new cognition that too will cease. Just as whatever arises must cease, so too whatever arises could just as well not have, had the conditions for its arising been absent; and they might have been absent because the conditions through which they would have arisen were absent, and so on. Thus whatever arises, might not have been, or might have been otherwise, or, more to the point, might have been *perceived* otherwise. There are many ways to interpret anything; there is always an otherwise to the way 'things look' now. This moment of 'black-on-white-visible' you, the reader, are now immersed in could have been otherwise, and will be otherwise soon. You might have been reading something else at this moment, or doing something else. You may understand this text in one way now, and another on some subsequent rereading. Likewise for all moments of sensation and cognition. Whatever could have been otherwise or might not have been, is *contingent.* Existentially, the marginal limits of consciousness are death or its own radical contingency.

Buddha is said to have engaged in a battle of wits with the god Brahma while sitting under the Bodhi-tree seeking Awakening. Brahma accused Buddha of arrogance and of having an inflated sense of self-importance since he (Buddha) believed he could solve the riddle of *duḥkha* and thereby save others. As a mere mortal he didn't even measure up to the puniest of gods, and even the gods lacked the knowledge that Buddha sought. Buddha responded, "You, Brahma, are considered a great God indeed. You are said to be eternal, immortal, beginningless and endless. They say that there was never a time when you were not, nor will there ever be a time when you will not be. Is that true?" Brahma proudly answered, "Yes, I am eternal." Buddha then asked, "Can you choose *not* to be?" Brahma reiterates, "No; I am eternal." Buddha then said, "Then I am greater than you, since I can choose not to be." Buddha defeats Brahma—and the pernicious view of eternality—by declaring and affirming his own contingency.[28]

In one sense, this story exemplifies a profound application of the Buddhist rejection of essentialism. As one delves deeper and deeper into the perceptual roots of experience, into the conditionality that constitutes it, no invariant, eternal essence is found. The structures of experience continually dissolve into more basic structures until even the matrices through which those structures arise also dissolve. This implies, among many other things, a radical contingency to the Buddhist notion of conditionality. Without essences, there can also be no necessary causes, but only contingent conditions which, within the parameters of a given structure (*loka*), function ineluctably. This contingency is the hinge between freedom and liberation *within* and not *from* conditions. The 'nothing' per se is not that freedom, but the simultaneous acknowledgment and emptying of contingency.

This nothing should not be construed as a mystical 'void,' much less a 'void-essence.' In language which sounds more like Mahāyānic Yogācāra than the Theravādin tradition it actually represents, Buddhaghosa's *Visuddhimagga* states:[29]

> [By paying] attention to the non-existence (*abhāva*), emptiness (*suññata*), and isolated mental-image (*vivittākāra*) of that same consciousness belonging to the base (*āyatana*) consisting of boundless *ākāśa* which became the object of the base of boundless consciousness

the meditator reaches the dhyāna of nothing. Here Buddhaghosa's primitive notion of *aufhebung* is clearly apparent, as is his use of important Mahāyānic terms such as suññata (S. *śūnyatā*) and *vivitta* (S. *vivikta*).[30]

For Buddhism, *ākiñcañña* involves the (positive) cognition of the (negative) 'emptied' aspects of the cognizing consciousness.[31] Etymologically it implies the absence of any cognition whatsoever. It is utter absence, but an absence conceived as the antidote to a ubiquitous, 'boundless' consciousness which acts as its base. Though it is nothing, because it arises only from the possibility of imagining the absence of what is already present, even as radical absence it never loses its relation to what it has erased and supplanted. As a cognized absence —a jhāna—it "appears" as the negation of its own cognizability. In a moment we will see that this impasse may indeed be deliberate, since the next dhyāna capitalizes on the ambivalence.

Having achieved this penultimate 'nothing,' which consists of emptying out all content whatsoever from the previous dhyānas and *lokas*, including anything resembling 'objective' or 'subjective' poles (the ākāśa and vijñāna realms, respectively), one is prepared to embark on the final dhyāna, radical marginality itself. This sequence of first emptying the objective pole, then the subjective pole (including consciousness itself), finally opening to an Awakened, non-polarized realization, is maintained to the letter in Yogācāra.[32]

4) *Naivasaṃjñānāsaṃjñā* (P. *nevasaññā nāsaññāyatana*)—Neither with nor without associative thinking (*saññā*, S. *saṃjñā*), already discussed as the third skandha. The name of this level sometimes also includes *vedanā*, i.e., neither with saṃjñā and vedanā nor without saṃjñā and vedanā. The *Vibhaṅga* describes this as:[33]

> By completely surmounting the base consisting of 'nothing' he enters and dwells in the base consisting of neither *saññā* nor *asaññā*...

Straddling the margins of thinking and non-thinking, of contentful and contentless awareness, of being aware and being unaware, this sphere of meditative activity bristles with the deconstructive dynamics of what Derrida has called (among other things) "the trace."[34] To flesh this out, let us first see how Buddhaghosa interprets this phase, and then examine it.

Gunaratana offers the following reading of Buddhaghosa:[35]

> The [fourth ārūpya] *jhāna* receives this name [reading *nevasaññā nāsaññā* as 'neither perception nor non-perception'] because on the one hand it lacks gross perception and on the other retains a subtle perception. Lacking gross perception, it cannot perform the decisive function of perception—the clear discernment of objects—and thus cannot be said to have perception (*neva saññā*). But yet this attainment retains an extremely subtle perception and thus cannot be said to be without perception (*nasaññā*). To make plain this ambivalent character of the *jhāna* it is named "the base of neither perception nor non-perception." Because perception as well as the other mental factors such as feeling [*vedanā*], consciousness, contact [*phassa*], and the rest, continue here reduced to the finest subtlety this *jhāna* is also named "the attainment with residual formations" (*saṅkhārasesa samāpatti*).
>
> ...A novice smeared a bowl with oil and an elder monk asked him to bring the bowl to serve gruel. The novice replied, "Venerable sir, there is oil in the bowl." Then the monk told him, "Bring the oil, novice, I shall fill the oil tube." Thereupon the novice said: "There is no oil, Venerable sir." In this tale what the novice said is true in both cases: there is no oil since there is not enough to fill the tube yet there is no utter absence of oil since some remains at the base of the bowl. Similarly, in this attainment perception cannot be said to be fully present since it is so subtle that it cannot perform the decisive function of perceiving; yet it cannot be said to be absent since it remains in residual form. [square brackets mine]

Buddhaghosa solves the dilemma of 'neither with saññā nor without saññā' by reinterpreting 'without saññā' to mean *subtle saññā* rather than no saññā at all. He views this subtle saññā as distinct from 'gross' or regular saññā in that it is too rarefied to function properly; normally saññā discerns cognitive objects more or less clearly, but rarefied saññā does not. Rarefied saññā is incapable of performing the role of saññā, just as having insufficient oil for cooking is like having no oil at all. But what does the term saññā means in its rarefied form, and isn't there a important difference between "there is no [oil]" and "there is not enough [oil]"? Wouldn't Buddhaghosa's example imply that *asaññā* is an overstatement, that in fact there is no absence of *saññā* but only a diminution of its functioning? Could the tension evoked by juxtaposing *saññā* and *asaññā* have been proposed so carelessly by the early Buddhists? What is the purpose of this paradoxical tension?

Buddhaghosa 'solves' the paradox by proposing two types of perception: (i) gross perception (P_1), or perception proper, which is defined as 'discerning objects,' and (ii) subtle perception (P_2), in which no objects appear, but nonetheless certain functions continue to operate[36], in particular, the operations of embodied-conditioning (*saṃskāra*, P. *saṅkhāra*). This is clever, but diffuses the radical nature of this dhyāna. It is as if Buddhaghosa is saying that *saññā*, along with the other nāmic skandhas (*vedanā, viññāṇa,* and the typical abhidhammic substitution of *phassa* for *rūpa*), are put on hold, or standby. 'Perception' is on, but not functioning as usual. He has reduced the tension between *saññā* and *asaññā* to the status of a hyperbolic expression denoting 'subtle *saññā,*' a *saññā* so faint that it can barely be called *saññā*. In fact, following his reasoning, it should be called *saṅkhāra,* which is an entirely different skandha! Moreover, his logic, which implies that two contradictories can both be true if viewed within different contexts, is reminiscent of Jaina logic (in particular, their notion of *anekāntavāda*) rather than Buddhist logic.

His analogy of residual oil also raises problems. Rather than splitting perception into two types, such that this dhyāna consists of P_2 while P_1 is absent —which implies (a) that normal perception consists of $P_1 + P_2$, (b) something, which remains unclear, has rent them asunder, (c) that an objectless subjectivity continues to function in P_2 even without P_1, (d) that the notion of *phassa* (S. *sparśa*) makes sense without an object[37], and (e) that *asaṃjñā* does not really mean *asaṃjñā*—it would be better to say there is no P_1 vs. P_2 dichotomy.

To maintain Buddhaghosa's explanation one would have to respond to the following problems: (1) Why should there be two such thoroughly different cognitive functions bearing the same name *saññā*? (2) Isn't there a difference between 'subtle saññā' and 'the absence of saññā'? Don't the differences merit clear terminological distinctions? Isn't there a difference between 'no oil' and 'not enough oil'? (3) What has rent these two types of saññā asunder, and why? Also how was this accomplished cognitively? What does it mean to say that subtle saññā is merely residual? How does that work? (4) If, as virtually every Buddhist text argues, in the absence of a cognitive-subject no cognitive-object arises, and in the absence of a cognitive-object no cognitive-subject can arise, what are the grounds for asserting that in this dhyāna such a cognitive impossibility occurs? (5) Similarly, if *phassa* is defined as the contact-point of the sensory interchange between a cognitive-subject and a cognitive-object (as every Buddhist would define it), the notion of an objectless *phassa* is equally impossible and absurd.

Putting Buddhaghosa's explanation aside, let us attempt to find a more satisfactory account. This dhyāna neither consists of P_1 nor does it lack P_1, nor is it other than P_1. Each of the ārūpya dhyānas constituted itself as if it were 'boundless' or 'infinite,' only to be exposed by the subsequent dhyāna as circumscribed by a horizon, a closure. Ākāśa seemed limitless until it was exposed as a mere horizon within consciousness. Likewise consciousness seemed limitless until its circumscriptive closure was revealed by the 'nothing' that contingently conditions it. This nothing now also is shown to be a closure, an inversion of the foundations of experience which, as an inversion, is entirely dependent upon and relative to those foundations.

The final dhyāna places itself on a vacillating margin, a switch-point, between a cognitively constructed world (*saññā*) and the erasure and negation of that world (*asaññā*). As such it is the effervescent contingency of the world, the switch-point where the world both is and isn't because it is in fact *always becoming otherwise*. *Saññāsaññā* means cognition that can make associations without being a product of associative-thinking. It discerns by observing margins in their contingency. It views them as they effervesce, a world-view that puts the whole world together this way, and another view that now puts the whole world together that way. This vision is not driven by one's past conditioning, rather it recognizes *how* things, views, realities become (*yathā bhūtam*). Still it is not completely *asaṅkhāta* (unconditioned). It is "like" nibbāna, but not yet nibbāna. It opens the closure of conditioned cognition, not by going elsewhere, but by making the margin between conditioning and non-conditioning fluid.

All the previous jhānas, once dissolved into higher subsuming jhānas, ultimately revealed themselves to be closures. This jhāna alone, constituted by a permeable, alternating margin, is never closed, but rather is itself the occasion through which cognitive worlds open and close. The neither/nor of this jhāna is the middle way that runs through all of Buddhism.

The four ārūpya-dhyānas form a sequence:

1. *Ākāśa* dissolves into consciousness. But what differentiates them? Isn't *ākāśa* merely consciousness' own self-objectification?
2. Boundless consciousness dissolves into its own contingency. The way to undo a limitless consciousness that subsumes the world by appropriating and eclipsing it, is to erase, negate that consciousness, but seeing it and the world it has subsumed from a vantage that is so radically otherwise, there is nothing at all.
3. A middle way emerges from this nothing in which awareness (*saṃjñā-vedanā*) cannot reassert itself full-blown ('boundlessly'), but instead flickers on the margins of its own contingency.

We shall see in a later chapter that this sequence reasserts itself as the *tri-*(*a-*)*svabhāva* doctrine in Yogācāra in the following manner.

(i) grappling with the confusion caused by not recognizing that so-called objective referents are actually projections of consciousness (*parikalpita*),
(ii) that consciousness itself is constituted by a contingent conditionality (*paratantra*), which
(iii) if conceived as an appropriational, substantive conditionality, needs to be effaced through the radical negation of the referents and procedures which produce and reify it (*pariniṣpanna*), resulting in
(iv) a conditionality marked by the absence of (i) in (ii) as a middle-way (purified *paratantra*).

Hence I am proposing a thematic continuity between the ārūpya model and the *trisvabhāva* model as follows:

(1) ākāśānantya *vis-à-vis* parikalpita;

(2) vijñānānantya *vis-à-vis* paratantra;
(3) akiṃcanya *vis-à-vis* parinișpanna;
(4) naivasaṃjñānāsaṃjñā *vis-à-vis* 'corrected' paratantra.[38]

Before turning to the last of the four models, some final remarks about the tri-dhātu model are in order. First, true to the Buddhist tendency towards a middle way, it is the middle dhātu, i.e., the rūpa-dhātu, rather than the 'highest' (i.e., ārūpya) dhātu, which is considered the most important for Awakening. This valuation is reinforced by the description of Buddha's death given in the Pāli *Mahāparinibbāna sutta.*[39] Buddha ascends through the rūpa-jhānas, then the five(!) ārūpya-jhānas, then descends back down to the beginning of the rūpa-dhātu again, and then begins to reascend.[40] When he reaches the top rūpa-jhāna, but not having re-entered the ārūpya-jhānas, he passes on into Nibbāna. These three dhātus or lokas together make up virtually the entire horizon of sentient experience. Whatever is of the world or in the world is *lokiya* (mundane). But Buddhism developed a vocabulary for breaking out of this closure. The highest attainments and Nirvāṇa itself were considered *lokuttara* (supra-mundane). These highest attainments (*samāpatti*), like Buddha's entry into Nirvāṇa, initially tended to be located near the upper margin of the rūpa-dhātu. Since Buddha himself, according to the tradition, entered final Nirvāṇa at precisely this juncture through this methodology, its importance for Buddhist praxis was assured.[41]

Noteworthy implications of the tridhātu model for Yogācāra include:

(1) The initial domain in which the human condition is located (*kāma-dhātu*) operates by a conative, affective economy. What here comes under the rubric of *kāma* (eros) will be repeated in Yogācāra vocabulary as the 'noetic-noemic appropriational economy' (*grāhaka-grāhya-upādāna*). Yogācāric analysis begins and ends with this economy. The bulk of one's ethical and moral practice occurs on this level. Hence even the provisional goal of experientially acquiring access to Maitreya's Tușita Heaven remains within this sphere.

(2) The appropriational problematic is ameliorated and gradually removed through meditation and the development of a formal, mental 'equalization' (*upekṣa*). What here has been labeled *rūpa* will become explicitly a matter of mental reductionism in Yogācāra. As we shall see, this transition is merely the fruition of factors already at play in Buddhist thought prior to Yogācāra.

(3) Yogācāra will reinforce that the search for substrata inevitably gives way to a realization of 'marginality.' Just as *vijñāna* (consciousness) serves as a substratum for spatiality, it too becomes contextualized by a 'nothing' that exposes its contingency. The context for that contingency is an indeterminable aporia between the presence and absence of *saṃjñā* and *vedanā.* The terms *vedanā, saṃjñā,* and *vijñāna*—three of the five skandhas—occur in the titles of ārūpya dhyānas. If we follow Buddhaghosa's synonym, the 'marginality' characteristic of the fourth ārūpya dhyāna involves *saṃskāra* (*saṇkhārasesa samāpatti*). Thus four of the five skandhas reconverge in the ārūpya-dhātu, which explicitly involves a mental search for horizonal roots. That search is

effected by separating from *rūpa*—the only skandha missing in this dhātu. Hence this sort of crucial, high-level exploration and discovery can only begin once one has disengaged from rūpa. These successive erasures, produced by identifying and then erasing horizonal margins, invoking a marginality that eclipses consciousness as well, finally hinges on the excess: what remains, and what does not. The term *vijñapti-mātra* was designed to invoke a similar sense of marginality. It, too, signifies a non-substrative margin—an alterity—that constitutes the ultimate human horizon.

To sum up, the human condition locates itself within three existential horizons, or regions (borrowing the term from Husserl) with multiple horizons: a cathexic region, a formal/structural region, and a region that dissolves its expansive horizons into marginality. None of these regions or horizons are ontologically prior to their denizens, nor do they survive without them. Each is entirely and utterly constituted by actions and the consequences of actions (*karma*). Both the horizons and those who occupy them are constituted through action, and have no other ontological status.[42]

Thus it is not surprising that the later Indian Buddhist schools considered efficient causality (*kāraṇa, karoti*) to be the only valid criterion for determining the 'realness' of something. Efficacy, not 'existence,' determines reality. Hence even a delusion which 'works,' i.e., which functions, is 'real'; and *as real* as any other concrete, empirical event, which itself must be measured (*pramāṇa*) against the efficacy criterion. Thus in the seminal Yogācāra text, *Madhyānta-vibhāga*, the *abhūta-parikalpa* ('that which schematically constructs and attaches to what is not actually there') is taken as a ubiquitous cognitive ground. The *Lotus Sutra*'s theory of *upāya* as beneficent deception derives from the same criterion.

Here, perhaps more radically than we see in Husserl, the noetic-noemic intentional process constitutes 'ontology'; it is not merely a 'reduction' or system of reductions from ontology. The world is not taken as a pre-established given; the world-as-lived is constituted by cognitive actions. Thus for Buddhism, ontology is always and everywhere nothing but an epistemological construction, constituted through action and/as cognition. Awakening or Enlightenment means to see clearly. Therefore *Buddhism is concerned with Seeing, not Being.*

In the first horizon/region (*kāma-dhātu*), cognition is primarily conative. In the second (*rūpa-dhātu*), conation decreases as cognition becomes increasingly formal, until it reaches a point where the conative thrust is neutralized. In the third region (*ārūpya-dhātu*), cognition seeks the limits of its own presuppositions. Realizing that the notion of 'being presuppositionless' is itself a presupposition, that this notion simultaneously produces and derives from other presuppositions, the middle way, as marginal trace, is/isn't cognized. Insofar as the delving into the ārūpya-dhātu was predicated on a search for cognitive grounds or origins, it results in the aporetic conclusion that the 'origin' is, in fact, a trace (*saṃskāra*).[43]

Two Zen accounts should help us put the theory of the 'Three Worlds' into proper Buddhist perspective. The first offers a reminder that one should be careful about adopting or clinging to any ontologies or cosmologies:[44]

> Sato-Kaiseki was very much disturbed by the implications of Copernicus' heliocentric theory, which, of course, was inconsistent with the old Buddhist cosmology in which Mount Sumeru occupies the center of the universe. He reasoned that if the Buddhist view of the cosmos proved false, the triple world [*tri-dhātu*] ... would be reduced to nonsense, resulting in the negation of Buddhism itself. Immediately he set about writing a book in defense of the Mount Sumeru position, sparing himself no effort as a champion of Buddhism.
>
> When he had finished the work, he took it at once to Master Ekido (1805-1879, Sōtō) and presented it to him triumphantly. After leafing through only the first few pages, however, the master thrust the book back and, shaking his head, said, "How stupid! Don't you realize that the basic aim of Buddhism is to shatter the triple world...? Why stick to such worthless things and treasure Mount Sumeru? Blockhead!" Dumbfounded, Kaiseki shoved the book under his arm and went quickly home.

Lin-chi (Jp: Rinzai), drawing on what Buddhism considers the three fundamental roots of *duḥkha*—viz. *rāga* (appropriational intent, passionate drives), *dveṣa* (aversion, hatred, despising) and *moha* (misconception, mental confusion), sometimes rendered greed, hatred and delusion—existentializes the *tri-dhātu* and drives the basic point home.[45]

> From everywhere you have come here; all of you eagerly seek the Buddha, the Dharma, and deliverance; you seek to escape the Three Worlds. You foolish people, if you get out of the Three Worlds, where then can you go? The Buddhas and patriarchs are only phrases of adoration. Do you want to know the Three Worlds? They do not differ from the sensation of your listening to the Dharma now! One of your passionate urges, however fleeting, is the world of desire. A momentary anger is the world of form.[46] And a second's foolish ignorance is the formless world. These are the furniture of your own house. The Three Worlds do not of themselves proclaim: We are the Three Worlds! Followers of the Way, it is the one clearly manifested and lively before your eyes, who perceives, weighs and measures the Three Worlds, and it is he who puts names to them.

With the move to the next model, we will have completed a transition from theory to practice: the skandha and *pratītya-samutpāda* models delineate primarily theoretic aspects for practice, while the *tri-dhātu* and *śīla-samādhi-prajñā* models are primarily emphasizing the practical side of theory. All four together indicate the spectrum of Buddhist praxis.

Notes

1 As will be demonstrated in more detail later, whereas the Abhidhamma texts repeatedly state that *rūpa* is entirely karmically neutral, that thought and matter exert no direct causal influence on each other, Buddhaghosa — working with an ambiguity he found in certain texts — nonetheless posits a direct karmic relationship between rūpa and thought, perhaps, in part, due to implications from the use of rūpa in the tridhātu model. His famous *citta-vīthi* (cognition moments-series) model is only one example of his efforts to posit intercausal relations between mental and rūpic phenomena. As I will suggest later, Buddhaghosa very probably was directly and profoundly influenced by Yogācāra thought, which was not only thriving in north India when he left it, but in southern India and Śri Lanka when he studied and wrote there. Hsüan-tsang, in his travelogue, describes the eminent reputation of contemporary Yogācāra studies there, and though he makes a sustained effort to visit Śri Lanka himself to witness them first hand, much to his regret, he was forced to abort his trip.

2 Some of these sources include: Winston King's *Theravāda Meditation: The Buddhist Transformation of Yoga* (University Park: Pennsylvania State University Press). See especially his diagrams on pp. 85f. Randy Kloetzli's *Buddhist Cosmology* includes seven charts of the tridhātu (pp. 33-39); ch. II discusses its structure and ch. IV discusses its function as a path. Also cf. the references he cites on p. 24 n. 1 and p. 33 n. 1. Alphonso Verdu's *Early Buddhist Philosophy* (Washington, D.C.: University Press of America) includes some insightful materials (cf. pp. 53-65 and 130-175, and the chart of pp. 171-175). Rahula's essay "A Comparative Study of Dhyānas, according to Theravāda, Sarvāstivāda and Mahāyāna" on pp. 101-109 of his *Zen and the Taming of the Bull* is concise and critical. Wayman's essay "Aspects of Meditation in the Theravāda and Mahīśāsaka", reprinted in his *Buddhist Insight* (Delhi: Motilal), pp. 69-98, is rich in detail and suggestive associations. Herbert Guenther's *Philosophy and Psychology in the Abhidharma* attempts a synthetic interpretation based on Pāli abhidhammic sources along with the *Abhidharmakośa, Abhidharmasamuccaya,* and Sthiramati's *-vṛtti, Triṃśikā-ṭīkā,* etc.; cf. esp. pp. 116-143. *Meditative States in Tibetan Buddhism* by Lati Rinbochay, Denma Lachö Rinbochay, Leah Zahler, and Jeffrey Hopkins is in two parts. The first is Zahler's translation of Lati's 'Oral Presentation,' and gives a moralistic cosmology as well as rudimentary meditational advice. The second part translates part of a nineteenth century Tibetan monk's (Paṇ-chen Sö-nam-drak-ba) commentary on Asaṅga's *Abhisamayālaṃkāra.* Why they chose this particular commentary to translate and present of all the possible texts available and in need of translation (e.g., Asaṅga's original text) is a mystery. For the most part, it records a sectarian dispute over whether certain features of meditative experience are already present in the stages prior to *rūpa-dhātu* and/or *arūpa-dhātu*, or not. As a sectarian document it can only provide hermeneutic confidence to those who uncritically accept the positional bias advanced there as textual dogma.

Another translation from a Tibetan source is Constance Hoog's *Prince Jiṅ-Gim's Textbook of Tibetan Buddhism* (Leiden: EJ Brill, 1983), her rendering of 'Phags-pa's *Śes-bya rab-gsal* (*Jñeya-prakāśa*). A Chinese translation of this text, which seems to differ occasionally from the Tibetan version, can be found at T.1645.32, pp. 226-236. This thirteenth century primer, composed for Kublai Khan's second son, begins with a detailed reiteration of the tridhātu cosmology as found in the *Abhidharmakośa.* Curiously, it follows this with the Buddhist evolutionary myth (found in the *Brahmajāla* and *Agañña suttas* of the *Dīgha Nikāya*, as well as in later works such as the *Mahāvastu*) of how 'sublime beings' originated and gradually grew coarser, until they became human. This is followed by a not entirely clear description of *pratītya-samutpāda*, and then a brief overview of the *Kośa*'s seventy-five dharmas. It acknowledges that Asaṅga and Vasubandhu offer a different account, but nonetheless seems to prefer and remain attached to the seventy-five dharma theory (cf. p. 57). It is nonetheless difficult to assign this text to a particular school, since elsewhere (p. 49) it is also critical of both the Vaibhāṣika and Sautrāntika schools. Its concluding sections cover the Path and the Fruit in typical Mahāyāna fashion (*sambhāra-mārga, prayoga-mārga*, the six pāramitās, etc.), and the last chapter recounts the seventy-five dharma version of *asaṃskṛta-dharmas*, though it indirectly implicates the Yogācāra version by mentioning *tathatā* (which the Yogācārins, but not the Vaibhāṣikas, considered an *asaṃskṛta-dharma*). Perhaps because it was intended as 'exoteric' exposition (of the bśad-mdzod genre), its presentation remained largely Hīnayānic while incorporating Mahāyānic elements. Interestingly 'Phags-pa also seems to have considered the four models of skandhas, pratītya-samutpāda, tridhātu, and (an expanded) śīla-samādhi-prajñā as the basic models for his handbook. This is interesting because I only discovered this work after having already written most of my analysis.

An impressive English language survey and critical appraisal of the tridhātu as used in Pāli Buddhist meditation is Henepola Gunaratana's *The Path of Serenity and Insight* which utilizes and coherently presents the doctrines propounded by Buddhaghosa in his Nikāya commentaries as well as his *Visuddhimagga*, combined with the eleventh century commentary on the *Dhammasaṅgaṇi* by Anuruddha, *Abhidhammatthasaṅgaha.* This latter has been translated three times: 1. along with the translator's own compendium of Abhidhamma thought by Jagdish Kashyap as *Abhidhamma Philosophy* (Delhi: Bharatiya Vidya Prakashan, rpt. 1982); 2. Nārada Mahā Thera's *A Manual of Abhidhamma* (Kuala Lampur: Buddhist Missionary Society, 1979 revised ed.), which includes the Pāli text and detailed charts and commentary; and 3. *The Compendium of Philosophy*, translated by Shwe Zan Aung for the Pali Text Society. The *Visuddhimagga* is the *classicus locus* for Theravādin speculations on tridhātu. Historically and doctrinally, between the early Pāli sources and the later revised Theravāda school as codified by Buddhaghosa, there is the Sarvāstivāda school. For a good account of their understanding of the tridhātu doctrine, see Nalinaksha Dutt's "Doctrines of the Sarvāstivāda School of Buddhism," *Indian Historical Quarterly,* 14, 1937, pp. 114-120, 799-812. Yogācāra texts that deal with tridhātu include Asaṅga's *Abhisamayālaṃkāra.* (mentioned above), the *Yogācārabhūmi, Daśabhūmika Sūtra*, as well as several others. The Yogācāra attitude, however, is summed up in the famous line from the *Avataṁsaka Sūtra* — "the three realms are only consciousness."

3 For an example, see the vivid descriptions in Mark Tatz and Jody Kent, *Rebirth: The Tibetan Game of Liberation* (NY: Anchor, 1977), pp. 66-75. This game is a kind of Buddhist 'chutes and ladders' which presents an accurate and informative overview of both Buddhist cosmology and the manner in which one 'transmigrates' the various paths (Sūtra, Tantra, etc.) through it towards Buddhahood. There are also East Asian versions of this game. See also MATSUNAGA Daigan and MATSUNAGA Alicia, *The Buddhist Concept of Hell* (New York: Philosophical Library, 1972); Bimala Churn Law, *Heaven and Hell in Buddhist Perspective* (Calcutta; Simla: Thacker, Spink & Co., 1925); Anne Swann Goodrich, *Chinese Hells: the Peking Temple of Eighteen Hells and Chinese Conceptions of Hell* (St. Augustin: Monumenta Serica, 1981).

4 *Buddhism: Its Essence and Development* (NY: Harper Torchbooks, 1959) p. 51.

5 Cf. *Wu-men Kuan* (Gateless Gate), case #2.

6 Present day Śri Lankan funerals seem to retain some of these ancient aspects, though the actual funeral goer is probably unaware of the non-Buddhist roots of the rituals and actions he or she is performing.

7 *Zen and the Taming of the Bull*, p. 49, paraphrasing *Majjhima Nikāya* III, p. 169 (PTS ed.).

8 The four kings rule the four directions from Mt. Meru, which in Buddhist cosmology stands at the center of the world. Kloetzli (*op. cit.*, p. 29) writes:

> Two classes of gods dwell on Mt. Meru; the Caturmahārājakāyika and the Trāyastriṃśa. Four classes of Caturmahārājakāyika gods inhabit the four terraces (*pariṣaṇḍa*) extending halfway up Meru. The Caturmahārājakāyikas are the most numerous among the gods and

also inhabit the palaces (*vimāna*) of the sun, moon and stars. The ruler of the Trāyastriṃśa is Indra or Śakra whose abode rests atop Mt. Meru.

Three of the four kingdoms are characterized in *Abhidharmakośa* as i. "always drunk" (inhabited by *sadāmattas*), ii. "bearing garlands" (inhabited by *mālādharas*), and iii. "bowl in hand" (inhabited by *karoṭapāṇis*).

9 Early Yogācāra, on its devotional side, developed an important Maitreya cult. This cult was still strong in Hsüan-tsang's day, and he makes reference to it and his participation in it, particularly in personal moments of crisis. That Amitābha worship eventually superseded Maitreya worship in China, and subsequently all of East Asia — crystallizing as Pure Land Buddhism — seems perhaps due more to political than strictly religious causes. Cf. Hardacre and Sponberg, eds., *Maitreya The Future Buddha* (Cambridge: Cambridge University Press, 1988).

10 Rahula, in *Zen...*, *op. cit.*, pp. 101-110, gives a marvelous, concise overview of this disparity, using the Pāli Nikāyas, Abhidhamma and commentaries, *Abhidharmakośa*, and Asaṅga's *Abhidharmasamuccaya*. He concludes that the Yogācāra model is closer to the original Nikāyas than either the Pāli Abhidhamma or Buddhaghosa. Wayman's article, "Aspects of Meditation...", *op. cit.*, also treats this issue, using more sources. Gunaratana, *op. cit.*, pp. 101-104, reiterates the standard Theravādin gloss, namely that the discrepancy between the four *dhyānas* and five *dhyānas* represents slightly different 'paths' that nonetheless begin and end identically. Guenther's synthetic approach in *Philosophy and Psychology...* incorporates the positions of the various major schools (Theravāda, Vaibhāṣika, Sautrāntika, Yogācāra, etc.) but tends to favor, implicitly, Buddhaghosa's *Aṭṭhasālinī* (his commentary on the *Dhammasaṅgaṇi*), since he considers it "based on the actual experience... so vividly described in words" (p. 121), whereas the other texts use abstract, textual, and etymological arguments. His interpretation differs from Rahula's, for instance, on the issue of whether 'one-pointed mind' should be included in all four (or five) rūpa-dhyānas or not. Rahula contends that this is only found in the Pāli Abhidhamma texts, not in the Suttas or Sanskrit texts, and its inclusion is misleading. Guenther, on the other hand, taking one-pointedness as a synonym for samādhi, accepts the importance of its presence in each of the dhyānas.

11 Treated as rebirth realms, they are collectively called the Brahma-lokas or 'Brahma-worlds,' though technically speaking Brahma only resides and rules in the lowest of the rūpa-dhātu heavens. There are several schema for classifying these life-worlds, but these will not be discussed in the present section. For details, see Kloetzli and Verdu. Also see the discussion in chapter six on the *samāpattis*.

12 This, of course, presupposes the common assumption that the *Sutta-piṭaka* is in fact older and more representative of the earlier tradition than the *Abhidhamma-piṭaka*, parts of which were known to have been composed at a much later date.

13 See note 69. Those works, including Gunaratana's, offer references to the various texts in which these models are discussed.

14 See previous note.

15 *Vivicc'eva kāmehi vivicca akusalehi dhammehi savitakkaṃ savicāraṃ vivekajaṃ pītisukhaṃ paṭhamajjhānaṃ*. Rahula, *ibid.*, p. 142 n. 8 notes the following locations in the Nikāyas where the "stereotyped formulas" for these four are given: *Dīgha N.* I, pp. 73-75, 183ff; II, pp. 78, 131, 222; *Majjhima N.* I, pp. 159, 181, 435f; *Aṅguttara N.* I, pp. 53, 168, 182; *Saṃyutta N.* II, pp. 210-211, IV, pp. 263ff, V, pp. 213ff.

For alternate renderings of the key terms in English, cf. Guenther, *op. cit.*: on *prīti* and *sukha*, see pp. 121f; on these and the rest cf. pp. 49-61. While his discussions contain helpful insights, his conflation of the various sources obscures some very real differences between the various systems. His seeming thoroughness is occasionally marked by omissions; e.g., he renders *samprajanya* as 'full awareness' (p. 124) and *prajñā* as 'intellectual acumen and appreciative analytical understanding' (p. 125) without noting that the *Vibhaṅga* and *Abhidharmakośa* both treat these terms as synonyms (cf. Rahula, p, 107).

16 *Vitakkavicārānaṃ vūpasamā ajjhattaṃ sampasādanaṃ cetaso ekodibhāvaṃ avitakkhaṃ avicāraṃ samādhijaṃ pītisukhaṃ dutiyajjhānaṃ.*

17 *Pītiyā ca virāgā upekkhako ca viharati, sato ca sampajāno, sukhar ca kāyena paṭisamvedeti, yaṃ taṃ ariyā ācikkhanti 'upekkhako satimā sukhavihārī'ti tatiyajjhānaṃ.* Note that the qualification of sukha as 'bodily' (kāyena) occurs only in the suttas; neither the Abhidhamma nor the later texts of other schools seem to have retained this explicitly, though insofar as the lived-body (kāya) is always the locus of experience, this qualification may have been implicitly understood, though unemphasized.

18 Sukhassa ca pahānā dukkhassa ca pahānā pubbe'va somanassa domanassānaṃ atthaṅgamā adukkhaṃ asukkhaṃ upekkhā sati parīsuddhiṃ catutthajjhānaṃ.

19 Following Rahula's chart, op. cit., p. 102. See his essay for the abhidhammic justifications for including ekaggatā (one-pointedness of mind) in each of the five levels.

20 Gunaratana, p. 99, writes:

> [The fourth] *jhāna* has two kinds of equanimity - [1] equanimous feeling, the affective tone which inclines neither towards pleasure nor pain, and [2] specific neutrality, the mental attitude of sublime impartiality free from attachments and aversion. Though the two are different factors, the one belonging to the aggregate of feelings (*vedanākkhandha*) and the other to the aggregate of mental formations (*sankhārakkhandha*), their concomitance is not fortuitous; for as specific neutrality becomes more and more refined it naturally tends to come into association with equanimous feeling, its hedonic counterpart.

He is drawing on the *Vibhaṅga* and Buddhaghosa for these distinctions.

21 On Hegel's notion of 'concept' as a synonym for the dialectical *aufhebung* process, cf. his "preface" to *The Phenomenology of Mind/Spirit.*

22 See Gunaratana, pp. 108f, 119-122.

23 *Iddhis* (S. *ṛddhi*) are the supernormal powers that accompany advanced spiritual attainments. Pāli texts usually list four: *chandiddhipādo, cittidhipādo, viriyiddhipādo, vimansiddhipādo,* i.e., 'the urge to do, active thought, being energetic, and the will to investigate.' For a good overview of the basic Pāli and Sanskrit literature and interpretations, see Har Dayal's *The Bodhisattva Doctrine in Buddhist Sanskrit Literature* (NY: Samuel Weiser, 1978 rpt. of 1932 ed.), pp. 104-106, 112-134. Cf. Warder, *Indian Buddhism,* p. 89. The so-called Āndhra schools that Warder identifies as the source of Mahāyāna claimed that the *ṛddhis* of the Buddha and his disciples "enables them to effect whatever they wish, regardless of the laws of nature" (*ibid.,* p. 327), prefiguring some of the more transcendentalistic interpretations of *upāya* in Mahāyāna. Cf. also Sten Konow, *The Two First Chapters of the Daśasāhasrikā Prajñāpāramitā: Restoration of the Sanskrit text, Analysis, and Index* (Oslo: 1941) for an early Mahāyānic reworking of this and other abhidhammic categories.

24 *Abhiññā* (S. *abhijñā*). On them, cf. Gunaratana, pp. 128ff; Dayal, *ibid.,* pp. 106-134. Conze's *Buddhist Scriptures,* pp. 121-133; *The Large Sutra on Perfect Wisdom,* tr. Conze, pp. 79-82. Jayatilleke, in his *Early Buddhist Theory of Knowledge,* argues that these five (or sometimes six) superknowledges and powers should not be considered supernatural, but rather as the empirically accessible spheres that are the specialized domain of meditation 'experts,' much as the finer mathematical and conceptual concerns of modern physics are accessible only to those specially trained in physics, though in principle accessible to anyone, and hence still empirical. In other words, these supernormal abilities are accessible to anyone with the discipline and abilities to acquire them; they are matters of training.

25 *Philosophy and Psychology...,* p. 127.

26 The notion of *avyākta-karma,* 'non-defined' or 'indefinite' karma (rendered in Chinese as 無記 *wu-chi,* lit. "non-recorded"), already important in the Abhidhamma schema, becomes a crucial Yogācāra distinction, that helps differentiate the seventh and eighth consciousnesses (which were Yogācāric innovations) from the first six consciousnesses. We will return to this when treating the *Triṃśikā.*

27 Cf. Merleau-Ponty's notion of *l'être sauvage et brut* (lit. 'savage and brutal Being,' usually translated 'wild ontology') in *The Visible and the Invisible.*

28 In other Pāli texts, such as the *Brahmajāla sutta*, we learn that Brahma's belief in his own primacy and eternality are simply erroneous views on his part.

29 P. 277. *Path of Purity*, p. 362. Cited and commented upon in Gunaratana, p. 115.

30 As stated above, Buddhaghosa lived after Vasubandhu, in a time when Yogācāra had already developed into a major Buddhist force. His writings thoroughly reflect a Yogācāric influence, though for obvious reasons his Theravādin commentators ignore or suppress this fact. Modern scholarship, whether emerging directly out of the Theravādin tradition or whether incorporating Buddhaghosa's writings into more intersectarian approaches, unfortunately also fails to take adequate note of this influence. I've only seen two works that even mention the possibility of Yogācāric influence on Buddhaghosa. One is Guenther in his *Philosophy and Psychology in the Abhidharma*, where on p. 133, while discussing the ārūpya-dhyānas primarily from the point of view of Buddhaghosa's *Aṭṭhasālinī*, Guenther writes:

> The author of the *Aṭṭhasālinī*, who is, as many passages in his work reveal, much indebted to the intellectual and spiritual acumen of the Vijñānavādins....

However, Guenther does not develop this observation, nor does he pick it up again later. The other is Kalupahana's *The Principles of Buddhist Psychology* (Albany: SUNY Press, 1987), where on pp. 114-115 he argues that Buddhaghosa was misguidedly influenced by the *Laṅkāvatāra Sūtra* — though, Kalupahana insists, *not* the Yogācāra of Asaṅga and Vasubandhu (Kalupahana's distinction is more a polemic than an adequately evidenced argument) — and that this introduced a host of improper metaphysical theories into subsequent Theravādin thinking. His point that Buddhaghosa (i) was influenced by Yogācāric thinking, whether from the *Laṅkāvatāra* or mainstream Yogācāra, and (ii) that this influence has profoundly altered the subsequent ways in which Theravādins have interpreted their own tradition is well taken.

31 It may be interesting to compare how a cognate term, *kaścid*, meaning 'anything' or 'any one,' is treated in its negative form (*na kaścid*, 'no thing' or 'no one') in Mahāyānic literature, for instance, in these kārikās from two separate chapters of Nāgārjuna's *Mūlamadhyamaka-kārikā* (MMK):

> (18.6) The Buddhas have heuristically taught (*prajñapitam...deśitaṃ*) ātman-theory (*ātmeti*) and anātman-theory (*anātmeti*). Also, they have not taught of anything (*na... kaścid...deśitaṃ*) as ātman or anātman.

> (19.6) If it is assumed that time exists depending upon an entity (*bhāva*), how can there be time without an entity? No entity whatsoever (*na ca kaścana bhāvo*) exists (*asti*). Whence does time become (*kutaḥ kālo bhaiṣyati*)?

Kaścid is an indefinite pronoun that, since it derives from the root term *ka* (an interrogative pronoun with negative overtones), carries both negative and interrogative associations. Buddha "teaches" provisionally, heuristically (*prajñapti*), using concepts and enumeration therapeutically, while cautiously refraining from teaching that such "things" have any actual referent. *Kaścid* is the most general, indefinite term available for denoting any possible referent — whether metaphysical, empirical, common-sensical, or whatever; it is "anything whatsoever". Thus we see that for Nāgārjuna, Buddha was not playing a sly game of *via negativa* allusion. The terms ātman and anātman have no referent whatsoever. Similarly, time "becomes" (*bhava*), but not from entities (*bhāvāḥ*) that exist (*asti*). "Entities", meaning 'anything whatsoever' (*kaścid*) that has an enduring identity or value (cf. 19.4!), do not exist and do not indicate anything — even in the most general, indefinite sense — that exists. Buddha, in other words, does *not* teach about existence and existents, but rather weaves a therapeutic web that, as Nāgārjuna repeatedly emphasizes throughout MMK, puts prapañca to rest.

32Yogācāra texts say: Negate the object, and the self is also negated (e.g., *Madhyānta-vibhāga*, 1:4, 8). Vasubandhu in two different texts offers a nearly identical formula, both hinging on two terms: upalabdhi, which means to 'cognitively apprehend,' i.e., to grasp or appropriate cognitively; and *artha*, 'referent' of a linguistic or cognitive act, i.e., that toward which an intentionality intends.s

> Apprehending vijñapti-mātra is the basis for the arising of the nonapprehension of artha. The nonapprehension of artha is the basis for the nonapprehension of vijñapti-mātra.
>
> *vijñapti-mātropalabdhim niśrityārthānupalabdhir-jayate. Arthānupalabdhim niśritya vijñapti-mātrasyāpi-anupalabdhir-jayate.* (*Madhyāntavibhāga-bhāṣya* I.7)
>
> By the apprehending of citta-mātra, there is the nonapprehension of cognized artha. By nonapprehending cognized artha, citta also in nonapprehended.
>
> *citta-mātra-upalambhena jñeyārthārthānupalambhatā. Jñeyārtha anupalambhena syāc-cittānupalambhatā.* (*Trisvabhāvanirdeśa* 36)

33 P. 254: *Sabbaso ākiñcaññāyatanaṃ samatikkamma nevasaññā nāsaññāyatanaṃ upasampajja viharati ti.*

34 The trace is one of Derrida's most complex and difficult concepts, drawing on the Hegelian and Nietzschian notions of aufhebung, as well as indications from others, such as Husserl's Logical Investigations and Heideggerian "Withdrawal". It is treated with ever more intricacy throughout his early and middle writings, and thus no single source could be cited for an adequate account. On the one hand, it evokes the question of what, in French, may be the implication of the phrase il se reste... which means "it remains," but more literally could be translated as "it leaves itself there," "it itself remains," or "it [is the agent of] its own remaining," or "it remains itself", etc. The question then is what notion or form of identity survives through the difference from one moment to the next, or from one level to the next (the "it" that oversees the "it" that changes from pre-remaining to post-remaining — but are they the same?), or the identity which both loses and gains itself through reflective reflexivity (the se makes the verb reflexive). On the other hand, a trace is what is present only by virtue of its marking an absence, by noting what is no longer (or possibly never was) there, like a footprint. Its presence is the evoking of an absence. The trace is that which survives radical negation, what survives the deconstruction of identity, but only insofar as it marks an erasure such that it may be re-traced, 're-traited,' 'remaining' as différance (another Derridean term, neither identical nor different from the actual word difference, i.e., it sounds the same but is written differently; a simulacrum of difference and deferral, of logico-spatial and temporal differings). I have already written on the trace in "Re-tracing the Human-Nature vs. World-Nature Dichotomy: Rereading Lao Tzu." An important, sustained discussion of the trace by Derrida can be found in "OUSIA et GRAMME: note sur une note de Sein und Zeit" in Marges de la philosophie (Paris: Les Editions de Minuit, 1972) and translated by Alan Bass as "Ousia and Gramme: Note on a Note from Being and Time" in Margins of Philosophy (University of Chicago Press, 1982).

Helpful for those intimidated by the demands made on the reader by Derrida's style, though difficult texts in their own right, are Rodolphe Gasché's "Joining the Text: From Heidegger to Derrida" in *The Yale Critics: Deconstruction in America,* ed. J. Arac, et al. (Minneapolis: University of Minneapolis Press, 1983), pp. 153-174, and chapter one of Robert Magliola's *Derrida on the Mend* (Indiana: Purdue University Press, 1984) (see my review of this book in *The Journal of Ecumenical Studies,* Fall 1986).

35 P. 118, citing Visuddhimagga p. 280 (Path of Purity, p. 366f).

36 The example of oil 'residue,' i.e., that which remains (il se reste) even after being emptied, has its corollaries in Yogācāra texts, and is part of the distinctively Yogācāric interpretation of śūnyatā. Cf., e.g., Vasubandhu's bhāṣya to v. 2 of Madhyānta-vibhāga.

37 Phassa means the contact between a sense-organ and its object; if there is no object, with what is an awareness in 'contact'?

38 The trisvabhāva model, often considered one of the primary Yogācāra models, will be considered later. I will there show why, according to the Ch'eng wei-shih lun, this model needs to be considered in four steps rather than three.

39 A translation with an introductory essay can be found in T.W. Rhys Davids, Buddhist Suttas (NY: Dover, 1969 rpt of 1881 Sacred Books of the East ed.) pp. xxix-136.

40 As mentioned previously, there are differing enumerations of the number and types of dhyānas and/or bhūmis in the triple-world system, and this sutta contains one of those variations. On p. 115, ibid., Rhys Davids translates the five post-rūpic meditations as

> [1] the infinity of space alone is present. And passing out of the mere consciousness of the infinity of space he entered into the state of mind to which [2] the infinity of thought is alone present. And passing out of the mere consciousness of the infinity of thought he entered into a state of mind to which [3] nothing at all was specially present. And passing out of the consciousness of no special object he fell into a state [4] between consciousness and unconsciousness. And passing out of the state between consciousness and unconsciousness he fell into a state in which [5] the consciousness both of sensations and of ideas had wholly passed away.

At which point Ānanda mistakes him for dead, though he is not dead yet. Cf. the description of meditative sequences on pp. 52ff, where the four rūpic jhānas are severely glossed allowing this list to still equal eight stages (three *rūpic* + five *arūpic*). In this version, our top level, which was the impasse between *saṃjñā* and *asaṃjñā*, is crowned with a higher stage, in which neither *saṃjñā* nor *vedanā* has survived. This is uncharacteristically nihilistic, but finds its corollaries in the *nirodha-samāpatti* as well as *nirvikalpa-jñāna*, both of which we shall have occasion to discuss later.

41 Buddhaghosa in the *Visuddhimagga* locates the pinnacle of the path at the top of the arūpa-dhātu in the nirodha-samāpatti. This will be examined later.

42 The *Ch'eng wei-shih lun* will suggest otherwise, however, apparently attempting to avoid some solipsistic consequences.

43 This aporia of precedence and consequence is reflected in the historical development of the theory of Awakening. While Buddha repeatedly claims in the Pāli texts that Awakening is consequent upon uncovering and removing the deep, underlying psycho-cognitive roots of *avidyā* (i.e., the *āsavas*, etc.), the Theravāda tradition, by arguing that the complete uncovering of presuppositions through meditative examination of the arūpa-dhātu was unnecessary, allowed the possibility of an Awakening that did not plumb the radical depths of the human condition. Later this controversy took several forms. While the Theravādins believed that Awakening was sudden, other non-Mahāyānic schools insisted that it was gradual. This debate is recorded in the *Katthā Vatthu*. Another form of the debate argued that if disentangling one's karmic condition involved the gradual activity of discovering and overcoming, piece by piece, one's karmic legacy, the task would be interminable, since each counter-karmic action is itself an action, and thus productive of further karma. Instead, certain schools proposed a sudden, disruptive experience that plucked out the problematic roots all at once without having to examine them centimeter by centimeter. Both the sudden/gradual and the modificatory/disruptive controversies reemerged in Ch'an (Sŏn and Zen). The polemical assault of the Southern School against the Northern School is well known, as are such later ramifications as Tsung-mi's and Chinul's notion of Sudden Awakening *followed by* Gradual Practice. Lin-chi, the founding patriarch of what in Japan is called the Rinzai school, himself came to Awakening in part by abandoning the modificatory model in favor of the disruptive model (cf. Irmgard Schloegl, *The Zen Teaching of Rinzai,* Berkeley: Shambhala, 1976, p. 35). The chiasm between previous and subsequent, i.e., the temporal implications of the *arché* being a trace, became one of the most striking features of Dōgen's

philosophy: against the claim that Awakening involved a once-and-for-all realization, or that Actualized Awakening merely involved the realization of an identity with Original Awakening (*hongaku*), Dōgen reiterated the aporetic chiasm by insisting that Awakening itself has to be dropped each and every moment in order that one may Awaken each and every moment. It goes beyond the scope of the present worked to examine these and other theories of Awakening further.

44 From *Zen: Poems, Prayers, Sermons, Anecdotes, Interviews,* ed. and tr. by Lucien Stryk and Takashi Ikemoto (NY: Doubleday Anchor Original, 1965) p. 113.

45 Schloegl, pp. 45-46.

46 Lin-chi seems to be treating this as *pratigha,* which means both 'aversion' and 'resistance' (rather than as *dveṣa*, 'hatred, aversion'). *Pratigha* is one of the standard definitions of rūpa. Cf. discussion above. How he became sufficiently aware of the Sanskrit terminology so as to construct this splendid pun (which is not at all apparent in the Chinese terms) is unclear.

Chapter Six

Model Four: Śīla-samādhi-prajñā (P. sīla-samādhi-paññā)

The trialectic interrelationship of 'behavioral discipline' (*śīla*), 'mental training through meditation' (*samādhi*) and 'cognitive acuity' (*prajñā*) forms the bedrock of Buddhist praxis. Their relationship is trialectic since as one endeavors to improve within one aspect, the other two automatically are involved and improve as well. The relation between the three is not isomorphic, but rather one of mutual influence.

For instance, progress made through behavioral discipline (*śīla*), such as gaining control over one's eating habits, necessarily involves focusing one's attention (*samādhi*) on the variety of food types, the types and intensities of one's hungers and thirsts, the conditions by which and surrounded by which one eats, etc. This then develops insight (*prajñā*) into the confluence of conditions we call 'eating habits' (the karma of eating). Further, as one's insight increases, the efficacy with which one implements the behavioral discipline and mentally observes and analyzes its conditions and consequences likewise improves. As discipline improves, so do meditation and insight. As meditation improves, so does discipline and insight. As insight improves, so will discipline and meditation. Thus one must make an effort in all three areas, knowing that accomplishments in any one area will prove beneficial in the others, which in turn will facilitate further accomplishments in all three.

Śīla

Scholars sometimes translate *śīla* as 'morality' because it involves not only a general sense of behavioral discipline, but it frequently signifies specific ethical injunctions and guidelines. The monastic rules and the rules for the laity, codified by the various schools in their respective *Vinaya* (the section of the canon dealing with the rules for the Saṅgha and the Buddhist community)[1] and *Pratimokṣa*[2] (initially a section of the *Vinaya* that at times came to signify the monastic rules themselves, particularly as ritually expressed), came under the rubric of śīla.

In this moralistic sense śīla may be simplistically reduced to either the so-called 'Five Precepts' for laypeople (*pañca-śīla*) or to what has sometimes been called the Buddhist Ten Commandments[3], the *daśa-kuśala-karma-patha*, 'the Tenfold Path of Advantageous Karma/Actions.'

The Five Precepts are abstain from (i) destroying life, (ii) stealing, (iii) adultery, (iv) lying, and (v) intoxicating drinks. The Five Precepts are expanded in the Tenfold Path of Advantageous Karma/Actions, which are expressed in negative and positive forms.

The negatives are: (i) don't kill, (ii) don't steal, (iii) refrain from sexual misconduct,[4] (iv) don't lie, (v) refrain from harsh speech,[5] (vi) backbiting,[6] (vii) and frivolous speech,[7] (viii) don't covet, (ix) refrain from malice or dishonest acts, and (x) relinquish wrong views.

The positive version is:

[1] the three bodily (*kāya*) advantageous activities, viz.
- (i) saving lives,
- (ii) giving, and
- (iii) sexual propriety;

[2] the four verbal (*vāc*) advantageous activities, viz.
- (iv) truthfulness,
- (v) reconciling disputes,
- (vi) gentle speech,
- (vii) speech conducive to Dharma; and

[3] the three mental (*manas*) advantageous activities, viz.
- (viii) compassionate attitude,
- (ix) generous attitude, and
- (x) right views.

Buddhists define karma as the intentional activities of body, speech and mind. The ten 'rules' are therefore karmic guidelines designed to influence one's activities of body, speech, and mind, thereby utterly reshaping the manner in which karma is produced and, by extension, its consequences. In other words, śīla involves a comprehensive program aimed at intercepting and reconstructing human actions (karma), particularly in respect to the recurrence and recidivism of habitualization. Since in order to fully evaluate and implement such changes one would have to undertake a systematic analysis of what exactly constitutes an acting person, here, quite clearly, the philosophical, epistemological, psychological, soteric, and ethical dimensions of Buddhism converge.

Also noteworthy is the importance given to language and its usage in these cardinal rules. Rules (iv) through (vii) of the negative version explicitly involve speech acts, and others, such as (ix) and (x), imply them. In the positive version, again (iv) through (vii) are explicitly associated with speech (*vāc*), while language and its functioning are implicit in most of the others. Language serves as a medium between bodily and mental acts, i.e., it mediates and interrelates thought and deed. Language is neither the ground of thought or action, nor does it simply derive from them. It is the communicative medium between them; and still it functions in its own sphere as well.

The relative importance of each of the three, viz. body, speech and mind, was apparently a matter of dispute in Buddha's day. Ergardt[8] offers the following summary of such a dispute at *Majjhima Nikāya* I:371-378:

> The debate starts on a controversial point concerning the problem of kamma. Whereas the Buddha talks about the neutral concept of kamma as connected with body, speech, and mind (*kāya, vacī, mano*) with mind as the most important, the Jainas talk about the more ethically readymade concept of daṇḍa, which contains something of activities worthy of penalty, of which they regard activities of body (*kāyadaṇḍa*) as more important than speech and mind.

It is interesting that here Buddhism is already espousing an ethical criterion which did not emerge in the West, including within Jewish and Islamic medieval Jurisprudence, until more than a thousand years later. While the Jains are arguing that one's 'actions' (*karma*) should be judged by what we do bodily, i.e., physically, Buddha is claiming the criterion of 'intention' (*manas*) is even more important. Thus the Jains (and many in the West) were hard put to differentiate between accidentally killing someone or something and doing so intentionally ("with premeditation"). As a consequence, Jains structured their activities around avoiding the accidental harming or killing of any embodied jīvas (living, omniscient forces) which they believed resided in virtually everything. While Buddhists also frowned on unintentionally harming things, they put more emphasis on rooting out the desire and intention to harm. Interception of the karmic problematic could be facilitated by 'neutralizing' (*upekṣa*) the conditioning extremities of pleasure and pain, or reward and punishment, though eventually even this neutrality must be overcome. Technically, unintentional harming may not even carry any karmic significance—a Buddhist would consider such actions *krīya*, 'sheer action devoid of moral or ethical significance.' On the other hand, intentional harming, in fact *any* intentional act, always carries karmic significance. We recognize the same distinction in our legal systems when we differentiate the declining severity from premeditated murder, to manslaughter, to accidental killing. Later Buddhists even went so far as to claim that intentions which do not show themselves in action are karmic and material (*rūpa*).

The degree to which śīla or various specific śīlic rules were considered either provisional or indispensable has been a bone of contention between Buddhist schools almost from Buddhism's inception.[9] The *Mahā-parinibbāna sutta* records this famous utterance, one of the last uttered by Buddha:[10] "When I am gone, Ānanda, let the Saṅgha, if it so wish, abolish all the lesser and minor precepts." Unfortunately there seemed to be no consensus as to which of the precepts were major and which were minor. Subsequently, according to tradition, the Second Council, which convened about a century after Buddha's death, produced the first major Buddhist schism, in which the Mahāsāṅghikas (lit. 'majority') split off from the Theras (Skt.: Sthaviras) or 'Elders.' The Buddhist tradition maintains that the issues of conflict between these groups revolved around whether to relax the precepts, though modern scholarship has concluded that this was not the primary motive behind the schisms.[11] Eventually different sects developed their own Vinaya.[12] Occasionally tendencies arose within Mahāyāna to jettison śīla altogether (e.g., some Mādhyamika thought and certain strains within Zen).[13]

However one's understanding of śīla should not be confined strictly to rules, ethical or otherwise. These rules are merely guidelines to help one comprehend and comprehensively reconstitute the processes through which one acts. Action (karma), methodically and methodologically reconstituted, lies at the core of Buddhist soterics or Mārga (path or method).[14]

Samādhi

Samādhi includes not only the dhyānas described earlier, but a vast score of practices from basic mindfulness (*smṛti*) of inhaling and exhaling, taking constant cognizance of what one is doing at every moment,[15] etc., to elaborate mental visualizations and sonorisations, such as tantric maṇḍala and yantra meditations[16] and mantras and dhāraṇī.[17]

Samādhi can be etymologically derived[18] from *sama* (the same, equalized, the convergence of two distinct things based on some commonality) + *adhi* (an emphatic, meaning something like 'higher,' 'better,' or 'most skillfully achieved'). Thus samādhi signifies the skillful unification of mind and object, or the mental equanimity conducive to and derived from attention perfectly focused on its object. Hence it is sometimes treated as synonymous with *ekacitta*, 'one-focused mind,' i.e., mind (*citta*) completely focused on and at one (*eka*) with its object. As such, every act of perception or cognition involves some degree of samādhi or meeting of mind and object; though usually this 'unity' is obscured by a host of distractions and diversionary conditions. As a technical term, then, Buddhists use samādhi only for those cognitions in which the diversionary conditions have been minimized or eliminated.

It can also be derived from *sam-* (to bring together) + *ādhi* (to place on, put, to impregnate, to give, to receive). In this sense, samādhi signifies the bringing together of cognitive conditions such that the mind is impregnated, or becomes the locus of the economy of those conditions. In this sense, the mind is not only the giver and receiver of the confluence of cognitive cognitions, but it is also understood as impregnated by and bringing to term deep seeded conditions.[19] Samādhi, then, involves bringing the buried latencies or *saṃskāras* into full view. The obscure and hidden become clear objects of cognition. This etymology also implies that samādhi itself may be the act of impregnation, the planting of advantageous (*kuśala*) seeds through unificatory mental practice. Meditation then is the womb through which insight is born. Cognitive acuity emerges from mental discipline.

In the threefold schema of śīla-samādhi-prajñā, the term samādhi also implies the entire range of *bhāvanā*, or 'mental cultivation.' Etymologically linked with the term *bhāva, bhāvanā* at once invokes a sense of process, becoming (cf. #10 of *pratītya-samutpāda*) as well as an uncovering of things (*bhāva*) as they are.[20] Like śīla, *bhāvanā* proceeds programmatically. Centered on the moment of actual experience, bhāvanā is methodical real-ization, i.e., training and practice that actualizes a method. It becomes a kind of experiential laboratory through which one focuses on the components of embodied experience while deconstructing that embodiment. Each school defines the structure and steps of the Mārga in terms of the order and procedures which that school deems necessary.[21] Texts such as Vasubandhu's *Abhidharmakośa*, Asaṅga's *Yogācārabhūmi* and Buddhaghosa's *Visuddhimagga*, illustrate how Buddhists could develop elaborate edifices to explicate the specifics of their methods/mārga in the minutist of categorial detail. The discussion of the two samāpattis in the next chapter will illustrate this more fully.

Samādhi provides the methodology and context within which experience is to be examined, which is to say, it is the focused situation in which experience examines itself. Samādhi, by training, focusing/collecting, cleansing and calming the mind (*cittabhāvana, cittaṃ ṭhapetabbaṃ/samāhitaṃ cittaṃ, cittaṃ paṭivāpeti, cittaṃ paṭipassaddha*, etc.), by examining the mind through the mind (*citte cittānupassī viharati*) and observing dharmas through dharmas (*dhammesu dhammānupassī viharati*), facilitates things being finally known (*jānāti*) and seen (*passati*) just as they are (*tathatā*). *Majjhima Nikāya* I:301 states *atha khvāssa pubbe va tathā cittaṃ bhāvitaṃ hoti yan-taṃ tathattāya upanetīti,* "and so, having developed his mind just-so, it brings him to 'just-so-ness.'" The term *tathatā*, frequently translated as Suchness or Thusness, usually taken to be a Mahāyānic term, here already occurs in a pre-Mahāyānic text in a manner wholly concordant with its later signification. Knowing and seeing things as they are (*yathābhūtaṃ*) means tathatā.[22]

Like śīla, samādhi deploys a methodological assault on karmic conditioning. Since conditioning arises through conditions, and according to Buddhism these conditions are always conditions of and in experience (i.e., Buddhism denies the existence of any non-experiential metaphysical factors[23]), the analysis, insight into, and elimination of karmic conditioning must occur within the locus of experience. Just as the mind is known through the mind (*citte cittānupassī viharati*) and thereby liberated (*cetovimutti*), so is experience understood through experience (*paṭisaṃvedeti*) and thereby de-conditioned (*asaṅkhata* [S. *asaṃskṛta*] = *vimoceti*).[24]

While change (*pariṇāma, vipariṇāma*) and relations (causal, formal, etc.) normally are not directly perceived, but only known through inference, Buddhists, by claiming that a necessary ingredient for Awakening is directly seeing *pratītya-samutpāda*, are in effect claiming that Awakening involves *a direct experience of change and relations* (though how this alters what then is understood by change and relations is a matter of some dispute between the different schools). The implications of the Buddhist claim that relations can be objects of direct perception has received little or no attention by modern scholars. In fact, some Buddhist texts claim that causal relations are *directly observable.* The *Aggivacchagotta sutta* of the *Majjhima Nikāya* has Buddha and Vacchagotta agree that they can 'see' certain types of fuels causing certain types of fire.[25] Since Buddha's enlightenment is intimately connected with his vision of pratītya-samutpāda, i.e., a causal chain, Buddha must have been able to *see* this causality. It seems unlikely that merely intellectually ruminating about causes would be sufficient for Buddha to declare himself enlightened.

Prajñā

While samādhi provides the situation for observing what needs to be observed, the act of successfully observing, insofar as it aims to produce 'knowing' as well as 'seeing,' involves knowledge (*jñāna*) both as a prerequisite and as a consequent condition.

Of the three terms in the model under current discussion, *prajñā* is undoubtedly the most important. Since *avidyā* is the etiological basis of duḥkha and saṃsāra, 'knowledge' (*vidyā, jñāna*) is its necessary cure.

Prajñā signifies pursuing and acquiring insight(s), as well as the intellectual and cognitive prerequisites needed to do that. The path/method (mārga) begins and ends with prajñā.[26] Prajñā connotes the full spectrum of Buddhist doctrine as doctrine, as well as the cognitive comprehension of those doctrines. Thus for us to spell out its contents would require reciting the totality of Buddhist doctrine in all its particulars. For the sake of overview, prajñā may be associated with four types of activities emphasized by Buddhism.

First, it signifies the clear and efficacious formulation and comprehension of Buddhist perspectives (*samyak-dṛṣṭi*). Not only must the correct views be engendered and nourished, but more importantly one must investigate how it is that views (*dṛṣṭi*) are engendered and nourished in the first place. Thus *dṛṣṭi*—from the root √*dṛṣ* 'to see'—signifies more than views or opinions, or even the mere holding of certain views. Etymologically implying a 'way of seeing,' 'point of view' or 'perspective,' *dṛṣṭi* is the imposition of limitations—imposed by the dynamics of the interrelation between horizons and a focal center—that invariably constitute any perspective. *Dṛṣṭi* signifies a partial vision, a limiting and limited perspective whose 'partiality' insists on appropriating by means of a reduction, in spite of the fact that what it appropriates can never be reduced to factors within the confines of its horizons. *Dṛṣṭi* implies a cognitive tropology, i.e., a program of tropological displacements and substitutions that ubiquitously reduces experience to an implicit, presupposed 'order of experience,' such that experience becomes reduced and constricted within the margins ascribed by the closure of that 'order.' This is conveyed by the important Yogācāra term, *parikalpa* 'imaginative construction' and especially its Chinese counterpart, *pien-chi* 遍計, which literally means 'everywhere schematizing.' *Dṛṣṭi* is not just a view about a certain thing, but the manner by which views constitute one's orientation to and understanding of whatever goes on in the world.

More simply put, a single perspective is necessarily incomplete. If I look at my hand, only part of it can be seen from a single perspective. If the back of my hand is fully visible, my palm remains outside my vision, and vice versa. As I turn my hand, what becomes visible and what becomes invisible changes; but some part of my hand always remains hidden from view. Whether my eye moves around the hand or the hand is rotated in front of my eye, the entire hand can never be seen all at once. My sense of 'order,' in this case a belief in the continuity of experience such that the 'hand' seen from multiple perspectives is in fact a single self-identical hand, allows me to infer that I have a hand which includes a back, a palm, sides, fingers, etc. This unified image of a 'hand,' however, is an abstraction, pieced together from disparate perspectives. Both the abstraction and the presupposed beliefs through which it is constituted are termed *dṛṣṭi*. The actual 'hands' that are perceived become displaced in my thinking by my abstracted, consolidated 'hand.' This abstraction is the "self"—the invariant essence of my "hand" independent of particular perceptions of it. Thus *dṛṣṭi* connotes the process through which we displace actuality with our supplementary interpretations of it. As such, *dṛṣṭi* can be taken as the *content* that avidyā produces. *Dṛṣṭis* are the defensive stopgaps we use in our attempts to fill in the gaping abyss of anxiety that marks our nescience. Confronting the void of our most profound ignorance, we desperately seek to plug it up with theories; we build massive theoretical constructions on a foundation of abysmal ignorance. Dispelling nescience thus necessitates plunging, without distractions or stopgaps, into the abyss. In this light, 'right view' (*samyagdṛṣṭi*) means the uncovering of the epistemological determinants conditioning our nescient cognitive constructions or interpretations such that the tendency to displace actuality with an interpretation is arrested. This type of prajñā can be called 'prescriptive epistemology.'[27]

The second type of prajñā is analytic scrutiny. The first step toward understanding something, according to Buddhism, involves focusing on it and then breaking it down into its functional components. This breakdown—whether clarifying the senses of a term or distinguishing the multitude of conditioning factors implicated in a phenomenal event—must be reasonable. Vitarka-vicāra (see section above on Rūpa-dhātu) and the Abhidharmic methods of dharmic analysis are examples of this type. It builds and investigates categories, though it remains constantly on the lookout for prajñaptic reifications. This type can be called 'categorial analysis.'

The third type falls under the heading of *pramāṇa*, i.e., establishing, validating and using 'valid means of knowledge.' In its most limited sense it means to conform to the rules of logic and proof. In its most general sense it means to set the standards and criteria by which any truth-claim may be evaluated. Insofar as it thus restricts what may or may not be affirmed or negated, and sets the rules by which such affirmation or negation may be implemented, it inevitably imposes a criteriological closure that demarcates 'acceptable claims' (and thus valid knowledge) from 'unacceptable claims' (invalid knowledge). The works of the Buddhist logicians from Dignāga on are examples of this approach to prajñā. This type of prajñā may be called 'proscriptive epistemology.'[28]

The fourth type can be called 'clear and penetrating insight.' Whether examining why and how the mind functions as it does, discerning the variety of factors involved in a given event, or just correctly cognizing an occasion, if one's cognitive acuity is on target, then it may be called prajñā. In meditative contexts, such penetrating insight is called *vipaśyanā* (P. *vipassanā*). This insight is never divorced from praxis, and thus in Mahāyānic contexts prajñā is often paired with *karuṇā* (compassion) while tantric contexts pair it with *upāya* (soteric efficacy). This insight doesn't penetrate into some 'other' mystical realm; it directly sees and knows things as they are. This knowing remains practical and practicable. It signifies the clear seeing that facilitates any task.

Prajñā thus means 'know-how.' Tying shoelaces requires prajñā (the requisite know-how) as well as the skillful action (*upāya*). To tie someone else's laces, or to teach that person how to tie his/her own, or to tie one's own in order to make oneself available to help others is karuṇā. To claim one knows how to tie shoelaces is meaningless unless one can demonstrate this 'knowledge' by actually doing it. Likewise, without upāya or karuṇā, there is no prajñā, since knowledge is only valid when it is demonstrable. Whether tying shoelaces or resolving the dukkhic dilemma, prajñā signifies the enabling insight.

Taking śīla, samādhi and prajñā together, the basis of Buddhist praxis is neither ultimately teleological—which would take these three as 'goals'—nor is it finally processional—which would take them as means only. Ends and means equally are absorbed into 'method.'[29]

In Part III we shall return to the problematic of 'means and ends' and the crucial role that that controversy played in the development of various strands of Buddhist thought. In particular, we shall see how one of the three trialectic terms, viz. prajñā, became privileged above the other two, and how this privileging was reflected in such developments as the notion of *prajñā-pāramitā* (perfecting of wisdom), the arising of essentialistic and progressionalistic interpretations of the Buddhist 'method,' and the narrowing of Buddhist praxis to cognitive and epistemic issues. As a result of that narrowing the Yogācāra school emerged.

We shall also see how the interplay of the four models outlined in Part II led to the deepening issues that Buddhism continually confronted, while at the same time setting the parameters within which those issues could be addressed and thought about. When, for instance, the five skandhas seemed to become too restrictive a notion to adequately account for a person, they could either be further subdivided into eighty nine, seventy five, or one hundred dharmas, etc.—as the abhidhammic and abhidharmic schools attempted—and thereby be extended to whatever new notions needed to be entertained and discussed; or the skandhas could be metaphorically reinterpreted through their nāma-rūpic aspects as some configuration of the problematic of the superimposition of 'nominal' characteristics onto neutral 'material/formal' causal chains; or they could be rejected outright as vestiges of a creeping substantialism, etc. However, no

Buddhist could claim to locate any part, aspect, essence or layer of the human being *outside* of the five skandhas without incurring the charge of heterodoxy.

In the next chapter we will begin to see how Buddhists deployed these models.

Notes

1 The Theravādin *Vinaya* texts have been translated into English and published by the Pali Text Society and the Sacred Books of the Buddhists series. These rules are found explicated there. The Vinaya presents the rules anecdotally, recounting the situations and persons that occasioned their original formulations. Typically an argument or issue arises between members of the Saṅgha or others, which is resolved by the establishment of some rule or set of rules. For Buddhaghosa's version of how those rules came to be codified and canonized in the First Council, see his *Vinayassa Bāhiranidānaṃ*. This has also been translated into English as *Inception of Discipline and Vinaya-Nidāna* by N.A. Jayawickrama (London: Sacred Books of the Buddhists XXI, 1962) which also contains the Pāli text romanized in the back. For a fascinating, if more legendary account of the process of canonization and its subsequent historical development, cf. Dhammakitti's *Saddhamma-saṅgaha*. Written centuries later, it differs frequently with Buddhaghosa's account. Dhammakitti's text has been translated by B.C. Law as *A Manual of Buddhist Historical Traditions* (Delhi: Bharatiya, 1980). Law's introduction is excellent. On the Theravāda vinaya rules for women, cf. Chatsumarn Kabil Singh's *A Comparative Study of Bhikkhunī Pāṭimokkha* (Varanasi: Chaukhambha Orientalia, 1984). Also cf. Mohan Wijayaratna, *Buddhist Monastic Life according to the texts of the Theravāda tradition*, tr. Claude Grangier and Steven Collins (Cambridge: Cambridge University Press, 1990).

2 On the term *pratimokṣa* (P. *pātimokkha*) and the various attempts by modern scholars to translate it, see John Holt, *Discipline*, p. 35f n. 1.

3 But see Sangharakshita's *A Survey of Buddhism* (Boulder: Shambhala, 1980) p. 127, in which he echoes the Pali Text Society's *Pali-English Dictionary* which rejects the term 'commandment'. Instead he proposes 'ten items of good character' or 'good behavior and training'. However he offers no specific reason for rejecting the term commandment. Of course, if taken in its literal, technical sense as a 'decree' or 'edict' from God or some other divine source, the term would have to be rejected by Buddhism. But if simply taken in a loose, popularistic sense as 'fundamental ethico-moral rubric,' then there should be no objections to the term.

4 *Brahmacarya*, which originally probably meant something like 'religious life' (cf. e.g. M I:522; and Jan Ergardt, *Man and His Destiny*, p. 57), came to mean complete sexual abstinence. While total abstention was insisted upon for the monastic community, the notion of brahmacarya was softened for lay followers to mean refraining from sexual misconduct such as adultery, incest or sexual activity with a member of the monastic community. A similar institutionalization of this term occurred in Jainism, at roughly the same time; in fact, this entire list of ten advantageous activities may reflect a revisionistic appropriation of the Jaina Five Vows. Cf. Chandradhar Sharma's *A Critical Survey of Indian Philosophy* (Delhi: Motilal, 1976) p. 66.

5 Rahula, in *What the Buddha Taught*, writes: "abstention...from harsh, rude, impolite, malicious and abusive language" (p. 47).

6 Rahula, *ibid.*, writes: "backbiting and slander and talk that may bring about hatred, enmity, disunity and disharmony among individuals or groups of people."

7 Rahula, *ibid.*, writes: "idle, useless and foolish babble and gossip."

8 *Op. cit.*, p. 69.

9 Cf. the discussion of this in Rahula's *The Heritage of the Bhikkhu*, pp. 8-12.

10 Ch. 6:3. P. 112 in *Buddhist Suttas, op. cit.*

11 For a quick summary of this and the other Buddhist councils, and the major issues in dispute, see *Buddhism: A Modern Perspective* Charles Prebish, ed. (Penn State UP, 1978) pp. 21-26. The Second Council is treated on pp. 23-25. The works by Buddhaghosa and Dhammakitti cited above also discuss the Councils.

12 Aside from the Theravādin *Vinaya*, only the Sarvāstivādin and Mahāsaṅghika *Vinayas* have received any sustained attention. See Charles Prebish's *Buddhist Monastic Discipline: The Sanskrit Pratimokṣa Sūtras of the Mahāsāṃghikas and Mūlasarvāstivādins* (Penn State UP, 1975). Such studies are only a beginning. The East Asian traditions considered the *Vinaya* to be a separate school, though to date study of this 'school' in Western scholarship can barely be called rudimentary.

13 The Mādhyamikan critique of śīla seems, ironically, never to have been institutionalized. For instance, whereas Candrakīrti's *Prasannapadā* exhibits some of these tendencies, his *Madhyamakāvatāra*, on the contrary, firmly grounds itself within the practice of the pāramitās. In subsequent Indian and then Tibetan forms of Madhyamaka, the anti-śīla rhetoric is entirely displaced by the syncretic blending of Prāsaṅgika Mādhyamika with other schools, such as Yogācāric, Sautrāntika and Svātantrika thought. The writings of such thinkers as Śāntideva, Śāntarakṣita, Kamalaśīla, and Tsoṅ-ka-pa amply illustrate this syncretism. Such synchretism was sufficiently intricate to lead present-day scholars to dispute to which school(s) these thinkers owed their allegiance.

As to Zen schools, the anti-śīla tendencies never became mainstream. The first Korean Ch'an master, Wu-hsiang 無相 (Kor: Musang; 684-762) was well known for his rejection of the precepts, including the requirement of 'sitting-meditation'. According to Tsung-mi, Musang influenced other masters, such as Wu-chu (714-774). The tension between following the 'rules' versus 'freedom from all conventions' reasserted itself periodically, but usually in the more restricted and subdued form of 'follow the scriptures' versus 'burn the scriptures.' On the early conflicts, cf. Yanagida Seizan's "The *Li-Tai Fa-Pao Chi* and the Ch'an Doctrine of Sudden Awakening" in *Early Ch'an in China and Tibet*, ed. by Whalen Lai and Lewis Lancaster (Berkeley: Berkeley Buddhist Studies, 1983) pp. 13-49. On the more normative Ch'an traditions concerning śīla and vinaya, cf. Martin Collcutt's "The Early Ch'an Monastic Rule: *Ch'ing kuei* and the Shaping of Ch'an Community Life" in *ibid.*. pp. 165-184. Tsung-mi was an important figure in these formative Ch'an debates; cf. Peter Gregory, *Tsung-mi and the Sinification of Buddhism* (Princeton: Princeton UP, 1992).

14 For one of the authoritative Yogācāra treatises on śīla, viz. the Śīla section of Asaṅga's *Yogācārabhūmi*; cf. the translation by Mark Tatz, *Asaṅga's Chapter on Ethics with the Commentary of Tsong-kha-pa*, Lewiston, NY: Edwin Mellen Press, 1986.

15 For Theravādin examples of such meditations, see e.g. Nyanaponika Thera's *The Heart of Buddhist Meditation* (NY: Samuel Weiser, 1973) which contains a translation and discussion of the *Mahā-satipaṭṭhāna sutta* of the *Dīgha Nikāya*; and Matara Sri Ñāṇārāma Mahāthera's *The Seven Stages of Purification and the Insight Knowledges* (Kandy: Buddhist Publication Society, 1983) which offers an overview of Buddhaghosa's *Visuddhimagga* from a practical orientation.

16 For an engrossing, if slightly theosophical discussion of these practices, based primarily on the Tibetan tradition, cf. Lama Anagarika Govinda's Creative Meditation and Multi-Dimensional Consciousness (Wheaton, Ill.: Theosophical Publishing House, 1976). For beautifully presented examples of Tantric art as preserved in the Japanese tradition, cf. Pierre Rambach's *The Secret Message of Tantric Buddhism*, tr. from French by Barbara Bray (NY: Rizzoli International Publications, 1979); R. Tajima (Ryujun) *Les deux grands mandalas et la doctrine de l'esoterisme Shingon*, Fukusei edition (Tokyo: Gokokuji: Hatsubaijo Nakayama Shobo Busshorin, 1984); Adrian Snodgrass, *The Matrix and Diamond World Mandalas in Shingon Buddhism* (New Delhi: Aditya Prakashan, 1988)

17 An excellent treatment can be found in Agehananda Bharati's *The Tantric Tradition* (NY: Samuel Weiser, 1975) chs. 5 and 6 and passim.

18 There are at least three ways to approach the question of Sanskrit etymology: 1. the so-called scientific approach, in which modern scholars use the best philological and historical tools to construct probable actual word-root histories. 2. Chronicle the claims made in traditional texts about the etymologies of technical terms (these often differ dramatically from the scientific versions). 3. Engage in the same sort of creative process as those recorded in 2. Most scholars, due to their training, are prejudiced toward the scientific approach, but the mentality as well as the conclusions reached through that method would have been alien to most ancient Indians, thus imposing elements and conclusions with a self-confidence not entirely appropriate, while frequently disdaining the etymological claims of traditional authors (Candrakīrti, in particular, gets singled out for such scorn, but all the medieval authors engaged in the same creative method). Chronicling traditional claims is worthwhile, but too detailed an endeavor for the generalistic approach being applied in this chapter. Thus I've chosen the somewhat riskier creative approach: engaging in nirukta (etymology). This is an effort to participate in the doing of Indian philosophy in the manner and style that they themselves employed. For them, doing etymology is doing philosophy. It is not a neutral, philological activity. I beg the indulgence of my scientific colleagues.

19 This prefigures the notion of an ālaya-vijñāna or warehouse-consciousness, which is the locus of the cognitive and affective economies. Like a warehouse, it takes karmically significant experiences in, stores them for awhile, and when the proper conditions arise, it sends those things back out. The ālayic economy will be described more fully in a later chapter.

20 Cf. Ergardt, op. cit. pp. 42ff for a discussion of the function in the Majjhima Nikāya of such cognate terms as *bhavati* (to become, to develop), *bhāveti* (to cause to become or develop), *bhāvanā* ([mental] development), *cittabhāvana* (mind-development), *bhāvitattā citassa* (developing the mind [to see things] as they are), etc. Cf. also p. 82, re: *bhāvehi* (the imperative 'Develop!'), and *passim.*

21 There are several ways that the various Buddhist schools are conventionally differentiated, such as by their opposing arguments on key epistemological or ontological concepts, by the structure and contents of their canon (which texts, and which reading of those texts they deem most important), etc. One rarely finds an attempt to differentiate and explicate the various schools using their respective mārgas as the criterion of comparison, though such a comparison would be quite valuable and instructive. Not only would this be illuminating for stark contrasts, such as between Madhyamaka and various forms of Pure Land, but perhaps even more revealing where the initial differences appear a bit more obscured, such as between various Pure Land schools, or the mārga of the *Abhidharmakośa* in light of the *Yogācārabhūmi* or *Cheng wei-shih lun*, etc. This approach might also prove useful in the difficult task of classifying those important thinkers who seem to straddle several schools, depending on who is describing them, such as Dignāga (Sautrāntika or Yogācārin), Śāntarakṣita (Mādhyamikan, Sautrāntika or Yogācārin), Bhartṛhari (Hindu, Buddhist, both, neither), etc. This might lead to such fascinating questions as 'Do Candrakīrti and Sthiramati actually share the same basic assumptions while expressing them through different methods?' A comparison of their respective mārgas (e.g., *Madhyamakāvatāra* vs. *Triṃśikā-ṭīkā*) might address that more directly than contrasting their rhetorical or logical stances.

22 By this, I mean not simply that *yathābhūtaṃ* and *tathatā* are synonyms, but rather that tathatā implies the convergence of 'knowing and seeing' (jānāti passati) with 'things just as they are' (yathābhūtaṃ). In Husserlian terms, whether this signifies a noetic-noemic unification or whether it signifies the erasure of any and all noetic-noemic closures such that transcendental conditions (for Husserl, these would be the transcendental object and the transcendental subject, but other transcendentals could be proposed) are dis-closed, has been disputed between differing Buddhist schools.

The problem of the noema, i.e., a cognized meaning noetically constituted from a hyle (fundamental sensorial 'stuff') or transcendental object (i.e., an object which participates in the constitution of a sensed-object, though not itself given within the actual cognition of that sensed-object) has parallels in Buddhist thought, such as arise with the terms *vastu, viṣaya* and *ālambana*. Though Indian literature is far from consistent in its use of these and related epistemic terms, later texts, particularly of the Sautrāntika and later Yogācāric schools, take these terms as sensorial objects, or more precisely as the *objective-pole* of an act of cognition. The frequent denial of the existence of external objects which occurs in these texts is aimed primarily at rebuking the tendency to assign ontological status to sensed-objects outside, behind or beyond the actual cognitive act. Hence, these schools would vigorously deny Husserl's notion of a transcendental object. What exactly a sensed-object *is* remains a point of contention, however; Is it merely a mental projection (*pratibimba*), or does it contain some non-mental material elements (*rūpa*)? Are correct cognitions composed of definitive perceptions (*savikalpa jñāna*) or are they entirely devoid of conceptualizable content (*nirvikalpa jñāna*)? Do Awakened persons still experience representational mental images (*sākāra*) or do they experience in a radically different manner, thoroughly devoid of any mental images (*nirākāra*)? Each of these positions has been accepted and argued by different Buddhist schools.

Though the debates between so-called Nirākāravādins and Sākāravādins peaked in India sometime after Hsüan-tsang, the seeds of this debate had already been planted, and thus a brief comment might not be out of order here. Though the debates grew complex, to some extent the distinction between *nirākāra* and *sākāra* may simply boil down to different styles of naming the distinction between (i) immediate direct perception as opposed to (ii) an indirect perception mediated by a conceptual background (*Ganzfeld*). The controversy then would hinge on the semantic ambiguity of the term *ākāra*. Both Sākāravādins and Nirākāravādins would agree that Awakened perception is direct and immediate. However the former would take *ākāra* as the 'configuration' of an act of immediate perception (shapes, sizes, textures, etc.) rather than as the percept *simplicitur*, whereas for the latter *ākāra* would signify a *conceptually derived* ordering of perception that is representational rather than presentational, and therefore indirect perception. Thus, at base, while they agree about the importance of differentiating between presentational and representational perceptions, and they also agree that enlightened cognition is presentational rather than representational, their dispute seems to fall squarely on how each defines and applies the term *ākāra* to that distinction. In part they seem, also, to differ on the extent to which a distinct and definite percept requires conceptual input in order to be re-cognizable. Thus, a very real distinction may be at play, since possibly some Sākāravādins would allow *sākāra* to be interpreted as 'representation,' i.e., the conceptual recognition of something. If so, those who assert that a correct, Awakened cognition involves definitive, representational mental content are, in effect, asserting that Awakened cognition is still noematic, whereas those who claim Awakened cognition is neither conceptual nor includes any formalized mental images (i.e., it involves no *ākāra*), are denying both ontological status to noema as well as declaring that there are no Noemata in Awakened cognition . For the latter groups, the noema is sometimes displaced by Tathatā, though exactly what that term signifies for each of them is arguable. As we will discover in a later chapter, the *Ch'eng wei-shih lun*'s position on this is quite striking.

23 Though it does make a distinction between direct and indirect experience.

24 Cf. Ergardt, pp. 50, 57, 68 and *passim* for the locations and functions in the Pāli texts of these terms.

25 Fire and fuel is a common Buddhist metaphor for desire (fire) and appropriation (fuel), which is quite poignant in Pāli and Sanskrit since the same word, *upādāna*, means both 'fuel' and 'appropriation.'

26 Cf. Sangharakshita's *A Survey of Buddhism* (*op. cit.*) pp. 156-157:

> In those texts wherein the steps of the Eightfold Path are distributed into three stages the order of stages is not, as one might expect, Morality, Meditation, Wisdom, but Wisdom,

> Morality, Meditation. Here by wisdom is meant "learning"; for intellectual comprehension of the Doctrine, though in itself powerless to effect Liberation, must precede any attempt to put into actual practice even its most elementary tenets.

For another description of the interplay between the threefold praxis and the Eightfold Path, cf. Lama Govinda's *The Psychological Attitude of Early Buddhist Philosophy* (NY: Samuel Weiser, 1969) ch. 4.

27 See my article "Ch'an and Taoist Mirrors" in *The Journal of Chinese Philosophy* 12 (1985) pp. 169-178, where I introduced the distinction between 'proscriptive epistemology' and 'prescriptive epistemology'. A proscriptive epistemology proscribes valid from invalid knowledge, valuable from nonvaluable meaning, good from bad, right from wrong, etc., by establishing criteria which demarcate the 'inner' and acceptable from the 'outer' and unacceptable/dangerous. It tends to be reductionistic and restrictive. Prescriptive epistemology, on the other hand, aims at uncovering the fundamental conditions of human knowing rather than insisting on or even recommending any particular criteriology of knowledge. It offers guidelines to facilitate the radical investigation, and is always open to new styles of investigation and reasoning, rather than clinging to restrictive rules for the sake preserving the security of an identity or theory.

28 See *ibid.* Jayatilleke's *Early Buddhist Theory of Knowledge* may be seen as an attempt to reduce prajñā to this third type, by arguing that the Early Buddhist criterion was a thoroughgoing empiricism. While he makes countless useful and insightful observations, he may finally have confused the requirement that a cognition be intersubjective with the claim that such knowledge is thereby empirical. Phenomenology, while also arguing for intersubjectivity, nonetheless is critical of empiricism. Husserl's critiques in *Ideas* and *The Crisis...* are well known. See also J. Douglas Rabb, "Empiricism from a Phenomenological Standpoint", *Philosophy and Phenomenological Research,* XLVI, 2, Dec. 1985, pp. 243-63. This is not the place to seek to determine exactly where the various strands of Buddhist thought would side in this debate, but we should remain aware that their options are larger than empiricism.

29 This is not to say that Buddhism never became ensnared in the tension between means and ends. Actually, an interesting topology of the relations between the various schools could be drawn according to which schools emphasized Buddhism as a means (e.g., Theravāda), which as an end (e.g., Pure Land), which took the means themselves as the end (e.g., Tendai and Dōgen), which denied the efficacy of means toward an end (e.g., Madhyamaka), etc. The Sudden vs. Gradual controversy in Ch'an plays on the same theme.

Chapter Seven

Asaṁjñī-samāpatti and Nirodha-samāpatti

This chapter will illustrate in part how the four models discussed in the previous chapters were deployed by Buddhists. As the sections of the *Ch'eng wei-shih lun* translated later in this chapter show, the models were often deftly interleaved rather than treated in pristine isolation.

How does one reach Awakening? As the texts examined here will show, Buddhists over time apparently developed different answers to that question. The aim of Early Buddhists was to eliminate the *āsavas* by undergoing a cognitive shutdown that consequently "cleansed" the senses. They deemed this shutdown to be penultimate to actual Awakening. Possibly because certain theoretical inconsistencies as well as pragmatic incoherencies adhered to these ideas as formulated (see below), later Buddhists radically revised them, displacing *āsavas* with *kleśa* as the prime problematic, and even then, treating kleśa as a secondary problem, undergirded by a deeper hindrance (*āvaraṇa*), namely the *jñeyāvaraṇa*, obstruction of the known, glossed in many later texts as a cognitive ignorance contaminated with the view of self-hood (*ātmadṛṣṭi*). The shutdown of cognitive functioning, which earlier had been the penultimate achievement of the mārga, was now separated into two distinct types of "attainments" (*samāpatti*), one disparaged as the vain pursuit of nonBuddhists (*āsaṁjñī samāpatti*), while the other (*nirodha-samāpatti*) was condoned but no longer retained its penultimate status.

This will be fleshed out in detail in this chapter. However, one additional model needs to be mentioned before proceeding.

Buddhism literally begins with the Four Noble Truths.[1] The four truths are structured according to a medical model still taught in Medical schools, called the pathological model: 1. Sympton, 2. Diagnosis, 3. Prognosis, 4. Treatment. Duḥkha is the symptom. Avidyā and tṛṣṇa are the causes of the symptom. The prognosis is that they are curable, the disease can be brought to an end. The way to cure the disease is the follow the mārga. All four truths point to the third Truth, *nirodha*, extinction. Buddhism is medicine for the sickness of duḥkha, and the three other Truths are designed to culminate in the Third, *the cure*, elimination of the sickness. The first Truth identifies the problem (symptoms), the second truth diagnosis it with causal analysis. The fourth Truth is Buddhism itself: the prescriptions, treatments, therapies, and methods that Buddhism employs to realize the third Truth, extinction. Nirvāṇa (or nibbāna)—another name for the goal of Buddhism—is often explained as deriving from nir + vā, "to blow, or blow out",[2] in other words, *extinguishing* the flames of desire.[3] The obvious questions are: What sort of extinction is this? and How is it accomplished?

Karma and Āsavas

Buddhism developed numerous models to assist people in their efforts to extinguish *duḥkha*. According to Buddhism humans are constituted by a nexus of causal conditions. The conditions of greatest interest and importance to Buddhists are karmic conditions. Karma consists of the intentional activities of body, language, and mind. Those activities can be advantageous (*kuśala*) or disadvantageous (*akuśala*) to resolving the problem of *duḥkha*. Disadvantageous conditions act as 'defilements' while advantageous conditions 'purify.' Since karma exclusively concerns *intentional* acts of body, language, and mind, karma is entirely cognitive. By "cognitive" I mean any act involving an intentionality of consciousness, which includes gestures, sensations, perceptions, affects, linguistic acts, and mental acts. Cognition, according to this usage, is a larger category than mind or mental acts, and therefore encompasses intentional actions of body and language as well as mind. Most of the models and paradigms employed in Buddhist psychology, philosophy, and homiletics are designed to clarify such karmic conditions and to make them amenable to intervention, improvement, and eventual obsolescence through practice. Such intervention, according to Buddhism, must ultimately lead to the cessation of karmic activity. Put another way, karma fundamentally consists of cognitive problems; hence, the solution must be resolved, at least in part, by addressing the issue of cognition. From this stems the strong emphasis on mind, consciousness, sensation, insight, and meditative experience; and the significance of terms derived from the root √jñā (to know, be aware), such as *vijñāna, prajñā, jñāna, saṃjñā, jñeyāvaraṇa*, and so on. Meditation, especially as developed by the early Buddhist practitioners, is a cognitive laboratory, a set of conditions in which cognitive activities can be viewed, altered, understood, focused, and modified.

Reviewing what has been discussed in the previous chapters, two of Buddhism's primary models—the five skandhas and pratītya-samutpāda—explain that pleasurable and painful sensations (*vedanā*) lead to attachment, desire, aversion, and the entire panoply of human emotions. What is pleasurable we desire to hold on to and repeat (*kāma, rāga, chanda*); the painful we desire to cut off and avoid (*dveṣa, pratigha*). Through this pleasure-pain conditioning we acquire the karmic habits that make us what we are: our daily behavior and attitudes, and ultimately the forms of life we become through countless rebirths (*bhava*). One term for this conditioning is *saṃskāra* (P. *saṅkhara*). It signifies our embodied conditioning, conditioning that is usually subliminal, latent, only reaching our awareness when it emerges as a volition (*cetanā*). Many texts treat *saṃskāra* and *cetanā* as synonyms.

Since conditioning results in *cetanā,* and *cetanā* is one way of defining *intentional* actions, the karmic causal chain becomes circular, perpetuating itself. As one is karmically conditioned by pleasurable and painful experiences—which will be cognized as painful or pleasurable in part due to prior experiences—these lead to subsequent intentional actions and reactions that generate further conditioning, which will ripen and mature eventually, leading to still further conditioned responses that will perpetuate and reinforce themselves, and on and on. For instance, a new acquaintance becomes so uncomfortable to be with that one is in pain while in the presence of that person. The fact that one is perceiving the actions or attitudes of that new acquaintance as uncomfortable will have something to do with one's prior experiences in similar or associatable circumstances, though those connections may only be subliminal during the experience of uncomfortableness. Because of the uncomfortableness, if one merely sees that person on some subsequent occasion, the feeling of uncomfortableness may reemerge, even if the two people don't stop to talk to each other. In the future, either seeing that person again, or finding oneself in a similar situation with someone or something else may rekindle similar negative feelings. This perpetuating, habitual cycle is karma. Or take an even more dramatic example of the bondage of karma. One meets a new acquaintance who is delightful. That person is so enjoyable to be with that one feels pain when separated from that person. One tries to be with that person as much as possible in order to feel the pleasure of their company. Of course, the fact that one finds this particular person pleasing will have something to do with one's past experience. Eventually one becomes attached to that person. But conditions change, and over time being with that person does not generate the same sort of pleasurable feelings. Frustrated, one tries to rekindle the pleasure, but the more one tries the more elusive it becomes. Finally neither person enjoys being with the other, since each is desperately seeking a permanent sensation that, due to impermanence, has already gone. The tenacity of karmic habit may keep these two people bound to each other for a long time after the pleasure that brought them together is gone. As their relationship grows more and more painful, they still cannot separate, since they are bound by their own habitual tendencies. At this point a therapist might step in and cast around terms like 'co-dependency.' These people are stuck together because of habits, ways of being in the world, that were formed or forming long before they met each other. Those habits, not the deliberative efforts of these two people, are determining their behavior. Breaking habits, especially those most deeply engrained—which Buddhism invariably identifies as ideas, perspectives, *dṛṣṭi*—is the most difficult task one can face.[4] Buddhist praxis is about extinguishing habitual reactions altogether. As we'll see a little later, this does not mean fleeing from sensation, but rather being able to sense in such a way that habits fail to become engendered.

One model that became popular in later Buddhism was the mind-stream (*citta-santāna*): the mind flows on like a polluted river until it is purified.[5] For some schools this meant returning to an original purity,[6] for others it meant achieving a total purity never before experienced.[7] In either case, purification involved eliminating pollutants and contaminants. Early Buddhism offered several 'purification' models, the most prominent of which is the jhāna method for 'destroying the āsavas' (*āsavānaṃ khayāya,* i.e., becoming *khīṇāsava*, one who has destroyed the āsavas; S: *kṣīṇāśravāṇām*)[8]. Āsava (S. āśrava)—a term that has been subjected to numerous misleading translations, such as cankers, outflows,[9] etc.—cannot be easily translated. The Buddhists borrowed the term from the Jains, who used it to describe the flow of karmic particles that stuck to and obstructed jīvas (omniscient life-forces), blocking their omniscience. Since Buddhists rejected the quasi-materialist karmic theory of Jainism, the term āsava—which for Jains denoted *the flow of particles* that were attracted by certain types of actions—never fit comfortably into Buddhism's own karmic theories. Instead the term functioned in Buddhism as an evocative emblem for the most fundamental karmic problems: given āsavas, one continues to act in such a way as to remain bound in saṃsāra; one becomes free from saṃsāra only by eliminating or 'destroying' (*khaya*) these āsavas. The *Mahāvastu* defines an Arhat this way:[10]

> ...all Arhats [are ones] who have destroyed the āśravas, who have kept the observances, whose minds have been liberated by Right Cognition, who have fully destroyed the fetters that bind one to existence, who have attained the goal.

What exactly is an āsava? Typically Pāli texts offer a list of either three or four āsavas:

1. *kāmāsava* - the āsava of craving sensory and aesthetic pleasure;
2. *bhāvāsava* - the āsava of craving existence;
3. *avijjāsava* - the āsava of ignorance; and sometimes
4. *diṭṭhāsava* - the āsava of (wrong) views

The āsavas, then, are deeply seated propensities that drive one to pursue and cling to pleasure, further existence, ignorance, and pernicious views and theories. They are the propensities that, due to ignorance and wrong views, compel us to desire and to become attached.

The Pāli texts speak of a meditative attainment, or *samāpatti*, that eliminates these āsavas. The Pāli suttas label it *saññā-vedayita-nirodha*, 'the cessation of associational-cognitions and pleasure-pain-neutral sensations," a term reminiscent of the third Noble Truth (*nirodha*) Later Buddhist writers called it *nirodha-samāpatti.* Several passages in the early texts treat this attainment as if it were either Awakening itself or at the very least the final threshhold to Awakening. However, the importance of nirodha-samāpatti progressively declined in later Buddhist formulations. This chapter, in part, will trace some features of that decline. Before turning to the texts that deal with this samāpatti, we should first mention some of the other terms used by Buddhists to denote impurities and contaminations, since these will become relevant later.

Impurities and Contaminants

Students of Abhidharma and later forms of Buddhism are well familiar with the terms *kleśa* (P: *kilesa*) and *upakleśa* (or *paritta-kleśa*, secondary kleśa), usually enumerated as lists of 'mental disturbances' that a Buddhist must learn to identify and overcome. The term *kilesa*, however, hardly appears in the Nikāyas at all. In fact, the use of the term *kleśa* seems to increase in direct proportion to the decrease in importance of the term āsava.

Abhidharmic[11] and Mahāyānic literature will still retain the term āsava, mis-sanskritized as *āśrava*,[12] to signify impure and contaminated cognitive events and 'seeds' (*bījā*), but the scope of the term was demoted to characterizing particular qualities of cognitive events, rather than designating the root problem itself. Its opposite, *anāśrava*, "uncontaminated" or "unpolluted," denotes 'purified' cognitive modes that come more and more to the fore as one progresses on the mārga. In Vaibhāṣika and Yogācāra literature one simply does not find *anāśrava* used to describe a once-and-for-all elimination of fundamental problems. On the contrary, *anāśrava* becomes a positive property, almost a positive entity that is struggling to realize itself. The Tathāgatagarbha tradition, in fact, understood it in precisely that way. Buddhaghosa, speaking for the Theravādin tradition, takes great pains to refute the claim[13] that Arhatship is merely a *paññati* (nominal designation; S: *prajñapti*) for the destruction of greed, hatred and delusion. He argues[14] that an actual Right View (*sammādiṭṭhi*) emerges from the elimination of wrong views, defilements, and subsequent khandhas upon attaining 'Stream-Entry'.[15] Moreover, he argues, the four Paths and the four Fruits[16] have a "measureless" object, and a "measureless state" (*appamaññā*).[17] Thus we see a tendency to reify or even substantialize the positive side of attaining cessation, a tendency that reached its most extreme form in the Tathāgatagarbha tradition which emphasized the parity of the Non-Empty with Emptiness, and defied the standard list of positional 'perversions' (*viparyāsa*)[18]—ways of seeing that obstructed one's progress to Awakening—by declaring the goal to be eternal, self, pure, and enjoyment (*nityā, ātman, viśuddha, sukha*).

Another important term for defilements in Pāli psychology is *anusaya* (S: *anuśaya*). These are inherent proclivities,[19] sometimes used as synonymns for kleśa (or upakleśa) and even the āsavas, though properly speaking they constitute a different set of mental problems, with some obvious overlaps. Pāli sources usually list seven anusayas:

1. Desire (*rāga*)
2. Aversion, hatred (*paṭigha*)
3. (Wrong) views (*diṭṭhi*)

4. Doubt (*vicchikicchā*)
5. Conceit, pride (*māna*)
6. Craving existence (*bhavarāga*)
7. Ignorance (*avijjā*)

This list overlaps and expands on another well-known list of fundamental problems, the Three Poisons (*tri-viṣāḥ*): Greed, hatred, and delusion (P: *rāga, dosa, moha;* S: *kāma-rāga, dveṣa* [or *pratigha*], *moha*). 'Delusion' means having fundamental misconceptions about the way things are, and thus is a correlate to ignorance and wrong views. The āsava list also contains greed and delusion (*kāma* and *avijjā/diṭṭhi*), but lacks a clear correlate for 'aversion' (though one may argue that craving existence, etc., implies an aversion for the contrary). However, the *Sammādiṭṭhi sutta* of the *Majjhima Nikāya* (#9), shortly after listing the standard three āsavas, describes their cessation through the noble eightfold path as having gotten rid of (1) addiction to attachment, (2) addiction to aversion, (3) addiction to the latent view 'I am,' and (4) ignorance. This suggests that *kāmāsava* consists of attachment *and* aversion, and that *bhavāsava* involves the view of self as real (*sakkāya-diṭṭhi*; S: *sat-kāya-dṛṣṭi*).[20] *Moha* and *avijjā* are synonyms, as already noted. The *Saṃyutta Nikāya,* in a passage to be cited below, explicitly links the destruction of the āsavas with the elimination of the Three Poisons.

The lists of kleśas and secondary kleśas offered by the Vaibhāṣikas and Yogācārins differ significantly from each other,[21] but most of the terms associated with the āsavas and anusayas can be found somewhere within them. The striking exception is *bhāvarāga*, craving existence, which is found nowhere in either the seventy-five dharma list of the *Abhidharmakośa* nor the one hundred dharma list of the Yogācārins.

The *Abhidharmakośa* devotes a lengthy chapter to expanding a basic list of six *anuśayas* into roughly one hundred.[22] The *Kośa*'s approach combines terminological psychology with rebirth cosmology. The first verse of this chapter begins: "The roots of existence [*bhava*], that is, of rebirth or of action, are the *anuśayas...*".[23] The six primary anuśayas are desire for (and attachment to) pleasure (*kāma-rāga*), anger, pride, ignorance, false views, and doubt.

The Pāli list of seven anusayas has become in the *Kośa* a list of six *anuśayas* by virtue of an extraordinary move: 'craving existence' (*bhavarāga*) has been elevated clear off the list to become its meta-rationale ("the roots of *bhava*"). Clearly, for the *Kośa,* anuśaya has replaced āsava as the foundational problem, and it has used one of the terms that the original Pāli anusaya list shared in common with the Pāli āsava list, 'craving existence,' to effect that usurpation. 'Craving existence,' as mentioned above, is the one item on the anusaya list that never appears in any of the dharma lists of the Vaibhāṣikas or Yogācārins. Since ostensibly the dharma lists are supposed to exhaustively enumerate all the basic factors affecting experience, the absence of 'craving existence' on these lists may signify either that it has become transcendentalized (as I am suggesting was the case for the *Kośa*), or that it has been reduced to an 'effect' of other, more basic dharmas. In either case, while the original Pāli list encourages the practitioner to grapple directly with the craving for existence, the later formulations have made such grappling indirect at best. *Bhava* is the consequence of the enumerated anuśayas, the *Kośa* is saying, and it is dealt with not directly but by eliminating those anuśayas.[24]

As for Yogācāra texts, especially those in Chinese, such as the *Ch'eng wei-shih lun*—and most other Chinese texts— kleśa (*fan-nao* 煩惱) and anuśaya (*huo* 惑) are used interchangeably.

Quickly reviewing two points:

1. The importance of the term āsava declines in direct proportion to the ascension in importance of the term kleśa.
2. Bhavāsava becomes either transcendentalized or rendered as something inconceivable in-itself, removing it from the list of things that one grapples with directly. Is this a veiled symptom of the reemergence of ātma-dṛṣṭi as conatus, the persistent desire for self-preservation?

Having surveyed some of the pertinent vocabulary, we are now ready to turn to the issue of the samāpattis.

Saññā-vedayita-nirodha (Nirodha-samāpatti) in the Nikāyas

Discussions of the cessation (or extinction) of associative-cognitions and pleasure-pain-neutral sensations (hereafter "cognitive and sensory cessation" for short) occur frequently in the Nikāyas, usually as part of standard formulas. These formulas are not always completely compatible with each other, or, if they are, it remains the task of the reader or commentator to draw out those connections.

Invariably cognitive and sensory cessation occurs as the ninth of a series of jhānas (technically only the first four are usually called jhānas). Usually, in the Nikāyas, it is treated as the culmination of Buddhist practice. Occasionally there is a suggestion of other practices that follow it. One standard formula is found at *Saṃyutta Nikāya* 36.2:[25]

> I have seen that the ceasing of saṅkhāras is gradual. [1] When one has attained the first jhāna, speech has ceased. [2] When one has attained the second jhāna, initial and sustained thought have ceased. [3] When one has attained the third jhāna, zeal has ceased. [4] When one has attained the fourth jhāna, inbreathing and outbreathing have ceased. [5] When one has attained the realm of unbounded spatiality, associative-cognition of [discrete] objects has ceased. [6] When one has attained the realm of unbounded consciousness, associative-cognition of the realm of unbounded spatiality has ceased. [7] When one has attained the realm of Nothing, associative-cognition of the realm of unbounded consciousness has ceased. [8] When one has attained the realm of neither associative-cognition nor

> non-associative-cognition, associative-cognition of the realm of Nothing has ceased. Both associative-cognition and pleasure-pain-neutral-sensations have ceased when one has attained 'cognitive and sensory cessation.' For the brother who has destroyed the āsavas, *rāga* is extinguished, *dosa* is extinguished, *moha* is extinguished.

Each succeeding level in some fashion erases the previous level, so that gradually[26] the saṅkhāras are eliminated until, in the ninth level, the ultimate saṅkhāras, the āsavas (*rāga, dosa, moha*), are eliminated.

Another formula frequently encountered is:[27]

> ...a monk, by passing beyond the plane of neither associative-cognition nor non-associative-cognition, enters on and abides in 'cognitive and sensory cessation;' and having seen by intuitive wisdom (*ñāṇa*), his āsavas are utterly destroyed... He has crossed over the entanglement of the world.

Such a one is also said to be "out of the reach of Māra".[28] The *Cūḷagosiṅga sutta* (Majj. #31; I.209) adds that practioners can enter this cessation "for as long as we like" and that "there is no other abiding... that is higher or more excellent than this abiding."

But the formula "having seen by intuitive wisdom (*ñāṇa*), his āsavas are utterly destroyed" is somewhat enigmatic. If this *nirodha* is considered to be totally bereft of any cognitive activities or content, how does 'knowledge' (*ñāṇa*) emerge from it, and more specifically, why does the ultimate soteric insight, the one that vanquishes the āsavas once and for all, arise from it? What makes the utter lack of cognizance and pleasurable-painful sensations so efficacious, especially if, as Paul Griffiths has suggested,[29] this samāpatti is little more than a catatonic state? Put bluntly, how does superior knowledge emerge from the utter absence of any cognition? Isn't that a non sequitur?

For the most part, the Nikāyas fail to give any response. They assume that this "cessation" automatically produces the definitive soteric moment. No mechanism or causal account is offered to explain how this happens. It seems clear that the later Buddhist tradition, even the later Theravādin tradition, was dissatisfied with this facile formula. Buddhaghosa will vacillate on the ultimacy of nirodha-samāpatti; the *Kośa* will consider it a high level, useful experience, devoid of any real soteric value; and the *Ch'eng wei-shih lun* seems to treat it as either a way to affirm the existence of manas and ālaya-vijñāna, or as a less than significant piece of business that needs to be accounted for before moving on to more important matters. But we are getting ahead of ourselves.

The inclusion of *vedanā* (pleasure, pain, and neutral sensations) in the name of the cessation (*vediyata* ≡ *vedanā*) seems to be a red herring, since being swayed by the extremes of pleasure and pain was already neutralized in the fourth jhāna, and acquiring the fourth jhāna is one of the preconditions for ascending the arūpa levels toward the level of cessation. In terms of the five khandhas, one khandha is explicitly excluded from the arūpa meditations (*rūpa*),[30] and three are explicitly mentioned in the names of the levels:

consciousness (*viññāna*), associative-cognition (*saññā*), and pleasure-pain (*vedanā*). The missing khandha is *saṅkhāra*, embodied conditioning. The various discussions of the meditations and their purpose makes clear, however, that uncovering and eliminating embodied conditioning is precisely what these meditations are all about. The answer to our question should, then, lie in what cessation does to saṅkhāra. Let us see what the suttas say.

The *Ariyapariyesana sutta* (Majj. #26) gives a lengthy autobiographical account of how Buddha studied in the forest prior to his Awakening, how he learned the neither associative-cognition nor non-associative-cognition meditation from Uddaka, Rāma's son, but dissatisfied continued to practice on his own until he achieved awakening. He is reluctant to teach others once he has become awakened until Brahmā Sahampati convinces him to survey the world with the awakened eye of compassion. His first audience is Upaka, the Naked Ascetic (a Jain), who is unimpressed by Buddha's teaching. Finally encountering the five 'monks' with whom he had been practicing for the six months prior to his awakening, he lectures them, and they listen. His lecture concludes with the formula

> by passing beyond the plane of neither associative-cognition nor non-associative cognition, he enters on and abides in 'cognitive and sensory cessation;' and having seen by intuitive wisdom, his āsavas are utterly destroyed... he has crossed over the entanglements in the world.

So this 'cessation' was the discovery made by Buddha that no one else in the forest had yet realized, and it was this discovery that made Siddhārtha Gotama a Buddha, a Tathāgata.[31] But how does it work? What and how did he "see" ("...having seen by intuitive wisdom...")?

One set of partial responses to this question is contained in scattered discussions of the 'signless' (*animitta*), which in some ways becomes as enigmatic as the discussions of 'cessation.' Sometimes the signless is included in a list of three things associated with the end of the path or nearing the end of the path, three things with which one has 'sensory-contact' (*phassa*): the empty (*suññata*), signless (*animitta*), and 'lacking intentionality' (*appaṇihita*).[32] These complicate the picture because each is sometimes cited as a distinct cause of its own type of liberation (*vimutti*), distinct from 'cessation' per se. Sometimes the signless is discussed independently of the other two. It is sometimes treated as something subsequent to 'cessation',[33] sometimes as prior to 'cessation',[34] and sometimes as simultaneous (synonymous?) with 'cessation'.[35] One text (Majj. #121) states that the three 'contacts' occur following the neither associative-cognition nor non-associative-cognition level (i.e., the eighth jhāna level) and lead to the destruction of the āsavas—without ever mentioning 'cognitive and sensory cessation' (the ninth level).

The version that seems to have most interested later Theravādins is the one where emptiness, signlessness, and wishlessness occur *after* 'cessation.' Majj. #44 gives the basic formula. When asked, What does one encounter (*phassa*, lit. 'sensory contact') upon emerging from 'cognitive and sensory cessation,' the nun Dhammadinnā (considered best of the Dhamma-teachers amongst the nuns) replies:[36]

> ... when a monk has emerged from the attainment of 'cognitive and sensory cessation' three 'contacts' confront him: contact that is empty, contact that is signless, and contact that is wishless.

Saṃyutta Nikāya VI.7[37] explains two of them:

> [Q] What, sir, is the liberation of mind (*ceto-vimutti*) by emptiness?
>
> [A] Herein, sir, a brother goes to the forest or the root of a tree or a lonely spot, and thus reflects: "Empty is this of self or of what pertains to self." This, sir, is called 'liberation of mind by emptiness.'
>
> [Q] And what, sir, is the liberation of mind that is signless?
>
> [A] Herein, sir, a brother, without thought (*saññā*) of all signs, reaches and abides in that tranquility of mind that is signless. This, sir, is called 'liberation of mind by the signless.'

Buddhaghosa glosses the three as arising from three different objects of meditation, namely the three marks of all conditioned things: impermanence, dukkha, and selflessness. Hence, concentration on impermanence leads to signless liberation (*animitta-vimokkha*), concentration on dukkha leads to wishless liberation (*appaṇihita-vimokkha*), and concentration on no-self leads to emptiness liberation (*suññata-vimokkha*). The Nikāyas, however, are not so orderly.

A more detailed exposition of the elimination of the āsavas (Majj. #121) omits 'cognitive and sensory cessation' altogether.[38] One proceeds through the meditative levels by seeing that the level that one is in is empty, while being 'disturbed' by the next highest one. One then moves into that one, empties it, and is disturbed by the next one. This continues until reaching the plane of neither associative-cognition nor non-associative-cognition.

> Ānanda, a monk, not attending to the perception of the plane of no-thing, not attending to the perception of the plane of neither associative-cognition nor non-associative-cognition, attends to solitude grounded on the concentration of mind that is signless. His mind is satisfied with... and freed in the concentration of mind that is signless. He comprehends thus: 'The disturbances there might be resulting from the perception of the plane of no-thing... from the perception of the plane of neither associative-cognition nor non-associative-cognition do not exist here. *There is only this degree of disturbance, that is, the six sensory fields that, conditioned by life, are grounded on this body itself.*' He comprehends: 'This perceiving is empty of the plane of no-thing... empty of the plane of neither associative-cognition nor non-associative-cognition. *And there is only this that is not emptiness, that is, the six sensory fields that, conditioned by life, are grounded on this body itself.*' ....' He regards that which is not there as empty... but in regard to what remains he comprehends: 'That being, this is.'

Thus, Ānanda, this too comes to be for him a true, not mistaken, utterly purified realisation of emptiness.

And again, Ānanda, not attending to... no-thing... neither associative-cognition nor non-associative-cognition, [he] attends to solitude grounded on the concentration of mind that is signless. His mind is satisfied with, pleased with, set on and freed in the concentration of mind that is signless. He comprehends thus, 'This concentration of mind that is signless is conditioned and thought out. But whatever is conditioned and thought out, that is impermanent, it is liable to cessation.' When he knows this thus, sees this thus, his mind is freed from the āsava of craving pleasure, and his mind is freed from the āsava of craving existence, and his mind is freed from the āsava of ignorance.... And *there is only this degree of disturbance, that is, the six sensory fields that, conditioned by life, are grounded on this body itself...* [he is empty of the three āsavas] *And there is only this that is not emptiness, that is, the six sensory fields...* 'That being, this is.' Thus, Ānanda, this comes to be for him a true, not mistaken, utterly purified and incomparably higher realisation of emptiness. [emphasis added]

What is even more intriguing than the failure to mention 'cognitive and sensory cessation' in this passage, is its explicit declaration that the six sense fields remain intact even after the climactic elimination of the āsavas; the six sensory fields are *not* empty. The continuance of the sense organs and sense objects is not a problem, but rather a condition that is "utterly purified," the highest "realisation of emptiness".[39] In fact, many suttas in the Nikāyas emphasize precisely this point. The *Saṃyutta Nikāya* offers a potent analogy:[40]

'The eye is not the bond of objects, nor are objects the bond of the eye, but that desire and lust that arise owing to these two. That is the bond. And so with tongue and mind [i.e., the other senses].

'Suppose, friend, two oxen, one white and one black, tied by one rope or one yoke-tie. Would one be right in saying that the black ox is the bond for the white one, or that the white ox is the bond for the black one?'

'Surely not, friend.'

'... But the rope or the yoke-tie which binds the two, that is the bond that unites them. So it is with eye and objects, with tongue and flavors, with mind and mental-states. It is the desire and lust which are in them that form the bond that unites them.

'If the eye, friend, were the bond of objects, or if objects were the bond of the eye, then this Brahmā-faring life for the destruction of dukkha could not be proclaimed....'

Elsewhere the *Saṃyutta Nikāya* states:[41]

There are objects cognizable by the eye, ...sounds ... by ear, ...scents ...by nose, ...flavors ...by tongue, ...tangibles... by body, ...mental-states ....by mind, ... desirable, pleasant, delightful and dear, passion-fraught, inciting to lust. If a

> brother is enamored of such... there comes a lure upon him. The arising of the lure... is the arising of dukkha. So I declare.
>
> But there are objects.... [I]f a brother be not enamored of such, if he welcomes them not, persist not in clinging to them, thus is not enamored, thus not persisting in clinging to them, the lure comes to cease. The ceasing of the lure... is the ceasing of dukkha. So I declare.

The point of practice, therefore, is the elimination of desire, not sensation. When the senses are 'purified,' 'controlled'—meaning that they operate without desire and without initiating desire—then one sees things as they are. Countless more passages of this sort could be cited, but one final citation will redirect the importance of this for the Nikāyas' conception of 'cognitive and sensory cessation.'

Two very similar passages, Majj. I.296 and S. 41.6.6,[42] discuss the meditative attainments in detail. Both mention the three 'contacts' on emerging from 'cessation.' They explain, in nearly identical terms that a meditator does *not* think, 'I am about to attain, am attaining, or have attained this cognitive and sensory cessation.' It arises not by will or self-consciously, but because 'his mind is so practiced that it leads him on to the state of being such.' Both state that meditative calm and insight (*samatha vipassanā*) are indispensible practices for attaining it. And both passages define the difference between a dead body and one in cessation. For a corpse, body and speech have ceased, "are calmed," life has run out, vital heat has ceased, and *the sensory faculties have dispersed.* For someone in cessation, body, speech, *and mind* have ceased, "are calmed," life and the vital heat remain, *and the faculties are clarified or purified.* In the light of what has been discussed so far, this last characteristic is the most significant. Somehow the meditative attainment of cessation was believed to *purify the sense faculties.* Purify them of what? Desire. As countless other suttas explain, desire only arises for someone who does not understand how the senses work, i.e., someone who is ignorant. Destroying the āsavas, it seems, is a synonym for purifying the senses from desire.

Eliminating the āsavas means to remove the saṅkhāras that infect the very act of perception, 'purifying' the senses such that they may roam the sensorium without being tempted or snared by the "lure." Awakening means to sense without desire, without the compulsions of intentionality, Wishlessly (*appaṇihita*).

Visuddhimagga on nirodha-samāpatti

There is another type of samāpatti that is devoid of mental activities which is discussed in later Buddhist texts, the *asaññi-samāpatti* (attainment of no-cognition, S: *āsaṃjñi-samāpatti*), but this samāpatti is never mentioned directly in the *Visuddhimagga.* Buddhaghosa does mention the no-cognition devas, or devas utterly devoid of any thought, usually in the context of rebirth consciousness (since they occupy a distinct heaven in the third rūpa-loka),[43] but the meditative practices that might land someone in the realm of thoughtless devas in a subsequent life are not discussed. We will have to wait until we turn to the *Abhidharmakośa* for that sort of discussion. The *Kośa* will sharply contrast *asaññi-samāpatti* with *nirodha-samāpatti.* The *Ch'eng wei-shih lun* also draws some contrasts between the two samāpattis, but not as severly as does the *Kośa.*

The title *Vissudhimagga* means 'path or method of purification.' Buddhaghosa says (I.5) that by 'purification' he means "nibbāna, which being devoid of all stains, is utterly pure. The Method of Purification is the method to that purification; it is the means of approach that is called Method." Since the attainment of that purity is also called *ceto-vimutti* (liberation of mind) or *paññā-vimutti* (liberation by wisdom), the *Visuddhimagga* is primarily concerned with methods for purifying the mind.

Buddhaghosa observes that the plane of neither-saññā-nor-non-saññā is the condition, or jumping off point, for nirodha-samāpatti (III.20). Neither-saññā-nor-non-saññā is the outcome of *samatha* (calm attentiveness), while fruition attainment[44] is the outcome of *vipassanā* (meditative observation and analysis). The attainment of cessation is the outcome of calm (*samatha*) coupled with insight (*vipassanā*) (IX.104).

So far Buddhaghosa has not claimed anything that obviously contradicts the Nikāyas. We now note his first divergence. He writes (XI.124):

> Āryas, having already produced the eight attainments, develop concentration thinking 'We shall enter upon the attainment of cessation, and by being without consciousness for seven days we shall *abide in bliss* (*sukha*) here and now by reaching the cessation that is nibbāna,' then the development of absorption (*appanā*) concentration (*samādhi*) provides for them the benefit of cessation.

Two elements in this description are immediately stunning. First, he seems to unequivocally equate nirodha-samāpatti with nibbāna. Second, he characterizes the cessational state, in which supposedly no mental activity is occurring, as "abiding in bliss." Moreover, earlier we saw explicit denials in both the *Majjhima* and *Saṃyutta Nikāyas* that one thinks "I shall enter this attainment, etc." How could Buddhaghosa so blatantly contradict this emphasized, repeated point? One possible source he could draw on is Majj. #43, *Mahāvedalla sutta.* This sutta explains that vitality depends on heat and heat depends on vitality, just as a flame depends on light to be seen, and the light depends on the flame to be seen. It explains *animitta ceto-vimutti* laconically as paying no attention to any signs while paying attention to the signless sphere.[45] To the question: "What are the conditions for persistence of *animitta ceto-vimutti*?" the answer given is: (i) pay no attention to signs, (ii) pay attention to the signless; and (iii) *prior preparation.* The sutta does not explain exactly what sort of prior preparation it means, but it likely means progressively developing along the *māgga.* Buddhaghosa seems to understand this as not simply *prior activities* that have prepared one for the samāpatti, but as cultivating a *prior intent* to enter cessation, even though the suttas reject such intent, especially if articulated as such.

Buddhaghosa actually quotes another part of Majj. I.302, one of the texts that precludes saying 'I will attain, I am attaining, etc.',[46] the part that explains that in 'cognitive and sensory cessation,' the saṅkhāras of speech, body and mind cease—in that order.[47] But according to Buddhaghosa this samāpatti still involves 'saṅkhāra consisting of saṅkhāta' (XVII.47), i.e., embodied-conditioning due to (prior) conditioning. While this might seem to contradict what the Nikāyas asserted, assuming that āsavas and saṅkhāras are somehow synonymous, if we remember that the body and senses are still intact when one emerges from cessation, then their persistence may be attributed to the endurance of certain saṅkhāras. Yet he seems to be saying more than that, namely that saṅkhāras are actually operating *during* cessation. Thus, while mental functions (*vedanā, saññā, viññāna*, etc.) have ceased, subliminal embodied-conditioning continues to function. In other words, three of the *nāma khandhas* have ceased, but the fourth, *saṅkhāra,* continues for the duration of the samāpatti. This is no different than the Yogācāra claim that the ālaya-vijñāna continues throughout nirodha-samāpatti, and Buddhaghosa may even have been influenced by the Yogācārins on this point.[48] But while the Yogācārins are not interested in exalting this samāpatti as the moment of final liberation, Buddhaghosa, as a Theravādin, does have such leanings, and the persistence of saṅkhāras in this samāpatti do not help his cause. Persisting saṅkhāras suggest something less than the utter eradication of the āsavas.[49] By using the term saṅkhata (conditioning), he is signaling that while he maintains that saṅkhāras from prior experiences are indeed operating during cessation, no new saṅkhāras are being generated at that time. Since saṅkhāras largely operate outside the purview of conscious awareness, this would still allow that *conscious* mental activity is absent even while unconscious mental activity continues.

At XXIII.16-52 he offers a detailed enumeration of cessation and its components: "attainment of cessation... is the non-occurrence of consciousness and its concomitants owing to their progressive cessation." (18) He then cites another of his own texts, the *Paṭisambhidāmagga* (i.97), for a list of prerequisites to cessation:

> Understanding that is mystery, owing to possession of two powers, to the tranquillization (*passaddhi*) of three formations, to sixteen kinds of exercise of knowledge, and to nine kinds of exercise of concentration, is knowledge of the attainment of cessation.

This is unpacked as follows:

The Two Powers are *samatha* and *vipassanā.*
The three saṅkhāras (formations):

> For one who has attained the 2nd jhāna, the verbal formations (*saṅkhāra*) consisting of vitakka and vicāra (initial and sustained applied thought) are quite tranquillized.

For one who has attained the 4th jhāna, the bodily formations consisting of in-breaths and out-breaths are quite tranquillized.

For one who has attained 'cognitive and sensory cessation,' the mental formations consisting of sensations and cognitions are quite tranquillized.

"...Being wearied by the occurrence and dissolution of formations, they attain it [i.e., attaining cessation] thinking 'Let us dwell in bliss by being without consciousness here and now and reaching the cessation that is nibbana'." (30)[50]

One who strives with calm (*samatha*) alone reaches the base (*āyatana*) consisting of neither associative-cognition nor non-associative-cognition and remains there, while one who strives with insight alone reaches the attainment of fruition and remains there. But it is one who strives with both, and after performing the preparatory tasks, causes the cessation of [consciousness belonging to] the base consisting of neither associative-cognition nor non-associative-cognition, who attains it. (31)

One can prearrange when one is to reemerge from the cessation by setting an inner alarm clock, and it will work infallibly (40). Cessation is accomplished by effort *and* preparation (43). If one gets to the fourth arūpa level without having done all the preparations, one cannot reach cessation, but drops back down to the "Nothing" level, i.e., the third arūpa level (44).

Cessation is defined as "the non-occurrence of consciousness and its concomitants owing to their progressive cessation".[51] How does this produce the requisite insight for Awakening?

His analysis of seclusion (*viveka*) and abandoning (*pahāna*) may provide some clues. According to Buddhaghosa, there are three types of seclusions:

1. bodily seclusion (*kāyaviveka*)
2. mental seclusion (*cittaviveka*)
3. seclusion by suppression (*vivekkhambhaṇaviveka*)

The bodily and mental seclusions can lead to *upadhi-viveka*, seclusion from the causative basis, which leads either directly to nibbāna, or indirectly to nibbāna by way of the five abandonings. The five are:

1. Abandoning by suppression (*vikkhambhanappahānaṃ*), which helps set up the various jhānas, since certain hindrances and mental problems need to be overcome or at least temporarily suppressed in order for jhānas to arise.
2. Abandoning by substitution of opposites (*tadaṅgappahānaṃ*) in which kusala (wholesome, advantageous attitudes and actions) replaces akusala (unwholesome, disadvantageous attitudes and actions). Yogācāra developed a parallel system of antidotes or counteractions (*pratipakṣa*), which not only exchanges good karma for bad, but offers a hermeneutic of counters and reversals that systematically recontextualizes all Buddhist doctrine and practice.
3. Abandoning by cutting off or eradicating (*samucchedappahānaṃ*) by which the fetters are cut off through activities along the transmundane

method/path. While suppression per se is temporary, 'cutting off' is irrevocable.

4. Abandoning by tranquilization (*paṭippassadhippahānaṃ*) signifies the subsiding of defilements at moments of fruition. In other words, as one practices, one's actions generate consequences that come to fruition when they reach maturity. Defilements can be 'tranquilized' as a result of certain practices, even if that specific defilement was not the explicit target of the practice.
5. Abandoning by Deliverance (*nissaranappahānaṃ*), i.e., ultimate release.

Buddhaghosa also speaks of *lokuttara-jhāna,* i.e., transmundane jhānas, which lead to *phala-samāpatti,* the fruit of meditative attainments. These become *vipāka,* or maturations of path/method consciousness. However, for him nirodha-samāpatti is *not* a jhāna. One enters nirodha-samāpatti from the Nothing level (seventh level). One prepares there, and then enters the eighth level for two moments, after which consciousness stops for however long a period one has predecided during preparation. As mentioned before, if one has not completed the requisite preparatory practices, one cannot rise above the eighth level, and will fall back into the Nothing level if one's attempt is premature.

It seems that for Buddhaghosa nirodha-samāpatti is, on the one hand, a reward (*vipāka*) for having practiced so effectively and so long on the Buddhist path, and, on the other hand, a special sort of practice that generates its own special rewards (e.g., it tranquilizes the defilements). It is either a vacation to nibbāna, a glimpse of nibbāna, or a nibbāna-like teaser. He does not seem to be sure which, and at different points treats it in all these manners. He does seem sure, however, that by itself it does not consist of abiding in nibbāna.

Throughout his discussion of cessation, one senses his enthusiasm for the subject as if were the very means for attaining nibbāna, as we saw above. However, Buddhaghosa fails to state that explicitly, and ultimately vacillates on this point.

Nirodha-samāpatti in the *Abhidhammattha sangaha* of Bhadanta Anuruddhā-cariya[52]

This text, a post-canonical Theravāda Abhidhamma work that ostensibly summarizes and reorganizes the *Visuddhimagga,* occasionally offers ideas not found in Buddhaghosa's text. For instance, in the *Abhidhamma sangaha, asañña* (being without associative thinking) is explicitly used to denote 'death proximate kamma,' i.e., one's thoughts at the time of death which determine one's next life.[53]

Nārada, in the commentary to his translation, writes:[54]

> [An] Anāgami [Nonreturner] or Arhant who has developed the rūpa and arūpa jhānas could, by will-power, temporarily arrest the ordinary flow of consciousness even for seven days continuously.... All mental activities cease although there exist heat and life, devoid of any breathing... The body [while in this state] cannot be harmed... [To enter this samāpatti, first one experiences] two moments of the 4th arūpa jhāna, then consciousness ceases.
>
> When he emerges from this state the first thought-moment to arise is an Anāgami fruit consciousness in the case of an Anāgami, or an Arhant fruit consciousness in the case of an Arhant. Thereafter, the stream of consciousness subsides into bhavanga. [square brackets mine]

The text itself says:[55]

> At the time of nirodha-samāpatti the 4th arūpa *javana*[56] runs twice and then contacts cessation (*nirodhaṃ phusati*). When emerging (from this samāpatti) either Anāgami Fruit-consciousness or Arhatta Fruit-consciousness arises accordingly. When it ceases there is subsidence into the continuum.

Nirodhaṃ phusati is an odd phrase. How does one make sensorial contact (*phassa*) with 'cessation'? The passage means that one enters nirodha-samāpatti by first entering the 4th arūpa level (neither associative-cognition nor non-associative-cognition), but only for two mental moments; one then enters nirodha-samāpatti. Emerging from it, one is or has become either a Non-Returner (Anāgamin) or an Arhat. This implies that only Non-Returners and Arhats can enter this samāpatti, since a Once-Returner would not be a Once-Returner if, within the same life, he suddenly became a Non-Returner. A Non-Returner could become an Arhat, though. An Arhat will reemerge still an Arhat (he cannot backslide).

While Buddhaghosa only admitted to certain conditioned saṅkhāras present in nirodha-samāpatti, Anuruddha goes further:[57]

> In the process of the attainments there is no regularity of thought-processes, as in the stream of life-continuum. Nevertheless, it should be understood that many (Sublime and Supramundane) *javanas* take place.

In other words, there is karmic activity taking place during cessation in the form of sporadic karmically-charged mental moments. Anuruddha has little else to say about nirodha-samāpatti.

Abhidharmakośa on Āsaṃjñi-samāpatti and Nirodha-samāpatti

As anyone familiar with the *Kośa* and its style would expect, its treatment of the samāpattis is both thorough and inextricably interwoven with a multitude of other issues and terms. In this chapter we can only review the most salient aspects of its discussion. As will be clear shortly, the *Kośa* draws a sharp line between the two samāpattis, denigrating one while praising the other. While he states that nirodha-samāpatti has something to do with Buddhas becoming Buddhas, he neglects to highlight it as the defining moment, and omits any direct discussion of the āsavas and their destruction, at least in the sort of terms we found in the Nikāyas.

One of the intriguing aspects of Vasubandhu's exposition, something we have not seen in precisely these terms so far, is the relation he posits not only between the eighth meditation and cessation, but between the seventh meditation—the level of Nothing—and cessation. His innovations may, at least in part, indicate his attempt to answer the question we asked earlier, namely, *how* does cessation work as a producer of knowledge? His answer will be: it doesn't.

The eighth level (i.e., the fourth Ārūpya-dhyāna) is given two names:

1. *Naivasaṃjñānāsaṃjñāyatana*, i.e., neither associative-cognition nor non-associative cognition, and
2. *Bhavāgra*, the highest level (*agra*) of existence (*bhava*).

Bhavāgra is the uppermost limit of the triple world (*tri-loka, tri-dhātu*), i.e., the worlds (*loka*) of desire (*kāma*), form (*rūpa*), and formless (*ārūpya*). To go beyond this limit is to leave the world (*loka*) and enter the transmundane world (*lokuttara*). The highest practices and attainments are considered transmundane. Some Buddhists maintained that Bhavāgra is an utterly pure realm in which karma is absent, but the Kośa rejects the view that there is no karma in Bhavāgra.[58] Since it is still part of the samsāric cycle, it must involve karma.

There are four dhyānas in the form world, each constituting a distinct meditative sphere (*dhyāna, āyatana*) as well as a distinct life-world in which beings are born and die.[59] In the fourth dhyāna level of the rūpa-loka are the āsaṃjñi-sattvas or āsaṃjñi-devas,[60] the thoughtless beings who occupy a realm in which no one thinks, perceives, or engages in any cognitive activity whatsoever. The moment a denizen of this realm has even the inkling of a thought, s/he instantly dies and is reborn elsewhere. Although this realm is counted as a heaven, it is obviously a place in which nothing is done, nothing is accomplished, and nothing whatsoever happens (aside from beings being born and dying there). In terms of progressing along the Buddhist path toward Awakening, this realm and the meditative state associated with it are singularly unproductive and useless. And that is precisely the attitude Vasubandhu takes toward it.

The Āsaṃjñikas are treated with utter contempt by the *Kośa*. The pursuit of either the meditative or rebirth status of āsaṃjñika is a misguided aspiration of Pṛthagjanas, ordinary people who are not practicing Buddhism. For Vasubandhu, the absence of saṃjñā is utter stupidity (*saṃmoha*).Those who pursue this sort of mindlessness mistake the stupidity of being utterly thoughtless for some sort of liberating experience. If they pursue that thoughtlessness, they will be able reach it in their misguided meditations. They can later, as a result of this experience, be born into that realm, which, because it is utterly devoid of thought, lacks any possibility for spiritual progress, and therefore can even prove counterproductive.[61] Āsaṃjñi-sattvas don't even breathe.[62]

How is the mind stopped? How does it restart once it has been interrupted? Vasubandhu says that certain meditations produce a dharma that temporarily blocks the production of cittas (apperceptive moments) and other mental states, like a dam that temporarily holds back water.[63] A related 'power' is the power of vows. Along the path, one can focus with determination on reaching something not yet attained. Progressing through the heavenly levels is never automatic. One can reach a certain level and, because of the type of heaven it is, be unable to reach another heaven, even a lower one, without first being reborn in much worst circumstances. At such times a prior vow or resolution can prove effective. The *Kośa* assures us that the power of *praṇidhāna* (vow; resolution) can produce pure fruit, meaning that when one is in a dhyāna, a previous vow can get one into one of the *lower* level pure states, even if—as in the case of an āsaṃjñika—one would otherwise be incapable in one's present state of accomplishing that.[64]

Nirodha-samāpatti is another name for saṃjñāvedita-nirodha (cessation of saṃjñā and vedanā). In contrast to āsaṃjñi-samāpatti, nirodha-samāpatti is cultivated only by Āryas, not Pṛthagjanas. It is always kuśala, never akuśala or neutral. Pṛtagjanas are prevented from attaining it by their fear that it would lead to their utter annihilation, and because it only arises through the practice of the Mārga.

According to the *Kośa*, it can be entered either from Bhavāgra or from the Nothing level.[65] The *Kośa* and Yogācāra literature are somewhat ambiguous about whether nirodha-samāpatti should be considered part of Bhavāgra or something beyond it. The conclusion seems to be that although nirodha-samāpatti and naivasaṃjñānāsaṃjñāyatana are distinct from each other as meditative experiences, they are nonetheless both associated with Bhavāgra; the latter as the direct experience of Bhavāgra, and the former as an experience of or in its margins. However, in stark contrast to some of the earlier claims made by by Buddhists, Vasubandhu states that since both Bhavāgra and the cessation levels suppress thinking, no defilements can be eliminated within them. "In Bhavāgra, it is by entering the Āryan absorption of Ākiṃcanya (the Nothing level) that one destroys the defilements".[66] In other words, whatever defilements are destroyed while one is engaging in meditations associated with the higher levels of the ārūpya-dhātu, will be destroyed while one is at the Nothing level, but not during cessation itself. The Nothing stage serves as a purifier; it strips away, reduces to nothing, erroneous thoughts and defilements. Further, "...the pure path can't be cultivated in Bhavāgra..."[67] In other words, this samāpatti is merely a glimpse of something nirvāṇa-like, not itself really efficacious. One has to return to the 'Nothing' stage to actually negate defilements.[68]

The *Kośa* implies, but does not state, that *experiencing* cessation produces knowledge of destruction (*kṣaya-jñāna*). And this knowledge leads to the knowledge of non-arising, which, because it brings samsāra to an end is the culminating knowledge offered by the *Kośa*. But how is a mindless state—and it is even *more* mindless than the āsaṃjñi-samāpatti, since it involves the suppression of vedanā as well as saṃjñā, while āsaṃjñikas only suppress saṃjñā—'experienced'? The *Kośa* says that the meditator experiences nirodha-samāpatti directly with body, not mind, i.e., he is a *kāya-sākṣin*, a "body witness".[69] Buddhaghosa defines a 'body-witness' (*kāya-sakkhi*) as "one who has realized nibbāna through experience," and includes it as one of the seven types of Āryas.[70] How does an insentient body 'experience'? Vasubandhu doesn't say.

Vasubandhu does says:[71]

> IT IS OBTAINED IN A SINGLE MOMENT... One takes possession of this absorption, not in the past, not in the future, but in one time period, that is, in the present, as is also the case for the *prātikmokṣa* discipline (iv.35). In the second moment of this absorption, and in all the moments that follow the obtaining of this absorption until the moment it ends, one possesses it in the past and in the present. On the other hand, since this absorption is not mind, it is impossible to acquire a future *prāpti* of this absorption.

In other words, no karmic consequences accrue (*prāpti*), either for good or for bad, as a result of this samāpatti. It remains related to its past, its moment of inception; it is obviously occurring in the present, but it never has a future. As such, it becomes a *bodily prelude to non-arising.* But while the Nikāyas were unclear about how this insentience resulted in knowledge, Vasubandhu folds this samāpatti into a correlative cognition.[72]

> The Buddha obtains the absorption of extinction at the moment when he becomes a Buddha, that is, at the moment of *kṣaya-jñāna* [knowledge of destruction] (vi.67). No quality of the Buddha is obtained through effort; all of his qualities are acquired through the simple fact of detachment: as soon as he wishes it, the mass of qualities arise at will.

But for others nirodha-samāpatti is produced through effort.[73] *Kṣaya-jñāna*, direct-cognition of destruction, is reminiscent of the destruction of the āsavas. Here it is being labelled explicitly as a cognition (*jñāna*). Nirodha-samāpatti is thus part of Buddha's Awakening, a correlate to it, but not its only condition.

While Sarvāstivādins consider the two samāpattis to be *dravya* (substantially real), the Sautrāntikas (and later, Yogācārins) consider them *prajñapti* (only nominal realities).

The salient contrasts between the two samāpattis according to the *Abhidharmakośa* are summarized in *chart 1* below.

Yogācāra passages on *nirodha-samāpatti*

Yogācāra accounts of nirodha-samāpatti arose at the tail end of a rich, minutely detailed discussion between a variety of abhidharmic schools, including the Vaibhāṣikas, Mahīśasikas, and so on. A lengthy discussion of nirodha-samāpatti occurs in the *Mahāvibhāṣā* 大毗婆沙論 (T.27.1545; fasc. 152-154), a major Vaibhāṣika Abhidharma text, but that is beyond the scope of the present work.

Sthiramati's commentary to Asaṅga's *Abhidharmasamuccaya*, the *Abhidharma-samuccaya-vṛtti* (阿毗達磨黑襰偷趋 *a-p'i-t'a-mo tsa-chi lun*), also called 雜集論 *Tsa chi lun* (T.31.1606) says:[74]

Āsaṃjñi-samāpatti	**Nirodha-samāpatti**
mindless (acitta)	tranquil
vipāka, hence neutral	good, because from good cause/root
produces no fruit (of the Mārga), but invariably leads to rebirth in the very next life as an āsaṃjñi-sattva in "mindless" realm	can lead to rebirth in 4th ārūpya-dhātu in next life, or good result in this life; one may now achieve nirvāṇa in *this* life (rendering other consequences moot)
entered from 4th rūpa-dhyāna	entered from 4th ārūpya-dhātu (Bhavāgra), but maybe also from 3rd ārūpya-dhyāna
cultivated by Pṛthagjanas	cultivated by Āryas
pursued because mistaken for type of deliverance (*niḥsaraṇa-mokṣa*)	pursued as dhyāna of (bodily) tranquility
a calamity	extremely high attainment. Pṛthagjanas can't attain it because (i) they fear annihilation, and (ii) it only arises through the Mārga.
counters (and suppresses) *saṃjñā*	suppresses *saṃjñā* and *vedanā*
obtained by producing a dharma that acts as a dam, temporarily blocking the arising of new cittas (pent up, they eventually reemerge/reassert themselves)	obtained by effort in Mārga, *not* detachment, that produces an obstructive dharma (like a dam).
void of experience/thought altogether	experienced by body, not mind

chart 1 - Contrasts between the Samāpattis in the *Abhidharmakośa*

> Already detached from the 'Nothing' āyatana, one goes far beyond (超過) the summit of existence (有頂, Bhavāgra); saṃjñā stops after a moment (暫息想) because of an intention previously made (作意為先故)[75] ... This is prajñaptically called cessation samāpatti (假立滅盡定).

Here one jumps from the 3rd ārūpya āyatana right past the 4th ārūpya āyatana (Bhavāgra) straight into nirodha-samāpatti. Saṃjñā exists for the first moment of this stage and then stops. The mechanism of the stopping is a prior intention.

The *Ch'eng wei-shih lun*'s treatment of the two samāpattis draws largely, though not exclusively, on the *Yogācārabhūmi śāstra* (hereafter YBh) of Asaṅga.[76] Some pertinent passages in the YBh are:

> ... This samāpatti is only able to make the pravṛtti-vijñānas cease (靜轉識); It is unable to make the ālaya-vijñāna cease.[77]
>
> It is *prajñapti-sat* (假有), not *dravya-sat* (非實物有).[78]
>
> When Śaikṣa āryas (有學聖者) can enter this samāpatti, that means they've realized the Anāgamin (nonreturning) body (不還身證). Aśaikṣa āryas can also enter it, meaning they are already fully liberated (*mokṣa*) (俱分解脫).

Ārya (lit. 'noble,' rendered in Chinese as *sheng* 聖, lit. 'sage') denotes someone who has progressed along the Buddhist way. A Śaikṣa is someone still in training on the Path; an Aśaikṣa is someone who no longer requires any training (e.g., Arhat, Pratyekabuddha, Buddha). Śaikṣa and Aśaikṣa are contrasted with Pṛtagjanas, ordinary people who have not begun practicing the mārga. This threefold distinction is already found in the Pāli sources: *puthujjana* (ordinary people), *sekha* (those in training), *asekha* (those who need no more training). The passage above is unclear about whetherx the Arhats entering the samāpatti must *already* have attained Arhathood, or whether, as a result of entering that samāpatti, they will now be Arhats. One would have to be at least an Anāgamin to enter nirodha-samāpatti, since only those very close to complete Awakening would be capable of achieving it. Another passage says:

> By wishing to go beyond the 'Nothing' (無所有處貪) level, one initiates the intent to fully stop (息止) saṃjñā (想); that is what is called the cessation stage (滅分位), heuristically designated as nirodha-samāpatti (建立滅盡定).[79]

Here, purified of desire in the 'Nothing' sphere, one initiates an intent to stop saṃjñā. This passage emphasizes that the labels 'cessation stage' and 'nirodha-samāpatti' are heuristic devices, prajñāptis (*chien-li* 建立).

Asaṅga's *Hsien-ch'ang lun* 顯揚論 (**Prakaraṇāryavākā śāstra*) states:

> With a desire to detach from the 'Nothing' āyatana, some enter the 'neither saṃjñā nor not-saṃjñā' samāpatti (非想非非想定). Some, again, advancing higher, enter the non-saṃjñā samāpatti (無想定). Again, some advance higher, to the temporary stopping of saṃjñā because of the upāya of an earlier intention. (Here) *ālambanas* (cognitive object-supports) have stopped (止息所緣); the sporadic (不恆) projective operations (現行) of *citta* and *caittas*, and *one part* of the perpetual operations (恆行) of *citta* and *caittas* cease.[80]

This passage seems to follow the nine-dhyāna model, in which the eighth dhyāna, 'neither with nor without saṃjñā,' is surpassed by a ninth dhyāna simply labeled 'non-saṃjñā.' Nirodha-samāpatti is above both of these. Here again a *prior* intent (not an intent contiguous with the attainment of cessation, as Buddhaghosa claimed) serves as the means. But we learn that mental activity has not stopped completely. While sense-objects no longer play a part (the *ālambanas* have stopped), and seven of the eight consciousnesses have temporarily shut down, the eighth consciousness, the ālaya-vijñāna continues to operate. The 'sporadic projective operations' signify the six consciousnesses; the 'perpetual operations' are manas and the ālaya-vijñāna. They are called that because the individual sense organs are sporadic, sometimes operating, sometimes not (e.g., they cease during deep sleep). The perpetual operations, on the contrary, are always functioning, even when we don't consciously notice them. 'One part of the perpetual operations' means that manas ceases but the ālaya-vijñāna does not. By this, Yogācāra also limits the ultimate efficacy of this samāpatti, since it only effects seven of the eight consciousnesses. The eighth does not cease during so-called cessation. Were the eighth consciousness to cease, one would be an Arhat, since the ālaya-vijñāna only stops at Arhathood (*tasya vyāvṛtir-arhatva*; *Triṃśikā* 5 [v. 4 in Hsüan-tsang's Chinese translation]).

Ch'eng wei-shih lun on the two samāpattis

In the *Ch'eng wei-shih lun* the samāpattis are *not* discussed in the section on ālaya-vijñāna, but rather in the manas and mano-vijñāna sections. What follows is a complete translation of all the relevant passages:

[from the *manas* section[81]]

Again, in accordance with what the Sutras say about the *āsaṃjñi-* and *nirodha-samāpattis* (無想滅定), some say that these (samāpattis) should be indistinguishable since defiled manas doesn't exist (in either). [However] this [indisinguishability should] refer [only to the fact] that there is no difference as to the cessation of the six consciousnesses and their caittas ... in those two samāpattis. (But) how could these two be distinguished [at all] if not that defiled manas exists in one but not in the other?[82]

Some say the difference (lies in their different) *prayoga* (加行 the prepatory stage) *dhātus*, *bhūmis*, *āśrayas*, etc. [*dhātu* = sphere/element of practice; *bhūmi* = the particular lived-world or station one inhabits; *āśraya* = the one practicing, lit. 'basis'], but logically this is not so, since the cause of these differentiations is due precisely to the existence (of manas in the āsaṃjñi-samāpatti but not in nirodha-samāpatti). If (manas) doesn't exist (in either samāpatti), then those causes as well wouldn't exist. Hence it is certain that what ought to distinguish them is the existence of manas.

Again, according to the Sutras, for Āsaṃjñi-sattvas (beings living in the Āsaṃjñi heaven) citta and caittas cease for the duration of one life span. If this consciousness (i.e., manas) doesn't exist, then those beings ought to be without defilements. [What] this [passage in the *Triṃśikā*, v.7, really] means [is that] during their entire life, the six *pravṛtti-vijñānas* don't exist.[83] (But) if there is no manas, then there would be no *ātma-grāha* (attachment to self). If no [*ātma-grāha* in that life], then in the remainder of the [future] lives they will live [even in other realms] they would be without *ātma-grāha* [since they would have extinguished it]. If there is no *ātma-grāha,* then (āsaṃjñī-samāpatti) would be like nirvana, and not what is rejected unanimously by āryas and worthies.

[An opponent (Sarvāstivādin) counters: Since *ātma-grāha*] exists at the very beginning and end (of an āsaṃjñi-sattva's life, guaranteeing the continuation of ātma-grāha in subsequent lives], our position is faultless.[84]

[We reply:] But since it does not exist *during* that life, your position is at fault.[85]

[The opponent counters:] Since it [i.e., *ātma-grāha*] exists in the past and future, our position is faultless.

[We reply:] Since [past and future] are neither present nor eternal,[86] (*ātma-grāha*) would be inexistent. Your position is at fault.

[An opponent (Mahāsaṅghika) counters:] Since the perceived is inexistent, the perceiver too is inexistent.[87] [i.e., there is no perceiver who could grasp for a self].

[We reply: What, then, do you propose acts as a conduit through which karma becomes reborn?] The *viprayukta-saṃskāras* have already been negated [so they (e.g., birth, etc.) cannot account for rebirth].[88] If the Storing Consciousness[89] (i.e., the ālaya-vijñāna) doesn't exist, then the vāsanās[90] don't exist as well [i.e., *where* would they be? The possibility that] any other dharma could receive vāsanās has already been disputed and [dismissed as] illogical.[91]

Hence you should [acknowledge that] the differentiation (between the two samāpattis rests on) the existence of defiled manas[92] which is perpetually producing ātma-grāha in the Āsaṃjñi-loka. Due to that, Worthies and Āryas unanimously reject that [realm].

The *Ch'eng wei-shih lun* goes on to discuss why manas serves as a necessary condition for the existence of *ātma-grāha* (grasping of selfhood), noting the seeming perpetuity of manas for Pṛthagjanas 異生, 'ordinary people.'

[from the *mano-vijñāna* section[93]]

... the ākāras (*hsing-hsiang* 行相, mental images, lit. 'operational forms') of the five pravṛtti consciousnesses are crude movements.[94] (The five consciousnesses) rely on conditions with which, often, they do not come into contact.[95] Hence sometimes many (sense-objects) arise, sometimes few.

Althought the sixth consciousness also (involves) crude movement, yet it relies on conditions with which at no time does it not come into contact. Hence when it doesn't arise, that is due to opposing conditions.[96] (I.e., something opposes or blocks it)

The ākāras of the seventh and eighth consciousnesses are minute and subtle; they rely on many conditions which exist at all times. Hence, generally, there is no condition which could obstruct them so as to make them inoperative.

Further, the five bodily consciousnesses are unable to think or cogitate, they only operate through external 'gates,' and since they rely on many conditions in order to arise, they are often interrupted; and seldom do they operate [uninterruptedly].

The sixth consciousness is able, on its own, to think and cogitate; it operates through inner and outer 'gates'; it doesn't rely on many conditions, and, with the exception of five cases, it is always able to project and produce. Hence, it is seldom interrupted, and frequently productive. That's why [the verse] didn't say that it projects and arises "following conditions."

What are the five exceptions?

Birth in the Āsaṃjñi-loka, etc.

Āsaṃjñi-devas are those who, by the force of cultivating that meditation (定) which suppresses crude thought, are born in a heaven blocking the sporadic operations of citta and caittas. Since the cessation of saṃjñā is considered the most significant (thing that is blocked), it's called āsaṃjñi-deva-loka (World of Nonthinking Gods). Thus, the six pravṛtti-vijñānas are cut off in this (loka).

THERE IS AN OPINION (*Yogācārabhūmi*, fasc. 13): Those in that heaven always lack the six consciousnesses because, the Āryan teachings say, they lack the pravṛtti-vijñānas. That is to say, they only have a rūpāṅga[97] [but not *nāma*-rūpa], which is why, they say, it is considered an *acitta* realm (a land devoid of mind).[98]

THERE IS ANOTHER OPINION: At the final stage of one's life in this heaven, one has to produce the pravṛtti-vijñānas just before this life ends, since there must be a desire that will moisten (latent karmic seeds) in order to produce a lower-level birth. The *Yogācārabhūmi śāstra* (fasc. 56) says once saṃjñā arises, those sentient beings sink down (from their heaven to a lower birth).

So if [some Sutras] say that [the āsaṃjñi-sattvas] are without pravṛtti-vijñānas, etc., it is the major duration of their life that is being talked about; that doesn't mean that [desire, etc.] are completely absent [for their entire life].

THERE IS ANOTHER OPINION: The pravṛtti-vijñānas also exist at the time of their birth, since they must possess them in order to produce and moisten the kleśas [that produce birth—both for their present life and the following one], just as in the other [realms] one initially must have pravṛtti-vijñānas originally [produced in a prior life].[99]

The *Yogācārabhūmiśāstra* (fasc. 12) says [on the contrary] that when born into that [realm], they only enter it, they don't produce [the pravṛtti-vijñānas, etc.], since, once saṃjñā arises, falling from that [realm immediately] follows.

If initially one lacks pravṛtti-vijñānas originally [produced in a prior life], how can this be called 'entering [āsaṃjñi-loka]'?

It is called "entering" [a mindless realm] because [the pravṛtti-vijñānas, etc.] existed previously, but after [entering] they do not exist.

A definitive passage [in the *Yogācārabhūmiśāstra* (fasc. 53) states that [when born into this realm] the citta and caittas that one is born with cease, and so it is called *asaṃjña*. The intent of this passage is to show that at birth [in this realm] one initially possesses, for a moment,[100] pravṛtti-vijñānas that are produced by *vipāka* [maturation of prior karma, karmic consequences], originally [produced in a previous life]. The power of these causes and conditions from a previous-life[101] [viz., the vipāka from experiences of āsaṃjñi-samāpatti in a previous life, is such] that [the pravṛtti-vijñānas arise at the moment one is born in this realm, but] do not arise again. Instead [the vipāka] leads to a distinctive stage— [itself] karmically indeterminate vipāka (*avyākta vipāka*)—that, differentiated, is called āsaṃjñi[-loka], just as the two samāpattis are called kuśala (advantageous, wholesome) [even though they are not really kuśala, but only avyākta, because of] the kuśala [previous life karma] that leads to them [i.e., they are named after their 'leading' causes[102]].

If this is not the case, i.e., none of the pravṛtti-vijñānas operate at all [at birth], why would the passage say that *only upon birth* [in this realm] does one attain cessation?

Hence, at the very beginning of this stage, the pravṛtti-vijñānas are momentarily produced.

This heaven is only contained in the fourth Dhyāna[103] since saṃjñā in the lower [dhyānas] is crude movement, difficult to cut off; and in the higher [Dhyānas], there is no āyatana for asaṃjñā-vipāka. It is precisely the *cetanā* (intention) that leads to the arising of āsaṃjñi-samāpatti that is able to bring about[104] the vipāka fruit of [birth in] that heaven.

[The *Triṃśikā* says] THE TWO *ACITTA* SAMĀPATTIS. This means that because both āsaṃjñi-samāpatti and nirodha-samāpatti are without the six consciousnesses, they are called *acitta* (無心).[105]

[*Āsaṃjñi-samāpatti*]

Āsaṃjñi-samāpatti means there are Pṛthagjanas[106] in Śubhakṛtsna[107] [a heaven in the third Dhyāna[108]] who have suppressed[109] 'appropriational intent' (*rāga*)but have not yet suppressed the higher defilements. Due to previously making (作) an intention to escape and detach from saṃjñā, [that intent] makes (令) the citta and caittas of sporadic saṃskāras cease.[110] Since this is primarily a cessation of saṃjñā, it is called *āsaṃjñi*. It makes (作) the body peaceful and harmonious (安和), and so it is also called *samāpatti*.

(Note, the *Kośa* claimed that while nirodha-samāpatti results in a tranquil body, āsaṃjñi-samāpatti *does not.*)

There are three levels to practicing this samāpatti.

[1] The lower level: The practitioner, on viewing this dharma,[111] necessarily retreats [from it], and is unable to quickly view it again. Later, when he is born into that heaven, his radiance is not very pure nor is his shape very large, and his death will certainly be premature.

[2] The middle level: The practioner, on viewing [this dharma], does not necessarily retreat, and even on retreat, is able to quickly regroup and view it again. Later, when he is born into that heaven, although his radiance is very pure and his shape large, they are still not at maximum. Although his death may be premature, that is uncertain.

[3] The higher level: The practitioner, on viewing [this dharma], necessarily does not retreat. After being born in that heaven, the purity of his radiance and vastness of his shape are at maximum. His death necessarily will not be premature; he will die only after having exhausted the full measure of his life.

This samāpatti is only encountered[112] in the fourth Dhyāna;[113] it is only kuśala, since that is what led to it; it does not exist in the higher or lower realms—as was previously explained.

These four[114] karmic [consequences] can be understood as three,[115] which are never experienced in the present.

THERE IS AN OPINION that this samāpatti only arises in the Kāma-dhātu, since it arises from the force of the teachings of the Tirthikas (Non-Buddhists), and because in humans wisdom and understanding are extremely astute.

THERE IS ANOTHER OPINION that those who have previously practiced in the Kāma-dhātu, after being born in the Rūpa-dhātu, are [then] able to view it. This excludes those (already) in the āsaṃjñi-loka, since that is the end (not the means).

Since this [samāpatti] is [motivated by] loathing toward saṃjñā and longing[116] for the fruit of entry, it is only *sāsrava* (contaminated), and not produced by Āryans.

[*Nirodha-samāpatti*]

Nirodha-samāpatti means there are Aśaikṣas or Śaikṣas who have already repressed or detached from the 'appropriational intent' (*rāga*) at the Ākiṃcanya (level, i.e., the Nothing level, the third ārūpya-dhātu); the 'appropriational intent' of the upper level (i.e., of Bhāvagra, the fourth ārūpya-dhātu) is indeterminate (i.e., it may or may not still be present[117]). Due to a previously made intention to stop saṃjñā, [that intention] makes the sporadic saṃskāras and the perpetual saṃskāras of defiled and impure citta and caittas cease. This establishes the term '*nirodha*' (cessation, 滅盡). Since it makes (令) the body peaceful and harmonious, it is also called *samāpatti*. Due to its inclination to reject *vedanā* and *saṃjñā*, it is also called the *saṃjña-vedita-nirodha-samāpatti* (attainment of the cessation of *saṃjñā* and *vedanā*).

There are three levels to practicing this samāpatti.

[1] The lower level: The practitioner, on viewing this dharma, necessarily retreats [from it], and is unable to quickly view it again.

[2] The middle level: The practioner, on viewing [this dharma], does not necessarily retreat, and even on retreat, is able to quickly regroup and view it again.

[3] The higher level: The practitioner finally does not retreat.

Initially the necessary prerequisite (*prayoga*) for entering into this *samāpatti* is uncontaminated (*anāśrava*) contemplation (*vipaśyanā*) in the Bhavāgra realm, since it occurs after the other *anupūrva-samāpattis*.[118] Although classified as included (屬) in Bhavāgra, it is categorized (攝) as 'uncontaminated.' Once one attains mastery in the cultivation of this *samāpatti*, one can subsequently make it present to one's mind, even from other realms.[119] Although classified as included in the *mārga-satya* (i.e., the fourth of the 4 noble truths, the Truth of Method/Path), it is categorized neither as Śaikṣa nor Aśaikṣa, since it is nirvana-like.[120]

The initial arising of this *samāpatti* only occurs in humans, since it arises from the power of the explanations of the Buddha and his disciples, and since in humans wisdom and understanding are most extremely astute. Subsequently, it may be experienced [from anywhere] in the two upper Dhātus (i.e., rūpa and ārūpya). This is confirmed by the *Udayi Sūtra* (鄔陀夷經) [which states that] Ārūpya [beings] are called "gods made by manas" (意成天, *mano-maya-devas*).

Those who have received but do not yet believe in the teachings on the Storing Consciousness, if they are born in the ārūpyā (realms), will not produce this *samāpatti*, since they will be afraid that the absence of rūpa and citta will entail their utter annihilation. If they already believe, then when born into those (realms) they will be able to experience (this *samāpatti*), knowing that, because the Store Consciousness exists, there is no annihilation.

The method for producing this *samāpatti* (requires) wanting to utterly extinguish (斷) (the defilements of) the Triple-World so that the *anuśayas* are utterly extinguished by Vision (*darśana*).[121] Since Pṛthagjanas are unable to repress or make the citta and caittas of Bhavāgra cease, this *samāpatti* is very subtle. Wanting to realize the two emptinesses (i.e., of self and dharmas) consequentially[122] leads to the arising [of this *samāpatti*].

THERE IS AN OPINION concerning which *anuśayas* (need to be) utterly extinguished in the cultivation of the eight prior levels (i.e., the Kāma-dhātu, Rūpa-dhātu, and the first three Ārūpya-dhyānas)(in order to attain cessation): those of the Kāma (realm need to be) completely extinguished, while the remaining may be either repressed or extinguished. This *samāpatti* [can only] initially arise after this has been achieved, since the two types of *anuśayas* of the Kāma-dhātu (non-advantageous and non-defined karmically) are troublesome and multifarious, and forcefully obstruct *samāpatti*. [The *Mahāyāna-saṃgraha śastra*] says that only the Non-returners, the Aśaikṣas of the Three Vehicles, and Bodhisattvas attain this *samāpatti*. Once one has attained it, one can re-produce it after being reborn in the upper eight levels.

THERE IS (ANOTHER) OPINION concerning which *anuśayas* (need to be) utterly extinguished during cultivation (in order to attain cessation): (Those of) the four lower levels (i.e., Kāma-dhātu and the first three rūpa-dhyānas) (need to be) utterly extinguished, while the remaining may be either repressed or extinguished. This *samāpatti* [can only] initially arise after this has been achieved, since the alterations (*pariṇāma*, 變) through different feelings (*vedanā*) together with the kleśic seeds forcefully obstruct *samāpatti*. Once one has attained it, one can reproduce it after being reborn in the upper five levels.

[Question:] If one who has (merely) repressed the lower anuśyas is able to produce this samāpatti, later, while not having utterly extinguished (the anuśayas), that one retreats to a birth in the higher levels (which became accessible through the attainment of this samāpatti); being born in a higher (level), will he have already actually extinguished (all) anuśayas below him?

[Answer:] There is no fault (in claiming that) they are extinguished, since this is like someone born in a higher (level) who extinguishes the lower anuśayas of the manas that he is born with (and yet manas per se remains).

Now the power of a Non-returner to oppose and control (his remaining anuśayas) is strong. Correctly 'moistening' (the seeds) of his (present) life, he doesn't produce any (new) kleśa; he (continues) to live only due to the moistening of the anuśaya seeds (remaining) from (previous lives in) the upper realms. Whether he retreated or didn't retreat from repressing his anuśayas (during earlier lives), the non-repressed (anuśayas) from the lower (realms led to) birth in higher realms. Hence (the argument) that without being born in the higher (realms) nevertheless the (anuśayas of the) lower (realm can be) extinguished fails.

If Bodhisattvas, while (practicing) in the previous two Vehicles (i.e., Śravaka and Pratyekabuddha), have already attained nirodha-samāpatti and then converted their mind (迴心) (to Mahāyāna), they will be able to produce this samāpatti in all the (subsequent Bodhisattva) stages (*bhūmi*, 位).

As for (Bodhisattvas for whom prior attainment of nirodha-samāpatti in the previous two Vehicles) is not the case, some may, upon reaching the full heart (滿心) of the seventh Bhūmi, become fully able to suppress all the kleśas. Even though they have not yet fully extinguished the anuśayas cultivated in the Kāmaloka,[123] yet it is as if they had already extinguished them; they are able to produce this samāpatti. The (*Yogācārabhūmi*) śāstra says: "Since they have already entered into the Dūraṅgana stage 遠位 (lit. "far-reaching" or "far-going" stage, i.e., seventh bhūmi), Bodhisattvas can produce nirodha-samāpatti."

There are some, like the Arhats, who subsequent to the first bhūmi are able to suppress all the kleśas so that in the rest of the ten bhūmis they may produce this samāpatti. Hence the (*Daśabhūmi*) Sūtra says: "Even Bodhisattvas in the first six bhūmis can produce nirodha-samāpatti."

Postscript

Even as such formulations became more refined and more finely etched, they were already becoming obsolete. The epistemo-logical wing of Yogācāra focused its energies on logic and epistemology, while the abhidharmic approach began to atrophy, becoming a matter of scholastic training in some Buddhist circles that at best provided students with rudimentary training, but by no means was considered adequate by itself to produce the higher fruits of Buddhist practice.

Starting with Dignāga, and more definitely after Dharmakīrti (7th century), the issues surrounding nirodha-samāpatti—such as the characteristics of pre-Awakening 'nirvana-like' cognition—were displaced by debates over *nirvikalpa-jñāna*, and sākāra-vādins vs. nirākāra-vādins (Awakened beings have or don't have mental images of things). The tri-dhātu meditational model itself was replaced by (1) rigorous epistemology, and (2) embellishments on the prajñāpāramitā as a path with multiple stages, such as the ten stages of Bodhisattva practive (*daśabhūmi*).

Chart 2 (next page) summarizes some of the differing notions of nirodha-samāpatti noted in this chapter.

Having now been introduced to the intricate, complicated style of abhidharmic literature, in Part Three we will step back to view some general Buddhist trends that will bear on our later examination of some different issues in the *Ch'eng wei-shih lun*. But first we will quickly review some salient features of the the four models.

Visuddhimagga	*Kośa*	YBh	CWSL
attained by: will-power, effort, thought; fulfilling prerequisite conditions (on the māgga); samatha + vipassanā	attained by: blocking cognitive processes, due to previous intent (vow); fulfilling prerequisites; Buddhas require no effort, but others do	arises in due course of progress in the Bodhisattva bhūmis (usually the 7th bhūmi, but exceptions)	attained by: eliminating anuśayas and fulfilling conditions (a variety of scenarios admitted) Must believe in ālaya-vijñāna only vipaśyanā
no thought or feeling, but still involves saṅkhāra of saṅkhata (embodied-conditioning from prior conditioning)	(dhyānas are not "bodily") but nirodha-samāpatti is experienced directly by body, not mind (*kāya-sākṣin*, body-witness)	ālaya-vijñāna operating, but the 6 pravṛtti-vijñānas and manas have stopped	samāpatti = tranquil body; ālaya operating, but the 6 pravṛtti-vijñānas and manas have stopped
beyond Bhavāgra (attained from 4th arūpa-jhāna)	beyond Bhavāgra (attained from 3rd or 4th ārūpya-dhyāna)	beyond Bhavāgra	uncontaminated Bhavāgra
nirodha is negative, but Arhathood is positive, hence it is nirvāṇa-like, but not the climactic, soteric moment, though penultimate, and seemingly a necessary condition for Awakening	must return to 'Nothing' level (3rd ārūpya-dhyāna) after nirodha to eliminate remaining anuśayas; Immediate condition for Buddhahood, but not sufficient condition	Nirodha attainable after 1st bhūmi, but becomes likely in 7th	Not the final soteric moment. Still need to traverse the remainder of the 10 bhūmis. Nirodha attainable after 1st bhūmi, but becomes likely in 7th
accessible by Anāgamins and Arhats	accessible by Anāgamins and Arhats (Śaikṣas and Aśaikṣas)	accessible by Śaikṣas and Aśaikṣas	Accessible by Anāgamins and Aśaikṣas of the 3 Vehicles (Śrāvaka, Pratyeka-buddha, Mahāyāna)

Chart 2

Notes

1 The Four satyas (lit., "actualities") are: 1. Duḥkha, all is 'suffering' (symptom); 2. Samudāya, suffering has a 'cause' (diagnosis); 3. Nirodha, the cause can be eliminated or 'extinguished' (prognosis); and 4. Mārga, the path or 'method' for extinguishing the cause (prescription,

treatment). According to tradition, Buddha announced these four 'actualities' in one of his first sermons after Awakening.

2 However that etymology is often challenged. The Pāli texts tend to prefer *vṛ* (to cover; i.e., putting out a fire by suffocating or smothering it) or *nis* + *vana* (without craving). Cf. Rhys-Davids and Stede, *Pāli-English Dictionary*, PTS, p. 362.

3 The Fire Sermon, in which Buddha declares that this whole world is aflame with desire, is traditionally taken, by the Theravādin tradition, to be his first sermon.

4 Axiomatic to Buddhism is that materiality itself is not a problem; it is the *ideas* one has about materiality, how one values or evaluates it, that leads to problems. More importantly, it is the ideas and notions that we cling to in order to constitute our own sense of identity, i.e., the ideas we identify with and with which we create our sense of identity, that lie at the root of all our problems. These ideas, *dṛṣṭi*—the most pernicious being *ātma-dṛṣṭi*, the idea of self—constitute the ignorance that blocks our awakening to things as they actually become (*yathā bhūtam*).

5 E.g., *Triṃśikā* 5: *...vartate srotasaugha-vat.*

6 The notion of Original Enlightenment (本覺, C: *pen-chüeh*, J: *hongaku*), an important feature of the Chinese apocryphal *Awakening of Faith*, strongly influenced the development of East Asian Buddhism, and eventually exerted influence in Tibet as well.

7 This is the orthodox Yogācāra position, and, as we'll see shortly, apparently also the position of Buddhaghosa.

8 A detailed list of occurrences in the Pāli Tipiṭaka of the terms *āsava, āsavānaṃ khaya*, etc., can be found in *Pāli-English Dictionary*, p. 115.

9 Edgerton's *Buddhist Hybrid Sanskrit Dictionary* offers the following questionable meaings: "evil influence, depravity, evil, sin, misery" (p. 111b).

10 *Mahāvastu* i.248.10f: *sarveṣāṃ arhatāṃ kṣīṇāśravāṇām uṣitavratānāṃ samyagājñāsu-vimuktacittānāṃ parikṣīṇabhavasaṃyojanānām anuprāptasva-kārthānām.* Cf. *Vinaya* i.183.24 for a similar formula.

11 I am using 'Abhidharma' to designate the literature of the Sanskrit-using Abhidharmists (Vaibhāṣika, Mahīśāsika, Saṃmitīya, etc.), as opposed to the Pāli Abhidhamma.

12 *Pāli-English Dictionary*, p. 114: "ā + sru would correspond to a [Sanskrit] *āsrava, cp. Sk. āsrāva. The B[uddhist Hybrid Sanskrit] āśrava is a (wrong) sanskritisation of the Pāli āsava..." [square brackets mine]. *Āsava*, in Sanskrit, means "distilling, distillation... liquor, juice," flower nectar (Monier-Williams, *A Sanskrit-English Dictionary*, p. 160c. An Āsāva is "a priest who presses out the Soma juice" (*ibid.*). *Āsrāva* means "flow, issue, running, discharge... suppuration... pain, affliction; a particular disease of the body... the objects of sense..." (*ibid.*, p. 162a), though apparently some of these meanings are derived from the Buddhist usage as well as Vedic sacrifice. *Āsrava* means "the foam on boiling rice... a door opening into water and allowing the stream to descend through it..." (*ibid.*).

13 Attributed to the Andhakas, who base their position on *Saṃyutta Nikāya* iv.252.

14 Citing the *Paṭisambhidāmagga* i.71, and *Dhammasaṅgaṇī* 1408.

15 In Theravādin and Abhidharmic literature one passes through four stages on the way to Awakening: 1. A Stream-Enterer, who is now on course toward Awakening. Some texts hold that upon entering this stage, one still has seven more lives to live before reaching the goal. 2. A Once-Returner, who will have to be reborn just one more time before achieving final Awakening. 3. A Non-Returner, who will achieve Awakening in this very life (though some later texts claim that even though a Non-Returner will not have to return to a human life before achieving Nirvana, he may be reborn in a Buddha-heaven to complete his studies). 4. An Arhat, a fully Awakened human.

16 The paths and achievements of the four types listed in the previous note.

17 This argument is suggestive, but not conclusive, since its cogency depends on what 'measureless' entails. Numerous passages from the Nikāyas could be cited here that would put such a positivist spin on the term 'measureless' into question, but this question is beyond the scope of the present discussion.

18 Literally, the "upside-down" or "reversals": 1. Seeing the impermanent as permanent, 2. seeing the selfless as having Self, 3. seeing the impure as pure, and 4. seeing duḥkha as happiness.

19 "Inherent" because acquired from previous experience, and in the cosmological formulations of Abhidharma, often discussed as acquired from previous lives.

20 In this sense, *bhavāsava* is retained in later Buddhist formulas as the fundamental problem, particularly by those who hold that the deepest problem is *jñeyāvaraṇa* (obstruction of the known) and that *ātma-dṛṣṭi* is a synonym for *jñeyāvaraṇa* (e.g., Śāntarakṣita's *Tattvasaṃgraha,* Hsüan-tsang's *Ch'eng wei-shih lun,* etc.).

21 See Appendix C.

22 *Kośa* chapter 5. Depending on how one counts, the *Kośa* lists either 98 or 108 anuśayas. The initial six proliferate by being subdivided. For instance, 'attachment' becomes two (attachment to pleasure and to existence), *dṛṣṭi* is subdivided into five dṛṣṭis, each counted as a distinct anuśaya, etc.

23 Leo Pruden's translation, *Abhidharmakośa-bhāṣyam,* v. 3, p. 767. Square brackets mine.

24 Even the later Theravādin tradition, while retaining the original terms, mystifies the process, thus also making it more indirect. For example, the commentary to *Majjhima Nikāya* (usually attributed to Buddhaghosa) at i.223f says:

> ...the āsavas of sense-pleasures and becoming are, through co-arising, the causes of ignorance... Ignorance is the cause, through co-arising, of the āsavas of sense-pleasures and becoming... This exposition of the āsavas is spoken of as an explanation of the conditions of that primary ignorance listed in *paticca-samuppāda.* By this exposition, the fact that the end of samsāric existence is *inconceivable* is proved. How? From the arising of ignorance is the arising of āsavas, from the arising of āsavas is the arising of ignorance. Having made the āsavas the cause of ignorance and ignorance the cause of the āsavas, the earliest point of ignorance is not perceptible, therefore the fact that the end of samsāric existence is *inconceivable* is proved." (cited in *Middle Length Sayings* I, p. 69, n. 2, slightly modified).

The subtle privileging of ignorance over the other āsavas combined with the air of inconceivability—something the Nikāyas would strenuously deny—leads to a mystification of the āsavas requiring indirect grappling. That there was, however, a tradition of generating dialectical pairings of nidānas was discussed in chapter four.

25 I have followed the translation in *Kindred Sayings* IV, p. 146, with some alterations. I have added the numbers in square brackets.

26 While later Buddhists in many countries came to argue about sudden vs. gradual, the Nikāyas uniformly and repeatedly insist that practice is gradual.

27 E.g., *Majjhima Nikāya* #25 (I.160). I have followed *Middle Length Sayings* I, p. 203, with alterations.

28 *Ibid.* Cf. also *Majjhima Nikāya* #26 (I.174-175).

29 *On Being Mindless* (La Salle, IL: Open Court, 1986) 11; he repeats that claim in "Indian Buddhist Meditation," in *Buddhist Spirituality,* ed. by TAKEUCHI Yoshinori (NY: Crossroads, 1995) 41.

30 Though some later Abhidharmists did argue that rūpa exists in the ārūpya-dhātu. The *Kośa rejects* the argument that there is some rūpa, even 'subtle rūpa, in the ārūpya-dhātus with detailed arguments. Cf. Pruden, *Abhidharmakośa Bhāṣya,* p. 1281 n. 21, for a discussion of various schools that claim that rūpa in rūpa- and ārūpya-dhātus arises from *karma.* Cf. p. 1286 n. 38; the *Vibhāṣā*: argues there must be rūpa in ārūpya-dhātu, otherwise there would be no way to restart rūpa when one is reborn in one of the other dhātus.

31 Aśvaghoṣa's *Buddhacarita* reiterates that Buddha's significant supplement to the meditative teachings in the forest was the discovery of this added level.

32 Conze renders *appaṇihita* as "wishless," and though it is far from a perfect rendering, I will use it in the following discussion since it is less awkward than 'lacking intentionality' (which is also imperfect) and is probably more familiar to English readers. *Appaṇihita* means not being directed toward or by desire while perceiving objects, i.e., having physical and mental sensations devoid of appropriational intent. The importance of this will be discussed below.

33 E.g., Majj. #44 (I.302); S. VI.6 (*Kindred Sayings* IV, pp. 200ff), etc.

34 S. VI.1 (*Kindred Sayings* IV, pp. 179ff).

35 Majj. #121; S. VI.7 (*Kindred Sayings* IV, pp. 204ff), etc.

36 *Middle Length Sayings* I, p.365, modified; Cf. S. VI.7: *suññato animitto appaṇihito phasso* (*Kindred Sayings* IV, p. 203).

37 *Kindred Sayings* IV, p. 205, modified.

38 *Cūḷasuññata sutta.* I cite *Middle Length Sayings* III, pp. 150ff, modified. Cf. S. VI ch. 40, which gives an extended account of Moggalāna's meditative attainments. Moggalāna was considered the most accomplished disciple in meditation (though Anuruddha was considered the most accomplished in clairvoyance, i.e., reading other minds; cf. *Middle Length Sayings* I, p. 262). Moggalāna does not mention 'cognitive and sensory cessation,' but climaxes his acquiring of the abhiññās (superknowledges) with *animitta ceto-samādhi* (concentration of mind on the signless). Cf. *Kindred Sayings* IV, p. 185.

39 Unlike the Mahāyānic mischaracterization of 'Hīnayāna' as only understanding the emptiness of self, but not the emptiness of dharmas, the Nikāyas speak explicitly about emptiness as applied to all the dharmas. Cf. e.g., *Kindred Sayings* IV, p. 2 and p. 29.

40 *Kindred Sayings* IV, pp. 101f, modified. Cf. pp. 157.

41 *Ibid.*, p. 34.

42 *Middle Length Sayings* I, p. 356; *Kindred Sayings* IV, pp. 200ff.

43 E.g., *Visuddhimagga* XVII.134. XVII.192: beings in this loka only has life-faculty (= rūpa) as their basis; *ibid.*.201, kamma-formation consciousness is a ...decisive-support condition (*nissaya paccaya*) for the rūpa of asaññisatta (no-thought beings). I have largely followed Bhikkhu Ñāṇamoli's translation, *The Path of Purification* (Kandy: Buddhist Publication Society, 1975) in the discussion that follows.

44 The Fruition attainments are the attaining of fruit (i.e., receiving effects) as a Stream-Enterer, Once-Returner, Non-Returner, or Arhat. These are the fruit from developing good kamma over many lifetimes.

45 The commentary, attributed to Buddhaghosa, glosses 'signless sphere' as the unconditioned (*asaṅkhāta*), i.e., nibbāna.

46 The commentary (M.A.ii.365) already subverts the point, by relocating such thinking in the past. Accordingly one *does* have such thoughts, but in a past moment sufficiently removed from the time one actually enters the samāpatti. One thinks: 'At that time I will become without mind.' This supplement becomes definitive for later Buddhist thought, and draws on comparable discussions of the arūpa-meditations elsewhere in the Majj. However, nowhere in the Nikāyas are such thoughts attributed to one entering 'cessation.' On the contrary, they are explicitly denied.

47 Speech ceases in the first jhāna; body in the fourth; and mind in nirodha-samāpatti.

48 Buddhaghosa lived well after Asaṅga and Vasubandhu, and in many places shows Yogācāric influence in his thinking. A systematic survey of his work for signs of such influence must remain a desideratum.

49 At XXIII.51 he does quote M.i.296: the three saṅkhāras of body, speech and mind cease, life is unexhausted, heat has not subsided, and one's faculties are quite whole - unlike death in which the latter three have subsided.

50 Again, even more directly contradicting the Nikāyas. Buddhaghosa explains "in bliss" as meaning "without dukkha".

51 XXIII.18: *Ya anupubbanirodhvasena cittacetasikānaṃ dhammānaṃ appavatti.*

52 I have used the text in Nārada Mahā Thera, ed. & tr., *A Manual of Abhidhamma*. Kuala Lampur: Buddhist Missionary Society, 1979, 4th revised edition, which contains the Pāli text, an English translation, and a running commentary by the translator. I have also consulted Jagdish Kashyap's treatment of the text in *Abhidhamma Philosophy* (Delhi: Bharatiya Vidya Prakashan, 1982).

53 Cf. p. 235f, for a detailed list of the denizens of the rūpa and arūpa lokas.

54 P. 227, based largely on Buddhaghosa.

55 4.11: *...nirodhasamāpattikāle dvikkhattuṃ catutthā ruppajavanaṃ javati. Tato paraṃ nirodhaṃ phusati. Vuṭṭhānakāle ca anāgāmi phalaṃ vā arahattaphalaṃ vā yathāraham' ekavāraṃ uppajjitvā niruddhe bhavaṅgapāto' va hoti.* (p. 224)

56 Ñāṇamoli translates *javana* as 'impulsion' -- it literally means 'speed' -- they are the initial moments in a thought-series that direct its karmic consequences.

57 *Sabbatthā' pi samāpatthivithiyaṃ pana bhavaṅgasote viya vithiniyamo natthi' ti katvā bahūni pilabbhanti ti. (veditabbaṃ) Op. cit.*

58 II.45b-bhāṣya; Pruden, p. 237.

59 The *Kośa* and other Abhidharma texts spend a great deal of time differentiating between what a particular realm is like for a meditator as against what it is like for one actually reborn there as a denizen. For instance, beings born in the first Dhyāna have all six senses, but that's not true of meditators who visit, since dhyānas are *not* bodily (*kāyena*); "The five consciousnesses are absent in a person who has entered into contemplation." VIII.9b-bhāṣya.

60 II.41b-42g-bhāṣya; Pruden, pp. 221-4, describes their abode in the 4th Dhyāna.

61 *Ibid.* Since it is vipāka, it is morally neutral, not good; therefore useless for the Path. But cf. IV.9b; Pruden, p. 574.

62 VI.13a-bhāṣya; Pruden, p. 924.

63 II.42-bhāṣya; Pruden, pp. 223-5.

64 VIII.16ab-bhāṣya; Pruden, p. 1246.

65 II.44de-bhāṣya

66 VIII.20ab.

67 *Ibid.*, bhāṣya.

68 This may be part of the *Kośa*'s notion of something positive coming at the culmination of the project, even though the final jñānas are negative: Knowledge of Destruction and Knowledge of Non-Arising.

69 VI.43cd-bhāṣya; Pruden, p. 1273-4.

70 *Visuddhimagga* XXI.77.

71 II.42g and bhāṣya; Pruden, p. 224.

72 II.44a-bhāṣya; Pruden, p. 226.

73 II.43g.

74 Translated by Hsüan-tsang in the late winter of 646, his second year back in China.

75 This is followed by a passage similar to the passage from Asaṅga's *Hsien-ch'ang lun* cited below.

76 Hsüan-tsang started his translation of this text soon after returning to China in 645, and completed it in 647. It is a voluminous, encyclopedic text; T.30.1579, 100 fascicles.

77 Fasc. 53, line 13ff. The pravṛtti-vijñānas are the first six consciousnesses, i.e., the five sense-consciousnesses and the mano-vijñāna. Sometimes the term includes manas as well.

78 This follows the Sautrāntikas, contra the Vaibhāṣikas.

79 Fasc. 56, line 1:

80 T.1602.21, 1st fasc., line 14.

81 T.31.1585.25b23-c9.

82 Cf. Tat, *Ch'eng Wei-shih lun*, pp. 330ff. However, a bit earlier CWSL argued that according to YBh, the ālaya-vijñāna always operates with at least one other consciousness. Since the six pravṛtti consciousnesses are clearly not present in nirodha-samāpatti, manas *must* be present, albeit in a purified form. CWSL, however, seems to overlook this theoretical inconsistency.

83 *Triṃśikā* 7 mentions three conditions in or for which manas does not exist: For an arhat, during cessation samāpatti, and in the supra-mundane path (*lokottara-mārga*). This verse does not mention āsaṃjñi-samāpatti, so the *Ch'eng wei-shih lun* is arguing that this omission is not accidental but an indication that manas does function during āsaṃjñi-samāpatti.

84 無如是失.

85 有過.

86 彼非現常.

87 'Perceived' renders *so-te* 所得 which literally means 'what is attained'; 'perceiver' translates *neng-te* 能得, lit. 'what is able to attain.' The *neng/so* construction is used in Chinese to distinguish subjective (doer, agent) and objective (passive, locus). This will be discussed in more detail in chapter sixteen. The present passage tersely argues something like this: Manas essentially consists of self-concern, ātma-grāha, the 'I, me, mine' propensity to appropriate. Therefore, in order to function, it must have something to appropriate. If there are no ālambana to appropriate, then it cannot function, and whatever doesn't function—according to Buddhist criteria (see chapter seventeen)—is nonexistent. Therefore, since āsaṃjñi-samāpatti is without object-content, it cannot have manas.

88 The *viprayukta-samskāras*, enumerated in the list of 100 hundred dharmas (see appendices 1 and 2), are considered mere prajñapti by the *Ch'eng wei-shih lun*, not real (*dravya*), and hence incapable of doing anything. They are merely nominal signifiers.

89 藏識.

90 熏習.

91 The argument here is this: The opponent has offered as axiomatic that in the absence of something grasped, a grasper does not exist. By extension, therefore, there can be no manas in āsaṃjñi-samāpatti. Non-Yogācāra schools do not recognize the ālaya-vijñāna, and so are left to account for things like the continuity of karma through multiple rebirths without it. The *Ch'eng wei-shih lun* exploits this to argue (i) that karma is transmitted by vāsanās (karmic impressions), and (ii) these can only reside in a consciousness. (iii) Since you, the opponent, only admit manas, but not the ālaya-vijñāna, manas must do the work of transmission of karma for you, and hence, according to your system, it must be present—which is what we Yogācārins claim anyhow. (iv) We have no difficulty with karmic transmission taking place without a manas, because it is transmitted by the ālaya-vijñāna. Implication: Why don't you become a Yogācārin and eliminate your doctrinal confusion?

92 染汙末那.

93 T.31.1585.37a24-38a21. Cf. Tat, pp. 480ff.

94 麤動.

95 所藉眾緣時多不具.

96 違緣.

97 有色支, rūpa+aṅga, i.e., the rūpa portion of nāma-rūpa.

98 為無心地.

99 如餘本有初必有轉識故. Yogācāra, and some other schools, use a seed metaphor to account for karmic continuance. Actions produce seeds, which are planted in the ālaya-vijñāna and then 'watered' (moistened) and nourished until they sprout as new actions, that will produce seeds in turn.

100 暫; temporarily = momentary.

101 宿因緣力.

102 引起. Generally karmic actions are either kuśala (advantageous, wholesome), akuśala (disadvantageous, unwholesome) or karmically neutral (avyākta). Neutral usually means that a particular action or mental condition is not intrinsically either kuśala or akuśala, but can become either kuśala or akuśala, depending on circumstances. Drowsiness, for instance, is karmically neutral, since if one has worked a hard day and needs some rest, sleepiness is good (kuśala); if one is driving a bus, severe drowsiness would be akuśala. This passage claims that the two samāpattis are honorifically labeled kuśala - because of the kuśala practices that led

to them - even though they are actually only avyākta. In the case of the samāpattis, since one cannot think or *do* anything, they can never be anything but neutral.

103 Lit.: 'stillness of anxious-thought' 第四靜慮.

104 Lit.: 'affect', 思能感.

105 Citta is sometimes a synonym for the ālaya-vijñāna, and sometimes a broader term covering all the consciousness. The *Ch'eng wei-shih lun* is arguing that *acitta* (no citta) in this passage does not mean absence of the ālaya-vijñāna, but only the absence of the pravṛtti-vijñānas.

106 異生.

107 遍淨

108 Usually the third class of rūpāvacara gods in the third dhyāna-bhūmi. The other two are Apramāṇaśubha and Parīttaśubha.

109 伏貪. 伏 is usually contrasted with 斷, the latter signifying utterly extinguishing the defilement, while the former means temporary suppression.

110 令不恒行心心所滅. This could also be translated: 'forces the cittas and caittas of the sporadic samskāras to cease.'

111 The samāpattis are counted among the one hundred dharmas. See appendix 1.

112 屬.

113 Lit.: 'stillness of anxious-thought' 第四靜慮.

114 Exactly what the 'four' are is not clear. Possibly: 1. premature death. 2&3. premature or not premature. 4. full life.

115 四業通三.

116 欣 , lit. 'delight,' 'happy'.

117 I.e., it would be present in those not yet Awakened but not present in those already Awakened.

118 *Anupūrva* means "narrowing," "successive process," "in the course of time" (cf. Edgerton, *Buddhist Hybrid Sanskrit Dictionary,* II, 30). *Anupūrva-samāpatti* is a designation for the sequence of eight (or nine) dhyānas starting in the rūpa-dhātu through to the top of the ārūpya-dhātu.

119 Unlike some of the previous theories, here nirodha-samāpatti is entered within Bhāvagra, in which it seems to form the highest vestibule. One can only get rid of desire in the Nothing sphere, which is one of the prerequisites for attaining cessation, but one has to be in Bhāvagra in a desireless state in order to enter nirodha-samāpatti. What the present passage is saying is that, once one has achieved mastery of the samāpatti, one can enter it from anywhere, not just from Bhāvagra.

120 似涅槃.

121 The Darśana-mārga is one of the crucial five stages in Yogācāra practice. This will be discussed in a later chapter.

122 *Pṛṣṭhalabdha,* 後得.

123 Again this plays on the opposition, common in Abhidharmic literature, between 伏 and 斷. See above.

Chapter Eight

Summary of the Four Models

The notion of skandhas (P. *khandha*) serves not only to decentralize what it is we consider to be a person by (i) denying that any part or aspect of that person remains constant, eternal, while other parts observably change, and (ii) asserting that persons are not self-contained wholes, but rather are conditioned and constituted by the aggregation of mutually dependent and changing parts. It also serves as a declaration against any metaphysical claims concerning 'personhood,' 'soul,' human 'nature or essence,' in short, it forecloses the possibility of asserting that anything lies behind or outside the economy of the human sensorium in which sensations and experiences are in perpetual fluctuation. Since everything experienced lacks true constancy, no constants may be asserted without violating the exhaustive givens of experience.

The sensorium, as stated earlier, includes mental and conscious acts (e.g., the mental apprehension of mental objects), as well as the activities of the five senses. Since the sensorium is all-inclusive—such that nothing which is incapable of being experienced may be admitted, and we are never located anywhere other than within it, and duḥkha arises by way of a non-recognition (*avidyā*) of the conditions (*hetu-pratyaya*) that enact and control the sensorial economy, viz. saṃsāra—epistemology became the crucial entry into and linchpin for Buddhist soterics. Epistemology in this sense includes not only general theories of knowledge, but it signifies a deliberate focus and sustained gaze on the intersection of the issues of perception, valuation, judgement, logic, validation, criteriology, psychology, etc., in short, the entire gamut of fields raised by the question 'How do we know?,' concisely encapsulated in Buddhist thought as the 'double obstructions,' viz. the cognitive and affective obstructions (*jñeyāvaraṇa* and *kleśāvaraṇa*) preventing us from seeing things as they actually become.

Moreover, since sensorial confusion is saṃskāric—i.e., driven by unconscious, presuppositional embodied conditioning—philosophy, psychology and linguistics become the critical sciences. Therefore the *nāma* side of the skandhas (as nāma-rūpa) takes precedence. The model was always tipped in this direction, since there are four nāmic skandhas to only one rūpic skandha. This imbalance increases. Abhidhammic discussions of the skandhas frequently replace the term *rūpa* with the term *phassa* (contact, S. *sparśa*), meaning that materiality could be reduced to considerations of how the four nāmic skandhas experienced and appropriated it. This is significant, since Yogācāra in the main treats rūpa as a viable category of karmic significance only to the extent it is understood as 'sensory contact'; their concern is with *how* rūpa is cognitively appropriated and how those appropriations affect and influence cognitive processes rather than what it might be in-itself.

Further, despite the seemingly empirical basis upon which Buddhism grounded itself, inferentials also had to be admitted. Things which were perhaps potentially perceivable, but not perceived at present, were knowable only through inference. For Early Buddhists this included not only places some particular person had never been, but Nirvāṇa and even the existence of Buddha himself.[1] In meditation practice, the realm of inferentials was dealt with as saṃskāras i.e., cognitive latencies. Like Husserlian transcendentals, saṃskāras by definition do not reveal themselves entirely within the moment in which they discharge their functioning. They carry the latencies and tendencies engendered and embodied from one moment into some subsequent moment. When the latencies do emerge, they emerge as volitions (*cetanā*), so that the abhidhammic literature often replaces the term *saṅkhāra* with the term *cetanā* when discussing the skandhas.

Most important, the skandhas are rarely if ever discussed in Pāli literature as if they were metaphysical components of a person, despite accusations to that effect in some Mahāyānic texts. More often than not they are discussed as *upādānakkhandha*, i.e., the 'appropriational aggregates.' Rupert Gethin, in a superlative article on the *khandhas*, states:[2]

> A *khandha-saṃyutta* passage states that the *khandhas* are to be considered *upādānakhandhas* only when they are with āsavas (*sāsava*) and subject to grasping (*upādāniya*).[3] In another passage that recurs several times in the *Nikāyas*, the question is asked whether *upādāna* should be considered the same as *upādānakkhandhas* or whether there is *upādāna* apart from them.[4] In reply it is stated that although *upādāna* is not the same as the five *upādānakkhandhas* there is no *upādāna* apart from them; *upādāna* is then defined as "whatever is will and passion (*chandarāga*) in respect to the five *upādānakkhandhas*".... The early *abhidhamma* texts clarify *upādāna*'s relationship to the *khandhas* under three principal headings: active grasping (*upādāna*), subject to grasping (*upādāniya*), and the product of grasping (*upādiṇṇa*). *Upādāna* as an active force is confined to *saṅkhārakkhandha*, although all five *khandhas* are potentially the objects of *upādāna*—that is, are *upādāniya*; similarly all five *khandhas* are said to be in some measure the products of *upādāna*—that is, *upādiṇṇa*.

Gethin offers the following note: "Four *khandhas* are not *upādāna*, *saṃkhārakkhandha* may or may not be; *rūpakkhandha* is *upādāniya*, four *khandhas* may or may not be; all five *khandhas* may or may not be *upādiṇṇa*, Vibh 67." For now we will merely note that according to the *Vibhaṅga* (the second abhidhamma text of the Pāli canon) (i) that whereas the four *nāmic* skandhas may or may not be graspable, rūpa *always* is, (ii) rūpa may be 'the product of grasping,' i.e., appropriation can give rise to materiality, and (iii) only *saṅkhāra* can 'actively appropriate.' This confers a special status on saṃskāra. Later in this paragraph Gethin writes:

> The early *abhidhamma* texts also state that *rūpakkhandha* is always considered to be with *āsavas* and subject to grasping, and that the only time when the four mental *khandhas* are not such—that is, in *nikāya* terminology, are not *upādānakkhandhas*—is on the occasions of the four *ariya* paths and fruits.

Yogācāra will expand on this, making 'appropriation' (*upādāna*) the cardinal problematic particularly as engendered in the grasper-grasped or noetic-noemic opposition (*grāhaka-grāhya*).

Pratītya-samutpāda should not exactly be taken as a *causal* formula, though it was sometimes pressed into service in that capacity by the Sarvāstivādin and Theravādin schools. By modern Western standards, pratītya-samutpāda might best be considered a case of a theory of 'conditionals,' which means it falls short of being a 'hard' causal theory.[5] The classic formula, "if P, then Q," with which *pratītya-samutpāda* is often encapsulated, is also the classic formula for logical conditionals. This should not disturb the Buddhist, who, despite the mass of modern literature that discusses 'Buddhist causality,' was invariably more interested and concerned with *conditions* (*pratyaya*) than with causes (*hetu*). Since the formula generally is applied to *conditioning factors and sequences* in the mental, psychological, cognitive sphere, rather than the domain of sheer matter—so that even matter is invariably viewed from the point of view of how it is cognized—pratītya-samutpāda should be understood as a formula or description of psychosophic conditioning.

That the twelve links form a circle, such that they encircle and recycle, indicates that, while operating, they form a *closure* in which there seems to be no absolute beginning or end. Nidāna #12 leads to #1 and #1 presupposes #12. That this 'encirclement' (*saṃvṛti*) is bondage (*sambandha*) suggests that the closure must be *erased*. Thus, when there is no avidyā, then there is no saṃskāra, and so on. The links, their configuration, how they relate to each other, how their descriptions interweave with each other, etc., all establish pratītya-samutpāda as a model designed to set coordinates for self-examination. But this self-examination does not aim at a metaphysical subjectivity that reflects on itself or its own intuitions. To examine the self by Buddhist methods, is to examine experiential conditions. *Pratītya-samutpāda* thus marks the crucial Buddhist doctrine: *conditionality*.

The *tri-dhātu* demarcates the existential horizons as they are constituted and deconstituted through experience and examination. As a paradigmatic tool its two major lessons are: (i) all experience is contextual, contextualized by the 'realm' (desire, formal, aformal) through which it and its meanings are generated, and (ii) that each context is constituted by a margin that breaks down into ever larger, more inclusive contexts until contextuality itself is revealed as nothing other than the activity of marginality. At the 'peak' of the ārūpya-dhyānas, two of the skandhas, viz. rūpa and vijñāna, are thoroughly eclipsed; the eclipse of rūpa is the condition for entering the **ā**-rūpa dhyānas initially, and the vijñāna horizon has been eclipsed by its own contingency at the Nothing level. At the 'peak' (in the Eight dhyāna version of the model) two other skandhas stand undecidably across the marginal chiasm, their efficacy and potency at once paralyzed and empowered by this marginal undecidability. With pain/pleasure perceptuality (*vedanā*) and associative-thinking (*saṃjñā*) thus stymied and stilled, the one remaining skandha, *saṃskāra*, the dynamic of causal and psychological conditionality, emerges in stark relief. Neither with nor without vedanā and saṃjñā, the margin which both separates these possibilities and is constituted by their mutually opposing impossibility eclipses itself as it becomes a penumbra to saṃskāra, which itself signifies the margin between conscious and unconscious, freedom and conditioning, karma and nirvāṇa. Buddhist meditation seeks insight into this dynamic.

The trialectic factors of śīla-samādhi-prajñā *prescribe* the 'attitudinal' basis for self-correction. As a model, they map the procedures for observing (*vipassanā*) and disrupting (e.g., the ana-gamin, lit. 'non-goer') and ultimately overcoming (*nirodha*) the karmic flow (*saṃsāra, saṃskṛta-sambandha,* etc.).

Indian Buddhism, at its core, provides a detailed analysis of sensation, the causes and consequences of interaction within the sensorium. Sparśa, 'impact'—often pictorially represented by an arrow piercing the eye—is the moment of collision between a poised, conditioned, intentional embodiment and the sensorial circumstances in which it is embedded and in which it moves and experiences.

Modern treatments of Buddhism—especially introductory works—tend to emphasize the moralistic side of Buddhism. For instance, the Four Noble Truths are often reduced to the second and fourth truths, with 'desire' rather than 'ignorance' identified as the cause of suffering; and the fourth truth is reduced to the Noble Eightfold Path with its concomitants, of which the moralistic aspects, such as right action and compassion, are emphasized. Sometimes treatments shroud Buddhism in a romantic haze, with a twinge of mystery, emphasizing the meditation side, as if that were either an end in itself, or the absolutely necessary prerequisite for attaining the Buddhist goal.The earliest Buddhist ethics and moralism were not aimed at providing a comprehensive social ethic, however, since, beyond some general rules of good behavior for the laity, the purpose of Buddhist ethics was not the construction of a better human society as much as achieving ultimate liberation from the vicissitudes of the human condition. The ideal type was the monk/nun or renunciant who lived a life best understood as located on the margins of society, both in a physical as well as philosophical sense. Physically, monks/nuns lived near, not in, villages, so as to facilitate daily begging for food as well as to be available to council and teach laypeople, and yet the bulk of their practice ideally took place in solitude, alone, in a quiet spot. The Theravāda Vinaya stipulates that monks and nuns have until noon to enter town and seek food, but by afternoon they were no longer allowed to eat, and instead were to retreat from town, find a quiet, uninhabited place, and engage in practice. They were neither full participants in normal community life, nor were they absolutely isolated from it: A middle way, a way of being in a margin. Curiously, in the early texts there seem to be at least as many practitioners reaching Arhathood during conversations and interactions with others (such as Buddha), as reached it during solitary practice. The story of Buddha's Awakening while sitting solitary under the Bodhi Tree, after he had left his home and family behind, however, stands as the obvious prototype for the solitary practitioner.

Prajñā is, above all, a *practical* knowledge (*jñā*), which is emphasized by the *pra-* prefix (cognate to *pro-* in English), indicating a 'moving towards.' What sort of knowledge is this? Generally it involves a breakdown of the factors of sensation and experience. These factors came to be called *dharmas*, 'upholders,' and were related to the sense of Dharma as 'Teaching, Norm, True Doctrine (*saddharma*),' in that they are the true factors revealed by proper analysis of the dynamics of mind and sensation. Analysis in Buddhism is always at least in part, self-analysis. One does not acquire knowledge or insight merely to know a fact, as if one were a disinterested or unaffected observer. Rather one analyzes and strives to know in order to improve oneself, to better understand how one has become what one is at this moment, and how one can move, change, in a manner that reduces and ultimately eliminates pernicious views and drives. One does this not only for one's own benefit, but in order to become more effective in assisting others to do likewise. The most potent and common description of what constitutes Awakening in the early literature is 'the *destruction* of the āsavas,' āsavas being the deep-core, embodied, conditioned proclivities that bind one to the sufferings of the rounds of saṃsāra. Even as later Buddhists replaced the term āsava with others (*kleśa, anuśaya, vāsanā*, etc.), the general program of rooting out and eliminating saṃskāra remained central.

Analysis of sensation—as laid out in the skandha and pratītya-samutpāda models, and extended to elaborate lengths (especially in Abhidharmic literature)—provides the key antidote to ignorance. And, as the pratītya-samutpāda model states: On the basis of ignorance, there is saṃskāra; in the absence of ignorance, there is no saṃskāra. Sensation is to be understood causally, or more accurately, as a web of conditions, a chain of causes and effects, or preconditions and consequences, in which all present experience is enmeshed and from which it arises. Hence this analysis is at once a *contextualization* of sensation (its causal background and history[6]) as well as an intense focus on the very moment of sensation itself.[7] This moment of sensation contains no essence that abides longer than the instant in which it occurs, an instant arising through the collision and collusion of sensorial and psychological factors already at play. These factors, when one's attention is brought to bear on them, reveal themselves to be webs of causal chains that are instantiated *as* the moment.

The instantaneous moment is key, since it is precisely here that Buddhism, for all its elaboration of causal determinants, escapes becoming a form of hard determinism. At the moment one recognizes the conditioning process for what it is—a pain/pleasure calculus shaped by previous experiences that sets the basis for subsequent attitudes, predilection, proclivities, experiences—one is free, detached from that chain's ineluctability. If such a moment of insight is fleeting or shallow, the old habitual patterns will reemerge. But if the insight is sufficiently radical, one can *at that moment*, detach from the chain, ceasing to be its locus. The chain thereupon expires, ceases, is eliminated. Moments of existential conversion (*bodhicitta*) in which one 'arouses' the aspiration to pursue the Buddhist path, as well as the moment of final Awakening, are described in such terms in Buddhist literature.

The factors that would normally engender conditioning lose their power when recognized for what they are. If one offers a piece of candy to a young child in order to motivate it to do something, the child's desire for the pleasure of the candy (reward) will become its motive force, motivating or moving the child to pursue a certain behavior. Repeated reinforcements (rewards) judiciously and consistently applied will eventually make that behavior automatic, habitual. But if one offers a thirty year old person a piece of candy to do something s/he might be inclined not to do, the thirty year old will not only fail to be moved, but the transparency of the pain/pleasure calculus will be evident as well. To motivate the thirty year old, other reinforcements may prove effective—threaten his job, or promise a new car, or a sufficient amount of money. However, the thirty year old is more likely to recognize such reinforcements for what they are, and can therefore exercise the choice of whether to accept or reject them (even though that choice itself will likely be conditioned by his prior conditioning). Moral dilemmas often arise from such situations, as do other dilemmas in which decisions between alternatives must be reached.

The middle way is a middle way between utter unconditionedness and determinism, between pleasure and pain, between any alternative and its contrary. While in most situations it is better, or even best, to do one thing rather than another, the middle way means that one does something not because of self-interest or principial self-denial, but rather because one recognizes the context of the action fully, thereby taking the action that is best for that situation. The underlying criterion is invariably the alleviation and removal of duḥkha. The absence of self-interest as a motivating factor does not entail that one willingly puts oneself in the position of victim, abandoning one's well-being to the vicissitudes of external demands or forces. One does not value oneself below others simply because they are Others. That would only be another form of dualistic extremism, and not a middle way. The best course of action may, in some circumstances, require one to defend one's own position, or attack an external problem. However the criteria by which one decides in such circumstances that this or that is the proper course, cannot themselves be motivated by self-interest. Since motives tend to conceal themselves, one must have deep self-understanding in order to avoid letting self-interest secretly make one's decisions for one. If someone, for instance, holds a dangerous or pernicious view by which she may harm herself or others, attacking that view in the most efficacious manner is best, even if on some levels that seems to involve advancing one's own view (truly correct views, however, are never really one's own; they would be true whether or not any particular individual saw or adhered to them). Conversely, one needn't perpetually adopt the interests or demands or others, as if they were one's own, either. That would demonstrate confusion rather than a middle way.

This self-analysis is balanced, in practice, by one's concern for the suffering of others. One does not acquire insight merely to improve one's own condition, but in order to help others see and improve theirs as well. As one understands one's own conditioning—thereby gaining deeper firsthand understanding of the process of conditioning—one gains skill at recognizing others' conditioning. As one learns how to intervene and interrupt chains of conditioning in oneself, one can likewise instruct or assist others to do so as well. However, each individual must ultimately unravel his or her own conditioning by themselves.

In this sense prajñā—as well as śīla—is at base ethical. It is about *action.* Thoughts are also considered actions (karma) in Buddhism.

In the next chapter we will begin by examining the notion of karma.

Notes

1 Cf. *Questions of King Milinda* III.5, where the king teases Nāgasena by applying a well-known argument used by Buddha against Brahmins to argue that Buddha himself does not exist. In the *Tevijja Sutta* Buddha discredits the Brahmins who blindly follow authorities they and their teachers have never met. The king now argues that since neither Nāgasena nor his teachers have met Buddha, (i) they cannot know whether Buddha existed and therefore (ii) "there is no Buddha!" Nāgasena replies that even though the king and his father have never seen the Whā river in the Himalayas, they definitely know it is there. The king agrees. The problem of 'how to know Nirvāṇa,' is discussed throughout the *Milindapañha.* Cf. e.g. IV.8, 61-88. The following section (book V) deals entirely with 'the problem of inference'.

2 "The Five Khandhas: Their Treatment in the Nikāyas and Early Abhidhamma", *Journal of Indian Philosophy* 14 (1986) pp. 35-53. The references offered in the next few notes are taken directly from Gethin's endnotes.

3 *Saṃyutta Nikāya* III.47.

4 *Majjhima Nikāya* I.299, *Saṃyutta Nikāya* III.100-1; cf. *Saṃyutta Nikāya* III 166-7.

5 On conditionals, see David H. Sanford, *If P then Q: Conditionals and the Foundations of Reasoning* (London and NY: Routledge, 1992).

6 History understood here, for instance, in the sense of Buddha's first watch of the night under the Bodhi Tree in which he views his past experiences and thousands of past lives, not for voyeuristic reasons, but in order to understand the causal chain of events that has brought him to this moment, and from which this moment arose.

7 One thinks, for instance, of the Theravāda practice of mindfulness (*sati*) in which one pays close attention to exactly what is happening in one's physical and mental experience at that very moment; or of Dignāga's focus on the primacy of the momentariness of perception.

Part Three

Karma, Meditation, and Epistemology

Chapter Nine

Karma

> If a cause [for an action] does not actualize (*asat*),
> the enacted (*kārya*) and activator (*kāraṇa*) are not found (*na vidhyate*).
> Those not having come to be (*abhāva*),
> activity (*kṛiya*), actor (*kartā*), and acting (*karaṇa*) are not found.
>
> Nāgārjuna, *Mūlamadhyamakakārikā* (8:4)

Karma: General Description

In Part III we will examine the notion of karma and related matters. Of special interest will be the role that mental functions (*manas, citta, viññāṇa,* etc.) play in the karmic process. Several other concomitant themes and topics will also be discussed, since it would be impossible to understand Yogācāra correctly without first coming to terms with these notions.

Buddhists tended to discuss karma in three distinct registers. The first is a mechanical theory of action, in which causes lead to effects, which in turn become causes of subsequent effects, and so on. The mechanics could include many components: agents, actions, various types of causes, etc. In general, however, this register treated 'action' as a type of physics, even if psychological components were included.[1] The second register is moral, i.e., karma as a moral theory of rewards and punishments aimed at shaping behavior. The third register envisions a soteric project in which karma is the villain. Buddhist practice aims at the elimination of karmic conditioning. These three were made to overlap, of course, but not always with comfort. Tensions between these registers led to some controversies, and some creative Buddhist thinking. In this chapter we will deal primarily with the karma as discussed in the first register. We will take up the other registers in the next chapter on Madhyamaka.

For Buddhism, karma is the prajñaptic term that came to signify all the determinants which manipulate and direct the course of sentient beings' existence. However karma was not always accorded such a preeminent role.

Initially Buddhists saw karma as only one of many determining factors which influenced the course of one's existence. Eventually all the determining factors were reduced, in one way or another, to karma.

Karma means 'action, doing, deeds' from the root √kṛ 'to do.' In a Buddhist context, karma denotes the cause and effect relations which obtain between an act and certain other acts which have preceded and will succeed it, particularly if any of those acts can be classified as *kuśala* (advantageous, beneficial, 'morally good') or *akuśala* (disadvantageous, harmful, 'morally bad'). In a moment we will discuss the significance of the *kuśala-akuśala* distinction, but first the causal, sequential nature of karma needs to be examined.

An act performed in the present is, in part, a consequence or effect of other acts which preceded it; it is also possibly a cause or contributing factor for some subsequent acts. For instance, learning to write involves all the previous actions which bring the learner into a situation where he can be taught to write. Depending on how rigorously one wishes to trace out the causal sequence, one could limit a description of these causes to such antecedent acts as (i) going to and arriving at the place of learning, (ii) procuring writing implements and materials on which to write, (iii) the learner becoming instilled with some sort of motivation to learn, (iv) familiarity with the language which will be written, and so forth. Each of these could be further subdivided into countless distinct acts—e.g., arriving would involve the many little acts, including breathing, walking, taking each breath, each step, looking where one is going, etc., which all together are lumped together by the words 'going to and arriving at;' additionally, breathing is a (partial) cause of walking, which is a (partial) cause of looking at what one is looking at, and so on. The remaining activities could be further subdivided along similar lines. In a more microscopic view, chemical, biological, molecular, subatomic, etc., factors would also need to be examined as causal contributors, since the actions occuring in each realm (chemical actions, molecular actions, etc.) contribute to and condition the behavioral 'action.' The chemical composition of the pen or pencil and its components, the production of the materials on which and with which one writes, and so on are also 'causes' contributing to a particular person learning to write. Moreover, in a more expansive view, the antecedent 'actions' would include the discovery, development and refinement of writing, including writing styles, calligraphy, literary history, pedagogical history, the development of writing materials from etchings to papyrus to silk to paper, etc.; preceding actions would include the development of language—both in the learner and among humans in general—and the person's previous experiences holding and manipulating implements and writing utensils (such as crayons for doodling or mankind's prehensile grasping), as well as all previous acts of learning which will now influence this particular learner's capacity to learn something new. And such lists could be expanded to virtual infinity. Similarly, each act involved in learning how to write will bear fruit each and every time the learner subsequently sets out to write. Whether the learner jots laundry lists or becomes a writer of the greatest novels of her century, all these subsequent actions are dependent upon the actions involved in learning to write. The causal history of writing, in fact, cannot be separated from the history of reading, which is equally complex, since writing and reading are of one fabric, each impossible and meaningless without the other. Furthermore, if the learner-turned-writer's writings are read and influence others, the causal chains resulting from this dissemination are also traceable and dependent upon the initial acts of learning to write. If the influenced reader subsequently also becomes an influential writer, or even if the reader influences himself or any one else in any way as a result of having read the learner-turned-writer's writing, the chain continues. And these are just the explicit causal chains. Uncountable auxiliary conditions, from political scenarios to mood swings, each with their own causal nexus, are also implicitly active in each and every so-called “simple act." Thus a seemingly simple act, such as taking a pencil in one's hand or typing at a keyboard, in fact marks the intersection of dizzyingly complex causal chains, even while the doer of the action remains largely oblivious to them.

What this means is that each and every act occurs within dense, far-reaching contexts, and those contexts largely determine that act. Causal chains are diachronic, and yet they synchronically intersect with countless other causal chains. Although Buddhists tend to differentiate proximate from remote conditions (*hetu* and *pratyaya* respectively), technically speaking they do not accept the notion of 'cause,' especially if by this one means a 'sufficient cause.' Buddhists instead propose a theory of conditionality, the precise definition of which varied from school to school.[2] Each moment marks the intersection of conditioned series of actions (bodily, verbal and mental)\. Each act, then, is the embodiment of a history: cultural, linguistic, sectarian, biographical, and so on. Each act is constituted by the intersection and actualization of various histories through a body. In fact, the 'body' is precisely that which is produced by the intersection of causal histories, whether a 'body of work' such as a writing *corpus*, or the sentient body which enacts prior conditioning as it is being conditioned and conditions situations around it. A body is neither an inanimate thing nor something insentient nor an isolatible entity; rather it constantly inter-acts with its environment, it constitutes a perspective, or a configuration of perspectives on the fields in and of which it is constituted.

In terms of the above example of 'writing,' the act of writing a text brings together and actualizes a multitude of histories, and the resultant text has neither a single author (except in the prajñaptic sense) nor is it an independent text. Its author is merely the occasion for the intersection of the histories and chains of discourse that converge in it, i.e., the author is a prajñaptic locus that has no voice, no contribution to the text other than participating in the intersection and actualization as the locus in which (histories of) ideas, (histories of) writing, (conceptual and material histories of) material composition, etc., converge. The author is the 'place' of the text, but only as it is being written.[3] Once written, the text has its own body, embodies its own set of intentionalities, and carries on its own commerce with its readers. Even while being written, a text has its own intentionalities, and the writer must listen to them while he writes. The text constantly interacts with other texts, other histories, such that its own history continues to unfold, just like our bodies, our speech, our cognitions continually interact with their environments, producing our continuance, our personal 'history.' We move through and eat, wear, admire, destroy, nourish, manipulate, fear, etc., our perceptual field, the lived-world inhabited by our body. We converse with and think about ourselves and each other, both of which are located in our perceptual field or what the *Bhagavad Gītā* calls *dharmakṣetra* ('the field of cultural coherence'; lit.: the field of Dharma). The greater the tension and play between the constitutive histories, that is, the more they seem to oppose each other, the more power the text embodies (the same principle applies to the tension between the histories which a reader brings to the text and the histories which the text inceptually embodied and has continued to accumulate).

Like texts, personal karma is intertextual, intersubjective. My actions affect you, and vice versa. But since karma was most frequently used by Indian schools as a model for establishing the moral accounting of individuals, i.e., how one's current moral actions will inevitably be requited by later moral consequences, the notion of 'collective karma' awaited such works as Vasubandhu's *Viṃśatikā* for adequate elaboration.[4]

By defining karma as the intentional action of body, speech or mind—*kāya, vāc, manas*—the Buddhists were making an important claim that later proved to be the *raison-d'être* for Yogācāra.[5] The significant contexts of an action qua karma are mental, cognitive, not material. A sheer action devoid of cognitive intent is called *krīya*, not karma. For the Buddhist not only is speech or language (*vāk*) cognitive, but the body (*kāya*) too is understood as a *sentient body*, that is, a sensing, feeling, aware, cognitional body, or to borrow the phenomenologists' term, a 'lived-body.'

For the sake of terminological clarity, in the present context I will use the term 'cognitive' to include the karmic modalities of body, speech, and mind, since each is considered karmic to the extent it engages in cognitive activies, i.e., is moved by intention. I shall restrict the term 'mental' to the karmic modalities of mind (*manas*). In this usage, cognitive is a larger term than mental; mental is included in cognitive, but bodily gestures (e.g., that may be unconscious habits) are not defined by Buddhists as necessarily 'mental.' Speech occupies a middle ground between body and thought, since it is thought expressed bodily, in audible utterance. The primary model of language that all Indian thinkers presupposed was speech as utterance (*vyañjana*), as sound (*śabda*). Speech is not only articulated by the body's vocal activity, it is also heard by the body's auditory activities. So the category of speech here includes not only what one says, but what one hears, how one listens, how one responds to what one hears, etc. That is why even when we silently talk to ourselves, we hear a voice in our head that articulates the words. The Indians, as did many cultures, considered writing to be artificial speech. Yet even writing and reading are at once physical (body) and mental, since we move our hand to write or move our eyes to read, and need to pay attention to understand or make sense.

Thus, in their understanding, speech participates in both the bodily and mental spheres, and yet is uniquely a sphere of its own at the same time. To repeat, then, 'cognition' as I will be using it includes all three karmic modes while 'mental' is restricted to the last of the three mode only.

The key to Yogācāra theory lies in the Buddhist notions of karma which it inherited and rigorously reinterpreted. As earlier Buddhist texts already explained, karma is responsible for suffering and ignorance, and karma consists of any intentional activity of body, language, or mind. Since the crucial factor is intent, and intent is a cognitive condition, whatever lacks intent is both non-karmic and non-cognitive. Hence, by definition, whatever is non-cognitive can have no karmic influence or consequences. Since Buddhism aims at overcoming ignorance and suffering through the elimination of karmic conditioning, Buddhism, they reasoned, is only concerned with the analysis and correction of whatever falls within the domain of cognitive conditions. Hence questions about the ultimate reality of non-cognitive things are simply irrelevant and useless for solving the problem of karma.

To be karmic, 'cognitive' implies that bodily and verbal actions arise from and produce intentions. Karmic actions, whether cognitive in the broad sense or strictly mental, are always intentional. From this it follows that the karmic dilemma is a dilemma of intentionality. This is so because 'intentional' implies 'desire,' intending or desiring toward something. Significantly, the Yogācārins defined the *ālaya-vijñāna* as non-intentional (i.e., prior to *manas*; also: *upekṣa-vedanā, anivṛtā, avyāktam,* etc.; cf. *Triṃśikā* v 4), meaning that it is karmically neutral, i.e., a recipient of karmic residue but never either the actual karmic agent (since it was not an agent-self) nor is it affected in itself by karma. Like a warehouse, it can hold and disperse all sorts of karmic goods, without the goods altering its warehouse structure. Goods come into the warehouse, are stored for awhile, and are sent back out when the 'economy' demands. It is the repository of karmic seeds and *vāsanās,* but is not itself polluted by the pollutants (*āśrava*) it houses and dispenses. The non-intentional status of the ālaya-vijñāna led to some disputes among Buddhists, such as whether its neutrality meant that it was pure in itself, or whether it needed to be overcome and erased. In China, the translator Paramārtha declared the ālaya-vijñāna 'defiled,' and posited a ninth pure consciousness (*amala-vijñāna*) that supplants it when one Awakens. The various Chinese Yogācāric schools of that time (sixth century) debated in earnest whether the ālaya was intrinsically pure (so that Awakening would consist of cleansing it of acquired, not intrinsic, impurities), partly pure and partly defiled (requiring that the defiled parts be eliminated and the pure parts increased), or whether it was completely defiled (requiring that it be utterly destroyed).

Incidentally, in the word 'cognitive,' the √gn root (e.g., *gnosis*) is cognate to √jñā (jñāna, vijñāna, vijñapti, and so on), as well as the English *know*. 'Cognitive' involves cognition, a knowing, a being conscious of, a *co-gnoscere* ('coming to know'), an acquaintance or cognizance which, though not exclusively mental in the sense of *manas*, is none the less sentient, conscious, and, thus in some sense, 'mental.'[6]

The three worlds (tri-dhātu) produced by karma are utterly cognitional. While only the ārūpya-dhātu is arguably exclusively 'mental' (since it involves the complete absence of rūpa), the other two dhātus are clearly also cognitional fields in which the drama of existential embodiment is played out. The three worlds, which in Buddhist jargon indicates any and all possible worlds, is intimately linked with karma and cognition. More than linked, they are utterly dependent on karma, they are produced by karma, by actions. When Vasubandhu says that the three worlds are nothing but vijñapti ("Mahāyāne traidhātukam vijñapti-mātram vyavasthāpyate." *Viṃśatikā* 1, *vṛtti*), he is actually saying that they are karmically constituted, as subsequent arguments in that text show. He is not arguing for metaphysical idealism. However while karma and the tri-dhātu are absolutely mutually dependent, such that each could not exist without the other, cognition (*jñāna*) is detachable from them, and there is, according to Buddhism, such a thing as a non-karmic cognition, e.g., the cognition of an arhat or the omniscience of a Buddha. Some Buddhists labeled nonkarmic cognition *nirvikalpa-jñāna*, non-discriminative direct-cognition. Since it is not at all clear what it would mean to have a cognition apart from the three worlds, one may argue that even a detached cognition is of the tri-dhātu. However, it may be precisely this implication, viz. that Awakened cognition still requires that there be a triple (hence karmic) world, that spurred the later Buddhist epistemologists to argue the validity or non-validity of *nirvikalpa-jñāna* (knowing devoid of conceptual constructions) and *nirākāra-jñāna* (cognition devoid of representational images). As we shall discuss presently, the issue of cognition and knowing was always quintessential for Buddhism; Awakening is, after all, a cognitive act! Without its theories of karma and cognition, Buddhism would be without a soteric dimension. Epistemology is a necessary cause of Awakening.

The most rudimentary of cognitive experiences is, according to the skandha theory, vedanā: pleasurable, painful or neutral experience. Through the repetitive conditioning of pain and pleasure, we acquire our karmic habits. 'Habit' means the automatic, unthinking repetition of an action—repeatedly performing a conditioned action. Breaking a habit, if the habit is deeply entrenched by thorough conditioning, generally requires more than a simple act of will or decision; sometimes entire behavioral constellations and associations related to the habit must be reorganized. For example, overeaters or smokers often need to consciously restructure more than basic eating or smoking activities to break their habits. Those habits spill over into, and are fed by so much other behavior that trying to eliminate only the problematic habit without also restructuring other concomitant behaviors can be difficult. From the karmic point of view, the distinction between addiction and habituation is merely one of degree, not of kind. Drug addicts have habits which are more deeply *embodied* than, for instance, a daily coffee drinker, but the structure and dynamics of both types of habits are basically the same. While with our

Cartesian models we tend to differentiate 'habit' from 'addiction' by saying that the latter is 'physical,' meaning it arises from and abides by material causes rather than mental causes (and arguably should be treated, or made to cease by same), from the Buddhist viewpoint any habit—precisely because it involves an intention or series of intentions which have become embodied and thus automatic, no longer requiring or even responding to intentions—is karmic whenever it is a true addiction.

To say that a physical addiction is "more deeply embodied" than a psychological habit may seem contradictory to the Buddhist emphasis on karma being primarily, or sometimes exclusively mental. However, physical addiction almost invariably is accompanied by psychological dependency, so that such simple distinctions are difficult to maintain. In most cases an addiction begins precisely because the addictive agent affords pleasurable (hence psychological) rewards, the 'physical' addiction arising only later. For instance, what makes heroin such a problematic drug is that it produces a very pleasurable state; if it produced unpleasant or painful effects there would be little temptation for anyone to chance becoming addicted to it in the first place. A single use of heroin or cocaine will not make one an addict. But seeking the repetition of the pleasure (*vedanā*) of the drug experience instills the desire (*tṛṣṇa*) to procure and appropriate (*upādāna*) more of the drug and its effects, until it becomes an actual impetus, a behavior pattern (*bhāva*). In other words, one first psychologically craves the drug, and later embodies that craving as physical addiction, thus making the physical addiction a deep-level by-product of the initial psychological habit.

Admittedly, drug-addiction and other types of addiction do not always transpire this neatly, and this only indirectly addresses the question of how something physical might be called karmically 'deeper' than something mental. The danger of giving this type of response is that the conclusion might be that physicality itself is a by-product of mentation, i.e., rūpa derives from nāma. While Buddhaghosa seems to entertain that line in his *Visuddhimagga*, and certain passages in the Buddhist scriptures might lend themselves to such a reading, and certain doctrines reinforce it (e.g., *mano-māya-kāya* or 'body fabricated by mind'), I do not think that this is the correct interpretation of Buddhism. The mental inevitably comes first and foremost, especially in karmic contexts, though the relation between karma and the material realm is far from unambiguous. I will offer what I understand to be the Yogācāra position later.

As we saw in the Part II, vedanic experience is embodied as conditioning, and this latency is called saṃskāra (P. *saṅkhāra*). The latency predisposes one to act or react in certain ways to certain situations. What we usually call 'intention' or 'will' is merely the surfacing of these latencies as dispositions, inclinations to do or choose some action over another. Hence in the Nikāyas and Abhidhamma, *saṅkhāra* is equated with *cetanā*, 'volitional intent.' Gethin writes:[7]

> The *nikāyas* define *saṅkhāras* primarily in terms of will or volition (*cetanā*); they also describe them as putting together (*abhisaṃkharonti*) each of the *khandhas* in turn into something that is put-together (*saṃkhāta*).[8] In this way *saṅkhāras* are presented as conditioning factors conceived of as active volitional forces. *Cetanā* is, of course, understood as *kamma* on the mental level [A III 415], and in the early *abhidhamma* texts all those mental factors that are considered to be specifically skilful (*kusala*) or unskilful (*akusala*) fall within the domain of saṃkhārakhandha.[9] Thus it is that the composition of *saṃkhārakhandha* leads the way in determining whether a particular arising of consciousness constitutes a skilful or an unskilful *kamma*. All this accords well with the *nikāyas'* singling out of *cetanā* as characteristic of the nature of *saṅkhāras*.

We shall see again later how saṃskāra is treated as the pivotal skandha. At this point, we simply take note that karma (particularly mental karma), intention/volition, the conditioning and the conditioned (*saṃskāra, saṃskṛta*, P. *saṅkhāra, saṅkhāta*), kusala and akusala (S. *kuśala, akuśala*) and the arising of consciousness all converge in saṃskāra, and fundamentally configure and are configured by saṃskāra.

Through this saṃskāric mulch, past experiences condition present experiences, which in turn are conditioning future actions. The succession of actions which constitute a life are strung like pearls on a karmic continuum.

Karma does not explain everything

But if present actions are determined by prior actions, are current enjoyments or displeasures necessarily and exclusively caused by previous pleasurable and unpleasurable experiences? When asked this question by Sīvaka Moliya, the Buddha replied[10]

> Certain experiences (*vedyita*), Sīvaka, arise here originating from bile,... from phlegm,... from wind,... resulting from the humours of the body,... born of the changes of the seasons,... of being attacked by adversities,... of spasmodic attacks,... of the coming-to-maturity of an action (*kamma-vipāka*). And this ought to be known by yourself, Sīvaka, that certain experiences arise here as originating from bile,... as born of the coming-to-maturity of kamma. And this is considered as truth by the world, that certain experiences arise here as originating from bile,... as born of the coming-to-maturity of kamma. Now, Sīvaka, those recluses and Brahmins who speak thus, who hold this view: "Whatever a human being experiences, whether pleasure, or pain, or neither pleasure nor pain—all this is by reason of what was done in the past," they go beyond what is personally known, and what is considered as truth in the world. Therefore, I say of these recluses and Brahmins that they are wrong.

From this passage we learn:

1) the claims that one makes about karma must be supportable either by personal experiences or through common knowledge. To offer a claim that violates both of those epistemic constraints is to be "wrong." This doesn't mean that these are two equally valid means of knowledge (*pramāṇa*). Buddha's point is that if one is *not* speaking from personal experience (the *only* sure-fire *pramāṇa* for Buddha), *and* what one says contradicts common experience and what is generally agreed upon, then on what grounds can one make such claims or believe such ideas? General knowledge is no equal or substitute for personal experience, but if one lacks personal knowledge in some area, one thereby also lacks the epistemic ground upon which to controvert general opinion in that area. What is derived neither from personal experience nor from common knowledge cannot come from an unambiguously reliable source. Therefore it is suspect at best, and to be treated as 'wrong.' The sequence of the passage is (i) 'X is the case,' (ii) you should personally 'know' that 'X is the case,' (iii) it is common knowledge that 'X is the case,' (iv) therefore those who assert non-X are wrong.
2) No one, except perhaps a few 'extremists' at that time in India thought that *all* of one's experiences were determined by past experiences. No one, including Buddha, thought that karma was all-determining. Karma did not denote an all-encompassing deterministic model of human behavior.
3) There were other recognizable and identifiable causes, aside from karma, for old age, sickness and death. "Bile..., phlegm..., wind..., bodily humours...., seasonal changes..., adversities..., 'spasmodic' attacks," as well as *vipāka-kamma* (maturation of kamma) contribute to present pleasant, painful and neutral experiences. Buddha was not making extravagant claims; he was not advocating a psychologistic reductionism. Psychological conditioning was only part of the human problem. Technically, we may even question whether *vipāka-kamma* and the saṃskāric re-enactment of *vedanā* are treated as synonyms is this passage. Based on virtually every other Pāli text which could be brought to bear on that question, we would have to answer that they do indeed act as synonyms.

Point (1) is intriguing in its own right, especially in the way it anticipates medieval developments in Buddhist epistomology, but for now points (2) and (3) demand our attention. Point (3) in particular raises some thorny issues for Buddhism. If the etiological, though mediate 'causes' of sickness, old age and death are—as *pratītya-samutpāda* and Buddhist doctrine insist—desire and nescience, and the overcoming of desire and the eradication of nescience are sought as means to overcome the dukkha of impermanence (sickness, old age, death), such that "accomplishing what needed to be accomplished, doing what needed to be done"[11] carries one beyond dukkha to become *amata* (lit. "deathless"),[12] then a question arises. What implications does this passage's admission that 'sickness, old age and death' may have other causes have for the standard version of the Buddhist project, in which behavioral and cognitive means are employed to eliminate karma *because* the elimination of karma is considered the elimination of duḥkha? Is the Buddhist mārga only for those whose problems (*dukkha*) are psychological in origin, but not others?

It may be argued that this is exactly the domain in which Buddhist thought locates itself. For instance, parallels with Stoicism have not gone unnoticed by modern scholars, and many contemporary interpretations of Buddhism either deliberately or inadvertantly make it out to be a kind of stoicism.[13] Does Buddhism aim merely at developing a change of 'attitude,' i.e., a psychological reorientation to the world, or do Buddhist transformative soterics aim at something more radical? Do they, in effect, involve a radical reconstruction of the entire manner in which one engages the world, a reconstruction whose radicality involves altering the world along with the one engaging it? It seems that this question underlies the entire critique of so-called Hīnayāna by Mahāyāna, though it was poorly formulated and articulated by them. A mere attitudinal change is restricted. It is private, personal, subjective; it effects no *social* change or justice. One saves oneself in a manner which remains impervious to the needs and plight of others, since its private, subjective nature makes it inaccessible to others. But true Awakening should involve, Mahāyāna would claim, an active re-engagement with the world, a fulfilment of the Bodhisattva vow that one's own achievements are meaningless unless they translate into assistance for others. As remarked earlier, initially Buddhism exhibited a powerful sense of social justice and reform, a sense which took shape in the world, for instance, by offering actual social alternatives to the stiffling and encompassing Brahmanical society and Caste structure. Cognitively, as well, Awakening involves a different manner of engaging the world of experience, specifically a manner of cognition which is non-appropriational. However, institutionally speaking, Mahāyāna, like Hīnayāna, failed to maintain in practice the disjunctive alterity between pre- and post-Awakening manners of engaging the world. In the name of patronage, it sold out its socially transformative voice.

Regardless, Buddhism cannot be reduced to a set of attitudes, theories or perspectives. If anything, it is the incessant criticism of such reductions that makes Buddhism what it is.

Is Buddhism a Psychologism?

We will now consider the degree to which Buddhism can be called psychologically grounded or even a psychologism. Buddhism, inasmuch as it concerns itself primarily with an analysis of and therapeutic prescription for the human condition, considers psychological matters—including perception, epistemology, knowledge, belief, motivation, interpretation, behavior, etc.—of the highest importance, and my term 'psychosophic' aims at emphasizing that. But this is not the same as admitting that Buddhism is a form of psychologism. Psychologism, most simply defined, is the reductionistic claim that psychological factors are the ultimate explanatory tools for understanding anything. Buddhism is not a psychologism. Even Yogācāra, which does propose to reduce karma and the entirety of the triple world to cognitive factors, is not a psychologism. This is because the point of Buddhist analysis is not the reification of a mental structure or theory of mind, but its erasure. Vasubandhu highlights the closure of cognitive horizons not because such a closure is either desirable or unalterable, but because the closure can only be opened once its all-encompassing complexity and ubiquity is understood and recognized. Yogācāra uses psychologistic arguments to overcome psychological closure, not to enhance it.

Labeling Buddhism as a psychologism presupposes that other, non-cognitive spheres can be demonstrably valid and independent of cognition, and thus cognition should be contextualized as a single, less than all-inclusive sphere amongst the other spheres of reality. This notion is asserted, predicated, defended and affirmed or denied *in cognition* and it is presupposed in the mind. To determine its status as either in or apart from cognition is again an act performed in cognition. As do some modern thinkers, Buddhists maintain that only a posteriori knowledge is valid or possible; a priori claims are claims which mask, ignore or are unaware of their presuppositions.

This issue is extremely familiar to Western thinkers, and frequently is argued in relation to the status of 'mathematical objects,' generally conceded to be the most ideal, necessary concepts we have. Mathematical relations are said to be timeless and true regardless of when or even if they are discovered by humans. Hence they are not contingent, not dependent on any temporal relation. Or are they? Whether a so-called mathematical object (e.g., a triangle) - and perhaps more importantly, its *properties* - has a reality independent of the mathematician that discovers it, such that the properties of a triangle are eternally true whether they had been discovered or not, and we, as humans, can merely acknowledge or acquiesce to their eternal truth but neither create nor alter them; or whether mathematical objects are simply human conceptual constructs, derived from experience, perhaps distorted or idealized (e.g., in ontic space and time no perfect circle exists), such that mathematics is an utterly temporal and historic phenomenon, an historical accretion; this debate has been argued countless times in countless ways. It was one of the issues that separated Frege from Husserl. Frege embraced the former position, while Husserl leaned toward the latter (actually, his position is complex and ambivalent). The charge levelled against Husserl and his phenomenology by the followers of Frege, viz. that phenomenology is only another form of psychologism, stems from this issue.[14] Husserl, of course, rejected that label and attacked psychologism on other grounds. Merleau-Ponty later pressed the counter-attack and argued that mathematical objects are indeed historical.[15]

The point for our discussion is that 'psychologism' and 'eternal essentialism' tend to constitute opposing poles. Since Buddhism rejects essentialism (*svabhāva*), its critics will respond with the charge of psychologism. Since essentialists conceive of, argue for and then religiously believe in what they conceive to be extra-conceptual, Buddhists retort that conceptions are never located anywhere else than within cognitive horizons, including the conception of a conception. Tellingly, the eternalists rarely shrink from calling their eternal, independent-of-cognition entities "concepts" (*Begriff*) or "ideas" (*eidos*), though they deny temporal origin to these entities. They concede that these 'objects' are mental, but for them mental connotes an eternal realm of eternal, immutable ideal ideas (though, to be fair, many contemporary Analytics are embarrassed by Frege's obvious Platonism). For Buddhists ideas are thoughts which arise, abide, decay and cease from moment to moment dependent on conditions. Like all conditioned things, they are impermanent.

Further, we may ask: Does the definition (essence) belong to the thing defined or to the one proffering and using the definition? While Husserl vacillated, arguing first in *Ideas I* that the essences obtained from phenomena through the phenomenological method belonged in an important sense to the things themselves, and then later in *Cartesian Meditations* arguing that the essence expressed and uncovered a transcendental self, Buddhism consistently denied that either the subject or the object were originary or primary. Instead of primary substantial entities, they envisaged only chains of conditions. A 'definition' is neither essence nor product, but rather a sedimentation of the nominalistic process (*prajñapti*) which accompanies and contributes to cognition (*vijñāna*). This is prapañca.

When instead of realizing that one sees X *as* Y, and instead argues and believes that X *is* Y, this is vikalpa or prapañca, or linguistic and cognitive projection (*pratibimba*).

The fundamental 'error' or problem, according to Buddhism, is not ontological, but epistemic, cognitive. And cognition is driven by intention; cognition also expresses intention (i.e., projection).

Karma: The Circuit of Intentionality

Karmic action is consequential action, action which receives its significance and meaning from those consequences which follow from it, which arise as a result (direct or remote) of its occurrence. Karma thus not only transmits the past to the present, by influencing and shaping current actions in the light of what has gone before. As historicality it is revisionistic, since the meaning of a current act is derived from consequences which will only occur later, in the future. It is the consequence in the future that gives a current or past act its meaning. The present, the immediate moment of action, becomes an open field (*kṣetra*) in which the determinative influences of the past and future collide; the karmic present merely signifies links of chains to before and after, chains for which karma constitutes the links. These links may mark a kind of durational continuity between a prior and a subsequent chain, or they may link chains in the manner of a train-track switch, shifting the trajectory of a past chain into a seemingly non-contiguous, dissimilar future chain, and vice versa. As the point of linkage between chains, karma may unite otherwise entirely disparate chains, revisionistically giving the disparities relationally common histories, or a common destiny. And the link marks a double causal flow; the future flowing toward (and through) the present into the past, and the past pushing through the present into the future.[16] Karma, thus, is thoroughly temporal.

Each action is involved in a rigorous, complex economy with its own past and future. The 'value' which accrues to an action within this temporal structure is a moral, ethical value. If an action leads to 'good' results, it is a good action, and inversely, a bad action is one which leads to 'bad' consequences.

As might be expected in systems which prize efficient causality over other forms of conditionality, the criterion for determining the meaning of 'good' and 'bad' is at once utilitarian and pragmatic. Actions are what they do, and if they produce benefits and advantages they are 'good,' *kuśala*. If they prove nonbeneficial, harmful, disadvantageous, then they are 'bad,' *akuśala*. If action P is an immoral act, it is immoral not because there is something intrinsically wrong with it as such, in itself; P is immoral because consequent Q ineluctably follows from P, and Q is harmful, *akuśala*. In recognition of the conditional relation between P and Q, P may also be called *akuśala*. However, perusal of Abhidhammic texts quickly dispels the notion that there exists any simple correspondence between the value of an act and its consequent. A number of permutations are possible. For instance, past action R, which was akuśala, may give rise to present action S, which is neutral (*upekṣa*, i.e., neither kuśala nor akuśala), whose influence on future action T is as yet indeterminate (*avyākta*). Or past action M, which was indeterminate, by somehow combining with action N, which is kuśala, effects current action O to be likewise kuśala, and predisposing future action P to also tend toward kuśala. In fact, a significant percentage of abhidharmic literature basically concerns itself with mapping important Buddhist terminology in terms of kuśala, akuśala, avyākta and vipāka, which is to say, abhidharma functions as, or codifies a 'karmic map.'

In terms of temporal relations between actions, various combinations of kuśala, akuśala and upek]a in relation to vipāka are theoretically possible. The defining characteristics (*lak]aṇa*) of specific *types* of situations and contexts (*dharmā*) determine the actual configuration. This categorization, then, is both rational and empirical. In order to develop the prescriptive, ethical guidance implicit in the Buddhist analysis of the human condition, all these possibilities were eventually traced out and codified, down to the smallest detail. The resulting maps are collected in Abhidhammic/Abhidharmic texts. It would not be unfair to categorize texts such as the *Abhidhammatthasaṅgaha* as the systematic classification of Buddhist terms and concepts in terms of kuśala and akuśala. Abhidharmic literature typically consists of (1) a listing and defining of the basic components required for Buddhistic analysis (skandhas, dharmas, bhūtas, etc.), generally grouped categorically (ex.: *viprayukta-dharmāḥ*) or functionally (ex.: *āyatanā* and *dhātu*), (2) classification of those components in terms of their kuśala or akuśala efficacy, and (3) an account of how manipulation of (2) results in Awakening. Not every abhidharmic text exhibits all three moves. Some are concerned with only one or another aspect; but they are all contextualized by their implicit presupposition of this tripartite movement. One categorizes in order to effect some karmically efficient corrections in one's karmic trajectory, and these corrections should ultimately lead to the complete and final overcoming of the karmic problematic.

We will not here enter into an examination of the intricacies of such classificatory schema. For our purposes, it is sufficient to note:

1) That such endeavors are basic to the Buddhist project, particularly for an analysis of karma.
2) That this project becomes one of the chief aims and activities of the Abhidhamma and Abhidharma literature, in whichever Buddhist schools deliberated with such literature.
3) The value and meaning of one's actions, and by extension, the value and meaning of a life lived as or through those actions is determined by these distinctions.
4) Any Buddhist school, if it attempts to be systematic, must locate itself within this criteriology, and be prepared to announce and explicitly recite which actions are kuśala, which are akuśala, and which are karmically neutral, and give reasons for so classifying each action.
5) The foundation of the prescriptive aspect of Buddhism is here, and Buddhism's claim to soteric efficacy is rooted in the correctness or insufficiency of this style of karmic analysis.

This last point is important. It is no accident that where, for various reasons, a Buddhist school rejects this style of karmic analysis, it must also relinquish claim to a large segment of Buddhist soterical rhetoric. For instance, Mādhyamika and Ch'an, once they have jettisoned karmic classification, are compelled to utter such non-soteric pronouncements as "no one obtains nirvana" or "there is nothing to attain", etc. Simply put, without karmic analysis any Buddhist soteric claim would be without foundation and incoherent. The curious claim/argument of Mādhyamika and Ch'an is that karmic analysis itself is incoherent! Buddhism, as such, must tread the middle way between these opposing options: If the analysis is overly reified, Buddhism degenerates into a determinism which further ensnares rather than liberates. If the analysis is rejected *in toto* and immediately, then one must thrash around without motivation or method, and, at least on one level, explicitly denounce and disclaim the goal/purpose/motive that is in fact immediately in-forming and necessitating the disclaimer. Honesty folds over into itself, away from itself. The allegorical foundation for this 'dis-honest' swerve is presented in the first part of the *Lotus Sutra*, viz. *upāya*. Subsequently, the notion of upāya is invoked every time a swerve from the actual, from the historical, from the presentative needs to be rationalized and justified. T'ien-t'ai, e.g., justifies Pure Land as an upāyic necessity, and Buddhism justifies its own institutionalization by an appeal to this same sense of 'upāyic' necessity.

Karma, then, is not only a causal theory or account of actions, an account through which the present action decenters and echoes in, as well as being echoed by previous and subsequent actions. It is a systematic criteriology by which actions receive their value, their 'karmic' meaning. Time moves, and each moment of action is merely transitional, on the way to future (or past) moments. Karma never arrives at itself, since to instantiate a karmic result (*vipāka*) usually requires or produces an action (karma), which necessitates future events in order that its vipāka reaches fruition. Action, karma, is a ceaseless relay team, a handing off of consequences from one durational situation to another. Its movement cannot be dammed (some schools will argue that it may be temporarily dammed), but its trajectory can be modified. The trajectory of akuśala-karma can be transposed into a kuśala-karmic trajectory. One's actions can ethically improve, which is to say that one's actions will lead to more and more beneficial consequences. Obviously the inverse can impede one's ethical development. Beneficial trajectories may be derailed, or converted into disadvantageous trajectories. The actual mechanics of this give and take economy vary from school to school, but insofar as they are karmic, the trajectories arise from activities of body, speech and mind, and it is through these factors that trajectories may be altered. Through *action* in the lived-world as a living, gesturing, cognating, communicative body, one's ethical situation en-acts. This 'situation' is neither strictly internal nor determinatively external. It is constituted through a dense, intricate economic karmic interchange, a 'circuit of intentionality'; and the diaphenous margin which arises *between* the lived-body and the lived-field is the birth-place of consciousness—or, as Buddhist terminology would put it, through the contact of a sense organ and a sense object, consciousness arises. In the Yogācāra school the complexities of this economy are metaphorically (*upacāra*) gathered into the image of a 'warehouse' consciousness, *ālaya-vijñāna*, which is given the nickname *vipāka*-vijñāna, the consciousness which handles the fruitional economy. The influence (*vāsanā*) and seeds (*bījā*) of all experiences traffic in and out of the ālaya, which stores them until conditions 'put in their orders,' and the stored influences and seeds are shipped out in the form of new experiences.

When karma is described in mechanistic terms the concomitance from cause to effect is treated as invariable, and each action invariably produces precisely its just desserts. By understanding karma as a *mechanical* process, interpreting its dynamics in a precise, mechanical way, it thereby becomes conducive to theoretical classification. Since B always and everywhere follows from A, and C from B, etc., the relation between A and C can be easily mapped. Mechanistic models, which function by a two-value logic system (in the Buddhist case an intermediate 'neutral' case is frequently added), tend to serve a will to univocality. In the case of karma, the mechanistic interpretation of action makes the meaning of an action theoretically univocal, nonambiguous. An action's meaning is simply and directly determined and defined by its result (*vipāka*). Seemingly ambiguous cases, i.e., actual situations which present themselves ambiguously, are, if properly analyzed and understood, nonambiguous. They need only be properly analyzed, viz. classified in terms of advantageous/disadvantageous consequences, and their singular value becomes apparent. No action can be examined in isolation, since all actions are thoroughly contextual. The relation between action and context, gestalt and Ganzfeld, then, is neither ambiguous nor vague. It is mechanically precise.

This univocal analysis is prescriptive and therapeutic inasmuch as it arises from a need to know what to do, how to cure and be cured, what to cure, how specifically to intercept a karmic trajectory and put it on a more beneficial course, and so on. It remains therapeutic only insofar as it actually works; thus such classificatory criteriological enterprises become meaningless abstractions if divorced from the pragmatic praxis for which they are designed.

Leaving aside the array of issues and problems such a brief description of the mechanics of karma might suggest, we turn instead to an issue which must be clarified in order for us to understand Yogācāra. The issue in question is the relation—or lack thereof—between karma and rūpa. In order to understand the Yogācāric move which is usually interpreted as the rejection of external objects in favor of a 'consciousness alone is real' idealism, we need to understand what, even prior to Yogācāra, the basic understanding of rūpa was. Once we know the place of rūpa in Buddhist soterics, the rationale and purport of the Yogācāric move will become apparent.

Karma and Rūpa

As noted in Part II, rūpa as a category is not without some ambiguity. As noted above in this chapter, it is always cognitional, and sometimes mental. As such, karma is always intentional, always an action that somewhere and somehow involves consciousness (*vijñāna, citta*) in some capacity. What is the relation between rūpa (materiality) and the cognitive intentionality (*nāma*) of karma? Does Buddhism address what Western philosophy has labeled the mind-body problem, and if so, with what results? If not, how was it avoided, and with what consequences?

Distinguishing the five skandhas into nāma and rūpa might suggest a mind-body split, but careful analysis does not bear this out. First, rūpa means *both* materiality and sentient materiality. Rūpa signifies, e.g., a visible object both insofar as that object is material and insofar as that object is visible, sensorial. It is never a materiality which can be radically separated or isolated from sentiency. Such a non-empirical category would appear ludicrous to the Buddhist. Its ability to be sensed is not accidental, but rather precisely its essence. The Pāli tradition manages to avoid substance-quality metaphysics, even in relation to 'matter.' rūpa is not a substratum or substance which has properties of sensibility; it functions as sensibility, perceivable physicality. 'Matter,' just like everything else, is finally defined in terms of its function, what it does, not what it *is*. Rūpa is sensed, since it is itself sensorial.

Nyanatiloka Mahathera, discussing how rūpa is treated in the Abhidhamma, writes:[17]

> Matter is viewed here only as a division in the range of cognizable objects, and as one among the constituents of so-called Personality, misconceptions about which it is the Abhidhamma's task to eliminate...

Secondly, the sensorial nature of rūpa is born out by the categorization of rūpa as the Four Great Happenings (*mahābhūta*, usually mistranslated 'Great Elements') as not simply Earth, Water, Fire and Air, but rather as sensorial qualities, viz. Solid, Liquid, Heat and Motion. The former (earth, water, fire, and air) are conceptual abstractions drawn from the sensorium in which one experiences solids, liquids, heat, and motion. Rūpa is defined by sensorial—and not metaphysically materialistic—typologies.

Let us examine what the Abhidhamma texts actually say. The *Dhammasaṅgaṇī* 595 states, and the *Vibhaṅga* (sec. 33) repeats verbatim:[18]

> "All form" (*sabbaṃ rūpaṃ*) is:
>
> [1] not 'root-cause' (*ahetu*), [2] not concomitant with 'root-cause,' [3] disassociated from 'root-cause' (*na hetu*), [4] involves conditions (*sappacayaṃ*, lit: 'with or having condition'), [5] conditioned (*sankhataṃ*), [6] rūpic (*rūpiyaṃ* or *rūpam eva*), [7] mundane (*lokiyaṃ*),
>
> [8] with *āsavas* (*sāsavaṃ*),[19] [9a] with the fetters (*saṃyojaniyaṃ*),[20] [9b] with the ties (*gantha*),[21] [9c] with the floods (*ogha*),[22] [9d] with the Bonds (*yoga*),[23] [9e] with the obstructions/hindrances (*nīvaraṇa*),[24] [10] perverted (*parāmaṭṭhaṃ*),[25] [11] appropriational (*upādāniyaṃ*), [12] (associated with) mental disturbances (*sankilesikaṃ*), [13] (karmically) indeterminate (*avyākata*),
>
> [14] without mental-object (*anārammaṇaṃ*), [15] not a mental-concomitant (*acetasikaṃ*), [16] disassociated from consciousness, [17] neither karmic-result (*vipāka*), nor productive of karmic-result, [18] not mentally-disturbed (itself, but capable of being) associated with mental-disturbances,[26]
>
> [19a] not 'with initial mental application' or 'with subsequent discursive reasoning' (*na savitakka-savicāraṃ*), [19b] not 'without initial application, but subsequent reasoning only,' [19c] neither 'initial application nor subsequent reasoning,' [20] not accompanied by intense joy (*pīti*), [21] not accompanied by pleasurable happiness (*sukha*), [22] not accompanied by neutrality (*upekkhā*),
>
> [23] not capable of being abandoned or eliminated by either perspectival orientation or cultivation (*dassanaṃ, bhāvanā*),[27] [24] not having a root-cause (*hetu*) capable of being abandoned or eliminated by either perspectival orientation or cultivation, [25] neither accruing nor dispersing (re: rebirth and death), [26] neither of discipleship (on the seven supra-mundane paths) or beyond, [27] trite and insignificant (*parittaṃ*),[28] [28] characteristic of the desire-realm (*kāmāvacaraṃ*), [29] [not][29] characteristic of the form-realm (*rūpāvacaraṃ*), [30] not characteristic of the formless realm, [31] is 'Included' (*pariyāpannā*, i.e., mundane and subject to appropriation),[30] [31] not 'Unincluded' (*apariyāpannā*),

> [32] no fixed or determined [consequences or results] (*aniyatā*), [33] not tending to be liberating,
>
> [34] presently arisen (*uppannaṃ*), [35] cognizable by the six cognitive modes (i.e., the six senses), [36] impermanent, [37] subject to decay.

I have added the numbers, and have grouped them to facilitate our discussion. The texts just list the items. The items on the list follow fairly closely the order of topics discussed in the *Dhammasaṅgaṇī* as a whole, and thus offer a sort of resume of that book. For that reason we cannot unpack this list exhaustively, since that would require unpacking the entire text, not just this section. The purpose of this section of the *Dhammasaṅgaṇī* is to show exactly where rūpa fits into the categorial grid of the Abhidhamma, so its meaning entails a full exposition of that grid. This would take us too far afield, but several salient points should be noted.

[1] through [5] define rūpa's status as participating in the realm of conditions. By *hetu* this text does not mean 'cause' or 'primary condition' in general, but rather a specific list of hetus, viz. *rāga, doṣa, moha* and their opposites. Rūpa has *nothing whatsoever* to do either with these hetus—the basic etiological sources of dukkha—nor with their antidotes. Rūpa is utterly irrelevant to the dynamics of the soteric field that Buddhism addresses. *Materiality, in other words, neither binds nor liberates.* Despite its karmic irrelevancy, it remains an important component of experience, and thus the text endeavors further descriptive analysis.

It functions by way of conditions, causes and effect, and is conditioned. It is important that this be stated overtly, because later in the matrix rūpa will start to share context with the transmundane realm and the unconditioned realm (nirvāṇa), since the former is at the fringe of and the latter is radically other than the karmic order. The reminder here that rūpa, though akarmic, functions in causal patterns—aside from being faithful to experience—makes it clear that whatever it might have in common with those realms, it is nonetheless entirely 'conditioned.' [6] and [7] reinforce this.

[8] through [13] define what it does or does not contribute to the saṃsāric dilemma. Although it is connected with the entire list of karmic problems (*āsavas*, fetters, etc.), [18] shows that it does not itself 'suffer' from these problems, it only contributes to them by proximity. For instance, while rūpa does not appropriate anything, it can be appropriated. Significantly, as [13] and [32] indicate, even though karmic problems may implicate rūpa, rūpa itself is entirely and utterly karmically neutral. It is neither produced by previous karma [13], nor will it lead to ineluctable karmic consequences [32]. [17] makes the same point. It is irrelevant to the entire process of vipāka, which is again to say it is altogether irrelevant to the karmic process.

[14] through [18] attempt to define aspects of its relation to cognition. Though itself the objective component of a cognitive act, it forms or takes no mental-object (*ārammana*). This is an interesting distinction, since later Indian schools will argue the status of the *ālambana*, i.e., Is the 'support' for the

cognitional object external to, or referred to by the cognition (i.e., is it an external 'object')?, or Is it constructed by cognition (*vikalpa, kalpanā*, etc.)? At least here we see that if rūpa is the cognitive 'support' which does not itself cognize, this would avoid an infinite regress of supports. [15] and [16] classify rūpa as neither consciousness nor *caitta*, (the 'felt texture' or 'ambiance field' of a cognitive moment), thus defining its otherness from the *nāmic* skandhas. The *Dhammasaṅgaṇī*, in fact, is primarily concerned with elucidating the system of eighty-nine 'classes of consciousness,' which involves fifty-two 'mental concomitants' (*cetasika* or *caitta*). In the appendices I have listed the Vaibhāṣika and Yogācāra lists of seventy-five and one hundred dharmas respectively. Their lists developed from the Theravādin list under discussion here, and the reader can see what they deemed as caittas. For the Theravāda lists Nyanatiloka's *Guide Through the Abhidhamma Piṭaka* (pullout between pp. 12 and 13) can be profitably examined.

To say that rūpa is neither citta nor caitta is not to say that it is apart or separate from the perceptual realm, the sensorium, as [35] makes plain. It means that rūpa is not reducible to the *mental* realm. As pointed out previously, that does not entail that it also be non-cognitive.

[19] through [22] indicate, interestingly, that rūpa cannot be reduced to the characteristics of the rūpa-dhātu. The relation and distinction to be drawn between rūpa and rūpa-dhātu need not detain us here, though it is not without its controversies and interpretive oppositions. Here we simply note that none of the mental reactions one acquires or loses in the rūpa-dhātu, including the neutrality that comes at the final stage, have anything to do with rūpa itself.

[23] through [33] reiterate the basic fact that rūpa is entirely foreign and irrelevant to the Buddhist task. Buddhist praxis, whatever it eliminates or overcomes, whatever it achieves or accomplishes, has nothing to do directly with rūpa. The mārga, the methodology, only concedes that rūpa is mundane, and desire appropriates it [28, 31, etc.]. While its susceptibility to being appropriated can complicate one's karmic problems [8-12], rūpa cannot remedy those problems in any way [23, 24, 25, 26, 31, 33].

Rūpa, moreover, has no distinctly purposeful connection adhering to its involvement in the rebirth-death cycle [25]. Rebirth involves, according to Buddhist definition, the coming together of nāma and rūpa, and death is their dissolution. But rūpa is entirely indifferent (= irrelevant) to the process of saṃsāra. This is a consequence of its karmic irrelevancy. It should be pointed out that this fact, the irrelevance of rūpa for the problem if rebirth, is thoroughly suppressed by Buddhaghosa in his commentaries and in his original works. His *Visuddhimāgga* is a long meditation and interrogation of the question of how, karmically, do nāma and rūpa come together to begin a life. How do they carry over from life to life and moment to moment? For him, rūpa *is* vipāka, it is a karmic result, produced by intentional actions. He is not entirely without scriptural foundation, since the texts do discuss the relation of karma and rūpa, but as we have just seen [17, etc.], to declare rūpa a vipāka is problematic, if not in fact 'heresy.' We will return to this problem momentarily.

[34] implies that rūpa arises from conditions, and is always and only in the present (past or future 'forms' can only exist in memory or imagination, which are mental, not 'material' activities). [35] overtly and explicitly declares that \f4all six senses cognize rūpa, and that its popular linguistic affinity with 'visible object' or 'tactile object' is merely metaphoric; it pervades the six-fold sensorium.[31] [36] and [37] remind us why attachment to rūpa is futile: impermanence and decay. Significantly, and for obvious reasons, the text does not say 'subject to death.' rūpa may not die, but it does not quite survive either.

Though this matrix seems eminently reasonable, serious tensions threaten its coherence. If rūpa is as vigorously and radically disassociated from the mental realm as [14-16] imply, by what means does it enter into proximity with the karmic problematics [8-13, etc.]? Is the distinction which was drawn earlier between cognitive (bodily and linguistic) and mental karma sufficient to carry this problematic? Rūpa is made to wear two hats: it is at once sensorial, cognitive, within the purview of eye-consciousness, ear-consciousness, and so on up to mental-consciousness (mano-vijñāna), and at the very same time emblematic of an entirely alien and remote etiology, a sign of all that is not sensorial, conscious, karmically derived and driven. It follows the same logic, the same grammar as the psycho-logical, cognitive functions, which is to say, it arises and ceases by an order of conditions, in a systematic fashion. It arises, like thought, from the concatenation of proper conditions, and disassembles by their dissolution. But its ceasing, unlike ours, is not a death. rūpa and the karmic world run a parallel course which never really becomes parallel. rūpa's impermanence is interminable, a kind of eternal flux. Unlike the cognitive individual who may terminate his saṃsāric journey by 'entering' final nirvana, rūpa has no telos, no terminus, no finality—and no problems!

Such ruminations on the implications of this formulation of rūpa—and they could be extended and deepened -problematize Buddhism itself. There is, in fact, an undercurrent discernible in a number of Pāli texts which intimate that the Buddhist solution to the problem of duḥkha may be something like identifying with rūpa or at least the rūpic-style of dynamics. To become 'neutral,' 'irrelevant' to the karmic process, to become outside or alien or radically other to the root-problems (*rāga, dveśa, moha*), and so on, is to 'solve' them. But rūpa, according to this text, is not even 'neutral' or 'indifferent' [22]. It cannot be anthropomorphized in that way.[32] Just as nirvāṇa resists anthropomorphic images. 'Rūpa' is utterly mindless, though sensorial.

It may be fair to say that despite the apparent complexity and sophistication of this system, at this stage Buddhism is still a form of naive realism. That an object can be radically other than consciousness, in terms of origin, function, structure, etc., and still be cognized by consciousness did not seem to them to be a problematic proposition. Perhaps their notion that something *can* be both sensorial and utterly mindless, if rigorously pursued, might lead one to produce a strong, coherent epistemology capable of adequately addressing and responding to the typical epistemological dilemmas which recur again and again as challenges to such a complacent assumption. If so, the Theravādins failed to develop it. Later abhidharmic systems, reacting to vastly more sophisticated and sensitive epistemological reflections, will rethink and reformulate the problems and the categories. To oversimplify, the Sarvāstivāda school will attempt a type of realist metaphysic, complete with substances (*dravya, vastu*), essential natures (*svabhāva*), qualities (guṇa), etc. Not only will rūpa substantialize, but even the mental dharmas will become essential, substantial, substrative 'reals.' This metaphysic will be attacked by Mādhyamika (not only for its substantialism, but for its metaphysicality) and Sautrāntika (who will collapse the entire metaphysical field into a single moment), as well as by others. The Yogācāric reaction was to simply reason:

1) The fundamental human problem, the problem that Buddhism addresses and cures, its central, fundamental concern, is karma.
2) Rūpa has nothing whatsoever to do with karma, except insofar as it becomes an object of appropriation and attachment (*upādāna, grāhya*).
3) This means the so-called rūpa which is considered to be karmically neutral, in fact, is neither actually neutral nor rūpa, but instead is an appropriational, and hence cognitive, mental construct. This construct *is* karmically active.
4) Therefore, rūpa can and should be ignored, since it, at best, is irrelevant, and at worse masks the psycho-cognitive appropriational activities which perpetuate the karmic problem.

Had we more time and space, this process could be diachronically traced out through the succeeding generations of texts. But such an ambitious, though crucial enterprise must await another occasion. Instead I shall try to bring into sharper focus the key issues that shaped the development of Yogācāra.

Above we noted that for Buddhaghosa rūpa could indeed be considered vipāka, despite the explicit claims to the contrary that we saw in the Abhidhamma texts. While the texts seem to insist that rūpa is not vipāka, i.e., it is not a karmic result, and that the causal chains of rūpa and the mental and cognitive (i.e., karmic) causal chains are radically distinct without any overlap or crossover, there are some texts which throw some ambiguity and confusion into this neat picture. The *Dhammasaṅgaṇī*, which we have been examining, offers us such an example.

The section on rūpa is divided into parts. The part we have cited presents rūpa as 'singular terms' (*ekakaniddeso*), and the succeeding parts present rūpa as 'double terms' (*duvidhena rūpa-sangaho*), 'triple terms,' and so on, up to 'elevenfold terms.' While discussing the 'triple terms,' the following statements are made. Asking what sort of rūpa is 'external and grasped at,' the text answers:

> [746] Woman-faculty, man-faculty,[33] life-force-faculty, or whatever other rūpa *exists through karma having been wrought*, whether it be in the spheres of

visible shape, odor, taste, or tactile, in the spatial or fluid element, in the integration or subsistence of rūpa, or in bodily nutriment. [emphasis added]

As for rūpa which is external but not grasped at, the text says:[34]

[747] The sphere of sound, bodily and vocal *viññati*,[35] the lightness, plasticity, wieldiness, decay, and impermanence of form, or whatever other rūpa *exists which is not due to karma having been wrought,* whether it be in the spheres of visible form, odor, taste or tactile, in the spatial or fluid element, etc....

Clearly, rūpa here is divided into that which is 'wrought' by karma and that which is not. The text gives no clue or insight into how, suddenly, rūpa may be considered as a karmic result, a vipāka.

Buddhaghosa treats the notion of kammically-produced rūpa as a given. He writes:[36]

'Related to a cause' (re: our [4], above: *sappacayaṃ*, 'involves conditions') means: matter sprung from kamma is caused by kamma, that sprung from nutriments, etc., is caused by nutriments, etc.

And again:[37]

In 'not due to kamma having been wrought,' matter sprung from another cause than kamma has been taken. In 'due to kamma having been wrought' only matter sprung from kamma has been taken.

Aside from this definitional tautology, he offers no clue as to *how* kamma might produce a rūpa. In fact, while discussing the two viññatis,[38] Buddhaghosa is careful to note that though they are discussed as 'sprung from consciousness,' in the 'ultimate sense' (*parāmattha*) it is only the dhammas on which the viññatis depend that can accurately be called 'sprung from consciousness,' not the viññatis themselves. One wonders why the same qualifications and caution were not tended to the claim of 'rūpa from kamma'?

This issue is not insignificant. Since the text allows one to maintain either that rūpa is or is not a karmic product, and there is no more basic concept for Buddhist soterics than karmic production, the positions different schools took on this issue become momentous. We can see a clear demarcation between the Theravādins and the Andhakas in the *Kathā vatthu* drawn precisely on this point.

Their respective positions on a wide range of topics all follow from whether they consider rūpa to be vipāka or not. Theravāda insists that rūpa is not vipāka, while the Andhakas (and Sāmmitiyas) claim that it is.[39]

Theravādins argue that rūpa lacks the necessary properties of a vipāka, viz. it is not vedanā, nor conjoined with vedanā, nor with mental reaction, nor with consciousness in its many phases, etc.; in other words, it lacks the 'mental' or cognitive prerequisites of a karmic 'result.' The Andhakas and Sāmmitiyas retort that just as consciousness and its concomitant attributes are rightfully considered to be vipāka, since they arise through actions done (*kamma*), so should rūpa which arises through actions done be considered vipāka. Clearly, their response begs the textual question.

Similarly, they dispute whether earth/land can be considered vipāka or not, and they split the same way, with the Theravādins saying "no" and the Andhakas saying "yes."[40] Again, the Theravādins argue that earth/land lacks all nāmic properties, while it possesses qualities foreign to a vipāka, such as the ability to expand, contract, be cut up, broken, bought, sold, located, collected, explored, be common to everyone, etc. They also argue over whether earth/land is a vipāka of collective karma, or whether many can 'share' the land owned by a world-monarch (i.e., do others share in his vipāka?). The Andhakas finally reply that there is action (*kamma*) to gain dominion over the earth, and action to gain sovereignty on the earth, and thus, the earth is a result of action. What is at issue here is not the metaphysics of rūpa, but instead its karmic status, which for the Andhakas simply means how it functions in the grasper-grasped dynamic. If it contributes to an appropriational economy, if it spurs the desire to appropriate, to gain power, to possess, to construct and expand a self through its appropriational desires, then it is karmic. If land becomes that which people struggle to possess, to dominate and be sovereign over, then land is a 'product' of those actions. This prefigures Yogācāric thinking.

Another argument sheds some light on the Theravādin understanding of vipāka. Disputing whether old age and death are a result of action, the Andhakas predictably maintain that they are, but the Theravādins do not respond with an outright denial.[41] They agree that vipāka does influence old age and dying, however, it is not the sole cause: *ūtū*, the 'physical order,' also contributes. Vipāka, they claim, is unlike other mental states (*nāma-khandha*), and therefore it is not strictly mental.

This is an interesting confession, considering their insistence during other arguments that vipāka should be deemed nāmic. But they fail to expound further how these two 'orders,' the cognitive (nāma) order and the physical order, intermix and precisely influence each other. They digress into a discussion of past vs. present *kusala* and *akusala*. We already know that the kusala/akusala categories apply to kamma, but this still does not account for the rūpic, or 'physical' dimension.

On their side, the Andhakas also display some sloppy thinking here. They argue, if karma conduces to the deterioration and curtailment of life, then their claim that old age and death are vipāka is true. This would be to take a contributing or even necessary cause to be a sufficient cause, which is invalid. What their argument does make clear is that the physical order, for the Theravādins, is not really vipāka, i.e., it is not kammic. The interrelationship of nāma and rūpa remains as problematic as ever.

Several more points need to be made before we move on to our next topic. The Theravādins were perhaps not entirely as unsophisticated as I have been trying to depict them. A move that occurs from time to time in the Nikāyas becomes normative for Abhidhammic texts. Recognizing that the importance of rūpa per se rests primarily in its being a sensorial object available for sensorial contact and cognitive (as well as physical) appropriation, most abhidhammic discussions that treat the five-fold skandha scheme displace the term *rūpa* with the term *phassa* (skt. *sparśa*), 'contact,' lit: 'touch.' The emphasis, the focus of the discourse, thus, moves to cognition, the hows and whys of perception and cognition, the appropriational and karmic interplay with the sensorium. Again and again the list becomes *contact*, pain-pleasure-neutral sensation, associational thinking, embodied-conditioning and consciousness,' instead of '*rūpa*, pain-pleasure-neutral sensation...,' etc. Such is the case in the opening sections of the *Dhammasaṅgaṇī*. Section one lists all the kusala dhammas, and where the five skandhas are listed, phassa replaces rūpa. Each of the five skandhas are discussed, one by one, at the beginning of the text. Sec. 2, which begins this ostensive overview of the five skandhas, in fact, offers a definition of phassa, *not* rūpa (the definition and discussion of rūpa doesn't occur until later, in the part of the text we discussed above, in a division of the text devoted entirely to rūpa, disconnected from the skandhic discussion by substantial intervening material); sec. 3 defines vedanā, and so forth. The seeds of the rigorous epistemological investigations which Buddhism later unleashed on all of Indian thought were planted here, in this simple, but astute displacement. It prefigures and sets the stage for the Yogācāric subsumption of rūpa into cognition.

A second displacement must also be noted. Not only does the abhidhamma systematically substitute sensorial contact (lit. 'touch') for rūpa, but the fourth skandha, saṃskāra (embodied-conditioning), is systematically displaced by *cetanā*, (volition, intentionality). Cetanā, inasmuch as it involves the mental determinations which shape and result in actions, is thoroughly kammic. Rather than emphasize the aspect of latency which 'embodied-conditioning' forefronts, the emerging of conditioning from its latency in or as conscious decisions, apparent predilections, conscious volitions, etc., becomes highlighted by the term *cetanā*. This move triggers two important consequences.

First, Theravādin accounts of unconscious, latent processes become inadequate. All explanation becomes surface, what is consciously present now and now only. For instance, in the *Kathā vatthu* they argue, against the Andhakas, that outbursts of *anuśaya* (latent biases) cannot take place unconsciously.[42] For an *anuśaya* to be 'unconscious,' they claim, that would mean that an anuśaya would have to be either rūpa, or nibbāṇa, or the five sense organs, or the five senses. For them, these categories and these categories alone are unconscious, i.e., devoid of nāma. This classificatory insistence, no doubt, is a by-product of the displacement of saṅkhāra by cetanā, i.e., replacing 'unconscious movement' with 'volitional manifestations.' They nonetheless, perhaps incoherently, maintain a series of 'potentials' which the arhat may realize, i.e., according to them, an arhat's cognitive ability is always enlightened even when he does not manifest that particular ability at some given moment.[43] How potentials, or even more pointedly, the latencies (anuśaya) are understood, where do they reside, by what mechanism are latencies and potentials stored and brought back to the surface, etc., remains unanswered by the Theravādins here.

The 'unconscious,' with the exception of the four 'non-consciousness' categories listed above (rūpa, nibbāṇa, and sense-organs and objects), is only real for them at the moment it is actually being cognized, which is to say when it is conscious; latent, embodied motivational and predispositional forces are only recognized by them when they emerge in the form of conscious volitions. This flattening out of the models of mental process led to theoretic difficulties. Kalupahana in his *Buddhist Psychology* argues that Early Buddhism (viz. his version of what the authentic Buddha taught) did not have a theory of the unconscious, that such theories were a later, unfortunate distortion of Buddha's teaching. An examination of the texts, however, might suggest a different scenario. What was originally a theory of an unconscious economy (*āsava, anusaya, kilesa, saṅkhāra,* etc.), in the process of abhidhammic codification, became a conscious economy, a conscious stream which was purely surface, no depth; but this 'economy' failed both to account for what lay outside the surface, or to explain *on* what the surface rested. The victory of the metaphysics of presence—the 'now,' apparent and conscious over the latent, embodied and unconscious—tipped the balance of the doctrinal scale, tilting it away from its 'middle way.' Negational discourse (ex.: Mādhyamika) arose as a corrective. Critics confused its method for its message, and interpreted it as a form of nihilism. The metaphysics of absence proved no less problematic. This dilemma, even at the early, pre-Mahāyānic stage, led some schools to posit substrata (substantial and otherwise) as compensation. Yogācāra offered the ālaya-vijñāna as a solution, and was hard pressed to differentiate it from an essentialistic substratum. This will be examined in a later chapter.

Second, cetanā makes the intentionality of consciousness thoroughly explicit. Consciousness is neither static nor passive, but ever actively intending, willing toward its objects. And this willing is never neutral, but always karmic. Intentionality itself becomes synonymous with karma. To overcome karma, then, involves overcoming intentionality. Since consciousness and intentionality are also synonymous, this means that consciousness too must be overcome. However, Yogācāra will add an interesting element to this formula. The ālaya-vijñāna will be defined as lacking intentionality, i.e., it is a non-intentional form of consciousness. However, the ālaya-vijñāna, too, must be overcome. Hence, intentionality, while symptomatic of deep-seated problems, is not the root or the most deep-seated. The karmic dilemma goes deeper. Exactly how this is worked out will be discussed in a later chapter.

Meditative intent (samādhi), focused as cetanā, rivalled prajñā in some camps as the most efficacious means of dealing with the karmic dilemma. These camps argued that insight (prajñā) alone is insufficient. It must be actualized, put into play in the world, in the situation it purveys. It intends its own betterment through a turning from akusala to kusala habits. But, again mārga, methodology holds the key. Since the problem concerns action and method, the question of 'how' to en-act, of praxis, becomes paramount. Hence prajñā must be conjoined with upāya.

Yogācāra karmic theory

In his *Karmasiddhi-prakaraṇa* (Exposition Establishing Karma), Vasubandhu challenged the views of the Vaibhāṣikas and any others who held that dharmas might be anything other than momentary. Momentariness basically explained the series of consciousness moments as a casual sequence in which each moment caused its successor. Recognizing that the theory of momentariness had difficulty explaining certain types of continuity—from one life to the next, the re-emergence of a consciousness stream after it has been interrupted in deep sleep or meditation, etc.—near the end of the treatise he introduces the Yogācāra notion of the *ālaya-vijñāna* (storehouse-consciousness) in which the 'seeds' of previous experiences are stored subliminally and released into new experiences. The metaphor of seeds being planted in the consciousness stream by experiences, only to sprout later (break through from the subliminal into conscious experience), possibly producing new seeds that are implanted to be sprouted later, provided a handy model that for Vasubandhu not only explained continuity between two separate moments of consciousness, but also provided a quasi-causal explanation for the mechanics of karmic retribution, i.e., it described how an action done at one time could produce 'fruit' at a another time, including across lifetimes. The *ālaya-vijñāna* also eliminated the need for a theory of a substrative, permanent self that is the doer and recipient of karma, since, like a stream, it is perpetually changing with ever new conditions from moment to moment. In this treatise Vasubandhu denies that something at $time_1$ can be identical to what might appear to be the same thing at $time_2$, since, he claims, it is undergoing changes every moment, even if so small as to go unnoticed. In good Buddhist fashion Vasubandhu argues that reality consists of a stream of changing causes and conditions with no permanent entities (such as God, soul, etc.) anywhere.

Previous Buddhists, especially in the Abhidharma schools, had developed a sophisticated metaphoric vocabulary to describe and analyze the causes and conditions of karma in terms of seeds (*bījā*). Just as a plant develops from its roots unseen underground, so do previous karmic experiences fester unseen in the mind; just as a plant sprouts from the ground when nourished by proper conditions, so do karmic habits, under the right causes and conditions, reassert themselves as new experiences; just as plants reach fruition by producing new seeds that re-enter the ground to take root and begin regrowing a similar plant of the same kind, so do karmic actions produce wholesome or unwholesome fruit that become latent seeds for a later, similar type of action or cognition. Just as plants reproduce only their own kind, so do wholesome or unwholesome karmic acts produce effects after their own kind. This cycle served as a metaphor for the process of cognitive conditioning as well as the recurrent cycle of birth and death (*saṁsāra*). Since Yogācāra accepts the Buddhist doctrine of momentariness, seeds are said to perdure for only a moment during which they become the cause of a similar seed that succeeds them. Momentary seeds are causally linked in sequential chains, each momentary seed a link in a chain of karmic causes and effects.

Seeds are basically divided into two types: wholesome and unwholesome. Unwholesome seeds are the acquired cognitive habits preventing one from reaching enlightenment. Wholesome seeds—also labeled "pure" and "unpolluted"—give rise to more pure seeds, which, as they reach full maturity, bring one closer to Awakening. In general Yogācāra differentiates inner seeds (personal conditioning) from external seeds (being conditioned by others). One's own seeds can be modified or affected by exposure to external conditions (external seeds), which can be either beneficial or detrimental. Exposure to polluting conditions intensifies one's unwholesome seeds, while contact with "pure" conditions, such as hearing the Correct Teaching (*Saddharma*), can stimulate one's wholesome seeds to increase, thereby diminishing and ultimately eradicating one's unwholesome seeds.

Another metaphor for karmic conditioning that accompanies the seed metaphor is "perfuming" (*vāsanā).* A cloth exposed to the smell of perfume acquires its scent. Similarly one is mentally and behaviorally conditioned by what one experiences. This conditioning produces karmic habits, but just as the odor can be removed from the cloth so can one's conditioning be purified of perfumed habits. Typically three types of perfuming are discussed: 1. linguistic and conceptual habits; 2. habits of self-interest and "grasping self" (*ātma-grāha*), i.e., the belief in self and what belongs to self; and 3. Habits leading to subsequent life situations (*bhāvāṅga-vāsanā*), i.e., the long-term karmic consequences of specific karmic activities.

Yogācāra literature debates the relation between seeds and perfuming. Some claim that seeds and perfuming are really two terms for the same thing, viz. acquired karmic habits. Others claim that seeds are simply the effects of perfuming, i.e., all conditioning is acquired through experience. Still others contend that "seed" refers to the chains of conditioned habits one already has (whether acquired in this life, in some previous life, or even "beginninglessly") while "perfuming" denotes the experiences one has that modify or affect the development of one's seeds.

Notes

1 Treating psychology as a type of physics was not unique to Buddhists. Western thought did the same, starting with the Greeks, and well past the Middle Ages. For instance Bk. II of Spinoza's *Ethics* treats the mind, perception, etc., as one at that time would have described the physical properties of material things, using the same type of language. We today owe a great debt to Freud and others, that we are no longer constrained to do so.

2 The Theravādins have a list of 'twenty-four conditions,' though the Theravādin abhidhamma literature discusses causality in many additional ways; the Vaibhāṣikas reduced those twenty four to seven or eight; Yogācāra in one sense reduced those further to four basic types of conditions; cf. chapter twenty, below. However beyond these four, they proposed multiple

categories of types of causes and conditions which they wove into a dense causal system. The *Ch'eng wei-shih lun* devotes a good deal of attention to the explication and application of this system. It is beyond the scope of the present work to examine the details. At the other extreme Mādhyamika eschewed the entire project of classifying conditions into typologies and, as Candrakīrti remarks in the first chapter of the *Prasannapadā*, *pratītya-samutpāda* means *pratyayatā mātreṇa*, i.e., utter conditionality.

3 Inasmuch as texts remain associated with their authors, such that, in the case of a strong text, the author is sometimes considered as if he were a property of the text (e.g., the author of the Fourth Gospel), and in cases of strong writers, particularly if they produced a large literary output, the text is considered a property of the author (e.g., Shakespeare and his works), the text and author share a proximity, a location, although one invariably encompasses and subsumes or possesses the other. Thus the 'author'—as that which belongs to the text, or that of which the text is an expression—remains beyond the actual moment of writing. It is much easier to see, though, that a long-dead, biographically ambiguous author (e.g., Pythagoras) is more prajñapti than flesh and bones. Such an 'author' is constructed out of the intersection of the histories embodied in the text (including readings of the text) and the histories embodied in the reader. In other words, the notion of 'author' is a hermeneutic construction.

Moreover, in a sense the text never ceases to be written, since each reader, through the unavoidable violence of reading and interpreting, perforce re-writes the text. Old texts are often revised or entirely revamped by editors, redactors, copyists, etc. It would be as impossible to state unequivocally how the first *Tao-te-ching* read, as to reconstruct what Aristotle's dialogues were like. Readers and subsequent writers have re-written, altered, and irrevocably lost much that has been written. But even texts whose syntagmatic and verbal integrity are unquestionable depend upon current readers for their 'sense,' their 'meaning,' their place in our history. What does the word 'Word' (*logos*) mean in *John* 1:1 anyway?

4 The *Viṃśatikā* (Twenty Verses) is commonly construed as an argument for ontological idealism, and much contemporary literature insists on reading it that way—despite (or maybe because of) the fact that such a reading makes the text incoherent.

5 While the early Buddhist theory of karma drew somewhat on contemporaneous Jaina theories, for the Jainas karma is a *material* category, i.e., the economy of the inflow (*āsava*) of karmic 'particles' that adhere to a *jīva*, (living-soul). By contrast, for the Buddhists karma is a mental category. This emphasis on mental rather than physical or metaphysical explanations for karma and the human problematic paved the way for Yogācāra's psycho-philosophic reinterpretation of the Buddhist mārga.

6 Interestingly, this is one word whose root or basic form remains recognizable in virtually all Indo-European languages: Skt: *jñāna*, Greek: *gnosis* or *gignoskein*, Latin: *gnoscere, noscere*; *cognitio*, French: *connaitre*, Eng: *know*, etc. The Sanskrit *jñ-* becomes *kn-* in English, as in German it became *kennen*, *Kenntnis* (Old High German: *bi-chāan*, Old English: *cnāwen*, Middle English: *knowen*). In other language groups such as Semitic (Hebrew: *da'ath*) or Chinese (*chih*), no similarities with the Indo-European root are found.

7 R. Gethin, "The Five Khandhas...," p. 37.

8 He cites *Saṃyutta Nikāya* III 59-60, 86-87

9 He offers the following note: "This is most simply expressed at Dhātuk 9 where the truth of arising and the truth of the path are said to be *saṃkhārakkhandha*; it is elaborated at Dhs 185-225, and at Vibh 63-9 where the various categories of unskilful *dhammas* are treated in terms of the *khandhas*."

10 *Saṃyutta Nikāya* IV.230-231. Cited in James McDermott, *Developments in the Early Buddhist Concept of Kamma/Karma*, Princeton University, 1970, PhD dissertation, p. 53 (recently published in India by Motilal, but page numbers given here will be from the original ms.).

11This, and other common formulae used to describe the arhat are discussed and classified in Jan Ergart, *Faith and Knowledge in Early Buddhism* (Leiden, 1977).

12 See an interesting discussion of the issue of *amata* in relation to nibbāṇa in Rune Johansson, *The Psychology of Nirvana* (Garden City, NY: Anchor, Doubleday, 1970) pp. 32-33, 103ff. To avoid substantialistic interpretations, Johansson translates *amata* as "freedom from death".

13 I can think of no more apt example of this genre than A. J. Bahm's *Philosophy of the Buddha* (NY: Collier Books, 1962). Focusing on Early Buddhism (entirely in translation), his argument is succinctly announced in the first paragraph of his first chapter:

> Gotama's Philosophy may be summed up in a simple, clear and obvious principle, which immediately compels belief once it is understood. The principle: Desire for what will not be attained ends in frustration; therefore, to avoid frustration, avoid desiring what will not be attained.

While this is certainly part of Buddha's message, Buddhism per se cannot be reduced to this or any other single simplistic formula. How, for instance, is one to know or determine what exactly *is* attainable? Bahm, incidentally, never once mentions the Stoics. It is nonetheless a frequently intriguing book.

14 Cf. ch. 2 of J. N. Mohanty's *Husserl and Frege* (Bloomington: University of Indiana Press, 1982).

15 Merleau-Ponty, *The Phenomenology of Perception* (London: Routledge & Kegan Paul, 1962), Part Two, Section 2, "Space". His argument, in part, is that when we perceive X *as* a geometric shape, that perception presupposes the history of the discovery/invention of that shape. We, unfortunately, confuse the 'as' for 'is.' For instance:

> If what I perceive is a circle, says the logician, all its diameters *are* equal. But, on this basis, we should equally have to put into the perceived circle all the properties which the geometer has been able and will be able to discover in it. Now it is the circle as a thing in the world which possesses in advance and in itself all the properties which analysis is destined to discover in it. The circular trunks of trees had already, before Euclid, the properties that Euclid discovered in them. But in the circle as phenomenon, as it appeared to the Greeks before Euclid, the square of the tangent was not equal to the product of the whole chord and its exterior position: the square and the product did not appear in the phenomenon, nor necessarily did the equal radii. (p. 273)

This argument takes perception as integral to geometric formulations in a way perhaps objectionable to those opposed to phenomenology. His full argument, which responds to this criticism, is too detailed to reproduce here and we needn't deal with it further. This snippet from an argument which continues for many pages is only brought in here for its suggestive evocation of the problem of prapañca as vikalpa in terms of historic embodiment (*saṃskāra*).

The ambivalence of Husserl's notion of geometric origins has been admirably explored by Derrida in his *Edmund Husserl's Origin of Geometry: An Introduction*, tr. by John P. Leavy, ed. by David Allison (Stony Brook: Nicolas Hays, 1978).

16 Interestingly, some Indian systems explicitly envision the flow of time by this alternate model. While we tend to assume that the 'natural' way to think about temporal direction is as a flow from the past toward the future, *from* birth *to* death, from Creation to Apocalypse—and even Heidegger has us being thrown by Being toward death, this movement, according to him, inscribing the parameters for all possibilities of our being authentic—this exclusivistic, unidirectional model meets not only such alternatives as circular (Eternal Return) and reiterative (Eternal Recurrence) time models; it meets its direct opposite, a model which in all seriousness has the meaningful flow of time flowing in the opposite direction. The Sarvāstivādin school, for instance, repeatedly envisions dharmas 'existing' in the future (i.e., harboring the potential for efficient causal activity), coming from the future into the present (i.e., discharging the efficient causal function), and then depositing itself in the past (i.e., a 'spent' dharma). It is the future which holds the possibilities for current action, not the past, according to this model. It would be interesting to work out how this reverse teleology, if

applied rigorously and systematically, alters the meaning and relation of such things as purpose, goal-oriented action, progress, desire (as a moving toward, a reaching for), conditionality, and so forth. Unfortunately it is hard to say whether the so-called Sarvātivādins themselves applied any systematic rigor to these questions since the state of their literature has so far discouraged most scholars from attempting any in depth studies of their thought. Few Sanskrit texts are extant; most of what we have in Sanskrit consists of problematized citations from Sarvāstivādin texts by texts from other schools, usually in the course of a critique of their tenets. Chinese translations probably constitute the largest extant collection of Sarvāstivādin texts, but due to terminological and other difficulties these have remained virtually unstudied by modern scholars.

17 Nyanatiloka Mahathera's *Guide Through the Abhidhamma-Piṭaka* (Colombo: Bauddha Sāhita Sabhā, 1957) p. 5.

18 Cf. *A Buddhist Manual of Psychological Ethics*, tr. of *Dhammasaṅgaṇī* by C.A.F. Rhys-Davids (London: Pali Text Society) pp. 155-157 and *The Book of Analysis* (*Vibhaṅga*), tr. P.A. Thiṭṭila (London: Pali Text Society) pp. 16f. I have drawn profitably on both, but follow neither translation. Cf. also Nyanatiloka Mahathera's *Guide Through the Abhidhamma-Piṭaka*, *ibid.*, pp. 20-21, where he briefly discusses and clarifies this mātikā.

19 Sec. 1096-1112 classifies the *āsavas* into four types: *kāmāsava* (desire-āsava), *bhavāsava* (rebirth-āsava), *diṭṭhāsava* (perspectivally closed-āsava), *aññāṇāsava* (ignorance-āsava). It then discusses which dhammas are āsavas, which can have āsavas, which aren't themselves āsavas but can have, etc.

20 Cf. sec. 1113-1134. These fetter or tie one to the wheel of rebirth. A list of ten 'fetters' is given and then discussed. The ten are: kāma, repulsion, conceit, diṭṭhi, perplexity, ritualism, desire for rebirth, envy, meanness and ignorance.

21 Cf. sec. 1135-1150. These are bodily-ties (*kāyagantho*) to the wheel of rebirth, and the text lists four: bodily-tie of craving (*abhijjhā-kāyagantho*), bodily-tie of ill-will, bodily-tie of ritualism and bodily-tie of dogmatism and proselytizing.

22 Four are listed, identical to the four āsavas.

23 Four are listed, identical to the four āsavas.

24 These were discussed elsewhere.

25 Cf. 1117-1184. Reiterates diṭṭhi-āsava and the nīvaraṇas.

26 This odd classification seems to mean: rūpa is one of the five skandhas, and, according to sec. 994 of the *Dhammasaṅgaṇī*, all five skandhas are not in themselves *kleśa*, but can produce or suffer kleśic consequences. Rhys-Davids translates 994 like this:

> Which are the states that are not corrupt but baneful?
>
> Good and indeterminate co-Intoxicant states [*sāsava*] taking effect in the worlds of sense, form and the formless; in other words, the *five* skandhas. (square brackets mine; italics hers)

I take this to mean that the skandhas per se are neutral in reference to the āsavas or kleśas, but that they may be swayed, or 'corrupted.' The later notion of *vāsanā* as a 'perfuming' - i.e., a cloth can absorb the odor of a perfume due to proximity, and will then smell like that perfume, although the cloth itself is not the perfume, and will not smell like that permanently - seems to evoke the same idea.

27 In his translation of this passage from the *Vibhaṅga*, Thiṭṭila offers: "Is not to be abandoned either by the first path or by subsequent paths," while Mrs. Rhys-Davids renders the terms more literally. *Dassana* and *bhāvanā*, i.e., 'perspectival orientation' and 'cultivation,' are the opening phases of the self-correcting practice prescribed and described by the abhidhamma. They signify becoming oriented and then sustaining practice on/as the beginning rungs of the 'path' (*māgga*). Having an orientation, an attitude toward disciplined cultivation, while cultivating and disciplining that attitude constitutes the initial methodological training. Cf. *Dhammasaṅgaṇī* 1002-1008, 1254-1267.

28 Cf. 1019. Rhys-Davids offers this note to 1019:

> Parittaṃ, understood as involving intellectual and ethical, as well as physical insignificance the connotation of the French term *borné*. The illustration chosen is that of a lump of cowdung! The essential quality is *appānubhāvatā*, i.e. of little importance of efficacy generally. Parittaṃ itself is ranked as an equivalent of the whole sphere of sense-experience.

By 'sense-experience' she means the kāma-dhātu.

29 A textual, as well as contextual issue is raised here. Rhys-Davids writes (p. liii):

> ...I have not followed the reading of the PTS. edition when it states that all form is kāmāvacaram eva, rūpāvacaram eva, that is, is both related to the universe of sense and also to that of form. The Siamese edition reads kāmāvacaram eva, na rūpāvacaram eva. It may seem at first sight illogical to say that form is not related to the universe of form. But the better logic is really on the side of the Siamese.

This 'logic' turns on her understanding 1281-1284 to be claiming "that the avacaras were mutually exclusive as to their contents" (p. liv). But no such claim is to be found there. The passages in question are attempting to define what is proper to each sphere, but it nowhere precludes overlap. Explicitly 'contents' such as the skandhas extend throughout the three realms. And rūpa, amongst other things, is one of the skandhas. Thiṭṭila's translation of this passage in the *Vibhaṅga* follows Rhys-David's reading. It is unnecessary for our present purposes to come to a decision about this textual aporia. For an important corrective to their interpretations, cf. Y. Karunadasa's *Buddhist Analysis of Matter* (Singapore: The Buddhist Research Society, 1989, 2nd ed.) chapter 1.

30 *Pariyāpannā* and *apariyāpannā* are shorthand terms for locations on the path. In a section of the text that discusses What is appropriational? What is appropriated and favorable to appropriation? What is not appropriated but favorable to appropriation?, when the question becomes What is neither appropriated nor favorable to appropriation?, the answer is: "The paths that are Unincluded, and the Fruits of the Paths, and unconditioned element." The Unincluded here means that which is located at the *transition point* between the mundane realm (*lokiya*) and the fruits of the transmundane realm (*lokuttara*), and hence 'not-included' in either. The ultimate 'unconditioned element' means nirvāṇa. 'Included' means included in the mundane realm, 'unincluded' means located at the switch point between mundane and transmundane realms.

31 Rūpa is sometimes taken to mean a *visible* object, or a color, etc. The Chinese term which translates rūpa is *se* 色, meaning not only 'form,' but also 'color,' 'aesthetically pleasing visual.' In other formulations rūpa becomes the object of 'body,' i.e., what body 'touches,' or 'body' itself (e.g., *rūpāṇi*, 'bodies').

32 But cf. *Atthasālinī*, p. 328; *The Expositor*, pp. 427f, where Buddhaghosa does define rūpic decay as 'aging,' offering 'hoariness' and 'wrinkling' as examples.

33 In Theravādin and Sarvāstivādin abhidharma, maleness and femaleness are defined as rūpic properties, and are included as such in their lists of dharmas.

34 C.A.F. Rhys-Davids' translation, p. 203, modified.

35 Viññati (Skt. *vijñapti*) is obviously an important term for Yogācāra. Here it means a gesture, whether bodily or linguistic, which has the capacity for communicating intention. My body language and what I say and how I say it offer clues, indications to what I internally intend. What becomes of interest to the Theravādins and Sarvāstivādins is its opposite, avijñapti-rūpa, i.e., the failure to produce a gesture capable of being understood by an external observer, i.e., either concealing one's intentions, or deliberately misleading others by conveying, through gestures or words, intentions other than the ones one actually harbors. The vijñapti and avijñapti-rūpas are considered karmic conduits, even though they are rūpic, not strictly mental or cognitive! By labeling them as rūpa, i.e., categorizing them as a material rather than

mental phenomena, the way was opened for some genuinely arcane debates and classifications. Yogācāra rejected the category of avijñapti-rūpa altogether, separated vijñapti from rūpa (in the process, conjoining vijñapti and prajñapti) and declared that the sensorium, including and especially the so-called neutral rūpic components, are nothing but vijñapti (*vijñapti-mātra*).

36 *Atthasālinī*, p. 304; *Expositor*, p. 400.

37 *Atthasālinī*, p. 337; *Expositor* p. 437.

38 *Ibid.* (*Expositor*, pp. 437f).

39 *Points of Controversy*, p.309.

40 *Ibid.*, pp. 205-207.

41 *Ibid.*, pp. 207-208.

42 *Ibid.*, p. 288.

43 *Ibid.*, p. 255. The question here is whether, if one is not immediately experiencing *ñāṇa*, even though *avijjā* (avidyā, nescience) is banished, is it correct to say that he is having thoughts not conjoined with *ñāṇa*? The Theravādins say 'no,' since if nescience is banished, *ñāṇa* must be present, or have been present, by definition. It is, they argue, *present even if not active.* Even if he is having thoughts which are not conjoined with *ñāṇa*, you should still say he has *ñāṇa*! To this pious outrage, the opponent sanely replies this would be granting him status based, at best, on a past insight (*ñāṇa*), not one presently active. Clearly what is at stake in this argument is the Theravādin's metaphysics of presence, here displaying its connection and inseparability from issues of authority, reverence and teleological identity.

Chapter Ten

Madhyamakan Issues

無為而無不為。
Lao Tzu, *Tao te ching*

聖人之見時，若步之與影不可離。
A sage can no more be seen as separate from his times,
as someone can walk away from his shadow.
Lü-shih ch'un-ch'iu 14:3.3

Madhyamaka and Karma

As mentioned previously, Buddhists discussed karma in three distinct registers:

1. The mechanics of action, in terms of cause and effect, doer and deed, the mechanics of rebirth, etc.;
2. Moral causality, how moral actions reap their rewards and punishments;
3. Karma, whether good or bad, as the underlying problematic that Buddhism, in its soteric dimension, is designed to overcome and eliminate.

In his *M?lamadhyamaka kārikā* Nāgārjuna devotes separate chapters to each of these registers. MMK 8, on *karma-kāraka* (action and actor) addresses the first register (mechanics of action), and as we'll see in a moment, is a remarkable chapter. MMK 16, on *bandhana-mokṣa* (bondage and liberation) takes up the third register (soteric theory), while the chapter that follows it, chapter 17, *karma-phala* (on karmic fruit), explores the second register (moral karma). In another chapter, MMK 13, on *saṃskāra*, Nāgārjuna takes up related issues concerning the inappropriateness of turning soteric psychology into a metaphysics. That chapter has strong implications for Yogācāra thought, so we will examine it after looking at the chapters on karma.

We have turned to this Madhyamaka text to present Buddhist theories of karma for three reasons. First, since the Buddhist karmic theories discussed here are encapsulated concisely in the MMK, often with variations explicated, the MMK chapters lend themselves more easily to our own encapsulation than would a longer, more elaborate text such as the *Abhidharmakośa*. Second, Madhyamaka being the 'other' Indian Mahāyāna school in India, as well as Yogācāra's predecessor, it exerted a profound influence on Yogācāra doctrine.

Yogācāra thought attempted to not only retain what was valuable in the schools that preceded it, but to do so in a way that would not violate the radical insights and warnings provided by Nāgārjuna. Thus, what Nāgārjuna says here had a bearing on Yogācāra thinking. Third, each of these chapters presents a radical critique of the theories it presents, highlighting the limits of each theory along with the issues in question that spurred debate among Buddhists. This is helpful for understanding what were the bones of contention among Buddhists when Yogācāra arrived.

Space precludes me from including the full texts of the four chapters of MMK to be discussed here, so the reader is encouraged to procure a copy of Nāgārjuna's text (in Sanskrit or translation) and follow my exegesis in tandem with those texts.

Karma-kāraka

MMK 8 revolves around the question of the relation between an agent (*kāraka*, lit. 'that which acts') and action (*karma*). The commonly-held view that Nāgārjuna challenges is that an agent is a distinct, autonomous source and initiator of the action. By this view, actions are performed by stable, identifiable entities whose existence and identities are always more than what is involved in the action. The criticism Nāgārjuna offers will aim at the independence and autonomy of the agent, an autonomy that, Nāgārjuna shows, not only separates and isolates the agent from the action (which is exactly the opposite of what someone proposing a theory of agency is trying to do), but also leads to a nihilistic view of action, such that all actions become pointless. In some interesting ways, Nāgārjuna's critique parallels Merleau-Ponty's critique of the beacon model of perception, in which noesis acts as the autonomous agent constituting noemata, which was discussed back in chapter two.

If the agent is really autonomous, it must have a fixed, invariant identity that exists apart from the action. If not, in what sense is it autonomous? Before proceeding further with the arguments in MMK 8, it will be useful to quickly contextualize the philosophical agenda of Nāgārjuna's philosophy. One of the primary targets of Nāgārjuna's philosophy is *svabhāva*, the idea that things have self-existent, self-caused, fixed, invariant, permanent, immutable, independent, autonomous identities. Theologies and philosophies, East and West, have not only argued for such things, but at least since Plato in the West and the Upaniṣads in India, they frequently elevate such svabhāvic things above the actual world in which we live, in which absolutely everything we encounter—including the way we encounter them—is variant, impermanent, and interdependent. In denial of this reality, people fabricate notions of eternality to which they then cling, in the hope that their identity can partake of the same eternality, and thus transcend their actual impermanent reality. Eternal things come to be more highly valued than things that are subject to generation and decay, i.e., impermanent things. Higher than this life are the eternal verities, the eternal 'truths.' Early Buddhism challenged the idea that persons possess svabhāvic selfhood, *ātman* (eternal, invariant identity). The term *svabhāva* was enlisted for this purpose later; early Buddhism labeled the denial of permanent, invariant, independent selfhood in a person the doctrine of *anātman* (no-self). One poses and clings to the idea of self for the deepest psychological reasons: One is afraid of death, impermanence, noncontinuance; sensing the absence of self is frightening, even terrifying. This fear generates an underlying anxiety—*duḥkha*—which we attempt to assuage by constructing theories of permanent selfhood. That is why many religions promise eternal 'life' after death: actual life is temporary, but death is true eternal life. Buddhism considered such promises pernicious since they masked the deep anxieties about impermanence and no-self that needed to be confronted in order to overcome duḥkha. Buddhists held this *ātma-dṛṣṭi*, 'view of selfhood,' to be the most deep-seated and pernicious view to which people cling. Devaluing actual life in order to imagine that death is more important—that death is, in fact, true life—is one of the *viparyāsas*, the perversions or reversals against which Buddhism warns, in this case, the *viparyāsa* of imagining the permanent in the impermanent.

Nāgārjuna recognized that the proclivities and propensities driving people to posit and cling to a notion of selfhood were subtle and ubiquitous, and not confined to people's speculations about themselves or other persons. They infected the way people thought about everything, though usually remaining in the background, as invisible presuppositions. Svabhāva, Nāgārjuna concluded, was not only an erroneous idea, but essentially incoherent as well, especially when pressed into the service of underwriting claims about the actual world, which was the primary reason people invented the notion in the first place. Starting with the incoherence of the basic definition of an invariant, independent, immutable, eternal, self-caused, self-existent entity,[1] Nāgārjuna repeatedly shows that such a thing could not, by definition, do anything, engage in any action, be altered or affected by any action, have any sort of relation with any other thing (especially another svabhāvic entity), etc., since all such things require mutability and dependence. Because of our ignorance and proclivities, some svabhāvic notion invariably creeps into our formulations concerning virtually everything, most evidently when we are trying our hardest to be reasonable and logical (though such presuppositions usually go unrecognized). Nāgārjuna, like iron filings to a magnet, zeroes in on the hidden svabhāvic assumptions in a position. Once disclosed, they are shown to be absurd, incoherent. The middle way between extremes, for Nāgārjuna, means a middle way between notions of eternality and annihilation, being and nonbeing, existence and nonexistence, identity and difference, and so on, since each side of these oppositions harbors svabhāvic presuppositions and is therefore extremist.

The svabhāvic entity that Nāgārjuna attacks in MMK 8 is the notion of agent as *sadbh?ta*, an actual, independent, permanent entity. As pointed out above, a svabhāvic entity cannot do anything, since that would require it to change. All actions involve change to some extent. Were an entity to change as a result of its relation with an action, then the entity would not be a permanent since the action has changed it. If the entity remains impervious to change, then it cannot be said to have a meaningful relation with variables such as actions. Simply, a doer must do, and doing involves change. Thus Nāgārjuna states (8:2) that a *sadbh?ta* can't do anything, and therefore no such agent can do an action. If agents are all *sadbh?ta*, then actions could not have agents. Further (8:3), as Garfield paraphrases,[2] "if the agent and action are totally nonexistent, there will be no cause for the action and no justification for calling the agent an agent." It is important to keep in mind that Nāgārjuna is not promoting this sort of nihilistic conclusion, but, on the contrary, he is warning us against it.

Nihilism, Nāgārjuna next argues, arises from clinging to svabhāvic premises, not from letting them go.

> If a cause [for an action] does not actualize (*asat*), the enacted (*kārya*) and 'efficient causal activity' (*kāraṇa*) are not found (*na vidhyate*).
> Those not having come to be (*abhāva*), activity (*kṛiya*), agent (*kartā*), and doing (*karaṇa*) are not found. (8:4)

An action must be caused by an agent. If the notion of agent contains svabhāvic elements, such as conceiving an agent as *sadbh?ta*, then such an agent cannot cause anything. In the absence of an agent, the action would have no cause. If, consequently, there is no cause, then the entire theory of action (karma) crumbles. The key terms in this verse are all derived from the root √*kṛ*, 'action, doing.' This is a key to the argument of the chapter, and draws on Indian sensibilities about language and grammar. A root term—which itself is an abstraction constructed by artificially differentiating some aspect or aspects of the altering flow of events—can be subjected to grammatical permutations. Each of those permutations, instead of being recognized as a mere permutation, a gesture of language, is given a life of its own. Each becomes an 'entity,' an existent, and people with metaphysicalizing tendencies will immediately latch on to each one, taking each as an element, a component, a distinct thing. Those elements will need to be classified, catalogued, defined, relations between them delineated, and so on. Moreover, the "root" is an abstraction of constructed commonality between, beyond, and behind these permutations. It is the generative matrix from which the variety of permutations derive. Hence, in some languages, the root form is treated as being its its most definitive and open-ended grammatical form when expressed as an 'infinitive,' implying it can take on infinite permutations. The root is not merely abstracted, but is frequently taken to be the 'word' or its essence in its purest, unmodified form. The root has an essential stability more real than its permutations. This grammatical metaphysics mirrors the ontologies and theologies of philosophers and religious thinkers, who also posit pure invarient essences as the generative matrices behind and beyond the fluctuating world of fleeting things and experiences.

This linguistic proliferation by which words and concepts become 'realities' overshadowing the actual conditions from which they are abstracted is called *prapañca.*

Translations of the above verse which offer distinct terms for each of the √*kṛ* derivatives, instead of demonstrating that they are cognates, miss the point. Nāgārjuna is not offering us a checklist of things that need to be found in order to satisfy some criterion. On the contrary he is showing that if one is unable to identify or locate a legitimate cause, one's demand that there be an understandable, teeming world of apprehendable conceptual realities will be frustrated, especially if one tries to reapply those ungrounded concepts to actual events. *Kārya* is 'what has been done, the effect, the accomplished act, the enacted'; *kāraṇa* is the efficient cause that brings something about, what makes something happen, the activator. Without something having been enacted (*kārya*) by efficient causal means (*kāraṇa*), talk of doers, deeds, and doing is groundless. Of what and through what means would they be doing anything?

> In the absence of a cause, there can be no enacted, no activator; no activity, no actor, and no acting.

A *sadbh?ta* cannot act, and hence cannot cause anything. Actions must have causes. If one clings to the notion of a svabhāvic agent, nihilism follows.

> If activity, and so on, do not come to be (*asaṃbhave*), then Dharma and Adharma are not found.
> If Dharma and Adharma don't actualize, then fruit (*phala*) arising from them is not found. (8:5)

> If fruit does not actualize, then neither a path to liberation nor a path to heaven is possible.
> All activities would fail to reach a goal (*nairarthakyaṃ*). (8:6)

In verse 5 Nāgārjuna demonstrates that discussions of karma in the mechanical register have implications for the moral register as well. Dharma here means the moral norm; Adharma signifies the chaos and 'evil' that arises when Dharma is not followed.[3]

Theories of action are usually constructed for some purpose, and in India that purpose was to provide a theory of action that explained how to act for social and/or spiritual goals, as well as provide an explanation for why such actions would be effective for reaching those goals. If there is no coherent theory of action, then there can be no coherent theory of social or spiritual activity, in other words, no ethics or morality. A religious moralism that relies on the promise of some future reward or punishment should be able to give a reasonable account of why the actions it promotes are good and lead to good consequences, while the actions it condemns will lead to bad consequences. However, lacking a coherent theory of action, moralism becomes incapable of compellingly conceiving—much less guaranteeing—how actions can produce the consequences, the fruits, moralists claim. Moral action becomes fruitless. Moral exhoratation becomes hollow.

And which fruits require the grandest claims? Afterlife promises. Verse 6 addresses the third register of karma, the soteric dimension. Svabhāvic moralists dangle promises of liberation or heaven in order to promote certain behavioral and institutional regimes. The types of activities advocated by moralism, moralists claim, are the most important, most meaningful, most directed toward the ultimate concerns and goals of humans. Their preferred behavioral program, they insist, should supersede all others, since it is the highest and most significant. The risk, however, is that, since their claims lie on an incoherent foundation—which is to say, no true foundation at all—whoever buys into their system becomes a potential nihilist, since she may come to realize that she has been persuaded to follow a path that turns out to be foundationless. Since she had thought that that path had been the most meaningful, the most important human endeavor, she is likely to conclude that *all* other paths must be even more meaningless, pointless, fruitless. All action becomes *nir-artha. Nir-* is a negational prefix. *Artha* means 'that towards which an intentionality intends,' or in this context, a goal. It also signifies 'meaning' or 'referent' (that towards which a linguistic intentionality intends, i.e., a word points to its referent). All action becomes pointless, fruitless, without purpose or goal. Life becomes meaningless.[4]

Again, Nāgārjuna is not promoting this bleak vision. He is warning against the svabhāvic presuppositions that lead to such desolute conclusions. It is necessary, Nāgārjuna is saying, for action to have a cause. If one chooses the wrong cause, all that follows from that wrong choice will also be wrong, even dangerous. So we should decide how to understand the causes of action seriously and carefully if we want to avoid all sorts of untoward consequences. In verse 12, after having eliminated some other incoherent possibilities for the relation of agent and action, Nāgārjuna offers a positive proposal.

> Agent *depends on* (*pratītya*) action, and action also *depends on* agent
> to occur (*pravartate*). We see no other way (*nānyat paśyāmaḥ*) of effectively establishing (*siddhi-kāraṇaṃ*) [them].

Like the dialectical circuit of intentionality between lived-body and perceived field with which Merleau-Ponty revised Husserl's theory of noetic constitution, Nāgārjuna proposes a dialectical solution that refuses to privilege either side of the dyad. The agent has no primacy over action, nor does action have primacy over the agent. They are mutually dependent (*pratītya*). An agent is an agent precisely in the moment it is causing an action—and at no other time or for any other reason; and an action is an action precisely at the moment an agent is engaging in it. In other words, the distinction between agent and action is finally only a matter of linguistic puffery. Agent and action are tautological; they can be distinguished conceptually, linguistically, but in actuality those words refer to an inseparability through which actions/agents occur (*pravartate*).

What has been negated or rejected by Nāgārjuna is the svabhāvic notion of agent, not the inseparability of agency and action.

The dialectical conclusion drawn here is all the more remarkable given Nāgārjuna's relentless critique elsewhere throughout MMK of all notions of simultaneity, convergence, confluence of conditions, and any sort of relations between things.[5] The notion of the mutual dependence of agent and action, stripped of all svabhāvic taints, is a rejection or leaving behind (*vyutsarga*) of the notion of agent as commonly conceived. Nāgārjuna wishes us to take away a lesson from this exercise:

> Even as karma and agent are left behind (*vyutsarga*), so should one understand 'appropriation' (*upādāna*).
> The [analysis of] agent and karma applies to the remaining existents (*bhāva*). (8:13)

There are several places in MMK where self-referentially Nāgārjuna states that something should be understood in the light of an argument or analysis carried out in another part of the text. He asks us to apply the analysis developed in this chapter to the remaining *bhāva*, that is, things containing explicit or implicit sva-*bhāva*. It is important that he explicitly encourages us to apply this analysis to appropriation, since, as we will see, appropriation lies at the core of all karmic problems.

Moral karma

MMK 17, on karma and its fruit (*karma-phala*), provides a summary of some basic Buddhist notions of moral karma and then subjects them to a critique. Very different opinions about which verses represent Nāgārjuna's own position are found in the literature on this chapter. This stems from the fact that, as is commonly the case in this type of literature, the positions and arguments of one's opponents are reproduced, but no graphic indicators are provided to sort out which statements are the author's and which represent an opponent. This feature reflects the roots in debate of this literature, since in Indian debate one usually was required to reiterate the opponent's argument before attempting to refute it. The ancients expected that everyone would be familiar with the stock arguments, so there was no need to explicitly identify them as such when citing them. Modern authors (and occasionally some of the ancient ones) don't always recognize such stock arguments. One's interpretation of an entire chapter can be radically affected if one attributes a position to the author, and endeavors to make that position consistent with what the author says elsewhere, when in fact that position or statement actually represents the opponent. Kalupahana, for instance, takes pretty much everything after verse 12 in this chapter to be Nāgārjuna's view.[6] Candrakīrti understood it otherwise; Kalupahana believes verse 14 is the crux of Nāgārjuna's view, whereas Candrakīrti attributes the view expressed there to the Sāṃmitīya, a Buddhist school associated with

Pudgalavāda thought. Obviously Candrakīrti and Kalupahana hold very different views about Nāgārjuna. For our purposes we needn't wade into this morass, since the reason we are looking at this chapter is to delineate some of the Buddhist views on karma; which source to attribute each view to is not our immediate concern.[7]

MMK 17 begins with a typical Buddhist moral maxim, not unlike the beginning of the *Dhammapāda*.

> Self-restraint (*ātma-saṃyamakaṃ*) and also benefiting others (*parānugraha*),
> is the Dharma of friendship (*maitra*). That is the seed giving fruit here [in this life] as well as the next. (17:1)

Curb oneself, while making oneself helpful to others is the Dharma of friendship. Maitra is a bond of intimate empathy and caring for others. Be a nice person, this verse says, and you will get your reward. Your reward will be here in the present as well as in future lives. This sort of friendship offers immediate rewards—friends and an engaged community. But moralism promises more than that. Moralism tends to be grounded in a promise. A promise is always a deferral of the present to the future. A desired objective will be achieved *later.* The promise puts what *is* in the service of what *might be.* Behavior becomes teleological.

The chapter now offers up a number of Buddhist karmic theories describing moral causes and the way they produce their fruit. These theories, which Nāgārjuna will ultimately deconstruct and dismiss, have at least one of two characteristics: They either begin to spin out and enumerate *categories*, or else they serve up novel *entities*—such as a seed theory or the promissory note (*avipraṇāśa*)—as supplements to the basic components of a simple mechanical karmic theory composed of doer and deed. Since, as we saw, these theories frequently fail to adequately ground themselves in reason (due to svabhāvic presuppositions), they insteald appeal to authority for the basis. These theories wrap themselves in the mantle of Buddha's authority, citing him as their source.

According to one theory, the Ultimate Sage (*paramā-ṛṣi*), the Buddha, said that karma consists of intention (*cetanā*) and intentionality (*cetayitvā*) (17:2). 'Intention' signifies mental karma, while 'intentionality' signifies bodily and linguistic karma (17:3). There are seven dharmas giving rise to karma, to wit:

1. voice or language (*vāc*),
2. physical activities (*viṣpanda*),
3. not resolving to avoid committing wrongdoing (*avirata*) while giving no external indication (*avijñapti*),
4. resolving to avoid committing wrongdoing (*virata*) without giving any indication (*avijñapti*),
5. Experiencing the (karmic results, *paribhoga*) of merit (*puṇya*) and
6. demerit (*apuṇya*), and

7. volition (*cetanā*) (17:4-5).

In Buddhist discussions of karma, the terms *vijñapti* and *avijñapti* mean 'gives indication' and 'gives no indication,' respectively.[8] There are several elaborations of this theory in Buddhist texts, but their simplest meaning is that some actions display or indicate their karmic significance in the very nature of the act, i.e., onlookers and observers can see what the intent of the person doing the action is (e.g., helping an old lady across the street, or hurling a racial epithet at someone). Actions with such indications are called *vijñapti* (lit. 'cause to be known'). Other actions, such as secretly resolving to do something while putting up appearances to the contrary, provide no indication. These are called *avijñapti* (lit. 'does not cause to be known). Dharmas 1 and 2 (verbal and physical actions) are vijñapti, while items 3 and 4 (resolving to either commit or desist from wrongdoing) are avijñapti, since one's actual resolve (or lack thereof) is concealed from others (unless expressed in verbal or physical actions, i.e., vijñapti)..

The point of verses 3-5 is that for Buddhists moral karma should be understood as causal and virtually ineluctable. From the moment the intent is set, or the moment a certain type of action is committed, the karma born at that moment continues uninterruptedly until it produces its fruit, until its consequences are 'enjoyed' (*paribhoga*), even if later one becomes distracted, or forgets about the original intent. If the continuity between deed and consequence were deemed to be any looser, then karmic fruit would not be guaranteed, the moral promise would go unfulfilled, and whether a particular intent or action led to some reward or punishment would be entirely arbitrary and happenstance. It is difficult to build a moral theory on such arbitrary foundations. One has to know that the causes lead to their fruit; otherwise why act in such a manner?

17:6 introduces a theoretical problem: Let's say that karma does reach its fruit. Thus the consequences of an action performed by person X will eventually come to fruition in person X at a later time. In the meantime karma must reside in the same locus, namely person X. What sense would it make for X to do an action if the consequences fall on Y? Such a theory would not engender any sense of personal responsibility, much less encourage anyone to pursue any particular course of action, since consequences would be entirely random. I do a job, and you get my paycheck. The svabhāvic problem is starting to rear its head (viz. imagining there are fixed stable identities such as X or Y in whom qualities such as karmic consequences inhere). Nāgārjuna points out that if karma remains in the same locus until it ripens, then it would seem to be permanent; if it has ceased, then could a fruit arise later? In other words, X does action Q. Does Q immediately disappear the moment it is performed? If so, then it is not around to produce a later fruit, and the fruit has no where to come from. If it perdures unchanged and stable until the fruit is produced—which in Buddhist theory could span many lifetimes—then it would come very close to looking like a permanent entity. Neither extreme is satisfactory, according to the middle way.

One attempt to respond to this problem is a theory developed initially by Sautrāntika Buddhists that was adopted (with some modifications) later by Yogācāra: a seed theory of karma as a metaphor for how the mental continuum conveys karma. This theory tries to circumvent the objection just raised by introducing an intermediate step or steps between the committing of the act and emergence of the fruit. In that way, karma per se is neither permanent (since the act itself does not endure), nor is it annihilational, since a series of events connect the initial act with the eventual fruit. A series, this theory holds, begins with a seed, which produces a sprout, which finally produces a fruit. Without the seed, the series could not develop (17:7). Since a series arises from a seed, and a fruit arises from a series, the relation between a fruit and the seed that precedes it, therefore, is neither interrupted nor eternal (17:8). In other words, the progression from seed to series to fruit is neither a single identity, nor an abortive discontinuity, and thus avoids the extremes of eternality and annihilationalism. In the same way, a consciousness stream or series (*citta-saṃtāna*) arises from an intention (*cetanā*), and a subsequent mental state develops (*cetaso'bhipravaratate*) from the series. Without the initial *citta* forming an intention, the fruit would not arise (17:9). The stream-series (*saṃtāna*) comes from the citta, and the fruit comes from the stream-series; so the progression from an earlier action to its fruit is neither interrupted nor eternal (17:10).

Emboldened, the theorist further enumerates: The ten pure paths of action (karma) are the means for achieving Dharma. The five qualities (*guṇa*) of pleasure (*kāma*) are the fruits of Dharma in this and future lives (17:11).[9]

Upon reading such a verse, the reader is probably curious to know what are the five x and the 10 y? Evoking that curiosity is precisely how such theorizing and its literature works. One wants to know more about each item, each category, and before long one has become so deeply enmeshed in the system that its vision has become one's own. The lure of the riddle and the promise of its explication pulls one in. Nāgārjuna deliberately intercepts that seductive lure by bluntly announcing that he will not engage in such silliness.

17:11 also strips bare another hidden assumption, one already embedded in the first verse of this chapter, the verse about present and future rewards deriving from the practice of friendship. The very notion of 'reward' as a motivation for behavior—whether moral or otherwise—implies a promise of *pleasure* (*kāma*). Do good, and pleasure is yours, now and in the future. As discussed in deatil in earlier chapters, the dichotomous pain-pleasure calculus had always been identified by Buddhism as pernicious. Pain-pleasure conditioning not only produces saṃskāras, but also underlies the deployment of 'heaven' and 'hell.' the promise of future punishment and reward, as moral incentive. To be self-restrained while caring for others *in order to reap some future pleasure* is not only selfish but a form of karmic ensnarement pursued in the name of better karma. One pursues karma rather seeking to eliminate it.

17:12 argues that this sort of speculative system building (*kalpanā*) is a great mistake.[10] Another theory, another kalpanā, this time wrapped in the authoritative mantel of "Buddhas, Pratyekabuddhas, and Śrāvakas," is presented: the *avipraṇāśa* theory. Avipraṇāśa is a promissory note, an I.O.U., a marker of a debt. One borrows money, and incurs a debt, and signs a promissory note promising to repay the debt at some future date. Once the promise is made a connection between the time of the initial loan and its repayment is established, no matter what sort of circumstances threaten to intervene in the interim. The text discusses several peculiarities of the avipraṇāśa theory which we can skip over (such as what connects a past life to a future life, what if anything one takes from one life to the next, and so on). There is some discussion about how one makes good on the debt or manages to cancel it, since Buddhist practice is supposed to eliminate the karmic debt one has accumulated over many lifetimes. Avipraṇāśa ceases as a result either of interrupting the development of its fruit, or due to death. The difference between these is determined by whether the person is *anāśrava* (without āśravas, [S. āśrava = P. āsava], i.e., without pollutants, pure) or *sāśrava* (with pollutants) (17:19). Someone anāśrava cuts off accumulated karmic debt in this life, and hence is not reborn, while someone sāśrava carries one, but not all karmic properties or debts into the next life. In other words the sāśrava is not forgiven his loan completely, but his payment amount is drastically reduced.[11]

The theorist tries to demonstrate how his position satisfies the middle way by claiming that emptiness is not annihilation, and saṃsāra is not eternal; so avipraṇāśa is the doctrine taught by the Buddha (17:20). Emptiness is not annihilation because there in nothing actual that it destroys or puts an end to. Emptiness only eliminates false ideas about the actual. Saṃsāra is not eternal because Awakening brings it to an end. This is a false middle way, however, false because it says only a single thing each about two unrelated terms, such that their predicates are opposed while the terms themselves are not real oppositions. This only provides an allusion of the middle way.

The correct middle way (*madhyama*) would need to avoid the extremes growing out of each term, not distribute one set of extremes between them. If S is a subject or term, and P is something predicated of a subject, the middle way would need to avoid positing P or -P (e.g., eternal vs. annihilational) of S. If T is another term, the middle way would require that neither P nor -P be predicated of it either. Instead, what Nāgārjuna's opponent has done here is claim: S is not P, and T is not -P. Since the relation between S and T is unclear at best, whatever else these statements signify, they do not satisfy the requirements of the middle way. We don't know, for instance, whether S is -P, or if T is P. Since P and -P are opposites, the principle of mutual exclusion dictates that if either of them pertains to an S, the other does not, and vice versa. That is, if S is -P, it should be P. Similarly, if T is P, then it cannot be -P. This is not the middle way, but an evasive acceptance of one extreme for each term. If P and -P pertain to S and T, both extremes—P and -P—would have to be rejected for each of them individually.

One could ask the opponent: Is emptiness eternal? Is saṃsāra annihilational?

At this point Nāgārjuna cuts off the theorist by taking the discussion back to its roots and performing radical surgery. Karma doesn't arise, he says, because it lacks self-nature. Since non-arisen, it doesn't perish (17:21). Note that, unlike his opponent, he negates the extremes predicated of the *same* term—karma—not two unrelated terms. The 'karma' that Nāgārjuna is claiming does not arise and does not perish is the 'theoretical construct karma.' What is that? Any attempt to posit an independent existent called karma removed from the *active* interplay of dependently co-arising events. Theorists create and extract a *concept* of karma that lies beyond or besides the actual moment of activity. They then give their theoretical construct a life of its own. As Candrakīrti says at this point, the theorists are building a city of Gandharvas and the walls are crumbling down. Gandharvas are deities who live in the clouds playing music; but this image is a favorite among Indian philosophers for indicating a fantasy with no basis in reality, much as we might say building castles in the clouds.

A svabhāvic concept of karma converts a moment of action into an occasion for constructing and differentiating svabhāvic existents (actor, act, agent, consequence, etc.). Nāgārjuna reminds us, if action is svabhāvic, then it must be eternal and uncaused, for the eternal is uncaused (17:22). Such a failure to successfully ground a theory of karma would evoke all the earlier problems of nihilism discussed above that arose once karma had no cause.

Misunderstanding Nāgārjuna's point by taking it to be a denial of action per se, such that one would desist from all action ("karma doesn't arise")—a misunderstanding that derives from being unable to distinguish between karma per se and the *concepts* of karma—an objector complains that if one desists from acting, there would always be a fear that one might be confronted later by something that one failed to do, that is, one may always have regrets about something one didn't do (17:23).[12] More gravely, all the human conventions that hold people and the social order together (*vyavahāra*) would be overturned; there would be no meaningful distinction, for instance, between meritorious and demeritorious actions (17:24). Anarchy would ensue.

To this Nāgārjuna replies that if a maturity of karma (*vipāka*) that has matured, matures again, and again, because action possesses a self-nature that determines and fixes its nature (*vyavasthita*), or certain types of action have certain qualities (such as good or bad) that are fixed and transfer from the deed to the maturing of its fruit, then karma would be hard determinism, and an interminable eternalism (17:25). Again, if karma is essentially kleśa, as some Buddhists claim, and these kleśas are not irreducible elements (*tattva*)—since kleśa can be broken down into other causal conditions—can such kleśas that themselves fail to be irreducible elements be cited as the irreducible elements of karma (17:26)? An infinite regress begins to loom. Moreover, the fact that kleśa is reducible to causitive factors that are not themselves kleśa means that moral karma is *not* a self-perpetuating closed system nor a form of hard determinism, since the production of negative karma derives from conditions that are not exclusively negative karmic conditions. In other words, the moral value of an action is not preset or pre-established by like-valued karmic factors exclusively. Pratītya-samutpāda, therefore, involves crossover in karmic value.

Instead of trying to envision karma and kleśa in terms of irreducibles, Nāgārjuna suggests that we see them as empty. Karma and kleśa are conditions (*pratyaya*) of bodies. If karma and kleśas are empty, what can be said about bodies (17:27)? The answer would be: Nothing. Once theorists start talking about bodies, they would convert living bodies into conceptual grist for their theoretical mills. Nāgārjuna is also subtly reminding his opponents that while they recite the formula that karma consists of actions of body, language, and mind, they invariably privilege the mind and focus their discussion there, while forgetting about the karmic body. The body is more than a repository for karmic residue—a job it does not do well in theory, since karma traverses across lives, and thus no body is adequate to the demands such a theory would place on it.

A sentient being, covered (*nivṛta*) in ignorance (*avidyā*) and fettered by craving (*tṛṣṇa*) is the one who experiences (*bhokta*, lit. the enjoyer); he is neither identical to nor different from the agent (17:28). People undergoing all the saṃsāric conditions of duḥkha may actually be enjoying themselves. The conditions by which one either enjoys or suffers are karmic, and thus promising rewards (or punishment) only perpetuates karma, since it defers and links present actions to future results. The one who later enjoys/suffers the fruits of a prior action done by an agent is neither the same nor different than that agent. We are not the same person we were before; but neither are we entirely otherwise. Svabhāvic identities are too rigid, too invariant, to adequately account for this. But when prapañca, the conceptual fantasy, is put to rest (*prapañcopaśama*) then the whole miserable construct with all it entails falls as well. Freedom from karma consists of seeing through the svabhāvic haze, which is the compulsive projection resulting from each person's clinging to ātma-dṛṣṭi. We invest everything with svabhāva in order to secure our own ātma-dṛṣṭi. When ātma-dṛṣṭi is overcome, so are all the karmic problems. This is a matter of insight, of losing one's dṛṣṭi, of eliminating ignorance; karma is not overcome by some form or another of systemic manipulation, especially when the system is nothing more than a svabhāvic fantasy.

Action is neither produced dependent on conditions (*na pratyaya samutpannam*) nor not produced dependent on conditions (*nāpratyaya samutthitam*); in the same way, the agent doesn't exist (17:29). Why? That action could arise independent of conditions is absurd and impossible, and would lead to all the problems that moral theorists are trying to avoid. That it cannot arise dependent on conditions follows from the fact that it is not a separate entity or *effect* of pratītya-samutpāda, but a conceptual isolation of what occurs as dependent co-arising. This being so, the entire theoretical enterprise has gone bankrupt, and therefore Nāgārjuna points out: If both agent and action are inexistent (*nāsti*), from where would the fruit born from action be born? With no fruit, where can an enjoyer (*bhokta*) be (17:30)?

Nāgārjuna makes one last attempt to explain to his opponents that what he is objecting to is not karma per se, but the *concept of karma* that the theorists have created and stubbornly cling to, a set of concepts which has taken on a life of its own. He offers the following analogy:[13] Just as a teacher by psychic power (*ṛddhi-sampāda*) creates an apparitional body (*nirmita*), and this apparitional body in turn creates another apparitional body, so also are the agent and his actions. The agent is like the apparitional form, and the action is like his creation (*kṛtam*). It is like a created form created by another who is created (17:31-32). Just as in this analogy the teacher is *real,* so also would the flow of events be real from which the concepts of agent and action were extracted. Thus, Nāgārjuna concludes, kleśa, karma, *dehā* (bodies), agents, and fruits are all like a city of Gandharvas, like mirages, like dreams (17:33).

Moralism consists of promises, wrapped in authority, grounded in confused svabhāvic presuppositions, built into a system that takes on a life of its own, eclipsing real life.

Karma and the soteric

From its early days Buddhism engendered a soteric myth of the entrapment of sentient beings within the seemingly endless rounds of saṃsāra, bound from life to life and moment to moment by karma. Until we reach Awakening, we accumulate karmic conditioning, saṃskāras, which bind us to the cycle, compelling us to ever new births in lives of additional appropriation. We move from one appropriational skandhic configuration to another. In MMK 16 Nāgārjuna demonstrates that this myth and the mechanics of karma do not sit well together.

Nāgārjuna raises one of the thorniest questions in all of Buddhist thought. In the absence of an invariant self, what transmigrates? The traditional Buddhist answer is saṃskāras, acquired karmic habits, conditioning that becomes embodied.[14] To this Nāgārjuna replies: If saṃskāras transmigrate (*saṃsaranti*), they don't do so as either permanent or impermanent entities. This also applies to sentient beings (16:1). This is common sense, and makes a similar point to 17:28 (the agent and the enjoyer are neither the same nor different). A permanent entity would not need to be reborn—it would simply remain the way it is. An impermanent entity would be incapable of rebirth (since, if what is 'born' later is the *same*, then it was not impermanent in the first place). So a saṃskāra cannot be an invariant thing that is the same from one moment to the next, or one life to the next.

If what transmigrates is not the self and it is not saṃskāra, what is it? What is the X that provides identity between some sentient being (P) in one life and a subsequent sentient being (R) in another life? In what sense can we say that R is P reborn?

This entire chapter of MMK is an attempt to get us to see that we have great difficulty even thinking about such questions without assuming such an X. That X is svabhāva personified.

Perhaps—without recourse to the notion of an invariant self—one can say, as some Buddhists did, that a *pudgala* (person)—which is neither the same nor different from the skandhas, but rather some quality of the whole that is not entirely reducible to the parts—is what transmigrates. Nāgārjuna responds: If it is the pudgala that transmigrates, but such a thing is not found in any of the skandhas, āyatanas, or dhātus within the five realms,[15] then the question still remains: what transmigrates (16:2)? Either the pudgala is *an entity in addition to* the components of the skandhas, āyatanas, and dhātus (which, according to basic Buddhist theories, includes all actual existent things), in which case the skandha, āyatana, etc., theory needs to be revised, or else it is a mere fiction, a prajñapti, in which case it would be utterly incapable of *doing* anything, much less transmigrate.[16]

As discussed earlier, the skandhas were called skandhā-upādāna, the appropriational aggregates. What binds together the aggregates is appropriation (upādāna). In each life, and in each moment, appropriation holds that life together and compels that life to continue, to persevere, to appropriate more. But what about *between* lives? Buddhists were divided on the question of whether rebirth is immediate or whether some intermediate state between lives needed to be traversed first. Nāgārjuna now raises a thorny issue in this interstice: While moving from one upādāna (appropriational configuration) to another upādāna—e.g., from one life to another, or from one body/embodiment to another—there would be no (skandhic) person, i.e., no skandha-upādāna. No person would be or would be becoming (*vibhavo bhavet*). Such an intermediate being, bereft of skandhas, would lack the concomitants of skandhas: appropriation and embodied existence. In other words, we would be talking about an entity, an identity, a something that is nonexistent/not-becoming (*vibhava*) and non-appropriational (*anupādāna*), i.e., devoud of 'becoming' and 'appropriation.' Where could such a thing transmigrate, he asks (16:3)?

One becomes (*bhava*) consequent on appropriation (*upādāna*), as the pratītya-samutpāda model explains. What sort of existence pertains *between* lives? For that matter, what sort of existence pertains *between moments* of skandhic configuration within a life? If 'existence' does not pertain, then neither can 'appropriation' (what would be appropriating?). Where could something that neither exists nor appropriates be reborn? And how? By what means or conditions?

Mechanically, appropriation is a necessary condition for continuance in life as well as continuance across lives. This is a moral as well as a mechanical question. If one deserves to transmigrate on the basis of being an appropriative being, why should a nonexistent being, who is temporarily outside of the inertia of becoming *and utterly nonappropriative*, deserve to be reborn? Where is he, this nonexistent thing, transmigratorily when between lives? Has he gone to nirvāṇa (even temporarily)? And if not, what is the difference between such nonbecoming, nonappropriativity, and nirvāṇa, since those are traditionally nirvanic characteristics?

The idea that saṃskāras can pass into nirvāṇa is unreasonable, since saṃskāras and nirvāṇa are mutually exclusive; the notion that sentient beings can pass into nirvāṇa is also unreasonable, since the myth holds that nirvāṇa is the absence of the conditions that create and bind sentient beings (16:4).

Reworking the standard Buddhist soteric theory by trying to make saṃskāras substrates (*dharmin*) onto which various life conditions rise and cease, or imagining that there is some life base that serves as a substrate for migrating saṃskāras won't work either, since saṃskāras, if they are substrates for arising and ceasing, are neither bound nor liberated (16:5). What is impermanent doesn't last long enough to be bound; what arises and ceases does so due to the compulsions of cause and conditions, and hence is not free. Neither free nor bound, it would be neither nirvanic nor samsaric. Nirvāṇa and saṃsāra are exhaustive categories. There can be no such third alternative apart from them. The saṃskāras cannot be impervious substrates of arising and ceasing, below or behind the changes; rather they precisely are what arises and ceases. In what X would they inhere? And how? So that attempt won't help.

Perhaps there is some entity that is not appropriation itself, but something that becomes linked with appropriation, that is to say, that appropriates appropriation. One would then distinguish between appropriation proper (*upādāna*) and that X that is 'with' appropriation (*sopādāna, sa + upādāna*). So there is a stable identity that can 'possess' appropriation while not itself entirely being appropriation. If not, liberation from appropriation would be impossible. The one who goes from life to life, our X, then, would be something different from appropriation itself. We already saw what happens when prapañca starts to proliferate categories. Nāgārjuna points out that if it is upādāna per se which is 'bondage,' then that X that is only 'with' upādāna is not itself bound, since it is something else. (If it were the same as upādāna, it couldn't be *with* upādāna, it would *be* upādāna.) Also, one who is *not* with upādāna is not bound. That simply follows from the definition. So, Nāgārjuna asks, if neither the one with appropriation nor the one without appropriation is bound, who is? In which status or state (*avastha*), if any, is one bound (16:6)? Of course, what is not bound does not transmigrate, so if one considers X to be nonbound, the entire discussion o transmigratory continuance becomes moot.

Since bound and liberated are mutually exclusive, someone who was actually bound could never be liberated (16:8). This would follow from either of these terms, bound and liberated, having svabhāvic definitions. If 'bound' is eternal and invariantly what it is, and can never be otherwise, and it is by definition the opposite of 'liberated' such that they are mutually exclusive and cannot appear simultaneously in the same locus, 'bound' could never be anything other than bound, and thus never liberated. Again, to try to salvage the myth, one feels compelled to reintroduce the X with some new twist, some new wrinkle. But we have been warned. Svabhāvic thinking is sneaky.

The myth itself is thoroughly infected with svabhāva and ātma-dṛṣṭi. Nāgārjuna warns: Whoever thinks that "I will be without upādāna, and thus transcend sorrow and attain nirvāṇa," is demonstrating *major* upādāna (*mahā-upādāna*) (16:9). Why? This would be the rawest form of ātma-dṛṣṭi: "I will get that."

Finally, he leaves us with this to think about: If nirvāṇa can't be brought about, because it is unconditioned, and saṃsāra cannot be cleansed of impurity (since saṃsāra, by definition, is the presence of impurity), what is it that is being discriminated (*vikalpyate*) as saṃsāra or nirvāṇa (16:10)?

The myth doesn't cure svabhāvic thinking; it embodies and reifies it.

Saṃskāra

As we have seen, Nāgārjuna has raised the stakes for Buddhists. The standard soteric myth proves to be not only incoherent, but an embodiment of precisely that which Buddhism should be seeking to overcome. It will no longer be sufficient for Buddhists to talk about *anātman*. Ātmanic, i.e., svabhāvic thinking has infiltrated Buddhist thought at every level, and keeps reasserting itself every time a new conceptual dilemma arises. It is our deepest and most ubiquitous (and invisible) proclivity. We seem incapable of thinking about anything without introducing svabhāva. When a term, or category, or relation fails to stand, we bring in a new svabhāva, whether a pudgala, an avipraṇāśa, or a substrate. We analyze by proliferating distinctions, and then svabhāvize each distinct component. This is ātma-dṛṣṭi at work; precisely what Buddhism should be designed to help us cure. But how, beyond bringing all this to our attention, does Nāgārjuna propose we overcome this?

MMK 13, on saṃskāra, provides a crucial look at the answer. It deals with two issues that are related to each other: delusion and the manner in which svabhāva overshadows our understanding of change. It is also one of the places in MMK where Nāgārjuna indicates rather explicitly what the purpose of the notion of *śūnyatā*, emptiness, should be.

Invoking the authority of the Buddha, a quasi-tautological syllogism is advanced: The Bhagavan said, That which is erroneous (*mṛṣā*) is a deluded thing (*moṣa-dharma*). All deluded things are saṃskāra; therefore, saṃskāra is erroneous (13:1).

Nāgārjuna immediately breaks us out of this syllogistic tautological closure by pointedly asking: Just *what* is it that one is deluded about? He then invokes the Bhagavan's authority on his behalf, answering the question thus: *That* is what the Bhagavan said emptiness reveals (13.2). Emptiness breaks us out of our deluded closure by revealing what it is we are deluded about. It should be noted that is *not* an ontological reply. The question 'What' usually elicits an ontological response. But 'what' we are deluded about is not a thing; nor is it a matter of some thing out there that we cannot yet see because we are deluded. It is our manner of seeing (*dṛṣṭi*) that constitutes delusion. The problem, as already evident from our discussion of the other chapters in MMK, is svabhāvic thinking.

An opponent tests whether Nāgārjuna is proposing an alternate metaphysics, one in which emptiness itself serves as the foundational svabhāva. Evoking a notion of alterity, the opponent contends: Because we perceive things becoming otherwise (*anyathā-bhāva-darśanāt*), we know that things are without svabhāva (*niḥsvabhāva*). Because of the emptiness of things (*bhāva*), a thing (*bhāva*) lacking the svabhāva (*asvabhāva*) of emptiness does not exist (*nāsti*) (13.3). The claim here is that the only svabhāva any thing really has is emptiness. Now this objection could be interpreted to mean that since emptiness means no more than the absence of svabhāva, this too is not an ontological statement, but a caution against svabhāvic delusion. Yogācāra will use that strategy to account for the three svabhāvas being actually three asvabhāvas (cf. *Triṃśikā* 24).

The key term in that verse is *anyathā*, 'becoming otherwise.' This will become an important component of the Yogācāra definition of *pariṇāma*, often mistranslated in Western works as 'evolution.' Evolution would imply the sort of svabhāvic continuity that Nāgārjuna has thoroughly problematized. Unlike Nāgārjuna, Yogācāra will emphasize that anyathā occurs due to causes and conditions that are different each moment. That something in one moment is neither the same nor different from something else another moment that has arisen through related causes and conditions marks an *alterity* that, when properly applied, avoids the extremes of identity/difference, or eternal/anihilation.

We know from our experience that the world and the things within it, including ourselves, are not fixed invariant entities. Everything is becoming otherwise, everything is changing, everything demonstrates alterity. But that way of understanding what we see—namely that *there are things* undergoing some process of change—reinstates the svabhāvic X. To say that X has changed is to assume that whatever was the case at $time_1$ is related to whatever is the case at $time_2$ in such a way that an invariant identity X has been carried over from one time to the other. The X at $time_1$ could be called X_1, while at $time_2$ it is called X_2. But the notion of change requires that the X in X_1 and the X in X_2 be the self-same X in at least some essential respects, or else X_2 cannot legitimately be called X. To talk about some-*thing* changing already assumes that that thing has an unchanging identity. That of course is the opposite of what we think we are saying. Svabhāvic thinking is pernicious and sneaky. The very notion of change makes no sense unless derived by way of contrast with a notion of constancy, one which it smuggles in and affirms at its core while pretending to do the opposite.

Nāgārjuna presents the options starkly. If there is no svabhāva, no enduring X, then what is becoming otherwise? In other words, of what is one predicating change? On the other hand, if there is svabhāva, which by definition is unchanging, what is becoming otherwise (13:4)? This highlights how deep-seated svabhāvic assumptions are in our thinking. We cannot even conceive of the opposite of svabhāva, namely change, without invoking and falling back into svabhāvic assumptions, even though we know that svabhāvic change is an oxymoron, an impossibility, and therefore our thinking, to the extent it is svabhāvic, is incoherent and impossible.

To drive the point home, the point being how deeply svabhāvic thinking has infiltrated even our most mundane, ordinary notions—and how impossible our way of looking at things is without assuming some svabhāva—Nāgārjuna deliberately tries to shock us by declaring: A youth doesn't become old; and even an old man doesn't become old (13:4). A youth, by definition, is young. A ten year old is never a seventy year old. Being ten and being seventy are mutually exclusive. To say a youth becomes old is to say there is a svabhāvic X that at one time inhabited the condition of being ten years old, and sixty years later that same X inhabited the conditions of being seventy years old. An old man, however, doesn't become old—he *is* old. In the case of the youth becoming old, an extra svabhāvic entity is assumed in order to make a connection between the youth and the old person. In the case of the old person, his condition itself is svabhāvized: oldness. He may or may not be something beyond the conditions of his age, but he is now defined by the definition of that age condition. The definition doesn't 'become.' The old person doesn't *become* old; he *is* old. One might wish to say 'he becomes *older*,' but then all the problems connected with the X above attach to the 'he.' What is the X undergoing aging?

Is there anything in the flux of conditions that remains invariant, that could stand up as the X? Nāgārjuna argues: If there were something nonempty and nonchanging amidst the changes, then 'empty' would be a something (13:7). If, in 'something,' one could separate out the empty from the nonempty, then the 'empty' part would have definable limits marked by where the nonempty begins and the empty ends, which would make 'empty' a circumscribed thing. Moreover, since emptiness would then be circumscribed, there must be that 'outside' its circumscription. All things would then be composed of two mutually exclusive parts: the empty and the nonempty. Not only would the empty part inhere, side by side, with a nonempty part in the same thing, but, since all "things" would necessarily have to contain these two parts—empty and nonempty—another absurd consequence follows. If everything has a double nature of being empty and nonempty, then that part of the thing which is empty, being itself a 'thing,' would also have to be both empty and nonempty, which leads to an absurd infinite regress composed of mutual oppositions. Nothing exists that is nonempty, however, so how could 'empty' be an existent (*bhāva*) (13:7)? The objection at 13:3 has been rejected.

Nāgārjuna finishes by returning to the question of what is delusion and what is it that one is deluded about, and offers one of the clearest statements in the MMK as to the purpose of the emptiness: The Jinas (conquerors, i.e., Buddhas and Awakened ones) have said, "Emptiness is the relinquishing of dṛṣṭis." Whoever holds emptiness as a view, as a dṛṣṭi, is said to be incorrigible (13:8).

Madhyamaka and the two satyas

The discussion of the relation between delusion and emptiness in MMK 13 did not settle the matter once and for all for Madhyamakans, nor for Yogācārins. We will now explore this further. Candrakīrti writes:[17]

> Is there then no reasoned argument (*upapatti*) for the wise?
>
> How could we say whether there is or there is not? The higher truth, for the wise, is a matter of silence (*tuṣṇīṃbhāva*).[18] How then would everyday language, reasoned or unreasoned, be possible in that realm?

Candrakīrti's passage concerning the 'higher truth' and 'everyday language' raises an issue of importance for all Mahāyānists, as well as other Buddhists: The problem of the two satyas. While there are earlier examples of Buddhists using the terms *vyavahāra* or (Pāli) *saṃmuti* in contrast to *paramārtha*, the two satya model, as it disseminated throughout Buddhism, is usually ascribed to Nāgārjuna, who in MMK 24:8-10 offers an account of the relation of each of these two satyas not only to each other, but to the attaining of nirvāṇa.

Despite the fact that *paramārtha* should not to be considered as something radically other than *saṃvṛti*—since it signals an epistemic shift of focus rather than a different set of ontological referents—again and again Buddhists could not resist entertaining and espousing dichotomous misinterpretations. For instance, in China before Hsüan-tsang's day, during the Liang Dynasty (502-557), the two satyas were already thoroughly separated and ontologized.[19]

In a very astute article on the two satyas that raises many of the issues we need to consider, Michael Broido traces out the following problematic in Indian and Tibetan Mādhyamika:[20]

> There is... the familiar though unclear Madhyamika relationship in which vyavahāra-satya is the basis or the means for the attainment of paramārtha-satya (MK XXIV.8, MMV [*Madhyamakāvatāra*] VI.80 &c.). This vyavahāra-satya is usually identified with saṃvṛti-satya. This identification gives rise to many... problems... The idea that ordinary everyday cognition is *really* (*paramārthatas, samyag-*) delusive, and that some quite different kind of cognition is *really satya* (paramārtha-satya) is an ancient one in India. The oldest sense of "vyavahāra-satya" is perhaps just that of ordinary everyday satya. [Broido has made no attempt yet to define 'satya'] The question arises as to how paramārtha-satya is possible... [Nāgārjuna at once denies that there can be any single or any series of ordinary cognitions which cause one to attain paramārtha-satya (MK XXIV.8), and yet] according to him, it is *only on the basis of ordinary everyday cognition* that paramārtha-satya is possible.... [emphasis Broido's] [T]o spell this connection out Candrakīrti [made] use of the notions of levels (*avasthā*) and stages (*krama*), distinguishing between saṃvṛti-satya for the ārya [nobles] and for the pṛthagjana [ordinary folk] and between saṃvṛti-satya and *mere* saṃvṛti (*saṃvṛti-mātra*). In this way "saṃvṛti-satya" acquired a sense different from the normal one of "vyavahāra-satya."... Saṃvṛti-satya became the preserve of more

advanced practitioners (bodhisattvas &c.) and was seen not merely as a necessary condition for paramārtha-satya, but as its cause. Treating the connection as causal (e.g. MMV VI.80)... introduces new problems; for instance it becomes difficult to understand what VI.23 could mean by saying that saṃvṛti-satya is delusive (*mṛṣa*). These problems were never properly resolved by Candrakīrti. In Tibet... the connection between the cognition of ordinary people and the saṃvṛti-satya of the āryas, which had been weakened by Candrakīrti, was now disrupted; the break in the chain of causal stages, which we already saw with Nāgārjuna, has reappeared.... Tsong-kha-pa held that it is implicit in Candrakīrti's theory of two satyas that two different senses of *satya* have to be kept in mind and distinguished, in addition to the straightforward one connected with ordinary veridical cognition. According to Mi-bskyod rDo-rje and Padma dKar-po, this disambiguation claim is little better than an admission that the interpretation is internally incoherent. [square brackets mine]

A little later Broido spells out some implications using the famous rope/snake analogy.

It may help to illustrate the Sanskrit and Tibetan vocabulary... if we outline the standard Indian example of a delusive perceptual situation, the rope/snake illusion. This example is normally treated from the point of view of the cognition of the ordinary person (pṛtagjana, byis-pa) and in terms of normal linguistic and other conventions (vyavahāra, tha-snyad). In conditions of poor illumination, at night perhaps, a person sees what is in fact a rope, but mistakes it for a snake. The non-existent snake is sometimes said to be an *abh?tavastu*; seeing it, the person may become nervous, and generally on this basis (*ālambana*, BHS [Buddhist-Hybrid Sanskrit] *ārambaṇa*) all sorts of mental activity (*abh?ta vastu nimittārambaṇa manasikāra*) may occur.[21] This perceptual situation and/or the associated cognition and/or the object of knowledge (*jñeya*, shes-bya, here the non-existent snake) and/or the referent of the cognitive state (*jñeyārtha*, shes-bya'i don, here probably the imagined snake) may all be said to be *delusive* (moṣa, mṛṣa; slu-ba, brdzun-pa). The idea of these English, Sanskrit and Tibetan words is always that although there appears to be a snake, in fact there is none; although the situation seems to yield knowledge of a snake, in fact it does not. The opposite of these words is *veridical* (satya, bden-pa); *these* words apply to perceptual situations and their referents &c in those cases which do, in fact, yield the knowledge which they seem to yield. As I said, the normal use of the rope/snake example is in the context of ordinary cognition. But it is also used *as a simile* for the delusiveness (*moṣa* &c) of ordinary cognition from a "higher" transwordly (lokottara, 'jig-rten-las 'das-pa) point of view. Paramārtha-satya, then, as our texts will say, is what is *really* (paramārthatas, don-dam-par; samyag-, yag-dar-par) non-delusive (apramoṣa &c) or veridical (satya); and as Tsong-kha-pa emphasized, there is the problem of saying coherently what this means. Here the rope/snake does not help much. For while we can make more explicit what it is for a cognition to be conventionally veridical (vyavahāra-satya, tha-snyad-kyi bden-pa), this explication is concerned with the relationships *among* ordinary everyday cognitions, and does not provide us with any basis for going outside the ordinary everyday realm to something else. This difficulty has made Nāgārjuna's assertion that vyavahāra-satya is the basis for paramārtha-satya into a puzzle for all later writers on Madhyamaka and has motivated the many attempts to introduce a notion of saṃvṛti-satya distinct, in some nontrivial sense, from ordinary everyday cognition or its referent.

Even with Broido's careful and sensitive reflection on the terms and the controversy,[22] Nāgārjuna's sense escapes him, as it apparently escaped some important Indian and Tibetan Buddhists before him. Like them, he assumes that some definitive separation of the two satyas is necessary. He construes Nāgārjuna's contention that "it is *only on the basis of ordinary everyday cognition* that paramārtha-satya is possible" to mean that saṃvṛti-satya is a springboard from which one jumps into the depths of paramārtha-satya. Saṃvṛti becomes something provisional that is elsewhere or elsewise to paramārtha. They are regarded and treated, according to this interpretation, as radically separate items.

Let us examine Nāgārjuna's actual words:[23]

Vyavahāram anāśritya paramārtho na deśyate |
paramārtham anāgamya nirvāṇaṃ nādhigamyate ||

If not based on the conventional (*vyavahāra*), paramārtha cannot be explicated (lit. 'taught').
If not comprehending paramārtha, nirvāṇa cannot be attained.

Notice, as Broido has mentioned, that the term used here is *vyavahāra*, not *saṃvṛti*, which suggests that Nāgārjuna is not referring to an 'enclosured' (*saṃvṛti*) realm, but rather to a conventional and communal means of expression and communication. Saṃvṛti is not automatically interchangeable with vyavahāhara, despite Broido's caution to the contrary and despite some opposing claims to the contrary profferred in the subsequent tradition. Broido's interpretation of this passage, that paramārtha is only *possible* on the basis of saṃvṛti may be confusing a claim about the function of language and communication for an ontological claim. Nāgārjuna does not seem to be saying that paramārtha *as such* depends on saṃvṛti; but merely that the linguistic and conventional expressions that will introduce and make coherent *the notion of paramārtha*—or better, that will lead one to an understanding that is paramārthic—depend on a commonly accepted conventional linguistic system. Otherwise efficacious communication—such as teaching the Dharma—would be impossible. Nāgārjuna is saying that should *an understandable explanation* that leads to an understanding of paramārtha not be available, it would be impossible to *reach an understanding* of paramārtha; as he says, paramārtha could not be *taught* (*na deśyate*). He is not claiming that saṃvṛti or vyavahāra are somehow ontological anchors or springboards to some realm called paramārtha. Paramārtha (*paramā* [superlative] + *artha* [referent]; ultimate referent) in most Buddhist discourse simply means 'stated most accurately and precisely.' There are prajñaptic ways of talking, e.g., referring to 'persons' when, in fact, the word 'person' is a heuristic for a complex web of causes and conditions. Were one to speak accurately, one would have to indicate with rigorous precision exactly all those causes and conditions and the intricate relations that obtain between them. Speaking in that manner would be paramārtha (and tedious). So what Nāgārjuna is saying is that without conventional discourse (*vyavahāra*), one cannot be taught a more precise discourse; and without the most precise discourse, in which the actual referents are precisely what the discourse identifies them to be, one cannot gain or master (*adhigama*) nirvāṇa. Vyavahāra points and orients; paramārtha is arriving at what vyavahāra was *ultimately referring to*; understanding paramārthically is nirvanic.

While this kārikā seems to be little more than a statement that in order to achieve nirvāṇa one must comprehend paramārthically, which is an understanding grounded on linguistic and conceptual conventions, nuances of this passage have generated material for controversy and debate ever since. Candrakīrti's illustration that saṃvṛti is like a container that holds the water (paramārtha) for the one who desires water, reinforces the impression that saṃvṛti is merely a provisional outer husk for some substantially separate, more highly valued, essential quencher of human thirst (*tṛṣṇa*).[24]

Moreover Broido's reading of Candrakīrti seems to presuppose that this separation must mark an opposition, since the only justification he offers for reading satya as 'veridical' is that 'veridical' is the opposite of the terms he has associated with saṃvṛti, and he virtually considers satya and paramārtha to be tautological synonyms ["paramārtha-satya... is what is *really* (paramārthatas...) non-delusive (apramoṣa) or veridical (satya)"]. Saṃvṛti-satya is differentiated from saṃvṛti-mātra by the fact that the former is observed, more or less, from the paramārthic perspective.[25] 'Veridical' is a clever, but thoroughly untextual proposal for either satya or paramārtha. This is all the more disappointing since Broido shows elsewhere in this article that he has a keen sense of the *textual* and *philosophical* nuances of a number of critical terms, as well as an ability and willingness to wrestle with the problems that arise when attempting to give due attention to the competing demands made by textual and philosophic concerns.[26] Both demand fidelity, though their demands may be mutually exclusive; at other times, only a keen philosophic sensibility will be able to open up a text's philological dimensions, while an accurate philological sensibility can guide philosophical ruminations away from idle speculations.

The assumed separation of paramārtha and saṃvṛti leads to the assumption that not only are they separate perspectives or ways of viewing things, but that their objects also differ. No matter how paramārtha and saṃvṛti are interpreted, as ontology or as epistemology, they cannot be separated from the issue of how experience is cognized and understood. In order to provide epistemological coherency, the respective 'objects' of saṃvṛti and paramārtha need to be defined. Almost immediately that question becomes confused (by Broido and some of his sources) with the question of genuine vs. delusive cognition, as if the question of saṃvṛti and paramārtha necessarily entailed nothing more than distinguishing true from false. Given such a dichotomous assumption, paramārtha necessarily must take the role of 'true,' which leaves saṃvṛti to bear the burden of falsehood.

That Buddhist discourse—including Bhāviveka's brand of Madhyamaka—treats vyavahāra (and saṃvṛti) as involving criteria for both true *and* false knowledge claims independent of paramārtha has gone unnoticed in the discussion. Taking paramārtha to be the sole arbiter of truth drastically underevaluates the role *vyavahāra* plays in Buddhist theory.

This lies at the core of Broido's stated difficulties with Candrakīrti's text ("it becomes difficult to understand what VI.23 could mean by saying that saṃvṛti-satya is delusive"). If saṃvṛti-satya is delusive it should not be the cognitive object of a paramārthic vision, though elsewhere Candrakīrti and subsequent commentators claim that it is.[27] But the demand that both claims cannot be properly offered at one and the same time revolves around a lack of semantic clarity about the use of 'delusion' (*mṛṣa*) in this context. 'Delusive' may be interpreted either as referring to (a) the context and value of a cognition, such that a delusive cognition is by definition *a mistaken cognition*—the cognizer either cognizes an object which is not actually present, or else fails to properly cognize an object which is. The cognizer, however, believes her cognition is true. Or 'delusive' signifies (b) the actual property of a type of cognition or perspective, such that the distortions or so-called delusory factors of the cognition are recognized as such to be intrinsic to the cognition or perspective. In the latter case the cognition, though involving a 'distorted representation,' remains clear about the fact of the distortion; it is an *accurate, non-mistaken cognition* whose content happens to be a distortion and recognized as such. For instance, when one knows a particular drawing is an optical illusion, one may still visually perceive the 'illusion' while no longer being mentally *fooled* by it.

Let's illustrate this with an example, the famous illusion in which a pencil or straight stick is partially submerged in a glass of water, producing the perception of a discontinuity between the unsubmerged and the submerged parts. The part in the water bends away at a different angle than the part above the water. To be 'fooled' is to think that what one sees is an accurate presentation of the condition of the pencil; this leads to interesting riddles when the pencil is gradually and repeatedly raised and lowered into the water. The pencil is continuously transformed by its baptism! Yet whatever part leaves the water returns to its pre-baptismal shape. Once we realize that the changes we perceive reflect the conditions by which the pencil is perceived rather than the pencil itself, we may begin to investigate the 'truth' of the illusion. One 'truth' of the perception is that water and air refract light differently. Water and air seem to share a common property, transparency, but that seeming commonality is the source of the illusion. It causes us to overlook that they will deliver light to us differently. The media, not the pencil have changed. But, unless we are thorough naive realists, we probably already knew that at the beginning, though we forgot to consider it, or perhaps we didn't 'scientifically' understand the media's refractive properties. But because of this illusion we discover and now know this to be the case. Hence the 'truth' of the illusion is that it demonstrates that for human vision the transparency of air and water are not equivalent.

Notice that coming to a realization about the 'truth' of the illusion does not affect how the immersed pencil appears to us. What has changed is how we understand what we see. We realize that the appearance of a discontinuous pencil is a precise demonstration of different refraction rates. If we are good Buddhists, then we would probably also note that what surprised and disturbed us initially about the illusion is that the constant identity we had assigned to the familiar pencil was being threatened. Pencils are supposed to be straight. That is their svabhāva, their essential nature, their invariant identity and appearance. We initially saw the illusion as if it were *the pencil itself* that was being bent, becoming discontinuous, whereas it was merely the difference between the refraction rates of air and water that was accurately being perceived. Once we let go of the need to perceive a constant, inviolable identity to the pencil, the 'truth' of the illusion becomes easy to see.

Similarly one may recognize a lie for what it is, which turns it into a kind of truth. When, for instance, someone lies about their age, they have at the same time told us a truth, or indeed several truths: What value they place on various ages, such as youth, etc.; How they wish to be considered by others; their sense of self-security or lack of it; their wish to be or be perceived as younger than they actually are; etc. If one knows how to look, the false proposition accurately and truthfully expresses a great deal about the person, much more than an accurate statement of age ever could. The lie expresses a truth.[28]

Broido is aware of these issues. He discusses the options outlined above as (a) 'mistaken cognition' and (b) 'cognition with distorted content recognized as such,' and he understands the need to "distinguish between a delusive referent and one experienced as delusive" (p. 43). He also recognizes that separating the two satyas leads to a correlative separation of their 'objects.' Tsong-kha-pa sometimes argued that though the referent-objects (*artha*) for saṃvṛti-satya and paramārtha-satya might be different, the *dharmin* (lit. 'what holds a dharma') of those arthas was the same in either case. Broido translates the following passage:[29]

> So what is the point of analyzing saṃvṛti-satya as attained by delusive cognition (MMV [*Madhyamakāvatāra*] VI.23)? It is attained by a conventional means of knowledge [**vyavahāra-pramāṇa*] which assesses a delusive object (artha). Out of the previously explained two svabhāvas or svarūpas, paramārtha-satya is the one which assesses the real object (artha) by means of a reasoned cognition and so reaches it, and this is explained under the verse "*vikalpitaṃ yattimiraprabhavāt...*" [MMV VI.29]. It is said that (of these two svarūpas) the one which is attained by a conventional means of knowledge which sees a delusive object (artha) is saṃvṛti-satya. Though the substrata [dharmin] attained

> in paramārtha and saṃvṛti-(satya) are spoken of separately, *they are attained as one and do not arise as two.* [emphasis Broido's; square brackets mine]

To follow Tsong-kha-pa's line of thinking, which met with much criticism in Tibet, the question of *where* to separate the two satyas becomes crucial. As perspectives they are distinct; and though their objects are superficially different, on a deeper, seemingly metaphysical level, the 'substrata' (*dharmin*) of these objects are identical. Since the almost universal understanding of paramārtha-satya took it as integrally connected with a culminating vision that was non-dual, the two satyas had to be ultimately identical as well as perspectivally different. The *Saṅdhinirmocana Sūtra*, which introduced many of the concepts that later come to be considered characteristically Yogācāric—such as tri-svabhāva and vijñapti-mātra—already wrestled with this issue, but managed to avoid this type of ontological speculation.[30]

If Broido's reading of Tsong-kha-pa is correct, then this metaphysicalized, substrative realm of identity is all that prevents Tsong-kha-pa from being labelled a dualist.[31]

> ...it is a brute fact that there are two kinds of object (artha): the ordinary one attained by a conventional cognition, and the "awareness-particular" (ye-shes-kyi khyad par, *jñānaviśeṣa) which is attained in paramārtha-satya; and so, since there are two kinds of object, there must be two kinds of cognition which cognize them.... [Since] Tsong-kha-pa insisted [that saṃvṛti-satya and paramārtha-satya as] two cognitions do have separate referents (artha)—even though they may be aspects of one and the same substratum (gzhi)—the balance of the evidence seems to be that he [Tsong-kha-pa] did regard the two cognitions as separate.

The cognizer and the cognized are different in cognition, but substratively identical! I do not think that Nāgārjuna would approve of such a metaphysical solution.

We have cited Broido's text at length for several reasons. First, it has quickly brought us close to the basic issues in a sophisticated manner. Secondly, his text does not merely state the problem, but also exemplifies it. Third, despite my critical remarks, I find this article to be one of the most insightful discussions of the two satyas in recent scholarship. Fourth, his formulation contains some undeveloped seeds that we can sprout here.

His article provides some useful semantic distinctions which help clarify the disputes that arose from differing interpretations of the two satyas.[32] Rather than discuss those interpretations in detail, which all developed later than Hsüan-tsang's visit to India, let us move into what is typically Yogācāric in his exposition, though he doesn't identify it as such.

The rope/snake analogy, a much beloved commonplace in Indian thought, is often used to explain and clarify the Yogācāra tri-svabhāva theory. But here we will only examine a Sanskrit term (or compound of terms) that Broido offered in his exposition, and unpack some of its significance. Re-citing what was quoted earlier:

> The non-existent snake is sometimes said to be an *abh?tavastu*; seeing it, the person may become nervous, and generally on this basis (*ālambana*, BHS *ārambaṇa*) all sorts of mental activity (*abh?ta vastu nimittārambaṇa manasikāra*) may occur.

He has alluded to possible connotations of most of the terms, but he has not explicated them precisely, and certain terms, such as *nimitta*, he ignores altogether. Let us examine the phrase *abh?ta vastu nimittārambaṇa manasikāra* carefully.

Abh?ta signifies the projection of a non-existent entity onto a locus in which it is not present, such that we perceive it to be present there (though it is not). Hence it means more than simply an inexistent or non-existent object. It also connotes (i) the place or locus of a projection, (ii) the desire that produces the projection; (iii) the act of projection, and (iv) a recognition that the so-called 'non-existent' projected object is only one of many factors responsible for its production. The so-called abh?ta-object need not necessarily be something a priori inexistent, such as impossibilities or chimeras like round squares, unicorns, etc. For a snake to be abh?ta does not mean that snakes per se are inexistent; such a claim would be obviously absurd. Moreover, the so-called illusion has *power*—one goes through the same physical and emotional fears and discomforts when encountering an imaginary snake as one would if encountering a real snake; the encounter is psychologically identical, only the ontological status of the referent of the experience is different. This arises from the fact that the one projecting the abh?ta takes the not-really-a-snake to be a real snake, even though the false snake is his own mental construction. Since we know snakes are dangerous, even lethal, our fear of dying impels us to devote all our attention to the 'snake.' Investing such attention allows the 'illusion' to grip us, to hold our attention. It is an illusion because, though dangerous snakes may be lurking elsewhere, the rope that is frightening us is not one of them. Abh?ta simply means that an object which seems to be cognized in such and such a place does not in fact actually exist in that place. The *abh?ta-parikalpa* or 'imaginative cognitive construction of inexistents [such that they occupy the place of "reality"]' is a key Yogācāra doctrine.[33]

Vastu is one of the many Sanskrit words usually translated as 'object,' and its semantic spread covers everything from 'thing' to 'substratum of a perception.' Its precise meaning must be determined within specific contexts, but in general *vastu* implies that the object has an ontological status not fully reducible to the role it plays in cognition, and that in fact the *vastu* itself may not be fully disclosed in cognition, raising issues similar to those connected with Kant's notion of a noumenon or an in-itself. More than any other Sanskrit term for object, *vastu* implies a mysterious ontological existence belonging to the object beyond what appears cognition. Here *abh?tavastu* means that the object of the cognition, which is presumed to be an actual external entity, lacks precisely this ontological status, since what seems to (objectively) underlie the cognitive object does not exist there in that locus. *Abh?tavastu* means that the actual object present in the cognition is, in fact, absent. The snake, though "perceived," is not in fact present in the locus in which it is being perceived.[34] Moreover, what does actually exist in that locus, namely the rope, fails to appear as such in the cognition. The rope participates in the cognition as a 'mysterious' object whose actual characteristics remain hidden or delusively cognized.

Nimitta signifies the characteristic sensorial marks of an object (e.g., a snake's color or shape, etc.), especially in the sense that such marks serve as the efficient cause (*nimitta-kāraṇa*) of the cognition of something that is observable. *Ārambaṇa* signifies the 'objective-pole' of a cognition, which, Husserl reminds us, is never outside consciousness, but is a formal requirement of consciousness to be consciousness (*Ideen I*). Since consciousness is always 'consciousness of,' it must always have an object shaping it. A cognition is, in part, shaped by its content. For someone who is not color blind, a red dress in proper light demands that it be seen as red. The conditions by which a cognition occurs (whether from the object-pole or noetically produced) necessarily shape the features of that cognition. A clear, unobstructed, spatially proximate, properly lit view of a rope by a calm individual will not yield a snake. Those 'content-conditions' which "support" a cognition are the *nimitta ālambana*. As both Husserl and Yogācāra remind us, the function of a content-condition can be fulfilled just as adequately by a hallucination, dream or non-veridical content, as by a veridical percept. In the *Viṃśatikā* Vasubandhu argues, for instance, that dreams can cause ejaculation (nocturnal emissions) just as effectively as erotic waking activities.[35] Hence neither the ālambana nor its nimitta need to be objectively external to the consciousness that cognizes it in order for it to function. Since functioning (i.e., producing an observable effect) is the Buddhist criterion for reality, we must entertain the interesting possibility that cognitions may be non-veridical and yet apodictic. However, this is not to say that the ālambana must *necessarily* be of an inexistent; only that it *may* be in some cases.

Manasikāra, from *manasi* (taking to heart [the locative of *manas*, 'intentional mentation']) + *kāra* (doing, making), i.e., making the mind intend [in] a locus, or 'the activity of mentally generating an intentional locus,' is usually translated simply as 'attention,' 'mental concern.' A place is filled with what is not actually there in such a way that one's attention notices little if anything else. Our imagined snake, though not actually there, obsesses us. It seizes our attention.

The compound could thus be paraphrased: what the mind pays attention to and becomes concerned with when the objective-pole's characteristic features are actually projections of things into a place where they do not exist. In other words, when something 'seems to be there' I cognitively and behaviorally respond to it *as there* because I believe something actually is there. Perceptually, emotionally, in every way, unquestioningly I know and feel that that thing is there, just as you know that this book is in front of you. The features that one perceives as being objectively there—which is to say, the characteristic of every perception to have an object or 'objective aspect'—are projections or cognitive constructions with which cognition displaces actuality, substituting concretizations of its own needs and fears.[36] Even when an actual object, a vastu, is contributing to the cognition, it is being understood, interpreted, perceived by terms and criteria established by noesis, by the 'grasper.' Yogācāra and other Buddhists call this cognitive displacement *vikalpa* (discrimination), *samāropa* (assertion), *khyāti* (something appears due to psycho-linguistic insistence), etc.

Closure and referentiality

Having said all this, what, finally, does saṃvṛti mean? Saṃvṛti is a statement, an evaluative categorization of the world (or worlds) of common experience, 'common' both in the sense of communal and ordinary. To say that such a world is saṃvṛti is to say that that world occurs within a closure, within limiting parameters and horizons. Insofar as that closure is constitutive of and constituted by communication, i.e., the intersubjective sharing of intentionalities, it can not be the property of a single solipsistic subjectivity. Though we may say that the world is noetically determined, the source of noesis is, according to Buddhism, never a transcendental subject (*ātman*), but rather a circuit of intentionality (*citta-santāna, ālaya-vijñāna*) which conditionally (*saṃskāra, saṃskṛta*) links previous and subsequent experiences (*saṃjñā*). Like Merleau-Ponty's 'circuit of intentionality,' noesis and noema or lived-body and perceptual field dialectically and mutually condition each other; neither has primacy.

Saṃvṛti's closure is not imposed from without. The closure arises through the operations of consciousness and language, or more precisely stated, the activity of consciousness and language is itself saṃvṛti's closure. According to Candrakīrti and other Buddhists, the word *saṃvṛti* literally means 'enclosed, enveloped, shut in and surrounded,' in other words: closure.

Language (*vāk*) is a system of referentiality. On the one hand, each sentence, each word, each syllable, each letter, each seme, is linguistic precisely because it endeavors to point beyond and outside itself toward something else. It refers, within the context of an utterance, to what it is not, i.e., to a referent which, by virtue of being a referent, a signified, must be something different than the signifier that pointed to it. On the other hand, each seme, etc., acts as an integral unit, a distinct, discrete unit whose identity is fixed by an invariable relation with that to which it refers. The word "tree" is, on the one hand, not actually a tree; on the other hand, its semantic identity is fixed and determined by its assigned concomitance with the notion or facticity of trees. The ambivalence of, for instance, the letter "e" in "tree" (which "e"? The first or second?), which is clearly unlike any tree and yet, as part of the English language system, invariably indicates trees when used in the word "tree," offers a hint at how closure operates. The act of referentiality implies a simultaneous identity and difference between signifier and signified such that they remain ultimately separable and inseparable from each other at the same time. Otherwise referentiality becomes impossible. Like the well known paradox of measuring subatomic particles—if measuring their velocity, their weight becomes undetectable, and vice versa, so that no particle can be said to demonstrably have weight and velocity simultaneously—in order for referentiality to function, a one-sided choice must be made, which automatically represses the other alternative. Reference, in order to be clear, should avoid ambiguity as much as possible, which involves repressing variant, marginal and overly connotative meanings. Each repression marks a limit; the closure of a word's semantic region. In order for a word to refer, it must repress, it must exclude. In order for a relation to obtain between signifier and signified, the act of signification must simultaneously repress and exploit the identity and difference of the signifier and its signified. The signifier shares an identity with the signified that must, by definition, be different from it. Without fixing such margins and thus establishing a closure, language cannot function. Without the implicit closure presupposed by linguistic referentiality—the class logic in which 'these signifiers' refer only to 'those signifieds' and not 'other signifieds,' in other words, the closure of a class or set—a word or seme, etc., could not fix or establish a stable meaning or set of meanings. Language constitutes and is constituted by closure. Contingency and even arbitrariness are displaced by necessary, absolute concomitance. Language gains precision as it approaches univocality. The contingent relation between a signified and its signifier must become an absolute and necessary relation in order for language to carry any power of literal referentiality. A necessary relation is a closed, unalterable relation.

The structure of consciousness operates in a similar manner. In a cognitive act consciousness refers to an object (*artha*). Consciousness (*vijñāna*) is differential. *Vi-* is similar to the English prefix 'dis-' (e.g., dis-criminate, dis-tinguish, dis-course, dis-cursive, etc.) which connotes the separating out of two things, or producing change through opposition. *Vi* + *jñāna* is the intentional cognitive activity of being cognizant of an object. What was said above about language is also true of consciousness. Its functioning depends on and produces cognitive closure. Not only does the noema depend on noetic constitution, but the noesis is neither operative nor self-reflective without a noema. The chiasmic ambiguity between the appropriator and the appropriated is both cause and effect of the closure of consciousness. Consciousness establishes its own limits qua objects in order to function; when limitless it becomes 'nothing,' as Sartre and the tri-dhātu model argue. For Buddhism, consciousness, insofar as it depends upon and is conditioned by saṃskāra,[37] is thoroughly dependent on memory, i.e., conditioning from previous experience.[38] The notion of a neutral, synchronically self-sufficient consciousness which cognizes in the present, independent of past cognitions, would be impossible for Buddhism. Past experiences influence and color present experience, and the restrictions this places on the possibility of novel experiences also contribute to the closure.

Buddhists are not hard determinists, and thus do not deny novelty—Awakening would be impossible without it—but the degree to which one is incapable of novelty while interpreting and responding to current situations is the degree to which one is karmically (habitually) determined. The problem of karma, as we will see shortly, turns on the appropriational nature of the seemingly innocent act of cognitive and/or linguistic reference. Breaking the referential cycle is part, if not all of the cure. As Nāgārjuna said: "When the citta-gocara (the intentionality circuit) stops operating, signifieds stop as well." (MMK 18:7) When the process of cognitive referentiality is disrupted, linguistic referentiality is likewise disrupted.

Consciousness, in its own depths, in the very manner in which it operates (*pravṛtti*), is constituted by and through significatory activity, viz. it generates signifiers (*abhidhāna*) and signifieds (*abhidheya*) by constructing an obstruction (*āvaraṇa*) between them, a *jñeyāvaraṇa* (obstruction of what's known due to clinging to ātma-dṛṣṭi, the view of selfhood), i.e., imposing what Lacan has called the sign's *barre*.[39]

In an important creative re-reading of Ferdinand de Saussure's discussion of the linguistic sign as a signifier (Sr) which refers to a signified (Sd), graphically representable as Sd over Sr, , divided like a fraction by a line or bar (French: *barre*),[40] Lacan has focused attention away from the Sr and Sd per se back to the line separating them that itself signifies their significatory relation. For Lacan this line represents the repressive margin between conscious and unconscious activities, both of which are thoroughly linguistic. One of the examples given by de Saussure for how the Sr signifies a Sd involves the word "tree" signifying a tree. In his text a simplistic drawing of a tree stands for the Sd, while the French word for tree, *arbre*, stands for the word. Lacan playfully reminds his reader that *barre* (i.e., the bar or line which both separates the Sr from the Sd and marks their significatory relationship) and *arbre* are anagrams, suggesting that the identity and difference between Srs and Sds mark a psychoanalytic economy, a repressive sundering via dissimulation, which is symptomatic of fundamental anxieties. For Lacan, the rearrangement of the letters in an anagram is emblematic of the way the unconscious rearranges conscious content, for instance, in dreams, Freudian slips or neurotic displacement. Language and consciousness converge through a referentiality that both presupposes and establishes the line of closure, the line which is neither identity nor difference and yet which must establish and maintain the identity and difference of what lies above and below it. Lacan insists, finally, that there is no independent agent called "the unconscious." The line marks the margin of repression, such that to focus on what is above the line involves suppressing and 'forgetting' what is below the line, and vice versa. Pushing memory out of view by exiling it to the forgotten, neglected side of the line is the activity of the unconscious. The unconscious is the product, not the agent, of an act whose oppositional components, viz. the parts above and below the line, are both linguistic and thus conscious. For Lacan as for Buddhism, language and consciousness are inseparable from closure.

Saṃvṛti means whatever occurs within the closure. The walls of the closure are mirrors aimed at each other, and directly or indirectly aimed towards the center. Saṃvṛti is the mirrored envelope in which consciousness folds back upon itself. Consciousness' self-referentiality, guided by the reflective paths of the mirrors, may be extremely indirect, and may thus incorporate all sorts of side-images and reflections. Significantly, the Sanskrit term for 'projection of consciousness' is *pratibimba*, which literally means 'reflected image, image in a mirror.'

The mirrored closured walls are *not solipsistic* constructions, but products of *communal* consent. Consciousness, in its very operations, constitutes the obstructions (*āvaraṇa*) which enclose and encircle it. As the seeming source of its own closure, it appears to itself as self-validating, self-justificatory, or to put this in social terms, communal assent comes to be accepted as the prerequisite and guarantor of certainty. For any conventional decision to become binding and regulative, its contingent origin must be at least partially repressed and forgotten, and it must assume the status of a law which always already was the case, and thus demands obedience.[41] Saṃvṛti operates within consensual truths.

But at the very instant saṃvṛti engages in its enclosuring, it is simulataneously interlinked with consensual discourse, with the 'other.' This is why in the *Mahāyānasaṃgraha*, Asaṅga details the undoing of the narcissism of the ālaya-vijñāna as caused by a linguistic packet imported from the ālaya-vijñāna's most vociferous other. *Mano-jalpa*, an engaged refutational mental activity aimed at tearing down stable structures, infiltrates the ālaya-vijñāna, destroying it from within while never being *of* the ālaya.[42] Saṃvṛti, then, is simultaneously a closure, and an powerful openness to the Other, an openness traversed by language and communication.

Saṃvṛti is also the tyranny of judgement, the measurement of self by other, and other by self; peer pressure, societal belonging, such that an individual stabilizes her own identity in terms of one or a series of communal identities which she appropriates, so that she *belongs* to that group, and it to her; the seeing of oneself through another's eyes; altruism and selfishness; etc., all this is saṃvṛti. The actuality of such a world, its facticity in the light of the conditions by which such a world is given is saṃvṛti-*satya*. Paramārtha-satya is the clear seeing of the actuality of saṃvṛti, i.e., saṃvṛti made transparent. It is paramārtha-satya or the 'actuality' of paramārtha because it is detached from saṃvṛti rather than caught up in the complex, obscured actualities of saṃvṛtic horizons. By "detached from" I don't mean that it is separated from or elsewhere than saṃvṛti, but only that it views saṃvṛti dispassionately (*virāga*), devoid of appropriational intent.

The two satyas should be understood as two distinct views of what seems to be the case: Saṃvṛti-satya determines 'what seems to be the case' through cognitive and linguistic referentiality, i.e., through the criteria of closure; paramārtha-satya sees 'what seems to be the case' *as closure* but not *by closure*. In other words the two satyas are: (1) The world as it actually functions and is cognized within the conditioned psychosophic closure, and (2) What is actually the case, what is simultaneously beyond reference (i.e., irreducible to the closure of referentiality) and the ultimate referent of what appears otherwise from within the closured perspective. This latter *satya* is not an ontologically transcendent truth, but rather simply and utterly what happens to be the case, which, like sensation, remains forever uncontainable by the closure of linguistic referentiality.

If what was argued about the tri-dhātu model in Part II is correct—namely that final margins do not mark a jumping off point to the radically and utterly other, but rather involve the uncovering of the conditions by which margins are constructed, thereby rendering the margins and the conditional factors they instantiate transparent—then this observation should be instructive for the current case as well. Paramārtha would not signify crossing the threshold of something utterly unlike what appears to be the case (*ābhāva*)—and Mahāyāna Buddhists insist that not an iota of distinction can be drawn between saṃsāra and nirvāṇa—but rather the very transparency of that margin.

Yogācāra was not interested in describing what the 'world in itself' might be, but rather how we karmically interact with the world, and, if that karmic interaction is the root human problematic, how precisely does it occur, by what law or economy does it become problematic, and how might it be cured? For them the interactive modality was karmic and interpretive; saṃsāra is saṃvṛti. To see and to experience interpretation *as* interpretation—and thus understand whatever is actually the case—is paramārtha. Thus even in order to understand what saṃvṛti-satya and paramārtha-satya signify and how they function in Buddhist thought, we must understand what karma is.

Concluding Remarks
Madhyamaka and the Four models

Technically speaking, in India there were only two distinct schools of Mahāyāna: Madhymaka and Yogācāra. Yogācāra attempted to retain what was useful in other forms of Buddhism, but to do so in a way that did not violate the warnings Madhyamakans leveled against Buddhists whom, they argued, had gotten so caught up in thinking 'like Buddhists' and promoting and reifying the 'truths' of Buddhism, that they had forgotten what Buddhism was really about. Just as one should go back to Buddhism's beginnings in order to understand Yogācāra properly, one also needs to examine what Madhyamaka brought to the table in order to appreciate its influence—which was profound—on Yogācāra.[43]

Although rarely recognized as such, Nāgārjuna uses an adapted version of the tri-dhātu model described in Part II, particularly the meditative program of the ārūpya-dhātu. The movement from 'infinite spatiality' to 'infinite consciousness' to 'nothing' to 'neither with nor without associative-thinking' is directly analogous to the movement through the 'four alternatives,' to his cognitive reductions (e.g., his highlighting of the notion of prapañca), to śūnyatic negations, to the neither/nor aporia of Madhyamic silence. Let's flesh this out a little.

The influence of the kāma-loka diminishes as one advances through the rūpa-loka, where 'objects' are characterized by their mutual 'resistance' (*pratigha*), their mutual obstruction. Even as the dichotomous extremes of vedanā are being neutralized (*upekṣa*), things are still ultimately constituted by their mutual resistance, by their boundaries, by the lines which are drawn between them. In ārūpya-loka the resistance, the mutual obstruction disappears into limitless spatiality, the matrix and ground of the possibility that there be any distinctions whatsoever.

Moving from rūpa-dhātu to ārūpya-dhātu is analogous to moving from the conceptual space of fixed, absolutistic, mutually exclusive positions to the matrix of conceptual possibilities, viz. the four alternatives (*catuṣkoṭi*),[44] since positions oppose each other by their mutual resistance, their mutual opposition. Instead of viewing 'possibility' through the metaphor of etheric spatiality (*ākāśa*), Madhyamaka considers 'possibility' in terms of the four propositional alternatives. The cosmological and meditational contexts of the model are sublimated in Mādhyamika. The soteric intent of the ārūpya-dhātu's cosmological and meditational strata becomes subsumed in a new soteric intent: The laying bare of the systematic myths and (seemingly) logical arguments with which we hide from anxieties. Abandoning the metaphor of a progressional ladder that the seeker climbs, the focus instead becomes the undermining of the proliferation of our linguistic, theoretical masks (*prapañca-dṛṣṭi*). The explicitly psychological character of early Buddhism shifts in Madhyamaka to a demonstration of the feebleness and incoherency with which we rationalize and become entrenched in our prejudices, such that the propensity to self-justify one's own prejudices in any and every sphere, from religion and politics to cosmology and economics, from musical tastes to food preferences, from the grandest ideals to the basest habits, from metaphysics to social structure, in all spheres, is irrevocably undermined.

Mādhyamika seeks to demonstrate that all views (*dṛṣṭi*) are ultimately false views, that all views arise through the use of the four alternatives. All positions, they argue, are simply fortified attachments to one of the four alternatives, and the four possibilities are inherently self-contradictory and thus fallacious. To master the four alternatives, then, is to master the possibilities of any and all positions. Since positions, just like the structure of rūpa-dhātu, are constituted by mutual resistance, animosity and aversion (*pratigha*)—and the vehemence with which people cling to their own views while assaulting and denigrating opposing views is the constant reminder that āsavas, not truth, are what compel people to propose logical formulations; logic, in this sense, is sublimated *pratigha*— Nāgārjuna astutely attacks this foundational condition composed of the interstices that bifurcate all extremest positions. 'Extreme' here means at either end of a pole, at either extreme; and since all positions are constituted by mutual opposition, all positions, insofar as they define themselves through their opposition or oppositional relation to an 'other' position, are extreme. To define themselves entirely apart from any other position, if not utterly impossible, still presupposes (i) other positions from which to be non-differentiated, and (ii) the opposition between self-contained (internal) and relational (external) explanations.

Positions are perspectives (*dṛṣṭi*) or points of view (*darśana*), arising from and feeding into experience (*gocara*). All possibilities are grounded in cognition (*vijñāna*), and cognition's propensity to super-intend, its insistence that there be possibilities so that it may express preferences and attach to these is ubiquitous, like the realm of boundless consciousness. One's preferential biases—expressions of one's conditioning—are projected everywhere, onto everything. For Nāgārjuna, this becomes most evident, and most problematic, in the linguistic sphere, in the manner by which we impose nominal and conceptual labels on everything. The propensity to do so he calls *prapañca*. This brings out the nāmic (nominalistic) qualities of cognitive activity.

Consciousness, in turn. is grounded in its radical contingency. Only because cognition is variable, i.e., able to change and alter, can it entertain cognitional possibilities. Were it constant, such that no difference in either content, mood, or focus ever occurred, not only would cognitions of the world disappear,[45] but cognition would be entirely divorced from any and all possibilities since an unaltering cognitive faculty could not keep track of or respond to an altering, changing sensorium. To be truly contant, it would have to remain unaltered and unaffected by anything that changes either internally or externally. To register some change, to notice something, is to already have been changed by that something, and thus no longer constant. Its contingency is its variability, and its variability is the source of its possibilities. The realization of this contingency is analogous to moving from limitless spatiality (the open possibilities of any position and the raw possibility that there be positions) to limitless consciousness (the cognitional economy in which positions occur and operate),[46] to the 'nothing' that undergirds consciousness. All cognitions are contingent, not only in the sense of human mortality, but because they could always be otherwise. Though I see a grey object at this moment, at some other time I may see something else. Had some other object been at hand, or had the light, or my eyes, or any number of conditions been otherwise, even at this moment I would be seeing something else. Cognition depends upon the cognitive object, the cognitive organ and the cognitive consciousness that arises through their contact. If one argues that while cognition is contingent for the reasons stated, on the other hand consciousness is not contingent, since its phenomenological structure, e.g., to be appropriative, to have horizons, to locate itself in a perceptual field, etc., are not contingent, but necessary, essential features of consciousness,[47] then the Buddhist would remind us that very existence of consciousness is contingent. The structure of consciousness is not self-defined; it arises dependent on other cognitory conditions. It is thoroughly contingent. Consciousness, the sheer fact that "experiencing" takes place, is neither permanent nor eternal; it arises in one moment dependent on conditions, and then ceases. In another moment, another consciousness arises.

That one moment conditions the next can be metaphorically expressed as a consciousness-stream (*citta-santāna*), which, like Heraclitus' river, because it is moving and changing, never retains any fixed identity beyond the moment in which it occurs.

Nāgārjuna, then, follows the tri-dhātu model. Conative (a.k.a. kāma-loka) and cognitive (a.k.a. rūpa-loka) barriers are attacked, exposing the conditions that constitute those barriers, viz. attaching (*kāma-loka*) to any of the four alternatives (*rūpa-loka*). The alternatives emerge from a web of possibilities (boundless ākāśa) underwritten by our ubiquitous prapañcic propensities (boundless consciousness). The psycho-cognitive-linguistic basis for these conditions, viz. *prapañca, vikalpa* (discrimination), etc., is attacked—which is to say 'emptied,' 'purified'—by marshalling the force of the nothing, the contingency, exposing all positions to the sheer fact that they could have been otherwise, and, if logically coherent, would be. The incoherency of all positions is precisely their contingency, i.e., that each embodies its own contradiction and undoing at its core in some essential way. Essence *as* essence provides its own problematic; it establishes itself on the grounds of its own erasure. Essential definitions are necessarily tautological. Linguistically, all 'necessary' statements are contingent, since all statements as statements imply and are contextualized by their contrary, their inverse. Language, and especially logic, doubles reality: for every x there logically inheres an affirmation *and* a negation, a true and a false. Its 'essence' is never apart from this duplicity. The two-valued logic which Nāgārjuna employs (or deploys) is a formal statement of contingency: yes or no, true or false, like so or otherwise. The negational flavor of Mādhyamika—which has terrified its opponents, prompting them to mislabel it as 'nihilism' (usually as an excuse for not having to deal with the thrust of Mādhyamikan arguments)—derives from the ārūpya-dhātu's 'nothing.'

The nothing gives way to utter marginality, to 'neither associative-thinking nor not-associative-thinking.' Similarly Nāgārjuna's 'Diamond Truth-shredder' negational logic gives way to aporetic living, to that special type of indeterminacy that is freedom. Attached to no position, one is free to play with all positions. Mādhyamika is often characterized as holding the 'neither-nor' position. If Mādhyamika was consistent, this would be impossible. However statements by Nāgārjuna, Candrakīrti and others can easily be construed this way: e.g., *MMK* 18.11, "without many meanings or a single meaning..."; or 25.10,[48] "The teacher has spoken of relinquishing both becoming [*bhavasya*] and other-[than-] becoming [*vibhavasya*]. Therefore, it is proper to assume that freedom is neither existence nor non-existence"; etc. Candrakīrti writes:[49]

> Is there then no reasoned argument (*upapatti*) for the wise?
> How could we say whether there is or there is not? The higher truth, for the wise, is a matter of silence (*tuṣṇīṃbhāva*).[50] How then would everyday language, reasoned or unreasoned, be possible in that realm?

He also writes:[51]

> Therefore all things are not to be taken either as devoid of being or as non-devoid; individuals are neither real beings nor unreal beings; this is the middle way.

Clearly he is taking the neither/nor formula as equivalent to the middle way (*madhyama*). And elsewhere he characterizes the neither/nor formulation as the most approximate to the 'truth,' formulated for those penultimate to full Awakening.[52] One could offer apologetic interpretations of such passages, but, there they are.

The penultimate—whether conceptual, samādhic, or linguistic—is characterized in both the tri-dhātu model and Mādhyamika as neither/nor, a neither-nor which is hulled from a series of radical negations.

Marginality, as 'neither saṃjñā nor asaṃjñā' (ārūpya-dhātu) or 'neither bhāva nor abhāva' (Mādhyamaka), becomes the penultimate realization. In the Theravādin tri-dhātu model the highest ārūpa-jhāna enables the nirodha-samāpatti which leads to the attainment of arhatship. In Madhyamaka, the neither/nor position becomes the least abhorrent propositional stance, the most correct way of saying something short of silence, the expression for and by the understanding of those just short of full Awakening. Marginality here means primarily the recognition of a margin without reifying that margin as the perimeter of a closure.

The following chart may help clarify the above discussion.

Tri-dhātu	Madhyamaka	Yogācāra
kāma-loka	propensity to assert and negate, attachment to views	grāhya-grāhaka
rūpa-loka	extremism, dṛṣṭi, opposition of views, either/or; **mutual exclusion**	vijñapti-mātra
ārūpya-loka		
boundless spatiality	web of 'logical' possibilities; **tautology**	ubiquitous parikalpita
boundless consciousness	prapañca, vikalpa; **infinite regress**	(defiled) paratantra
Nothing	emptying views, all views are contingent, not absolute	parinispanna
neither with nor without saṃjñā	neither/nor	purified paratantra

Notice I have included Yogācāra correspondences as well. We will examine these important Yogācāra terms more fully later, but I have included them here to show that even at this level Yogācāra and Madhyamaka have a great deal in common, and that commonality is something directly traceable to early

Buddhism. This chart may also help clarify the therapeutic structure of the Madhyamakan approach to Buddhism, a point which is often either overlooked by modern treatments, or seems hard to find for some. Religions, philosophies, political persuasions, in short, any ideology, imposes its identity in the world through assertion and negation. This is a proclivity, a compulsion, derived from and symptomatic of clinging to views. We identify with the views to which we cling, so that a challenge to the viability of those views is perceived as a direct assault on one's essential identity. Views become what they are by opposing other views: opposition, resistance, extremism, *pratigha*, etc. By coming to recognize that the fierce 'logical' battles one wages, often somewhat unawares, in order to create and maintain an identity are really rationalizations masking proclivities, and that these logical edifices are drawn from a web of possibilities grounded in one's discriminative and psycho-linguistic compulsions (*vikalpa, prapañca*), one can empty these views, finally attaching to neither this nor that view, but recognizing all views for what they are: desperate attempts to establish a permanent identity where no such thing exists or can exist.

Nāgārjuna's *prāsaṅgika* (reductio ad absurdum) tactics are also displayed in the chart. Nāgārjuna uses three basic strategies to negate an opponent's position:

(i) Demonstrate that the position is mutually exclusive from something else the opponent holds as true, or with an integral aspect of itself;
(ii) demonstrate that the opponent's position rests on a tautology, which means it begs the question;[53] and
(iii) reduce the position to an infinite regress, which means it never establishes or validates itself.

The rūpa-dhātu, constituted of *pratigha* which is the resistance between two forms such that they cannot occupy the same space at the same time, is therefore by definition in its deepest constitution a place of mutual exclusion. Tautology occurs when two apparently different things turn out to be identical, homogenous, like ākāśa, which is homogeneity par excellence. Consciousness, especially when implicated in the question of selfhood, is infinite regress, since it distinguishes itself by reflecting on itself; reflexivity becomes bottomless. I perceive something; I perceive myself perceiving something; I perceive that I have perceived myself perceiving something. And so on. There is no end to such reflexivity. The question of the self trying to find its true self—which Buddhists contend does not exist, making such a quest pointless and interminable—is integrated into the very structure of consciousness, as will be discussed in a later chapter.[54] Thus, Nāgārjuna's three strategies are seen to derive from the tri-dhātu model. Employing these strategies brings one to the Nothing, the emptying of all dṛṣṭi, the purification of the saṃskāric residue that generates the compulsions that need to be negated. Once dṛṣṭis are emptied, the middle way, neither/nor, emerges, in which one becomes free *in* conditions, not *from* conditions.

In order to make the chart comprehensible, the Yogācāric terms now will be briefly explained. *Grāhya-grāhaka* (grasped-grasper) signifies the appropriative circuit that Yogācāra identifies as the primary problem. Vijñapti-mātra signifies the displacement of the actual world behind a psychosophic projection compeled by the need to appropriate, just as rūpic materiality is displaced by formal mental operations during dhyāna in the rūpa-loka. The four levels of the ārūpya-dhātu correspond to the four aspects of the three self nature theory of Yogācāra (*trisvabhāva*). Parikalpita is the ubiquitous projection of delusionary views that one mistakes for the world; this is like ākāśa not only because it is ubiquitous, but, as the *Ch'eng wei-shih lun* and other Yogācāra texts point out when discussing ākāśa, ākāśa is a purely mental construction. Paratantra (lit. 'dependent on others') signifies *pratitya-samutpāda*, i.e., causality in which nothing produces itself, but everything arises dependent on other conditions (and therefore are 'empty' of own-being, *svabhāva*). Consciousness arises dependent on the contact of sense-organ and sense-object, and ideas—whether accurate or erroneous—arise dependent on conditions as well. Given certain conditions, such as adherence to erroneous views or the compulsions of self-interest, one is deluded and experiences the world falsely. Defiled paratantra is different from parikalpita in that parikalpita is simply viewing the world erroneously, while defiled paratantra is an account of the conditions that produce that erroneous vision. Parinişpanna, the Yogācāra correlate to Madhyamakan 'emptiness,' is the antidote to parikalpita. It is the Nothing that empties parikalpita from paratantra. The result of that emptying is purified paratantra, in which causality occurs without delusionary consequences.

Notes

1 For instance, the idea of 'self-caused' is incoherent because it is impossible for something to cause itself. To cause itself, it would *already* have to exist prior to when it does exist, in order to be there to cause itself. If it is already existent, it is no longer necessary or possible for it to cause itself, since it would already have been caused. This has not prevented theologians from arguing for centuries that God is *sui generis*, self-caused.

2 Jay Garfield, *The Fundamental Wisdom of the Middle Way* (Oxford: Oxford University Press, 1995), p. 179.

3 See Ariel Glucklich, *A Sense of Adharma* (Oxford: Oxford University Press, 1994) for a treatment of this concept in Classical Hinduism. Cf. Also the *Bhagavad Gītā*, esp. chs. 2-4, for classical statements on Dharma vs. Adharma.

4 That the deepest nihilism comes from clinging to the highest metaphysical ideals which, when they lose their veracity, drain one's life of meaning, leaving a *nihil* in place of the former ideals, has been more eloquently discussed by Nietzsche than I can attempt here. Cf. *Will to Power*, and other works.

5 E.g., cf. especially MMK 9 (negates the two extremes of prior and posterior, as well as middle [where would it be?]), 14 (on *saṃsarga*, 'connecting together,' in which Nāgārjuna provides a rigorous deconstruction of the notion of 'difference'), 20 (on *sāmagrī*, 'coordinating causes and effects'), 21 (on *saṃbhava-vibhava*, 'confluence and dissolution').

6 Streng, more or less following Candrakīrti, attributes verses 1 through 5 to one opponent, 6 through 11 to another opponent, and 12 through 20 to a third opponent, with Nāgārjuna joining the discussion at verse 21.

7 That this chapter presents some difficulties is reflected in the fact that most of the available translations contain serious flaws, especially regarding the earlier verses (such as 4 and 5) in which Buddhist karmic theory is presented. Nāgārjuna provides a list of what he calls the "seven dharmas producing karma," but an English reader would be hard pressed trying to figure out which terms are counted among the seven in either Kalupahana, Garfield, or Streng; and while Inada distinguishes the seven correctly, his translation of some of the terms themselves are less than helpful. The stunning exception—stunning because it was published long before the others—is Étienne Lamotte's rendering of Candrakīrti's commentary to this chapter, accompanying his translation and analysis of Vasubandhu's *Karmasiddhi prakaraṇa.* Lamotte knew the Buddhist literature on the issues discussed by Nāgārjuna and Candrakīrti in this chapter very well.

8 This derived in part from the Pratimokṣa ritual in which monks or nuns periodically made public confessions to a full group of their fellow clerics concerning their wrongdoings with vows to improve. But while they are offering a public display of their contrition, performing all the correct physical gestures and uttering all the correct formulas, and maybe even half believing what they are doing, what are they *really* thinking? To all appearances they may be performing acts of contrition, but in actuality they may be laying karmic seeds even at that moment leading to a repetition of the wrongdoing or some other wrongdoing. Some Buddhists developed an odd materialistic theory to account for that sort of duplicity, calling it *avijñapti-rūpa*, i.e., a physical element, a rūpa, that does not reveal itself, but nonetheless contains karmic efficacy and traverses the time from when the initial seed of the act was developed until the act reaches final fruition. This was applied to a number of spheres. For instance, if person X puts out a contract to have person Y murdered, person X can give the appearance that he is good friends with Y, and by giving no external indication, X may seem to all who observe them, to have no animosity toward Y. Nor does X personally kill Y. Does X carry karmic responsibility nonetheless? Yes, according to this theory, from the moment he incurred the desire to kill Y until the moment Y is killed by someone else, X has had an avijñapti-rūpa that connects him directly to the murder act itself.

9 Nāgārjuna does not elaborate on what these numbers signify, but Candrakīrti explains that the ten pure paths are the 3 bodily and 4 linguistic dharmas (alluded to in verse 4), plus the 3 mental dharmas (alluded to in verse 5 by the term *cetanā*), totaling 10. The three are: nongreed, nonhatred, and correct views. The five qualities of pleasure are the five types of sense objects: visibles, audibles, etc. Cf. *Abhidharmakośa-bhāṣya*, ch. 4, on karma, starting around v. 3c.

10 The position Kalupahana attributes to Nāgārjuna begins here. He was perhaps drawn to that conclusion by the use of the first person in 17:13. Regardless, I think Candrakīrti is right to see this as yet another mistaken attempt at system building, explicitly marked in the text by the use in 17:13 of the term *kalpanā.*

11 The avipraṇāśa (promissory note), the recasting of karma in terms of debt, etc., are clear evidence of the growing relation between Buddhists and the mercantile classes that were becoming important patrons. Buddhists congregated in Northwestern India, the hub of the Indian portion of the world trade routes. Buddhism disseminated beyond Indian borders by following the merchants along the Silk Road that brought them to various regions of Central Asia and China and beyond. Just as the 'seed' metaphor was an effective heuristic for an audience steeped in agriculture, the mercantile metaphors would have been comparably effective for the monied class Buddhism was growing increasingly intimate with. Notions that developed around the same time, such as the Sambhoga-kāya, or Recompense Body, also trade on mercantile thinking (rewarded future luxury for hard work now).

12 This argument also implies a critique of Jain karmic theory which extols total inaction as the highest form of karmic divestment.

13 This type of analogy to a magical act is quite popular in Buddhist literature. Cf. Bhikkhu Ñānananda, *The Magic of the Mind: An Exposition of the Kālakārāma Sutta* (Kandy: BPS, 1985) for a discussion of the Theravāda applications of these analogies. See Vasubandhu's *Trisvabhāvanirdeśa* vs. 34-35, for a Yogācāra application of the magic analogy.

14 New Age Buddhists prefer to think that consciousness is what transmigrates, since 'consciousness' has become a 'good' term in their conceptual universe. Buddha, however, flatly denied that in the *Tevijja-vacchagotta sutta* of the *Majjhima-Nikāya.*

15 This was how the Pudgalavādins defined it. On skandhas, āyatanas, etc. see Part Two. The five realms are the rebirth regions of the kāma-loka minus the Āsuras.

16 It is important to note that the so-called Pudgala-vādins *did* view the pudgala as a prajñapti. Cf. Bhikshu Thich Thiên Châu, *The Literature of the Personalists of Early Buddhism* (Delhi: Motilal Banarsidass, 1999); also Leonard Priestley, *Pudgalavāda Buddhism* (Toronto: University of Toronto, 1999).

17 *Prasannapadā,* p. 57; Sprung, p. 50.

18 *Tuṣṇīṃbhāva* might also be rendered 'pacifying nāmic tendencies.'

19 See Whalen Lai, "The Sinitic Understanding of the Two Truths Theory in the Liang Dynasty ((502-557): Ontological Gnosticism in the Thought of Prince Chao-Ming," *Philosophy East and West,* 28, no.3, July 1978, pp. 339-351.

20 Michael Broido, "Veridical and Delusive Cognition: Tsong-kha-pa on the Two Satyas," *Journal of Indian Philosophy,* 16, 1988, pp. 30-32.

21 Broido offered the last Sanskrit phrase as a single compound, but I have broken it up for easier readability. I will discuss its components shortly.

22 Broido is the first to publish certain English correspondences for technical Sanskrit terms which for several years I thought I alone was proposing (though I do not agree with all of his suggestions). For instance, he takes *artha* as "referent," and even offers an endnote to a passage in his translation of Tsong-kha-pa's text which says

> This use of *artha* (don) is very common in both Sanskrit and Tibetan and seems to have the dictionary sense of "that towards which something is directed," that is, the object of an intentional state. The latter phrase probably best taken in the sense of Husserl...

a reading of artha not unlike the one I offered above. I take his article as a sign that Buddhist scholarship in the West is healthy, astute and on the right track.

23 *Madhyamika-kārikā* 24.10.

24*Prasannapadā,* p. 494; Sprung, p. 232.

25 Note the usage of -mātra here. It is a demeaning, restrictive term, not a reifying honorific. That is how it is invariably used by Buddhists, making the idealist interpretation of the term vijñapti-*mātra* all the more improbable. We will return to this later.

26 He addresses the question 'How does one translate while attempting to remain faithful to the demands of textual and philosophic accuracy?' on pp. 30ff, and in his notes.

27 Ibid., passim.

28 I owe this example to Holmes Welch, *Taoism: The Parting of the Way* (Boston: Beacon, 1966).

29 Op. cit., p. 47; from Tsong-kha-pa's *dgongs-pa rab-sal* (lHa-sa ed., Delhi rpt.) 108b2. I've deleted Broido's transcribed Tibetan, or substituted Sanskrit equivalents.

30 See *Saṅdhinirmocana Sūtra,* ch. 1.

31 Broido, op. cit., pp. 47-48.

32The distinctions he draws are (p. 40):

paramārtha = samyagartha, the real or proper intentional object;
saṃvṛti*= obscured (cf. āvaraṇa, sgib-pa; āvṛti, bsgribs-pa);
saṃvṛti# = vyavahāra, conventional

satya* = veridical (non-delusive, mi-slu-ba) in primary sense
satya# = neither veridical nor delusive in primary sense.

Accordingly Tsong-kha-pa's view is:
Buddha-cognition is paramārtha-satya*
āryas' cognition is typically saṃvṛti*-satya#
pṛtagjana's cognition is typically mere saṃvṛti#, and he rejects the Svātantrika view that it is saṃvṛti#-satya*.

Broido characterizes Tsong-kha-pa's opponent, Padma dKar-po, as:
Buddha and ārya both have paramārtha-satya* and saṃvṛti*-satya*, they differ in the intensity and stability of these cognitions.
pṛtagjana's cognition is mere saṃvṛti* (not saṃvṛti#).

Candrakīrti is schematized:
Buddha-cognition is paramārtha-satya
ārya cognition is typically saṃvṛti-satya
pṛtagjana's cognition is typically mere saṃvṛti.

33 See, e.g., *Madhyānta-vibhāga*, ch. 1; for a translation of this basic text with rudimentary comments, see the appendix to Lusthaus, *A Philosophic Investigation...* 1989.

34 Tsong-kha-pa's metaphysical substratum can be reduced to this notion of vastu. Both saṃvṛti-satya and paramārtha-satya see something: the former sees a 'snake' (delusion) as its artha; the latter's artha is the rope. He may have actually had just this analogy in mind when formulating his argument. Buddhists have found it hard, understandably, to discuss the problem of appearance and reality without sounding ontological or metaphysical.

35 *Viṃśatikā* 4 and *-bhāṣya.*

36 This Yogācāric notion was later adopted and modified by Śaṅkara to explain how *māyā* displaces Brahman, and he called his revised version of the theory *adhyāsa.* We shouldn't confuse the Vedāntic version of cognitive displacement and its absolutistic metaphysical agenda with the epistemo-psychological theory of the Yogācārins.

37 Links #2 and #3 in the pratītya-samutpāda model.

38 Here we see an important difference between the Buddhist notion of recurrent, karmic experience and Nietzsche's notion of eternal recurrence. While for Nietzsche eternal recurrence was a solution, a way of synchronizing all that remains beyond one's present ability to affect or change with one's will that it be so (that is, accepting or acquiescing to history, but on one's own terms), for Buddhism eternal recurrence is a symptom of the problem, viz. karma's habituality. Eternal recurrence, for Buddhists, would signify what needs to be overcome, not reified.

39 Jacques Lacan, "The agency of the letter in the unconscious or reason since Freud," in *Écrit*, tr. by Alan Sheridan (NY: Norton, 1977), pp. 146-178, esp. p. 154: "(The anagram of '*arbre*' and '*barre*' should be noted.)" Cf. also Anthony Wilden's discussion of Lacan's reworking of Structuralism in his essay "Lacan and the Discourse of the Other," in Lacan's *The Language of the Self*, tr. and comm. by Anthony Wilden (NY: Delta, 1968), pp. 159-311, esp. pp. 204-249

40 Ferdinand de Saussure, *Cours de linguistique générale* (Paris: 1916); English tr. by Wade Baskin, *Course in General Linguistics*, ed. by Charles Bally, et al. (NY: Philosophical Library, 1956). The section relevant to our present discussion is also reproduced in *The Structuralists: From Marx to Lévi-Strauss*, ed. by Richard and Fernande De George (NY: Doubleday Anchor, 1972), pp. 69-79.

41 Even in Twentieth Century American jurisprudence, the system of law by, of and for the people, though explicitly considered a conventional product authored by all too human disputants, and hewn from their cantankerous disputes, grounds itself in the Constitution, which even as its name indicates was 'constituted' by political hands. But the Constitution frequently is venerated as if it were a sacred, timeless absolute document that stated eternal inalienable

rights beyond reproach or revocation (though the phrase "inalienable rights" is found in the Declaration of Independence, not the Constitution). The Constitution may be amended, i.e., supplemented, but to actually erase part of the Bill of Rights or an existing amendment is still today utterly unthinkable (in practice one gets around this by adding amendments that alter or negate previous amendments; one does not simply erase a ratified amendment). When it becomes thinkable, the Constitution will no longer function as the binding document it appears to be today.

42 I delivered a paper on this topic at the Conference on Yogācāra in China, Leiden University, in June 2000: "Notes on the Hermeneutics of Asaṅga: Language, Saṃskāras, Appropriation." Chs. 1 and 3 of the *Mahāyānasaṃgraha* focus most especially on the mano-jalpa's pivotal role in undoing the ālaya-vijñāna. On the term *jalpa*, which is a technical term in Indian logic, cf. Vātsyāyana's *bhāṣya* to *Nyāya Sūtra* I.1 and I.2.1-3.

43 The discussion of Madhyamaka offered here is somewhat abstract and high level, not introductory in the usual sense of the term (though I will attempt to introduce a new context for understanding Madhyamaka). For something a bit more introductory, see my entry on 'Nāgārjuna' in *Great Thinkers of the East*, Ian P. McGreal, ed., (NY: HarperCollins, 1995).

44 There have been many attempts to reduce the fourfold alternatives to a basic model or a formal logical expression. Generally it appears in some permutation of the following two (simplified) schemata:

(1) x, (2) -x, (3) x and -x, (4) neither x nor -x;

or

(1) x $\cap$ [y], (2) x $\not\subset$ [y], (3) x both $\cap$ [y] and $\not\subset$ [y], (4) x neither $\cap$ [y] nor $\not\subset$ [y].

45 A great deal of experimental psychology has amply studied and documented this point. Our eyes, for instance, are in constant movement, oscillating over a thousand times a second. Experiments have shown that if a light shines directly on the same part of the retina uninterruptedly for over forty-five seconds, the light disappears from view (though still shining on the retina). By implication, if the visual field were in a constant fixed position *vis-à-vis* the eye—with neither the eye nor the field altering or moving in any way—then the world would literally disappear from sight! If we are subjected to a constant sound (either tonally or rhythmically constant), such as the hum of a machine or the ticking of a clock, after forty-five seconds to a minute we 'habituate' to the sound and not only don't consciously acknowledge or hear it, but EEGs show that our brains are no longer registering the sensation. Only a change in sound, a disruption of its constancy, will make us aware of it. We've all had the experience of being in a room where a loud machine went unnoticed until it suddenly turned off. The contrast between the resulting quiet and the previous unnoticed noise is so stark that we suddenly realize how loud it had been. Similar experiments have been done with other senses, all indicating that perception requires variability, change, and contrast; perception disappears with constancy. Epistemology has recognized this for a long time, and it is reflected in such riddles as: If the universe is doubling in size every second, and we, as part of the universe, are doubling in size at the same rate, how would we know? Since this 'change' would be constant, it would necessarily be imperceptible.

46 It cannot be overstressed that positions (*dṛṣṭi*), from a Buddhist point of view, are not simple, neutral abstract collections of propositions, but charged, passionate interpretations of experience which thoroughly color and flavor - literally - our every thought, sensation and action. They are produced by and produce embodied-conditioning (*saṃskāra*), and are thus symptoms of our conditioning rather than neutral alternatives from which one can innocently and naively choose. This all follows from the Buddhist analysis of *avidyā* and *jñeya-āvaraṇa*.

47 This, to some extent, is precisely the position taken by Husserl in *Logical Investigations* and *Ideas*. Husserlian Phenomenology, let's not forget, began as a search for essences (*Wesen*).

48 Kalupahana's tr., p. 361. Square brackets mine.

49 *Prasannapadā*, p. 57; Sprung, p. 50.

50 See n. 18 above.

51 *Ibid.*, p. 445; Sprung, p. 202.

52 *Ibid.*, p. 358; Sprung, p. 176. Cf. his commentary to *MMK* 18.8; *Ibid.*, pp. 369ff; Sprung's tr. (p. 181f) is somewhat misleading in parts.

53 The tautologies are usually not obvious until Nāgārjuna's analysis reveals them. For instance, for Nāgārjuna, 'fire and fuel' are not two distinct entities, but a tautology, since without fuel there is no fire, and without fire, fuel would be something else. Similarly 'Devadatta cooks' is for Nāgārjuna a tautology, since the Devadatta that walks is not the same thing as the Devadatta that cooks, and Devadatta's cooking would be impossible without Devadatta. In other words, differentiating nouns from verbs is a linguistic fiction, since no noun is conceivable without verbs (x must be doing something, if only 'existing' or 'not existing'), and no verbs are conceivable without nouns (who or what would *do* them?).

54 This is one of the reasons that Yogācāra considers consciousness to be the problem, not the solution. The urge to appropriate is born from the compulsion to have a rock-solid self.

Chapter Eleven

The Privileging of *Prajñā*: Prajñā-pāramitā

"Only don't know."

Korean Sŏn Master
Seung Sahn

That Buddhists pair *prajñā* and *upāya* highlights that not only are means (*upāya*) also ends—since the purpose of Awakening, especially in Mahāyānic thinking, involves acquiring the ability to Awaken others by means of *upāya*—but the ends (*prajñā*) themselves are simply means, since *prajñā* is the necessary condition for performing *upāya*. Moreover, Buddhist texts often treat prajñā—as opposed to *jñāna*—as a 'means' for acquiring knowledge, rather than as the end-product itself.[1] Buddhist texts resonate with a profound ambivalence on the problem of means and ends. Like Taoism, which had to 'explain' how one acts without acting, or tries without trying (*wu-wei*), Buddhism often felt compelled to account for how its 'goal' was not teleological, or how one achieves desirelessness (*apraṇihita*) without finally desiring it.[2]

The ambivalence between means and ends engendered major Mahāyānic controversies, emerging in various doctrinal and formulaic contexts, from Nāgārjuna's argument that if the Unconditioned (*asaṃskṛta*) can be attained by fulfilling conditions (*saṃskṛta*) then it cannot be considered Unconditioned, to the Ch'an debate between Sudden vs. Gradual Awakening and/or practice. The tension and dissonance is often in evidence even between different works by one and the same author. For example, Candrakīrti's so-called Prāsaṅgika version of Mādhyamika displays this tension when comparing his two major works: the *Prasannapadā* (his commentary on MMK) can be read as a virulent and rigorous attack on the use of means to establish and achieve ends, while on the other hand, his *Madhyamakāvatara* contextualizes his critiques of other schools as part of an exposition on the development of the means of the Bodhisattva Path/Practice (*mārga*), i.e., the cultivation of *prajñā-pāramitā*.

This ambivalence between means and ends can be brought to the forefront by focusing on the key term *prajñā-pāramitā*. Since, at least in India, this term is synonymous with the advent of Mahāyāna, a close look at both parts of this compound term may be helpful for tracing some of the changing contours of Buddhist thought.

First, note that prajñā is singled out as the factor around which the other pāramitās are oriented, which is to say that it is by or through prajñā, and for the purpose of developing prajñā, that one practices the pāramitās. The significance of assigning this special status to prajñā will be discussed presently.

The term prajñā-pāramitā is usually rendered in English as '*Perfection* of Wisdom' which accurately reflects the Sanskrit grammatical structure of *pāramitā* as an abstract noun connoting a completed or accomplished set of conditions. However, in Buddhism one *practices* the pāramitās as a means of both self- and other-improvement. One progresses along the Buddhist mārga (path *qua* method) by practicing the pāramitās and one also offers aid to other sentient beings by means of the pāramitās. This would suggest that, based on meaning rather than grammar, it might also be translated as *perfecting*. One actively engages in the 'perfecting' of *prajñā* (or perhaps *through prajñā*) rather than abiding in a static state of 'perfected' *prajñā*.[3] There are reasons for preferring a philosophical rather than philological translation of this term.

While in English 'perfection' implies an accomplished state, a non-variative fixed state, 'perfecting' suggests an ongoing process. The notion of prajñāpāramitā, as used in Buddhist literature, straddles both possibilities. The term 'perfection' lends itself to a kind of essentialism (which, as we will see, despite repeated Buddhist refutations of essentialism, nonetheless frequently and problematically crept into Buddhist thought) while 'perfecting' suggests a kind of process or progressionalism (which also had its Buddhist advocates and opponents).

At this point two important but distinct issues have emerged, and both need to be addressed. The first is the privileging of prajñā and the implications of that move. Secondly, the conflict of interpretations signalled by the essentialist vs. the progressionalist controversy must be sorted out and clarified. The first point basically concerns developments in India, while the second point, though already addressed in India, re-emerges as a critical problem in China, and as such is most germane to the subject-matter of the present work. Since the argument I wish to set out here is complex, and will require lengthy evidence, it will be presented in four parts. In order to give a concrete sense of the elaborate centrality of 'knowledge' and examine the issue of essentialism vs. progressionalism, we will (1) quickly cite the six pāramitās, (2) examine the inordinate importance given to one of its terms, viz. prajñā, (3) examine correlative developments in some detail, and (4) finally return to the essentialist vs. the progressionalist controversy. This will hopefully help explain—not historically but philosophically—the emergence of the notion of prajñā-pāramitā as a basic 'cognitive soteric methodology.' By offering non-Mahāyānic formulae which likewise envision a kind of prajñā-pāramitā, we will be suggesting that this development, though characteristic of Mahāyāna, nonetheless reflects a similar orientation in non-Mahāyānic Buddhism.

The fourth of the Four Noble Truths, viz. mārga, is often summarized as the Noble Eight-fold Path (*aṣṭāngika mārga*), which is:

[1] correct view (*samyag-dṛṣṭi*);
[2] correct conceptualization (*samyak-saṃkalpa*);
[3] correct speech (*samyak-vāk*);
[4] correct action (*samyak-karmānta*);
[5] correct livelihood (*samyag-ājīva*);
[6] correct effort (*samyag-vyāyāma*);
[7] correct recollection/mindfulness/remembrance (*samyak-smṛti*); and
[8] correct meditation (*samyak-samādhi*).

Mahāyāna Buddhism in effect reduced[4] the Eightfold Path, which was a cornerstone of early Buddhist thought, to Six pāramitās. The six[5] are:

[1] giving (*dāna*);
[2] behavioral discipline (*śīla*);
[3] patient tolerance (*kṣānti*);[6]
[4] energetic effort (*vīrya*);
[5] meditative contextualization (*dhyāna*); and
[6] cognitional insight (*prajñā*).

If we substitute samādhi for dhyāna, the fifth term of the pāramitā list, we immediately notice that the three members of our trialectic scheme, śīla-samādhi-prajñā, are explicitly highlighted (viz. the second, fifth and sixth pāramitās). There have been various approaches for matching up the eight parts of the Eightfold Path with the three trialectic factors, and similarly the three factors have been applied to the six pāramitās.[7] We needn't review such efforts here, but merely take note that the attempts have all been made because both the Eightfold Path and the Six pāramitās were unfailingly seen as extensions of the trialectic factors, which in turn were invariably considered foundational.

As pointed out earlier, the development of the pāramitā system in Buddhism finally raised prajñā above śīla and samādhi, and this privileging was marked by the production of the *prajñā-pāramitā* literature which both ushered in and consolidated the Mahāyānic Buddhist schools. Of all the perfections/perfectings, the sixth one, viz. the perfecting of prajñā, became explicitly the most crucial.

Prajñā's ascendancy to importance manifested on many fronts. For instance, in theTheravādin *Milindapañha* (*Questions of King Milinda*), which may roughly be dated at near the time of the earliest Prajñā-pāramitā Sūtras,[8] Buddha begins to be treated as omniscient (*sabbaññutā*)[9] despite the fact that in earlier texts, such as the *Tevigga Sutta* of the *Dīgha Nikāya*, Buddha explicitly rejects possessing any such capacity. Under the aegis of these later Buddhists, Buddha's cognitive mastery, as well as the range of that mastery, became greatly extended.[10] Since Buddha had become the example *par excellence* for Buddhists to imitate and emulate, this shift also reflected a change in Buddhist practice. The mārga was now seen as a pursuit of cognitive mastery.

Similarly, the Mādhyamika school focused on *avidyā* (nescience, ignorance), particularly as expressed through its cognitive corollary, *dṛṣṭi* (theoretical perspectives), as the cardinal problematic that needed to be overcome. Life's problems arise, according to this view, due to insufficient cognitive acuity, or, more precisely, due to over-reliance on inappropriate cognitive constructions. This school also drew inspiration and authority from the *Prajñā-pāramitā Sūtras*. Many prajñā-pāramitā texts were pseudepigraphically attributed to this school's founder, Nāgārjuna, even though a good number were written centuries after he died. Buddhist legend holds that Nāgārjuna recovered the *Prajñā-pāramitā Sūtras* from the Dragons (*nāgās*) who kept them concealed at the bottom of the ocean. This implied that the prajñā-pāramitā literature contained vital teachings which had been hidden since the time of Buddha, The privileging of prajñā reflected the hidden, latent core of the original Buddha's teaching though concealed until Nāgārjuna uncovered it.

Correlatively, concepts and terms involving the root √jñā (knowing, knowledge) became increasingly dominant within Buddhist discourse—e.g. *vijñāna, prajñapti, vijñapti, prajñā, jñāna,* etc.—and Buddhist praxis became increasingly concerned with correct cognition and theories of knowledge. All these developments are symptomatic of the privileging of prajñā. Yogācāra emerges amid the revisionistic readings of Buddhist doctrine entailed by this privileging. Like Mādhyamika, it too grounded itself in the Prajñā-pāramitā Sūtras. Also like Mādhyamika, Yogācāra focused on the overcoming of a cognitive problematic—which they labeled *vijñapti*—as the crucial and basic concern of Buddhist soterics.

Privileging prajñā in this manner signaled a change in the way the notion of 'Awakening' (*bodhi*) had come to be conceived. Increasingly it began to revolve around epistemic issues. Prajñā and jñāna no longer simply denoted means or conditions for attaining Awakening,[11] but began to serve as powerful, frequently cited synonyms for Awakening itself. Doctrinally the focus of Buddhist praxis narrowed (even as the practices themselves proliferated), and Awakening became primarily and explicitly seen as some sort of *cognitive* acuity, a Seeing of reality just as it is (*tathatā*). The language of the early Nikāyas, which was frequently more psychological than technically epistemological, was displaced by a rigorous philosophical and epistemological language. The descriptions of Awakening as 'overcoming the *āsavas*' or drying up the flood of deep-seated affective disorders, gave way to discourses aimed at reorienting or deconstructing the fundamental cognitive structures through which we attempt to perceive, evaluate and relate to ourselves and the world.[12] Consequently śīla and samādhi came to be seen more and more as prerequisites for prajñā rather than as factors in parity with it.

Privileging *Ñāṇa* in the Pāli Abhidhamma

Signs of this change, of an equivalence between Awakening and a sheer cognitive act, already appear in the *Kathā-vatthu*, the fifth book of the Theravādin Abhidhamma.[13] The *Kathā-vatthu* is a repository of controversial doctrinal opinions argued between some of the leading pre-Mahāyāna schools. Tradition (and most contemporary scholarship) holds it was composed following Aśoka's Council of Patna, ca. 246 B.C.E., as a record of actual debates which occurred at that council, though the possibility of later additions has to be considered. Its form typically consists of: (i) a controversial doctrinal position is stated, (ii) the arguments advanced by non-Theravādin schools are cited (the various schools are usually identified in the commentary, not the main text), (iii) the Theravādin rejoinder is offered, and (iv) sometimes the debate continues for extra rounds. While the Theravādin tradition would maintain that their own position invariably triumphs, an impartial reader may readily conclude that on more than a few occasions the opponents' argument displays greater merit. The text is an invaluable source for the study of Buddhist doctrinal development, particularly in the early schools.

The question arose as to whether *ñāṇa* (S. *jñāna*), 'knowledge,' is or is not equivalent to *vimutti* (S. *vimukti*), 'liberation.' The Andhakas[14] claimed the two were equivalent; in other words, 'knowing' itself constitutes liberation. The Theravādins, still resistant to this new claim, attempt to rebut it. They counter on the ground that equating *ñāṇa* with vimutti does not adequately distinguish between different types of knowledge (*ñāṇa*), and that only one specific type of *ñāṇa* may appropriately be deemed equivalent to liberation. The commentary clarifies the distinctions:[15]

> Four sorts of knowledge (or insight, *ñāṇa*) are grouped under knowledge of emancipation [*vimutti-ñāṇa*], to wit, [1] insight or intuition, [*ñāṇa-dassana*; 2] path-knowledge, [*magga-ñāṇa*; 3] fruit-knowledge, [*phala-ñāṇa*; 4] reflective knowledge [or 'reviewing-knowledge' *paccavekkahana-ñāṇa*]. In other words, emancipation considered as (1) freedom from perceiving things as permanent or persisting, or through perceiving the opposite [i.e., things as impermanent and non-persisting]; (2) the severance and renunciation effected by the Paths [i.e., 'methods,' *magga*]; (3) the peace of fruition [*phala paṭissaddhi vimutti*]; (4) contemplation of emancipation as such. [all square brackets mine]

The gist of the Theravāda argument is that only the third, viz. the peaceful liberation (*paṭissaddhi vimutti*), which is the fruit or effect (*phala*) of the path/method, can properly be called 'liberation'; the other three *ñāṇas* fall short of this. It should be noted that this fourfold scheme was elsewhere expanded by the Theravādins into more complex enumerations of *ñāṇa*, such as is found in Buddhaghosa's *Visuddhimagga*.[16]

Buddhists constructed elaborate road maps of the path to liberation, specifying every nook and cranny along the way. This literary genre became very popular, and one of the ways a school asserted its difference from other schools was to draw a different map. These tended to be intricate, scholastic enterprises, densely packed with terms and categories. Yogācāra was no exception. The best known Yogācāra contribution to this genre, the vast *Yogācārabhūmi śāstra,* is possibly the most comprehensive, but not the only Yogācāra offering. We are about to dip into a Theravāda version of this genre.

The four *ñāṇa*s just cited from the *Kathā vatthu* commentary become subsumed in the last three 'stages' of the seven stages that Ñāṇārāma extracts from the *Visuddhimagga.*[17] A summary of these stages will prove useful for later, when the comparable Yogācāric formulations will be discussed.

The fifth of these seven stages,[18] 'purification by **knowledge** and vision of what is path and not-path' (*maggāmagga* ***ñāṇa*** *dassana visuddhi*), establishes one in correct meditation through 'knowledge by comprehension' (*sammasana ñāṇa*) and by overcoming the 'ten secondary mental disturbances (that pervert) insight' (*dasa vipassan 'upakkilesā*). Interestingly, aside from the tenth 'disturbance,' the list of 'secondary disturbances' involves terms which one usually finds in a list of positive qualities. They are: (1) illumination (*obhāsa*), (2) knowledge (*ñāṇa*) [!], (3) enjoyment (*pīti*), (4) calmness (*passaddhi*) [which is cognate to *paṭissaddhi*, 'peacefulness,' i.e., the type of *ñāṇa* which Theravādins accept as equivalent to vimutti!], (5) happiness (*sukha*), (6) zealous worship and proselytizing (*adhimokkha*), (7) energy (*paggaha*), (8) assurance and confidence (*upaṭṭhāna*), (9) equanimity (*upekkhā*), and (10) attachment (*nikanti*). The tenth

> is latent in [the other nine] imperfections. The unskilful meditator conceives a subtle attachment to his insight which is adorned with such marvelous things as illumination; thus he is carried away by craving, conceit and view. The skilful meditator uses his discerning wisdom [*ñāṇa*?], and frees himself from the influence. (p. 42)

The sixth stage, 'purification by **knowledge** and vision of the way' (*paṭipada* ***ñāṇa*** *dassana visuddhi*), clarifies the three 'mundane' (*lokiya*) 'total understandings' (*pariññā*), which are:

1) Fully understanding the 'known' (*ñāta pariññā*), which includes comprehensive knowledge of the individual characteristics, functions, causes, etc. of all dhammas; technically, this involves the first four stages.
2) Fully understanding through investigating (*tīraṇa pariññā*), which includes the fifth and the beginning of the sixth stages. Here 'knowledge' proceeds from individual dhammas (the subject matter of the previous 'total understanding') to their general characteristics, viz. that they are all impermanent, dukkha, and without-self.
3) Fully understanding through abandoning (*pahāna pariññā*), which proceeds through the remainder of the sixth stage. It

> involves the systematic abandoning of defilements by the method called substitution of opposites (*tadangappahāna*), i.e. by the development of particular insights which eclipse defiled erroneous notions from the mind. (p. 44)

The method of erasure through opposites is retained in Yogācāra and called *pratipakṣa*, 'antidote' or 'counteracting.'

The sixth stage is further subdivided into eight (or nine) stages of knowledge (*ñāṇa*):

i. Knowledge through contemplation of arising and ceasing (*udayabbay-ānupassanā ñāṇa*), which is the culmination of (2) above, and corresponds to the first *ñāṇa* listed in the *Kathā vatthu* commentary. Everything is seen as impermanent, dukkha, and not-self; as rūpa and nāma (i.e., the khandhas); and as arising, abiding and ceasing. The false prajñaptic unities are deconstructed into their conditioned components: this insight is called *ghana-saññā*, 'perceiving the basics' (lit. 'perception of the compact'). The four types of 'false unities' are: (1) compactness as a continuity (*santati ghana*), (2) compactness as a mass (*samūha ghana*), (3) compactness as a function (*kicca ghana*), and (4) compactness as a cognitive-object (*ārammaṇa ghana*). In other words, by viewing the discontinuous as continuous, by taking an aggregation to be a 'whole,' by believing that functioning involves durational continuity and relational continuity of agent and product, and by amalgamating discrete perceptual spheres into trans-sensorial objects, we impose a conceptual 'compactness' onto experience. Under careful meditative scrutiny, these prajñaptic 'compacts' deconstruct. In this stage, for instance, one discerns that

> The characteristic of impermanence is concealed by continuity. The characteristic of suffering is covered up by the change of postures [since the physical discomfort of holding a specific seated posture for long stretches of time is the most immediate form of 'suffering' of which the meditator is aware]. The characteristic of not-self is overcast with compactness. (p. 47)

ii. **Knowledge** through contemplation of dissolution (*bhaṅgānupassanā* ***ñāṇa***), which is the beginning of (3) above. At this stage not only does the object of meditation 'dissolve' (due to impermanence), but the meditator also reflects on the reflective-thought itself, such that it, too, dissolves. Since both the cognitive object as well as the reflective apprehension of that cognition 'vanish,' as it were, leaving no trace, either latent or apparent, this arrests the production of saṅkhāras.

iii. **Knowledge** through 'appearance as terrifying' (*bhay'upaṭṭhāna* ***ñāṇa***), in which the ubiquitous dissolutions become terrifying. Here one's understanding of impermanence moves beyond intellection and observation, and enters the existential, affective sphere. With everything dissolving, all possibilities of continuity, stability, grounding, or denial of death become radically inaccessible, and one has nowhere to turn and nothing to hold on to. The terror of this abyss eventually subsides by concertedly observing it.

iv. **Knowledge** through contemplation of danger (*ādīnavānupassanā* ***ñāṇa***), in which the meditator realizes that these terrifying dissolutions arise from saṅkhāra, and that it is saṅkhāra that perpetuates the wheel of saṃsāra.

Realizing the 'dangers' of embodied-conditioning and conditioning itself (P. saṅkhāra and saṅkhāta; S. saṃskāra and saṃskṛta), detachment arises, which leads to

v. **Knowledge** through contemplation of disenchantment (*nibbidānupassanā **ñāṇa***). This is a critical stage in which the meditator finds everything, including his practice, distasteful and annoying. A deeply nihilistic sense overcomes him; everything seems meaningless. He becomes restless and agitated.

> [The teacher] should recognize that the real source of the meditator's dissatisfaction is his insight into the dangers of [saṅkhāras], and that this discontent has only been *displaced and transferred* to other things. (p. 53f; brackets and emphasis mine)

The saṅkhāric latent, subconscious proclivities, resisting the disclosing and dissolving gaze of the meditator, mobilize defense mechanisms which deflect that gaze.[19] Since the saṅkhāras thereby stubbornly persist, the restlessness continues into

vi. **Knowledge** through desire for deliverance (*muñcitukamyatā **ñāṇa***). The intense unease accompanying the nihilistic restlessness, once it is seen as deriving from embodied-conditioning (*saṅkhāra*), engenders a desire for resolution of all tensions.

vii. **Knowledge** through contemplation of reflective-thinking (*paṭi-sankhānupassanā **ñāṇa***) involves bringing the affective back into a cognitive, intellectual realm. One's theoretical knowledge is now fully 'lived-experience.' Thinking is no longer abstract, but fully experiential. What was abstractly known before (e.g., impermanence, etc.) now becomes directly and fully known and understood. Just as an older student returning to the university after years in the 'real' world may appreciate and understand things better due to his experience, so does the meditator here achieve a deeper understanding of Buddhist theoretics due to his lived-experience of the problematics arising from the influence of the saṅkhāras.

viii. **Knowledge** through 'neutralizing' embodied-conditioning (*sankhār'-upekkhā **ñāṇā***) arises with the understanding of *suññatā* (emptiness), which in the Theravādin context means

> that everything is void of self or what belongs to self....*Suññamidam attena vā attaniyena vā.* [*Majjhima Nikāya*, II, 263].
>
> ...Reflection on [saṅkhāras] now goes on effortlessly.... The object presents itself to the reflecting mind without any special effort. It is as if the mind is propping up its objects.... Even if an attractive or repulsive object is presented to him...it will simply roll away from his mind without stimulating greed or hatred. There is equanimity [*upekkhā*] at this stage because the meditator *understands objects in terms of the four elements.* Owing to the absence of defilements, the meditator's mind seems pure like an arahat, though at this point the suppression

> of defilements is only temporary, effected by the 'substitution of opposites' through insight. (pp. 56-57) (brackets and emphasis mine)

Note that in this stage two distinctly Mahāyānic themes are given prominence. The idea of emptiness, though here restricted to 'self and what belongs to self,' when applied both to one's self and another's self, and indeed all things, became the hallmark of Mādhyamikan discourse. The notion of an equanimous mind which, like a mirror, reflects all objects as they are without appropriational overtones or undertones, and which, especially in Tantric texts becomes associated with rūpa, became an important component of Yogācāric thought. Again, the *pratipakṣa* (antidotes) are mentioned.[20]

Understanding objects to be merely the four elements can only be efficacious for achieving *upekkhā* if rūpa is karmically neutral. Like a materialist who rids his world of psychological ghosts by stripping them of ontological status, the meditator here becomes detached from the reward and punishment, pain and pleasure of experience by noting that these experiences are no more than the transpiring of material causal networks. Without his embodied-conditioning coloring his perceptions, he sees the causal chains clearly. Since embodied-conditioning is only temporarily arrested at this stage, the able meditator moves on to the next stage.

ix. Conformity **knowledge** (*anuloma* ***ñāṇa***) stabilizes the previous eight 'knowledges,' and establishes the beginning of the Thirty-Seven Factors of Awakening.[21] At this stage the practitioner understands conditioned things (*saṅkhāta dhammā*) well, and begins to *infer* as to the Unconditioned (*asaṅkhāta* = *Nibbāna*). This leads him to the threshold of the final, supra-mundane stage. This threshold is called 'Insight Leading to the Emergence [of the Supra-mundane Paths]' (*vuṭṭhānagāmini vipassanā*), which is threefold:
   (i) fully matured **knowledge** about the neutralization of embodied-conditioning,
   (ii) conformity **knowledge**, and
   (iii) Change-of-Lineage **Knowledge** (*gotra-bhū* ***ñāṇa***).

   The meditator 'transforms' from the lineage of ordinary worldlings (*puthujjana*) to the lineage of a 'noble one' (*āriya*).[22] This change constitutes a middle position between the mundane (*lokiya*) knowledges which precede it and the supra-mundane (*lokuttara*) Paths/methods which will presently arise.

In the seventh and final stage, the object of meditation no longer is conditioning (saṅkhāra and saṅkhāta), but Nibbāna. No longer merely 'inferring' it, the meditator cognizes it directly. This stage, called 'Purification by **Knowledge** and Vision' (***Ñāṇa*** *dassana visuddhi*), has four levels, each of which is subdivided into two parts, a path/method (*magga*), and the Fruition (*phala*) of that magga.

> The Path lasts for only a single moment of consciousness, whereas the Fruition occurs for either two or three mind-moments. (p. 65)
>
> ...Each Path arises only once... [and] has its own particular range of defilements to burst. When a path arises, immediately, *by the power of knowledge,* it bursts the defilements within its range. (p. 67) (brackets and emphasis mine)

The four Supra-mundane Paths are:

> The Path of Stream-entry, breaks the three fetters of personality-view [*ātta-diṭṭhi*], doubt, and clinging to rules and rituals. One who passes through this Path and its subsequent Fruition becomes a Stream-enterer (*sotāpanna*).... He has entered the stream of Dhamma, is forever liberated from the possibility of rebirth in the four lower [*Kāma-dhātu*] planes, and will at most be reborn seven more times in the human or heavenly worlds before reaching the final goal.
>
> The second Path, the Path of Once-return, does not eradicate any defilements completely but greatly reduces the roots—greed [*rāga, lobha*], hatred [*dosa*], and delusion [*moha*]. One who dies as a Once-returner (*sakadāgāmi*) will be re-born in the human world only one more time before attaining deliverance.
>
> The third Path, the Path of Non-return, bursts the two fetters of sensual desire [*rāga*] and aversion [*paṭigha, dosa*]. One who passes away as a Non-returner (*anāgāmi*) will not be reborn at all in the sense-sphere realm [Kāma-dhātu]; he is reborn only in the higher Brahma worlds where he attains final deliverance.
>
> The fourth Path, the Path of Arahatship, eradicates the five subtle fetters—desire for fine-material existence (in the Brahma worlds), desire for non-material existence (in the formless worlds), conceit [*māna*], restlessness [*uddhacca*], and ignorance [*moha*]. The Arahat or liberated one is free from all bondage to the round of saṃsāra. He lives in the full attainment of deliverance.
>
> (p. 67, square brackets mine)

Recalling the four *ñāṇas* cited in the commentary to the *Kathā vatthu,* clearly the second and third types, viz. knowledge by the severance and renunciation effected by the Paths as well as the crucial 'Peace from Fruition' (*phalam paṭipassaddhi vimutti*) occur in these stages. The fourth *ñāṇa* corresponds to the 'Reviewing Knowledge' (*paccavekkahana ñāṇa*) which follows each Fruition.

> This Reviewing Knowledge takes [saṅkhāras] as its object, not Nibbāna as do the Fruits and Paths. (p. 65)
>
> After Fruition there occurs reviewing knowledge. With this knowledge the meditator reviews five things: the Path, its Fruition, the defilements abandoned, the defilements remaining, and Nibbāna. Such is the case for Stream-enterers, Once-returners, and Non-returners. But the Arahant has no review of remaining defilements as he has cut them off entirely. (p. 68, square brackets mine)

This lengthy overview of a Theravādin meditative system has highlighted the following points for us:

1) We have seen how the four knowledges mentioned in the *Kathā vatthu* were expanded and/or incorporated into a much larger system of knowledge-

acquisition. They occur in the sixth stage, subsection (i), and in the various divisions of the seventh stage. Had our overview been even more inclusive, many more types of knowledge would have been cited.

2) The unmistakable concern of virtually the entire system is the ferreting out of embodied-conditioning (saṅkhāra, saṃskāra). This is due to the importance of conditioning for the Buddhist theory of karma. Meditation in this context simply means making one's unconscious, latent conditioning, i.e., saṃskāra, accessible to conscious scrutiny and intervention through procedures which sharpen, focus and alter the mind (*citta*). It is thus a kind of self-psychoanalysis that employs intellect and reason (knowledge) to cure what seemingly functions unreasonably.

3) As such, the Thervādin system displays the symptoms and signs of having privileged *ñāṇa*. The stages, paths and fruits are characterized by what stands as their ultimate cognitive objects: saṅkhāras or nibbāṇa. Awakening involves the correct cognition of the correct cognitive object.

4) We have noted several features of this formulation which are more than a little suggestive of issues that also arose in Mahāyānic thought.

5) This expansive systematization of knowledge parallels the 'magga leading to fruit' relation mentioned in the seventh stage. Since the magga consists of the details elaborated in this 'map,' and the magga leads to its fruit, this genre viewed itself as synonymous with ultimately attaining the goal of Buddhist practice. Discussing the 'concentration with immediate result' (*ānantarika samādhi*) that invariably follows from each Fruition, Ñāṇārāma writes, "This indescribably keen concentration enables wisdom to cut through the range of defilements and purify the mental-continuum." (p. 68) Knowledge and wisdom become the primary agents of Awakening. Śīla and samādhi are relegated to secondary importance; they establish the conditions for prajñā (or jñāna). One the one hand, knowledge is product, while śīla and samādhi are the means. On the other hand, knowledge eventually becomes both the ends and the means. Buddhist soterics, even in this late Theravādin formulation, revolves entirely around producing 'liberating knowledge.'

Tathatā: Essentialism or Progressionalism?

But what exactly does such knowledge come to know? What is its object (*prameya*)? In the Theravādin system just described, the actual goal or object of the practice is described, if at all, in negative terms. There are specific types of knowledges concerning specific situations on the path, and one acquires and outgrows them as one progresses. But an expository characterization of the final telos, the final object of knowledge is stunningly absent. One reaches the arhat stage, which is marked by the *absence* of saṅkhāras, and almost immediately one is past that; one becomes reflective, retrogressively reflective, one looks back. The text states that the proper object during the path and its fruition is nibbāṇa, not saṅkhāras. But in what sense? The objects of one's cognitions during retrospective moments are saṅkhāras. How can nirvāṇa be a cognitive object or meditative object, which is to say, a contributary *condition* to cognitive acts, and yet be considered 'unconditioned' (*asaṅkhāta*)? Can a condition be unconditioned? What sort of knowledge is that all-important knowledge, the one for which the entire path and the subsidiary knowledges were directed, the one which contextualizes and gives meaning to the path itself, the one which marks the terminus, the one of which it is said upon achieving: "he has done what was to be done"?

The Theravādins referred to this 'knowledge' not only in negative terms (absence of embodied-conditioning, nibbāṇa, deathless, the absence of kamma, kilesa, āsava, etc.). They also used the term *yathā-bhūtam*, 'just as it is,' or better, 'just as it has become.' We cited a Pāli passage which suggested the term *tathatā*, often translated 'suchness' or 'thusness.' Claiming that nirvāṇa is a cognitive object is problematic. More commonly Buddhists, especially in Mahāyāna, use the term *tathatā* to denote the object of Awakened cognition. *Tathatā* assumes a pivotal, prominent place in the literature, and signifies the objective-pole in an act of knowing which is free from any and all obstructions and interference. The original imperative to see things in the exact way they actually become (*yathābhūta*), rather than how our desires incline us to perceive them, was reinforced with the emergence of the term *tathatā* as the catch-all word signifying everything positive that Buddhism offered as ultimate.

Tathatā, an abstract noun form of the indexical *tat* (that, this), indicated the immediate, direct knowing of anything or everything. Though some texts claim tathatā is non-conceptual (*acintya*) and non-linguistic (*anabhilāpya*), it nevertheless is invariably treated as inseparable from knowledge (*jñāna*).

The hypostatization of the indexical *tat* ("this", "that")—first as Tathāgata ("Thus-come" and "Thus-gone"; the cardinal epithet for the Buddha), then as *tathatā* (just-so-ity), and finally as *tathāgata-garbha* (Tathāgata-embryo)—occurred as a consequence of the Buddhist attempt to force language to point directly at non-linguistic reality. Though they tried to 'index' words responsibly, to silence the prajñaptic problematic by taking recourse to indexicality (*tathatā*), the index itself was mistaken for what was to be indexed, and once more Buddhist gazes fixated on the finger and forgot about the moon. Yet, even the final hypostatization, the Tathāgata-garbha, is considered the *active functioning* of one's potential for Buddhahood. It indicates and marks the trajectory toward the realization of tathatā.

Tathatā means seeing everything, *including* so-called appearance, just as it is. As countless Buddhist texts repeat, tathatā does not so much involve the eradication of delusion as such, as much as it involves seeing delusion *as delusion*.[23] Rather than denoting an immaculate, transcendental realm absolutely devoid of cognitive misapprehension, the term tathatā invokes a comprehensive (in both senses: encompassing and comprehending) experience of the full range of lived-experiences. When a delusion is recognized as a delusion, in an important sense it no longer functions as a delusion. Instead its delusive power is neutralized and it is understood simply as a phenomenon. A phenomenon, however, is understood by the Buddhist as a complex web of conditionality. Thus, properly understood, tathatā is synonymous with pratītya-samutpāda, i.e., conditionality.

Though tathatā is that which is known (*jñeya*) through the instrument of prajñā, properly speaking it is not an 'object' of knowledge (*prameya*). In Husserlian terms, the noema is never independent of noesis but always noetically constituted. Noetic functions, when looked at such that they in turn become noemata, inevitably become displaced by that reflective act.[24] The looker who sees himself, always sees a 'looker' other than the original looker, just as one who looks at his own reflection in a mirror sees only that reflection, but not the one looking at it. Noesis, *while it is actually functioning*, is always (in Husserl's sense of the term) transcendental. The sheer, immediate seeing of things as they are (*tathatā, yathābhūtam*), however, must continue to include the noetic constituents without either (i) reducing them to noemata, or (ii) allowing them to remain transcendental and thus not immediately given. Hence, while inclusive of the noetic-noemic structure, tathatā cannot be reduced to it, much less to one or the other component of that structure. As sheer knowing (*jñāna*), tathatā is epistemic, though not (proscriptively) epistemological. Incapable of being either objectified or subjectified, it defies ontologization.

Prajñāpāramitā: Essentialism or Episteme?

We are now ready to return to the question: Should *prajñā-pāramitā* be understood as connoting an essentialistic understanding of tathatā or should it be understood as connoting an epistemic process? Both positions have had their adherents within the Buddhist tradition. Since this controversy stands at the heart of the East Asian appropriation of Buddhist thought, and has determined many important parameters for doctrinal developments in China, Korea and Japan, closer examination of its features is in order. Yogācāra, in particular as disseminated in China, polarized around this opposition, and in part Hsüan-tsang's project can be seen as a systematic refutation of the essentialist position as advocated by Paramārtha and others.

If Awakening, at least provisionally, is considered to be a goal, and sheer knowing is that goal's necessary (and perhaps sufficient) condition, the question arises: Is the goal something essentially existent, such that the epistemic method (*jñāna-mārga*) uncovers it; or, does the method subsume the goal, such that the goal's provisionality is exposed, revealing not an essential truth, but rather an insight into the epistemic process itself? In the first case, knowledge (*jñāna*) will be considered the means or agent for attaining some-*thing* which in itself is impervious to or indifferent to the vicissitudes of epistemological approaches, though made accessible through such approaches. In the second case, nothing relevant exists outside or apart from the dynamic, progressive sphere of knowledge; Awakening here would mean that knowing (*prajñā, jñāna*) becomes transparent to itself. Again, the former implies an absolute, objective

Truth, while the latter implies a progressional unfolding that never posits anything apart from the process itself.

In Buddhist terminology, the former (the Essentialist) posits Buddhahood as a distinct realm, distinct precisely because it is accessible only to Buddhas, and hence somehow essentially other than the realms accessible to the remainder of sentient beings. At best, non-Buddhas might contain a germ or seed (*tathāgatagarbha*) that offers the *potential* of entry into the distinct Buddha-realm, but they are considered non-Buddhas precisely because they have not yet actualized this potential. Here, as in other philosophical contexts, essentialism inscribes itself through the discourse of 'potential/actual.' Buddhahood and its corollaries—tathatā, sambodhi, etc.—would signify an ultimate, transcendental Reality.

The latter (the Progressionalist) would argue that the process of Awakening can never be separable from the Bodhisattva path[25], and that (i) the pre-Awakening striving, (ii) the Awakening realization and (iii) the post-Awakening aid offered to other sentient beings can never be seen apart from the saṃsāric process in which that path occurs; moreover, saṃsāra is able to proceed only in virtue of its emptiness (*śūnyatā*).[26] The full career of the Bodhisattva is nothing other than this process. During (i), the Bodhisattva's progress is largely determined by saṃsāric and saṃskāric conditions, though efforts are made to overcome these determinants through theory and practice. During (ii), theory and practice converge, such that the inseparability of saṃsāra and nirvāṇa, or process (*pratītya-samutpāda*) and emptiness, infuse the whole of the Bodhisattva's life-world. The remedied process continues and disseminates in (iii).

Practical considerations also arise from this problem. If Awakening unfolds through a process, then to some extent this unfolding is temporal. These temporal aspects necessitate that practice towards Awakening be gradual. If, on the other hand, a ready-made transcendental realm already exists, then what is essential about Awakening remains entirely separate from temporal considerations, and entry into it may be 'sudden,' i.e., nondependent on any temporal considerations.

Pāli Texts on Sudden and Gradual

Even in the early texts, one can find signs of this ambivalence between sudden vs. gradual Awakening. In the *Potthapāda sutta* of the *Dīgha Nikāya*, Buddha explains the sequence of meditations ascending through the tri-dhātu. When he reaches the description of the ārūpya-dhātu, his discussion of each of the first three levels of this dhātu—viz. *ākāsānañcāyatana*, *viññāṇañcāyatana*, and *ākiñcaññāyatana*—concludes with the refrain:[27]

> Thus also is it that through training one idea [*saññā*], one sort of consciousness [*viññāṇa*], arises; and through training another passes away....

The final ārūpya transition, the one from *ākiñcaññāyatana* to *nevasaññā-nāsaññāyatana*, is described, in part, as follows:[28]

> So from the time, Potthapāda, that the Bhikkhu is thus conscious in a way brought about by himself (from the time of the first [jhāna]), he goes on from one stage to the next, and from that to the next until he reaches the summit of consciousness.[29] And when he is on the summit it may occur to him: "To be [associatively] thinking at all is the inferior state. 'Twere better not to be [associatively] thinking. Were I to go on conditionally-compounding[30] (*Abhisaṅkhareyyaṃ*) [associative] thought, these ideas, these states of consciousness, I have reached to, would pass away, but others, coarser ones, might arise. So I will not conditionally-compound [associative] thought any more." And he does not.[31] And to him neither [associatively] thinking any more, nor conditionally-compounding, the ideas, the states of consciousness, he had, pass away; and no others, coarser than they, arise. So he enters *abhisaññā nirodha* (the cessation of associative thought). Thus it is, Potthapāda, that the attainment of the cessation of conscious ideas [*saññā nirodha samāpatti*] takes place *step by step* [emphasis mine].

The refrain cited above that came at the conclusion of each of the previous arūpa-jhānas, "that through training one idea [*saññā*], one sort of consciousness [*viññāṇa*], arises; and through training another passes away" does *not* occur here at this point. The intimate relation between the impermanence of arising and ceasing and the gradual, "step by step" character of its undoing is then brought into highlight:

> Now what do you think, Potthapāda? Have you ever heard, before this, of this *gradual attainment* of the cessation of conscious ideas? [emphasis mine]

Potthapāda replies "no", and after repeating the passage just cited he asks the following question:

> And does the Exalted One teach that there is one summit of consciousness, or that there are several?

Considering the fact that according to what Buddha has just said the 'summit of consciousness' is not the pinnacle of practice, but merely the foundation from which one jumps off, as it were, into the abyssal dissolution of cognitive chains, this may appear to be a misguided question. Nonetheless, it provides Buddha with an opportunity to explicate further how, through a gradual process that is identical to impermanence, one arrives at the overcoming of impermanence. The text continues:

> 'In my opinion, Potthapāda, there is one, and there are also several.'
>
> 'But how can the Exalted teach that there both is one, and that there are several?'
>
> 'As he attains to the cessation (of one idea, one sort of consciousness) after another, so does he reach, one after another, to *different summits up to the last*

> [emphasis mine]. So it is, Potthapāda, that I put forward both one summit and several.'

These summits cannot be a final telos, but rather signify a vantage point that encompasses a certain lived-word parameter. Existential horizonal limits (i.e., what are viewed from the "summits") coalesce and fixate, then are deconstructed, and then reinstitute new, more inclusive limits. Each limit marks an horizon, a lived-world closure. This deconstructive 'expansion' continues up to the final margins of the ārūpya-dhātu. Those margins, constituted by the undecidability of the fourth level—the sphere of neither with nor without associative thinking (*nevasaññā nāsaññāyatana*)—as pointed out previously, are fluid, permeable, and thus avoid closure.

Remembering that even the last 'summit' is only a springboard to a deconditioned sphere which the text does not reinscribe within a new 'summit,' the apparent point of gradual training would be the progressional deconstruction of ever-broader closures, until one reaches a closure-less (de-)condition. Being closure-less, one is in, but not *of* the conditioning determinants of the tri-dhātu. In Yogācāric terminology, to be closure-less means to be without appropriational involvement, to be devoid of the *grāhya-grāhaka* (appropriated-appropriator) structure. One neither possesses nor is possessed by conditions, though one is thoroughly enmeshed in them.

The text then makes the temporal aspect of this gradual training even more explicit:

> [Potthapāda asks] 'Now is it, Sir, the idea, the state of consciousness, that arises first, and then knowledge [*ñāṇa*; S. *jñāna*]; or does knowledge arise first, and then the idea, the state of consciousness; or do both arise simultaneously, neither of them before or after the other?'
>
> 'It is the idea, Potthapāda, the state of consciousness, that arises first, and after that knowledge. And the springing up of knowledge is dependent on the springing up of the idea, the state of consciousness. And this may be understood from the fact that a man recognizes: "It is from this cause or that that knowledge has arisen to me."'

The Saḷāyatana section of the *Saṃyutta Nikāya*, at IV, 216, reiterates the same message. A monk asks Buddha to explain the three vedanās, viz. pleasure, pain and neutral, in light of the saying "Whatsoever is experienced, that is dukkha." Buddha responds:[32]

> This saying of mine was uttered concerning the impermanence of conditioned things (*saṅkhāra*).... [It] was uttered concerning the perishable, transient nature of conditioned things, of their nature to fade away and cease.
>
> Now, brother, I have seen that *the ceasing of saṅkhāras* is gradual. When one has attained the first jhāna, speech has ceased. When one has attained the second jhāna, vitakka and vicāra have ceased. When one has attained the third jhāna, zest (*pīti*) has ceased. When one has attained the fourth jhāna, inbreathing and outbreathing have ceased.

Note this text differs somewhat from the description offered previously of the rūpa-dhātu. Whether the fourth jhāna involves an actual cessation of breathing or just a lack of attention to it has been a matter of controversy. The text continues with *five* stages for the ārūpya-dhātu, making nine (instead of eight) jhānas all together:

> When one has attained the realm of infinite space, 'associative thinking' on [discrete] objects has ceased. When one has attained the realm of infinite consciousness, the 'associative thinking' on the realm of infinite space has ceased. When one has attained the realm of nothingness, the 'associative thinking' on the realm of infinite consciousness has ceased. When one has attained the realm of "neither associative thinking nor non associative thinking", the 'associative thinking' of the realm of nothingness has ceased. Both associative thinking and vedanā have ceased when one has attained *saññā vedayita nirodha* (cessation of associative thinking and pleasure-pain-neutral feelings). For the brother who has destroyed the āsavas, craving (*lobha*) is extinguished, aversion (*dosa*) is extinguished, radical-misconception (*moha*) is extinguished.

In this manner the text very quickly summarizes the jhānas. Each succeeding stage involves the cessation of the previous stage's characteristics, which, if we follow context, are to be considered saṅkhāras.[33] The *āsavas* are the saṅkhāric root. Sometimes treated as synonymous with 'nescience' (*avijjā*, S. *avidyā*), the first link of the *pratītya-samutpāda* chain, āsava is the root condition of saṃskāras. The Theravāda tradition has understood the term to signify the constant 'outpouring' of conditions, but an outpouring that distorts itself through the prism of craving, aversion and radical-misconceptions. Āsava was also taken to mean a cankerous sore, something festering, or the putrification process of fermentation (and thus also implies intoxication). Traditionally it carries strong negative connotations of something diseased, festering, oozing, enveloping the mind like an intoxicant. It is also noteworthy that this passage explicitly states that saññā (Skt. *saṃjñā*, associational-thinking) is operating at the Nothing level. This would mean that even that level could not be a cognitive void.

The text then repeats the nine-part formula, this time beginning "Again, brother, I have seen that the *mastery of saṅkhāras* is gradual. When one has attained the first jhāna, speech is mastered...." and so on, all the way through mastery of moha. In the short summation which closes that passage, six 'calmings' are listed. The four rūpa-dhātu cessations are each counted separately, but the entire ārūpya-dhātu is reduced to one calming, the *saññā vedayita nirodha*. The sixth reads: "For the brother who has destroyed the āsavas, lobha, dosa and moha are calmed down."

The passages just examined from the *Dīgha* and *Samyutta Nikāyas* both advocate a gradual path aimed at removing saṃskāric conditioning. The gradual path was explicitly defined as temporal in the first passage; more importantly, Awakened knowledge (*ñāṇa, jñāna*) can only arise dependent on temporal experience. But if we turn to another text, the *Kathā-vatthu*, part III sec. 4,[34] we find the Theravādins denying that *vimutti* (liberation) is a gradual process, and instead arguing that it is sudden. Their argument, however, is not that Awakening involves something atemporal, but rather they wish to emphasize the radical specificity of this particular temporal moment. To claim vimutti is gradual, they argue, would imply gradations. Gradations would imply that at some point, at some moment one might be partly liberated and partly non-liberated, which, they say, is absurd. Liberation, like pregnancy, is an all or nothing proposition. Much hinges on how one understands what happens mentally in the very moment of Awakening. What happens to the mental stream, the stream of citta, that marks a transition from a serious of nonAwakened citta to Awakeneing? It would not be an ordinary mental moment, but, by Theravādin theory, a mind composed and focused as in meditation. They ask: Is *eka-citta* (the singular apperceptive vector) already free when it arises, and then in the process of becoming free when it ceases? Both claims, they argue, are patently absurd, violating the temporal sense of the momentary arising and ceasing of citta, and the relation between arising and ceasing and vimutti.

The problem of the process of temporal succession, of what, if anything, continues from one moment to the next, lies at the bottom of this and many similar Buddhist controversies. The 'absurdities' alluded to in their argument are perhaps more clearly recognized in a different, but related argument.[35] Do new skandhas arise *before* the skandhas that are seeking rebirth cease? In other words, what precisely is the relation between a previous and subsequent conditioned factor? How contiguous must conditioned factors be in order to validly claim that they involve continuity? The greater the contiguity and the more proximate, the greater the continuity; the less contiguous and more approximate, the greater the discontinuity. A cause and its effect can neither be identical nor utterly different. Can they, must they share the same moment? If the temporal gap between them is too large, by what means can they be said to influence each other? If there is no gap at all, if they share the same moment, then there is no succession, and again continuity is thrown into question. But what reasonable position exists between these extremes?

To the question about skandhas, the Theravādins state that if the new skandhas arise before the rebirth seeking skandhas have ceased, then there would be ten skandhas all together, not merely five, which is absurd. Even if one were to claim only a single (or more) specific extra skandha, there would still be six (or seven, etc.) instead of five.

The opponent (the commentary mentions Andhakas) retorts: When the five skandhas seeking rebirth cease, does the Path [automatically] arise?

The Theravādin replies affirmatively.

The opponent then raises the problem of cessation as continuity/discontinuity with: "What! do the dead, does one who has ended his days develop the Path?"[36]

The Theravādin is caught in a dilemma. If the skandhas overlap, then there will be some moment when there will be more than five. If they don't overlap, their discontinuity should, by definition, signal their utter dissolution and extinction, and the Path, defined as what arises when the appropriative skandhas cease (again, the problem of the negative definition) should automatically, spontaneously occur. That would mean that every death is vimutti. Not carrying the presuppositions of a Western eschatological framework, to them such a claim was patently and utterly absurd (it would make all praxis meaningless, since death would accomplish everything automatically).

Another implication: mere cessation cannot produce the Path. If it could, *any* disruption of continuity, any rupture in the temporal, conditioned flow would automatically set one on the Path. While such 'cessations' were helpful, useful, and frequently sought as part of practice (e.g., *nirodha-samāpatti*), they were not substitutes for Awakening. The Theravādin argues[37] that attaining cessation (*nirodha-samāpatti*) is not asaṅkhāra (S. asaṃskṛta, Unconditioned), since it follows from conditions.[38]

The *Kathā vatthu* revisits these issues, in a variety of guises, again and again. What is the duration of consciousness?[39] The Andhakas claim that the duration of consciousness is one day, and in certain deva lokas (heavens) it lasts for an entire life (remember that lives in the deva lokas have beginnings and ends, just as elsewhere). The Theravādin insists that it is momentary, and has only two of the three characteristics of conditioned things, viz. the arising and ceasing characteristics (*uppāda* and *vaya, bhanga*), not the characteristic of abiding. The duration of life and the duration of consciousness are never identical, and we certainly don't die with the same consciousness as the one with which we are born. Life is invariably longer.

The same problems arise in such different questions as: Is samādhi confined to a momentary consciousness unit, or is it coextensive with a durational stream of consciousness (*citta-santati*)?[40] Do sensations follow each other in an unbroken fused sequence, or are they radically discrete?[41] The problem of continuity and discontinuity is unavoidable for Buddhists precisely because Buddhism is concerned fundamentally with the question of conditioning. And conditioning is only coherent if some relational continuities obtain between distinct items. Further, the question of conditioning is raised by Buddhists in order to discover how to disrupt that continuity, how to rupture saṃsāra. Thus not only does the tension between continuity and discontinuity arise out of the incoherency of that opposition—as Nāgārjuna shows—but the centrality which that opposition receives in Buddhism intensifies it.

Arguably the entire Buddhist project is nothing but the systematic putting into question of the issue of continuity/discontinuity, which rests on its critique of identity/difference or logocentrism/differentialism. Existentially approached, the problem of identity is always a problem in or of time: of mortality, of temporal finality, of the perdurance of moral and social responsibility, of the appropriative war between Time and person (does radical time 'take' man, or does man 'take' the time? Does he existentially appropriate Time by *identifying* with it, as for instance is suggested in the eleventh chapter of the *Bhagavad Gītā*), of the continuity or dissolution of *my* identity, etc. To where and to what does my identity extend, and where and by what is it delimited? The 'my' conatively, loudly (yet hidden), exuberantly insists on its continuity; it infects each and every gaze with a professed continuity, an identity that self-evidences itself (*Selbstverständlichkeit*). And by the sheer power of its conative desire that there be continuity, the 'my' privileges the continuous over the discontinuous in every sphere, in every cognition, in every discourse, in every desire. Conation, thus, is always attempted self-perpetuation, as Spinoza and Nietzsche noted. Buddhism is designed to disrupt that economy.

Essentialism vs. Progressionalism

As Mahāyāna Buddhism developed, the essentialist vs. progressionalist controversy peaked. One text which preserves the tensions is the *Lotus Sūtra*. The first half deals with *upāya*, the provisional, deceptive character of Buddhist doctrine and practice. The 'truths' of Buddhism are mere provisional ploys designed to bring one to a place where ploys are no longer necessary nor possible. The second half presents the 'True Buddha,' an ahistorical, unborn, undying, mythologically omniscient and omnipresent Power or Being. Centuries later East Asian schools, such as Tendai and Nichiren, rightly asked and debated which of these two visions of Buddhism contextualized which? If the first half gives the 'truth,' then the second half should be seen as an elaborate upāyic ploy. If the second half gives the 'truth,' then the ploys of the first half are merely indirect, pedagogical instruments for reaching this truth, for reaching this ontological realization.

Beyond the *Lotus Sūtra* the essentialist vs. progressionalist opposition is found shaping Buddhist methodology, which is to say, the mārga, the Path. Those taking Buddhism to hold an ontological nature as its essence, who conceive of Buddhism as grounded in Being, develop their essentialism by understanding prajñā-pāramitā as 'perfect-ion,' and posit that perfection as an ontologically primal and definitive 'tathatā'; i.e., a 'suchness' which is the universal, sacred, perfected nature of all things. Suchness becomes a cosmic essence, the primal, originary scene. Buddha is no longer a teacher who perfected himself, but the universal essence of all things, the potential perfection ontologically concealed behind a veil of transmigratory appearance. And yet, the veil and what it veils are united in essence. It is this interpretation which reads Nāgārjuna's statement that not an iota of distinction can be drawn between saṃsāra and nirvāṇa (an epistemic observation) as if it were an ontological claim, a statement of essentialistic identity: saṃsāra *is* nirvāṇa.[42]

On the other hand, those who take the progressionalist stance displace the notions of nature and essence with a theory of perdurance, of continuity which, precisely because it is grounded in neither identity nor difference, can engender progress and betterment (or worsening). Prajñā-pāramitā here means 'perfecting,' as that which perdures becomes that which it is not, without ever being totally other than itself. The path is tread, and as with Heraclitus' river, the foot never truly stands on the same ground twice. The doctrines of the four gatins (stream-enterer, once returner, etc.), the bodhisattva career of ten or eighteen or fifty-two stages (*bhūmi*), etc., all exemplify the progressionalist attitude.

But like the *Lotus Sūtra*, one way of dissipating the tension is to accept and attempt to harmonize both extremes. Thus hybrids arose: progressive essentialists claimed that one progresses *toward* the essence, and that the progress itself was grounded in the essence (*tathāgatagarbha*); essentialistic progressives mounted elaborate schema in which one ultimately progressed beyond essentialisms by working through them (*tattva, vastu, bhūta, dharma svalakṣaṇa, svarūpa, svabhāva,* etc.). Yogācāra was a case of this last type of hybrid.

Finally, is tathatā, 'indexicality,' indicative of liberating universals, or repetitive, reiterative particulars? Given the incompatibility of essentialist universals and śūnyatā, tathatā must remain ontologically open. It is entirely without conceptual (*kalpita, vikalpa, kalpanā,* etc.) ontological commitments. For the *Ch'eng wei-shih lun*, tathatā is a mere prajñapti.

Implications: Rūpa and the Three Worlds, Again

Let us review the meaning of 'progress' through the tri-dhātu. First, one quiets the erotic, appropriative urge and its lived-field (kāma-dhātu), and rises through this sublimation to the rūpa-dhātu. Then, like rūpa, one becomes 'neutral'; or, again, one neutralizes rūpa; or, the stoic commitment that rūpa is neutral (decathexed), follows from the very characteristics of rūpa as karmically neutral. The meditative mastering of the rūpa-dhātu is capped by upekṣa-vedanā, the neutralization of all affective bifurcations.

With such neutrality, on enters the ārūpya-dhātu in search of the roots of thinking, the conditions by which cognition occurs. A broad vista opens, a series of expansive, nāmic horizons one by one are mastered and overcome, each in turn becoming the grounding condition for the next horizon, until the sequentialism folds in on itself.

The rūpa-dhātu (with the kāma-dhātu) becomes, in the later, de-cosmologized schools of Buddhist thought, the *kleśa-āvaraṇa*, the hindrance and obstruction from emotional and mental disturbances. These obstructions are what prevent us from cognizing what is as it is, or what becomes as it becomes (*tathatā*). Kleśāvaraṇa, in turn, is grounded in *jñeya-āvaraṇa*, the cognitive, theoretic obstruction, identified in many texts as the perspectivality (*dṛṣṭi*) of self (*ātman*). At the root of thinking, its inceptual error consists in assigning selfhood, essences, self-definitions to the objects of thought as well as the thinker. Uproot this obstruction, and only clear, direct seeing, purified of all obstructions, occurs. Many later Buddhist texts echo Jain rhetoric, saying that with the elimination of obstructions, one becomes omniscient (*sarvajñā*), one's insight radiating, penetrating, illuminating everywhere.

This methodology advises 'detach from rūpa,' and then plummet the cognitive depths. Yogācāra took this very seriously, following this advice not only in terms of tri-dhātu meditation, but for establishing the parameters of its phenomenology. Rūpa is indeed jettisoned, and the Yogācāric gaze concentrates and investigates the cognitive depths.

If rūpa is considered to arise and cease in a causal region or sphere all its own, that is, that the causal sequences of rūpa occur in a domain radically separate from the domain of nāma, such that nāma and rūpa constitute parallel causal chains (though not strictly isomorphic in the Spinozean sense, since physical conditions can affect mental dispositions), then detaching from the karmic appropriation of rūpa is nāmically cleansing, 'purifying.' Cleansing the vijñāna-stream (*saṅtāna*) of its karmic 'defilements' (i.e., habitual determinants, predispositions) has always been at the core of Buddhist praxis. Following the stream metaphor, the consciousness stream flows torrentially, driven by karmic motive forces (kleśas, the āvaraṇas, etc.). The flow continues unabated until nonbeneficial karma (akuśala) is transmuted into beneficial karma (kuśala), thereby filtering, purifying the stream's water. Nonetheless it rages on until abruptly, and with finality, it is dissipated in the arhat stage. This helps explain the concern in Early abhidhamma with classifying dhammas in order to ascertain which were rūpic and which weren't.

One of the stated goals of Buddhist praxis in the early texts is to become 'deathless,' *amata*. Remember that Buddha begins his meditation under the Bodhi tree on the night of his Awakening asking "Why is there Death"? The *pratītya-samutpāda* formula, according to this account, arose as the answer to that question. Overcoming 'death' was pivotal, and one of the epithets for an Awakened one, was that he/she was *amata*. What does amata really mean, since it never seems to have been taken in a literal fashion. Buddha and the first generation of arhats die, like all impermanent things, and yet they continue to be called 'deathless.' Let me suggest an interpretation. To be undying means to not arise, to not arise means 'unborn' (*anutpāda*) in the sense of not constrained by conditioning, not condemned to habitually repeat previous experience, to have one's experience determined by the moment by moment 'arising of conditions' (*utpāda*). "I don't die" means (1) there is no self which undergoes death (but this is strictly formulaic, not existential), and (2) it connotes asaṃskṛta, in the sense that Chinese translated that term, viz. *wu-wei*, i.e., the non-conditioned spontaneity and freedom of *tzu-jan*. Further, it meant to not suffer loss due to impermanence, to remain unaffected by loss and gain. Impermanence (e.g., in terms of rūpa) continues unabated, but it is now upekṣa, i.e., no longer experienced *as loss*. *Amata* is thus an epistemic change, not ontological. Awakening is thus an epistemic, not ontological transformation!

The term *anutpāda* (Ch.: *wu-sheng* 無生), non-arising, non-birth, etc. is a clever rejection of the Buddhist attachment to causational (arising-ceasing) theories. Buddha's formula for the solution to duḥkha took the form: When X does *not arise* (anutpāda), then Y also does not arise. Hence non-arising suggested that if avidyā, etc., did not arise, then there would and could be no duḥkha, no problems. However, if nirvāṇa itself is non-arising, then how does it avoid hypostatization? Candrakīrti, while explaining that *asvabhāva* (absence of essential, self-nature) and *pratītya-samutpāda* are synonyms, writes:[43]

> As it is said in the verse by the illustrious one, 'Whatever is born of conditions, that is not born; it does not come to be in self-existence. Whatever is dependent on conditions is said to be devoid of a self-existent nature. Whoever understands the absence of self-existence is wise.

With the privileging of prajñā, the ārūpyadhātu in its samādhic function is displaced by epistemology and psychology. Meditation at most becomes a tool for epistemological clarity, for psychological insight. This is most strikingly evident in the blending of the Yogācāra and Sautrāntika schools, where the problematic aspects of Yogācāra doctrine, such as the ālaya (considered by other Buddhists to be too suggestive of a substrative ātmanic self) and the abhidharmic schema (considered too catechismic), are discarded and the logical and epistemological approaches to Buddhism predominate. These changes occurred after Hsüan-tsang's return to China, and thus do not directly concern what we shall be discussing in the following chapters, since he was unaware of them. But he left India at the moment Indian Buddhism was on the threshold of these changes, and thus the Buddhism he brings back to China carries the seeds of this development. That he was ultimately unsuccessful at introducing this change to China, that he failed to establish a Chinese Buddhist logical tradition, even after translating two pivotal logic texts (one by Dignāga), may eventually help shed some light on why the *Ch'eng wei-shih lun* assumed the important role and position it did in East Asian thought.

Notes

1 For a discussion of the difference between prajñā and jñāna, see Genjun H. Sasaki's *Linguistic Approach to Buddhist Thought* (Delhi: Motilal, 1986) pp. 90-105. Also, see below.

2 Sangharakshita translates *apraṇihita* as 'Aimlessness,' while Conze uses 'Wishless,' and writes in *Buddhist Thought in India* (Ann Arbor: University of Michigan Press, 1967) p. 67:

> The word *a-pra-ṇi-hita* means literally that one 'places nothing in front,' and it designates someone who makes no plans for the future, has no hopes for it, who is aimless, not bent on anything, without predilection or desire for the objects of perception rejected by the concentration on the Signless [*ānimitta*]. This raises the problem whether Nirvana can be desired.

Predictably he answers this by saying that the Nirvana one desires is one's own mistaken conception of Nirvana, not Nirvana itself, which is defined as the absence of craving or desire. See his very helpful discussion of the 'Three Doors to Deliverance,' viz. *śūnyatā* (emptiness), *ānimitta* (signless), and *apraṇihita*, in *ibid.* pp. 59-69. Doctrinally, if not in terms of praxis, Conze is correct in noting that "the Wishless [is] very much less important for

Buddhist thought than Emptiness and the Signless..." (p. 67). Nonetheless, whether always explicitly doctrinalized (e.g., as non-attachment) or not, 'wishlessness' invariably looms large within Buddhist practice. However, the picture Conze draws of one who is wishless sounds more like someone lethargic and depressed than a joyful, energetic treader of the supermundane path; he has possibly confused disengagement for detachment. On 'disengagement' (*nibbida*), see below. The *Triṃśikā* alludes to the notion of *apraṇihita* in verse 27.

3 This problematic of means and ends became one of the most important issues addressed by the various schools of East Asian Buddhism. Some of the hottest and thorniest controversies grew out of it, though garbed in a new phraseology. Questions such as "If I already have Buddha-nature, and Buddha-nature means (Original) Awakening, then why do I have to practice?," or "What is the difference between 'Original Awakening,' 'Non-Awakening,' 'Initial Awakening,' 'Final Awakening,' and 'the inception of Faith'?," recur incessantly in the T'ien-t'ai, Hua-yen, and Ch'an schools. Some Ch'an traditions, picking up on a suggestion by Nāgārjuna, simply sidestep the issue by declaring "nothing is attained." The patriarch of Japanese Sōtō Zen, Dōgen, puzzled for many years by this dilemma, drew on both Ch'an and Tendai formulations of the problem, and offered one of the famous 'solutions,' namely that practice itself *is* Awakening. Predictably, these ongoing controversies led to entirely novel positions and formulations, as, for instance, some T'ien-t'ai sects arguing that to differentiate any potentially actual Awakenings from the 'actually potential' Original Awakening violated Awakening's non-dual nature. See Chan-jan's *Shih Pu-erh men* ("The Ten Gates of Non-duality"), T46.1927.702-4, and Chih-li's commentary on it, *Shih Pu-erh men Chih-yao-ch'ao* ("On the Main Points in 'The Ten Gates of Non-duality'"), T46.1928.704-20.

4 'Reduced' is perhaps too strong a word, since it is the centrality of the Eightfold Path which becomes displaced, not the list itself. The Eightfold Path re-emerges as part of the list of Thirty-Seven Factors of Awakening, which is adopted by Mahāyāna through the Prajñāpāramitā literature which in turn compiled it from the Abhidharmic literature. The seven factors of Awakening (*sattabojjhaṅga*) which constitute the cause and condition of the arising of knowledge and insight, mentioned in the *Saṃyutta Nikāya* (see Jayatilleke, *Early Buddhist Theory of Knowledge*, p. 422 and n. 2) are expanded in the Mahāsaḷāyatanika Sutta of the *Majjhima Nikāya* (III, 287 ff) into Thirty Seven Factors (for a list, cf. Conze, *The Large Sutra on Perfect Wisdom*, p. 671; for a discussion of these, see Har Dayal, *The Bodhisattva Doctrine in Buddhist Sanskrit Literature*, Delhi: Motilal, rpt. 1978, pp. 80-164; for an excellent, detailed book length study, see Rupert Gethin, *The Buddhist Path to Awakening: A Study of the Bodhi-Pakkhiyā Dhammā*, Leiden: EJ Brill, 1992).

5 Sometimes ten pāramitās are listed, adding [7] skillful and advantageous implementation of upāya (*upāya-kauśalya*); [8] commitment (*praṇidhāna*); [9] power (*bala*); and [10] knowing (*jñāna*) to the list of six. The *Ch'eng Wei-shi lun* uses the list of ten.

6 For a helpful and critical appraisal of the meanings of the Sanskrit term *kṣanti* in terms of how it sometimes deviates from the original Pāli Buddhist term *khanti* (a 'willingness' to calmly engage all things/theories along with their implications, in a way which incurs no detriments) as well as the further implications raised by the Chinese terms used to translate *khanti* and *kṣānti*, cf. Genjun H. Sasaki's *Linguistic Approach to Buddhist Thought* (Delhi: Motilal, 1986) pp. 64 n. 1, 101f, 133-140.

7 Sangharakshita, *op. cit.*, makes such an effort on pp. 123-169, 419-452. Lama Govinda, in *The Psychological Attitude...* ch. 4, offers a different configuration. In CWSL, Hsüan-tsang records that the cultivation of the pāramitās involves the two categories of *puṇya* (merit) and *prajñā* (wisdom), which were applied in different ways by different thinkers to the six. It is also possible to correlate the three trialectic factors with the three major sections of the Buddhist canon, i.e., śīla with Vinaya, samādhi with Sutra, and prajñā with Abhidharma. However such correlations should be taken as reflecting relative tendencies rather than

absolute or hard and fast distinctions between them, since the entire canon deals with all three factors.

8 Cf. Ergardt, *op. cit.*, pp. 88f.

9 *Milindapañha*, PTS ed., edited by V. Trenckner, p. 105.

10 The issue of Buddha's alleged omniscience gradually assumes a more central place in Buddhist thought. Dharmakīrti, who probably lived shortly after Hsüan-tsang's trip to India, attempted to divert the issue by arguing that Buddha only knew Dharma (*Dharmajñā*), not each and every thing, either collectively or individually. Śāntarakṣita, however, in his *Tattvasaṃgrāha*, a compendium of Buddhist philosophy aimed primarily at rebuking the attack on Dignāga and Dharmakīrti by Kumārila's Mīmāṃsā school, revitalizes the position that Buddha is omniscient (*sarvajñā*), and his concluding chapter, which underlines and highlights the entire book, is precisely his argument for this omniscience. Once Mahāyāna emerges, the Sūtra as well as Śāstra literature continually refer to Buddha's omniscience; this has been mentioned above.

11 Cf. Sasaki, *op. cit.*, pp. 90-105, on the distinction between *prajñā* and *jñāna*. According to Sasaki prajñā primarily means 'knowledge to be practiced,' while jñāna means 'knowledge achieved,' i.e., the 'product' of prajñā.. He reviews several salient moments in the history of these terms. He also notes that they become unified as or in the *ākāra* (mental image):

> [The *ākāra*] represents the mental disposition in which *prajñā* and *jñāna* come into unity. In other words, *prajñā* denotes the essential nature of *ākāra* and the basis of *jñāna*. The [*Abhidharmakośa*] states that "the essence of *ākāra* is *prajñā*." (p. 103)

Note the essentialistic language.

12 Cf. Dayal, *op. cit.*, p. 109.

13 English translation: *Points of Controversy*, tr. by Shwe Zan Aung and Mrs. Rhys Davids (London: Pali Text Society, 1960 rpt), p. 173. S.N. Dube's *Cross Currents in Early Buddhism* (Delhi: Manohar, 1980) offers a useful overview of the *Kathā-vatthu*.

14 A.K. Warder, in his *Indian Buddhism* (Delhi: Motilal, 1980 revised ed.), argues that the Andhakas constitute the prototype for the later-to-emerge Mahāyāna. They do indeed seem to hold positions that Yogācāra will later develop. For instance, the Andhakas deny the existence of Hell guardians, a position Vasubandhu echoes in his *Viṃśatikā*. However, significant differences also must be noted, on issues major and minor, e.g., on the duration of a moment of consciousness (the Andhakas argued it lasted for a full day; Yogācāra accepted the orthodox notion of momentariness). The most significant corollary between Andhaka and Yogācāra theories is the insistence on the centrality of karma as necessitating the reduction of *rūpa* and other supposedly non-mental categories to their mental implications.

15 *Points of Controversy*, p. 173

16 An excellent overview of the Theravādin Path (*magga*) as formulated by Buddhaghosa can be found in Ñāṇārāma Mahāthera's *The Seven Stages of Purification* (Kandy: Buddhist Publication Society, 1983) from which the following summary will be extracted. The exact author of the commentary to the *Katha-vatthu* is uncertain; Buddhaghosa or one of his contemporaries is often credited with it. If so, these four *ñāṇas* could be his own simplified list.

17 See previous note.

18The first four stages are:

1) Behavioral purification (*sīla visuddhi*);
2) Mental purification (*citta visuddhi*), involving overcoming the ten impediments (*palibodhā*), six obstacles (*vodāna*) and five hindrances (*pañcanīvaraṇa*) (see ibid. ch. 2), as well as developing samādhic proficiency through (a) *Upacāra-samādhi* (holding a clear mental image while the hindrances are suppressed), (b) *Āppanā-samādhi* (entering the rūpa-dhātu jhānas) and (c) *khaṇika-samādhi* (clearly seeing 'momentariness')—(a) and (b) involve *samatha*, 'calm,' and (c) involves *vipassanā*, 'clear insight';

3) Purification of Theories (*diṭṭhi visuddhi*), which includes sixteen types of knowledge (ñāṇa) to be obtained in sequence (see ibid. ch. 3).

4) Purification by overcoming doubt (*kankhāvitaraṇa visuddhi*) see ibid. ch. 4.

19 The saṅkhāric maneuver in which the saṅkhāras 'defend' themselves by 'displacing and transferring' the insightful gaze of the meditator on to other things, of course, is very evocative of the Freudian notions of displacement and transference. In both the Buddhist and Freudian formulations, the Unconscious attempts to avoid being scrutinized and exposed by marshalling defense mechanisms that divert scrutiny away from the 'truth,' truth being the hidden, repressed etiological source of whatever problem underlies the apparent symptoms that prompted the scrutiny in the first place. A further irony should be noted in the Buddhist formulation: the saṅkhāras are in fact fighting for their very existence, i.e., for the preservation of their 'self.' If exposed, they would disappear and lose their power to generate and perpetuate the saṃsāric cycle of existence. This is also a metaphor for the persistent clinging to a 'notion of self' (*ātma-dṛṣṭi*) that Buddhism identifies as the root problematic of the duḥkhic dilemma. Just as one generates all sorts of cognitive fantasies (*prapañca, vikalpa, kalpanā*, etc.) to avoid admitting that no permanent self exists, saṅkhāras generate this displacive smoke-screen in order to prevent the insight which dissolves them, an insight that evaporates their darkness with its glaring light. This process is also what lies behind the mythical descriptions of Clear Seeing, Awakening or Enlightenment dissipating the distractive 'temptations' of Mara in the story of Buddha's Awakening.

20 Interestingly, at this stage Ñāṇārāma offers a Theravādin retort to the Mahāyānic notion of a Bodhisattva vow, though his point is made indirectly. Mahāyāna practice involves four vows that all aspirants must make at the inception of their entry into Buddhist practice. One vow is directly aimed against 'Hīnayāna.' Since Mahāyāna sees the pursuit of the individual attainment of nirvāṇa as a 'selfish' Hīnayāna practice, all Mahāyānist practitioners must vow not to enter nirvāṇa until all sentient beings are ready to likewise enter. As a consequence of this vow, the highest stage to which a Mahāyānic Bodhisattva can aspire is the tenth Bodhisattva stage (*bhūmi*), which is just short of Buddhahood, in order to await the ripening to Buddhahood in all sentient beings. Ñāṇārāma writes:

> Some meditators are unable to go beyond the Knowledge of Equanimity about Formations due to some powerful aspirations they have made in the past, such as for Buddhahood or Pacceka Buddhahood, Chief Discipleship, etc. In fact, it is at this stage that one can ascertain whether one has made any such aspiration in the past....

In a conciliatory tone, Ñāṇārāma finally says:

> However, even for an aspirant to Buddhahood [i.e., a Mahāyānic Bodhisattva!] or Pacceka Buddhahood, Knowledge of Equanimity about Formations will be an asset towards his fulfilment of the Perfection of Wisdom [i.e., prajñā pāramitā]. This Equanimity of Formations is of no small significance when one takes into account the high degree of development in knowledge at this stage. (p. 57)

21 See note 4 above. The Thirty Seven Factors of Awakening (*bodhi pakṣika dharmā*) are:

- The Four Abodes of Mindfulness (*smṛti upasthāna*)

Focusing mindfulness/recollection on (i) body, (ii) sensations, (iii) mind, and (iv) things (dharmas).

- The Four Correct 'Efforts' [or literally 'Abandonments'] (*samyak prahāṇa*)

(i) effort not to initiate dis-advantageous (*akuṣala*) actions which have not yet occurred,

(ii) effort to eliminate (repetition of, or consequential continuation of) dis-advantageous actions which have already occurred,

(iii) effort to initiate advantageous (*kuśala*) actions which have not yet occurred,

(iv) effort to further strengthen and expand advantageous actions which have occurred.

[I follow Thurman in accepting Dayal's argument that *prahāṇa* (lit. 'abandonment') is a mis-Sanskritization of the Pāli *padhāna* (struggle, effort); cf. Dayal, *op. cit.*, pp. 102-3)]

- The Four Bases of Magical Powers (*ṛddhipāda*)

(i) Harnessing a strong desire/will (*chanda*) to the saṃskāric energy engendered by meditative concentration (*samādhi*) and 'effort' (*prahāṇa*) (*chanda samādhi prahāṇa saṃskāra samavāgaṭ*).

(ii) Harnessing mind (*citta*) to the saṃskāric energy engendered by meditative concentration and 'effort.'

(iii) Harnessing vigorous energy (*vīrya*) to the saṃskāric energy engendered by meditative concentration and 'effort.'

(iv) Harnessing analytic-method (*mīmāṃsā*) to the saṃskāric energy engendered by meditative concentration and 'effort.'

- The Five [metaphorical] Cognitive-Organs (*indriya*)

(i) faith (*śraddhā*), (ii) vigorous energy (*vīrya*), (iii) mindfulness/recollection (*smṛti*), (iv) meditative concentration (*samādhi*), and (v) cognitive acuity (*prajñā*).

[Cf. Dayal, pp. 141-147 for a fascinating discussion of the textual history of how 'faith' (*śraddhā*) eventually displaced 'desire/will' (*chanda*) from this list.]

- The Five Powers (*bala*)

The dynamic functioning of the Five Cognitive-Organs.

- The Seven Factors of Awakening (*saṃbhodhyaṅga*)

(i) Mindfulness/recollection, (ii) investigating the teachings (*dharma pravicaya*), (iii) vigorous energy, (iv) joy (*prīti*), (v) tranquility (*praśrabdhi*), (vi) meditative concentration, (vii) equanimity/'neutralization' (*upekṣā*).

- The Eightfold Noble Path (*aṣṭāṅga-* or *aśṭāṅgika mārga*)

[Listed above]

22 Initially the notion of 'changing lineage' carried political connotations, in particular, one's liberation from the confines and determinations of the caste system and other societal conditionings. Entering the saṅgha (Buddhist community) provided basic behavioral and peer conditions for disengaging from caste society. It marked part of the Buddhist rejection of Caste distinctions by announcing a novel social and religious status, while providing a practical alternative. To change 'lineage' meant that liberation from societal conditions had been fully actualized, i.e., that one's politics had made one a new type of person. Eventually the notion of change-of-lineage acquired intricate Buddhological significances. So far the only comprehensive study of the notion of *gotra* is the brilliant study in French, drawing on Indian and Tibetan sources by David Seyford Ruegg, *La Théorie du Tathāgatagarbha et du Gotra* (Paris: 1969).

23 As an example in addition to ones provided earlier, see Nāgārjuna's *Śūnyatāsaptati* (Eng. tr. and romanized Tib. text in C. Lindtner, *Nagarjuniana*, Copenhagen: Akademisk Forlag, 1982, pp. 31-69), especially verses 36, 40-42, 51, 59-60, 64, 66, and 73. This is a curious text. Though the style of its argumentation is Mādhyamikan, much of its vocabulary and basic concerns evoke Yogācāric issues (e.g., *pariklp-* in verse 61, etc.). Closer study of such texts would do much to help modern scholars close the presumed gap between these schools. On the issue of 'cessation' and 'delusion,' Nāgārjuna's *Yuktiṣaṣṭikā* verse 7 is instructive:

> While [thc ignorant] imagine that annihilation (*nirodha*) pertains to a created thing (*bhāva*) which is dissolved (*naṣṭa*), the wise (*sat*), however, are convinced that annihilation (*nirodha*) of [something] created (*kṛtaka*) is an illusion (*māyā*).
>
> (Lindtner's translation, p. 105, all insertions his)

In Candrakīrti's commentary to this verse, he conjures up the analogy of an artificial elephant produced by magic. When eliminated, nothing real has been destroyed.

Verses 15 and 16 also address this:

15. ...The world, devoid of a previous and final limit (*pūrvaśaścimāntarahita*), appears like an illusion (*māyāvat*).

16. When one thinks that an illusion (*māyā*) arises or that it is destructed, one who recognizes the illusion is not bewildered by it but one who does not recognize it longs for it (*paritṛṣ-*).

(*Ibid.*, p. 107)

These themes recur throughout Mahāyānic literature.

24 On this, cf., e.g., Husserl's *Ideas I*, ch. 4, secs. 37-38, (pp. 109-113 in Gibson's English translation). For a fascinating study and critique of this problem from within the framework of Neo-Kantian discourse, see Nishida Kitaro's *Intuition and Reflection in Self-Consciousness*, trs. V. Vigielmo, Takeuchi T., and J. O'Leary (Albany: SUNY Press, 1987).

25 Even in extreme cases, like the traditional story of Hui-neng's Awakening, this rubric remains in place, if tacitly. The story goes that while still a young and unlearned firewood seller, Hui-neng was carrying some wood through the street when he overheard someone chanting a line from the *Diamond Sūtra*. Immediately upon hearing it, he was Awakened. Wouldn't that be a case of Awakening without recourse to the Bodhisattva Path? Perhaps, but it should be noted that the most common traditional 'explanation' of how that occurred is that Hui-neng was ripe for Awakening at that moment due to the merit and practice he accumulated in previous lives, i.e., he *did* have recourse to the Bodhisattva Path, albeit in the 'past.' Whether this explanation merely reflects a conservative spirit concerned with preserving Buddhist institutions, or says something else about what Buddhists, Ch'anists in particular, consider Awakening to be is an open question. After all, the notion of acquiring experience and merit in previous lives which come to fruition in the present life has had a continuous history since Buddha himself, as evidenced in the Jātaka tales, etc.

26 Nāgārjuna's *Vigrahavyāvartāni* eloquently argues that rather than negating the possibility that there be a world, śūnyatā (emptiness) constitutes the very possibilities of the world. Without śūnyatā the actual world is inconceivable and impossible.

27 T.W. Rhys Davids' translation, my interpolations; from *Dialogues of the Buddha* (London: Luzac & Co., 1956 rpt) I, pp. 250-1.

28 *Ibid.*, p. 251. Square brackets mine.

29 As will be clear in a moment, 'the summit of consciousness' means the horizonal margins, i.e., an awareness which knowingly extends up to its fullest limits.

30 *Abhisaṅkhareyyaṃ*. Rhys Davids has 'fancying,' which is clearly wrong, but offers a footnote suggesting "perhaps 'perfecting' or 'planning out.' *Samkhāra* (S. *saṃskāra*), which we defined above as 'embodied conditioning,' implies the 'bringing together of conditions,' or 'compounding conditions.' *Abhi-* is an emphatic prefix. The sense in this passage seems to be something like dredging up the deepest or most remote latent saṃskāras. Since at this stage in training the impact of new conditioning would be virtually arrested, only the vestiges of previous, deeply embedded conditioning would still be functioning and exerting any influence. Despite the impression one might get from Rhys Davids' translation, which I have modified slightly, the Bhikkhu here is not lamenting 'thinking' per se. He is now aware that *saññā* is 'associative thinking,' and therefore is dependent on conditions, including his unresolved saṃskāras. Since in early Buddhism Awakening explicitly involves breaking saṃskāric (i.e., karmic) conditioning, the Bhikkhu is merely noting that as long as 'associative thinking' keeps arising through 'embodied conditions' (i.e., *saṃjñā* arises from *saṃskāra*), the karmic dilemma has not yet been resolved.

31 Remarkably, this text seems to be saying that at this stage, progress is made through sheer decision.

32 Woodward's translation, in *The Book of the Kindred Sayings* (London: Luzac & Co., 1956 rpt) IV, pp. 145-146; slightly modified. Parentheses and emphasis mine.

33 See previous note.

34 Cf. *Points of Controversy*, pp. 145f.

35 *Ibid.*, p. 243.

36 We see from where Nāgārjuna borrowed this argument. Cf. discussion of MMK 16:3 in chapter ten.

37 *Ibid.*, pp. 190f.

38 They concede to their opponent that it cannot be categorized as conditioned either. They say here that in entering cessation speech, action and then consciousness cease. Emerging from cessation follows the opposite order, i.e., consciousness recommences, then activity, then speech. They ask, could one come out of the unconditioned? Under what conditions? Thus, *nirodha-samāpatti* is still karmic, while nibbāṇa is not.

39 *Ibid.*, pp. 124-127.

40 *Ibid.*, pp. 260f.

41 *Ibid.*, pp. 285f.

42 This may be the most famous case of misreading or erroneous citation in Buddhism. In the Nirvāṇa chapter of MMK (ch. 25), Nāgārjuna writes:

[19] Na saṃsārasya nirvāṇāt kiṃcid asti viśeṣaṇaṃ/
na nirvāṇasya saṃsārāt kiṃcid asti viśeṣaṇam //
[20] Nirvaṇasya ca yā kotiḥ kotiḥ saṃsaraṇasya ca/
na tayor antaraṃ kiṃcit susūkṣmam api vidyate//

[19] There is no thing by which saṃsāra is distinguished from nirvāṇa,
there is no thing by which nirvāṇa is distinguished from saṃsāra.
20] Nirvāṇa's horizonal-limit (koti) and the horizonal-limit of saṃsāra,
there is not even the subtlest thing between them.

In his *Prasannapadā* Candrakīrti also seems to fall momentarily into the essentialist camp, writing: "And so there is no specifiable difference between the everyday world (*Saṃsāra*) and *nirvāṇa* with respect to one another, because, on being thoroughly investigated, they are basically of the same nature." (Sprung's translation, pp. 259-260)

43 Sprung, *Ibid.*, p. 229; *Prasannapadā*, p. 491.

Part Four

Triṃśikā and Translations

唯 識 三 十 頌

Wei-shih San-shih sung

Vasubandhu

世 親

Shih-ch'in

Part IV focuses on several versions of the *Triṃśikā*, the thirty verses by Vasubandu on 'vijñapti.' A Sanskrit version that included the commentary of Sthiramati was discovered early in the twentieth century by Sylvain Lévy. Its title is *Triṃśikā-vijñapti-bhāṣya* (Commentary on the Thirty [verses on] vijñapti).

In the sixth century the Indian translator, Paramārtha—who was a committed Yogācārin, but to a different style of Yogācāra than Hsüan-tsang—produced a translation in which Vasubandhu's root text was seamlessly buried amidst Paramārtha's explanations. Paramārtha was one of the most influential Buddhist translators. Paramārtha's understanding of Yogācāra was idiosyncratic (from the point of view of the orthodox Indian tradition), and is known for having introduced the idea of a ninth consciousness, beyond the standard eight consciousnesses in Yogācāra, which he called the Amala-vijñāna (Pure Consciousness). For him, the ālaya-vijñāna is defiled and must be eliminated in order to let the Pure Consciousness reveal itself. He also allied his thinking with tathāgatagarbha ideas. He translated numerous Yogācāric, Abhidharmic, and other texts, many of which, like the *She lun* 攝論 (*Mahāyānasamgraha śāstra*, T.1593), have remained influential throughout East Asia. The *Chuan-shih lun* 轉識論 (T.1587), which contains the thirty verses, was one of his minor works, interesting today mainly as a counterpoint to Hsüan-tsang's version, which itself has remained influential in East Asia.

In 648 Hsüan-tsang produced a thirty verse version in Chinese of Vasubandhu's root text. Later, instead of translating various Sanskrit commentaries on Vasubandhu's text separately—which was his usual *modus operandi*—he was persuaded to combine the commentaries into one translation, adding comments on their relative merits: thus was the *Ch'eng wei-shih lun* born in 659. The story behind the *Ch'eng wei-shih lun* is critically discussed in Part V, chapter 15.

This section contains the following:

Triṃśikā — Vasubandhu's Sanskrit text
English translation of the Sanskrit, by Richard H. Robinson (unpublished ms.)
Paramārtha's Chinese translation of the *Triṃśikā*, extracted from *Chuan-shih lun* (T.15870)
English translation of Paramārtha's Chinese version
Hsüan-tsang's Chinese translation of the *Triṃśikā* (T.1586)
English translation of Hsüan-tsang's Chinese version

The translations are followed by a comparative discussion. More technical matters are taken up in the notes to the translation.

VERSE 1

[Vasubandhu's Sanskrit]

Ātma-dharma-upacāro hi vividho yaḥ pravartate |
Vijñāna-pariṇāmo'sau pariṇāmaḥ sa ca tridhā || 1

[Robinson's Translation]

The metaphor of 'Self' and 'Elements', which functions in several ways
Is upon the transformation of consciousness. This transformation is of three kinds;

[Paramārtha's Chinese Translation]

識轉有二種。一轉為眾生。二轉為法。[...] 次明能緣有三種。

Shih *chüan yu erh chung. Yi chüan wei chung-sheng. Erh chüan wei fa.*
[...]
Tz'u ming neng-yüan yu san chüan.

There are two types of "**Consciousness** Revolving":
1. Revolving into sentient beings,
2. Revolving into dharmas [...]

Next, [I will] clarify subjective-conditions (*neng-yüan*); there are three types:

[Hsüan-tsang's Translation]

由假說我法　有種種相轉
彼依識所變　此能變唯三

Yu chia shuo wo fa, *yu chung chung hsiang chuan,*
pi yi ***shih*** *so pien,* *ts'u neng pien wei san.*

Due to the provisional expressions (*chia-shuo*) "ātman and dharma,"
there is the proliferation of their mutual operations (*hsiang-chuan*).
They [i.e., the interactions between self and its perceptual field] depend upon **consciousness** for their alterations.
That which actively alters (*neng-pien*) is only three:

VERSE 2

[Vasubandhu's Sanskrit]

Vipāko mananāca **vijñaptir**-viṣayasya ca I
Tatra-ālayākhya **vijñānam** vipākaḥ sarvabījakam II 2

[Robinson's Translation]

(1) Retribution, (2) Mentation, and (3) perception of the sense-fields,
Among them, retribution is the so-called store-consciousness, which has all the seeds.

[Paramārtha's Chinese Translation]

一果報識。〔即是阿梨耶識〕。二執識 。〔即是阿陀那識〕。
三塵識。〔即識六識〕。[...] 亦名藏 識。一切種子隱伏之處。

Yi kuo-pao ***shih****. (chi-shih a-li-yeh-****shih****).*[1] *Erh chih* ***shih****. (chi-shih a-t'o-na-****shih****). San ch'en* ***shih****. (chi-shih liu* ***shih****).* [...] *Yi ming tsang-****shih****. Yi-ch'ieh chung-tzu yin-fu chih chu.*

1. Fruit-recompense consciousness (i.e., *ālaya* consciousness);
2. Attachment consciousness (i.e., *ādāna* consciousness)[2];
3. Dust consciousness (i.e., the six consciousnesses). [...]

[The first is] also called the "storehouse consciousness," where all the seeds are concealed.

[Hsüan-tsang's Translation]

謂異熟思量	及了別境識
初阿賴耶 識	異熟一切種
Wei yi shou ssu liang,	*chi* ***liao pieh*** *ching* ***shih*** [?!]
ch'u a-lai-yeh ***shih****,*	*yi shou yi ch'ieh chung*

...the **consciousnesses** (*shih*) that are called "differently maturing" (*vipāka*)[3], "willing and deliberating,"[4] and "**distinguishing** (*liao-pieh* , *vijñaptir*) sense-objects (*ching*, *viṣaya*)."[5]
The first, the *ālaya-vijñāna*, matures-at-varying-[times] (*vipāka*) all the seeds.

VERSE 3

[Vasubandhu's Sanskrit]

Asaṃviditakopādisthāna-**vijñaptikam** ca tat |
Sadā sparśa-manaskāra-vit-sañjñā-cetanā-avitam || 3

[Robinson's Translation]

Its appropriation and its perception of location are not discerned consciously.
It is always associated with contact, [attention],[6] sensation, ideation, and volition.[7]

[Paramārtha's Translation]

相及境不可分別 [...] 一觸。二作意。三受。四思惟。五想。

Hsiang chi ching pu-k'e fen-pieh [...] *Yi ch'u. Erh tso-yi. San shou. Ssu ssu-wei. Wu hsiang.*

Its characteristics[8] and sense-objects cannot be discriminated [...] 1. Contact, 2. paying attention, 3. pleasure/pain/neutral (*vedanā*), 4. volition, 5. conceptualizing (*saṃjñā*).[9]

[Hsüan-tsang's Translation]

不可知執受	處了常與觸
作意受想思	相應唯捨受
Pu k'e chih chih shou,	*ch'u* ***liao*** *ch'ang yü ch'u*
tso-yi shou hsiang ssu,	*hsiang-ying wei she shou*

Unknowable [is what and how] it appropriates[10] and
where it **discerns**;[11] always with 'sensation' [#9],
'attention' [#13], 'pleasure/pain [#10], 'conceptualization' [#12], 'volition' [#11],
it corresponds only with neutral[-ized] 'pain/pleasure.'[12]

VERSE 4

[Vasubandhu's Sanskrit]

Upekṣā vedanā tatra-anivṛtā-avyāktam ca tat I
Tathā sparśa-ādayas-tacca vartate srotasaugha-vat II 4

[Robinson's Translation]

In it, the sensation is indifference and it is pure[13] and morally neutral.
The same for contact, etc. It flows on like the current of a river.

[Paramārtha's Chinese Translation]

受但是捨受 [...] 此 識及心法。但是自性無記。念念恆流如水流浪。

Shou tan shih she-shou [...] *Tz'u shih chi hsin-fa. Tan shih tzu-hsing wu-chi. Nien-nien heng liu ju shui liu-lang.*

Vedanā (associated with the ālaya-vijñāna) is only neutral-vedanā (*upekṣa-vedanā*). [...] This consciousness and [its] mental dharmas (i.e, *caittas*) only have the non-karmically-defined (*avyākta*) self-nature.[14] Moment by moment (or: thought-instant after thought-instant[15]) it is constantly flowing, like water flowing in waves.

[Hsüan-tsang's Translation]

是無覆無記　　觸等亦如是
恆轉如暴流　　阿羅漢位捨

Shih wu fu wu chi,　　*ch'u teng yi ju shih*
heng chuan ju pao liu,　　*a-lo-han wei she.*

It [i.e., ālaya-vijñāna] is non-covered and non-recording.[16]
Sensation, etc. [in relation to ālaya] are also like this.
Constantly operating like a wild torrent.[17]
[in] the arhat stage [it is] abandoned/neutralized.

VERSE 5

[Vasubandhu's Sanskrit]

Tasya vyāvṛtir-arhattve tad-āśritya pravartate I
Tad-ālambam mano-nāma **vijñānam** mananātmakam II 5

[Robinson's Translation]

Its reversal takes place in the state of Arhatship. Based on it, there functions,
with it as object, the consciousness called mind, which consists of mentation.

[Paramārtha's Chinese Translation]

乃至得羅漢果 [...] 依緣此 識有第二執識。此識以執著為體。

Nai chih te lo-han kuo [...] *Yi yüan tz'u* ***shih*** *yu ti-erh chih-****shih****. Tz'u* ***shih*** *yi chih-chu wei t'i.*

[...] until reaching the fruit of Arhathood.[18] [...] Dependent on conditions, this consciousness has a second—the attachment consciousness. This consciousness takes attachment as its essence.

[Hsüan-tsang's Translation]

次第二能變	是識名末那
依彼轉緣彼	思量為性相
Ts'u ti erh neng pien,	*shih* ***shih*** *ming mo-na*
yi pi chuan yüan pi,	*ssu-liang wei hsing hsiang.*

Next, the second that actively alters:
this **consciousness** is named *manas.*
Dependent on that [i.e., the ālaya] it turns around and objectifies it;[19]
its nature is characterized as 'willing and deliberating.'[20]

VERSE 6

[Vasubandhu's Sanskrit]

Kleśais-caturbhiḥ sahitam nivṛta-avyākṛtai sadā I
ātma-dṛṣṭi-ātma-moha-ātma māna-ātma-sneha-sañjñitai II 6

[Robinson's Translation]

It is always accompanied by four passions which are impure but morally neutral,
Known as notion of self, delusion of self, pride of self, and love of self.

[Paramārtha's Chinese Translation]

與四惑相應。一無明。二我見。三我慢。四我愛。
此識名有覆無記。

Yü ssu huo hsiang ying. Yi wu-ming. erh wo-chien. San wo-man. Ssu wo-ai. Tz'u shih ming yu-fu wu-chi.

And four delusions (= *kleśa*)[21] interact with it: 1. Ignorance [!?][22], 2. 'self' view, 3. 'self' arrogance, 4. 'self' love. This consciousness is termed 'covered' and 'non-defined.'

[Hsüan-tsang's Translation]

四煩惱常俱 謂我癡我見
并我慢我愛 及餘觸等俱

Ssu fan-nao ch'ang chü, wei wo-ch'ih wo-chien
ping wo-man wo-ai, chi yu ch'u teng chü

[Manas] is always together with the four *kleśas,*[23]
called self-delusion, self-belief/view,
self-arrogance, and self-love;
and the rest, [i.e.] sensation [#9], etc., are together [with it].

VERSE 7

[Vasubandhu's Sanskrit]

Yatrajas-tanmayair-anyaiḥ sparśa-ādyaiś-cārhato na tat ǀ
na nirodha-samāpattau mārge lokottare na ca ǁ 7

[Robinson's Translation]

With those from where it is born, also with others—contact, etc. It doesn't exist in the Arhat,
In the attainment of cessation, nor in the supra-mundane path.

[Paramārtha's Chinese Translation]

至羅漢位究竟滅盡。及入無心定亦皆滅盡 [...] 得出世道 [...]
究竟滅盡 [...]

Chih lo-han-wei chiu-ching mieh-chin. Chi ju wu-hsin-ting yi chieh mieh-chin [...] *te ch'u-shih tao* [...] *chiu-ching mieh-chin* [...]

(Upon) reaching the Arhat stage, it finally ceases completely. Also, (when one) enters the mindless (*acitta*) samāpattis it completely ceases [...] Attaining the lokuttara-mārga (transmundane path) [...] it finally ceases completely [...]

[Hsüan-tsang's Translation]

有覆無記攝　　隨所生所繫
阿羅漢滅定　　出世道無有

Yu fu wu chi she,　　*sui so sheng so chi*
a-lo-han mieh ting,　　*ch'u-shih tao wu yu.*

[Manas] has the classification 'covered and non-recording (karmically)'.
It follows from where it is born and bound.
[For] the *arhat*, [during] *nirodha-samāpatti*,
and [on] the supra-mundane way, it does not exist.

VERSE 8

[Vasubandhu's Sanskrit]

Dvitīyaḥ pariṇāmo'yam tritīyaḥ ṣaḍ-vidhasya ya ǀ
viṣayasya-upalabdhiḥ sa kuśala-akuśala-adva ya ǁ 8

[Robinson's Translation]

This is the second transformation. The third is the sixfold. Perception of the sense-field, which is good, bad, or neither.

[Paramārtha's Chinese Translation]

第三塵識者。識轉似塵。更成六種識轉似塵 [...] 體通三性。

Ti-san ch'en ***shih*** *che.* ***Shih****-chüan ssu-ch'en. Kung ch'eng liu-chung* ***shih****-chüan ssu-ch'en* [...] *t'i t'ung san hsing.*

Third, Dust **Consciousness**. **Consciousness** revolving[24] [into] the appearance of dust [i.e., the six sensory realms], immediately establishes the six types of revolving-**consciousness** [as] the appearance of dust [...][25] Essentially they are understood as [having] three natures (i.e., good, bad, neutral).

[Hsüan-tsang's Translation]

次第三能變　　差別有六種
了境為性相　　善不善俱非

Ts'u ti san neng pien,　　ch'a-pieh yu liu chung
liao ching wei hsing hsiang, shan pu shan chü fei

Next, the third [mano-vijñāna], which actively alters,
is distinguished into six types:
its nature is characterized as 'discerning objects' (*liao ching*).[26]
[It can be] advantageous, disadvantageous, and neither.

VERSE 9

[Vasubandhu's Sanskrit]

Sarvatra-gair-viniyataiḥ kuśalaiś-cetasair-asau I
samprayuktā tathā kleśair-upakleśais-trivedanā II 9

[Robinson's Translation]

And associated with the universal mental (elements), specially determined, and good,
And also with the passions and sub-passions. It has three sensations.

[Paramārtha's Chinese Translation]

十善惡。并大小惑具三種受。

Shih shan o. Ping ta hsiao huo chu san-chung-shou.

The Ten Good and Bad [Dharmas]. And the Major and Minor Delusions (*kleśa*) together with the three types of Vedanā.[27]

[Hsüan-tsang's Translation]

此心所遍行　別境善煩惱
隨煩惱不定　皆三受相應

Ts'u hsin so pien hsing, pieh ching shan fan-nao
sui fan-nao pu ting, chieh san shou hsiang-ying

These [are its] mental associates (*caittas*): the Always-active [#9 - 13],
the Specific [#14 - 18], the Advantageous [#19 -29] and Mental Disturbances [*kleśas*, #30 - 35],
Secondary Mental Disturbances [#36 - 55], and the Indeterminate [#56 - 59].
All three *vedanā*-s [i.e., pain, pleasure, neutral] mutually interact[28] [with these six categories].

VERSE 10

[Vasubandhu's Sanskrit]

Ādyāḥ sparśādayas-chanda-adhimokṣa-smṛtayaḥ saha |
samādhi dhībhyām niyataḥ śraddhā-atha hrīr-apatrapā || 10

[Robinson's Translation]

The first are contact, etc. Desire, decision, memory, Concentration, and intelligence are determined. Faith, conscience, shame,

[Paramārtha's Chinese Translation]

觸等 [...] 但此為最粗也。後五者。一欲二了三念四定五慧 [...] 一信二羞三慚

Ch'ü teng [...] *tan tz'u wei tsui ts'u yeh. Hou wu che. Yi yü erh liao san nien ssu ting wu hui* [...] *yi hsin erh hsiu san tsan*

Contact, etc. [...] But these are considered the most crude.[29] The next five are (1) desire (*chanda*), (2) discernment (*adhimokṣa*), (3) mindfulness (*smṛti*), (4) samādhi, (5) wisdom (*dhī*) [...] (1) faith, (2) shame, (3) embarrassment

[Hsüan-tsang's Translation]

初遍行觸等　　次別境謂欲
勝解念定慧　　所緣事不同

Ch'u pien-hsing ch'u teng, ts'u pieh-ching wei yu
sheng-chieh nien ting hui, so yuan shih pu t'ung

First, the Always-active, [i.e.,] 'sensation', etc.
Next, the Specific, called 'desire' [#14],
'confident resolve' [#15], 'memory' [#16], 'meditative concentration' [#17], and 'discernment' (*prajñā*) [#18];
[their] conditioned occasions[30] are not identical.

VERSE 11

[Vasubandhu's Sanskrit]

Alobha-ādi trayam vīryam praśrabdhiḥ sa apramādikā |
ahiṃsa kuśalāḥ kleśa rāga-pratigha-mūḍhayaḥ || 11

[Robinson's Translation]

Greedlessness, with the two others, energy, serenity, vigilance's companion (indifference),
And harmlessness are the good (elements). The passions are lust, ill-will, delusion,

[Paramārtha's Chinese Translation]

四無貪五無瞋六精進七猗八無放逸九無逼惱十捨 [...] 大惑有十種者。一欲二瞋三癡。

ssu wu-t'an wu wu-ch'en liu ching-chin ch'i yi[31] *pa wu-fang-yi chiu wu-pi-nao shih she* [...] *ta-huo yu shih chung che. Yi yü erh ch'en san ch'ih.*

(4) absence of greed (*alobha*), (5) non-hatred (*adveṣa*), (6) being energetic (*vīrya*), (7) reliability (?)[32] (*praśrabdhi*), (8) non-careless (*apramāda*), (9) non-compulsive (?) (*ahiṃsa*), (10) equinimity (*upekṣa*) [...] There are ten types of great delusion (*kleśa*): (1) desire (*rāga*), (2) aversion (*pratigha*), (3) confusion (*mūdha*)...

[Hsüan-tsang's Translation]

善謂信慚愧　　無貪等三根
勤安不放逸　　行捨及不害

Shan wei hsin ts'an k'ui, *wu t'an teng san ken*
ch'in an pu-fang-yi, *hsing-she chi pu-hai*

The Advantageous are called 'faith' [#19], 'shame' [#20], 'embarrassment' [#21];
'absence of greed' [#22], etc., which are the three roots;[33]
'diligence'[34] [#25], 'tranquility' [#26], 'carefulness' [#27],
'equanimity' [#28] and 'non-injury' [#29].

VERSE 12

[Vasubandhu's Sanskrit]

Māna-dṛk-vicikitsāś-ca krodha-upanahane punaḥ ǀ
mṛkṣaḥ pradāśa īrṣyā-atha mātsaryam saha māyayā ǁ 12

[Robinson's Translation]

Pride, wrong views, doubt, anger, resentment, Dissimulation, sarcasm, envy, avarice, along with deceit,

[Paramārtha's Chinese Translation]

四慢。五五見。十疑。[...] 小惑 [...] 一忿恨。二結怨。三覆藏。四不拾。五嫉妒。六慳惜。

ssu man. Wu wu chien. Shih yi. [...] *hsiao huo* [...] *yi fen hen. Erh chieh yüan. San fu-tsang. Ssu pu-she. Wu chi tu. Liu lin hsi. Chi ch'i k'uang. Pa ch'an ch'ü.*

...(4) pride (*māna*), (5) [-(9)] the five views (*dṛṣṭi*)[35] [and] (10) doubt (*vicikitsa*). [...] The minor delusions (*upakleśas*): (1) anger (*krodha*), (2) ill-will (*upanāha*), (3) hiding faults (*mrakṣa*), (4) non-equinimity (*pradāsa*), (5) envy (*īrṣyā*), (6) stinginess (*mātsarya*), (7) deceptiveness (*māya*), (8) flattery (*śāthya*)

[Hsüan-tsang's Translation]

煩 惱 謂 貪 瞋	癡 慢 疑 惡 見
隨 煩 惱 謂 忿	恨 覆 惱 嫉 慳
Fan-nao wei t'an ch'en, *sui fan-nao wei fen,*	*ch'ih man yi erh chien* *hen fu nao chi ch'ien*

The Mental Disturbances (*kleśa*) are called 'appropriational intent' [#30], 'aversion' [#31],
'stupidity' [#32], 'arrogance' [#33], 'doubt' [#34], and 'wrong perspectives'[36] [#35].
The Secondary Mental Disturbances are called 'anger' [#36],
'enmity' [#37], 'resisting recognizing one's own faults' [#38, lit. 'concealing'], '(verbal) maliciousness' [#39], 'envy' [#40], 'selfishness' [#41],

VERSE 13

[Vasubandhu's Sanskrit]

Asaṭyam mado'vihiṃsā-hrīr-atrapā styānam-uddhavaḥ |
aśraddhām-atha kausīdyam pramādo muṣitā smṛtiḥ || 13

[Robinson's Translation]

Hypocricy, vanity, violence, lack of conscience, shamelessness, torpor, dissatisfaction,
Unfaith, laziness, carelessness, forgetfulness,

[Paramārtha's Chinese Translation]

九極醉十逼惱十一無羞十二無慚十三不猗十四掉戲十五不信十六懈怠
十八忘念

...chiu chi tsui. Shih pi-nao. Shih-yi wu-hsiu. Shih-erh wu-ts'an. Shih-san pu-yi. Shih-ssu tiao hsi. Shih-wu pu-hsin. Shih-liu hsieh-tai. Shih-chi fang-yi. Shih-pa wang-nien.

(9) conceit (*mada*), (10) injury (*vihiṃsa*), (11) shamelessness (*āhrīkya*), (12) lack of embarrassment (*anapatrapya*), (13) non-reliability[37] (*sthyāna*), (14) falling into playfulness[38] (*auddhatya*), (15) lacking faith (*aśraddha*), (16) laziness (*kausīdya*), (17) indulgence (*pramāda*), (18) forgetfulness (*muṣita-smṛta*)

[Hsüan-tsang's Translation]

誑 諂 與 害 憍　　無 慚 及 無 愧
掉 舉 與 惛 沈　　不 信 并 懈 怠

K'uang ch'an yü hai chiao, wu ts'an chi wu k'ui
tao chü yü hun ch'en, pu hsin ping hsieh tai

'Deceit' [#42], 'guile' [#43], and 'injury' [#44], 'conceit'[39] [#45],
'shamelessness' [#46], and 'non-embarrassment' [#47],
'restlessness' [#48] and 'mental fogginess' [#49],
'lack of faith' [#50] and 'laziness' [#51],

VERSE 14

[Vasubandhu's Sanskrit]

Vikṣepo'samprajanyam ca kaukṛtyam middhameva ca I
Vitarkaś-ca vīcāraś-ca-iti-upakleśa dvaye dvidhā II 14

[Robinson's Translation]

Distraction, wrong judgement, remorse, torpor,[40] Reflection and investigation are the sub-passions, two pairs in two ways.

[Paramārtha's Chinese Translation]

十九散亂。二十不了。二十一憂悔。二十二睡眠。二十三覺。二十四觀。

Shih-chiu san-luan. Erh-shih pu **liao**. *Erh-shih-yi yu hui. Erh-shih-erh shui-mien. Erh-shih-san chüeh. Erh-shi-ssu kuan.*

(19) distraction (*vikṣepa*), (20) misunderstanding (*āsamprajñā*), (21) remorse (*kaukṛtya*), (22) torpor, (23) awakening [!] (*vitarka*), (24) 'contemplative observation' [!] (*vicāra*)[41]

[Hsüan-tsang's Translation]

放逸及失念　　散亂不正知
不定謂悔眠　　尋伺二各二

Fang-yi chi shih-nien,　　*san-luan pu-cheng chih*
pu-ting wei hui mien,　　*hsün ssu erh ke erh*

'Carelessness'[42] [#52] and 'forgetfulness'[43] [#53],
'distraction'[44] [#54], 'lack of correct knowledge'[45] [#55].
The Indeterminate[46] are called 'remorse' [#56] (and) 'torpor' [#57],
'initial mental application' [#58] (and) '[sustained] discursive thought'[47] [#59];
(these) two (pairs)[48] are named in two (ways).

VERSE 15

[Vasubandhu's Sanskrit]

Pañcānām mūla-**vijñāne** yathā-pratyayam-udbhavaḥ I
Vijñānānām saha na vā taraṅgāṇām yathā jale II 15

[Robinson's Translation]

On the fundamental consciousness, the five consciousnesses originate according to conditioning factors,
Whether all together or otherwise, as the waves arise upon the water.

[Paramārtha's Chinese Translation]

五識（於等六意識及）本識（報識。於此三根中）隨因緣。或時俱起或次起。[...] 亦如浪同集一水。
Wu ***shih*** *(yü teng liu yi-shih chi) pen* ***shih*** *(pao-shih, yü tz'u san ken chung) sui yin-yüan. Hou shih chu ch'i. Hou tz'u ts'e ch'i* [...] *yi ju lang t'ung chi yi shui.*

The five **consciousnesses** (for the sixth, mano-vijñāna and) the fundamental **consciousness** (and the attachment consciousness [i.e., manas]. These three roots[49] [i.e., the ālaya-vijñāna, manas, and manovijñāna] follow from causes and conditions, sometimes arising together, other times arising separately [...] like many waves gathered together in one water.

[Hsüan-tsang's Translation]

衣止根本 識　　五識隨緣現
或俱或不俱　　如濤波依水

Yi chih ken pen ***shih****,*　　*wu* ***shih*** *sui yüan hsien*
huo chü huo pu chü,　　*ju t'ao-po yi shui*

Depending on and resting in the 'root' **consciousness**,[50]
the five **consciousnesses**[51] accord with the objective conditions that appear,[52]
sometimes [the five senses working] together, sometimes not together.[53]
Like waves depend on water [so do these five depend on the mūla-vijñāna].[54]

VERSE 16

[Vasubandhu's Sanskrit]

Mano-**vijñāna**-sambhūtiḥ sarvadā-asañjñikad-ṛte |
samāpatti-dvayān-mūrchanād-api acittakāt || 16

[Robinson's Translation]

There is co-existence of mental consciousness always except in non-ideation,
the two cessations, and torpor and fainting, where there is no awareness.

[Paramārtha's Chinese Translation]

此意識於何處不起 [...] 離無想定及無想天。熟眠不夢醉悶絕心暫死離。此六處餘處恆有。

*Tz'u yi-**shih** yü ho ch'u pu ch'i* [...] *Li wu hsiang ting chi wu hsiang t'ien. Shou mien pu meng, tsui men chüeh hsin chan szu li. Tz'u liu ch'u yü ch'u heng yu.*

Where does mano-**vijñāna** not arise? [...] It is separate from [1] [those who practice] asaṁjñi-samāpatti; and [2] [beings in the] asaṁjñi-heaven; [3] during the ripening of dreamless sleep; [4] drunken stupor; [5] when mind is cut off (*chüeh hsin, acitta*); and [6] the moment(s) before death.[55] These six are where [it doesn't arise]. Elsewhere it always exists.

[Hsüan-tsang's Translation]

意識常現起　　除生無想天
及無心二定　　睡眠與悶絕
Yi-shih ch'ang hsien ch'i, ch'u sheng wu hsiang t'ien
chi wu hsin erh ting, shui-mien yü men chüeh

Mano-vijñāna is always projecting and arising,
except [for] those born in the non-conceptual heavens [#77],
and [during] the two mindless (*acitta*; *wu-hsin*) *samāpattis* [#75, 76],[56]
[and also in] sleep and total unconsciousness.

VERSE 17

[Vasubandhu's Sanskrit]

Vijñāna-pariṇāmo'yam vikalpo yad-vikalpyate I
tena tan-nāsti tena-idam sarvam **vijñapti**-mātrakam II 17

[Robinson's Translation]

The transformation of consciousness is imagination. What is imagined
By it does not exist. Therefore everything is representation-only.

[Paramārtha's Chinese Translation]

如此識轉（不離兩義）一能分別。二所分別。所分別既無 [...] 以是義故唯識義得成。

Ju tz'u ***shih****-chüan (pu li liang yi). Yi neng fen-pieh. erh so-fen-pieh. So-fen-pieh chi wu* [...] *Yi-shih yi ku wei-****shih*** *yi te ch'eng.*

Like this, **consciousness** revolves. (It is not separate from the two 'principles,' namely) (1) the discriminator[57] and (2) the discriminated. The discriminated is already inexistent[58] [...] For this reason, the principle of **consciousness**-only is proven.

[Hsüan-tsang's Translation]

是諸識轉變　　分別所分別
由此彼皆無　　故一切唯識

Shih chu ***shih*** *chuan pien, fen-pieh so-fen-pieh*
*yu ts'u pi chieh wu,　　ku yi-ch'ieh wei-****shih***

These are the various **consciousnesses** [i.e., the eight consciousnesses]
whose alterity (*vijñāna-pariṇāmo* ; Ch.: *shih-chuan-pien*)
discriminates and is discriminated.
As this and that are entirely nonexistent,
therefore all is **Psycho-sophic** closure.[59]

VERSE 18

[Vasubandhu's Sanskrit]

Sarva-bījam hi **vijñānam** pariṇāmas-tathā tathā I
yāti-anyonya-vaśād yena vikalpaḥ sa sa jāyate II 18

[Robinson's Translation]

For consciousness is the seed of everything. Transformation in such and such ways
Proceeds through mutual influence, so that such and such imagination is born.

[Paramārtha's Chinese Translation]

一切法湩子識。如此如此造作迴轉。或於自於他。互相隨逐。起種種分別及所分別。

Yi-ch'ieh fa chung-tzu ***shih****. Ju tz'u ju tz'u chao tso hui chuan. Huo yü tzu yü t'a. Hu hsiang sui chu. Ch'i chung-chung fen-pieh chi so-fen-pieh.*

Consciousness is the seed for all dharmas. Like this, like this, constructing and revolving, sometimes into a self or into an other. By the reciprocal interacting [of self and other] there arises the proliferation of discriminations and discriminateds.

[Hsüan-tsang's Translation]

由一切種 識　　如是如是變
以展轉力故　　彼彼分別生

Yu yi-ch'ieh chung ***shih****, ju shih ju shih pien*
yi chan chuan li ku, pi pi fen-pieh sheng

Due to the all-seeds **consciousness**,
altering [now] like this [and now] like this,
[and] by the power of its sequential unfolding (*chuan-li*),
discriminating that from that arises.

VERSE 19

[Vasubandhu's Sanskrit]

Karmano vāsanā grāha-dvaya-vāsanayā saha I
kṣīṇe pūrva-vipāke 'nyad vipākam janayanti tat II 19

[Robinson's Translation]

The impressions from action, together with the impressions from the twofold grasping
When the former retributions are exhausted, produce other retributions.

[Paramārtha's Chinese Translation]

由二種宿業熏習及二種習氣。能為集諦。成立生死。

Yü erh chung su yeh hsün-hsi chi erh chung hsi-ch'i. Neng wei chu ti. Cheng li sheng szu.

Due to two types of latent karmic vāsanās and two types of [kleśic] vāsanās,[60] which become the 'collective truth',[61] establishing life and death.

[Hsüan-tsang's Translation]

由諸業習氣 二取習氣俱
前異熟既盡 復生餘異熟

Yu chu yeh hsi-ch'i, erh ch'ü hsi-ch'i chü
ch'ien yi shou chi chin, fu sheng yu yi shou

Due to the various karmic 'perfumings'[62]
'perfuming' both of the graspings[63] [i.e., the grasped and grasper],
[even as what has] previously matured is already exhausted,
again [they] give rise to further maturings.

VERSE 20

[Vasubandhu's Sanskrit]

Yena yena vikalpena yad yad vastu vikalpyate I
parikalpita-eva asau svabhāvo na sa vidyate II 20

[Robinson's Translation]

Whatever thing is imagined by whatever imagining
Is of an *imaginary* own-nature, and non-existent.

[Paramārtha's Chinese Translation]

如是如是分別。若分別如是如是類。此類類名分別性 [...] 此所顯體實無。

Ju shih ju shih fen-pieh. Jo fen-pieh ju shih ju shih lei. tz'u lei-lei ming fen-pieh hsing [...] *tz'u so hsien t'i shih wu.*

Discriminating this from this, like discriminating this type from this type. These types are called the 'discrimination nature' [...] What is disclosed by this is that the essence (*t'i*) [of these things] is truly inexistent.[64]

[Hsüan-tsang's Translation]

由彼彼遍計　　遍計種種物
此遍計所執　　自性無所有

Yu pi pi pien-chi,　　*pien-chi chung chung wu*
ts'u pien-chi-so-chih,　　*tzu hsing wu so yu*

Due to that and that 'everywhere schema-tized',[65]
'everywhere schema-tizing' proliferates things.[66]
The self-nature (*svabhāva*) of this 'Everywhere schema-tizing what is grasped' (*parikalpita*),[67]
is nonexistent.

VERSE 21

[Vasubandhu's Sanskrit]

Paratantra-svabhāvas-tu vikalpaḥ pratyaya-udbhavaḥ I
niṣpannas-tasya pūrveṇa sadā rahitatā tu yā II 21

[Robinson's Translation]

The *relative* own-nature is an imagination arising out of conditioning factors.
The *absolute* is the latter when it is forever separated from the former.

[Paramārtha's Chinese Translation]

此分別者因他故起立名依他性。此前後兩性未曾相離。即是實實性。

Tz'u fen-pieh che yin t'a ku ch'i li ming yi t'a-hsing. tz'u ch'ien hou liang hsing wei tseng hsiang li. Chi-shih shih shih hsing.

Because these disciminations are caused to arise by [things] other [than themselves], the term 'dependent on others nature' is established. The former and latter natures are inseparable from each other. This precisely is the really real nature.[68]

[Hsüan-tsang's Translation]

依他起自性　　分別緣所生
圓成實於彼　　常遠離前性

Yi-t'a-ch'i tzu-hsing,　　*fen-pieh yüan so sheng*
yüan-ch'eng-shih yü pi,　　*ch'ang yüan li ch'ien hsing*

The 'Dependent on others to arise' self-nature (*paratantra-svabhāva*)[69]
is produced by discriminative conditions.
The 'Perfectly Accomplished Real [nature]'[70] is when that [i.e., the *pariniṣpanna in* the *paratantra*]
is permanently remote and detached from the previous [i.e., *parikalpita*] nature.

VERSE 22

[Vasubandhu's Sanskrit]

Ataḥ eva sa na-eva-anyo na-ananyaḥ paratantrataḥ ।
anityatā-ādi-vad vācyo na-adṛṣṭe asmin sa dṛśyate ॥ 22

[Robinson's Translation]

Thus it is neither other than nor not other than the relative.
It must be considered like impermanence, etc. When the one hasn't been perceived, the other isn't perceived.

[Paramārtha's Chinese Translation]

是故前性於後性不一不異 [...] 如無常 [...] 若不見分別性則不見依他性。

Shih ku ch'ien hsing yü hou hsing pu yi pu yi [...] *ju wu-ch'ang* [...] *ju pu chien fen-pieh-hsing tse pu chien yi-t'a-hsing.*

This is so because the former nature and the latter nature are neither the same nor different [...] like impermanence [...] If one doesn't see the discriminated nature then one doesn't see the dependent on other nature.[71]

[Hsüan-tsang's Translation]

故此與依他	非異非不異
如無常等性	非不見此彼
Ku ts'u yü yi-t'a,	*fei yi fei pu yi*
ju wu-ch'ang teng hsing,	*fei pu chien ts'u pi*

Therefore this [i.e. *parinispanna*] and 'Dependent on others' (*paratantra*) are neither different nor not different;
like impermanent (things), etc. and (their abstracted) nature (i.e., impermanency),[72]
it is not the case that you don't see[73] 'this' [i.e. *paratantra*] and yet can see 'that' [i.e. *parinispanna*].

VERSE 23

[Vasubandhu's Sanskrit]

Tri-vidhasya svabhāvasya tri-vidhām niḥsvabhāvatām I
sandhāya sarvadharmāṇām deśitā niḥsvabhāvatā II 23

[Robinson's Translation]

The no-own-nature of all the elements was only preached in connection with
The threefold no-own-nature of the threefold own-nature.

[Paramārtha's Chinese Translation]

如來衆生説法無性。亦有三種。

Ju-lai chung-sheng shuo fa wu-hsing. Yi yu san chung.

The Tathāgata taught the Dharma of no-nature to sentient beings. Moreover, there are three types.

[Hsüan-tsang's Translation]

即依此三性　　立彼三無性
故佛密義説　　一切法無性

Chi yi ts'u san hsing,　　*li pi san wu hsing*
ku fo mi yi shuo,　　*yi-ch'ieh fa wu hsing*

Always-already[74] dependendent on these three natures,
the three non- [self] natures are established.[75]
Thus Buddha's secret intention is to explain that[76]
all dharmas are without [self-] nature.

VERSE 24

[Vasubandhu's Sanskrit]

Prathamo lakṣaṇena-eva niḥsvabhāvo'paraḥ punaḥ I
nasvayam-bhāva etasya iti-apara niḥsvabhāvatā II 24

[Robinson's Translation]

The first is without own-nature by its very characteristic. The second
Is so because it does not exist by itself. The third is without own-nature.

[Paramārtha's Chinese Translation]

分別性名無相性。無體相故。依他性名無生性，體及因果無所有。
[...] 真實性名無性性。（無有性無無性）

Fen-pieh-hsing ming wu-hsiang hsing. Wu t'i hsiang ku. Yi-t'a-hsing ming wu-sheng hsing.T'i chi yin-kuo wu so yu. [...] *Chen-shih-hsing ming wu-hsing hsing.* (*Wu-yu-hsing wu wu-hsing*)

Discrimination nature is termed 'without-characteristics nature,' since it is characterized as having no essence.[77] The Dependent on other nature is termed 'non-arising nature.' Its essence is that cause and effect do not exist in it.[78] [...] The Truly Real nature is termed 'natureless nature.' It neither has nor does not have a nature.[79]

[Hsüan-tsang's Translation]

初即相無性　　次無自然性
後由遠離前　　所執我法性

Ch'u chi hsiang wu hsing, ts'u wu tzu-jan hsing
hou yu yüan li ch'ien, so chih wo fa hsing

[the three natures are considered non-natures because]
The first [i.e. *parikalpita*] is characterized precisely as not having [self-] nature.
The next [i.e. *paratantra*] is without a self-originating[80] nature.
The last [i.e. *parinispanna*], due to its remoteness and detachment from the previous one's [i.e. *parikalpita*]
attachment to the [self-]nature of *ātman* and *dharmas*.[81]

VERSE 25

[Vasubandhu's Sanskrit]

Dharmāṇām paramārthaś-ca sa yatas-tathatā-api saḥ I
sarva-kālam tathā-bhāvāt sa eva **vijñapti-mātratā** II 25

[Robinson's Translation]

Because it is the absoluteness of the elements and their suchness,
Because it is 'so' forever. It alone is perception-only-ness.

[Paramārtha's Chinese Translation]

是一切法真實 **[...]** 名常 **[...]** 明唯識義也。

Shih yi-ch'ieh fa chen-shih [...] *ming ch'ang* [...] *ming* **wei-shih** *yi yeh.*

It is the True Reality of all dharmas [...] termed 'eternal' [...] elucidating the meaning of **consciousness-only.**[82]

[Hsüan-tsang's Translation]

此諸法勝義	亦即是真如
常如其性故	即唯識實性
Ts'u chu fa sheng yi,	*yi chi shih chen-ju*
ch'ang ju ch'i hsing ku,	*chi* **wei-shih** *shih hsing*

Ultimately (*paramārtha*) the various dharmas
also are precisely 'truly-like [this]' (*tathatā*).[83]
Because their [(non-)self-] nature is always like [this]
their real nature[84] precisely is **Psychosophic closure**.

VERSE 26

[Vasubandhu's Sanskrit]

Yāvad **vijñapti-mātratve vijñānam** na-avatiṣṭhati |
grāha-dvayasya-anuśayas-tāvan-na vinivartate || 26

[Robinson's Translation]

So long as consciousness does not remain in the state of representation-only,
The residues of the twofold grasping will not cease to function.

[Paramārtha's Chinese Translation]

未住此唯識義者。二執隨眠所生眾惑不得滅離。

Wei chu tz'u ***wei-shih*** *yi che. Erh chih sui mien so-sheng chung huo pu te mieh li.*

[One is] not yet abiding in the meaning of **consciousness-only** [because] of the multitude of delusions produced by the proclivities of the two attachments [to self and dharmas] which one has not gotten rid of or away from.

[Hsüan-tsang's Translation]

乃至未起 識　　求住唯 識性
於二取隨眠　　猶未能伏滅

Nai chih wei ch'i ***shih****,*　　*ch'iu chu* ***wei-shih*** *hsing*
yü erh ch'ü sui-mien,　　*yu-wei neng fu mieh*

As long as there has not yet arisen a **consciousness**,[85]
seeking to abide in **Psychosophical-closure**-hood,
[there remain] proclivities (*anuśayas*) from the two attachments [to *ātman* and *dharmas*]
which means [one] has not yet been able to be suppress or destroy [them].[86]

VERSE 27

[Vasubandhu's Sanskrit]

Vijñapti-mātram-eva-idam-iti-api hi-upalambhataḥ ǀ
sthāpayan-agrataḥ kiṃ-cit tanmātre na-avatiṣṭhate ǁ 27

[Robinson's Translation]

Even in recognizing 'it is representation-only'
of whatever you make stop before you, you fail to remain in 'that only'.

[Paramārtha's Chinese Translation]

若謂但唯有識現前起。此執者。若未離此執。不得入唯識中。

Ju wei tan ***wei*** *yu* ***shih*** *hsien-ch'ien ch'i. Tz'u chih che. Ju wei li tz'u chih. Pu te ju* ***wei-shih*** *chung.*

If someone says: 'Whatever arises before me exists **only** in **consciousness**,' whoever holds (or is attached to) [such an idea] will not attain entry into **consciousness-only** until he lets go of this opinion.[87]

[Hsüan-tsang's Translation]

現前立少物 謂是唯識性
以有所得故 非實住唯識

Hsien ch'ien li shao wu, *wei shih* ***wei-shih*** *hsing*
yi yu so te ku, *fei shih chu* ***wei-shih***

If you set up before yourself some little thing,[88]
and say: "This is **Psychosophical Closure-hood**,"[89]
since [you are] taking 'something' to be attainable/attained
that is not really abiding in [seeing through] ***Psychosophic closure***.

VERSE 28

[Vasubandhu's Sanskrit]

Yadā tu-ālambanam jñānam na-eva-upalabhate tadā ǀ
sthito **vijñāna-mātratve** grāhya-abhāve tad-agrahāt ǁ 28

[Robinson's Translation]

But when consciousness no longer recognizes an object,
Then it rests in representation-only, because when there is nothing to grasp, there is no grasping.

[Paramārtha's Chinese Translation]

若智者。不更緣此境。二不顯現。是時行者名入唯識。**[...]** 是名無所得...

Ju chih che. Pu kung yüan tz'u ching. Erh pu hsien-hsien. Shih shih hsing che ming ju ***wei-shih****.* [...] *shih ming wu so te...*

If the knower doesn't directly apprehend the objective-condition (*ālambana*) of this perceptual-object, then neither of the two (i.e., the knower or the object) appears. At this moment the practitioner is said to have entered **consciousness-only.**[90] This is called 'Nothing is attained...'

[Hsüan-tsang's Translation]

若時於所緣　智都無所得
爾時住唯 識　離二取相故

Jo shih yü so yüan,　*chih tou wu so te*
erh shih chu ***wei-shih****,*　*li erh ch'ü hsiang ku*

If, at [some] moment, of objective conditions (ālambana)[91]
nothing whatever is attained/acquired by a cognition (*jñāna*),
you, at that moment, abide in '**consciousness-only**',
since you have detached from the characteristics of the two attachments.

VERSE 29

[Vasubandhu's Sanskrit]

Acitto'nupalambho'sau jñānam lokottaram ca tat I
āśrayasya parāvṛttir-dvidhā dauṣṭulya-hānitaḥ II 29

[Robinson's Translation]

It is without thought, without cognition, supramundane knowledge,
Revolution of the basis through elimination of the two kinds of denseness,

[Paramārtha's Chinese Translation]

...非心非境。是智名出世 [...] 亦名轉依麤重及執二俱盡故。

...fei hsin fei ching. Shih chih ming ch'u-shih [...] *Yi ming chuan-yi ts'u chung chi chih erh chü chin ku.*

...neither mind nor sense-object. This cognition is called supra-mundane. [...] Moreover, it's called 'overturning [the basis on which the ātma-dharma circuit] depends' (*āśraya-paravṛtti*) since the gross impediments and the two attachments are both utterly exhausted.

[Hsüan-tsang's Translation]

無得不思議　　是出世間智
捨二麤重故　　便證得轉依

Wu te pu-ssu-yi,　　*shih ch'u-shih chien chih*
she erh ch'u chung ku,　　*pien cheng te chuan-yi*

Non-acquirable,[92] non-conceptual
is cognition in the supra-mundane [realm].
Since [it] has neutralized the two crude barriers,[93]
[it] immediately realizes and attains 'overturning [the basis on which the ātma-dharma circuit] depends.'[94]

VERSE 30

[Vasubandhu's Sanskrit]

Sa eva-anāśravo dhātur-acintyaḥ kuśalo dhruvaḥ I
sukho vimukti-kāyo'sau dharmākhyo-'yaṃ mahā-muneḥ II 30

[Robinson's Translation]

It is the uncontaminated, inconceivable, good, immutable and blessed realm,
The Liberation body (i.e., Dharma) of the great sage.

[Paramārtha's Chinese Translation]

是名無流界。是名不可思惟。是名真實善。是名常住果。是名出世樂。是名解勝身。於三身中即法身。

Shih-ming wu-liu chieh. Shih-ming pu-k'e-ssu-wei. Shih-ming chen-shih shan. Shih-ming ch'ang-chu kuo. Shih-ming ch'u-shih le. Shih-ming chieh-sheng shen. Yü san shen chung chi fa-shen.

This is called 'the non-flowing realm' (*anāśrava-dhātu*); this is called 'the unthinkable' (*acintya*); this is called 'Truly Real goodness' (*kuśala*); this is called 'the eternally abiding fruit (*dhruva*)[95];' this is called 'supra-mundane happiness' (*sukha*); this is called 'liberation body' (*vimukti-kāya*); Among the three bodies, it is the Dharma-kāya.

[Hsüan-tsang's Translation]

此即無漏界	不思議善常
安樂解脫身	大牟尼名法
Ts'u chi wu-lou chieh,	*pu-ssu-yi shan ch'ang*
an-le chieh-t'uo-shen,	*ta mu-ni ming fa*

This precisely is the uncontaminated realm,[96]
non-conceptual,[97] advantageous, constant,
blissful,[98] the Liberation-body,[99]
[what the] Great (Śakya-) Muni [= Buddha] called Dharma.

Notes to *Triṃśikā*

1 The passages in parenthesis are explanatory phrases from the *Chuan-shih lun* that, while not directly from the *Triṃśikā*, offer some illumination into Paramārtha's interpretation.

2 執識 is sometimes also rendered 執持識, *chih-ch'ih-shih* (grasping-and-holding consciousness). *Ādāna* means to grasp or cling; *ādāna-vijñāna*, 'attachment consciousness,' is a common epithet for the 7th consciousness, i.e., manas.

3 Hsüan-tsang is overliteral in his translation of *vipāka*, rendering the 'vi-' as *yi* ("different"). This has already been noted by Sponberg in his dissertation on K'uei-chi, (see bibliography). "Differently maturing" implies the seeds (*bījās*) are maturing or coming to fruition at various/different times; in other words, present *effects* arise through latent causes. As will be stated presently, this describes the functioning of the ālaya-vijñāna.

4 The compound *ssu-liang* can mean 'thinking and deliberating' or simply 'thinking'. However, when taken as separate characters, *ssu* is used to translate *cetanā*, which can be rendered "volition" or "willing." This compound is used—rather ingeniously—by Hsüan-tsang to render *mananākhyaśca*, over which various translators are in some disagreement ("thinking," "always reflecting," "mentation"). It describes the functioning of Manas.

5 *Liao-pieh* and *shih* are both used by Hsüan-tsang as equivalents for *vijñapti*. The Sanskrit text uses the term *vijñaptir* only once in this line, which makes Hsüan-tsang's use of *shih* either redundant or problematic. Either it denotes, for a second time, *vijñaptir* or it is meant to qualify all three 'names' by implying the three types of 'consciousnesses' [and hence to be understood as vijñāna and not as vijñapti here] announced at the end of the previous verse, i.e., "differently maturing [-consciousness]," "willing and deliberating [-consciousness]," and "discriminating or discerning objects consciousness." Tat, in fact, reads it in precisely this way. However we choose to understand it here, it becomes clear that in both the Sanskrit and Hsüan-tsang's Chinese text, vijñapti ('making known,' discerning') is used to denote the function of the sixth consciousness (mano-vijñāna), with which it is specially connected in several verses of the *Triṃśikā*. It does not, at least in those verses, stand for the entire consciousness process, much less all of 'reality'. In verse 3 vijñapti will be mentioned in conjunction with the ālaya-vijñāna, but precisely in terms of the *lack* of discernment (*vijñapti*) in the ālaya-vijñāna.

6 Robinson's translation inadvertently omits *manaskāra*.

7 Kochumuttom offers the following paraphrase:

> ālaya-vijñāna (store-consciousness) is the individual unconscious, which carries within it the seeds of all past experiences. It has within itself the representations of consciousness of unknown objects (*upādi*, literally meaning 'what one grasps,' or 'clings to') and places (*sthāna*). It is invariably associated with the experiential categories such as touch (*sparśa*), attentiveness (*manaskāra*), knowledge (*vid* = awareness), conception (*sañjñā* = idea), volition (*cetanā*) and feeling (*vedanā* = sensation). None of these experiences at this stage is particularly pleasant (*sukha*) or unpleasant (*duḥkha*). Therefore, they are all equally indifferent (*asukha-aduḥkha* = *upekṣā*). The ālaya-vijñāna is not yet obscured by *āvaraṇas*, whether *kleśa-āvaraṇas* or *jñeya-āvaraṇas*, and therefore, is described as unobscured (*anivṛtam*). Nor can it be defined

as either good *(kuśala)* or as bad (*akuśala*), and, therefore, it is described as undefined (*avyākṛtam*). The ālaya-vijñāna, which is like a torrent of water (*srotasaugha-vat*), ceases to exist [!] only at the attainment of *arhattva*. (p.135f)

8 Diana Paul assumes that *hsiang* means *ākāra* in this verse, but it is unclear whether Paramārtha is thinking of *hsiang* as *lakṣaṇa* or *ākāra* or *nimitta* (it is used for all of them)—or perhaps none of the above—since there is nothing corresponding to it in the Sanskrit. Also note that Paramārtha has provided no equivalent for the *vijñapti* found in the Sanskrit text.

9 In his explanation, Paramārtha asks: If it cannot be discerned, how do we know it exists? His answer is, By inference from what it produces. One infers what is the case from its effects. The ālaya-vijñāna, he says, is not known itself; it is never an object of knowledge.

10 *Chih shou* literally means "attachment/grasping + feeling/receiving," hence appropriation of or through one's feelings. *Shou* when used in a technical sense is the equivalent for *vedanā*, the pain/pleasure principle. Hsüan-tsang is using *chih shou* to translate *upadhi*, 'what is appropriated'. *Upadhi* is suggestive of the ninth nidāna in the *pratītya-samutpāda* model, viz. *upādāna* which means 'appropriation'.

11 'Discerns' translates *liao* which is used here by Hsüan-tsang to translate *vijñapti.*

12 *She shou* literally means 'cut off or abandon feelings,' and here translates *upekṣā vedanā. Shou,* again, translates *vedanā. Upekṣā* means neutral or neutralized or equalized (in the sense of equalizing/neutralizing opposites). It is #28 on the Hundred Dharma list (see appendix).

The numbers in brackets following sensation, etc. are the traditional numbers assigned these dharmas on the standard list of 100 dharmas. Note that they don't always appear in the *Triṃśikā* or its translations in the same order as the standard list.

13 For *avyakṛtam* Robinson's manuscript has "undefiled" and "without covering"—both acceptable translations—crossed out with "pure" left in their place.

14 "Self-nature" is Paramārtha's addition.

In this verse Paramārtha uses 自性 *tzu-hsing* for svabhāva, although 'svabhāva' does not occur in the Sanskrit. In later verses, where svabhāva does appear in Sanskrit, Paramārtha uses several terms in Chinese, including 性 *hsing* and 體 *t'i* to render it.

However in this verse he omits *anivṛta*, non-covered.

15 *Nien-nien* can refer to moments or thought-instants. Though there is nothing corresponding in the Sanskrit, it is a useful embellishment.

16 *Wu chi*, lit. 'non-recording,' i.e., morally neutral. 'Non-covered' (*wu-fu*) means not obstructed or impeded by the two āvaraṇas, viz. cognitive obstruction and affective obstruction, *jñeyāvaraṇa* and *kleśāvaraṇa*, respectively.

17 Cf. #85 on the 100 dharma list, *pravṛtti. Pao-liu* may in part be a pun for *liu-chuan.*

18 Paramārtha neglects to mention explicitly that the ālaya-vijñāna actually ceases (*vyāvṛti*) on reaching Arhathood, though it is inferable in that the flow mentioned in v.4 ends here. He directly joins this passage to the wave metaphor, and claims

that

> the basic consciousness (*mūla-vijñāna*, which in Chinese becomes *pen-shih*, "original consciousness"—suggestive of "original enlightenment, original nature," etc.) is the [water] flow, the five dharmas [caittas?] are like the waves. UNTIL REACHING THE FRUIT OF ARHATHOOD, the flow and waves of dharmas seem to never cease. Hence it's called the "first [=primary] consciousness." [T.31.1587.62a12-13]

Diana Paul mispunctuates, and hence misinterprets the passage as a denial of the cessation of the ālaya-vijñāna. Cf. Paul, p. 155, though there is enough ambiguity in Paramārtha's phrasing to open the door to her reading.

19 This might also be read (in concert with both Chinese grammar and Yogācāra doctrine) 'it depends upon that (the ālaya-vijñāna) or turns around [and depends upon] objective conditions'.

20 *Ssu-liang* can also be read as a compound meaning 'deliberation.'

The words *hsing hsiang* have no correlate in the Sanskrit text. *Hsing* (lit. 'nature') implies *svabhāva*; and *hsiang*, as noted above, implies *lakṣaṇa* or *nimitta*. This entire line is an attempt to render the word *mananātmakam*, which simply means 'essence of mentation'. The *Ch'eng wei-shih lun* makes clear that *hsing-hsiang* are deliberate insertions, meant to signify *svabhāva* and *ākāra*, respectively. The relevant passages are translated and discussed in Part V. Nonetheless, here I have translated Hsüan-tsang's phrase, bringing it in line with the sense of the Sanskrit, as "its nature is characterized as 'willing and deliberating'."

21 Paramārtha uses *huo* (delusion) for *kleśa*.

22 He glosses *ātma-moha* (self-conceptual-confusion) by substituting 'ignorance' (*avidyā*), which suggests that for him, the primary 'ignorance' that Buddhism addresses is precisely the confusion about 'self'.

Both Paramārtha and Hsüan-tsang reverse *ātma-moha* and *ātma-dṛṣṭi* from the Sanskrit order. Hsüan-tsang begins the next verse with 'covered' and 'non-recording,' instead of including that in this verse.

23 This line is unclear in both the Sanskrit and Hsüan-tsang's version; Paramārtha simply omits it. In Hsüan-tsang's Chinese this line literally reads: 'follows (or accords with) where born, where bound' or 'follows (or accords with) what is born, what is bound'. *So* can be understood as 'place' (which is what the Sanskrit intends) or as signaling the passive case.

Kochumuttom offers:

> "...touch (*sparśa*), attentiveness (*manaskāra*), knowledge (*vit*), conceptions (*sañjñā*) and volition (*cetanā*). These associates are of the same nature as the region (*dhātu-bhūmi*) in which one is born (*yatrajas-tan-maya*)." (p.137)

Since the term *dhātu-bhūmi* does not occur in either Sanskrit or Chinese, relying on it to interpret this line is problematic. Kochumuttom relies on Sthiramati's commentary, which says: *Tan-mayair-iti yatra dhātau bhūmau vā jātas-tad-dhātukaiḥ tad-bhūmikair-eva ca samprayujyate, na-anya-dhātukair-anya-bhūmikair-vā*.

24 Here Paramārtha uses 轉 *chüan* for *pariṇāma*. Hsüan-tsang uses 變 *pien*. *Upalabdhi* of *viṣaya* = P. 似塵 *ssu-ch'en* (the appearance of dust); HT. 了境 *liao-ching* (discerning sense-objects).

25 The six 'dusts' are the six senses; the six 'appearances of dust' are the six types of sense realms.

26 *Liao* in this verse does **not** translate *vijñapti*. It translates *upalabdhi* (cognitively apprehending), showing that for Hsüan-tsang *vijñapti* was not only interchangeable with *vijñāna*, but with *upalabdhi* as well. Vijñapti thus denotes cognitive, discriminative discernments. The number 'six' refers to the six categories listed in the next verse.

27 Paramārtha omits the 'Always-active' (General) and 'Specific' categories here, though he mentions the General in the next verse. The classic Yogācāra list of Kuśala Dharmas includes eleven, not ten items (see appendix). Vaibhāṣika Abhidharma has an Akuśala category in its Dharma list, but the Yogācāra list does not. Hsüan-tsang includes *aniyata* (indeterminate) in this verse, but that category is not listed in the Sanskrit until later.

28 *Hsiang ying* ('mutually interact') has no counterpart in Sanskrit, and is Hsüan-tsang's gloss for the fact that in mano-vijñāna all three vedanās are operating.

29 Paramārtha uses *tsui-ts'u* (literally 'most crude or coarse'] for what is usually labeled 'general' (*samanya*). By this he no doubt intends 'most primitive, most basic,' but *ts'u* implies a negative valuation, with a sense of vulgarity.

30 *So-yüan-shih*, lit. 'objective-conditions affairs'. Usually *so-yüan* translates *ālambana* (the objective-pole of a cognition), but there seems to be nothing in the Sanskrit that corresponds to this line by Hsüan-tsang. Its meaning possibly supplements the gloss at the end of the previous verse. While all six categories associated with mano-vijñāna interact with the three vedanās, the actual province of each sense, as experienced through mano-vijñāna, is distinct. Hence 'memory' of a sound is different from 'memory' of a smell, and so on. This means that although the senses all share a common structure, namely the classification of 'sensation, etc.' into pain, pleasure, or neutral, the cognitive objects of each sense remains distinct. In other words, Hsüan-tsang's glosses seem to imply a kind of 'form/content' distinction *vis-à-vis* the six senses ('mind' [*mano-*] being the sixth sense), such that their 'form' is the vedanā structure while their contents are the discrete domains of each sense.

31 Possibly a corrupt substitution for the similar 倚 *yi*, reliability.

32 See previous note.

33 I.e., #22, 23, 24. The Sanskrit does not call these the three "roots"; this is a gloss by Hsüan-tsang which reflects Vasubandhu's categorization. 'Lack of greed,' 'lack of hatred' and 'lack of delusion or misconception' are called 'the three roots' because (a) greed, hatred and delusion/misconception are the three root *āśravas*, or root mental problems according to all Buddhist schools, and (b) #22-24 are their 'antidotes' or 'counter-agents' (*pratipakṣa*), i.e., the means by which the root problems are corrected or eliminated. The notion of 'antidote' is crucial for the Yogācāra project, and forms a fundamental theme of the seminal text *Madhyānta-vibhāga*. However, cf. Vasubandhu's *Pañcaskandhaka-prakaraṇa*, where he says that 'carefulness' (#27) alone is the root antidote (English translation in Anacker's *Seven Works of Vasubandhu*, p.67).

Notice also that the traditional terms for these three root āśravas, viz. *rāga*, *dveṣa*, *moha*, are somewhat altered in the 100 dharma list of kleśas as *rāga* (#30), *pratigha* (#31) and *mūḍhi* (#32), while the terms *dveṣa* and *moha* are preserved in their negated forms (i.e., *a-dveṣa*, *a-moha*) as #23-24. The negative form for *rāga* is given as *alobha* (#22). See appendix.

34 Hsüan-tsang translates *vīrya* (vigor) with *ch'in* (diligence, industriousness). This is not the term used for *vīrya* in the standard 100 dharma list, though Hsüan-tsang already used *ch'in* for *vīrya* in his translation of the *Abhidharmakośa*. Cf. the 75 dharma list, #24.

35 Paramārtha does not enumerate the five views in his text, but a standard version of the list includes: (1) view of self (*ātma-dṛṣṭi*); (2) extremist views of eternalism or annihilationalism; (3) the view that nothing is real or nothing exists; (4) mistaking the bad or disadvantageous for the good or advantageous; and (5) misapplied *śīla*.

36 Hsüan-tsang has reversed the order of 'perspectives' and 'doubts' from the Sanskrit. The 100 dharma list follows Hsüan-tsang's order. Also, the adjective 'wrong' preceding 'perspectives' is Hsüan-tsang's gloss; however, it is implicit in Vasubandhu's text. Whether Yogācāra, like Mādhyamika, considers all *dṛṣṭi* ('perspectives,' 'theories,' 'ways of seeing') to be 'wrong,' or whether it allows for a 'correct' *dṛṣṭi* is explored elsewhere.

Note also that Hsüan-tsang has included the end of the Sanskrit v.11 in his v.12, while the last term of the Sanskrit v.12 (*māya*) begins Hsüan-tsang's v.13. This allows v.11 to be entirely devoted to Kuśala dharmas and v.12 to begin the Kleśa dharmas.

37 On 猗 *yi* as a substitute for 倚 *yi* see above.

38 An odd translation for 'restlessness.'

39 Hsüan-tsang has reversed the order of 'injury' and 'conceit' from the Sanskrit. The 100 dharma list follows his order.

40 Robinson's ms. indicates he was considering changing his translation of *anapatrāpya* in v.13, since in v.14 he wanted to use 'torpor' for *middha*. Since he did not indicate, at least on the copy I have, what his alternate translation of the latter would be, I have left it as it appears in his text.

41 The terms Paramārtha uses for *vitarka* (initial application of attention to an object in meditation) and *vicāra* (continued meditative attention to that object) are unusual in that Buddhists generally use these Chinese terms for other things. For *vitarka* he uses *chüeh*, which means 'awakening' and is usually used by Paramārtha and others for Awakening or Enlightenment. *Kuan*, which he is here using for *vicāra*, commonly renders *vipaśyanā* or other types of meditative contemplation (originally used in a related sense in *Tao te ching* ch. 1, 16, etc.).

42 May also be rendered 'negligence, indulgence'. Hsüan-tsang begins v.14 with the end of the Sanskrit v.13.

43 The Chinese words for 'forgetfulness' literally mean 'losing memory'. *Nien*, here denoting 'memory,' also carries the connotations of the other Sanskrit term it translates here, i.e., *smṛti*, which in a Buddhist context can mean 'mindfulness' or 'concentration/recollection,' as well as 'memory'. It also came to denote (1) visualizing or worshipping a Buddha or Bodhisattva, and (2) chanting Buddha's name (*nien-fo*) in Pure Land practice (ex., *Namu A-mi-t'o Fo*; in Japanese, *Namu Amida Butsu*). Hence to a Chinese reader *shih-nien* might imply not just loss of memory, but losing concentration, or the inability to retain sufficient mental presence (= memory and/or meditative recollection) to perform Buddhist practice.

44 Lit. 'dispersal and confusion,' i.e., the destruction of concentration.

45 I have translated the Chinese literally. *Pu-cheng-chih* can also be read as 'non-discernment' or 'no correct knowledge'. In his *Pañcaskandhaka-prakaraṇa* Vasubandhu defines *asaṃprajanya* thus: "It is a judgement connected with afflictions [*kleśa*], by which there is entry into not knowing what has been done by body, voice, or manas." (Anacker's translation, p.70, my interpolation)

46 Indeterminate means karmically neutral, i.e., neither advantageous (*kuśala*) nor disadvantageous (*akuśala* or *kleśa*) in and of themselves; rather their karmic value must be judged contextually, or in other words, by things or situations other than themselves.

47 *Vitarka* and *vicāra* are already important terms in the earliest Buddhist texts, and receive special attention in the first of the Pāli Abhidhamma texts, the *Dhammasaṅgaṇī*. They are the means by which one begins to understand the constitution of experience within the temporal flow, or put in Western terms, they are the opening moments of reflective thinking. *Vitarka* is how one initially pays attention to something one wishes to analyze, and *vicāra* is engaging in discursive analysis.

48 The two pairs are 'remorse and torpor' and '*vitarka* and *vicāra*'. This line means that these two pairs can be either kleśic or kuśala, hence two pairs in two ways.

49 Paramārtha uses *ken* (root) for the three main consciousnesses. *Ken* usually translates *indriya*, sense-organ, or more literally '(sensory) capacity.'

50 *Mūla-vijñāna*; Ch.: *ken-pen-shih*, a synonym for the ālaya-vijñāna. This model of a root or fundamental consciousness underlying and projecting the conventional sensorium is possibly the closest parallel to the Sāṃkhya theory of the higher Puruṣa and Prakṛti projecting the conventional realm of the *indriyas*, *tanmātras*, etc. in their model of twenty-five *tattvas*. Judging by Hsüan-tsang's account of his stay in India, the most significant and heated debates between Buddhists and Hindus at that time were between Yogācāra and Sāṃkhya. He recounts some of his own debate victories, and the issues that he raises are directly related to the Yogācārin attempts to distance themselves from the Sāṃkhyan doctrine. Dharmapāla is known to have written several disparaging tracts against Sāṃkhya, only a portion of which still survive. Cf. Honda, Megumu, "Dharmapāla's Report on Sāṃkhya", *IBK*, 17, no.1, 1968-69, pp.445-440 (1-6). Though his translations are often questionable, the original Chinese passages are included for easy comparison. He lists as the four extant works of Dharmapāla, all which survive only in Chinese: (1) T.1571.30 a gloss on the second half of Āryadeva's *Catuḥśataka*, translated by Hsüan-tsang ; (2) T.1585.31 his comm. on the *Triṃśikā*, i.e., the *Ch'eng Wei-shih lun* 'translated' by Hsüan-tsang (!); (3) T.1591.31 a gloss on the *Viṃśatika*, translated by I-ching; (4) T.1625.31 gloss on Dignāga's *Ālambanaparīkṣā*, translated by I-ching.

51 I.e., the five sensory consciousnesses, viz. seeing, hearing, smelling, tasting, touching. Generally Buddhists divide 'sensation' into three parts, consisting of the sense organ, the sense object and the consciousness which links them, or more accurately, the consciousness which arises as a result of the contact between organ and object. All three are necessary conditions for a sensation to arise. Adding mind (manas) as the sixth sense organ, along with dharmas (mental objects, thoughts, cogitations, 'experiential factors') and mano-vijñāna (thinking, cogitation) as the consciousness which links manas to dharmas, the six senses are described as the 'eighteen [experiential] elements' (*dhātu*).

Yogācāra disrupts this model by separating the sixth level from the five senses level, setting mano-vijñāna up as something akin to a cross between an empirical ego and an Aristotelian 'common sense' (i.e., that which organizes the disparate sense fields into a 'sense' of commonality, or in other words, what makes an 'object' of seeing, hearing and touching, for instance, though sensed independently by each of those senses, seem to be one and the same object)—thus substituting mano-vijñāna for what traditionally had been the function of manas—and completely reformulating the role and function of manas, opening entirely new dimensions for Buddhist deep-level psychology and philosophy. The addition of the ālaya-vijñāna to this scheme is, of course, their most famous innovation.

52 *Yathā-pratyayam-udbhavaḥ*, 'as the conditions [through which] things arise;' Ch: *sui-yüan-hsien*. *Hsien* is often translated as 'manifesting' or 'showing,' but I would argue that in many Buddhist texts, especially those with strong Yogācāra backgrounds, it is most properly translated as '[mental] projection.' Here I have translated it neutrally as 'appear.'

53 How senses include or exclude the other senses was, for various reasons, an important issue in Abhidharmic and subsequently Yogācāric thought. Cf. e.g., the section on *apratisaṃkhyānirodha* in Skandhila's *Abhidharmāvatāraśāstra* [ch. VIII; translated into French by Marcel Van Velthem as *Le Traité de la Descente dans la Profonde Loi de l'Arhat Skandhila* (Louvain: Institut Orientaliste de Louvain) 1977, p. 78. He also includes the Tibetan and Chinese texts in the back]. Also, cf. *Abhidharmakośa* I.45 and ff. See also the following note.

54 Paramārtha emphasizes the unity of the water, while Vasubandhu and Hsüan-tsang focus on the *dependence* of the distinct senses (or waves) on the mūla-vijñāna (or water). This will be discussed more fully in the analysis following the translation.

55 This is purely Paramārtha's addition; nothing in Vasubandhu or Hsüan-tsang corresponds to it.

56 The two *samāpattis*, especially *nirodha-samāpatti*, have been discussed in great detail in an earlier chapter.

57 Paramārtha uses *fen-pieh* to indicate the 'discriminator' although *fen-pieh* only means 'discrimination.' Following his usage elsewhere in the text, he could have used *neng-fen-pieh* to indicate 'discriminator. The second term in the pair listed in this verse, *so-fen-pieh*, does mean 'what is discriminated.' The Sanskrit says: *vikalpo yad-vikalpyate*, which literally means 'discrimination and what is discrimination,' so Paramārtha's translation is literally correct. Hsüan-tsang follows Paramārtha and renders the terms as *fen-pieh* and *so-fen-pieh*, respectively. In the *Chuan-shih lun* Paramārtha uses *fen-pieh* in both senses, as 'discrimination' and as 'discriminator.' This opens interesting interpretive possibilities for his use of *fen-pieh-hsing* 'discrimination nature' *or* 'discriminator nature' as a synonym for *parikalpita-svabhāva*.

58 Paramārtha adds: "The discriminator, too, is inexistent. If there is no object which can be grasped, an arising of consciousness does not obtain." 能分別亦無。無境可取識不得生。 This statement clearly demonstrates that even for Paramārtha Yogācāra does not entail idealism, since consciousness arises dependent on objects, *not* the other way around. This also shows that, despite Diana Paul's claims to the contrary, Paramārtha exactly follows Sthiramati's outlook.

59 'Psychosophic closure' is my translation of Vijñapti-mātra.

My translation of Hsüan-tsang here accords well with Robinson's translation of the Sanskrit. Other translators, such as Anacker and Kochumuttom, seem to follow Sthiramati's interpretation of this verse, but Hsüan-tsang appears to be reading this differently. See Sponberg's *K'uei-chi...*, p.98 and p.185 n. 75. See also Vallée-Poussin's *Vijñapti-mātratā-siddhi*, p.46. The meaning(s) of this verse are analyzed in Part V.

60 In Chinese Paramārtha uses the two common renditions of *vāsanā*—*hsün-hsi* and *hsi-ch'i*—as if they denoted different terms, which they do not: (1) latent karmic vāsanās (*hsün-hsi*) and (2) [kleśic] vāsanās (*hsi-ch'i*). He also clearly applies *dvaya* ('two-fold') to both types of vāsanā, instead of only the second. Paramārtha's ensuing discussion of these two sets of pairs is complex and one of the more important sections of the *Chuan-shih lun* for understanding his philosophy. He tries to explain this verse using a concatenation of oppositions based on many of the categories introduced so far together with a couple of new ones, including *saṃvṛti-* and *paramārtha-satyas*, *neng* and *so*, discriminative nature and dependent on others nature, *kleśas*, *vāsanās*, *vāsanās* from prior karma and attachment to the images of *vāsanās* from prior karma, sense-objects and consciousness, etc. For instance, the *vāsanās* of prior karma are what is discriminated, hence associated with sense-objects and the 'discrimination nature' (i.e., parikalpita-svabhāva), while *attachment* to the *vāsanās* of prior karma is the discriminator, equated with consciousness and the other-dependent nature (since it depends on the previous nature). Basically Paramārtha asserts that kleśas projecting past impressions are the objects we attach to. There is some room for confusion in his account, however. For instance, as noted previously, he equates the bare term *fen-pieh* (discrimination) with the 'one who discriminates' or 'discriminator.' Now while 'what is discriminated' should be dependent on the act of discrimination that creates them *as* discriminated cognitive or sensory objects, Paramārtha here reverses the order of dependence, equating attachment to one's projection of prior impressions with consciousness and paratantra, while making these latter equations dependent on what is discriminated. Clearly attachment to impressions would depend on there being impressions to which one may attach, but to make the discriminator and consciousness dependent on the discriminated and sense-objects is to argue in a circle, in a chicken-and-egg manner. Looked at from another perspective—possibly one closer to Paramārtha's own thinking—the key identification in all this is consciousness with attachment, since the role of consciousness gets focused on whether one should or shouldn't attach to one's own impressions.

61 *Chi-ti* (collected truth) usually stands for the second of the four noble truths, *samudaya*, the truth of the cause of suffering, but Paramārtha's use here and in his comments suggests it (also?) implies *saṃvṛti* or *vyvahāra-satya*, i.e., truth reached by consensus or communally (俗諦). He explicitly contrasts *chi-ti* with *chen-ti* 真諦, which is a standard Chinese rendition of *paramārtha-satya*.

62 'Perfumings,' or *vāsanā*, evokes an image of a cloth that has absorbed the smell of a perfume or odor that it has been in proximity with, such that the cloth now gives the appearance that this aroma is intrinsic or an inherent characteristic of the cloth, when the aroma is only an acquired characteristic from which the cloth can be purified. In karmic theory, *vāsanā* are the 'habit energies' planted and carried in the ālaya-vijñāna, signifying karmic dispositions acquired through experience.

63 The 'two attachments' or 'two graspings' are (1) grasper (*grāhaka*) and (2) grasped (*grāhya*), Vasubandhu's favorite terms for subject-object, i.e., the relation between an appropriator and his appropriation (*upādāna*). What is key is that it is not the subjective and objective poles of a cognition that are being challenged, but rather the *appropriational intent* that circulates between them, i.e., the intention or karmic intent that binds one to the other through appropriational desire.

64 Paramārtha interprets *parikalpita-svabhāva* as if it were *vikalpa-svabhāva*. Discrimination-nature discriminates one thing from another, then divides them up into types. In other words, for Paramārtha, the sheer act of making distinctions is sufficient to render parikalpa a problem. By Yogācāra standards, that sort of analysis is somewhat unsophisticated.

65 *Pien-chi* is Hsüan-tsang's translation for both *vikalpena* and *vikalpyate* (what is discriminated and what discriminates). *Vikalpa* (discrimination is related to other terms derived from √*kḷp*—e.g., *kalpanā* ('imagination,' 'mental construction'), *saṃkalpa* ('together imagined,' 'imagined conglomerate'), *vikalpa* ('discrimi-nation,' 'making false distinctions'), and *parikalpita*.

66 'Things' in Chinese is *wu* 物. This is Hsüan-tsang's translation for *vastu*. There are many terms in Sanskrit for components and factors in perception and cognition, most of which have no direct correlate in Western theories, and hence are both hard to translate and to pin down denotatively. Determining their precise meaning becomes more difficult as one scans the various usages these terms receive in different texts, and it is not at all certain that any one definitive meaning can be asserted as adequate or representative for all the texts. In the *Triṃśikā* so far we have encountered at least three terms which can be rendered in a general sense as 'cognitive object,' viz. *viṣaya*, *ālambana*, and now *vastu*.

Some texts, such as the *Laṅkāvatāra-sūtra*, seem to treat *vastu* as a quasi-mysterious term, signifying those 'objects' which remain outside the closure of cognitive misperception, and hence are the 'objective' ground of object-experience, though directly cognizable only by one who is Awakened. Hence in Chinese translations of the *Laṅkāvatāra*, *vastu* was rendered by *pen-yu* 本有 'original existents,' *miao-wu* 妙無 'wondrous-mysterious thing,' etc.

It is unclear from Vasubandhu's verse whether he means that *vastu* is nothing but the consequence of 'imaginative-rationalizing construction' (*parikalpita*) or whether imaginative construction is 'superimposed' upon actual *vastus* . Different traditions have used this ambiguity to import their own answers. For instance, the Vedāntic school of Hinduism opted, in part, for the latter interpretation, generating a theory of *māyā* and 'superimposition' (*adhyāsā*) from it; however, they displaced *vastu* as the actual existent upon which superimposition imposes itself, instead asserting that the 'real existent' is Brahman.

67 This is the 'long-form' of parikalpita. Literally it reads: *pien* (everywhere, universally, pervasive) + *chi* (calculating, scheming, planning) + *so* ('what is..' [or passive case]) + *chih* (attachment, seizing, grasping). Hence 'everywhere schema-tizing that to which one is attached,' or 'being attached to what is everywhere schema-tized. *Chih*, which literally means to seize or hold on to something, also is used by Hsüan-tsang to signify an opinion, i.e., a position or claim that someone "holds." This implicitly reinforces the affinity between attachment and *dṛṣṭi*, the tenacious clinging to theory.

68 For Paramārtha *pariniṣpanna* marks the inseparability of *parikalpa* and *paratantra*.

For Vasubandhu and Hsüan-tsang, however, *pariniṣpanna* signifies the absence of *parikalpita* in *paratantra*.

69 The 'long-form' for *paratantra-svabhāva*.

70 I.e., *pariniṣpanna*. The Chinese literally reads: *yüan* (round, complete, entire, perfect [*yüan* is a euphemism for synthetic totality, and hence connotes 'what has been perfected, unified']) + *ch'eng* (to complete, accomplish, to perfect [this is the same *ch'eng* used in the title *Ch'eng wei-shih lun*]) + *shih* (real, solid, full). Hence, 'perfectly accomplished realness' or 'what is really there for those who are perfectly accomplished.'

Notice this 'real' nature is not a separate, independent 'higher' nature, but rather the 'accomplished' or perfectly cognized aspect of the paratantra, or as Vasubandhu puts it, the absence (*rahitatā*) of parikalpita in paratantra. Cf. Lusthaus, "Returning to the Sources" in Hubbard and Swanson, eds., *Pruning the Bodhi Tree*.

71 While for Vasubandhu and Hsüan-tsang the subject of this verse is the lack of identity or difference between paratantra and *pariniṣpanna*, Paramārtha takes it to be maintaining the non-difference of *parikalpita* from paratantra. This has the effect of privileging *pariniṣpanna*, keeping it aloof from the limitations of the first two svabhāvas. The Sanskrit explicitly names *paratantra* but refers to the remaining nature indirectly, implying the subject of the verse is the last mentioned subject of the previous verse, which was *pariniṣpanna*.

72 The Sanskrit defers to a stock argument, which Hsüan-tsang barely sketches out. The term *anityatā* (impermanency) is the principle of impermanence, an abstraction drawn from observing particular impermanent items. The stock question was: What is the relation between impermanent (things) (*anitya*) and impermanency (*anitya-tā*)? Since the latter is an abstraction from the former, they are neither identical nor different. *Hsing* (nature) renders the -*tā* suffix, which in Sanskrit signifies an abstract noun (e.g., *śūnya* 'empty' -> *śūnya-tā* 'emptiness'). So the Chinese seems to be saying: This is like *anitya*, *śūnya*, and so on, being treated abstractly with a -*tā* suffix, i.e., principial abstractions drawn from particulars. An important Yogācāra text, to which Vasubandhu wrote a commentary, deals with this topic: *Dharma-dharmatā-vibhāṅga*.

73 "See" (*chien*) is dṛṣṭi, which though literally meaning 'to see,' also implies 'point-of-view,' 'perspective,' 'way of seeing,' '*theoria.*' The point of the verse is that pariniṣpanna cannot be 'seen' without first 'seeing' paratantra. This is reminiscent of the famous line in Nāgārjuna's *Madhyamaka-kārikās* that without vyavahāra†one cannot learn about paramārtha, and without understanding paramārtha one cannot attain nirvana (*MMK* 24:10).

74 'Always-already' is my translation of chi 即. *Chi* is a most important term, being the strongest copula available in Chinese. Usually translated as 'precisely,' '(x) exactly is...,' etc., it seems that the term 'always-already'—particularly with the metaphysical and demetaphysicalizing connotations that phrase has received from Husserl, Heidegger (*immer schon*) and Derrida (*toujours déjà*)—may be, in certain contexts, the most appropriate modern translation. *Chi* is sometimes used to signal 'identities' that become only apparent to the Awakened, such as the famous passage from the *Heart Sūtra*, "Form always-already is śūnyatā, śūnyatā always-already is form." Even in ordinary experience, when we 'wake up,' we sense that the world has been always already awake, even as we slept. See Takeuchi's

The Heart of Buddhism, pp. 77, 158, and passim, where he discusses *chi* (*soku* in Japanese), and amongst other things, compares it with Heidegger's *Ereignis* in the context of *pratītya-samutpāda.*

75 That non-svabhāvic nature is 'grounded' in svabhāvic nature is a typical claim from the Prajñāpāramitā literature. Cf. e.g., the *Diamond Sūtra*'s famous 'formal logic:' x is not-x, therefore it is x.

76 The phrase 'Buddha's secret meaning' is Hsüan-tsang's gloss, and has no corollary in the Sanskrit.

77 The distinction between *t'i* (essence) and *hsiang* (characteristics) plays a crucial role in the *Awakening of Faith*, a text closely associated with Paramārtha. As will be seen in a later chapter, this is a distinction that Hsüan-tsang also adopts when differentiating the *svabhāva* from the *ākāra* of the various consciousnesses. In this verse, however, Paramārtha is using two different terms to render *svabhāva*, *t'i* (essence) and *hsing* (nature), somewhat diffusing the original argument. Also, neither the Sanskrit nor Hsüan-tsang's rendition claim that paratantra is devoid of causality altogether, but only that it isn't *self* caused (since it signifies things being caused by others). In what sense is the discriminative nature understood to be without characteristics or formless? Its characteristics or forms (*hsiang*) are all without svabhāva. Why is this labeled 'without character nature' rather than 'without svabhāva characteristic'?

78 Paramārtha follows Sthiramati in labeling the first two natures *niḥlakṣaṇa* and *anutpāda.*

79 The *Triṃśikā* and Hsüan-tsang both state that pariniṣpanna is *niḥsvabhāva* (lacking in self-nature) because by definition it signifies the absence of parikalpita in paratantra, i.e., it essentially denotes an absence of svabhāva rather than the presence of something, and has no 'reality' apart from that emptying of paratantra. In other words, the third self-nature is defined precisely as the absence of self-nature. Paramārtha takes a different tact, arguing that it is the Truly Real Nature because it rejects the two extremes of (i) erroneous conceptions of svabhāvic existence (in self or dharmas) as well as (ii) the equally erroneous nihilistic alternative of their sheer nonexistence. Pariniṣpanna is the Yogācāric version of the notion of emptiness. Paramārtha is reciting standard Mahāyāna doctrine in which the claim that self and dharmas are both empty, such that neither self nor dharmas have self-nature, should not be misconstrued as a claim of utter nonexistence.

80 Hsüan-tsang has translated *svayam-bhāva* (roughly 'self existent,' or 'existent by/through itself') with *tzu-jan*, a term loaded with Taoist connotations. Literally meaning 'self-so' or 'self-ly,' it often is used to signify the spontaneous unique naturalness of each and every thing, especially as used by Lao tzu and Chuang tzu .

Kuo Hsiang's commentary on the *Chuang tzu* introduced a new conception of *tzu-jan.* For Kuo Hsiang, *tzu-jan* meant each and every thing always and everywhere self-creating themselves, again and again, without recourse to or dependence on anything outside themselves. Buddhists borrowed the term and used it to designate "self-caused" as opposed to "caused by something other." Judging by his use of the term here, in Hsüan-tsang's day Kuo Hsiang's interpretation must have been both general knowledge and the 'orthodox' meaning of *tzu-jan*, since only that notion of 'independently self-creating' would yield the appropriate connotation.

81 The second half of this verse is a gloss by Hsüan-tsang. It is indeed curious how

both Paramārtha and Hsüan-tsang deviate from the simplicity of the Sanskrit verse, especially concerning the third non-self-nature. The Sanskrit simply says of it: It is non-svabhāva-ness (*niḥsvabhāva-tā*).

82 While I translate *ch'ang* as 'always' for Hsüan-tsang's use of it in this verse, for Paramārtha, following his own comments, 'eternal' seems more appropriate. His full text reads: "Because it is taken to be apart from existence, it is termed 'eternal'."

83 *Tathatā*, usually translated as 'Suchness' or 'Thusness,' may also be rendered 'as-it-is-ness.' It signifies the Awakened (non-)perspective of directly perceiving *yathā-bhūtam*, things 'just as they have become,' without the cognitive misperceptions characteristic of unAwakened beings. The Chinese translation is *chen-ju*. *Chen* means 'true,' 'truly'; *ju* can signal a simile and mean 'like,' 'as,' or it can signify 'just so, just like this.' Hence 'true-like' or 'truly-just-like-this.' *Ju* is a soft way of indicating 'just like that, or just so,' softer than a copula. The stronger and more common term for 'just so' in Chinese would be *jan* 然. In the next line Hsüan-tsang uses *ju* to translate *tathā*.

84 Here Hsüan-tsang has not only used *hsing* (nature) to render the *-tā* suffix (in *vijñapti-mātra-tā*), he has offered the valorizing compound *shih-hsing* (real nature). The problem of rendering *-tā* with *hsing* is discussed in "Phenomena and Reality in Vijñaptimātra Thought (I): On the usages of the suffix 'tā' in Maitreya's Treatises" by Shoko Takeuchi, in *Buddhist Thought and Asian Civilization*, ed. Kawamura and Scott (CA: Dharma Publishing) 1977, pp. 254-267. This issue will be addressed below.

85 According to the *Ch'eng wei-shih lun* this is the stage of 'accumulating merit,' sometimes translated 'moral provisioning' (*saṃbhāra*).

86 The Chinese terms *fu* and *mieh* connote "suppress" (*prahāna*) and "cessation" (*nirodha*), respectively. These two terms are frequently distinguished in Abhidharmic literature: "suppression" meaning the temporary putting out of action of some defilement, and "cessation" meaning its ultimate, irreversible extirpation. This verse, which begins the description of how to attain Nirvāṇa, presents the first stage, the next gives the second stage, and so forth through five stages.

87 This is Paramārtha's most anti-idealist statement.

88 *Shao wu*, lit. 'small thing,' implies a small part of a larger matter to be understood, and so also means 'little understanding.' It is Hsüan-tsang's rather ingenious translation of *tanmātra*. *Tanmātra*, originally a Sāṃkhyan term denoting the basic, simple elements of the experiential realm, is composed of two parts: *tan* (= *tat*) 'that' + *mātra* 'only;' hence 'that-only,' or 'that which cannot be reduced further.'

89 Hsüan-tsang has *wei-shih-hsing*—implying *vijñapti-mātra-tā*—but the Sanskrit only has *vijñapti-mātra*.

90 See the discussion of this verse in the analysis following the translation.

91 *So-yüan* translates *ālambanam*. Sometimes translated 'objective-support,' it generally signifies the objective pole of a perceptual moment. Whether this objective pole derives from an actual object, is generated by consciousness, or arises through a combination and cooperation of object and consciousness, became a point of controversy between various Buddhist schools. Hsüan-tsang's text is open to any of these interpretations.

92 *Wu-te* can also be translated 'non-attainable' or 'nothing acquirable/attainable.'

Note that what was translated as 'nothing whatsoever is attained/acquired' in verse 28 was *tou wu so-te*, while what is here translated as 'non-acquirable' is *wu te.*

93 The 'two crude barriers'—namely *kleśāvaraṇa* (obstruction through conative, affective mental problems) and *jñeyāvaraṇa* (obstruction through cognitive, metaphysical and ontological assumptions and presuppositions)—are the basic obstacles or obstructions preventing one from clearly seeing the closure for what it is. The two crude barriers are also sometimes interpreted as the attributing of self-hood or svabhāva to self and dharmas.

94 *Āśraya-paravṛtti* in Chinese literally reads 'overturning dependence.' *Āśraya-parāvṛtti* might be translated 'reversal of the basis' or 'overturning the basis.' D.T. Suzuki understood this term to refer to shifting one's metaphysical dependence from *pravṛtti-vijñāna* (i.e., the six consciousnesses from *mano-vijñāna* down through the five senses) upward towards the *ālaya-vijñāna.* Whatever the merits of that interpretation might be for the *Laṅkāvatāra-sūtra*, in the case of the *Triṃśikā* the *paravṛtti* or 'turning around' seems to mean the transformation from *vijñāna* to *prajñā.* The most thorough examination of the history of the concept of *āśraya-paravṛtti* is Ronald Davidson, *Buddhist Systems of Transformation: āśraya-parivṛtti/-paravṛtti Among the Yogācāra*, unpub. Ph.D thesis, UC-Berkeley, 1985.

95 *Dhruva* means firm, unmovable, fixed, as well as permanent, and is associated with the fixed polar star. Whether *dhruva* here means, as Paramārtha takes it, the attainment of an eternal reward, or whether it might better be understood as an allusion to attaining the *vajrasamādhi* stage in the eighth bhūmi, which is also called *acala* (unmovable, steadfast, imperturbable), is an open question.

96 *Anāśravo-dhātur*, i.e., the *dhātu* (experiential realm) of *anāśrava* (uncontaminated, non-defiled). In other words, where one's perceptual field is no longer contaminated by karmic projections.

97 Hsüan-tsang uses *pu-ssu-yi*, which in the previous verse translated *acitta*, to here translate *acintyah.*

98 *An-le*—here translating *sukha* (pleasure or happiness)—is often used for the Sanskrit *ānanda* 'blissful,' and can also connote the Pure Land of Amitabha.

99 Notice that even at this, the highest stage, one is described as a *body.* The notion of 'body' in Buddhism, particularly its phenomenological implications, has barely been noticed as yet, most discussion of 'body' centering around the history of the tri-kāya doctrine. However from the Pāli *Brahmajāla sutta* onwards, Buddhism has consistently argued that the limits of the body are the limits of reality. The *vimukti-kāya* or 'Liberation-body' is that body which is liberated from the saṃsāric, psychosophical closure.

Comparative Analysis of the Three Translations

This section is not designed to offer a comprehensive analysis of the full *Triṃśikā*—the entire *Ch'eng wei-shih lun* attempts that, and that work is encyclopedic. Instead I intend to take note of some of the differences between the three renderings—Vasubandhu's original Sanskrit verses, Paramārtha's Chinese rendition, and Hsüan-tsang's Chinese version—while offering some comments about the basic ideas and terms found in the *Triṃśikā.* Even a cursory glance at the three versions, however, reveals important variations. Both Chinese versions add terms and concepts to Vasubandhu's terse verses. Since those additions reflect the interpretive orientations of the translators, they are useful markers for delineating differences between them that highlight some of the crucial details of those orientations.

While these three texts are the main focus, we are actually dealing with five translations: Aside from Vasubandhu's original Sanskrit text, there are two Chinese translations, and three English translations offered in the preceding section, one by Robinson and the other two by me. I deliberately chose to include Robinson's translation of the Sanskrit for two reasons. First, it has never been published and deserves an audience. Second, and more germane to the purpose of this section, it serves as a touchstone for my interpretations of the Chinese texts. While Robinson's translation is sound, there are many things that I would have rendered differently. And that is the point. My translation would have revealed how I interpret the Sanskrit text, which clearly would not be the only way that text could be read, since we already have several English translations available (e.g., Anacker, Kochumuttom, etc.), most of which are sound—but differ from each other on many points. My interpretative orientation undoubtedly already colors to some extent how I've rendered the Chinese versions. If one compares my rendition of Hsüan-tsang's text with those of Wei Tat[1] or Wing-tsit Chan,[2] or those two translations with each other, one will find many places where we all differ. The same can be said for my translation of Paramārtha's version compared to the one done by Diana Paul.[3] Were I to offer only my own version of all three texts, it would be hard for the reader—or even me—to be sure where interpretive bias has crept in and where the thought of the three writers has been most accurately portrayed. Robinson's translation, therefore, acts as a touchstone against which to compare my understanding of the many Yogācāric terms and concepts that are packed into these thirty terse verses.

It is also not the purpose of this section to provide a detailed philological comparison. The notes to the translations discuss some of those details.

Brief Historical Context

At the start of the sixth century an event occurred that set the tone for much of what happened over the next two centuries with Chinese Buddhism. Two Indian translators, Bodhiruci and Ratnamati, were brought together by Imperial command to collaborate on a translation of the *Daśabhūmi-sūtra śāstra*, Vasubandhu's *Commentary on the Ten Stages Sutra* (*Ti lun* 地論, for short, in Chinese). The *Daśabhūmi-sūtra* was influential not only in Yogācāra circles through Vasubandhu's commentary, but later was incorporated into the *Hua Yen Ching* (*Avataṁsaka sūtra*). Before long the two translators were feuding over interpretive issues. Bodhiruci—who went on to translate about forty additional texts, some of which became very influential—took a relatively orthodox approach to the text. Ratnamati, on the other hand, was attracted to tathāgatagarbha thought, and wanted to translate the *Ti lun* in conformity with his understanding. Their differences became irreconcilable. Ratnamati eventually participated in half a dozen other translation projects, while promoting his understanding of the *Ti lun*. According to traditional Chinese Buddhist history the two interpretations circulated and each acquired adherents. Though at best an oversimplification, these supposed two camps were called the Northern Ti Lun and Southern Ti Lun schools.

When Paramārtha arrived in China in the mid-sixth century, Yogācāra controversies ostensibly linked to the Ti Lun debates were already occupying Chinese Buddhists. His own brand of Yogācāra, which had some affinities with Ratnamati's tathāgatagarbha leanings, attracted admirers, who came to be called the *She lun* school, after the title of one of his most influential translations, the *She ta-sheng lun* 攝大乘論 (*Mahāyānasamgraha*).

Among the texts that Paramārtha translated was a partial version of Asaṅga's massive *Yogācārabhūmi* (T.1584) in ten fascicles. When Hsüan-tsang first expressed his wish to travel to India, the reason he gave was to procure the remainder of the *Yogācārabhūmi* so that he could translate it and put to rest the many doctrinal disputes that pervaded the Chinese Buddhism of his day. Like many of his contemporaries, he too had been an avid student of Paramārtha's translation of the *Abhidharmakośa*, and before leaving for India Hsüan-tsang had made a reputation for himself in Chang-an, the Chinese capital, by outsmarting even the most learned pundits with his knowledge of this text and its implications—to which he apparently developed an innovative interpretation. Hsüan-tsang also apparently admired *The Awakening of Faith*, a work purporting to be a translation by Paramārtha from a Sanskrit original written by Aśvaghoṣa. It would be fair to say, then, that early in life Hsüan-tsang must have been an admirer of Paramārtha's works.

That changed once he arrived in India. Before long he realized that Buddhism as it had developed in China did not accord with Buddhism as practiced in India. As he grew more familiar with the Sanskrit texts, studying with various teachers throughout India, including a couple of years at the famous Nālandā University—then the center of Buddhist learning in the world and, at that time, a Yogācāra stronghold—it dawned on him that the problems in Chinese Buddhism were due to causes much deeper than a missing section of the *Yogācārabhūmi.* There were profound problems with the earlier translations, translations which had become entrenched in Chinese Buddhism *as scripture.* Important turns in Buddhist doctrine had developed out of disputes about passages that had no Sanskrit counterpart, or that were misleading. When he returned to China he devoted himself to translation: retranslating works that Paramārtha and others had already made popular, as well as introducing new materials that, he hoped, would recontextualize Chinese Buddhism, bringing it closer to its Indian origins. For instance, he not only retranslated the *She lun* (T.1594), but also translated the commentaries on it by Vasubandhu (T.1597) and *Asvabhāva (T.1598), so that students of that text would have access to a more accurate rendition and thereby avoid misconceptions. Hsüan-tsang did not publicly attack his predecessors, but hoped that his translations would do the work for him. His attitude concerning his predecessors can be detected, however, in some of the commentaries of his disciple, K'uei-chi, who, in works like his commentary (T.1835) on Hsüan-tsang's rendition of the *Madhyānta-vibhāga* (T.1600), repeatedly points out errors in the earlier translations—usually accurately.

General Features of the Two Chinese Versions

Hsüan-tsang's version, while occasionally glossing some terms, stays fairly close to Vasubandhu. A few times the contents of a Sanskrit verse are carried over into contiguous verses in Chinese (these are documented in the notes to the translation), undoubtedly due more to the rigors of his trying to maintain the poetic meter of five-character semi-verses than to any semantic considerations.

The same cannot be said for Paramārtha's rendition. The verses of the *Triṃśikā* are embedded within the *Chuan-shih lun* in such a way that they are not recognizable as either verses or as imports from another text. The pieces of the *Triṃśikā,* though they appear in the correct sequence, are broken up and seamlessly interspersed within the full text, as if the *Chuan-shih lun* were itself a single integral text, not a root text encased in a commentary. When Paul translated the text, she attempted to separate the content of the original *Triṃśikā* from the material provided by Paramārtha, and, as a comparison of my rendition with hers will show, she was sometimes unsuccessful. Determining where Paramārtha stops and Vasubandhu begins in the *Chuan-shih lun* is complicated by the fact that the original verses often are broken up, a

Vasubandhu phrase used as part of one sentence, and the next phrase of the verse, several sentences later, used as part of that other sentence. In my translation I marked these with ellipses inside square brackets. What occurs in these ellipses may be a short gloss, or an extended discussion drawing on terms or concepts not found in the *Triṃśikā*. I presented the extracted portions attributable directly to the *Triṃśikā*, not the material it is encased in (with a few exceptions that appeared in parentheses).

Analysis of the Verses

The thirty verses of the *Triṃśikā* can be grouped as follows:

(1) **Verse 1**

Statement of the basic thesis, viz. that what we experience as self and other, me and things, subjective and objective cognitive vectors (*ātman* and *dharmā*), etc., are actually linguistic displacements (*upacāra*) produced by a threefold alteration (*pariṇāma*) of consciousness (*vijñāna*). The Yogācāra theory of Alterity.

(2) **Verses 2-16**

Abhidharmic discussion of the Eight Consciousnesses

(2a) **Verses 2-4**[4]

The ālaya-vijñāna

(2b) **Verses 5-7**

Manas

(2c) **Verses 8-16**

Mano-vijñāna and the pravṛtti-vijñānas

(2c.1) **Verses 8-9**

Mano-vijñāna

(2c.2) **Verses 10-14**

A listing of the caittas, i.e., the General, the Specific, the Advantageous (*kuśala*), the basic and secondary Mental Disturbances (*kleśa* and *upakleśa*) and the Indeterminate (*aniyata*).[5]

(2c.3) **Verse 15**

The Five Sense-Consciousnesses: They depend on the root consciousness (*mūla-vijñāna* = ālaya-vijñāna), and they sometimes work in tandem, sometimes not

(2c.4) **Verse 16**

Conditions in which mano-vijñāna does or does not occur

(3) **Verses 17-19**

Recasting *pariṇāma* (alterity) in terms of discrimination (*vikalpa*) and karmic conditioning (*vāsanā, grāha-grāhya, vipāka*, etc.)

(4) **Verses 20-25**

The Three (non-) Self-natures (*tri-[a-]svabhāva*)

(5) **Verses 26-30**

Descriptions of the five stages of realization

Another way of grouping the verses is to graft them onto the Four Noble Truths.

1. The first Noble Truth is a statement of the problem, i.e., the symptoms. For the *Triṃśikā* that would be the *parināṃa* (alteration) of consciousness into self and dharmas by means of linguistic, conceptual imprecision (*upacāra*). That is the topic of v.1 of the *Triṃśikā.* Self and dharmas are set up in an appropriational economy, which for Yogācāra is the root problem, namely *grāhya-grāhaka*, grasped and grasper.
2. The second Noble Truth is the diagnosis, the reason for the symptoms. Verses 2-16 provide a detailed categorization of the various consciousnesses, their characteristics, in which conditions they cease to operate, and a classificatory discussion based on the Yogācāra abhidharma system. According to Sthiramati and *Ch'eng wei-shih lun*, vs. 1-16 are themselves *upacāra*, imprecise metaphors or metonymies.

Vs. 17-19 recast the issues raised in v. 1 in a different language, one more focused on logic and analysis than on classification. This comes as a sort of philosophical rupture, an intermission in the trajectory of the *Triṃśikā*'s presentation. Listing and sorting items gives way to thinking about the dynamics underlying them: The discriminative process that sorts, the compulsions and proclivities that motivate the discriminations, etc. Sthiramati and Hsüan-tsang call this section the 'proofs' section. Since the portion of the *Ch'eng wei-shih lun* dealing with these verses is the most significant philosophically, and the aim of this work is to investigate Yogācāra philosophy, the analysis and discussion of the *Ch'eng wei-shih lun* beginning in chapter sixteen will concentrate largely on this section, drawing in other parts of the *Ch'eng wei-shih lun* that have bearing on the issues dealt with there.

3. The third Noble Truth offers the prognosis, i.e., a decision about whether what was diagnosed can be cured. The prognosis, according to Buddhism, is good. Vs. 20-25 deal with the trisvabhāva theory. By applying the proper antidotes (*pratipakṣa*), the problem of svabhāva can be emptied when recognized for what it is. In the jargon of trisvabhāva, pariniṣpanna is the antidote to the parikalpic pollution of paratantra; pariniṣpanna empties parikalpita from paratantra.
4. The fourth Noble Truth is the treatment plan, the prescription. Vs. 26-30 each deal with one of the five stages of Yogācāra practice.

The *Triṃśikā*, and consequently the entire *Ch'eng wei-shih lun* seeks to discuss one thing: *vijñāna-pariṇāma*, the alterity of consciousness.

Comments on the Verses

Verse 1

Vasubandhu and Hsüan-tsang both explain that 'due to *upacāra*' the proliferation of alterations of consciousness (*pravṛtti*) occur in the form of 'self' and 'dharmas.'

Upacāra denotes a linguistic concoction, something which has linguistic, but not actual reality. Hsüan-tsang uses 假說 *chia-shuo* to translate *upacāra. Chia-shuo* is more commonly used to translate *prajñapti.* An example Hsüan-tsang gives in the *Ch'eng wei-shih lun* of an *upacāra* is the term 'eye-consciousness' (*cakṣur-vijñāna*) for vision. Even though vision as a cognition is something different in kind from the physical eye, it borrows the word 'eye', according to Hsüan-tsang, imprecisely, based on association, and can serve as an understandable metonymy for vision (which in Sanskrit and Buddhist Chinese actually is referred to as 'eye-consciousness'), but should not be taken literally. The implication for this verse is that 'self' and 'dharmas' are imprecise metonymies that have, through the constructive force of language (=conceptualization), acquired an erroneous sense of reality. They are metonymies, according to the second half of the verse, for three types of alterations of consciousness (*vijñāna-pariṇāma*), which the subsequent verses will define as the ālaya-vijñāna, manas, and mano-vijñāna.

'Dharma' here does not mean, as some translators have misleadingly suggested, 'things.' Dharma specifically refers to the abhidharmic dharma list. The classic Yogācāra version, enumerated in a text by Vasubandhu titled *The Hundred Dharma Treatise*, consists of one hundred dharmas (see appendix). The *Triṃśikā* lists many of these, but not all one hundred. These dharmas are not things, but factors of experience, from conditions or styles of cognition, to emotions, to factors with positive or negative karmic values, to felt textures framing the way one experiences.

The first thing one notes about Paramārtha's version is that he entirely omits *upacāra*. Also, instead of 'self' (*ātman*) he offers 'sentient beings.' Sentient beings may believe they have a self (at least most humans do), but these terms are hardly synonymous. Vasubandhu and Hsüan-tsang are framing a cognitive, conceptual issue; Paramārtha frames the issue in cosmological terms instead. Paramārtha uses the ambiguous word 為 *wei* which means both 'becomes' as well as 'is deemed,' so that consciousness is either (or both) *deemed* to be sentient beings and dharmas (possibly by some linguistic, conceptual means), or it 'becomes' them.

Hsüan-tsang's version more clearly stipulates that the *upacāras* proliferate through *mutual* interaction (*hsiang-chuan*). For Paramārtha consciousness is a transcendent (rather than transcendental) third term that "turns into" 轉 actual beings and dharmas so that beings and dharmas are treated as dependent by-products of three types of consciousness. The problem does not arise, in his reading, from the way selves and their experience interact, but rather by fiat or a mere derivative of a bifurcation of consciousness. How or why consciousness should do this becomes a mystery.

Paramārtha uses 轉 *chuan* (revolving) for both *pravartate* and *pariṇāma* (or else he omits *pariṇāma* altogether). Hsüan-tsang uses 變 *pien* for *pariṇāma* and considers *chuan* 轉 (qua *pravartate*) to be a 'reciprocal' (相 *hsiang*) interaction between ātman and dharmas that proliferates an upacāric world.

Paramārtha talks about a threefold "subjective-condition" (能緣 *neng-yüan*). For Paramārtha there are basically two types of *chuan*: i. *chuan* as sentient beings and *chuan* as dharmas. Of these it is the 'subjective conditions' (*neng-yüan*) that are threefold. Hsüan-tsang draws a subjective-objective or active-passive pole by differentiating 能變 *neng-pien* (active, subjective alterations, the alterer) from *so-pien* (所變 what is altered).

Verse 2

This verse begins the abhidharmic classification of the eight consciousnesses. The *Triṃśikā* at first characterizes the three main consciousnesses—*ālaya-vijñāna, manas,* and *mano-vijñāna*—by their definitive characteristics.

Paramārtha has basically ignored the semantic interpretations offered by the *Triṃśikā* for the eighth, seventh, and sixth consciousnesses, and substituted his own, albeit with common glosses. "Fruit-recompense" is appropriate for vipāka, but the *Triṃśikā* defines the seventh consciousness (*manas*) as (as Robinson puts it) "mentation" (*mananāca*), while Paramārtha substitutes the common characterization of it as ādāna-vijñāna (attachment consciousness). Hsüan-tsang renders 'mentation' as *ssu-liang* which can be translated literally (as I have done in the main text) "willing and deliberating," or more loosely as "intellection" or "cogitating." Hence Paramārtha treats manas as "attachment consciousness," while Hsüan-tsang and the *Triṃśikā* define it as "mentation." While the *Triṃśikā* defines the sixth consciousness (or possibly the six consciousnesses) as discerning (*vijñapti*) cognitive-objects (*viṣaya*), Paramārtha substitutes "dust consciousness," completely ignoring the use of *vijñapti* in this context. "Dust" is a common euphemism for sense-objects in Buddhist and Chinese literature, originally signifying the billowing dust of the bustling marketplace, i.e., being encompassed by the realm of mundane concerns that obstruct one's vision of things as they are.

Verse 3

For the Sanskrit *asaṃvid...vijñaptikam* Paramārtha offers "cannot be discriminated" (*pu-k'e fen-pieh*) and Hsüan-tsang has "unknowable... discerns" (*pu-k'e chih... liao*). Neither clearly indicates the presence of the term *vijñapti* in the Sanskrit. It becomes "discrimination" (*fen-pieh*) in Paramārtha's version, and "discerning" (*liao*) in Hsüan-tsang's. *Upadhi, sthāna, vijñapti* are lumped together by Paramārtha as "characteristics and sense-objects." Paramārtha also reverses the order of *saṃjñā* (associative-thinking) and *cetanā* (volition).

Asaṃviditak- means 'imperceptibility' or 'not discerned consciously.' Hsüan-tsang's *pu-k'e chih*, while capable of being read in the same way, more strongly implies an utter "unknowability." While Vasubandhu's phrase seems only to be claiming that the *ālaya-vijñāna* operates subconsciously, Hsüan-tsang's phrase suggests that it cannot (*pu k'e*) be known at all. Hsüan-tsang may have been influenced in this by Paramārtha, for whom the sort of cognitions the ālaya-vijñāna has—if any—lack sense-objects and distinguishing characteristics. Paramārtha will return to this theme of undifferentiated awareness in vs. 18 and 28-29. His is not an obvious interpretation of the *Triṃśikā* and thus represents Paramārtha's own ideology. Significantly, even though Hsüan-tsang follows him here somewhat—including using the implications of this verse to determine that the ālaya-vijñāna is not directly cognizable as an object but can be known through inference because of its effects—he rejects Paramārtha's version of undifferentiated pure consciousness emerging at the fulfillment of the path.

The issue of how something sub-conscious can be brought into consciousness goes to the heart of the Yogācāra problematic. Buddhism in fact is compelled to develop a vocabulary that describes modalities of 'knowing' (*jñāna*) which are not within the closure of consciousness (such as *nirvikalpa-jñāna, prajñā*, etc.).

None of the translations—neither Robinson's nor the Chinese versions—preserves clearly the threefold structure of the ālaya-vijñāna in this verse.

Nonetheless, analyzed carefully, Hsüan-tsang's Chinese rendition contains fundamental clues for determining what the upper three vijñānas, viz. [1] *ālaya-vijñāna* ,[2] *manas*, and [3] *mano-vijñāna*, mean. In verse 2 they are described as:

[1] varyingly maturing (*vipāka*),
[2] thinking and deliberating (*mananāca*), and
[3] discerning and distinguishing sense-objects (*vijñapti*, 了別 *liao-pieh*), respectively.

In this verse, they are described as:

[1] grasping and 'feeling' things (*upadhi* 執受, *chih-shou*),
[2] locus (*sthāna* 處, *ch'u*), and
[3] discerning (*vijñaptika* 了, *liao*), respectively

with the point being that all three operate within ālaya-vijñāna, but subconsciously.

To gloss:

[1] ālaya-vijñāna 'holds' experience,
[2] manas localizes experience through thinking, and
[3] mano-vijñāna is the discriminating discernment of sense objects (*viṣaya*).

Connecting manas with localization is interesting since manas is also associated with self-interest, selfishness, arrogance, etc., all of which can phenomenologically derive from experiencing oneself as the center of the world, and identifying oneself as the *place* at the center of *my* experience. This makes all experience, and the world that appears in it, *my* world, *my* experience.

Note that in the Sanskrit the term *vijñapti* has been twice explicitly identified as a synonym for mano-vijñāna. Paramārtha's version provides no indication whatsoever that the term *vijñapti* plays a role here, much less what that role is. Hsüan-tsang uses two distinct terms for *vijñapti*—*liao-pieh* and *liao*—which both use *liao* (discern, understand). However neither term has any obvious connection with *shih* 識, which Hsüan-tsang uses for *vijñāna* as well as *vijñapti* (elsewhere). Hence the close etymological link between *vijñāna* and *vijñapti* becomes an identity when *shih* is used, an identity that doesn't allow any differentiation between them, while *liao* and *liao-pieh* remain entirely distinct from *shih* and provide no hint that one term, *vijñapti*, lies behind all three. Additionally, when speaking about *vijñapti-rūpa* and *avijñapti-rūpa*, Hsüan-tsang uses 差別 *ch'a-pieh* for *vijñapti*, again preventing a Chinese reader from recognizing the terminological connection. The semantic range of *vijñapti* is lost in Paramārtha's text, while diffused and diluted in Hsüan-tsang's.

Verse 4

Paramārtha omits the term *anivṛta* (covered by obstructions). By this omission Paramārtha remains silent on whether the *ālaya-vijñāna* has *āvaraṇas* (karmic obstructions) or not. Hsüan-tsang correctly translates that it doesn't. Possibly Paramārtha's stance on the question of whether the *ālaya-vijñāna* is impure or not, which was a hot topic of debate in China in the sixth century when he was there, colored his translations. Paramārtha held that the *ālaya-vijñāna* was impure and needed to be superseded by a ninth consciousness, a "pure" consciousness. Conceding that the *ālaya-vijñāna* was *anivṛta* might have complicated his position.

The Sanskrit and Hsüan-tsang speak of the ālaya-vijñāna as a torrential waterflow, an allusion to a perduring continuity that from instant to instant reconstitutes its identity, thus never retaining a single, self-same identity. Paramārtha substitutes an allusion to waves, an image found in many Buddhist texts. The wave metaphor is a famous feature of The *Awakening of Faith*, a text whose "translation" is attributed to Paramārtha, though current scholarship is virtually unanimous in holding it to be a Chinese creation with no Indian counterpart. The *Awakening of Faith*'s wave metaphor holds that ignorance is like wind creating waves on the surface of the sea that may obscure the water's true nature of "wetness" (i.e., "original enlightenment"); when the sea becomes calm, its true nature is revealed, though it was always present. The waves also signify the mind is "moved" by adventitious conditions and ignorance, i.e., waves of thought arising and ceasing due to the winds of ignorance. This "original nature" or "original enlightenment" theory became dominant in East Asian Buddhism, but is not part of the thinking of the *Triṃśikā* and was opposed (along with the tathāgatagarbha thought that accompanied it) by Hsüan-tsang. The *Triṁśikā* does employ an image of waves later in v. 15, but there as well Paramārtha seems to be rewriting the image for a different agenda.

Wu chi, lit. 'non-recording,' i.e., morally neutral. 'Non-covered' (*wu-fu*) means not obstructed or impeded by the two āvaraṇas, viz. cognitive obstruction and affective obstruction. 'Non-recording' means that even though the ālaya-vijñāna is produced by karma, it does not itself produce further karma. This is derived from the Abhidhammic notion that *vipāka*, or the fruition of prior karma, is itself karmically neutral. Were it not, karma would become hard determinism since, for instance, bad karma would perpetuate itself endlessly. The analogy of a tape-deck can illustrate this. A previously recorded tape can now play back what was recorded before without at the same time re-recording any new material, i.e., making new recordings and registering new impressions. Hence, though playing something recorded previously, it is now 'non-recording.' Liberation would mean to erase the tape, i.e., put the ālaya-vijñāna out of commission (*vyavṛti*).

That the *ālaya-vijñāna* was defined as (1) the conveyor of karmic seeds such that its constitution is nothing but karmic continuity and process, while (2) nonetheless it was considered in itself karmically 'neutral,' led in part to the Chinese controversies over the 'nature' of the ālaya: Was it pure and unending or tainted and hence to be superseded by a ninth vijñāna which would be pure, etc.? According to the *Ch'eng wei-shih lun* and numerous other Yogācāra texts the ālaya-vijñāna holds the karmically contaminated seeds until they are ready to sprout, but it does not become contaminated itself. It performs its functions ineluctably, mechanically, and with utter karmic neutrality.

Verse 5

While the Sanskrit might be understood to claim that objective conditions (*ālambana*) 'develop' or 'come to operate' (*pravartate*) out of the ālaya-vijñāna, Hsüan-tsang's version can be understood (and I have so translated it) to be claiming that the objective conditions are in fact objectifications of the ālaya-vijñāna itself, objectifications produced through a process of 'turning around' (*chuan*), i.e., "reversing" the cognitive process such that, on the one hand, the object-supports (*ālambana*) are perceived as if independent of the ālaya-vijñāna which conditions all such cognitions, and, on the other hand, though the *ālambana* are displays of the ālaya-vijñāna, they shield the ālaya-vijñāna from being an object of direct cognition since one perceives the ālambana and not the ālaya-vijñāna in itself. In this reading *pravartate* would then refer to mistaking *interpretations* of ālaya-vijñāna for 'reality'; hence the *āśraya-parāvṛtti* ('turning around of the basis'), which in Yogācāra thought signifies the radical psycho-cognitive change characteristic of Awakening, would actually be an un-reversal, a removal of the interpretive projections that have been mistakenly taken for naive-realist or metaphysical grounds. *Chuan* (*pravṛtti, pravartate,* 流轉 *liu chuan*) is *chuan*-ed (*parāvṛtti,* 轉依 *chuan-yi*).

Paramārtha offers a somewhat inexplicable reading: he claims that objective-conditions (*ālambana*) are the conditions by which the manas arises, i.e., the arising of manas is precisely the forming of attachments to objective-conditions. This is inexplicable because Paramārtha has not explained where these so-called objective-conditions have come from, nor in what manner or by what they have been cognized. For the ālaya-vijñāna to be dependent on objective-conditions, they must have originated independently of it.

Verse 7

Vasubandhu gives the three cases in which there is no manas. The first is the extinction of *kleśāvaraṇa*, which defines (according to Sthiramati and the *Ch'eng wei-shih lun*) the achievement of Awakening for the 'Hīnayānic' practitioner, viz. the arhat.

The second is *nirodha-samāpatti*, the meditative attainment of cessation, which was thoroughly discussed in chapter seven, above. For Vasubandhu and Hsüan-tsang *nirodha-samāpatti* entails the absence of manas; *āsaṃjñī-samāpatti* suppresses mano-vijñāna, but not manas. Paramārtha says "(manas) ceases completely upon entering the *acitta-samāpattis*." Since *acitta-samāpatti* (*wu-hsin-ting*) usually includes both nirodha- and āsaṃjñī-samāpatti, Paramārtha seems to be diverging from Vasubandhu (and Hsüan-tsang) by including the āsaṃjñī-samāpatti in this verse. Vasubandhu and Hsüan-tsang reserve āsaṃjñī-samāpatti for v. 16 which lists the conditions under which mano-vijñāna ceases. See comments on v. 16, below.

The third, which is beyond the *ārūpya-dhātu* and hence lokuttara, i.e., "beyond the 'three worlds'" (viz. the worlds of desire, form, and formless), can be understood to signal a breaking out from the karmic closure. What exactly constitutes lokuttara is defined differently in different texts, but it plays an important role in Abhidharmic, Prajñāpāramitā, and Yogācāra literature. Some texts say that up to the eighth bhūmi (Bodhisattva stages) one is on the *lokiya* (mundane) path (*mārga*), while beyond the eighth, one practices the *lokuttara* (supra-mundane) mārga.

Verse 8

This verse begins a discussion of the sixth consciousness, the mano-vijñāna. The *kuśala* (advantageous) group of the 100 Dharmas (#19-29) and its opposites are associated with this vijñāna. To summarize the basic classification so far:

1) ālaya-vijñāna is non-covered and karmically neutral ('non-recording');
2) manas is covered but karmically neutral;
3) mano-vijñāna can be either karmically advantageous, disadvantageous, or neutral.

What this apparently means is that although all three are karmically derived, ālaya-vijñāna is a neutral embodiment of karmic seeds, from which, within its own perspective, it remains detached (and hence offers the conditions by which one can become detached from one's karmic stream). Although manas is a product of negative karma ('covered'), it produces no negative karma by itself—or put another way, though its operations establish the conditions for the production of negative karma, in themselves the operations are neutral. Mano-vijñāna has the capacity to produce either positive, negative, or neutral karmic effects.

The ālaya-vijñāna was characterized as having only neutral vedanā. In the description of Manas, no mention of vedanā was made at all. Polarized vedanā, i.e., the bifurcating tension of conditioning/conditioned experience qua pain and pleasure, only operates in the mano-vijñāna, and by implication, in the five sensory consciousnesses which are part of its domain.

What is interesting and problematic so far is that manas, though separate from the karmic problems of conditioning, and thus logically and psychologically prior to karmic experience (kuśala, akuśala, etc.), nonetheless is karmically 'covered' (*nivṛta, fu*) and associated with kleśa, or, as Sthiramati writes, it is *kliṣṭamanas* ('defiled-manas'). This gives kleśa—as an abstraction—primacy over karmic conditioning understood as pain/pleasure conditioning. In fact, kleśa becomes a necessary condition for such conditioning. This reinforces that the notion of *kleśa* has replaced the notion of *āsava* expounded in the earlier Theravāda texts. This means that the definition of karmic conditioning as understood in previous schools of Buddhism, and as formalized in the pratītya-samutpāda model, underwent a serious re-evaluation leading to an investigation of the sources and origins of karmic conditioning beyond vedanic (pain/pleasure) conditioning. One result is that the status of the *bījā* ('seeds') in the ālaya-vijñāna becomes a crucial issue—do they precede the consciousness-stream (are they beginningless?) or are they produced through the stream's experiences. These abstracted issues defer investigation away from empirical experience and onto the ālaya-vijñāna, which becomes simultaneously a singular, personal consciousness stream (*santāna*) and an intersubjective stream undergoing continuous rebirth. *Ch'eng wei-shih lun* addresses this most directly during its discussion of seeds and vāsanās. See comments to v. 19 below.

Verses 9-14 enumerate dharmas from the Abhidharma list. See Appendix 1. The basic caitta categories are:

General: These caittas are always involved in every cognitive act.
Specific: These only occur in certain cognitions.
Advantageous: These are associated with positive karmic results
Mental Problems (*kleśa*): These are roots of negative karma
Secondary Mental Problems: These are components of negative karma secondary to Mental Problems
Indeterminate: For instance, initial mental application could be kuśala if applied to the right object, but conducive to negative karma if focused on a detrimental object.

Verse 14

Indeterminate, i.e., karmically indeterminate, does not mean that these dharmas cannot have karmic significance, but only that their significance is not determined by these dharmas themselves, but rather by their circumstances. They are neither advantageous (*kuśala*) nor disadvantageous (*akuśala* or *kleśa*) in and of themselves; rather their karmic value must be judged contextually, i.e., by things or situations other than themselves. *Middha* (ch: *mien*), 'torpor,' is karmically neutral since drowsiness or tiredness may be either beneficial (e.g., when rest is needed in order to recover from an illness) or non-beneficial (e.g. when alertness is required, such as while driving). Simply put, torpor is not in itself good or bad. Its value in any situation must be judged by context. Likewise for the other three Indeterminates.

It should be noted that 'sloth' and 'torpor' were not always considered indeterminate in Buddhism. In the Pāli Abhidhamma, 'sloth and torpor' (*thīnamiddha*) were initially considered a single term but later were distinguished from each other. More importantly this term was part of the list of the Five Basic Obstructions (*pañcanīvaraṇā*), and thus negative. The five are: (1) *kāmacchanda* (eros), (2) *byāpāda* (resentment), (3) *thīnamiddha* (sloth and torpor), (4) *uddaccakukkucca* (restlessness and worry), and (5) *vicikicchā* (doubt).[6]

Verse 15

Here we have a wave metaphor. The analogy of mind:thoughts::water:waves already occurs in the Pāli Nikāyas.[7] The wave metaphor in the *Awakening of Faith* is probably the most famous example in East Asian Buddhist literature. However, Sthiramati is probably right when he writes that Vasubandhu had in mind the wave analogy from the *Saṅdhinirmocana-sūtra* (5.5).

The *Ch'eng wei-shih lun* in fact says of this line only the following:

> The so-called five consciousnesses, [in reference to the] body, internally they depend on the root consciousness; externally they accord with 'attention' [lit. 'what is intended'; manaskāra], 'the five sense organs,' 'sense-objects' [*viṣaya*], etc.; all these various conditions intermix and coalesce in the space one projects before oneself [*chung yüan ho-ho fang te hsien ch'ien* 眾緣和合方得現前].
>
> Dependent on these [conditions], sometimes (the five) arise together, sometimes not together, because the coalescing with external conditions may be sudden or gradual. Like water and waves, 'according to varying conditions' [*sui-yüan*] (there may be) many or few. This and similar analogies are explained in the [*Saṅdhinirmocana*] *sūtra*.

Kochumuttom has this to say on Sthiramati's technical discussion of this verse:

> If sense-consciousness is the result of the co-operation of sense, object and consciousness, how can it still be called a transformation of consciousness (*vijñāna-pariṇāma*)? ...Waves arise on water only under certain atmospheric conditions. In other words, the arising of waves depends not only on water but also on the atmospheric conditions. But, that the waves arise depending on the atmospheric conditions, does not make it impossible to say that those waves are just modifications (*pariṇāma*) of water on which they arise. Similarly, consciousness depending on certain factors such as sense-organ and object, transforms itself into sense-consciousness. However, that the sense-organ and object co-operate with the consciousness in producing the sense-consciousness,

does not in any way contradict the fact that the latter is a transformation of consciousness.

Sthiramati, too, finds it necessary to refer to objects (*ālambana*) for adequately explaining the emergence of sense-consciousness. According to him the point of comparison between 'five sense-consciousnesses on *mūla-vijñāna* ' and 'waves on water' is that just as waves can together or separately arise on the same water, so the five sense-consciousnesses can arise together or separately on/from the same *mūla-vijñāna* . There are two kinds of causes at work in both cases: antecedent causes (*samanantara-pratyaya*) and objective causes (*ālambana-pratyaya*). The former of these, for example, water or *mūla-vijñāna*, remaining always the same, the latter keeps changing. It is according to the number and nature of the [objective] causes available (*yathā-pratyayam*) [*Yathā-pratyayam-udbhavaḥ iti yasya yasya yaḥ pratyayaḥ sannihitas-tasya tasya niyamena-udbhavaḥ ātma-lābhaḥ]*, that waves or sense-consciousness arise together or separately. By the objective cause (*ālambana-pratyaya*) of any consciousness is meant the object of that consciousness. But in the case of sense-consciousness it has got to be external objects, not the so-called internal objects such as seeds (*bīja*) left behind in the ālaya-vijñāna by past experiences, *saṃskāras* and *vāsanās*. For, while those internal objects remain always the same, the external objects can keep changing from time to time, and from place to place, and thus can provide for different and multiple-sense-consciousnesses... (pp. 142-144)

I'm not sure that Kochumuttom has sufficiently understood Sthiramati's point. Kochumuttom's attempt to explain embodied-conditioning as constant while external objects are variable is highly problematic from a Yogācāric viewpoint.

Anacker offers the following note on this line:

The multiplicity of waves in water depends on the force of the prior agitation of water: in the same way the extent to which the evolving consciousnesses occur depends on the force of prior agitation in the citta-series. (pp. 189f n. 7)

Paramārtha sharply differentiates the sea from the waves, emphasizing the *underlying unity* of the different consciousnesses, rather than accepting that sometimes they work in tandem, and sometimes they don't. He presses as hard as he can for the primacy of unity. Vasubandhu and Hsüan-tsang seem more interested in the six senses themselves, while Paramārtha keeps his focus on the three parināṃas, which he uses in part to 'unify' the senses. An underlying unity in consciousness is not a requisite for Vasubandhu or Hsüan-tsang, especially not in terms of the five senses. Even the wave metaphor is made to champion the idea of a unitive base by Paramārtha,

Vasubandhu's original point may simply be the same as what, in general, *the Awakening of Faith* states. Waves (sensory experience) arise on water (deep mind) due to the interplay of conditions (*Awakening of Faith* identifies 'wind' with *avidyā*); they are the perceptible surgings of what lies beneath them.

Verse 16

This verse lists the conditions in which mano-vijñāna ceases. Each of the three versions gives a different list. Paramārtha, for instance, omits nirodha-samāpatti, but adds 'the moment before death.' Hsüan-tsang pushes *acitta* to near the top of the list (otherwise following Vasubandhu's order). As we saw in the earlier chapter on nirodha-samāpatti, which included part of the *Ch'eng wei-shih lun*'s discussion of this verse, Hsüan-tsang is at pains to argue that the *acitta* mentioned in this verse does not involve the absence of the ālaya-vijñāna (citta is often a synonym for the ālaya), since his theory of ālaya-vijñāna requires that it still operate during the samāpattis. The following chart shows the differences in the respective lists of each text.

CONDITIONS IN WHICH MANO-VIJÑĀNA CEASES

Vasubandhu	**Paramārtha**	**Hsüan-tsang**
1. asaṃjñi	asaṃjñi-deva (mindless gods)	asaṃjñi-deva
2. samāpattis (asaṃjñi)	asaṃjñi-samāpatti	*acitta*
3. " (nirodha)	dreamless sleep	asaṃjñi-samāpatti
4. deep sleep	drunken stupor	nirodha-samāpatti
5. fainting (stupor)	when the mind is cut off (*acitta*)	sleep
6. no awareness (*acitta*)	moment before death	total unconsciousnes s

Let me summarize some of the points covered so far:

The operations of vijñāna-pariṇāma (the alterity of consciousness) are described in a tripartite manner. This following simplified schematic gives the basic relations between these three operations of consciousness as described in verses 1-16. Verses 17-20 clarify these distinctions and introduce the term *vijñapti-mātra.* Verses 20-24 will redescribe these operations in terms of the *tri-svabhāva* theory. Verses 25-30 will then give an account of the soteric resolution of the psycho-sophical closure.

Ālaya-vijñāna	Manas	Mano-vijñāna
differently maturing *vipāka*	willing and deliberating *mananākyaśca*	discerning objects *vijñaptir-viṣayaya*
appropriating *upadhi*	localizing *sthāna*	discerning *vijñapti*
non-covered *anivṛta*	non-covered *anivṛta*	apprehending objects *viṣayasya-upalabdhi*
karmically indeterminate *avyakṛtam*	karmically indeterminate *avyakṛtam*	either kuśala, akuśala, or indeterminate
neutral[ized] pleasure-pain *upekṣa-vedanā*	———	pleasure-pain-neutral *tri-vedanā*
ceases in: arhathood *arhattva*	**ceases in:** arhat, nirodha-samāpatti, Supramundane Path *arhat, nirodha-samāpatti, lokuttara-mārga*	**ceases in:** asaṃjñi-denizen, the two samāpattis, sleep, total unconsciousness *asaṃjñika, samāpatti-dvaya, acittikā, mūrchā*
caittas #9-13, but only neutral vedanā	**caittas** #30-35, 9-etc.	**caittas** #9-13, 14-18, 30-35, 36-55, 56-59

Verse 17

Since this verse will be discussed in some detail in Part V, chapter 16, only a few comments will be offered here. First, while Robinson translates *vikalpa* and its derivatives in this verse as 'imagination,' the more common translation is 'discrimination.' The Chinese for *vikalpo yad vikalpyate* (discrimination and what is discriminated), used by both Paramārtha and Hsüan-tsang, is 分別 *fen-pieh* and 所分別 *so-fen-pieh*, respectively. Already in early Chinese texts, such as the *Chuang Tzu*, *fen-pieh* meant to discriminate, to cut apart (both *fen* and *pieh* contain the 'knife' radical).

The verse says that all sorts of things are discriminated by acts of consciousness; these things have no existence apart from those acts: Hence they 'all belong to vijñapti-mātra' (*sarvam vijñapti-mātrakam*). Paramārtha will continue to stress the distinction between discrimination and what is discriminated in the following verses, retaining the terms *fen-pieh* and *so-fen-pieh*, while Hsüan-tsang will use a different term than *fen-pieh* to represent *parikalpita*. See v. 19.

Verse 18

Here Robinson and Paramārtha seem to be on the same wavelength, while Hsüan-tsang (and arguably Vasubandhu) see things differently. For Robinson and Paramārtha, consciousness is the seed of everything, or all dharmas (these are not necessarily the same thing). For Hsüan-tsang, this verse is only talking about the 'all-seeds-consciousness'—a euphemism for the ālaya-vijñāna—not about the seed of everything. For Hsüan-tsang the deployment of seeds by the ālaya-vijñāna is responsible for *discrimination*, not for that upon which discrimination acts.

To complicate matters, Anacker, who consulted the Tibetan as well as Sanskrit text, renders this line: "Consciousness is only all the seeds..." which limits, rather than unleashes the parameters of consciousness. Kochumuttom, working only from the Sanskrit, offers the neutral phrase "the consciousness contains all seeds..." Since *sarva* (all) modifies seeds (*sarva-bījam*) and not dharmas or things (neither term occurs in Sanskrit), Paramārtha and Robinson have taken some interpretive liberty with the text. Robinson's rendition sounds like idealism; but it does so by saying something the text doesn't say. Paramārtha's rendition might be idealist if all that exists are dharmas, or the dharmas that emerge from the ālaya-vijñāna's seeds are the only kinds of dharmas. But Hsüan-tsang (and Vasubandhu) are talking about mental closure, not the ontological composition of the universe.

Paramārtha and Hsüan-tsang both offer interesting interpretive readings of Vasubandhu's "mutual influence" (*yāti-anyonya-vaśād...*). Paramārtha not only turns it into "constructing and revolving" (*chao-tso hui-chuan*), but adds what is constructed by the 'revolutions,' viz. 'self and other.' Hsüan-tsang renders 'mutual influence' with *chan-chuan li*, which can mean 'reciprocal, mutual,' but also strongly implies the unfolding of a sequential order. Paramārtha and Hsüan-tsang both use *chuan* 轉, which implies 'revolving, turning around.' Paramārtha reinforces that sense forcefully with the compound *hui-chuan* 迴轉, since *hui* also means 'to spin around, revolve, rotate.' See comments to v. 1 above on *chuan.*

If read in the tripartite manner laid out in the second chart under v. 16 above, this verse might be read as saying: (1) ālaya-vijñāna is the all-seeds consciousness (2a) which, as viewed by manas, is subject to perpetual active alterations, (2b) while, if manas 'turns around' to look at the mano-vijñāna and the sensorium, the ālaya-vijñāna unfolds its operating force, until (3) mano-vijñāna discriminates that from that.

If this reading is correct, then *vikalpa* (discrimination) is synonymous with *vijñapti* as the latter term functioned in earlier verses, that is, as the basic activity of mano-vijñāna. As the chart above makes clear, for Vasubandhu mano-vijñāna best exemplified the term *vijñapti*—a fact completely lost in the Chinese versions. This being the case, vijñapti-mātra, far from meaning 'true cognition' or 'consciousness is real' or some such valorizing affirmation, would simply mean consciousness-experience is nothing but [false] discriminations, imaginings.

Kochumuttom gives the following account of Sthiramati's interpretation:

> According to Sthiramati this stanza says how the various kinds of subject-object distinctions in the absence of any extra-mental means comes to actuality from *ālaya-vijñāna*, which is itself without a basis...by referring to the context in which the subject-object distinctions arise, namely the interaction between *ālaya-vijñāna* and *pravṛtti-vijñāna*. "The consciousness that contains all seeds" is obviously *ālaya-vijñāna*; and "its such and such transformations" refer to *pravṛtti-vijñāna*. The latter keep arising by the mutual influence of itself and *ālaya-vijñāna*. This statement might sound [like] a vicious cycle. But the point is that the actual origination of *pravṛtti-vijñāna* is occasioned by the coming-together (*sannipāta* = *sparśa*) of *indriya*, viṣaya and *vijñāna*.... (p.148)

In other words, pravṛtti-vijñāna arises from the confluence of sense-organs (*indriya*), sense-objects (*viṣaya*) and their respective types of consciousnesses. The point of this interpretation, then, would be to indicate that this confluence is not a mere mechanical sensation, with consciousness merely a byproduct. Rather the confluence, as experienced in consciousness, is itself infused and deeply influenced by prior experiences ("seeds") retained and deployed by the ālaya-vijñāna.

Verse 19

Kochumuttom's commentary on this verse goes right to the point:

> *Vipāka*...[i.e., the *ālaya*]...gets exhausted (*kṣīṇa*) in the course of time. But it continues to exist, so to say, through the *vāsanās* (habit-energies) left behind by the deeds (*karma*) it promoted, and by the *grāha-dvaya* (the twofold grasping) it exercised. *Vāsanās* are the impressions or habits, or characters, or traces, or habit-energies, left behind by past experiences. They are also capable (*samartha*) of producing future experiences. They are like seeds (*bījas*) which are produced by trees, and are also capable of producing future trees. For Sthiramati vāsanā means ability (*sāmarthyam*).
>
> There are two factors that produce *vāsanās*, namely *karma* (deed) and *grāha-dvaya* (the twofold grasping). Of them *grāha-dvaya* means the idiosyncrasy for subjectivity and objectivity. 'The two graspings are (i) the grasping of the graspable, and (ii) the grasping of the grasper. Among them the grasping of the graspable is the belief that there are graspables independent of consciousness, although in fact they are what the stream of consciousness projects itself. The belief that such graspables are apprehended or known or grasped by the consciousness is the grasping of the grasper. And the habit-energies of the twofold grasping are the seeds, which being produced by the earlier graspings of graspable and grasper, are now capable [of] engendering fresh graspings of graspable and grasper of the same kind.' [Sthiramati: *Grāha-dvayam. Grāhyo-grāho grāhaka-grāhaś-ca. Tatra vijñānāt-pṛthag-eva sva-santāna-adhyāsitam grāhyam-asti-iti-adhyavasāyo grāhya-grāhaḥ. Tac-ca vijñānena pratīyate vijñāyate gṛhyate iti yo'yam niścayaḥ sa grāhaka-grāhaḥ. Purvotpanna grāhya-grāhaka-grāha-ākṣiptam-anāgata-taj-jātīya-grāhaka-grāha utpatti bījam grāha-*

> *dvaya-vāsanā*]...What particularly interests me at this point is Vasubandhu's suggestion that the habit-energies of karma can produce the next *ālaya-vijñāna* only in collaboration (*saha*) with the habit-energies of the twofold grasping...This implies that the continuity of *ālaya-vijñāna* and of the consequent saṃsāric existence depends decisively on the subject-object idiosyncrasy. Therefore no wonder that Vasubandhu is advocating its eradication as the means of attaining nirvāṇa. (p.150f)

Paramārtha provides a complicated (and somewhat confusing) discussion of this verse in the *Chuan-shih lun,* involving categorizing things in terms of saṃvṛti vs. paramārtha distinctions,[8] *neng-so* distinctions (active/passive, subjective/objective), discrimination nature (i.e., parikalpa) and dependent on others nature (paratantra), kleśas, objects and consciousness, vāsanās from past karma and attachments to those vāsanās, and so on. He basically asserts that past impressions (*vāsanās*) *are* the kleśas that project the objects we attach to. Cf. comments to v. 8 above.

Verse 20

This verse again uses grammatically differentiated forms of the word *vikalpa*: *vikalpena* and *vikalpyate*. Related to other terms derived from √*kḷp*—e.g., *kalpanā* ('imagination,' 'mental construction,' 'theoretical proposal'), *saṃkalpa* ('totally imagined'), *vikalpa* ('discrimination,' 'making false distinctions'), and *parikalpita*—they mean 'what is discriminated' and 'what discriminates.' *Pien-chi* is Hsüan-tsang's translation for both *vikalpena* and *vikalpyate.* He also uses *pien-chi* as the short version of *parikalpita.* Paramārtha continues to employ the *fen-pieh* and *so-fen-pieh* distinction that he has already entrenched in the *Chuan-shih lun.*

This verse concerns parikalpita-svabhāva so Hsüan-tsang is trying to indicate the etymological affinities between *pari-kalp-ita, vi-kalp-ena* and *vi-kalp-yate.*

Paramārtha indicates the affinity between the three terms by retaining *fen-pieh* throughout. For him, parikalpita is discrimination nature, which discriminates and then divides up the discriminations into types. For him the sheer act of discrimination is sufficient to render parikalpita a problem. According to Paramārtha's understanding of the first line of the *Triṃśikā,* the discrimination of consciousness into two types set all the problems in motion. This is a somewhat unsophisticated approach by Yogācāra standards.

In the trisvabhāva (three self-natures) scheme parikalpita signifies the delusional svabhāva. The trisvabhāva scheme, whose earliest textual appearance seems to be the *Saṅdhinirmocana-sūtra,* came to be considered a fundamental Yogācāra doctrine. It receives significant treatment in the works of Asaṅga (e.g., the *Mahāyānasamgraha* or *She-lun*), Vasubandhu (who also devoted an entire text to it, viz. *Trisvabhāva-nirdeśa*), as well as basic Mahāyāna texts such as the *Laṅkāvatāra-sūtra,* etc.

Hsüan-tsang's rendering of *parikalpita* literally reads *pien* ('everywhere,' 'generally,' 'universally') + *chi* ('calculate,' 'plan,' 'scheme'). Other Chinese translators had sometimes rendered parikalpita as *wang-chi* 妄計 ('erroneous calculation'). The 'long-form' in Hsüan-tsang's Chinese for parikalpita is *pien-chi-so-chih* 遍計所執 (being attached to what is schematized everywhere). Hsüan-tsang's term implies that this 'erroneous discrimination' applies itself everywhere as a mental elaboration or as a determinative cognitive grid. It is not simply that one discriminates, or allows one's imaginative constructions to pervade one's experience. One becomes deeply attached (*so-chih*) to these constructions. In other words, parikalpita constitutes a cognitive closure that intrudes into the very process of knowing/perceiving one's self and the world, or anything in cognition. In fact, since parikalpita's basic assumption is that whatever it discriminates has substantialistic existence (svabhāva), it basically functions as that which 'discriminates' the world into 'self' and 'perceived components,' i.e., ātman and dharmas. What renders parikalpita erroneous is not simply the fact that it discriminates, but more importantly, that these discriminations instigate and fuel attachment to 'self' and 'dharmas.'

My term 'schema-tize' is an attempt to preserve the calculative, plotting, scheming aspects of the Chinese *chi*. However this should not be misunderstood to imply that parikalpita is always a deliberate, consciously exercised activity. The 'schemata' may be entirely presuppositional, unconscious, and yet play out as a 'rationalized,' (previously) elaborated grid that comes to be applied piecemeal by an agent who is unaware of its 'karmic' (i.e., conditioned) origins. It might also be rendered as 'rationalizations projected everywhere,' but that could be misconstrued to imply that the process is more consciously constructed than the Buddhists intend. While 'rationalizing'—both in the psychological sense and as the activity of utilizing *ratio* (reason) to construct intricate logical 'rationalizations' (dṛṣṭi)—is included in the notion of parikalpita, the term carries a much wider scope, virtually 'covering' (*saṃvṛti*) the entire range of non-Awakened human cognitions.

Verse 21

Vasubandhu, Robinson, and Hsüan-tsang are of one mind concerning this verse, but Paramārtha has his own ideas. For all but Paramārtha this verse means that paratantra (dependent on others) is the linchpin. The 'others' that paratantra is defined by, namely causation by other-nature (*parabhāva*)—which, like sva-bhāva, was criticized as untenable by Nāgārjuna—are only considered truly 'others' with their own svabhāva if one is thinking parikalpically, if one is assuming that things have such natures as self-nature and other-nature. Paratantra, though, is simply the realm of conditional arising (*pratyaya-udbhava*), i.e., pratītya-samutpāda. When imagined in terms of self- and other-natures, it is infected by parikalpita. Pariniṣpanna is paratantra devoid of parikalpita. So parikalpic-paratantra is a deluded or defiled paratantra, while pariniṣpannic-paratantra is a purified paratantra from which all parikalpita has been flushed away, cleansed.

Paramārtha has a different idea. For him parikalpita and paratantra are inseparable. Recognizing their inseparability is pariniṣpanna. This is a radically different idea than the one described above. Here pariniṣpanna is a transcendent realm, forever removed from and apart from the other two natures. They, to use his terms, are simply variations of discrimination. Parinişpanna, which he doesn't translate (as does Hsüan-tsang) as 'perfected or accomplished' nature, but as 'really real nature' or 'truly real nature,' signifies for him a unitive, nondiscriminative realm beyond the world of difference, cognitions, and conditions. The 'truth' for him, then, would be to float above the two lower natures, since they are forever incurably entangled in discrimination.

Verse 22

Here again Paramārtha strikes out on his own with a unique interpretation. For Vasubandhu and Hsüan-tsang the subject of this verse is the fact that parinişpanna and paratantra are "neither different nor not different from each other," reinforcing the point of the previous verse, namely that parinişpanna is paratantra cleansed of parikaplpita. Paramārtha, however, takes this verse as maintaining the non-difference of *parikalpita* from paratantra, rather than *parinişpanna* from paratantra. He neglects to mention that the two items are "neither different nor not different," but only points that out that they are not different, hence implying that they are the same while suppressing whatever sense differentiates them. By substituting parikalpita for parinişpanna, and lumping parikaplita and paratantra together, he has again privileged parinişpanna, keeping it aloof from the limitations of the first two svabhāvas. The Sanskrit explicitly names paratantra but refers to the remaining nature indirectly, implying the subject of the verse is the last mentioned subject of the previous verse, which was parinişpanna.

"On impermanence, etc." This is a standard Buddhist argument about what is neither the same nor different. Particular things which are all impermanent (*anitya*) and the principle of impermanency (*anityatā*) are neither the same nor different. The *-tā* suffix makes a term an abstract noun, comparable to -ness or -ity in English. Hsüan-tsang indicates the *tā* suffix in Chinese with *hsing* 性 (nature); 無常 *wu-ch'ang* = impermanent, 無常性 *wu-ch'ang-**hsing*** = impermanence. Things are neither reducible to principles, nor are principles exactly identical with things, though the intimacy of their relation is sufficient to conclude that they are not completely different from each other either. Just as 'impermanence' is an abstraction, or general category, which like all 'universals' must be unreal (according to most Buddhist schools), the categories of paratantra and parinişpanna are also ultimately unreal. One must be careful about applying general categories (*sāmānya-lakşaṇa*) to unique individuals (*svalakşaṇa*). For instance, the general category 'impermanency' is, as such, unreal—only each and every entity uniquely not being permanent can be called 'real' (at least by Sautrāntikas). A corollary is that when one says X and Y are impermanent, this cannot be taken as a statement of identity between X and Y. The Yogācāra text, *Dharma-dharmatā-vibhāga*, as its title suggests, addresses this issue in greater detail.[9]

Anacker (p.190 n. 11) takes a different tact:

Impermanence is neither exactly the interdependent (which looked at "as a whole" may not be impermanent), nor does it exist anywhere except in the interdependent. Actually, neither the constructed nor the fulfilled are exactly different or non-different from the independent, since the constructed is basically the interdependent constructed and constricted, and the fulfilled is basically the interdependent unconstructed and unconstricted.

Verse 23

Hsüan-tsang follows the Sanskrit closely, but adds "secret intention (is to) explain" 密義說 *mi-yi shuo*, where the Sanskrit only says *deśitā* (preach, teach). The notion that the niḥsvabhāva version (the non-self-natures) of the trisvabhāva theory, or other doctrines in Buddha's discourses reflect a 'secret intention' in Buddha's teaching, i.e., that some doctrines give the appearance of saying something, but actually are provisional means for getting to a different, deeper point, is presented in the *Saṅdhinirmocana sūtra*, and referred to by Vasubandhu in his *Viṃśatikā*. By "secret" they don't mean esoteric, but rather a meaning not evident or explicit on the surface which accounts for the motive behind the explicit teaching.

Paramārtha neglects to mention that the principle of the three non-self-natures (*tri-niḥsvabhāva-tā*) is only taught in relation to the three svabhāva theory. For the trisvabhāva to be effectively understood, one must avoid reifying them. The positive and negative versions of the trisvabhāva are inseparable. Thus the full trisvabhāva theory is neither naively affirmational, nor nihilistically negative.

Verse 24

This verse explains how the three self-natures are also simultaneously three non-self-natures. The 'Everywhere schema-tizing' is by definition without self-nature, since it is pure fictitious construction. As Sthiramati points out, it is of the 'nature' of a purely psycholinguistic chimera, and hence is no more real than a round square or the son of a barren woman (he uses the stock example of 'sky-flower'). Hence it lacks an 'essence.'

Paratantra also lacks essence in that paratantric entities can't define themselves, generate themselves, or make themselves exist independently of other 'entities.' They all depend on conditions other than themselves. Whatever is not self-originating cannot have its 'own' nature (***sva**-bhāva*), since its 'nature' is shaped and conditioned by things external to itself.

Pariniṣpanna is without self-nature by definition, since its specific purpose is to remove the mistaken svabhāvic thinking of parikalpita from paratantra. Ultimately everything is without svabhāva. Pariniṣpanna functions in Yogācāra theory as the antidote (*pratipakṣa*) for parikalpic delusions. Initially paratantra—signifying the realm of causes and conditions, pratītya-samutpāda—is infected with parikalpita. That is 'defiled paratantra.' Pariniṣpanna serves as the antidote, cleansing paratantra of all parikalpic pollutants, resulting in 'purified paratantra,' which means one has become Awakened, with Awakened cognitions.

Hsüan-tsang translates parinișpanna literally as 'accomplished or perfected' (*ch'eng-yüan*) while Paramārtha metaphysicalizes it as 'Truly Real' (*chen-shih* 真實) or 'Really Real' (*shih-shih* 實實). This treats the notion as a substance, since *chen-shih* also is used to translate *dravya*, substance. Paramārtha's term, then, implies not only 'truth', but 'substance.' Later Chinese Buddhists, such as Fa-tsang, continue in that tendency, glorifying parinișpanna as a transcendent reality divorced from parikalpita and paratantra (rather than 'remote' from parikalpita *in* paratantra). Note that while the Sanskrit explicitly and flatly states that the third (parinișpanna) is 'non-self-nature-hood' (*niḥsvabhāva-tā*), Paramārtha resists conceding that and instead asserts that "it neither has nor does not have a nature." While he avoided a neither/nor notion in the last verse that the Sanskrit did assert, here he introduces one where it is absent in the Sanskrit. This sort of neither/nor claim is common in other works by Paramārtha, especially when he makes ultimate claims about true reality (*chen-ju* 真如, etc.).

Verse 25

'Ultimate Referent' is a literal translation of both the Sanskrit *paramārtha* and the Chinese 勝義 *sheng-yi*, Hsüan-tsang's rendering of *paramārtha.* Paramārtha uses the same term for paramārtha that he used for parinișpanna, 真實 *chen-shih,* reinforcing his treatment of *paramārtha* and *parinișpanna* as synonyms. The term *paramārtha* has suffered an unfortunate history of mistranslation and misinterpretation in much modern scholarship, East and West, and as we see here that tendency has had a long history. The term *paramārtha* does not mean 'Ultimate Truth' or 'Supreme Reality' or 'Absolute Truth,' etc., though it is usually rendered with terms such as these. Robinson uses "absoluteness" to render *paramārtha* in this verse. *Paramā-* signifies the superlative case. *Artha* can mean 'referent,' 'meaning,' 'object,' 'an objective,' or even 'attained material objectives (i.e., wealth).' In other words, it always signifies that towards which intentionality intends.

In opposition to *saṃvṛti*—which literally means 'enclosed,' 'surrounded by,' 'closure'—*paramārtha* announces the non-closure, the breaking out from saṃvṛti. Normal acts of referentiality—a word referring to its referent—are usually either prajñapti (heuristic, in which what is being referred has only linguistic reality) or saṃvṛti (or *vyavahāra*, conventional designation, in which a word points to something considered 'real' by conventional criteria). Paramārtha exceeds these conventional acts of reference. Thus it is an ironic and even paradoxical term, for it implies that its referent is beyond referentiality or at least normal reference. Hence it is always an indirect referral, or one not enacted by language. The 'ultimate referent' is thus no referent at all, since it can never be referred to directly. In part it defies reference because it is not a thing, or even a no-thing. More to the point, it exploits language's own self-referentiality to break out of language, to refer or defer language beyond itself.

This function parallels the ironic intent behind the Yogācāric term Vijñapti-mātra. Like paramārtha, it is used not to reify or self-affirm itself, but in order to expose the anxieties, needs, and resultant complexes through which a need for such a term becomes engendered.

Since, as was explained in an earlier chapter, paramārtha means 'explicating with total precision rather than loosely,' I have turned it into an adverb in my translation of Hsüan-tsang's verse: 'ultimately.'

Tathatā, introduced in this verse and associated with *vijñapti-mātra-tā* (psychosophical closure-hood), will be discussed in later chapters.

Verse 26

The last five verses characterize the five stages of practice. Different Buddhist texts, and even different Yogācāra texts, offer different enumerations of stages. The *Yogācārabhūmi*, e.g., has seventeen stages. The *Ch'eng wei-shih lun*, following the *Triṃśikā*, details these five stages.

The first stage is called "provisioning" (*sambhārāvasthā*) since this is the stage at which one collects and stocks up on "provisions" for the journey. These provisions primarily consist of orienting oneself toward the pursuit of the path and developing the proper character, attitude and resolve to accomplish it. It begins the moment the aspiration for enlightenment arises (*bodhicitta*). The next stage is the "experimental" stage (*prayogāvasthā*), in which one begins to experiment with correct Buddhist theories and practices, learning which work and which don't, which are true and which are not. One begins to suppress the grasper-grasped relation and begins to study carefully the relation between things, language, and cognition. After honing one's discipline, one eventually enters the third stage, "deepening understanding" (*prativedhāvasthā*). Some texts refer to this as the Path of Corrective Vision (*darśana-mārga*). This stage ends once one has acquired some insight in nonconceptual cognition (*nirvikalpa-jñāna*).

Nonconceptual cognition deepens in the next stage, the Path of Cultivation (*bhāvanā-mārga*). The grasper-grasped relation is utterly eliminated as are all cognitive obstructions. This path culminates in the Overturning of the Basis (*āśraya-paravṛtti*), or Awakening. In the "final stage" (*niṣṭhāvasthā*), one abides in Unexcelled Complete Enlightenment (*anuttara-samyak-sambodhi*) and engages the world through the five immediate, direct sense cognitions. All one's activities and cognitions at this stage are "post-realization." As a Mahāyānist, from the first stage one has been devoting oneself not only to one's own attainment of enlightenment, but to the attainment of enlightenment by all sentient beings. In this final stage that becomes one's sole concern.

According to the *Ch'eng wei-shih lun* this verse indicates the stage of 'accumulating merit,' sometimes translated 'moral provisioning' (*saṃbhāra*). *Saṃbhāra* may also be translated as 'preparation.' Cf. Kamalaśīla's *Bhāvanākrama* ch.1, where, for instance, he quotes the *Akṣayamati-nirdeśa* as saying "...even as duḥkha is the antecedent cause of the lived-body (*jīvitendriya*), just so the bodhisattva's great compassion is the antecedent cause of 'acquiring the equipment' (*saṃbhāra*) of Mahāyāna..."

Although even in Theravādin texts śīla (behavioral self-discipline, 'morality'), samādhi (meditation), and prajñā (Awakened discernment) are given parity such that each reinforces and depends on the others for its development (i.e., developing śīla will benefit samādhi which will benefit prajñā which will benefit śīla and samādhi which will benefit prajñā and śīla, and so on), nonetheless the Abhidhamma, with some justification from the Pāli suttas, developed a progressional scheme that hierarchized them. According to this hierarchy, the three jewels constitute stages: one goes from śīla to samādhi to, ultimately, prajñā.[10]

The 'stage of accumulating merit or moral provisioning' is a hold-over in Mahāyāna of considering śīla to be the initial stage of serious practice. However, this becomes qualified through the inclusion of samādhi and prajñā in the six pāramitās, the pāramitās being the core of Mahāyānic śīla practice. The *Ch'eng wei-shih lun* says:

> At this stage [i.e., saṃbhāra], one has not yet realized vijñapti-mātra tathatā (the psychosophy of closure as-it-is). Depending on the power of 'confident resolve' [dharma #15] to cultivate the various perfecting practices...[one solidifies his faith into] the stage of understanding practice.
>
> What are the defining characteristics of the perfecting practices (pāramitās) being cultivated?
>
> In general there are two types, which are called 'merit' and 'discernment' (*puṇya* and *prajñā*; Ch: *fu* 福 [lit. 'happiness, felicity'] and *chih* 智). Of the perfecting practices, whichever are of the nature of wisdom (*hui*) are called 'discernment' (*chih*), and the rest are called 'merit.' The six pāramitās, at bottom, are all characterized by these two. The breakdown is: the first five are called 'meritorious virtues or qualities' (*fu te* 福德) and the sixth is called Prajñā (*hui-chih*). Or again, sometimes they are broken down as only the first three are 'meritorious virtue,' the last one alone is Prajñā, and the remaining [two, viz. (4) vigor and (5) samādhi] are a mixture [of the other] two.

According to the *Ch'eng wei-shih lun* this stage is still prior to overcoming the two *āvaraṇas*, viz. *kleśāvaraṇa* (the deep-seated psychological obstructions) and *jñeyāvaraṇa* (the root-level cognitive obstructions). Since Mahāyāna generally grants the so-called 'Hīnayānic' Arhat the status of having overcome the *kleśāvaraṇa* (but not *jñeyāvaraṇa*), this would indicate that this stage is even prior to the "Lesser Vehicle's" Awakening, or in other words, this is an entirely unAwakened stage.

The Chinese terms *fu* and *mieh* used by Hsüan-tsang in his translation connote "suppress" (*prahāna*) and "cessation" (*nirodha*), respectively. These two terms are frequently distinguished in Abhidharmic literature: "suppression" meaning the temporary putting out of action of some defilement, and "cessation" meaning its ultimate, irreversible extirpation.

Paramārtha translates verses 26-30 with minimal interpolations, though some interpretive deviations will be noted below.

Verse 27

This is the next stage, the "experimental" stage (*prayogāvasthā*).

Hsüan-tsang has *wei-shih-hsing*—implying *vijñapti-mātra-tā*—but the Sanskrit only has *vijñapti-mātra*. This again reminds us to be cautious in following Vallée-Poussin's rendering of the title of this text as *Vijñapti-mātra-tā-siddhi* rather than using the actual Sanskrit title found on Sthiramati's text, *Triṃśikā-vijñapti-bhāṣya* (Commentary on Triṃśikā-vijñapti), which is the only extant Sanskrit text. *Ch'eng wei-shih lun* would literally render into Sanskrit as *Vijñapti-mātra-siddhi-śāstra*, not Vijñapti-mātratā. At the end of the *Ch'eng wei-shi lun* an alternate title for the text is given (not an uncommon practice in Chinese translations), which also fails to justify *Vijñapti-mātra-tā-siddhi*. It is: *Ch'ing wei-shi* 淨唯識 (Purifying Vijñapti-mātra, *Vijñapti-mātra-viśuddhi*). The title of the text on which the *Ch'eng wei-shih lun* was based, according to the *Ch'eng wei-shih lun*, was *Wei-shih san-shih* 唯識三十, which literally translates as *Triṃśikā-vijñapti-mātra*, a ringer for Sthiramati's title.

But why did Hsüan-tsang choose to add *hsing* (nature) here? That's an intriguing question. It may be a deliberate move on his part to distinguish the reified *vijñapti-mātratā* as a "small understanding" (*shao-wu*, lit. 'small thing') from *vijñapti-mātra* as non-reifiable. To turn *vijñapti-mātra* into 'something attained' (*yu so-te*) is, according to this verse, a misguided reductionism ("small understanding"), i.e., *grasping* at abstractions. The Sanskrit verse emphasizes the inability to fixate on, or "fix" (stop) (*na-avatiṣṭhate*) *vijñapti-mātra* as an object of cognitive apprehension (*upalambhataḥ*). Interestingly, the Sanskrit does not repeat *vijñapti-mātra*—as does Hsüan-tsang—but instead uses *tan-mātra* in the second half of the verse. *Tanmātra* (*tat* + *mātra*) is used by Sāṃkhya and other Hindu schools to denote the subtle material elements of existence. The term *tanmātra* (lit.: nothing but that) implies nonreducibility, or what is irreducible, hence a basic element. It is these irreducible elements that are components of experience which cannot be frozen, made to stay put in an abiding present of understanding (*sthāpayan-agrataḥ kiṃ-cit tanmātre*), that remain as non-reducible to the cognitive act that declares (*eva-idam iti*) "that which I am cognizing is only nothing-but vijñapti."

Paramārtha's version emphasizes that one must get rid of the idea that everything is consciousness-only in order to actually 'enter' vijñapti-mātra, in which neither an objective-support (*ālambana*) nor a cognizer has arisen. Why is that 'consciousness only'? Because it demonstrates that consciousness is the condition for objects to appear, be experienced. The transition from negating the object, which also negates the knower (without an object, a consciousness cannot arise), to entering where neither appears, is comparable to the first three levels of the ārūpya-dhyānas, i.e., in the absence of objects (equivalent to ākāśa), consciousness (second level) becomes Nothing (third level). This is a repeated theme in Yogācāra texts. For instance, *Madhyānta-vibhāga*, 1:4 and 8 stress that when one negates the object, the self is also negated.

That this is the motive behind the denial of external objects is reinforced by Vasubandhu who, in two texts, offers a nearly identical formula, both hinging on two terms: *upalabdhi*, which means to 'cognitively apprehend,' i.e., to grasp or appropriate cognitively; and *artha*, 'referent' of a linguistic or cognitive act, i.e., that toward which an intentionality intends.[11]

> Apprehending vijñapti-mātra is the basis for the arising of the nonapprehension of *artha*. The nonapprehension of *artha* is the basis for the nonapprehension of vijñapti-mātra.
>
> *vijñapti-mātropalabdhim niśrityārthānupalabdhir-jayate. Arthānupalabdhim niśritya vijñapti-mātrasyāpi-anupalabdhir-jayate.* (*Madhyāntavibhāga-bhāṣya* I.7)

> By the apprehending of citta-mātra, there is the nonapprehension of cognized *artha*. By nonapprehending cognized *artha*, citta also in nonapprehended.
>
> *citta-mātra-upalambhena jñeyārthārthānupalambhatā. Jñeyārtha anupalambhena syāc-cittānupalambhatā.* (*Trisvabhāvanirdeśa* 36)

By recognizing that those things which appear in an act of cognition as if they were other than consciousness are actually appearing *in consciousness*, and thus cannot be cognitively 'apart' from it, that is, that cognitive-objects appear to exist apart from cognition only within an act of cognitive construction, one ceases to grasp at one's own construction as if it were a graspable entity 'out there.' One does not reject the 'object' or noema in order to reify or valorize noesis or noetic constitution. On the contrary, because one ceases to grasp at the noema, noesis too ceases to be grasped. The circuit of grasped and grasper (*grāhya-grāhaka*) is disrupted, and the type of cognition that endeavors to seize and 'apprehend' its 'object' ceases. This bears repeating. Not only is the object, the *artha*, negated, but that which noetically constitutes it (*vijñapti-mātra, citta-mātra*) is also negated.[12] Vijñapti-mātra or citta-mātra are provisional antidotes (*pratipakṣa*), put out of operation once their purpose has been achieved. They are not metaphysically reified or lionized.

Verse 28

The three versions of this verse offer some interesting differences. For Vasubandhu the argument is a simple and typical one: Since, in the absence of an object, a consciousness doesn't arise, in the absence of grasping an object, consciousness doesn't grasp either, hence abiding in vijñapti-mātra means here cognition devoid of attachment and grasping. For Paramārtha, the knower and its object both seem to disappear or melt into a non-cognitive state called Consciousness-only. Hsüan-tsang is closer to Vasubandhu, maintaining that at the moment one is in objective conditions (*ālambana*) without attaching to or 'attaining' any of them, one has entered an understanding of psychosophical closure, since one can now cognize without grasping or attachment, having eliminated the two graspings (for self or things). While for Vasubandhu and

Hsüan-tsang cognitions continue to occur, except now devoid of attachment, for Paramārtha nothing at all seems to 'manifest' (*hsien-hsien*) or appear, so that 'consciousness-only' must signify for him either an entirely non-cognitive state or one in which only an undifferentiated consciousness exists. The latter seems closest to him. As he will comment on the next verse: "Non-discriminative cognition (*nirvikalpa-jñāna*) is when sense-object and cognition are undifferentiated" 無分別智。即是境智無差別. This resonates with his insistence on consciousness as unitive back in v. 18.

The verse is saying there is a moment of insight in which the psychosophic closure makes itself transparent (and hence no longer en-closuring) and which utterly and instantaneously neutralizes the root problematic of karmic continuity through detachment from the dual appropriations, viz. 'grasper and grasped.' In other words, the appropriational duo—by being exposed for what they are—viz. karmically potent mental fabrications, become impotent, and thus see-able as the fictitious malignancies (*āśrava*) they really are.

The structure of this sentence suggests some interesting readings. Word-for-word it reads:

chih 'wisdom,' '[correct] knowledge,' etc. (while often used in Buddhist texts as an equivalent for prajñā, Hsüan-tsang sometimes differentiates *prajñā* [wisely discerning] from *jñāna* [direct, immediate cognition] by using *hui* for the former and *chih* for the latter) +
tou—'all,' 'the whole,' 'in its entirety' +
wu—'nothing,' 'there is not,' 'without,' 'absence of' +
so—location, 'objective' and/or passive case +
te—'attain,' 'acquire.'

Hence the first two lines of this verse might also be translated 'if, at the very moment one is within objective conditions one knows that all of this, in its entirety, is nothing which is attainable or acquirable...'

What does this mean? If, during the experiential continuum, there comes a moment when the sensorium—which is inclusive of all sensations, whether pleasurable, painful or neutral, whether subjective or objective, etc.—is directly, intuitively, and without any doubt or ambivalence whatsoever, known (*jñāna*) in such a way that it is void of any appropriational characteristics, this constitutes the experience of 'consciousness-only.' 'Consciousness-only' here means that the appropriative dynamic that had pervaded and permeated cognition (reaching out toward and holding on to cognitive objects) is gone, and all that *was* nothing but the way consciousness normally acts. Entering an understanding of consciousness-only does not mean entering a realm in which consciousness exists alone by itself (how lonely and solipsistic!), but rather stepping back from consciousness' appropriational circuit, losing the vi-jñāna that distances itself from things in order to make them appropriatable, so that *jñāna*—direct, immediate cognition, shorn of the *vi*—emerges. The objective pole, which includes subjective 'sense-supports' that have been objectified as 'objects' of perception, is "entirely without anything to be acquired."

Does this necessitate that the ālambana themselves are non-existent, or that everything is created by mind? Not at all. It only means that the appropriational characteristics, i.e., those aspects of experience which perpetually, from a horizon, condition experience to present itself appropriationally—as 'I-mine,' as 'my truth,' 'my experience,' as things, ideas, theories and objects which can be taken to hand, which can be taken—only these appropriational characteristics are emptied from experience. One no longer grasps at anything, since everything is non-graspable, non-acquirable, in a profound way non-attainable. It is a kind of meta-objectivity that sees things as they actually are, a kind of meta-perspectivality that Sthiramati calls *sarvajña*, 'omniscience.' 'Things' are not presented, or represented, or given to/in experience. They are directly known devoid of appropriational tendencies, and hence devoid of karmic capacity. Since nothing is acquired, no seeds can accumulate, and the ālaya-vijñāna is broken. The destruction of the ālaya-vijñāna becomes a metaphoric means of describing in experiential terms the disruption and final elimination of karma. Since language itself, in this view, is no more than an instrument and instantiation of the appropriational tendencies (*prajñapti*); whatever might be the experiential case in or subsequent to this insight must necessarily be 'beyond' language.

If any justification can be made for Hsüan-tsang using (*shih* 識) for both vijñāna and vijñapti, this line is it. Vasubandhu writes here that you are abiding in VIJÑĀNA-mātra, not vijñapti-mātra. This is because vijñāna is *not* 'making things known' (*vijñapti*) at this point. What was vijñapti—what was being made known by consciousness, i.e., posing objectifications for appropriation, i.e., *abhūta-parikalpa* (as the *Madhyānta-vibhāga* calls it)—has ceased, revealing that all that *was* only the appropriative agenda and structure of consciousness (*vijñāna-mātra*). Obviously, the Chinese reader, unaware that the original text has distinguished vijñapti from vijñāna, would have no clue at this point that wei-shih has switched referents.

Note, also, that one abides in consciousness-mātra and not consciousness-*mātra-tā*.

In the *Ch'eng wei-shih lun*, Hsüan-tsang writes of this verse:

> 'You, at that moment' refers to what is called really abiding in the truly paramārthic nature of psychosophical closure which always-already realizes as-it-is-ness. *Jñāna* and *tathatā* are thoroughly equalized because both are detached from the characteristics of grasper and grasped. The grasper-grasped characteristics (*grāhaka-grāhya-lakṣaṇa*) together constitute the discriminations (*vikalpa*) of attainable existents (i.e., the appropriational attitude), [which are actually nothing but] prapañcic mental projections.

Vijñāna-mātra can be understood in two ways:

1) that the entire experiential realm as constituted in the closure of non-Awakened experience is 'nothing but a fabrication of the operations of consciousness,' and since everything so far has aimed at eliminating this, the idea of 'consciousness-only' should not be reified, or

2) this verse signals a stage towards Awakening, but not Awakening itself, so this stage consists of the emptying of the so-called objective realm of its svabhāvic 'essences,' leaving 'nothing but consciousness remaining.' If the latter interpretation is to be followed, then the next stage would be the emptying of any svabhāvic 'essence' from consciousness itself. Finally, by neutralizing the objective and subjective poles, tathatā alone remains, that is, things are known for what they are without the slightest interpretive interpolation. The subsequent discussion in the *Ch'eng wei-shih lun* gives credence to both of these readings.

In the passage just cited, the *Ch'eng wei-shih lun* states that the grasper and grasped are replaced by *jñāna* (direct cognition) and *tathatā* (the experiential realm just-as-it-is, devoid of mental projections). Hence subject and object in the most general sense remain, but are purified of appropriational intent, and thus 'equalized.'

Paramārtha seems to prefer a more mystical version of the second option, understanding consciousness-only as a realm of pure, undifferentiated consciousness. While for the *Ch'eng wei-shih lun* the knower and known remain as *jñāna* and *tathatā*, Paramārtha claims that the knower and known both fail to appear at all. Whereas the Sanskrit and Hsüan-tsang both state that it is the grasper-grasped relation that disappears, Paramārtha asserts that it is the nonappearance of knower and object that is called "nothing is attained." As elsewhere, the Sanskrit and Hsüan-tsang are offering psychosophical and epistemological observations which Paramārtha converts into metaphysical and cosmological assertions.

Verse 29

Hsüan-tsang's translation of the first few words of this verse might seem problematic from the point of view of the later developments of Chinese Buddhism. *Wu-te* must be translated 'non-acquirable' because the issue here is the elimination of the appropriational attitude, not a hyperbolic genuflection to some mystical Other. It translates *anupalambho*, which means 'cannot be known through the senses or ordinary means of knowledge.' As mentioned in a note on v. 8, *upalabdhi*, at least to Hsüan-tsang, was considered in some ways synonymous with *vijñapti*. If *upalabdhi* and *upalambho* can be taken as virtually synonymous terms, then this may be tantamount to claiming that realization of *vijñapti-mātra* is itself devoid of *vijñapti* (*anupalambha*), i.e., 'discriminating-understanding-only' means no longer 'discriminating-understanding'!

The next phrase, *pu-ssu-yi*, meaning 'non-conceptual,' 'inscrutable,' translates the Sanskrit *acitta* which means absence of *citta*, 'non-citta.' *Acitta* can be understood here in at least two ways: (1) insentience in the ordinary sense, meaning the absence of a subjective vector within or behind any non-perceptual moment, such as, for instance, in deep sleep or utter unconsciousness; (2) the absence of a subjective vector within an experiential field of awareness, such that subjective and objective poles, i.e., noesis (*grāhaka*) and noema (*grāhya*), are neither constituting experience nor being constituted by it. The 'experience' of Nirvāṇa and the not-yet-fully-Awakened experience penultimate to Nirvāṇa (i.e., nirodha-samāpatti as the experiencing of *saṃjñā-vedayita-nirodha* [#76 and #99 on the Hundred Dharma list]) are said to be this type of *acitta*. The latter signifies the release from the closure of what texts like the *Laṅkāvatāra-sūtra* call *citta-mātra-dṛśya*, 'seeing only what is projected by mind (*citta*).'

Besides reversing the order of the terms from the Sanskrit, Hsüan-tsang has left unremarked an important aspect of Yogācāra thought which eventually came to be overlooked by many East Asian Buddhists as well as most modern scholars. This line is describing the jñāna that goes beyond the 'three worlds' (*jñānam lokottaram*). Since, as the famous line from the Hua-yen sūtra says (and similar lines can be found throughout this type of literature[13]), "The three worlds are nothing but citta," this line indicates that (1) vi-jñāna becomes just jñāna, i.e., 'consciousness' becomes 'direct-knowing'—and thus the assertion that Yogācāra holds a position of 'only consciousness (vijñāna) is ultimately real' becomes untenable—(2) this jñāna not only is no longer a vijñāna, it is also explicitly declared to no longer be a citta.

While Hsüan-tsang often becomes overly literal (e.g. his translation of *vipāka*), in this case his 'non-conceptual' (*pu-ssu-yi*) for *acitta* removes the crucial term *citta*. In v.16 Hsüan-tsang does literally translate *acitta* with *wu-hsin*. 'Non-conceptual' is a justifiable reading of *acitta* if 'citta' is taken in the sense of 'generic thought;' hence *a-citta* would mean 'unthinkable.' Nonetheless, by interpreting rather than literally translating this term, Hsüan-tsang has not allowed this verse to enter into a debate that came to the fore shortly after his death between his disciple K'uei-chi and the Hua-yen patriarch Fa-tsang on the supposed distinction between *wei-shih* (consciousness-only; meaning Hsüan-tsang's 'school') and *wei-hsin* (mind-only; meaning Fa-tsang's position). Since most of the important Chinese Buddhist schools such as T'ien-t'ai, Hua-yen, and some forms of Ch'an, came to be known as *wei-hsin* (*citta-mātra*) due to their affirmation of citta as a metaphysical ground beyond any ultimate negation or cancellation, this crucial line of the *Triṃśikā* might have radically altered the course of Chinese Buddhism by arguing unambiguously that Awakening involves the superseding of citta, i.e., that Awakening consists of breaking the ālaya-*vijñāna* (by turning it into *jñāna*) and eliminating citta. Citta, in its most precise abhidharmic and Yogācāric formulation means the momentary, subjective point or vector within any cognitive moment. Some meditational practices, such as nirodha-samāpatti, aim precisely at the elimination of citta from the experiential stream. For Vasubandhu, this practice did not go deep enough, because the 'stream' itself, namely the ālaya-vijñāna which becomes the Yogācāric metaphor for 'karmic continuity,' remains unaltered and fully functioning even after this samāpatti. For Vasubandhu only the full transformation from 'consciousness' (which includes the ālaya-vijñāna and the 'subjective' citta) to 'immediate-knowing' effectively uproots the karmic dilemma. For Hsüan-tsang, the ālaya-vijñāna operates even during nirodha-samāpatti.

While we may rely on the Sanskrit verse to conclude safely that *chih* 智 here translates jñāna, a Chinese reader necessarily would remain uncertain as to whether *chih* is translating *jñāna* (cognition) or *prajñā* (wisdom). These two terms are often conflated by Chinese Buddhists as a result.

Paramārtha's final words in the *Chuan-shih lun* are:

> If cognition doesn't condition a sense-object, then both [the cognition and the sense-object] do not appear, since the sense-object is precisely a consciousness-only sense-object. This is what is confusing about consciousness-only. Since the sense-object is nonexistent, consciousness is nonexistent. Consciousness already being nonexistent, the mind of consciousness-only that is able to [produce] conditions is also nonexistent. Thus [the verse] says: THE TWO DO NOT APPEAR. The two are simply consciousness and the sense-objects that appear to it. Since the sense-object is already nonexistent, this is called 'consciousness revolving.'

Paramārtha seems to differentiate between consciousness per se (or consciousness-only) and a "mind of consciousness-only." This yields a three-tiered negation. The sense-object does not appear, and so is nonexistent (in experience—this needn't be interpreted ontologically). The object being nonexistent, its consciousness is also nonexistent, since consciousness is always *consciousness of*, and cannot arise without an object. The third tier is the *mind* of consciousness-only, which is also (亦) nonexistent since consciousness is nonexistent.

It is unclear what Paramārtha gains in this context by adding this extra tier, since he negates it as soon as he introduces it.

Notes

1 See bibliography.

2 Chan offers a complete translation of the thirty verses in his *Source Book in Chinese Philosophy*, Princeton: Princeton University Press, 1963, ch. 23.

3 See bibliography.

4 Since there are some minor discrepancies between the Chinese and Sanskrit verses as to which phrases are placed in which verse, this schematic follows the Chinese. For instance, verse 5 in the Chinese begins with the discussion of manas, whereas in the Sanskrit it first completes discussing the ālaya-vijñāna and then begins manas.

5 Following Vasubandhu's classifications in the *One Hundred Dharmas Śāstra* (*Śatadharmaśāstra*, *Pai-fa lun* 百法論), Hsüan-tsang lists remorse, torpor, initial mental application and discursive thought as the four Indeterminates, whereas the *Triṃśikā* seems to include these four as part of the secondary Mental Disturbances (*upakleśa*). Sthiramati's commentary also treats them as upakleśa.

6 For a lucid discussion of these five nīvaraṇas see Henepola Gunaratana's *The Path of Serenity and Insight* (Delhi: Motilal, 1985) pp. 28-48, and my Part II, above. Also Cf. Appendices 2 and 3, below.

7 Cf. *Saṃyutta Nikāya* 5:121-24 (Eng. tr. Kindred Sayings, V, p.106).

8 He uses the term 集諦 *chi-ti* to contrast with 真諦 *chen-ti* (paramārtha), rather than 俗諦 *ssu-ti* (saṃvṛti), even though *chi-ti* usually signifies the second of the four noble truths. He also distinguishes two types of kleśa and then says that the two kleśas are *paramārtha-satya*!?

9 A critical edition of the Tibetan version of this text, accompanied by analysis and a German translation was announced: Klaus-Dieter Mathes, *Unterscheidung der Gegebenheiten von ihrerm wahren Wesen (Dharmadharmatāvibhāga) - Eine Lehrschrift der Yogācāra-Schule in tibetischer Überlieferung* (Indica et Tibetica Verlag, Swisttal-Odendorf, 1996), but I have not seen this work, nor an earlier translation from the Tibetan, *Distinguishing Phenomena and Pure Being by Maitreya with Mipham's commentary Distinguishing Wisdom and Appearance as taught by Khenpo Tsultrim Gyamtso Rinpoche* , translated by Jim Scott (Kathmandu: Marpa Translation Committee)(Printed in Singapore by International Press Co. Pte. Ltd.) 1992.

10 See, e.g., Lama Govinda's *The Psychological Attitude of Early Buddhist Philosophy*, pp. 67-70; and Gunaratana's *The Path of Serenity and Insight*, pp. 11-14.

11 The double sense of *artha* as both a linguistic referent ('meaning') and a sensorial object is poignantly reinforced in *Trisvabhāvanirdeśa* by the repeated use of the term *khyāti* 'cognitive appearance.' *Kyāti* actually means a 'statement,' or 'theoretical assertion,' or something asserted to be the case (Monier-Williams, p. 341a: "'declaration,' opinion, view, idea, assertion... perception, knowledge... name, denomination, title..."); in other words, something which appears to be the case because it has been linguistically, conceptually asserted as such. The explication and disruption of this linguistic-cognitive construction is one of the primary subtexts of *Trisvabhāvanirdeśa.*

12 While some later traditions in China and Tibet differentiated sharply between *vijñapti-mātra* (Ch. *wei-shih*) and *citta-mātra* (Ch. *wei-hsin*), it is clear from passages such as these that Vasubandhu countenanced no such distinction.

13 Cf. *Viṃśatikā-vṛtti* 1: "*...traidhātukam vijñapti-mātram...*" (the triple world is nothing but vijñapti).

Part Five

The *Ch'eng Wei-Shih Lun* and the Problem of Psychosophical Closure: Yogācāra in China

Chapter Thirteen

Background Sketches

In Part Five, we will first look at important trajectories in Indian and Chinese Buddhism which can be seen intersecting in the *Ch'eng wei-shih lun.* Our aim is to properly contextualize Hsüan-tsang's general project in order to locate with some clarity the place of the *Ch'eng wei-shih lun* in that project. Having set the Sinitic context, we will then rejoin the discussion begun in the previous four Parts, and examine carefully the relevant positions defined and debated in the *Ch'eng wei-shih lun.* It contains, organizes and evaluates a vast range of Buddhist doctrinal minutia. Stylistically it is at once concise —sometimes to the point of elliptical obscurity—and redundant—rehearsing and rerehearsing terms and models in one permutational aggregation after another.

Due to the size and complexity of the *Ch'eng wei-shih lun* our treatment can in no way be exhaustive. We will instead (1) summarize how the *Ch'eng wei-shih lun* treats the Thirty Verses, (2) discuss some of the less familiar doctrines and paradigms used throughout the *Ch'eng wei-shih lun*, and (3) investigate the significance of the concept and experience of *vijñapti-mātra* (*wei-shih*). As this last issue stands at the core of the Yogācāric system, particularly as expounded in the *Ch'eng wei-shih lun*, an adequate understanding of *wei-shih* is the unavoidable prerequisite for any serious reflection on the Yogācāra system. Whether Yogācāra is or is not a form of idealism, whether the goal of Yogācāra is the reification or erasure of mind and consciousness, in what way or ways does Yogācāra intend its texts to be read, interpreted and used, etc.? The answers to all serious questions of this sort depend on what one understands *vijñapti-mātra* to signify. This Part will have been successful if, by its conclusion, the reader will be able to address these and similar questions in a manner consistent with Hsüan-tsang's Yogācāra.

As Buddhism trickled into China via the Central Asian trade routes and by sea, it came dressed in a variety of garbs. Pious businessmen with portable altars for worshipping a variety of bodhisattvas and deities introduced a devotional, practice-oriented Buddhism. Pious monks representing various schools and interpretations of Buddhism from various regions[1] brought and translated Buddhist texts. While non-Mahāyānic Buddhism apparently predominated in Central Asia,[2] in China after the fifth century Buddhism was almost exclusively Mahāyānic. The earliest 'schools,' depending on limited access to Indian thought—limited by the number and quality of translated texts, and the language abilities of translators (many 'translators' apparently spoke or wrote little or no Chinese; they expounded a text, and their disciples and translation committees would render those expositions into literary Chinese)—constructed positions whose vestigial slogans in many cases indicate a closer affinity to Taoism than Buddhism.[3] The first clear-cut Chinese Buddhist schools (as distinct from communities of foreign Buddhists in China) were probably those groups that have come to be called the Prajñā schools. They will be discussed shortly.

The dissemination of Buddhism in China leading up to the T'ang produced a variety of schools and positions among whom inevitable contradictions and conflicts arose. If there is one Dharma, why are there so many conflicting schools, texts and doctrines? This was the underlying, pressing question that all Chinese Buddhists in the sixth and seventh centuries attempted to resolve. Hsüan-tsang's project, as well, should be seen in the light of that agenda.

Eventually the Chinese settled on two types of 'answers' to this question. The first was the synthetic, syncretistic conflation of doctrine, most notably as proffered in the text *Ta-ch'eng ch'i hsin lun* (*Awakening Mahayanic Faith*). This text provided a theoretical foundation for the impulse expressed in other texts such as the *Lotus Sutra* that aimed at subsuming the multiplicity of schools into one-vehicle (*eka-yāna*; Ch.: 一乘 *yi-ch'eng*)

The second 'answer,' related to the first, deploys a hierarchical classification of doctrines that are often correlated with the presumed chronological order in which Buddha taught those doctrines. Known as *p'an-chiao* 判教, this classificatory strategy became a way for all Chinese schools to concede some upāyic validity to rival schools while positioning themselves in the highest slot—which in China came to mean possessing the most totalistic perspective, the most subsuming, the "Roundest" approach. *P'an-chiao* strategy involved privileging whatever particular text or ideology the evaluating school held as most important. The Sinitic Mahāyāna schools—T'ien-t'ai, Hua-yen, Ch'an and Ch'ing-t'u (Pure Land)—all rest on foundational (or at least cornerstone) *p'an-chiaos*. T'ien-t'ai grounded itself in the *Lotus Sūtra*, declaring its *eka-yāna* (One Vehicle) to be the Prime Way for which all other schools are vestibules. According to its *p'an-chiao*, the *Lotus Sūtra* was Buddha's penultimate sermon, given just prior to his final sermon (the Mahāyāna *Nirvāṇa Sūtra*) and entrance into nirvāṇa. Hua-yen privileged the *Avataṃsaka Sūtra* (a fusion of distinct Indian sūtras into one text), which they believed expressed the immediate content of his Awakening, as it was delivered, according to their *p'an-chiao*, during the first weeks following his Awakening under the Bodhi tree. T'ien-t'ai also accepts this account of the *Avataṃsaka*; however, for them, Buddha gushed it out, it was too immediate, too intense, too removed from ordinary experience to be of pedagogic value for beginners. To bring people up to a level where they would be able to understand and utilize the teachings expressed in *Avataṃsaka*, Buddha generated a succession of increasingly more profound teachings that culminated, in full maturity and with a honed pedagogical precision, in the *Lotus Sūtra*. According to tradition Ch'an—while eventually replacing 'textual grounding' with a 'scriptureless transmission' from master to disciple (though Ch'an never really abandons texts, either its own or standard Buddhist texts)—originally grounded itself in the *Laṅkāvatāra Sūtra*, and with Hui-neng, the Sixth Patriarch, switched to the *Diamond Sūtra*. Ch'ing-t'u (Pure Land) also initially treated the *Lotus Sūtra* as foundational, but, focusing on Amitābha and his Pure Land, it turned to the scriptures devoted to describing them (*A-mi-t'o ching, Wu liang shou ching*, etc.).[4] Their *p'an-chiao* emphasized a theory of history in which understanding of the Dharma and the ability of practitioners to implement the Dharma teachings, progressively declines. The 'degeneration of Dharma' theory (*mo-fa*, Jp: *mappō*) posits that the further one gets from the time of the Buddha, the more degenerate the age and the more distorted the understanding of the Dharma. For them, the age had already become so degenerate that no one would be able to achieve Awakening through his/her own efforts, and only the grace of a Buddha or a Bodhisattva's transfer of merit would prove to any avail.

The T'ang dynasty (618-906) dawned during Hsüan-tsang's lifetime (600-669). Though Buddhism already had been disseminated in China for over six centuries and had gained sporadic support from Emperors and intellectuals, especially in the Northern Dynasties during the period of disunion, it was not until the T'ang that Buddhism became a dominant cultural force throughout China. Hsüan-tsang played a key role in that ascendance, even though virtually every major Chinese Buddhist thinker—from Chih-I to Chi-tsang, Ching-ying Hui-yüan to Hui-neng, Paramārtha to Fa-tsang—lived within a hundred years of Hsüan-tsang and many were his contemporaries. Chih-i, the major foundational thinker of T'ien-t'ai, lived in the century just prior to Hsüan-tsang. Chih-yen and Fa-tsang, foundational thinkers for the Hua-yen school, were Hsüan-tsang's contemporaries. Ch'an and Ch'ing-t'u emerged as distinct systems shortly after Hsüan-tsang died. Often the T'ang has been considered the Golden Age of Buddhism in China.

Notes

1 Many—likely a majority—of the early monk translators were not Indian, but hailed from a variety of locations in Central Asia, such as Parthia, Sogdiana, Bactria, Khotan, etc. As a field, Central Asian Buddhism is only recently receiving attention by Western scholars outside the Soviet Union.

2 Especially the Sarvāstivāda, Mahāsaṅghika, Mahīśāsika, etc. schools. Nattier discussed this in her paper, and Hsüan-tsang's travelogue confirms it. On his journey to India through Central Asia, he was surprised by the dearth of Mahāyānic monasteries along the way. They became more numerous as he approached India proper.

3 Cf. TSUKAMOTO Zenryū, *A History of Early Chinese Buddhism: From its Introduction to the Death of Hui-Yüan*, tr. from Japanese by Leon Hurvitz (Tokyo: Kodansha) 1985, 2 vols.

4 On early Pure Land and its literature, cf. Kenneth Tanaka, *The Dawn of Chinese Pure Land Buddhist Doctrine* (Albany: SUNY Press, 1990); Young-Ho Kim, *Tao-sheng's Commentary on the Lotus Sutra* (Albany: SUNY Press, 1990); Julian Pas, *Visions of Sukhāatī: Shan-Tao's Commentary on the* Kuan Wu-Liang-Shou-Fo Ching (Albany: SUNY Press, 1995); Luis

Gomez, *The Land of Bliss: The Paradise of the Buddha of Measureless Light: Sanskrit and Chinese Versions of the* Sukhāvatīvyūha Sutras (Honolulu: University of Hawaii Press, 1996).

Chapter Fourteen

Seven Trajectories

By the sixth and seventh centuries Buddhism, both in India and China, had become thoroughly pluralistic. Varying and often opposing interpretations vied for legitimacy and adherents. The psychosophical trajectory called Buddhism had splintered into numerous sub-trajectories.

Seven such sub-trajectories are particularly worthy of note:

1) **Categorial matrices.** Although found throughout all Buddhist literature, this trajectory took two main forms. (a) the Abhidharmic matrices (*mātṛkā*), and (b) the Prajñāpāramitā reworking of those matrices. The categories, or lists, such as the 75 or 100 dharmas, the thirty-seven Factors of Enlightenment, the ten (or seventeen, or fifty-two) Bodhisattva stages, etc., grew more intricate and involved with the passing centuries. Novel doctrinal developments were produced by recombining sets of these lists or subdividing categories differently or more minutely than one's rivals. For Hsüan-tsang the *sine qua non* text of this genre was the *Yogācārabhūmi*. In fact, Hsüan-tsang's avowed purpose for going to India was to procure a more complete and accurate version of this text, since he believed that all the discrepancies and doctrinal wranglings—which had made the Buddhism of the China of his day something less than a harmonious coherent tradition—would be resolved by the complete *Yogācārabhūmi*. A huge text (100 *chüan*), it is among the first he translated after returning to China in 645.
2) **Reasoning and logic.** Although logical acumen is already evident in Nāgārjuna, and even earlier[1], it was not until Yogācāra emerged that logic, particularly syllogistic logic, received a firm foundation. Vasubandhu's *Vādavidhi*, though still a 'debate' text and not strictly speaking a 'logic' text, takes the first steps that his primary disciple in the field of logic, Dignāga, later expanded on and developed.[2] Hsüan-tsang introduced Indian logic to China by translating Indian logic texts for the first time.[3]

Dignāga had already been introduced to Chinese readers, but as an epistemologist, not as a logician. Paramārtha had translated the *Ālambana-parīkṣā-vṛtti* (T.31.1619), *Hastavāla-prakaraṇa-vṛtti* (T.31.1620)[4] in the sixth century, both texts more concerned with epistemology than logic. Hsüan-tsang translated *the only two Indian logic texts ever rendered in Chinese*:[5] Dignāga's *Nyāyamukha* (T.32.1628) and a primer on Dignāga's logic by Śaṅkarasvamin, *Nyāyapraveśa* (T.32.1630). He also retranslated the epistemological *Ālambana-*

parīkṣā (T.31.1624). I-ching, roughly half a century after Hsüan-tsang, also translated the *Ālambana-parīkṣā* (T.31.1623) as well as Dharmapāla's commentary on it (T.31.1625); *Nyāyamukha* (T.32.1629), and *Upadāya-prajñapti-prakaraṇa* (T.31.1622). A treatise on Prajñāpāramitā attributed to Dignāga (T.25.1518) was translated into Chinese during the Sung Dynasty by Dānapāla (10th century), et al. Hsüan-tsang's translations of the two logic texts did spur East Asian monks to compose commentaries for several centuries, but from the standpoint of Indian logic itself, these efforts are decidedly unimpressive and inaccurate. Dignāga's *Pramānasamuccaya* was never translated into Chinese. Neither were *any* works by such pivotal figures as Dharmakīrti, Candrakīrti, Śāntarakṣita, etc., despite the fact that translator monks continued to arrive in China through the 13th century. Thus this rich and pivotal tradition never took hold—in fact, it barely appeared—in China.

3) **Soteric systematics**. Including basic formulations like the Four Noble Truths and the Noble Eightfold Path, but developed into detailed, rich systematics. As with the matrices mentioned above in (1), the key text for the Yogācāra school was the *Yogācārabhūmi*. In China, all the important texts were interpreted in terms of soteric systematic enumeration, i.e., the *She-lun, Ti-lun, Hua-yen ching,* etc. were viewed, in part, as step by step guides to enlightenment. Even the critical Madhyamakan negations become soteric systematics—i.e., a hierarchy of soteric achievements—in the hands of their most important Chinese commentator, Chi-tsang. The massive creative work of the T'ien-t'ai foundational thinker, Chih-I, can also be seen as an elaborate and highly original soteric systematic that attempts to synthesize all the various Buddhist theories and practices known in China at that time into a step by step manual. Not surprisingly, different texts offered different systematics, and the differences were sometimes irresolvable. Resolving, or at least harmonizing the differences became a primary objective for most Chinese Buddhist thinkers, and the development of Sinitic Mahāyāna must be viewed in this light.
4) **Dialectical-deconstructive critique**. Like (2) above, this involves a logical, reasoned approach to matters of importance for Buddhism, but unlike debate and logic, its concern is not to construct a more adequate or more accurate description, much less suggest prescriptive axioms. Its aim—whether overtly as in Prāsaṅghika Mādhyamika, or implicitly as in the Sautrāntika discussion of time or the Yogācāra critique of 'externality'—is the falsification of whatever theory it takes under discussion. This 'method,' first expounded by the Buddha in the *Brahmajāla sutta* of the *Dīgha Nikāya*,[6] is sharpened by Nāgārjuna and adopted and applied by all subsequent Buddhist schools to attack their Buddhist and non-Buddhist opponents. While the syllogistic tradition never really takes root in China, dialectics were readily accepted and appropriated, in part due to the fact that there already existed a sharp dialectical tradition in China (e.g., Lao Tzu, Chuang Tzu) prior to Buddhism's entry.

Note that (1) and (3) are both classificatory, and thus *expansive*, in the sense that they function through the promulgation of ever more divisive distinctions and bifurcations. A categorial approach, by definition, proliferates itself. On the contrary, (2) and (4) are reductive, i.e., they either reduce what they treat to general classes (*samānya*), or else they reduce (false) propositions to absurdity. By definition, the subject of a logical proposition can never be a distinct particular, but will always be a member of a general, universalistic class. For example, a tree can only be the subject of a logical investigation insofar as it participates in categories indicative of what remains outside of or besides the particularity of a specific tree, such as 'tree-ness,' biological and physical laws, etc.; logic deals in general laws, and can only approach a particular case to the degree that that case is reducible to 'appropriate' general principles. Deconstructing a claim—whether by demonstrating internal inconsistency, by revealing hidden assumptions, by *petitio principii, reductio ad absurdum,* etc.—reduces a claim and whatever edifice has been made to rest on that claim to an untenable assertion. Inasmuch as it reduces a set of claims to either untenable claims, or no claims at all (depending on the rigor of the critique), it, like logic, is *contractive.*

5) **Psychologistic reductionism**. By fixating on karma as the key problematic, and defining karma as the intentioonal cognitive and mental activity of lived-body, language and mentation, Buddhist analysis considers anything *outside* the cognitive-mental sphere of experience to be utterly irrelevant to its soteric goals and/or undemonstrable. Since karma and intentionality are considered, from the beginning, to be synonyms, all experience—insofar as it is always directed by a gaze imbued with intentionality—is reduced to a play of intentionality, a play in which even the subtlest and most sublimated intentionalities are viewed as expressions of appropriational intent (*upādāna, rāga, taṇha,* etc.).

There are, however, two very important non-intentionalistic types of cognition admitted by the Yogācārins. The first is Awakened cognition. The other exception to this intentionality-reduction is the notion of the ālaya-vijñāna. According to Yogācāra the ālaya-vijñāna is non-obstructed (*anivṛtā*, Ch: *wu-fu*) and non-recording (*avyakṛta*, Ch: *wu-chi*), which means it is non-intentional (cf. *Triṃśikā* v. 4). This categorization serves several functions: It announces that there is such a thing as karmically neutral experience, i.e., neutral in the sense of the absence of appropriational intent. It also signifies one of the important roles the ālaya-vijñāna plays as vipāka-vijñāna, 'consciousness as the maturation of karmic seeds,' since *vipāka* is classified as always karmically neutral. Most importantly, since the ālaya-vijñāna is the root consciousness (*mūla-vijñāna*) upon which the interactions of the other seven consciousnesses depend, this non-intentionalistic characterization of the ālaya-vijñāna indicates that appropriationless experience lies at the core of all experience. This, in turn, promises the feasibility and possibility of Awakening. If *all* experience, all thought, cognition, etc. were inextricably intentional, and thus bound in and by (causally and logically) unalterable 'necessary' cognitive causal chains, there would be little if any chance of breaking those chains, or put more directly, if experience were utterly determined, freedom would forever be impossible. If all is reduced to consciousness, and consciousness itself is an impotent victim of hard determinism, then Awakening *qua* the breaking of the karmic habitual conditioned chains (*saṃbandha*) would be impossible. The notion of an ālaya-vijñāna free from intentionality answers this difficulty.

However, positing a non-intentional consciousness was not without its perils either. Chinese Buddhists, particularly in the sixth century, drew sectarian lines along the question of whether the ālaya-vijñāna was (i) defiled, (ii) not defiled, or (iii) partly defiled and partly non-defiled. The *Ch'eng wei-shih lun* argues that (i) and (ii) are extremist positions, and thus opts for a version of position (iii).

This issue is quite vital. On the one hand, it produced the historical positions and rhetoric that Buddhists for a century leading up to Hsüan-tsang had to deal with, such as the so-called Ti-lun and She-lun schools and especially Paramārtha's ninth consciousness. On the other hand, it stands at the core of what perhaps is the *Ch'eng wei-shih lun*'s major internal inconsistency, which, incidentally also marks a clear distancing of the *Ch'eng wei-shih lun* from the original text of the *Triṃśikā*. The *Triṃśikā* claims that the ālaya-vijñāna is destroyed (*vyāvṛti*, Ch: *she* 捨; vs. 5), the *Ch'eng wei-shih lun* qualifies this by saying that the *shih-t'i* 識體 ('consciousness itself' or 'the essence of this consciousness') is *not* destroyed.[7] Instead the function of the ālaya-vijñāna (as a storer of seeds, etc.) is eliminated. Hsüan-tsang opened a can of worms that included, among other things, the question of whether Yogācāra is or is not ultimately an idealism. Vasubandhu clearly has in mind that the ālaya-vijñāna, in virtue of its being one of the *saṃskṛta-dharmas* (conditioned dharmas) and not *asaṃskṛta* (unconditioned), must be cut off. Hsüan-tsang's revision of Vasubandhu's position is not done unthinkingly, and in fact entails a radical reappraisal of the notion of *asaṃskṛta*; specifically that 'unconditioned' does not refer to any real dharma, but rather is a mere prajñapti for tathatā, which itself is a prajñapti.[8]

Linguistic reductionism, like mental reductionism, carries psychologistic tendencies. Like Husserl, the Yogācārins took great pains to distinguish what they did *as a phenomenology* from mere psychologism. This is not always (or we should say, ever) easy. Husserl, for instance, grappled with this distinction throughout his career. In his final work, the *Crisis of European Sciences*, he returns again and again to the distinctions between psychologism, transcendental philosophy and transcendental psychology. Though he limits psychology (as practiced) to a prescientific naive worldview incapable of transcendentalizing or overcoming its presuppositions concerning empiricism,[9] he nonetheless concedes[10]

> But if the universal epoché, which encompasses all having-consciousness-of-the-world, is necessary, then the psychologist loses, during the epoché, the ground of the objective world. Thus pure psychology in itself is identical with transcendental philosophy as the science of transcendental subjectivity. This is unassailable....
>
> Pure psychology simply knows nothing other than the subjective; to admit into it something objective as existing is already to abandon pure psychology. [Phenomenology, on the other hand, "can return from the reorientation into the natural attitude"] ...This, systematically developed through the most vigorous of all conceivable methods—that is, the method of transcendental subjectivity reflecting apodictically upon itself and apodictically explicating itself—is precisely transcendental philosophy; thus pure psychology is and can be nothing other than what was sought earlier from the philosophical point of view as absolutely grounded philosophy, which can fulfill itself only as phenomenological transcendental philosophy.

This momentary 'identity' between pure psychology and transcendental philosophy leads Husserl to assert that pure psychology is thus different "from every other positive [and natural] science,"[11] in that it, by definition, eschews the so-called objective or natural world except insofar as that world is a world "for-me," that is, appropriated by and belonging to the subject. If we remind ourselves that perhaps Husserl's most radical insight consisted of 'seeing-through' the notion of "Nature,"[12] i.e., recognizing 'nature' as a construct rather than an ontological foundation, the immense importance of this confession about the relationship of pure psychology to transcendental philosophy becomes clearer. Earlier in the same text Husserl had written[13]

> Whatever may be the chances for realizing, or the capacity for realizing, the idea of objective science in respect to the mental world (i.e., not only in respect to nature), this idea of objectivity dominates the whole *universitas* of the positive sciences of the modern period, and in the general usage it dominates the meaning of the word 'science.' This already involves a naturalism insofar as this concept is taken from Galilean natural science, such that the scientifically "true," the objective, world is always thought of in advance as nature, in an expanded sense of the word. The contrast between the subjectivity of the life-world and the "objective," the "true" world, lies in the fact that the latter is a theoretical-logical substruction, the substruction of something that is in principle not perceivable, in principle not experienceable in its own proper being, whereas the subjective, in the life-world, is distinguished in all respects precisely by its being actually experienceable.
>
> ...All conceivable verification leads back to these modes of self-evidence because the "thing itself".. lies in these intuitions themselves as that which is actually, intersubjectively experienceable and verifiable and is not a substruction of thought; whereas such a substruction, insofar as it makes claim to truth, can have actual truth only by being related back to such self-evidences.

The Yogācāra position, employing a slightly different vocabulary, is not very different from this. It is in Husserl's notion of a transcendental subject that Yogācāra would be cautious about careless comparisons. If Husserl's notion of 'transcendental' is interpreted merely to indicate self-evidencing (*Evidenz*), then it would be accepted by at least some Yogācārins, viz. those who accept the third and/or fourth *bhāgas*, i.e., the *svasaṃvid-* (*tzu-cheng* 自證) and *saṃvid-svasaṃvid-bhāgas* (*cheng-tzu-cheng fen* 證自證分). These precisely are 'self-evidencing' and 'evidencing-self-evidencing' respectively. The *Ch'eng wei-shih lun* lists four bhāgas: *nimitta-bhāga* (the objective portion of a cognition), *darśana-bhāga* (the subjective portion of a cognition), *svasaṃveda* (reflexive portion, which can step back and observe and reflect on the *darśana-bhāga*), and the *saṃveda-sva-saṃveda* (which can step back from the self-reflection of the *sva-saṃveda* and observe it introspectively). Though it lists all four, the *Ch'eng wei-shih lun* says that there are really only two bhāgas—nimitta and darśana—while the remainder are figurative.

If, however, the transcendental subject (and/or object) is understood as either substrative, as a stable or permanent identity, as an autonomous world-constituting 'self,' or in any sense as a 'transcendent' (rather than 'transcendental') entity, then Yogācāra would immediately deny it. Another trend associated with Yogācāra, the Tathāgatagarbha tradition, as well as some Yogācāra texts such as the *Mahāyānasūtrālaṅkāra* (attributed to Asaṅga), do lend themselves to the substrative transcendent position. Tellingly, Hsüan-tsang did *not* translated the *Mahāyānasūtrālaṅkāra* though he studies it India.

6) **Differentialism vs. non-differentialism**. One trend, evident in such schools as the Vaibhāṣika and Sautrāntika, proffered differentialism as the ultimate descriptive mode, to that end offering doctrines such as atomism, momentariness (a kind of temporal atomism), and lists of irreducible dharmas or *bhūtas*. Unique, discrete particulars—each momentary concrescence self-defining itself momentarily (*svalakṣaṇa*)—became the ultimate 'reals' (*paramārtha dravya-sat*). On the other hand, a universe or pluriverse(s) composed of radically discontinuous particularities that cease the moment they arise, that are so violently impermanent that they verge on annihilationalism, other schools saw as extremist. Difference, no matter how radical, becomes incoherent without at least a modicum of 'continuity,' even if such continuity is itself identity-less and constituted by difference. Thus a middle way between *identity and difference* was sought. Mādhyamika dismissed both categories as incoherent. Yogācāra tread a more restrained route and tried, with the notion of the consciousness stream (*citta-saṅtāna, ālaya-vijñāna*), to offer an account of 'continuity' that avoided both the identity and difference extremes. While agreeing with Madhyamaka that it is fallacious to assert that 'identity X' exists such that X is the self-same X at t_1 and t_2, they also insisted that to fall into the opposite position, viz. that no X (or anything) has ever existed, that is to say, that *nothing exists*, is just as fallacious. To be sure, Madhyamaka never accepts the nihilistic

proposition that nothing exists either, but by hesitating to say what if anything did exist, their hesitation and silence could and often was construed by their opponents as a denial of existents altogether, despite Madhyamakan disclaimers and counterarguments. Thus Madhyamaka was consistently miscast by its opponents as 'nihilism.' We will later look at the original way in which Yogācāra proposes a kind of logical 'crossover' between 'exist' and 'not exist' as a way of implementing the 'middle way.'[14]

This grouping may also be delineated in another way, as 'reified differentialism' vs. 'non-reifying differentialism,' that is, the reifiers construct, argue for, and maintain a 'substructed' ontology, while the non-reifiers deconstruct attachment to any ontological framework. For the non-differentialists—inasmuch as they agree with all Buddhists that the primary and deepest obstruction to seeing things as they are is the logocentric imputation of 'identity' (*ātman, svabhāva*) into cognition and experience—some sort of differentialism must remain at least provisionally privileged over any identity thesis, no matter how provisional or earnest, in turn, that identity thesis is claimed to be. The absence of identity necessarily invokes suspicion that difference is affirmed. In its rejection of identity (logocentricity) *qua ātman* or *svabhāva*, Buddhism is committed, by default, to some sort of differentialism. That this differentialism can itself become an extremist trap leads to the 'middle way' attempts at avoiding either extreme.

7) **Progressionalism vs. Essentialism**. This opposition, already introduced in Parts Two and Three, became the central *differend*[15] of East Asian Buddhism. Readings of (1) and (3) above suggested progressionalism, while the dangers contained in the universalistic propensities of language (2) tended toward essentialism. Ironically, rigorous negations sometimes produced a kind of conceptual 'afterglow,' and thus (4) as well had its essentialistic interpreters[16]

These seven trajectories obviously did not always coexist equally in every text or system. But they do markedly converge in Yogācāra. In India, logic and abhidharma converge most noticeably in Vasubandhu's writings[17], and the *Triṃśikā*, although predominantly *āgamic* (i.e., discoursing from the scriptural rather than logical tradition), clearly is trying to balance both aspects. Sthiramati, in his commentary on the *Triṃśikā*, claims that the first sixteen verses, which are the abhidharmic verses, are merely *upacāra* (metaphorical heuristics) for describing *pariṇāma* (the alterity of consciousness), and that the text shifts gears at verse 17, now offering 'proofs.' Though Hsüan-tsang ostensibly divides the text differently, he, too, when beginning his discussion of verse 17 states that here begin proofs for *wei-shih* (*vijñapti-mātra*). Paramārtha also interprets those verses as 'proofs.' By Sthiramati's time, logic was already winning out over the abhidharmic (hence his devaluation of the first sixteen verses as mere heuristics).

Incidentally, this is only one of many examples in the *Ch'eng wei-shih lun* where Hsüan-tsang implicitly follows Sthiramati without announcing that he is doing so. K'uei-chi usually seems unaware of these tacit borrowings. The traditional belief, fostered by K'uei-chi's commentary, that Hsüan-tsang has taken Dharmapāla as authoritative while rejecting Sthiramati as erroneous becomes suspect when the *Ch'eng wei-shih lun* is carefully compared with the Sanskrit version of Sthiramati's commentary, a comparison only possible in this century because of the rediscovery of the Sanskrit ms. of Sthiramati's commentary to the *Triṃśikā* by Sylvain Lévy.[18] This is the only one of the ten original commentaries currently available to us. The next chapter will address this more fully.

The Failure of Indian Logic in China

Dignāga, whose profound influence had permeated Indian thought a century before Hsüan-tsang's visit, radically reoriented Buddhist thinking. For instance, he shifted the notion of *pramāṇa* (criteria for valid knowledge) from 'scripture' and 'reason'—which are accepted in Vasubandhu's writings as well as *Ch'eng wei-shih lun*—to 'perception' and 'inference' (i.e., rejecting 'scripture' or testimony, *śruti* or *śabda*, as an independent valid *pramāṇa*). After Dignāga, in part due to the new positional possibilities opened up by his epistemology and logic, and in part due to the stinging critique leveled at Yogācāra by other Buddhist schools (cf. e.g., Candrakīrti's *Madhyamakāvatāra*, ch. 6), the Abhidharmic classificatory schemata were converted into an epistemo-psychology, one which from then on constituted a field of discourse that is shared by virtually all Indian (and, subsequently, Tibetan) Buddhist schools: Madhyamaka, Yogācāra, Sautrāntika, etc.[19] By the time Dharmakīrti's writings were being disseminated in India, which must have been shortly after Hsüan-tsang's visit to India,[20] both the ālaya-vijñāna psychology and the Abhidharma had been jettisoned from Yogācāra thinking in favor of a critical epistemology that drew heavily on Sautrāntika and Madhyamakan methods. Thus the convergence of Abhidharma and logic in Vasubandhu initially splinters into two types of Yogācāra, the abhidharmic and the logical, with the latter eventually eclipsing the former entirely.

Chinese Buddhism never made this shift from psychology to logico-epistemology. Instead it further developed the psychology into a meta-psychology, an elaborate descriptive and prescriptive examination of the mind. This is partly due to the fact that the forms of Buddhism to which the Chinese were introduced and toward which they displayed any sustained interest—which then became definitive—all preceded the important developments in logic that occurred in India. Thus, as mentioned earlier, Candrakīrti's *Prasannapadā* was never translated into Chinese; Dharmakīrti, Śāntarakṣita, Ratnakīrti, etc. remained virtually unknown in East Asian Buddhism. This cannot be attributed solely to historical circumstance since monks continued to arrive and translations continued to be made well into the eleventh and twelfth centuries. Newer developments in India continued to reach China via Tibetan and Central Asian contacts (e.g., the Lamaism of the Yüan Dynasty[21]). For instance, Tantra passed right through China in the seventh through ninth centuries, leaving the barest esoteric trace there while engendering the Shingōn school which continues to flourish in Japan today.[22] Hsüan-tsang introduced the Indian syllogism to China, but it never caught on. Thus we are forced to conclude that circumstance alone does not explain why the logico-epistemological shift never occurred in China. Rather, we must look to other factors.

This shift was basically alien to Chinese interests and the contemporaneous Chinese thought. Fa-tsang's eventual victory over K'uei-chi for the patronage of Empress Wu—which marked the triumph of Sinitic Mahāyāna over Indian-styled Buddhist schools in China, most notably Hsüan-tsang's Yogācāra—signaled not so much the arising of a new set of doctrines or teachings as much as a restatement of the old, pre-Hsüan-tsang Buddhist concerns articulated by Paramārtha and others.[23] In rejecting the Buddhism that Hsüan-tsang had brought back from India, China also rejected the roots of the shift that decisively altered the course of Indian Buddhism and the Tibetan Buddhism that was later to follow it. It is at this juncture, more than at any other, that Indo-Tibetan Buddhism and East Asian Buddhism diverge into separate traditions that will go their own ways, progressively sharing less and less common concerns or vocabulary. The cross-influences between Chinese and Tibetan Buddhism, though apparent, have not been thoroughly studied yet, in part due to the Tibetan myth that it early on rejected Chinese Buddhist ideas in favor of authentic Indian ones, codified in the story of the Lhasa debates.[24] The Chinese, too, made efforts to downplay or deny the influence of foreign ideas. Even today many Chinese still consider Buddhism a 'foreign religion.'

These are, then, two crucial moments in which the variety of Buddhist trajectories initially converge and then fatefully part: (1) The convergence (in Vasubandhu) and ultimate eclipsing of the Abhidharmic by Logic (in Dignāga, Dharmakīrti, etc.), and (2) the attempt to bring Chinese Buddhism into line with Indian Buddhism by Hsüan-tsang, which, at least partly because of his failure to instill a willingness on the part of the Chinese to engage in logic and epistemology, failed to establish the conditions there that produced the shift in India from abhidharmic—and ālaya-vijñāna—psychology to logico-epistemology.

For Hsüan-tsang, the Buddhism of his day—and by extension, that which preceded it in China—had seriously deviated from the 'authentic' teachings promulgated in India. His travels had shown him that what lay at the core of the doctrinal incoherencies and the rampant disputes between the Chinese schools[25] was not simply due to a few missing chapters from the *Yogācārabhūmi*, but rather a systematic misreading and misrepresentation of Buddhist thought, encoded in faulty translations and exaggerated through faulty hermeneutics grounded on those translations. He thus envisioned his mission as a direly needed corrective, designed to put Chinese Buddhism back on track. His "correctives" took several forms: (1) re-translating whatever crucial texts had been erroneously rendered—these included not only the *Yogācārabhūmi-śāstra*, but *Vimalakīrti-nirdeśa-sūtra*, *Mahāyāna-saṃgrāha* (*She-lun*), *Abhidharmakośa-bhāṣya*, *Mahāprajñā-pāramitā Sūtra*, *Diamond Sūtra*, *Heart Sūtra*, and a host of others—and (2) to introduce new or overlooked texts to re-contextualize the reading of familiar texts and introduce the Chinese audience to a fuller sense of the range of issues at play in the Indian scene. The *Ch'eng wei-shih lun*, along with a list of other texts, notably Abhidharma texts and Yogācārin commentaries,[26] are included in this category.

While some of his retranslations failed to replace earlier versions (even K'uei-chi chose to write a commentary to Kumārajīva's version of *Vimalakīrti* rather than Hsüan-tsang's!), many of his works became seminal, such as his rendition of the *Heart Sūtra*, the *Medicine Buddha Sūtra* (T.15.450),[27] etc. In an appendix, I have listed all of Hsüan-tsang's translations, which the reader will discover cover a wide range of genres, from devotional texts, to Dhāranī texts, to Hindu treatises, to key Sūtras, to Yogācāra commentaries on Madhyamaka texts, to Āvadāna ("biographical" legends) texts, to logic manuals, and so on.

The last three trajectories mentioned above (psychological reductionism, differentialism vs. nondifferentialism, and progressionalism vs. essentialism) are clearly discernible in Chinese Buddhist thought. The psychologistic reduction, infused by a deeply ingrained native tradition culled from dominant figures like Mencius and Chuang Tzu, becomes the normative underpinning for all Sinitic Mahāyāna.[28] The plethora of Yogācāric theories that dominated Chinese Buddhist thinking in the sixth and seventh centuries—certainly the most innovative period for Chinese Buddhism—all coalesce in the syncretic text *Awakening of Mahāyānic Faith* and its doctrine of One Mind. Though emblematic of the type of psychologistic fallacy that he would eventually challenge and seek to correct, the *Awakening of Faith* apparently deeply impressed Hsüan-tsang. While in India, discovering that no Sanskrit version of the text existed and that no one there had ever heard of it, Hsüan-tsang translated it from Chinese into Sanskrit. That version is no longer extant.[29] All East Asian Buddhist schools hold the *Awakening of Faith* in the highest regard, and with it, its psychologistic reductionism. It holds an esteemed place in Korean Buddhism comparable to the preeminence given the Lotus Sutra in Japan.

The tensions of differentialism vs. nondifferentialism dominate the formulations of Chih-i, who equates enlightened mind-nature with any deluded thought-instant, and who, in a variety of ways, searched for a middle way between provisional theories (differentialism) and emptiness (nondifferential). In a later chapter we will examine Hsüan-tsang's response to an extreme form of Madhyamakan nondifferentialism.

The progressive vs. essentialist trajectory appears in countless forms in East Asian Buddhism, and is part of what has driven the recent critique of essentialistic, substrative forms of Buddhism by Hakamaya and Matsumoto, labeled by the term coined by Hakamaya: Critical Buddhism (*Hihan Bukkyō*).[30] The tension between these two approaches is perhaps best encapsulated in the

Hua-yen contention that the arising of faith that marks the initial moment of entering onto the Bodhisattva path of fifty-two stages is *essentially* already identical to achieving the culmination of the path (since the culmination is a necessary consequence that gives the initial insight its meaning and context), though the stages still need to be traversed. That formula gets reworked in countless ways by other schools, such as the Ch'an school's tension between sudden enlightenment and gradual practice.

The Prajñā Schools

The emergence of a psychologistic reduction—that coincides with a heavily ontologized notion of self—already is apparent in the early Prajñā schools of the fourth century.[31] While major figures in the Chinese Buddhist tradition, such as Seng-chao and Chi-tsang, took turns refuting these schools, the Prajñā schools already had serious disputes among themselves. In some important ways they set a certain tone that has echoed in much of the later East Asian Buddhist tradition. Hence it may be worthwhile to take note of these formative moments.

Others have already offered detailed overviews of these schools, so that needn't be repeated here.[32] These schools are called Prajñā schools because they ostensibly built their theories on the early translations of Prajñāpāramitā texts. An insightful article by Whalen Lai[33] outlines these schools. To summarize part of Lai's article: The monk Fa-shen formulated the Pen-wu 本無 ('original emptiness') school early in the fourth Century. He (1) interpreted 'emptiness' (*wu* 無) as a quasi-neo-Taoist nothingness that has cosmogonic and metaphysical primacy to *yu* 有 ('being'), and (2) treated emptiness as basically an external matter, since he viewed the inner self (*shen* 神 lit. 'spirit') as immortal and not empty. The Pen-wu school clearly had a distorted view of Buddhism, since, according to even the most derogatory Mahāyānic polemic, even the 'Inferior Vehicle' knows that the self is empty. Though Lai doesn't mention it, this suggests Taoistic motives behind the early Chinese acceptance of Buddhism, viz. Buddhism was adopted to help clarify and realize (practice) Taoist cosmology as a soteriology in pursuit of becoming an immortal (*hsien* 仙). Buddhism was seen as providing, in detail and with precision, the *means*—meditation, chanting, yoga, etc.—for achieving Taoist goals. Taoists and quasi-taoists of the time were looking for 'methods,' whether meditational, alchemical, dietary, calisthetic, etc. They seemed to find the Buddhist materials being introduced into China more comprehensive and systematic than native treatises and practices, and so were drawn to them. Taoist texts, for instance, exhorted and insisted that one should accord with Tao, act 'without acting' (*wei-wu-wei* 為無為), be a True Man, a sage, practice 'mind-fasting,' etc., but exactly how one might accomplish any of this was frequently left to the reader's imagination,[34] or embedded in vague suggestions. What methods had been suggested in Taoist circles were scattered throughout many difficult-to-acquire sources, as Ko Hung repeatedly complains in his *Pao p'u tzu*.[35]

The Taoist texts, and Mencius as well, had already decided that the basic soteric and ontological region in which humans achieve their ultimate realizations is the region of mind (*hsin* 心) qua nature (*hsing* 性).[36] By the Han Dynasty, that notion became axiomatic for all subsequent Chinese thinking.

Fa-shen entertained various oppositions such as the pairing of full and empty—while privileging the empty and equating the full with form, which clearly reflected Taoist concerns already established in the Lao Tzu.[37] While Taoism placed form and emptiness in a disymmetric dialectical relation of inseparability, Buddhism ultimately went a step further, positing the absolute non-difference between form and emptiness. For Buddhism, emptiness and form are identical, they share the same referent, though they may be conceptually distinguished. Lao Tzu's empty/full dialectic still admits a preference for one over the other, and treats them as *different* things, while the Buddhists deconstructed the dialectical tension, rendering 'form' and 'emptiness' as simply two ways of talking about the same thing, viz. the flux of causes and conditions. Distinguishing the empty from the full took several rhetorical forms, of which the most significant in the Buddhist context[38] was the question: What does 'form is emptiness and emptiness is form' mean? Taoists, on the other hand, posited a primordial Nothing (*wu*) from which things emerge and return. For Buddhism, there is no Nothing/Something fluctuation; things are nothing other than emptiness while emptiness is nothing other than things.[39]

In response to the Pen-wu school, Min-tu retorted that the self is also empty. Moreover, he argued, Buddhist emptiness is not nothingness, and can't be reduced to Taoist categories. The Prajñā schools—and later Tao-an and Hui-yüan as well—didn't wish to concede this. Despite the doctrinal soundness of Min-tu's points, amazingly, his objection was 'refuted' not by either logical or scriptural counterpoint, but through *ad hominum* slanders.[40] Despite the *ad hominum* dismissals, the force of Min-tu's Hsin-Wu 心無 ('Mind-empty') school was double-barreled: Since it was clearly based on and in concert with the available literature of that time and, as Lai contends, it was persuasively argued, it thus compelled those in the Pen-wu school to adjust and modify their own arguments. Lai's article chronicles these attempts. At each turn the 'modifiers' attempted to reassert *shen* or some other form of immortal, eternal self (emblemized in the slogan: *shen pu-mieh* 神不滅 'spirit is not destroyed').

The schools that arose in response to further wrinkles in these debates were:

1) Huan-hua school 幻化宗 (the 'Māyā or illusion' school) claimed that *shen* was immaterial, hence not subject to arising and ceasing, and thus paramārthically immortal. This was their ingenious way of "saving" the notion of an immortal self.
2) Yüan-hui school 緣會宗 ('confluence of conditions school') rather Hīnayānically argued that the confluence of conditions causes 'being' (lower truth), and the reduction of being to emptiness is the Highest truth. While

getting closer, they are still separating conditions from emptiness, failing to recognize that emptiness *is* conditionality.

3) Shih-han school 識含宗 ('subsuming of consciousness' school)

> cleverly distinguishes *shih* (consciousness, or *hsin*, mind) from the higher *shen* (spirit). It either proposes *Shih-han*, that is, the world of objects is subsumed (*han*) under the function of consciousness (*shih*); or *Han-shih*, that is, such a consciousness is subsumed (*han*) under the spirit... it is clear that the *hsin* that is emptied is the deluded mind and that a transcendental *shen* always remains as the immortal soul and guarantor of enlightenment, as *paramārtha*.

Here the efforts to save *shen* grow even more sophisticated and intricate. When centuries later Fa-tsang will differentiate his approach from Hsüan-tsang's by pointing to mind as a metaphysical ground (see below), he will be echoing the Shih-han approach.

4) Chi-se school 即色宗 argued a kind of Chuang-tzu-like 'going along with forms.' Lai argues *chi* should not be read as the copula 'always-already,' but in its secondary sense of 'according with.' Reviewing Seng-chao's critique[41] of Chi-se (as well as other critiques) Lai shows that this school did not see the identity of form and emptiness, but merely thought that emptiness could be found in forms, insofar as forms do not self-create (i.e., this school rejects the Kuo Hsiang thesis of *tzu-jan* 自然 as spontaneous self-generation), but are dependent on other things. However the Chi-se school does seem to argue that 'consciousness is always consciousness of.' Emptiness understood as causal dependence is much closer to actual Buddhist positions formulated in India than were the theories of any of the previously mentioned schools.

Hence the Prajñā schools grappled with concerns that established the course of Chinese Buddhism, viz. the efforts to accept and affirm an immortal mind-self-nature, with the appropriation and dispatching of Buddhist rhetoric for that purpose. Again and again the passages Lai quotes begin with insightful, faithful Buddhist positions (the Shih-han school in particular seems very close to an authentic Yogācāra position, if it would let go of *shen*), only to hermeneutically twist and contort those positions into heretical, onto-metaphysical positions that Chinese Buddhism never fully abandoned. That each of the Prajñā schools was driven by an agenda to find something eternal that transcended the fluctuating world of cause and conditions is clear. What they struggled with was deciding the role that mind, consciousness, and emptiness played in that agenda, with each subsequent variation of the Prajñā schools configuring the relationship between those terms and the eternal in somewhat different terms. One also sees much of the later Chinese Buddhist rhetoric already emerging in slogans such as 'elevating the origin and repressing the subsequents,' etc.[42]

Deviant Yogācāra

The subsequent development of Buddhism in China is better known, e.g., Kumārajīva, Seng-Chao, San-lun (Chinese Madhyamaka), so-called Northern and Southern Ti-lun, She-lun, etc. Regardless, too much space has already been devoted here to pre-*Ch'eng wei-shih lun* history. In terms of the *Ch'eng wei-shih lun*, only two of these later developments are vital to keep in mind at this stage:

1) Virtually every Chinese school in the century preceding Hsüan-tsang as well as in his own century was either Yogācāric (She-lun, Ti-lun, Ch'an *qua* Laṅkāvatāra school, etc.) or strongly Yogācāra-influenced (Pure Land *qua* Maitreya cult, T'ien-t'ai, Hua-yen, Chi-tsang's reading of the San-lun texts as well other texts).[43] The popular formula: T'ien-t'ai comes from Mādhyamika and Hua-yen comes from Yogācāra is too simplistic, to the point of being wrong and misleading. Garma Chang[44] showed persuasively that the Madhyamakan notion of śūnyatā as an interpretive entry into the *Heart Sūtra*'s famous line "form is emptiness, emptiness is form" lies as much at the heart of Hua-yen as any other statement in Buddhist literature, and exerts a greater influence there than the Yogācāra theory of 'mind-only.' I have elsewhere argued that Chih-I was as influenced by Yogācāra as he was by Mādhyamika, and that, e.g., his famous formula, 'provisional, empty, middle,' though explicitly addressing Nāgārjuna's MMK 24:18, is actually Chih-I's fourfold formula derived from the Yogācāric Trisvabhāva theory (the 'four' involving a doubling of paratantra as either parikalpic or pariniṣpannic).
2) All these schools, especially those textually grounded in Paramārtha's translations, had deviated from genuine Buddhism according to Hsüan-tsang, and thus his efforts aimed directly and indirectly at replacing those earlier supplementary, displacive misreadings of Indian (and thus 'authentic') Buddhist thought.[45] His "new translations" (as the vocabulary and style of his work came to be called) was, in effect, an attempt to "supplement the supplements" by supplanting them, as they had already supplanted authentic Indian ideas. The most striking deviation found in Paramārtha's translations is the introduction of a ninth consciousness—which he labeled the *amala-vijñāna* (Pure Consciousness)—beyond the standard eight discussed in Yogācāra texts. This ninth consciousness was considered a pure consciousness ultimately only accessible to enlightened beings. When the other eight, including the ālaya-vijñāna, were extinguished, this pure consciousness would emerge, eternal, resplendent. The original Sanskrit texts into which Paramārtha inserted this novel consciousness when 'translating' them never mention it. This is purely Paramārtha's supplement.[46] What it effectively does is resurrect the eternal *shen* notions we found the Prajñā schools struggling to maintain, though wrapping them in a new vocabulary. Historically speaking, these notions must have

resonated well with their Chinese audience, since they continually reasserted themselves.

The notion of Buddha-Nature, another Chinese supplement, offers an additional example of the yearning for an eternal *shen*. The question of the Chinese origins of the term "Buddha-nature" is too complex to develop here, but a few comments are in order. The Chinese term 佛性 (*Fo-hsing*, Buddha-nature) coalesced from a variety of sources, including some implications in Tathāgatagarbha ideology and certain Sanskrit terms such as *buddhatva* (Buddhahood), *buddha-gotra* (Buddha-family), etc. At some point in history, which I have not yet completely identified, Chinese translations and original texts containing the term *buddha-gotra* as 佛姓 (*fo-hsing*) were "revised," substituting the homonym *hsing* 性 (nature) for *hsing* 姓 (family). Tun-huang texts, apparently put into storage *before* this revisionistic moment, clearly use the "family" *hsing*, but the standard editions of these same texts, such as the *Platform Sutra,* all have the "nature" *hsing* in its place. When scholars study and translate these materials today they reflexively treat the "family" *hsing* as a graphical mistake and invariably "restore" the "nature" *hsing* in its place. In terms of the *Ch'eng wei-shih lun*, the traces of this revisionistic rewriting can be clearly seen in several places, such as the section on "seeds", in which the context unmistakably denotes seed "families," not natures, and yet there are in circulation some manuscripts (but *not* all) that have converted "family" into "nature." Again, where and when these revisions were instituted is as yet unclear, but the reason for it is not. That reason is the promotion of "nature" as an emblem for the *shen*-like transcendent self. Not counting the versions of *Ch'eng wei-shih lun* that replace *hsing*-family with *hsing*-nature, the term 佛性 *fo-hsing* (Buddha-nature) appears about twenty-six times in Hsüan-tsang's translations.[47]

As for developments within Sinitic Mahāyāna—that is to say, those schools that were beginning to establish themselves around the time Hsüan-tsang lived—we see the dialectic between differentialism and non-differentialism in such things as the T'ien-t'ai notion of 'a single thought-instant in three thousand worlds' and Hua-yen's mutual interpenetration of all particulars. In the latter especially, great pains are taken to give a rigorous account of how all distinct, unique events or things (*shih shih* 事事) interpenetrate, such that they constitute a whole, a totality, but without sacrificing one iota of their individual uniqueness.[48]

The sinitic schools, following Fa-tsang's classification, all came to identify themselves as Dharma-*Nature* schools, meaning that they all wrestled with the adoption of a rehabilitated *shen*-notion qua Buddha-nature—that is, essentialism. One well known example of this tension is the Sudden vs. Gradual controversy which clearly and explicitly wrestles along the fissure of the progressionalism vs. essentialism dichotomy.[49] But in strictly Yogācāric terms the issue lies elsewhere: Does nature (*hsing*), whether Buddha-nature, mind-nature, or whatever, have an 'essence' (*svabhāva*, in Chinese *tzu-hsing* 自性, lit. 'own-nature' or 'self-nature'), or is the notion of 'nature' merely a provisional, prajñaptic (*chia ming* 假名) device devoid of any real, fixed essence? While all Buddhists, to remain consistent with basic Buddhist doctrine, should accept the latter description and reject the former, some nonetheless hypostatized nature, particularly the *nature* of mind and consciousness, reifying it as an essence. Even some statements in Hsüan-tsang's *Ch'eng wei-shih lun* lend themselves to this interpretation, though in the main he seems to have taken great pains to challenge the essentializing tendency present in the Chinese Buddhism of his day.

Hsiang hsing 相性 ("characteristic and nature") in the *Ch'eng wei-shih lun*

Perhaps the most significant instance of Hsüan-tsang's 'essentialism' is his use of *hsiang hsing* 相性 'characteristic and nature' in his translation of the *Triṃśikā*, as noted in Part IV.[50] These lines, which distinguish *hsiang* from *hsing*—though no such corresponding terminology occurs in Sanskrit—reflect a foundational distinction in East Asian Buddhism. Both Tat and Wing-tsit Chan insist on the extreme importance of this distinction in their translations of Hsüan-tsang's version of the *Triṃśikā*.[51] Apparently neither noticed the absence of any Sanskrit correspondences. In fairness to Chan and Tat, it should be pointed out that Hsüan-tsang drew this distinction between *hsiang* and *hsing* deliberately, and even provides an account of it in the *Ch'eng wei-shih lun*. Commenting on a line in verse 8 of the *Triṃśikā* that defines *mano-vijñāna* and the five sense consciousesses, Hsüan-tsang writes:[52]

> Next, there are the words: "DISCERNING PERCEPTUAL-OBJECTS IS ITS NATURE AND CHARACTERISTIC (*hsing hsiang*)." [see Part IV for a translation that stays closer to the Sanskrit] This pair discloses the self-nature (*tzu-hsing* 自性) and activity-characteristic (*hsing hsiang* 行相 = *ākāra*)[53] of the six consciousnesses. The Consciousnesses take DISCERNING PERCEPTUAL-OBJECTS as their self-nature, and again their 'activity-characteristic' (*ākāra*) is precisely the functioning (*yung* 用) of that [nature]...

Hsüan-tsang has converted the Chinese paradigm of *t'i-yung* (體用 structure and function) into *svabhāva* and *ākāra*, taking the latter term as *an activity*, as a *hsing* 行 (not to be confused with *hsing* 性 'nature,' an entirely different word). Though his translations are usually accurate and faithful to the Sanskrit (sometimes even reproducing Sanskrit, rather than Chinese, syntax) there are such occasional divergences that are noteworthy. Here he generates new categories in Chinese. In the second verse of the *Triṃśikā* he translated *vijñapti* as *liao-pieh* 了別, while here he has used *liao* 了 (both mean 'discern') to translate *upalabdhi*, as if *vijñapti* (lit.: cause to be known) and *upalabdhi* (perceptually grasp) were synonyms. Here we have clear evidence of Chinese interests and paradigms overshadowing and possibly obscuring the thoughts expressed in the Sanskrit text.

Earlier, he had already defined the seventh consciousness, *manas*, in terms of *svabhāva* and *ākāra*:[54]

> The [fifth] verse says [of manas]: "WILLING-DELIBERATING IS ITS NATURE AND CHARACTERISTIC." [see Part IV for a different translation.] This pair discloses the self-nature and activity-characteristic (*hsing hsiang*) of this consciousness. Manas takes WILLING-DELIBERATING as its self-nature, and again its 'activity-characteristic' is precisely the functioning of that [nature].

He has used the same phraseology for both definitions. Both passages go on to state that distinguishing the eight consciousnesses in terms of each's distinctive *svabhāva* and *ākāra* is what allows different *names* to be assigned to these consciousnesses, i.e., these 'natures' and 'functions' define each consciousness as unique, as different from the ālaya-vijñāna and each other. Manas, like the Sāṃkhyan *buddhi*, is reflective,[55] while mano-vijñāna and the five sense-consciousnesses discern and discriminate cognitive objects. It is easy to lose sight of the fact that Hsüan-tsang is saying that what a consciousness is in itself (*svabhāva*) is nothing but what it does (*ākāra*). *Ākāra*, as he uses it here, means the cognitive characteristics—such as size, texture, color, even affective tone, etc.—that are apprehended in a cognitive act, or more generally, the mental images of our cognitions. The nominal distinctions between the eight consciousnesses are determined on the basis of their functions, their activities, since their 'self-nature' is nothing more than a formal declaration of those functions.

Ironically, this very distinction became one of the major rhetorical weapons used by Fa-tsang against Hsüan-tsang's school, calling them "[the mere] fa-hsiang" (Dharma-Characteristics) school against his own Sinitic "fa-hsing" (Dharma-Nature) school. This distinction became so important that every Buddhist school originating in East Asia, including all forms of Sinitic Mahāyāna, viz. T'ien-t'ai, Hua-yen, Ch'an, and Pure Land, came to be considered Dharma-nature schools. In Korea, one of the foundational Buddhist schools actually called itself the Dharma-nature school (Pŏpsŏngjong), and it is probably fair to say that all subsequent developments in Korean Buddhism owe some allegiance to this school. By contrast, the Dharma-Characteristics school—defined by Fa-tsang as exclusively the interpretation and texts of Hsüan-tsang and K'uei-chi—became almost universally disparaged in East Asia as 'pseudo-Hīnayāna' or 'quasi-Mahāyāna,' a polemically demeaning pejorative that one still finds frequently repeated by some modern scholars in the East as well as the West as if this were objective history.[56]

In one form or another, all seven trajectories converge in the *Ch'eng wei-shih lun*. Given its large size and its even larger scope, we will not be able to deal with all the trajectories, but have had to make judicious choices. For instance, abhidharmic disputes, important and integral to the *Ch'eng wei-shih lun* as they are, will remain relatively ignored. Only those aspects of the trajectories that are of the greatest philosophic importance will be examined. Hence what will be explored will be those portions of the text that bear on:

1) the question of idealism (yes-or-no?), or what precisely is or isn't the case according to *Ch'eng wei-shih lun*: What is a human? A sentient being? Tathatā? Conscious-ness(es)? Perception? The status of objects? Externality? Closure? Intersubjectivity?
2) What passes for an argument? A proof? Criteriology?
3) The soteric systematics, with emphasis on *systematics*, especially in terms of philosophic grounding and justification (i.e., reasonability).

We will only be discussing such "yogācāric" mainstays as the eight consciousnesses and one-hundred dharmas in passing or as needed (following Sthiramati's suggestion that they are *upacāra*), and the same applies to the Three (non-)Self-natures theory, though to many these particular theories *are the essence of Yogācāra*. On the contrary, by shifting our focus away from a concerted explication of these models onto the other philosophic concerns addressed by the text, a more informed and responsible interpretation of those models will become possible, since an understanding of their fuller context and applications will impose an informed restriction on speculation. The task I have set out to achieve here is to recover the original orientation of the *Ch'eng wei-shih lun* sufficiently to facilitate an accurate reading of those models. In other words, this work might be seen as a prolegomena to the foundational Yogācāra models, not their definitive exposition. Rather we are focusing on whatever clarifies the philosophic issues.

More could be said about these sub-trajectories and their effect on the *Ch'eng wei-shih lun*, but we will now let that slip into the background as we begin to look more closely at the *Ch'eng wei-shih lun* itself.

Notes

1 For instance, according to Theravāda tradition, Buddha's two leading disciples, Sariputta and Moggallana, joined him after having studied with the leading 'skeptic' of the day, Sanjaya, and his 'skeptical' rhetoric and reasoning found their way into the early Buddhist teachings; or the Ājīvikas (cf. A.L. Basham, *History and Doctrines of the Ājīvikas*, Delhi: Motilal, 1981 rpt); or the pseudo-logic of the *Kathā-vatthu* as discussed in Part Three above; or Jaina logic, though technically speaking their logic arose in response to Buddhist logic. Early Jain thinkers, such as Umāsvāti (44-85 C.E.), Samantabhadra (2nd-3rd century C.E.) or Kundakunda (127-179 C.E.) were debaters, commentators, and doctrinal formulators, but hardly proficient logicians. Although Āryarakṣita's *Anuyogadvāra Sūtra* (1st century) already broached epistemological themes such as the *pramāṇas* (means of valid cognition), it is not until the fourth or fifth century (e.g., Siddhasena Divākara) that Jaina epistemology achieves a rigorous logic. Many of the early Jaina logicians arose in response to Buddhism, and are known and respected in Jaina history for their refutations of Buddhist arguments; e.g., Mallavādī 4th-5th Century, defeated Buddhists at the court of King Śilāditya; Pātrakesarī -

(5th-6th Century) his *Trilakṣaṇa-kadarthana* refuted Buddhist causation theories [not extant]; *Mallavādī* [II] - 700-750 C.E., wrote a commentary on Dharmottara's commentary on Dharmakīrti's *Nyāyabindu*; etc.). But generally

> Akalaṅka [8th Century] is said to be the pioneer in the field of Jaina logic. It is believed that the science of logic was given a definite shape in his time. (Yuvacarya Mahaprajna. *Jaina Nyaya Ka Vikasa,* tr. into Eng. by Nathman Tatia as *New Dimensions in Jaina Logic,* Rajasthan: Jaina Vishva Bharati, 1984, p. 163)

His biography bears a marked resemblance to the Mīmāṃsika Kumārila Bhaṭṭa, down to the family name.

> 'Bhaṭṭa' was [Akalaṅka's] family title. His brother's name was Niṣkalaṅka. Once the two brothers lived in a Buddhist monastery to study Buddhist logic. It was leaked there that they were Jaina. Niṣkalaṅka was killed; but Akalaṅka somehow escaped. After getting the status of an *ācārya* for himself he had a debate with the Bauddhas in the court of Himaśītala, the king of Kaliṅga. The opponents installed goddess Tārā in an earthen pot and by virtue of her power became invincible. Akalaṅka knew this secret. He invoked the deity of his order and after breaking the pot defeated the Bauddhas in the debate. (*ibid.,* p. 163).

This violent and fanciful story shows both where Jainas had to go in order to learn logic, and how serious a matter it was for them.

2 Cf. translation and discussion in Anacker, *Seven Works of Vasubandhu*, pp. 29-48.

3 Cf. Richard Chi's *Buddhist Formal Logic* (Delhi: Motilal, 1984 rpt of 1969 Royal Asiatic Society of Great Britain ed.) which discusses, in great analytic detail, one of these texts, the *Nyāyapraveśa* along with K'uei-chi's (Hsüan-tsang's leading disciple) commentary on it. I've given two papers on the reception of the Indian syllogism by the Chinese: (1) the Annual Conference of the International Society for Chinese Philosophy, Hilo, Hawaii, July 25, 1989; and (2) at the Fall 1989 Annual Meeting of the American Academy of Religion (both unpublished).

4 For an English translation, with the Tibetan and Chinese texts, and a reconstructed Sanskrit text, see: F.W Thomas and UI Hakuju, "The Hand Treatise, a Work of Āryadeva," *Journal of the Royal Asian Society*, 1918, pp. 367-310 (the text is misattributed to Āryadeva in the Tibetan tradition).

5 Not counting Paramārtha's translation of *Ju shih lun* 如實論 (T.32.1633), **Tarka-śāstra*, sometimes attributed to Vasubandhu, which hardly qualifies as a rigorous logic text. The only other translation of a logic text was a second translation of *Nyāyamukha* by I-Ching, but not only was this a text already translated by Hsüan-tsang, I-Ching's version was largely ignored by the East Asian tradition since it offered no advantage over Hsüan-tsang's rendition, and is frequently more obscure.

6 As part of his delineation and rejection of the sixty-two extreme views.

7 This echoes the *Awakening of Faith*. Cf. T.32.1666.578a7: 唯心相滅非心體滅. "Only the characteristics of mind cease; not the *t'i* of mind."

8 We will deal with this more fully later when discussing how Hsüan-tsang interprets the claim that consciousness is not empty.

9 Cf. *The Crisis of the European Sciences*, tr. by David Carr, Evanston: Northwestern University Press, 1970, pp. 203-208.

10 *Ibid.*, pp. 258f.

11 *Ibid.*, p. 260.

12 "Nature" is not a pregiven or even a given to which men simply adapt, but a concept, an idea, or set of ideas, which are interpretations, constructions, theories, that have not only gained currency but have become embodied worldviews, 'sedimented' in us so that we "see" the world as nature, and assume that seeing it that way is 'natural.'

13 *Ibid.*, p. 127f.

14 This 'crossover' idea is derived from the *Madhyānta-Vibhāga.* While Yogācāra proper only takes this crossover procedure one step, it may be argued that Hua-yen, and in some ways T'ien-t'ai, extended the crossover indefinitely or infinitely, so that Hua-yen's infinite mutual interpenetration of all events or T'ien-t'ai's 'provisional and empty' culminating in the 'middle', etc., can be seen as the working out of Yogācāric implications.

15 The term 'differend' was coined by Jean-François Lyotard. His fascinating book, *The Differend: Phrases in Dispute,* tr. from French by Georges Van Den Abbeele (Minneapolis: University of Minnesota Press, 1988), drawing expertly on the philosophical tradition from Plato and Aristotle to Kant to Wittgenstein to Heidegger and Russell, etc., proposes a deconstructive ethic to deal with how, in an age without metaphysical certainty, where opposing, contradictory moral and ethical claims lead to logical impasses and aporia (his explicit theme is Auschwitz, i.e., in an age where the referent cannot be reached for testimony - how can one answer, in an ethically compelling manner, the contemporary defender of Nazidom who simply denies the reality of, i.e., the referent 'Auschwitz', and who claims that the imposition of Nuremburg justice is only doing to the loser what the loser himself is accused of doing, viz. imposing a dominant will and sense of right and wrong on a weaker party?), how, in the milieu of undecidability, does one make decisions with integrity? He begins to define 'differend' on p. xi:

> As distinguished from a litigation, a differend [*différend*] would be a case of conflict, between (at least) two parties, that cannot be equitably resolved for lack of a rule of judgement applicable to both arguments. One side's legitimacy does not imply the other's lack of legitimacy. However, applying a single rule of judgement to both in order to settle their differend as though it were a mere litigation would wrong (at least) one of them (and both of them if neither side admits this rule)...

16 Not only do the obvious Hindu appropriations of Buddhist thought come to mind, such as Gaudapāda's utilization of Madhyamaka and Yogācāra thought to reinterpret the Upaniṣads, or Śaṅkara's appropriation of the Yogācāric notion of cognitive displacement as the basis for his theory of adhyāsa *qua* māyā; but perhaps even more importantly the persistence by both Buddhist and Western scholars to read notions like *śūnyatā* in Vedāntic or onto-theological registers needs to be recognized and addressed. *Śūnyatā* is not a *via negativa* for revealing or uncovering the 'True Ground of Being' or any other such fantasy; nor is *śūnyatā* itself that ground. The term signifies the activity of 'emptying out' such notions, not merely as concepts, but in terms of the festering inner compulsions which lead one to posit such things in the first place. Emptiness is not an ontological ground, but a methodological tool to be discarded, i.e., 'emptied', when its task is completed. Such, at least, I would argue, is the authentic Yogācāra or Madhyamaka sense of the term. That is not to say that all Buddhists at all times and in all places have unequivocally explained it in precisely this way. In terms of the *Ch'eng wei-shih lun* no other understanding of emptiness than the one given here is to be found. Some illustrative passages will be cited later. It should be noted, however, that the ontologization of emptiness did not occur first in modern scholarship, but has a Buddhist pedigree in East Asia. Tibetan varieties include the Dzog Chen and Shentong traditions. S.K. Hookham's *The Buddha Within* (Albany: SUNY Press, 1991) provides an exposition and defense of the Shentong position.

17 Dignāga wrote a commentary on the *Abhidharmakośa* which survives only in Tibetan.

18 Louis de la Vallée Poussin apparently consulted the Tibetan version of Sthiramati's commentary, not the Sanskrit, for his French translation of the *Ch'eng wei-shih lun.* Though he reads it well (i.e., he has good instincts as to what Sanskrit terminology lies behind the Tibetan) some discrepancies have apparently crept in. Despite his vast erudition and unblinking command of a dizzying array of sources, he doesn't show a sense of Sthiramati as an integral thinker with a cohesive position spread among a range of texts. Despite his conferring with

Sthiramati's commentary in Tibetan, he seems in several places to defer too readily to K'uei-chi's appraisal. One example will be discussed later.

19 This 'psychology' revolves around notions of *prapañca, vikalpa, abhūta-parikalpita*, etc., as root problematics, and some sort of knowledge, most frequently *nirvikalpa-jñāna*, as their corrective. Many details of this psychology stay in contention between the various schools, but the basic gist underwrites their thinking.

20 Dating Indian thinkers is a notoriously uncertain enterprise. According to Tāranātha's *History of Buddhism in India* (tr. from Tibetan by Lama Chimpa and Alaka Chattopadhyaya, Simla: Indian Institute of Advanced Study, 1970) Candrakīrti, Candragomī and Dharmapāla are contemporaries (cf. pp. 198-207, 209, 213, etc.). However while Tāranātha says that Dharmapāla succeeds Candrakīrti, he also claims that Dharmapāla's commentary on *Mādhyamika- kārikās* is *older* than Candrakīrti's (p. 213). Dharmakīrti is supposedly initiated by Dharmapāla (p. 229). Since Candragomī is also said to have received one-time instruction in Sūtras and Abhidharma-piṭaka from Sthiramati (p. 210), all these thinkers would have to be contemporaries. Yet elsewhere he claims that Sthiramati lived in an earlier period, contemporaneous with Dignāga, Buddhadāsa, Buddhapālita, Bhāvaviveka, and others (p. 177). Putting Tāranātha further into doubt are Hsüan-tsang's own writings, especially the (*Ta T'ang*) *Hsi-yü-chi* (大唐)西域記 (*Journey to the West during the Great T'ang Dynasty*). Having visited India centuries earlier than Tāranātha's writing, and thus closer to the time of the original events, his writings are more definitive, particularly in terms of what or who is *absent* from his account. Since he aims to be somewhat comprehensive, the failure to mention someone is a good indication that that person has either not yet made his mark, or that that person is not yet living. According to Hsüan-tsang, Dharmapāla was challenged by Bhāvaviveka to debate, but declined. Dharmakīrti and Candrakīrti are not mentioned at all (Beal, *Buddhist Records of the Western World*, NY: Paragon Book, 1968 rpt, p. i.189-90 n. 76, notes that some have associated a 'Deva Bodhisattva' mentioned in the text with Candrakīrti, but he rejects that identification). Though Sthiramati is mentioned, there is no indication that he and Dharmapāla were contemporaries (cf. Beal, p. ii.171, which in fact suggests that they were not). In I-ching's account of the curriculum at Nālandā (*Nan-hai chi-kuan nai fa chuan* 南海寄歸內法傳, ch. 34), Dharmakīrti's writings are given prominent mention, indicating that Dharmakīrti must have risen to prominence during the decades between Hsüan-tsang's return from India (645) and I-ching's stay there (671-691). This timetable tantalizingly suggests that Hsüan-tsang and Dharmakīrti may have known each other at Nālandā, before the latter had yet made his mark.

21 The cross-pollination between Chinese and Tibetan Buddhism has not been adequately explored by modern scholars. Self-interests and nationalistic prides on both the Chinese and Tibetan sides have dampened attention to any indebtedness one might owe the other. Mongolian histories have yet to be fully factored into these accounts. Official Chinese histories, disdaining dynastic periods during which non-Chinese ruled China, such as the Mongol and Manchu dynasties, have downplayed achievements during those dynasties, at times ignoring positive events almost entirely in favor of emphasizing negative events that helped justify and rationalize the superiority of Chinese rule. Court histories, since usually compiled by Confucian historians, tended to downplay or ignore events that primarily concerned Buddhists or Taoists unless those events directly impinged on the court. As a result, important developments in Buddhism during the Yüan dynasty, including a special intensification of contact between Central Asian and East Asian forms of Buddhism through the auspices of the Khans and by other means have been neglected. Chinese Buddhists in the Ming period following the Yüan were better served by not emphasizing borrowings or influences from "foreign" forms of Buddhism, since Buddhism itself was still frequently accused of being a foreign religion.

22 The fate of Tantra in China is, I suspect, more complex than this. Not only is there the Mongol and Tibetan influence, which perhaps due to nationalistic pride rarely receives serious

attention from Chinese scholars; closer examination of some late Chinese Buddhist writings, such as Han-shan Te-ching's autobiography written during the Ming Dynasty, indicates the presence of Tantric elements and themes (e.g., his 'dreams') which go unannounced as such. Further, Vairocana, central to the Hua-Yen Sūtra and thus to the Hua-Yen school, is also a key Tantric deity. Much more work needs to be done to clarify these and other indications which have so far remained 'between the lines' in Chinese Buddhism.

As for Shingōn in Japan, Kūkai (a.k.a. Kobodaishi) is venerated as one of Japan's most influential thinkers, credited not only with bringing Tantra from China, but with developing the katakana alphabet and instituting many new cultural directions, which Japan has nurtured ever since. On Kūkai, see Yoshito Hakeda's *Kūkai: Major Works* NY: Columbia UP, 1972; on Shingōn, see Minoru Kiyota's *Shingōn Buddhism: Theory and Practice* (Los Angeles-Tokyo: Buddhist Books International, 1978), and Pierre Rambach, *The Secret Message of Tantric Buddhism*, op. cit.

23 To date, the two best sources on the state of Buddhism in sixth and seventh century China - particularly in terms of the ubiquity of Yogācāra schools and their subsumation by Hua-yen - are unpublished dissertations. Robert Gimello's *Chih-yen (602-668) and the Foundations of Hua-Yen Buddhism*, Columbia University, 1972, gives a thorough account of the Buddhism of Hsüan-tsang's day (Hsüan-tsang's dates are 600-669, making him and Chih-yen precise contemporaries). Ming-wood Liu's *The Teaching of Fa-tsang An Examination of Buddhist Metaphysics*, UCLA, 1979, covers, among other things, the polemic disputes between Fa-tsang and Hsüan-tsang's brand of Yogācāra in great detail. It is lamentable that neither of these works, both first class, has been published and made more readily available. What they examine bears directly on the *Ch'eng wei-shih lun* and the matters under discussion here, but I must refer the reader to them, as space does not permit me to replicate them here.

24 On the Lhasa debate story and its polemical uses, see David Seyfort Ruegg, *Buddha-nature, Mind, and the Problem of Gradualism in a Comparative Perspective: On the Reception of Buddhism in India and Tibet* (London: School of Oriental and African Studies, University of London, 1989).

25 Chang-yueh, in his preface to Hsüan-tsang's *Hsi-yü-chi*, paraphrasing chapters 38 and 20 of Lao tzu, expresses it thus:

> At this time the schools were mutually contentious; they hastened to grasp the end without regarding the beginning; they seized the flower and rejected the reality; so there followed the contradictory teaching of the North and South [Ti-lun schools], and the confused sounds of "Yes" and "No," perpetual words! (Beal's translation, *op. cit.*, p. i.5, square brackets mine)

26 E.g., Sthiramati's commentary to Asaṅga's *Abhidharmasamuccaya*, T.1616.31. The existence of such texts suggest that Hsüan-tsang's opinion of Sthiramati may not have been as negative as is usually asserted. K'uei-chi, in fact, wrote a commentary to this text, and its ideas show up in K'uei-chi's commentary to the *Ch'eng wei-shih lun*. We'll return to this in the next chapter.

27 A translation can be found in Raoul Birnbaum, *The Healing Buddha* (Boulder: Shambhala, 1979) 151-172.

28 To even begin to catalogue all the forms and varieties of psychologistic reductions found in Chinese, Korean and Japanese Buddhism is beyond the scope of this present work. T'ien-t'ai's 'contemplating mind' (*kuan-hsin* 觀心) or chilicosms of thought-instants (*nien* 念); Ch'an's direct pointing at mind, no-mind, etc.; the *Hua-yen Sūtra*'s "the three worlds are only mind," etc.; are all only the obvious, visible tip of the iceberg.

29 The only other text Hsüan-tsang is known to have translated into Sanskrit was the *Lao Tzu*.

30 On Critical Buddhism, see *Pruning the Bodhi Tree*, eds. Jamie Hubbard and Paul Swanson (Honolulu: University of Hawaii Press, 1997).

31 On these schools, cf. TSUKAMOTO Zenryū, *A History of Early Chinese Buddhism: From its Introduction to the Death of Hui-Yüan*, op. cit. This is Hurvitz' translation of *Chūgoku Bukkyō*

Tsūshi v. 1 (Shunjūsha: 1979). Unfortunately TSUKAMOTO died before completing a full history, so these volumes end with Hui-yüan. Hence it stops short of the Yogācāric expansion in China and the subsequent explosion of Sinitic Mahāyāna. Hsüan-tsang's predecessor and foil, the translator Paramārtha, e.g., is only mentioned once. However, it is a fairly thorough survey of the material it covers. It is long on history and sometimes short on philosophy and doctrine; historically critical, but rarely philosophically critical. Hurvitz's notes provide an indispensable supplement.

Hurvitz' translation, as always, is very professional. An index, primarily of Chinese names with the characters, is at the end of the second volume. The original audience of the book was to be the Japanese layman (with an understanding that Hurvitz would make it available to English readers), so the material is accessible with a minimum of technical vocabulary. Many important texts are cited. No other work available in English even approaches its scope and detail.

For a different (perhaps more accurate) interpretation of these schools, cf. Whalen W. Lai, "The early Prajñā schools, especially 'Hsin-wu', reconsidered", *Philosophy East and West*, 33, no. 1, January 1983, pp. 61-77.

32 Along with Tsukamoto and Lai, a translation and discussion of Chi-tsang's refutation of the Prajñā schools can be found in Paul Swanson, *Foundations of T'ien-t'ai Philosophy* (Berkeley: Asian Humanities Press, 1989; Leon Hurvitz was nearing publication of a translation of Chi-tsang's refutation along with the Japanese monk Ancho's commentary (Swanson also makes use of Ancho), when he died.

33 *Op. cit.*

34 For instance, see *Alchemy, Medicine & Religion in the China of A.D. 320: The Nei P'ien of Ko Hung*, tr. and ed. by James Ware (NY: Dover, 1981). The theme of the text is precisely the uncertainty of what to do, what will work, which 'elixirs' and practices are lethal or dangerous, etc., coupled with an intense desire to experiment. It was from these often mortally fateful uncertainties that 'neo-Taoists' turned to Buddhism as a method, a way, a Tao.

35 Cf. *Pao p'u Tzu: Hsin-yi* 抱朴子：新譯. Li Chung-hua 李中華 and Huang Chih-min 黃志民, eds. Taipei: Sanmin, 1997, 2 vols.

36 Cf., e.g., *Chuang Tzu* ch. 16 (p. 41, line 9 in the Harvard- Yenching Concordance edition). Although I have not found the actual compound *hsin-hsing* in the Chuang Tzu, both terms are crucial. E.g., on the relation of Mind and Form (another *hsing* 形) cf. ch. 4 (p. 9, ln. 28), ch. 23 (p. 62, ln. 19), ch. 5 (p. 12, ln. 2), etc. On Mind and Nature (*hsing* 性) cf. ch. 16 (p. 41, ln. 9). For Mencius mind and nature are also crucial: cf. 2:1.2 and passim on 'the unperturbed mind' (lit. 'not-moved mind', *pu-tung hsin* 不動心, a term later adopted by Buddhists for *āneñjya* or *akopya* mental states, i.e., implacable mental states such as arise in the eighth *bhūmi*), and the famous dispute with Kao-tzu on the meaning of Nature, 6:1.3: *Sheng* (生 the inborn, innate, lit. "born, arising, producing") is *hsing* (性 nature), playing on the etymology of the character for *hsing*, which is a compound of *hsin* 心 'mind, heart' and *sheng* 生. While the appearance of Chuang Tzu's language and thought in Chinese Buddhist writings is generally recognized (though an exhaustive detailed study has yet to be written in a Western language), Mencius' influence is rarely discussed, if noticed. In a study of the *Lin-chi-lü* which I am preparing, Mencius' contribution to Ch'an will be explicitly acknowledged and examined.

37 Cf. *Tao te ching*, chs. 11, 12, 14, etc.

38 This was usually posed in reference to the famous line in the Heart Sūtra: "Form is emptiness, emptiness is form; form is not different from emptiness, emptiness is not different from form."

39 See my essay "Chinese Buddhist Philosophy" in *The Routledge Encyclopedia of Philosophy* for further discussion.

40 For instance, Hui-yüan uses a pun drawn from the *I-ching* concerning *shen* (spirit) being quick to show anger. This pun is reminiscent of a later Zen story (and may be its source). Cf. Lai's article for Hui-yüan's pun. The Zen story is:

One day Tesshu, the famous swordsman and Zen devotee, went to Dokuon and told him triumphantly he believed all that exists is empty, there is no you or me, etc. The master who had listened in silence suddenly snatched up his long tobacco pipe and struck Tesshu's head.

The infuriated swordsman would have killed the master there and then, but Dokuon said calmly, "Emptiness is quick to show anger, isn't it?"

Forcing a smile, Tesshu left the room.

from *Zen: Poems, Prayers, Sermons, Anecdotes, Interviews*, ed. and tr. by Lucien Stryk and Takashi Ikemoto (NY: Doubleday Anchor, 1965), p. 121.

41 Cf. Swanson and Hurvitz, *op. cit.*

42 Cf. also Whalen Lai, "*Hu-Jan Nien-Ch'i* (Suddenly a Thought Arose): Chinese Understanding of Mind and Consciousness", *Journal of the International Association of Buddhist Studies*, 3, no. 2, 1980, pp. 42-59, which deals with, amongst other topics, the notion of *shih* (consciousness) in the *Feng-fa-yao*, the treatment of *hsin* (mind) and *shih* (consciousness) in the Prajñā schools and the *Ch'eng-Shih* (*Satyasiddhi*) masters' speculations on *Citta-santāna* (consciousness-stream); cf. also Whalen Lai, "Before the Prajñā Schools: The Earliest Chinese Commentary on the *Aṣṭasāhasrikā*," *Journal of the International Association of Buddhist Studies*, 6, no. 1, 1983, pp. 91-108, which deals with the Neo-Taoist/early-Chinese Buddhist (ca. 312-385 CE, the time of Tao-an) interpretations of *śūnyatā* by way of the *Prajñāpāramitā-Sūtra* of 8000 lines and the *Ming-tu* commentary. The last section contains this quote (Lai's translation) with his comment:

(My teacher says) '...The *Mahāsattva* courses (in the perfection of wisdom) and sees that as being identical with life and death. Saṃsāra and the (Nirvanic) Way are the same. All dharmas being empty, all things are equal. This path of equality is one that would not abandon the ill of any sentient existence in an aspiration only for the originally pure. Rather, it is to bear the pain of life and death in order to guide others on to the Great Way so that the path of the Buddha can continue with no end.' (p. 482a14-15 [in T])

That is neither Hīnayāna Psychology nor Taoist philosophy, and can never be reduced to them.

43 A number of papers presented at a conference on "Yogācāra in China" held at the University of Leiden, June 8-9, 2000, organized by Chen-kuo Lin (Cheng-chi University, Taipei) documented this. E.g., Hans-Rudolf Kantor, "Zhiyi's (538-597) Reception, Interpretation and Criticism of Dilun and Shelun Thought"; Nobuyoshi YAMABE, "The Influence of Xuanzang's Yogacara Texts over the Nothern School of Chan.;

44 *Buddhist Teaching of Totality* (University Park: Penn State University Press, 1977).

45 For a good example of the critique of Paramārtha's translations, cf. K'uei-chi's commentary to Hsüan-tsang's translation of the *Madhyānta Vibhāga*, in which he exploits every opportunity to ridicule and attack Paramārtha's earlier translation. His criticisms, it should be pointed out, are invariably justified and pertinent. Texts such as these should be consulted by those scholars, mainly Japanese, who blindly repeat each other when they attempt to assert that Paramārtha's translations are 'better' than Hsüan-tsang's. Paramārtha's may at times be more readable or literary (since Hsüan-tsang often chose to emulate Sanskrit syntax, and the Chinese of his day was syntax-dependent for meaning rather than grammar-dependent, hence making his texts difficult to read, especially in the absence of a Sanskrit original or at least some knowledge of Sanskrit and its syntax), but they are almost never more *accurate*.

46 In the original Sanskrit, when available, one never finds mention of a ninth consciousness, though the term *amala-vijñāna* does occur in a few instances (e.g., in the *Ratnagotra-vibhāga*, a Tathāgatagarbha text considered as a Yogācāra text in the Tibetan tradition). When comparing sections of Paramārtha's translation with Hsüan-tsang's translations of the same texts, one finds no mention in Hsüan-tsang of an *amala-vijñāna*. Instead other terms, such as

āśraya-paravṛtti (overturning the basis), occur. Cf. Diana Paul, *Philosophy of Mind in Sixth-Century China*, pp. 139-150.

47 E.g., T.7.220.895b27, 2895c1, 895c5; 220.1036b5, 1036b25; T.31.1606.748a21, 749c2.; the remainder are also in T.220, Hsüan-tsang's massive translation of the *Mahāprajñāpāramitā Sūtra.* T.1606 is a translation of Sthiramati's commentary on *Abhidharmasamuccaya.* In other words, all his uses of *fo-hsing* are restricted to two texts. Tellingly, Chu Fei-huang's 朱芾煌 *Yogācāra (Fa-hsiang) Dictionary* (法相大辭典, Taipei, 1988, 2 vols.), which defines "fa-hsiang" terms with extended passages from Chinese Yogācāra texts, does not include *fo-hsing* (Buddha-Nature) among its more than 30 compounds for *fo* (Buddha).

48 Ch'eng-kuan, the so-called "fourth" patriarch of Hua-yen, especially worked hard at establishing this relation, as well as offering numerable ways of approaching this. *Shih-shih wu-ai* 事事無礙 (the non-obstruction of event and event) alludes to a totality constituted not out of the elimination or overlooking of actual distinctions, but out of the total accumulation of all possible perspectives, contexts, realms of discourse, etc., such that all possible distinctions are made possible and actualizable, but only insofar as they all mutually depend on each other and are mutually constitutive, i.e., 'empty.' Fa-tsang poses this as a going beyond identity and difference. For examples of this in translation, see Garma Chang's *The Buddhist Doctrine of Totality* (University Park: Pennsylvania State UP, 1971), pp. 187-230.

This rigorous affirmation of both the *totality* and the distinct *individual* carries interesting political implications, though Hua-yen does not draw them out. It offers a theory by which the State and the Individual both achieve integrity and freedom without 'obstructing' or impeding the other. In fact, this may indicate the influence of Chinese political thinking, albeit unconscious and in all likelihood completely unnoticed, in the development of Hua-yen as Sinitic Mahāyāna. The harmonization of self and society, citizen and ruler, family-member and family-whole — graphically inscribed in the character for the Chinese virtue *yi* 義 ('righteousness', 'justice', ethic of social interaction) whose parts consist of a 'herd, flock of sheep' 羊 and below that 'I, me' 我, thus signifying the interrelation of the self with the herd, i.e., how do I and society interact — looms high on the agenda of Chinese thought at least since the time of Lao Tzu and Confucius. Hua-yen has ontologized and existentialized this ethico-political problematic. In Ch'an the ontology is dropped while the existential dimension is developed in terms of pedagogy, particularly that which obtains in the relation between teacher and student. A full fleshing out of this sketch must await another occasion.

49 Some noteworthy works dealing with this issue are *Sudden and Gradual: Approaches to Enlightenment in Chinese Thought*, ed. by Peter Gregory (Honolulu: University of Hawaii Press, 1987) and John McRae, *The Northern School and the Formation of Early Ch'an Buddhism* (Honolulu: University of Hawaii, 1986).

50 Cf. vs. 5, 8, etc.

51 Cf. Wing-tsit Chan's translation and note in *Source Book in Chinese Philosophy* (Princeton: Princeton University Press, 1963), p. 384.

52 T.31.1585.26a-b; Ch.5:11A-B. References to the Taishō edition will be by volume number, text number, page number, page-section (a, b, c), and sometimes to row and character-place number. So T.31.1585.26a-b indicates: Taishō, volume 31, text number 1585, page 26, section blocks a and b. Since I also relied heavily upon the Nanjing blockprint editions of several of the texts discussed here, including the *Ch'eng wei-shih lun*, K'uei-chi's commentaries, *Hsi yü chi*, etc., I have occasionally also included references for these as well. The blockprint editions are bound in traditional style, meaning that the left hand page and its obverse side share the same page number. Hence I have called the left side of a page "A" and the page when turned over "B". *Ch'eng wei-shih lun* has 10 fascicles (*ch'üan*), and begins numbering pages anew with each fresh *ch'üan*, so reference will be to ch'üan, page, side, and occasionally column. E.g., the first verse occurs at ch.1:1B,5-6, i.e., first ch'üan, page 1, side B, columns 5 and 6. So Ch.5:11A-B means fascicle five, page 11, sides A and B.

53 *Hsing-hsiang* usually translates *ākāra*; cf. Hirakawa's *Index to the Abhidharmakośa*, v.2, pp. 89-90; in Sanskrit, *ākāra* means the form, shape, representational texture of a cognized object.

54 T.31.1585.22a20.8-23; Ch4:18A.3-6; Tat, p. 286, VP p. 254.

55 See my article, "Sāṅkhya", in the *Routledge International Encyclopedia of Philosophy*, 1997.

56 The unfairness of Fa-tsang's criticism becomes obvious when recognizing that the term *fa-hsiang* (dharma characteristic) occurs 647 in Hsüan-tsang's translations, while *fa-hsing* (dharma nature) occurs 4887 times.

Chapter Fifteen

The Legend of the Transmission of the *Ch'eng wei-shih lun*: Dharmapāla versus Prasenajit

According to K'uei-chi the *Ch'eng wei-shih lun* incorporates ten distinct Sanskrit commentaries into its discussion and exposition of the *Triṃśikā*. K'uei-chi champions one of the ten, the one written by Dharmapāla, as the most authoritative, and thus, he claims, it is the source of the orthodox positions accepted by the *Ch'eng wei-shih lun*. K'uei-chi presents himself as part of a direct line of transmission from Dharmapāla, thus endowing himself with the authority of a lineage. Despite the fact that there are no independent confirmations for any of these claims from any other source—including from within the *Ch'eng wei-shih lun* itself—the East Asian tradition has accepted K'uei-chi's assertions without question. A number of contemporaneous documents and incidents, however, suggest another scenario. Neither Dharmapāla's nor eight of the other commentaries are extant. But one of the so-called ten commentaries was rediscovered in the twentieth century, namely Sthiramati's *Triṃśikā-vijñapti-bhāṣya*, allowing us for the first time in many centuries to compare an actual commentary with what K'uei-chi says about it in his own commentaries to the *Ch'eng wei-shih lun*.

In the present chapter we will first sketch the traditional (= K'uei-chi's) version of the background and composition of the *Ch'eng wei-shih lun* This will include a translation and discussion of the transmission story in K'uei-chi's *Ch'eng wei-shih lun shu-yao*. After examining how this story problematizes itself, we will focus on the problem of connecting Dharmapāla with the *Ch'eng wei-shih lun* and with *Triṃśikā* commentaries in general. From there we turn to the question of Hsüan-tsang's actual "lineage" as described in his biography, which will further problematize K'uei-chi's claims about Dharmapāla. Instead a figure virtually ignored until now will emerge as a key player, a certain hermit-scholar named Prasenajit, who both instructed Hsüan-tsang in the *Triṃśikā* and "fulfilled" his mission to India. If, as I will try to show, both K'uei-chi's claims about the background of the *Ch'eng wei-shih lun* and his fastidious attributions of passages and positions within it to the various ten commentaries become unreliable, what implication does that have for any reading of the *Ch'eng wei-shih lun*? This chapter will end with some reflections on this question.

K'uei-chi's Situation

The unquestioned assumption for many centuries has been that the *Ch'eng wei-shih lun* utilizes the ten commentaries in the following manner: For each of the thirty verses of the *Triṃśikā,* the ten commentaries were correlated; those which held identical or similar views were grouped together, usually reducing the views of the ten commentaries to two or three, sometimes four, distinct views. These were then presented and critiqued according to the position of one of the commentators, Dharmapāla, who was invariably given the authoritative and final voice. It is not uncommon to find East Asian scholars citing the entire *Ch'eng wei-shih lun* as Dharmapāla's commentary.[1]

This view has its roots in K'uei-chi's commentaries to the *Ch'eng wei-shih lun*,[2] especially his *Ch'eng wei-shih-lun-shu-yao.* The dates when his various commentaries were written are unknown, but based on internal evidence they appear to have been written after Hsüan-tsang's death. Hsüan-tsang composed the *Ch'eng wei-shih lun* in 559, only five years before he died.[3] According to the *shu-yao* K'uei-chi was privy to Hsüan-tsang's oral instructions at the time the *Ch'eng wei-shih lun* was being translated[4] and by his own account he even seems to have been more than a little instrumental in determining its final structure and style. This being the case, his declarations and interpretations were accepted unquestioningly by the East Asian tradition. After all, who better than K'uei-chi would be in a position to know such things?

K'uei-chi's authoritative position was bolstered by the fact that he succeeded Hsüan-tsang after the latter's death. He then established the Wei-shih school (**vijñapti-mātra-vāda,* also known as the Fa-hsiang school or **dharma-lakṣaṇa-vāda,* though, because this label was attached to the school by Fa-tsang during his diatribes against it, the school itself considered the label pejorative). K'uei-chi, *not* Hsüan-tsang, is considered the first patriarch of this school. Thus K'uei-chi's pronouncements became the authoritative voice of the school itself. Rather than taking his interpretations and commentaries of the *Ch'eng wei-shih lun* and other texts as simply "K'uei-chi's interpretation," they have been regarded by the East Asian tradition as *the* voice of Wei-shih, as the definitive exposition of that school's views.

But both K'uei-chi's rise to prominence and his tenure as the school's leader are not without their controversies. First, it seems clear that the monks participating in the translation committee that assisted Hsüan-tsang[5] were often in disagreement about the meaning of the texts they worked on. The most famous example is Fa-tsang—later to become one of the foundational thinkers of the Hua-yen school—who briefly joined Hsüan-tsang's translation committee in the early 660s (a few years after K'uei-chi himself joined Hsüan-tsang), drawn by Hsüan-tsang's eminent and authoritative reputation, only to quit due to severe disagreements with Hsüan-tsang's understanding of Buddhism.[6] At another time, when Hsüan-tsang was translating the *Nyāyapraveśa*, a manual on Indian Buddhist logic, ten monks involved in the translation, including K'uei-chi, wrote commentaries on it, based on Hsüan-tsang's oral explanations of the text. Far from exhibiting a univocal interpretation of the text, the commentaries were so diverse and incommensurate that the *Nyāyapraveśa* quickly earned a reputation in the capitol for representing the epitome of undecipherability. A Taoist court official, Lü Ts'ai 呂才, bragged he could understand and quickly master anything difficult, so the Buddhists challenged him to make sense of the *Nyāyaprraveśa*. He applied himself to the challenge and wrote his own commentary, miscontruing its logic system as an expression of Taoist cosmological principles (e.g., 'affirmation and negation' are applications of 'yin and yang,' etc.). Once completed he boasted of his accomplishment, even though the Buddhists quickly recognized that his 'interpretation' was wide of the mark. Conflict and confrontation broke out between Buddhists and Taoists at Court, until Hsüan-tsang was prevailed upon by the Emperor to render a verdict as to the veracity of Lü Ts'ai's work. Reluctantly Hsüan-tsang declared it worthless.[7]

This incident suggests that not only were Hsüan-tsang's teachings interpreted in conflicting ways by his immediate students, but that he apparently exercised *no censorial control over his disciples' literary output.* Given the dizzying timetable he required to produce his own prolific translations (usually working on several texts at the same time), it is understandable that he had little if any time to inspect the writings of his students, much less offer minute corrections. Incidentally, K'uei-chi's commentary to the *Nyāyapraveśa* contains a number of logical errors and misunderstandings, and it displays awkward misapplications of Indian logical operations, some so blatant that, considering Hsüan-tsang's reputation as a perspicacious debater at Nālandā, it would be hard to attribute these errors to Hsüan-tsang himself.[8]

As to the *Ch'eng wei-shih lun* itself, we know of at least one major dispute between K'uei-chi and another of Hsüan-tsang's prominent students, the Korean monk Wŏnch'ŭk (Ch.: Yüan-ts'e 圓測, 632-696). Wŏnch'ŭk is perhaps best known for his commentary on the *Saṅdhinirmocana sūtra*, which became so renowned that it was translated into Tibetan (its tenth fascicle survives only in Tibetan) and which apparently greatly influenced the preeminent Tibetan reformer Tsoṅ-kha-pa.[9] After Hsüan-tsang died, K'uei-chi and Wŏnch'ŭk locked horns on a number of issues, most notably their incompatible interpretations on the question of mental seeds (*bījā*), i.e., latent karmic conditioning, which, perhaps directly due to the prominent role it played in their disputes, came to be considered one of the *Ch'eng wei-shih lun*'s key doctrines (though it occupies a relatively small space in the text itself). K'uei-chi's own disciples and his successor, Chih-chou 智周 (668-723), the third patriarch of the Wei-shih school,[10] ultimately drove Wŏnch'ŭk out of the orthodox Wei-shih school, labeling his theories 'heterodox.' Unfortunately Wŏnch'ŭk's commentary on the *Ch'eng wei-shih lun* is lost, but the debate was important enough for the main issues to be recorded and described in some detail by other sources.[11] While K'uei-chi assumed leadership of the Tz'u-en Monastery 慈恩寺 after Hsüan-tsang's death, Wŏnch'ŭk became abbot of the Hsi-ming monastery 西明寺, each gathering disciples who contested the interpretations of the other. Hsüan-tsang had spent time in both monasteries, and both had come to be identified with him.[12]

The dispute between the interpretations of K'uei-chi and Wŏnch'ŭk apparently continued until well after their deaths, but lost significance once the Wei-shih school collapsed in China during the eighth century. The *Hsü kao-seng chüan* (*Further Biographies of Eminent Monks*, T.50.2060.457c-58a) reports what may be an apocryphal story concerning the dispute over who had legitimate authority to interpret the *Ch'eng wei-shih lun* According to this story Wŏnch'ŭk hid in order to overhear Hsüan-tsang's private instruction on the *Ch'eng wei-shih lun* to K'uei-chi, only to subsequently go public with what he had overheard. K'uei-chi was reportedly outraged at this bit of espionage. Although the author of this account, Tao-hsüan, would have been a contemporary to these events which reportedly took place in his monastery (Hsi-ming ssu), it is unclear whether he reports it as he does (assuming this story was not inserted by a later hand) because of his own affinities with K'uei-chi (despite the fact that both he and Wŏnch'ŭk lived in the same monastery) or because he is merely reporting the facts.[13] It is telling that the one who is outraged is K'uei-chi, not Hsüan-tsang, suggesting either that Hsüan-tsang was not upset by the incident or, more likely, that it occurred after Hsüan-tsang died. Since only K'uei-chi would have known what actually transpired between he and Hsüan-tsang in private, the matter comes down to a question of K'uei-chi's word against Wŏnch'ŭk's. If, as we suspect, the incident occurred after Hsüan-tsang's death, it would be symptomatic of K'uei-chi's struggle to be accepted as the successor to Hsüan-tsang's *authority*. The story seems designed to demonstrate that K'uei-chi's interpretation should be taken as authoritative because he alone received the complete "secret" teachings concerning the *Ch'eng wei-shih lun* However, the story also concedes that Wŏnch'ŭk's "interpretation," at least for those parts he overheard, would also be correct and accurate. Therefore it does little to resolve their conflicting interpretations of the *Ch'eng wei-shih lun* since the teachings Wŏnch'ŭk overhears are authentic. Rather the story serves as an elaborate ad hominum attack on Wŏnch'ŭk's character. If nothing else, the dispute between K'uei-chi and Wŏnch'ŭk stands as a reminder that even in his own day K'uei-chi's interpretation of Hsüan-tsang's works, and especially the *Ch'eng wei-shih lun,* were not accepted unequivocally. At least one viable alternative presented itself.

After Hsüan-tsang's death the Imperial esteem and patronage he had enjoyed did not automatically transfer to K'uei-chi. In fact, it was virtually withdrawn.[14]

> Even before Hsüan-tsang's interment in the fourth month of 664 Kao-tsung [the Emperor] decreed: 'Now that the Master Hsüan-tsang of the Yü-hua-ssu is gone, all translation activities should cease.... Disciples of Hsüan-tsang as well as those monks assisting him in the translation of the scriptures who do not properly belong to the Yü-hua-ssu are each to return to his own monastery.'

K'uei-chi would have to earn his own patronage. Although he was not without experience at the Court,[15] the situation changed dramatically during his tenure as founding patriarch of the Wei-shih school.

Because the Imperial Court had found Hsüan-tsang's knowledge of the outlying regions of China and Central Asia through which he had traveled a useful asset for its own political and military ambitions, it had patronized and supported him, hoping to exploit his knowledge for its own benefit. That, combined with the reputation he garnered as a unique Chinese link with the home of Buddhism, made him the most renowned Chinese Buddhist of his day. His prominence drew monks from Japan and Korea as well as from throughout China. While Hsüan-tsang was alive and favored by the Court, he was unassailable. But once he died the field opened for others to compete at Court for the favor he had held. Kao-tsung, Emperor when Hsüan-tsang died, had been gradually turning away from Buddhism towards Taoism,[16] but in fact it was his consort, Wu Chao, who actually ruled, first surreptitiously from 660 to 684 (Kao-tsung died in 683), and then outright until 705. Her religious interests lay in Buddhism, not Taoism, and Buddhists from all over China came to her court to win her favor, particularly after 684. Many foreign translators as well as native monks received her support, Shen-hsiu, the Northern Ch'an master depicted in Southern Ch'an literature as Hui-neng's rival, being one of them.[17]

According to Hua-yen tradition Empress Wu's "favorite" monk was Fa-tsang. Fa-tsang was posthumously declared the third patriarch of Hua-yen by the "fourth patriarch," Cheng-kuan, and in at least one respect he was a faithful follower of Chih-yen, whom Cheng-kuan dubbed the "second patriarch." Chih-yen had lived near the capitol during Hsüan-tsang's heyday, but, since he was an outspoken critic of Hsüan-tsang's brand of Yogācāra, preferring the *Tathāgata-garbha* laced Yogācāra promulgated by Paramārtha in the sixth century, he had to bide his time while Hsüan-tsang's version of Yogācāra reigned supreme.

Fa-tsang continued the critique of Wei-shih leveled by Chih-yen, thus becoming a vicious rival to K'uei-chi. His success at wooing Empress Wu effectively contributed to the eclipsing of the "Fa-hsiang" school. With a polemic that both pined for a return to the 'old-style religion' of Paramārtha, (whose work was the leading, though not sole, source of the 'misinformation' that Hsüan-tsang had endeavored to rectify with his 'new' translations), and an appeal to ontological issues close to the Chinese heart since the time of Mencius and Chuang Tzu (such as Mind-Nature and Returning to the Source—which had already become increasingly part of the fabric of Chinese Buddhism itself), Fa-tsang decisively determined the course of all future East Asian Buddhism.[18] He argued that the Wei-shih school was merely *Fa-hsiang* 法相,

i.e., concerned with the 'characteristics of dharmas,' while True Buddhism (viz. Fa-tsang's interpretation) was *Fa-hsing* 法性, i.e., concerned with the 'nature of dharmas,' this latter position being, in Fa-tsang's view and the view of most subsequent East Asian Buddhists, ontologically 'deeper.' As a corollary, he argued that the "Fa-hsiang" school only understood 'wei-shih' 唯識 (*vijñapti-mātra*), i.e., defiled consciousness, while he and the more ontologically oriented Chinese schools understood 'wei-hsin' 唯心 (*citta-mātra*), i.e., the ultimately real, metaphysical One Mind spoken of in *The Awakening of Faith* and elsewhere. This is not the place to evaluate the validity of Fa-tsang's claims; what is important here is that, historically speaking, Chinese, Korean, and Japanese Buddhists found them very convincing indeed. Thus, while the project of Wei-shih had consisted in overcoming the limitations of mental (= karmic) problems by erasing (*vyāvṛtī*) the mind and its closure (*vijñapti-mātra, saṃvṛti,* etc.), after Fa-tsang the telos of East Asian Buddhism shifted, such that it now consisted of returning to and recovering the metaphysically Pure Mind.[19] Even while it may be appropriate to label some of the subsequent East Asian developments as 'idealism,' as I argue throughout this work, the position of Hsüan-tsang's *vijñapti-mātra* school—reflecting the Yogācāra tradition derived from Vasubandhu—should not be interpreted idealistically. It engaged in epistemological investigations in order to overcome cognitive closure (*vijñapti-mātra*), not to reify it. In any event, it was during K'uei-chi's stewardship that the Wei-shih school was eclipsed, and it never again rose to prominence in China.[20]

K'uei-chi had to fight for authority both within the Wei-shih school (against Wŏnch'ŭk and his followers) and against other Buddhists for Royal patronage. While successful in the first venture, he failed at the latter.

K'uei-chi's Transmission Story

K'uei-chi's *Ch'eng-wei-shih-lun shu-yao* begins with a recital of the transmission of Buddhism from Buddha to Nāgārjuna to Āryadeva to Asaṅga to Vasubandhu to Dharmapāla. He offers a short *précis* on each until he comes to Dharmapāla, at which point his writing takes on detail and literary flourish. At this stage he makes no mention of any other Yogācāra figures, such as Sthiramati or Dignāga. He says of the lineage, beginning with Nāgārjuna:

1. Nāgārjuna introduced the Mahāyāna teaching of emptiness without marks (*wu-hsiang k'ung chiao* 無相空教), composed the *Chung lun* (*Mūlamadhyamaka-kārikā*), and so on; he refuted the [erroneous] view of 'existence.'
2. Āryadeva composed the *100 Treatise* (*pai lun*), etc., expanding the great meaning (of Nāgārjuna's emptiness). Due to this, people became attached to an [erroneous] view of 'emptiness.'[21]
3. Asaṅga introduced the first stage [of Yogācāra teachings]. He realized the Dharma when the great spiritual light of Maitreya appeared to him expounding

the treatises... All who practice hard can attain Bodhi. Each must realize it on one's own.

4. Vasubandhu (*Fa-ssu-p'an-t'u* 筏蘇畔徒), Asaṅga's half-brother; at first followed Hīnayāna teachings (*hsiao chiao* 小教), until he heard the *Daśabhūmika* section of the *Avataṃsaka Sutra,* and the Mahāyāna section(s) of the *Abhidharmasamuccaya.* He then turned/converted (*kuei* 歸) to the wondrous principle (*miao-li* 妙理), and composed commentaries on Mahāyāna texts. He wrote these two Mahāyānic treatises (i.e., *Triṃśikā* and *Viṃśatika*).... 10,000 images (*hsiang* 象) are contained in a single word (*tz'u* 辭), 1000 explanations are compressed into one word (*yen* 言)... illuminating the scriptures (*sheng* 聖))

(translation)

[1:4A.6] Afterwards, there were Bodhisattvas such as Dharmapāla and so on, who carefully examined the verse text (of the *Triṃśikā*), each offering [his own] interpretation. Although each of these lofty peaks[22] has its high points, one of these commentaries [alone is] the "precious branch";[23] One alone shines brighter than the rest; It alone has [a special] fragrance—this one being none other than [the commentary of] that unique person, Dharmapāla.

Though in previous eras who accomplish the Bodhi Fruit [i.e., reach Awakening],[24] far exceed present-day Worthies, that cherished thing[25] was secreted away (in his bosom) awaiting the right circumstances to be revealed.[26] At the age of 29, he knew that the time for the coming to an end of his karmic development[27] [was near].[28] Weary of impermanence, he practiced meditation[29] and swore not to leave the Bodhi-tree.[30] His [life] ended at the age of thirty.

Whenever he took a break from his meditation and ritual-practice,[31] he would concentrate on annotating[32] those commentaries [on the *Triṃśikā*]. The text [he produced] surpassed [the others] with its far-reaching implications, and his original insights became renowned.[33] Whether to hold or reject [various positions] was settled with a single word (*yen* 言), eliminating the confusion of conflicting inter-pretations with half a verse.[34] Their texts [i.e., of the other 'Bodhisattvas' who wrote *Triṃśikā* commentaries] are as different as water and fire, but [Dharmapāla's] interpretation glued them back together.

Its meaning traverses the rivers and lakes [of the world, i.e., it is all-encompassing] effectively [distinguishing] the clear from the turbid.[35] [Reading his commentary feels like one is traveling] from the low plains of the remotest outskirts of the ends of the universe and suddenly rarefied elevations zoom up to[36] the Milky Way; then, cascading down[37] to the teaming river ports, from which again [one ascends to] the commanding heights; and from the lofty vaults back down to the level open plains.[38] If you bend to peer into its depths,[39] it is bottomless. If you gaze upwards at its heights,[40] it is limitless. His commentary is simple, but its meaning branches out extending endlessly. The quality of his majestic sentences reaches the highest possible limit.[41] His merit [for writing it] exceeds that of a thousand other sages, [since it will promote] the Tao [as effectively] as one hundred [virtuous] kings combined.

At that time, there was a layperson, Hsüan-chien 玄鑑 (lit. "profound/ mysterious mirror"!?)[42] who could recognize the difference between phoenix and pheasant feathers,[43] and could easily track the footprints of a unicorn [on land] or a dragon hidden on the sea bottom[44] (i.e., he could see that Dharmapāla was special, though ordinary to look at). He put whatever he had of value at [Dharmapāla's] disposal.[45] His sincerity and honesty grew ever deeper through the years. Bodhisattva [Dharmapāla] guided him through the many doctrines[46] and answered [all his questions] with this commentary.[47] Then he commanded him, saying:

"After I die, from whomever comes to observe [me],[48] take one tael of gold. Use your ability for discerning spiritual talents[49] to recognize that special one who will be able to teach and understand [this commentary]".[50]

The final end of that Profound Guide[51] (i.e., Dharmapāla) gradually drew near. The Bodhisattva's fame rose in India, and one heard about his treatises and interpretations in other lands as well. Who, with any sort of spiritual sensitivity,[52] could fail to cherish his magnificence? [Since] if one hears it in the morning, one can die in the evening [fulfilled],[53] who would be too stingy [to offer] gold and jewels [to behold him]?[54]

[After he died, the place] was bustling with the thoroughfare of hordes coming to see the Worthy, and soon valuables were piled as high as the Five Sacred Mountains. A steady line of spectators streamed in from the five regions of India [in such mass] as had never before been seen.[55]

The Great Master [Hsüan-tsang] visited all the sacred places, and he had the natural gift[56] for knowing the genuine from the false. [When he arrived at Dharmapāla's shrine, he said,][57] "This lacks even a trace of spirituality and is utterly sacrilegious. How could you leave [Buddhist] teachings so open to ridicule?"[58]

Upon hearing such marvelous reasoning[59] [the layman[60]] humbly approached and listened further [to Hsüan-tsang]. The layman, recalling the previous sage's [i.e., Dharmapāla's] last words, [thought] "Now this Worthy must be the right one!" So he gave [Hsüan-tsang] this 'humble' text along with [a copy of] Dharmapāla's Commentary to the *Pañcaskandha-prakāraṇa*.[61]

The Great Master read it carefully, and it was as if he were gazing at [Dharmapāla's] sagely appearance [or "face" itself]. He knew that what he held in his hands was the true explanation.[62]

Just as the moon in the west traverses to its home in the East [unseen],[63] so once again[64] this expansive, far-reaching subtle 'fish trap'[65] was passed on in secret. Its message is so "potent" [lit. appreciated] it transports your spirit to other [i.e., heavenly] mansions; its brilliance eclipses the sun; it purifies the ears and eyes in order to think most deeply;[66] it can shake up your mental spiritual-potency and offers a clue to the wondrous.[67]

And so [Hsüan-tsang?] now said, "[this text] alone can please my mind."

Hsüan-ni (i.e., Confucius)[68] said, "I have a beautiful jade here. Should I now hide it away in a jewelry case? Or should I see whether someone offers a good price and sell it?"[69]

[I, K'uei-]chi, in my previous life [before becoming a monk], was orphaned at the age of nine, and mourned for my parents. Being [disconsolate] in this way, an aspiration [to overcome life's grief] flared up in me.[70] And so I donned the black robes.[71] This fleeting worldly dust bestows youth and then cuts down sentient [beings]![72] At the age of seventeen, I went to a Buddhist monastery.[73] By imperial edict I became a doorman. I was satisfied to be part of [the monastic community] of three thousand, but immediately became overjoyed when [asked to be] included within the circle of the seventy (of Hsüan-tsang's translation committee).

After taking the necessary vows I began receiving instruction directly at the feet of the master, and could think about nothing else. I then became the official "oral commentary checker."[74] My job was to write down what [was said] as we savored the (oral instructions) we received concerning these treatises.

At first [Hsüan-tsang] endeavored to translate each of the ten commentaries [on the *Triṃśikā*] as separate works. Fang, Shang, Kuang, and [K'uei-]chi were the four men who received these treatises. [We would, respectively] polish [Hsüan-tsang's oral translation], write [the polished version] down, collate and check [it against other works], and annotate it.[75]

[Hsüan-tsang] had already insisted that his translation rules required that each [of the texts] must be dealt with on its own. After a few days, [I, K'uei-]chi sought to withdraw [from the translation project]. The Great Master earnestly asked me why.

Somberly I responded, "All night I dreamt of a golden appearance (or face),[76] and the next morning I was riding a white horse. It was formidable, and from its long mane there suddenly emerged a "brilliance"[77] [astride its] shoulders. As I awoke to the morning wake-up call, my mind was in prayer.

"I grasp the 'eight Aggregates'[78] but can only see them dimly. Although we have obtained the lees and scum[79] of the dharma-gates, nonetheless we are losing the pure living-kernel of the profound source. Now in the east [i.e., China] we have been granted [too many] books that equally bear witness to the profoundest principles.[80] Fortunately, this one alone stands out, superior to anything we have seen since the ancient times. There is no merit to be gained from lees and scum, so go against your tendency [to translate them all separately, and utilize this special text].

"Furthermore, each and every one of these sagely authors is famous in India. Even if their writings were to be transmitted on countless pages, the [definitive] meaning would still not be contained in a single text. Sentient [beings] will see that each of them is different, [and interpret according to their] own dispositions, while having no basis [for deciding which is correct]. This will make it all very difficult for people to understand. If you combine the various works all into a single text, then they will have guidelines to be able to determine what's true and what's untrue."

After a long time, he acquiesced.

And this is how this treatise (i.e., the *Ch'eng wei-shih lun*) came to be written.[81] The Great Master assigned the other three [other duties], and transmitted this book to "stupid"[82] me alone.

This treatise incorporates secrets from many sutras, and includes the interpretations of many sages. How could it be stagnant rather than interfused? If there is no darkness, then there is no [need for] a candle. If you look upwards, it is limitless. Bend down, it is bottomless. If you look too far afield, then you'll be without wisdom; but if you examine [this text] closely, then you will have discernment.[83] It implicitly contains [explanations] of the "five knowledges"[84] and explicitly exposits the Eightfold Scriptures.

A barrier of darkness conceals [the truth] from everyone who has not yet penetrated the Profound Path. [This text] is like the illuminative brilliance [that shines once one realizes the non-difference in size] between the tip of a hair and a mountain;[85] it warms the frigid ice in which is amassed the fertile waters that will luxuriate (the land).[86] Trust in the Great Night's silver brightness (i.e., the moon), when the golden mirror (i.e., the sun) reaches dusk.[87]

Even though, once again, these texts come from India, nonetheless [the *Ch'eng wei-shih lun*] is not a haphazard collection of their explanations. Directly from the ten masters, it collects their most difficult points. Moreover, there has never been a secret[88] text like this [revealed previously]. And that is the reason this treatise [i.e., *Ch'eng wei-shih lun,* was written].

[K'uei-chi. *Ch'eng wei-shih lun chu-shu* T.43.1831.608.a-09c]

K'uei-chi's sometimes hyperbolic prose style in this passage – dramatically different from the sober, prosaic style of the actual commentary that follows as well as the bulk of K'uei-chi's other writings – is typical of late Sui and early T'ang writers. Thus we needn't make much of his embellishing a story about Indian events with frequent allusions to Chinese texts such as the Confucian *Analects* and *Chuang Tzu.* Displaying one's literary erudition was considered *de rigueur.* Rather we need examine more closely what K'uei-chi says about Dharmapāla and his commentary.

The Twelve Royal Symbols

Before doing that, however, it may be helpful to highlight a crucial but easily overlooked subtext, one so effectively concealed that it remains virtually subliminal. From early Chinese history twelve "symbols" have been associated with the Imperial power of the Emperor and these have frequently been the main motifs on Imperial robes.[89] The twelve symbols are stars, sun, moon, mountains, dragons, pheasants, flames, water-weeds, grains, cups, an axe, and an obscure symbol[90] called *fu* that looks like a squared-off numeral three with its mirror-image behind it. In fact it was precisely

> [d]uring the T'ang dynasty that the meaning of these symbols was reinterpreted. Instead of being considered as representations of elements in nature, collectively forming a kind of cosmic plan, they were now explained as being purely symbols of the emperor's superior qualities". [91]

Though this reevaluation became 'official' very shortly after K'uei-chi's time, it was during K'uei-chi's time that the symbols had come under reconsideration. Very likely one of the motives that courtiers, officials, or clergy had for attributing these cosmic qualities to the Emperor was to flatter him so that he and the court would show a kindly disposition, and even patronage, toward one's cause.

Nine of the twelve symbols are explicitly found in K'uei-chi's text. The Milky Way is composed of "Stars." "Sun" and "moon," because they describe a circuit-journey, are used to describe the journey of Dharmapāla commentary to China ("Just as the moon in the west traverses...its brilliance eclipses the sun"). "Mountains" occur already at the beginning ("...each of these high peaks...") and recur again later ("...commanding heights of the lofty vaults...," etc.). The "dragon" and "pheasant" are used to describe Dharmapāla's lay-patron ("difference between a phoenix and a pheasant... track a unicorn or dragon..."). "Flame" and "water-weeds" describe the text and its effects on a reader ("If there is no darkness, then there is no need for a candle [or flame].... amassed the fertile waters...that will luxuriate the land."). They also depict the brilliance of his commentary ("split apart water and fire"). K'uei-chi uses "grains" to describe the condition of Chinese Buddhism at that time ("Although we have obtained the lees and scum of the dharma-gates, the pure living-kernel...").

This leaves only three symbols not explicitly mentioned by K'uei-chi: Cups, axes, and *fu.* The other nine symbols all designate things of nature; these three are not natural, but artificial. One might strain to impute the first two items into his text. For instance, 'cups' may be implied by the obscure reference to a kiln in which ceramic utensils such as cups are produced.[92] Though awkward, it may be the "axe" of wisdom that "shattered the opinions with one word." Or possibly an axe or similar chopping tool is implied in the sentiment "this fleeting worldly dust bestows youth and then cuts down sentient [beings]!" These efforts are admittedly a stretch.

Fu, on the other hand, coincides strikingly with K'uei-chi's subtext, since *fu,* in K'uei-chi's day, signified a revealed text and the process or procedures by which 'divine' texts were revealed to mortals. In medieval usage the term *fu* denoted talismans or sacred emblems revealed by spirits or deities to worthy mortals. As religious Taoism began to produce texts ascribed to spirits or long-dead ancient sages who would either 'visit' a worthy and dictate a text to him, or more mysteriously 'inspire' a worthy to compose a treatise by spirit-writing (a type of mediumship in which texts were written whose authorship was ascribed not to the medium but to the inspiring agent, usually a deity or past sage), the term *fu* came to designate this mode of text production. As Robinet notes[93]

> At first, these treasures were magic objects such as the *fu-ying* ("auspicious responses") ... which, as talismans and lucky objects, appeared in response to the virtue of a sage king. These objects possessed the power of good omens and confirmed the heavenly mandate (*ming*) which the king had received....
>
> Afterwards, the magical objects became texts which played a similar role....
>
> The term *fu*, which refers to the magic charms or talismans of the Taoists, originally meant a contract, and the testimonial document, that united two parties.... *Fu* is a term that is particularly associated with the word *hsin* meaning "faith," "credit," and "sincerity"....
>
> The *fu* especially testified to the feudal bond wherein a vassal promises loyalty and the lord pledges himself to reward his vassals for services rendered. In this sense, a lord regularly held feudal assemblies where he "united the *fu*" (*ho-fu*) so as to attest to the contract sworn between himself and his vassals. Later on the *fu* served as letters of credit, as signs of identification, and as insignia of function....
>
> In the mythical and political history of China, *pao* ['treasures,' another kind of early talismanic object] and *fu* are also auspicious objects because they *testify to an abundance of power and prestige associated with the special protection of a deity or lord.* The *fu* is the *token of a contract by which a donor binds himself to his donee.* [emphases and square brackets added]

Like *fu*, K'uei-chi's story of the transmission of the Dharmapāla commentary from Dharmapāla to his lay patron to Hsüan-tsang and finally K'uei-chi concerns confirmation of a mandate embodied in a text, that involved contractual and testimonial relations between the four members of the 'lineage.' The *Ch'eng wei-shih lun*, to the extent it represents a Chinese embodiment of that commentary, served for K'uei-chi as his letter of credit, his sign of identification, his insignia of function, i.e., the emblem of his authority and legitimacy inherited, precisely with this text, from Hsüan-tsang. It was also, according to K'uei-chi, a testimony of the prestige he hoped to receive on its basis, guaranteed as it were by its association with a sacred, spiritual transmission. It is a token of the contract or agreement reached between Dharmapāla and his patron donor. The *Ch'eng wei-shih lun* is *fu* because it is a revealed text, one with a spiritual pedigree that lifts it above the realm of other texts.

If K'uei-chi is indeed employing these symbols, that would suggest that the intended audience—at least for the preamble to his commentary, which, again, is written in an ornate, typically literary Chinese (not Buddhist) style—was the Court, and not merely his fellow Buddhists. Since Emperors wrote (and on occasion read) prefaces to Buddhist texts, a strategy that aimed at suggesting that Dharmapāla's commentary was not only the supreme Buddhist text—one which K'uei-chi himself had exclusive access to!—but one which conformed to and perhaps enhanced the power and divine context of the Emperor him/herself, would be a shrewd one indeed. It is a plea for patronage wrapped in flattery. Because he had "exclusive rights" to Dharmapāla's commentary, the more he elevated Dharmapāla's importance, the greater importance he garnered for himself. This provides a very strong motive for glorifying Dharmapāla. In effect, the *Ch'eng wei-shih lun,* combined with the elevated authority of Dharmapāla, becomes K'uei-chi's claim to authority. This story can be read as his plea for patronage and recognition.

K'uei-chi's Catechism and 'Secret' Lineage Transmission

There is no evidence that Hsüan-tsang considered the *Ch'eng wei-shih lun* a special text, much less the preeminent text for Buddhist thought and practice. His writings and biography suggest, on the contrary, that three other texts were of cardinal importance to him: The *Yogācārabhūmi*, for which he went to India and which was one of the first texts he endeavored to translate upon his return to China; the *Heart Sutra*, which he found to be the most efficacious *dhāranī* for protection during his journeys and which his biography reports he chanted on his deathbed; and the *Mahāprajñāpāramitā Sūtra*, which he devoted the last years of his life to translating and of which, according to his biography, he offered much public praise. K'uei-chi, not Hsüan-tsang, chose the *Ch'eng wei-shih lun* as the foundational text for the Wei-shih school.

An element of the story that a number of later scholars have found disturbing is the "secrecy" surrounding Dharmapāla's commentary. By K'uei-chi's own account, Dharmapāla's *Triṃśikā* commentary was entirely unknown in India, even to those who revered him. Since the text left India with Hsüan-tsang who received it in secret, it remained unknown there. This provides a convenient excuse for the fact that no one—except K'uei-chi—would have ever heard of the text, including the Buddhist missionaries who continued to arrive in China from India, as well as those Chinese pilgrims that made their way to India. Though the obvious intent of K'uei-chi's hagiographic account is to elevate Dharmapāla, Hsüan-tsang and the *Ch'eng wei-shih lun*, while simultaneously attempting to account for why no one familiar with the texts that were actually circulating in India at that time would have heard of a Dharmapāla *Triṃśikā* commentary, the effect of K'uei-chi's story does just the opposite. It immediately raises the suspicion that the so-called Dharmapāla commentary may not be genuine at all. Similarly, since it is K'uei-chi's commentary— and not either the *Ch'eng wei-shih lun* or Hsüan-tsang— that tells us there were originally ten Sanskrit commentaries of which Dharmapāla's is the most eminent, we must look elsewhere to allay or confirm our suspicions.

How plausible is K'uei-chi's account, putting aside the hagiographic embellishments? He reports that the commentary was written by Dharmapāla who entrusted it to his patron while he was steadfastly practicing under or near the Bodhi-tree, where he finally died. Hsüan-tsang, in his *Hsi-yu-chi* (Record of Western Lands), associates Dharmapāla with three locales: 1. Kāñchīpura in Drāviḍa where he was born and from which he fled when marriage was imminent, settling elsewhere (unspecified) to become a Buddhist monk.[94] 2. Nālandā, where Śīlabhadra meets and studies with him.[95] 3. the Bodhi-tree, where according to Hsüan-tsang the Madhyamakan Bhāvaviveka came to debate him, but Dharmapāla declines, in effect saying that he had outgrown such things.[96] Though Hsüan-tsang does not explicitly set the time at the Bodhi-tree as a later period in Dharmapāla life, the tenor of the stories suggests that.

Problems with a Śīlabhadra 'lineage'

The problematic story is the one concerning Śīlabhadra, who is curiously omitted from K'uei-chi's account (and thus, despite the repeated claims of scholars, he was not included in K'uei-chi's lineage). Śīlabhadra was the leader at Nālandā when Hsüan-tsang stayed there, and so is counted as one of Hsüan-tsang's important teachers. According to the account in the *Hsi-yu-chi* concerning Śīlabhadra's meeting with Dharmapāla, Śīlabhadra was so struck by Dharmapāla's insight that he became his disciple. Later, when a *tīrthika* from the south came to challenge Dharmapāla to a debate, "Disciple (*men-jen*) Śīlabhadra" volunteered to stand in for him. The other disciples were upset due to Śīlabhadra's "youth" and inexperience, but reassured by Dharmapāla, they let him engage in the debate where he acquitted himself admirably.

The problem is with Śīlabhadra's alleged "youth." Hsüan-tsang says in his account of that story that Śīlabhadra was thirty years old at that time. Dharmapāla is said by K'uei-chi to have died when he was only thirty. Obviously this story, in which Śīlabhadra is a neophyte disciple of Dharmapāla, would have to have taken place sometime before Dharmapāla died. So the assembly should not have been concerned about Śīlabhadra's age since Dharmapāla had not yet gone to spend his last years at the Bodhi-tree and thus must have been considerably younger than thirty himself. Either Hsüan-tsang or K'uei-chi must have been confused about someone's age. Since K'uei-chi's only source of information on either Dharmapāla or Śīlabhadra must have been Hsüan-tsang, it would seem the confusion was K'uei-chi's. But the problem is not that simple.

Though Śīlabhadra is usually considered by the East Asian tradition to be the disciple of Dharmapāla, no doubt as a direct result of Hsüan-tsang's account in the *Hsi-yu-chi*, in fact they were initially contemporaries. While dating Indian thinkers and texts is a notoriously precarious task, the general consensus based on all the available materials points to the following conclusion: Dharmapāla (530-561) died quite young, but Śīlabhadra reputedly lived well over a hundred years (529-645!) and was already quite old when Hsüan-tsang met him in India. Having been born a year earlier than Dharmapāla, he was actually his senior, though in the monastic community seniority is established in terms of when one enters the order, not birth date. We do not know the respective years in which each joined the order.

A little later we will discuss the *Fo-ti ching lun* (*Buddhabhūmyupadeśa*, T.26.1530)—a text translated by Hsüan-tsang in 649, just four years after his return to China—that is believed by some scholars to actually contain two distinct commentaries on the *Buddhabhūmi sūtra*, (T.16.680, translated by Hsüan-tsang in 645). One of the commentaries in the *Fo-ti ching lun* scholars attribute to Śīlabhadra and the other to Dharmapāla. Neither name is mentioned in the text or elsewhere by Hsüan-tsang in relation to this text. Since the sections of this text that scholars attempt to attribute to Dharmapāla contain virtually verbatim parallel passages to the *Ch'eng wei-shih lun*, and those passages when appearing in the *Ch'eng wei-shih lun* are attributed by K'uei-chi to Dharmapāla, this will be relevant to our current concerns. At this stage we need only point out that there is no cross-referencing or citation of either section to the other. Neither acts as a subcommentary on the other. However, scholars generally agree that the part of the *Fo-ti ching lun* allegedly written by Dharmapāla came *after* the part allegedly written by Śīlabhadra, since certain statements it makes presuppose points made there. If so, perhaps we should consider Dharmapāla to be Śīlabhadra's disciple, instead of the other way around. To further anticipate a later argument, the assumption that Dharmapāla's views constituted the authoritative position at Nālandā *in all matters* during Śīlabhadra's tenure as its head may be another 'exaggeration' by K'uei-chi, one which, incidentally, Hsüan-tsang's biography does not really support.

Hsüan-tsang does offer a passage in the *Hsi-yu-chi* naming some of the great Worthies connected with Nālandā, names which those coming to Nālandā who were successful in gaining admittance (only two or three out of every ten who try) would be able to link with their own. But the list is not a list of either historical succession or graded importance. Rather its organizing principle seems to be initially paired groupings of names that share a common Chinese character, ending with miscellaneous names. The names are (in the order Hsüan-tsang presents them):[97]

Dharmapāla (Hu-fa 護法), Candrapāla (Hu-yüeh 護月);
Guṇamati (Te-hui 德慧), Sthiramati (Chien-hui[98] 堅慧);
Prabhamitra (Kuang-yu 光友), Jinamitra (Sheng-yu 勝友);
Jñānacandra (Chih-yüeh 智月); Ming-min 明敏 (?); and Śīlabhadra (Chieh-hsien 戒賢); and others whose names are already forgotten.

This passage does suggest that rather than feeling himself to be part of a distinct lineage from Dharmapāla, Hsüan-tsang thought of himself as an inheritor of the grand, accumulated prestige of Nālandā as a whole.

One might ask: If, like K'uei-chi, Hsüan-tsang considered Dharmapāla's *Triṃśikā* commentary to be the preeminent text, such that "Only this text can comfort my mind," why then did K'uei-chi have to argue so forcefully to convince him abandon independent translations of the other nine *Triṃśikā* commentaries? As the story goes, it K'uei-chi a substantial period of time, perhaps weeks, from the time he withdrew from the translation project until Hsüan-tsang relented and agreed to produce a catechism rather than independent translations. Why did Hsüan-tsang take so long to finally yield to K'uei-chi's request for a decisive catechism? Correlatively, one might ask, if this text was so special to Hsüan-tsang, why did he wait so long to translate it, having translated over sixty other texts since returning to China in 645, only taking this one up in 659? If it was so important him, why wouldn't he have translated it earlier?

The fact that Hsüan-tsang was initially resistant to K'uei-chi's demand that the commentaries be translated together, rather than separately, is significant. K'uei-chi insisted that translating the ten texts separately, as Hsüan-tsang planned to do, would only add to the doctrinal confusion already rampant in Chinese Buddhism. Instead, according to K'uei-chi's own account, he demanded that Hsüan-tsang translate all ten together as a single text, so that Hsüan-tsang might indicate clearly which of the varying interpretations should be considered 'correct'. At first Hsüan-tsang refused, but after K'uei-chi threatened to leave the translation committee altogether unless he got his way, Hsüan-tsang finally relented, and so the *Ch'eng wei-shih lun* was written. By focusing on the special transmission of Dharmapāla's *Triṃśikā* commentary and his own role in convincing Hsüan-tsang to establish an authoritative position, K'uei-chi implies both that Dharmapāla's views overshadow those of the other commentaries, as well as giving himself an active and significant link with Dharmapāla. It is he, not Hsüan-tsang, who conceives of the *Ch'eng wei-shih lun* as an occasion for declaring Dharmapāla views. As the lone recipient of this "secret" teaching, he becomes Dharmapāla's direct heir through Hsüan-tsang. Thus, from the start, the parameters of the *Ch'eng wei-shih lun* reflected K'uei-chi's concerns and not the project originally envisioned by Hsüan-tsang. It takes its shape and form in response to K'uei-chi's insistent request for a doctrinal catechism. As we shall see shortly, it is K'uei-chi's commentary that gives the *Ch'eng wei-shih lun* its catechismic flavor, not the *Ch'eng wei-shih lun* itself.

Hsüan-tsang's Reticence

As already mentioned, the *Ch'eng wei-shih lun* is unique among Hsüan-tsang's works in that it does not purport to present a faithful, strict translation of an original text. Hsüan-tsang believed that the problems and misunderstandings that had become prevalent in Chinese Buddhist thought were a direct result of the many liberties that previous translators had taken with their materials. His goal was to set Chinese Buddhism aright by replacing the earlier misconceptions with new, accurate translations. To that end he retranslated works made famous by his predecessors and introduced new works in an effort to introduce Chinese Buddhists to the full Indian Buddhist context. While the *Ch'eng wei-shih lun* may be seen as an attempt to present the debates and stock arguments he encountered at Nālandā and elsewhere on his journeys, finally it is not a faithful translation of any particular text. There is reason to believe that Hsüan-tsang had qualms about this, misgivings that did not disappear when he eventually stopped resisting K'uei-chi and acceded to his insistent request for a catechism rather than a translation. In 660, the very year following his composing the *Ch'eng wei-shih lun*, when considering whether to produce an abridged translation of the *Prajñāpāramitā sūtra*, he experienced an ominous dream warning him to translate the full sūtra. This was another situation in which his students (perhaps including K'uei-chi) encouraged him to produce something other than a complete, faithful translation. His biography states:[99]

> On the first day of the first month in the spring of the fifth year (A.D. 660), he started the translation of the *Mahāprajñāpāramitā Sūtra*. The original Sanskrit text had a total number of 200,000 verses. Since it was such an extensive work, *his disciples suggested that he should make an abridgement of it* [emphasis added]. The Master complied with their wishes and intended to translate it the way Kumārajīva translated the Buddhist texts, expunging the tedious and repetitionary parts. When he cherished this thought he dreamed in the night some very terrible things as a warning to him. He dreamed he was climbing over a precipitous peak and some wild animal was trying to catch him. He trembled with perspiration and managed to escape from the dangerous position. After awakening he related his evil dream to the people and decided to translate the entire text of the sūtra. That night he dreamed he saw Buddhas and Bodhisattvas emitting a light from between their eyebrows that shone over his body and made him feel comfortable and happy. He also dreamed that he offered flowers and lamps to the Buddhas; that he ascended a pulpit to preach the Dharma for the people who surrounded him, some praising and admiring him, some offering him delicious fruits. When he awoke he felt happy, and he thought no more of making any abridgement but made the translation in exact accordance with the original Sanskrit text.

Hsüan-tsang took dreams very seriously: They mark both his key decisions and reveal his primary aspirations.[100] Nor should it go unremarked that apparently K'uei-chi knew full well the importance that Hsüan-tsang attached to dreams, since an important cornerstone of K'uei-chi's argument to Hsüan-tsang consists of a dream – somewhat obscure in imagery – that is, in fact, mirrored to some extent by Hsüan-tsang's own dreams persuading him to translate the *Prajñāpāramitā sūtra* faithfully and fully. In both Hsüan-tsang's dreams and in K'uei-chi's, some sort of discomfort or disturbance is alleviated by the emitting of light. Whether K'uei-chi's account of his own dream is an accurate retelling of actual events that transpired between Hsüan-tsang and himself, or a story invented later perhaps to counteract the story of Hsüan-tsang's *Prajñāpāramitā sūtra* dreams, a story that would have been widely known amongst Hsüan-tsang's living disciples, is hard to say.

The *Prajñāpāramitā* dreams reinforce the fact that Hsüan-tsang, even after deviating from his usual translation regime to compose the *Ch'eng wei-shih lun*, preferred full, accurate translations rather than 'translations' done in the collated, selective style of the *Ch'eng wei-shih lun* It would not be unreasonable to conclude that these dreams and his reaction to them may be a sign of his retrospective remorse at not having translated the *Triṃśikā* commentaries separately and completely.

Thus, from its inception, the *Ch'eng wei-shih lun* represents K'uei-chi's aspirations, not Hsüan-tsang's, and it is K'uei-chi who has invested it with catechismic significance. How did K'uei-chi transform the *Ch'eng wei-shih lun* into a catechism?

Virtually all attributions of positions to authors or sects is done in the commentaries, not the *Ch'eng wei-shih lun* itself.[101] While the *Ch'eng wei-shih lun* does present divergent views on various and sundry topics, it rarely identifies the sources of those views. Most importantly, the various interpretive stances presented and/or evaluated in relation to those divergent views are never identified with any of the ten commentators by the *Ch'eng wei-shih lun* itself. Further, while the *Ch'eng wei-shih lun* does take definitive stands on many of the topics it raises, on others its own position is less than clear. Sometimes it seems that the presentation of alternative views is done quite aporetically: Some say X, while some say Y, while some say Z; and all may be viable.[102] Rather than ten distinct opinions on anything, most commonly one finds no more than two or three, occasionally four, distinct opinions on any issue in the *Ch'eng wei-shih lun.* If there were ten commentaries it seems that at most only four of them would disagree or diverge on any single issue at a time. That seems unlikely.

It is K'uei-chi who supplies us with the supposed names of the sources and who invariably declares one position to be the only 'correct' position. Until the recovery of Sthiramati's commentary in its original Sanskrit by Sylvain Lévy in 1922, we had no choice but to accept K'uei-chi's pronouncements, since none of the other commentaries has survived independently of their implication in the *Ch'eng wei-shih lun* by K'uei-chi.

Even a cursory comparison between Sthiramati's text and the various positions that K'uei-chi attributes to Sthiramati throughout the *Ch'eng wei-shih lun* reveals major discrepancies. Positions not found at all in Sthiramati's text are attributed to him by K'uei-chi. Positions found in the *Ch'eng wei-shih lun* but attributed by K'uei-chi to others are actually espoused by Sthiramati. Further, some of the positions that K'uei-chi accepts as 'correct' (all of which he attributes to Dharmapāla) are actually found in Sthiramati, though K'uei-chi will have attributed one of the other positions to Sthiramati.

Because of K'uei-chi's systematic denigration of Sthiramati (and the other eight commentators) coupled with his lionization of Dharmapāla, the East Asian Buddhist tradition has tended to view Sthiramati and Dharmapāla as opponents, complete with a list of issues on which they differ. Since, according to K'uei-chi, the *Ch'eng wei-shih lun* champions Dharmapāla, the tradition has also considered the 'official' position of the *Ch'eng wei-shih lun* and the Wei-shih school to faithfully reflect Dharmapāla. Without Dharmapāla's own commentary available for comparison, it is difficult to determine just where the

Ch'eng wei-shih lun and Dharmapāla agree and where they part company. But, as just noted, some of the 'official' positions of the *Ch'eng wei-shih lun* turn out to be Sthiramati's.

Why should K'uei-chi have chosen to systematically elevate Dharmapāla above the others? Even if his ulterior motive may have been to acquire Hsüan-tsang's authority and prestige, he might just as easily have selected one of the other "ten" commentators for that honor. This is a difficult question, especially given the fact that K'uei-chi, in one of his own original works, the *Ta-ch'eng fa-yüan i-lin-chang* 大乘法苑義林章 (T.45.1861), shows considerable influence from Sthiramati. K'uei-chi had written a subcommentary[103] on Hsüan-tsang's translation of Sthiramati's commentary to the *Abhidharmasamuccaya*,[104] and ideas developed in his subcommentary reappear in the *Ta-ch'eng fa-yüan i-lin-chang.*[105] As S. Takasaki has pointed out, Sthiramati incorporated passages of his *Abhidharmasamuccaya* commentary into his *Triṃśikā* commentary.[106] Thus K'uei-chi's own thought is much closer to Sthiramati's than the traditional accounts would lead one to believe. Given this influence, why did he assign the 'authoritative' positions in the *Ch'eng wei-shih lun* to Dharmapāla?

Is Dharmapāla's Interpretation the Prominent One? Evidence from the *Fo-ti ching lun*

Even though we only have Sthiramati's text as an independent standard against which to judge K'uei-chi's attributions, it is sufficient to throw many of those attributions into doubt, and with them, the notion of Dharmapāla's preeminence. KATSUMATA Shunkyo's efforts to recover the 'original' Dharmapāla commentary by finding passages in two other texts translated by Hsüan-tsang—the *Fo-ti ching lun* 佛地經論 (T.26.1530, *Buddhabhūmyupadeśa*) and Dharmapāla's *Ta-ch'eng kuang-pai lun shih-lun* 大乘廣百釋論 (T.30.1571)—that parallel passages in the *Ch'eng wei-shih lun,* while illuminative, tend to lead one to the opposite conclusion from the one Katsumata desires.[107] Let us consider the issue for a moment, since it may reveal precisely the sort of 'attribution problem' the *Ch'eng wei-shih lun* entails.

As mentioned above, the *Fo-ti ching lun* is a commentary on the *Buddhabhūmi sūtra* (T.16.680). Although, as stated above, some scholars treat the *Fo-ti ching lun* as incorporating two separate commentaries which they attribute to Śīlabhadra and Dharmapāla, the version translated by Hsüan-tsang preserved in the Chinese canon attributes the text to "Bandhuprabha, etc." The Tibetan version of another commentary on the *Buddhabhūmi sūtra,* titled the *Buddhabhūmi vyākhyāna* (Peking ed., 5498), is attributed there to Śīlabhadra. Roughly half of Bandhuprabha's commentary (i.e., the *Fo-ti ching lun*) corresponds to the commentary preserved in Tibetan attributed to Śīlabhadra. Because the Tibetan version attributes this to Śīlabhadra, scholars infer that those portions of the *Fo-ti ching lun* that correspond to it must also be

Śīlabhadra's work. Since the *Fo-ti ching lun* contains *more* than the so-called Śīlabhadra commentary, the inference would be that it was compiled later than the composition of Śīlabhadra's text. The portions of the *Fo-ti ching lun* that do not correspond to the Śīlabhadra text appear to be a cogent, but separate commentary on the *Buddhabhūmi sūtra.* While a distinct commentary, it seems in places to draw on the Śīlabhadra text, suggesting that it came later. The amalgamation of the two commentaries into a single text would have come later still. If Bandhuprabha was not the author of either of these, then perhaps he was the editor or redactor who brought them together (though why Hsüan-tsang would list his name rather than that of the author(s) is unclear).

More intriguing, a number of sizable passages contained in the Bandhuprabha commentary which do not correspond to the Tibetan, and thus would not be by Śīlabhadra (assuming that he is indeed the author of the text preserved in Tibetan that corresponds to part of the *Fo-ti ching lun*), are near verbatim parallel passages to the *Ch'eng wei-shih lun*, specifically passages that, in his commentaries to the *Ch'eng wei-shih lun*, K'uei-chi assigns to Dharmapāla. Consequently, scholars such as Katsumata have concluded that these parallel passages were written by Dharmapāla, thereby reducing Bandhuprabha to the role of an editor who compiled two commentaries on the *Buddhabhūmi sūtra*, one by Dharmapāla and the other by Śīlabhadra, into a single commentary. These "Dharmapāla" parallels are strong enough that it is obvious that either the *Ch'eng wei-shih lun* borrowed from the *Fo-ti ching lun*, or vice versa. Vallée Poussin believed, I think rightly, that the *Ch'eng wei-shih lun* borrowed from the *Fo-ti ching lun.* However, Katsumata and Keenan argue that the *Fo-ti ching lun* borrowed from the *Ch'eng wei-shih lun.* Keenan offers two arguments to support this (the second of which he attributes to Katsumata), which I shall quote in full, as they bring us to the vortex of the problem.[108]

> If the *Vijñaptimātratāsiddhiśāstra* [i.e., the *Ch'eng wei-shih lun*] were dependent on the *Buddhabhūmyupadeśa* [*Fo-ti ching lun*], then the present form of that *Buddhabhūmyupadeśa* would have existed as an independent text before the *Vijñaptimātratāsiddhi.* In such a case it is extremely unlikely that the *Vijñaptimātratāsiddhi* would have restricted its borrowing to only those passages that are not shared by the *Buddhabhūmivyākhyāna*, without ever quoting a passage that is shared by both texts. Furthermore, as Katsumata Shunkyo argues, the internal evidence of a number of passages strongly suggests that the *Buddhabhūmyupadeśa* assumes that the doctrinal content of the passages it shares with the *Vijñaptimātratāsiddhi* are already known and need not be explained at length. Thus it can be concluded that the *Buddhabhūmyupadeśa* of Bandhuprabha has drawn upon the *Vijñaptimātratāsiddhi* of Dharmapāla in order to bring it within the circle of his thinking.

Let us start with the second argument, i.e., that the *Buddhabhūmyupadeśa* (*Fo-ti ching lun*) assumes that its doctrines are already familiar, implying they are familiar from Dharmapāla's commentary on the *Triṃśikā*. First, let us remember that according to K'uei-chi Dharmapāla's *Triṃśikā* commentary was unknown in India and secretly transmitted to China by Hsüan-tsang. Thus, the *Fo-ti ching lun* in India could not have presupposed any Indian readers familiar with it. Moreover, it can be argued with equal, perhaps even greater, force that when those parallel passages appear in the *Ch'eng wei-shih lun* they also presuppose a prior familiarity. Moreover, I would argue that if one compares the parallel passages *in situ* with an eye to how well or awkwardly they fit the surrounding context in each text, the appearances in the *Ch'eng wei-shih lun* often seem almost cryptic, marginally related at best to the ostensive *Triṃśikā* verse under discussion. Bare terms such as *śruta-vāsanā* drop from the sky with no explanation or exposition. By way of contrast, these same passages always fit seamlessly into the places where they occur in the *Fo-ti ching lun* and are usually accompanied by an edifying explication. In fact, a good way to figure out what these unclear passages mean in the *Ch'eng wei-shih lun* is precisely to consult the parallel occurrences in the *Fo-ti ching lun* for further edification and illumination.

Second, Hsüan-tsang translated the root text *Buddhabhūmi sūtra* (*Fo-ti ching*) in 645, the first year of his translation effort. He translated the Bandhuprabha commentary, *Buddhabhūmyupadeśa* (*Fo-ti ching lun*), in 649. He didn't 'translate' the *Ch'eng wei-shih lun* until 659, eleven years later.[109] K'uei-chi precludes that the *Triṃśikā* commentary could have contextualized the *Fo-ti ching lun* for Indian readers. What about Chinese readers relying on Hsüan-tsang's translations? A Chinese reader may have been expected to already be familiar with the *Buddhabhūmyupadeśa* when the *Ch'eng wei-shih lun* appeared, but not the inverse. Though this is hardly evidence to argue which text was first written in India, it may indicate to some extent which text Hsüan-tsang himself thought was required as background for which.

Third, the Katsumata-Keenan argument hinges on the assumption that Dharmapāla did indeed write an independent treatise on the *Triṃśikā,* and that the *Ch'eng wei-shih lun* presents all or most of it intact. Rather, as I have been suggesting, one can raise serious doubts about whether Dharmapāla ever wrote a *Triṃśikā* commentary. We can assume that he did, not because the *Ch'eng wei-shih lun* provides any evidence whatsoever in that regard—it clearly does not—nor because we blindly trust K'uei-chi's assertion that he did. The only seemingly solid evidence that Dharmapāla composed a *Triṃśikā* commentary appears in Hsüan-tsang's translation of the *Triṃśikā* (T.31.1586), a separate text from the *Ch'eng wei-shih lun* translated back in 648, in which Hsüan-tsang includes in his prefatory remarks this statement: "Dharmapāla and other Bodhisattvas have composed *ch'eng wei-shih* (establishing vijñapti-mātra) on these thirty verses",[110] assuming that these supplementary remarks were not added later by K'uei-chi or someone else, and were indeed written by Hsüan-tsang himself. Whether *Ch'eng wei-shih* is meant as a formal title of a single text, or a general name for a class of works is unclear, though clearly a connection can be drawn between this title and the *Ch'eng wei-shih lun* (treatise on establishing vijñapti-mātra).

On the basis of a comparison of the *Ch'eng wei-shih lun* with Sthiramati's commentary as well as with the many other texts of non-*Triṃśikā* provenance that are liberally incorporated into the *Ch'eng wei-shih lun*, it seems very clear that in the *Ch'eng wei-shih lun* Hsüan-tsang (1) was more likely to paraphrase the commentaries he used than translate them verbatim, and (2) that many texts other than ones directly related to the *Triṃśikā* were included in the *Ch'eng wei-shih lun*'s discussions. Major passages from the *Yogācārabhūmi, Abhidharmakośa, Viṃśatikā, Madhyānta vibhāga*, as well as other texts are quoted or paraphrased throughout the *Ch'eng wei-shih lun.* Was Hsüan-tsang only citing materials already quoted by the supposed commentators he was "translating," or may we assume that he was freely drawing on a broad range of Buddhist literature to encapsulate his own understanding of the issues raised, tempered by the exegesis he had received at Nālandā and elsewhere? Because of the sheer mass of cited material, the sources for which are sometimes given by name but frequently are not, I tend toward the latter assumption.

Were it the case that Hsüan-tsang drew *exclusively* on *Triṃśikā* commentaries to compose the *Ch'eng wei-shih lun* , then it would be obvious why Śīlabhadra's portion of the *Fo-ti ching lun* is absent from the *Ch'eng wei-shih lun.* But Hsüan-tsang drew on a wide range of literature besides *Triṃśikā* commentaries whenever he considered passages in those other texts relevant to the topic at hand. As to what criteria he may have used in deciding which portions of the *Fo-ti ching lun* to include and which to exclude, that remains unclear since it would not have gone against his grain to use a point raised by Śīlabhadra had he thought it pertinent. Keenan is right to make that an issue, but it only ultimately complicates the picture, first because of what the omission of Śīlabhadra suggests about Hsüan-tsang's view of Śīlabhadra, and second because of the supposed distancing of the views of Śīlabhadra and Dharmapāla entailed in thus distinguishing their respective commentaries. Śīlabhadra becomes the odd man out, whichever way you look at it. As we've pointed out, K'uei-chi also effectively excluded Śīlabhadra from the *Triṃśikā* lineage, skipping him by way of a layman who transmits the text directly to Hsüan-tsang from Dharmapāla. Śīlabhadra, who enjoys a good historical reputation primarily due to his association with Hsüan-tsang (the Tibetan *Buddhabhūmi* commentary is, as far as I can determine, the only known text of his to survive with his name attached to it), may have been the recipient of Hsüan-tsang's affection,[111] but whether he also received Hsüan-tsang's intellectual respect is less certain, as will be clearer shortly.

Fourth, Keenan's argument assumes, even more problematically, that the parallel passages in the *Buddhabhūmi* commentary belong to Dharmapāla. There is no direct evidence from Hsüan-tsang, his biography (see below), or any other source for this attribution. This assumption is made entirely on the basis of the parallelism with the *Ch'eng wei-shih lun.* Since K'uei-chi's attribution of those passages in the *Ch'eng wei-shih lun* is problematic, this assumption begs the question. If we suspend belief in K'uei-chi's claims of attribution, we don't even know, for instance, whether there were actually ten *Triṃśikā* commentaries, or more, or less. Ten, of course, is a very typical, auspicious Chinese number. Since, as far as I can tell, no where does the *Ch'eng wei-shih lun* lay out ten distinct views on anything, that claim is at least dubitable. More to the present point, again, we have only K'uei-chi's authority that those passages in the *Ch'eng wei-shih lun* which Katsumata has found in common with the *Buddhabhūmi* commentary were authored by Dharmapāla. Since the *Buddhabhūmi* commentary is attributed to "Bandhuprabha, etc.", but not Dharmapāla, K'uei-chi becomes our sole source for identifying the parallel passages with Dharmapāla at all.

To repeat an earlier point, if one evaluates the parallel passages in terms of context, i.e., to which of the two root texts—the *Triṃśikā* or the *Buddhabhūmi sūtra*—the commentarial passages are most pertinent, the *Buddhabhūmyupadeśa* wins hands down. The commentary there rather tightly follows the themes advanced by the root text, while the *Ch'eng wei-shih lun* constantly veers off into one digression after another, many of which are only connected tenuously at best to the explicit themes raised in the verses of the *Triṃśikā* proper. The *Buddhabhūmi sūtra* would have presented Dharmapāla (or whomever) with a better occasion for expounding the passages in question than the *Triṃśikā.*

The other Dharmapāla text mentioned above that shares common passages with the *Ch'eng wei-shih lun,* the *Ta-ch'eng kuang-pai lun shih-lun* (translated in 650), is a commentary on Āryadeva's *Śataka śāstra.* As such its theme and content are primarily Madhyamakan (with Yogācāra rejoinders), and the parallel passages reflect Madhyamakan issues. The *Triṃśikā* does not invoke any explicit Madhyamakan themes at all (even the ubiquitous Mahāyāna term *śūnyatā* is absent), thus leading again to the conclusion that these passages were brought into the *Ch'eng wei-shih lun* from the *Śataka* commentary and not vice versa. Hsüan-tsang uses the *Ch'eng wei-shih lun* to rehearse some of his own arguments for the non-difference of Madhyamaka and Yogācāra, and he seems to have found some of Dharmapāla's points useful. The *Śataka śāstra* commentary is Dharmapāla's refutation of Bhāvaviveka's Madhyamakan critique of Yogācāra which he performs in the context of his own commentary to a major Madhyamakan text. By implication and by explicit argument, then, he is not refuting Madhyamaka per se, but rather Bhāvaviveka's position; and he is doing so by attempting to show that his own Yogācāra position concords more directly with Āryadeva's Madhyamaka than does Bhāvaviveka's. This approach, rebuking Madhyamakan critiques while insisting on the non-difference of Yogācāra and Madhyamaka, was the same approach Hsüan-tsang took while at Nālandā. He successfully debated Madhyamakans with this approach and wrote a text in Sanskrit while in India on the non-difference between the two schools. He was lauded for both efforts by Śīlabhadra and his peers at Nālandā. In fact, as I shall argue presently, for Hsüan-tsang—and I suspect for Nālandā as a whole—Dharmapāla's importance lay squarely and almost exclusively in the domain of Madhyamaka-Yogācāra disputes. Hence it is no accident that this one text—the commentary on Āryadeva that rebuts Bhāvaviveka—is the *only* text of Dharmapāla that Hsüan-tsang translated; at least the only one, aside from the *Ch'eng wei-shih lun*, to which Dharmapāla's name was explicitly attached .

Hsüan-tsang and Dharmapāla

The East Asian tradition assumes that Hsüan-tsang and K'uei-chi are part of a Yogācāra lineage, beginning of course with Asaṅga and Vasubandhu, and then developing into a sectarian lineage starting with Dharmapāla who is succeeded by Śīlabhadra, who transmits it to Hsüan-tsang, from whom K'uei-chi acquired it. K'uei-chi then passes it on to Hui-chao 慧沼 (650-714) and Chih-chou 智周 (668-723), etc. (the Japanese Hossō lineage traces itself primarily to Hsüan-tsang and Chih-chou). K'uei-chi, not Hsüan-tsang, is considered the first patriarch of the Wei-shih school; Hui-chao the second patriarch; Chih-chou, the third. This assumed lineage is one of the bedrocks of East Asian interpretations of the *Ch'eng wei-shih lun* and Hsüan-tsang's teachings. We have already seen that Śīlabhadra's position in this "lineage" is problematic.

The Chinese Buddhist preoccupation with lineages begins during the T'ang dynasty and reached the status of central importance for all Chinese Buddhist schools by the Sung dynasty. For the most part, as Twentieth Century scholarship has shown, these lineages were largely fabrications retroactively imposed on previous generations, frequently distorting the actual historical lines of influence and transmission. In this respect it is intriguing to consider that K'uei-chi may have been among the first important Chinese Buddhists to engage in this activity, an activity often considered one of the defining characteristics of the 'sinitic' Buddhist schools (T'ien-t'ai, Hua-yen, Ch'an, and Pure Land)—since, with some prejudice, those sinitic schools often constructed their own lineages in such a way as to intentionally exclude the Wei-shih school (though it emerges contemporaneously with them) despite the fact that all of them owed some debt to Hsüan-tsang's translations, a debt which very soon was forgotten and hidden by lineages that excluded him. Since the Chinese penchant for constructing lineages (i.e., tracing the transmission of a school's authority through a sequence of masters to its alleged "root" or patriarch) intensified proportionate to the self-distancing of the sinitic schools from their actual Indian roots (which, in part, explains the exclusion of the Wei-shih school from 'sinitic' status—it was deemed 'too Indian'), the project of lineage-construction is both ironic and telling. Designed to provide a historical ground for a school's claim, it instead subverts history and problematizes that school's ideological ground. The professed lineages of the Ch'an schools, Hua-yen and Pure Land are being overturned by modern scholarship, sometimes radically.[112] That K'uei-chi might have been one of the early practitioners of "lineage construction" is indeed ironic.

Returning to the question of authorship of the *Fo-ti ching lun*, the notion of lineage raises some problems here as well. Assuming that the Tibetan attribution of the *Buddhabhūmi vyākhyāna* to Śīlabhadra is accurate, it is then curious that Śīlabhadra nowhere seems to quote Dharmapāla, assuming, again, that Dharmapāla might be the author of the other *Buddhabhūmi* commentary contained in the *Fo-ti ching lun*. If Dharmapāla was either his contemporary or especially if he considered himself Dharmapāla's disciple, this omission would seem quite incongruous. Since, as Katsumata as others state, if either of the two commentaries contained in the *Fo-ti ching lun* is drawing upon the other, it is the one they are attributing to Dharmapāla that is derivative of the one they attribute to Śīlabhadra, this is a curious reversal of lineage. While it might not be completely unthinkable that a 'master' composed a text after one of his students, and drew from that student's work, in the case of Dharmapāla and Śīlabhadra as outlined above, this seems odd, given Dharmapāla's young death, and Śīlabhadra's fawning admiration for his adopted teacher.

As Keenan points out, the parts of the *Fo-ti ching lun* being attributed by scholars to Śīlabhadra are not echoed in the *Ch'eng wei-shih lun*. Thus not only doesn't the *Ch'eng wei-shih lun* quote the commentary of Śīlabhadra to the *Buddhabhūmi sūtra* (another curious fact, since while Hsüan-tsang never met Dharmapāla, he did study with Śīlabhadra and considered him one of his mentors), but Śīlabhadra fails to cite a commentary that would have been written by his supposed mentor. Conversely, Dharmapāla does not really cite Śīlabhadra either. Since, as noted above, it is the Tibetan tradition that associates part of the *Buddhabhūmi* commentary with Śīlabhadra, and not Hsüan-tsang's Chinese version (which only explicitly names Bandhuprabha), modern scholars who have inferred that the other part of the *Buddhabhūmi* commentary should be attributed to Dharmapāla do so primarily on the basis of its parallelism with the *Ch'eng wei-shih lun* passages attributed by K'uei-chi to Dharmapāla. We may, and perhaps should continue to question both attributions, but we may as well allow that the Tibetan tradition has correctly attributed the text to Śīlabhadra since, though Śīlabhadra is mentioned in Buddhist histories as an important Nālandā figure, he was not generally considered an important author, and so would not be a typical candidate for pseudepigraphic attribution. Regardless, for our present purposes the matter may remain moot.

A careful reading of Hsüan-tsang's biography further problematizes Śīlabhadra's role in the Dharmapāla "lineage." For that matter, it also problematizes Dharmapāla. To bring this out we need to examine in some detail what Hsüan-tsang studied, when, and where.

Prior to leaving China, Hsüan-tsang was already expert in the *She lun* (*Mahāyānasaṃgraha*) and *Abhidharmasamuccaya*, and he is known to have lectured on them on his way to the Capitol prior to leaving for India. Once at the Chinese capitol, Chang-an, he studied the *Abhidharmakośa*, which, according to his biography, he mastered in one reading, fathoming its 'inner meaning,' such that no one could compete with him. "There was more than one point on which he had his own particular view."[113] This very clearly indicates that he was not a slave to tradition and did not hesitate to offer his own original insights.

The *Triṃśikā* is not mentioned in the biography until Hsüan-tsang has already arrived in India. Hsüan-tsang stayed 14 months with Vinitaprabha (probably in Kashmir, ca. 631-33), who had written commentaries on the *Triṃśikā* and the *Pañcaskandha prakāraṇa.*[114] This *Triṃśikā* commentary, incidentally, is not included in K'uei-chi's list of ten commentaries. A list of texts that Hsüan-tsang studied with Vinitaprabha is given in the biography, but it is not clear whether the *Triṃśikā* commentary was among them.

When he finally reached Nālandā (ca. spring 637) he announced to Śīlabhadra that he has come to study the *Yogācārabhūmi.* He studied with Śīlabhadra for fifteen months, attending three series of lectures on the *Yogācārabhūmi.*[115] He also attended Śīlabhadra's lectures on the *Madhyamaka-kārikā, Śata-śāstra* (three series each); *Abhidharma-nyāyānusāra, *Prakāraṇāryavācā śāstra* 顯楊聖梨阿論頌,[116] *Abhidharmasamuccaya* (one series each); *Nyāyapraveśa, Nyāyamukha, *Śabdavidyā śāstra* (i.e., Sanskrit grammar) 聲明論, and **Samuccaya-pramāṇa śāstra* 集量論 (two series each). While, as we can see from the titles of the texts that were the subjects of those lectures, he evidently studied Madhyamaka, logic and other topics with Śīlabhadra, neither the *Triṃśikā* nor its commentaries were included in the curriculum.[117] Since the only Madhyamakan texts Hsüan-tsang subsequently translated were the *Śataka śāstra* of Āryadeva (T.30.1570), Dharmapāla's commentary on it (T.30.1571) and Bhāvaviveka's *Karatalaratna* (T.30.1578), we may infer that (1) Hsüan-tsang's Madhyamaka studies focused on the Yogācāra-Madhyamaka debate as formulated by the disputes between Dharmapāla and Bhāvaviveka,[118] and (2) that Dharmapāla's 'authority' at Nālandā, at least in the eyes of Śīlabhadra, may have been confined to his contributions to that debate.

Later, while again traveling around India, he visited Dharmapāla's home town (ca. February, 640; see above). At that point the biography attributes the following works to Dharmapāla:

> The *Śabdavidyā Anthology Treatise* 聲明雜論, in 25,000 verses; a commentary on the *Catuhśataka*; the *Wei-shih lun*; Logic texts; and some tens of miscellaneous books.

Presumably the *Wei-shih lun* 唯識論 (*Vijñapti-mātra śāstra*) mentioned here implies the *Triṃśikā* commentary used in the *Ch'eng wei-shih lun*, but this title is vague enough to also imply either (1) a commentary on Vasubandhu's *Viṃśatika* (Twenty verses treatise), (2) a work commenting on both the *Triṃśikā* and *Viṃśatika*, or (3) it could mean a general treatise (or treatises) on *vijñapti-mātra*. We know that Dharmapāla did write a commentary on the *Viṃśatika*, since that was translated into Chinese by I-ching (T.31.1591) in the late seventh or early eighth century. The passage above occurs in the biography as background on Dharmapāla, and does not indicate anything concerning when or where Hsüan-tsang may have acquired or studied these texts. Also note, no mention is made here of a *Buddhabhūmi* commentary, though the *Śataka śāstra* commentary *is* mentioned (i.e., *Catuhśataka*). There is also no mention at all of any lay-patron, nor of Hsüan-tsang's having received a secret *Triṃśikā* commentary.

Shortly after this list, a truly revealing passage occurs. Hsüan-tsang meets two Siṃhalese monks and quizzes them on the *Yogācārabhūmi,* but "they could not give a better explanation than Śīlabhadra".[119] This might initially be taken as saying that Hsüan-tsang held Śīlabhadra's explanation so highly that he measured all others against it. But read in context, and perhaps peering a bit between the lines, it actually suggests that Hsüan-tsang was not completely satisfied with Śīlabhadra's exposition. He was still looking for a "better explanation." This is reinforced by the next point.

Prasenajit

Awhile later he encountered a hermit śāstra master named Prasenajit 勝軍 who, despite being virtually ignored by both the Wei-shih school and the East Asian tradition in general, should probably be considered *the Indian teacher that most profoundly influenced Hsüan-tsang* and with whom he became most intimate. According to the biography Prasenajit's credentials were impressive: He had studied the *Yogācārabhūmi* with Śīlabhadra; he had studied logic with Bhadraruci; he had studied Śabdavidyā and "Hīnayāna and Mahāyāna śāstras" with Sthiramati (!); and he was "exhaustively" well versed in the key Indian sciences of Vedas, astronomy, medicine, geography, and math. If he did indeed study with Sthiramati, Prasenajit must have been quite old, since Sthiramati preceded Dharmapāla (with whom apparently he did *not* study).[120] Unlike Dharmapāla, whom K'uei-chi depicts as closely associated with a wealthy patron, Hsüan-tsang's biography emphasizes Prasenajit's utter refusal to be placed in the position of a donee.[121] When King Purṇavarman of Magadha repeatedly invites Prasenajit to become the royal teacher, Prasenajit replies:[122]

> "I have heard that if one accepted the gifts of others, one would have to share their responsibilities. Now as I am urgently engaged in my work for the liberation of rebirth, how can I have time to attend to the king's affairs?"

Though he remained outside the political and Buddhist institutional mainstreams, Prasenajit was not a solitary hermit, since the biography states that he was well known and respected by the people for his virtue, and he always had several hundred students, "both monks and laymen," studying with him at Staff-forest Hill where he lived.

Hsüan-tsang became Prasenajit's companion for two years (by way of contrast, he only studied with Śīlabhadra for fifteen months), during which time they traveled together away from Nālandā. With Prasenajit he studied the *Explanatory Treatise on Vijñapti-mātra* (*Wei-shih chüeh-tse lun* 唯識決擇論), *Treatise on Doctrinal Theories* 義理論, *Abhayasiddhi śāstra* (Establishing Fearlessness Treatise 成無畏論), *The Non-abiding Nirvana Treatise*

(不住涅槃), *Treatise on the Twelve* [links of] *Pratītya-samutpāda* (十二因緣論), and *Mahāyānasūtrālaṃkāra śāstra* (莊嚴經論).[123] Although he did not know it yet, Hsüan-tsang was nearing the end of his stay in India when he met Prasenajit, and yet here we find only the second mention of a *Triṃśikā* commentary in the biography (assuming, again, that *wei-shih* here means *Triṃśikā* and not the *Viṃśatika* or *vijñapti-mātra* in general). This is the first time the biography states explicitly that Hsüan-tsang actually studied it. Unfortunately, exactly whose commentary or commentaries they studied together is unknown.

The biography also says that Prasenajit solved for Hsüan-tsang some doubtful points on the *Yogācārabhūmi*, confirming (1) that Hsüan-tsang had not been fully satisfied with Śīlabhadra's teaching, and (2) that finally, in Prasenajit, he had found the teacher he had been seeking, since it was the pursuit of a complete understanding of the *Yogācārabhūmi* that had brought him to India in the first place.

The stories presented of the two of them in the biography depict them as intimate friends with none of the diplomatic formalities found in most of Hsüan-tsang's other dealings, including those with Śīlabhadra. Whereas throughout the rest of the biography Hsüan-tsang is usually portrayed as devout to the point of gullibility—a character trait so distinctive that it becomes the key feature of the Hsüan-tsang caricature in the popular novel *Journey to the West* that retells his pilgrimage to India accompanied by a mischievous but heroic monkey[124]—with Prasenajit we see him sharing moments of healthy skepticism. Here is how the biography tells it:[125]

> According to the custom of the western countries [i.e., India and its neighbors], the Buddha's relic-bone in Bodhi Monastery was exhibited in this month [the first month of the Chinese calendar, i.e., ca. February]. The monks and laymen of the various countries all came to worship it. Thus the Master [Hsüan-tsang] and Prasenajit went together to the Bodhi Monastery and saw that some grains of the relic-bones were large and some small, and the larger ones were like pearls with a pink-white hue. There were also flesh relics, as large as peas with a red lustre. The relic-bones were replaced in the stupa when innumerable devotees had offered flowers and incense and paid homage to them.
>
> After about the first watch of the night, Prasenajit discussed about the unusual size of the relic-bones with the Master and said: "I have seen relic-bones at other places and they were only as large as grains of rice. How is it that they are so large at this place? Don't you also have some doubt about it?"
>
> The Master replied: "I also have some doubt about it."

In the biography Hsüan-tsang visits many sacred sites, some offering items far more incredible than oversized relics, but Hsüan-tsang invariably treats those sites and their displays with utmost reverence and piety. Hence his admission to Prasenajit of harboring doubts on this occasion is uncharacteristic and startling. The unusual candor shared between Hsüan-tsang and Prasenajit suggests a personal and intellectual intimacy between them that one does not find elsewhere in the biography.

Even as they share their moment of doubt, the dominating ethos of the biography reasserts itself, and piety ultimately prevails, even in this account, as the story continues:[126]

> A little while afterwards the lamp in their room suddenly became dim, and it was very bright inside and outside the house. Being amazed they went out to see and saw the stupa of the relic-bone issuing a bright light that shone toward the sky. It was a colored light and illuminated the sky and earth so brightly that the moon and the stars became darkened, and they also smelled an unusually fragrant scent which filled the courtyard. Thus the people told one another, saying that the relic-bones were showing a great miracle. Having heard this they assembled again to worship the relic-bones and praised it as a rare occurrence. After about a meal's time the light gradually diminished, and when it was about to disappear, it wound around the container of the relic-bones for several times and finally entered into it. The sky and earth became dark again and the stars reappeared. When the people had seen this sight, they had no more doubt about the relic-bones in their mind.

In K'uei-chi's account of Hsüan-tsang's visit to Dharmapāla's tomb, Hsüan-tsang's vocal complaints about such a sacred site becoming a crass tourist amusement with an admission price is rewarded by his receiving Dharmapāla's secret commentary on the *Triṃśikā*. In the relic story the skepticism of Prasenajit and Hsüan-tsang is requited with an impressive light show. In both cases an initial disapproving doubt is replaced by a strengthening of Hsüan-tsang's faith in the Dharma. Did K'uei-chi perhaps conflate these stories?

It was while he was with Prasenajit that Hsüan-tsang finally felt he had accomplished his mission in India. This realization became clear to him in a dream—which he discussed the next day with Prasenajit—that he interpreted to mean his time to return to China had arrived. As noted above, dreams marked important milestones and decisions in Hsüan-tsang's life.[127] It was Prasenajit, not Śīlabhadra, who, in Hsüan-tsang's mind, had fulfilled his mission.

Unfortunately for K'uei-chi's purposes, since Prasenajit was considered a hermit scholar rather than an authoritative voice at Nālandā, he hardly provided good lineage material. Under different circumstances a hermit monk might provide just the right sort of mysterious source for the introduction of a new tradition. But K'uei-chi was *not* trying to start a new tradition. On the contrary, he was attempting to characterize himself as the recipient of a well-known, well-established recognizable tradition with unimpeachable credentials. He was striving to be the voice of orthodoxy. For K'uei-chi to inherit the mantle of Hsüan-tsang's orthodoxy and preeminence, the lineage he received from Hsüan-tsang would have to be fully authoritative and mainstream. Were he to attempt to legitimize a new tradition, that would throw the onus of legitimizing that tradition squarely back on K'uei-chi; a new tradition would still be seeking to acquire authority through the promotion of its own merit (i.e., K'uei-chi's efforts) rather than by simply inheriting authority from a recognized, established authority such as Hsüan-tsang. The purpose behind K'uei-chi's story, I believe, is precisely to claim Hsüan-tsang's authority, and in particular to be recognized as such by Empress Wu, thereby becoming the recipient of her favor and patronage, as had Hsüan-tsang of the emperors who ruled during his time.

While K'uei-chi did try to lend the Dharmapāla commentary a special aura of revealed secrets only entrusted to the truly worthy, and he did claim *unique access* to a Dharmapāla commentary not previously in general circulation, nonetheless, he did not do so to confer esoteric status on it—on the contrary, he wished it to be considered mainstream. This may account for the ambivalence in his story as to whether Dharmapāla's *Triṃśikā* commentary brought widespread renown or was subject to a secret transmission. K'uei-chi appears to have wanted it both ways: Wide renown on the basis of an exclusive inheritance. K'uei-chi's claim was that Dharmapāla's teachings were the official, orthodox teachings at Nālandā, and that Śīlabhadra, as Dharmapāla's disciple, was their upholder and transmitter (even if he could never have seen the text, according to K'uei-chi's transmission story). In this way K'uei-chi could claim that he had come to possesses the most important piece of that lineage, one entrusted only to Hsüan-tsang and now himself, namely Dharmapāla's commentary. That would put K'uei-chi directly in line with the most orthodox of Indian Buddhist authority, a status unavailable from a hermit monk. As possesser of the preeminent, exclusive text for mainstream authority, passed to China by the most preeminent Buddhist in East Asia (i.e., Hsüan-tsang), not only would be K'uei-chi himself now be the next in a line of preeminences, but the mainstream authority he represented should be of special interest to an Emperor who, herself, represented the mainstream.

Before departing India for China, Hsüan-tsang returned to Nālandā. Śīlabhadra then asked him to lecture on the *She lun* (*Mahāyānasaṃgraha*) and the *Triṃśikā* commentary! Whether or not this commentary was Dharmapāla's (the biography gives the same title as the one [or ones] Hsüan-tsang studied with Prasenajit: *wei-shih chüeh-tse lun*), it is clear that Śīlabhadra was not a party to its transmission (unless his receiving instruction *from* Hsüan-tsang qualifies him for lineage membership). Since Prasenajit had originally studied the *Yogācārabhūmi* with Śīlabhadra, in some sense he could be construed as Śīlabhadra's disciple: However, he also studied with other masters (including Sthiramati?), and, judging by Hsüan-tsang's biography, had surpassed Śīlabhadra's understanding of the *Yogācārabhūmi* since studying it with him.

During this final stay at Nālandā, Hsüan-tsang debated some Madhyamakans (defeating them of course), and as a result, as previously stated, he composed, in Sanskrit, a treatise on the non-mutual-exclusion of Yogācāra and Madhyamaka in 3000 verses,[128] which Śīlabhadra encouraged the other monks to study. Though this treatise has not survived, some of its arguments may be detected in the *Ch'eng wei-shih lun*, and, indeed, here is one of the places where we do seem to find Dharmapāla's influence with some certainty (e.g., the parallel passages from Dharmapāla's commentary on Āryadeva's *Śataka śāstra*). Dharmapāla apparently was valued at Nālandā for having given the most effective Yogācāric response to Madhyamakan thought. The tensions between these two Mahāyāna schools preoccupied Buddhist philosophers for several centuries, starting with the polemics between Sthiramati, Bhāvaviveka, and Dharmapāla prior to Hsüan-tsang's visit to India, and continuing through Dharmakīrti (Hsüan-tsang's contemporary and possible classmate at Nālandā), and, after Hsüan-tsang left India, Candrakīrti, Śāntarakṣita, and so on.

Just before leaving, he paid homage to Śīlabhadra saying, "...Since my arrival I have been privileged to learn the *Yogācāra-bhūmi śāstra* from your Reverence, and thus all my doubts have been solved".[129] In the context of the preceding discussion, this should not be taken as anything more than typical Chinese politesse. Śīlabhadra and the others at Nālandā were trying to persuade Hsüan-tsang to stay in India. In order to decline their entreaties diplomatically, he had to insist that *they* had already fulfilled his mission, so that he might now return to China with the teachings he had received from them.[130]

In short, the notion of a Dharmapāla lineage as advanced by K'uei-chi and institutionalized by Chih-chou seems to be as problematic as his erroneous Sthiramati attributions in the *Ch'eng wei-shih lun.*

If Not Dharmapāla, What Authorities inform this *Triṃśikā* Commentary?

K'uei-chi's account of how Hsüan-tsang came into possession of Dharmapāla's *Triṃśikā* commentary would seem to rule out Prasenajit as the source, since he was a hermit monk, not a "rich benefactor." If I am right that Prasenajit was Hsüan-tsang's main *Triṃśikā* source, these two stories become incommensurate.

Why is Prasenajit ignored by K'uei-chi? Since Prasenajit doesn't appear to have written any commentaries himself, it is understandable why Hsüan-tsang, who basically translated written texts, lacked the occasion and opportunity for making Prasenajit better known to his Chinese audience. Hsüan-tsang does seem to have translated most of the texts he had studied with Prasenajit.[131] He also translated the sūtra in which Buddha instructs King Prasenajit (T.14.515), his mentor's namesake.

It is worthy of note that according to Buddhist legend King Prasenajit was not only a contemporary of Buddha, but a sort of lay-alter-ego for Buddha. They are supposedly born in the same year; when Gotama leaves home to pursue Dharma, Prasenajit ascends to his throne; and so on. He eventually becomes a devotee of the Buddha, a Cakravartin (Wheel-turning Monarch). But reading King Prasenajit's story is like reading a "what-if" alternate account of what might have been the Buddha's life had he chosen to accept his father's kingdom rather than leaving home to pursue Dharma.

It is not unlikely that in the two years they spent together, Hsüan-tsang and Prasenajit might have discussed this famous legend, piqued by the common name. Hsüan-tsang's Prasenajit seems also to have acted as his alter-ego, someone who shared the same concerns, skepticisms, sense of humor, etc. In terms of the *Ch'eng wei-shih lun*, Hsüan-tsang's biography leaves little room for doubt that Hsüan-tsang's own interpretation of the *Triṃśikā* was decisively influenced by Prasenajit.

Sthiramati's independent commentary on the *Triṃśikā* throws further light on the composition of the *Ch'eng wei-shih lun*. A careful comparison of this commentary with the *Ch'eng wei-shih lun* indicates that Hsüan-tsang did not follow the structure of the commentaries section by section, i.e., correlating what all had to say about verse one, then moving on to verse two, etc. Rather we find positions and arguments that only occur very late in Sthiramati's commentary being brought to bear already near the beginning of the *Ch'eng wei-shih lun*.[132]

Further, at certain critical junctures, we find the *Ch'eng wei-shih lun* presenting ideas that Sthiramati introduced in other texts, such as his threefold distinctions for each of the two *satyas* (found in Sthiramati's commentary to the *Madhyānta vibhāga*). However K'uei-chi does not identify the source.[133]

This reinforces our earlier claim that Hsüan-tsang used the *Ch'eng wei-shih lun* as an occasion to air many key Yogācārin disputes, and he used his broad-ranging command of the full complement of Yogācāric (and non-Yogācāric) literature to focus those positions from diverse sources into topical arguments. Thus the *Ch'eng wei-shih lun* is less a correlation of commentaries on the *Triṃśikā* than an overview of Yogācāric doctrines that draws on a wide range of sources (including, but not restricted to *Triṃśikā* commentaries) that uses the *Triṃśikā* as a skeleton on which those topics could be fleshed out. In conjunction with K'uei-chi's commentaries, it serves as a sort of Yogācāra catechism.

That the *Ch'eng wei-shih lun* became the central text of the Wei-shih school owes more to the esteem heaped on it by K'uei-chi than to any particular attention given it by Hsüan-tsang, who seems to have preferred a number of other texts (e.g., the *Yogācārabhūmi*, *Prajñāpāramitā sūtra*, *Heart Sutra*, etc.). As Nakamura indicates:[134]

> The formation of the *Fa-tsang* [sic for 'Fa-hsiang'] *wei-shih* school after his return to China is often spoken of as a matter of course; but, in fact, it is very curious, judging from his motives for going to India as well as from the works he translated after his return and the studies of them made by his students, that a school centered around the Yogācāra theory did not develop instead of one around the *ch'eng wei-shih* theory. It is probable that Hsüan-tsang tried to teach a philosophy centered around the *Yogācārabhūmiśāstra* and that his disciples studied it, but the peculiar conditions led to its transformation into a wei-shih philosophy. The *Yogācārabhūmiśāstra* was not suitable for Chinese scholars of that time.

While this formulation of the question of the centrality of the *Ch'eng wei-shih lun* for K'uei-chi's school may not be the best way of framing it, the basic question is right, viz., why did this text, of all the texts translated by Hsüan-tsang, get singled out by K'uei-chi as the cornerstone of *his* school? Whether Chinese scholars were prepared for the *Yogācārabhūmi* at that time, and precisely what differentiates the *Ch'eng wei-shih lun* from that text (in Nakamura's mind) are unclear to me since, for the *Ch'eng wei-shih lun* itself, the text that really seems at issue again and again is not so much the *Triṃśikā*, but the *Yogācārabhūmi*. Hsüan-tsang repeatedly presents passages from the *Yogācārabhūmi* (occasionally identified as such, more often merely offered with the phrase "the treatise says") and then lays out a number of different ways those passages may be or have been interpreted. Occasionally he even concludes that the *Yogācārabhūmi* itself is at fault in its pronouncements.[135] Thus, it would not be unfair to characterize the *Ch'eng wei-shih lun* as a hermeneutic exercise on the *Yogācārabhūmi*.

The *Ch'eng wei-shih lun*, though a sizable, far-ranging text, is written in a very concise, frequently elliptical style. Therefore, for centuries readers have turned to K'uei-chi to help fill in the ellipses. But if K'uei-chi could be wrong or misleading about some things, he might also be wrong about others. As a consequence, I have brought K'uei-chi's interpretation into my discussion of the *Ch'eng wei-shih lun* only very sparingly. It seems to me that we will be better able to see the *Ch'eng wei-shih lun* for what it is if we can disengage it from the influence of K'uei-chi and whatever we suppose is the contribution of Dharmapāla. In any event, neither is in a position to act as an unquestionable authority.

Notes

1 The Taishō edition (31.1585) gives the author(s) as "Bodhisattva(s) Dharmapāla, etc."

2 These are the *Ch'eng wei-shih lun shu-chi* (T.43.1830), which is a line by line commentary on the *Ch'eng wei-shih lun*, and the *Ch'eng wei-shih lun chang-chung shu-yao* (T.43.1831), which concentrates on difficult passages in the *Ch'eng wei-shih lun* and the *Ch'eng weiOshih lun shu-chi*, and from which the story of transmission will be translated; *Ch'eng wei-shih lun shu-chi k'o-wen*, an incomplete version of which is found in *Sung-tsang i-chen* (Rare Books of the Sung Tripitaka) 5.2; and *Ch'eng wei-shih lun pieh-ch'ao*, an incomplete version of which is found in the *Dainihon zokuzōkyō* 1/77/5. I also have blockprint editions from the Nanching Blockprint reprinting project of the *-shu-yao* and the *-pieh-ch'ao* which offer different readings than the Taishō and *Dainihon zokuzōkyō* versions. Only the *-shu-yao* will concern us in the present chapter.

3 This is the usual date assigned to the *Ch'eng wei-shih lun*, but some have dated it slightly later. E.g., W. Pachow, based on his calculations from the *Hsü Kao-seng chuan* (T.50.2060), writes: "Round about 660-663 when Hsüan-tsang completed the translation of the [*Ch'eng wei-shih lun*]..." (*A Study of the Twenty-Two Dialogues on Mahāyāna Buddhism*, Taipei: The Chinese Culture, 1979, p. 22). Pachow's latest date (663) is unlikely since the *Ch'eng wei-shih lun* would have been completed only one year before Hsüan-tsang died (664), which, considering the fact that some eight or nine other translations, including the monumental *Prajñāpāramitā Sūtra*, were completed *after* the *Ch'eng wei-shih lun*, seems impossible.

4 This seems to be confirmed by the *Hsü Kao-seng chuan* which was written by Tao-hsüan, a contemporary of Hsüan-tsang's and K'uei-chi's who died in 667 and who was part of Hsüan-

tsang's translation committee for a time. He lived at Hsi-ming monastery, one of the monasteries where Hsüan-tsang worked, and which became the center for the Wŏnch'ŭk 'school' that rivaled K'uei-chi's school (centered in the Ta-tz'u-en monastery, another place were Hsüan-tsang had worked) after Hsüan-tsang's death. He is one of the sources for the story about Wŏnch'ŭk spying on K'uei-chi receiving private instruction from Hsüan-tsang on the *Ch'eng wei-shih lun*. More on this in a moment.

5 Monks and laymen, some not even Buddhist, were assigned to the translation committee in 648 by order of Emperor T'ai-tsung, who held Hsüan-tsang in the highest regard, making Hsüan-tsang the most eminent Chinese Buddhist of his day. The personnel of the committee varied over the years, and at some points exceeded seventy people. One noteworthy participant was the monk Hsüan-ying 玄應, a leading lexicographer, who later compiled the first major Buddhist dictionary of technical terms, the *I-ch'ieh-ching yin-i* 一切經音義 (T.54.2128), that glossed terms from 434 texts, including the *Yogācārabhūmi*. After his death, the work was completed by Hui-lin 慧琳 who extended its coverage to 1220 texts.

While the Emperor (and, when he died, his son and successor, Kao-tsung) seemed to have had an affection for Hsüan-tsang—supporting him, building a pagoda to house the Sanskrit texts he had brought to China (which still stands today and is a major tourist attraction), commemorating the Ta-tz'u-en Monastery in honor of Hsüan-tsang, instituting the translation committee and ordering monks and laymen from near and far to participate in it, insisting that Hsüan-tsang stay near the capitol despite his repeated requests to be allowed to remove himself to a more secluded, less cosmopolitan environment in which to pursue his translations, etc.—another reason has been suggested in the early accounts as to why Hsüan-tsang found such favor. The Emperor apparently had dreams of spreading his empire westward into Central Asia, and Hsüan-tsang was the only trustworthy voyager he knew who had been there. Thus he pressed him for information: population cites, geopolitical data, troop size and deployment, etc. Hsüan-tsang, not wishing to contribute to such martial exploits, resisted the Emperor's entreaties, but finally 'compromised' by writing his aforementioned travelogue, which is rich in detail, but not very useful for military purposes. Cf. Stanley Weinstein, *Buddhism Under the T'ang* (Cambridge: Cambridge University Press, 1987), p. 24.

6 See Yoshihide Yoshuzi, *Kegon ichijō shisō no kenkyū* (Tokyo: Daitō-shuppan-sha, 1991), pp. 102ff.

7 I have presented two papers on this confrontation and the issue of the Chinese reaction to Indian logic raised by it: "Attitudes Toward Logic in Chinese Philosophy," International Society for Chinese Philosophy, Hilo, Hawaii, 1989; "Chinese Reception of Buddhist Logic," American Academy of Religion, Anaheim, CA, 1989. Only the preface to Lü Ts'ai's commentary is extant, preserved in the 8th fascicle of Hsüan-tsang's biography, *Ta-tz'u-en-ssu san-tsang fa-shih chuan*, op. cit. This section is not included in the English translation by Li Yung-hsi, but I included a partial translation in the latter paper. The new translation by Li Rongxi, *A Biography of the Tripitaka Master of the Great Ci'en Monastery of the Great Tang Dynastu* (Berkeley: Numata, 1995) does contain a complete translation of the preface on pp. 237-244. For an overview of Lü Ts'ai's life and works, cf. the second chapter of *Chung-kuo ssu-hsiang-t'ung shih* (History of Chinese Philosophy), ed. Hou Wei-lu (Taipei, 1959); Part Four, pp. 108-140.

8 T.44.1840. On K'uei-chi's commentary, cf. Richard Chi's *Buddhist Formal Logic* (Delhi: Motilal, 1984). On problems in Hsüan-tsang's translation, particularly concerning the notion of *eva* ("only"), cf. Tom Tillemans' "Some Reflections of R.S.Y. Chi's *Buddhist Formal Logic*," *Journal of the International Association of Buddhist Studies*, 11, 1, pp. 155-171. For more on the problem of 'eva,' which has received a great deal of scholarly attention in reference to the works of Dignāga and Dharmakīrti, cf. Richard Hayes and Brendan Gillon, "Introduction to Dharmakīrti's Theory of Inference as Presented in *Pramāṇavārttika Svopajñavṛtti* 1-10," *Journal of Indian Philosophy*, 19, 1991, pp. 1-73, and the sources cited therein.

9 Cf. John Powers, "Lost in China, Found in Tibet," *Journal of the International Association of Buddhist Studies*, 15, 1, 1992, pp. 95-105.

10 The second patriarch was Hui Chao 慧沼 (650-714).

11 The key source is *Ch'eng wei-shih lun liao-i-teng* (T.43.1832) compiled by Hui-chao. The third patriarch, Chih-chou, wrote his own commentary on the *Ch'eng wei-shih lun*, the *Ch'eng wei-shih lun yen-pi* (T.43.1833), which supported the interpretation in K'uei-chi's *Ch'eng wei-shih lun shu-chi*. Shōtarō Iida has championed Wŏnch'ŭk's position over K'uei-chi. Cf. his "Who best can re-turn the Dharma-cakra? a controversy between Wŏnch'ŭk (632-696) and K'uei-chi (632-682)," *Indogaku Bukkyōgaku Kenkyū*, 34, 1986, pp. 984-941 (11-18); "A MuKung-hwa in Ch'ang-an—A Study of the Life and Works of Wŏnch'ŭk...," *Proceedings of the International Symposium Commemorating the 30th Anniversary of Korean Literature*, Korea, 1975, pp. 225-251; "Another Look at the Mādhyamika vs. Yogācāra Controversy concerning Existence and Non-existence," in *Prajñāpāramitā and Related Systems*, ed. Lewis Lancaster (Berkeley: University of Berkeley Press, 1977), pp. 341-360; "The Three Stupas of Ch'ang An," *Papers of the 1st International Conference on Korean Studies*, The Academy of Korean Studies, Seoul, Korea, 1980, pp. 484-497.

12 Incidentally, the *Ch'eng wei-shih lun* was not translated at either of these two, but at a third monastery, Yü-hua ssu 玉華寺, where he completed many of his translations.

13 Since the *Ch'eng wei-shih lun* was not translated at Hsi-ming Monastery, it is hard to imagine how the events reported by Tao-hsüan could have happened there.

14 Stanley Weinstein, *Buddhism Under the T'ang* (Cambridge: Cambridge UP, 1987), p. 31.

15 He was sent to the capitol to procure an Imperial Preface for Hsüan-tsang's translation of the *Prajñāpāramitā Sūtra*. Cf. *ibid.*, p. 30.

16 *Ibid.*, pp. 34-37.

17 *Ibid.*, pp. 44-47.

18 Fa-tsang's critique of Wei-shih was more far-ranging than this summary might suggest, and he returns to that theme numerous times throughout his works. Cf. e.g., T.35.1733.346-47 and T.45.1861.258-59 for two different lists of '10 types of wei-shih' by Fa-tsang, with relevant discussions. A discussion of the main points of the dispute between Hsüan-tsang's Yogācāra and Fa-tsang's revisionism can be found in Ming-wood Liu's Ph.D. dissertation, *The Teaching of Fa-tsang—An Examination of Buddhist Metaphysics*, (unpub.).

19 There are elements of this valorization of pure mind even in a number of texts translated by Hsüan-tsang (e.g., the *Buddhabhūmyupadeśa*), which seem to indicate a blending of Yogācāra and Tathāgatagarbha thought, though the latter term rarely if ever appears in his translations. See Keenan, *A Study of the Buddhabhūmyupadeśa*, Part Two, chs. 1-2, unpub. Ph.D. dissertation. However, at most, one can say that Hsüan-tsang is ambivalent about these elements, and, for instance, where comparable discussions occur in the *Ch'eng wei-shih lun*, the term *tathāgatagarbha* is conspicuous in its absence.

20 According to Weinstein, *op. cit.*, it was during the time of the third Fa-hsiang patriarch that the school declined, not while K'uei-chi was at the helm. Without going into a long argument, I will only say here that Empress Wu began to assert her power at the end of Hsüan-tsang's life, but her inordinate fondness for Fa-tsang blossomed (and thus patronage of him and his ideas) while K'uei-chi headed the Fa-hsiang school. Its eclipse may have more or less finalized during the third partriarch's tenure, but clearly the writing was already on the wall, since, at least in the eyes of Empress Wu (and the preponderance of East Asian Buddhists ever since), K'uei-chi made a poor show of himself against Fa-tsang.

The later Tantric developments in China are sometimes considered part of the Yogācāra school partly because Tantra involved "yoga" practice and partly because they headquartered in the same monasteries (Hsi-ming ssu and Tz'u-en ssu) as Hsüan-tsang. Tantra in China peaked in the eighth century. When Vajrabodhi (ch. Chin-kang-chih 金剛智), considered the fifth patriarch of the Esoteric school, came to China from India in 720, he initially stayed at the Ta-tz'u-en monastery, which was the Yogācāra monastery dedicated to

Hsüan-tsang and from which K'uei-chi's other name, Tz'u-en, is derived. It was during the time of his successor and student, Amoghavajra (ch. Pu-k'ung 不空), i.e., the mid-eighth century, that this tantric form of Yogācāra, or yoga practice, reached its zenith. The relation between this practice-oriented esoteric 'yoga' school, steeped in magical incantations and visualizations, and the exoteric Yogācāra school exemplified by Hsüan-tsang is not clear and deserves further study. Hsüan-tsang did translate a number of tantric texts (or, more precisely, dhāranī and ritual texts), but it seems the later Chinese and Japanese traditions were less than approving of his efforts. Cf. e.g., Kūkai's commentary on the *Heart Sutra* (T.2203), in which, during his review of the various Chinese translations, he declares Hsüan-tsang's inadequate, specifically complaining that its concluding mantra is "ineffective."

21 The 'erroneous view of existence' involves mistaking what does not exist, such as an eternal self, for something truly existent. The 'erroneous view of emptiness' means to mistake emptiness for a form of nihilism or the utter denial that anything exists. That Madhyamaka negates false views of existence but itself may lead to the opposing false view of nihilism—hence requiring Yogācāra to 'correct' the wrong views by returning to the Middle Way between extremes—is already suggested in *Saṁdhinirmocana Sūtra*.

22 I.e., each of the Bodhisattvas, alluding to the supposed ten commentators that Hsüan-tsang is said by K'uei-chi to have taken into account when composing the *Ch'eng wei-shih lun*.

23 A magical corral branch taken from a fairyland tree (*ch'iung-chih* 瓊枝) with salvific properties. Cf. *P'ei wen yün fu*, v. 2, 1189.3.

24 By K'uei-chi's day, many Buddhists believed that those who had been contemporaries of the Buddha were vastly superior beings to their own contemporaries, since the Sutras tell of people reaching complete Awakening by just hearing a few words from Buddha, while later Buddhists needed to practice and study diligently for a mere shadow of that understanding.

25 *Fu-wu* 撫物, alluding to the Bodhi-fruit.

26 This sentence seems to mean that Dharmapāla was destined to outshine his contemporaries in terms of his degree of Awakening. It also implies that Dharmapāla's depth of Awakening was equal to that of the greatest 'Worthies' and that he had been cultivating it through many lives since that time.

27 *Hsi-hua chih yu ch'i* 息化之有期, i.e., his days of wandering in Samsara were coming to an end.

28 I.e., that he would soon die and enter Nirvana.

29 *Ch'an-hsi* 禪習.

30 An obvious allusion to the Buddha Siddhārtha's own pledge to remain seated under the Bodhi-tree until reaching complete Awakening. Here it has a figurative meaning, i.e., that Dharmapāla made a solemn vow to practice uninterruptedly and without distraction until achieving enlightenment. But other sources indicate that Dharmapāla did indeed practice at the Bodhi-tree by Bodh-gaya at the end of his life, so it should probably be taken literally here as well.

31 *Ch'an li chih hsia* 禪禮之暇. This could either mean, as translated above, "taking a break from *ch'an* and *li*," or "amidst the ease of *ch'an* and *li*."

32 *Chu-ts'ai* 注裁 which usually means to produce marginal notes. Note, K'uei-chi is depicting Dharmapāla as already composing a composite text based on the previous commentaries. The *Ch'eng wei-shih lun* is such a composite text, but, as we'll see later in this story, it did not become so merely by imitating Dharmapāla's text.

33 But cf. n. 50 below.

34 Note that K'uei-chi is characterizing Dharmapāla's commentary as a sort of catechismic assortment of the previous commentaries, again a feature of the *Ch'eng wei-shih lun*. But as we'll see, this is a feature that K'uei-chi himself had to argue and persuade Hsüan-tsang to implement. If Dharmapāla's commentary already exemplified this approach, K'uei-chi's arguments would have been superfluous.

35 Alluding both to being able to discern the better and worse qualities of the other commentaries as well as being able to see the principles expounded by Dharmapāla operating everywhere. Note his deft mixing of the literary phrases "traversing rivers and lakes" (which euphemistically means to cover the whole world) with "clear and turbid", denoting clear water distinguished from muddy water (a euphemism for separating out the pure, clean, transparent, calm, etc. from the dirty, murky, stirred, etc.).

36 *Chieh* 接 which means "to receive in hand, take charge of, connect, join." Hence it connotes both joining up with the Milky Way as well as implying control over it. This is reinforced in the next phrase (*o-o* 峨峨) which means both "a high, dignified presence" *and* "commanding."

37 The blockprint text has the rare character *t'ui* (another form of 隤) meaning "to collapse, drip, fall down." This would suggest a pouring down or effusing from the heights. The *Taisho* text has *tui* 堆 here, meaning "to heap up, a pile, a mass," suggesting a different image. I have tried to suggest both possibilities by rendering the *t'ui* as "cascading down" and the *tui* as "teeming."

38 *Tui pu o-o yi ch'iung-lung yi t'an tang* 堆埠峨峨夷穹窿以坦蕩. The point of this and the surrounding lines is to give some sense of how one feels reading Dharmapāla's commentary, i.e., exhilarating, surprising, far-ranging, etc. In this sentence *Tui pu o-o* also suggests stylistic alterations, i.e., 'high and low' is a 'flowery' style alternating between difficult and easy; and *yi ch'iung-lung yi t'an tang* is 'level,' implying a lucid, simple style. It also connotes an open-minded composure.

39 "Depths" (*sui* 邃, lit. "deep, abstruse") picks up on a subtle pun impossible to capture in English. The second term of the compound just translated as "lofty vaults" (*ch'iung-lung*), i.e., *lung*, when not used in that compound, means "cavity, hole."

40 K'uei-chi has used several different words throughout this passage which basically mean "heights" or "lofty," (*sung ts'eng feng* 聳層峰*... o-o i ch'iung-lung....* and now *kao* 高).

41 The oblique reference to a kiln (*t'ao-chen*) in this sentence is obscure—*Hao-chü hung-tsung t'ao-chen yu chi* 浩句宏宗陶甄有極—— though *t'ao-chen* here probably only means 'manage, regulate.'

42 An unlikely Sanskrit name: Hsüan-chien = *Gambhirādarśa? *Hsüan* 玄 is a significant, ubiquitous Chinese term (the same *hsüan* as in Hsüan-tsang's name), frequently used in Chinese Buddhist names during this period, but lacking any clear Sanskrit equivalent. *Chien* 鑑 (mirror or mirroring) might be *ādarśa* or *(prati-)bimba.* The name seems likely to be a Sinitic concoction.

43 Allusion to a Chinese story of a merchant who, to gain favor with the King of Ch'u, searched for a phoenix guided only by its description. He was conned into accepting a pheasant in its place since the two have similar descriptions, and he had never seen either one. Thus the story signifies differentiating the authentic from a facsimile, the dangers of searching for something based only on its description, etc. Most importantly for what follows in the story, it denotes his ability to see the extraordinary in the ordinary.

44 Like the previous allusion, this is a way of saying that he was of unusual intelligence and sensitivity to spiritual matters. The unicorn leaves her tracks on dry land, but is elusive; the dragon's tracks are hidden under the sea and hard to reach. It implies he could recognize Dharmapāla's special spiritual qualities despite his ordinary appearance.

45 I.e., he was a wealthy patron of Dharmapāla.

46 *To-tuan* 多端 can also mean "in many ways."

47 Could also mean "with these commentaries." If singular, then only the *Triṃśikā* is meant. If plural, than that plus his commentary on the *Viṃśatika* would be implied. Although K'uei-chi's story seems to focus exclusively on the former, he prefaced the story by mentioning both. Hsüan-tsang never translated the *Viṃśatika* commentary. That was translated by I-ching half a century later.

48 It is unclear exactly what sort of pilgrimage "spectator display" is intended here, whether viewing of the body (such as the "mummy" traditions in Ch'an and Tibet), a stupa of his relics,

or some other form of homage. Hsüan-tsang does report visiting Dharmapāla's stupa while in India in his *Hsi-yü chi* but makes no mention of a layman or text transmission.

49 *Shen-ying* 伸穎 lit., "spiritual acuity."

50 I.e., the commentaries. Note, while K'uei-chi earlier claimed that Dharmapāla becomes famous as a result of his *Triṃśikā* commentary, the commentary itself, we now read, remains secret. Thus, it would seem that Dharmapāla's renown in India can have nothing to do with that commentary. Cf. n. 33.

51 *Hsüan-tao* 玄導.

52 *Yu ling* 有靈, lit. 'having spiritual-potency.'

53 A paraphrase of *Analects* 4:8.

54 This is a clue to the intent of the command he gives the layman above.

55 This sentence contains the word for crane (*hao* 鶴), which, I have ignored in the translation. I don't know what the oblique use of the word "crane" (usually a Chinese symbol of longevity) signifies here. Perhaps it is a subtle allusion to the Crane Grove where, according to tradition, the Buddha Siddhārtha died.

56 *Jui-fa t'ien-tzu* 叡發天資.

57 The Chinese does not specify either who speaks or to whom the following is said. By context, it is clearly Hsüan-tsang who is speaking, but his audience could be the spectator crowd in general—of whom the layman is a part—or the layman directly.

58 His argument is that this mockery (running the stupa like a carnival sideshow for profit) will reflect poorly on the teachings that Dharmapāla represents, namely Buddhism. If people judge Buddhism by this travesty, they will dismiss it as crass and spiritually unworthy.

59 *Miao-li* 妙理.

60 But cf. note 57 above. Again, it may be the entire crowd that receives Hsüan-tsang's pronouncement this way, which catches the attention of the layman, or perhaps the exchange is simply between the layman and Hsüan-tsang. In the latter case, it is a quiet affair, conducive to the secret transmission of texts. In the former case, Hsüan-tsang's actions would have been an overt and unmistakable sign of his own "spiritual acuity."

61 An Abhidharmic text by Vasubandhu.

62 *Chen-shuo* 真說用.

63 A very literary phrase: *Tzu hsi fei yü-tieh, tung ch'ih su-hsia* 自西霏玉牒, 東馳素象.

64 "Once again" here means: just as Dharmapāla handed the text in secret to the layman, so did the layman give it in secret to Hsüan-tsang. The west to east movement also alludes to Hsüan-tsang's returning to China (east) from India (west).

65 An allusion to the *Chuang Tzu*, end of ch. 26 (Harvard/Yenching ed. 75/26/48-49; Watson's tr., p. 302), where it says: "You use a fish trap to catch a fish; once the fish is caught, you may throw away the trap.... You use words to capture the intent (meaning); once the intent is caught, you may throw away the words." Hence "fish trap" here means "meaning." For "fish trap" K'uei-chi uses *ch'üan* 筌 while Chuang Tzu uses its homonym 荃 (they differ only as to their respective radicals on top).

66 *Yüan-ssu* 淵思.

67 *Yi-miao* 繹妙.

68 *Analects* 9:12. The quoted passage is spoken by Tzu-kung, not Confucius. Legge translates the full passage as:

> Tsze-kung said, 'There is a beautiful gem here. Should I lay it up in a case and keep it? or should I seek for a good price and sell it?' The Master [i.e., Confucius] said, 'Sell it! Sell it! But I would wait for one to offer the price.'

According to Confucian tradition this passage is a veiled way of discussing eagerness to seek office, i.e., make one's talents available. K'uei-chi seems to be using this passage to justify Dharmapāla's "strategy" for transmitting his *Triṃśikā* commentary. 宣尼 (Hsüan-ni) is an epithet dating from the Han dynasty, when Confucius received the nickname "Duke of

Hsüan." Since the character *ni* was appropriated by Buddhists to indicate "nuns" (signaling the addition of *-ni* to *Bhikṣu* [monk] to make it *Bhikṣuni* [nun]), this may be a subtle denigration of Confucius by K'uei-chi, albeit one with a traditional Confucian history.

69 This interlude—in which a decision is reached to make public a hitherto secret text—also acts as a transition from the story of how Hsüan-tsang came to receive the text to K'uei-chi's autobiographical discussion of how he came to be involved in its "translation."

70 Lit., "smoked or fumed up."

71 *Tzu fu* 緇服 appears to have a double meaning: *Tzu* means black robes, such as a novice monk wears. *Fu* means mourning garb. In other words, he joined the Order as an expression of his mourning the tragic impermanence of life.

72 This phrase is hard to translate without being misleading. To cut off feelings doesn't mean to repress emotions, but to lose sentience, the feelings which make one alive.

73 Lit. "black-robed forest," *Tzu-lin* 緇林.

74 *Sui-wu-yi-liao* 隨伍譯僚.

75 K'uei-chi now depicts himself as the annotator, the one of the four most in command of the *meaning* of the texts. However he has just said that he was merely the scribe or stenographer. Perhaps he is implying another promotion? Or perhaps we can harmonize the discrepancy by saying that his job was to annotate the scribed translations based on Hsüan-tsang's oral commentary. This division of translation labor into four roles was common enough that some Tibetan translators are reported to have used the same system.

76 Suggestive of the "appearance/face" of Dharmapāla seen earlier by Hsüan-tsang.

77 *Ling-chih* 靈智, lit. Spiritual-potency Wisdom.

78 Probably the Eight Skandhas refers to the eight sections of the Abhidharma.

79 Another allusion to Chuang Tzu, ch. 13 (Harvard/Yenching ed., 36/13/70f; Watson, pp. 152ff.—"chaff and dregs") where trying to learn the ancient ways from the writings of the ancients is fruitless, since their writings are nothing more than "the lees and scum of bygone men," devoid of their true living art.

80 This may also mean: "Now, finally, in China there appears a book (or stratagem) that certainly bears witness to the profoundest principles (*Hsüan-tsung* 玄宗)."

81 Could also mean: "Therefore to do the treatise [this way] is appropriate."

82 Common self-deprecating form of self-address in Chinese.

83 Could also mean: "If you stay far away from it, you'll have no wisdom; if you draw near to it, you will have discernment."

84 *Pañcavidyā-sthānāni*: the traditional five fields of knowledge in India were: 1. grammar, 2. mathematics, 3. medicine, 4. logic, and 5. internalizing (memorizing and embodying) scripture.

85 Allusion to *Chuang Tzu* 17, etc.

86 Cf. *Analects* 9:27; and *Chuang Tzu* 28/65 (Watson, p. 319).

87 The allusion is unclear, but seems to mean that even as things grow dark, have faith, for the light will come.

88 The word for secret here, *yu* 幽, has been translated as "darkness" above.

89 On the twelve symbols, see Schuyler Cammann's "Types of Symbols in Chinese Art," in Arthur Wright, ed., *Studies in Chinese Thought* (Chicago: University of Chicago Press, 1953), pp. 195-231, esp. pp. 204-208. For beautiful color prints of some Imperial robes incorporating these symbols see John E. Vollmer, *Five Colours of the Universe* (Edmunton: Edmunton Art Gallery, 1980).

90 Of the *fu* Cammunn writes: "...[it] was so old that its original significance was apparently forgotten even before the T'ang." (p. 205)

91 *Ibid.*

92 Cf. note v.

93 Cf. Isabelle Robinet, *Taoist Meditation*, tr. Julian Pas and Norman Girardot (Albany: SUNY Press, 1993), pp. 24-25.

94 *Ta-t'ang hsi-yu-chi*, T.51.2087.931c; Ch.10:22A (Nanching Blockprint edition); cf. Beal ii.229f.

95 *Ibid.* T.51.914c; Ch.8:15A-B; cf. Beal ii.110-112.

96 *Ibid.*, T.51.930c-931a; Ch.10:18A-B; cf. Beal ii.223f.

97 *Ibid.* T.51.923c-924a; Ch.9:18A-B; cf. Beal ii.171.

98 The more common Chinese rendition of Sthiramati is *An-hui* 安慧.

99 *Ta-tz'u-en-ssu san-tsang fa-shih chüan*, (T.50.2053.275c-276a) Ch.10.2A-2B. I am quoting Li Yung-hsi's translation from *The Life of Hsüan-tsang* (Beijing: The Chinese Buddhist Association, 1959), pp. 260-261, slightly modified.

100 I presented a paper on the role of dreaqms in Hsüan-tsang's biography at the Southeast Regional Meeting of the American Academy of Religion, Savannah, GA, Jan. 1997, titled "On Portents and Dreams: Xuanzang's Dreams." A few examples of the role of dreams in Hsüan-tsang's life will illustrate this. (1) On his way to India, he dreams of the Bodhi-tree under which Buddha realized Awakening, and he interprets the dream as a prediction that he, too, will become Awakened when arriving there. To his profound disappointment, his subsequent visit to the Bodhi-tree fails to produce the anticipated result. (2) When Hsüan-tsang arrives at Nālandā, he is greeted by Śīlabhadra, who treats him auspiciously, claiming that he himself had a dream predicting Hsüan-tsang's coming. (3) After his two years with Prasenajit (cf. below), Hsüan-tsang has a dream which he interprets as a sign that it is time to return to China. Interestingly, this dream portends that a 'Dharma-drought' will befall India, making it imperative that the seeds of Buddhism be well planted elsewhere (viz. China). Prasenajit takes this in stride, injecting that all things are impermanent. However, everyone, including Hsüan-tsang, apparently understood the dream as signaling that Buddhism's decline in India would be temporary. In the seventh century, it seems, no one could quite envision exactly how true and definitive Hsüan-tsang's dream really was. (4) Hsüan-tsang's dream concerning the *Prajñāpāramitā sūtra* gains extra significance when we consider how important this sūtra was to him. It was the largest text he translated (600 fascicles, filling three entire volumes in the Taisho edition). Only two other texts rivaled it in importance to him: (1) the *Yogācārabhūmi*, which he went to India for, and (2) the *Heart Sutra*, which he first learned from a sick man he treated on his way to India. When beset by demons in the 'Mo-ho-yen' desert, he discovered it was more efficacious for dispelling them than chanting Kuan-yin's name (on the practice of chanting to Kuan-yin, especially during traveling calamities, cf. Cornelius P. Chang, "Kuan-yin Paintings from Tun-huang: Water Moon Kuan-yin," *Journal of Oriental Studies*, XV, 2, July 1977, pp. 141-160, esp. pp. 143-145). Hsüan-tsang chanted this sutra often, and his biography records that he chanted it on his death bed. On the prajñāpāramitā dream and its relevance for ascertaining the nature of Hsüan-tsang's project, cf. Hakamaya Noriaki's *Genjō*, [a critical biography of Hsüan-tsang, in Japanese] (Tokyo: Daizō Shuppan, 1981), p. 301. Hakamaya considers some of the questions that I am raising in this section (cf. esp. pp. 311-312).

101 Occasionally major texts, such as the *Yogācārabhūmi*, *Abhidharmasamuccaya* and *Laṅkāvatāra Sūtra*, are mentioned by name. Usually they are being cited as proof texts for various positions, but (1) the holders of the positions are never identified, and (2) more often than not the passages from the identified texts are used as occasions for laying out different hermeneutic approaches to those passages themselves, not to the *Triṃśikā* or in any obvious immediate sense a commentary on the *Triṃśikā* ; again, the sources or 'authors' of those approaches are not identified.

102 This is a very important issue, unfortunately too complex to be discussed here fully. Briefly, most of the so-called positional differences come down to disputes on how to either define or categorize certain key terms. Early in the *Ch'eng wei-shih lun* Hsüan-tsang offers some discussion on his theory of language, which deals in part with the problems of referentiality and precision in definition. Some of this will be translated in a later chapter. Hsüan-tsang draws a distinction between (1) properly defining something i.e., the definition is neither too

narrow to preclude adequately circumscribing its topic, nor too broad to become inclusive of things aside from what is to be defined—and (2) the more figurative use of language, such as calling visual consciousness 'eye-consciousness' (which is how it is said in Sanskrit and Chinese). Although visual consciousness is not itself part of the physical eye, 'eye' can be used to 'define' vision by metonymy (but not synecdoche). Many of the later disputes seem to turn on this distinction, that is, when an opinion is neither blatantly wrong (i.e., it does not violate logic or scripture) nor poorly formulated (i.e., it is not incoherent or inconsistent with other aspects of the position), then it may simply be a case of allowing a looser standard of language. As long as the appropriate standard is recognized, the position may be viable, though perhaps 'one-sided.' It would take us beyond our present concerns to flesh this out further here.

103 *Tsa-chi-lun shu-chi* (in *Dainihon Zokuzōkyō* 74.603/4-5.

104 T.31.1606.

105 Cf. Alan Sponberg, *The Vijñaptimātra Buddhism of K'uei-chi*, unpub. Ph.D. dissertation, p. 34.

106 *Indogaku Bukkyōgaku Kenkyū*, 4, 1, 1956, pp. 116ff.

107 *A Study of the Citta-Vijñāna Thought in Buddhism* (in Japanese) (Tokyo: Sankibo-Busshorin, 1961), chs. 3 and 5. Katsumata also devotes a long chapter to Sthiramati's commentary in comparison with the *Ch'eng wei-shih lun*'s account of it, but, though he recognizes the problem of K'uei-chi's attributions, he does not follow this through to its full implications. Katsumata draws on the work of UI Hakuju, *Anne Gohō Yuishiki Sanjūju Shakuron* (Commentaries by Sthiramati and Dharmapāla on Vasubandhu's *Triṃśikā Vijñapti-mātra*), Tokyo, 1952. Since Katsumata pays little attention to how the *Ch'eng wei-shih lun* incorporates Sthiramati's text out of the order of the original commentary (his discussion proceeds verse by verse through the *Triṃśikā*), his treatment tends toward superficiality, and he seems to let nothing deter him from his stated purpose throughout most of the first half of the book—recovering Dharmapāla's original commentary. Fukihara Shōshin's *Gohōshu Yuishikiko* (Examination of the Vijñaptimātratā Doctrine in the Dharmapāla School), Kyoto: Hōzōkan, 1955, compares the 'assumed' Dharmapāla commentary with Sthiramati's and Paramārtha's *Chuan shih lun.*

108 Keenan, Ph.D. diss., *op. cit.*, pp. 364f.

109 The order of translation unfortunately offers little help in determining the order of original composition. Sometimes when Hsüan-tsang would translate a root text that required commentarial exposition, he would translate the commentary *first.* For instance, he translated Asvabhāva's commentary to the *She lun* (T.31.1598) in 647; Vasubandhu's commentary to this text (T.31.1597) in 648; and the *She Lun* itself, *sans* commentary, later that same year. At other times, a commentary would be translated after the root text. For example, he translated the *Triṃśikā* (the Thirty Verse root text behind the *Ch'eng wei-shih lun*) in 648 (T.31.1584), but didn't compose the *Ch'eng wei-shih lun* until 659.

110 護法等菩薩。約此三十頌造成唯識。 T.31.1586.60a.20.

111 There are a number of endearing exchanges between Hsüan-tsang and Śīlabhadra provided in the biography, as well as a letter Hsüan-tsang sent to India after learning of Śīlabhadra's death. Apparently an Uigurish Turkish translation of the letter appeared in the tenth century. It is unclear whether that was made from the Chinese version in Hsüan-tsang's biography or from an extant copy of the original Sanskrit letter sent to India, though most likely the former. An English translation of the "Turkish" version appears in S.Y. Goyal's *Harsha and Buddhism* (Meerut: Kusumanjali Prakashan, 1986), pp. 61-67, taken from D. Devahuti, *Harsha: a Political Study* (Oxford: Oxford UP, 1983). Goyal also mentions a critical edition with German translation by Annemarie von Gabain, but offers no bibliographic data. Alexander Mayer informed me of an ongoing project, in German, "editing the Uigur manuscripts of the *Ci'en zhuan* (Klaus Roehrborn), as well as critical studies and translations from the Chinese, entitled 'Xuanzang: Übersetzer und Heiliger', for which five volumes are already available. His own

contributions include *Cien-Biographie VII. Xuanzang. Übersetzer und Heiliger.* (Teil 2) Wiesbaden, 1991 (223 p.) and *Xuanzangs Leben und Werk. Xuanzang. Übersetzer und Heiliger.* (Teil

1) Wiesbaden , 1992 (388 p.)

112 That T'ien-t'ai has so far been spared this upheaval may be due more to the fact that attention to it commensurate to what the other schools have received is still forthcoming. One of the first examples of lineage construction is Kuan-ting's version of the T'ien-t'ai succession in his *Sui T'ien-t'ai Chih-che ta-shih pieh-chuan* (T.50.2050). Though the precise relationship between Chih-i and his T'ien-t'ai "predecessor," Hui-ssu, has been questioned, so far nothing comparable to Yanagida Seizan's devastating undermining of the Ch'an lineages has emerged.

113 *The Life of Hsüan-tsang*, tr. by Li Yung-hsi (Peking: The Chinese Buddhist Association, 1959), p. 10. Cf. *Ta-tz'u-en-ssu san-tsang fa-shih chuan*, T.50.2053.222b; Ch.1:7B.

114 *Ibid.* T.50.232a; Ch.2:21B. The *Triṃśikā* commentary is entitled 唯識三十論釋 *Wei-shih san-shih lun shih* (Explanation of the *Triṃśikā Vijñapti* Treatise).

115 *Ibid.* T.50.238c-239a; Ch.3:19B.

116 T.31.1603; cf. T.31.1602. Hsüan-tsang translated both during his first year back in China (645).

117 A few other texts, primarily abhidharmic, are mentioned, which Hsüan-tsang studied informally during this period, just to "clarify doubtful points." He also studied Sanskrit grammar rigorously at this stage. The biography gives the title of the Sanskrit mneumonic that was used for a basic textbook as *Vyākaraṇa*. Its description sounds like Pāṇini's *Grammar*. I-ching, a Chinese pilgrim who traveled to India from 671-695, describes the grammar texts used as standard curriculum during his stay there, which included Pāṇini's *Aṣṭādhyāyī* as well as a series of commentaries on it, and three texts by Bhartṛhari that culminate in a text whose verses were written by Bhartṛhari accompanied by a commentary written by Dharmapāla. Cf. I-ching, *Nan-hai chi-kuei nai-fa chuan*, chapter 34; English translation available in J. Takakusu, *A Record of the Buddhist Religion* (New Delhi: Munshiram Manoharlal, 1982 rpt.).

118 Both sought an expanded use of the notion of *saṃvṛti-satya* (the validity of conventionalized discourse) applied to important Buddhist doctrines, but differed over where to draw the line between *saṃvṛti, paramārtha,* and *prajñapti* (linguistic appropriation of sensation). Thiw will be taken up in a later chapter.

119 *The Life of Hsüan-tsang*, op. cit., p. 135; cf. T.50.2053.241c; Ch.4:7A.

120 There is another intriguing possibility: The biographers may have slightly distorted the situation, believing Prasenajit studied with the *person* Sthiramati, when in fact he just may have been a student—and follower—of Sthiramati's *teachings*. If so, and if, as I argue, his influence on Hsüan-tsang was the most profound of Hsüan-tsang's Indian teachers, then Hsüan-tsang himself might be considered a follower of Sthiramati rather than Dharmapāla. This may not be as absurd as it sounds, though that would certainly challenge the doxographies that have been constructed around these figures.

121 Cf. T.50.2053.244a; Ch.4:15B; *The Life of Hsüan-tsang*, p. 149.

122 *Ibid.*

123 T.50.2053.244a; Ch.4:15B.

124 This famous and very popular Chinese novel has the same name as Hsüan-tsang's travelogue, *Hsi yu chi*, and is probably best known in the West through Arthur Waley's partial but colorful translation, *Monkey: A Folk Novel* (NY: Grove, 1963). A complete, if less exhuberant, translation of the novel is Anthony Yu's *Journey to the West* (Chicago: University of Chicago Press, 1977-1983, 4 vols.

125 *The Life of Hsüan-tsang*, p. 151. Cf. Ch.4:16B

126 *Ibid.*, pp. 151f.

127 See n. 100 above.

128 *Ibid.* 244c; Ch.4:17B. The passage reads:

He harmonized [or fused] the two schools, [since] their words are not mutually exclusive. And so he composed the "Harmonizing the Schools Treatise" in 3000 verses.

129 *The Life of Hsüan-tsang*, p. 165. Cf. T.50.2053.246b; Ch.5:2B.

130 The full passage illustrates Hsüan-tsang's firm but gentle diplomacy:

> As this country is Buddha's birthplace, it is certainly not that I wouldn't love to stay. But I came here with the intention to acquire the great Dharma for the benefit of all living beings. Since my arrival I have been privileged to learn the *Yogācāra-bhūmi śāstra* from your Reverence, and thus all my doubts have been solved. I have visited the various holy places and studied the teachings of the different schools to my great content so that I feel I have not come in vain. Now I wish to return home to translate the books that I have learned into Chinese, so that others may have the good fortune to study them also. In this way I wish to repay the kindness of my teacher, and that is why I do not wish to linger here any longer. (*Ibid.* modified)

131 Since many of the text titles given in the biography are not exact matches with the standard Chinese titles, determining concurrence is in a few cases difficult. Of those texts mentioned in the biography that Hsüan-tsang studied with Prasenajit, the only one that Hsüan-tsang definitely did *not* translate is the *Mahāyānasūtralaṃkāra*, perhaps because, of all the seminal Yogācāra texts, it is closest to Tathāgatagarbha ontology. The *Wei-shih* text, whether *Triṃśikā* or *Viṃśatika* (or both), he translated. *The Treatise on Doctrinal Theories* may be either the *Hsien-ti sheng-chiao lun* [*sung*],T.31.1602, [T.31.1603], both translated in 645, the first year of his translation work, or Vasumitra's *I-pu-tsung lun lun* (T.49.2031, translated in 662). *The Treatise on Pratītya-samutpāda* might refer to any number of texts, from Nāgārjuna's *Pratītya-samutpāda hṛdaya kārikā* (which Hsüan-tsang did not translate), to *The Treatise of the Superlative Introductory Dharma-Gate Discriminating Pratītya-samutpāda* (T.16.717, translated in 650), to a commentary on the *Pratītya-samutpāda sūtra* (T.2.124, translated in 661). Hsüan-tsang did not translate any text titled *Ch'eng wu-wei lun* (Treatise Establishing Fearlessness).

132 E.g., Sthiramati's distinction between the enlightenment of Arhats, Pratyekabuddhas and Bodhisattvas on the basis of the two *āvaraṇas* occurs near the end of his text, but is introduced in the opening lines of the *Ch'eng wei-shih lun.*

133 K'uei-chi was not the only one to miss the source of the threefold distinction. Vallée Poussin, in his French translation, *Vijñaptimātratāsiddhi, La Siddhi de Hiuan-tsang*, (Paris: Paul Geuthner, 1929, pp. 549-553) goes to great lengths to try to account for the distinctions, citing virtually every important Buddhist text and author except Sthiramati. Cf. Sthiramati's *-ṭīkā* in *Madhyānta Vibhāga Śāstra*, ed. R.C. Pandeya (Delhi: Motilal Banarsidass, 1971), p. 94.

134 *Op. cit.*, p. 277 n. 37.

135 In a lengthy section discussing the disputes between various interpretations of how the four conditions, fifteen *adhiṣṭhānas*, ten causes, six causes and two causes are to be defined and correlated, he writes:

> The [*Yogācārabhūmi*] treatise says that the *hetu-pratyaya* (causal condition, the first of the four conditions) is categorized as the generative cause (*janaka-hetu*); the *adhipati-pratyaya* (miscellaneous condition, the fourth of the four) is the facilitative cause (*upāya-hetu*); the two [remaining] conditions are included in the 'collected-into-experience cause' (*parigraha-hetu*).

To which he immediately adds:

> Although the last three conditions [viz., the *samanantara-pratyaya*, *ālambana-pratyaya* and *adhipati-pratyaya*, or 'immediately-antecendent condition,' 'cognitive-support condition' and 'miscellaneous conditions'] are included in the facilitating [cause], yet the adhipatis

are so numerous [that they are treated metonymically or hyperbolically by the *Yogācārabhūmi* passage]; thus that is a one-sided explanation.

T.31.1585.42a. Cf. Tat p. 562. For now, one needn't unpack the categorial complexity of this passage to recognize that Hsüan-tsang is declaring the *Yogācārabhūmi* to be 'one-sided,' the usual Chinese euphemism for biased, prejudiced, or simply wrong.

Chapter Sixteen

Alterity: *Pariṇāma*

As noted in Part IV, the *Triṃśikā*, and consequently the entire *Ch'eng wei-shih lun* seeks to discuss one thing: *vijñāna-pariṇāma*, the alterity of consciousness.[1] Hsüan-tsang subtly introduces a terminological distinction in the first verse whose full import will not become clear until the *Ch'eng wei-shih lun*'s commentary to v. 17.[2] The distinction both announces and instantiates alterity. The Sanskrit to v. 1 says:

> ...*vijñāna*-***pariṇāmo*** *'sau* ***pariṇāmaḥ*** *sa ca tridhā.*

Two different grammatical forms of the word *pariṇāma* occur in this line. The first *'pariṇāma'* is locative, the second nominative. Hsüan-tsang inscribes this grammatical distinction into the Chinese by rendering the first as *so-pien* 所變 and the second as *neng-pien* 能變. *Pien* means "to change; to *alter*; to transform; metamorphosis;..."[3] and here stands for *pariṇāma*-in-general. *Pariṇāma* means 'change, alteration, transformation into,' etc.[4] The *neng-so* distinction in Chinese, here used to denote the distinction between nominative and locative, has two primary senses: (1) *Neng* means 'ability to, capability for' and thus signals the active case, while *so* signals the passive case; and/or (2) *Neng* denotes the agent of an action, the subjective, active doer while *so* denotes the recipient of an action, the objective, passive field manipulated by a doer. *Neng-pien* would then imply 'he who alters,' 'that which alters,' 'that which has the ability to alter,' and *so-pien* would indicate 'what is altered.' Since *so* also means 'place,' 'locus,' it is an appropriate indicator of the locative. However, Hsüan-tsang's choice of the opposition between active and passive, doer and what is done (*neng-so*), subjective and objective, creates a much neater distinction in Chinese than the distinction between locative and nominative would suggest in Sanskrit. After all, Sanskrit still has six other declensions to choose from (ablative, genitive, etc.), whereas the *neng-so* dyad does not imply even a third case, much less a number of others. More significantly, the locative/nominative distinction not only lacks any clear oppositional tension, but suggests an entirely different notion of identity and difference than that implied by *neng-so*, as will be demonstrated momentarily. What is actually at issue here?

The first verse also implicates *upacāra*, metaphor or metonymy, at the root level of the problematic to be explored. The first words, appearing as a compound, are: "*ātma-dharma-upacāro...*" Linguistic problems, in other words, are part of what sets everything in motion. Based on the proliferating interactions of two upacāras, 'self' and 'dharmas,' everything follows. These interactions occur in consciousness, which is threefold. Self and dharmas generate the problem, but the so-called 'self and dharmas' are linguistic fictions, ostensibly experienced in consciousness as distinct, mutually interactive things. 'Dharmas' refers to the factors of experience enumerated in the Abhidharmic lists. Yogācāra provides one hundred dharmas, which include not only physical elements (rūpa), but emotional, cognitive, psychological, and linguisitic factors which constitute the *felt textures* of a cognition. Dharmas such as attention, anger, tranquility, jealousy, and so on, describe how a cognitive moment *feels*, how one is experiencing it. Our experience 'feels' like an interaction of self and dharmas, both in terms of perceiving a so-called external world as well as how we internally feel during perceptual and cognitive moments. Since this basic framework built into the way we cognize is misleading, unreal—these upacāras are mistaken interpretations of activities within consciousness—our experience from the beginning presents itself as other than it actually is. Experience as perceived by those who have not yet understood what constitutes experience, has gone through some alteration, some difference, some alterity between what actually constitutes it (conscious activities) and what appears to be constituted (and constitutive), viz. self and dharmas.

There are at least three issues converging here: (1) Terminological implications of the Sanskrit text. (2) Similar use of the *neng-so* distinction by Paramārtha in his earlier glossy translation and paraphrase of the *Triṃśikā*, the *Chuan-shih lun*.[5] (3) Issues apparently related to Dharmapāla's thought, since Hsüan-tsang similarly uses *neng-so* in other translations of Dharmapāla, suggesting that this distinction in Chinese evoked, at least in Hsüan-tsang's mind, a significant issue in Dharmapāla's form of Yogācāra.

Two key terms in the first verse, *pariṇāma* and *pravartate* (i.e., *pravṛtti*), were taken over by Yogācāra from Sāṃkhya. In Hindu thought,[6] both terms connote an evolutionary, developmental cosmology or ontology. The world as we experience it, they claim, 'evolves' from *prakṛti* (i.e., the three guṇas) and *pariṇāma* and *pravṛtti* describe important elements of that process. Sāṃkhya was still a vigorous school in the seventh century, and Hui-li's biography reports in detail on debates between Hsüan-tsang and a Sāṃkhyan.[7] One may detect some anxiety on the part of Yogācāra about its theoretic proximity to Sāṃkhyan thought. Great pains were taken to distinguish the 'incoherency' of the svabhāvically conceived prakṛti that Sāṃkhya advanced from the non-svabhāvic ālaya-vijñāna which Yogācāra affirmed. The crucial distinction was whereas prakṛti was at once eternal and unchanging while somehow connected to and even *identical* with the changing world, ālaya-vijñāna was constituted of a series of mental moments neither absolutely identical nor absolutely different from the moments which preceded and followed them. Like a stream (*santāna*), the moments perdured without either fixed identity or such radical difference that mental continuity would go unaccounted for. The mental continuum *altered* every moment.

For Sāṃkhya *pariṇāma* involved a theory of evolution, of things evolving out of a primordial nature (*prakṛti*) whose essence remained unchanged even as the equilibrium of its modifications (*guṇas*) fluctuated. For Yogācāra *pariṇāma* meant sheer alterity, the radical self-otherness through which each cognitive moment constitutes itself as itself (*svalakṣaṇa*) precisely by being other than it was or will be momentarily. Its self *is* its self-otherness. Its uniqueness refers directly to its self-difference as well as its difference from what is other to it, since, inasmuch as it is momentary, it is always becoming different from itself—which is to say, that the 'it' and the 'itself' of this sentence do not refer to an enduring substance or identity or substratum, but rather assign a linguistic constant (*upacāra*) heuristically to a flow of 'altering' variables.

Sthiramati, in his commentary on the *Triṃśikā*, makes this point strikingly clear:[8]

> What is named 'pariṇāma'? It is "becoming otherwise" (*anyathātvam*, i.e., alterity). Pariṇāma means 'self-appropriation' (*ātma-lābha*) by an effect (*karya*) that, by definition, is different from what was at the moment of cause, occurring in the moment the cause ceases.

A similar definition of pariṇāma is also found in the *Abhidharmakośa*[9]

The momentariness of causes and effects insures that alterity, i.e., 'becoming otherwise,' is perpetual. Each moment is an intersection of cause and effect, in which, for causes to be causes and effects to be effects, the cause *must be different from* the effect. In the very same moment that something arises and ceases (and, according to Buddhism, that lasts only a moment), there is a "becoming otherwise" into which "self-appropriation" insinuates itself. There is an attempt to seize, to grasp and hold on to that moment, in order to install upon it a stable self, an identity. But the moment itself is simply a moment of 'becoming otherwise,' an identity that is always already inscribed as alterity.

In Western philosophy "alterity" connotes a variety of themes, including: (1) the Other, (2) transcendence (especially of self or solipsistic attitudes), (3) the alter-ego, (4) that which opposes, stands against, or is other to a subject (either a metaphysical subject or a perceptual subject). The Other thus conceived may *also* be viewed as a perceiving subject or similar metaphysical subject. It is by seeing that the Other is like me, and that I am like the Other, that we constitute, limit, and define each other; each subjectivity transcends itself by recourse to understanding the Other. Alterity involves recognizing the Other *as* oneself and, conversely, recognizing that which constitutes oneself as the Other. Each of these themes is predicated on the assumption of a fundamental divide between a subject and its other, even if the point of thinking about alterity is to somehow ameliorate or overcome that divide. But in Buddhism, alterity is conceived in different terms. Since Buddhism rejects the notion of the metaphysical self entailed in the self/other, self/transcendent, etc., dichotomies, alterity, for Buddhists, means the perpetual, moment-by-moment 'becoming other-than-it-was' of a self, which is to say, a non-self, since this becoming other precludes the possibility of an invariant identity. In fact, Buddhist alterity requires a "self" so radically lacking in stable, invariant identity that it can never be a self. A (non-)self that cannot be defined by any essential unchanging characteristic *except* that whatever essential defining feature (*svalakṣaṇa*) one can determine of it at any given moment, even in that same moment, in and as its most vital function, it is becoming other to itself, it is altering—alterity. And, as Sthiramati reminds us, this process of perpetual alterity does not occur in a vague, mysterious manner, but as a direct consequence of the play of causes and conditions insofar as they are definable as causes distinct from effects. Sthiramati is speaking about "efficient causes" (*kāraṇa*), not abstractions. Humans (and everything else) are loci of attempted self-appropriations within moments of alterity, caused by a perpetual nostalgia to grasp at each moment once it has passed, as if, could one only stop time and causality, one might then finally attain an invariant identity, an eternal self. Recognizing those causes and conditions, and becoming liberated from the appropriational impulse, is the task Buddhism sets before us.

Alterity (*pariṇāma*) is constituted of durational *projectories*, i.e., trajectories constructed through projections. While a projection may denote a single event, or the constitution of a single object, or a single goal (to take on a project, in the Sartrean sense), a projectory requires duration, such that it subtends any number of distinct projections through and within its movement. A goal, a telos may only arise within a projectory. But these projectories, though internally constituting goals, such that they seem to have direction and purpose, when viewed from without, are seen to be utterly without direction, a view shared from within at the culminating moment in which a goal is achieved. Though the tension of anticipation has been relieved, though the desire and the goal finally coincide, the victory, the achievement is instantaneously hollow.[10] Another projectory must immediately be installed to conceal the abyss. For Buddhism, projectories are saṃsāra, the cycle of duḥkha. Disadvantageous and disturbing projectories (*akuśala, kleśa*) may be supplemented and displaced by soterically advantageous projectories, though ultimately these are as empty and saṃsāric as those for which they are the antidote. The arising of a soteric directionality in place of directionless projectories is called *cittotpāda* (*fa-hsin* 發心), 'arising [of a soterically directional] mind.'

Projectories, in virtue of the manner in which they are constructed, involve closure, since the durational trajectory must close itself off from whatever might distract or deter its directionality (the alternative is to lose its 'identity'). *By defining themselves teleologically, projectories automatically relinquish their full range of possibilities.* Rather than facing the future as a field of infinite possibilities, all potentialities are yoked and constrained toward approaching whatever goal is set up on the horizon. To be a great musician—in virtue of the requirement that one must practice many hours a day—involves a personal closure; for during those practice hours one *cannot do something else*, and thus some other potential, some other talent lies undeveloped. After many years, the other talent, indeed perhaps many talents, may have atrophied to the extent that their realization and actualization remain no longer possible—that is, what was possible has been sacrificed and is no longer possible (many possibilities have been reduced to one, and the one achieved only at the expense of the many). The pursuit of a telos, while perhaps the necessary (but not sufficient) condition for achieving that telos, always involves the denial and putting out of operation of the possibility of many more teloi. This *fore*-closure of possibilities always already arises at the instant a projectory arises, and thus marks the inscription of every projectory within its own closure, and each closure as the horizonal inscription of a projectory.

Since a consciousness stream incorporates many projectories, the structural absoluteness of each projectory's closure often goes unnoticed; perspectives shift from one projectory to another—in another sort of dance of alterity, thus avoiding the claustrophobic horizon of any singular closure.[11] When conflicting projectories cease to mutually interpenetrate (i.e., allow perspectival shifting easily back and forth between them) and instead crash head-on, the consciousness-stream, forced to identify itself simultaneously with opposing identities, opposing teloi, is thrown into crisis. That we live always amid crisis-provoking trajectories, even when the crises remain latent, Buddhism labels *duḥkha*.

Alterity 'operates,' i.e., it spins around (*pravartate*).[12] *Pra-vṛit* (*-vartate*) means to roll or go onwards, set in motion or going, issue, originate, arise, be produced, be intent on or occupied with; round, globular; circulated (as a book); going to, bound for; happened, occurred; purposing or going to, bent upon; giving or devoting one's self to; inclination or predilection; conduct, behavior or practice. While *pravṛtti* connotes a 'rolling towards,' a becoming intent upon, a reaching for, a happening or occurrence that will lead to a tendency, that will take on a projectorial trait, *pariṇāma* implies an aporia, a movement unsure of its direction. *Pari-* means round, around, about; fully, abundantly, richly; *against, opposite to.*[13] √*Nam* (the root) means[14] to bend or bow; *to turn away, to turn toward*; to aim at, to yield to. *Pariṇāma* is a rich turning about of many directions, a pursuing and yet aversionary movement. Its conative quality also announces a deep alterity. When engaged, it can go in either direction. When reflecting on the *meaning* of a direction, i.e., questioning 'why' to go that way instead of this, it may produce ambivalence.

Before *fa-hsin* can occur, i.e., before one can collect, marshal, nurture and 'moisten' the pure seeds that lie latent in the consciousness stream,[15] 'projectoriality' must be disclosed, at least sufficiently to allow the thought, "I can do otherwise; I can alter or exchange projectories." This insight—which, by placing 'choice' at the core of the possibility of freedom, marks Buddhism as fundamentally a system of 'ethics'—initiates the soteric project, ritually notarized in Mahāyāna with the Bodhisattva vows. *Fa-hsin* is the determinative initiation (*niyata-raśi*). 'Initiation' here signifies to initiate, begin, to bring to inception, to start to make something happen (*pravartate*). The saṃsāric trajectory—which is a karmic concatenation of multiple projectories—becomes absorbed, changed, altered. *Fa-hsin* names the beginning of a soteric projectory, a projectory which 'begins' precisely because it installs an otherness to other, previous trajectories, and an inbred ability to perpetually become other to itself, i.e., an ability to change, to develop, to engender sequential change aimed at a telos. It is alterity through and through. *Fa-hsin* marks the end of randomness, directionlessness in the projectories through and within which one lives; and it marks the beginning of a directive, purposeful movement. It installs what for Buddhism is the only genuine telos, *anuttara-saṃyak-saṃbodhi*. *Fa-hsin*'s alterity achieves a focus, a focal point, a soteric direction but, unlike non-genuine teloi, its directionality aims at the cancellation of its own telos.

Generally we aim at a goal, and either become frustrated by falling short of that goal, or dissatisfied by the post-climax, the after-effect of having achieved it. Achieving a goal means that one must quickly establish a new goal; otherwise one's clinging to the moment of triumph becomes increasing frustrating or pathetic as the moment of that success grows increasingly remote. Buddhism attempts to pre-empt this frustration by (1) promising from the beginning that the telos of Buddhism is self-canceling, and (2) by clarifying from the outset that the absolutely necessary condition for achieving the goal is losing the desire to achieve the goal—but losing it within the context of mārga, which is to say, within a methodology that itself has a telos, a trajectory guided by and aimed at its final cause. Thus mārga means methodology, but a methodology that has a direction, a soteric telos. Nonetheless this is a telos whose most essential ingredient is nothing other than the negation of teleology and teleological thinking, and all forms of life driven by teleological premises. Nirvāṇa is the cessation of teleology, not because the 'goal' has been reached so that one need no longer strive for what has already been accomplished (hence the Zen rhetoric of 'nothing attained,' etc.), but rather it is such because the affective and cognitive problems which generate the teleological (= appropriational) mode of existing for a world, such that a world exists for me (*grāha-grāhya*), have altogether been uprooted.

Between the first verse in Sanskrit and its Chinese rendition a linguistic alterity has emerged.

> *...Vijñāna-**pariṇāmo** 'sau **pariṇāmaḥ** sa ca tridhā.*

Robinson translates this line "...is upon the transformation of consciousness. This transformation is of three kinds." Justifiably, even though the first *pariṇāma* is locative and the second nominative, he considers them to refer to the same referent, the same 'transformation.' He marks the locative with the awkward phrase "it is upon the transformation," as if pariṇāma signified a platform onto which something could be placed. Grammatical alterity—though altering a word, turning a root seme into a semantic element in a sentence, giving it differing sounds and graphic shapes, 'evolving, developing' words from their root (*pariṇāma, pravṛtti*)—assumes a continual identity that survives changing verbal forms. The seme is assumed to possess an "essential meaning" that remains substantially (*dravya*) the same, even as grammatical alterations modify (*paryāya*) its appearance. This substance/modification ontology, while central to Jain and certain Hindu systems, was often rejected or, when accepted, severely qualified by Indian Buddhists. Nonetheless it does occur in a number of Sūtras through a variety of analogies, the most repeated of which is the one reiterated in the Chinese apocryphal *Awakening of Faith* as the waves (modifications) and Sea (unalterable essence) metaphor. The *Ch'eng wei-shih lun* also on occasion invokes a substance/modification model (particularly in its discussion of language, to be translated and analyzed in another chapter), but its basic position—following the *Triṃśikā*—is that the ālaya-vijñāna flows on torrentially, like a stream, until it ultimately ceases, thus confounding the wave-sea metaphor.

Nominal declensions, verbal case endings, gerundival constructions, in short, the full range of grammatical alterations—for which Sanskrit has a particular genius and meticulous order—announce language itself as a field of alterity. In the Yogācāric context a most striking example would be the rules of *saṅdhi*, i.e., the system of substitutions whereby two adjoining letters are replaced by a single letter. There are internal saṅdhi, or substitutions within a single word, and external saṅdhi, or substitutions based on the contraction of the last and first letters of contiguous words. The term *saṅdhi* denotes a joint, a linkage, something flexible between two things that joins and modifies them. Its grammatical sense was applied to other spheres. Already in Pāli Buddhism, *saṅdhi* denoted the linking of a previous to a subsequent consciousness-stream (*paṭisandhi-viññāṇa*), i.e., what links a previous life to a subsequent life. The earliest text to appear with distinctively Yogācāric themes is the *Saṅdhi-nirmocana Sūtra*, whose title alludes to, amongst other implications, the alterations of consciousness, particularly insofar as they are implicit (*nīyartha*), i.e., unconscious. *Saṅdhi* here signifies the *explicit traces* of *implicit substitutions*, the series of rules, of alterations of words and mental/cognitive situations, such that the underlying operations become masked by what appears on the surface. Understanding the apparent word, however, requires determining those 'hidden' operations.

A grammatical example: A word ending with *-a* followed by a word beginning with *a-* ; the two words are linked and *ā* is substituted for the two a-s. Hence the long a (*ā*) is the explicit trace of two short a-s (*-a* + *a-*). The most famous case of ambiguation arising from the substitution of a long 'a' for two short 'a'-s is the word *Tathāgata*, an epithet for Buddha. What lies "behind" that long 'a'? It could mean either *tathā* + *gata* or *tathā* + *agata*. The first option means "Thus gone" while the second means "Thus come." But which? The Chinese translate Tathāgata as *ju-lai* 如來, meaning 'thus come,' but Buddhist literature has no shortage of readings of Tathāgata as "Thus gone" either. Another example: *-a* + *u-* = *o*; *citta* + *utpāda* => citt-o-tpāda (*cittotpāda*). The 'o' appears on the surface, but to a knowledgeable reader the 'o' acts as a surface mark for the -a+u- that it has displaced.

The mind similarly works by systematic substitutions, displacements, concealing and revealing, highlighting foreground from background, etc. To understand the movement means to recognize in what is present (i.e., what is presented in consciousness) that which is absent, that which has been displaced by substitution (i.e., the background, the unconscious). The *Saṅdhinirmocana Sūtra* proposes, therefore, a kind of Psychoanalysis that maps the language of the unconscious, the grammar of displacive substitutions with which conscious life articulates and expresses, as well as binds and liberates, itself. But if there are no invariant substances, then the modifications themselves *are* the words, and the invariant root seme becomes a mere prajñaptic abstraction devoid of originary status. In either case, stated paradoxically, *pariṇāme* (loc.) and *pariṇāmas* (nom.) are different yet the same, or neither different nor the same.

In Chinese, as noted above, an opposition is created: The locative *pariṇāme* (a.k.a. *pariṇāmo*) becomes *so-pien* (what is altered), and the nominative *pariṇāmas* (a.k.a *pariṇāmaḥ*) becomes *neng-pien* (that which, or he who alters). An active/passive, subjective/objective bifurcation has been installed in the ambiguous space between the alterity of the two *pariṇāmas*. Since the Sanskrit terms appear in the verse in grammatically recognizable forms that are nonetheless different from the 'pure' versions of those grammatical forms (*pariṇāme* a.k.a. *pariṇāmo*, *pariṇāmas* a.k.a *pariṇāmaḥ*), this too marks an alterity of Sanskrit grammar, in which words appear through their alter egos. Conditions and circumstances *alter* things according to regular amd definite principles. Translational alterity means that just as Hsüan-tsang's translation alters the text, and one seeks to see through it to the original, just so when reading the English translations one attempts to see through them to the originals. Alterity, therefore, signifies attempting to approach, to apprehend an object, a referent, a meaning (*artha*)—whether in a hermeneutic register, or within consciousness, or linguistically. Each register is motivated by a desire to apprehend and grasp an objective.

The initial opposition of *neng/so* (a.k.a. *pariṇāmo...pariṇāmaḥ*) is highlighted by another dyadic opposition, *pi* 彼 and *ts'u* 此 ('that' and 'this'). To paraphrase the first verse: 'That,' i.e., the proliferation of the mutual turning around (*hsiang chuan* = *pravartate*) of what derives from the upacāric 'self' and 'dharma,' depends on consciousness *qua* 'what is altered' (*so-pien*). Consciousness, in its capacity as passive, as acted upon, as a locus on or in which cognition occurs, is *that* upon which the 'provisional expressions' (*chia-shuo*) of 'self' and 'dharmas' interact, proliferating a cognitive world in which self and dharmas are constructed. 'This' able-to-alter (consciousness) is only threefold. 'That' points out the passive, objective perceptual field of consciousness (*pi... so-pien*); 'this' introduces the active, subjective conscious agent (*ts'u neng-pien*). The active, subjective consciousness is threefold, viz. the ālaya-vijñāna, manas and mano-vijñāna.[16] If we interpret *so-pien* as noema and *neng-pien* as noesis, this might be taken to imply that these three 'active' consciousnesses take caittas (noemata) as their passive field. However, this can hardly be, since we later learn in the *Ch'eng wei-shih lun* that the consciousnesses take each other as objects.[17] Thus, technically speaking, each of the three must be both *so-pien* and *neng-pien*. What then is the issue for Hsüan-tsang? Why has he introduced in his translation this additional alterity?

The answer comes with the *Ch'eng wei-shih lun*'s discussion of v. 17. The verse reads:

> *Vijñāna-**pariṇāmo** 'yam vikalpo yad-vikalpyate* /
> *tena tan-nāsti tena-idam sarvam vijñapti-mātrakam* //

The alterity (*pariṇāma*, this time rendered in Chinese as *chuan-pien*) of the consciousnesses[18] discriminates (*vikalpa, fen-pieh*) what is discriminated (*yad-vikalpyate, so-fen-pieh*). The alterity of consciousness discriminates the discriminated. The second part of the verse, in Chinese, translates as "since [the discriminated] 'this' and 'that' are all inexistent, therefore all is psychosophic-closure." The meaning of the verse, by this reading, would be: The alterity of consciousness (*vijñāna-pariṇāma*) discriminates what is discriminated. Since everything that is discriminated ("this" from "that"), and perhaps even the discriminator, are entirely inexistent, thus it all belongs to nothing but consciousness. One way of reading this is: The interplay of discriminator and discriminated are epiphenomenal occurrences (waves) subsumed by the *vijñāna-pariṇāma* (the Sea). *Vijñāna-pariṇāma* stands behind these epiphenomena and remains ultimately unaltered by the variations and fluctuations of *vikalpa* and *vikalpyate*.

Sthiramati reads the verse differently, putting a break after the first *vikalpo*, which gives the sense:

> *Pariṇāma-vijñāna* is *vikalpa*.
> Whatever is discriminated, that does not exist.
> Therefore everything is *vijñapti-mātra*.

Rather than retaining the tautological closure of 'discrimination-discriminated' as a definition for pariṇāma-vijñāna, Sthiramati associates *vijñāna-pariṇāma* only with the first term, 'vikalpa,' discrimination. Vijñāna-pariṇāma does not stand outside or behind the tautological interaction of discrimination and discriminated, but *is itself* the discrimination. Discrimination *is* the alterity of consciousness (*vijñāna-pariṇāma*); it is the discriminated (but not the discrimination) that is inexistent. Though stylistically questionable in terms of disrupting the meter, his reading is intellectually satisfying. He has turned the verse into a syllogism:

(i) 'alterations of consciousness' is discrimination;
(ii) what is discriminated does not exist (as such, independent of discrimination);
(iii) therefore everything is, strictly speaking, nothing but consciousness (i.e., conscious discriminations).

In syllogistic fashion he has generated a different tautology, viz. that 'alterity of consciousness' is 'nothing but psychosophical closure,' the important middle term being the minor premise, to wit: the denial of external, substantial 'existence' to whatever is produced by discrimination. In other words, this is an argument which though reminiscent of Kantian epistemology, is actually more radical, more extreme. It claims an exclusively noetic constitution of cognitive

(= discriminative) experience. It is tautological in the sense that Sthiramati has said 'alterations of consciousness' are 'nothing but consciousness,' but it is not merely tautological inasmuch as it *explicitly* rejects the influence of something *outside* consciousness as responsible for those changes. Discriminations are epistemically produced, they arise from consciousness; they are not ontologically determined correspondences of 'things out there' (and hence the habit by some scholars of using the Kantian term *Vorstellung*, re-presentation, to denote the Yogācāra cognitive theory is misleading). Vijñāna-pariṇāma is a name for the propensity to discriminate. That everything is vijñapti-mātra clearly means here that consciousness is engaged in producing cognitions that are erroneous because they divide up, discriminate experience inappropriately. Thus everything appearing in consciousness that one holds on to as a distinct thing, is really just made to be known (*vijñapti*) as such by consciousness' propensity to discriminate, to imagine distinctions. Sthiramati is not lauding consciousness here as a glorious reality, but is pointing directly at its most basic propensity while accusing it of causing the problems that need to be overcome. The term *vijñapti-mātra*, in other words, does not signify a happy realization and affirmation of consciousness as a reality, but rather becomes an indictment of the problems the activities of consciousness engender. Consciousness is the problem, not the solution. Recognizing the problem for what it is is the first step in the cure.

Hsüan-tsang seems to read the verse differently. Discrimination and that which is discriminated (implying once again the *neng-so* distinction), as they dialectically interact, interchange, are themselves consciousness' alterity. In this verse Hsüan-tsang terminologically conflates *pariṇāma* and *pravṛtti* by translating pariṇāma as *chuan-pien*. *Chuan*—which in the first verse translated *pravartate*—means to turn around, to revolve, to spin. Alterity (*pien*) means spinning in place, flipping over, which implies now noetically constituting a noema through discrimination, and then flipping again and making the previous noesis a noema for current discrimination. *Fen-pieh*, literally 'to apportion into distinct parts,' and *so-fen-pieh*, 'what is (passively, objectively) apportioned into distinct parts,' mutually condition each other, mutually turn around on each other. That 'turning' *is* the alterity of consciousness, which is to say, it indicates the same proliferative dynamic as the 'self and dharmas' of the first verse. What was primarily linguistic (*chia-shuo*) there has become cognitive here. But why is Hsüan-tsang *altering* the words?

The *Ch'eng wei-shih lun* states:[19]

> We have already examined discrimination (*fen-pieh*) [in terms of] the characteristics of the three [consciousnesses that are] 'able-to-alter' (*neng-pien*), regarding them as that upon which the two divisions (*bhāga*, *fen*) of 'what is altered' (*so-pien*) depend.

The subjective, active side (*neng*) is thus threefold—ālaya-vijñāna, manas, mano-vijñāna—while the passive, objective side (*so*) is twofold—the noetic-noemic components of cognition. But as the text continues we see that the *darśana-bhāga* (noesis), *nimitta-bhāga* (noema) distinction is also applied to or derived from the *neng* side of alterity.

> 'What are altered' dependent on consciousness (*yi shih so-pien*, 依識 所變 *vijñāna-pariṇāme*, i.e., 'consciousness-altered'), namely the figurative expressions (*upacāra*) 'ātman and dharmas,' are not distinct, real (*shih* 實, *dravya*, substantial) existents, but [to show] that these are all only [indicative of] the existence of consciousness, the verse says:
>
> THIS IS THE CONSCIOUSNESSES TURNING-AROUND AND ALTERING, DISCRIMINATING AND DISCRIMINATED; SINCE THIS AND THAT ARE ALL INEXISTENT, THEREFORE THEY ARE ALL NOTHING-BUT-CONSCIOUSNESS (psychosophic-closure).
>
> "THE CONSCIOUSNESSES" refers to what was previously described as 'the three (ways in which) consciousness alters (能變識 *neng-pien shih*)' and "THAT" [refers to] their caittas.
>
> [1] All that is 'able-to-alter' (能變 *neng-pien*) appears as two *bhāgas*, viz. the darśana-bhāga (the 'seeing part,' the noesis) and the nimitta-bhāga (the 'cognitively-produced part,' the noema).[20] So the term *pariṇāma* (轉變 *chuan pien*, TURNING-AROUND AND ALTERING, 'alterity') is established.
>
> [2a] The *darśana-bhāga* 見分 of 'what is altered' explains the term "DISCRIMINATION" (*vikalpa*, 分別 *fen-pieh*), because it is characterized as noesis (*grāhaka*, 能取 *neng-ch'ü*, 'grasper').
>
> [2b] The *nimitta-bhāga* 相分 of 'what is altered' is termed "[what is] DISCRIMINATED" (所分別 *so-fen-pieh*) because it is a noetically constituted noema (*grāhya*, 所取 *so-ch'ü*, 'what is grasped').
>
> For this reason [although] those ātmans or dharmas [may be asserted or believed to be] real (實 *shih*) apart from the consciousnesses 'that are altered' (*vijñāna-pariṇāma*), they are all determined to be non-existent. Since apart from noesis and noema (*neng so ch'ü*, *grāha-grāhya*, grasper-grasped) there are no distinct things (*wu pieh wu ku* 無 別 物 故) [or no distinguishing of things], thus there are no existent real things apart from these two characteristics. Therefore everything, whether conditioned (*yu-wei*, *saṃskṛta*) or unconditioned (*wu-wei*, *asaṃskṛta*) [i.e., any of the 100 dharmas], whether real (*shih*) or nominal (*chia* 假, *prajñapti*),[21] none is apart from consciousness.

This reinforces Sthiramati's point that cognitive distinctions reflect an epistemic, not an ontological source.

> The word(s) "NOTHING-BUT" (*mātra*, *wei*, in "NOTHING-BUT CONSCIOUSNESS") [serves to] deny that there are any real things apart from consciousness, but not [to exclude or claim that] the caittas, etc., are apart from consciousness.

K'uei-chi assigns this interpretation of the verse to Dharmapāla. What does this position maintain?

The subjective-active pariṇāma and the objective-passive pariṇāma of the first verse have been expanded. We could chart this as:

The Alterity of Consciousnesses

(1) What actively-alters (*neng-pien*) => (2) What is altered (*so-pien*)

|⇒ (a) ālaya-vijñāna — (2a) noesis ⇒ (2b) noema

|⇒ (b) manas

|⇒ (c) mano-vijñāna

(2a) *vikalpa* = *darśana-bhāga* = *grāhaka* = noesis
(discrimination = 'seeing-part' = grasper)

(2b) *vikalpyate* = *nimitta-bhāga* = *grāhya* = noema
(discriminated = 'sense-mark-part' = grasped)

What is curious so far is that both the noetic and the noemic sides of cognition are grouped with 'what is altered,' i.e., consciousness as passive and objectified. The *darśana-bhāga*—which would seem to be an active, subjective constituent of perception—is classified here as a passive, objective product of the threefold active 'alterers'.[22] In other words, that aspect of cognition which we would call 'subjective,' the perceiver, is being treated here as an objectified by-product of activities among consciousnesses (viz. ālaya-vijñāna, manas, mano-vijñāna) that can neither be reduced to simple subjective nor objective components. This will shortly lead us into a labyrinth of categories, but let us momentarily put this and the chart aside and examine "Dharmapāla's" statement. It will plunge us directly into the core question of the *Ch'eng wei-shih lun*'s relation to idealism.

Is "Vijñapti-mātra" an Ontological or Epistemological Notion?

Dharmapāla (if this 'position' accurately reflects his lost text) claims that apart from the grasper-grasped relationship there are no distinct things. Why should this be? Does he mean that distinctions are affectively motivated by the need to grasp; or, perhaps, the need to grasp actually generates distinct things? The coherency of Dharmapāla's reading of this verse hinges on which of these claims he is making, and thus, we should examine the text carefully.

First, he has equated 'existent real things' (*yu shih wu* 有實物) with 'distinguishing things' *or* 'distinct things' (*pieh wu* 別物). Much rides on how we interpret *pieh* in the latter phrase. It lends itself to both an ontological and an epistemological reading. If read as a verb, i.e., as "distinguishing," then the emphasis is epistemic. If read as an adjective, i.e., as "distinct," then the emphasis would appear to be ontological. Since no grammatical principle leaps to our assistance in determining which reading to prefer, each being equally plausible, we turn to the full context of the argument in order to see if some clue is forthcoming.

Dharmapāla argues that since there can be no distinct things apart from the economy of noesis-noema, and nothing real exists outside of these two characteristics, nothing whatsoever exists apart from consciousness. His point hinges on the word *shih* 實 (real, *dravya*). *Shih* etymologically means 'full, solid, real, substantial.' Hsüan-tsang often uses it to translate *dravya*, 'substance.' The argument here would be that there are no real, solid substantives which can be determined (*ting* 定) a priori through and within consciousness to exist independently of consciousness. Since the question of determination itself arises in consciousness, and would have to be settled within consciousness, to posit something that is determined *in and by* consciousness as being outside of or radically other than consciousness would be methodologically untenable, if not completely absurd. Hence, if the argument is epistemological, it is valid; consciousness cannot declare its own determinations to be other than *its own determinations* without undermining the epistemological foundation of that declaration. If the argument pretends to be ontological, it merely begs the question. It becomes an unsupported assertion that consciousness, and not external objects, is responsible for whatever actual 'real' distinct objects appear in cognition. Hence, if this is designed to argue for ontological idealism, it is a poor argument. Finally, if the argument is taken merely to be an example of the 'psychological reduction,' then, while it may be valid, it would nonetheless be strictly tautological and trivial.

The question of whether to read *pieh*, and by extension the entire passage, as an epistemological, ontological or psychological argument is grammatically undecidable. But, if my characterization of the force of the various readings of the argument is correct, the epistemological reading becomes preferable. No thing cognized within consciousness can be declared in and by consciousness to be otherwise than consciousness. Since, by definition, everything knowable must be knowable through consciousness, nothing knowable can be declared to be 'real' apart from consciousness. Notice that this argument does not entail the further stipulation that consciousness alone exists while objects do not, but merely that the sensed *externality* of any cognized objects is an illusion that arises *within* consciousness. In the phrase 'external object,' what Yogācāra challenges is the sense of 'external,' not the notion 'object' per se (see chap. 19).

Looking at what follows in the *Ch'eng wei-shih lun* reinforces this reading. Another (Nanda?)[23] explains pariṇāma (*chuan-pien* 轉變) thus:

> The internal consciousnesses spin around (*chuan*), projecting (*hsien* 現) the characteristics of what seem to be ātman and dharmas as external perceptual-fields (*viṣaya, ching* 境). It is precisely this 'alterer' (*neng chuan-pien* 能轉變, i.e., noetic constituter) that is termed DISCRIMINATION (*vikalpa, fen-pieh* 分別), because it prajñaptically discriminates (*chia fen-pieh*) [by ascribing] svabhāva to the three dhātus, citta and the caittas. The perceptual-field to which it is attached

is termed THE DISCRIMINATED (*vikalpyate, so-fen-pieh*), which is precisely what is falsely attached to as the 'real' [self-] nature of ātman and dharmas. Due to these discriminative alterations (*fen-pieh pien*) the characteristics of the prajñaptic ātman and dharmas appear as external perceptual-fields.[24] That which is discriminated as the 'real' [self-] nature of ātman and dharmas most definitely does not exist, as has been previously demonstrated [with proofs from both] scripture and reason (*chiao li* 教 理).

Therefore everything is "only existent in consciousness" (*shih ku yi-ch'ieh chieh wei yu shih* 是故一切皆唯有識), since the existence of erroneous false discriminations is (thereby) ultimately established.[25]

"ONLY" does not deny dharmas as long as they are not separate from consciousness, hence the truly empty,[26] etc., also thereby have an existent [self-] nature.... This establishes the meaning (referent, *artha*) of PSYCHOSOPHIC-CLOSURE (*wei-shih*) in accord with the Middle Way.[27]

Dharmas—which include colors, shapes, sounds, etc., as well as emotional and cognitive textures—are not being denied, *as long as* they are not considered "separate from consciousness." While Dharmapāla (the first reading) seems to be denying externality outright, this second reading (Nanda?) seems to bracket it. His internal/external distinction elicits the same objections as Dharmapāla's position, unless, again, his argument is made on epistemological rather than ontological grounds. 'Internal' then should be understood not as an ontological locale. Internal here means 'phenomenological,' i.e., within consciousness. All experience is *of* consciousness. But consciousness does not mean subjectivity. Self and things, i.e., ātman and dharmas are *both* considered 'external.' Clearly consciousness and 'self' are not synonymous. While autonomy is clearly denied to the objective aspect of experience (where *in* consciousness would that be?), subjectivity, as well, is merely a prajñaptic by-product. What then is 'consciousness'?

'Consciousness' means cognizance, discerning, the awareness that arises due to contact between a cognitive faculty (a sense organ) and its corresponding perceptual-object (*viṣaya*, the objects of which the perceptual-field is composed).[28] There are those discernings which are 'conscious,' i.e., aware of what presently appears to it, and those which are 'subconscious,' i.e., latent or non-apparent projectories. In either case, discernment involves intentionality, a movement of intent (*cetanā*) toward a referent. The ālaya-vijñāna is an intentionally neutral economy of conscious/subconscious alterities, which appears subjective only when appropriated as such by manas (*Triṃśikā* v. 6).

The *Ch'eng wei-shih lun* continues with two sorts of proofs: *Śruti* (textual support) and *yukti* (reason). After citing several passages from a number of texts which support the claim of *wei-shih*,[29] four types of cognitions (*jñāna* 智) are discussed.[30] These are:

(1) *Hsiang-wei shih-hsiang chih* 相違識相智, Cognitions characterized by mutually exclusive consciousnesses, which refers to the range of possible ways a single locus may be cognized by different perceivers. If the object

originates its own meaning, they argue, mutually exclusive perceptions of the identical spatio-temporal locus should be impossible; but, on the contrary, depending on differing karma, i.e., different habits of perception, different types of beings perceive different sorts of objects in the same locus.[31] In other words, people can hold mutually exclusive interpretations of the 'same' object based on their own immediate experience. "How could this be if perceptual-objects are substantially [svabhāvically] existent (*shih-yu* 實有, *dravya*)?"

(2) *Wu so-yüan shih chih* 無所緣識智, Cognition involving a consciousness without an ālambana, which means that certain conditions, such as dreams, past and future 'objects.' mental images, etc., can appear as noema, as mental objects, though obviously an external corresponding object is absent. "Since those perceptual-fields are inexistent, the rest should be as well." This, of course, is a very weak argument. It opens the possibility, but by no means mandates that perceptual fields necessarily be constructed of non-externally-existent objects. That some X is P does not mean that all X is P, much less that any Y is P. However, dreams and so on do provide clear examples of cognitions that require no external object, thus 'proving' that an external object is not absolutely necessary for the cognition of an object 'as external.' While consciousness is a necessary condition for such a cognition, an external object is not (giving consciousness an epistemological, if not ontological, priority).

(3) *Tzu ying wu-tao chih* 自應無倒智, Cognition in which one reacts unimpededly [to a perceptual-field or an 'other']. The text is slightly ambiguous, and two plausible readings emerge. The first: If perceiving external objects only involves a correspondence between a subject and an object, such that the 'natural' perception of a naive realist achieves an authentic cognition of what actually is the case, then liberation would be effortlessly attained even by morons, since liberation only requires seeing things as they are. This argument is clearly rhetorical and somewhat circular, and hinges on the assumption that the average person is not liberated *because* she is unable to perceive things just as they are. Hence Awakened cognition *must* be qualitatively different from the way we normally perceive; otherwise we would already be Awakened. The second: Direct seeing involves cognitive non-confusion, non-impediment (*wu tien-tao* 無顛倒)[32] between the cognizer and the cognized, which, due to the closure of consciousness, does not characterize the perceptions of the foolish. Such direct seeing, without impediment, is liberation. Hence liberation arises from the overcoming of the closure of consciousness, "closure" signifying the solipsistic, narcissistic inability to see things in any way except as cases for projecting self-interest. The basic underlying argument is the same, but this version is less rhetorical or circular.

(4) *Sui san-chih chuan-chih* 隨三智轉智, The "Overturning Cognition" that follows from the three-cognitions. "Overturning" signifies *āśraya-paravṛtti*, the overturning of the basis on which non-enlightened cognition operates,

which elsewhere the *Ch'eng wei-shih lun* discusses in great detail. We will return to it in a later chapter. The "three cognitions" mentioned in this passage are:

(4a) *Sui tzu-tsai-che chih chuan-chih* 隨自在者智轉智, 'Overturning Cognition' that follows the cognitions of those who are self-masters [i.e., free].[33]

For the one who has already realized and attained mental self-mastery (*cetovaśitā*), lands [and things], etc., alter (*chuan-pien, pariṇāma*) according to his desires.[34] If those perceptual-fields were substantially existent [independent of consciousness],[35] how could such alterations be possible?

Does 'mastery' here imply that one's mind actually creates realities independent of one's consciousness (which would defeat the point of the example), or is something being said about one's ability to control how one's mind projects its perceptual-field? A *cetovaśitā* is often interpreted as, amongst other things, someone who has acquired the ability to create physical bodies with his mind, these mentally created bodies being called *mano-maya-kāya*. Theravādins, Sarvāstivādins, and other Buddhists—not just Yogācārins—accepted this ability as fact. The passage here includes the ability to project entire phenomenal realms. It is by this ability, incidentally, that the various Buddhas are said to establish their respective Buddha-Lands (such as Amitābha's Pure Land). Hence, the Yogācārin asks, how could that be possible if it is impossible to mentally project phenomenal realms? By asserting that "lands, etc." are generated in this manner, the charge that such mental activity might be mere solipsistic fantasy is deflected, since these lands are intersubjective.

(4b) *Sui kuan-ch'a-che chuan-chih* 隨觀察者轉智, "Overturning Cognition" that follows from observation and investigation (*pravicaya*).[36] According to K'uei-chi, this cognition characterizes the Śrāvakas and Pratyeka-Buddhas. Achieving an excellent meditative observational investigation of dharmas, one observes multiple characteristics appearing before one within even a single object. In other words, as we examine something we discover different and novel aspects (*ākāra*) in it. If not, the very reason for investigating anything would be pointless. "If the object is real (*shih*, i.e., independent of consciousness), how could it follow mental alterations (*chuan*)?"

What is changing here? As in the previous case, though more explicitly here, the issue concerns mental control over how one projects an objective sphere. If one passively observed external objects, one could not control the perceptual alterations to which the 'object' may be subjected. While a materialist might try to attribute all the changing characteristics of a cognitive object to material conditions (changing light, variations in spatial location, etc.), some changes, nonetheless, render such an account inadequate. For instance, an object may appear innocuous but, after some trauma associated with or associatable with that object, it may become frightening. Or a fragrance that one may be neutral towards or find only mildly pleasant, may send one into romantic reveries if one begins to associate it with someone one loves or has passionate feelings for. Such attitudes and reactions cannot be reduced to purely physical factors.

The philosophical implications may be made clearer by reference to a distinction between Frege and Husserl. Frege differentiated sense (*Sinn*) from referent (*Bedeutung*). While the sense could be altered, or a single referent could have multiple senses, the 'meaning' or referent itself remained absolutely objective and univocal. The referent is always either true or false. Husserl challenged this differentiation, and argued that the Meaning *was* its *Sinn*, that a phenomena's essence was its *Sinn*, and though it may have *an* essence, that essence is constituted of multiple senses. In fact, Husserl defines essence as the invariant structure that perdures throughout all the variations of sense (*Sinnen*). Hence he proposed a method of eidetic variation, i.e., the deliberate proliferation of senses, with which to recover essences.

Like Husserl, Yogācāra rejects the notion of a univocal referent independent of sense. They also deny, however, that cognitive variation produces an invariant identity, or essence, or that multiple senses produce a synthetic invariance. *Pravicaya* is a kind of Buddhist eidetic variation, an investigational study of dharmas within the context of meditation, that scrutinizes them in terms of characteristics such as impermanence, suffering, non-self, emptiness, arising, etc. The object, as something grasped in cognition, palpably changes as a result of such meditations. An object, for instance, at one time charged with attractiveness, which powerfully instigates longing, may, through pravicaya, be divested of its appeal, so that it henceforth 'feels' (*vedanā*) different.

(4c) *Sui wu-fen-pieh-chih chuan-chih* 隨無分別智轉智, "Overturning Cognition" that follows from non-discriminative-cognition (*nirvikalpa-jñāna*).

> This means that with the arising (*ch'i* 起) of the realization of the real (*cheng shih* 證實) non-discriminative cognition, the characteristics of all objects are not projected before one. If the objects are real, why are their appearances (*jung* 容) not projected (*pu-hsien* 不現)?

Since *wei-shih* is synonymous with *vikalpa*, the notion of a cognition that is *nirvikalpa* warns us that ultimately something other than the reification of consciousness or its alterity is the goal.

Notes

1 As an aside, I offer some French cognates of *alter* to help set up a semantic resonance: *altérant* - adj., thirst-producing; *altération* - adulteration, deterioration, debasement, faltering (voice), heavy thirst [*soif*]; *altercation* - f., altercation, dispute; *altérer* - to alter, to change, to adulterate, to spoil, to fade, to make thirsty; *s'altérer* - to undergo a change, to alter, to degenerate, to deteriorate; *alternance* - f., alteration, rotation (agriculture); *alternatif*

alternate, alternative; *alternative* - alternative, option; *alterner* - v., to alternate, to rotate. Notice the connotations of 'rotating,' turning over the soil; this parallels well with the Sanskrit and Chinese terms. Note also the implication of 'thirst', *tṛṣṇa*. Rather than suggesting an evolutionary betterment, however, these words suggest spoilage, deterioration. Note as well that this semantic field constitutes the grounds for any ethic that requires choice, the ability to choose *alternatives*.

2 For the Chinese text to *Ch'eng wei-shih lun* I have relied primarily on the Nanking blockprint edition recently made available again by the People's Republic of China: *Ch'eng wei-shih lun* (金陵刻經處識 *Chin-ling k'o-ching ch'ü shih*, 2 vol., 1897). It is a boon to have this and other prints of many important Buddhist texts again being produced in the PRC, since they are generally reliable editions, often superior to (or at least different from) the Taishō. I have also used the reprint editions of other texts likewise made available from PRC, such as K'uei-chi's commentary to the Twenty Verses, *Wei-shih erh-shih lun shu-chi* 唯識二十論述記 (光緒刻經處校刊 *Kiangsi k'o-ching ch'ü hsiao-k'an*, 2 vol., 1438); the *Yogācārabhūmiśāstra*, Hsüan-tsang's translations of *Madhyānta Vibhāga*, *Saṅdhinirmocana Sūtra*, *Mahāyānasaṃgrāha*, etc., as well as his travelogue, *Hsi-yü-chi*. These have begun to appear in Taiwanese reprint editions in recent years. For *Ch'eng wei-shih lun* I also consulted the Taishō edition and Wei Tat's bilingual edition. Though the Taishō lists variants while the blockprint offers only a single reading, I have found a number of places where the blockprint gave a reading not mentioned by the Taishō. Its punctuation was often superior as well. There are also several places where the Taishō gives a better reading. Aside from the punctuation differences, however, few if any significant semantic differences emerged between the various texts.

3 Giles, character #9210, my emphasis.

4 Monier-Williams, p. 594. It also means development, evolution; digestion; aging; result, consequence; a figure of speech by which the properties of an object are transferred to that with which it is compared, etc. It is clear, though, that the primary meaning(s) of *pariṇāma* and *pien* coincide.

5 T.31.1587. A translation and study of this text can be found in Diana Paul, *Philosophy of Mind in Sixth-Century China* (Stanford: Stanford UP, 1984). My own translation of the actual verses, compared with the Sanskrit and Hsüan-tsang's version can be found in Part IV.

6 Especially Sāṃkhya, but Sāṃkhya thought influenced other Hindu schools; cf., e.g., Patañjali's *Yoga Sūtras*. In *Yoga Philosophy of Patañjali: Containing his Yoga Aphorisms with Vyāsa's Commentary in Sanskrit and a Translation...*, by Sāṃkhya-yogāchārya Swāmi Hariharānanda Āraṇya, rendered into English by P.N. Mukerji (Albany: SUNY Press, 1983). A glossary is offered at the back (pp. 465f):

> *pariṇāma* - Result; effect; fluctuation; transformation
> *pravṛtti* - clear mode of mind; inclination to worldliness (e.g. in Pravṛtti-mārga); conation; supersensuous perception.

7 *Ta-tzu-en-ssu san-tsang fa-shih chuan*, by Hui-li (completed by Yen-tsung), (T.50.2053). I primarily used the edition published in Nanking (Chin-ling k'o-ching ch'ü tsang-pan, 1954) ch.4:19A-20B (cf. T.50.2053.245a-245c), ch.5:7A-8B (cf. T.50.2053.247b-248a). English tr.: *The Life of Hsuan-Tsang*, Compiled by Monk Hui-li, translated under the auspices of the San Shih Buddhist Institute (Peking: Chinese Buddhist Association, 1959), pp. 154-160, 174-176. The English is generally reliable, but incomplete. Hsüan-tsang might have drawn on the arguments against the Sāṃkhyan notion of *pariṇāma* in the *Abhidharmakośa-bhāṣya* to 50a.

8 *Ko 'yam pariṇāmo nāma | anyathāthvam kāraṇa-kṣaṇa-vilakṣaṇa kāryasyātmalābhaḥ pariṇāmaḥ...* Cf. *Abhidharmakośa* II.36d-*bhāṣyā* for a similar definition. (English translation in Leo Pruden, *Abhidharmakośa Bhāṣyam*, vol. 1, p. 211; French translation, Vallée-Poussin, *L'Abhidharmakośa de Vasubandhu*, vol. 1, p. 185.)

9 For the *Kośa-bhāṣya*, since pariṇāma means change, it is also a synonym for duḥkha: *vipariṇāma eva duḥkhatā.* (6.3 *bhāṣya*).

10 This may be viewed in terms of Kierkegaard's description of reason as a 'passion' which, once it spends itself, nonetheless inevitably begins again; or Freud's notion of life as irresolvable tension, a tension that only ceases at death; or as the constant round of rebirths, ever engendering another life, another birth which is produced by the blending of one's desire for life (*bhava-āśrava*) with one's parents' desire for pleasure (*kāma-āśrava*); or in countless other ways.

11 This sort of hermeneutic straddling has functioned in some contemporary literary criticism as an emblem of freedom, i.e., the undecidability or aporia of a text becomes glorified as the essence of the freedom of the reader, the hermeneutic freedom of textual openness. While the ambiguous or aporetic do mark (resistance to) the encoding of a revolutionary spirit that challenges any text's claim to univocality or fixed determinateness, these pockets of resistance are still thoroughly parasitic on textual determinations, and thus are merely emblematic of freedom, not actual freedom. A 'free' reading must be able to thrive not only in a text's ambiguities, but within determinateness itself. As Yogācāra would say, this involves being able to see through closures, looking through any (textual) limit, 'seeing' the limit as a transparency.

12 Cf. Monier-Williams, pp. 693-694.

13 *Ibid.*, p. 594.

14 *Ibid.*, p. 528.

15 'Moistening' the seeds, i.e., activating the seeds by providing productive conditions, is part of the *Ch'eng wei-shih lun*'s vocabulary for causality.

16 On how the *Triṃśikā* treats these terms, see the Part IV and its notes.

17 This is already implied, or at least is one possible reading of *Triṃśikā* v. 15-16. An explicit discussion of how the various consciousnesses become perceptual object-supports (*ālambana*) for each other is discussed at T.31.1585.42c; Ch.8:5B-6A. Cf. Tat, p. 570. This will be translated below.

18 Hsüan-tsang has made them plural in Chinese—*chu-shih* 諸識—though *vijñāna* is singular in Sanskrit.

19 T.31.1585.38c-39a; Ch.7:12A-13A; Tat, pp. 502-504. In the perennial dilemma that faces all translators, readability vs. literal accuracy, I have opted for the latter. Taking the text seriously as a philosophical treatise involves, I believe, treating its vocabulary as technical terms, as well as regarding its general usage of language to be a mirror of its form of thinking. Tat's translation is very free, generally following Vallée Poussin's French translation (without the latter's erudite and helpful annotations). While their translations will certainly be more 'readable' than mine, that readability often comes at the expense of faithfulness to the text. To be fair, the text is often overly concise, elliptical, and the wholesale filling in of the "blanks" by Vallée-Poussin, his interpretive expansions of the text, etc., are frequently insightful and justifiable. But no matter how insightful an interpretation or emendation might be, it remains precisely that, an interpretation or embellishment. While no translation can avoid being an interpretation, it can try to convey to the reader a sense of the flow of the original text, with as accurate a representation of the original's terminology as is possible. In the end, there are crucial dimensions in which Vallé-Poussin's reading is *not* justified. One critical example, his treatment of *chih* 質, as "archetypes"—wholly unjustified—stands at the core of his interpretation of *Ch'eng wei-shih lun* as a form of idealism. This will be examined in greater detail in a later chapter. The *Ch'eng wei-shih lun* is not a 'pretty' text, even in Chinese, and to make it such in English would thus be to perform a certain kind of violence. I apologize if this makes the reader's task more difficult, but my aim was accuracy not elegance. I hope in this I was successful.

20 *Nimitta*, Monier-Williams, p. 551: a butt, mark, target... cause, ground, reason, motive,... *caused or occasioned by,...* etc. In Buddhist texts, *nimitta* means the sensorial marks by which

a sense-object is cognized and characterized as what it is, e.g., color, shape, texture, etc. For Yogācāra it means the cognitive sensorial marks by which a projection of consciousness assumes an objective quality. *Nimitta* also carries some "causal" connotations, since an object is what is in virtue of *causing* itself to be perceived in certain ways, i.e., according to its 'qualities' (*guṇas*). As might be expected, this aspect of *nimitta* plays less of a role in Yogācāric thinking than it does for other Indian schools.

21 While the word *chia* generally means 'provisional' in Chinese Buddhist texts, Hsüan-tsang clearly establishes an opposition between 'real' and 'nominal', and thus uses the term *chia* as his equivalent for *prajñapti*. On *prajñapti*, see Parts II and III above.

22 This may seem less problematic if we keep in mind that Dharmapāla is said to have accepted altogether four bhāgas, not just these two, so that the 'seer' and the 'nimitta' are subtended by two other cognitive constituents, though it is not clear whether either of these are actually 'neng-pien' (that which alters) either.

23 K'uei-chi assigns this position to Nanda.

24 Note that both Dharmapāla and Nanda consider ātman as well as the dharmas to be 'external objects'.

25 *Hsü-wang fen-pieh yu chi ch'eng ku* 虛妄分別有亟成故 which seems to mean 'consciousness' is inclusive of everything, including whatever is falsely discriminated. This point seems trite.

26 *Shih k'ung* 實空 could also mean "tathatā (*chen-ju*) and śūnyatā."

27 This last line offers a clue to Hsüan-tsang's attempted harmonization of Yogācāra and Mādhyamika. He reportedly wrote a treatise while in India, in Sanskrit, arguing the non-difference of these two schools. Tathatā and śūnyatā become affirmational and negational means of establishing the same proposition. Significantly, as we shall see shortly, both as-it-is-ness and emptiness are declared to be prajñapti by the *Ch'eng wei-shih lun*.

28 I will be translating *ching* 境 (*viṣaya*) as 'perceptual-field' unless the context shows that a singular object is indicated, in which case I will translate it 'perceptual-object'. A related term, *ālambana* (*so-yüan* 所緣), which in Chinese literally means 'objective condition', in Sanskrit signifies the objective 'support' of a cognition, i.e., what lies at the objective pole of a perception or cognition that supports or upholds that particular perception. In realist systems it signifies the object as perceivable; in systems with more critical epistemologies it signifies what is being perceived *as* an object. I will translate *so-yüan* either back into Sanskrit as ālambana or into English as 'objective-[cognitive]-support', depending on context.

29 E.g.: *Daśabhūmika*: "The three dhātus are *wei-shih*." *Saṅdhinirmocana Sūtra*: "The ālambana is projected by *wei-shih*." *Laṅkāvatāra Sūtra*: "There are no dharmas apart from citta."

30 Vallée Poussin [hereafter VP], p. 421-22 Sanskritizes them as follows: (1) *viruddha vijñāna nimitta jñāna*; (2) *anālambana vijñāna pratyakṣopalabdhi jñāna*; (3) *anabhisaṃskārāviparīta[tva] jñāna*; (4) *trividha jñānānuvartaka jñāna*: (4a) *vaśitājñānānuvartika jñāna*; (4b) *pravicaya jñānānuvartaka jñāna*; (4c) *nirvikalpaka jñānānuvartaka jñāna*.

31 This argument is drawn in part from Vasubandhu's *Viṃśatika*..

32 *Tien* means to overturn; *tao* means hindrance, impediment. As a compound *tien-tao* means to confound, to confuse (e.g., right with wrong).

33 VP, p. 422 n. 3, points out that this knowledge is associated with the tenth *vaśitā* according to the *Daśabhūmika-sūtra* and the *She-lun*. For K'uei-chi, this knowledge marks the accomplishment of the Eighth Bhūmi.

34 Literally: As his desires alter (turn and change), lands, etc., all are established (*ch'eng*).

35 *Shih yu* 實有 here implies 'stable entities'.

36 Akira HIRAKAWA'S *Index to the Abhidharmakośabhāṣya* (Tokyo, 1977) 3 vols., especially v. 2, Chinese-Sanskrit, has been indispensable. The *Index* correlates both Hsüan-tsang's and Paramārtha's terminology in their respective translations of the *Kośa* with the Sanskrit original. Though neither maintained constant correspondences, a sense of their usage, of the

semantic spread they imputed into terms is discernible. Many passages in the *Ch'eng wei-shih lun* which might otherwise have remained entirely unclear or which I might have thoroughly misunderstood, became more readily comprehensible when I discovered the likely Sanskrit terms. VP, who worked without the advantage of such an *Index*, becomes all the more amazing when one sees how often his Sanskrit reconstructions are on the mark. He identifies *kuan-ch'a* as *pravicaya* (investigation, examination). Cf. *Index* p. 72, where a number of correspondences are noted, including pravicaya's cognate term *vyavacāraṇāvasthā* (stage of pondering over or considering). Cf. Monier-Williams, pp. 691 and 1033. (All references to the *Index* will be to volume 2, unless otherwise noted).

Chapter Seventeen

Why Consciousness Is Not Empty

A crucial subtext has gone unremarked up to this point. At issue in the distinctions drawn in the last chapter, as well as further distinctions to be drawn soon, is the question: What is real (*shih* 實)? Before offering the *Ch'eng wei-shih lun*'s reply to that question, we should first look at the theories of two Madhyamakans, since Hsüan-tsang seems as interested in addressing their objections as he is in reciting Sautrāntic and Yogācāra positions.

While Hsüan-tsang was at Nālandā in India, the form of Mādhyamika being studied there as the orthodox version was Bhāvaviveka's. Apparently at that time Buddhists were also concerned with rejoinders that Dharmapāla made to Bhāvaviveka. Hsüan-tsang's study of Madhyamaka no doubt occurred in that context. The only translation by Hsüan-tsang unambiguously attributed to Dharmapāla is the latter's commentary on *The Hundred Treatise* (T.30.1571), in which we find some of those rejoinders laid out. He also translated Bhāvaviveka's *Karatalaratna* (T.30.1578). While I question the orthodoxy that K'uei-chi attributes to Dharmapāla for Hsüan-tsang's understanding of Yogācāra in general and the *Triṃśikā* in particular, I do think that Hsüan-tsang found Dharmapāla's interpretation of Madhyamaka important and was influenced by it. Thus the section of the *Ch'eng wei-shih lun* that I will be translating and discussing in this chapter may indeed be one that is culled from or heavily indebted to Dharmapāla's writings. Whether those writings are exclusively a commentary on the *Triṃśikā* is another question, one I have dealt with previously.

In India Bhāvaviveka's orthodoxy would eventually be superseded by Candrakīrti, whose interpretation of Nāgārjuna came to be labeled by Tibetans as Prāsaṅgika-Madhyamaka. Candrakīrti was severely critical of both Bhāvaviveka and Yogācāra. Since we find no mention of Candrakīrti by either Hsüan-tsang or I-ching, we should assume that Candrakīrti rose to prominence after I-ching had already left India at the end of the seventh century. It is likely, however, that before Candrakīrti other Madhyamakans were already developing some of the arguments and positions that have come to be associated with him. Indeed, he traces the orthodoxy of his own position back to Bhāvaviveka's predecessor, Buddhapalita (whose works survive only in Tibetan). Thus, even though Hsüan-tsang would have been unfamiliar with Candrakīrti's writings, he seems to have been aware of some of the arguments later to be developed in them. The Madhyamakans that Hsüan-tsang debated and defeated in India seem, on the basis of their positions, to have professed ideas quite close to Candrakīrti on several issues. Hence, for illustration, Candrakīrti will be included in our discussion.

Saṃvṛti, Paramārtha, and Language According to Bhāvaviveka

Lindtner[1] and Harris[2] have presented a good overview of Bhāvaviveka's breakdown of 'true' and 'false' according to his interpretation of the two *satyas.* I won't repeat their work here, but instead offer Lindtner's chart.[3]

```
                    sakalpa (delusive mental constructs)
                    /
         mithyā (erroneous; false)
           /   \
          /      akalpa (heterodox theories)
       /
saṃvṛti-satya (conventional perspective)
       \
          \   neyārtha (non-definitive texts/interpretations [=Yogācāra])
            \  /
         tathya (true) → saparyāya-paramārtha (penultimate\perspective)
                    \
                    nītārtha (definitive) --- [Madhyamaka]
                                          \
                                          aparyāya-paramārtha (ultimate perspective)
```

Briefly, Bhāvaviveka takes *saṃvṛti* as the foundation of his system. Everything stems from it. *Saṃvṛti* is subdivided into two general aspects: 1. The false (*mithyā*), which he further subdivides into erroneous mental cognitions, such as mirages, and unreasonable, illogical theories; and 2. the true (*tathya*), which is subdivided into *neyārtha* and *nīthārtha* aspects. *Neyārtha* means something requiring further elucidation, and when referring to statements or Buddhist literature, denotes statements which are provisionally true, but are only fully understood by further clarification or explanation. For example, for Yogācāra (as we'll see shortly), statements attributed to the Buddha about ten of the twelve āyatanas being rūpa are *neyārtha* statements; they are not exactly untrue, although one does not appreciate the true meaning of Buddha's words about rūpa until they are properly contextualized by an understanding of his purpose for offering statements that are actually not literally true. *Nīthārtha* statements, on the contrary, are exact, true statements requiring no further explication or qualification. Bhāvaviveka distinguishes between (i) *neyārtha* theories of Śrāvakas and Yogācārins, which are 'truths' wrapped in conventional discourse requiring further unpacking, and thus primarily saṃvṛti, and (ii) *nīthārtha* 'truths' that are fully paramārthic; paramārtha is further subdivided into two types: *saparyāya-paramārtha* and *aparyāya-paramārtha. Paryāya* here means a 'methodic way,' a 'means,' a methodology that is deliberately set out and followed. For Bhāvaviveka, Madhyamakan statements are paramārthic in the sense of *paryāya*, i.e., they are a deliberate, methodic means, a path to be followed. They are 'true guidelines,' as well as what validates the Buddhist path in its struggle to terminate karma. Full apprehension of *paramārtha*, however, is solely the province of full Buddhas. That is *aparyāya* because it no longer requires a method; Buddhas are already fully realized.

We take note of two things. First, Bhāvaviveka differentiates *within saṃvṛti* between true and erroneous cognitions as well as between true and erroneous statements. There may be overlap, but a clear distinction can be drawn between language and cognition at least in some, if not all cases. Second, language intrudes into *paramārtha*, i.e., there are paramārthic statements, specifically the *nītārtha* Madhyamakan statements (which for Bhāvaviveka includes syllogistic arguments) as well as whatever might be included in paramārthic *paryāya* statements. The *aparyāya* is both nonlinguistic and nonconceptual (*nirvikalpa*), so the 'highest' level of *paramārtha* is devoid of language, but language does play a role on the 'lower' *paramārtha* level(s).

Candrakīrti apparently assigns much greater scope to language. For him, what is 'true' cannot be separated from the truth-claims which posit and defend that *as* true. The prāsaṅgika interpretation of MMK reads that text as problematizing *all* truth-claims. Since truth-claims are problematic, the status of 'truth' is likewise problematized. Candrakīrti, in other words, endeavors to demonstrate that all criteria, and all efforts to set up criteria—whether for truth-claims, valid knowledge, valid distinctions, etc., i.e., *all valuations*—are chimeric, absurd and impossible linguistic fictions, like round squares. For him, karma is only another case of these linguistic fictions.

Candrakīrti's Chimera

Criteriology seeks to establish the axioms by which discourse, especially ontological discourse operates. In his commentary to vs. 26-30 of MMK 17, Candrakīrti associates these verses with distinct axiomatic criteria for determining whether something exists or not, and he takes these verses to be refutations of those axioms.[4] For the sake of our present concern, we will leave aside the details of his critique and only look at the axioms themselves, which may be schematized as follows:

axiom criterion	**counterexample**	
1. X exists because it is caused (refuted by MMK 17.26)	unlike hairs of a tortoise, i.e., what violates something's essence, definition	definition, essential
2. X exists because it effects (refuted by MMK 17.27	unlike sky-flower, i.e., unfindable, incapable of being verified by perception v. 27)	perceptual, empirical
3. X exists because its fruit has an enjoyer (refuted by MMK 17.29-30)	unlike mango-fruit growing in space, i.e., a mirage	pragmatic, achievability

The first axiom claims that real existent things can be differentiated from unreal inexistent things, because existent things have determinable causes. To prove something is real, according to this criterion, requires determining the causes of that thing. For instance, a certain pot can be said to exist because the clay, the potter, etc., are its causes. However, in his discussion Candrakīrti limits the sense of cause here to what in Western philosophy is called 'formal cause,' which is to say, its definition, what it is by nature. Hence the hairs of a tortoise are unreal because they would violate the definition, the essence, of what a tortoise is. Formal cause is the assertion of formal properties, properties essential to or invariant within whatever has this cause, or definition. The essence of a thing is its nature. What follows from a thing's nature, i.e., what its nature causes, is real and can exist; what cannot follow from its nature, cannot be caused to exist. Dogs cannot give birth to kittens, nor cats to puppies. Each thing is 'caused' by its own nature. This axiom might also be understood to be claiming that whatever lacks a cause (of any type) does not exist. That existence is thoroughly causal, and thus the determinant of something's existence must be an identifiable cause, was an axiom accepted by all non-mahāyānic schools. The Four Noble Truths, for instance, presuppose this axiom.

But formal definition, if it is to be applied to concrete instances—i.e., be real—requires an examination of *effects.* A tortoise may be defined as a shelled reptile devoid of hair only because these characteristics, and not others, are observable. To offer formal definitions a priori without a posteriori confirmation is to risk positing pure fictions. One might posit a seemingly logical definition to which nothing 'real' corresponds (e.g., the teeth of a crow, or a unicorn, which are not logically precluded, but nonetheless do not exist). Thus the essentialist criteria fails because it still requires confirmation by observation.

The second axiom states that what exists does so in virtue of producing observable effects (hence solving the problem of the first axiom). This criterion is perceptual, empirical. Things like sky-flowers or unicorns are unreal because they cannot be observed anywhere. But hallucinations are 'observed' and yet are not real, i.e., the objects observed in an hallucination do not actually exist.

The third axiom claims that something exists if the effect it produces can be 'enjoyed,' i.e., it has fulfilled some purpose. This criterion straddles pragmatism and teleology. A mirage (Candrakīrti's example: "the fruit of a mango tree which grows in space") though perhaps perceptually present under certain hallucinatory conditions (and hence satisfying the second criterion), cannot be enjoyed. When one sees an oasis-mirage in the desert, one wishes to quench one's thirst with its water. Since one cannot drink the 'water' that one perceives in the mirage, it fails this third criterion. Were one able to drink the water at an oasis, the water would be real.

This third criterion was accepted by the Sautrāntikas and Yogācārins and is one of the cornerstones of Dharmakīrti's philosophy. Candrakīrti, however, accepts as axiomatic the conclusions, reached elsewhere in MMK, about the impossibility of posing an adequate theory of causality. In the realm of theory, according to Candrakīrti, one must sound like a nihilist.

Elsewhere in the *Prasannapadā* he offers this tantalizing comment:[5]

> There is no identity of insight or of explanation between the Mādhyamikas who have fully realized the real nature of things as it is (*vastusvarūpa*) and who expound that, and the nihilists who have not fully realized the real nature of things as they are, even though there is no difference in their theory of the nature of things.

Almost paradoxically, Candrakīrti seems here to be making a claim about truth and the relation of truth to statements, but his claim resists being taken as a truth-claim. We will return momentarily to this conundrum, but first we take note of the fact that Candrakīrti seems to allow for at least three levels of truth-claims:

1) Some claims are unambiguously chimeric ('the son of a barren woman'). These chimera are pure linguistic fictions.
2) Some claims are conventionally 'real,' but ultimately chimeric (the three axiomatic criteria). On this level no distinction is drawn between experience and language. For Candrakīrti, these sorts of claims are all like mirages. In effect, this treats *saṃvṛti* and language as synonyms. (Nāgārjuna's use of *vyavahāra*, which implies linguistic conventionalism, as a synonym for *saṃvṛti* lends Candrakīrti some textual support).
3) And some truth-claims (the distinction between Mādhyamika and nihilism), in fact precisely those which save Mādhyamika from nihilism, can be explicitly asserted (as Candrakīrti did above), but are intrinsically incapable of being either formally proposed or defended.

This last type is ultimately real. But since the 'claims' of this level are incapable of being positively and coherently formulated in propositional language, and thus remain indefensible, they are not claims at all, but promises, articulated 'silent' promises. To claim what cannot be claimed is chimeric. What differentiates Candrakīrti from a nihilist is experience, how what one says, does, etc., is grounded in an experience that refuses to be reduced to linguistic approximations. Since this level demands silence, its relation to language and any expression of it in language must necessarily be chimeric. For one lacking the requisite experience, what is chimeric yet ultimately true can only serve as a promise. It remains a matter of faith, no matter how many counterarguments are reduced to rubble. Candrakīrti, however, would not be comfortable with these implications. He would reject the privileging of faith over knowledge on the grounds that the distinction is incoherent. And in his treatment of MMK 17, Candrakīrti soundly thrashes the notion of the 'promise' (*avipranāśa*), which is one of that chapter's major topics.[6]

Candrakīrti's threefold distinction bears a notable affinity to the Yogācāra *trisvabhāva* doctrine, which may have contributed to it. The utterly false and erroneous (*parikalpita*) gives way to causal existences (axioms 1 and 2), i.e., *paratantra,* which itself culminates in an axiom defining fulfilment or accomplishment (*pariniṣpanna*) of a purpose. It is beyond the scope of the present work to speculate on the role that model may have played in the formulation of the philosophies of Dharmakīrti and Candrakīrti.

It may be fair to argue that in this third level Candrakīrti has left behind philosophy as well as philosophical discourse. However sympathetic one may be with such a move, it raises a problem for prāsaṅgika as a project: What fails to conform to philosophical discourse cannot be used as a philosophical refutation. Since the *Ch'eng wei-shih lun* will exploit this issue, we will return to it shortly.

What is *Real* in Yogācāra?

Throughout the *Ch'eng wei-shih lun* the term 'real' (*shih* 實, *dravya*) is contrasted with two other terms: *hsü-wang* 虛妄 and *chia* 假 (*prajñapti*). *Hsü-wang* literally means 'unreal and false' or 'erroneous.' In the *Abhidharmakośa* Hsüan-tsang used *hsü-wang* to translate two different Sanskrit terms:[7] (1) *abhūta* and (2) *kalpanā-mātra*. Both terms imply the first of the three (a)svabhāvas, viz. *parikalpita-(a)-svabhāva*, which the *Madhyānta-vibhāga* describes in terms of *abhūta-parikalpa* (imaginatively constructing and projecting something into a locus in which it is not; e.g., seeing a snake where there is only a rope) and other texts, such as *Saṅdhinirmocana Sūtra*, discuss as *kalpanā-mātra* (nothing but imaginative construction).[8] *Hsü* may also translate *mṛṣā* (untrue, false, misleading).[9] *Wang* translates *mithyā* (erroneous, false, deceitful).[10] Hence when they occur later I shall translate *hsü-wang* as 'unreal and false,' though this should only be taken as a sort of prajñaptic shorthand for these terms.[11]

'Real' here means a substantial entity that participates in a moment of efficient causality (*dravya*). What exists nominally, the text contends, is not 'real.' *Prajñapti* depends on language, and, as will be seen in a later chapter on the *Ch'eng wei-shih lun*'s theory of language, while the sounds and sensory aspects of language are considered 'real,' language itself is not. In part language per se is not *dravya* because it is not momentary, and Yogācāra follows the Sautrāntikas in asserting that *dravya* is momentary. Language as a communicative medium is considered a purely cognitive phenomena, and while the cognitive components on which it depends may include some *dravya* (the sound, the sense organs, etc.), nominal existence itself lacks such substance. This implies that 'real' means to be non-linguistic and substantive.

Prajñapti displays at least nominal, heuristic existence, but whatever is 'unreal and false' does not exist at all, though it may appear in certain types of erroneous cognitions to be the case (e.g., mistaking a rope for a snake).

'Real,' then, is opposed to either 'nominal' or 'false.' Something real is something existent (*asti*), substantial (*dravya*), and momentary (*kṣanika*). What if anything could be considered 'real' by this criterion? That will be answered shortly.

In the *Ch'eng wei-shih lun*, *chia* is consistently used as an abbreviation for *chia-ming* 假名, and thus invariably translates *prajñapti*, 'nominal reality' (this is noteworthy, since *chia* is often used in other East Asian Buddhist texts in the sense of 'provisional,' which does not denote the same semantic range as *prajñapti*, especially concerning its relation to language). According to the *Ch'eng wei-shih lun* nominal 'realities' lack causal efficacy (*kāraṇa*), whereas what is 'real' (*shih* = Skt. *dravya*) discharges observable causal efficacy.

Thus we have three types of 'things':

1) Things which are utterly false and erroneous;
2) Things which are nominally 'existent' but not demonstrably operative; and
3) Things which are 'real,' meaning, according to the *Ch'eng wei-shih lun*, that they are momentary, causally effective, and capable of being cognized. This sort of 'reality' is also accepted in similar formulas by the Sautrāntikas and Bhāvaviveka.

A further qualification is given concerning the third type: It is *saṃvṛti*, not *paramārtha*. Bhāvaviveka would agree with this qualification.

How do these three (un-)realities compare with the three discussed by Candrakīrti?

What is utterly false (*hsü-wang*), such as a round square, must be so essentially, by definition. It lacks any essential or generative cause. This corresponds to the first axiom, though here that is used to define the chimera, not differentiate it from what is real.

A nominal "existent" is something that may be identifiable as an integral entity by conventional description (e.g., a pot or something abstract such as "aging"), but is in actuality either a heuristic for a concatenation of causes and effects (the pot is constructed by a potter out of clay, etc.) or an abstraction describing a process or thing that appears to be the case from a naive viewpoint (such as "aging"), but for which, in actuality, no singular, integral *thing* corresponds. As such, while a nominal existent may have the ability to produce observable effects attributed to it by convention ("Aging is the cause of his rheumatism"), it is not the nominal entity itself that is causing those effects, but the concatenation of actual causes that the nominalization subsumes and conceals. Since the nominal entity itself is a fiction that can cause nothing, it thus matches the counterexample of Candrakīrti's second axiom.

Just like Candrakīrti, the *Ch'eng wei-shih lun* would consider these first two types of 'truths' chimeric, though not equally so. *Prajñaptic* reality, while lacking the requisite causal characteristics, remains nonetheless psychologically potent. Fictions are ultimately false, though capable of evoking a full range of powerful emotional and cognitive reactions. One may here think of those people who write hate or love letters to soap opera stars, confusing the fictional roles with the actual people playing those roles. The saṃsāric problem is, according to Yogācāra, a *prajñaptic* event. Though driven by causes and conditions (*paratantra*), in saṃsāra one recognizes only the fantasies of one's own projections (*parikalpita*) rather than the actual conditions. That is why the *Triṃśikā* defines *pariniṣpanna* as the absence of *parikalpita* in *paratantra.*

The third items on both lists hold the key to the difference between Candrakīrti and Hsüan-tsang. To say something is causally efficient and observable is comparable to saying that a fruit (produced by causal efficiency) has an enjoyer (observer). Though initially this sounds like Candrakīrti's second axiom, the Yogācāric understanding of causal efficacy moves it into the third axiom.[12] Causal efficacy here means achieving some purpose in an observable manner, i.e., in such a way that it can be 'enjoyed.' The observer is integral, and the observer's intent is integral—meaning that the purpose of an event consists of an intersection between the purpose or desire of the observer and the chain of effects which occur. For instance, a farmer whose purpose is to cultivate a field and the field which seasonally produces a crop must coincide in some causal sense in order for the 'fruit' to be enjoyed. Even a seemingly simple act of perception is, for Yogācāra, a complex process of projection and appropriation, an active apprehending and grasping of a cognitive object (*viṣaya*). The grasper and the grasped (*grāhaka-grāhya*) are mutually produced, and hence inseparable.

The further stipulations—namely that when saying 'X is real,' X must be momentary and the statement is merely a conventionalism, not a statement of ultimate reality—effectively shield this criterion from Candrakīrti's criticism (though Candrakīrti might protest that momentariness and the conventional are incommensurate, since an ordinary person does not apprehend his/her experience as radically momentary).

The *Ch'eng wei-shih lun* lacks a critical discussion of the distinction between veridical and erroneous cognition, perhaps because it was written prior to Dharmakīrti's important examination of that question. Erroneous cognition for the *Ch'eng wei-shih lun* would be exhaustively included in the first two 'types.'

Perhaps the most important difference between Yogācāra and Candrakīrti is that for Candrakīrti all *saṃvṛti* is linguistic and thus chimeric or susceptible to the Mādhyamikan critique. For Yogācāra language is only one aspect of *saṃvṛti*, and truth-claims can be made on the condition that they are understood to be *saṃvṛtic*, and not mistaken for paramārthic or metaphysical claims, a position similar to Bhāvaviveka's.

As Nāgārjuna wrote, without recourse to *vyavahāra*, conventional discourse, deeper understanding and nirvāṇa remain unattainable. For Yogācāra, it is *because* things are empty and that 'truth' needs to be understood, that Yogācārins speak. To hear the *saddharma* (the true teaching) can change the projectories of someone's life. Emptiness, therefore, cannot reduce a Yogācārin to silence, but, on the contrary, emptiness compels him to speak.

While Candrakīrti seems to imply that the only 'proper' ways of speaking are silence (*paramārtha*) or magical fictions (*saṃvṛti*), since whatever masquerades as rational discourse is, under examination, nothing more than deceptive chimera—thus ultimately reducing all discourse to the same chimeric level, or, at best, different levels of chimera, some more explicitly chimeric than others—Yogācāra, on the other hand, attempts, as did Candrakīrti's 'opponent,' to maintain clear-cut distinctions between those things which are conventionally real and those things which are truly chimeric. What is paramārthic should not be a matter of truth claims; but that doesn't foreclose making saṃvṛtic truth-claims.

Means of Valid Knowledge in the *Ch'eng Wei-shih lun*

The *Ch'eng wei-shih lun* frequently offers 'proofs' based on citation or appealing to authoritative texts, viz. the Sūtras. When it initially offers proofs for the validity of the doctrine of wei-*shih* these sorts of authoritative texts are appealed to. Eventually Buddhist epistemology would accept only perception (*pratyakśa*) and inferential reasoning (*anumāna*) as valid means for acquiring knowledge (*pramāṇa*), but these standards were only beginning to take root in India while Hsüan-tsang was there. They were not yet fully institutionalized. Prior to that shift the two acceptable means were scriptural testimony (*śruti*) and reasoning (*yukti, anumāna*). It was Vasubandhu's disciple, Dignāga,[13] after all, who had proposed perception and inference as the two valid *pramāṇas*, thus undermining the status of scripture. The context of that shift was not merely logical, or epistemological, but in the interest of intertraditional debate (*siddhānta*). For two rival schools to address each other, they must first have a common language, they must share some common axioms or modes of discourse; otherwise they will talk past, not to each other. What 'reasonable men' have least in common interreligiously is scripture, since each will hold a different set of texts up to the privilege of being scripture. To cite a scripture that the opponent doesn't accept as authoritative is a useless, meaningless gesture since that scripture carries no weight as an authority for such a person. Buddhists further argued that to validate a claim from scripture requires inference, i.e., one has additionally to *prove* the notion of scriptural validity as well as *prove* any particular claim based on scripture. Hindus tried to justify the notion of scriptural validity, but never to the satisfaction of the Buddhists. If a scripture makes a claim, it may or may not be true. Whether it is or not can only be determined by inference, i.e., by determining whether such a claim is or isn't reasonable or plausible, or by perception. If, as is the case, the Bible claims that rabbits chew their cud, then the Bible cannot be the arbiter of the truth of that claim. Examining actual rabbits (which, in fact, have no cuds) determines that the Bible's claim is untrue.[14] Scripture is a species of the genus 'hearsay,' which is to say, it requires external validation, and that validation will only come from perception or inference. This is the case when speaking to someone *outside* the tradition. When addressing someone *inside* the tradition, someone who accepts the validity of the same scriptures that you do, who expects what is true to not violate what the scriptures—which record 'true sayings'—present, who uses scripture as the limit case of what can be claimed, then you must show that what you propose is neither heterodox nor transgressional. In India after Dignāga, scripture itself was subject to interrogation and 'measurement' by the other two *pramāṇas.* A claim was not deemed true because it accorded with scripture; rather scripture was deemed true if it accorded with perception and/or reason. Thus a claim is not true because it is Buddhist, but rather it is Buddhist because it is true. In China, Ch'an similarly 'defrocked' scriptural authority, making experience, existential realization[15] the arbiter of doctrine, and not *vice versa.*

To be fair to the *Ch'eng wei-shih lun* and Buddhist epistemology as a whole prior to the shift of pramāṇic grounding, scripture as a means of knowledge functioned primarily as a limiting case rather than as a revelational fountainhead. For a Buddhist school or thinker to make a claim that appeared novel and/or odd to the other Buddhist schools, it became incumbent upon them to show that this claim does not contradict or violate established scriptural statements. The Yogācāra claim of *vijñapti-mātra* was perceived by other schools as a novel, odd, even wrong-headed notion, so it was incumbent on the Yogācārins to demonstrate that the idea (i) did not violate scriptural limits, and (ii) that, in fact, scriptural authority could be mustered in support of the claim. Of course, they drew on a range of Yogācāric 'scriptures,' especially texts such as *Saṅdhinirmocana Sūtra*, *Laṅkāvatāra Sūtra*, *Prajñāpāramitā Sūtras*, *Daśabhūmi-sūtra*, the 'sūtras' of Maitreya, etc., which had strong Yogācāric content.

Some of these texts raise an interesting but presently unanswerable historical question. Some of these texts *pre-dated* Asaṅga and Vasubandhu, indicating that many and perhaps even all of the 'novel' concepts associated with Yogācāra were in fact around for quite some time before either of the two half-brothers founded the school. Where did these ideas come from? From what did they arise? While the answers to these questions are as yet indeterminable, hopefully the discussion in the previous chapters will help show that the so-called Yogācārin ideas arise out of a faithful and close interpretation of Buddhism, as it developed from its inception. They brought to fruition and order notions which were basic to Buddhism from the beginning, such as karma being grounded in the cognitive-mental register, from which followed concerns such as the importance of analyzing cognition, the problem of continuity and discontinuity of self and dharmas, etc.

Returning to the text, the *Ch'eng wei-shih lun* now offers 'proofs' based on reasoning (*yukti, li* 理).[16] This is an important section for understanding what happens elsewhere in the text, and thus bears a careful reading. The text mounts a simple, direct, yet crucial argument.[17]

Each of the five sense organs, such as the eye, ear, etc., has a corresponding consciousness. Visual consciousness and the eye are linked, such that the eye does not see sounds but sees colors, shapes, and contours. Similarly the ear does not hear colors, but hears sounds. And so on for the other three sense organs (nose, tongue, body) and their corresponding consciousnesses (olfactory-, gustatory- and tactile-kinesthetic-consciousnesses). Each only cognizes perceptual conditions (such as color) that are of its own type; it has no awareness of perceptual spheres apart from its own. Nor do any of the consciousnesses ever actually perceive their respective spheres as in any way apart from themselves, i.e., in the act of perception, the perceptual-field of a particular consciousness must, by definition, be the content of that consciousness, and cannot be 'apart' from it. Since to speculate on cognition is for them merely another form of sensory cognition, one performed by manas or mano-vijñāna, no contrary case can be conceived.

As for the remaining consciousnesses besides the five sensory ones, such as the mano-vijñāna, these are just like the five sense organs and their respective consciousnesses, i.e., each only cognizes perceptual conditions that are of its own type; they have no awareness of dharmas other than those of their own sphere. Nor do any of these consciousnesses ever perceive their respective spheres as apart from themselves.

> The immediately cognized ālambana (*tz'u ch'in so-yüan* 此親所緣) are definitely never separate from [their corresponding consciousness].[18]

The ālambana are part of the economy of consciousness, part of the dualism arising from upacāra. The duality of perceiver and perceived, grasper and grasped, noesis and noema—in each of the consciousness spheres—derives from a splitting apart, an activity by *vi*-jñāna, prior to which there is neither self nor dharma. The ālambana and ālambaka, i.e., the cognitive supports of the objective and subjective poles, are reflectively separated out from an experience that originally has only consciousness as its 'locale,' not opposing poles or even opposing sides of the same pole. For an object of experience (*ālambana*) to truly be *of* experience, it must be *in* consciousness.

> Hence, the ālambana-dharmas, like the dharmas associated with citta (*saṃprayukta-dharmas*, see appendix, 100 dharmas), definitely are not separate from citta and caittas.

What has this 'reasoned' argument argued? First we must emphasize what it did *not* argue: viz. it did not attempt to give an idealist's argument for objects, things, etc. being 'created by' or made by consciousness. It made no attempt to establish any causal relation between consciousness(es) and its (their) objects. On the contrary, by discussing distinct spheres of consciousness in terms of their respective faculties, it concedes that conditions cause consciousness. This bears repeating. We have now seen several examples of arguments in which, should the Yogācārins have wished to offer an idealist argument about metaphysical foundations or causation, they could have, *but they didn't.* Instead, Yogācāra consistently restricts its arguments to epistemological issues. What we know we only know through cognition. Cognition is the karmic realm, and thus, of the gravest importance. But cognition is such that while everything we know appears nowhere else in cognition, things in cognition appear *as if* they were external to cognition. Cognition disowns its own objects in the very act of cognizing them. That is one dimension of *abhūta-parikalpa.* Why does consciousness disown its objects and distance itself from its own constructions? In order to conceive of them as external, as other than consciousness, so that consciousness can appropriate them. We will return to this later when discussing the Yogācāra critique of externality.

We also will look a little later at exactly what sort of account of causal dependence the *Ch'eng wei-shih lun* gives. What is argued here, and quite well, is not an ontological, metaphysical or causational idealist theory, but something more modest, and from a Buddhist perspective more important. The argument simply demonstrates that whatever is known, insofar as it must be known through cognition, i.e., through one of the senses or consciousness spheres, is inconceivable apart from cognition. To 'know' it, whether in immediate perception or through some mental mediation, is to have awareness of it *in consciousness.* Nothing whatsoever is known except through sensation, through consciousness. Consciousness is always consciousness of, and whatever is knowable, is thus *of* consciousness. This harks back to Buddha's definition of *sabba* (all) in the *Saṃyutta-Nikāya* as simply the twelve āyatanas. "Aside from these, there is nothing."

The entire argument might be summed up in one word: *phenomenality.* Whatever is determined (*ting* 定) to be 'real,' must be determined as such in and by consciousness, and hence it is phenomenal, never apart from consciousness. The citta and caittas, i.e., the momentary apperceptive vector and its feeling-tonal-fields *are* experience. Nothing occurs apart from them; hence all is vijñapti-mātra. Q.E.D.

Why Consciousness is not Empty

This raises the question of whether consciousness itself is 'real.' The Mādhyamikan notion of emptiness might seem to prohibit such a claim. All is empty. But Yogācāra attempts to steer another course through the 'Middle Way' (*mādhyamika* versus *madhyānta*). Hence the *Ch'eng wei-shih lun* continues:[19]

> Self and dharmas are not existent.
> Emptiness and consciousness are not inexistent.
> Neither existent nor inexistent,
> hence, corresponding to the Middle Way.

While *ātman* and *dharmas* are negated, emptiness and consciousness are not (it is their negations which are negated). Notably, consciousness is placed on the same soteric, corrective level as emptiness, signifying the Yogācāric supplement to Mādhyamika.[20]

Mādhyamika uses the term emptiness in at least two senses:

1) as a methodical dialectical corrective which 'empties' false views, and
2) as a statement of what precisely is the case, namely the mutually dependent conditions through which everything occurs (MMK offers arguments for this, but Nāgārjuna's *Vigrāhavyavārtani* most explicitly develops that aspect of emptiness).

Yogācāra retains the term emptiness for the first sense, which it also calls *parinispanna*, but substitutes the term *paratantra* for the second sense. Thus, one might argue, when Yogācārins say that consciousness is *paratantra*, they are saying that consciousness is empty, but in their own rhetoric. Nonetheless, as we will see in a moment, they refuse to say that consciousness is empty.

How can the negation of self and dharmas together with the negation of the negation of śūnyatā and consciousness be considered a Middle Way? In a previous chapter we saw that Nāgārjuna would not recognize as legitimate a formulation of the 'middle way' in which two distinct things (X and Y) were treated as if in accord with the middle way when opposite predicates (P and -P) were separated out, with one predicate applied to one thing while its opposite predicate is applied to the other (X is P, Y is -P). How did Yogācāra sidestep that objection? The *Ch'eng wei-shih lun* cites the *Madhyānta Vibhāga*, I.2-3 as scriptural *and* reasoned proof:[21]

> The *Abhūta-parikalpa* (*hsü-wang fen-pieh*, lit: 'unreal and false discrimination') exists.
> In this, duality is entirely non-existent.
> In this, only emptiness exists.
> In that (i.e., emptiness) this also exists. [2]
>
> Hence, it is said all dharmas
> are neither empty nor non-empty.
> Existence, non-existence and hence existence;

> this accords with the Middle Way. [3]
>
> These verses are expressions of defiled paratantra; In reality (*li shih*) there is also a pure paratantra.

We leave aside the significance of the doubling of *paratantra* for now. The imaginative construction of the unreal—which here Hsüan-tsang has translated as *fen-pieh*, as if it were a species of *vikalpa* (*parikalpa* is, after all, its cognate)—is in emptiness just as emptiness is in it. Hence neither the *abhūta-parikalpa* nor *śūnyatā* definitively define the world as either strictly existent nor inexistent. The *abhūta-parikalpa* is as much a part of emptiness as emptiness is a part of the *abhūta-vikalpa*. The world, as we experience it, is emptiness; emptiness is the world as we experience it. A dialectical process, from existence (*sat*) to non-existence (*asat*) to a different sense of existence (*sat*), similar to that found in the *Diamond Sūtra*,[22] constitutes a middle way in which everything can be said to be both empty and non-empty, though in practice, only some things can properly be called empty (e.g., duality), whereas others can properly be called non-empty (e.g., consciousness). The first half of chapter 1 of the *Madhyānta-vibhāga* lays this out in some detail. It is the specificity and propriety with which certain things should be labeled in certain ways that is at issue in this section.

The *Ch'eng wei-shih lun* has an opponent raise the following objection:[23]

> [If all is 'only-consciousness'] Why did the World-Honored One teach the twelve *āyatanas*?

The twelve *āyatanas* consist of the six sense organs with their six corresponding sense objects. Ten of these twelve are considered by Buddhist theory to be *rūpa*, sensate form, not consciousness. The force of this objection then is, if Buddha considered five of the sense-organs (eye, ear, nose, mouth, skin) and five of the sense-objects (visibles, audibles, smellables, tastables, and touchables) to be rūpic, and only the mental-organ (*manas*) and its mental-objects (*viṣaya*, *dharmas*) to be mental or consciousness proper, how can the Yogācārins subsume the first ten in the last two? Why would the Buddha call them *rūpa* if they are, as the Yogācārins insist, actually mental? The *Ch'eng wei-shih lun* answers:

> These [twelve] depend on altered-consciousness [to function cognitively]. They are not substantially-real (*shih* 實) existents separate [from altered-consciousness]. The two pairs of six were taught in order to enter [an understanding of] the emptiness of self [i.e., to break down the notion of a central, unified self into conditions], just as the continuity (*saṃbandha*) of sentient beings was taught to refute the annihilationalist view [though, properly speaking, there are no continuing 'identities']. In order to enter [the understanding of] the emptiness of dharmas, again, consciousness-only was taught, so that you would know that external dharmas do not exist.

This passage[24] shows one of the Yogācāric strategies for reinterpreting and revaluating previous Buddhist doctrine. Buddha offered certain doctrines as correctives for specific wrong views. If the problem is an erroneous belief in self, the antidote (*pratipakṣa*) consists of applying decentering reinterpretations of a person, such as the twelve *āyatanas*. If the problem is annihilationalism, posit continuity. If the problem is non-recognition of the emptiness of dharmas and a belief in their externality, propose 'consciousness-only'. The proposal of consciousness-only is compared to Buddha's proposal of continuity. This needs to be emphasized, since Yogācārins, like the Sautrāntikas, accept the analysis of dharmas as momentary, not continuous. Continuity here functions as a corrective for a specific problem; by extension, then, the notion of consciousness-only should be a corrective for a specific problem, not an ontological, absolute entity.

What is interesting in this exchange is the reduction of the non-mental components of the eighteen dhātus[25] to their roles in consciousness—precisely because they are empty. But here the text does not say they are empty; it says they do not exist, i.e., *external* dharmas do not exist. The word 'external' is pivotal. The question is, external to what? The immediate answer is: Consciousness. And again we see the point is phenomenality, not ontological idealism. What has happened to the standard Buddhist claim that consciousness itself arises from the contact (*sparśa*) of sense-organ and sense-object? Curiously, nothing. It stands, with one radical qualification. The collision of organ and object *is* consciousness. Consciousness is not a third party, a spark set off when two material 'sticks' are rubbed together. Perception itself is intentional, and hence the organ and the object are always already producing consciousness because consciousness is 'producing,' intending itself through and towards them.

The middle way between eternalism and annihilationalism is "entered into" by way of prajñaptic teachings that offer specific antidotes or counter proposals. While, according to Mahāyāna polemics, Hīnayānists recognize that self is empty (*anātman*), but fail to recognize that dharmas are empty, this passage is claiming, following the *Saṅdhinirmocana Sūtra* and other Yogācāric texts, that the prajñaptic teaching concerning consciousness-only arose as a way to bring Hīnayānists to Mahāyāna by helping them "enter" the understanding that dharmas too are empty. Hsüan-tsang is thus making the Yogācāric notion of Vijñapti-mātra a symbol for Mahāyāna. For Mahāyāna, recognizing that both self and dharmas are empty is axiomatic.

But if the Mahāyāna view consists of the insight that all dharmas are empty, as even this passage admits, isn't consciousness empty as well?[26]

> No.
>
> Why?
>
> Because that is not what we hold 非所執故.[27] What this means is that, when, due to consciousness altering 依識變成,, one erroneously 妄 clings to 執 [seemingly] substantially-real dharmas that are in principle unattainable

(理不可得 *nopalabdhi*), those dharmas are considered empty. Because [they are unlike] *vijñapti-mātratā* which is [1] not inexistent 非無, [2] apart from language 離言 [and hence not prajñaptic], and [3] realized by correct cognitions 正智所證 [and hence not 'unreal and false' or chimeric, therefore] these [aforementioned false] dharmas are said to be empty.

This passage clearly articulates the three sorts of things, viz. the utterly false, the nominal and the real. *Vijñapti-mātratā*—the principle that experience arises through the operations of consciousness—is not utterly false and inexistent; it is not merely prjñapti; and it can be directly cognized, i.e., become apparent *in* experience, if one cognizes correctly. What must not be overlooked is that the key issue is attachment, or "holding" to a position, a *dṛṣṭi*. What one attaches to must be emptied, as must attachment itself. What is not attached to need not be emptied. Consciousness, i.e., phenomenality, is not attached to; it is existent, non-linguistic and comprehended through correct cognition. Consciousness-only-ness (*vijñapti-mātratā*) is not a false projection (*abhūta*) one tries to appropriate; it is incapable of being attached to in that way. Remembering that *abhūta-parikalpa* and *prajñapti* were the two opposites of 'real,' this passage is arguing what is empty is such by virtue of its being 'unreal,' insubstantial, and, as is added here, inexistent. More to the point, the term 'empty' is used as a device, as an antidote to attachments that cling to false mental constructions. As in the previous verse, emptiness and consciousness-only together serve as correctives.

This does not accord with orthodox Madhyamaka usage of the term 'emptiness,' since for them emptiness has nothing to do with existence or non-existence, or validity or invalidity. Emptiness is a synonym for conditionality, in which distinct entities involved in the conditional process do not need to be isolated and identified. For Yogācāra, however, the term 'emptiness' should be reserved for specific pedagogic purposes. Their reason for doing so is thoroughly Madhyamakan, however. The notion of emptiness is a weapon that should only be deployed when attachment to a false dravya is at issue. Emptiness should not be used as an ontological commitment, or a universal ontological theory. Any Madhyamakan or Buddhist who does so has forgotten that emptiness also needs to be emptied (MMK 13:8, etc.). It is emptiness in the sense of nonexistent or unreal that Yogācāra is denying one should attribute consciousness. They are not claiming that consciousness enjoys some special privileged existence apart from causes and conditions, but they are denying that the facticity of consciousness can be rejected out of hand.

Hsüan-tsang remains sensitive to the Mādhyamikan concern that whatever is not emptied may undergo objectification, substantialization, reification and thus conceptual attachment from which Yogācāra is claiming *vijñapti-mātra* is exempt. Emptiness, according to that view, provides the only effective inoculation against falling into such erroneous *dṛṣṭi*. Hence, in language strongly reminiscent of MMK 24:10 ("Without relying upon convention [*vyavahāra*], *paramārtha* is not taught. Without understanding *paramārtha*, nirvana is not attained."), Hsüan-tsang reminds us that what is at stake here is not a theory or ontology of 'what is,' but a bottom-line recognition of the fact, *the facticity of phenomenality* (*vyavahāra* = *saṃvṛti* = *vijñapti* = consciousness).

> If this consciousness were inexistent, that would make *saṃvṛti-satya* inexistent; if *saṃvṛti-satya* is inexistent, then *paramārtha-satya* would also be inexistent, since *paramārtha* and *saṃvṛti* depend on each other to be established. (ibid.)

This passage explicitly equates consciousness with *saṃvṛti* . To deny the existence of consciousness is to deny *saṃvṛti* since the entire phenomenal sphere occurs no where else than in consciousness. *Paramārtha* is not a radically separate region inaccessible from or incommensurate with *saṃvṛti*. On the contrary, *paramārtha* and *saṃvṛti* establish each other, they are mutually dependent. *Paramārtha* is not separate from *saṃvṛti*—on the contrary, it is a special perspective *on saṃvṛti*. Likewise, *paramārtha* depends on *saṃvṛti*, since it is learned through the language and experience one has in *saṃvṛti*. To deny phenomenality (*vijñapti-mātra* = *vyavahāra* = *saṃvṛti*) is to deprive oneself of anything and everything, not the least of which is *any* basis for knowledge. Without some acceptance of the facticity which is never anything or anywhere other than consciousness, nothing whatsoever can be affirmed or denied, nothing can be known or understood. Knowability, by definition, requires consciousness, i.e., an amenability to awareness. Without some basis for knowledge, not a single determination can be made about the form or content of one's experience. Even Candrakīrti must concede this if he doesn't want to be a nihilist. And he did concede that, despite an identity in rhetoric and polemic between nihilists and Madhyamakans, they differed as to *experience*. Even if one denies any basis to knowledge (as does the Mādhyamikan critique of *pramāṇa* in the opening chapters of the *Prasannapadā*), one is still incapable of knowing, recognizing, or being aware of that epistemologically 'ungrounded' world anywhere else than in consciousness. It is extremely significant that in this passage consciousness is made equivalent to *saṃvṛti*, that is, cognitive closure (*saṃvṛti* means, according to Candrakīrti's etymology, to be enclosed, obstructed). *Vijnapti-mātra* is not a paramārthic claim! It is a means, not the end of insight. Without consciousness, a mundane or conventional world cannot appear (where and what would it be?). Without the conventional, enclosured experiential domain, of what would one have *paramārthic* insight, what would emptiness make transparent?

But what if the two *satyas* are themselves inexistent, vacuous fantasies of some Buddhist's overactive imagination? Aren't they, as well, 'empty?' While a commentary on MMK—ascribed to Asaṅga, that survives only in Chinese[28]—makes precisely that argument, the *Ch'eng wei-shih lun* takes a firm stand against this nihilistic move. Hsüan-tsang's argument again echoes MMK. MMK 24:11 states:[29]

> A wrongly perceived emptiness ruins a person of meager intelligence. It is like a snake that is wrongly grasped or knowledge that is wrongly cultivated.

Compare MMK 13:8:[30]

> The Victorious Ones have announced that emptiness is the relinquishing of views. Those who are possessed of the view of emptiness (*śūnyatā-dṛṣṭi*) are said to be incorrigible.

The *Ch'eng wei-shih lun* states:

> To dismiss the two *satyas* as inexistent, is to grasp emptiness in a depraved way, [a sickness that] the Buddhas said was incurable. You should know that dharmas are both empty and non-empty.

Candrakīrti offers a similar statement (*PP* 445; Sprung 202):

> Therefore all things are not to be taken as either devoid of being or as non-devoid. Individuals are neither real beings nor unreal beings; this is the middle way.

At first glance there seems to be a clear difference between the Yogācāric notion derived from the *Madhyānta-vibhāga* and the Mādhyamikan notion expressed by Candrakīrti. While Candrakīrti says that neither being nor non-being may be predicated of 'individuals,' Yogācāra seems to be saying that emptiness *can* be predicated of some (not all) things, and non-emptiness can be predicated of other (the remaining?) things. Candrakīrti's statement thus has universal application, whereas the Yogācāra position divides that which can be predicated into two distinct classes. But, examining the *Madhyānta-vibhāga* more carefully we see that such simplistic distinctions don't really apply. For the *abhūta-parikalpa*, though existent, has śūnyatā 'within it.' Saying that "no duality is found"—though explicitly intended as a refutation of *grāhya-grāhaka*—by implication also puts us on alert that the duality between *abhūta-parikalpa* and *śūnyatā* is itself "not found," even while "even in this, that is found." The *Madhyānta-vibhāga* knows that this is the implication. Hence, the amazing aporia of its third verse reiterates not only the actual dual distinction between the *abhūta-parikalpa* and *śūnyatā*, but reinforces their non-duality, the elimination of their duality—in language not unlike Candrakīrti's, and equally 'universal':

> Neither empty nor non-empty, thus is everything described; due to its existence (or being, *sat*), its non-existence, and again its existence, this is called the middle way.

The middle way, then, requires the inseparability of *paramārtha* and *saṃvṛti*. Understanding (i) what exists and doesn't exist, as well as (ii) what is and isn't the case (i and ii are not necessarily the same thing) implies the mutuality of the two *satyas*. In different ways Madhyamakans and Yogācārins insist that discourse about 'existence or nonexistence' occurs in a completely different register from discourse about emptiness (and non-emptiness). To say something is empty has nothing to do with whether that thing exists or doesn't. To claim something exists or doesn't exist need not entail any cognizance of emptiness (as when non-Buddhists make claims about the existence of something). For Candrakīrti, existence and non-existence are both chimeric assertions built on incoherent epistemological foundations. For Yogācāra, existence and non-existence are not ontological assertions, but phenomenological descriptions. For Madhyamaka, emptiness is the ultimate analytic device; for Yogācāra, it is one of several corrective tools, one which points to the conditionality (*paratantra*) out of which phenomenality (*saṃvṛti, vijñapti*) is constructed.

According to Yogācāra, this phenomenality is necessarily entailed in the Madhyamakan notion of two *satyas*. *Paramārtha* cannot be understood except on the basis of experience; what one hears and learns, what one cognizes and analyzes, etc.

Should the Mādhyamikan be willing to jettison the two-*satya* notion, not only is his (non-) position then placed in jeopardy, but his ability to criticize others is also undermined—for he can no longer say that he is able to take on his opponent's axioms and propositions to demonstrate their fallacies and thus needs none of his own.[31] In order to appropriate another's assumptions, even for the purpose of falsifying them, one must already presuppose *vyavahāra*, i.e., a conventional arena of discourse in which meanings are communicable. Without such an assumption, there can be no communication. And if there is no communication, no one can be critiqued or negated, since, first of all, the negator would be incapable of understanding the position to be negated, and those subject to the negations would be incapable of appreciating the critique. On the other hand, should the Mādhyamikan reply that he will allow the two-*satya* theory to stand 'un-negated,' the Yogācārin can retort that this very two-satya theory itself presupposes an experiential sphere in which conventional communication takes place. Hence, logically speaking, *without Yogācāra, there can be no Mādhyamika*. Again, if he should deny the two-*satya* theory, not only has he transgressed Nāgārjuna's prescription, he has reduced himself to a form of meaningless solipsism.

But when the Yogācārin says that consciousness is not empty, isn't he confusing *saṃvṛti* with *paramārtha*? If consciousness is apart from language, how can it be *vyavahāra*? The *Ch'eng wei-shih lun* replies:[32]

> Since *citta* and *caittas* depend on other things to arise (*paratantra*), they are like a magician's trick, not truly substantial ('real') entities 真實有. But so as to oppose false attachments to the view that external to *citta* and *caittas* there are perceptual-objects (*ching* 境, *viṣaya*) [composed of] real, substantial entities 真實有, we say that the only existent is consciousness 説唯有識. But if you become attached to the view that *vijñapti-mātra* is something truly real and existent, that's the same as being attached to external perceptual-objects, i.e., it becomes just another dharma-attachment [and definitely not liberating].

In thoroughly explicit language the *Ch'eng wei-shih lun* declares that consciousness is *not* a true dravya. The claim that consciousness is the only existent is made for epistemological and therapeutic, not ontological reasons. We are strongly warned against holding a view that vijñapti-mātra indicates some reality. On the contrary, it is "like a magician's trick." The claims made in the name of *vijñapti-mātra* are only antidotes to a specific, deep-rooted, ubiquitous type of attachment, one that invovles positing an external world ripe for appropriation. Emptiness is posited as an antidote to attachment; and *vijñapti-mātra* is charged with the same task.

Vyavahāra, for Yogācāra, is larger than the sphere of language. It involves the entire range of lived experience, of which language is certainly a part, but not the full extent. *Vyavahāra* is phenomenality. To see phenomenality as it is (*paramārtha*), is to see without attachment. Thus merely critiquing propositions, as Mādhyamika does, inevitably fails to reach the source of the problem that generates those propositions (*prapañca*). To do that, according the *Ch'eng wei-shih lun*, one must contemplate one's own mind (*tzu kuan hsin* 自觀心).

The *Ch'eng wei-shih lun* declares elsewhere that the five *asaṃskṛta-dharmas*, including *tathatā*, are all mere *prajñapti*, not truly real. Does that mean that *tathatā* is non-existent, or unreal? Not exactly. The term is a *prajñapti*, but it serves an upāyic soteric function.

> To refute the claim that it [*tathatā*] is inexistent 無, it is said to be considered 'existent' 有.
>
> To refute attachment to its being considered existent, it is said to be considered 'empty.'
>
> So it won't be called vacuous or illusory 虛幻, it is said to be considered 'real' 實 (*shih*).
>
> Since reason neither falsifies nor contradicts it 理非妄倒, it is termed *chen-ju* 故名真如.
>
> We are not like the other schools (who claim) that apart from *rūpa, citta,* etc., there exists a real, permanent dharma 有實常法 called by the name of '*tathatā*.' Instead, we say the unconditioned dharmas definitely are *not* real-substantial existents 故諸無為非定實有.

We will examine *tathatā* and the *asaṃskṛta-dharmas* more fully later. I've included this passage here in order to further illustrate the manner in which claims that may initially appear to be ontological or metaphysical assertions of Truth, are in fact provisional statements that need to be handled carefully.

Like a chess master, Hsüan-tsang has checkmated his Mādhyamikan opponent. If the Mādhyamikan objects to the Yogācāra claim that consciousness is real (*saṃvṛtically* real), then either he must reject *saṃvṛti* itself or he is relying on an incoherent and eccentric notion of *saṃvṛti*. If he chooses the first option, then not only has he distanced himself from Nāgārjuna (MMK 24:10), but he loses even the vague differentiation he assumes between himself and the skeptic. While on the surface the Mādhyamikan's 'theory' looks the same as the skeptic's, it is different in virtue of a different "insight" into *vastusvarūpa* such that though the Mādhyamikan's "explanation" is expressed in identical terms to that of the skeptic, its significance bespeaks a "realization" that the skeptic lacks. In other words, what differentiates them is a cognitive experience, a *paramārthic* insight into *saṃvṛti*. Moreover the Mādhyamikan's negation game is really an "explanation." Without *saṃvṛti* he has no way of explaining how he can critique a false position, much less insist that such negation is meaningful. If the Mādhyamikan rejects *saṃvṛti*, he has backed himself into a corner, fatally undermining any efficacy to Mādhyamika whatsoever. Thus, from the Yogācārin perspective, emptiness compels language to speak, but to speak therapeutically.

If, on the other hand, the Mādhyamikan accepts the notion of *saṃvṛti*, he will have no ground for criticizing Yogācāra, since the notion of *saṃvṛti* is meaningless without phenomenality and intersubjective communication, the two key characteristics of consciousness (and expounded as such at length in Vasubandhu's *Twenty Verses*).

If he rejects *saṃvṛti*, he negates Mādhyamika. If he accepts *saṃvṛti*, he must likewise accept Yogācāra.

Candrakīrti is confused about *saṃvṛti*.[33] He vacillates between seeing it as conventionalism and seeing it as inherently false and unreal. Yogācāra retorts emphatically that *saṃvṛti* is neither inherently false nor unreal; it is not chimeric. It circumscribes a qualified 'reality.' It entails domains each of which possesses clear and discernible criteria for evaluating the veracity and functionality of whatever occurs within it. To say that they are not 'ultimately' true is not the same as saying that they are utterly false. Candrakīrti is rushing to collapse these extremes.

If the Madhyamakan merely resents the Yogācārin use of *vijñapti-mātra* as an *upāya* (beneficent deception), he needs to defend his own use of emptiness. Just as Nāgārjuna insists that finally emptiness too must be emptied, Yogācārins repeatedly state that finally consciousness, the cittas and caittas, and the *ālaya-vijñāna* are made to cease. *Vijñapti-mātra* is no less self-negating than *śūnyatā*.

Why then does Yogācāra supplement emptiness with *vijñapti-mātra*? For them one must be cautious about proclaiming a conclusion too hastily. For them, Candrakīrti too quickly leaps from the obviously chimeric to a position of no position. Between these two extremes, they argue, lies a domain in which reason and order remain reasonable. While there are thoroughly erroneous notions (such as a round square) and a paramārthic perspective through which the erroneous can be negated and overcome, there nonetheless remains a middle way, which is neither a riddle-laden collection of paradoxes nor a metaphysical apex. It is simply reasonability, that is, experience and language that recognize valid causes and reasons (*hetu*). Puppies come from dogs, not cats, and because where there is smoke there is fire, if smoke is observed on the hill, one may reasonably infer that fire exists there concomitantly. This reasonability precludes nonsense passing as 'Truth,' and remains valid only to the extent that it recognizes its own conventionality. It is *saṃvṛti*, not absolute. It is a middle way between absurdity (non-sense, gibberish) and Truth (Absolute Metaphysical claims).

If the Mādhyamikan refuses to accept such conventional reasonability, he can say nothing, for he is thereby refusing the very conditions of his own discourse. In short, the *vijñapti-mātra* supplement signifies that both experience and language display a rationality that, even while ultimately conventional, nonetheless provides an order, a sense of true and false, a moral distinction between good or advantageous (*kuśala*) and bad or disadvantageous (*akuśala*), a reasonability with which one may discern a path and tread it (*mārga*).

Vijñapti-mātra also emphasizes that it is within one's own experience—one's envelopment in phenomenality as well as the linguistic constructs one uses to make sense out of that phenomenality—that one realizes what is the case (*yathābhūtam, tathatā*). Exploring and negating all views may be one way of reaching realization; but one need not pursue such an extensive, possibly interminable course. Simply realizing what a moment of cognition entails (a grasper, a grasped, and an appropriational consciousness; *grāhaka-grāhya-vijñāna-upadāna*) in that moment of cognition as it arises is sufficient to make cognition itself (*jñāna*) transparent (*śūnyatā*).

Finally, to follow the Mādhyamikan course may lead to a reduction of experience to language, or *vijñāna* to *dṛṣṭi*, of cognition to propositions concerning cognition, of what is the case to an interpretation of what is the case. Mādhyamika attacks that reductionism, as it should, but since it forecloses any rational discourse whatsoever concerning cognition, it suggests to the linguistically minded that consciousness itself is merely a linguistic entity, rather than something 'more real' than language. Conscious experience arises through causes and conditions, the understanding of which constitutes 'realization.' Just as Nāgārjuna equates *pratītya-samutpāda* with *śūnyatā*, Yogācāra defines *vijñāna* in terms of *paratantra*. Both agree that we must be on our guard against reducing our experience to a theory of experience, but they offer distinct methods for doing that: Mādhyamika, by challenging the theories and the theorization process (*prapañca, kalpanā, dṛṣṭi*); Yogācāra, by plumbing the depths of experience itself. Initially Mādhyamika negates theorization while Yogācāra affirms experience. But they meet in the middle. Both must at least implicitly agree that experience is larger than language.

As a commentary on Mādhyamika, Yogācāra insists that we not mistake phenomenality for the language games it circumscribes. Enlightenment is experiential. For Yogācāra it requires mastering the hermeneutics of experience. Though the problem of language can neither be ignored nor underestimated, one must be careful to properly distinguish between the linguistic components of experience and the facticity that language invariably attempts to appropriate through its pretext of referentiality; language appropriates experience by referring to it, by placing experience at a distance from the discourse that desires it and intends toward it. As it reaches across the distance that it has put into place, it confuses itself for what it attempts to grasp. To confuse language for experience, i.e., to reduce experience to the theoretical discourse that tries to have experience, to own experience, is to fail to understand both experience and appropriation.

Finally, despite some real points of controversy, in the end perhaps Bhāvaviveka and Hsüan-tsang agreed on the most important things. In the *Jewel In the Hand Treatise* Bhāvaviveka writes:

> In reality (*paramārthatāḥ*) conditioned things are empty because they are produced from conditions, like a magical production; the unconditioned is not real because it is not produced, like a sky-flower.

Notes

1 Christian Lindtner, "Bhavya's Critique of Yogācāra in the *Madhyamaka-ratnapradīpa*, Ch. IV," in Matilal and Evans (eds.), *Buddhist Logic and Epistemology* Dordrecht, 1986.

2 Ian Charles Harris, *The Continuity of Madhyamaka and Yogācāra in Indian Mahāyāna Buddhism*, Leiden: EJ Brill, 1991, esp. ch. six.

3 For a fuller discussion, see ibid.

4 Candrakīrti may have derived these distinctions from Dharmakīrti, who offers similar criteria.

5 Sprung's tr. in *Lucid Exposition of the Middle Way*, p. 180. Cf. Vallée Poussin's Sanskrit edition of *Prasannapadā*, p. 369 (on *Ātman-parikṣa* ch.18).

6 *Avipranāśa* is a 'promissory note.' The term was used by some of the Abhidharmika schools as part of their account of karma and its retributive powers. See Part Three, Chapter Ten.

7 Hirakawa, *Kośa Index*, p. 128.

8 On how the *Triṃśikā* treats this and the other two svabhāvas (self-natures), see vs. 20-25.

9 *Index*, p. 127. Cf. Monier-Williams, p. 831.

10 *Index*, p. 468. Cf. Monier-Williams, p. 817. In the *Kośa* Hsüan-tsang used *wang* in other ways as well; e.g., the compound *wang-wei* 妄謂 for *dṛṣṭi*.

11 According to the *Index*, p. 193, *shih* carries a number of implications: *dravya* (substance), *asti*, *as-* (is, exists), etc.

12 It was Dharmakīrti who finally distinguished these two, and to whom Candrakīrti is responding. Since Dharmakīrti was probably writing at or near the time Hsüan-tsang was in India, nascent versions of this distinction may have already been in the air, awaiting Dharmakīrti to give them full articulation. Since Candrakīrti claims to already find the distinction being addressed by Nāgārjuna, this is not unlikely.

13 There is no agreement among scholars about whether Dignāga actually studied with Vasubandhu or if he was merely a later disciple of Vasubandhu's works, in the way Candrakīrti was a disciple of Nāgārjuna, though removed from him by five or so centuries. There are some logic texts attributed to Vasubandhu that may have influenced Dignāga; he is reputed to have written a short commentary on the *Abhidharmakośa* that only survives in Tibetan.

14 This example caused some problems for missionaries in Africa who preached that God was all-knowing, and that every word in scripture was absolutely true. When the claim about rabbits chewing their cuds came up, the natives pointed out that rabbits have no cuds. The missionaries, ignorant of rabbit anatomy, kept insisting that if the Bible says so, it must be true. The natives decided the missionaries and their God didn't know what they were talking about, until, exasperated, the missionaries finally decided that the Bible was talking about special rabbits at the time of the Bible, now extinct.

15 This existentialization derives, to a large extent from Mencius, who centuries before had existentialized Confucius' teachings; e.g., redefining the Five Constants in terms of the Four

Beginnings, the latter being existential lived-world examples of what lies at the basis of the former, which, because they are experiential (*hsin*) are to be taken as indicative of human nature (*hsing*). I hope to write more on this on another occasion.

16 T.31.1585.39a23-40a2; Ch.7:13B-16B; Tat, p. 508-524.

17 T.31.1585.39a23-39b7; Ch.13B-14A; 508-510. VP: I.423-424. The Chinese text is extremely terse. VP's translation is, as a consequence, very free, and he incorporates so much of K'uei-chi's commentary that it would not be inaccurate to say that he has translated the latter rather than the *Ch'eng wei-shih lun* itself. Tat virtually repeats VP, though he rearranges the order of presentation. Since the terseness will not yield a useful translation, I have decided to paraphrase peppered with translated phrases.

18 VP, I.423 interprets the next line, which only says rather cryptically (using only four characters), "since two accord with one," as referring to a later discussion (VP, II:445) concerning two types of ālambana, viz. the immediate object (*sākṣāt-ālambana*) which is always integral to a consciousness, never apart from it; and the remote object, which may seem to be separable from the cognizer, as a sort of hyle that produces the nimitta-bhāga which the darśana-bhāga perceives. He 'translates' the phrase "since two accord with one" thus:

> ...parce qu'il est un des deux Bhāgas (à savoir le *nimittabhāga*) de ces Vijñānas; tout comme la partie du Vijñāna qui connait (à savoir le *darśanabhāga*) n'est pas distincte du Vijñāna puisqu'elle est Vijñāna de sa nature.

Not bad for four Chinese characters! The 'two' of the above phrase, then, would refer to the two bhāgas, and the 'one' would be consciousness itself.

19 T.31.1585.39b4-7; Ch.7:14A; Tat, p. 510.

20 This may seem similar to what in chapter Ten we treated as an illegitimate version of the middle way, since it opposed predicates of unrelated terms, rather than dealing with oppositional terms themselves. In other words it claims self and dharmas are strictly inexistent; emptiness and consciousness are strictly existent. Hence it would seem that self and dharmas fall into the annihilational extreme, while consciousness and emptiness allude to the eternalist extreme. But, Yogācāra counters, that isn't so because, since self and dharmas have never existed, they cannot be annihilated; since emptiness and consciousness only exist saṃvṛtically, not paramārthically, they are not eternal realities. Rather the latter pair are used as antidotes to the former pair, and therefore this opposition is a therapeutic application of the middle way.

21 I have translated the Chinese literally. The Sanskrit reads:

> *Abhūta-parikalpo 'sti dvayam tatra na vidyate, śūnyatā vidyate tu-atra tasyām-api sa vidyate.* ll 2
>
> *Na śūnyam na-api ca aśūnyam tasmāt sarvam vidhīyate, sattvād-asattvāt sattvac-ca madhyamā pratipac-ca sā.* ll 3

I would translate this as:

> [Though] abhūta-parikalpa (m., mental construction of the non-real) exists, no duality is found. But śūnyatā (f) is found there, even in this (m), there is that (f). [2]
>
> Neither śūnya nor aśūnya, thus is everything described; due to its existence (*sat*), its non-existence (*asat*) and again its existence (*sat*), This is called the Middle Way. [3]

The most significant difference between the Chinese and Sanskrit is the clue that gender gives to the meaning of v. 2.

22 For instance: "...the harmonies of Buddha-fields, Subhuti, as no-harmonies have they been taught by the Tathāgata. Therefore he spoke of harmonious Buddhafields." (Conze's translation, modified, in *Buddhist Wisdom Books*, NY: Harper, 1972, p. 46) This three-step formula—X is not X, therefore X—is repeated throughout the *Diamond Sutra* applied to a variety of topics and terms.

23 This argument is paraphrased from Vasubandhu's *Viṃśatika.*

24 The argument that one needs Yogācāra thought in order to understand madhyamaka or emptiness properly is first made in the *Saṅdhinirmocana sūtra.*

25 The 'mental' components, technically, include not only the six consciousnesses, but manas and mano-dhātu, the former being grouped with the six organs and the latter with the six objects

26 T31.1585.39b; Ch.7:14B.

27 This phrase could also be translated: "Since that is not what we hold (to be true)."

28 *Hsun chung lun* 順中論, T.30.1565, translated by *Gautama Prajñāruci in the early sixth century. There is some evidence of Yogācāric concerns in this commentary, but its ascription to Asaṅga is uncertain. Curiously, I have found no strictly Madhyamakan text that makes this claim.

29 Kalupahana's translation.

30 Kalupahana's translation.

31 That was the standard Madhyamakan reply to the accusation that they weren't fit for debate, since they only criticized others, but offered no positive counterproposals. In effect, they replied that they didn't need to make counterproposals; they merely tested the coherency and validity of the opponents' positions by the criteria accepted by the opponent.

32 T.31.1585.6c; Ch.2:4B.

33 This subject was already broached in Chapter ten.

Chapter Eighteen

On Rūpa

Assuming that the Mādhyamikan objections have been satisfactorily silenced, the *Ch'eng wei-shih lun* turns to a more pressing issue concerning the manner in which consciousness operates.[1]

> If the rūpic *āyatanas* are basically consciousness itself (*shih-wei-t'i* 識為體), what accounts for the fact that [consciousness] discloses itself (*hsien-hsien* 顯現) by appearing with the characteristics of rūpa, [namely]
>
> (i) Homogeneous,
>
> (ii) firmly abiding, and
>
> (iii) in a continuous series (*saṃbandha*) that keeps 'flowing on' (*chuan*[2])?

While what we experience is always experienced *in* consciousness, it is also the case that the contents of consciousness are not experienced *as* consciousness. Rūpa has certain characteristics: Homogeneity, i.e., typological or morphological or phylogenic similarities, etc.; stability (a tree retains a stable appearance across moments, and it presents itself as 'solid,' whereas consciousness, by comparison, seems ephemeral); continuity (whereas mind fluctuates from thought to thought, moment to moment, rūpic entities appear to continue in a stable, homogeneous fashion). Implied here are the four 'elements': "air" is homogeneous; "earth" is stable, solid; "water" rolls on, flows in a continuous stream; and "fire" illuminates things, making them visible, giving them color (*rūpa*), discloses appearances. How is it that consciousness takes on these 'characteristics' (*lakṣaṇa*)?[3]

Types of Vāsanā

> [These rūpic characteristics] arise because of the power (*shih-li* 勢力) of the vāsanās (*hsün-hsi* 熏習) of 'names and words'.

The *Ch'eng wei-shih lun* elsewhere lists three kinds of vāsanās:[4]

(1) Vāsanās of 'Names and words' or 'terms and words' 名言習氣 *ming-yen hsi-ch'i,* which means 'latent linguistic conditioning,' which are of two types:

  (1a) 'Terms and words indicating a referent' (*piao-yi ming yen* 表義名言), through which one is immediately able to express (*ch'üan*

詮) meanings (*yi* 義, *artha, referent*) by the differentiation of vocal sounds (*yin-sheng ch'a-pieh* 音聲差別).[5]

(1b) 'Terms and words revealing perceptual-fields' (*hsien-ching ming wen* 顯墓名言), through which one immediately discerns (*liao* 了 = *vijñapti* or *upalabdhi*) perceptual-fields (*viṣaya*) as citta and caitta dharmas.

These seeds, planted [in the root consciousness] by 'terms and words' are the causes and conditions of each saṃskṛta dharma.

(2) Vāsanās of self-attachment (*ātma-grāha-vāsanā, wo-chih hsi-ch'i* 我執習氣), meaning the false attachment to the seeds of 'me' and 'mine.' Self-attachment is two-fold:

(2a) Inherent self-attachment (lit.: 'what one is born with'). This attachment to 'me' and 'mine' is destroyed in the *bhāvanā-* [*mārga*][6].

(2b) Self-attachment from discrimination. This attachment to 'me' and 'mine' is destroyed in the *darśana-* [*mārga*].[7]

These seeds, planted [in the root consciousness] by self-attachment, differentiate self from other sentient beings.

(3) Vāsanās which link existences (*bhāvāṅga-vāsanā, yu-chih hsi-ch'i* 有支習氣),[8] meaning the karmic seeds, 'differently maturing' (*vipāka*), that carry over (*chao* 招)[9] from one existence to another in the three worlds. The *bhāvāṅga* (linkage from one life to the next) is twofold:

(3a) Contaminated [yet] advantageous (*sāśrava-kuśala, yu-lou shan* 有漏善) i.e., actions (karma) which produce desirable (*k'e-ai* 可愛) fruits.

(3b) Disadvantageous, i.e., actions which produce non-desirable fruits.

Vāsanās—the karmic 'perfuming' of the consciousness stream—are conditioning. Experiences produce vāsanās that are 'planted' in the ālaya-vijñāna, latently conditioning subsequent experiences until the planted vāsanā comes to fruition. Then, depending on the type of fruit produced (kuśala, akuśala, or neutral), new vāsanās are produced which get planted. In this way karmic conditioning cyclically continues until broken. Yogācāra focuses on three types of vāsanās in particular: 1. linguistic vāsanā, self-attachment vāsanā, and linkage vāsanās.

Linkage vāsanās account for karmic continuity between lives and between moments. Since vāsanās are karmic conditioning, they are sāśrava, 'with āśravas,' though they can be either kuśala or akuśala, leading to better or worse karmic consequences, better or worse births, and so on. Self-attachment vāsanās come in two types: those produced by differentiating oneself from others, imposing a sense of mine against yours (or theirs); and those which one already bears when one is born. The latter is a deeper sense of selfhood, and thus requires deeper meditative intervention and extirpation.

As for linguistic vāsanā, one type is specifically language oriented, in which words directly indicate their referents (*artha*). This vāsanā is our propensity towards language. Since words are used to refer to meanings, i.e., language pointing toward language, this indicates the self-referentiality of language. As such, it marks a linguistic cycle of closure. The other linguistic vāsanā is more far-reaching. It is conceptual conditioning, which produces linguisitically conditioned experience *as* certain types of citta and caittas. Due to this type of vāsanā one actually sees and experiences the world in certain ways, and one actually becomes a certain type of person, embodying certain theories which immediately shape the manner in which we experience. A dialectical materialist, for instance, who has embodied a theory of dialectical materialism, actually sees the world as an occasion of dialectical economic forces in which people—including oneself—are instantiations of economic principles, such as class conflict, alienation, structures of production, and so on. A psychiatrist, embodying certain psychological theories, sees her patients as enactments of those theories, and may notice things about her patients that others don't see. Linguistic conceptual conditioning shapes how things (*viṣaya*) appear, and also the modes through which we approach experience (*citta-caitta*).

Returning to the previous argument, rūpic characteristics are formulated out of linguistic conditioning, which is conditioning that is embodied, either from birth or acquired through linguistic activity. Language, then, is not merely an ephemeral string of sounds or concepts that waft ghostlike through and within the field of concrete experience. That field is itself, in part, linguistic conditioning, embodied language. The cognition of the characteristics of rūpa arises, according to the *Ch'eng wei-shih lun*, through habitual linguistic conditioning.[10] The *categorial fixations* which we call 'physical sensate stuff' are linguistic projections; the world of experience, as *recognizable* entities, involves a high degree of linguistic embodiment; but the projectorial activity is neither deliberate nor conscious. We are driven to project the world, which is to say, we are also projected by the world. Birth and death occur within a whirling stream of intentionality (*pravṛtti-pariṇāma, chuan-lun* 轉輪). Trapped, dragged along by the current, by the torrential flow (*srotasaugha-vat, pao-liu* 暴流), we seem doomed to be the duḥkhic occasion of an endless flow going nowhere. Or are we? Why, we may ask again, does Yogācāra say that consciousness is not empty?

Yogācāra is not interested in doing ontology. While *vijñapti-mātra* invites an epistemological attitude, the epistemological attitude it invites is not the one that constructs methods with which to measure and validate what is. Rather, it engenders an attitude of self-deconstruction, self-examination, predicated on the absence of an ultimate self who either watches or is viewed. It is an invitation to become aware of the psychosophical torrents that proscribe and circumscribe the horizons—as well as vacuous core—of what/where we are. What is at stake in the notion of rūpa for a Yogācārin is not its ontological or ontic status. In either case such a notion of 'rūpa' would reduce experiential content to graspable entities, graspable by a self which is their grasper. The notion of an ontic or ontological rūpa invests the perceiver with the power of appropriation (*upādāna*), specifically the power to appropriate rūpa. Rūpa becomes a case of intentionalistic reference, it becomes karmic. But all 'grasping' is not equal. Some teloi immerse one deeper in the current, they may even drown one; whereas other *teloi*, if provisionally and expediently applied, may help extricate one from the cycle, the whirlpool. Thus there is 'value' in different sorts of actions, not because the referents, addressees, addressors, or senses carry *intrinsic* value in-themselves, but because the expedient application of poison may result, in that *particular* situation, in the poison becoming medicine. Context is important. We are thus not cured by the Truth, but by efficacious deceptions (*upāya*). Medicine is poison re-contextualized. Thus the original argument in *Ch'eng wei-shih lun* continues:[11]

> [Why do we cognize rūpic qualities?] Because they are the locus (*adhiṣṭhāna*) on which occur the defiled and pure dharmas. That is to say, if [rūpa] were inexistent, then there would be no *viparyāsa*,[12] which would then make for no mixed, defiled and no pure dharmas. This is why the consciousnesses and what seems to be rūpa are projected.

Has he actually said that rūpa is non-existent while consciousness does exist, or that consciousness is the ontological ground (rather than epistemic cloak) of rūpa? On the contrary, *he is positing the inseparability of consciousness and rūpa*! A line from the *She-lun* is then cited to drive the point home:

> It is like the verse [from the *Mahāyānasaṃgrāha* which] says: "The mark of confusion[13] and confusion itself, it should be conceded, are rūpa-consciousness and non-rūpa-consciousness. If one does not exist, the other can not either."[14]

What sort of consciousness, other than these two, could there be? Rūpa, even if it were ontologically real, would not be known except through consciousness. What is known *as* rūpa is, in fact, a categorial projection onto what is *given* (and which we then—as graspers, appropriators, *grāhaka* —'take'). Rūpa (i.e., rūpic-consciousness) is a necessary condition for appropriation (*upādāna*). Rūpa here signifies the full sensorium, that which is given *as object* in an act of cognition. Were there no rūpic consciousness, in fact, there would be no non-rūpic consciousness—which is to say, there would be *no consciousness*. Surprisingly, not only has the *Ch'eng wei-shih lun* refrained from ever explicitly declaring that consciousness *creates* rūpa, it actually argues that rūpa—though a rūpa *in consciousness*—constitutes consciousness.[15] Rūpic-consciousness is a necessary condition for consciousness itself. What then is the distinction between (1) rūpa, (2) rūpic-consciousness and (3) non-rūpic-consciousness?

This delivers us into a philosophical maelstrom no less virulent today than it was fifteen hundred years ago in India and China. What is the material object apart from our cognition of it? How can one even assert that it 'exists'? To assert or offer proofs always already involves the reduction of that which is to be asserted or proved to the cognitive sphere; i.e., to 'prove' matter, is to reduce matter to a cognitive category, either directly (i.e., offer cognition or cognizability in one form or another as the standard of proof) or indirectly (the domain of proofs is never other than the cognitive domain). The 'belief' in matter may be predicated, made reasonable, made probable, perhaps even made imperative, but matter itself, insofar as it remains truly material, can never be the subject of a (cognitive) proof.

Interlude: Some Ideas about the "cognitive object" in Western Philosophy

The status of the cognitive object has underwritten Western philosophical thought at least since Descartes. Thinking he had grounded certainty in cognitive self-reflectivity, Descartes tried to jump from the cognitive 'substance' to the other substance, the 'extensional' substance; but, his method and conclusions (the pineal gland!) have proved less than satisfying to virtually every subsequent thinker of note. Spinoza eliminated one aspect of the bifurcation by claiming there was only one substance, and that cogitation and extension were two of the infinite attributes of that substance. But since attributes are, by his definition, "that which the intellect perceives of substance as constituting its essence,"[16] cogitation becomes privileged since extension is grounded in intellect, not materiality. Berkeley explicitly challenged the notion of materiality, calling himself an 'immaterialist,' and Hume challenged the epistemological foundations of material and causal thinking. Kant attempted to reground experience in a real world, but the gap between the cognizer and what he cognizes had now grown so vast, that the object per se, in-itself, was at best vague, unclear, a noumenon. Whatever is clearly and distinctly perceived or conceived (the criterion of 'reality' for the Rationalists) is phenomenal, i.e., a cognitive construction shaped by innate mental categories and judgments through which all experience is filtered. Hegel declared the 'idea' supreme, that 'reality' amounted to reason itself as a movement of the idea searching for itself such that the 'concept' (involving the three dialectical moments resulting in an *aufhebung*) recoincides with itself. Marx accused Hegel of losing track of material history, and offered the supplement of material dialectics, while Kierkegaard accused Hegel of losing sight of true subjectivity, and offered a 'reality' divorced from objective constraints. Similarly Schopenhauer shifted the 'idealist' focus away from reason, and Protestantized it as 'will.'[17]

Brentano developed the notion of intentionality, which attempted to sort out the array of categorial confusions that had accrued to the question of the status of the cognitive object. In the introduction to his translation of Husserl's *The Idea of Phenomenology*, Nakhnikian writes:[18]

> An intentional act, said Brentano, is always "about" or "of." I think of or about. I desire this or that. And the peculiarity of intentional acts is that their objects do not *have* to exist. An intentional act may have as its object an existentially mind-dependent entity, for example, the *idea* of a mermaid; or its object may be something physical; or it may be an impossible thing such as the round square; or

> it may be something possible but unactualized, such as a golden mountain. Any mode of mentality (loving, desiring, believing) may have as its object an "intentionally inexistent" entity, namely, an entity that is neither physical nor existentially mind-dependent. The *idea* of a mermaid is, being an idea, existentially mind-dependent. But the *mermaid* which is the intention of the idea is neither a physical thing nor is it existentially mind-dependent. In contrast to this, no physical action requiring an object can be performed upon an intentionally inexistent entity. Kicking a football requires a football; but thinking of a football does not. I may think of a football that never existed. Brentano identified the mental with any intentional state, that is, with any state that *could* be directed to an intentionally inexistent entity.

He supplements this characterization of Brentano with the following footnote:

> This, however, is only one possible interpretation of Brentano's view of intentionality as presented in Chapter I of *Psychologie vom empirischen Standpunkt.* It is also possible to interpret Brentano as saying that on *every* occasion of a mental act, whether there be a physical thing as referent or not, there is an intentionally inexistent entity; so that, for example, when I desire the apple in front of me, the apple is the object of my desire in the sense of the word "object," namely, as the thing that could satisfy my desire; but there is also another object, the intentionally inexistent apple which is the common and peculiar object in all desires of apples.... The sense-datum is to the intentionally inexistent object what the perceptual object, if there is one, is to the material referent, if there is one, of the intentional act.... Husserl's work... strongly suggests that his conception of the mental is in line with the second interpretation.

The proliferation of ātman and dharmas, indeed! 'Sense-data,' 'intentionally inexistent objects,' 'perceptual objects,' 'material referent'—one might be tempted to continue to introduce all the other metaphors and titles for 'cognitive object' in use over the last hundred years: signified, addressee, sense, gestalt, etc.—and they all, including the concept of a "material referent," are cognitive categories.

Above I said that "the 'belief' in matter may be predicated, made reasonable, made probable, perhaps even made imperative." By 'imperative,' I am thinking of 'physical' arguments, such as bodily striking the non-materialist, or withholding food, etc. Broken bones and starvation carry a certain persuasive force. One may even try to argue that these 'arguments' are no longer cognitive reductions but actual physical arguments, but this, of course, is just begging the question. What would make these arguments successful would not be their raw physicality at all, but their cognizability by the addressee of the argument. Lack of food is not experienced; *hunger* is cognized. The symptom pain is not experienced as 'broken bone.' The cognitive connection *qua* presupposed causal theory, etc., is precisely the issue in question. Even were I to strike someone repeatedly, and should that cognizer experience pain concomitant with each strike, that still lacks the force of a proof. Hume and Mill have already demonstrated that consistency does not produce certainty, but only expectation. Thus its cognizability and its status as an expectation still grounds so-called 'materiality' in the cognitive.

Yogācāra on Rūpa, Again

To be sure, Yogācāra never claims that rūpa does not exist because it doesn't function (*karaṇā*). Rather it attempts to point out that what we think are external things exhibiting these functions need not be any more real than the seemingly external objects that appear in dreams. Yogācārins are *not*, however, saying that dreams are entirely fictitious realms with no connection to a 'real' world. Quite to the contrary, the key example offered in Vasubandhu's *Twenty Verses* is a wet dream, which is to say, based on fictitious factors (the erotic imagery in a dream) an actual physical event (seminal emission) which carries ethical and moral consequences has transpired.[19]

What is important about this example is that it is *not* claiming that dream images 'function' solely in terms of or within the dream context. That we respond to dream images *as if* they were actual, real things external to our activity of cognitive projection is obvious. But the example points to more than that. Not only do dream images discharge their function within the context of the dream, they may produce observable effects, physical effects in other realms, other contexts as well. The seemingly physical world to which we respond is like a dream: WE are projecting it, interacting with the turmoils and desires of our own displaced intentionalities. The cognitive object is thick, encrusted with the sediment of projected characteristics, qualities, attributes; it becomes the locus into which we project our universal categories, our assumptions, fears, needs, predilections. In Yogācāric language, rūpa is a case of *abhūta-parikalpa*. The object is the screen on which the film of our desire is projected. Thus the *Ch'eng wei-shih lun* asked: How, if it is something independent of cognition, can the 'material' object change with the alterations of mind? Nonetheless even as we thrash about in our dreams, real consequences are being produced elsewhere, in a realm or realms which we cannot even dream about until we have awakened. This does not necessarily entail the existence of transcendent 'other' realms, but rather an awareness of *this* realm devoid of the blindness of cognitive closure. That would mean seeing not just what appears within the limited closured horizon encircling the borders of a projectory, but directly cognizing the conditionally interdependent 'nature' (paratantra-svabhāva, *pratītya-samutpāda*) that holds that closure together.

But if dharmas are empty, and no substrative self exists that would serve as the source of these projections, from what do they arise?

What is at stake in the *Ch'eng wei-shih lun*'s argument is not a causal claim (certainly *not* that consciousness creates rūpa), but rather the inseparability of consciousness and rūpa. Rūpa is a 'locale,' a locative base (*adhiṣṭhāna*), the location on/in which defilement/purity occurs. It is the locus of the fundamental cognitive reversal—that is to say, it is that about which the most fundamental cognitive 'perversions' (*viparyāsa*), reversals, *take* place (i.e., take their place, locate themselves appropriationally). 'Rūpa' is, then, a cognitive reversal—seeing what is *of* consciousness as something external to consciousness. It makes experience a place in which cognitive objects can be grasped, taken, pointed at, referred to and seized. It is the field of appropriation.

Cognizing rūpa is the putting into play of embodied linguistic conditioning. Why language? Language is the sphere of universals, of universal classes, of the cognitive linking of one particular cognitive object with another based on definable identities and differences. What is (the notion of) rūpa if not another case of a universal category into which certain cognitive objects can be collected as class members? When we cognize a 'pencil,' for instance, we collate what appears to our various senses as certain colors, textures, solidity, etc., and impute into the aggregation an identity such that it belongs to a class of objects named 'pencil.' Moreover, the clarity with which we discern the various characteristics such as color, texture, etc., will also implicate those characteristics themselves as universal categories (yellowness, hardness, blackness, etc.). The pencil's 'materiality' is only another genus, another class into which we group our aggregated perception. Whatever offers sensorial or spatial resistance (two material objects cannot occupy the same place at the same time) belongs, by definition, to the category 'rūpa.' We overlay the particular (*svalakṣaṇa*) with universals, generalities (*samānya*), and 'cognize' those generalities *as* the particular.[20] Thus we say that we see 'a pencil,' which is a prajñapti for a complex field of synthesized cognitive conditions; only synthetically, i.e., having defined and prejudged our cognition in terms of a universal class (or universal classes) to which we can associate it (*saṃjñā*), can a 'pencil' appear in cognition. But this 'class' through which the cognition was filtered is not 'real;' it is a linguistic construction (*prajñapti-mātra*). Rūpa is a case of cognitive displacement (*viparyāsa adhiṣṭhāna*), and the condition for this displacement is embodied linguistic conditioning. Just as with Kant's categories, we are born with certain predilections to cognize in terms of certain universal categories, and these, inasmuch as they are universal, are linguistic. Rūpa, then, is a case of prajñapti.

The distinction between consciousness and rūpa is itself a *viparyāsa*. "Consciousness and what seems to be rūpa are projected," i.e., experience becomes dichotomized. This dichotomization establishes the anxious gap between cognizer and cognized that we attempt to fill in with acts of appropriation. This appropriation serves as the ground condition for both defilement and purity, duḥkhic entrapment and liberation—these all hinge on the rolling around, the direction of the reversal.

Both rūpa *and* consciousness are projections. Alterity of consciousness turns, rolls, cycles; the moments and movements of history as well as of each individual percipient are constituted and determined in these reversals. Duḥkha and the elimination of duḥkha are its turnings, as is the turning of the wheel of

Dharma. Yogācāra proposes a soteric resolution to the duḥkhic dilemma through the expedient application of *pratipakṣa*, 'antidotes,' 'counteractives,' intellective-affective reversals.[21]

For Yogācāra the root problematic is 'appropriation.' Rūpa is a metaphor for the appropriational dynamics. The same issues are involved here as were discussed previously in reference to the phrase *abhūta vastu nimittārambaṇa manasikāra*.[22] If we lose sight of the centrality of appropriation as the root Yogācāra problematic, we risk utterly misunderstanding everything that Yogācāra attempts.

In an earlier section the *Ch'eng wei-shih lun* states explicitly why, for Yogācāra, consciousness-only is asserted, and equally important, what sort of misunderstanding should be avoided concerning that claim. Even though I introduced this passage earlier, it is important enough to bear repeating. The passage occurs precisely where the notion of *grāhya-grāhaka*, noema-noesis, the division of cognition into a grasper and grasped, i.e., an appropriational dynamic, has been introduced:[23]

> Since cittas and caittas depend on others to arise (*paratantra*), they are like a magician's trick, not truly substantial entities (*fei chen shih yu* 非真實有) . But so as to oppose false attachments [to the view that] external to citta and caittas there are perceptual-objects [composed of] real, substantial entities (*shih yu ching* 實有墓), we say that the only existent is consciousness (*wei yu shih*). But if you become attached to *wei-shih* (consciousness-only, vijñapti-mātra, psychosophic closure) as something truly real and existent (*chen shih yu* 真實有), that's like being attached to external perceptual-objects, i.e., it is just another dharma-attachment [and definitely not liberating].

The *Ch'eng wei-shih lun* could not have made its claim more explicit. Wei-shih is posited as an antidote to attachment to external objects. Its purpose is the interruption of the appropriational economy, the magic show we take for 'true cognition.'

As we've shown above, consciousness itself is not immediately canceled since phenomenality must be retained in order for any communication, any knowledge, any method to function. Further, it is not rūpa per se which is rejected, but, as we will see in a moment, *externality*. After examining the *Ch'eng wei-shih lun*'s position on externality, we will examine more closely what it is that the *Ch'eng wei-shih lun* argues is real, and what is not.

Notes

1 T.31.1585.39b25-39c3.7; Ch.7:15A; Tat, p. 518.

2 轉 *chuan*, as noted earlier, literally means to roll around, to turn, but is used in this sort of literature to mean 'operate.'

3 *Ibid.*

4 T.31.1585.43a-43b; Ch.8:7B-8A, Tat, p. 582-584. In this passage vāsanā is rendered *hsi-ch'i*, while in the passage just cited it was rendered *hsün-hsi*. These terms are interchangeable. The first connotes 'perfumed or smoked habit', the second 'habitual force'. *Hsi* means 'what is acquired through repetition', hence 'habit' or 'practice', etc.

5 *Index*, p. 195: *ch'a-pieh = viśeṣa, prakāra, prabheda, bhid-*.

6 These two mārgas, and the other three presented in the *Ch'eng wei-shih lun* were outlined in Part IV. The darśana-mārga precedes the bhāvanā-mārga, and the former involves gaining conscious control over *how* one cognizes, while the latter involves practice and cultivation that deepens the insights gained during the former, embodying them. Hence, 'discrimination' (i.e., how current experience reflects and produces conditioning) is dealt with in the former, and the long term conditioning, the conditioning that one is born with, i.e., is carried over from previous existences. One uproots this inherent conditioning in bhāvanā mārga.

7 See previous note.

8 VP, p. ii.479:

> Vāsaṇā of the *bhavāṇga* (*bhava* = the triple existence, *aṅga* = *hetu*) : The Bījas which proceed from the act, *karmabījas*, which creates the retribution of the three Dhātus (*traidhātukavipāka*). - The Bhavāṅga is of two sorts: impure but good, *sāśravakuśala*, the acts which create the agreeable fruits; bad, *akuśala*, the acts which create a disagreeable fruit. [my translation, as will be all subsequent translations from his French version]

9 Chao 招 means 'to hail, beckon, call', but is used (*Index*, p. 248) for *abhi-nir-vṛt-* ('to result from', 'proceed from').

10 VP, p. 478; Vallée Poussin links the linguistic vāsanā to a discussion in the section on the Ten and the Two Hetus and Fifteen Adhiṣṭhānas, his p. 454 (re: T.31.1585.41b; Ch.8:1A; Tat, p. 552). He reads the relevant passage thus:

> Anuvyavahārahetu (*sui-shuo-yin* 隨說因) and vacana- or vāgadhiṣṭhāna (*yü-yi-ch'u* 語依處).
>
> The vāgadhiṣṭhāna has for its nature vāc, speech, which is produced by dharma, nāman and saṃjñā [the word vāgadhiṣṭhāna is thus a karmadhāraya and signifies: the Adhiṣṭhāna which consists of vāc : this is the explanation of the *Yogācārabhūmiśāstra*]. Vāc or speech is produced by the thing (dharma) that it names [VP adds this note: The thing that one names is a nimitta, a mental image which proceeds from previous speech], the name and the notion.
>
> One establishes the *Anuvyavahārahetu* relative to this Adhiṣṭhāna. - In effect, it is because of speech and in conformity with it that is in line with experience (*vyavahāra*) of all things (*artha*) that are seen, heard, thought, known (*dṛṣṭaśutamatavijñāta...*). - The denomination (*abhilāpa, neng-shuo* 能說, i.e., the speech which denominates) is the cause of the denominable (*abhilāpya, so-shuo* , i.e., all the dharmas). [my translation from VP's French rendition]

The text mentions another theory as well, in which the *sui-shuo-yin* (lit: 'Cause *qua* following from language') is taken as a *tatpuruṣa* signifying 'Adhiṣṭhāna of Vāc', i.e.,

> The supports of speech are known as *nāman, saṃjñā* and *dṛṣṭi*: since it is by reason of, and in conformity [with *nāman*], that one names [an object, with *saṃjñā*] that one seizes [the object's] characteristics, [with *dṛṣṭi*] that one becomes attached to it. [my translation from the Chinese]

According to K'uei-chi, this latter position entails that the three dharmas - name, associative-thinking, and viewpoint - are the cause, such that *vāc* is their fruit. That interpretation seems rather incoherent. How can 'name', etc., be the *cause* of language?

11 T.31.1585.39b25-39c3.7; Ch.7:15A; Tat, p. 518.

12 *Tien-tao* 顛倒, lit. 'to turn around, reverse, flip over, make contrary.' (Cf. *Index*, p. 342: *viparīta, viparyaya,* which also mean 'turned around, reversed, opposite, contrary, reversal.') Traditionally Buddhism lists four viparyāsas or 'perversions', i.e., reversals of what is correct. The four are: Taking what is impermanent as permanent; taking what is selfless as having self; taking what is impure as pure; taking what is suffering as happiness. These 'perversions' are reversals which correct seeing must again reverse, or turn back. The *āśraya-paravṛtti* ('foundational reversal' or 'turning around of the basis') in part derives from this notion. That exemplifies the privileging of the cognitive dimension, which is required in order to engage in an analysis of what is problematic as well in order to devise prescriptions for a cure.

13 VP, p. 428, interprets *luan*, which means 'confusion, chaos, anarchy' (i.e., psychological, political, cosmological, etc. confusion) as corresponding to *bhrānti*, 'á cognitive error, an erroneous cognition.' But cf. *Index*, p. 487: *bhrānti* does not occur there, but among the correspondences listed is *viparyāsa*. Other terms are *ākula-*, *mūrchā-*, *vikṣipta*, etc.

14 VP, *ibid.*, offers the following gloss:

> That is to say: The illusion (or thought) which is *arūpavijñāna*, immaterial Vijñāna (the *darśanabhāga*), has for a cause the *rūpavijñāna*, the material Vijñāna, the Vijñāna appearing as Rūpa (the *nimittabhāga*). There is no *viṣayin*, subject, if there is no *viṣaya*, object.

VP is taking *hsiang*, *lakṣaṇa*, 'mark or characteristic', in this context as 'cause' (*nimitta-karaṇā* ?).

15 To be more precise, at T.31.1585.9b (Ch.2:14B, Tat, p. 128) the *Ch'eng wei-shih lun* states that

> the (*bījās*) lead to their own fruit, i.e., rūpa (*bījās*) lead to rūpic fruit, and citta (mind) (*bījās*) lead to citta fruits, each leading to the production of its own particular kind... This refutes the theory which the Sarvāstivādins are attached to, viz. that rūpa and citta reciprocally act as causes and conditions for each other.

Does this mean that no reciprocal relation is posited? No. What is being denied is an ontological status for rūpa, i.e., if one accepts that it is on a causal parity with citta, then one is implicitly conceding that there is an external thing, independent of consciousness, which shapes cognition. K'uei-chi, in his commentary to this line is quick to point out that rūpa and citta *do act as adhipatipratyaya*. The *Ch'eng wei-shih lun* accepts four categories of conditions; the *adhipatipratyaya* is the fourth type, a sort of miscellaneous grab-bag of whatever is to be considered a 'condition' (*pratyaya*) but was not included in the first three categories. The four pratyayas will be outlined later, particularly the third, the *ālambana-pratyaya*.

16 *Ethics* I.def4, Shirley's translation.

17 The Reason vs. Will debate predates Protestantism, e.g., with the Dominican vs. Franciscan debates of the Middle Ages, but Luther establishes Protestant theology firmly on a foundation of Will *qua* faith, and it is this feature, especially as it relates to the problem of free-will and determinism, that marks the movement away from Catholicism and towards the notion of a morally autonomous individual, the Protestant hallmark. On this, cf. the Luther-Erasmus debates, which were a decisive moment in the formation of the Reformation: *Erasmus-Luther: Discourse on Free Will*, tr. and ed. by Ernst Winter (NY: Continuum, 1988).

18 Tr. by William Alston and George Nakhnikian (Hague: Martinus Nijhoff, 1964), p. xiv.

19 *Viṃśatikā* 4-bhāṣya. Wet dreams have moral consequences for monks since they violate the celibacy rules to which monks are avowed. This attitude about wet dreams was present in all Indian forms of brahmacārya practice (celibacy). In his autobiography Gandhi anguished over the fact that over the years he had had a few wet dreams, defiling his brahmacārya practice.

20 Cf. T.31.1585.7b; Ch.2:7A; Tat, p. 94:

The 'true' (*chen*) is the *svalakṣaṇa* (*tzu-hsiang*). Prajñaptic knowledge and language (*vāc*) do not [cognize such] an object. Prajñaptic knowledge and language don't attain the svalakṣaṇa, but only the operation of samānya-lakṣaṇa (general or universal characteristic) of dharmas.

21 Cf. *Madhyānta-vibhāga*, ch. 3, and passim.

22 Cf. Chapter Ten.

23 T.31.1585.6; Ch.2:4B; Tat, p. 86.

Chapter Nineteen

Externality

The *Ch'eng wei-shih lun* continues by entertaining the following objection to its position:[1]

> [That] rūpic external perceptual-objects are distinct [entities is] clearly evident and realized[2] in immediate cognition and is perceived [as such].[3] How can you deny that, and consider them inexistent?

The text replies:

> At the moment [they are] immediately cognized and realized, [one] doesn't hold them to be external. Only afterwards, mano-[vijñānic] discrimination falsely produces the notion of externality (*wei-hsiang* 外想).[4] Thus, the perceptual-object immediately cognized is altered consciousness, and is [consciousness's] own nimitta-bhāga, and can be said to exist [in this sense]. Mano-vijñāna is attached to external substantialistic rūpas, etc., falsely schematizing (*pariklp-*, *wang-chi* 妄計) them as existents. Hence we consider them to be inexistent.

Again, the crucial factor is attachment. In immediate experience, externality as such is not perceived; rather it is retrospectively read into, imposed on immediate experience. This cognitive overlay is not done out of some inexplicable cosmic flaw (such as Hinduism's *māyā*) or because of a cognitive mistake (*pariklp-*, *wang-chi* 妄計). It is generated by discriminative, appropriational intent. In order for appropriation to appropriate there must be that which is appropriable, i.e., 'external.' Thus in the positing of external objects what, for Yogācāra, is problematic is not the positing of objects as such. The problem lies in positing *externality*, the idea or notion of the external (*wei-hsiang*). Externality is the necessary condition for appropriation.

What is at stake should not be confused or misconstrued as a question of ontological description. Yogācāric 'phenomenological description' does not aim at delineating ontological regions, but rather psychosophical regions. Yogācāra is concerned with *how* and *why* we construct for ourselves, out of our collective karma, the kind of world or *Lebenswelt* that we do. Its ontic or ontological 'reality' is of no particular interest except insofar as that reflects on our karmic circumstances. They are interested in *why* we do ontology, what compulsions drive us to affirm and negate this or that type of world or object.

Husserl claimed that his phenomenological method did not deal with real 'facts,' empirical entities, but rather aimed at 'essences,' invariant structures that had no necessary relation to empirical 'reality.'[5] The essence might be of an imaginary figure (or even a chimera) just as well as of an empirical event. Yogācāra, too, considers imaginary events (*parikalpita*) to be of equal phenomenological interest to whatever may be determined to be non-imaginary (*pariniṣpanna-paratantra*), though, unlike Husserl, they do not seek essences. Given their soteric orientation, they seek to uncover and remedy the conditions given which we bind and condition ourselves to suffer the kind of mental-cognitive tortures entailed in our coursing through saṃsāra.

Because the fundamental human problem is karma, and karma is constituted entirely within and as a cognitive-mental domain, a domain grounded on intent and intentionality, the only arena of phenomenological interest for Yogācāra is the field of consciousness. While Husserl chose in *Ideen I* to concentrate on consciousness as a specialized region for phenomenological inquiry as one of many possible regions for fruitful inquiry,[6] though a foundational region to be sure, for Yogācāra a soteric investigation of karma could begin or end nowhere else.

What does the denial of externality entail? If consciousness is always consciousness of, everything must be *of* or within consciousness. What exactly, according to the *Ch'eng wei-shih lun*, is consciousness?

Back at the beginning of the text we are given the following definition of the character *shih* 識, which, to anticipate a terminological alterity, is used throughout the *Triṃśikā* and Hsüan-tsang's other writings as a translation for either *vijñāna* (consciousness) or *vijñapti* (lit. 'cause to be known'):[7]

> 'Consciousness' (*shih: vijñāna, vijñapti*?) refers to 'discerning distinctions' (了別 *liao-pieh*). The word 'consciousness' includes the caittas, since they mutually interact [with it].

First, here as in many other places in the *Ch'eng wei-shih lun*, the text is quick to point out that 'consciousness-only' (*vijñāna-mātra, vijñapti-mātra, wei-shih*) never means an isolated citta or a single solitary consciousness, but always includes the caittas, the felt, lived textures and cognitive fields within which cognition occurs and from which its characteristics (e.g., angry, doubtful, attentive, etc.) are inscribed. Consciousness is never apart from its caittas, and thus 'consciousness only' never means that only a subjective projector exists; what is discriminated, perceived, objective, etc., also exists, but the term 'exists' will be qualified to include only that which can be experienced (directly or indirectly), i.e., only that which exerts some efficient causal effect which is (in principle) observable can be said to 'exist.' For that reason, the *citta viprayukta dharmas* (those dharmas not directly perceived by citta, such as aging and language; cf. appendix 1) are said by the *Ch'eng wei-shih lun* to not be 'real' but rather prajñapti.

Further, consciousness does not refer to a thing or a substance, but an activity. The activity is 'discerning, cognizing distinctions.' In *Triṃśikā* 2, *liao pieh* translates *vijñapti*, and *shih* translates *vijñāna*. I translated *liao-pieh* there as 'distinguishing;' it is used to describe the characteristic function of the sixth consciousness, the mano-vijñāna. *Triṃśikā* 2 says that *viṣaya* ('sense-objects') are what *liao-pieh* discerns.

So the 'definition' runs something like: consciousness and/or discerning means discerning, i.e., vijñapti means vijñapti. Or, *vijñapti* and *vijñāna* are synonyms. But does this imply that all consciousnesses, ālaya-vijñāna included, are reducible to the sixth-consciousness or its function (discerning, distinguishing sense-objects)? In *Triṃśikā* 3, the ālaya-vijñāna is indeed discussed in terms of *vijñapti*, here translated by Hsüan-tsang by the single character *liao* (discerning, distinguishing). The verse enumerates a number of 'unknowable' (*pu-k'e-chih, asaṃviditaka*) aspects of the ālaya-vijñāna; the locus of its discernments is one of them (*sthana*). Another is its appropriational involvement (*upadhi*). This implies that, while like the sixth consciousness it discerns or distinguishes (*vijñapti*), the locus of such distinctions is unclear. It would be hard to locate what we ordinarily associate with a perceptual object alongside or amongst these 'unknowables.' Thus, 'discern' or 'distinguish' (*liao*) here does not mean simply the distinguishing of 'distinct objects,' but an appropriating into consciousness of that which it perceives (the third unknowable). To cognize, discern is to appropriate; this is the Yogācāra equivalent of the Husserlian phrase 'consciousness of.'

Thus *shih* (*vijñāna* or *vijñapti*) means vijñapti (*shih, liao-pieh, liao*). At least one other equivalent for vijñapti is found in the *Ch'eng wei-shih lun*. While discussing the classificatory system of the Sarvāstivādins, in particular the Seventy Five Dharmas as explained in the *Abhidharmakośa*, two forms of rūpa are examined: *avijñapti-rūpa* and *vijñapti-rūpa*. The Chinese character used there for vijñapti is *piao* 表, which means 'to manifest, to make evident.'[8]

Altogether then ***vijñapti*** is translated by Hsüan-tsang as (1) 識 *shih* (know, understand, recognize; consciousness = vijñāna); (2) 了別 *liao-pieh* (discerning or distinguishing distinctions); (3) 了 *liao* (discern, comprehend);[9] (4) 表 *piao* (indicate, manifest, make explicit or evident).

Rejection of the "One Mind" theory: Other Minds

Consciousness is consciousness of, which is to say, all experience involves a discerning, appropriational movement. But does the denial of externality thus entail that everything is *located within* consciousness, such that consciousness is a substance within which ontologies may be established or fabricated? Wouldn't that entail that there be ultimately a single consciousness within which everything is located, since, as Yogācārins insist, experience is intersubjective? Should Yogācāra respond affirmatively to these questions, then they would unquestionably be idealists.

But the text seeks to nip this type of misreading in the bud. The *Ch'eng wei-shih lun* affirms the existence of other minds.[10] The opponent, recognizing that acceptance of other minds entails rejecting a solipsistic idealism, asks:[11]

Since already [you admit] a sense-object different [from your own consciousness, viz. another's mind which can be cognized], how can [your position] be called 'consciousness-only'?

The text responds:

How extremely opinionated! You have doubts about where to locate [the distinct factors involved in] contact (*sparśa*).[12]

Traditionally, *sparśa* (lit. 'touch') is defined as the meeting, contact, encounter, 'touch' between a sense organ and a sense-object, implying the organ is internal and the object is external; consciousness is that which arises due to this contact. The opponent has doubts about the location of the object of contact, i.e., what is within and what is outside consciousness. Since the point is not to locate things and perceivers on an ontological spatial map, but to analyze the manner in which we cognize, the question is wrongheaded, since for Yogācāra to say that all experience is of consciousness or even in consciousness—vijñāna straddles the genitive ["of"] and locative ["in"], and the conflation of vijñāna with vijñapti invokes the instrumental ["by, with"], dative ["for, in pursuit of"], ablative ["from, because"], etc.—is only to therapeutically rephrase the tautological proposition that all experience is experiential. The text continues:

How could the *Wei-shih* teaching only espouse a single consciousness? That's not the case. And why not?

Once and for all a very common misconception concerning Yogācāra as an idealism can be put to final rest. Yogācāra does not posit any single overarching 'mind' or 'consciousness' as the source or solitary existent of or in the world. There is no 'Cosmic ālaya-vijñāna' of which we are all parts or manifestations. There is no One Mind subtending the universe. The world is populated, according to Yogācāra, by a multitude of distinct sentient beings, each with its own consciousness system (*citta-kalāpa*). The *Ch'eng wei-shih lun* is as explicit on this point as it can be.

You should examine[13] and alertly listen. If there were only a single consciousness how could the ten directions, the sages and ordinary folk, causes and effects, and so on, be distinguished? Who would look for [the teachings] and who would espouse them? What [would differentiate] the Dharma from its seeker?

Thus, the words 'wei-shih' have a deep meaning. The word *shih* (consciousness, vijñapti, vijñāna) in general reveals that all sentient beings each have [their own] eight consciousnesses, six types of caittas,[14] altered [consciousness] (*so-pien*) *qua nimitta-* and *darśana-*[*bhāgas*], distinguishing divisions,[15] and *tathatā* which is disclosed through the principle of emptiness.

Since the self-characteristics (*svalakṣaṇa*) of the consciousnesses, [the dharmas] associated with consciousness, the two altered [*bhāgas*], the three divisions,[16] and the four real natures [of the preceding categories][17], as well as all other dharmas, are never separate from consciousness, we have established the [sense in which we use the] term *shih*.

In other words, *vijñāna* and *vijñapti* designates the inseparability of what is experienced from its medium, viz. consciousness. Nowhere here—once again it should be noted—did the text make any causative or primordial claims. The issue clearly and simply is one of cognitive inseparability.

> The word *wei* (*mātra*, only, nothing but) is only [used to reveal what is] concealed from the fools who are attached to [the idea that] apart from the consciousnesses there are real, substantial, entitative rūpas, etc.

The denial of externality once again is aimed at overcoming an attachment.

But does denial of externality mean that nothing whatsoever exists outside of my consciousness? On the one hand, Yogācāra enjoys arguing away the existence of externals, primarily because epistemologically realism is difficult if not impossible to establish unequivocally. Since the more Yogācāra undermined the security of their opponents' epistemological grounding, the more insistent, agitated and vociferous their opponents became, it grew more and more obvious that what drives the realist to posit and validate externality is a deep inner anxiety, a psychic need, and not the dry detached attitude with which they they would like to pretend. Revealing these inner *āśravas* is the whole point of the Yogācāra analysis. To prove 'only mind exists' as a sort of doctrine or dogma, a position to take because it is the 'correct' position, is to thoroughly miss the Yogācārin's point. By eliminating the projected status of what can be grasped, the grasper as well is thrown into question. Consciousness has a quality—beyond its ubiquity—that makes it suitable for this therapeutic task. Consciousness itself is in and as itself impossible to grasp, rendering it less susceptible to the psychosophic abuses that an external, physical, possessible world is prone to, or even encourages. One can cling to ideas, but not a fleeting moment of consciousness.

The therapeutic effectiveness of this strategy is recounted in the famous (though most likely apocryphal) story of Hui-k'o, who was to become the second Ch'an patriarch, and Bodhidharma (the first patriarch). This story illustrates the sort of soteric power made available by these tactics. Hui-k'o, originally a Confucian scholar, became convinced of the efficacy of Buddhism and became equally convinced that Bodhidharma should be his teacher. He approached Bodhidharma for instruction while the latter was at the Shao-lin monastery, but Bodhidharma was less than receptive.[18]

> In order to prove his sincerity and thus receive the teachings, Hui-k'o stood near where Bodhidharma was meditating and waited for hour upon hour in earnest supplication. Snow began to fall from the cold winter sky, but Hui-k'o was undaunted. Over the course of the evening the snow accumulated to Hui-k'o's knees, but when Bodhidharma finally noticed the supplicant and discovered why he was there, the Indian sage only warned him about the difficulty of practicing the "unsurpassable, wondrous path of the Buddhas."
>
> Finally, in a surge of zealous desperation and with thoughts of the trials of former enlightened ones, Hui-k'o took a knife and cut off his left arm, placing it

> in front of Bodhidharma. Permitted at last, through this extraordinary (if macabre) demonstration of self-sacrifice, to receive the teaching, Hui-k'o asked Bodhidharma: "My mind is not at peace; please pacify it for me."
>
> To this Bodhidharma replied: "Bring your mind here and I will pacify it for you."
>
> Hui-k'o: "I have searched for my mind, but it is completely unobtainable (i.e., imperceptible; or "I cannot find it anywhere")."
>
> Bodhidharma: "I have [now] completely pacified your mind for you."
>
> Although Bodhidharma's final reply might appear as a neat piece of sophistry to a modern reader, it was enough, according to the traditional account, to inspire Hui-k'o to a great realization or enlightenment experience.

According to other early sources, Hui-k'o's arm was actually lost to robbers and not symbolically 'sacrificed,' but the story shows how the intangible, ungraspable characteristic of mind can be used soterically; how its resistance to appropriation may incur *prapañcopaśama*, the pacification or bringing to rest of the linguistic-cognitive excesses, the anxieties which we see *as* the world in the place of the actual world itself (*abhūta-parikalpita*).[19] Bodhidharma is administering some applied Yogācāra theory. This instance of Ch'an praxis instantiates the Yogācāric method for realizing the emptiness of mind. Bodhidharma after all was said by tradition to have taken the *Laṅkāvatāra Sūtra* as his root text, thus indicating that his approach was steeped in Yogācāra.

The denial of externality constitutes part of a process, aimed at emptying not only 'the grasped,' but the grasper as well. Neither transcendental object nor transcendental subject survive Yogācāra's phenomenological method.

As we have just seen, Yogācāra does not advocate solipsism. Consciousness is intersubjective; karma is communal as well as personal. Therefore, the existence of other minds is affirmed. The above cited passage from the *Ch'eng wei-shih lun* is crucial, since it unequivocally discusses the perception by a consciousness of that which is other (i.e., external) to that consciousness. Not only is no attempt made to reduce 'other minds' to mere projections of one's own, but the very core of Buddhism—the teaching of Dharma by one sentient being to another—is made absolutely contingent on there being consciousnesses external to and yet perceptible by other consciousnesses. In other words, *the entire point of Yogācāra phenomenology rests on both the necessity and possibility that there be communication between distinct minds.* Consciousness, to say it again, is thoroughly intersubjective.

There are many consciousnesses. The text will avoid using the argument that one consciousness views another by inference based on observation of what the other is bodily, physically doing—though that is implied, and becomes later in Dharmakīrti's time the standard Buddhist response to the theory of other minds.[20] Nonetheless, it does portray the mind as a mirror that reflects a world around it. The cited passage walks a thin descriptive line. It implies that something besides the mind is reflected in the mind, but it remains excruciatingly silent about the rūpic status of that something. Other minds are known by what? What is it that one observes as the other? The other's own immediate thoughts to him/herself? Or a more corporeal, gestural, behavioral exhibition of what that other thinks and intends?

The opponent asks:[21]

> [Even if] external rūpa is substantially inexistent (*shih wu* 實無), [it is still] possible that perceptual-objects (*ching*) are not within consciousness. [If] other minds substantially exist (*shih-yu* 實有) [and all that really exists must be perceived, and thus within consciousness], why aren't they ālambana (*so-yüan* 所緣, lit. 'objective condition'; in Skt: 'cognitive support') for one's own [consciousness, i.e., why aren't they perceived directly]?
>
> Who says that the other's consciousness is not a perceptual-object for one's own consciousness? We only refuse to say that it is an 'immediate ālambana' (*sākṣāt-ālambana*) [i.e., it is not perceived directly, but indirectly].[22] This means that when [another's] consciousness arises [in your awareness], it is neither substantial [i.e., not tangible, etc.] nor made to function [by you] (*tso-yung* 作用, *kāritra*). [Your consciousness, when perceiving another mind] is not like a hand, for instance, which immediately/directly grasps an external [tangible] thing, nor like the sun which extends its radiance immediately-directly illuminating external perceptual-objects.

The examples of 'hand' and 'sun' are interesting illustrations. The example of the hand carries two implications. First, I can move my hand by conscious intent (*cetanā*), so *my* hand acts out my bodily karma (*kāyika-karma*). You can't move someone else's mind (or hand) the way you can move your own, since it has an independent cetanā. Secondly, hands grasp tangible things. But consciousness does not 'grasp' (執 *chih*, appropriate) other minds, implying that minds are intangible. Again we see the text emphasizing consciousness' resistance to being appropriated. The second example, the sun, alludes to the *prakāśa* model of perception, which was common in India. *Prakāśa* implies that consciousness shines, radiates, illuminates objects, i.e., perception is not the passive reception of light from visible objects by the eye, or sounds by the ear, etc., but the active illuminating by consciousness of that which is perceived. Consciousness shines on everything, making all appear. But the *Ch'eng wei-shih lun* clearly is rejecting this model. The sun shines (*prakāśa*) on each object, lighting each up so as to make it colorful and visible. Similarly, an idealist might claim that consciousness illumines objects, bestowing its light (*prakāśa*) on them; that to perceive something means to shine a mental spotlight on it. But while discussing other minds, minds which are other than one's own consciousness, which operate independently (i.e., they are not made to function or behave as they do by *me*), the text reinforces their independence by reminding us that we don't 'generate' or create other minds (or objects) by illuminating them.

Does this mean that it would be proper to call other minds 'external' to consciousness? Since, as we've seen, the Yogācārins are taking external to mean 'radically separate from consciousness,' the answer would have to be negative, not only because the 'external' consciousness would itself be a consciousness, but because, though in some sense it is independent of me, I still do perceive it, even if not directly. It is not separated from my consciousness, though distinct.[23]

This specialized sense of the denial of externality must be kept in mind if one wishes to correctly interpret the thrust of the Yogācāra argument. Nothing whatsoever, especially if it can be appropriated by conversation or cognition, can properly be said to be radically separate from consciousness. This does not entail the absurd consequence that my consciousness and my consciousness alone has thoroughly and utterly constructed the entire Lived-world in which I locate myself as a self. While there are things that operate in ways that are significantly independent of my consciousness, their independence does not imply externality. I perceive other minds as moved by wills and intents other than my own. But I *perceive them.* Does this non-external 'external' mind establish a perceptual pattern that might equally be applied to other things? In other words, if Yogācāra grants that there exist consciousnesses besides my own, which I can only perceive remotely, not directly, then might there not also be other sorts of things and 'perceptual-objects' (*viṣaya*) in my perceptual field whose 'existence' (or intentionality) is likewise independent of me? If so, then all shreds of metaphysical idealism will have been precluded from the Yogācāra position.

The 'Mirror' metaphor

The text, having rejected the 'grasping' model of perception (like a hand) and the illuminational model (*prakāśa*), now proffers the Yogācāra model:

> It is only like a mirror, which 'perceives' what appears [within it as] external objects. [This kind of perception is the type we] term 'discerning (*liao*) other minds,' though they can't be immediately-directly discerned. What is discerned immediately-directly is [one's consciousness'] own alterations (*so-pien*). Hence the [*Saṅdhinirmocana*] *Sūtra* says: There is not the slightest dharma which can grasp the remaining dharmas; only when consciousness arises does one project/perceive the appearance of that, which is called 'grasping that thing.'

Does the mirror-mind, then, only perceive itself and other minds, or does it also perceive rūpa, etc.? The very next line, which concludes the argument is:

> Other mind is this sort of condition; rūpa, etc. are the same case.

This is tantamount to admitting that rūpa exists independently, though not separate from my mind. It is known indirectly, it is a remote ālambana. How could such a crucial passage have gone unnoticed for so long?

Vallée Poussin's "Idealist" interpretation

We may look at Vallée Poussin's 'explanation' as an example of precisely how a reading of the *Ch'eng wei-shih lun* can itself be precisely an instance of what the *Ch'eng wei-shih lun* in its entirety is warning against, namely, the imposition of one's presuppositions onto or into something such that one misreads or mistakes one's (erroneous) interpretation for the thing interpreted. Vallée Poussin's leading presupposition, which he already announces on his first page, is that Vijñapti-mātratā is idealism. He takes every opportunity available to interpret and translate the *Ch'eng wei-shih lun* in concert with that assumption. To be fair, it was the universal assumption of his generation, and thus, had he assumed that vijñapti-mātra stood for some other, non-idealist position, that would have been both surprising and noteworthy.[24] When he arrives at the passage just cited above, though, he recognizes that to equate 'other minds'—which are clearly identified as originating and operating independently of the consciousness to which they are other—with rūpa disrupts the idealist position. What does he do?

To support an idealistic reading he offers the following gloss on the meaning of rūpa in the line just discussed:[25]

> The Rūpa which is the *nimittabhāga* of the other mind (*de la pensée d'autrui*) (the body of the other, developed from the Vijñāna of the other), and also the Rūpa which is the development of an other Vijñāna of the same person (*de la même personne*). [That is to say: the cakṣurvijñāna (darśanabhāga) has for an immediate *ālambana* its own *nimitta*, which is a reproduction of the Rūpa developed from the Ālaya-vijñāna.]

This is quite fanciful, and, at best, partially faithful to the *Ch'eng wei-shih lun*. Indeed, all we know directly and immediately (*sākṣāt*) is the alterity of our own consciousness. This can be illustrated by a physiological example of tactile perception.

Technically speaking, when I 'touch the table' I do not actually feel the table. My feelings, my tactile sensibility *qua* feeling is produced by nerves, and the nerves are *within* my skin, not on or outside the dermal surface. My nerves never come into direct contact (*sparśa*) with the table. My nerves interpret alterations of my skin *as* the texture of an external object, when it is only the inside of my own skin that I am feeling, that I perceive directly. The texture of the table is perceived—but remotely. Knowing another mind (or any rūpa), the *Ch'eng wei-shih lun* is arguing, follows the same pattern. I know of other minds remotely. All I know directly is what happens immediately within my own consciousness. In other words, *consciousness is always and everywhere a case of cognitive closure.* But the closure can never be absolute. What is not *of my consciousness* in the genitive and generative sense (i.e., what does not exist simply in virtue of my consciousness either possessing or creating it) may still exert an influence on me, it may still be perceived remotely, i.e., filtered through my cognitive apparatus. No matter how far away, it may still arise on the surface of my 'mental mirror,' and appear there as of equal depth as everything else reflected/projected (*pratibimba*) there. But before we examine what Yogācāra means with its use of the mirror metaphor, let us further examine Vallée Poussin's gloss.

He recognizes that what is perceived of the other mind is not a disembodied consciousness, but an embodied behavioral configuration. Now the phrase *de la même personne* is ambiguous. *Même* can mean 'same,' or it can mean 'one's own,' i.e., *même personne* can mean either that the rūpa is developed by the 'same person,' i.e., the perceiver of the other mind, or that it is developed by 'its own person,' i.e., the other person him/herself. This is a tantalizing ambiguity, since the first option is unabashedly idealist—in fact solipsistic, a position which we have already seen the *Ch'eng wei-shih lun* reject—while the second option opens other possibilities. Vallée Poussin tries to straddle both options. His illustrative example of the *cakṣurvijñāna* (*darśanabhāga*) comes to hinge on a single word: "reproduction." Although he is not specific about whose ālaya-vijñāna has 'developed' the initial rūpa, the perceiver's or the other mind's, the perceiver's perceptual field (*nimittabhāga*) contains as its content "a reproduction of the Rūpa developed from the Ālaya-vijñāna." Assuming he means that the rūpa is produced by the other mind, when I see your 'mind,' I am actually seeing a reproduction of the rūpa that your mind has produced. He has made the causative metaphysical argument—i.e., consciousness alone creates the world—despite the fact that, as we noted above, the *Ch'eng wei-shih lun* consistently refrains from making such an argument, even when such a claim would expedite its cause. On what does Vallée Poussin base his interpretation?

At the end of his gloss he writes: "See p. 446." If one turns to that page looking for a declarative pronouncement on the ability of the ālaya-vijñāna to create rūpa, one will be sorely disappointed.[26] The discussion underway there concerns *ālambana-pratyaya*, i.e., what sort of cognitive condition is an ālambana. On Vallée Poussin's page the only mention of 'other minds,' much less rūpa being created by an ālaya-vijñāna, comes in the first of three arguments concerning what, if anything, the ālaya-vijñāna takes for an ālambana-pratyaya. The *Ch'eng wei-shih lun* will reject the position laid out there as 'unreasonable.' Since this section of the text discusses another significant Yogācāric notion which has been thoroughly misconstrued—the *chih* 質 or hyle that Vallée Poussin and many since have translated, incredibly, as "archetype"—it would be worthwhile examining it in some detail.

Notes

1 T.31.1585.39b25-39c3.7; Ch.7:15A; Tat, 520.

2 *Fen ming hsien-cheng* 分明現證. The compound *hsien-cheng* translates *sākṣāt-kārin* (*Index*, p. 122). *Sākṣāt-kāra* implies being put in front of one's eyes, making evident to the senses;

"evident or intuitive perception, realization" (Monier-Williams, p. 1198), and signifies the same thing as the English phrase "seeing it with my own eyes." It is tempting to think of Husserl's notion of *Evidenz*, but as this form of 'believing' is about to be criticized as bespeaking a naive viewpoint, I have translated *hsien-cheng* more literally. In Chinese *hsien* means 'to make evident, become manifest, to (be) see(n)' and in Yogācāra literature frequently signifies 'projection.' *Index*, p. 121, gives a number of Sanskrit correspondences: *ābhāsa-prāpta, ut-PAD, upa-LABH, DṚŚ, pratyutpanna, pratyupasthita, madhyama, varttamān*, etc. *Cheng* means 'realization.'

3 *Hsien liang so-te* 現量所得. *Liang* translates *parimāṇa*, 'measure, measuring out', "measure of any kind, e.g. circumference, length, size, weight, number, value, duration... having measure, measurable" (Monier-Williams, p. 599). It is cognate to *pramāṇa*, means of cognition; I have translated it here as 'cognition.' *So-te* often translates *upalabdhi*, 'perceptually grasp.'

4 The text says *yi* (manas) and not *yi-shih* (mano-vijñāna), but VP, p. 428-429, notes that this section "follows very closely the *She-lun*. For this line VP has: [During immediate knowing] "color isn't conceived as external (because the Pratyakṣa attains the svabhāvas). It is later that the Manovijñāna (the reflexion of Manas: *manovikalpa*) falsely creates the notion of externality (*bāhyasaṃjñām* or *bāhyabuddhiṃ janayati*)." His use of the word svabhāvas is questionable; his justification comes from a section of the text (his p. 87; Tat, pp. 92-94; T.31.1585.7b; Ch.2:6B-7A) that discusses svalakṣaṇa, but not svabhāvas. VP equates them (p. 87, "svalakṣaṇa = svabhāvas"). But the discussion there concerns unique particulars revealed in perception in opposition to the generalities indulged in by language and reasoning which, properly speaking, is a matter of *svalakṣaṇa* in opposition to *samānya*, and not *svabhāva*..

5 *Ideas*, op. cit., e.g., introduction, part I, and *passim*.

6 *Ideas, ibid.*, ch. 4, pp. 101ff. As to his intent, he writes on p. 101, in reference to the *epoché*:

> The disconnecting of the world does not as a matter of fact mean the disconnecting of the number series, for instance, and the arithmetic relative to it.
>
> However, we do not take this path, nor does our goal lie in its direction. That goal we could also refer to as *the winning of a new region of Being, the distinctive character of which has not yet been defined*, a region of *individual* Being, like every genuine region. We must leave the sequel to teach us what that more precisely means.

It is, no doubt, to this passage that Merleau-Ponty, in the introduction to his *Phenomenology of Perception*, elliptically refers when he writes of Heidegger, "...the whole of *Sein und Zeit* springs from an indication given by Husserl." (*Phenomenology of Perception*, tr. by Colin Smith, NJ: Humanities Press, 1962, p. vii) Merleau-Ponty begins his own definition of phenomenology by saying, "Phenomenology is the study of essences: the essence of perception or the essence of consciousness, for example." (*ibid.*)

7 T.31.1585.1a-1b; Ch.1:2A; Tat, p. 10.

8 Cf. T.31.1585.4c; Ch.1:14A; Tat, pp. 54-56.

9 *Liao* carries another meaning which is interesting in our context. It marks bringing something to a conclusion. As 'comprehending', then, it involves an understanding that comes at the conclusion of a process. As conclusion it implies bringing things to a close, bringing a pursuit or endeavor to *closure*, e.g., closing a legal case ("this case is closed").

10 Some of the *Ch'eng wei-shih lun*'s statements on the existence of other minds will be translated below, immediately after the argument currently under discussion.

11 T.31.1585.39c; Ch.7:16A; Tat, pp. 522-524.

12 Tat translated this sentence as "And how sceptical you are regarding all things that you come into contact with!" i.e., the 'contact' being contact with the Wei-shih teachings! It could be read that way, but only as a reinforcing irony which plays on the notion of 'contact' I am about to outline.

13 'Examine' = *ti* 諦 elsewhere used for the *satyas*, e.g., *saṃvṛti-satya* and *paramārtha-satya*, as well as the four noble "truths."

14 General, Specific, Advantageous, Mental Disturbances, Secondary Mental Disturbances and Indeterminate. See appendix 1.

15 The reference is unclear. Tat, following VP (p. i.431), takes it to refer to the *viprayukta-dharmas.*

16 Reference is to whatever was the referent of the previous note. VP interprets the three to indicate caittas, rūpa and the *viprayukta-dharmas.*

17 Again unclear. I am following VP, as does Tat.

18 I've transcribed this account from McRae's *The Northern School and the Formation of Early Ch'an Buddhism*, pp. 15-16.

19 The coincidence of the Indian Buddhist notion of *prapañcopaśama* or the 'making peaceful' (*upaśama*) of prapañca and Mencius' notion of pacifying the 'perturbed' (lit. 'moving') mind marked a point of consolidation between Chinese Buddhism and Confucianism.

20 Cf. Dharmakīrti's *Santānāntara-siddhi, with Vinītadeva's Commentary*, translated [freely] from T. Stcherbatsky's Russian version into English by Harish C. Gupta, in *Papers of Th. Stcherbatsky, Indian Studies Past & Present* (Calcutta, 1969), pp. 71-121.

21 T.31.1585.39c; Ch.7:15B-16A; Tat, pp. 520-522.

22 The *Ch'eng wei-shih lun* differentiates two types of ālambana: Immediate or direct ālambana (*ch'in so-yüan* 親所緣) and remote ālambana (*shu so-yüan* 疏所緣). Cf. Tat, pp. 542-544; VP pp. 445f, and below.

23 Hsüan-tsang does not reproduce Vasubandhu's arguments concerning other minds from the *Viṃśatikā*, possibly because the issue had acquired a more sophisticated treatment by the time he arrived in India. According to Vasubandhu, we can know other minds, but, while UnAwakened, in an unclear way. He reminds us that we hardly know our own minds, much less anyone else's, because we still have not overcome the obstruction of grasper-grasped. Buddha, however, knows other minds more clearly than we know our own. Hence, when one becomes Awakened, other minds become easy to discern. *Viṃśatikā-bhāṣya* 21.

24 Tuck, in *Comparative Philosophy and the Philosophy of Scholarship: On the Western Interpretation of Nāgārjuna* (Oxford: Oxford University Press, 1990), ch. 2, chronicles the influence of German Idealism on Buddhist studies during this period. Cf. J.W. de Jong, *A Brief History of Buddhist Studies in Europe and America* (Tokyo: Kosei, 1997), ch. 2.

25 VP p. i.430. Countless examples could be collected from other works about the *Ch'eng wei-shih lun* or Yogācāra as well. For instance, Tat, on p. 547, 'translates': "The five material Indriyas or organs. They have as their essential nature the subtle Rupa (eyes, etc.) which is the manifestation of Mulavijnana, etc." Has the *Ch'eng wei-shih lun* finally said that ālaya-vijñāna 'manifests' rūpa? In Chinese not only is there no word for 'manifest', but the passage reads quite differently from Tat's causative-idealist 'interpretation':

> The five rūpa organs, which alterations (*so-pien*) in the mūla-vijñāna, etc., take in through the eyes, etc. Pure rūpa 淨色 *ching-se*) is regarded as their nature.

The passage actually says that their nature is 'pure rūpa'. One sees a visible object (rūpa) through the eye, and that visible experience of 'pure rūpa' is registered as "alterations in the mūla-vijñāna, etc." Far from implying a causative idealist theory, the ālaya-vijñāna (a.k.a. mūla-vijñāna) and other consciousnesses are passive recorders (*so-pien*) of the activities of the visual organ and its corresponding object.

26 VP pp. ii.446f; cf. T.31.1585.40c-41a1.6; Ch.7:19B-20A; Tat, p. 544.

Chapter Twenty

The Four Conditions

The *Ch'eng wei-shih lun* accepts four types of conditions (*pratyaya*), and discusses them in some detail.[1] They are:

Hetu-pratyaya 因緣 *yin-yüan*

Samanantara-pratyaya 等無間緣 *teng wu-hsien yüan*

Ālambana-pratyaya 所緣緣 *so-yüan yüan*

Adhipati-pratyaya 增上緣 *tseng-shang yüan*

Hetu-pratyaya

Hetu-pratyaya includes the saṃskṛta-dharmas that directly en-act their fruit (effect; *phala*, 果 *kuo*). There are two types of hetu-pratyaya:

1a) Seeds (*bījās*) residing in the *mūla-vijñāna* (fundamental consciousness) having the power to 'differentiate' (*ch'a-pieh* 差別) "the advantageous and the defiled, the non-recording, the various realms and lands, etc." This is again subdivided into two types, (i) those seeds which produce the same species as themselves in a subsequent effect or series, and (ii) those which produce the same seeds simultaneously.

1b) Exactly how to translate this 'causal-condition' is unclear. The Chinese is *hsien-hsing* 現行, lit. 'projecting/perceiving activity,' implying what is operating or present in one's perceptual field. *Hsing*, which literally means 'walking,' is also the Chinese equivalent for *saṃskāra* (embodied conditioning). *Hsien* means 'present,' so that this could be read as saṃskāras that have emerged from their latent potentiality, that have become actual. That seems to be the thinking behind the interpretation of Vallée Poussin and Tat. Tat, following Vallée Poussin renders it "actual dharmas," but neither of the Chinese terms technically means either 'actual' or 'dharma.' Hsüan-tsang used the term *hsien-hsing* to translate a number of Sanskrit terms in his rendition of the *Abhidharmakoṣa*.[2] These are: *kriyā-*, *vṛtr-*, *samudācāra*, *saṃmukhī-bhāva*, *saṃmukhī-bhūta*. In the *Yogācārabhūmi* he also used *hsien-hsing* for *adhyācāra*, *pracāra*, and *pratipadyamāna*.[3] The semantic range covered by these terms is highly suggestive of a number of intriguing possibilities.

Let us look briefly at these terms to see what, if anything, they share in common, since Hsüan-tsang apparently understood them all as *hsien-hsing*.

Kriyā means a strictly physical activity that occurs without either intent or karmic consequence. Since Yogācāra phenomenology concerns only the karmic realm, *kriyā* seems unlikely here, especially since this type of hetu-pratyaya is defined as the operation of the seven consciousnesses (i.e., all but the ālaya-vijñāna). This would suggest *vṛtr*, or more accurately, *pravṛtti*, the turning around and operating of the six consciousnesses, since the six consciousnesses are called *pravṛtti-vijñāna*. But that would leave out the seventh consciousnessess, manas. Moreover, Hsüan-tsang has already established other terms in the *Ch'eng wei-shih lun* for *pravṛtti*, so it would not be necessary to inject a new one (though, as we saw with the term *vijñapti*, Hsüan-tsang was not incapable of proliferating terminological correspondences).

Samudācāra means 'a presentation, offering, entertainment (for a guest); proper or correct usage or conduct or behavior; intention, purpose, design, motive.'[4] This term provides everything that *kriyā* lacked! This term is a very reasonable candidate: the seven consciousnesses are like a presentation, an offering, an entertainment for or from the ālaya-vijñāna. The seven consciousnesses are thoroughly intentional, so that 'intention, purpose, design, motive' also serve well descriptively.

But the last term is stunning. *Saṃmukhī* means 'to place facing, to make something one's chief aim.'[5] The term found in the *Kośa* is not just *saṃmukhī*, but *saṃmukhā-bhāva*. *Saṃmukhā-bhū* means 'to be or stand face to face or opposite, to be opposed to,' i.e., to be *con-fronting*. To project an *artha* before one, or to confront that which is before one: But which? Both? The term *sammukhin* mediates: it means 'a looking-glass, a mirror.' Again, perception is conceived of on the model of a mirror.

Adhyācāra, pracāra, pratipadyamāna imply what is useful because of being ready to hand.

We needn't choose between these Sanskrit options. Hsüan-tsang may have had all of them in mind (though in general, *samudā-√car* and *adhyācāra* would most commonly be used in this context). Hetu-pratyaya may actually implicate the connotations of all of them. What, then, is *hsien-hsing*?

If the first type, the bīja hetu-pratyaya, involves effects that arise out of one's own ālaya-vijñāna, effects which are of the same 'species' (*tzu lei* 自類) as the seed, then, logically speaking, this other type of causal condition (*hsien-hsing*) should be either (i) what produces effects which are of a different species than their causes, (ii) causes other than seeds, or (iii) causes arising elsewhere than from the ālaya-vijñāna; or some combination of the three.

The text notes that the two types of hetu-pratyaya interact in three ways: (i) seeds producing seeds, (ii) seeds producing *hsien-hsing*, and (iii) *hsien-hsing* producing seeds. Significantly, *hsien-hsing* producing *hsien-hsing* is not listed, probably because these would be completely outside the ālaya-vijñāna and thus not cognizable, and thus not producing *effects in experience, in cognition*. Again we must remember that Yogācāra is doing cognitive phenomenology, not metaphysical ontology. Yogācāra is talking about discernible effects in experience, not constructing metaphysical causation theories.

Seeds producing other seeds describes latent karmic conditioning, which takes place unconsciously. Seeds, according to Yogācāra, are momentary, so karmic continuity proceeds through causal chains of seeds that arise and cease each moment, being perpetually replaced with seeds of the same kind. Hence an akuśala seed, for instance, does not lie dormant, intact, until some later date when it reaches fruition, but perpetuates itself by continually regenerating new seeds of the same type that replace it in a sequence that runs until the fruit is produced. The theory of seed-series was discussed in Part III, chapter ten.

Seeds producing *hsien-hsing* would mean seeds coming to fruition as the experiential content one con-fronts, en-counters. Latent anger or passion, for instance, comes to fruition when a certain situation fructifies it. *Hsien-hsing*—since they are the content of the perceptual field already inflected with the felt textures of one's prior conditioning—can engender further seeds, planting the conditioning of an experiential moment back in the ālaya-vijñāna, beginning a new seed-series.

Put another way, in terms of experience or karma, the *fact* that a certain object in my proximity possesses certain properties or qualities is karmically insignificant. It is my perception and interpretation of that object—in terms of the intentions brought to bear on it—that holds all the karmic significance. The object *in my experience* is the one ālayically interpreted, not the abstraction some metaphysics will posit out there for me. Objects *as experienced* are already interpreted—Merleau-Ponty would say they already embody intentionalities—and that interpretation is what appears to me as the object. Buddhists have been clear about that since coining *saṃjñā* (associative-thinking) as their crucial term for 'perception.' The notion of the ālaya-vijñāna provided the Yogācārins with a way to flesh out (literally and figuratively) the dynamics and details of this perceptual interpretive economy.

Samanantara-pratyaya

The second condition is the *samanantara-pratyaya*, the immediately antecedent condition. This condition is employed to solve two problems: the problem of continuity, and the problem of what breaks saṃsāric continuity upon entrance into nirvāṇa.

At first the antecedent condition seems like a repeat of the hetu-pratyaya, since it produces repetitions of the same 'species' sequentially, though here the emphasis is on the same species immediately following from its antecedent condition, in contiguous moments. As one condition discharges its efficient causal force, it disappears and is immediately replaced with its effect, a subsequent condition. The disappearing condition, which existed momentarily, is the 'antecedent condition.' According the the *Ch'eng wei-shih lun*, this is unlike the seeds, since seeds may operate simultaneously with their effect, while the antecedent condition is always contiguous but sequentially prior. Moreover the seeds of a species operate at all times (i.e., their series tend to be perpetual, continuous), while the antecedent condition is always momentary.

The eight consciousness are likewise not antecedent to each other since they don't conditionally intermix in this fashion (i.e., for example, manas doesn't disappear in order for visual consciousness to arise; the disappearance of one consciousness is not the cause of the others). Like seeds, the consciousnesses 'continue' through time, and don't utterly disappear (though in a sense they do, since the consciousnesses are neither substances—and hence ungraspable—nor substrata). They structurally and functionally perdure.[6]

> Caittas and citta always operate together, and since they interact in such a way that they harmonize into a single envisioning (*tādṛśa*), they cannot be prajñaptically separated or differentiated, and thus their interaction constitutes a samanantara-pratyaya.

The Chinese translation of *samanantara-pratyaya* literally reads: 'same with-no-gap condition,' i.e., not the slightest gap intrudes between the disappearance of the antecedent and the arising of the subsequent condition. Cittas and caittas mutually produce each other, but so seamlessly, that they can be called 'antecedent.'[7]

The nirvāṇa issue is addressed as follows:[8]

> When entering (the nirvāṇa) without remainder[9] the mind grows extremely faint and rarefied, and is unable to open [another path] or lead the way onward. It cannot produce another antecedent dharma, and so it is not this [sort of] condition.

Continuity, which has perpetuated the cycle of saṃsāra as well as carried one through the projectory of the stages of the mārga, is here radically and utterly disrupted. All continuity occurs on a background of radical momentariness, but a momentariness that replaces and replenishes itself from moment to moment durationally. The movement ultimately stops once and for all at the 'entrance' to nirvāṇa without remainder.

There ensues a detailed discussion of the *ādāna-vijñāna* (the 'taking or grasping consciousness,' another name for the ālaya-vijñāna[10]) as samanantara-pratyaya, and into which realm within the tridhātu one is reborn according to which sort of antecedent condition. While an impure or contaminated (*sāśrava*) *ādāna* can engender a pure or uncontaminated (*anāśrava*) *ādāna*, the inverse cannot occur, since the Great Mirror Cognition, once attained, is never cut off. This offers an optimistic, progressional view. By implication, 'good,' over countless kalpas, by the law of probability, must eventually triumph, since good can arise from bad antecedent causes, but not the other way around. Similar discussions are given concerning the remaining consciousnesses. Since each consciousness has its own sort of object, one of the consciousnesses may be anāśrava while another may be sāśrava. The discussion turns to what conditions are antecedent to which key attainments along the path to nirvāṇa, i.e., which conditions immediately precede which? The background issue is: What condition, if any, is *the sine qua non* condition for the attainment of nirvāṇa? The answer: *none*! Since nirvāṇa is asaṃskṛta (unconditioned), no condition can be given which would produce it. Thus it is attained negatively, i.e., by cutting off, destroying obstructions. Nirvāṇa is never a presence, and is 'attained' only by making obstructions absent, that is, by eliminating them. Neither arising nor ceasing (*anutpāda-anirodha*), nirvāṇa cannot be produced by any means.

Ālambana-pratyaya

The most important condition for Yogācāra phenomenology is the *ālambana-pratyaya*, the 'objective-condition condition,' to translate the Chinese literally. The *Ch'eng wei-shih lun* initially defines this condition thus:[11]

> The ālambana condition means if there exists a dharma,[12] [it will have such-and-such] an appearance;[13] the mind will sometimes correspond with it (*hsiang-ying*), [such that it will] be cognized and perceptually-grasped.[14]

Again we see the *Ch'eng wei-shih lun* assigning some responsibility for the characteristics of a cognition to a seemingly autonomous dharma or objective-condition. If a dharma exists, it will have its own certain style of appearance, its own *ākāra*. If the mind happens to correspond with it (*samprayukta*), that *ākāra* will be cognized and grasped. Technically, this would be limited to the five basic types of samprayukta caittas.[15] The dharma itself, apparently, is not cognized directly, but is perceptually grasped in terms of its 'appearance' (*ākāra, tai-hsiang*). K'uei-chi points out that *hsiang*, which usually stands for *lakṣaṇa* or *nimitta* (images, forms), here stands for the thing-itself (*t'i-hsiang* 體相) and not its image (*hsiang-hsiang* 相象).[16]

There are two types of ālambana conditions:

1) the immediate-direct (*sākṣāt, ch'in* 親, lit: 'intimate, familially related'), and
2) the remote (*shu* 疏, lit: 'estranged').

What distinguishes them?

The text gives the following definitions:[17]

> If [what is] given to the cognizor[18] is itself (*t'i*) not separated from him, [i.e., it is] internally cognized and perceptually-grasped[19] as being of the darśana-bhāga, [nimitta-bhāga], etc., that you should know is the immediate-direct ālambana.
>
> If [what is] given to the cognizor is itself separated from it (i.e., the cognizor), [i.e., it is] internally cognized and perceptually-grasped such that it is considered to have arisen from a hyle,[20] that you should know is the remote ālambana.

In other words, if what is perceived is exhaustively and transparently given through the lived-body (*darśana-bhāga*) and perceptual-field (*nimitta-bhāga*), then the ālambana is 'immediate.' If the thing-in-itself is not exhaustively given, but seems to have arisen from a hyle, then the ālambana is remote. Both the immediate and the remote ālambana involve the interaction of the *nimitta* and *darśana bhāgas*, such that something is being perceptually grasped within a cognition. What differentiates the immediate from the remote ālambana is simply that the remote one is "separate" from the cognizor. Is this another way of saying 'external' object, a way which avoids conceding anything in a cognition is external to that cognition? What is this hyle?

The Hyle (*Chih* 質)

Chih 質 means[21]

> matter, as opposed to [*ch'i*, vital force or breath]. Substance, or elements of which anything is composed; stuff; material; constitution. Disposition. Solid; real, as opposed to [*wen*, fictitious]. To confront; to call to witness.

It is the basic, solid, non-fictitious *stuff* of which things are made. Thus it would seem that the *Ch'eng wei-shih lun* is affirming some sort of material stuff, 'remote' (if not 'external') to the consciousness which perceives it indirectly, at a distance. The translation 'archetype' offered by Vallée Poussin and repeated by Tat would appear to be a deliberate and deceptive effort to preserve an idealist reading by suppressing or altering all textual contrary evidence. But it is not that simple.

The Sanskrit term most likely being rendered by *chih* is *bimba*[22] (or *pratibimba*). *Bimba* means[23] 'the disc of the sun or the moon,' i.e., source-light and reflected light in round, orb form; 'an image, shadow, reflected or represented form, picture, type; a chameleon.' *Bimba-pratibimba* signifies an "object of comparison and that with which it is compared," an 'original and counterfeit,' etc. *Bimbita* means "mirrored back, reflected;" and *bimbinī* means "the pupil of the eye." *Chih* and *bimba* do not overtly overlap semantically, except in their secondary meanings: each has a secondary sense of 'contrasting, confronting, standing over against.' Putting aside this secondary correlation, which is subliminal at best, why did Hsüan-tsang choose *chih* to translate *bimba*? Was he intentionally attempting to address the idealistic misreading?

The distinction drawn between the immediate and the remote ālambanas comes very close to the distinction drawn by Kant, Hegel, Sartre, et al., between the in-itself and the for-others. Cognition involves the appropriation of 'cognitive objects' by my consciousness. These objects, as appropriated, are 'for-me'; the other's ālaya-vijñāna, for instance, is known by me but not directly. I neither think his/her thoughts as s/he does, nor does my will move his/her body or set up his/her cognitive life. There is inevitably something about the other's mind that remains remote, opaque to me, no matter how clearly I discern his/her mental workings or how deeply I understand him/her. That aspect or aspects of the other's mind which remain remote from me—I don't perceive the world through his/her body, etc.—are the hyle or that person's mind in-itself. What I observe, always partially colored and filtered by the latent 'seeds' that predispose me to cognize my experience as I do, is that aspect of the other's mind that is for-me. But this does not only concern the problem of other minds. Even as I look into my own mind, the same dichotomy arises: there are aspects even of my own mind which remain opaque, which act as hyles, which are in-themselves, which are *chih*. The hyle is the in-itself of what is for-me. Like Husserl's hyle (see chapter 2.II), this 'substance' is not matter in the materialist sense, but rather a cognitive substance, a 'stuff' out of which noemata are constructed. Its ontological status is indeterminable. We will see in a moment how the *Ch'eng wei-shih lun* describes the interaction of these 'conditions.'

The text continues:[24]

> All cognizors (能緣 *neng-yüan*) have an immediate-direct ālambana pratyaya, since they necessarily could not arise apart from [something being] internally cognized and perceptually-grasped [i.e., consciousness is always consciousness of; without an immediate perceptual-object, no cognizor arises].
>
> Some cognizors have a remote ālambana pratyaya, since they may also arise even apart from externally cognized and perceptually-grasped (things).

Cognition constantly, by definition, involves an inner cognitive sensibility. 'Inner' here simply means 'within a cognitive act,' i.e., within consciousness. A cognition *may or may not have an actual corresponding remote object*. In the absence of some cognitive object, a 'cognizer' cannot arise.

K'uei-chi says that the remote ālambana referred to in this passage are mentally constructed objects, such as past or future events, or notions of a substantial self to which one becomes attached, and so on, i.e., basically nonexistent things (無本質 *wu pen chih*). He is arguing, it seems, that only direct ālambana are legitimate cognitive objects. Remote ālambana are 'made up' by consciousness, since consciousness needs an object in order to arise.

The *Ch'eng wei-shih lun*'s use of the notion 'remote ālambana' suggests that it is more properly understood in a more obvious way. Remote ālambana are those cognitive conditions that do originate from or within oneself exclusively, which one takes cognizance of, such that they affect one.

The text quickly shows that the key point in the distinction does not in fact revolve around internal vs. external. Some hold the opinion, it states, that the ālaya-vijñāna only has immediate-direct ālambana pratyaya, i.e., experience is entirely subjectively produced through the force of [one's own] karmic causes.

> There is [another] opinion, that [the ālaya-vijñāna] also definitely has remote ālambana, since it is the influence of others' changes (他變 *t'a-pien*) that is the hyle directing one's own changes (自方變 *tzu feng pien*).

The text then declares[25]

> There is [another] opinion which says that both [previous theories] fail to accord with reason. Self and other, (lived) body and (perceptual) field[26] are able to

mutually experience each other, since the other's alterations become one's hyle [and vice versa].

Since reason [indicates] that the other is not experiencing one's own seeds, to consider the other's alterations as [an enactment of one's own seeds] does not accord with reason. All sentient beings do not have the same or equivalent seeds.

One should say concerning this case (of whether the ālaya-vijñāna has) remote ālambana pratyaya, at all stages (whether one is an ignorant slug or an enlightened Buddha), whether there is or there is not (a remote ālambana pratyaya) is indeterminate.

Hsüan-tsang has brought us into the vicinity of Merleau-Ponty's intentional arc. The relation between oneself and the hyles that act as remote ālambana are thoroughly dialectical (互 *hu*), without a hyle becoming fully transparent to me. My intentionality intends toward it, while it intends toward me, each of us mutually influencing each other. Through my lived-body I can perceive you in my perceptual field, and you likewise can perceive me in your perceptual field. We don't become the same person simply by virtue of sharing reciprocal intentionalities. We remain remote to each other, even as we influence each other. We can cognize each other, just as one hand can touch the other. More importantly, we can communicate with each other. Your ideas affect me, and vice versa. But I will always be an in-itself for you, while you will be an in-itself for me. And though we may share common intentionalities, there is always a disjunction between us. You are never simply a projection of my 'seeds,' nor am I entirely your projection. Just as what I am for you will in part be shaped by your seeds—what you are predisposed to notice, whatever biases, prejudices, or positive expectations you may project onto me, etc., I will inevitably do the same when I perceive you. My seeds are my own, just as yours are your own. Each of us has acquired, utilized, exhausted, nourished, buried, planted, etc., countless seeds, and, for Yogācāra, individuality is defined for the most part by the economic status of one's seeds.

The text does not simply address this dialectical conditioning in terms of 'self and other,' in which case one might be tempted to reduce the dialectical relation to minds interacting. It also explicitly mentions 'bodies and lands,' indicating that hyle are not just people but things, environments, perceptual *fields*.

Whether, within a particular cognition, there are remote ālambanas is indeterminate, which could mean either that it is indeterminate because it is sometimes the case and sometimes not (the text implies but does not explicitly announce this reading), thus leaving one the task of making the determination for each distinct situation; or, it could mean that the very status of remote conditions is itself indeterminate. As the reader may have noticed, the *Ch'eng wei-shih lun* assiduously avoids defining the ontological status of ālambana or 'remote' objects.

The text then looks at the remaining seven consciousnesses in terms of remote ālambana. Manas, the seventh, prior to undergoing the *āśraya-paravṛtti*—

the turning over of that upon which one stands—always has a remote ālambana pratyaya since it must have an external hyle. Since the manas appropriates the activity of the ālaya-vijñāna as its 'self' (*ātman*), and then clings to that self as its object, and the self is never an 'immediate' cognitive object (because it is merely nominal), the manas is always attached to a remote object. After the *āśraya-paravṛtti*, the remote ālambana (i.e., the *ātmanic* appropriation of the ālaya-vijñāna) no longer exists. "When tathatā is the [cognitive] condition, there is no external hyle." Again, tathatā is not a thing or entity, but a descriptive term for the activity of cognizing things just-as-they-are. Hence, when we cognize things just as they are, nothing any longer remains opaque. 'Things' are transparent, the in-itself is penetrated, and the opposition between in-itself and for-others no longer applies.

The mano-vijñāna in all stages (from the lowest to Buddhahood; i.e., both before and after the *āśraya-paravṛtti*

> operates freely, autonomously (*tzu-tsai* 自在), and it is sometimes confronted, sometimes not confronted by an external hyle. Whether it does or doesn't have a remote ālambana is indeterminate.
>
> The five sensory consciousnesses, prior to the āśraya-paravṛtti are crude and gross, and so they must be confronted with an external hyle, and so are determined to have remote ālambana conditions. After the āśraya-paravṛtti stage, it is not definite [when they do and when they don't] have [a remote ālambana], since if the [cognitive] condition is, for example, a past or future [dharma], then they are without an external hyle (無外質故).

Remote ālambana are 'external hyle.' Why, given the critique of externality detailed earlier, are these called 'external'? Because, by calling them hyle, they are inscribed within cognitive acts; they participate in cognitions, and are therefore not 'external' to a cognitive act (consciousness), even though their source is somewhere outside the consciousness that cognizies them, such that they remain somewhat opaque to that cognition's gaze. Again we see that the Yogācāra's point is epistemological, not ontological.

Adhipati-pratyaya

The fourth pratyaya is the *adhipati-pratyaya* which is basically a miscellaneous category for whatever conditioned occurrences were left uncovered by the other three. In fact, this grouping is all inclusive and subsumes the other three types of conditions, as well as whatever additional conditional factor one might wish to add to those three.[27] Its primary significance lies in the role it plays in mapping different moments along the Path. Compared to the importance given this pratyaya in both Theravādin literature and the *Abhidharmakośa*, the discussion in the *Ch'eng wei-shih lun* is remarkably brief and curt.

In the *Ch'eng wei-shih lun* this category is used to establish milestones and events along the mārga, such as the darśana-mārga and bhāvanā-mārga, etc. It is subdivided into twenty-two 'roots' reminiscent of the *Abhidharmakośa*: the five material sense organs, the two sexual organs, the *jīvitendriya,* the five kuśala roots, and (perhaps most importantly) the ability to learn, and so on. The description basically summarizes what is found in the *Yogācārabhūmi* fascicle 57.

Some Implications of the Four Pratyayas

Clearly the most important of the four 'conditions' for our discussion is the *ālambana pratyaya.* In a later section the following list is given:[28]

> The vikalpas (discriminations) by sentient beings toward each other can be ālambana- and/or adhipati-pratyaya, but not samanantara-pratyaya.

A samanantara-pratyaya involves *immediate* succession of cause by an effect occurring in *virtually* the same temporal and spatial locus. Occurring in an instant, it must remain within each single distinct consciousness stream; I don't have your memories, nor am I suddenly experiencing through your body or you through mine, etc., therefore we don't share this pratyaya. The hetu-pratyaya is not associated with vikalpa at all; it only concerns actual efficient causes, not imaginary existents.

> Within a single person the eight consciousnesses between themselves are adhipati-pratyaya. They may or may not be ālambana-pratyaya.

Then a detailed list is offered:

1- the ālaya-vijñāna is the ālambana of the other seven consciousness.
2- the seven are *not* the ālambana of the eighth, since they are not the hyle on which the eighth is based. (cf. 5)
3- the seventh is the ālambana of the sixth, but not the other five.
4- the first six are *not* the ālambana of the seventh.
5- the sixth is not the ālambana of the five, since the five consciousnesses perceptually-grasp (*t'o* 託) only the eighth's *nimitta.* (i.e., the hyle of the five senses are the nimitta of the eighth consciousness, and not external things; while the ālaya-vijñāna is the five's ālambana, they are not its ālambana; cf. 2)
6- the five are the ālambana of the sixth.

Before leaping to conclusions about the apparent inconsistency over the hyle—i.e., earlier the text said that when I perceive another mind as a hyle the other is not reducible to seeds in my own ālaya-vijñāna, while here it seems to be saying that the other would have to be a product of my own ālaya-vijñāna—an important contextual distinction must be taken into account. Previously the text was describing the basis on which the other is perceived. In the present context the text is describing (1) how one's own eight consciousnesses relate to each other, not their relation to whatever is other than themselves, and more importantly, (2) the context here is *vikalpa*, not accurate cognition or hetu-pratyaya. Vikalpa, in relation to perceiving the other, precisely means *not* perceiving the other, but being distracted by one's own vikalpic projections, i.e., one's ālayic seeds. The present description concerns the closured operation of the eight consciousnesses, not their 'dis-closured' operation.[29]

> The causes and effects of vikalpa are fully established by reason and scripture to conditionally arise mutually between and within the consciousnesses. Being attached to external conditions and then claiming that they exist is useless. [Since] that contradicts both reason and scripture, why would you wish to remain attached to such an opinion?

Notes

1 T.31.1585.40a6.11-41b6.6; Ch.7:17A-21B; Tat, p. 534-550; VP ii.436-452. The four conditions are only the tip of the iceberg for the *Ch'eng wei-shih lun*'s analysis of causality. Drawing on the *Yogācārabhūmi* and other texts, it lays out a dense list of intricate causal categories (e.g., ten hetus, fifteen adhiṣṭhānas, etc.) which it then analyzes in terms of the interactions of various members of the various causal category lists. Space limitations prohibit exploring these further in the present work, though they are important for understanding Yogācāra causal theories more adequately than current scholarship addresses. I plan to explore this more fully elsewhere.

2 *Index*, p. 121.

3 Yokoyama, Koitsu. *Index to the Yogācārabhūmi.*

4 Cf. Monier-Williams, p. 1167.

5 *Ibid.*, p. 1180.

6 T.31.1585.40a21.11-40b5.1; Ch.7:18A; Tat, p. 536.

7 VP and Tat (who has translated VP in this section, not the Chinese text) claim that the citta is the antecedent of the subsequent caitta, but properly speaking, they should be producing each other. Here again, the assumption they make that the mind, a.k.a. the citta is 'creating' the world has colored their interpretation.

8 T.31.1585.40b5.2-b8.4; Ch.7:18A; Tat, p. 536-38.

9 Buddhism discusses two types of nirvāṇa: nirvāṇa-with-remainder and nirvāṇa-without-remainder. the former means that even after attaining nirvāṇa, though one has stopped producing and accumulating new karma, one still has not burned off all the karma acquired up to then; this residual karma is responsible for the continuance of the enlightened one's body, etc. To enter parinirvāṇa means that no residuals, no body, nothing remains.

10 Generally Yogācāra literature associates ādāna-vijñāna with attachment by way of seeds and sensory organs. Cf. *Yogācārabhūmi* fasc. 76, line 1; Hsüan-tsang's *She lun*, fasc. 1, line 3; etc.

11 T.31.1585.40c12.1-40c23.7; Ch.7:19B; Tat, p. 542.

12 *Yu-fa* 有法, *saddharma.*

13 *Tai-chi-hsiang* 帶己相, *tadākāratā. Tai* means 'to take, lead; close, connected with, carry with; girdle, zone.' VP, pp. ii.444f discusses this and a number of terms we will be discussing momentarily, since their usage in this literature does not always accord easily with their general Chinese meanings. The *Index*, once again, demonstrates the accuracy of VP's reconstructive efforts. For *tai-chi-hsiang* he offers *qui naissent semblables à elle* (which is born resembling it), and later renders *tai* alone as *en s'attachant intimement* (intimately

connected). *Tadākāratā*, which he recognizes is the equivalent for *tai-hsiang*, means 'having such-and-such an appearance'.

14 'Cognized' = *so-lü* 所慮. In Chinese this literally means 'object of concern' or ''what is thought about.' VP, *ibid.*, offers 'qui est connue' ou 'perçue' (what is known or perceived). He writes:

> The image in the mirror is supported by (*s'appuie*) the thing reflected: this thing is the *pratyaya*, the condition of the image; but not its ālambana-pratyaya, because it isn't "known" or "perceived" by the mirror.

S'appuie translates *so-t'o* 所託, which in this passage I translated as 'perceptually-grasped.' *Index*, p. 328, gives two correspondences for Hsüan-tsang, *upalabhya* (cognitively grasp) and *adhīna* (resting on or in, situated, depending on, subject to, subservient to), and several for Paramārtha: *abhi-ni-viś-, avakram, pratisaṃdhi, praviś-*. Apparently VP took it as *adhīna*. The preponderance of meanings, and the philosophical context of the *Ch'eng wei-shih lun*, however, dictate that the term carries important implications of 'attachment, grasping.' In Chinese *t'o* means 'entrust, request, to engage,' but it is associated with its homonym 托 which means 'to support, as with the hand; the length of one's two arms extended; and hence a fathom' (Giles #11,366).

15 The general, specific, kuśala, kleśa, upakleśa, and aniyata; see appendix 1.

16 Cf. VP, p. ii.445.

17 T.31.1585.40c12.1-40c23.7; Ch.7:19B; Tat, p. 542.

18 *Neng-yüan* ,能緣 lit: active-subjective condition.

19 *Nei so lü t'o* 內所慮託.

20 *Chih* 質, an important term we will examine presently.

21 Giles, #1892, p. 237f.

22 *Index*, p. 291.

23 Monier-Williams, p. 731.

24 T.31.1585.40c21.1-40c23.7; Ch.7:19B; Tat, p. 544.

25 T.31.1585.40c23.7-41a1.6; Ch.7:20A; Tat, p. 544.

26 *Tzu-t'a shen-t'u* 自他身土. Has Hsüan-tsang been reading Merleau-Ponty?

27 Though important for explaining the Yogācāra's soteric map, this material is beyond the scope of the current study. Cf. T.31.1585.41a; Ch.7:20-21B; Tat, p. 546-551 The term 增上緣 occurs only eighteen times in the entire *Ch'eng wie-shih lun*, mostly concentrated in the section between 1585.42b-43b where it is applied to mārga classification.

28 T.31.1585.42c; Ch.8:5B-6A; Tat, p. 570.

29 T.31.1585.42c27.5-43a9; Ch.8:6B; Tat, p. 574.

Chapter Twenty-One

Mirror Knowing: Soteric Alterations

What function does the mirror model play in Yogācāra thought? We saw it used above to explain ordinary cognition. But Yogācāra is a soteric phenomenology, which means that it does not merely describe in order to describe. Description, for Yogācāra, carries soteric significance. While Husserl, for instance, certainly hoped that his phenomenological method would provide benefits beyond mere description, such as giving a firm philosophical foundation to the 'groundless' European *Wissenschaften*, he did not go so far as to claim that description itself is intrinsically transformative, or, what would amount to its descriptive corollary, that by means of perfecting the descriptive method, that which is described, viz. consciousness, would become so radically altered that an entirely new description—perhaps even a new method—would be required. But Husserl's reticence in this regard is symptomatic of Western thought as a whole.[1] The line between descriptive and prescriptive discourse—between describing what is and prescribing what ought to be—frequently becomes blurred in practice. But that blurring is never theoretically justified.[2] Put in Kantian terms, the 'pure' and the 'practical' styles of reason remain largely incommensurate, while 'aesthetic' reason remains enigmatic.[3]

How does Yogācāra overcome or circumvent this incommensurability? Their phenomenological description concerns *alterity*: The alterations of consciousness in terms of its appropriation of cognitive objects, the alterations in projectories as consciousness restructures itself, what alters and is altered as consciousness disassembles and reassembles its habit-projectories (*vāsanā-saṅtāna*), the karmic alterations switching projectorial tracks (tracts, traits, traces) as *kuśala* and *akuśala* linkages conditionally displace and substitute for each other, etc. All this is grounded on the radical alterity of consciousness itself, i.e., the absence of an abiding, persistent, unchanging self, which is to say, it (never) rests on a consciousness that is always becoming other than itself, which always *is* other than itself. Alterity is the cognitive counterpart to the doctrinal notion 'impermanence' and the existential horizon of 'death' and personal limits. The upacāras *ātman* and *dharma* are responses to and symptoms of a denial and rejection of impermanence, death and limitation. Yogācāra, as a product of the privileging of the cognitive dimension, tackles the source of this futile denial in cognitive terms. Thus, its description and analysis focus on consciousness and cognition, and it identifies the root problematic as distinctly cognitive. *jñeyāvaraṇa* (obstruction of the knowable). To know clearly, fully, precisely, exactly, without hindrance or obstruction is *buddhi* (awakening, enlightenment, clear intellect).

The alterity of consciousness is, according to Yogācāra, not an endlessly repeated structure that remains structurally identical while only functionally changing. Its very structure, lacking a self (= essence = invariant structure = *ātman* = *svabhāva* = permanent identity) alters radically, and it is this radical alterity which both causes saṃsāra to be experienced as duḥkha and which provides the conditions that allow consciousness to change so as to no longer either be 'consciousness' or duḥkhic. Nāgārjuna had already indicated this in his *Mūla-madhyamaka-kārikā*, 25:9:[4]

Ya ājanaṃ-javī-bhāva upādāya pratītya vā,
so 'pratītyānupādāya nirvāṇam upadiṣyate.

That which is the rushing in and out [of existence] when dependent or conditioned,
this, when not dependent or not conditioned, is taught to be nirvāṇa.

Yogācāra develops an elaborate vocabulary to describe the alterity between rushing in and out of existence conditionally and doing so without conditions (i.e., without appropriational intent). They call the climactic alteration *āśraya-paravṛtti*, the overturning of the basis on which one stands, the upheaval of the (false) under-standing.[5] Buddhism is the concerted effort to bring the trajectory of alterities under control (*fu* 伏, *viṣkambhana*) in order to fundamentally and decisively extinguish (*tuan* 斷, *prahāṇa*) projectorial (i.e., teleological) conditioning.[6]

When the ālaya-vijñāna undergoes āśraya-paravṛtti, it ceases and is replaced by the Great Mirror Cognition (*mahādarśa-jñāna*). The cognitive components of Mirror Cognition, being devoid of delusion, is labeled *tathatā*. The *Ch'eng wei-shih lun* lists ten types of tathatā (*chen-ju*)[7] and bases its further discussion on them. They are:

(1) Pervasive activity tathatā (*p'ien-hsing chen-ju* 遍行真如). This tathatā is so-called because it is disclosed by the two *śūnyatās* (of ātman-dharma), such that not a single dharma [anywhere] is excluded.

(2) Most excellent tathatā (*tsui-sheng chen-ju* 最勝真如). This tathatā is so-called because, of all the unlimited [excellent] qualities in all dharmas, it is considered the most excellent.

(3) Excellent flow tathatā (*sheng-liu chen-ju* 勝流真如). This tathatā is so-called because the Dharma teachings that flow from it, of all other Dharma teachings, this is considered the most excellent.

(4) Not-categorized by cognitive-reductions tathatā (*wu-she-shou chen-ju* 無攝受真如). This tathatā is so-called because it is not tied to any category;[8] nor can self-grasping depend on it to grasp (anything).

(5) Non-differentiation of classes tathatā (*lei wu-pieh chen-ju* 類無別真如). This tathatā is so-called because classes are not differentiated, unlike eyes, etc., that have different [classes of objects].[9]

(6) Neither defiled nor pure tathatā (*wu-jan-ching chen-ju* 無染淨真如). This tathatā is so-called because its original nature is undefiled, so it can't be said that afterwards it has been purified.

(7) Non-separation of the Dharma tathatā (*fa-wu-pieh chen-ju* 法無別真如). This tathatā is so-called because although there are many Dharma teachings proliferating and being established, yet they are not different.

(8) Neither increasing nor decreasing tathatā (*pu-tseng-chien chen-ju* 不增減真如). This tathatā is so-called because it is detached from the appropriational [economy of] increase and decrease, i.e., it isn't increased or decreased by purity or defilement. This [tathatā] is also called 'the tathatā on which depends mastery of (cognitive) characteristics and (perceptual) fields.'[10] This means that once this tathatā is realized and attained, perceiving/projecting (*hsien*) characteristics and perceiving/projecting fields is completely mastered.

(9) That on which mastery of cognition depends tathatā (*chih tzu-tsai so-yi chen-ju* 智自在所依真如), which means once one has realized and attained this tathatā, one has already attained mastery of unobstructed understanding.[11]

(10) That on which mastery of action (karma) depends tathatā (*yeh tzu-tsai-teng so-yi chen-ju* 業自在等所依真如). Once one has realized and attained this tathatā, then all the *abhijñās* are enacted, as are the *dhāraṇā-mukhas* and *samādhi-mukhas*. they are all mastered.[12]

Although already in the first bhūmi one can 'see through' all of them,[13] still one's ability to realize and practice it has not yet been fully developed. So that in order to progressively fully develop [complete insight, these ten tathatās], are asserted and established.

These ten tathatās are respectively associated with the ten bhūmis,[14] such that in the eighth bhūmi, for instance, the eighth tathatā is realized, and so on.

Immediately the text introduces six types of *āśraya-parāvṛtti*. It is the sixth which is most important, and K'uei-chi claims that it is this type which the *Triṃśikā* primarily discusses.[15] The text says of this one:[16]

6. Vipula-parāvṛtti (*kuang-ta chuan* 廣大轉) 'Broad or extensive overturning,' which is the Mahāyāna stage. [Unlike the Hīnayānists, who strive only for their own enlightenment, longing for nirvāṇa while detesting saṃsāra] the great Bodhisattvas act for the benefit of others, neither detesting nor delighting in either life-and-death (i.e., saṃsāra) or nirvāṇa. They are able to fully penetrate and see through the two emptinesses (self and dharmas) [which disclose] tathatā [though the Hīnayānist only comprehends self-emptiness]. They utterly cut off the seeds of the *jñeyāvaraṇa* [the source of both *āvaraṇas*], and suddenly realize *anuttara* [*saṃyak saṃ-*] *bodhi* (unexcelled, correct complete Awakening) and nirvāṇa. They have the excellent profound abilities [to perform any upāya anywhere], and so this is called the 'broad or extensive overturning.'

The *Ch'eng wei-shih lun* then distinguishes four components of the *āśraya-paravṛtti*, discussing each in turn. They are (1) The method (*mārga*, *tao*) which turns [the basis] around; (2) The basis which is turned; (3) what is cut off in the turning; and (4) what is attained in the turning. We will now turn to the fourth component.[17]

The fourth is divided into two parts: (1) what is disclosed, uncovered by the turning, and (2) what arises from the turning. What is disclosed is *mahāparinirvāṇa*, which is further subdivided. All we need note here is:[18]

> What's termed 'attaining nirvāṇa,' since it depends on tathatā and is detached from the obstructions and prajñaptis, its 'body'(*t'i*) is always already the pristinely pure dharma-dhātu.

The dharma-dhātu, though sometimes presented through a rhetoric of descriptive mystifications, simply and solely means the experiential realm. In Yogācāra literature it can denote either the sensorium with its defilements, or, in some instances, the cognitive field cleansed of prajñaptic misconceptions. That the latter meaning is meant here is made clear my explicitly adding the qulifiers "pristinely pure." This pristine cognitive field is *this* world perceived directly and immediately just as it is (*yathā bhūtam*). Thus nirvāṇa is a prajñapti for clear perception.

'What arises from the turning' is *mahābodhi*, great Bodhi.[19] This arises from latent seeds which had been prevented from blossoming by the āvaraṇas. These are the Four Cognitions (*jñāna*, *chih* 智) characteristic in the Yogācāra system of an enlightened one.

Vi-jñāna is converted into *jñāna*, which is to say that 'dis-tinguishing, discriminating, dis-cerning' (*vi-jñāna*) loses its dichotomous, bifurcational nature (the *vi-* prefix)—the dualism here is not simply any and all duality in a vague sense, but specifically the appropriational dichotomy between grasper and grasped, *grāhaka-grāhya*, noesis and noema. Knowing, cognizing becomes immediate, direct—hence the absence of 'remote ālambana.' The eight consciousnesses which so far constituted the full extent of Yogācāric phenomenological description are suddenly 'overturned,' and displaced by four jñānas.

Awakening consists in bringing the eight consciousnesses to an end, replacing them with enlightened cognitive abilities (*jñāna*).[20] Overturning the Basis turns the five sense consciousnesses into immediate cognitions that accomplish what needs to be done (*kṛtyānuṣṭhāna-jñāna*). The sixth consciousness becomes immediate cognitive mastery (*pratyavekṣaṇa-jñāna*), in which the general and particular characteristics of things are discerned just as they are. This discernment is considered nonconceptual (*nirvikalpa-jñāna*). *Manas* becomes the immediate cognition of equality (*samatā-jñāna*), equalizing self and other. When the ālaya-vijñāna finally ceases it is replaced by the Great Mirror Cognition (*Mahādarśa-jñāna*) that sees and reflects things just as they are, impartially, without exclusion, prejudice, anticipation, attachment, or distortion. The grasper-grasped relation has ceased.

It should be noted that these "purified" cognitions all engage the world in immediate and effective ways by removing the self-bias, prejudice, and obstructions that had prevented one previously from perceiving beyond one's own narcissistic consciousness. When 'consciousness' (*vijñāna*) ends, true knowledge (*jñāna*) begins. One more Yogācāra innovation was the notion that a special type of cognition emerged and developed *after* enlightenment. This post-enlightenment cognition was called *pṛṣṭhalabdha-jñāna*. Since enlightened cognition is nonconceptual (*nirvikalpa-jñāna*) its objects cannot be described.

The *Ch'eng wei-shih lun* says concerning the overturning of the eighth consciousness:[21]

> (1) The Great Perfect Mirror Cognition, (*ta yüan ching chih* , 大圓鏡智 *mahādarśajñāna*) associated with the mind (*samprayukta citta-varga*). Separated from discriminations (*vikalpa*), its ālambana and *ākāra* are very subtle, difficult to know, [and yet] it doesn't forget, doesn't mis-take the characteristics of any perceptual-object. Its nature and characteristics are pristinely pure, detached from adventitious defilements (*āgantuka-kleśa*)... [it is] able to project/perceive and able to produce lived-bodies and perceptual-fields, knowing their reflections (*ying* 影, *pratibimba*)... like a great mirror projecting/perceiving rūpas and pratibimbas (material things and their reflections, *se hsiang* 色像).[22]

The most important part of this description might easily be overlooked. That which the mirror reflects is not simply projected mental phantasms...it is *rūpa*! "Lived-bodies, perceptual-fields, he knows their reflections."

Does Yogācāra actually confirm *rūpa to* be 'real'? In an earlier section while determining which of the three (non-) self-natures were 'real' and which only nominal, the *Ch'eng wei-shih lun* says:[23]

> Mind (citta), mental-associates (caittas) *and rūpa*, since they arise from conditions, are considered to be *real existents* (為實有 *wei shih yu*). If there were no real dharmas, there would be no prajñaptic dharmas either, since the prajñaptic (*chia* 假) depends on a real cause, viz. prajñapti (*shih-she* 施設). [emphasis added]

Thus rūpa, because it operates causally, is real.

The notion of a mirror mind already occurred in Chinese literature prior to the introduction of Buddhism. The mirror, as Chuang Tzu already wrote, is both all-embracing and detached:[24]

> The Perfect Man uses his mind like a mirror—going after nothing, welcoming nothing, responding but not storing. Therefore he can win out over things and not hurt himself.

Neither welcoming, anticipating things as they approach, nor pining or running after things when they leave, the mirror simply reflects things accurately and without prejudice or partiality. It 'responds but doesn't store.' The ālaya-vijñāna is also named the 'storage-consciousness' or 'warehouse-consciousness' (*tsang-shih* 藏識) because it stores the seeds. To respond without storing, the ālaya-vijñāna must be cut off, the seeds—whether advantageous or disadvantageous—must be exhausted, extinguished; then mirror-cognition blooms. The mirror reflects things just as they are. The *Ch'eng wei-shih lun* says:[25]

> If, after the arising of Vajropama-samādhi, there no longer exists a perfumable eighth consciousness (the Vipākavijñāna), and if pure dharmas no longer grow and increase, the Bodhisattva has attained Buddhahood. The four Cognitions will then be in manifestation.

This is the terminus of the progressional path, the culmination of the method, where one "has done what had to be done."

The eight consciousnesses are listed as the first eight dharmas on the list of one hundred dharmas (see Appendix One). They, and all the dharmas which follow up until the ninety-sixth dharma, are *saṃskṛta-dharma*, conditioned dharmas. Since, as Nāgārjuna stated, nirvāṇa—i.e., seeing things as they are—means the "rushing in and out [of existence] when... not dependent and not conditioned," the ālaya-vijñāna (*saṃskṛta*) and nirvāṇa (*asaṃskṛta*) are mutually exclusive. Hence the *Triṃśikā* (Skt. v. 5; Hsüan-tsang's v. 4) says that the ālaya-vijñāna must be cut off (*vyāvṛti, she* 捨).

To be free of the determination of seeds (in Yogācāric language) means to overcome historical conditioning, to dissolve each and every layer of sedimentation, of embodied history (in phenomenological language). The ālaya-vijñāna is the 'repository-consciousness' (藏識 *tsang-shih*) which 'accumulates and stores (*cīyate*) and attaches to (*ālīyante, grāhya-grāhaka, abhiniveśa*)' experience. Its 'repositoriness' signifies the manner in which it is thoroughly pervaded by attachment. Mirror cognition is its antithesis. Just as a mirror neither anticipates what will come into its purview, nor chase after what has gone, the Great Mirror Cognition clings to nothing, reflects the present as it is, and owes to history only the structure of its constitution; a structure which has been rendered transparent.

Does this jñāna have the same ālambana as the ālaya-vijñāna? The text says:[26]

> When its (cognitive) condition is tathatā, it is nirvikalpa; when its (cognitive) conditions are other perceptual-objects (*viṣaya*), it is grouped with *pṛṣṭhalabdha jñāna* (post-Awakening cognition); its *t'i* 體 is one, but it is divided into two according to functions (用 *yung*). Since [even when] discerning the mundane (了俗 *liao-su*, vijñapti-saṃvṛti?), [this cognition does so] due to having realized tathatā, it is considered [Cognition] 'After [Complete Awakening] was Attained' (*pṛṣṭhalabdha jñāna*, i.e., post-Awakening cognition).

The same type of argument is made for the other three jñānas, which are:

1) *p'ing-teng-hsing chih* 平等性智, *samatā jñāna* (sameness or equalizing cognition)
2) *miao-kuan-ch'a chih* 妙觀察智, *pratyavekṣanā jñāna* (wondrous exploring cognition)

3) *ch'eng so-tso chih* 成所作智, *kṛtyānuṣṭhāna jñāna* (accomplishing what is to be done cognition).

Manas becomes the Equalizing Cognition. Rather than cling to self (*ātma-dṛṣṭi*, etc.), carving up the world into opposing values of me and you, us and them, etc., the equalizing cognition sees the same emptiness of self and dharma in all things, in oneself as well as in others. Mano-vijñāna becomes the Wondrous Exploring or Investigative Cognition. Rather than compart-mentalize the world into grasping and graspable entities, as does the mano-vijñāna, this investigative cognition explores everything in their particularities (*svalakṣaṇa*), devoid of attachment. The five sense-consciousnesses become the cognitions that accomplish what needs to be done. Even the fully Awakened being acts in the world. Hence the *Ch'eng wei-shih lun* rejects any theories that place either these cognitions or their objects entirely outside the saṃvṛti world. As grounded in tathatā, they are paramārthic; as grounded in saṃvṛti viṣaya, they are pṛṣṭhalabdha-jñāna .

If the overturned consciousnesses are cognitions, ways of knowing, that now perceive reality as it is, what is real? Are saṃskṛta dharmas real? Asaṃskṛta dharmas? Tathatā? Citta?

Notes

1 There are a few notable exceptions, such as Levinas, post-70s Derrida, Lyotard and so on, but their ethical efforts only shine in contrast to the lacuna of competing formulations.

2 Which is not to say that we lack efforts to bridge that gap. The Neo-kantians tried to bridge it, as did Kant himself, and a number of current analytic philosophers have taken a stab at it (e.g., Morton White's *What Is and What Ought to Be Done*, NY: Oxford University Press, 1981), but none have managed to satisfactorily link epistemology with ethics. The Western philosophical predilection to do ontology and consider it the most important of the philosophical disciplines has effectively crippled the development of a coherent Western ethic. Epistemology becomes ontology's handmaiden, and ethics is castigated as a pathetic attempt at moral epistemology. Hegel's indirect 'solution,' collapsing what ought to be into his notion of what is, by declaring the 'idea' *qua* ideal to be the crux of reality led to Marxism, whose most famous indictment of Hegel and the style of philosophy it exemplified was given by Marx in the 11th thesis of his *Theses on Feuerbach*:

> The philosophers have only *interpreted* the world, in various ways; the point, however, is to *change* it.

The tension between ontological thinking and ethical engagement has been particularly haunting in the Twentieth Century. One thinks of the 'Heidegger question' (or Carl Jung, or Paul deMan); the crucial but uneasy Marxist supplement to French existentialism, structuralism and phenomenology; etc. The sheer wasted politico-ethical thought of so many of our leading philosophers, either neglecting to oppose Nazi fascism (unless directly assaulted by it) or embarrassingly supporting Stalinist totalitarianism, merely highlights the poor and misguided quality of contemporary ethical thought.

3 Lyotard and Deleuze have led the effort in France that is attempting to unify these three parts of the Kantian system. Giles Deleuze's *Kant's Critical Philosophy: The Doctrine of the*

Faculties, tr. by Hugh Tomlinson and Barbara Habberjam (Minneapolis: University of Minnesota Press, 1984) is a particularly noteworthy effort at seeing all three critiques (pure reason, practical reason and judgment) from the Kantian corpus as a unified architectonic structure. As interesting as these efforts are, the three critiques remain largely incommensurate.

4 Streng's translation, slightly modified.

5 The *Ch'eng wei-shih lun* discusses the āśraya-paravṛtti in numerous, intricate ways. We have neither time nor space to deal with them all here. Rather some salient portions will be extracted and highlighted. The criterion of saliency that I used, in part, considered the degree to which the context of a particular passage had been adequately established by our previous discussion. As a corollary, passages that clearly contributed to the arguments being made were of course included.

6 On *fu* 伏 and *tuan* 斷, cf. T.31.1585.54c15-55a10.5; Ch.10:4A-4B; Tat, p. 752; VP pp. 662ff. *Viṣkambhaṇa* carries the double meaning of 'holding back or impeding' (such as by bolting a door) *and* 'a means of tearing open.' *Vikambh* means to firmly fix, prop up, to support something (like a support beam) *and* to hurl, cast, come forth, escape. Thus it connotes at once holding back and thrusting forth. *Fu* means 'to fall down; humble; suffer; to lie in ambush; to sit, as a bird on eggs; to yield or give way.' *Prahāṇa* means to eradicate; *tuan* means to break or cut off. Together they imply a kind of cathartic crescendo: One holds back, building to a climax (*viṣkambhana*), which culminates in a final release (*mokṣa*) that eliminates and resolves (*prahāṇa*) all the previous tensions. That this 'process' is amenable to a Freudian reading should be obvious.

7 T.31.1585.54b9.5-54c3.10; Ch.10:2B-3A; Tat, p. 746-748.

8 *Wu so-chi shu* 無所繫屬. *Shu* can mean 'to belong, to be ranked, sorted, allied with, grouped with, classified as, depend on,' and implies being located somewhere in a family chain. It thus implies the classificatory principle behind such schema as phylogeny, ontogeny, morphology, taxonomy, and Abhidharma.

9 The example of the eye is not clear. Does it mean there are different types of eyes (brown, blue, etc.; human, cow, fly, etc.; round, slanted, etc.; open, closed; etc.)? Or that eyes differentiate by color, size, shape, etc.? The contrast between this *chen-ju* and the previous one seems to be that the other involves the family-hierarchy principle on which classes and their members are located, and this one concerns the actual placement of members within a class. Or, perhaps, that the previous *chen-ju* implies 'genus' and this *chen-ju* involves species.

10 *Hsiang-t'u tzu-tsai so-yi chen-ju* 相土自在所依真如.

11 This 'understanding', achieved in the ninth bhūmi, is thoroughly linguistic and hermeneutic. Earlier the text described the āvaraṇas which are cut off in the 9th stage. Tat translates this section thus (pp.739-741):

> ...the ninth Bhumi cuts off, with their *dausthulya*, two delusions:
>
> (1) A triple *dharanivasitamoha* ([*sic*; Tat never ends this parenthesis] delusion of impeding the first three Pratisamvids: (a) of *artha* (meaning, i.e., unhindered power of interpreting the meaning of the Dharma, the Law); (b) of *dharma* (the letter of the Law, i.e., unhindered power of interpreting the letter of the Law); and (c) of *nirukti* (language or form of expression, i.e., unlimited power of interpreting or understanding the language).
>
> a. By 'mastery of the innumerable dharmas preached by the Buddha' is meant the Arthapratisamvid (unhindered power of interpretation with reference to the meaning of Dharma). In other words, it is the 'mastery of all that can be explained', which makes it possible for all meanings to appear in one Meaning.
>
> b. By 'mastery of the innumerable names, sentences, clauses, phrases and words' is meant the Dharmapratisamvid (unhindered power of interpretation with reference to the letter of the Law). In other words, it is the 'mastery of all that can explain or express meanings', which makes it possible for all names-phrases-syllables to appear in one name-phrase-syllable.

c. By 'mastery of all methods or repeated and continuous explanation and exposition' is meant the Niruktipratisamvid (unhindered power of explaining and understanding languages and forms of expressions). In other words, it is the 'mastery of all methods of repeated and continuous exposition and elucidation of verbal expressions and vocal sounds', which renders it possible for all sounds-notes to appear in one sound-note, thus enabling one to understand in the language of one country the languages of all countries.

(2) The *pratibhanavasitamoha* (delusion impeding the mastery of the power of argumentation) which impedes the Pratisamvid of *pratibhana* (argument, i.e., unhindered power of argumentation), skilfulness in discourse which proceeds from a thorough knowledge of the natural qualifications of the sentient beings to be converted.

12 The *abhijñās* are the super-cognitive abilities acquired though meditation. Most texts attribute the acquisition of these powers to meditations in the arūpya-dhyānas. The *dhāraṇāmukhas* are liberations acquired through chanting *dhāranīs;* the samādhimukhas are liberations acquired through *samādhi.*

13 "See through" = *ta* 達, which also means 'to understand; to open, inform.' 'See through' evokes the sense of transparency that the *Ch'eng wei-shih lun* associates with Awakened cognition.

14 The ten bhūmis are the ten stages of Bodhisattva practice, common to all forms of Mahāyāna. On the ten bhūmis, see Dayal, *The Bodhisattva Doctrine...*, ch. VI.

15 The other five are:

1. Destroying the power [of defiled seeds] and increasing the ability [of good seeds]-paravṛtti (gradually 'controlling' the seed's projectories).
2. Prativedha-paravṛtti (partial āśraya-paravṛtti during darśana-mārga, that sees through the gross aspects of the two āvaraṇas.
3. Bhāvanā-paravṛtti (gradual progress through practice and cultivation, *bhāvanā*, of the ten pāramitās, etc., finally extinguishing the two crude āvaraṇas).
4. Full development of the fruit-paravṛtti (the fruition of three mahākalpas of practice, suddenly, in the *vajropama samādhi* —which occurs, according to some passages in the *Ch'eng wei-shih lun,* between the tenth stage and Buddhahood, and according to other passages, in the eighth stage—one utterly cuts off the two āvaraṇas, and henceforth always assists other sentient beings).
5. Inferior-paravṛtti (for Śravakas and Pratyekabuddhas).

16 T.31.1585.54c; Ch.10:4A; Tat, p. 752; VP pp. 662ff.

17 A brief outline of the rest:

(1) the method which turns [the basis] around.

(1a) Suppresses or controls (*viṣkambhana*) the influential power of *anuśayas* (latent tendencies) that actualizes the two āvaraṇas.

(1a.1) Preparatory knowledge (*prayoga-jñāna*);

(1a.2) Fundamental knowledge (*mūla-jñāna*);

(1a.3) Post-awakening knowledge (*pṛṣṭhalabdha-jñāna*).

(1b) Decisively extinguishing (*prahāṇa*) the two āvaraṇa's *anuśayas.* "The *anuśayas* which involve 'deluded theories' (*mi-li* 迷理) can only be extinguished by the fundamental knowledge *qua nirvikalpa-jñāna.* The remaining *anuśayas* which involve 'deluded praxis' (*mi-shih* 迷事) are extinguished by the preparatory and post-Awakening knowledges.

(2) The basis which is turned.

(2a) the basis which holds the seeds, viz. the ālaya-vijñāna.

(2b) the basis of delusion and awakening.

(3) What is cut off in the turning.

(3a) cutting off (*she* 捨) what is extinguished (*fu*, *prahāṇa*), i.e., the antidote to the *āvaraṇas*, which stops the projection of parikalpita.

(3b) cutting off what is rejected (*so-ch'i* 所棄), i.e., at the moment of the *vajropama samādhi*, the Diamond Samādhi associated with the eighth bhūmi (the crucial stage on the path from which one doesn't backslide, and in which one's Awakening is fully stable; the remaining two bhūmis merely involve perfecting the insight gained here by more experience practicing upāya, etc.) both contaminated and non-contaminated seeds are utterly rejected and cut off, which leads to 'a supremely perfect, lucid, simple, pure mūla-vijñāna that won't 'support' (*āśraya*) them, though some traces of the seeds remain —enough to remain in saṃsāra.

(4) What is attained in the turning.

18 T.31.1585.55b; Ch.10:6A; Tat, p. 758.

19 Hsüan-tsang transliterates 'bodhi' here, rather than translating it.

20 On ādarśa-jñāna, see *Mahāyanasūtralaṃkara*, T.31.1604.606c26-607b26; 大乘本生心地 觀經 (tr. by Prajñā, T'ang Dynasty) T.8.261.912a6; 大乘理六波羅蜜達多經 (tr. by Dānapāla, Sung Dynasty) T.12.346.175b-177a; 佛說大方廣善巧方便經 (tr. Dānapāla, Sung Dynasty) T. 12.346.175b-177a; *Suvarṇaprahāṣa* (tr. I-Ching, T'ang Dynasty) T.16.665.408a6; *Buddhabhūmi sūtra* (tr. Hsüan-tsang) T.16.680.721b12-c25; *Buddhabhūmiśāstra* (tr. Hsüan-tsang) T.26.1530.291b15, 294b2, 301b8-304a21, 306b3, 309a19-313b18, 315a7, 317a4-318c1, 321a9-326c5; Vasubandhu's comm. on *Mahāyānasamgraha* T.31.1596.314a19-20 (Dharmagupta's tr.), T.31.1597.372a13-14 (Hsüan-tsang's tr.); Āsvabhāva's comm. on *Mahāyānasamgraha* (Hsüan-tsang's tr.) T.31.1598.438a15; 集大乘相論 (tr. Buddhavijñānan, Dānapāla, Sung Dynasty) T.32.1637.148b28-c28; *Diamond Yoga Samādhi Heart Treatise* (tr. Amoghavajra, T'ang Dynasty) T.32.1665.573c24; the commentary on the *Awakening of Faith* attributed to Nāgārjuna, T.32.1668.618a22, 631b26.

21 T.31.1585.56a; Ch.10:8B; Tat, p. 766.

22 *Ying* = pratibimba or chāyā ('shadow, reflection') (*Index*. p. 478); *hsiang* = pratibimba (*Index*, p. 308).

23 T.31.1585.47c; Ch.8:23B; Tat, p. 650.

24Burton Watson's translation, *Chuang Tzu: Basic Writings*, NY: Columbia UP, 1964, p. 95

25 T.31.1585.56b; Ch.10:9B-10A; Tat, p. 772. This is Tat's translation (virtually pirated from VP pp. 685f), diacriticals added.

26 T.31.1585.56c; Ch.10:11A; Tat, p. 776.

Chapter Twenty-Two

Language, Avijñapti-rūpa and Vijñapti-rūpa

Early in the *Ch'eng wei-shih lun*, while reviewing and critiquing the seventy-five dharma system of the Sarvāstivādins (see appendix 2), some definitive statements concerning the Yogācāra orientation are made.

The Sarvāstivādins propose to define *saṃskṛta-dharma* as a dharma whose essence (*svabhāva*) consists of the four marks (*lakṣaṇa*) of all conditioned things: arising, abiding, decaying, ceasing. Thus, for the Sarvāstivāda, these marks are *svabhāvic*, i.e., the essential factor or essence of saṃskṛta. The *Ch'eng wei-shih lun* refutes these claims and then says:[1]

> Saṃskṛta-dharmas (*yu-wei-fa* 有為法), because of the power of causes and conditions, are originally inexistent (*pen-wu* 本無), now existent (*chin-yu* 今有), briefly existent (*chan-yu* 暫有), and then once again inexistent (*hai-wu* 還無). [In order to] indicate (*piao* 表, *vijñapti*?) their difference from asaṃskṛta (dharmas, which are not affected by causes and conditions), the four marks are nominally established.
>
> The stage of existence (*yu-wei* 有位) [from] originally inexistent [to] now existent is termed 'arising.' The stage of arising to briefly settling for an instant[2] is termed 'abiding.' While abiding [the dharma] is distinguished from what precedes and follows it (or: its previous and subsequent conditions; i.e., it is *changing*), and so again it is given a different name [namely, decaying, or 'briefly existing']. Briefly existing, then once again inexistent: When it becomes (again) inexistent, that is termed 'cessation.'
>
> Since the first three are existents, they involve the identity of presence (or, abide in the present);[3] since the last one is inexistent, it abides in the past.

Dharmas, then, are what come in and out of existence, as Nāgārjuna wrote (*ājanaṃ-javī-bhāva upādāya pratītya*). The four marks are nominal labels. The text continues:[4]

> 'Arising' indicates (*piao*) there is a dharma that previously didn't exist. 'Cessation' indicates there is a dharma that subsequently is inexistent. 'Decay' (in Chinese, lit: 'difference') indicates that this dharma does not congeal.[5] 'Abiding' indicates this dharma briefly exists and functions.

Hence these four marks of conditioned dharmas are simply terms for indication (*ming-piao* 名表); and yet they may indicate different [things]. They may be the nominal four marks of a *kṣanika* (moment), or for any length of temporal duration nominally established.

First [coming into] existence is termed 'arising.' Subsequent inexistence is termed 'cessation.' The mark of having already arisen and appearing to be sequentially continuous (*saṃbandha*) is termed 'abiding.' And precisely the alterity (*chuan-pien* 轉變) of the sequential continuity is termed 'difference' [i.e., 'decay'].

To be 'conditionally real' means to appear durationally (even for an instant) in a conditioned series which at its core perpetually self-deconstructs, whose only consistent 'identity' is *alterity*. Impermanence, non-self and duḥkha—the three marks of all conditioned things according to the earliest Buddhist texts—all converge into this one 'characteristic.' Alterity means impermanence; it means no univocal self; it means the radical absence of the least shred of stability and security either in oneself or in the world, and hence is the *sine qua non* of *duḥkha*. Alterity is the play of radical difference; and it is 'deteriorative' or productive of 'decay' only to the extent that one possesses the expectation that there exist stable entities and identities such that any sign of instability is a sign of decay. That notion presupposes that change itself *is* decadence. Buddhism, properly understood, can abide no conservatism, since there is nothing stable to hold and conserve. At best one may manipulate projectories, but only in order to radically open them up to their own history, their own conditioning.

On Language and Reality

But some conditioned dharmas are not even real in a conditional sense. The Sarvāstivādin next tries to argue that *nāma-pada-vyañjana* (name, sentence, utterance) are independently real substances (*dravya*). The *Ch'eng wei-shih lun* refutes this. In response to a proof text offered by the Sarvāstivādin, the *Ch'eng wei-shih lun* responds "this Sūtra doesn't say that different from *rūpa, citta, caittas,* there exists a real [thing] called *nāma*, etc."[6] Notice that rūpa is included here in the accepted group of real things, alongside citta and caittas. The *Ch'eng wei-shih lun* repeats this phrase continuously.[7]

But while accepting rūpa per se, the *Ch'eng wei-shih lun* insists on redefining it.[8] As phenomenologists, the Yogācārins insist that the only rūpa of which we can speak is phenomenological rūpa, which is to say, rūpa that occurs within consciousness. What we perceive *as rūpa* is actually alterations within our perceptual stream, as was noted in the example earlier on touching a table. Rūpa is admitted; its *externality* to the cognitive activity in which it occurs is denied. This is a phenomenological reduction, not a metaphysical claim. The distinction between these may be illustrated by returning to the debate between the Sarvāstivādins and the *Ch'eng wei-shih lun.*

There ensues a vigorous debate concerning where in a speech act meaning resides, the Sarvāstivādin trying to locate it in the names, sentences and utterances themselves, and the *Ch'eng wei-shih lun* arguing that such theories undermine language's ability to connote, to imply reference.[9]

> If names, sentences and utterances are real existents (*shih-yu*) different from sound (*sheng* 聲), then, like color and (other real things different from sound), they would be real (things) incapable of linguistically-connoting (*ch'üan* 詮).
>
> [If, on the other hand] sound is that which is able to produce names, sentences and utterances, then this sound must (already) have phonological inflections (音韻屈曲 *yin-yun ch'ü-ch'ü*) (lit. *ch'ü* 屈 'bend, oppress,' *ch'ü* 曲 'crooked, perverse').

Are the three viprayukta-dharmas that deal with language—viz. names, sentences, and utterances—substantially real entities distinct from sound, or does sound itself account for the communicative and referential functions of language?

If 'names, sentences, and utterances' are substantial entities that, in some essential way, are different from sound, then they would be like the other substantial *dravya* that are different from sound, such as color, tastes, and so on, which, of course, lack the capacity to linguistically connote or refer. They don't speak. Without sound the three linguistic viprayukta dharmas cannot exercise linguistic functions, and hence would be oxymoronic.[10]

A linguistic sound must be different from mere noise. It must be capable of producing phonological inflections, i.e., meaningful human speech. Indians, since ancient times, not only considered communicative, meaningful 'language' to be intimately connected with sound; they developed detailed 'sciences' analyzing the phonological features of language, as well as the grammar, syntax, prosody, etc., initially in an attempt to penetrate the meaning embodied in the linguistic structure of the Vedas. Noting where in the mouth each sound was produced, Indians developed an alphabet that was phonologically grounded—unlike Western alphabets which are random in order, vestiges of historical accidents—starting at the back of the throat and working forward through diphthongs, palatals, linguals, dentals and labials, concepts which the Indians themselves were the first to discover and which were millenia later introduced to Europe via European scholars studying Sanskrit who learned these principles from the Indians. The transmission of these principles initiated the modern Western science of linguistics. Writing, for Indians, merely encoded the meanings encoded in the sounds of speech (*vāc*). Mantras and dhāranī developed from the same notion. The famous mantric syllable, OM, for instance, actually spelled AUM, signifies the totality of the roughly fifty letters of the Sanskrit alphabet uttered quickly, starting at the back of the throat ("A"), closing and forming the sound as it pushes forward ("U"), and sealing it with the lips ("M"). As the totality of the sonic alphabet, AUM is powerful because it doesn't merely *represent* the totality of sounds and thus reality itself; the utterance of AUM *enacts* the totality of reality. Phonological analysis in India, as mentioned, explored many other facets as well, such as grammar, intonation, song, chant, and so on.

Phonology was also understood in India (and China) as involving tones (*yin* 音) (as well as many other phonological features, such as the rules of saṅdhi, etc.). Modern Mandarin Chinese has four (or five) tones which are crucial for reducing the otherwise impossibly confusing homophonic possibilities created by a language of monosyllabic words. Cantonese, which retains older phonetic features than Mandarin, has nine tones. Sanskrit has tones (*svara*) as well, i.e., high, middle, and low. *Yin-yun* means "phonology," i.e., the study of speech sounds and their analysis in phonetics and phonemics.

The inflections (*ch'ü-ch'ü*) can be grammatical, semantic, syntactic, tonal, etc. They are variations, or deployments of linguistic permutations that articulate different nuances of meaning. The analysis of alterity in the Sanskrit and Chinese articulations of *pariṇāma* and *pravṛtti* offered in Chapter Sixteen illustrated one form of this. We can offer another example here, one which might even be a subtext to this passage. The compound *ch'ü-ch'ü* is composed of two terms, both of which mean 'bend, crooked.' They 'bend' the sounds, creating inflections. On the one hand the two terms are homophonic (both uttered in the first tone), and form a compound literally implying bent or crooked (their shared connotation). But the second term may also be pronounced in the third tone, thus receiving *a different meaning,* namely 'songs, ballads,' thus reinforcing the importance of *vocal* intonation for producing meaningful sounds. The point being made by the *Ch'eng wei-shih lun* is that meaning is related by and to the human voice (*vāc, yü* 語).[11]

If meaning is found in sounds themselves, then already sound is connotative, evoking and indicating something other than itself. This would make the so-called 'realities'—names, sentences, and utterances—superfluous.[12]

> Since these [phonologically inflected sounds] are sufficient to connote [meanings], of what use are [the superfluous categories] names, etc.?
>
> If you say that the sounds mentioned above, i.e., the phonological inflections, precisely are the real entities (實有 *shih-yu*) 'names, sentences and utterances' and that these are different from sound, [this is like saying of] a rūpa (= form = color) which is seen that the variations (*ch'ü-ch'ü*) of shape and size would be different from their rūpic locus (*rūpāyatana*), and have their own separate substantial body (*pieh yu shih t'i* 別有實體).

This displacive ontological proliferation of substantial real 'entities' over and above what is actually experienced is, of course, precisely the problem that Yogācāra seeks to eliminate. Sound and color are phenomenological facticities. They are sensate. Positing additional abstract entities over and above them is sheer imagination.

In what way are sounds the same or different from linguistic meaning? Does meaning derive from a realm distinct from the sounds, or is it identical to the sounds? Or, do the sounds themselves somehow connote meanings?

> If you say that the sounds mentioned above, i.e., phonological inflections, are like the sounds of stringed or reed instruments,[13] which are unable to connote [linguistic meanings], then like those [instrumental] sounds, these would not produce distinct names, etc.

In other words, if sound lacks the ability to produce meaningful intonations, then it would, by definition, be incapable of producing meaningful linguistic semes, which is absurd. The argument continues, until the text finally insists that meaning must come from the *human* voice, from human discourse (*vāc, yü* 語 = discourse, language, words). Meaning does not reside in distinct, separate entities called 'names, sentences,' etc., nor in inchoate sounds. Discourse and connotation are inseparable. "Humans and devas universally discern [this to be the case]."[14]

The text then advances the 'correct view.'

> Depending on discursive sounds (語聲 *yü sheng*), distinct contexts (*wei* 位, lit: stages, seats) are differentiated (*ch'a-pieh* 差別) and name-, sentence- and utterance-bodies are prajñaptically established and asserted. 'Names' signify self-natures (*svabhāvāḥ*); 'sentences' signify differentiations (*ch'a-pieh* 差別); 'utterances' precisely are the words (*tzu* 字)[15] on which the other two are supported. Although these three have no 'body' (*t'i*) apart from sound, yet [in terms of] prajñapti they are really different, not the same as sound.

Prajñaptically, 'names' is how we refer to things in themselves (*svabhāva*). 'Sentences' construct meanings out of relations between words, differentiating words by syntactical, etc., differences, and differentiating their referents according to the categories linguistically assigned to them. These two types of expressions—things (e.g., nouns, subjects) and predicates—are 'supported' or conveyed by 'utterances.' In the connotative sphere the three viprayukta dharmas are 'really' different from sound, though they are not different from sound in any 'real' way. Linguistically meaningful and referential sound is only different from noise, instrumental music, the whistling of the wind, and so in, in that it is the *sound of the human voice.* Human sound can embody and convey intentionalities and meanings. Meaningful reference when communicative is discourse. Discourse, of course, is one of the three modes of karma (activities of body, discourse and thought). But does the *Ch'eng wei-shih lun* understand sound, which is the root of discourse, to be rūpic? Yes, but in the modified sense of rūpa discussed above, i.e., as never separate from consciousness.

Vijñapti-rūpa and Avijñapti-rūpa

Earlier the text critiqued the Sarvāstivādin notion of rūpa. Sarvāstivādins claim two types of rūpa, (1) rūpa which gives resistance (*pratigha-rūpa, yu-tui* 有對) and (2) non-resistant rūpa (*apratigha-rūpa, wu-tui* 無對). The first is denied by the *Ch'eng wei-shih lun* because, as defined by Sarvāstivādins, it depends on some sort of atomic theory and the *Ch'eng wei-shih lun* points out that those theories involve irremedial logical incoherencies.[16] Note that it is not the cognitive facticity of rūpa that is being rejected here, but the *theoretical* constructions to which those cognitions may be reduced. It is the erroneous interpretation of cognition, not the content of cognition, that is being criticized.

Then the rūpic theories of other schools are likewise critiqued.[17]

The Sarvāstivādin's non-resistant rūpa is then discussed.[18] It is of two kinds: *vijñapti-rūpa* and *avijñapti-rūpa.* In this part of the text Hsüan-tsang uses 表 *piao* (indication) to translate *vijñapti. Vijñapti-rūpa* is again subdivided into two: bodily vijñapti-rūpa and vocal vijñapti-rūpa. *Avijñapti-rūpa* is likewise doubled.[19] For Yogācāra these activities—which are rūpic *and* karmic for the Sarvāstivādins—can only be non-rūpic, since they *are* karmic. Vijñapti-rūpa is said to be gestural or vocalized activity which indicates or conveys its meaning from one person to another. Avijñapti-rūpa is non-indicative, it does not convey its sense. When, for instance one pretends to befriend someone, giving every indication by word and bodily gesture that one is a friend, while in actuality disliking and plotting against that person, the 'intent' which is not gesturally transmitted is *avijñapti-rūpa.* The earlier texts usually discussed these special rūpas in terms of ritual or confession. When one does a certain rite, for instance, the assembly has no way of knowing what sort of intention or mindfulness the actor is performing the rite with. The action itself, they thought, might have karmic consequences. This would be a singular case of a non-intersubjective karmic act. Such speculation led to all sorts of theoretical 'actions' which were rūpic, and not cognitive.

The *Ch'eng wei-shih lun* says:[20]

> The yoga masters,[21] using a prajñaptic conceptual cognition (*yi chia hsiang hui* 以假想慧),[22] [thought about] the characteristics of gross rūpa, and gradually, progressively divided and split it (*ch'u hsi* 除析) until it could no longer be divided. [This indivisible unit they gave] the *upacāra* 'the smallest' (lit. 'supremely tiniest,' i.e., atom, *t'ai-wei* 太微). Although this 'smallest' refers to something that has been methodically divided (*feng fen* 方分) until it could no longer be divided, if [you try to] split it further, then all you would see is empty [space], so that it could no longer be considered rūpa. Hence what is called 'the smallest' is rūpa's final limit.[23] Due to this you should know that the rūpas which resist are all perceived/projected (*hsien*) alterations of consciousness (*shih-pien*), and not [actually] achieved 'smallest' units.

This tiniest atom, in other words, is a mental construct devised by a method that draws short of reaching its logical conclusion—emptiness. The 'limit' is a conceptual limit, not a physical limit divorced from the cognitive methodology that produced it. Pushed to its extreme, the method would undermine that which it seeks to establish. In order to ground rūpa in an indivisible unit, that unit must be asserted via a paring down of physical forms to that beyond which they can no longer be divided. That limit itself is only another cognitive construct, so that the atom is deconstructed by the very process through which it is conceived. Geometrically speaking, if a point lacks magnitude (as atoms were argued to lack, since if they had any magnitude, they could be further subdivided, and hence would not be the smallest irreducible unit), then it would be impossible to build three dimensional objects from them, no matter how many magnitude-less you heaped together (whatever 'heaping things devoid of magnitude' would mean). If it has magnitude, it can be further subdivided, since it would necessarily still have distinct parts (top, bottom, one side, the other side, etc.).

The *Ch'eng wei-shih lun* concedes that Buddha did teach about atoms, but only in order to help those attached to notions of gross matter overcome their attachment. "Atom" is a prajñapti (假說極微), constructed prajñaptically in thought, noetically (以假想慧), in the manner described above.

The point that the *Ch'eng wei-shih lun* is trying to drive home is that rūpa is sensorial, i.e., that it is a phenomenological appearance. The theoretical categories constructed to account for rūpa in a nonsensorial way, that treat rūpa as some sort of non-experiential materiality, are abstractions and themselves cognitive constructions. "Due to this, we definitely know that it is what is altered of one's own consciousness (自識所變) that gives the appearance of the characteristics of rupa, and so on (似色等相). This is what is deemed the ālambana-pratyaya." What we perceive *as* rūpa depends on our own cognitive capacity. That we see a shape *as* a certain *type* of shape, or a color as a certain hue, depends on our cognitive capacity. Consciousness doesn't invent the ālambana out of nothingness. "Perception (*darśana*) arises from taking that (i.e., the appearance of the ālambana), since it holds that as its object (*nimitta*)" (見託彼生，帶彼相故). Consciousness superimposes itself on the perceptual.

> Now when consciousness alters, what suddenly appears (is taken to be) large or small according to (how consciousness) sizes it up into a single characteristic; it is not that apart from what is constructed in (such) alterations, there are numerous subtle atoms combined to establish a single thing.

Having dealt with pratigha rūpa, the *Ch'eng wei-shih lun* now turns to apratigha-rūpa, which, since even to modern ears these sound more like psychological conditions than 'material' entities, the argument begins

> As for what's left, the non-resistant rūpa, [either] it is the same sort of thing [as the resistant rūpa], and thus not a real existent (非實有 *fei shih yu*), or it is like the citta and caittas, and hence definitely not really rūpa (*fei shih se* 非實色).

We needn't rehearse the full series of arguments here. As might be expected, they will attempt to demonstrate that what passes for vijñapti- and avijñapti-rūpa are actually strictly mental or cognitive activities (karma). It is mind which synthesizes and unites discrete moments and things, and labels them 'continuous,' related, etc. A physical gesture has *meaning* only for consciousness. In fact, it is precisely because of the intentionality of consciousness that a physical movement becomes a 'gesture.' The meaning that a gesture carries and conveys is intentionality. This kind of rūpa—i.e., a theoretic construct which is not actually rūpa, but a theory of rūpa— *is caused* by the mind. It is precisely the karmic (= intentional) characteristic of this 'rūpa' which makes it what it is, not the metaphysical creativity of a mind.[24]

> [Bodily vijñapti-rūpa should not be considered caused by rūpic conditions, such as the āyatanas, etc.] but rather mind (citta) should be considered the cause. Now as consciousness is altered, rūpic characteristics such as the hand, etc., arise and cease in a sequential, continuous series (*saṃbandha*), operating (*chuan*) agreeably in the space around it, appearing to have movement and activity. Since [what has synthesized temporal sequence, causal sequence, spatial continuity, foreground-background, what has motivated the hand, etc., what has interpreted and collected discrete particular events and given them a durational meaning] indicates and reveals the mind [at work], the term 'bodily indication' (*kāya-vijñapti*) is [only] a prajñapti.

A little later, after refuting both types of rūpa, the *Ch'eng wei-shih lun* makes its point explicit:[25]

> [The opponent objects]: The Bhagavat (World-Honored One) says in the sūtras that there are three [types of] karma. You deny the bodily and linguistic karma [while accepting only mental karma]. How can you contradict the sūtras?
>
> We don't deny them, or claim they don't exist. We only say that they are not rūpic. The volition (思 *ssu, cetanā*) with the capacity to move the body is what is called bodily karma; the volition with the capacity to give rise to speech (*vāc*) is what is called speech karma; the two volitions 'judgement' and 'decision' (審決 *shen chueh*), since they are associated with intention (*ssu-yi* 思意), with the capacity to motivate intention (意 *yi*), are called intentional (mental) karma.

Yogācāra reaffirms that karma is intentional, volitional. What moves the body is motive; what produces speech is intent. What synthesizes sounds into meaningful units is always mind. Phenomenologically, the region of meaning is always already inscribed within sedimented structures, i.e., seeds and 'perfumings,' and experience *qua* experience is the conscious discerning of distinctions *qua* meanings.

Does Yogācāra posit some 'true' reality, something transcendental or 'otherwise' than the paratantric conditional (*saṃskṛta*) realm of historical embodiment? What, for them, is *asaṃskṛta* ?

Notes

1 T.31.1585.6a; Ch.2:1B; Tat, p. 74-76.

2 *Chan t'ing chi* 暫停即. *Chan* means 'briefly, shortly, temporarily;' *t'ing* means 'stop, settle, delay, rest;' *chi* means 'an instant.'

3 *T'ung tsai hsien tsai* 同在現在.

4 T.31.1585.6a; Ch2:2A; Tat, p. 76.

5 *Fei ning jan* 非凝然. *Ning* means 'to congeal, freeze,' hence the dharma does not freeze in time or space.

6 *Ibid.*

7 Cf. T.31.1585.5a, 5b, 52a, etc.; Ch.1:15A-B, 1:16B-17A, 9:16B, etc.

8 T.31.1585.4a; Ch.1:12A ff; Tat, pp. 46ff.

9 T.31.1585.6a-6b; Ch2:2A-2B; Tat, pp. 76-78.

10 The presupposition of the inseparability of language from sound (rather than identifying language with the visual abstraction of writing, as we tend to do today) goes back to Vedic times in India. Language was sound, utterance; writing merely a secondary record of the sounds. This assumption, of the primacy of aural over written language, was pervasive in most cultures, at least until Derrida challenged the notion by arguing that writing is primary to speech. Cf. his *On Grammatology* and other early works.

11 VP i.69 offers the following correspondences: *yin yün* = *svara* (sound, noise, *tone*); *Ch'ü ch'ü* = *ākuñcana* (bending, e.g., a limb). It seems to me that retranslating *Ch'ü ch'ü* into Sanskrit misses part of the point.

12 *Op. cit.*

13 Prior to modern musical instruments, there were only three basic types of instruments: (1) Stringed instruments, (2) instruments made from reeds or tubes, such as flutes, and (3) percussion (drums, etc.). The first two required a tonal theory, i.e., a theory or *pramāṇa* with which to determine which tones were 'valid' and which were to be suppressed (percussion instruments often participated in tuning theory as well, e.g. Chinese musical stones in which not only each successive stone in a series took up the 'next' note of the scale, but each part of each stone—such as the various edges—also was attuned to a specific tone). Once holes were carved in a reed the tones it could produce were fixed, unalterable. Stringed instruments, since they played varying tones, were scrupulously designed to produce just the right tones. Confucius' high regard for music reflects this use of tuning theory as the criteriological means of access to the cosmic pattern, since musical ratios (the mathematics of tuning theory) made concrete the otherwise 'invisible' patterns that moved and roused men's hearts and minds, patterns isomorphic to the celestial, cosmological, cosmogonic, etc., patterns of the universe. They were the standards against which man and society were to be measured and 'tuned.' The instrument, person and society were to be tuned to the same ratios. The Pythagoreans and Plato (e.g., *The Republic*) explicitly shared this view, and it is likely that some form of musicological theory was widespread throughout the Ancient and Medieval worlds (e.g., the Music of the Spheres). Chuang Tzu's reflections on music (e.g., beginning of Ch. 2), the section on music in the *Li Chi* (Book of Rites), etc., all point to the vital role that tonal theory played in Chinese thought. This subject is much too complex to adequately address here, and nothing definitive has yet been written. A good first step is Kenneth DeWoskin's *A Song for One or Two: Music and the Concept of Art in Early China* (Ann Arbor: Center for Chinese Studies, 1982). The centrality of music *qua* sound models of reality in other cultures has been more adequately addressed, though more needs to be done. Cf. the works of Ernest McClain, e.g. *The Myth of Invariance: the Origin of the Gods, Mathematics and Music from the Ṛg Veda to Plato* (NY: Nicolas Hays, 1976); *The Pythagorean Plato: Prelude to the Song Itself*

(NY: Nicolas Hays, 1978); *Meditations through the Quran: Tonal Images in an Oral Culture* (NY: Nicolas Hays, 1981); also cf. Antonio De Nicolas, *Avatāra: The Humanization of Philosophy Through the Bhagavad Gītā* (NY: Nicolas Hays, 1976); also, for another perspective of how music, sound provides a different ontology, a different philosophy than that which sight models (which predominate in our culture) create, cf. Victor Zuckerkandl's *Sound and Symbol: Music and the External World* (Princeton: Bollingen, 1969) and *Man the Musician: Sound and Symbol*, v. II (Princeton: Bollingen, 1973).

14 *Ibid.*

15 The Chinese *tzu* usually indicates a written word!, whereas *vyañjana*, the Sanskrit term it is translating, means 'utterance,' but in this context denotes 'basic syllables.' Cf. *Abhidharmakośa-bhāṣya* 2.47a-b.

16 Cf. T.31.1585.4a-4c; Ch.1:12A-14A; Tat, pp. 46-54. Several Yogācāra texts offer refutations of atomism; cf. e.g., Vasubandhu's *Twenty Verses*, etc.

17 They are reduced to four basic theories, and these theories are then refuted. Cf. *ibid.*

18 T.31.1585.4c-5a; Ch.1:14A-15A; Tat, p. 54-58.

19 Cf. Part III. chapter ten, for a review of these categories in MMK 17.

20 *Ibid.*

21 According to K'uei-chi, this means Yogācārins.

22 Chia-hsiang was sometimes used by Hsüan-tsang to translate saṃjñā, associative conceptual thinking.

23 "Final limit" = *pien-chi* . Pien means 'the side, bank, edge, margin, frontier'; chi means 'border, limit.' *Index* p. 427: Pien-chi = *anta, anta-kṛiyā, kāla-niyama, paryanta, prānta-koṭika*, which all signify some sort of edge, border, end, boundary, limit.

24 T.31.1585.5a; Ch.1:14B; Tat, p. 56.

25 T.31.1585.5a; Ch.1:15A; Tat, p. 58.

Chapter Twenty-Three

Is What Is Ultimately Real Itself Ultimately Real?

What are real dharmas? The *Ch'eng wei-shih lun* says:[1]

> The claim that there are unconditioned dharmas apart from rūpa, citta and [the caittas], which are definite real existents, is not supported by reason. There are three types of dharmas determined to exist:
>
> (1) dharmas known through direct perception, such as rūpa, citta, etc.[2]
>
> (2) dharmas whose functions are enjoyed through direct perception. such as pitchers and clothes.
>
> The whole world universally knows that these two types of dharmas exist; they don't need to be established by reason.
>
> (3) dharmas that actively function, such as the eye, ear, etc.; due to their functioning, one realizes and knows that they exist.

The first two are immediately known through perception, and thus do not require additional inferential proofs. The third is inferential. For instance, even though the eye can not see itself, the sheer fact that one can see at all demonstrates that one has eyes. One can determine the role of the eyes by covering them up, or closing them, and trying to see. This knowledge is inferential, but still directly tied to immediate experience. Thus we see, that even though explicitly the *Ch'eng wei-shih lun* treats scripture and reasoning as the basic pramāṇas, when determining which dharmas are real, perception and inference alone count. The inferential category is important for Yogācāra, since things like the ālaya-vijñāna, like the eye, cannot be perceived directly, and can only be known through inference concerning its observable effects.

It again bears emphasis that rūpa is accepted as a real dharma *because it is known through cognitive acts.*

Empirical 'reality' is accepted, not denied. What *is* denied is any claim that we *know* of it or that it exists *for us* anywhere else than *within* acts of cognition. 'Consciousness' is a name for what arises through such acts. Empirical 'laws,' commonality, causal relations, and so on, are all mental constructs, ways of 'knowing.'

Unconditioned dharmas are not directly perceived, nor do they exhibit observable effects in the empirical world; so the *Ch'eng wei-shih lun* does not accept them as ultimately real.

> Unconditioned dharmas are not universally known by the whole world as definitely existing, since they lack active functions, unlike the eye, ear, etc. If [one could prove or demonstrate] they had a function, [this action would arise and cease within a temporal sequence, and thus] they would have to be impermanent. Hence [the view] that unconditioned dharmas definitely exist cannot be held. However, since the nature of unconditioned dharmas is known, and since that nature is sometimes revealed by rūpa, citta, etc., like rūpa, citta, etc., one shouldn't hold the opinion that apart from rūpa, citta, etc., [there are] unconditioned dharmas.

The unconditioned dharmas (*asaṃskṛta-dharma*) are non-empirical, by definition, and hence, since the criterion of reality is the ability of a dharma to discharge its efficient causality, they cannot be real. Their 'nature' is sometimes disclosed in the way the dharmas engaged in cognition—such as rūpa, citta, and the caittas—operate cognitively. Principles (i.e., natures) can be generalized by inference from particular occurrences. Since the unconditioned dharmas are not accessible or knowable apart from how they are implicated in cognitions, the *Ch'eng wei-shih lun* insists that "apart from rūpa, citta, etc., [there are no] unconditioned dharmas." Like rūpa and externality, unconditioned dharmas cannot be divorced from the realm of cognition in which they are constructed and 'known.' For Yogācāra, all is reducible to phenomenality, and the *idea* that something exists outside or beyond that is only an idea that occurs within phenomenal cognitions.

The text then turns to each of the dharmas professed to be unconditioned, such as *ākāśa* (spatiality), etc. (see appendices 1-3 for lists of asaṃskṛta-dharmas).[3]

> The sūtras say that "the unconditioned dharmas, such as *ākāśa*, etc., exist."
>
> Generally there are two types:
>
> (1) Dependent on alterations of consciousness (*shih-pieh*) they are prajñaptis which one assumes exists (假施設有). [For instance] one has heard the terms *ākāśa,* etc., and subsequently one [imaginatively] discriminates (*vikalpa*) the characteristics of *ākāśa*. Because the power of these ruminations becomes habitual, the mind, etc., at some point, produces what appears to be *ākāśa*, etc., projecting/perceiving (*hsien*) the [learned] 'unconditioned' characteristics. Since the projected/perceived characteristics appear without alterity (i.e., they don't change), they are prajñaptically labeled 'permanent' (常 *ch'ang*).
>
> (2) Dependent on dharma-nature (*dharmatā*), they are prajñaptis which one assumes to exist. Tathatā is disclosed by the emptiness [of dharmas] and no-self. [This tathatā] is neither existent nor inexistent. The paths of mind and language are cut off (心言路絕 *hsin yen lü chüeh*); it is neither the same nor different from all dharmas, etc. It is the true principle of dharmas, and so it is called *dharmatā*

The Five Asaṃskṛta Dharmas are then explained in terms of what they prajñaptically signify.[4]

> Since it is apart from obstructions and obstacles, it is called 'spatiality' (*ākāśa*).
>
> Due to the power of *pratisaṃkhyā* (deep understanding), the cessation of confusion and impurity [or heterogeneous defilements] is ultimately realized and acquired, and hence it is called *pratisaṃkhyā-nirodha* (cessation through understanding).
>
> [If tathatā] is disclosed, not due to the power of understanding, but because of the absence of any [obstructive] conditions [to block] the pristinely pure original nature, this is termed *apratisaṃkhyā-nirodha* (cessation without understanding).
>
> Since the feelings of pain and pleasure (*duḥkha* and *sukha*) cease, it is termed *āniñjya* (unperturbed, lit: 'non-moving').
>
> Since *saṃjñā* and *vedanā* don't operate, it is termed *saṃjñā-vedanā-nirodha* (cessation of associative-thinking and pain-pleasure).
>
> These five (unconditioned dharmas) are all prajñaptis established in dependence on tathatā; and tathatā also is a prajñaptic name (依真如假立。真如亦是假施設名).

This passage is crucial. Tathatā it turns out, is also prajñapti.

Before we pointed out that the *Ch'eng wei-shih lun* utilizes an opposition between 'real' (實 *shih, dravya*) and 'nominal' (假〔實〕 *chia* [*-shih*], *prajñapti*). Does this mean that tathatā is non-existent, or unreal? Not exactly. Adhering to the middle way that avoids extremes means to not leap to the affirmation of one extreme when the other extreme is negated. The term 'tathatā' *is* a prajñapti, but it serves an upāyic soteric function.[5]

> To refute the claim that [tathatā] is inexistent, it is said to be considered 'existent.'
>
> To refute attachment to its being considered existent, it is said to be considered 'empty.'
>
> So that it won't be called vacuous or illusory, it is said to be considered 'real' (實 *shih*).
>
> Since reason neither falsifies nor contradicts it, it is termed *'chen-ju'* 真如 (*tathatā*).
>
> We are not the same as the other schools (who claim) that apart from rūpa, citta, etc. [i.e., the caittas], there exists a substantial permanent dharma called by the name of 'tathatā. Instead, [we say] the unconditioned dharmas definitely are not real existents.

In case one became confused by the seeming vacillation suggested by this middle way—to fully affirm or deny would be extreme—the text has reiterated the basic fact: tathatā and the other so-called unconditioned dharmas are linguistic fictions. They can be conjured either by having once heard about them, and then letting one's mind and imagination flesh out the ideas, developing those impressions into actual 'perceptions,' i.e., a kind of wish-fulfillment; or by 'disclosing' the dharma-nature which is neither identical to nor different from actual dharmas. Like tathatā, dharmatā is a prajñaptic device, not an 'ultimate reality.' The text continues:[6]

> ...To oppose false attachment [to the view that] external to citta and caittas there are real existent perceptual-objects (*ching*, *viṣaya*), we say that only consciousness exists (唯有識 *wei yu shih*). If you attach to "only consciousness" as something truly real and existent, that is like being attached to external sense-objects, i.e., just another dharma-attachment.

Tathatā is not a 'real thing, nor is vijñāna/vijñapti. It is a merely descriptive term for what occurs in a cognition 'purified' of karmic defilements and cognitive obstructions. Emptiness is posited as an antidote to attachment; and 'consciousness-only' is charged with the same function.

Psychosophic closure cannot be reified. The closure undergoes erasure; the obstructions become transparent. Descriptive discourse crosses over into prescriptive discourse not because of an imperative or imperialistic insistence. Language is brought to its own margins, its own dislocations. The description itself plays the dance of language, it enacts the appropriational urge without which words would fail to seek a referent. The grasper-grasped is exposed immediately and ubiquitously in every moment of cognitive apprehension; the 'given' loses its innocence and is exposed as the 'taken'; the appropriational economy is everywhere revealed for what it is: a consciousness that 'hangs onto' (*ālambana*) whatever it can, even and especially its own creations. Consciousness discerns sense-objects, cognitively embraces them, and then 'dwells' on them.

First externality is challenged. The external is not ontologically significant, i.e., it is not actually external *to* me; it is external *for* me, to define my limits, such that I contruct and operate myself appropriationally.

The very end of the text repeats the salient points one final time:[7]

> The word 'only' (*mātra*, *wei*) refutes externality, but it doesn't deny the perceptual-fields within...

It is consciousness-only and not 'perceptual-object-only' because consciousness cannot be externalized, whereas objects not only can, but often are. To return us to our own experience, to the intentionality that connects us with our world, to bring us to understand precisely what cognition is, how it functions, and how to smash the closure that narcissistically traps us in our own consciousness, so that we reflect the world like a mirror, rather than our own anxieties and predilections; to uncover and strip away the presuppositions which blind us; for these reasons Yogācāra has offered a phenomenological system for self-analysis. The details of that system, such as the interplay of the various caittas, etc., the antidotal application of the three non-self-natures, have been suggested but far from exhaustively expounded here.[8]

There are those foolish ones; deluded, they attach to perceptual-objects. Karmic mental-disturbances (*kleśa*) arise, and the [foolish ones] are engulfed and drowned in the [cycle of] birth and death (i.e., saṃsāra). Not understanding contemplating mind (*kuan-hsin* 觀心), who seeks to transcend and detach from it? Out of a deep inner sympathy for those [who suffer thus], the words '*vijñapti-mātra* are expounded, so that you may contemplate your own mind (*tzu kuan hsin* 自觀心) and be liberated from saṃsāra.

Notes

1 T.31.1585.6b; Ch.2:3A-3B; Tat, pp. 80-82.

2 Tat, *ibid.*, translates K'uei-chi's comment to this passage as: "Dharmas known by evidence, like Rupa which is known by the five consciousnesses, and like mind and its caittas which are known by the 'knowledge of other minds."

8T.31.1585.6c6-12; Ch.2:4A-B; Tat, p. 82-84.

4 *Ibid.* 6c12-17.

8 *Ibid.* 6c17-20.

6 *Ibid.* 6c24-26.

7 1585.59a8-9.

8 1585.59a11-14. *Kuan-hsin*, which became an important term in T'ien-t'ai, Ch'an, etc., as well, appears five times in *Ch'eng wei-shih lun*, twice in this passage (once as *tzu-kuan-hsin*), and also at 49b26, 49c6, and 54a16.

Conclusions

When Yogācārins deny 'external objects,' what are they rejecting and what, if anything, are they affirming? Yogācāra employs many words to designate types of cognitive objects—*viṣaya, artha, ālambana, vastu, ākāra, prameya, jñeya, viṣaya-gocara, rūpa-pratibhāsa, grāhya, nimitta,* etc. We lose access to the nuances of their phenomenology when we homogenize their discourse by using the single English term 'object' for all these (and more). Many of these terms are never rejected at all by Yogācārins. As we have seen repeatedly Yogācārins do not reject the category of *rūpa* (matter); eleven of the one hundred dharmas in Yogācāra abhidharma are rūpa-dharmas. They also employ a technical, phenomenological vocabulary for the sorts of cognitive activities in which cognitive objects appear—*pratyakṣa, upalabdhi, grāha, khyāti, pratibhāsa, pratibimba, vijñapti, parināṃa, viśeṣa-prāpti, pravṛtti, abhūta-parikalpa,* etc. Without some understanding of what these cognitive activities entail, it would be difficult to decide what they include or exclude and why.

Yogācāra is not Metaphysical Idealism

Yogācāra (yoga practice) doctrine received that name because it provided a 'yoga,' a comprehensive, therapeutic framework for engaging in the practices that lead to the goal of the bodhisattva path, namely enlightened cognition. Meditation served as the laboratory in which one could study how the mind operated. Yogācāra focused on the question of consciousness from a variety of approaches, including meditation, psychological analysis, epistemology (how we know what we know, how perception operates, what validates knowledge), scholastic categorization, and karmic analysis.

Yogācāra doctrine is often encapsulated by the term *vijñapti-mātra*, "nothing-but-noetic constitution" (often rendered "consciousness-only" or "mind-only") which has sometimes been interpreted as indicating a type of metaphysical idealism, namely, the claim that mind alone is real and that everything else is created by mind. *Vijñapti-mātra* and its corollaries *vijñāna-mātra* and *citta-mātra* have repeatedly been interpreted by Western and Asian scholars as promoting metaphysical idealism. *Mātra* ("only"), according to this interpretation, acts as an approving affirmation of mind as the true reality. However, the Yogācārin writings themselves argue something very different. Consciousness (*vijñāna*) is not the ultimate reality or solution, but rather the root problem. This problem emerges in ordinary mental operations, and it can only be solved by bringing those operations to an end.

Why has Yogācāra been misinterpreted as idealism? The common way of interpreting *mātra* so as to valorize 'consciousness' is striking since those same interpretors never impute such implications to *mātra* on the many other occasions it is used by Buddhists or Yogācārins. For instance, the closely allied term *prajñapti-mātra* ("only nominally real") has never led a modern interpretor to speculate that Language is the metaphysical reality behind the world of experience; on the contrary, those prone to idealist interpretations tend to privilege ineffability and yearn for a realm beyond language and conceptions. Similarly, terms found in Yogācāra texts such as *kalpanā-mātra* (nothing but imaginative construction),[1] *bhrānta-mātra* (nothing but cognitive error),[2] *ākāra-mātra* (nothing but a noema),[3] *ākṛti-mātra* (nothing but construction),[4] and so on, have never led interpretors to speculate that the terms accompanying *mātra* in those instances should be treated as metaphysical realities. It is commonly recognized that terms such as kalpanā, bhrānta, etc., are emblematic of the problems Buddhism seeks to overcome—namely ignorance and misconceptions (*avidyā, moha*, etc.)—so that they cannot signify a positive reality. That the term *vijñapti-mātra* has been valorised while no one would dream of valorizing the other *-mātra* compounds is perhaps a testament to the pernicious persistence of *bhāvāsava*, the compulsion to assert something existent to which one can cling. That is one of two extremes from which the middle way is designed to steer us (nihilism is the other). Yogācāra is deeply concerned about the human propensity to posit things we can appropriate.

Yogācāra tends to be misinterpreted as a form of metaphysical idealism primarily because its teachings are taken to be ontological propositions rather than epistemological warnings about karmic problems. The Yogācāra focus on cognition and consciousness grew out of its analysis of karma, and not for the sake of metaphysical speculation.

Yogācāra

Tellingly no Indian Yogācāra text ever claims that the world is created by mind. What they do claim is that we mistake our projected interpretations of the world for the world itself, i.e., we take our own mental constructions to be the world. Their vocabulary for this is as rich as their analysis: *kalpanā* (projective conceptual construction), *parikalpa* and *parikalpita* (ubiquitous imaginary constructions), *abhūta-parikalpa* (imagining something in a locus in which it does not exist), *prapañca* (proliferation of conceptual constructions), *samāropa* (assertive reification), *khyāti* (appearance according to conceptual, linguistic assertions), *pratibimba* (projection), to mention a few. Correct cognition is defined as the removal of those obstacles which prevent us from seeing dependent causal conditions in the manner they actually become (*yathā-bhūtam*). For Yogācāra these causal conditions are cognitive, not metaphysical; they are the mental and perceptual conditions by which sensations and thoughts occur, not the metaphysical machinations of a Creator or an imperceptible domain of inchoate or insensate material. What is known through correct cognition is euphemistically called *tathatā*, "suchness," which Yogācāra texts are quick to point out is not an actual thing, but only a word (*prajñapti-mātra*).

What is crucial in the forgoing for understanding Yogācāra is that its attention to perceptual and cognitive issues is in line with basic Buddhist thinking, and that this attention is epistemological rather than metaphysical. When Yogācārins discuss "objects," they are talking about *cognitive* objects, not metaphysical entities.[5] Rather than offer one more ontology, they attempt to uncover and eliminate the predilections and proclivities (*āśrava, anuśaya*) that compel people to generate and cling to such theoretical constructions. Since, according to Yogācāra, all ontologies are epistemological constructions, to understand how cognition operates is to understand how and why people construct the ontologies to which they cling. Ontological attachment is a symptom of cognitive projection (*pratibimba, parikalpita*). Careful examination of Yogācāra texts reveals that they make no ontological claims, except to question the validity of making ontological claims.[6] The reason they give for their ontological silence is that were they to offer a metaphysical description, that description would be appropriated by its interpreters who, due to their proclivities, would project onto it what they wish reality to be, thereby reducing the description to their own presupposed theory of reality. Such projective reductionism is the problem. That is what *vijñapti-mātra* means, viz., to mistake one's projections for that onto which one is projecting. Vasubandhu's *Thirty Verses* (*Triṁśikā*) states that if one clings to one's projection of the idea of *vijñapti-mātra*, then one fails to truly dwell in an understanding of *vijñapti-mātra* (verse 27). Enlightened cognition free of all cognitive errors is defined as *nirvikalpa-jñāna*, "cognition without imaginative construction," i.e., without conceptual overlay. Ironically, Yogācāra's interpreters and opponents nevertheless could not resist reductively projecting metaphysical theories onto what Yogācārins did say, at once proving Yogācāra was right and at the same time making actual Yogācāra teachings that much harder to access. Interpreting their epistemological analyses as metaphysical pronouncements fundamentally misconstrues their project.

The arguments Yogācāra deploys frequently resemble those made by epistemological idealists. Recognizing those affinities Western scholars early in the twentieth century compared Yogācāra to Kant, and more recently scholars have begun to think that Husserl's phenomenology comes even closer. There are indeed intriguing similarities, for instance between Husserl's description of noesis (consciousness projecting its cognitive field) and noema (the constructed cognitive object) on the one hand, and Yogācāra's analysis of the (cognitive) grasper and the grasped (*grāhaka* and *grāhya*) on the other hand. But there are also important differences between those Western philosophers and Yogācāra. The three most important are: Kant and Husserl play down notions of causality, while Yogācāra developed complex systematic causal theories it deemed to be of the greatest importance; there is no counterpart to either karma or enlightenment in the Western theories, while these are the very *raison d'être* for all Yogācāra theory and practice; finally, the Western philosophies are designed to afford the best possible access to an ontological realm (at least sufficient to acknowledge its existence), while Yogācāra is critical of that motive in all its manifestations. To the extent that epistemological idealists can also be critical realists, Yogācāra may be deemed a type of epistemological idealism, with the proviso that the purpose of its arguments was not to engender an improved ontological theory or commitment, but rather an insistence that we pay the fullest attention to the epistemological and psychological conditions compelling us to construct and attach to ontological theories.

Karma, Matter, and Cognitive Appropriation

The key to Yogācāra theory lies in the Buddhist notions of karma which it inherited and rigorously reinterpreted. As earlier Buddhist texts already explained, karma is responsible for suffering and ignorance, and karma consists of any intentional activity of body, language, or mind. Since the crucial factor is intent, and intent is a cognitive condition, whatever lacks intent is both non-karmic and non-cognitive. Hence, by definition, whatever is non-cognitive can have no karmic influence or consequences. Since Buddhism aims at overcoming ignorance and suffering through the elimination of karmic conditioning, Buddhism, they reasoned, is only concerned with the analysis and correction of whatever falls within the domain of cognitive conditions. Hence questions about the ultimate reality of non-cognitive things are simply irrelevant and useless for solving the problem of karma. Further, Yogācārins emphasize that categories such as materiality (*rūpa*) are cognitive categories. "Materiality" is a word for the colors, textures, sounds, etc., that we experience in acts of perception, and it is only to the extent that they are experienced, perceived and ideologically grasped, thereby becoming objects of attachment, that they have karmic significance. Intentional acts also have moral motives and consequences. Since effects are shaped by their causes, an act with a wholesome intent would tend to yield wholesome fruits, while unwholesome intentions produce unwholesome effects.

In contrast to the cognitive karmic dimension, Buddhism considered material elements (*rūpa*) karmically neutral. The problem with material things is not their materiality, but the psychology of appropriation (*upādāna*)—desiring, grasping, clinging, attachment—that permeates our ideas and perceptions of such things. It is not the materiality of gold that leads to problems, but rather our *ideas* about the value of gold and the attitudes and actions we engage in as a result of those ideas. Those ideas have been acquired through previous experiences. By repeated exposure to certain ideas and cognitive conditions, one is conditioned to respond habitually in a similar manner to similar circumstances. Eventually these habits are embodied, becoming reflexive, presuppositional. For Buddhists this process by which conditioning becoming embodied (*saṁskāra*) is not confined to a single life-time, but accrues over many life-times. *Saṁsāra* (the continuous cycle of birth and death) is the karmic en-act-ment of this repetition, the reoccurrence of cognitive embodied habits in new life situations and life forms.

For all Buddhists this follows a simple sensory calculus: Pleasurable feelings we wish to hold on to, or repeat. Painful feelings we wish to cut off, or avoid. Pleasure and pain, reward and punishment, approval and disapproval, and so on, condition us. Our karmic habits (*vāsanā*) are constructed this way. Since all is impermanent, pleasurable feelings cannot be maintained or repeated permanently; painful things (such as sickness and death) cannot be avoided permanently. The greater the dissonance between our actual impermanent experience and our expectations for permanent desired ends, the more we suffer, and the greater tendency (*anuśaya*) toward projecting our desires onto the world as compensation. Though nothing whatsoever is permanent, we imagine all sort of permanent things—from God to soul to essences—in an effort to avoid facing the fact that none of us has a permanent self. We think that if we can prove something is permanent, anything, then we too have a chance for permanence. The anxiety about our lack of self and all the cognitive and karmic mischief it generates is called several things by Yogācāra, including *jñeyāvaraṇa* (obstruction of the knowable, i.e., our self-obsessions prevent us from seeing things as they are) and *abhūta-parikalpa* (imagining something—namely permanence or a self—to exist in a locus in which it is absent).

The karmic cause of the fundamental dis-ease (*duḥkha*) is desire expressed through body, speech, or mind. Therefore Yogācāra focused exclusively on cognitive and mental activities in relation to their intentions, i.e., the operations of consciousness, since the problem was located there. Buddhism had always identified ignorance and desire as the primary causes of suffering and rebirth. Yogācārins mapped these mental functions in order to dismantle them. Because maps of this sort were also creations of the mind, they too would ultimately have to be abandoned in the course of the dismantling, but their therapeutic value would have been served in bringing about enlightenment. This view of the provisional expediency of Buddhism can be traced back to Buddha himself. Yogācārins describe enlightenment as resulting from Overturning the Cognitive Basis (*āśraya-paravṛtti*), i.e., overturning the conceptual projections and imaginings which act as the base of our cognitive actions. This overturning transforms the basic mode of cognition from consciousness (*vi-jñāna,* discernment) into *jñāna* (direct knowing). Direct knowing was defined as non-conceptual (*nirvikalpa-jñāna*), i.e., devoid of interpretive overlay.

The case of material elements is important for understanding one reason why Yogācāra is not metaphysical idealism. No Yogācāra text denies materiality (*rūpa*) as a valid Buddhist category. On the contrary, Yogācārins include materiality in their analysis. Their approach to materiality is well rooted in Buddhist precedents. Frequently Buddhist texts substitute the term "sensory contact" (Pāli: *phassa,* Sanskrit: *sparśa*) for the term "materiality." This substitution is a reminder that physical forms are sensory, that they are known to be what they are through sensation. Even the earliest Buddhist texts explain the four primary material elements are the sensory qualities solidity, fluidity, temperature, and mobility; their characterization as earth, water, fire, and air, respectively, is declared an abstraction. Instead of concentrating on the fact of material existence, one observes how a physical thing is sensed, felt, perceived. Yogācāra never denies that there are sense-objects (*viṣaya, artha, ālambana,* etc.), but it denies that it makes any sense to speak of cognitive objects occurring outside an act of cognition. Imagining such an occurrence is itself a cognitive act. Yogācāra is interested in why we feel compelled to so imagine.

The Crux

Everything we know, conceive, imagine, or are aware of, we know through cognition, including the notion that entities might exist independent of our cognition. The mind doesn't create the physical world, but it produces the interpretative categories through which we know and classify the physical world, and it does this so seamlessly that we mistake our interpretations for the world itself. Those interpretations, which are projections of our desires and anxieties, become obstructions (*āvaraṇa*) preventing us from seeing what is actually the case. In simple terms we are blinded by our own self-interests, our own prejudices (which means what is already prejudged), our desires. Unenlightened cognition is an appropriative act. Yogācāra does not speak about subjects and objects; instead it analyzes perception in terms of graspers (*grāhaka*) and what is grasped (*grāhya*).

Yogācāra at times resembles epistemological idealism, which does not claim that this or any world is constructed by mind, but rather that we are usually incapable of distinguishing our mental constructions and interpretations of the world from the world itself. This narcissism of consciousness Yogācāra calls *vijñapti-mātra,* "nothing but conscious construction." A deceptive trick is built into the way consciousness operates at every moment. Consciousness projects and constructs a cognitive object in such a way that it disowns its own creation—pretending the object is "out there"—in order to render that object capable of being appropriated. Even while what we cognize is occurring within our act of cognition, we cognize it *as if* it were external to our consciousness. That self-deception folded into the very act of cognition is what Yogācārins term *abhūta-parikalpa.* Realization of *vijñapti-mātra* exposes this trick intrinsic to consciousness's workings, catching it in the act, so to speak, thereby eliminating it. When that deception is removed one's mode of cognition is no longer termed *vijñāna* (consciousness); it has become direct cognition (*jñāna*).

Consciousness engages in this deceptive game of projection, dissociation, and appropriation because there is no "self." According to Buddhism, the deepest, most pernicious erroneous view held by sentient beings is the view that a permanent, eternal, immutable, independent self exists. There is no such self, and deep down we know that. This makes us anxious, since it entails that no self or identity endures forever. In order to assuage that anxiety, we attempt to construct a self, to fill the anxious void, to do something enduring. The projection of cognitive objects for appropriation is consciousness's main tool for this construction. If I own things (ideas, theories, identities, material objects), then "I am." If there are permanent objects that I can possess, then I too must be permanent. If I can be identified with something permanent, then I too must have a permanent identity. To undermine this desperate and erroneous appropriative grasping, Yogācāra texts say: Negate the object, and the self is also negated (e.g., *Madhyānta-vibhāga*, 1:4, 8).

That this is the motive behind the denial of external objects is reinforced by Vasubandhu who, in two texts, offers a nearly identical formula, both hinging on two terms: *upalabdhi*, which means to 'cognitively apprehend,' i.e., to grasp or appropriate cognitively; and *artha*, 'referent' of a linguistic or cognitive act, i.e., that toward which an intentionality intends.[7]

> Apprehending vijñapti-mātra is the basis for the arising of the nonapprehension of *artha*. The nonapprehension of *artha* is the basis for the nonapprehension of vijñapti-mātra.
>
> *vijñapti-mātropalabdhim niśrityārthānupalabdhir-jayate. Arthānupalabdhim niśritya vijñapti-mātrasyāpi-anupalabdhir-jayate.* (*Madhyāntavibhāga-bhāṣya* I.7)

> By the apprehending of citta-mātra, there is the nonapprehension of cognized *artha*. By nonapprehending cognized *artha*, citta also in nonapprehended.
>
> *citta-mātra-upalambhena jñeyārthārthānupalambhatā. Jñeyārtha anupalambhena syāc-cittānupalambhatā.* (*Trisvabhāvanirdeśa* 36)

By recognizing that what appears as something apart from an act of consciousness only assumes that appearance within an act of consciousness, that is, that cognitive-objects appear to exist apart from cognition only within an act of cognitive construction, one ceases to grasp at one's own construction as if it were a graspable entity 'out there.' One does not reject the 'object' or noema in order to reify or vaorize noesis or noetic constitution. On the contrary, because one ceases to grasp at the noema, noesis too ceases to be grasped. The circuit of grasped and grasper (*grāhya-grāhaka*) is disrupted, and the type of cognition that endeavors to seize and 'apprehend' its 'object' ceases. This bears repeating. Not only is the object, the *artha*, negated, but that which noetically constitutes it (*vijñapti-mātra, citta-mātra*) is also negated.[8] Vijñapti-mātra or citta-mātra are provisional antidotes (*pratipakṣa*), put out of operation once their purpose has been achieved. They are not metaphysically reified or lionized.

Conclusions

Yogācārins deny the existence of external objects in two senses:

1) In terms of conventional experience they do not deny objects such as chairs, colors, and trees, but rather they reject the claim that such things appear anywhere else than in consciousness. It is *externality*, not objects per se, that they challenge.

2) While such objects are admissible as conventionalisms, in more precise terms there are no chairs, trees, etc. These are merely words and concepts by which we gather and interpret discrete sensations that arise moment by moment in a causal flux. These words and concepts are mental projections. The point is not to elevate consciousness, but to warn us not to be fooled by our own cognitive narcissism. Enlightened cognition is likened to a great mirror that impartially and fully reflects everything before it, without attachment to what has passed nor in expectation of what might arrive. What sorts of objects do enlightened ones cognize? Yogācārins refuse to provide a detailed descriptive answer aside from saying it is purified from karmic pollution (*anāśrava*), since whatever description they might offer would only be appropriated and reduced to the habitual cognitive categories that are already preventing us from seeing properly.

Notes

1 Trisvabhāvanirdeśa 2.

2 *Ibid.* 15.

3 *Ibid.* 27.

4 *Ibid.* 29.

5 This becomes clear as soon as one examines the rich vocabulary Yogācārins employ to denote 'objects' and their place in cognitive acts. This vocabulary will be briefly examined shortly.

6 Instead of making ontological claims, Yogācāra texts tend to offer a discourse on "purity" (*viśuddhi, vyavadāna. anāśrava*, etc.), which will be discussed later.

7 The double sense of *artha* as both a linguistic referent ('meaning') and a sensorial object is poignantly reinforced in *Trisvabhāvanirdeśa* by the repeated use of the term *khyāti* 'cognitive appearance.' *Kyāti* actually means a 'statement,' or 'theoretical assertion,' or something asserted to be the case (Monier-Williams, p. 341a: "'declaration,' opinion, view, idea, assertion... perception, knowledge... name, denomination, title..."); in other words, something which appears to be the case because it has been linguistically, conceptually asserted as such. The explication and disruption of this linguistic-cognitive construction is one of the primary subtexts of *Trisvabhāvanirdeśa.*

8 While some later traditions in China and Tibet differentiated sharply between *vijñapti-mātra* (Ch. *wei-shih*) and *citta-mātra* (Ch. *wei-hsin*), it is clear from passages such as these that Vasubandhu countenanced no such distinction.

Appendices

The One Hundred Dharmas

I. The Eight Consciousnesses Citta-dharma 心法，八識

1. Seeing-consciousness	*cakṣur-vijñāna*	眼識
2. Hearing-consciousness	*śrotra-vijñāna*	耳識
3. Smelling-consciousness	*ghrāṇa-vijñāna*	鼻識
4. Tasting-consciousness	*jihvā-vijñāna*	舌識
5. Tactile/kinetic consciousness	*kāya-vijñāna*	身識
6. Empiric-consciousenss	*mano-vijñāna*	意識
7. Focusing	*manas*	意
8. Warehouse consciousness	*ālaya-vijñāna*	阿賴耶識

II. Mental Associates caitta, caitasika-dharma 心所法
citta-samprayukta-dharma 心相應法

A
Always-active Sarvatraga 遍行

9. Sensory contact	*sparśa*	觸
10. Pleasure/pain/neutral	*vedanā*	受
11. Volition	*cetanā*	思
12. Associative-thinking	*saṃjñā*	想
13. Attention	*manaskāra*	作意

B
Specific Viniyata 別境

14. Desire	*chanda*	欲
15. Confident Resolve	*adhimokṣa*	勝解
16. Memory/mindfulness	*smṛti*	念
17. Meditative concentration	*samādhi*	定
18. Discernment	*prajñā*	慧

C
Advantageous Kuśala 善

19. Faith/trust	*śraddhā*	信
20. [inner] Shame	*hrī*	慚
21. Embarrassment	*apatrāpya*	愧
22. Lack of Greed	*alobha*	無貪
23. Lack of Hatred	*adveṣa*	無瞋
24. Lack of Misconception	*amoha*	無痴
25. Vigor	*vīrya*	精進
26. Serenity	*praśrabdhi*	輕安
27. Carefulness	*apramāda*	不放逸

28. Equanimity	*upekṣa*	行捨
29. Non-harmfulness	*ahiṃsā*	不害

D
Mental Disturbances Kleśa 煩惱

30. Appropriational intent	*rāga*	貪
31. Aversion	*pratigha*	瞋
32. Stupidity	*mūḍhi*	痴
33. Arrogance	*māna*	慢
34. Doubt	*vicikitsā*	疑
35. Perspectivality	*dṛṣṭi*	惡見

E
Secondary Mental Disturbances Upakleśa 隨煩惱

36. Anger	*krodha*	忿
37. Enmity	*upanāha*	恨
38. Resist recognizing own faults	*mrakṣa*	覆
39. [verbal] maliciousness	*pradāsa*	惱
40. Envy	*īrṣyā*	嫉
41. Selfishness	*mātsarya*	慳
42. Deceit	*māyā*	誑
43. Guile	*śāṭhya*	諂
44. Harmfulness	*vihiṃsā*	害
45. Conceit	*mada*	憍
46. Shamelessness	*āhrīkya*	無慚
47. Non-embarrassment	*anapatrāpya*	無愧
48. Restlessness	*auddhatya*	掉舉
49. Mental fogginess	*styāna*	惛沈
50. Lack of Faith/trust	*āśraddhya*	不信
51. Lethargic negligence	*kausīdya*	懈怠
52. Carelessness	*pramāda*	放逸
53. Forgetfulness	*muṣitasmṛtitā*	失念
54. Distraction	*vikṣepa*	散亂
55. Lack of [self-]Awareness	*asaṃprajanya*	不正知

F
Indeterminate Aniyata 不定

56. Remorse	*kaukṛtya*	悔
57. Torpor	*middha*	隨眠
58. Initial mental application	*vitarka*	尋
59. [subsequent] Discursive Thought	*vicāra*	伺

III. Form — Rūpa-dharma 色法

60. Eye	*cakṣus*	眼
61. Ear	*śrotra*	耳
62. Nose	*ghrāṇa*	鼻
63. Tongue	*jihvā*	舌
64. Body	*kāya*	身
65. [visible] form	*rūpa*	色
66. Sound	*śabda*	聲
67. Smell	*gandha*	香
68. Taste	*rasa*	味
69. Touch	*spraṣṭavya*	觸
70. 'Formal' Thought-objects	*dharmāyatanikāni rūpāni*	法處所攝色
a. Concrete form analyzed to minutest extent		極略色
b. Non-concrete form (space, color) analyzed to grandest extent		極逈色
c. Innermost impression of perceptual form		受所引色
d. Forms arising through False Conceptual Construction		遍計所起色
e. Forms produced and mastered in Samādhi		定所生自在色

IV. Embodied-conditioning Not Directly [perceived] by Citta
Citta-viprayukta-saṃskāra-dharma 心不相應行法

71. (karmic) Accrual	*prāpti*	得
72. Life-force	*jīvitendriya*	命根
73. Commonalities by species	*nikāya-sabhāga*	眾同分
74. Differentiation of species	*visabhāga*	異生法
75. Attainment of Thoughtlessness	*asaṃjñi-samāpatti*	無想定
76. Attainment of Cessation	*nirodha-samāpatti*	滅盡定
77. [realm of] Thoughtless [beings]	*āsaṃjñika*	無想果
78. 'Name' body	*nāma-kāya*	名身
79. 'Predicate' body	*pada-kāya*	句身
80. 'Utterance' body	*vyañjana-kāya*	文身
81. Birth/arising	*jāti*	生
82. Continuity/abiding	*sthiti*	住
83. Aging/decaying	*jarā*	老
84. Impermanence	*anityatā*	無常
85. Systematic Operation	*pravṛtti*	流轉
86. Determinant (karmic) Differences	*pratiniyama*	定異
87. Unifying	*yoga*	相應
88. Speed	*jāva*	勢速
89. Seriality	*anukrama*	次第
90. Area	*deśa*	方
91. Time	*kāla*	時
92. Number/calculation	*saṃkhyā*	數
93. Synthesis	*sāmagrī*	和合性
94. Otherwiseness	*anyathātva*	不和合性

V. Unconditioned Dharmas Asaṃskṛta-dharmas 無為法

95. Spatiality	*ākāśa*	虛空
96. Cessation through Understanding	*pratisaṃkhyā-nirodha*	擇滅無為
97. Cessation without Understanding	*apratisaṃkhyā-nirodha*	非擇滅無為
98. 'Motionless' Cessation	*āniñjya*	不動滅無為
99. Cessation of Associative-thinking and Pleasure/pain	*saṃjñā-vedayita-nirodha*	想受滅無為
100. Ipseity	*tathatā*	如來

Appendix Two

75 dharmas

Rūpāṇi (Form)

1. Cakṣus	eye
2. Śrotra	ear
3. Ghrāṇa	nose
4. Jihvā	tongue
5. Kāya	body
6. Rūpa	visibles
7. Śabda	sound
8. Gandha	smell
9. Rasa	taste
10. Spraṣṭavya	touch
11. Avijñapti-rūpa	gesture unrevealing of intent

Citta (Mind)

12. Citta	mind

Mahābhūmika (Major Groundings)

13. Vedanā	pleasure/pain/neutral
14. Saṃjñā	associative-thinking
15. Cetanā	volition
16. Sparśa	sensory contact
17. Chanda	desire
18. Mati (= prajñā)	discernment
19. Smṛti	memory/mindfulness
20. Manaskāra	attention
21. Adhimukti (= adhimokṣa)	confident resolve
22. Samādhi	meditative concentration

Kuśala-mahābhūmika (Advantageous Major Groundings)

23. Śraddha	faith/trust
24. Vīrya	vigor
25. Upekṣa	equanimity
26. Hrī	(inner) shame

27. Apatrāpya	embarrassment
28. Alobha	lack of greed
29. Adveṣa	lack of hatred
30. Ahiṃsā	non-harmfulness
31. Praśrabdhi	serenity
32. Apramāda	carefulness

Kleśa-mahābhūmika (Mental Disturbance Major Groundings)

33. Moha (= mūḍhi)	confusion
34. Pramāda	carelessness
35. Kausīdya	lethargic negligence
36. Āśraddhya	lack of faith/trust
37. Sthyāna	mental fogginess
38. Auddhatya	restlessness

Akuśala-mahābhūmika (Nonadventageous Major Groundings)

39. Āhrīkya	shamelessness
40. Anapatrāpya	non-embarrassment

Paritta-kleśa-mahābhūmika (Secondary Mental Disturbance Major Groundings)

41. Krodha	anger
42. Upanāha	enmity
43. Śaṭṭhya (= śāṭhya)	guile
44. Īrṣyā	envy
45. Pradāsa	[verbal] maliciousness
46. Mrakṣa	resist recognising own faults
47. Mātsarya	selfishness
48. Māyā	deceit
49. Mada	conceit
50. Vihiṃsā	harmfulness

Aniyata-mahābhūmika (Indeterminate Major Groundings)

51. Vitarka	initial mental application
52. Vicara	[subsequent] discursive thought
53. Kaukṛtya	remorse
54. Rāga	appropriational intent
55. Māna	arrogance
56. Pratigha	aversion
57. Vicikitsā	doubt
58. Middha	torpor

Citta-viprayukta-saṃskāra-dharmāḥ (Embodied-conditioning dissociated from Mind)

59. Prāpti	(karmic) accrual
60. *Aprāpti*	(karmic) divestment
61. Sabhāgatā	commonality of species
62. Asaṃjñika	[realm of] Thoughtless beings
63. Asaṃjñi-samāpatti	attainment of Thoughlessness
64. nirodha-samāpatti	attainment of Cessation
65. Jīvita (= jīvitendriya)	life-force
66. Jāti	birth
67. Sthiti	continuity/abiding
68. Jarā	aging/decay
69. Aniyatā	impermanence
70. Nāma-kāya	'Name' body
71. Pada-kāya	'Predicate' body
72. Vyañjana-kāya	'Utterance' body

Asaṃskṛta-dharmāḥ (Unconditioned Dharmas)

1. Ākāśa	spatiality
2. Pratisaṃkhyā-nirodha	Cessation through understanding
3. Apratisaṃkhyā-nirodha	Cessation without understanding

Appendix Three

Comparison of 75 and 100 dharmas

There are only 2 dharmas that appear exclusively in the 75 Dharma list:

1. *Avijñapti-rūpa* (#11), and
2. *Aprāpti* (#60)

The rest are either found in common on both lists, or exclusively in the 100 Dharma list. Their order and categorization differs as follows:

LEGEND

(symbols comment on terms to their left in the charts)

∞ classified as *aniyata-mahābhūmika* in the 75 dharma system
• classified as *kleśa-mahābhūmika* in the 75 dharma system
≈ classified as *parittakleśa-mahābhūmiks* in the 75 dharma system
¶ classified as *akuśala-mahābhūmika* in the 75 dharma system
- absent from the 75 dharma system

(#n) is number in 75 dharma system
(n) is number in 100 dharma system
(i) is number within specific category of 75 dharma system

§§

100 Dharmas		**75 Dharmas**
Citta-dharmāḥ		**Citta** (#12)
1. Seeing-consciousness	*cakṣur-vijñāna*	i. Citta (mind)
2. Hearing-consciousness	*śrotra-vijñāna*	
3. Smelling-consciousness	*ghrāṇa-vijñāna*	
4. Tasting-consciousness	*jihvā-vijñāna*	
5. Tactile/kinetic consciousness	*kāya-vijñāna*	
6. Empiric-consciousenss	*mano-vijñāna*	
7. Focusing	*manas*	
8. Warehouse consciousness	*ālaya-vijñāna*	

II. Mental Associates caitta, caitasika-dharmāḥ citta-samprayukta-dharmāḥ

Always-active Sarvatraga **Mahābhūmika** (#13-22)

9. Sensory contact	*sparśa*	i. Vedanā
10. Pleasure/pain/neutral	*vedanā*	ii. Saṃjñā
11. Volition	*cetanā*	iii. Cetanā
12. Associative-thinking	*saṃjñā*	iv. Sparśa
13. Attention	*manaskāra*	

Specific Viniyata

14. Desire	*chanda*	v. Chanda
15. Confident Resolve	*adhimokṣa*	vi. Mati (= prajñā) (18)
16. Memory/mindfulness	*smṛti*	vii. Smṛti
17. Meditative concentration	*samādhi*	viii. Manaskāra (13)
18. Discernment	*prajñā*	ix. Adhimukti (= adhimokṣa) (15)
		x. Samādhi (17)

Advantageous Kuśala **Kuśala-mahābhūmika** (#23-32)

19. Faith/trust	*śraddhā*	i. Śraddha
20. [inner] Shame	*hrī*	ii. Vīrya (25)
21. Embarrassment	*apatrāpya*	iii. Upekṣa (28)
22. Lack of Greed	*alobha*	iv. Hrī (20)
23. Lack of Hatred	*adveṣa*	v. Apatrāpya (21)
24. Lack of Misconception	*amoha*	———
25. Vigor	*vīrya*	vi. Alobha (22)
26. Serenity	*praśrabdhi*	vii. Adveṣa (23)
27. Carefulness	*apramāda*	viii. Ahiṃsā (29)
28. Equanimity	*upekṣa*	ix. Praśrabdhi (26)
29. Non-harmfulness	*ahiṃsā*	x. Apramāda (27)

Mental Disturbances Kleśa **Kleśa-mahābhūmika** (#33-38)

30. Appropriational intent	*rāga*	∞	i. Moha (= mūḍhi) (32)
31. Aversion	*pratigha*	∞	ii. Pramāda (52)
32. Stupidity	*mūḍhi*	•	iii. Kausīdya (51)
33. Arrogance	*māna*	∞	iv. Āśraddhya (50)
34. Doubt	*vicikitsā*	∞	v. Sthyāna (49)
35. Perspectivality	*dṛṣṭi*		vi. Auddhatya (48)

Akuśala-mahābhūmika (#39-40)

	i. Āhrīkya (46)
	ii. Anapatrāpya (47)

Secondary Mental Disturbances

Upakleśa **Paritta-kleśa-mahābhūmika** (#41-50)

36. Anger	*krodha*	≈	i. Krodha
37. Enmity	*upanāha*	≈	ii. Upanāha
38. Resist recognizing own faults	*mrakṣa*	≈	iii. Śaṭṭhya (= śāṭhya, 43)
39. [verbal] maliciousness	*pradāsa*	≈	iv. Írṣyā (40)
40. Envy	*īrṣyā*	≈	v. Pradāsa (39)
41. Selfishness	*mātsarya*	≈	vi. Mrakṣa (38)
42. Deceit	*māyā*	≈	vii. Mātsarya (41)
43. Guile	*śāṭhya*	≈	viii. Māyā (42)
44. Harmfulness	*vihiṃsā*	≈	ix. Mada (45)
45. Conceit	*mada*	≈	x. Vihiṃsā (44)
46. Shamelessness	*āhrīkya*	¶	
47. Non-embarrassment	*anapatrāpya*	¶	
48. Restlessness	*auddhatya*	•	
49. Mental fogginess	*styāna*	•	
50. Lack of Faith/trust	*āśraddhya*	•	
51. Lethargic negligence	*kausīdya*	•	
52. Carelessness	*pramāda*	•	
53. Forgetfulness	*muṣitasmṛtitā*	-	———
54. Distraction	*vikṣepa*	-	———
55. Lack of [self-]Awareness	*asaṃprajanya*	-	———

Indeterminate Aniyata **Aniyata-mahābhūmika** (#51-58)

56. Remorse	*kaukṛtya*	∞	1. Vitarka (58)
57. Torpor	*middha*	∞	2. Vicara (59)
58. Initial mental application	*vitarka*	∞	3. Kaukṛtya (56)
59. [subsequent] Discursive Thought	*vicāra*	∞	4. Rāga (30)
			5. Māna (33) [kleśa in the
			6. Pratigha (31) 100 list]
			7. Vicikitsā (34)
			8. Middha (57)

III — Form Rūpa-dharma **Rūpāṇi** (#1-11)

60. Eye	*cakṣus*	1. Cakṣus
61. Ear	*śrotra*	2. Śrotra
62. Nose	*ghrāṇa*	3. Ghrāṇa
63. Tongue	*jihvā*	4. Jihvā
64. Body	*kāya*	5. Kāya
65. [visible] form	*rūpa*	6. Rūpa
66. Sound	*śabda*	7. Śabda
67. Smell	*gandha*	8. Gandha
68. Taste	*rasa*	9. Rasa
69. Touch	*spraṣṭavya*	10. Spraṣṭavya
70. 'Formal' Thought-objects	*dharmāyatanikāni rūpāni*	11. *Avijñapti-rūpa*

IV — Embodied-conditioning Not Directly [perceived] by Citta
Citta-viprayukta-saṃskāra-dharma (#59-72)

71. (karmic) Accrual	*prāpti*		1. Prāpti (71)
72. Life-force	*jīvitendriya*		2. *Aprāpti*
73. Commonalities by species	*nikāya-sabhāga*		3. Sabhāgatā (73)
74. Differentiation of species	*visabhāga*	-	4. Asaṃjñika (77)
75. Attainment of Thoughtlessness	*asaṃjñi-samāpatti*		5. Asaṃjñi-samāpatti (75)
76. Attainment of Cessation	*nirodha-samāpatti*		6. nirodha-samāpatti (76)
77. [realm of] Thoughtless [beings]	*āsaṃjñika*		7. Jīvita (= jīvitendriya, 72)
78. 'Name' body	*nāma-kāya*		8. Jāti (81)
79. 'Predicate' body	*pada-kāya*		9. Sthiti (82)
80. 'Utterance' body	*vyañjana-kāya*		10. Jarā (83)
81. Birth/arising	*jāti*		11. Aniyatā (84)
82. Continuity/abiding	*sthiti*		12. Nāma-kāya (78)
83. Aging/decaying	*jarā*		13. Pada-kāya (79)
84. Impermanence	*anityatā*		14. Vyañjana-kāya (80)
85. Systematic Operation	*pravṛtti*	-	
86. Determinant (karmic) Differences	*pratiniyama*	-	
87. Unifying	*yoga*	-	
88. Speed	*jāva*	-	
89. Seriality	*anukrama*	-	
90. Area	*deśa*	-	
91. Time	*kāla*	-	
92. Number/calculation	*saṃkhyā*	-	
93. Synthesis	*sāmagrī*	-	
94. Otherwiseness	*anyathātva*	-	

V — Unconditioned Dharmas Asaṃskṛta-dharmas (#73-75)

95. Spatiality	*ākāśa*		1. Ākāśa
96. Cessation through Understanding	*pratisaṃkhyā-nirodha*		2. Pratisaṃkhyā-nirodha
97. Cessation Not through Understanding	*apratisaṃkhyā-nirodha*		3. Apratisaṃkhyā-nirodha
98. Motionless Cessation	*āniñjya*	-	
99. Cessation of Associative-thinking and Pleasure/pain	*saṃjñā-vedayita-nirodha*	-	
100. Ipseity	*tathatā*	-	

Appendix Four: Hsüan-tsang's Translations and Works

A survey of Hsüan-tsang's prolific translations demonstrates that he was anything but a narrow sectarian. His translations cover the gamut of Buddhist literature including: sūtras and śāstras of interest to Yogācāra; Madhyamaka texts; Pure Land texts; Sarvāstivādin Abhidharma works; Tantric texts; a Hindu Vaiśeika text; works on logic and epistemology; Abhidharma texts; Dhāranī texts; Avadāna texts; Mahāyāna sūtras; Vaipulya sūtras; Sūtras concerned with pratītya-samutpāda, Buddha's teachings just before his parinirvāṇa, instructions to rulers; Pratimokṣa texts; Prajñāpāramitā texts; his travelogue; Adbhūtadharma texts; texts devoted to Avalokiteśvara, Maitreya, Bhaiṣajya-guru (the Medicine Buddha), Kṣitigarbha, Amitābha; etc. His works are spread throughout the *Taishō* edition of the Chinese Buddhist canon, which is organized according to literary or sectarian type, demonstrating that he contributed to every genre. Some of his translations, such as the *Heart Sutra* and *Diamond Sutra*, have remained at the center of East Asian Buddhist study and devotion. Others, such as his translation of the *Vimalakīrti-nirdeśa sūtra*, were overshadowed by translations done by others. Some are very short works, others are of unparalleled length (his translation of the *Mahāprajñāpāramitā sūtras* fills three *Taishō* volumes! No other Chinese Buddhist text comes close).

The list is chronological. For some texts we have very precise dates, but for others there is little or no information. There are some controversies concerning the place or date of certain texts; some of these I have noted, others I have ignored.

For each work I have provided most or all of the following: the Chinese title; the number of fascicles; the Sanskrit title when it is known (reconstructed Sanskrit titles are preceded by an asterisk); in most cases an English translation of the title (if the meaning of the Chinese title differs from the known Sanskrit title, or represents only one possible interpretation of the Sanskrit, I have translated the Chinese); the *Taishō* number (volume, followed by text number); the date and place of translation (or where the text was completed); the original author; and annotations placing the text in context and/or indicating whether English (or French) translations exist. Full references for the English and French translations noted here can be found in the Bibliography.

Year **645**

1. *Ta p'u-sa tsang ching* 大菩薩藏經 (20 fasc)
Bodhisattva piṭaka-sūtra.
(Sutra of the Scriptural-Basket of the Great Bodhisattva)
(included in T.11.310 [sūtra 12] secs. 35-54)
Hung-fu (Vast Prosperity) Monastery 弘福寺

NOTE: Part of the *Ratnakūṭa sūtra*. The brunt of the *Ratnakūṭa* was translated by Bodhiruci (706) and Dharmarakṣa (313), though many other translators contributed selections. According to Hsüan-tsang's biography, the last text he was asked to translate was the complete *Ratnakūta*. He began, but sickness and old age prevented him from getting very far. Since *Ta p'u-sa tsang ching* was the first text he translated upon returning to China, that brought his work full circle.

2. *Hsien-yang sheng-chiao lun sung* 顯揚聖教論頌 (1 fasc)
**Prakaraṇāryavākā*
(Exposition of the Ārya Teachings, Verse Treatise)
T.31.1603 (cf. 5 below) July 8, Hung-fu Monastery
Author: Asaṅga 無著

NOTE: Asaṅga text based on the *Yogācābhūmi* (see 10, below). Dignāga is said to have written a commentary, titled *Yogāvatāra*, not extant, on its ninth chapter.

3. *Fo ti ching* 佛地經 (1 fasc)
Buddha-bhūmi sūtra
(Buddha-Stage Sutra)
T.16.680 (cf. 30 below) August 12, Hung-fu Monastery

4. *Liu-men t'o-lo-ni ching* 六門陀羅尼經 (1 fasc)
Saṇmukhi-dhāranī
(Six Gates Dhāranī Sutra)
T.21.1360 October 11, Hung-fu Monastery

NOTE: The Six Gates are the senses; Dhāranī, like mantra, is an enabling chant or invocation.

5. *Hsien-yang sheng-chiao lun* 顯揚聖教論 (20 fasc)
(Exposition of the Ārya Teachings)
T.31.1602 (cf. 2 above) Oct 645-Feb. 646, Hung-fu Monastery
Author: Asaṅga 無著

NOTE: Asaṅga's exposition on the verses of **Prakaraṇāryavākā* (2 above).

Year **646**

6. *Ta-sheng a-p'i-t'a-mo tsa-chi lun* 大乘阿毗達摩雜集論 (16 fasc)
Abhidharmasamuccaya-vyākhyā
(Mahāyāna Abhidharma Mixed-Collection Treatise)
(T.31.1606) (cf. 47 below) Feb. 7-April 19, Hung-fu Monastery
Author: Sthiramati 安慧

NOTE: Sthiramati's commentary (called *Tsa-chi lun* 雜集論 for short) to Asaṅga's *Abhidharmasamuccaya* (called *Chi lun* 集論 for short, cf. #47 below). This is the only text by Sthiramati translated by Hsüan-tsang. K'uei-chi wrote a commentary on it (*Zokuzōkyō* 74.603). The Tibetan tradition attributes the *Tsa-chi lun* to Jinaputra.

7. (*Ta-T'ang*) *Hsi-yü chi* （大唐）西域記 (12 fasc)
(*Great T'ang*) *Record of Western Regions*
T.51.2087
Hung-fu Monastery
Author: Hsüan-tsang 玄奘

NOTE: Written at the behest of the Emperor, this is Hsüan-tsang's travelog of his journey through Central Asia and India. It remains one of our most valuable records of those regions in the seventh century. Includes abundant material on customs, Buddhist legends, population, etc. "Great T'ang" signifies the T'ang Dynasty, and in a broader sense China. English translation in Beal (*Buddhist Records of the Western World*) and Li Rongxi (*The Great Tang Dynasty Record of the Western Regions*).

Year **647**

8. *Ta-sheng wu-yun lun* 大乘五蘊論 (1 fasc) *Pañcaskandhaka-prakaraṇa*
(Mahāyāna Treatise on the Five Skandhas)
T.31.1612 April 4, Hung-fu Monastery
Author: Vasubandhu 世親

NOTE: A proto-Yogācāra work by Vasubandhu. English translation from Tibetan in Anacker. Also French tr. by Lamotte, rendered into English by Pruden.

9. *She ta-sheng lun wu-hsing shih* 攝大乘論無性釋 (10 fasc)
**Mahāyānasaṁgrahopani-bandhana*
(*Asvabhāva's commentary on the *Mahāyānasaṁgraha*)
T.31.1598 (cf. 18, 19)
April 10, 647-July 31, 649,

Ta-tz'u-en (Great Compassion) Monastery 大慈恩寺
Author: *Asvabhāva 無性

NOTE: *Asvabhāva's commentary on Asaṅga's *Mahāyānasaṁgraha*, one of several versions of the *Mahāyānasaṁgraha* translated by Hsüan-tsang as part of his effort to correct the misunderstandings among Chinese Buddhists derived from Paramārtha's translations. The *Mahāyānasaṁgraha*, or *She-lun* 攝論 for short, was a key text for Paramārtha's followers. Lamotte includes substantial portions of this comm. in his tr. *Somme du Grand Véhicule.*

10. *Yü-ch'ieh shih-ti lun* 瑜伽師地論 (100 fasc)
Yogācārabhūmi śāstra
(Stages of Yoga Practice Treatise)
T.30.1579 July 3, 646-June 11 648
Hung-fu & Ta-tz'u-en Monasteries
Author: Maitreya 彌勒

NOTE: This massive work, attributed in the Chinese tradition to Maitreya and in the Tibetan tradition to Asaṅga, served as the grand Yogācāra encyclopedia for Hsüan-tsang, who originally went to India to procure a complete copy of this text. Paramārtha had done a partial translation (T.30.1584). The section on Śrāvakabhūmi has been translated from a Sanskrit ms. into English by Wayman; other partial English translations, from the Tibetan version, include Tatz and Willis. A complete translation from Hsüan-tsang's Chinese version is now underway for the Numata Center translation series.

11. *Chieh shen mi ching* 解深密經 (5 fasc)
Saṅdhinirmocana sūtra
(Sutra Explaining the Deep Secret)
T.16.676 August 8, Hung-fu Monastery

NOTE: The *Saṅdhinirṃocana* was translated into Chinese several times, including by Bodhiruci (in 514, T.16.675), Paramārtha (in 557, T.16.677), and Guṇabhadra (in 435-43, T.16.678 and 679). There is a French translation, drawing on Hsüan-tsang and the Tibetan versions, by Lamotte. An English translation from the Tibetan by Powers.

12. *Yin ming ju cheng-li lun* 因明入正理論 (1 fasc)
Nyāyapraveśa
(Introduction to Logic)
T.31.1630 · Sept. 10, Hung-fu Monastery
Author: Śaṅkarasvāmin 商羯羅主

NOTE: The first Indian Logic text ever translated into Chinese. It offers an overview of Dignāga's logic. Ten monks associated with Hsüan-tsang during its translation wrote commentaries on this text which were incommensurate. A Court Taoist, Lü

Tsai, wrote his own applying yin-yang and Chinese cosmological principles, which outraged the Buddhists, leading to a Buddhist vs. Taoist conflict in the capital that only dissipated after Hsüan-tsang, pressed by the Emperor to render judgement, confirmed that Lü's commentary was erroneous. English translation with Sanskrit text in Musashi.

Year **648**

13. *T'ien ch'ing-wen ching* 天請問經 (1 fasc)
Devatā sūtra
(Divine Explanation Sutra)
T.15.593 April 17, Hung-fu Monastery

14. *Shih-chü yi lun* 十句義論 (1 fasc)
Vaiśeṣika-daśapadārtha śāstra
(Treatise on the Ten Padārthas)
T.54.2138 June 11, Hung-fu Monastery
Author: Maticandra 慧月

NOTE: A Hindu Vaiśeṣika text. *Padārthas* are the basic components of reality. Vaiśeṣikas more commonly list nine, rather than ten, *padārthas*. English translation in Ui.

15. *Wei-shih san-shih lun* 唯識三十論 (1 fasc)
Triṃśikā
(Thirty Verses on Vijñapti-mātra Treatise)
T.31.1586 June 25, Hung-fu Monastery
Author: Vasubandhu 世親

NOTE: The root text on which the *Ch'eng wei-shih lun* expounds. The Chinese title would literally translate into Sanskrit as *Triṃśikā-vijñapti-mātra śāstra*. Translated in Part Four of this book. Other translations, from Sanskrit, found in Anacker and Kochumuttom.

16. *Chih-kang po-lo ching* 金剛般若經 (1 fasc)
Vajracchedikā sūtra
(Diamond Sutra)
T.7.220 Ta-tz'u-en Monastery

NOTE: There are several Chinese translations of the Diamond Sutra, including by Kumārajīva (401), Bodhiruci (509), Paramārtha (558), and I-ching (703), but Hsüan-tsang's rendition became the standard in East Asia. Conze translated the *Diamond Sutra* from Sanskrit.

17. *Pai fa ming-men lun* 百法明門論 (1 fasc)
Mahāyāna śatadharmā-prakāśamukha śāstra
(Lucid Introduction to the One Hundred Dharmas)
T.31.1614 December 7, Hung Fa Hall 弘法院
Author: Vasubandhu 世親

NOTE: Vasubandhu's enumeration of the Yogācāra One Hundred Dharma list, divided up by categories. See Appendix 1.

18. *She ta-sheng lun shih-ch'in shih* 攝大乘論世親釋 (10 fasc)
Mahāyānasaṁgraha-bhāṣya
(Vasubandhu's commentary on the *Mahāyānasaṁgraha*)
T.31.1597 (cf. 9 and 19)
Northern Palace 北闕 and Ta-tz'u-en Monastery
Author: Vasubandhu 世親

NOTE: French tr. included in Lamotte, *Somme...*

Year **649**

19. *She ta-sheng lun pen* 攝大乘論本 (3 fasc)
Mahāyānasaṁgraha
(Encyclopedia of Mahāyāna)
T.31.1594 (cf. 9 and 18) Jan. 14-July 31, Ta-tz'u-en Monastery
Author: Asaṅga 無著

NOTE: Paramārtha's version of this text by Asaṅga had become very popular in the sixth century and its influence was still pervasive in Hsüan-tsang's day. That Hsüan-tsang chose to translate complete commentaries on the *She lun* 攝論 (9 and 18 above), including one by Vasubandhu, before translating the root text indicates his purpose was to replace misconceptions engendered by erroneous ideas introduced to China by Paramārtha's translation. Before offering a different version of the text, Hsüan-tsang provided authoritative commentaries undermining Paramārtha's emendations. English translations of the versions by Hsüan-tsang, Paramārtha, and Tibetan versions of the tenth chapter of the *Mahāyānasaṁgraha* are in Griffiths, et al. Hsüan-tsang's version is very close to the Tibetan; Paramārtha's is much looser. The Sanskrit for this text is no longer extant. English translation of Paramārtha's complete text in John P. Keenan, *The Summary of the Great Vehicle by Bodhisattva Asaṅga translated from the Chinese of Paramārtha* (Numata Translation Series).

20. *Yüan-ch'i sheng-tao ching* 緣起聖道經 (1 fasc)
Nidāna sūtra
(Sutra of Ārya Teachings on Conditioned Arising)

T.16.714 (cf. 34, 71) Feb. 17, Hung Fa Hall

NOTE: A sutra on *pratītya-samutpāda*.

21. *Shih-shen tsu lun* 識身足論 (16 fasc)
Abhidharma Vijñāna-kāya pāda śāstra
(Discourse on Consciousness Body)
T.26.1539 March 3-Sept. 19
Hung Fa Hall and Ta-tz'u-en Monastery
Author: Devakṣema 提婆設摩

NOTE: The third text of the Sarvāstivāda Abhidharma canon. Summary of contents in Frauwallner, *Studies in Abhidharma Literature*, pp. 28-31. Cf. Willemen, pp. 197-205; and Potter (ed.), *Abhidharma*, pp. 367-74.

22. *Ju-lai shih-chiao sheng chün wang ching* 如來示教勝軍王經 (1 fasc)
Rājavavādaka sūtra
(Sutra in which the Tathāgata Reveals Teachings to King Prasenajit)
T.14.515 (cf. 26) March 24, Ta-tz'u-en Monastery

NOTE: Buddha teaches King Prasenajit how to be a good king. For Hsüan-tsang this sutra probably had at least two implications. First, his Indian friend and pivotal teacher was also named Prasenajit 勝軍 (see Chapter Fifteen). King Prasenajit was Buddha's contemporary and alter-ego: born the same day as Buddha, he inherited his own father's throne, unlike Buddha who rejected his to become a mendicant; King Prasenajit eventually becomes Buddha's disciple. Second, it served as an exemplar of how a Buddhist advises a ruler, and so provided a response to the Chinese emperor who, due to military ambitions, had been pressuring Hsüan-tsang for information about the territories to the West of China. The *Hsi-yü chi* (see 7, above) was one response, providing detailed information on monasteries, geography, and customs, but little that would be of military use.

23. *Shen hsi yu ching* 甚希有經 (1 fasc)
**Adbhūtadharma-paryāya sūtra*
(Sutra of Marvels)
T.16.689 July 2
Ts'ui-wei Palace 翠微宮, Chung Nan Mt. 終南山

NOTE: *Adbhūtadharma* is one of the twelve genre divisions of Buddhist scriptures, concerned with tales of marvels.

24. *Po-lo hsin ching* 般若心經 (1 fasc)
Prajñā-pāramitā hṛdaya sūtra
(Heart Sutra)
T.8.251 July 8, Ts'ui-wei Palace

NOTE: Full title: *Po-lo po-lo-mi-ṭo hsin ching*般若波羅密多心經. Translated many times into Chinese, Hsüan-tsang's version has become the standard version. Very popular in China, Korea and Japan, this version has been chanted daily throughout East Asia by clerics and laypeople for over a thousand years. There are many English translations.

25. *P'u-sa chieh chieh mo* 菩薩戒羯磨 (1 fasc)
(An Elaboration of On Conferring the Bodhisattva Vinaya)
T.24.1499 (cf. 28) August 28, Ta-tz'u-en Monastery
Author: Maitreya 彌勒
NOTE: This text is drawn from the *Yogācārabhūmi* (see 10 above, and 28 below).

26. *Wang fa cheng-li ching* 王法正理經 (1 fasc)
(Sutra of [Maitreya's] Correct Principles of Royal Rule)
T.31.1615 (cf. 22) August 31, Ta-tz'u-en Monastery
Author: Maitreya 彌勒

27. *Tsui wu-pi ching* 最無比經 (1 fasc)
(Supreme Incomparable Sutra)
T.16.691 Sept. 1, Ta-tz'u-en Monastery

28. *P'u-sa chieh pen* 菩薩戒本 (1 fasc)
**Bodhisattva-śīla sūtra*
(On Conferring the Bodhisattva Vinaya)
T.24.1501 (cf. 25) Sept. 3
Ta-tz'u-en Monastery (or Ts'ui-wei Palace in 647)
Author: Maitreya 彌勒
NOTE: Bodhisattva Pratimokṣa attributed in China to Maitreya, and in Tibet to Asaṅga. This served as the Yogācāra *pratimokṣa*, a routinely performed communal confession for monks and nuns. The *chieh mo* (25, above) expands on this root text.

29. *Ta-sheng chang chen lun* 大乘掌珍論 (2 fasc)
Karatala-ratna
(Mahāyāna Jewel in the Palm Treatise)
T.30.1578 Oct. 19-24, Ta-tz'u-en Monastery
Author: Bhāvaviveka 清辯
NOTE: The first Madhyamaka text translated by Hsüan-tsang. The debates between Madhayamaka and Yogācāra that were in full swing when Hsüan-tsang was at Nālandā, focused on the teachings of Bhāvaviveka (representing Madhyamaka), on the one hand, and Sthiramati and Dharmapāla (representing Yogācāra) on the other hand.

30. *Fo ti ching lun* 佛地經論 (7 fasc)
Buddhabhūmi-sūtra śāstra
(Treatise on the Buddha-Stage Sutra)
T.26.1530 (cf. 3 above) Nov. 12, 649-Jan. 2, 650
Authors: Bandhuprabha 親光, etc.

NOTE: Contains combined commentaries on the *Buddha-bhūmi.* Since some of the passages reappear in the *Ch'eng wei-shih lun*, some speculate that these parallel passages should be attributed to Dharmapāla (though neither this text nor the *Ch'eng wei-shih lun* explicitly does so). A Tibetan translation of a commentary to the *Buddha-bhūmi* also parallels passages in this text; Tibetans attribute that commentary to Śīlabhadra, the head of Nālandā while Hsüan-tsang was there. Translated by John Keenan (unpub. PhD Diss).

Year **650**

(first year of Kao Tsung's 高宗 reign as emperor. His father T'ai Tsung 太宗 had strongly supported Hsüan-tsang. Kao Tsung continued the support, but with less enthusiasm.)

31. *Yin-ming cheng-li men lun pen* 因明正理門論本 (1 fasc)
Nyāyamukha
(Gateway to Logic)
T.31.1628 Feb. 1, Ta-tz'u-en Monastery
Author: Dignāga 陳那

NOTE: One of Dignāga's basic texts on logic. English translation in Tucci.

32. *Ch'eng-tsan ching-t'u fo she-shou ching* 稱讚淨土佛攝受經 (1 fasc)
Sukhāvatī-vyūha sūtra
(Sutra In Praise of the Pure Land)
T.12.367 Ta-tz'u-en Monastery

NOTE: Important Pure Land Sutra commonly known as the *Smaller Sukhāvati Sutra*. Separate English translations of Sanskrit and Chinese versions of the *Larger* and *Smaller Sukhāvati Sutras* are offered in Luis O. Gomez, *The Land of Bliss: The Paradise of the Buddha of Measureless Light: Sanskrit and Chinese Versions of the Sukhāvativyūha Sutras* (Honolulu: University of Hawaii Press, 1996). Gomez uses the Kumārajīva version of the *Smaller Sutra*, with some reference to Hsüan-tsang's version.

33. *Yü-ch'ieh shih-ti lun shih* 瑜伽師地論釋 (1 fasc)
Yogācārabhūmi-śāstra-kārikā
(Explanation of the Stages of Yoga Practice Treatise)
T.30.1580
Author: Jinaputra 最勝子

NOTE: Jinaputra's commentary on the *Yogācārabhūmi* (10). There is a Sanskrit edition, translated into French by Sylvain Lévy, 2 vols., Paris, 1911.

34. *Fen-pieh yüan-ch'i ch'u-sheng fa-men ching* 分别緣起初勝法門經 (2 fasc)
** Vikalpa-pratītya-samutpāda-dharmottara-praveśa sūtra*
(Sutra on The Primacy of the Dharma Gate Distinguishing Conditioned Arising)
T.16.717 (cf. 20, 71) March 10, Ta-tz'u-en Monastery

NOTE: Another sutra on *pratītya-samutpāda*.

35. *Shuo Wu-kou ch'eng ching* 說無垢稱經 (6 fasc)
Vimalakīrti-nirdeśa sūtra
(Sutra of the Teachings of Vimalakīrti)
T.14.476 Ta-tz'u-en Monastery

NOTE: This sutra—always popular in China because its hero is an enlightened layman who outsmarts all of Buddha's highest bodhisattva disciples, demonstrating that laypeople could reach higher attainment than monks—was translated five times before Hsüan-tsang's version: Kumārajīva (406), Chih-ch'ien (223-228), Dharmarakṣa (308), Upaśūnya (545), and Jñānagupta (591). Kumārajīva's version remained the popular one, due largely to its literary merits. Charles Luk translated the Kumārajīva version into English, as did Richard Robinson (unpublished); Thurman translated from the Tibetan, taking advantage of Robinson's rendition from Chinese; Burton Watson also translated the Kumārajīva version. Lamotte took all editions, including Hsüan-tsang's, into account in his thorough translation of *Vimalakīrti* into French (*L'enseignement de Vimalakīrti*, 1962); his version has been translated into English by Sara Boin (PTS, 1976).

36. *Yao-shih (liu li kuang ju-lai) pen-yüan kung-te ching*
藥師（流璃光如來）本願功德經 (1 fasc)
Bhaiṣajya-guru-vaiḍūrya-prabhāsa-pūrvapraṇidhāna-viśeṣa-vistara
(The Meritorious Original Vow of the Medicine Master [Lapis Lazuli Radiance Tathāgata] Sutra)
T.14.450 June 9, Ta-tz'u-en Monastery

NOTE: An important sutra on the Medicine Buddha. English translation in Raoul Birnbaum's *The Healing Buddha* (Boulder: Shambhala, 1979) 151-72. In Japan, in the Nara period, the Medicine Buddha was intimately associated with Yogācāra (Hossō), and one of the main Nara Hossō temples, Yakushi-ji, named after the Medicine Buddha, still houses a huge statue of the Medicine Buddha in its main hall.

37. *Ta-sheng kuang pai lun pen* 大乘廣百論本 (1 fasc)
**Catuḥśataka*
(Mahāyāna-Vaipulya One Hundred Treatise)
T.30.1570 (cf. 38) July 13, 650-Jan. 30, 651, Ta-tz'u-en Monastery
Author: Āryadeva 聖天

NOTE: A major Madhyamaka text by Āryadeva, Nāgārjuna's first major disciple.

38. *Ta-sheng kuang pai lun shih-lun* 大乘廣百論釋論 (10 fasc)
(Commentary on the Mahāyāna-Vaipulya One Hundred Treatise)
T.30.1571 (cf. 37) July 30, 650-Jan. 30, 651, Ta-tz'u-en Monestary
Authors: Āryadeva 聖天, Dharmapāla 護法

NOTE: Dharmapāla's commentary on Āryadeva's text, i.e., a Yogācāra commentary on a Madhyamaka root text. Some passages from this text reappear in the *Ch'eng wei-shih lun*. English translation of the tenth chapter in John Keenan, *Dharmapāla's Yogācāra Critique of Bhāvaviveka's Mādhyamika: Explanation of Emptiness: The Tenth Chapter of Ta-Ch'eng Kuang Pai-Lun Shih Lun, commentary by Dharmapāla.* Edwin Mellen Press, 1997.

39. *Pen shih ching* 本事經 (7 fasc)
Itivṛttaka sūtra
(Sutra on the Original Events)
T.17.765 Oct. 10-Dec. 6, Ta-tz'u-en Monastery

NOTE: Hagiographic treatment of the Buddha and his contemporaries.

40. *Chu-fo hsin t'o-lo-ni ching* 諸佛心陀羅尼經 (1 fasc)
Buddha-hṛdaya-dhāranī
(Sutra of the Dhāranī of the Heart of the Buddhas)
T.19.918 Oct. 26, Ta-tz'u-en Monastery

Year **651**

41. *Shou ch'ih ch'i fo ming-hao (so-sheng) kung-te ching*
受持七佛名號（所生）功德經 (1 fasc)
(Receiving Merit [produced by] the Seven Amitābha Buddhas)
T.14.436 Feb. 4, Ta-tz'u-en Monastery

NOTE: The honorific title, *ming-hao* 名號, is a standard epithet for Amitābha.

42. *Ta-ch'eng ta-chi-ti-tsang shih lun ching* 大乘大集地藏十輪經 (10 fasc)
Daśa-cakra-kṣitigarbha sūtra
(Ten Cakras of Kṣitigarbha, Mahāyāna Great Collection Sutra)

T.13.411 Feb. 18, 651-Aug. 9, 652

NOTE: According to Nakamura, this sūtra was a compiled by priests who spoke Iranian languages.

43. *A-p'i-t'a-mo hsien tsung lun* 阿毘達磨藏顯宗論 (40 fasc)
**Abhidharma-samayapradīpika* or **Abhidharmakośa-śāstra-kārikā-vibhāṣya*
(Revealing the Tenets of the Abhidharma Treasury)
T.29.1563 April 30, 651-Nov.26, 652
Author: Saṅghabhadra 尊者眾賢

NOTE: This and the *Nyāyānusāra* (49 below) are two Abhidharmic commentaries by Saṅghabhadra (a younger Sarvāstivādin contemporary of Vasubandhu) translated by Hsüan-tsang. This work criticizes Vasubandhu's *Kośa* (44 below) from an orthodox Sarvāstivādin position. Cf. Willemen, pp. 240-49.

44. *A-p'i-t'a-mo chü-she lun* 阿毘達磨俱舍論 (30 fasc)
Abhidharmakośa-bhāṣya
(Treasury of Abhidharma)
T.29.1558 (cf. 45) June 3, 651-Sept. 13, 654, Ta-tz'u-en Monastery
Author: Vasubandhu 世親

NOTE: Vasubandhu's most important pre-Yogācāra work, called *chü-she lun* 俱舍論 for short in Chinese (俱舍 in early T'ang pronunciation apparently transliterated the Sanskrit sounds *kośa*). Consisting of verses (also translated separately as 45 below) with exposition, the *Kośa* organizes and condenses primarily Sarvāstivāda Abhidharma teachings, but not without being critical, and hence adopting positions associated with other Buddhist schools, such as the Sautrāntikas. It was this intellectual restlessness that eventually led Vasubandhu to become a Yogācārin. Vallée Poussin translated Hsüan-tsang's version into French (6 vols.) before a Sanskrit version was rediscovered in this century. Leo Pruden translated the French version into English, though some errors were introduced. Subhadra Jha's *The Abhidharmakośa of Vasubandhu* (Patna: K.P. Jayaswal Research Institute, 1983) offers separate English translations of the Sanskrit version (as edited by Prahlad Pradhan) and Vallée Poussin's rendition of Hsüan-tsang, but he stops with Chapter Two (the *Kośa* has nine chapters). Further volumes of Jha's work have not been announced.

45. *A-p'i-t'a-mo chü-she lun pen-sung* 阿毘達磨俱舍論本頌 (1 fasc)
Abhidharmakośa
(Treasury of Abhidharma, verses)
T.29.1560 (cf. 44) Ta-tz'u-en Monastery
Author: Vasubandhu 世親

NOTE: The *Kośa* verses sans *bhāṣya.*

46. *Ta-sheng ch'eng yeh lun* 大乘成業論 (1 fasc)
Karma-siddhi-prakaraṇa
(Mahāyāna Treatise Establishing Karma)
T.31.1609 Sept. 24, Ta-tz'u-en Monastery
Author: Vasubandhu 世親

NOTE: An intermediate work of Vasubandhu that shows how his ideas were developing since writing the *Kośa* but not yet employing the full Yogācāra palette. English translation from Tibetan in Anacker, and an English translation (by Pruden) from Lamotte's French version of Hsüan-tsang's version.

Year **652**

47. *Ta-sheng a-p'i-t'a-mo chi lun* 大乘阿毘達磨集論 (7 fasc)
Abhidharmasamuccaya
(Mahāyāna Abhidharma Compendium)
T.31.1605 (cf. 6) Feb. 11-April 3, Ta-tz'u-en Monastery
Author: Asaṅga 無著

NOTE: An important Yogācāra treatise by Asaṅga, called *chi lun* 集論 for short. A French transkation from Sanskrit by W. Rahula.

48. *Fo lin nieh-p'an chi fa-chu ching* 佛臨涅槃記法住經 (1 fasc)
(Sutra of the Abiding Dharma Recorded Just Prior to Buddha's Nirvana)
T.12.390 May 17, Ta-tz'u-en Monastery

Year **653**

49. *A-p'i-t'a-mo hsun cheng-li lun* 阿毘達磨順正理論 (80 fasc)
Abhidharma-Nyāyānusāra śāstra
(Abhidharma in Accord with Reason Treatise)
T.29.1562 Feb.3, 653-Aug. 27, 654
Author: Saṅghabhadra (尊者)眾賢

NOTE: Orthodox Sarvāstivāda Abhidharma treatise by the same Saṅghabhadra who wrote a critical commentary on the *Kośa* (see 43 above). Longer, more comprehensive and more sophisticated than the *Kośa.* Cf. Willemen, pp. 240-249.

Year **654**

50. *Ta A-lo-han nan-t'i-mi-to-lo so-shuo fa-chu chi* 大阿羅漢難提蜜多羅所說法住記 (1 fasc) *Nandimitrāvadāna*

(Nandimitra's Record of the Abiding Dharma Explained to the Great Arhats)
T.49.2030 June 8

NOTE: Excerpt—called *Fa-chu li* 法住立 (Setting Up the Abiding Dharma) for short —from the *Mahāparinirvāṇa sūtra* (cf. 48 above) in which Nandimitra recounts how Buddha, just before his Nirvana, entrusted the Abiding Dharma to sixteen Great Arhats and their disciples, charging them to protect and preserve it.

51. *Ch'eng-tsan ta-sheng kung-te ching* 稱讚大乘功德經 (1 fasc)
(Sutra on the Merit of Extolling Mahāyāna)
T.17.840 July 24, Ta-tz'u-en Monastery

52. *Pa-chi k'u nan to-lo-ni ching* 拔濟苦難陀羅尼經 (1 fasc)
(Sutra of the Dhāranī that Carries One Over Suffering and Adversity)
T.21.1395 Oct. 15, Ta-tz'u-en Monastery

53. *Pa-ming p'u-mi t'o-lo-ni ching* 八名普密陀羅尼經 (1 fasc)
(Sutra of the Dhāranī of the Universal and Esoteric Eight Names)
T.21.1365 Nov. 11, Ta-tz'u-en Monastery

54. *Hsien wu-pien fo-t'u kung-te ching* 顯無邊佛土功德經 (1 fasc)
Tathāgatāṇaṃ Buddhakṣetra-guṇokta-dharma-paryāya (*sūtra*)
(Sutra Revealing the Qualities of the Infinite Buddha-Lands)
T.10.289 Nov. 12, Ta-tz'u-en Monastery

55. *Sheng ch'uang pei yin t'o-lo-ni ching* 勝幢臂印陀羅尼經 (1 fasc)
(Sutra of the Dhāranī for Bearing the Banners and Seals)
T.21.1363 Nov. 13, Ta-tz'u-en Monastery

56. *Ch'ih-shih t'o-lo-ni ching* 持世陀羅尼經 (1 fasc)
Vasudhāra-dhāranī
(Sutra of the Dhāranī for Upholding the World)
T.20.1162 Nov. 24, Ta-tz'u-en Monastery

Year **655**

(Hsüan-tsang was too ill to work)

Year **656**

57. *Shih-yi-mien shen-chou hsin ching* 十一面神咒心經 (1 fasc)
Avalokiteśvaraikādaśamukha-dhāranī
(Sutra of the Spiritual Mantra of the Eleven-Faced [Avalokiteśvara])
T.20.1071 April 17, Ta-tz'u-en Monastery

58. *A-p'i-t'a-mo ta-p'i-p'o-sha lun* 阿毘達磨大毘婆沙論 (200 fasc)
(*Abhidharma*) *Mahāvibhāṣa*
(The Great Abhidharma Commentary)
T.27.1545 Aug. 18, 656-July 27, 659
Authors: The 500 Great Arhats

NOTE: This huge work, crucial for Sarvāstivāda Abhidharma, fills an entire *Taishō* volume. Consisting of 8 divisions with 43 chapters, it is a commentary on the *Jñānaprasthāna* (cf. 59) probably composed in Kashmir. The 500 Arhats, discussed in such Mahāyāna works as the *Lotus Sutra* and *Nirvana Sutra*, and venerated especially by Pure Land and Zen sects, were believed to have compiled the *Mahāvibhāṣa* four hundred years after Buddha's Nirvana during a Council convened by Kaniṣka for that purpose. Two other translations exist in Chinese: T.28.1546, tr. ca. 425-27 by Buddhavarmin, et al., originally 110 fasc., but 50 fasc. were lost during the Liang Dynasty; and T.28.1547 (20 fasc.), tr. in 383, by Seng-ch'ieh-pa-ch'eng 僧伽跋澄 (Saṅghabhadra or Saṅghadeva). Cf. detailed summary by Ichimura, Buswell, et al., in Potter, *Abhidharma*, pp. 511-568; cf. Willemen, pp. 229-239.

Year **657**

59. *A-p'i-t'a-mo fa-chih lun* 阿毘達磨發智論 (20 fasc)
(*Abhidharma*) *Jñānaprasthāna śāstra*
(Treatise on the Arising of Wisdom through the Abhidharma)
T.26.1544 Feb. 14, 657-June 20, 660
Yü-hua (玉華 Jade Flower) Monastery
Author: Katyāyanīputra 迦多衍尼子

NOTE: The seventh volume of the Sarvāstivāda Abhidharma piṭaka, often considered — along with the *Mahāvibhāṣa* which is a commentary on it — the central canonical text of the Sarvāstivādins. Cf. Willemen, pp. 221-229; Potter, *Abhidharma*, pp. 417-449.

60. *Kuan so-yüan yüan lun* 觀所緣緣論 (1 fasc)
Ālambana parikṣa
(Treatise Contemplating Objective Conditions)
T.31.1624

Ta-nei-li-jih Hall (Great Inner Elegance Sun Hall) 大內麗日殿
Author: Dignāga 陳那

NOTE: A work on epistemology by Dignāga that had been translated earlier into Chinese by Paramārtha. French translation by YAMAGUCHI Susumu from Chinese and Tibetan versions; English tr. by Shastri.

Year **658**

61. *Ju a-p'i-t'a-mo lun* 入阿毘達磨論 (2 fasc)
Abhidharma-āvatāra-prakaraṇa
(Treatise on Entering Abhidharma)
T.28.1554 Nov. 13, Ta-tz'u-en Monastery
Author: Skandhila 塞建陀羅

NOTE: According to Nakamura, Tocharian fragments and the Tibetan version of this text suggest that Hsüan-tsang translated it "arbitrarily." French translation, using the Tibetan and Chinese versions, by Van Velthem. Cf. Willemen, pp. 282-285.

Year **659**

62. *Pu-k'ung chüan-so shen-chou hsin ching* 不空羂索神咒心經 (1 fasc)
Amoghapāśahṛdaya śāstra
(Essential Scripture of Amogha's Ensnaring Spiritual Mantra)
T.20.1094 May 15, Ta-tz'u-en Monastery

63. *A-p'i-t'a-mo fa yün tsu lun* 阿毘達磨法蘊足論 (12 fasc)
Abhidharma-dharmaskandha pāda śāstra
(Treatise on Dharmas and Skandhas according to the Abhidharma Path)
T.26.1537 Aug. 20-Oct 5, Ta-tz'u-en Monastery
Author: Mahāmāudgalyāyana (尊者)大目乾連

NOTE: The Fifth work of the Sarvāstivāda Abhidharma canon, traditionally attributed to one of Buddha's disciples — either Mahā-Maudgalyāyana or Śariputra — but probably composed two or three centuries after Buddha. Summary of its contents in Frauwallner, *Studies in Abhidharma Literature*, pp. 15-21; Potter, *Abhidharma*, pp. 179-187; cf. Willemen, pp. 181-189.

64. *Ch'eng wei-shih lun* 成唯識論 (10 fasc)
**Vijñapti-mātra-siddhi śāstra*
(Treatise Establishing Vijñapti-mātra)
T.31.1585 Oct. or Nov., Yü Hua (玉華 Jade Blossom) Monastery
Author: Hsüan-tsang, traditionally ascribed to "Dharmapāla, et al."

NOTE: K'uei-chi's linkage of this text with Dharmapāla is problematic (see Chap. 15). This is the only translation by Hsüan-tsang that is not a direct translation of a text, but instead a selective, evaluative editorial drawing on several (traditionally ten) distinct texts. Since K'uei-chi aligned himself with this text while assuming the role of Hsüan-tsang's successor, the East Asian tradition has treated the *Ch'eng wei-shih lun* as the pivotal exemplar of Hsüan-tsang's teachings. Vallée Poussin's French translation incorporates material from the SAEKI edition and the commentaries by K'uei-chi while embedding his reading in a heavily idealistic interpretation. Wei Tat's English rendition of Vallée Poussin's translation omits most of Vallée Poussin's extensive explanatory notes. Ganguly offers an abridged version of the *Ch'eng wei-shih lun*. Most recently translated in full by Cook.

Year **660**

65. *Ta po-jo p'o-lo-mi-t'o ching* 大般若波羅蜜多經 (600 fasc)
Mahā-prajñā-pāramitā-sūtra
T.5-7.220 Feb. 16, 660-Nov. 25, 663
Yü Hua Kung (玉華宮 Jade Blossom Palace) Monastery

NOTE: This massive work, six hundred fascicles filling three entire *Taishō* volumes, includes such well known works as the Heart Sutra and Diamond Sutra, and is one of the most complete collections of Prajñāpāramitā sutras available. Hsüan-tsang considered abridging his translation to avoid repetition, but was dissuaded by a dream, and thus translated the Prajñāpāramitā corpus *in toto*. Conze's translations of Prajñāpāramitā texts — *The Large Sutra on Perfect Wisdom with the Divisions of the Abhisamayālaṅkāra* (Berkeley: University of California Press, 1975), *Perfect Wisdom: The Short Prajñāpāramitā Texts* (*Perfection of Wisdom in 500 lines, 700 lines, Heart Sutra, Diamond Sutra*) (Devon, England: Buddhist Publishing Group, 1993), *The Perfection of Wisdom in Eight Thousand Lines & Its Verse Summary* (Bolinas: Four Seasons Foundation, 1973) — though taken from the Sanskrit, not Chinese versions of these texts, provides a sampling of their style and content.

66. *A-p'i-t'a-mo p'in-lei tsu lun* 阿毘達磨品類足論 (18 fasc)
Abhidharma-prakaraṇa-pāda
(Treatise of Classifications according to the Abhidharma Path)
T.26.1542 Oct. 10-Nov. 30, Yü Hua Monastery
Author: Vasumitra (尊者)世友

NOTE: Second work of Sarvāstivāda Abhidharma canon; a compendium of terms, categories, and positions. Summary of contents in Frauwallner, *Studies in Abhidharma Literature*, pp. 32-37. Summary by Lindtner in Potter, *Abhidharma*, pp. 375-379 and in Willemen, pp. 212-221.

67. *A-p'i-t'a-mo chi yi men tsu lun* 阿毘達磨集異門足論 (20 fasc)
Abhidharma-saṅgītī-paryāya pāda śāstra
(Collection of Different Aspects of the Abhidharma Path Treatise)
T.26.1536 Jan. 2, 660-Feb. 1, 664, Yü Hua Monastery
Author: Śariputra (尊者)舍利子

NOTE: First work of Sarvāstivāda Abhidharma canon, attributed in the Tibetan tradition to Mahā-Kauṣṭhila, and by Yaśomitra (in his commentary to the *Kośa*) to Pūrṇa. Numerically groups doctrines. Summary of contents in Frauwallner, *Studies in Abhidharma Literature*, pp. 14f. Cf. Lindtner's summary in Potter, *Abhidharma*, pp. 203-216 and in Willemen, pp. 177-181.

Year 661

68. *Pien chung pien lun sung* 辯中邊論頌 (1 fasc)
Madhyānta Vibhāga kārikā
(Treatise on Distinguishing Between Middle and Extremes, Verses)
T.31.1601 (cf. 69) June 3, Yü Hua Monastery
Author: Maitreya 彌勒

NOTE: The Verses of a key Yogācāra text, attributed to either Maitreya or Asaṅga.

69. *Pien chung pien lun* 辯中邊論 (1 fasc)
Madhyānta Vibhāga bhāṣya
(Treatise on Distinguishing Between Middle and Extremes)
T.31.1600 (cf. 68) June 12-July 2, Yü Hua Monastery
Author: Vasubandhu 世親

NOTE: Expository commentary, attributed to Vasubandhu, on the verses of 68 above. Translation from Sanskrit and Tibetan in Anacker; translation of the first chapter from Sanskrit, with reference to Sthiramati's commentary in Kochumuttom.

70. *Wei-shih erh-shih lun* 唯識二十論 (1 fasc)
Viṁśatikā-vṛtti
(Twenty Verses on Vijñapti-mātra Treatise)
T.31.1590 July 3, Yü Hua Monastery
Author: Vasubandhu 世親

NOTE: One of Vasubandhu's most philosophically important Yogācāra works. Hamilton translated Hsüan-tsang's version with K'uei-chi's commentary. Translations not from Chinese include Anacker and Kochumuttom.

71. *Yüan-ch'i ching* 緣起經 (1 fasc)
Pratītya-samutpāda divibhaṅga-nirdeśa sūtra
(Sutra on Conditioned Arising)
T.2.124 (Cf. 20, 34) Aug. 9

NOTE: A sutra on *pratītya-samutpāda* with some affinities to *Majjhima Nikāya* 33, Mahāgopalaka Sutta.

Year **662**

72. *Yi pu-tsung lun lun* 異部宗輪論 (1 fasc)
Samaya-bhedoparacana cakra
(Treatise of the Wheel of the Different Divisions of the Tenets)
T.49.2031 Sept. 2, Yü Hua Monastery
Author: Vasumitra (according to Tibetan tradition)

NOTE: Overview of Twenty schools from the Sarvāstivāda viewpoint.

Year **663**

73. *A-p'i-t'a-mo chieh shen tsu lun* 阿毘達磨界身足論 (3 fasc)
Abhidharma Dhātu-kāya pāda śāstra
(Treatise on Body Elements According to the Abhidharma Path)
T.26.1540 July 14, Yü Hua Monastery
Author: Vasumitra (尊者)世友

NOTE: Fourth canonical text of Sarvāstivāda Abhidharma, concerned with enumerating mental categories. Summary of contents in Frauwallner, *Studies in Abhidharma Literature*, pp. 21-28. Cf. Buswell's summary in Potter, *Abhidharma,* pp. 345-358 and in Willemen, pp. 206-212.

74. *Wu shih p'i-p'o-sha lun* 五事毘婆沙論 (2 fasc)
**Pañca-vastuka-vibhāṣa*
(Five Phenomena Vibhāṣa Treatise)
T.28.1555 Nov. 18, Ta-tz'u-en Monastery
Author: Dharmatrāta (尊者)法救

NOTE: An abhidharmic discussion of rūpa, citta, and caittas. Similar to first chapter of *Prakaraṇapāda* (#66 above). Cf. Willemen, pp. 213f.

75. *Chi chao shen pien san-mo-ti ching* 寂照神變三摩地經 (1 fasc)
Praśānta-viniśaya-prātihārya-samādhi sūtra
(Sutra on the Samādhi of Singularly Radiant Spiritual Alterations)
T.15.648 Feb. 1, 664 (or Feb. 12, 665), Yü Hua Monastery

Year **664**

76. *Chou wu-shou ching* 咒五首經 (1 fasc)
(Mantra of Five Heads Sutra)
T.20.1034 Feb. 2, Yü Hua Monastery

---

77. *Pa-shih kuei-chu sung* 八識規矩頌

(Verses on the Structure of the Eight Consciousnesses)

Author: Hsüan-tsang 玄奘

(Date uncertain)

NOTE: This text written by Hsuan-tsang (as opposed to translated from an Indian original) is not found in the *Taishō*, though a commentary on it by P'u-t'ai 普泰 that reiterates the root text is found at T.45.1865.467-476, entitled *Pa-shih kuei-chu pu-chu* 八識規矩補註. It covers similar topics to the *Ch'eng wei-shih lun*, but organized somewhat differently. An English translation of Hsüan-tsang's root text by Ronald Epstein can be found on his Web site:

<http://online.sfsu.edu/~rone/Buddhism/Yogacara/Basiccontents.htm>.

Select Bibliography

Abbreviations:

ed.	Editor or Edition
IBK	*Indogaku Bukkyōgaku kenkyū*
JIP	*Journal of Indian Philosophy*
JIABS	*Journal of the International Association of Buddhist Studies*
PEW	*Philosophy East and West*
PPR	*Philosophy and Phenomenological Research*
PTS	Pali Text Society
rpt.	Reprint
T	*Taishō shinshū dai zōkyō* 大正新脩大蔵経. TAKAKUSU Junjirō 高楠順次郎, WATANABE Kaigyoku 渡辺海旭, et al. (eds.), 100 vols. Tokyo: Taishō Issaikyō Kankōkai, 1924-1932 (ex.: T.26.1540 = *Taishō* volume 26, text no. 1540)
tr.	Translator or Translated by; Eng. tr(s). = English Translation(s)
ZZ	*Dainihon Zokuzōkyō* 大日本続蔵経. (vol. number, first page of text)

Abhidharma-dhātukāya-pādaśāstra. by Vasumitra. Hsüan-tsang's translation 阿毘達磨界身足論 T.26.1540. Eng. tr. Swati Ganguly, *Treatise of Groups of Elements: The Abhidharma-dhātukāya-pādaśāstra.* Delhi: Eastern Book Linkers, 1994

Abhidhammattha-sangaha (PTS edition); Eng. tr.: *Compendium of Philosophy*. tr. by Shwe Zan Aung, London: PTS, 1972 rpt. of 1910 ed.

Ameriks, Karl. "Husserl's Realism." *The Philosophical Review*, 86(4), October 1977, 498-519.

Anacker, Stefan. *Seven Works of Vasubandhu: the Buddhist Psychological Doctor. Delhi*: Motilal Banarsidass, 1984.

Anguttara-Nikāya.Eng. tr: *Gradual Sayings*, 5 vols., [vols. 1,2 and 5 tr. by F. L. Woodward, vols. 3 and 4 tr. by E. M. Hare], London: PTS, 1979-1988 rpts.

Annambhaṭṭa. *Tarkasaṃgraha* (with *Dīpikā*), text and translation by Swami Virupashananda. Madras: Sri Ramakrishna Math, 1980

Arac, J., et al. *The Yale Critics: Deconstruction in America,* Minneapolis, University of Minnesota Press, 1983.

Aramaki, Noritoshi. "*Paratantrasvabhāva* (I) - A Diagrammatic Account,"*IBK*, 15(2), 1966-67, 955-941 (40-54).

————. "*Paratantrasvabhāva* (I) - A Diagrammatic Account (continued)" *IBK,* 16(2), 1967-68, 968-956(29-41).

Asaṅga 無著. *Abhidharmasamuccaya* (Hsüan-tsang's tr. T. 1605, see Appendix Four).

————. *Asaṅga's Chapter on Ethics With the Commentary of Tsong-Kha-Pa,* The Basic Path to Awakening, *The Complete Bodhisattva.* tr. Mark Tatz. Lewiston: Edwin Mellon Press, 1986

————. *Bodhisattvabhūmiḥ, being the XVth section of Asaṅga's Yogācārabhūmi.* Nalinaksha Dutt, ed., Patna: K.P. Jayaswal Research Institute, 1978.

———. *Le compendium de la super-doctrine (philosophie) (Abhidharmasamuccaya) d'Asaṅga*. traduit et annoté par Walpola Rahula. 2ème ed., Paris: École Française d'Extrême-Orient, 1980

———. *Mahāyāna-Sūtrālaṃkāra, exposé de la doctrine du Grand Vehicule selon le système Yogācāra*. Ed. et tr. d'apres un manuscrit rapporté du Nepal, par Sylvain Lévi. Paris: H. Champion, Bibliothèque de l'École des Hautes Études, 1907-11, 2 vols.

———. *Mahāyānasaṃgraha. She-lun* 攝論. (1) Chinese trs.: 攝大乘論, Buddhaśānta's [T. 31.1592]; 攝大乘論, Paramārtha's [T.31.1593]; 攝大乘論本, Hsüan-tsang's [T.31.1594]; 攝大乘論釋論 , Dharmagupta's [T.31.1596;. Tr. of Vasubandhu's *bhāṣya* by Hsüan-tsang 攝大乘論釋 [T.31.1597]; Tr. of *Asvabhāva's commentary by Hsüan-tsang 攝大乘論釋 [T.31.1598]; (2) French tr.: Étienne Lamotte, *La Somme du Grand Véhicule d'Asaṅga,* 2 vols., Louvaine: Institut Orientaliste, 1973 rpt of 1938 ed.; (3) Eng. tr. John P. Keenan, *The Summary of the Great Vehicle by Bodhisattva Asaṅga translated from the Chinese of Paramārtha.* Berkeley, CA: Numata Center for Buddhist Translation and Research, 1992

———. *Mahāyānasūtrālaṁkāra.* (1) *Mahāyānasūtrālaṁkāra of Asaṅga.* S. Bagchi (ed.). Dharbhanga: Mithila Institute, 1970; (2) *Mahāyānasūtrālaṁkāra by Asaṅga.* Sanskrit text and English tr. by Surekha Vijay Limaye. Delhi, India: Sri Satguru, 1992; (3) *Ta-sheng chuang-yen ching lun* 大乘莊嚴經論 (*Mahāyāna-sūtrālaṃkāra*). Tr. Prabhākaramitra 波羅頗蜜多羅 (T.31.1604) (Yogācāra text, with Tathāgatagarbha leanings never translated by Hsüan-tsang, though he studied it in India. Prabhākaramitra was an Abhidharma teacher at Nālandā who arrived at Ch'ang-an in 627, after spending time with Turkic tribes)

———. *The Realm of Awakening: a Translation and Study of the Tenth Chapter of Asaṅga's Mahāyānasangraha.* translation and notes by Paul J. Griffiths, HAKAMAYA Noriaki, John Keenan, et al. New York: Oxford University Press, 1989.

———. *Uttaratantra* [or *Ratnagotravibhāga*]; Eng. tr.: E Obermiller, *Uttaratantra or Ratnagotravibhaga: The Sublime Science of the Great Vehicle to Salvation.* tr. from Tibetan, Talent, Oregon: Canon, 1984 rpt. of *Acta Orientalia* IX, 1931

———. *Yogācārabhūmi-śāstra.* (1) 瑜伽師地論, Hsüan-tsang's version, T.30.1579 (see Appendix Four); (2) *Bodhisattvabhūmi, Being the XV Section of Asaṅgapāda's Yogācārabhūmi,* ed. by Nalinasksha Dutt, Patna, 1966; (3) Janice Dean Wills. *On Knowing Reality: the Tattvārtha Chapter of Asaṅga's Bodhisattvabhūmi. NY*: Columbia University Press, 1979; (4) Alex Wayman, *Analysis of the Śravakabhūmi Manuscript*, Berkley: University of California Press, 1961 [translated outline of this part of *-bhūmi*, with some complete sections]; (6) *Śravakabhūmi of Ācārya Asaṅga.* Karunesha Shukla (ed.), Patna: K.P. Jayaswal, 1973

Bahadur, K.P. *The Wisdom of Nyaaya.* New Delhi: Sterling Publishers, 1978

Bapat, L. *Buddhist Logic: A Fresh Study of Dharmakīrti's Philosophy.* Delhi: Bharatiya Vidya Prakashan, 1989

Barrett, T.H. *Taoism Under the T'ang.* London: Wellsweep, 1996

Barua, Amal. *Mind and Mental Factors in Early Buddhist Psychology.* New Delhi: Northern Book Center, 1990

Basham, A.L. *History and Doctrine of the Ājīvikas. Delhi*: Motilal Banarsidass, 1981 rpt.

Bataille, Georges. *Theory of Religion.* tr. by Robert Hurley. NY: Zone Books, 1989

Baum, A.J. *Philosophy of the Buddha.* NY: Collier Books, 1962

Beal, Samuel. *Buddhist Record of the Western World: Translated from the Chinese of Hiuen Tsiang [A.D. 629].* NY: Paragon Book Reprint, 1968, 2 vols. in one [tr. of *Hsi-yu-chi*]

———. *The Life of Hiuen-Tsiang.* Delhi: Munshiram Manoharlal, 1973 (rpt. of 1911 Kegan Paul ed.) (partial tr. of early sections of *Biography* of Hsüan-tsang)

Bechelard, Suzanne. *A Study of Husserl's Formal and Transcendental Logic.* tr. by Lester Embree. Evanston: Northwestern University Press, 1968

Bell, David. *Husserl.* London: Routledge, 1990

Bendall, Cecil, and Louis de la Vallée Poussin. "Bodhisattva-Bhūmi: A Textbook of the Yogācāra School. An English Summary with notes and illustrative extracts from other Buddhistic works." *Le Muséon* 7, 1906, 213-230.

Benn, Charles D. *The Cavern-Mystery Transmission: A Taoist Ordination Rite of A.D. 711.* Honolulu: University of Hawaii Press, 1991

Berkeley, George. *George Berkeley: Principles, Dialogues, and Philosophical Correspondence,* ed. by Colin Turbayne, Indianapolis: Bobbs-Merrill, 1965

Bernet, Rudolf, Iso Kern, and Eduard Marbach. *An Introduction to Husserlian Phenomenology.* Evanston: Northwestern University Press, 1993

Bharati, Agehananda. *The Tantric Tradition.* NY: Samuel Weiser, 1975

Bhattacharya, Sibajiban. *Gaṅgeśa's Theory of Indeterminate Perception: Nirvikalpavāda.* Part II (text and notes). New Delhi: Indian Council of Philosophical Research, 1993

Bhattacharya, Vidhushekhara. "Evolution of Vijñānavāda." *Indian Historical Quarterly,* X(1), March 1934, 1-11

Bhikkhu Bodhi. *The Discourse on the All-Embracing Net of Views: The Brahmajāla Sutta and its Commentaries,* Kandy: Buddhist Publication Society, 1978

Bhikkhu Ñāṇamoli, tr. *The Path of Purification: Visuddhi Magga* [by Buddhaghosa], Kandy: Buddhist Publication Society, 1984

Bhikkhu Ñāṇananda. *Concept and Reality in Early Buddhist Thought: An Essay on 'Papañca' and 'Papañca Saññā Saṅkha.'* Kandy, Sri Lanka: Buddhist Publication Society, 1971

————. *The Magic of the Mind: An Exposition of the Kālakārāma Sutta,* Kandy: Buddhist Publication Society, 1985

Biography of Hsüan-tsang. (see Hui-li; Beal; Li Rongxi)

Birdwhistell, Anne D. "An approach to verification beyond tradition in early Chinese philosophy: Mo Tzu's concept of sampling in a community of observers." *PEW,* 34 (2), April 1984, 175-183

Bloom, Harold, ed. *Sigmund Freud: Modern Critical Views.* NY: Chelsea House, 1985

————. et al. *Deconstruction & Criticism.* NY: Continuum, 1979

————. *A Map of Misreading.* NY: Oxford University Press, 1975

————. *Kabbalah and Criticism.* NY: Continuum, 1975

————. *The Anxiety of Influence.* NY: Oxford University Press, 1973

Bond, George D. "The Netti-Pakarana: A Theravāda Method of Interpretation." *Buddhist Studies in honor of Walpola Rahula,* London: Gordon Fraser, 1980, 16-28

————. *The World of the Buddha: the Tipitaka and its Interpretation in Theravāda Buddhism,* Colombo, Sri Lanka: Gunasena, 1982

Boquist, Ake. *Trisvabhāva: a Study of the Development of the Three-Nature-Theory in Yogācāra Buddhism.* edited by Tord Olsson. Lund, Sweden: Dept. of History of Religions, University of Lund, 1993

Brahmajāla Sutta (Dīgha-Nikāya) Eng. trs.: (1) T.W.Rhys-Davids, *Dialogue of the Buddha,* Vol. I, *SacredBooks of the Buddhists,* London: Luzac, 1956 rpt of 1899 ed., pp. xxv-55; (2) Bhikkhu Bodhi, *The Discourse on The All-Embracing Net of Views: The Brahmajāla Sutta and its Commentaries,* Kandy, Sri Lanka: Buddhist Publication Society, 1978; (3) Maurice Walshe, *The Long Discourses of the Buddha.* Boston: Wisdom, 1995, 67-90

Brentano, Franz. *Sensory and Noetic Consciousness: Psychology from an Empirical Standpoint III.* tr. by Margarete Schättle and Linda McAlister, ed. by Oscar Kraus. NY: Humanities Press, 1981

Broido, Michael M. "Veridical and Delusive Cognition: Tsong-kha-pa on the Two Satyas." *JIP,* 16, 1988, 29-63

Bronkhorst, Johannes. *The Two Traditions of Meditation in Ancient India.* Delhi: Motilalal Banarsidass, 1993

Bu-ston, *Chos-hbyung* ; Eng. tr.: *History of Buddhism* by Bu-ston. tr. E. Obermiller. Heidelberg, 1931, 2 vols.

Buddhadasa Bhikkhu. *Teaching Dhamma by Pictures.* Bangkok: Social Science Review, 1968

Buddhaghosa. *Atthasālinī* (PTS edition); Eng. tr.: *The Expositor.* tr. by Ma Aung Tin. London: PTS, Vol.I, 1920, Vol. II, 1921, rpt.1958

————. *Bāhiranidāna* (the introductory chapter to his *Samantapāsdikā* comm. to Vinaya). Eng. tr.: N.A. Jayawickrama. *The Inception of Dicipline and the Vinaya Nidāna*, London: Luzac & Co., 1962
————. *Visuddhimagga* (see Bhikkhu Ñānamoli)
Burke, B. David. "On the measure of '*parimaṇdala*." *PEW*, 33 (3), July 1983, 273-284
Buswell, Jr., Robert (ed. and tr.). *The Collected works of Chinul: The Korean Approach to Zen*. Honolulu: University of Hawaii Press, 1983
———— (ed.). *Chinese Buddhist Apocrypha*. Delhi: Sri Satguru, 1990
————. *The Formation of Ch'an Ideology in China and Korea: The* Vajrasamādhi-Sūtra, *a Buddhist Apocryphon*. Princeton: Princeton University Press, 1989
————. *The Zen Monastic Experience*. Princeton: Princeton University Press, 1992
Buzo, Adrian and Tony Price. *Kyunyŏ-jŏn: The Life, Times and Songs of a Tenth Century Korean Monk*. Sydney: University of Sydney, 1993
Cammann, Schuyler. "Types of Symbols in Chinese Art." in Arthur Wright (ed.). *Studies in Chinese Thought*, Chicago: University of Chicago Press, 1953, 195-231
Candrakīrti. *Madhyamakāvatāra*. C.W. Huntington (tr.).*The Emptiness of Emptiness*. Honolulu: University of Hawaii Press, 1989
————. *Prasannapadā*. Partial Eng. tr.: Mervyn Sprung, *Lucid Exposition of the Middle Way: The Essential Chapters from the Prasannapadā of Candrakīrti*, Boulder: Prajna Press, 1979
————. *Yuktiṣaṣṭikāvṛtti: Commentaire à la soixantaine sur le raisonnement ou Du vrai enseignement de la causalité par le Maître Çandrakīrti*. Cristina Anna Scherrer-Schaub (tr.). Bruxelles: Institut Belge Des Hautes Études Chinoises, 1991
Catalog of the *GRAND EXHIBITION OF SILKROAD BUDDHIST ART*. Tokyo: Yomiuri Shimbun sha, 1996
Chakravarti, Uma. *The Social Dimensions of Early Buddhism*. Delhi: Oxford University Press, 1987
Chan, Wing-Tsit. *A Sourcebook in Chinese Philosophy*. Princeton: Princeton University Press, 1963
Chang, Garma C.C. *The Buddhist Teaching of Totality*. University Park: Pennsylvania State University Press, 1971
Chatterjee, Ashok Kumar. *Readings on Yogācāra Buddhism*. Benares: Banares Hindu University, 1971
————. *The Yogācāra Idealism*. Delhi: Motial Banarsidass, 2nd ed. 1972
Chatterjee, S.P. *The Mission of Wang Hiuen Tse in India*. tr. from M. Sylvain Levi's French version, ed. by B.C. Law. Calcutta: Sri Satguru, 1987, 2nd ed.
Chattopadhyaya, D.P., Lester Embree, and Jitendranath Mohanty (eds.). *Indian Philosophy and Phenomenology*. New Delhi: Motilal Banarsidass, 1992
Chaudhuri, Sukomal. *Analytical Study of the Abhidharmakośa*, Calcutta: Sanskirit College, 1976
Chegwan, *T'ien-t'ai Buddhism: An Outline of the Fourfold Teachings*, ed. and tr. by David Chappell, et al., Tokyo, 1983 [Chinese text and tr.]
Chen, Kenneth. *Buddhism in China: A Historical Survey*. Princeton: Princeton University Press, 1974
Ch'en Fei-fan 陳飛凡 and Huang Szu-lang 黃俟郎, eds. *Ta-T'ang Hsi Yu Chi: hsin yi* 大唐西域記：新譯 ([Hsüan-tsang's] *Record of the Western Regions during the Great T'ang: New Explanations*). Taipei: Sanmin, 1999
Ch'eng Wei-shih lun 成唯識論. Hsüan-tsang (compiler, author). Among versions used:
(1) T.31.1585.1-59;
(2) Blockprint edition, Nanjing: Chin-ling k'o-ching ch'ü shih, 2 vols. (This print became available in various bound editions in Taiwan in the 1990s);
(3) (French tr.) Louis de la Vallée Poussin. *Vijñaptimātratāsiddhi: La Siddhi de Hiuan-Tsang*. 2 vols., Paris, 1928;
(4) (Eng. tr.) Wei Tat. Ch'eng Wei-Shih Lun: The Doctrine of Mere Consciousness. [text and translation], Hong Kong, 1973;
(5) See Saeki, Jōin;

(6) see Cook, Francis.
(7) see Han T'ing-chieh.
(8) in addition to commentaries on *Ch'eng wei-shih* lun cited elsewhere in this bibliography (cf. K'uei-chi, Chih-chou, Chih Hsü, Chih Ssu, Ling Tai, Ming Yü, Ta Hui, T'ai Hsien, Tao Yi, Wang K'en-t'ang), T.65-68 contains eight commentaries (#2260-2267), and T.85.2804 is a commentary on the *Triṃśikā.*

Chi, Richard S.Y. *Buddhist Formal Logic: a Study of Dignāga's Hetucakra and K'uei-chi's Great Commentary on the Nyāyapraveśā.* Delhi: Motilal Banarsidass, 1984 rpt. of Royal Asiatic Society 1969 ed.

Chih-chou 智周 (T'ang Dynasty). *Ch'eng wei-shih lun liao-yi teng chi (tan hsien-tsun)* 成唯識論了義燈記 但現存. ZZ.78.409

————. *Ch'eng wei-shih lun yen-mi* 成唯識論演祕. (T.43.1833)

————. *Ch'eng wei-shih lun chang chung shu yao-chi (tan hsien-tsun)* 成唯識論掌中樞要記但現存. ZZ.78.100

Chih Hsü 智旭 (Ming Dynasty). *Ch'eng wei-shih lun kuan-hsin fa yao* 成唯論觀心法要. in Chih-hsü. *Fa-hua-ching hui-yi/Ch'eng wei-shih lun kuan-hsin fa yao.* Taipei: Chin Wen Fung, 1993; (also: ZZ.82.393)

————. *Wei-shih san-shih lun chih-chieh* 成唯識論直解. ZZ.83.267

Chih Ssu 智素 (Ch'ing Dynasty). *Ch'eng wei-shih lun yin-hsiang pu yi k'e* 成唯識論音響補遺科. ZZ.82.709

Chinchore, Mangala R. *Dharmakīrti's Theory of Hetu-centricity of Anumāna.* Delhi: Motilal Banarsidass, 1989

————. *Santāna and Santānāntara.* Delhi: Sri Satguru, 1996

————. *Vādanyāya: The Nyāya Buddhist Controversy.* Delhi: Sri Satguru, 1988

Chou, Hsiang-Kuang. *The History of Chinese Buddhism*, Allahabad: Indo-Chinese Literature Publications, 1956

Chu, Fei-huang 朱芾煌. *Fa-hsiang ta tz'u-tien* 法相大辭典 (Great Dictionary of Yogācāra). Taipei: Shin Wen Fang, 1988

Chuang, Tzu. *A Concordance to Chuang Tzu*, Harvard-Yenching Institute, Cambridge: Harvard University Press, 1956. Eng. tr.: Burton Watson, *The Complete Works of Chuang Tzu.* NY: Columbia University Press, 1968; A.C.Graham, *Chuang Tzu: The Inner Chapters*, London: George Allen & Unwin, 1981

Chuang Tzu: Kuo Hsiang chu 莊子：郭象註. Taipei: Yi Wen Yin, 1984

Ciyuan 辭源. Beijing: Shangwu yinshu guan, 1989

Collins, Steven, *Nirvana and other Buddhist felicities.* Cambridge: Cambridge University Press, 1998

————. *Selfless Persons: Imagery and Thought in Theravāda Buddhism*, Cambridge: Cambridge University Press, 1982

Conze, Edward, tr. *The Large Sutra on Perfect Wisdom with the Divisions of the Abhisamayālaṅkāra.* Berkeley: University of California Press, 1984 [compendium tr. of the 100,000, 25,000, 18,000 etc. version of the *Prajñāpāramitā*]

————. *Buddhist Thought in India*, Ann Arbor: University of Michigan Press, 1967

————. *Buddhist Wisdom Books: The Diamond Sutra and The Heart Sutra.* NY: Harper Torchbooks, 1972

————. *The Perfection of Wisdom in Eight Thousand Lines and Its Verse Summary*, Bolinas: Four Seasons Foundation, 1973

Cook, Francis. *Hua-yen Buddhism: the Jewel Net of Indra.* University Park: Pennsylvania University Press, 1977

————. *Three Texts on Consciousness Only.* Berkeley: Numata Center, 1999 (trs. of *Ch'eng wei-shih lun, Triṃśikā,* and *Viṃśatikā*)

Cooper, Barry. "Hegel and the genesis of Merleau-Ponty's atheism." *Studies in Religion, Sciences Religieuses*, 6(6), 1976-1977, 665-671

Cousins, L.S. "Buddhist *Jhāna*: Its nature and attainment according to the Pali Sources." *Religion*, III (2), 1973, 115-131

Cowell, E.B. tr. *The Aphorisms of Sāṇdilya, with the Commentary of Swapneśwara*, Bibliotheca Indica, Vol. 84, Calcutta: Asiatic Society of Bengal, 1878; rpt. in West Germany, 1981

Cunningham, Suzanne. *Language and the Phenomenological Reductions of Edmund Husserl*. The Hague: Martinus Nijhoff, 1976

Davidson, Ronald Mark. *Buddhist Systems of Transformation: Āśraya-Parivṛtti/Paravṛtti among the Yogācāra*, Unpublished doctoral dissertation, Berkeley, 1985

Dayal, Har. *The Bodhisattva Doctrine in Buddhist Sanskrit Literature*. Delhi: Motilal Banarsidass, 1978 rpt.

de Saussure, Ferdinand. *Course in General Linguistics*. tr. by Wade Baskin. NY: Philosophy Library, 1956

De Silva, C.L.A. *A Treatise of Buddhist Philosophy or Abhidharma*. Delhi: Sri Satguru, 1988 (rpt. of 1937 ed.)

de Silva, Patmasiri. *An Introduction to Buddhist Psychology*. NY: Barnes & Noble, 1979

———. *Buddhist and Freudian Psychology*, Columbo: Lake House Investments Ltd., n.d.

Deleuze, Gilles. *Expressionism in Philosophy: Spinoza*. tr. Martin Joughin. NY: Zone Books, 1992

———. *Kant's Critical Philosophy: The Doctrine of the Faculties*. tr. by Hugh Tomlinson & Barbara Habberjam, Minneapolis: University of Minnesota Press, 1984

———. *Spinoza: Practical Philosophy*. tr. by Robert Hurley, San Francisco: City Lights, 1988

Della Santini, Peter. *Madhyamaka Schools in India*. Delhi: Motilal Banarsidass, 1986

Demiéville, Paul. "Le chapitre de la *Bodhisattvabhūmi* sur la Perfection du Dhyāna." *Schayer Commemorative Volume* (Warszawa: Panstwowe Sydawnictwo Naukowe, 1957), *Rocznik Orientalistyxzny*. Polaska Akademai Nauk. Tome XXI, 1957, 109-128

———. "La *Yogācārabhūmi* de Saṅgharakṣa." *Bulletin de l'École Française d'Extrême-Orient*, XLIV, 1954, 339-436

DeNicolas, Antonio, review of "The *Bhagavad Gītā* by Winthrop Sargeant." in *PEW*, 31(1), January 1981, 98-101

———. *Avatāra: The Humanization of Philosophy Through the Bhagavad Gītā*. NY: Nicolas Hays, 1976

———. *Meditations Through the Ṛg Veda*. NY: Nicolas Hays, 1976

Derrida, Jacques. "On an Apocalyptic Tone Recently Adopted in Philosophy." tr. by John P.Leavey, Jr., in *Semeia* 23, 1982

———. *Aporias*. tr. Thomas Dutoit. Stanford: Stanford University Press, 1993

———. *Archive Fever*. tr. Eric Prenowitz. Chicago: University of Chicago Press, 1995

———. *Dissemination*. tr. by Barbara johnson. Chicago: University of Chicago Press, 1981

———. *Edmund Husserl's Origin of Geometry: An Introduction*. tr. by John P. Leavey, Jr., Stony Brook: Nicholas Hays, 1978

———. *Given Time: 1. Counterfeit Money*. tr. Peggy Kamuf. Chicago: University of Chicago Press, 1992

———. *Margins of Philosophy*. tr. by Alan Bass. Chicago: University of Chicago Press, 1981

———. *Of Grammatology*. tr. by Gayatri Spivak, Baltimore: The Johns Hopkins University Press, 1982

———. *Of Spirit: Heidegger and the Question*. tr. Geoffrey Bennington and Rachel Bowlby. Chicago: University of Chicago Press. 1989

———. *On the Name*. tr. David Wood, John P. Leavey, Jr., and Ian McLeod. Stanford: Stanford University Press, 1995

———. *Politics of Friendship*. tr. George Collins. London and NY: Verso, 1997

———. *Positions*. tr. by Alan Bass. Chicago: University of Chicago Press, 1981

———. *Resistances of Psychoanalysis*. tr. Peggy Kamuf, Pascale-Anne Brault, and Micheal Naas. Stanford: Stanford University Press, 1998

————. *Signéponge: Signsponge.* tr. by Richard Rand [bilingual ed.]. NY: Columbia University Press, 1984
————. *Specters of Marx.* tr. Peggy Kamuf. London and NY: Routledge, 1994
————. *Speech and Phenomenon and Other Essays on Husserl's Theory of Signs.* tr. by David Allison. Evanston: Northwestern University Press, 1973
————. *Spurs: Nietzsche's Styles.* tr. by Barbara Harlow [bilingual ed.]. Chicago: University of Chicago Press, 1984
————. *The Archaeology of the Frivolous: Reading Condillac.* tr. by John P. Leavey, Jr. Pittsburgh: Duquesne University Press, 1980
————. *The Gift of Death.* tr. David Wills. Chicago: University of Chicago Press. 1995
————. *The Post Card: From Socrates to Freud and Beyond.* tr. by Alan Bass. Chicago: University of Chicago Press, 1987
————. *The Truth in Painting.* tr. by Geoff Bennington & Ian McLeod. Chicago: University of Chicago Press, 1987
————. *Writing and Difference.* tr. by Alan Bass. Chicago: University of Chicago Press, 1978
Dessein, Bart. *Saṃyuktābhidharmahṛdaya: Heart of Scholasticism with Miscellaneous Additions.* Delhi: Motilal Banarsidass, 1999, 3 vols.
Dewoskin, Kenneth. *A Song For One or Two: Music and the Concept of Art in Early China*, Ann Arbor: Center for Chinese Studies, 1982
Dharmakīrti. *Santānāntara-siddhi, wtih Vinītadeva's Commentary.* tr. into English from T. Stcherbatsky's Russian version by Harish C.Gupta, in Papers of Th. Stcherbatsky, Indian Studies Past and Present, Calcutta, 1969
Dharmamasangaṇī [first work of Theravāda Abhidamma] ; Eng. tr.: *A Buddhist Manual of Psychological Ethics.* tr. by C.A.F.Rhys Davids, London: Pali Text Soceity, 1974, 3rd ed.
Dharmapāla 護法. *Dharmapāla's Yogācāra Critique of Bhāvaviveka's Mādhyamika Explanation of Emptiness: the Tenth Chapter of Ta-ch'eng Kuang pai-lun shih, commenting on Āryadeva's Catuḥśataka chapter sixteen.* tr. by John P. Keenan. Lewiston, NY: Edwin Mellen Press, 1997.
————. (see also Yi-ching)
Dharmasema Thera. *Jewels of the Doctrine: Stories of the Saddharma Ratnāvaliya.* tr. by Ranjini Obeyesekere. Albany: SUNY Press, 1991
Dignāga. *Ālambanaparikṣa and vṛtti (with the commentary of Dharmapāla), restored into Sanskrit from the Tibetan and Chinese versions and edited with English translations and notes and with copious extracts from Vinītadeva's commentary*, by N. Aiyaswami Sastri. Madras: Adyar Library, 1942
————. *Ālambanaparīkṣa.* French tr.: Susumu Yamagushi, *Dignāga. Examen de l'Objet de la Connaissance [Ālambanaparīkṣa] - Textes Tibétain et Chinois et Traduction des Stances et du Commentaire.. d'aprés le commentaire Tibétain de Vinītadeva*, Paris: Librarie Orientaliste Paul Guethner, 1929
————. *Nyāyamukha* ; Eng. tr.: Tucci, Giuseppe, *The Nyāmukha of Dignāga*, Taiwan: Chinese Materials Center, 1978 rpt of 1930 Heidelberg ed. [based on Hsüan-tsang's tr., T.1628, consulting Tibetan texts]
————. *Pramāṇasamuccaya* ; Eng. tr.: Masaaki Hattori. tr. *Dignāga, On Perception: being the Pratyakṣaparicchada of Dignāga's Pramāṇasamuccaya*, Cambridge: Harvard University Press, 1968
————. (see also Appendix Four; and Yi-ching)
Doboom Tulku, ed. *Mind Only School and Buddhist Logic: a Collection of Seminar Papers.* New Delhi: Tibet House and Aditya Prakashan, 1990
Donner, Neal, and Daniel Stevenson. *The Great Calming and Contemplation: A Study and Annotated Translation of the First Chapter of Chih-I's* Mo-ho Chih-kuan. Honolulu: University of Hawaii Press, Kuroda Institute, 1993
Dragonetti, Carmen. "Some Notes on the *Pratītyasamutpāda hṛdayakārikā* and the *Pratītyasamutpāda hṛdayakārikāvyākhyāna* Attributed to Nāgārjuna." *Buddhist Studies.* Delhi, no.6, 1979, 70-73.

Dreyfus, Georges. *Recognizing Reality: Dharmakīrti's Philosophy and Its Tibetan Interpretations.* Albany: SUNY Press, 1997

Dīgha-Nikāya. (PTS ed.); Eng. trs.: (1) *Dialogues of the Buddha.* tr. by T.W.Rhys Davids, 3 vols., *Sacred Books of the Budhists,* vols. 2-4, London: Luzac, 1956 rpt.; (2) *The Long Discourses of the Buddha.* Maurice Walshe (tr.). Boston: Wisdom, 1995

Dube, S.N. *Cross Currents in Early Buddhism.* Delhi: Manohar, 1980

Duerlinger, James. "Candrakirti's denial of the self." *PEW,* 34(3), July 1984, 261-272

————. "Vasubandu on the Vātsīputrīya's fire-fuel analogy." *PEW,* 32(2), April 1982, 151-158

Dutt, Nalinaksha. *Buddhist Sects in India.* Delhi: Motilal Banarsidass, 1978

————. *Mahāyāna Buddhism.* Delhi: Motilal Banarsidass, 1978

Dvivedi, Radhey Shyam Dhar (ed.). *Bauddhavijñānavāda: Cintana Evam Yogadana.* Varanasi: Kendriya Ucca Tibbati-Siksha-Samsthana, 1983

Eckel, M. David. *To See the Buddha.* Princeton: Princeton Paperbacks, 1994

————. *Jñānagarbha's Commentary of the Distinction Between the Two Truths,* Albany: SUNY Press, 1977

Edgerton, Franklin. *Buddhist Hybrid Sanskrit Grammar and Dictionary,* 2 vols. Delhi: Motilal Banarsidass, 1985 rpt.

Elliston, Frederick & Peter McCormick, eds. *Husserl: Expositions and Appraisals,* Notre Dame: University of Notre Dame Press, 1977

Ergardt, Jan. *Faith and Knowledge in Early Buddhism.* Leiden: EJ Brill, 1977

————. *Man and His Destiny: The Release of the Human Mind - A Study of Citta in Relation to Dhamma in Some Ancient Textts,* Leiden: E.J.Brill, 1986

Evans, Fred and Leonard Lawlor. *Chiasms: Merleau-Ponty's Notion of Flesh.* Albany: SUNY Press, 2000

Evola, J. *The Doctorine of Awakening.* tr. from Italian by H.E.Musson, London: Lusac, 1951

Fa-sheng 法勝 (*Dharmaśrī). *Abhidharmahṛdaya* (阿毘曇心論 *A-p'i-t'an Hsin Lun*) T. 1550. tr. into Chinese in 391 CE by Saṃghadeva and Hui-Yüan. (cf. T. 1551 and 1552); French tr.: *Le Coeur de la Loi Suprême: Traité de Fa-Cheng, Abhidharmahṛdayasástra de Dharmaśrī.* traduit et annoté par I. Armelin, Paris: Paul Guethner, 1978; Eng. tr.: Charles Willemen, *The Essence of Metaphysics: Abhidharmahṛdaya,* Brussels: 1975

Factor, R. Lance. 'What is the "logic" in Buddhist logic?' *PEW,* 33(2), APRIL 1983, 183-188

Falk, Maryla. *Nāma-Rūpa and Dharma-Rūpa,* Calcuta: University of Calcutta, 1943

Feer, M.L. *A Study of the Jātakas.* tr. by G.M. Foulkes. Calcutta: Susil Gupta, 1963

Fenner, Peter G. "Candrakīrti's refutation of Buddhist idealism." *PEW,* 33(3), July 1983

Flint, Thomas Kemp. *Causality in Yogācāra Buddhism: a Whiteheadian Perspective.* Unpub. M.A. Thesis, Colorado State University, 1978.

Fo-kuang ta tz'u-tien 佛光大辭典 [Fo-kuang Encyclopedic Dictionary (of Buddhism)]. Hsing Yun (ed.). 8 vols. Taiwan: Fo-kuang, 1989.

Foucher, A. "Notes Sur L'Itinéraire de Hiuan-Tsang en Afghanistan." *Études Asiatiques,* 1925, 257-284

Franco, Eli. "Once Again on Dharmakīrti's Deviation from Dignāga on Pratyakṣābhāsya." *JIP,* 14, 1986, 79-97.

————. *Perception, Knowledge and Disbelief: A Study of Jayarāśi's Scepticism.* Delhi: Motilal Banarsidass, 1994

Frauwallner, Erich. "Die Erkenntnislehre des Klassischen Sāṃkhya-systems." *Weiner Zeitschrift für die Kunde Sud- und Ostasiens,* 2 (1958), 3-58

————. *Studies in Abhidharma Literature and the Origins of Buddhist Philosophical Systems.* tr. by Sophie Francis Kidd. Albany: SUNY Press, 1995

Galloway, Brian. "A Yogācāra Analysis of the Mind, Based on the *Vijñāna* section of Vasubandhu's Pañcaskandhaprakaraṇa with Guṇaprabha's Commentary." *JIABS,* 3(2), 1980, 7-20.

Ganguly, Swati. *Treatise in Thirty Verses on Mere-consciousness: a Critical English translation of Hsüan-tsang's Chinese version of the Vijñāptimātratātrimsika with notes from Dharmapāla's commentary in Chinese.* Delhi: Motilal Banarsidass, 1992

————. (see also *Abhidharma-dhātukāya-pādaśāstra*)

Gasché, Rodolphe. *Derrida and the Philosophy of Reflection,* Cambridge: Harvard University Press, 1986

Gernet, Jacques. *Buddhism in Chinese Society: an Economic History from the Fifth to the Tenth Centuries.* tr. Franciscus Verellen. NY: Columbia University Press, 1995

Gethin, Rupert. "The Five Khandhas: Their Treatment in the Nikāyas and Early Abhidhamma." *JIP*, 14, 1986, 35-53

————. *The Buddhist Path to Awakening: A Study of the Bodhi-Pakkhiya Dhammā.* Leiden: EJ Brill, 1992

Giles, Herbert. *A Chinese-English Dictionary*, Taipei: Ch'eng Wen Publishing Co., 1972 rpt.

Gimello, Roberrt. *Chih-yen (602-668), and the Foundation of Hua-yen Buddhism,* Unpublished doctoral dissertation, Columbia University, 1972

Gimello, Robert, and Peter Gregory (eds.). *Studies in Ch'an and Hua-yen.* Honolulu: University of Hawaii Press, Kuroda Institute, 1983

Glucklich, Ariel. *A Sense of Adharma.* Oxford: Oxford University Press, 1994

Gokhale, Pradeep P. *Hetubindu of Dharmakīrti (A Point of Probans).* Delhi: Sri Satguru, 1997

————. *Inference and Fallacies Discussed in Ancient Indian Logic, with special reference to Nyāya and Buddhism.* Delhi: Sri Satguru, 1992

————. *Vādanyāya of Dharmakīrti: The Logic of Debate.* Delhi: Sri Satguru, 1993

Gokhale, V.V. "What is Avijñaptirūpa (Concealed Form of Activity)." *New Indian Antiquary*, I, 1938, 68-73

————. "Yogācāra Works Annotated by Vairocanarakṣita." *Annals of the Bhandarkar Oriental Research Institute*, Poona, 1977

Gómez, Luis O. *The Land of Bliss: The Paradise of the Buddha of Measureless Light, Sanskrit and Chinese Versions of the* Sukhāvatīvyūha Sutras. Honolulu: University of Hawaii Press, 1996

Govinda, Lama Anagarika. *Creative Meditation and Multi-Dimensional Conciousness*, Wheaton, IL: Quest, 1976

————. *Foundation of Tibetan Mysticism.* NY: Samuel Weiser, 1969

————. *The Psychological Attitude of Early Buddhist Philosophy.* NY: Samuel Weiser, 1969

Goyal, S.R. *Harsha and Buddhism.* Meerut, India: Kusumanjali Prakashan, 1986

Gradinarov, P.I. *Phenomenology and Indian Epistemology: Studies in Nyāya-Vaiśeṣika Transcendental Logic and Atomism.* Delhi: Ajanta Books, 1990

Gregory, Peter (ed.). *Sudden and Gradual: Approaches to Enlightenment in Chinese Thought.* Honolulu: University of Hawaii Press, Kuroda Institute, 1987

———— (ed.). *Traditions of Meditation in Chinese Buddhism.* Honolulu: University of Hawaii Press, Kuroda Institute, 1986

———— (ed.). *Sudden and Gradual: Approaches to Enlightenment in Chinese Thought.* Honolulu: University of Hawaii Press, 1987

————. *Inquiry into the Origin of Humanity: An Annotated Translation of Tsung-mi's* Yüan jen lun *with a Modern Commentary.* Honolulu: University of Hawaii Press, Kuroda Institute, 1995

————. *Tsung-mi and the Sinification of Buddhism.* Princeton: Princeton University Press, 1991

Griffiths, Paul. "On being Mindless: The debate on the reemergence of consciousness from the attainment of cessation in the *Abhidharmakośabhāṣyam* and its commentaries." *PEW*, 33(4), October 1983, 379-394

————. *On Being Buddha.* Albany: SUNY Press, 1994

————. *On Being Mindless: Buddhist Meditation and the Mind-Body Problem*, La Salle, IL: Open Court, 1986

Grosnik, William. "*Cittaprakṛti* and *Ayoniśomanaskāra* in the *Ratnagotravibhāga*: A Precedent for the *Hsin-Nien* Distinction of *the Awakening of Faith*." *JIABS*, 6 (2), 1983, 35-47

————. "Nonorigination and *Nirvāna* in the Early *Tathāgatagarbha* Literature." *JIABS* 4, 1981, 33-43

Guenther, Herbert V. *Philosophy and Psychology in the Abhidharma*. Berkeley: Shambhala, 1976

Guha, Dinesh C. *Navya Nyāya System of Logic*. Motilal Banarsidass, 1979

Gunaratana, Henepola. *The Path of Serenity and Insight*. Delhi: Motilal Banarsidass, 1982

Gurwitsch, Aron. *Studies in Phenomenology and Psychology*. Evanston: Northwestern University Press, 1966

Hagiwara, Unrai 萩原雲来. *Sanjūju ryō besshaku* 三十頌了別釋. in *Hagiwara Unrai bunshū* 萩原雲来文集, 628-677, Tokyo: Taishō Daigaku Shuppen, 1938

Hakamaya, Noriaki 袴谷憲昭. "Araya-shiki sonzai no hachi ronshō ni kansuru shobunken." (アーラヤ識存在の八論証に関する諸文献) *Komazawa daigaku bukkyōgakubu kenkyūkiyō*, 36, 1-26

————. "Asvabhāva's Commentary on the *Mahāyānasūtrālaṃkāra* IX. 56- 76." *IBK*, 39, Dec. 1971, 473-465

————. "*Nirodhasamāpatti* - Its Historical Meaning in the *Vijñaptimātratā* System." *IBK*, XXIII (2), March 1975, 1074-1084 (33-43)

————. "The Realm of Enlightenment in *Vijñapti-mātratā*: The Formulation of the 'Four Kinds of Pure Dharmas'." tr. from Japanese by John Keenan, *JIABS*, 3(2), 1980, 21-41

————. *Yuishiki no kaishaku gaku "Kaishin Mitsukyō" wo yomu* 唯識の解釈学ー『解深密経』を読む. Tokyo: Shunjōsha, 1994

————. see KUWAYAMA Shoshin

Hakeda, Yoshito. *Kūkai: Major Works*. NY: Columbia University Press, 1972

Haldar, Aruna. *Some Psychological Aspects of Early Buddhist Philosophy Based on Abhidharmakośa of Vasubandhu*, Calcutta: Asiatic Society, 1981

Han-shan De-ch'ing 憨山德清. *Han-shan ta-shih meng-yu chi* 憨山大師夢遊集. Taipei: Hsin Wen Fung, 1974

Han T'ing-chieh 韓廷傑. *Ch'eng wei-shih lun* 成唯識論. Taiwan: Fo Kuang, 1997 (Original text with modern annotations and commentary)

Hansen, Chad. *A Daoist Theory of Chinese Thought*. Oxford: Oxford University Press, 1992

————. "Linguistic skepticism in the *Lao Tzu*." *PEW*, 31(3), July 1981, 321- 336

Harris, Ian Charles. *The Continuity of Madhyamaka and Yogācāra in Indian Mahāyāna Buddhism*. Leiden; New York: E.J. Brill, 1991

Hashimoto, Tetsuo. "The Concept of Loka in Early Buddhism (IV)." *IBK*, 33 (2), March 1985, 861-855 (9-15)

Hattori, Masaaki. *Dignāga, On Perception*. Cambridge: Harvard University Press, 1968

Hayes, Richard. *Dignāga on the Interpretation of Signs*. Dordrecht: Kluwer, 1988

————. "Principled Atheism in the Buddhist Scholastic Tradition." *JIP* 16 (1988) 5-28

Hazra, Kanai Lal. *The Rise and Decline of Buddhism in India*. New Delhi: Munshiram Manoharlal, 1995

Heng-Ching Shih, in collaboration with Dan Lusthaus. *A Comprehensive Commentary on the Heart Sutra (Prajñāpāramitā-hṛdaya-sūtra) by K'uei-chi*. Berkeley: Numata Center, 2001

Hirabayashi, Jay & Shotaro Iida. "Another Look at the Mādhyamika vs. Yogācāra Controversy Concerning Existence and Non-existence." L. Cousins, et al., eds., *Buddhist Studies in Honor of I.B.Horner*, Dordrecht: D. Reidel, 1974, 341- 360

HIRAKAWA Akira 平川彰, *Bukkyō tsūshi* 仏教通史 (Outline of Buddhist History), Tokyo: Shunjūsha, 1980

————. *Daijō kishinron* 大乘起信論. Tokyo: Daizō Shuppan, 1989

————. *A History of Indian Buddhism: From Śākyamuni to Early Mahāyāna.* tr. and ed. Paul Groner. Honolulu: University of Hawaii Press, 1990

————. *Index to the Abhidharmakośabhāṣya.* vol. 1: Sanskrit-Chinese-Tibetan; vol. 2: Chinese-Sanskrit-Tibetan. Tokyo: Daizō Shuppan, 1973, 1977

HIRAKAWA Akira, KAJIYAMA Yuichi, TAKASAKI Jikido, et al. *Yuishiki shisō* 唯識思想. Tokyo: Shunjusha, 1995.

Hoffman, Frank J. *Rationality and Mind in Early Buddhism.* Delhi: Motilal Banarsidass, 1987

Holt, John C. *Discipline: The Canonical Buddhism of the Vinayapitaka. Delhi*: Motilal Banarsidass, 1981

Honda, Meguma. "Sāṃkhya Reported by Paramārtaha in the Buddhist Canon." *IBK*, XXII (1), Dec. 1972, 501-490 (7-18)

————. "Dharmapāla's Report on *Sāṃkhya*." *IBK*, 17(1), 1968-69, 445- 440(1-6)

————. "Sāṃkhya in the *buddhagotra*." *IBK*, XVIII (1), Dec. 1969, 441- 434 (1-8)

————. "The Essence of the Sāṃkhya by Vijñāna Bhikṣu." *IBK*, XIX (1), Dec. 1970, 489-477 (1-13)

————. "The Essence of the Sāṃkhya II." *IBK*, XX (1), Dec. 1970, 488- 474 (8-22)

————. "[K'uei-] chi's Statement of Sāṃkhya." *IBK*, XXXV (1), Dec. 1976, 516-512 (9-13)

Hoog, Constance. tr. & annot. *Prince Jin-Gim's Testbook of Tibetan Buddhism,* Leiden: E.J.Brill, 1983 ['Phags-pa's Ses-bya rab-gsal (Jñeya-prakāsa); [cf. T. 1645]

Hopkins, Jeffrey. *Emptiness in the Mind-Only School of Buddhism.* Berkeley: University of California Press, 1999

————. *Emptiness Yoga.* Ithaca: Snow Lion, 1987

Hsüan-tsang. (For a complete, annotated list of all his translations and writings, see Appendix Four)

Hui-chao 惠沼(. *Cheng-wei-shih-lun liao-yi-teng* 成唯識論了義燈. (T.43.1843)

Hui-li 慧立 (completed by Yen-ts'ung 彥悰). *Ta-t'ang ta-tz'u-en-ssu san-tsang fa-shih chuan* 大唐大慈恩三藏法師傳. (Biography of Hsüan-tsang) (T.50.2053); (1) Abridged Eng. tr. by Li Yung-hsi, *The Life of Hsuan tsang: The Tripitaka-Master of the Great Tzu En Monastery*, Peking: Chinese Buddhist Association; (2) First half translated in Beal, *The Life of Hiuen-Tsiang* (see Beal); (3) (see also Li Rongxi for complete translation).

Huntington, Jr., C.W. 'A "nonreferential" view of language and conceptual thought in the work of Tson-kha-pa', *PEW*, 33 (4), October 1983, 325-329

Huo T'ao-hui 霍韜晦. *An-hui "San-shih wei-shih shih" yüan-tien yi-chu* 安慧『三十唯識釋』原典議註 (Sthiramati's Commentary on *Triṃśikāvijñapti*: A Chinese Translation with Notes and Interpretation). Hong Kong: Chung Wen Ta-hsüeh, 1980

Hurvitz, Leon. tr. *Scripture of the Lotus Blossom of the Fine Dharma (Lotus Sutra).* NY: Columbia University Press, 1976

Husserl, Edmund. *Cartesian Meditations: An Introduction to Phenomenology.* tr. by Dorion Cairns. The Hague: Martinus Nijhoff, 1977

————. *Experience and Judgement.* tr. by James Churchill & Karl Ameriks, revised & ed. by Ludwig Landgrebe. Evanston: North Western University Press, 1973

————. *Formal and Transcendental Logic.* tr. by Dorion Cairns. The Hague: Martinus Nijhoff, 1978

————. *Ideas: General Introduction to Pure Phenomenology*, [*Ideas I*] tr. by W.R.Boyce Gibson. NY: Collier Books, 1962

————. *Ideas Pertaining to a Pure Phenomenology and t o a Phenomenological Philosophy: First Book.* [*Ideas I*] tr. by F. Kersten. Dordrecht: Kluwer, 1982

————. *Ideas Pertaining to a Pure Phenomenology and t o a Phenomenological Philosophy: Second Book.* [*Ideas II*] tr. by R. Rojcewicz and A. Schuwer. Dordrect: Kluwer, 1989

————. *Logical Investigations.* tr. by J.N. Findlay. NY: Humanities Press, 1970, 2 vols.

————. *On the Phenomenology of the Consciousness of Internal Time (1893-1917)*. tr. by John Barnett Brough. Dordrecht: Kluwer, 1991

————. *Phenomenological Psychology: Lectures, Summer Semester; 1925*. tr. by John Scanlon. The Hague: Martinus Nijhoff, 1977

————. *The Crisis of European Sciences and Transcendental Phenomenology*. tr. by David Carr. Evanston: Northwestern University Press, 1970

————. *The Ideas of Phenomenology*. tr. by William Alston & George Nakhnikian. The Hague: Martinus Nijhoff, 1964

————. *The Paris Lectures*. tr. by Peter Koestenbaum. The Hague: Martinus Nijhoff, 1967

————. *The Phenomenology of Internal Time-Consciousness*, ed. by Martin Heidegger. tr. by James Churchill. Bloomington: Indiana University Press, 1964

I-Ching 義淨 (tr.). *Ken-pen shuo yi-ch'ieh you pu p'i nai yeh* 根本說一切有部毘奈耶. ([*Mūla-Sarvastivāda*] *Vinaya-vibhaṅga*)(T.23.1442)

————. *Nan-hai Chi kuei nei fa ch'uan* 南海奇歸內法傳s (T.54.2125) (Eng. tr. see Takakusu, Junjirō)

————. *Ta-t'ang Hsi-yu ch'iu-fa kao-seng ch'uan* 大唐西域求法高僧傳. (Eng. tr., see Lahiri, Latika)

————. (See Dharmapāla)

Ichigo, Masamichi. "A Synopsis of the *Madhyamaka alaṁkāra* of Sāntarakṣita (1)." *IBK*, XX (2), March 1970, 995-989 (36-42)

Ichimura, Shohei. "A New Approach to the Intra-Mādhyamika Confrontation over the Svātantrika and Prāsaṅgika Methods of Refutation." *JIABS*, 5 (2), 1982, 41-52

Iida, Shotaro. "A Mukung-hwa in Ch'ang-an - A Study of Life and Works of Wonch'uk (613-696), with Special Interest in the Korean Contributions to the Development of Chinese and Tibetan Buddhism." *Proceedings of the International Symposium Commemorating the 30th Anniversary of Korean Liberation*, Republic of Korea: National Academy of Sciences, August 11-20, 1075, 225-251

Inazu, Kizow. "The Concept of *Vijñapti* and *Vijñāna* in the Text of Vasubandhu's *Viṃśatikā-vijñaptimātratā-siddhi*." *IBK*, 15 (1), 1966-67, 474-468 (1-7)

————. "*Vijñapti-mātratā* Doctrine as Systematical Explanation of Bodhisattva's Life." *IBK*, 16 (2), 1967-68, 996-992 (1-5)

Ingalls, Daniel H.H. *Materials for the Study of Navya-Nyāya Logic*. Delhi: Motilal Banarsidass, 1988

Iwata, Ryōzō 岩田良三. *Shindai no amare-shiki setsu ni tsuite* 真諦の阿摩羅識說について. Tokyo: Suzuki Research Foundation, 1971

Jackson, Roger. *Is Enlightenment Possible? Dharmakīrti and rGyal tshab rje on Knowledge, Rebirth, No-Self and Liberation*. Ithaca, NY: Snow Lion, 1993

Jagchid, Sechin. "The Mongol Khans and Chinese Buddhism and Taoism." *JIABS*, 2 (1), 1979, 7-28

Jaini, Padmanabh S. "On the Sarvajñatva (Omniscience) of Mahāvīra and the Buddha." L. Cousins, et al. eds., *Buddhist Studies in Honor of I.B. Horner*, Dordrecht: D. Reidel, 1974, 71-90

————. "Prajñā and dṛṣṭi in the Vaibhāṣika Abhidharma." L. Cousins, et al., eds., *Buddhist Studies in Honor of I.B. Horner*, Dordrecht: D. Reidel, 1974, 531-547

————. "The Development of the Theory of the Viprayukta-Saṃskāras." *Bulletin of the London School of Oriental and African Studies*, 22, 1959, 531- 547

Japanese-English Buddhist Dictionary, R.H. Blyth, et al., Tokyo: Daito Shuppansha, 1965

Jayasuriya, W.F. *The Psychology and Philosophy of Buddhism (being an Introduction to the Abhidhamma)*, Colombo: Y.M.B.A. Press, 1963

Jayatilleke, K.N. *Early Buddhist Theory of Knowledge*. Delhi: Motilal Banarsidass, 1980

Johansson, Rune. *Pali Buddhist Texts*. Sweden: Studentlitteratur, 1973

————. *The Psychology of Nirvana*. NY: Anchor, 1970

Joshi, Lal Mani. *Studies in the Buddhistic Culture of India (During the 7th and 8th Centuries A.D.)*. Delhi: Motilal Banarsidass, 1977, 2nd revised ed.

Kabilsingh, Chatsumarn. *A Comparative Study of Bhikkhunī Pāṭimokkha.* Delhi: Chaukhambha Orientalia, 1984

Kajiyama, Yūichi. "Bhāvaviveka, Sthiramati and Dharmapāla." *Wiener Zeitschrift für die Kunde Sud- und Ostasiens und Archiv für Indische Philosophie*, #12, 13, 1958, 193-203.

————. "Controversy between the *sākāra-* and *nirākāra-vādins* of the Yogācāra School - some materials." *IBK*, 14 (1), 1955-56, 429-418 (26-37)

————. "The Atomic Theory of Vasubandhu, the Author of the *Abhidharmakośa.*" *IBK*, XIX (2), March 1971, 1006-1001 (19-24)

————. "Three Types of Affirmation and Two Kinds of Negation in Buddhist Philosophy." *Wiener Zeitschrift für die Kunde Sud- und Ostasiens und Archiv für Indische Philosophie*, 17, 1973, 161-175

Kalupahana, David. *The Principle of Buddhist Psychology*, Albany: SUNY Press, 1987

Kamalaśīla. *Bhāvanākrama.* French tr.: *La Progression dans la Méditation.* traduit du Ṣanscrit et du Tibétain par José Van Den Broeck, Bruxelles: Institut Belge des Hautes Études Bouddhiques, 1977

Kamata, Shigeo 蒲田茂雄. *Chung-kuo fa-chiao shih* 中國佛教史. Tr. into Chinese by Kuan Shih 關世. Taipei: Hsin Wen Fung, 1983

Kanaoka, Shuyu. "Sāntideva's attitude towards *Vijñāna* Theory." *IBK*, 10 (2), 1962, 749-744 (34-39)

Kant, Immanuel. *Critique of Judgement.* tr. by J.H. Bernard. NY: Hafner Press, 1951

————. *Critique of Pure Reason.* tr. by Norman Kemp Smith. NY: St. Martin's, 1965

Kar, Bijayananda. *The Theories of Error in Indian Philosophy: An Analytical Study.* Delhi: Ajanta, 1978

Karunadasa, Y. *Buddhist Analysis of Matter.* Singapore: The Buddhist Research Society, 1989

Kashyap, Jagdish. *Abhidhamma Philosophy.* Delhi: Bharatiya Vidya Prakashan, 1982 rpt.

Kathā-vatthu. (PTS edition). Eng. tr: *Points of Controversy.* tr. by Shwe Zan Aung & Mrs. Rhys Davids, London: PTS, 1979 rpt.

Katsumata, Shunkyō 勝又俊教. *Bukkyō ni okeru Shinshiki-setsu no kenkyū* 仏教における心識説の研究 (*A Study of the Citta-Vijñāna Thought in Buddhism*). Tokyo: Sankibo, 1961

————. "Yugashijiron ni okeru shikan" 瑜伽師地論における止觀. in Sekiguchi Shinda, ed., *Shikan no Kenkyū.* Tokyo: Iwanami, 1975

————. *Yuishiki shisō to mikkyō* 唯識思想と密教. Tokyo: Shunjusha, 1988.

Katz, Nathan. "*Prasaṅga* and deconstruction: Tibetan hermeneutics and the yāna controversy." *PEW*, 34 (2), April 1984, 185-204

Kaul, Adaitavadini. *Buddhist Savants of Kashmir and their Contribution Abroad.* Kashmir: Utpal Publications, 1987

Kawamura, Leslie (ed.). *The Bodhisattva Doctrine in Buddhism.* Canada: Wilfred Laurier University Press, 1978

————. "The *Dharma-Dharmatā-vihāga.*" *IBK*, XXXII (2), March 1984, p. 1114-1107 (10-17)

————. *Vinītadeva's Contribution to the Buddhist Mentalistic Trend*, [comm. on *Triṃśikā*] Unpublished doctoral dissertation, University of Saskatchewan, 1975

Keenan, John P. "Original Purity and the focus of Early *Yogācāra.*" *JIABS*, 5 (1), 1982, 7-18

————. *A Study of the* Buddhabhūmyupadeśa*: The Doctrinal Development of the Notion of Wisdom in Yogācāra Thought.* Unpub. Ph.D. Dissertation. University of Wisconsin-Madison, 1980

Kieschnick, John. *The Eminent Monk: Buddhist Ideals in Medieval Chinese Hagiography.* Honolulu: University of Hawaii Press, 1997

King, Winston. *Theravāda Meditation: The Buddhist transformation of Yoga.* University Park: Penn State University Press

Kiyota Minoru, ed. *Mahāyāna Buddhist Meditation: Theory and Practice.* Honolulu: University of Hawaii Press, 1978

————. *Shingon Buddhism: Theory and Practice*, Los Angeles-Tokyo, Buddhist Books International, 1978

Klein, Anne. *Knowing, Naming, and Negation: A Sourcebook on Tibetan Sautrāntika.* Ithaca, NY: Snow Lion, 1991

————. *Knowledge and Liberation.* Ithaca: Snow Lion, 1986

Kloetzli, Randy. *Buddhist Cosmology.* Delhi: Motilal Banarsidass, 1983

Klostermaier, Klaus K. "Time in Patañjali's *Yogasūtra*." *PEW*, 34 (2), 1984, 205-210

Knaul, Livia. "Kuo Hsiang and the Chuang Tzu." *Journal of Chinese Philosophy*, 12, 1985, 429-447

Kochumutton, Thomas A. *A Buddhist Doctrine of Experience: A New Translation of the Works of Vasubandhu the Yogācārin.* Delhi: Motilal Banarsidass, 1982 [Sanskrit and English for *Madhyāntavibhāga* ch. 1; *Trisvabhāva-nirdeśa; Triṃśikā; Viṃśatikā*; with analysis]

Kohn, Livia. *Laughing at the Tao: Debates among Buddhists and Taoists in Medieval China.* Princeton: Princeton University Press, 1995

Kolakowski, Leszek. *Husserl and the Search for Certitude*, New Haven: Yale University Press, 1975

Komito, David Ross. *Nāgārjuna's "Seventy Stanzas": A Buddhist Psychology of Emptiness.* Commentary by Geshe Sonam Rinchen. tr. by Tenzin Dorjee and David Ross Komito. Ithaca, NY: Snow Lion, 1987

————. *Nāgārjuna's "Seventy Stanzas": A Buddhist Psychology of Emptiness.* Ithaca: Snow Lion, 1987

Konow, Sten. *The Two First Chapters of the Daśasākasrikā Prajñāpāramitā: Restoration of the Sanskrit Text, Analysis, and Index*, Oslo, 1941

Koseki, Aaron K. "Chi-tsang's *Sheng-man pao-k'u*: The true dharma doctrine and the bodhisattva ideal." *PEW*, 34 (1), January 1984, 67-83

————. "The Concept of Practice in San-lun Thought: Chi-tsang and the 'Concurrent Insight' of the Two Truths." *PEW* 31, 4 (October 1981) 449-466

————. "Later Mādhyamika' in China: Some Current Perspectives on the History of Chinese *Prajñāpāramitā* Thought." JIABS, 5 (2), 1982, 53-62

————. "*Prajñāpāramitā* and the Buddhahood of the Non-Sentient World: The San-Lun Assimilation of Buddha-Nature and Middle Path Doctrine." JIABS, 3(1), 1980, 16-33

Kritzer, Robert Benjamin. *Pratītyasamutpāda in the* Abhidharmasamuccaya*: Conditioned Origination in the Yogācāra Abhidharma.* Unpub. Ph.D. Dissertation, University of California. Berkeley, 1995

Kuang Chung 光中. *T'ang Hsüan-tsang san-tsang chuan shih hui-pien* 唐玄奘三藏傳史彙編. Taipei: Tung Ta, 1990

K'uei-chi 窺基. *Ch'eng wei-shih lun chang-chung shu-yao* 成唯識論掌中樞要. (T.43.1831) (Nanjing Blockprint alternate title: *Ch'eng wei-shih lun chu-shu san-chung* ||||著述三種)

———— *Ch'eng wei-shih lun pieh-ch'ao* 成唯識論別鈔. Nanjing Blockprint, 2 vols., 1960

————. *Ch'eng wei-shih lun shu-chi* 成唯識論述記. (T.43.1830)

————. *Cheng-wei-shih-lun liao-chien* 成唯識論了義. (T.44.1836)

————. *Hsin-ching lüeh-shu* 心經略疏. (T.33.1710)

————. *Pien chung-pien lun shu-chi* 辯中邊論述記 (T.44.1835)

————. *Wei-shih erh-shih-lun shu-chi* 唯識二十論述記. (T.43.1834)

————. *Yin-ming ju cheng-li lun shu* 因明入正理論疏 (T.44.1840)

————. *Yu-ch'ieh-shih-ti-lun lüeh-tsuan* 瑜伽師地論略纂. (T.43.1829)

Kung Chiung 龔雋. *"Ta-sheng ch'i hsin lun" yü fo-hsüeh chung-kuo hua* 『大乘起信論』與佛學中國化. Taipei: Wen Chin, 1994

Kunst, Arnold. "Some Polemics in the *Laṅkāvatārasūtra*." in *Buddhist Studies in Honor of Walpola Rahula*, London: Gordon Frazer, 1980, 103-112

KUWAYAMA Shoshin 桑山正進. *Genjō* 玄奘. (with HAKAMAYA Noriaki). Tokyo: Daizō Shuppan, 1981

Lacan, Jacques. *Écrits.* tr. by Alan Sheridan. NY: Norton, 1977

Lahiri, Latika. *Chinese Monks in India: Biography of Eminent Monks Who Went to the Western World in Search of the Law During the Great T'ang Dynasty*. Delhi: Motilal Banarsidass, 1986. (Tr. of Yi-Ching's *Kao-seng-chuan*, T.2066, includes Chinese Text.)

Lai, Whalen. *The Awakening of Faith in Mahayana* (Ta-ch'eng ch'i-hsin lun); *A Study of the Unfolding of Sinitic Motifs*, Unpublished doctoral dissertation, Harvard, 1975

————. "Before the Prajña Schools: The Earliest Chinese Commentary on the *Aṣṭasāhasrikā*"." JIABS, 6 (1), 1983, 91-108

————. "Chou yung vs. Chang Jung (on *Śūnyatā*); The *Pen-mo Yu-wu* Controversy in Fifth-Century China." JIABS, 3 (2), 1979, 45-65

————. "A Clue to the Authorship for the *Awakening of Faith:* Śikṣānanda's Redaction of the Word '*Nien*'." JIABS, 3, 1980, 34-53

————. "The Defeat of Vijñaptimātratā in China: Fa-tsang on Fa-Hsing and Fa-Hsiang." *Journal of Chinese Philosophy*, 13, 1986, 1-19 [contains translation of Fa-tsang's *Wu chiao chang* (Five Teachings chapter) T.45, 484c-485b.]

————. "The Early Prajñā schools, Especially 'Hsin-wu', Reconsidered." *PEW*, 33 (1), January 1983, 61-77

————. "*Hu-Jan Nien-Ch'i* (Suddenly a Thought Arose): Chinese Understanding of Mind and Consciousness." JIABS, 3 (2), 1980, 42-59.

————. "Kao Tzu and Mencius on mind: Analyzing a paradigm shift in classical China." *PEW*, 34 (2), April 1984, 147-160

————. "Limits and Failure of *Ko-I* (Concept-matching) Buddhism." *History of Religions* 18, 3, Feb. 1979, 238-257

————. "The Meaning of 'Mind-only' (*wei-hsin*): an Analysis of a Sinitic Mahāyāna Phenomenon." *PEW*, 27 (1), 1977, 61-77

————. "Nonduality of the Two Truths in Sinitic *Mādhyamika*: Origin of the Third Truth." JIABS, 2 (2), 1979, 45-65

————. "Sinitic Speculations on Buddha-nature: The Nirvāṇa School (420-589)." *PEW*, 32 (2), April 1982, 135-149

Lai, Whalen & Lewis Lancaster, eds. *Early Ch'an in China and Tibet. Berkeley*: Berkeley Buddhist Studies, 1983

Lalithambal, K.S. *Dharmakīrti's Rūpāvatāra: A Critical Study*. Delhi: Sri Satguru, 1995

Lama Chimpa & Alaka Chattopadhyaya. *Tāranātha's History of Buddhism in India*. translated from the Tibetan, Simla: Indian Institute of Advanced Study, 1970

Lamotte, Étienne. "Conditioned Co-production and Supreme Enlightenment," in *Buddhist Studies in Honor of Walpola Rahula*, London: Gordon Frazer, 1980, 118-132

————. "Passions and Impregnations of the Passions in Buddhism," L. Cousins, et al., eds., *Buddhist Studies in Honor of I.B. Horner*, Dordrecht: D. Reidel, 1974, 91-104

————. "Conditioned Co-production and Supreme Enlightenment." in *Buddhist Studies in Honour of Walpola Rahula*, 1980

————. *History of Indian Buddhism: From the Origins to the Śaka Era*. English tr. by Sara Webb-Boin. Louvain-La-Neuve: Université Catholique de Louvain, 1988

————. *Karmasiddhiprakaraṇa: the Treatise on Action by Vasubandhu*. English translation by Leo M. Pruden. Berkeley, CA: Asian Humanities Press, 1988

————. "Passions and Impregnations of the Passions in Buddhism." in Lance Cousins, et al. (eds.), *Buddhist Studies in Honour of I. B. Horner*, 1974

————. *La Somme du Grand Véhicule D'Asaṅga (Mahāyānasaṃgraha)*. 2 vols. Louvain: Institut Orientaliste Louvain-la-Neuve, 1973

————. *Śūraṃgamasamādhisūtra: The Concentration of Heroic Progress*. tr. Sara Boin-Webb. Surrey: Curzon Press, 1998

————. *The Teaching of Vimalakīrti*. tr. Sara Boin-Webb. Oxford: Pali Text Society, 1994

————. *Le Traité de la Grande Vertu de Sagesse de Nāgārjuna (Mahāprajñāpāramitāśāstra)*. 5 vols. Louvain: Institut Orientaliste Louvain-la-Neuve, 1970-81

Lancaster, Lewis. *The Korean Buddhist Canon.* With collaboration of Sung Bae Park. Berkeley: California University Press, 1979
Lancaster, Lewis (ed.). *Prajñāpāramitā and Related Systems: Studies in Honor of Edward Conze.* Berkeley: Berkeley Buddhist Studies Series, 1977
Lancaster, Lewis, and Whalen Lai. *Early Ch'an in China and Tibet.* Berkeley: Asian Humanities Press, 1983
Lao Tzu Chu-tzu so-yin 老子逐字索引 *(A Concordance to the Laozi).* Hong Kong: Commercial Press, 1996. (contains *Tao-tsang* edition of Wang Pi version, with Wang Pi's commentary; Ho Shang-kung version with Ho's commentary)
Lapointe, Francois H. "The Existence of Alter Egos: Jean-Paul Sartre and Maurice Merleau-Ponty." *Journal of Phenomenological Psychology,* 6 (2), Spring 1976, 209-216
Larrabee, M. J. "The one and the many: Yogācāra Buddhism and Husserl." *PEW,* 31 (1), January 1981, 3-15
Larson, Gerald, and Ram Shankar Bhattacharya (eds.). *Sāṃkhya: A Dualist Tradition in Indian Philosophy.* Encyclopedia of Indian Philosophies. Princeton: Princeton University Press, 1987
Lati Rinbochay & Elizabeth Napper. *Mind in Tibetan Buddhism,* Valois, NY: Snow Lion, 1980
Law, Bimala Churn.*The Buddhist Conception of Spirits.* Varanasi: Bhartiya Publishing, 1974 (rpt. of 1934 ed.)
———. *Concept of Buddhism.* Amsterdam: H.J. Paris, 1937
———. *Concepts of Buddhism.* Leiden: Kern Institute, 1937
———. *Kṣatriya Clans in Buddhist India.* Delhi: A. Sagar Book House, 1993 (rpt. of 1922 ed.)
———. *The Legend of the Topes (Thūpavaṃsa).* New Delhi: Munshiram Manoharlal, 1986 rpt.
———. *The Life and Work of Buddhaghosa.* Delhi: Nag Publishers, 1976 rpt.
——— (tr.). *A Manual of Buddhist Historical Traditions.* Delhi: Bharatiya Publishing House, 1980 [tr. of Dhammakirti's *Saddhamma Saṃgaha*]
Legge, James (tr.). *A Record of Buddhistic Kingdoms: Being an account by the Chinese Monk Fa-Hien of his travels in India and Ceylon (AD 399-414)...* NY: Dover, rpt. of 1886 ed.
Lenk, Hans, and Gregor Paul. *Epistemological Issues in Classical Chinese Philosophy.* Albany: SUNY Press, 1993
Lessing, Ferdinand D. "Structure and Meaning of the Rite Called the Bath of the Buddha According to Tibetan and Chinese Sources," in *Studia Serica: Bernhard Karlgren Dedicata,* Soren Egerod & Else Glahn, eds., Copenhagen: 1959, 159-171
Lessing F. D. & Alex Wayman. *Introduction to the Buddhist Tantric Systems.* Delhi: Motilal & Samuel Weiser, 1980 rpt. of 1968 ed. [tr. of Mkhas-grub-chos-rje's *Rgyud sde spihi rnam par gzag pa rgya par brjod*]
Levinas, Emmanuel. *Basic Philosophical Writings.* Adriaan T. Peperzak, Simon Critchley, and Robert Bernasconi (eds.). Bloomington: Indiana University Press, 1996
———. *Beyond the Verse: Talmudic Readings and Lectures.* tr. Gary D. Mole. Bloomington: Indiana University Press, 1994
———. *Collected Philosophical Papers.* tr. Alphonso Lingis. Dordrecht: Kluwer, 1993
———. *Difficult Freedom: Essays on Judaism.* tr. Seán Hand. Baltimore: Johns Hopkins University Press, 1990
———. *Entre Nous: Thinking-of-the-Other.* tr. Michael B. Smith and Barbara Harshav. NY: Columbia University Press, 1998
———. *Existence and Existents.* tr. Alphonso Lingis. Dordrecht: Kluwer, 1988
———. *In the Time of the Nations.* tr. Michael B. Smith. Bloomington: Indiana University Press, 1994
———. *Nine Talmudic Readings.* tr. Annette Aronowicz. Bloomington: Indiana University Press, 1990

————. *Otherwise Than Being Or Beyond Essence.* tr. by Alphonso Lingis. The Hague: Martinus Nijhoff, 1981

————. *Outside the Subject.* tr. Michael D. Smith. Stanford: Stanford University Press, 1994

————. *The Theory of Intuition in Husserl's Phenomenology.* tr. by André Orianne. Evanston: Northwestern University Press, 1969

————. *Time and the Other.* tr. Richard A. Cohen. Pittsburgh: Dusquesne University Press, 1987

————. *Totality and Infinity: An Essay on Exteriority.* tr. by Alphonso Lingis. Pittsburgh: Dusquesne University Press, 1969

Lévy, Sylvain. *Matériaux pour l'étude du systeme Vijñaptimātra.* Paris: Bibliothèque de l'École des Hautes Études, 1925

Li Jun-sheng 李潤生,. *Wei-shih san-shih sung tao-chiang* 唯識三十頌導講 (Reading Guide to the Thirty Verses on Consciousness-Only). Honk Kong: Vajrayana Buddhism Association, 1994

Li Rongxi (tr.) *A Biography of the Tripiṭaka Master of the Ci'en Monastery of the Great Tang Dynasty.* Berkeley: Numata Center, 1995 (tr. of Hui-li's *Ta-t'ang ta-tz'u-en-ssu san-tsang fa-shih chuan*)

————. *The Great Tang Dynasty Record of the Western Regions.* Berkeley: Numata Center, 1996 (tr. of Hsüan-tsang's *Hsi yu chi*)

Li Yün-p'eng 李雲鵬. *Wei-shih erh-shih sung chiang-chi* ; *Pa-shih kuei-chü sung* 唯識二十頌講記：八識規矩頌 (Explanation of the twenty verses on consciousness-only; Verses on the regulation of the eight consciousness). With explanation by Dharma-master Yen P'ei 演培. Taipei: Tien Hua, 1991

Lin, Chen-Kuo. *The Saṃdhinirmocana Sūtra: a Liberating Hermeneutic.* Unpub. Ph.D. Dissertation, Temple University, 1991

Lin-chi 臨濟. *Lin-chi lü* 臨濟錄 (T.47.1985).
Eng. trs.: (1) Ruth Fuller Sasaki. *The Record of Lin-Chi.* Heian International Publishing, 1975; (2) Irmgard Shloegl, *The Zen Teaching of Rinzai.* Berkeley: Shambhala, 1976; (3) Burton Watson. *Zen Teachings of Master Lin-chi.* Boston: Shambhala, 1993

Lindtner, Christian. *Nāgārjuniana.* Delhi: Motilal Banarsidass, 1987

————. *Nagarjuniana: Studies in the Writings and Philosophy of Nāgājuna.* Copenhagen: Akademisk Forlag, 1982 [tr. and summaries of major and minor texts attributed to Nāgāruna with Tibetan and Sanskrit text romanized; the Motilal Banarsidass ed. is not identical to this one]

Ling Tai 靈泰 (Ming Dynasty). *Ch'eng wei-shih lun shu-ch'ao tan-ch'ien* 論疏 抄但欠. ZZ 80.201

Lipman, Kennard. "The cittamātra and its Madhyamika critique: Some phenomenological reflections." *PEW*, 32 (3), July 1982, 295-308

Liu, Ming-wood. "The Doctrine of the Buddha-Nature in the Mahāyāna *Mahāparinirvāṇa-sūtra.*" JIABS, 5 (2), 1982, 63-94

————. *Madhyamaka Thought in China.* Leiden: EJ Brill, 1994

————. *The Teaching of Fa-tsang - An Examination of Buddhist Metaphysics.* Unpublished doctoral dissertation, UCLA, 1979

Lopez, Jr., Donald. *A Study of Svātantrika.* Ithaca, NY: Snow Lion, 1988

———— (ed.). *Buddhist Hermeneutics.* Honolulu: University of Hawaii Press, 1988

Lü-shih Ch'un-ch'iu 呂氏春秋. Taipei: Chung Hwa, 1980

Lusthaus, Dan. "Chinese Buddhist Philosophy." in the Routledge *Encyclopedia of International Philosophy*, 1998

————. *A Comprehensive Commentary on the Heart Sutra (Prajñāpāramitā-hṛdaya-sūtra) by K'uei-chi.* Tr. in collaboration with Heng-Ching Shih. Berkeley: Numata Center, 2001

————. "Critical Buddhism: Back to the Sources," in *Pruning the Bodhi Tree*, ed. by James Hubbard and Paul Swanson. Honolulu: University of Hawaii Press, 1997

————. "Hsüan-tsang." In *Great Thinkers of the Eastern World*, Ian P. McGreal, ed., HarperCollins, 1995

————. "Lao Tzu." In *Great Thinkers of the Eastern World*, Ian P. McGreal, ed., HarperCollins, 1995
————. "Nāgārjuna." In *Great Thinkers of the Eastern World*, Ian P. McGreal, ed., HarperCollins, 1995
————. "Reflections on the Mirror Metaphor in Hui-neng, Chuang Tzu and Lao Tzu." *Journal of Chinese Philosophy* 12, June 1985, 169-178
————. "Retracing the Human-Nature vs. World-Nature Dichotomy in Lao Tzu." *Journal of Chinese Philosophy* 17, June 1990, 187-214
————. "A Brief Retrospective of Western Yogācāra Scholarship of the Twentieth Century." in *Chinese Philosophy Beyond the Twentieth Century*, edited by Vincent Shen and Wen-Sheng Wang. Taipei: Wu-nan, 2001
————. "Sāṃkhya." in the Routledge *Encyclopedia of International Philosophy*, 1998
————. "Vasubandhu." In *Great Thinkers of the Eastern World*, Ian P. McGreal, ed., HarperCollins, 1995
————. "Yogācāra." in the Routledge *Encyclopedia of International Philosophy*, 1998
Lyotard, Jean-Francois. *Libidinal Economy*. tr. Iain Hamilton Grant. Bloomington: Indiana University Press, 1993
————. *The Differend: Phases in Dispute*. tr. by Georges Van Den Abbeele, Minneapolis: University of Minnesota Press, 1968
————. *The Post-Modern Condition: A Report on Knowledge*. tr. by Geoff Bennington & Brian Massumi, Minneapolis: University of Minnesota Press, 1988
Lyotard, Jean-François & Jean-Loup Thébaud. *Just Gaming*. tr. by Wlad Godzich, Minneapolis: University of Minnesota press, 1985
Mabbett, I.W. "Nāgārjuna and Zeno on motion." *PEW* 34 (4) Oct. 1984, 401-420
Madison, Gary Brent. *The Phenomenology of Merleau-Ponty*. tr. from the French by the author. Athens: Ohio University Press, 1981
Magnin, Paul. *La Vie et L'Ouevre de Huisi* 慧思 *(515-577)*. Paris: École Française d'Extrême-Orient, 1979
Mair, Victor. *T'ang Transformation Texts*. Cambridge: Harvard University Press, 1989
Majjhima Nikāya (PTS ed.); Eng. trs.: (1) *The Middle Length Sayings*, 3 vols. tr. I.B. Horner, PTS, 1954; (2) *The Middle Length Discourses of the Buddha*. Bhikkhu Ñāṇamoli and Bhikkhu Bodhi (trs.). Boston: Wisdom, 1995
Makransky, John. *Buddhahood Embodied*. Albany: SUNY Press, 1997
Mangvungh, Gindallian. *Buddhism in Western India*. Meerut, India: Kusumanjali Prakashan, 1990
Mano, Ryūkai. "On 'Abhisamaya'." *IBK* 17 (2), 1968-69, 917-911 (47-53)
————. "On the 'Three *Jñatās*'." *IBK* 18 (2), March 1970, 1042-1036 (21-27)
Marasinghe, E.W. *The Bimbamāna of Gautamīyaśāstra as Heard by Śāriputra*. Delhi: Sri Satguru, 1994
————. *The Citrakarmaśāstra*. Delhi: Sri Satguru, 1991
Marsh, James. *Post-Cartesian Meditations*. NY: Fordham University Press, 1988
Martin, Mike W. *Self-Deception and Morality*. Lawrence, KS: University Press of Kansas, 1986
Mathews, R.H. *Mathew's Chinese-English Dictionary*. revised American Edition, Cambridge: Harvard University Press, 1979
Matilal, Bimal Krishna. "A Critique of Buddhist Idealism." in L.S. Cousins, et al. (eds.), *Buddhist Studies in Honor of I.B. Horner*, Dordrecht: D. Reidel, 1974, 139-169
————. "Error and truth—Classical Indian theories." *PEW* 31(2), April 1981, 215-224
————. *Logic, Language and Reality*. Delhi: Motilal Banarsidass, 1985
————. *Perception: An Essay on Classical Indian Theories of Knowledge*. Cambridge: Oxford University Press, 1986
————. *The Character of Logic in India*. Ed. by Jonardon Ganeri and Heeraman Tiwari. Albany: SUNY Press, 1998
Matilal, Bimal Krishna, and Robert Evans. *Buddhist Logic and Epistemology: Studies in the Buddhist Analysis of Inference and Language*. Dordrecht: D. Reidel, 1986

Matsuda, Kazunobu 松田和信. "*Abhidharmasamuccaya* niokeru jūnishiengi no kaisahku" (*Abhidharmasamuccaya* における十二支縁起 の解釈). in *Shinshū sogo kenkyūshō kiyo* 1, 1983.

————. "Seshin *engikyōshaku* (PSVy) niokeru arayashiki no teigi" 世親 [縁起経釈] (PSVy) におけるアラヤ識の定義. *IBK* 61, 1982.

————. "Vasubandhu kenkyū nōto (1)" (Vasubandhu 研究ノ ート). *IBK* 64, 1984

Matsumoto, Shirō 松本史朗. "Dharmapāla no nitai setsu" (Dharmapāla の二諦説), *IBK* 27, 2 (March 1979) 184-185

————. "Yuishiki-ha no ichi jō shisō nitsuite" (唯識派の一乗思想につ いて). in *Komazawa Daigaku Bukkyōgakubu Ronshū* 13, 1982.

McClain, Ernest. *The Myth of Invariance: The Origin of the Gods, Mathematics and Music from the Ṛg Veda to Plato.* NY: Nicolas Hays, 1976

————. *The Pythagorean Plato: Prelude to the Song Itself.* NY: Nicolas Hays, 1978

McDermott, A. Charlene S. "Asaṅga's Defense of *Ālaya-vijñāna*—Of Catless Grins and Sundry Related Matters." *JIP*, 2, 1973, 167-194

————. (tr. and ed.) *An Eleventh-Century Buddhist Logic of 'Exists': Ratnakīrti's* Kṣaṇabhaṅgasiddhi Vyatirekāmikā. Dordrecht: D. Reidel, 1969

McDermott, James. *Developments in the Early Buddhist Concept of Kamma/Karma.* Ph.D. Dissertation, Princeton, 1970

McRae, John. *The Northern School and the Formation of Early Ch'an Buddhism.* Honolulu: University of Hawaii Press, Kuroda Institute, 1986

Melville, Stephen W. *Philosophy Beside Itself: On Deconstruction and Modernism.* Minneapolis: University of Minnesota Press, 1986

Mencius (Meng Tzu 孟子). (1) *Meng-tzu yin-te* 孟子引得 (Harvard-Yenching Concordance to Meng Tzu), Taipei, 1966. (2) *The Works of Mencius.* James Legge (tr.). NY: Dover, 1970

Mensch, James Richard. *Intersubjectivity and Transcendental Idealism.* Albany: SUNY Press, 1988

Merleau-Ponty, Maurice. *Adventures of the Dialectic.* tr. by Joseph Bien. Evanston: Northwestern University Press, 1973

————. *Consciousness and the Acquisition of Language.* tr. by Hugh Silverman. Evanston: Northwestern University Press, 1973

————. *Humanism and Terror: An Essay on the Communist Problem.* tr. by John O'Neill. Boston: Beacon, 1969

————. *In Praise of Philosophy and Other Essays.* tr. by John Wild, et al. Evanston: Northwestern University Press, 1963

————. *L'Union de L'Ame et du Corps chez Malebranche, Biran et Bergson* (notes prises au cours de Merleau-Ponty à l'École Normale Superiere, 1947-1948). Jean Deprun (ed.). Paris: Librarie Philosophique J. Vrin, 1968

————. *Phenomenology of Perception.* tr. by Colin Smith. NJ: Humanities Press, 1978

————. *The Primacy of Perception.* tr. by James Edie. Evanston: Northwestern University Press, 1978

————. *The Prose of the World.* tr. by John O'Neill. Evanston: Northwestern University Press, 1973

————. *Résumés de Cours* (College de France, 1952-1960). Paris: Gallimard, 1968

————. *Sense and Non-Sense.* tr. by Hubert and Patricia Allen Dreyfus. Evanston: Northwestern University Press, 1964

————. *Signs.* tr. by Richard McCLeary. Evanston: Northwestern University Press, 1964

————. *The Structure of Behavior.* tr. by Alden Fisher. Boston: Beacon, 1967

————. *Texts and Dialogues.* Hugh Silverman and James Barry, Jr. (eds.). NJ: Humanities Press, 1992

————. *The Visible and the Invisible.* tr. by Alphonso Lingis. Evanston: Northwestern University Press, 1968

Mijuskovic, Ben. "Brentano's Theory of Consciousness." *PPR*, 38, 3, March 1978, 315-324

Mikogami, Esho. "Some Remarks on the Concept of Arthakriyā." *JIP*, 7, 1979, 79-94

Miller, Izchak. *Husserl: Perception and Temporal Awareness*. Cambridge: MIT Press, 1984

MIMAKI Katsumi. *Blo Gsal Grub Mtha': Chapitres IX (Vaibhāṣika) et XI (Yogācāra) édités, et Chapitre XII (Mādhyamika) édité et traduit*. Kyoto: Zinbun Kagaku Kenkyusyo, 1982

————. "Le chapitre du *Blo gsal grub mtha' sur les Sautrāntika*: Présentation et édition." *Zinbum*, 15, 1979, 175-210

Ming Yü 明昱 (Ming Dynasty). *Ch'eng wei-shih lun ssu-chüan* 成唯識論俗詮. ZZ.81.1

————. *Wei-shih san-shih lun yueh-yi* 唯識三十論約意. ZZ.83.251

Mirsky, Jeanenette (ed.). *The Great Chinese Travelers*. Chicago: University of Chicago Press, 1964

Mistry, Freny. *Nietzsche and Buddhism*. Berlin and NY: Walter de Gruyter, 1981

Mitomo, Kenyo. "Anuśaya as conceived in Abhidharma-Buddhism." *IBK* 22 (1) Dec. 1973, 501-497 (32-36)

Mittal, Kewal Krishnan (ed.). *Vijñānavāda (Yogācāra) and its Tradition*. Delhi: Dept. of Buddhist Studies, University of Delhi, 1993

Mizuno, Kōgen. *Buddhist Sutras: Origin, Development, Transmission*. Tokyo: Kōsei Publishing, 1982

Mochizuki, Shinkō 望月信亨. *Bukkyō dai jiten* 仏教大辭典. 10 vols., Kyoto: Seikai Seiten Kankō Kyōkai, 1954-1963 rev. ed.

Mo Tzu Chi-chieh 墨子集解. Chang Ch'un-yi 張純一 (compiler). Taipei: Wen Shih, 1994

Mohanty, Jitendranath N. *Edmund Husserl's Theory of Meaning*. The Hague: Martinus Nijhoff, 3rd ed., 1976

————. *Essays on Indian Philosophy*. ed. by Purushottama Bilimoria. Delhi: Oxford University Press, 1993

————. *Gaṅgeśa's Theory of Truth, containing the text of Gaṅgeśa's* Prāmāṇya (jñapti) vāda. Delhi: Motilal Banarsidass, revised ed., 1989

————. *Husserl & Frege*. Bloomington: Indiana University Press, 1982

————. *Transcendental Phenomenology: an Analytic Account*. Cambridge, MA: Basil Blackwell, 1989

Mokṣākaragupta. *Tarkabhāṣā*. (1) Singh, B.N. *Bauddha Tarkabhāṣā of Mokṣākaragupta*. Varanasi: Asha Prakashan, 1985; (2) Kajiyama, Yuichi. *An Introduction to Buddhist Philosophy: An Annotated Translation of the Tarkabhāṣā of Mokṣākaragupta*. Memoirs of the Faculty of Letters, Kyoto University, no. 10, 1966

Monier-Williams, Sir Monier. *A Sanskrit-English Dictionary*. Delhi: Motilal Banarsidass, 1986 rpt.

Morohashi, Tetsuji 諸橋轍次 , *Dai Kan-wa jiten* 大漢和辭典 (ed). 13 vols., Tokyo: Taishūkan Shoten, 1958-1960.

Mukherjee, B.N. *India in Early Central Asia*. New Delhi: Harman Publishing House, 1996

Mukherjee, Prabhatkumar. *Indian Literature in China and the Far East*. Calcutta: Greater Indian Society, 1930

Murti, T.R.V. *The Central Conception of Buddhism*. London: Unwin, 1980

————. *Studies in Indian Thought: The Collected Papers of T.R.V. Murti*. Harold Coward (ed.). Delhi: South Asia Books, 1983

Musashi, Tachikawa (see Śaṅkarasvāmin)

Nagao, Gadjin 長尾雅人. *Chūkan to yuishiki* 中観と唯識. Tokyo: Iwanami Shoten, 1979

————. *An Index to Asaṅga's Mahāyānasaṃgraha*. 3 vols., I. Tibetan-Sanskrit-Chinese, II. Sanskrit-Tibetan-Chinese, III. Chinese-Sanskrit. Tokyo: The International Institute for Buddhist Studies, 1994

————. *Madhyamaka and Yogācāra: a Study of Mahāyāna Philosophies*. Edited, collated, and translated by L.S. Kawamura in collaboration with G.M. Nagao. Albany: State University of New York Press, 1991

————. *Madhyānta-vibhāga-bhāṣya, a Buddhist Philosophical Treatise Edited for the First Time from a Sanskrit Manuscript.* Tokyo: Suzuki Research Foundation, 1964

Nāgārjuna. *On Voidness*, by Fernando Tola and Carmen Dragonetti, (contains translations of *Hastavāla-nāma-prakaraṇa-vṛtti* of Āryadeva; *Yuktiṣaṣṭi-kārikā*; *Śūnyatā-saptati-kārikā*; and *Catustava*). Delhi: Motilal Banarsidass, 1995;

————. *Mahāyānaviṃśaka*. English tr. in Vidhusekhara Bhattacarya, *Mahāyānaviṃśaka of Nāgārjuna.* Calcutta, 1931 (includes two Tibetan texts, restored Sanskrit, Chinese text, English translation, and notes)

————. *Mūla-madhyamaka-kārikā.* (1) *Mūlamadhyamakakārikāḥ.* J.W. de Jong (ed.), Madras: Adyar Library and Research Center, 1977; (2) 中論. Kumārajīva (tr.). (T.30.1564); Eng. trs.: (3) Frederich Streng, *Emptiness: A Study in Religious Meaning.* NY: Abingdon, 1967; (4) Kenneth Inada, *Nāgārjuna: Mūlamadhyamakakārikā.* Tokyo: Hokuseido Press, 1970; (5) David Kalupahana. *Nāgārjuna: The Philosophy of the Middle Way.* Albany: SUNY Press, 1986; (6) *The Fundamental Wisdom on the Middle Way.* trans. and commentary by Jay Garfield. Oxford: Oxford University Press, 1995

————. *Nāgārjuna's Ratna Mala.* Pushpendra Kumar (tr.). Delhi: Nag Publishers, 1980 (Sanskrit and English)

————. *Pratītyasamutpāda-hṛdaya-kārikā.* Eng. tr.: L. Jamspal and Peter Della Santini, "The Heart of Interdependent Origination of Ācārya Nāgārjuna with Commentary by the Author: Translated into English from the Tibetan." *Buddhist Studies.* Delhi, March 1974, 17-31 (includes Devanāgri text)

————. *Rājaparikathā-ratnamālā.* Eng. tr.: Jeffrey Hopkins, Lati Rimpoche, and Anne Klein. *The Previous Garland.* NY: Harper and Row, 1975

————. *Vaidalyaprakaraṇa.* in Tola and Dragonetti, *Nāgārjuna's Refutation of Logic (Nyāya): Vaidalyaprakaraṇa.* Delhi: Motilal Banarsidass, 1995

————. *Vigraha-vyāvartanī.* (1) [text and Eng. tr.] K. Bhattacharya, et al., *The Dialectical Method of Nāgārjuna: Vigrahavyāvartanī.* Delhi: Motilal Banarsidass, 2nd ed., 1986; (2) 迴諍論. trs. Vimokṣaprajñā 毘目智仙 and Prajñāruci 瞿曇流支. (T.32.1631); (3) Eng. tr. Richard Robinson (unpub)

————. *Yuktiṣaṣṭi-kārikā.* (1) (see Nāgārjuna *On Voidness*; and Candrakīrti, Scherrer-Schaub, above); (2) 六十頌如理論. tr. Dānapāla 施護. (T.30.1575)

————. (see also Lindtner)

Nagasawa, Jitsudō 長澤実導. "Kamalaśila's Theory of Yogācāra." *IBK* 10 (1), 1962, 371-364

————. "*Upacāra* to *Prajñaptī*" (*Upacāra* と *Prajñapti*), *IBK* 2, 2, 1954.

————. *Yugagyo shisō to Mikkyō no kenkyū* 瑜伽行思想と 密経の研究. Tokyo: Daitō Shuppansha, 1978

Nakamura, Hajime 中村元. *Bukkyōgo daijiten* 仏教語大辞典. Tokyo: Tokyo Shoseki, 1976

————. *Indian Buddhism: A Survey with Bibliographical Notes.* Tokyo: KUFS Publication, 1980

————. "The Theory of 'Dependent Origination' in its Incipient Stage." in *Buddhist Studies in Honour of Walpola Rahula,* London: Gordon Fraser, 1980, 165-172

Ñāṇārāma Mahathera, Matara Sri. *The Seven Stages of Purification and The Insight Knowledges.* Kandy: Buddhist Publication Society, 1983

Natanson, Maurice. *Edmund Husserl: Philosopher of Infinite Tasks.* Evanston: Northwestern University Press, 1973

Nattier, Jan. *Once Upon a Future Time: Studies in a Buddhist Prophecy of Decline.* Berkeley: Asian Humanities Press, 1991

Naudou, Jean. *Les Bouddhistes Kaśmīriens au Moyen Age.* Paris: Presses Universitaires de France, 1968

Nietzsche, Friedrich. *Sämtliche Werke.* 15 vols. Berlin: Walter de Gruyter, 1999

Nishida, Kitaro. *Intuition and Reflection in Self-Consciousness.* tr. by Valdo Viglielmo, et al. Albany: SUNY Press, 1987

Norris, Christopher. *Derrida.* Cambridge: Harvard University Press, 1987

Nyanaponika Thera. *Abhidhamma Studies: Researches in Buddhist Psychology.* Kandy: Buddhist Publication Society, 1965

Nyanatikoka Mahathera. *Guide Through the Abhidhamma Piṭaka.* Columbo: Buddhist Literature Society, 1957

O'Brien, Paul Wilfred, S.J. "A Chapter on Reality from the *Madhyāntavibhāgaśāstra.*" *Monumenta Nipponica*, 9 (1-2), 1953, 277-303

————. "A Chapter on Reality (*Tattva*) from the *Madhyāntavibhāgaśāstra.*" *Monumenta Nipponica*, 1941

Obermiller, E. *The Doctrine of the Prajñā-pāramitā as Exposed in the* Abhisamayālaṃkāra *of Maitreya.* Talent, OR: Canon Publications, 1984 (rpt. of *Acta Orientalia* XI, 1932)

————. *Prajñāpāramitā in Tibetan Buddhism.* Harcharan Singh Sobti (ed.). Delhi: Classics India Publications, 1988

Oliver, Curtis Forrest. *The Yogācāra Dharma List: a Study of the* Abhidharmasamuccaya *and its Commentary,* Abhidharmasamuccayabhāṣya. Unpub. Ph.D. Dissertation, University of Toronto, 1982

————. "Perception in Early Nyāya." *JIP* 6 (1978) 243-266

Ortega y Gasset, José. *An Interpretation of Universal History.* tr. by Mildred Asams. NY: Norton, 1973

Orzech, Charles. *Politics and Transcendent Wisdom.* University Park: Pennsylvania State University Press, 1998

Osaki, Akiko. "What is meant by destroying the *Ālayavijñāna*?" *IBK* 26 (2), March 1978, 1069-1064

Pachow, W. *A Study of the Twenty-Two Dialogues on Mahāyāna Buddhism.* [Tun-huang texts], Taipei: The Chinese Culture, 1979

————. *Chinese Buddhism: Aspects of Interaction and Reinterpretation.* Lanham, MD: University Press of America, 1980

Padhye, A. M. *The Framework of Nāgārjuna's Philosophy.* Delhi: Sri Satguru. 1988

Pao p'u Tzu: Hsin-yi 抱朴子：新譯. (eds.) Li Chung-hua 李中華 and Huang Chih-min 黃志民,. Taipei: Sanmin, 1997, 2 vols.

Paramārtha 真諦 (tr.). *Chuan-shih lun* 轉識論. (T.31.1587)

———— (tr.). *Chung pien fen-pieh lun* 中邊分別論 (*Madhyānta-vibhāga*). (T.31.1599)

————. *P'o-sou-p'an-tou fa-shih chuan* 婆藪槃豆法師傳 (Biography of Vasubandhu). (T.50.2049)

———— (tr.). *She ta-sheng lun shih* 攝大乘論釋 (*Mahāyāna-samgraha*). (T.31.1595)

————. *Ta-sheng ch'i-hsin lun* 大乘起信論. (T.32.1666) (translation attributed to Paramārtha; text attributed to Aśvaghoṣa).

Park, Sung Bae. *Buddhist Faith and Sudden Enlightenment.* Albany: SUNY Press, 1983

Parrott, Rodney J. "The Problem of Sāṃkhya Tattvas as Both Cosmic and Psychological Phenomena." *JIP* 14, 1986, 55-77

Pas, Julian. *Visions of Sukhāvatī: Shen-Tao's Commentary on the* Kuan Wu-liang-Shou-Fo Ching. Albany: SUNY Press, 1995

Pasnau, Robert. *Theories of Cognition in the Later Middle Ages.* Cambridge: Cambridge University Press, 1997

Paul, Diana. *Philosophy of Mind in Sixth-Century China: Paramārtha's* 'Evolution of Consciousness.' Stanford: Stanford University Press, 1984

Perdue, Daniel E. *Debate in Tibetan Buddhism.* Ithaca: Snow Lion, 1992

Perrett, Roy W. "The Problem of Induction in Indian Philosophy." *PEW* 34 (2), April 1984, 161-174

Pfänder, Alexander. *Phenomenology of Willing and Motivation.* tr. Herbert Spiegelberg. Evanston: Northwestern University Press, 1967

Piatigorsky, Alexander. *The Buddhist Philosophy of Thought: Essays in Interpretation.* NJ: Barnes & Noble, 1984

Pieris, Aloysius, S.J. "The Notions of Citta, Ātta and Attabhāva in the Pāli Exegetical Writings." in *Buddhist Studies in Honour of Walpola Rahula.* 213-222

Potter, Karl (ed.). *Abhidharma Buddhism To 150 A.D.* Encyclopedia of Indian Philosophies. with Robert Buswell, Padmanabh Jaini, Noble Ross Reat, Collet Cox, et al. Delhi: Motilal Banarsidass, 1998 rpt.

Potter, Karl (ed.). *Indian Metaphysics and Epistemology: The Traditions of Nyāya-Vaiśeṣika up to Gaṅgeśa.* Encyclopedia of Indian Philosophies. Princeton: Princeton University Press, 1977

Potter, Karl, and Sibajiban Bhattacharya (eds.). *Indian Philosophical Analysis: Nyāya-Vaiśeṣika from Gaṅgeśa to Raghunātha Śiromaṇi.* Encyclopedia of Indian Philosophies. Princeton: Princeton University Press, 1992

Powers, John. *Hermeneutics and Tradition in the* Saṃdhinirmocana-sūtra. Leiden: EJ Brill, 1993

————. *Two Commentaries on the* Saṃdhinirmocana-sūtra *by Asaṅga and Jñānagarbha.* Lewiston, NY: Edwin Mellen Press, 1992

————. *Wisdom of the Buddha: the Saṃdhinirmocana Mahāyāna Sūtra.* Berkeley, CA: Dharma Publishing, 1995

————. *The Yogācāra School of Buddhism: a Bibliography.* Metuchen, N.J.: American Theological Library Association; London: Scarecrow Press, 1991.

Prasad, Hari Shankar. "Time in Nyāya-Vaiśeṣika and Vaibhāṣika-Sautrāntika." *Buddhist Studies*, 5. Delhi, May 1978, 34-47

Prebish, Charles S. *Buddhist Monastic Discipline: The Sanskrit Prātimokṣa Sūtras of the Mahāsāṃghikas and Mūlasarvāstivādins.* University Park: Penn State University, 1975

Priestley, Leonard C.D.C. *Pudgalavāda Buddhism: The Reality of the Indeterminate Self.* Toronto: University of Toronto, 1999

Puggala-paññati (Fourth work of Theravāda Abhidhamma). Eng. tr.: Bimala Charan Law. *Designation of Human Types.* London: PTS, 1959 rpt. of 1924 ed.

Ra, Lang E. *The T'ien-t'ai Philosophy of Non-Duality: A Study of Chan-jan and Chih-li.* Unpub. Ph.D. Dissertation. Temple University, 1988

Rabb, J. Douglas. "Empiricism from a Phenomenological Standpoint." *PPR,* 46, 2, Dec. 1985, 243-63

Rabgay, Lobsang. "The Mind Only School of Thought." *Tibetan Review,* 12, 1, Jan. 1977

Rahula, Walpola. *The Heritage of the Bhikkhu.* NY: Grove Press, 1974

————. *Zen and the Taming of the Bull.* London: Gordon Fraser, 1978

Ramanan, K. Venkata. *Nāgārjuna's Philosophy.* Delhi: Motilal Banarsidass, 1978

Rambach, Pierre. *The Secret Message of Tantric Buddhism.* tr. from French by Barbara Bray. NY" Rizzoli, 1979

Randle, H.N. *Fragments from Diṅnāga.* Delhi: Motilal Banarsidass, 1981 rpt. of 1926 Royal Asiatic Society ed.

Rapp, Roger. *The Yogācāra Conception of Reality as Expounded in the Eleventh Chapter of the Mahāyānasūtrālaṅkāra.* M.A. Thesis, University of California, Santa Barbara, 1979

Rastogi, Navjivan. "Theory of Error According to Abhinavagupta." *JIP* 14 (1986) 1-33

Ratnakaya, Shanta. "Metapsychology of the *Abhidharma.*" *JIABS.* 4, 1981, 76-88

Ratnapala, Nandesena. *Crime and Punishment in the Buddhist Tradition.* New Delhi: Mittal Publications, 1993

Reat, N. Ross. *The Śālistamba Sūtra.* Delhi: Motilal Banarsidass, 1993

Régamey, Konstanty. *Philosophy in the Samādhirājasūtra.* Delhi: Motilal Banarsidass, 1990 rpt. of 1938 ed.

Remis, David Raphael. *Continuity and Change: a Study of the Ālaya-consciousness in the Indian "Yogic Practice" (Yogācāra) Tradition.* Unpub. M.A. Thesis, University of Virginia, 1993

Rhys Davids, T.W., and William Stede (eds). *Pali-English Dictionary.* London: PTS, 1986 rpt.

Ricouer, Paul. *Freedom and Nature.* tr. Ezraim V. Kohak. Evanston: Northwestern University Press, 1966

————. *Husserl: An Analysis of His Phenomenology*. tr. Edward G. Ballard and Lester E. Embree. Evanston: Northwestern University Press, 1967

Rizzi, Cesare. *Candrakīrti*. Delhi: Motilal Banarsidass, 1988

Robinson, Richard (tr.). *Chinese Buddhist Verse*. London: John Murray, 1954

————. *Early Mādhyamika in India and China*. Madison: University of Wisconsin Press, 1967

Ruegg, D. Seyfort. "Ahiṃsā and Vegetarianism in the History of Buddhism." in *Buddhist Studies in Honour of Walpola Rahula*. 234-241

————. *La Théorie du Tathāgatagarḇha et du Gotra: Études sur la Sotériologie et la Gnoséology du Bouddhisme*. Paris: École Française d'Extrême-Orient, 1969

Sadakata, Akira. *Buddhist Cosmology: Philosophy and Origins*. Tr. Gaynor Sekimori. Tokyo: Kosei, 1997

Saeki, Jōin 佐伯定胤 *Shindō Jo-yuishiki-ron* 新導成唯識論. Nara: Shōsōgaku Seiten, 1940

Sakuma, Hidenori S. *Die Āśrayaparivṛtti-Theorie in der Yogācārabhūmi*. Stuttgart: F. Steiner, 1990. 2 vols.

Saṃdhinirmocana sūtra. Hsüan-tsang's tr. T.16.676 (see Appendix Four); French tr.: *Saṃdhinirmocana Sūtra: L'explication des Mystères*. tr. by Étienne Lamotte, Louvain, 1935. (for Eng. tr., see Powers, John)

Saṃmitīya-nikāya śāstra. 三彌底部論 *San-mi-ti pu lun* (T.32.1649). Eng. tr.: "*Saṃmitīyanikāya śāstra*." tr. by K. Venkataramanan. *Viśva-Bharati Annals*, 6, 155-243

Saṃyutta-Nikāya (PTS edition). Eng. tr.: *The Book of Kindred Sayings*. 5 vols., PTS, 1950

Sanford, David H. *If P then Q: Conditionals and the Foundations of Reasoning*. London and NY: Routledge, 1992

Sangharakshita. *A Survey of Buddhism*. Boulder: Shambhala, 1980

Sankalia, Hasmukh. *The University of Nālandā*. Madras: B.G. Paul & Co., 1934

Śaṅkarasvāmin. *Nyāyapraveśa*. Hsüan-tsang's tr. T.31.1630 (see Appendix Four); Eng. tr.: Musashi, Tachikawa. "A Sixth-Century Manual of Indian Logic (A Translation of the *Nyāyapraveśa*)." *JIP*, 1, 1971, 111-145 [Sanskrit text included]

Śāntakarkṣita. *The Tattvasaṅgraha of Shāntarakṣita with the Commentary of Kamalashīla*. tr. by Ganganatha Jha. 2 vols. Delhi: Motilal Banarsidass, 1986 rpt.

Śāntideva. *Śikṣa-samuccaya: A Compendium of Buddhist Doctrine*. tr. Cecil Bendall and W.H.D. Rouse. Delhi: Motilal Banarsidass, rpt.

Sarachchandra, Edirivira R. "From Vasubandhu to Śāntarakṣita: a critical examination of some Buddhist theories of the external world." *JIP*, 4, 1976, 69-107

————. *Buddhist Psychology of Perception*. Colombo: Ceylon University Press, 1958

Sasaki, Genjun H. *Linguistic Approach to Buddhist Thought*. Delhi: Motilal Banarsidass, 1986

————. *A Study of Abhidharma Philosophy: a historical and critical study of Buddhist Realism*. Tokyo: Kobundo, 1958

————. *A Study of Kleśa*. Tokyo: Shimizukobundo, 1975

Sastri, N. Aiyaswami. "*Pañcavastuka Vibhāṣā* of Bhadanta Dharmatrāta." *Brahmavidya, The Adyar Library Bulletin*. Madras, 20, 1956, 234-46

Schenk, David. "Merleau-Ponty on Perspectivism, with Reference to Nietzsche." *PPR*. 46, 2, December 1985, 307-314

Schmithausen, Lambert. *Alayavijñāna: on the Origin and the Early Development of a Central Concept of Yogācāra Philosophy*. Tokyo: International Institute for Buddhist Studies, 1987.

————. "The *Darśanamārga* Section of the *Abhidharmasamuccaya* and its Interpretation by Tibetan Commentators (with Special Reference to Bu Ston Rin Chen Grub)." in Ernst Steinkellner and Helmut Tauscher (eds.), *Contributions on Tibetan and Buddhist Religion and Philosophy*. Vienna, 1983, vol. 2, 259-274

————. "On Some Aspects of Descriptions or Theories of 'Liberating Insight' and 'Enlightenment' in Early Buddhism." in Klaus Bruhn and Albrecht Wezler (eds.),

Studien zum Jainismus und Buddhismus: Gedenkschrift für Ludwig Alsdorf. Wiesbaden: Franz Steimer, 1981

Schopen, Gregory. *Bones, Stones, and Buddhist Monks.* Honolulu: University of Hawaii Press, 1997

Schroeder, William Ralph. *Sartre and His Predecessors: the Self and Others.* London: Routledge & Kegan Paul, 1984

Shah, Nagin J. *Akalaṅka's Criticism of Dharmakīrti's Philosophy.* Ahmedabad: L. D. Institute of Indology, 1967

————. "Essentials of Dharmakīrti's Theory of Knowledge (based on the *Pramāṇavārtikka*)." in Klaus Brahn and Albert Wezler (eds.), *Studien zum Jainismus und Buddhismus: Gedenkschrift für Ludwig Alsdorf.* Wiesbaden: Franz Steiner, 1981

Shaner, David E. *The Bodymind Experience in Japanese Buddhism: A Phenomenological Study of Kūkai and Dōgen.* Albany: SUNY Press, 1985

Sharma, Dhirendra. *The Differentiation Theory of Meaning in Indian Logic.* The Hague and Paris: Mouton, 1969

Sharma, T.R. *Vijñaptimātratāsiddhi (Viṃśatikā), with Introduction, Translation and Commentary.* Delhi: Eastern Book Linkers, 1993

Shastri, D.N. *The Philosophy of Nyāya-Vaiśeṣika and its Conflict with the Buddhist Dignāga School.* New Delhi: Bharatiya Vidya Prakashan, 1976 rpt.

Shastri, Mool Chand. *Buddhist Contributions to Sanskrit Poetics.* Delhi: Parimal, 1986

Shastri, N.A. "Store-Consciousness (Ālaya-vijñāna)—A Grand Concept of Yogācāra Buddhism." *Bulletin of Tibetology,* IX (1), Feb. 1972

Shastri, Yajneshwar S. *Mahāyānasūtrālaṅkāra of Asaṅga: A Study in Vijñānavāda Buddhism.* Delhi: Sri Satguru, 1989

Shinohara, Koichi, and Gregory Schopen. *From Benares to Beijing: Essays on Buddhism and Chinese Religion.* NY: Mosaic Press, 1991

Silk, Jonathan. *Wisdom, Compassion, and the Search for Understanding: The Buddhist Studies Legacy of Gadjin M. Nagao.* Honolulu: University of Hawaii Press, 2000

Silverman, Hugh. "Re-Reading Merleau-Ponty." *Telos,* 19, Fall 1976, 106-129

Sinha, Braj M. "The Abhidharma Notion of *Vijñāna* and its Soteriological Significance." *JIABS,* 3, 1980, 54-57

————. *Time and Temporality in Sāṃkhya-Yoga and Abhidharma Buddhism.* New Delhi: Munshiram Manoharlal, 1983

Sinja, Jadunath. *Indian Epistemology of Perception.* Calcutta: Sinha Publications, 1969

Skandhila. *Abhidharmāvatāraśāstra.* French tr.: *Le Traité de la Déscente dans la Profonde Loi (Abhidharmāvatāraśāstra) de l'Arhat Skandhila.* traduit et annoté par Marcel van Veltham. Louvain: Institut Orientaliste, 1977 (French tr. of Hsüan-tsang's T.1554 collated with the Tibetan version)

Skinner, B.F. *About Behaviorism.* NY: Vintage, 1976

Smith, Joseph H., and William Kerrigan (eds.). *Taking Chances: Derrida, Psychoanalysis and Literature.* Baltimore: Johns Hopkins University Press, 1988

Sokolowski, Robert. *Husserlian Meditations.* Evanston: Northwestern University Press, 1974

Soothill, William Edward, and Lewis Hodous. *A Dictionary of Chinese Buddhist Terms: with Sanskrit and English Equivalents and a Sanskrit-Pali Index.* Taipei: Hsin Wen Fung, 1983 rpt. of 1937 Kegan Paul ed.

Sparham, Gareth. *Ocean of Eloquence: Tsong kha pa's Commentary on the* Yogācāra Doctrine of Mind. Albany: SUNY Press, 1993

Spinoza, Baruch. *Opera Quotquot Reporta Sunt.* Ed. by J. Van Vloten and J.P.N. Land. 3rd ed., 2 vols. The Hague: Martinus Nijhoff, 1914

Sponberg, Alan. "Dynamic Liberation in Yogācāra Buddhism." *JIABS,* 2 (1), 1979, 44-64

————. "Meditation in Fa-hsiang Buddhism." in *Traditions of Meditation,* Peter Gregory (ed.), 1986, 15-43

————. *The Vijñaptimātratā Buddhism of the Chinese Buddhist monk K'uei-chi (A.D. 632-682).* Unpub. Ph.D. Dissertation, University of British Columbia, 1979

Śrīmālā-devī sūtra. Guṇabhadra's tr. T.12.353; Bodhiruci's tr. T.11.310 (sūtra 48). Eng. trs.: (1) Wayman, Alex. *The Lion's Roar of Queen Śrīmālā*. NY: Columbia University Press, 1974; (2) *A Treasury of Mahāyāna Sūtras: Selections from the Mahāratnakūta Sūtra*. Garma C.C. Chang (ed.). University Park: Pennsylvania State University Press, 1983, 363-396

Staten, Henry. *Wittgenstein and Derrida*. Lincoln: University of Nebraska Press, 1984

Stcherbatsky, Th. *Buddhist Logic*. 2 vols. NY: Dover, 1962 rpt. of 1930 *Bibliotheca Buddhica* ed.

Steinkellner, Ernst. "The *Ṣaṣṭitantra* on Perception, a Collection of Fragments." *Asiatische Studien/Études Asiatiques*, 53.3 (1999), 667-77

Sthiramati. *Madhyāntavibhāgaṭīkā*. (1) Yamaguchi, Susumu (ed.). Nagoya: Librairie Hajinkahu, 1934; (2) R. Pandeya (ed.). Delhi: Motilal Banarsidass, 1971; (3) Eng. tr. Friedman, D.L. *Sthiramati Madhyāntavibhāgaṭīkā*. Utrecht: 1937 (only translates the first two chs. of the *-ṭīkā*, poorly conjectured translation).

————. *Ta-sheng A-p'it'a-mo tsa-chi lun* 大乘阿毘達磨雜集論 (Commentary on *Abhidharmasamuccaya*). tr. Hsüan-tsang. (T.31.1606)

————. *Triṃśikā-vijñapti-bhāṣya*. (1) Edited by Sylvain Lévy. in *Matériaux*. Paris: Bibliothèque de l'École des Hautes Études, 1932. (2) Eng. trs.: Chatterjee, K.N. *Vijñapti Mātratā Siddhi*. Varanasi: Kishor Vidya Niketan, 1980; (3) Kawamura, Leslie, *A Study of the Triṃśikā-Vijñapti-Bhāṣya*. Unpub. M.A. Thesis, Kyoto University, 1964; (4) (See Huo T'ao-hui)

Straus, Erwin (ed.). *Phenomenology: Pure and Applied*. Pittsburgh: Dusquesne University Press, 1964

Strong, John. *The Legend of King Aśoka*. Princeton: Princeton University Press, 1983

Stryk, Lucien, and Taskashi, Ikemoto. *Zen: Poems, Prayers, Sermons, anecdotes, Interviews*. NY: Doubleday anchor, 1965

Suganuma, Akira. "The Examination of the External Object in the *Tattvasaṃgraha*." *IBK*, 10 (2), 1962, 732-726

Suguro, Shinjō 勝呂信静. *Shoki Yuishiki shisō no kenkyū* 初期唯識思想の研究 (Studies on Early Vijñaptimātra Philosophy). Tokyo: Shunjū-sha, 1989

Sutton, Florin Giripescu. *Existence and Gnosis in the Laṅkāvatāra-sūtra: a Study in the Ontology and Epistemology of the Yogācāra School of Mahāyāna Buddhism*. Albany: SUNY Press, 1986

Suzuki, D.T. *The Laṅkāvatāra Sūtra*. Boulder: Prajñā Press, 1978, rpt.

————. *Studies in the Laṅkāvatāra Sūtra*. Boulder: Prajñā Press, 1981 rpt.

Swanson, Paul. *Foundations of T'ien-t'ai Philosophy*. Berkeley: Asian Humanities Press, 1989

Ta Hui 大惠 (Ming Dynasty). *Ch'eng wei-shi lun tzu-k'ao* 成唯識論自考. ZZ.82.89

T'ai Hsien 太賢 (T'ang dynasty). *Ch'eng wei-shih lun hsüeh chi* 成唯識論學記. ZZ.80.1

T'ai Hsü 太虛. *Fa-hsiang wei-shih hsüeh* 法相唯識學. Shanghai: Commercial Press, 1936, 2 vols.

Takakusu, Junjirō. *The Essentials of Buddhist Philosophy*. Wing-Tsit Chan and Charles A. Moore. Westport, CN: Greenwood Press, 1973 rpt. of 1956 ed.

———— (tr.). *A Record of the Buddhist Religion as Practiced in India and the Malay Archipelago, A.D. 671-695, by I-Tsing*. [i.e., I-Ching]. New Delhi: Munshiram Manoharlal, 1982 rpt.

Takasaki, Jikidō 高崎直道. "A Comment on the Term *Ārambaṇa* in the *Ratnagotravibhāga*, I.9." *IBK*, 10 (2), 1962, 757-750 (26-33)

————. "*Dharmatā, Dharmadhātu, Dharmakāya* and *Buddhadhātu*—Structure of the Ultimate Value in Mahāyāna Buddhism." *IBK*, 14 (2), 1955-56, 919-903 (78-94)

————. *Nyoraizō shisō no keisei* 女来蔵思想の形成. Tokyo: Shunjū-sha, 1974

Takemura, Makio 竹村牧男. *Yuishiki no kōzō* 唯識の構造 . Tokyo: Shunjū-sha, 1985

Takeuchi, Shokō 竹内紹晃. *Yugagyo yuishikigaku no kenkyū* 唯識学の研究. 1979.

Takeuchi, Yoshinori. *The Heart of Buddhism*. tr. by James Heisig. NY: Crossroad, 1983

Taminiaux, Jacques. *Dialectic and Difference: Finitude in Modern Thought*. NJ: Humanities Press, 1985

Tananaka, Kenneth. *The Dawn of Chinese Pure Land Buddhist Doctrine: Ching-ying Hui-yüan's Commentary on the* Visualization Sutra. Albany: SUNY Press, 1990
T'ang, Yung-t'ung 湯用彤. *Han Wei Liang Chin Nan Pei chao Fo-chiao shih* 漢魏兩晉南北朝佛教史 (History of Buddhism in the Han, Wei, Liang, Chin, Southern and Northern Dynasties). Taiwan: Taiwan Shang Wu Yin Shu, 1992
Tao Lun 道倫 (T'ang Dynasty). *Yu-ch'ieh-shih-ti-lun chi* 瑜伽師地論記 (Commentary on *Yogācārabhūmi-śāstra*). Taiwan: Hsin Wen Feng, 1991, 2 vols.
Tao Yi 道邑 (T'ang Dynasty). *Ch'eng wei-shih lun yi-yun* 成唯識論義蘊. ZZ.78.763
Tat, Wei. *Ch'eng Wei-shih Lun: The Doctrine of Mere Consciousness.* Hong Kong: Ch'eng wei-shih lun Publication Committee, 1976
Tharchi, Geshe Lobsang, et al. *The Logic and Debate Tradition of India, Tibet, and Mongolia.* NJ: n.d.
Thich Thiên Châu, Bhikshu. *The Literature of the Personalists of Early Buddhism.* tr. Sara Boin-Webb. Delhi: Motilal Banarsidass, 1999
Thrangu Rinpoche, Khenchen. *The Uttara Tantra: A Treatise on Buddha Nature: A Commentary on the Uttara Tantra Śāstra of Asaṅga.* tr. by Ken and Katia Holmes. Delhi: Sri Satguru, 1994
Tillemans, Tom J.F. *Scripture, Logic, Language: Essays on Dharmakīrti and his Tibetan Successors.* Boston: Wisdom, 1999
————. "Some Reflections of R.S.Y. Chi's *Buddhist Formal Logic.*" *JIABS*, 11 (1), 155-171
Tin, Pe Maung. *Buddhist Devotion and Meditation: An Objective Description and Study.* London, 1964
Tito, Johanna Maria. *Logic in the Husserlian Context.* Evanston: Northwestern University Press, 1990
Tiwary, Mahesh. "*CITTA-VĪTHI, course of cognition.*" *Buddhist Studies.* Delhi, 7 March 1983, 84-95
Tripathi, Chhote Lal. *The Problem of Knowledge in Yogācāra Buddhism.* Varanasi: Bharat-Bharati, 1972
Tsukamoto, Zenryū. *A History of Early Chinese Buddhism: From its Introduction to the Death of Hui-Yüan.* tr. from Japanese by Leon Hurvitz. 2 vols. Tokyo: Kodansha, 1985
Tucci, Giuseppe, *On Some Aspects of the Doctrines of Maitreya[natha] and Asaṅga.* San Francisco: Chinese Materials Center, 1975 (rpt. of Calcutta: University of Calcutta, 1930 ed.)
————. *Minor Buddhist Texts I and II.* Delhi: Motilal Banarsidass, 1978 rpt.
————. *Rati-līlā: An Interpretation of the Tantric Imagery of the Temples of Nepal.* tr. James Hogarth. Geneva: Nagel, 1969
————. *The Theory and Practice of the Mandala.* tr. A.H. Brodrick. NY: Samuel Weiser, 1970
T'ung Jun 通潤 (Ming Dynasty). *Cheng wei-shih lun chi-chieh* 成唯識論集解. ZZ.81.303
Tung Yüeh. *Tower of Myriad Mirrors: A Supplement to* Journey to the West. tr. Shuen-fu Lin and Larry Schulz. Berkeley: Asian Humanities Press, 1978
Ueda, Yoshifumi 上田義文. *"Bonbun yuishiki sanjūju" no kaimei* 梵文唯識三十ケ|の解明. Tokyo: Daisan Bunmeisha, 1987.
————. *Yuishiki shisō nyumon* 唯識思想入門. Kyoto, Asoka Shorin, 1977.
Ui, Hakuju 宇井伯寿. *Bonkan taishō bosatsuji sakuin* 梵漢對照菩薩地索引 (an Index to the Bodhisattvabhūmi, Sanskrit and Chinese). Tokyo: Suzuki Foundation, 1961
————. "Maitreya as an Historical Personage." *Indian Studies in Honor of Charles Rockwell Lanman,* Cambridge: Harvard University Press, 1929, 95-101
————. "On the Author of the Mahāyāna-sūtrālaṃkāra." *Zeitschrift für Indologie und Iranistrik,* Leipsig, 1928, 215-225
————. "On the Development of Buddhism in India." *The Eastern Buddhist,* 1 (5-6) 1922, 303-315
————. *Yugaron kenkyū* 瑜伽論研究. Tokyo: Iwanami Shoten, 1979

Ui, Hakuju and F.W. Thomas. "'The Hand Treatise,' A Work of Aryadeva." *Journal of the Royal Asiatic Society of Great Britain and Ireland,* April 1918, 267-310

Umino, Takanori. "The *vijñaptimātratā* theory of Ratnakaraśānti in the *Prajñapāramitopadeśa*— on the concept of '*ākāra*'." *IBK* 17 (1), 1968-69, 267-310

Vallée Poussin, Louis de la. "La Controverse du Temps et du Pudgala dans le Vijñānakāya." *Études Asiatiques,* 1925, 343-376

————. "Note sur l'Ālayavijñāna." *Mélanges Chinois et Bouddhique.* Louvain, vol. 3, 1934-35, 145-255

————. *The Way to Nirvana.* Delhi: Sri Satguru, 1982 rpt.

————. *Vijñaptimātratāsiddhi, Le Siddhi de Hiuan-tsang: Index.* Paris: Librairie Orientaliste Paul Geuthner, 1948

————. (see *Ch'eng wei-shih lun*; *Abhidharmakośa*; and Bendall, Cecil)

Varagnat, Jean, 1885-1948. *Les hauts-pouvoirs spirituels par la pratique du Yogācāra.* Paris, Editions Dangles [1964]

Varma, Chandra B. *Buddhist Phenomenology: A Theravādin Perspective.* Delhi: Eastern Book Linkers, 1993

Vasubandhu 天親 or 世親. *Abhidharmakośa-bhāṣya.*

(1) Gokhale, V.V. (ed.). "The Text of the *Abhidharmakośa-bhāṣya* of Vasubandhu." *Journal of the Bombay Branch of the Royal Asiatic Society,* 22, 1946, 73-102;

(2) Chinese translations (*A-p'i-ta-mo-chu-she-lun* 阿毘達磨俱舍論): Hsüan-tsang's T.29.1558; Paramārtha's T.29.1559;

(3) French tr., *L'Abhidharmakośa de Vasubandhu,* traduit et annoté par Louis de la Vallée Poussin. Paris: Paul Greuthner, 1931, 7 vols. (based on Hsüan-tsang's version);

(4) Eng. tr., *Abhidharmakośabhāṣyam,* from Vallée Poussin's French Version. tr. Leo Pruden. 4 vols., Berkeley: Asian Humanities Press, 1988-90;

(5) partial Eng. tr., Jha, Subhadra. *The Abhidharmakośa of Vasubandhu.* Patna: KP Jayaswal Research Institute, 1993 (trs. first two chapters of *Kośa,* with separate English renditions of the Pradhan Sanskrit text and Vallée Poussin's French tr. of Hsüan-tsang's Chinese);

(6) (also see Griffiths, *On Being Mindless,* 184-192, for discussion of *Kośa* editions and related texts)

————. *Madhyānta-vibhāga-bhāṣya.* (1) *Madhyānta vibhāga śāstra.* R.C. Pandeya (ed.). Delhi: Motilal Banarsidass, 1971; (2) (see Nagao, Anacker, Kochumuttom, and Sthiramati); (3) Chinese versions: Hsüan-tsang's T.1601 (verses only) and T.1600 (with *-bhāṣya*); Paramārtha's T.1599; (4) Eng. tr.: Th. Stcherbatsky, *Madhyānta-Vibhānga.* Osnabrück: Biblio Verlag, 1970 rpt.

————. *Three works of Vasubandhu in Sanskrit manuscript: the* Trisvabhāvanirdeśa, *the* Viṃśatikā *with its* Vṛtti, *and the* Triṃśikā *with Sthiramati's commentary.* Edited by KATSUMI Mimaki, MUSASHI Tachikawa, and AKIRA Yuyama. Tokyo, Japan: Centre for East Asian Cultural Studies, 1989

————. *Trisvabhāvanirdeśa.* (1) Sujitkumar Mukhopadhyaya (ed. and tr.). *The Trisvabhāvanirdeśa of Vasubandhu: Sanskrit Text and Tibetan Versions, edited with an English Translation, Introduction, Vocabularies.* Calcutta: Visvabharati, 1939; (2) Eng. trs. also in Anacker and Kochumuttom. (Never translated into Chinese)

————. *Viṃśatikā.* (1) Lévy, Sylvain (ed.). "*Viṃśatikā-vṛtti.*" in *Matériaux.* Paris: Bibliothèque de l'École des Hautes Études, 1925, 241-245; (2) Hsüan-tsang's tr. T.1587; (3) Eng. trs. in Anacker and Kochumuttom; (4) Eng. tr. and Chinese text of Hsüan-tsang's version with commentary of K'uei-chi, Clarence Hamilton. *Wei Shih Er Shih Lun or The Treatise in Twenty Stanzas on Representation-Only by Vasubandhu.* New Haven: American Oriental Society, 1938

Vasumitra (尊者)世友. *A-p'i-t'a-mo chieh shen tsu lun* 阿毘達磨界身足論 (*Abhidharma Dhātu-kāya pāda śāstra*)(Treatise on Body Elements According to the Abhidharma Path). Hsüan-tsang's tr. T.26.1540; (Eng. tr. see Ganguly)

————. *A-p'i-t'a-mo p'in-lei tsu lun* 阿毘達磨品類足論 (*Abhidharma-prakaraṇa-pāda*) (Treatise of Classifications according to the Abhidharma Path). Hsüan-tsang's tr. T.26.1542

————. *Yi-pu-tsung lun lun* 異部宗輪論, [Hsüan-tsang's tr. of Vasumitra's treatise on the doctrines of the different schools] (T.49.2031); Eng. tr.: Masuda, Jiryo, *Origin and Doctrines of Early Indian Buddhist Schools*, Leipzig: 1925

Vattanky, John, S.J. *Nyāya Theory of Language.* (Viśvanātha Pañcāna's *Muktāvalī* with Dinakara's *Dinakarī*). Delhi: Sri Satguru, 1995

Verdu, Alfonso. *Dialectical Aspects in Buddhist Thought: Studies in Sino-Japanese Mahāyāna Idealism.* University of Kansas: Center for East Asian Studies, 1974

Vibhaṅga (second work of Theravāda Abhidhamma) (PTS edition). Eng. tr. *The Books of Analysis.* tr. Paṭhamakyaw Ashin Thiṭṭila. London: PTS, 1969

Vinītadeva. *Nyāyabindu-ṭīkā, Sanskrit Original reconstructed from the extant Tibetan version, with English translation and annotations.* by Mrinalkanti Gangopadhyaya. Calcutta: Indian Studies Past and Present, 1971

Vollmer, John E. *Five Colours of the Universe.* Edmunton: Edmunton Art Gallery, 1980

Vyas, C.S. *Buddhist Theory of Perception with special reference to* Pramāṇa vārttika *of Dharmakīrti.* New Delhi: Navrang, 1991

Waley, Arthur. *Monkey: A Folk Novel of China by Wu-Ch'eng-en.* NY: Evergreen, 1958

————. *The Real Tripitaka.* NY: Macmillan, 1952 (biography of Hsüan-tsang)

Walleser, M. *The Life of Nāgārjuna from Tibetan and Chinese Sources.* New Delhi: Asian Educational Services, 1990 rpt.

Wang K'en-t'ang 王肯堂 (Ming Dynasty). *Ch'eng wei-shih lun cheng-yi* 成唯論證義. ZZ.81.645

————. *Yin-ming ju cheng-li lun chi-chieh* 因明入正理論集解. ZZ.87.105

Wang, Ting-chih 王亭之. *Ta-sheng ch'eng yeh lun* 大乘成業論 (The *Karmasiddhi-prakaraṇa*). Hong Kong: Vajrayana Buddhist Association, 1994

Warder, A.K. *Indian Buddhism.* Delhi: Motilal Banarsidass, 2nd rev. ed. 1986

Watanabe, Fumimaro. *Philosophy and its Development in the Nikāyas and Abhidharmma.* Delhi: Matilal Banarsidass, 1983

Wayman, Alex. *Buddhist Insight.* George R. Elder (ed.). Delhi: Motilal Banarsidass, 1984

————. *A Millenium of Buddhist Logic.* Delhi: Motilal Banarsidass, 1999

————. "A Reconsideration of Dharmakīrti's 'Deviation' from Dignāga on Pratyakśabhāsa." *Annals of the Bhandarkar Research Institute,* Poona, 1978

————. "A Report on the *Akṣayamatinirdeśasūtra*:" *Studies in Indo-Asian Art and Culture,* 6, ed. Lokesh Chandra. New Delhi: International Academy of Indian Culture, 1980, 211-232

————. *Untying the Knots in Buddhism.* Delhi: Motilal Banarsidass, 1997

————. *Yoga of the Guhyasamājatantra.* Delhi: Motilal Banarsidass, 1980

Wei shih san shih lun yao shih: Tun-huang pen 唯識三十論要釋：敦煌本. Hong Kong: Fa chieh hsüeh yüan, 1966

Weinstein, Stanley. "The Ālaya-vijñāna in Early Yogācāra Buddhism—a Comparison of Its Meaning in the Saṃdhinirmocana-sūtra and the Vijñapti-mātratā-siddhi of Dharmapāla." *Transactions of the International Conference of Orientalists in Japan,* Tokyo: Toho Gakkai, 1958, 46-58

————. "A Biographical Study of Tz'u-en." *Monumenta Nipponica,* 15, 1-2 (1959) 119-49

————. *Buddhism Under the T'ang.* Cambridge: Cambridge University Press, 1987

————. *The Kanjin Kakumushō* 觀心覺夢鈔 [of Ryōhen 良遍]. Unpub. Ph.D. Dissertation, Harvard University, 1965.

Whirford, Margaret. *Merleau-Ponty's Critique of Sartre's Philosophy.* Lexington, KY: French Forum, 1982

Whiteside, Kerry H. *Merleau-Ponty and the Foundation of an Essential Politics.* Princeton: Princeton University Press, 1988

Wijayaratna, Mohan. *Buddhist Monastic Life According to Texts of the Theravāda Tradition.* tr. by Claude Grangier and Steven Collins. Cambridge: Cambridge University Press, 1990

Willemen, Charles. Bart Dessein and Collett Cox. *Sarvāstivāda Buddhist Scholasticism.* Leiden: EJ Brill, 1998

Williams, Paul. *The Reflexive Nature of Awareness: A Tibetan Madhyamaka Defense.* Surrey: Curzon, 1998

Wŏnch'ŭk 圓測. *Hsin-ching-tsan* 心經贊. (T.33.1711)

————. *Jen-wang ching shu* 仁王經疏. (T.33.1708)

Wriggins, Sally Hovey. *Xuanzang: A Buddhist Pilgrim on the Silk Road.* Boulder: Western Press, 1996

Wright, Arthur. *Buddhism in Chinese History.* Stanford: Stanford University Press, 1959

————. *Studies in Chinese Buddhism.* Ed. by Robert M. Somers. Hew Haven: Yale University Press, 1990

———— (ed.). *Studies in Chinese Thought.* Chicago: University of Chicago Press, 1953

Yamada, Isshi. "Premises and Implications of Interdependence." in *Buddhist Studies in Honour of Walpola Rahula,* 1980, 267-293

Yamaguchi, Susumu. *Mahāyāna Way to Buddhahood.* tr. and ed. by Buddhist Books International, Los Angeles and Tokyo, 1982

————. (see also Dignāga [Yamagushi]; Sthiramati, *Madhyāntavibhāga-ṭīkā.*)

Yamakami, Sōgen. *Systems of Buddhist Thought.* Calcutta: Calcutta University Press, 1912

Yan P'ei 演培. *Pa-shih kuei-chü sung/Wei-shih san-shih sung* 八識規矩頌／唯二十頌 Taipei: T'ien Hua, 1990

Yang Hui-nan 揚惠南. *Fo-chiao ssu-hsiang hsin lun* 佛教思想新論. Taipei: Tung Ta T'u Shu, 1982

Yang, Hsüan-chih. *A Record of Buddhist Monasteries in Lo-yang.* tr. Yi-t'ung Wang. Princeton: Princeton University Press, 1984

Yang Pai-yi 楊白衣. *Wei-shih yao-yi* 唯識要義 (the meaning of consciousness-only). Taipei: Wen Chin Publ., 1996

Yaśomitra. *Sphuṭārtā: Abhidharmakośa-vyākhyā of Yaśomitra, [reconstructed Sanskrit kārikās and vyākhya].* Edited [with English introduction] by Narendra Nath Law and Nalinaksha Dutt. Calcutta: Oriental Book Agency, 1957

Yeh A-yueh 葉阿葉. "The Problems of the 'Ātyantika' in K'uei-chi's *Prajñāpāramitā-hṛdaya-sūtra-vṛtti.*" *Chung-Hwa Buddhist Journal.* no. 3, April, 1990, 381-401

————. *Yuishiki Shisō no kenkyū* 唯識思想の研究. Tokyo: Kokusho Kankōkai, 1975

Yi-ching 義淨. *Ch'eng wei-shih pao sheng lun* 成唯識寶生論. T.31.1591 (tr. of Dharmapāla's commentary on the *Viṃśatika*)

————. *Kuan-suo-yüan lun shih* 觀所緣論釋. T.31.1625 (tr. of Dharmapāla's commentary on Dignāga's *Ālambana-parikṣa*)

————. *Kuan-tsung-hsiang lun sung* 觀總相論頌. T.31.1623 (tr. of Dignāga's *Ālambana-parikṣa*) (cf. Hsüan-tsang's tr., T.31.1624, 觀所緣緣論)

————. *Nan-hai chi-kuei nei-fa ch'uan* 南海寄歸內法傳 (Soujourn through the Southern Seas to Take Refuge in the Dharma). T.54.2125 (Eng tr. see Takakusu, Junjirō)

————. *Ta-t'ang Hsi-yü ch'iu-fa kao-seng ch'uan* 大唐西域求法高僧傳 (Great T'ang Journey to Western Lands in Search of the Dharma and Eminent Monks). T.51.2066 (Eng tr. see Lahiri, Latika)

Yokoyama, Koitsu. *Index to the Yogācārabhūmi, Chinese-Sanskrit-Tibetan* Tokyo: Sankibo Busshorin Pub. Co., 1996

Yoshihide Yoshizu 吉津宜英. *Kegon ichijo shisō no kenkyū* 華嚴一乗思想の研究. Tokyo: Daitō-Shuppan-sha, 1991

Yu, Anthony. *Journey to the West.* 4 vols. Chicago: University of Chicago Press, 1977-83

Yü Ling-po 于凌波. *Wei-shih san-sung chiang-chi* 唯識三頌講記. Taiwan: Fo Kuang, 1998

Yüan Hsiang 圓香. *Sheng-seng Hsüan-tsang ta-shih chuan* 聖僧玄奘大師傳. (Teachings of the Holy Monk Great Master Hsüan-tsang). Kao-Hsiung, Taiwan: Fo Kuang, 1993

Yuasa, Yasuo. *The Body: Toward an Eastern Mind-Body Theory.* tr. Nagatomo Shigemori and Thomas Kasulis. Albany: SUNY Press, 1987

Yūki, Reimon 結城令聞. "Genjō to sono Gakuha no seiritsu 玄奘とその学派の成立." in *Sōritsu jugo shunen kinen ronshu II* 創立十五周年記念論集 2 , Tokyo: Tokyo daigaku tōyō bunka kenkyūjo, 1955
———. *Seshin yuishiki no kenkyū* 世親唯識の研究. Tokyo: Aoyama Shoin, 1956
———. *Yuishiki sanjūju* 唯識三十頌 . Tokyo: Daizō Shuppan, 1991
———. *Yuishikigaku tensekishi* 唯識学典籍志. Tokyo: Daizō shuppan, 1962
Zürcher, Erik. "Buddhist Influence on Early Taoism: A Survey of Scriptural Evidence." *T'oung Pao* LXVI, 1-3, 1980, 84-148.
———. *The Buddhist Conquest of China. The Spread and Adaptation of Buddhism in Early Medieval China.* Leiden: EJ Brill, 1972.
Zürcher, Erik, and Chun-chieh Huang. *Time and Space in Chinese Culture.* Leiden: E.J. Brill, 1995

Index

30290381R00355

Made in the USA
Lexington, KY
26 February 2014